Chad Carpenter presents:
The Really Big TUNDRA Treasury

Written & Illustrated by Chad Carpenter
Co-written by Darin Carpenter & Mark Dickerson
Published by **Tundra & Associates**

Copyright © 2001 by Chad Carpenter

All "TUNDRA" comic strips copyright © 1991, 1992 1993, 1994, 1995, 1996, 1997, 1998, 1999, 2000, 2001

All other artwork & photographs copyright © by Chad Carpenter All rights reserved, including the right to reproduce this book or portions thereof in any form.

Published by Tundra & Associates
P.O. Box 770732
Eagle River, Alaska 99577

For additional volumes of this or other Tundra books, as well as calendars, shirts, mouse pads, screen savers, etc. please visit THE OFFICIAL TUNDRA WEBSITE at:

www.tundracomics.com

or email us at:

tundra@arctic.net

Official Tundra photographer - Darin Carpenter
Official Tundra prufe reeder - Kim Kellogg

Library of Congress Catalog Card Number: 2001117653
First printing: July 2001
ISBN 1-57833-149-8
Printed in the USA

This Book is dedicated to
my family & friends.

You know who you are.

- except for crazy Uncle Larry, who hasn't known who he was since 1967.

BLANK PAGE:
Please tear out and recycle

The Official Tundra Foreword

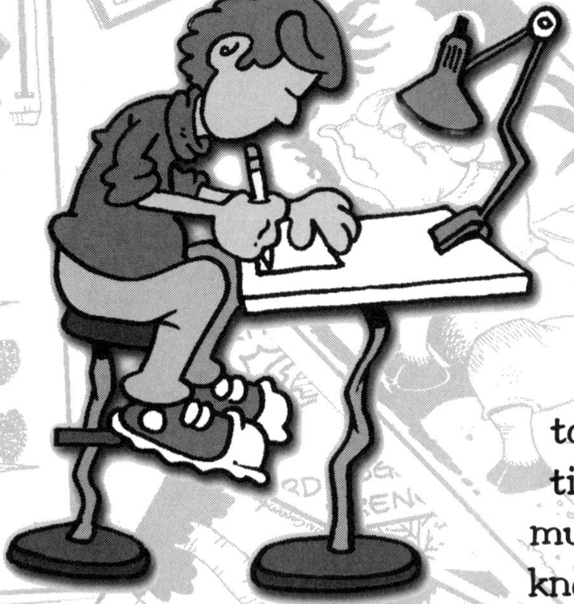

One of the first things that became quite apparent when I decided to put together "THE REALLY BIG TUNDRA TREASURY," was the important task of beginning it with an appropriately crafted foreword. I spent many long hours trying to think of a suitable introduction to a body of work that may very well go down in literary history as a complex reflection of our life & times. Many a sleepless night was spent mulling over my extensive list of options. I knew that it was vitally important that the method chosen equal the importance of the bejeweled piece of literature it was to introduce, but what path to take?

Should I have some internationally famous fellow cartoonist write up words of praise for my strip and the contributions it has made to the world of art & humor? Or maybe I should have some powerful political leader express his admiration for the economic stability & world harmony Tundra has helped forge. Or, possibly, just simply have one of this century's gifted poets write a few paragraphs regaling that which is Tundra. My chore was truly daunting. The decision I would make would have lasting repercussions. I must choose wisely.

In an effort to meet this challenge, I scoured dozens & dozens of other books (well, two or three others, anyway) in the hope of gleaning some guidance to the correct path. And, after copious amounts of extensive research, like a butterfly emerging from its cocoon, the truth of it all was made clear to me - forewords suck. They're all boring. No wonder I've never read a foreword before.

So, because of this, I have decided to share with you something that is far more useful - my mother's potato soup recipe. Trust me, it's better than any foreword you will ever read - and much more tasty.

— Chad Carpenter

Mom's Potato Soup

Ingredients:

10 medium sized potatoes
1 medium onion (chopped)
Water (enough to cover)
1 tsp. Salt
Pepper
1 stick of butter or margarine
1 or 2 cups of milk
1/2 lb. Chopped, cooked bacon

Peel & cube potatoes. Add chopped onion and enough water to cover. Cook over medium heat. While potatoes are cooking, chop & fry bacon until crisp. Drain well and put aside. Cook potatoes until they start to fall apart. Mash slightly leaving lots of lumps. Add butter/margarine and stir until melted. Add one cup of milk – If too thick pour in 2nd cup of milk. Stir in bacon. Salt & pepper to taste.

MMM, Yummy!

Introduction:

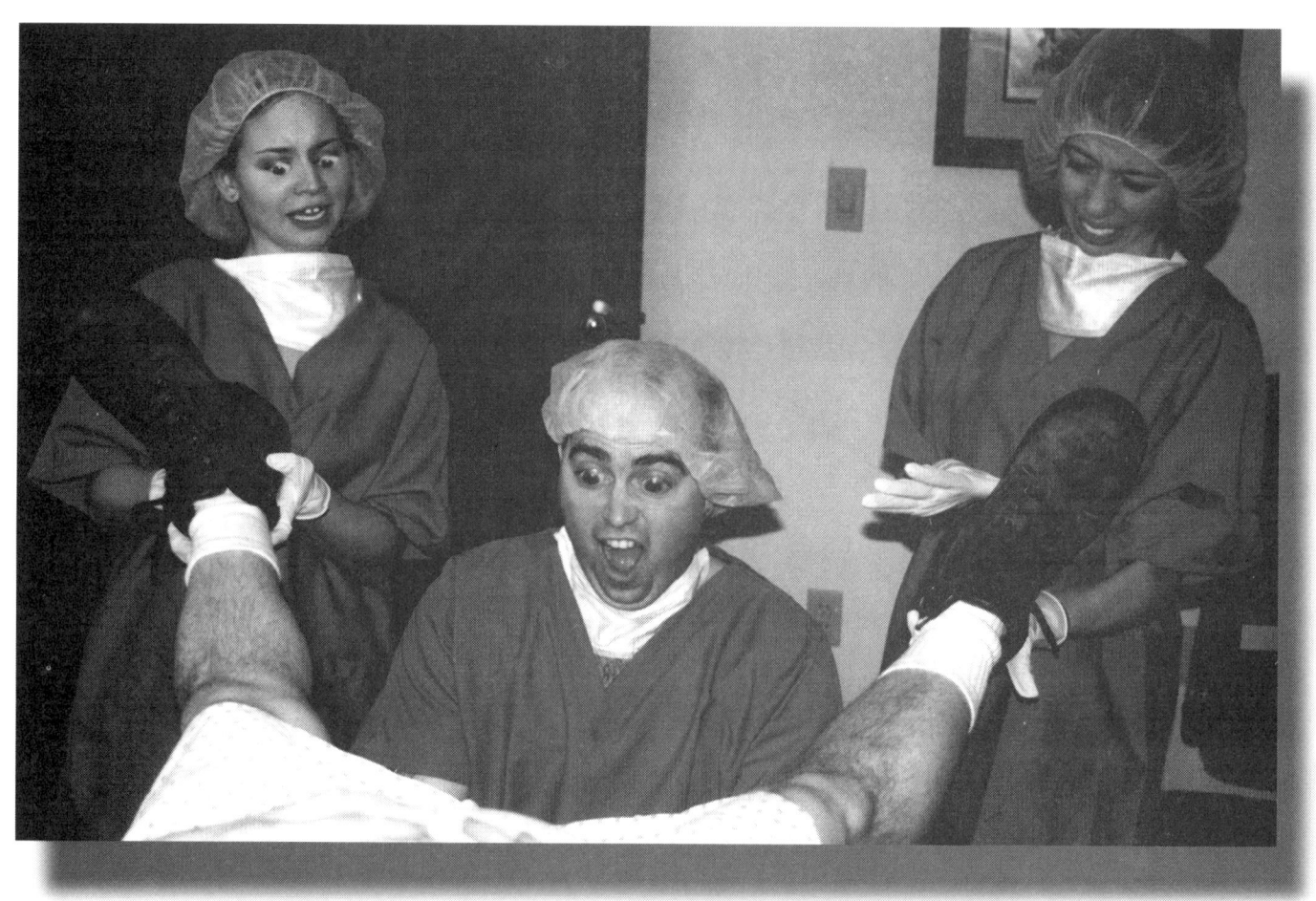

THE BIRTH OF TUNDRA

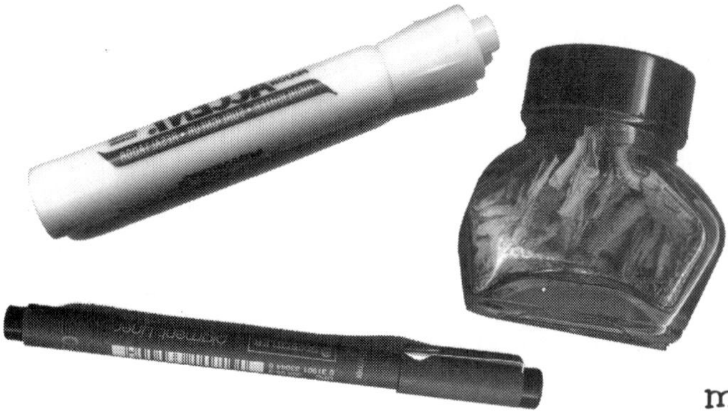

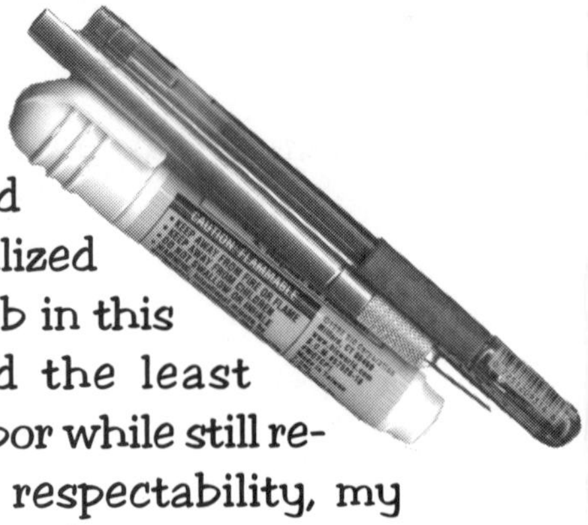

I have always enjoyed drawing, but when I realized that it was the one job in this world that required the least amount of physical labor while still retaining a modicum of respectability, my mind was set. I'm sure the fact that it was my only marketable skill had something to do with it as well, but either way, I knew what my path would be.

When first approaching this book, one might be struck by the fact that this exceptional cartoon has managed to maintain its sharp and brilliant humor for ten whole years. Either that or you are simply amazed that newspapers have continued printing it for that long. Regardless, one sure ponders where and how Tundra originated. From whence did this stream of humor first spring forth? Toss aside the visions of Alaskan wilderness and inspirational northern vistas, and instead look to the balmy and art-infested land of Sarasota, Florida. The year was 1988.

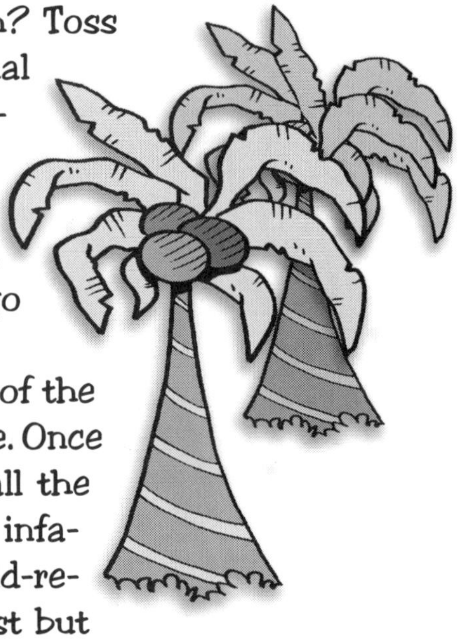

Sarasota is, what some might call, the cartoonist Mecca. Other people might say it is where old people's parents go to retire. They're both correct. I traveled to this land, from my home in Alaska, in hopes of encountering some of the giants of the cartoon world that were rumored to live there. Once in Sarasota, the land of cartoon legends, I found that all the stories were true. Among many others, there were the infamous Garfield creator, Jim Davis, Dik Browne, the world-renowned artist responsible for Hagar the Horrible, and last but definitely not least, there was the Pulitzer Prize-winning author of Mother Goose and Grimm, Mike Peters.

At that time, Sarasota played host to a charity benefit known as the "Cartoon Classic." It was while attending this function that I was fortunate enough to rub elbows with the aforementioned literary geniuses, not to mention steal the scraps off their dinner plates. Granted, while I didn't have the opportunity to have in-depth, philosophical conversations with any of these famous attendees, I'll never forget the brief exchanges of conversation my mentors and I shared. I can almost hear, with giddy

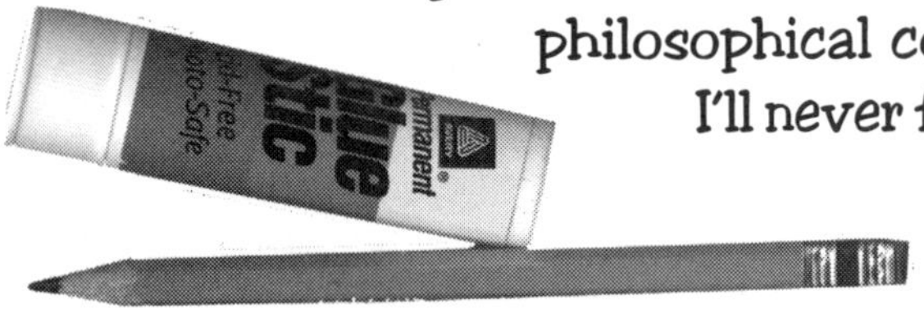

exhilaration, Dik Browne telling me to quit touching all the meatballs, or Jim Davis telling me to stay away from his wife or when Mike Peters pretended to call security and two men actually showed up and escorted me from the building. Ahh, the wacky hijinx of those funny guys. Yes, ladies and gentlemen, I had reached the cartoonist nirvana.

Shortly after the Cartoon Classic (and after I was bailed out) I had the good fortune of running into Dik Browne on a golf course. Fate was surely smiling on me that day - not only did I manage to slip by disguised as a caddie (thus avoiding a greens-fee) but Mr. Browne didn't recognize me as the meatball-fondler from the previous evening. I spoke with Mr. Browne for a short while about my quest to be a cartoonist, and he was kind enough to give me his number to set up an appointment to visit him in his studio. I must admit that I was quite excited. So excited in fact that I began to jump around a bit. Unfortunately, in all my exuberance, I slipped on Mr. Browne's golf ball. It rocketed up into the sky as I did a backwards somersault with a half-twist and landed square on my side. Only a second later, the offending golf ball rapidly descended and planted itself in my right ear. Mr. Browne, evidently being a strict observer of the rules & etiquette of golf, insisted that he play it where it lay. It was a fantastic 300-yard drive. And, ever the gentleman, he promptly replaced the divot.

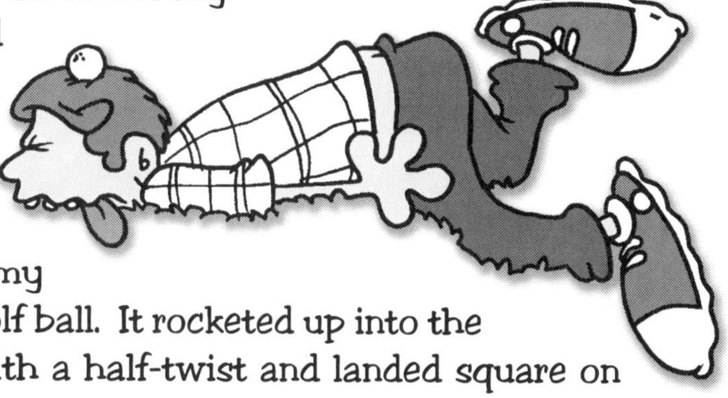

At first, Mr. Browne was a little difficult to get a hold of, always out of town burning and pillaging (research for his strip, his secretary called it). However, after showing up unannounced when I "just happened to be in the area," I was finally able to spend some time with him in his studio where he proceeded to show me the tricks of the trade. That is to say, he enlightened me to the inner circle of cartoonist knowledge. For example, the types of pens and paper to use, the correct format of a comic strip, and most importantly, that a well-organized drawing table is by no means necessary. It was that last part that I cling to to this day as sacred.

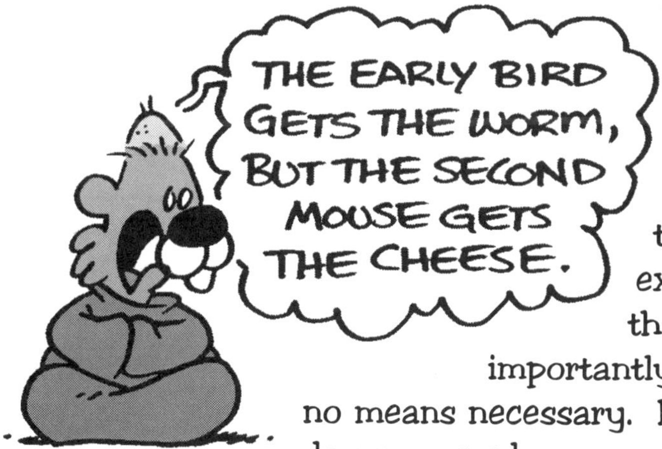
THE EARLY BIRD GETS THE WORM, BUT THE SECOND MOUSE GETS THE CHEESE.

Chad gleans wisdom from the professionals

So now I had some tools in my arsenal and was thinking of trying to make a go of this cartoonist gig. It was a second run-in with Mike Peters at the following Cartoon Classic that clinched my decision to avoid real jobs and draw funny pictures for a living. Having been a fan of both his political cartoons as well as Mother Goose & Grimm, I was especially thrilled with the opportunity to get some cartooning advice. I asked him how one comes up with a comic strip subject that can be drawn day after day, year after year, without burning out? He told me four simple words that would inspire me to develop Tundra - those words - "Draw what you know." I have always been grateful for those four words; after all, he could have said a lot of four-word sentences that wouldn't have had near the impact - such as - "Get off my leg." or "Who let you in?"

It was about this time that an oil tanker by the name of "Exxon Valdez" had an itsy-bitsy fender bender back home in Alaska. You may have heard of it. In any case, due to the demand of duty and love of country, I traveled back to Alaska to do my part in cleaning up the oil spill (not to mention Exxon was paying everyone big bucks!).

I quickly landed a job with Exxon as a security guard, thus proving that their background checks weren't very thorough. I was to be stationed in the tiny town of Valdez. Upon reaching the "tiny" town of Valdez, it didn't take long to realize that it wasn't as tiny as it had been only a few weeks earlier. Due to the spill, Valdez's population had grown from about 3,000 to 10,000. The place had taken on a decidedly "gold-rush" atmosphere. Being the base of operations for the spill cleanup, it was teeming with thousands of workers involved in one way or another with the cleanup effort.

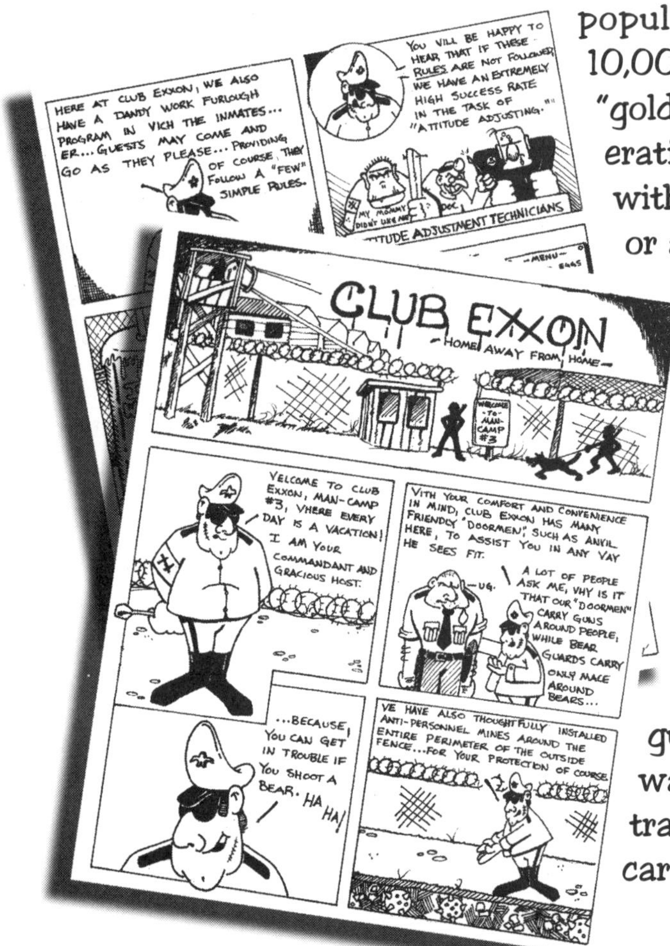

HERE AT CLUB EXXON, WE ALSO HAVE A DANDY WORK FURLOUGH PROGRAM IN VICH THE INMATES... ER... GUESTS MAY COME AND GO AS THEY PLEASE... PROVIDING OF COURSE, THEY FOLLOW A "FEW" SIMPLE RULES.
YOU VILL BE HAPPY TO HEAR THAT IF THESE RULES ARE NOT FOLLOWED WE HAVE AN EXTREMELY HIGH SUCCESS RATE IN THE TASK OF "ATTITUDE ADJUSTING."
MY MOMMY DIDN'T LIKE ME
DOC
TUDE ADJUSTMENT TECHNICIANS
CLUB EXXON
-HOME AWAY FROM HOME-
WELCOME -TO- MAN-CAMP #3
VELCOME TO CLUB EXXON, MAN-CAMP #3, VHERE EVERY DAY IS A VACATION!
I AM YOUR COMMANDANT AND GRACIOUS HOST.
VITH YOUR COMFORT AND CONVENIENCE IN MIND, CLUB EXXON HAS MANY FRIENDLY "DOORMEN", SUCH AS ANVIL HERE, TO ASSIST YOU IN ANY VAY HE SEES FIT.
UG.
A LOT OF PEOPLE ASK ME, VHY IS IT THAT OUR "DOORMEN" CARRY GUNS AROUND PEOPLE, WHILE BEAR GUARDS CARRY ONLY MACE AROUND BEARS...
...BECAUSE, YOU CAN GET IN TROUBLE IF YOU SHOOT A BEAR. HA HA!
VE HAVE ALSO THOUGHTFULLY INSTALLED ANTI-PERSONNEL MINES AROUND THE ENTIRE PERIMETER OF THE OUTSIDE FENCE...FOR YOUR PROTECTION OF COURSE.

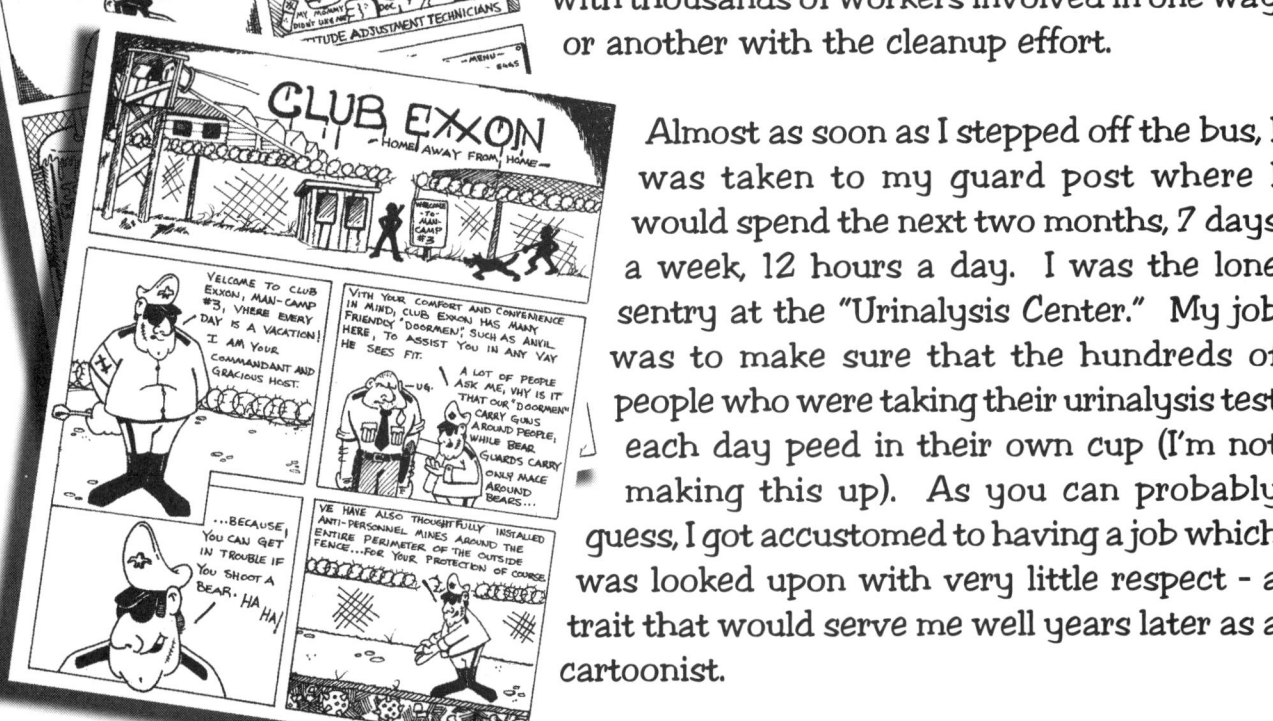

Almost as soon as I stepped off the bus, I was taken to my guard post where I would spend the next two months, 7 days a week, 12 hours a day. I was the lone sentry at the "Urinalysis Center." My job was to make sure that the hundreds of people who were taking their urinalysis test each day peed in their own cup (I'm not making this up). As you can probably guess, I got accustomed to having a job which was looked upon with very little respect - a trait that would serve me well years later as a cartoonist.

The Exxon company, like the rest of the country at that time, was plagued by a disease known simply as *political correctness.* A disease that still exists today but was at its peak in the late 80's & early 90's. One symptom of this was, in an effort to foster pride in one's duties, a lofty job title was given to the thousands of sweaty raincoat-clad folks scrubbing tar off the beaches. They were known as "Oil Recovery Technicians." In fact, it seemed that every person involved in the spill, regardless of what his or her job was, had the word "Technician" somewhere in their title. I'm pretty sure the cook's assistants were "Potato Peeling Technicians" and the folks that did the laundry were "Garment Decontamination Technicians." Well I figured if anyone needed a glossy job title to make them feel proud of what they did, it was me. I decided that I would be known simply as the "Urine Recovery Technician."

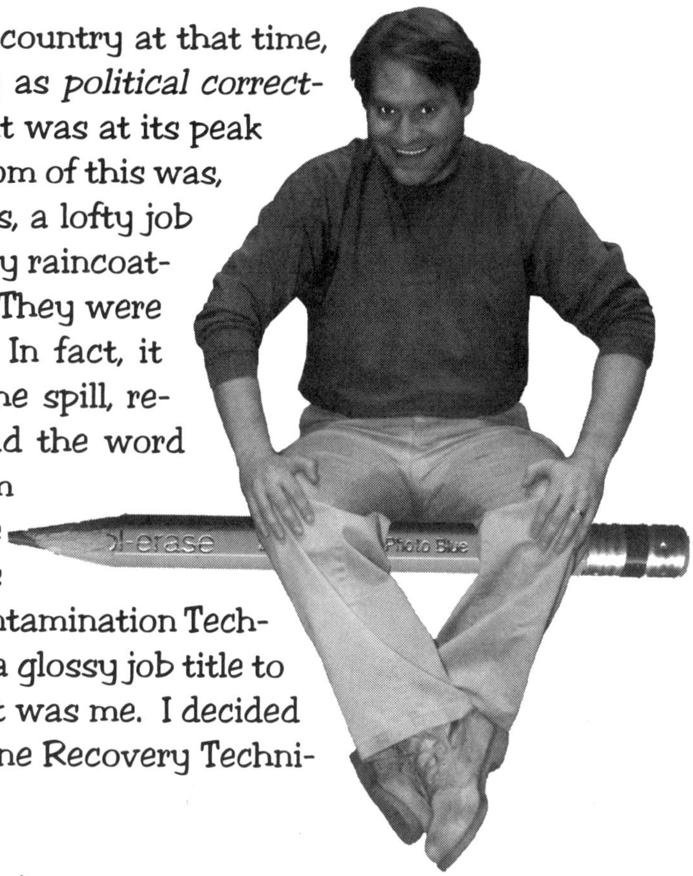
Photo Blue

The whole oil-spill situation, while tragic in most every way, was also ripe with opportunities to be made fun of. I decided now was a good time to try my hand at this whole cartooning gig. It was thus that "Club Exxon" was born.

As with most political cartoons, Club Exxon was a pleasant mix of parody with a heaping portion of truth thrown in for good measure. Club Exxon was a sarcastic look at the ridiculous living conditions of what was known as "Man Camp #3." Man Camp #3 was a sort of dormitory consisting of stacks and stacks of Atco trailers piled on top of each other forming large barracks. The hundreds of workers, myself included, who worked directly in the town of Valdez lived in these structures. One of the many bizarre aspects of Man-Camp #3 was that its perimeter was surrounded by a large fence whose entrances & exits were patrolled by armed guards around the clock. These weren't dime-a-dozen, rent-A-cops such as myself, not that I should have been armed for my job in the first place (I can just see it, "Step away from the cup of urine or I'll have to shoot!"). These guards were Exxon's full-timers. The elite. Kind of like Iraq's "Republican Guards." What made this particularly ironic was that the subcontracted guards, who were stationed out on the beaches and in charge of protecting the Oil Recovery Technicians from bears,

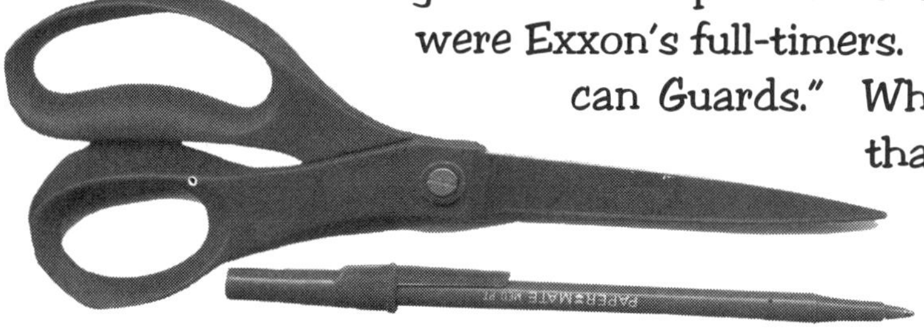

weren't allowed to carry guns. They were only armed with a large can of "bear-mace." It was because of this and many other ludicrous situations & rules that I decided to create my "Club Exxon" series. Although it was not published directly, Club Exxon developed quite a large circulation, mysteriously appearing in hundreds of photocopies & faxes and showing up on desks, walls and windows around the big burg of Valdez. Soon after, everywhere I went, people were telling me how much they loved it and asking when the next installment was coming out. It was at this time that I first tasted the fame and the pain of cartooning. Club Exxon was becoming wildly popular with the workers and wildly unpopular with the management. Needless to say when it came time for layoffs, I was in the first group to go. I took pride in the fact that I had enough of an audience to be censored, but at the same time I was disappointed that I no longer had an audience. At first I didn't know what direction to go - then I remembered Mike Peters' words, "Draw what you know."

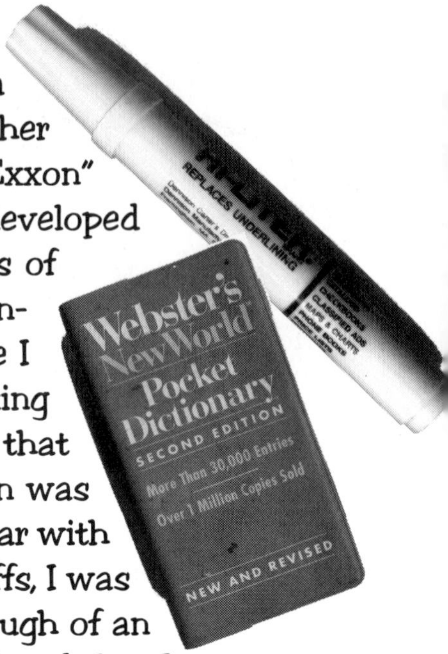
REPLACES UNDERLINING
Webster's New World
Pocket Dictionary
SECOND EDITION
More Than 30,000 Entries
Over 1 Million Copies Sold
NEW AND REVISED

I moved back to Sarasota and began working on a strip that would fit those words. Having grown up in Alaska and having been surrounded by animals & nature, I decided that those very subjects would be a logical theme. I figured that the best way to pursue my dream was to move back to Alaska with my idea, draw some strips and present them to the Anchorage Daily News. That's exactly what I did.

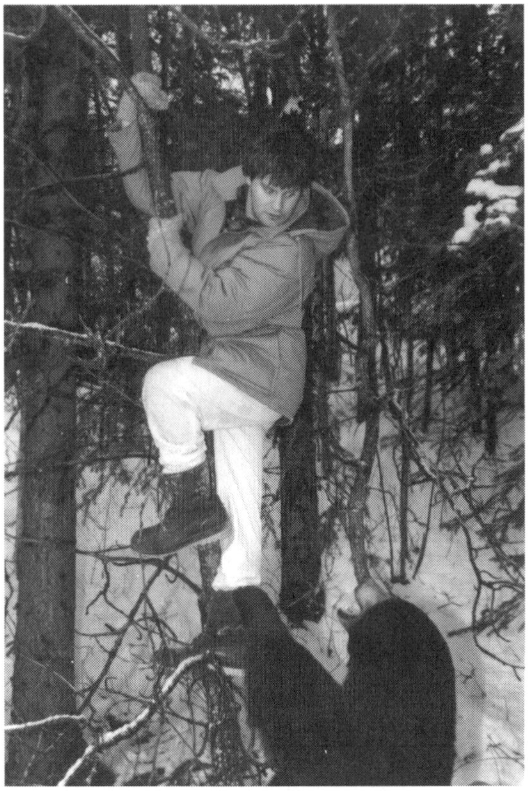

Chad does some research for his Alaskan strip to "Draw what he knows."

In November of 1991, I made an appointment with Mike Campbell, the entertainment editor of the Anchorage Daily News. I brought with me the 36 comic strips that I had thus far completed as well as the single word title of "Tundra." He looked at them, made some copies, and said he would give me a call and let me know. I don't know if I hit them on a good day, or if they were just swayed by the singing aardvark telegram, but they agreed to run my comic strip.

A week or so later, on December 2nd, 1991, Tundra began running in the Anchorage Daily News.

The first Tundra strip that appeared in the Anchorage Daily News

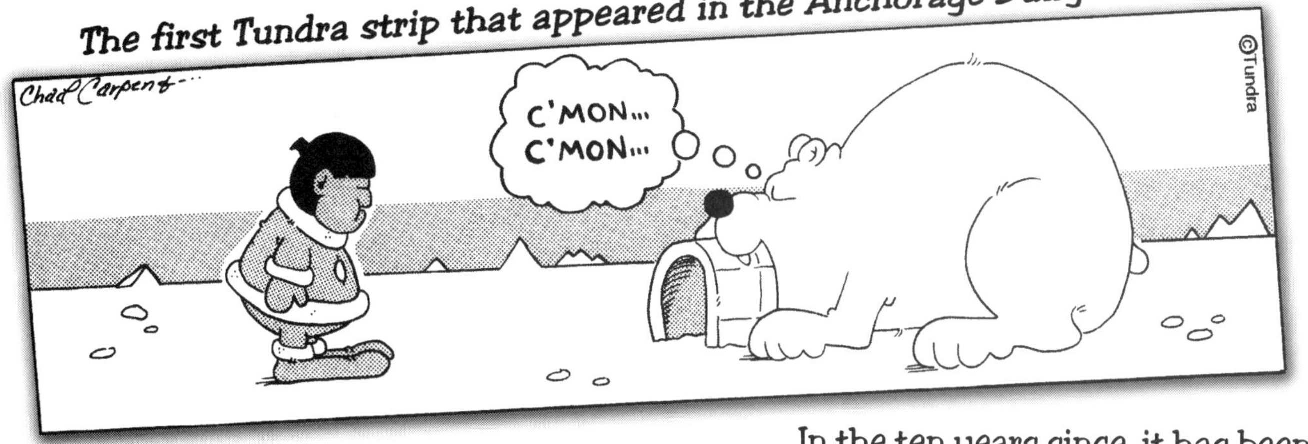
Chad Carpenter
C'MON...
C'MON...
©Tundra

In the ten years since, it has been picked up by other newspapers and printed in dozens of magazines throughout the United States, Canada & Europe. It has also culminated in seven compilation books as well as two spin-off books, many different calendars, t-shirts, mouse pads, coffee mugs, note cards, a CD-ROM and any other item I can make a buck off.

Over the past decade, the Tundra strip has also seen the formation of many reocurring characters. The main comic strip inhabitants include Dudley the Bear, Sherman the Squirrel, Andy the Lemming, Whiff the Skunk, Chad the Cartoonist, a gang of moose nugget mercenaries and several "part-timers." Oddly enough, when I first began drawing these guys, I didn't have any specific personality or characteristics in mind for them. Over time, they just seemed to develop all of that by themselves. Since their creation, they have become a very important part of my life - just short of me actually talking to them when I'm in public. One of the questions people frequently ask me is where do the Tundra characters live? Out of the 3,000 Tundra strips I've drawn, it has never been mentioned. Strangely enough, in my mind, I've always had a name for the community that is home to the Tundra dwellers and their outrageous escapades. So, for the first time in print, I will now take this opportunity to share with you the name of the Tundra gang's little town -

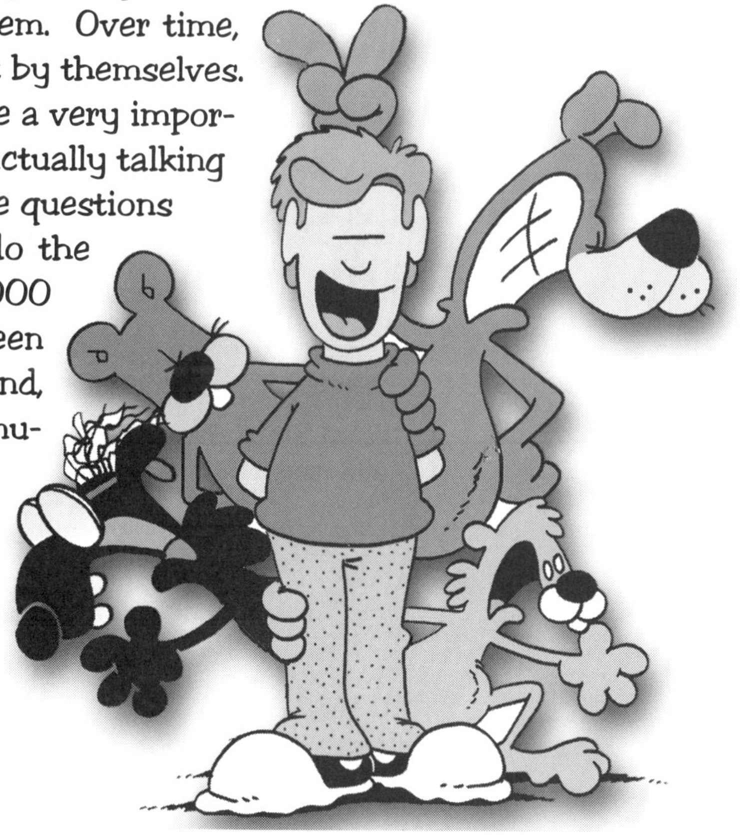

Gangrene Gulch

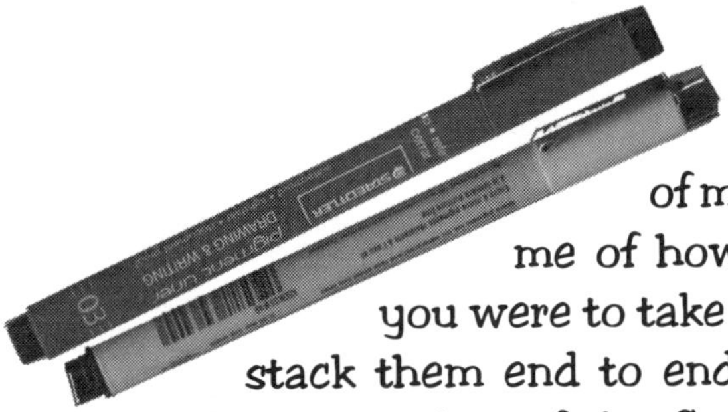

Recently I was looking through a stack of my past cartoons, when the realization hit me of how much I've drawn this past decade. If you were to take all of the Tundra cartoons I've drawn and stack them end to end, they would reach a height more than twelve times that of the Statue of Liberty, more than fifty-six times taller than the Great Sphinx, and three times taller than the Empire State Building. Upon reflecting on these numbers, I realized two things - **1)** *Calculators are really cool* - and - **2)** *It's going to take me 349,184 years to draw enough cartoons to reach the moon* - which means, of course, I need to stop writing, and get busy drawing...

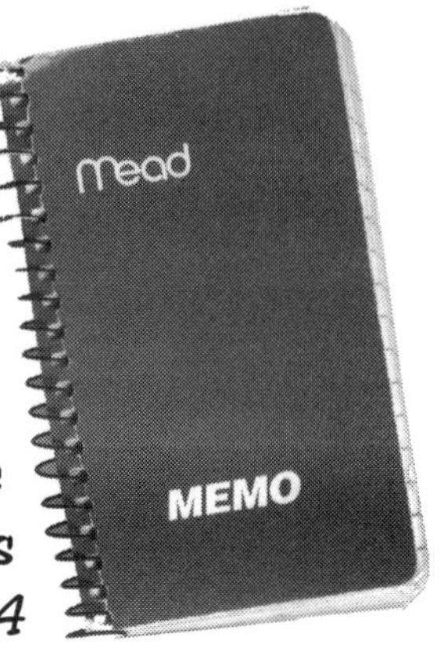
Mead
MEMO

-Chad Carpenter

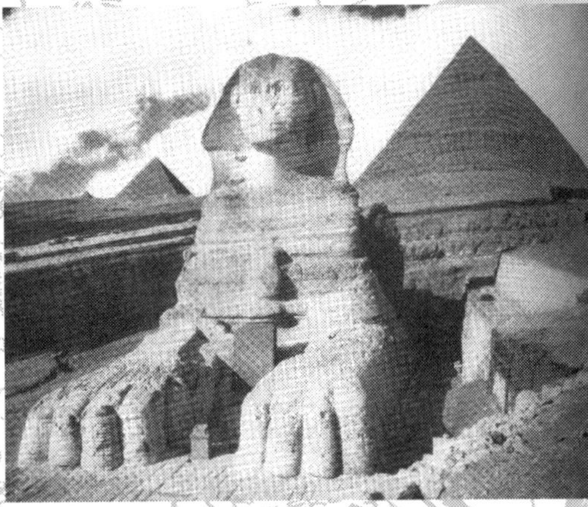

56 times taller than the Great Sphinx

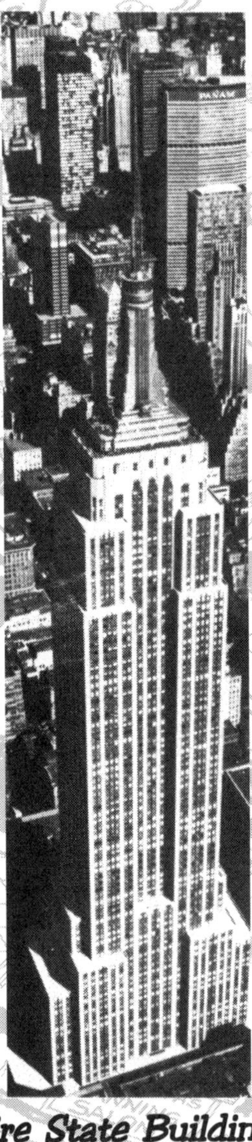

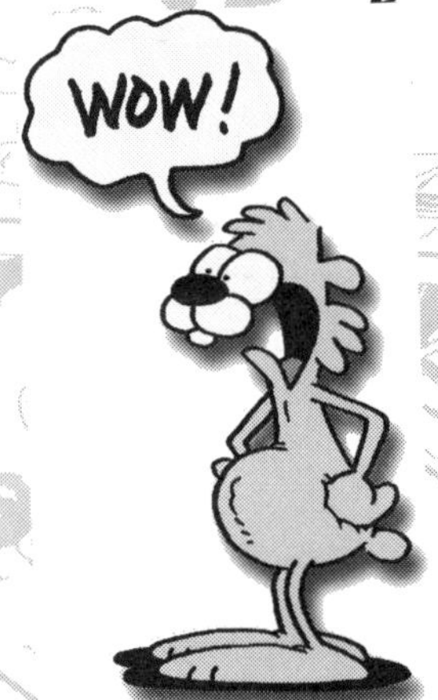
WOW!

12 times taller than the Statue of Liberty

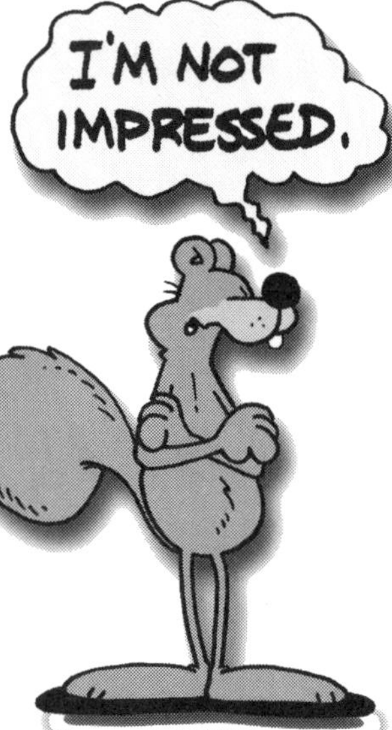
I'M NOT IMPRESSED.

3 times taller than the Empire State Building

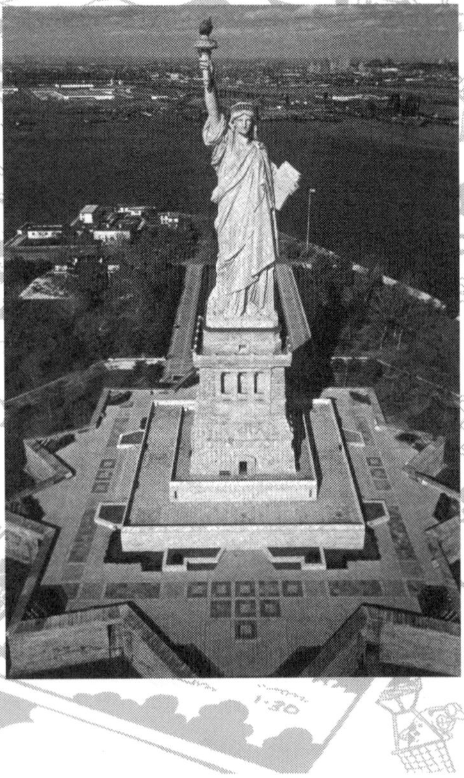

Chapter One

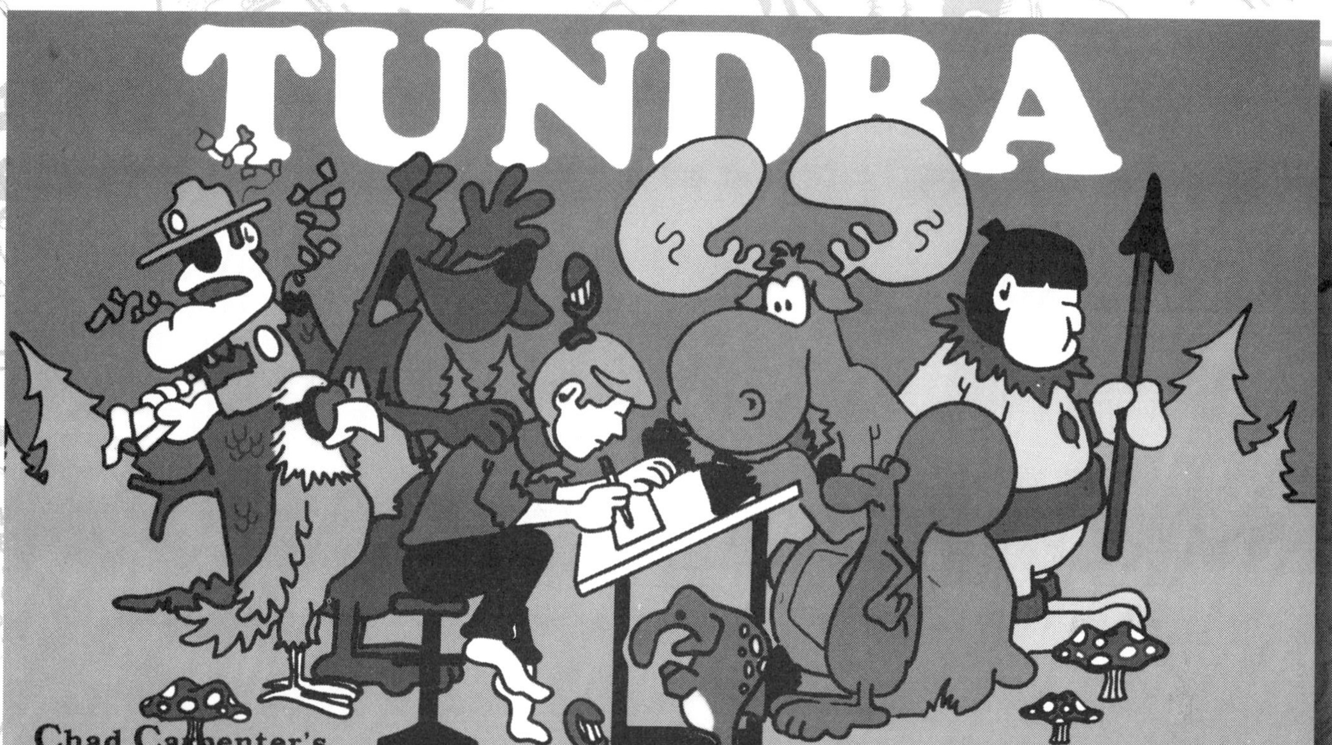
TUNDRA
Chad Carpenter's
CARTOONS FROM THE LAST FRONTIER

First Printing: February 1993

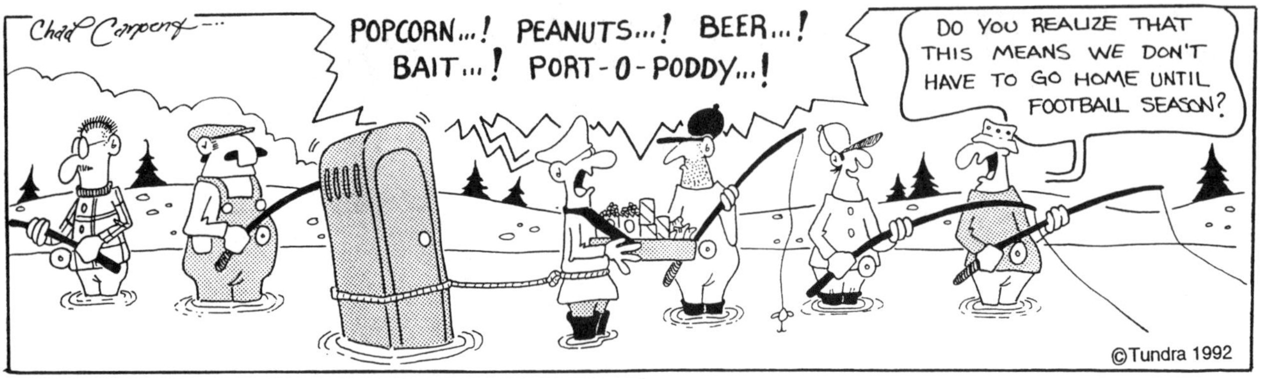
POPCORN...! PEANUTS...! BEER...! BAIT...! PORT-O-PODDY...!
DO YOU REALIZE THAT THIS MEANS WE DON'T HAVE TO GO HOME UNTIL FOOTBALL SEASON?
©Tundra 1992

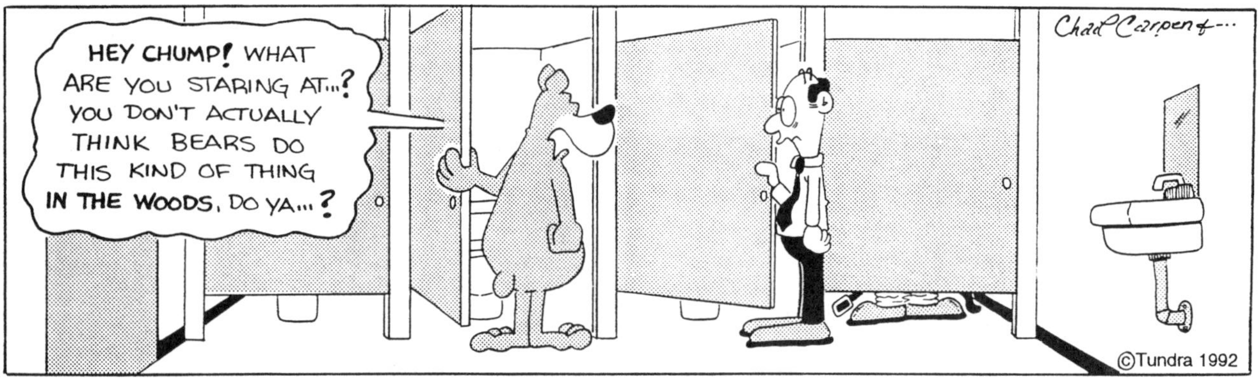
HEY CHUMP! WHAT ARE YOU STARING AT...? YOU DON'T ACTUALLY THINK BEARS DO THIS KIND OF THING IN THE WOODS, DO YA...?
©Tundra 1992

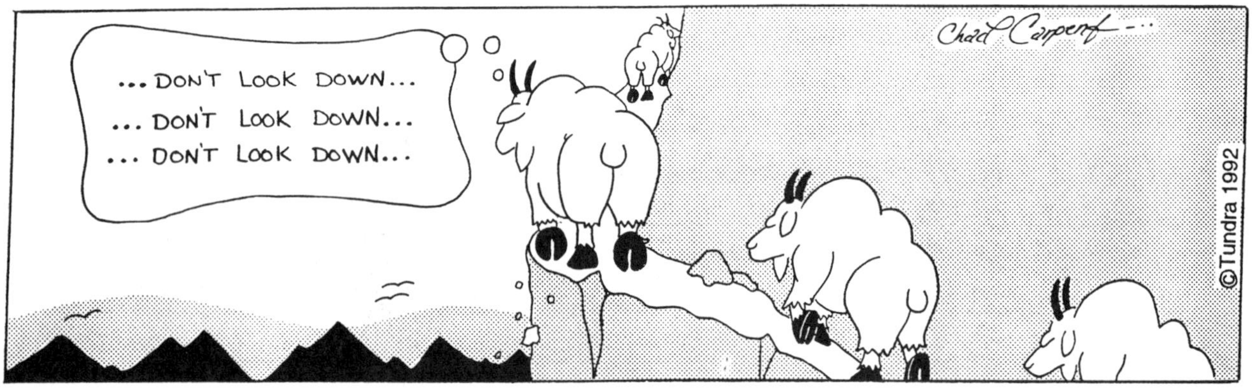
...DON'T LOOK DOWN...
...DON'T LOOK DOWN...
...DON'T LOOK DOWN...
©Tundra 1992

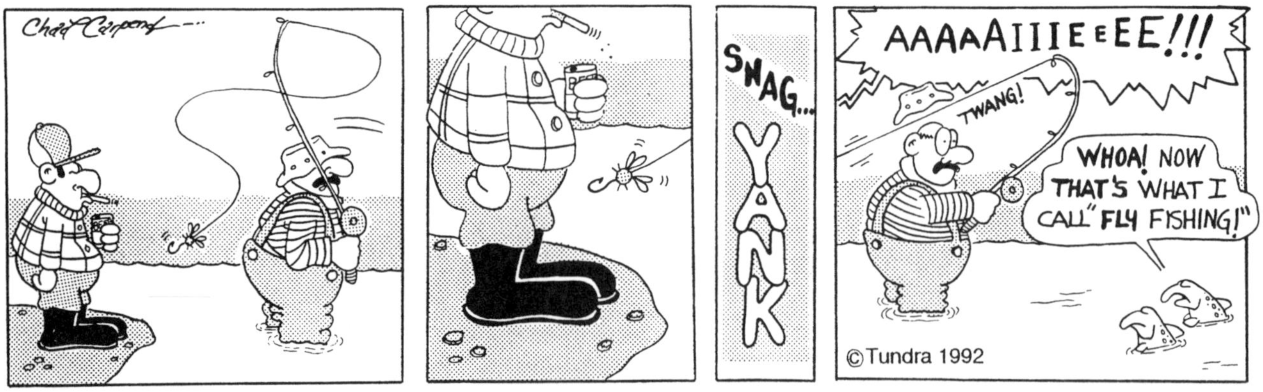
SNAG...
YANK
AAAAAIIIEEEE!!!
TWANG!
WHOA! NOW THAT'S WHAT I CALL "FLY FISHING!"
©Tundra 1992

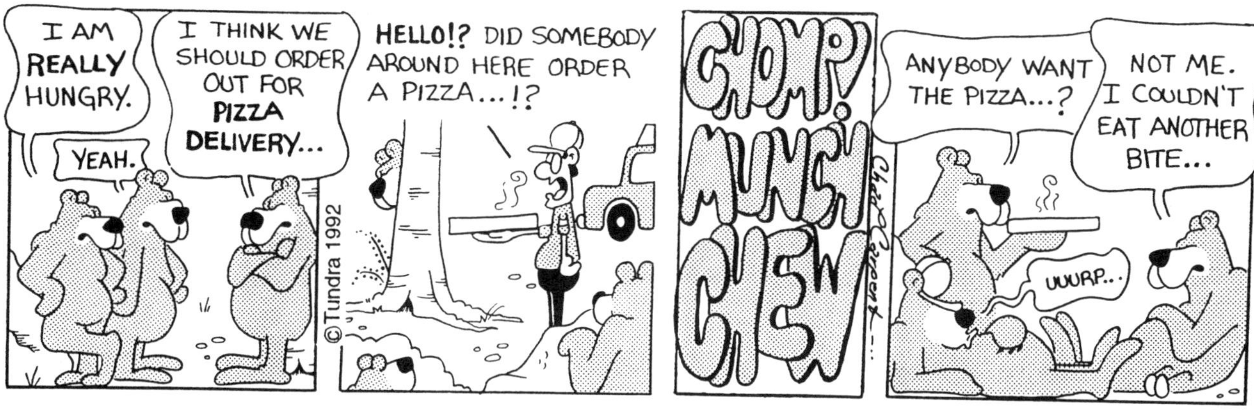
I AM REALLY HUNGRY.
YEAH.
I THINK WE SHOULD ORDER OUT FOR PIZZA DELIVERY...
©Tundra 1992
HELLO!? DID SOMEBODY AROUND HERE ORDER A PIZZA...!?
CHOMP! MUNCH CHEW
ANYBODY WANT THE PIZZA...?
NOT ME. I COULDN'T EAT ANOTHER BITE...
UUURP...

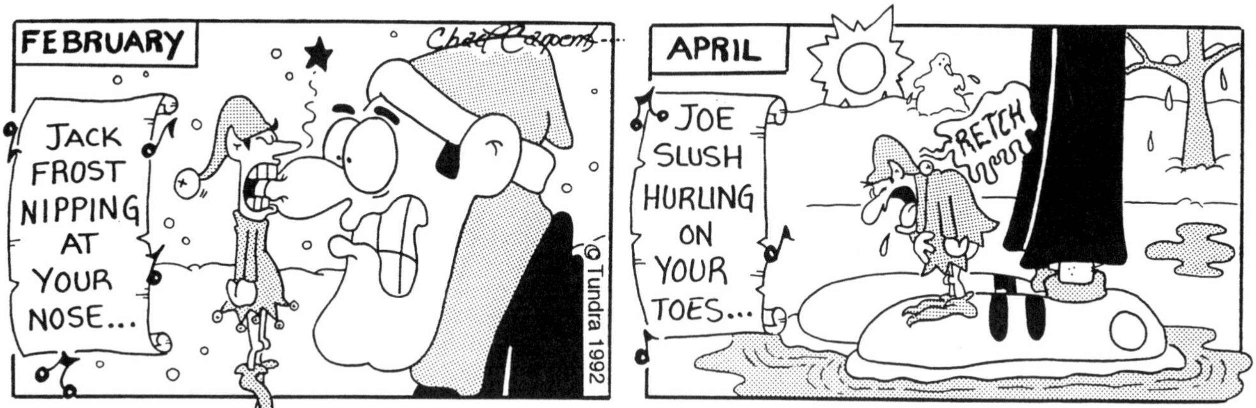
FEBRUARY
JACK FROST NIPPING AT YOUR NOSE...
©Tundra 1992
APRIL
JOE SLUSH HURLING ON YOUR TOES...
RETCH

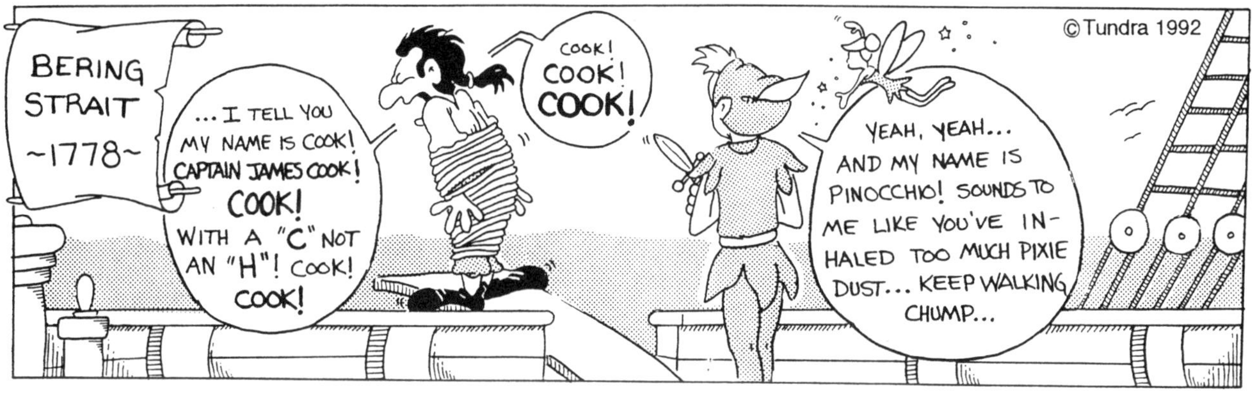
BERING STRAIT ~1778~
...I TELL YOU MY NAME IS COOK! CAPTAIN JAMES COOK! COOK! WITH A "C" NOT AN "H"! COOK! COOK!
COOK! COOK! COOK!
YEAH, YEAH... AND MY NAME IS PINOCCHIO! SOUNDS TO ME LIKE YOU'VE IN-HALED TOO MUCH PIXIE DUST... KEEP WALKING CHUMP...
©Tundra 1992

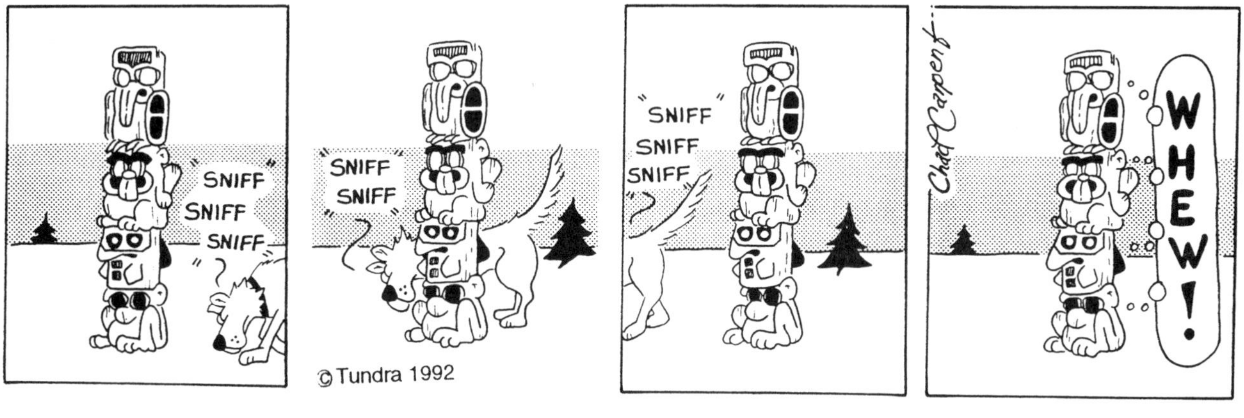
SNIFF SNIFF SNIFF
SNIFF SNIFF
©Tundra 1992
SNIFF SNIFF SNIFF
WHEW!

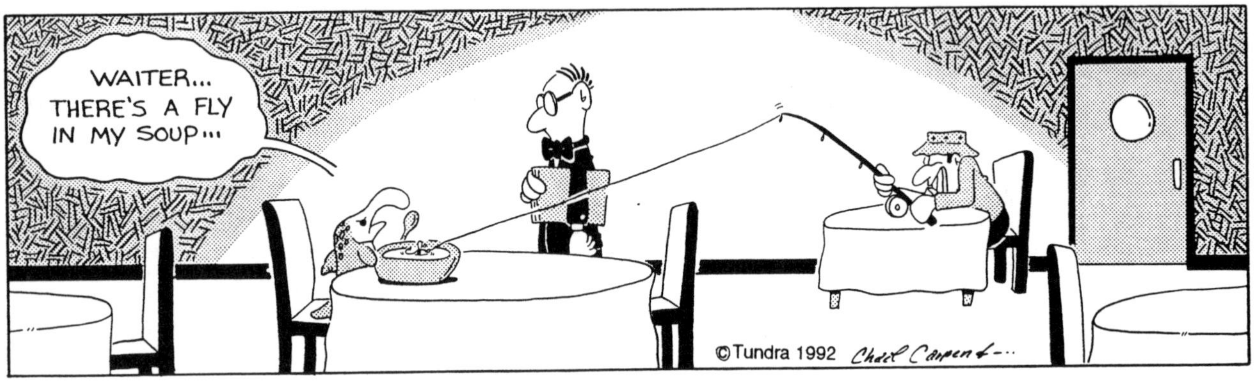
WAITER... THERE'S A FLY IN MY SOUP...
©Tundra 1992

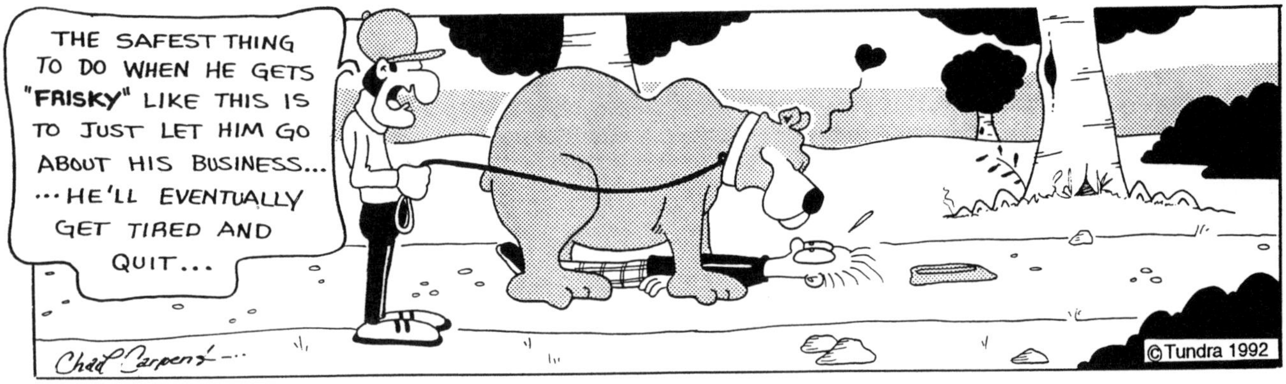
THE SAFEST THING TO DO WHEN HE GETS "FRISKY" LIKE THIS IS TO JUST LET HIM GO ABOUT HIS BUSINESS... ...HE'LL EVENTUALLY GET TIRED AND QUIT...
©Tundra 1992

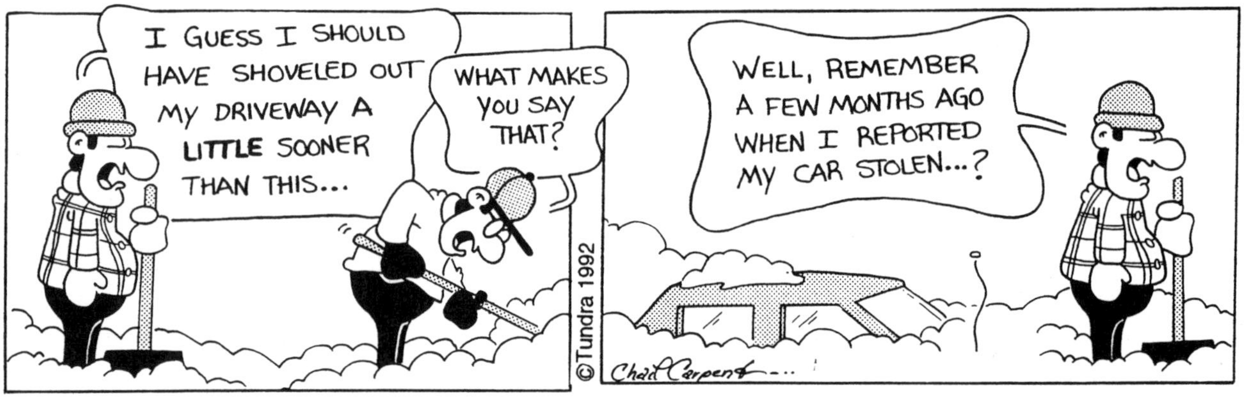
I GUESS I SHOULD HAVE SHOVELED OUT MY DRIVEWAY A LITTLE SOONER THAN THIS...
WHAT MAKES YOU SAY THAT?
WELL, REMEMBER A FEW MONTHS AGO WHEN I REPORTED MY CAR STOLEN...?
©Tundra 1992

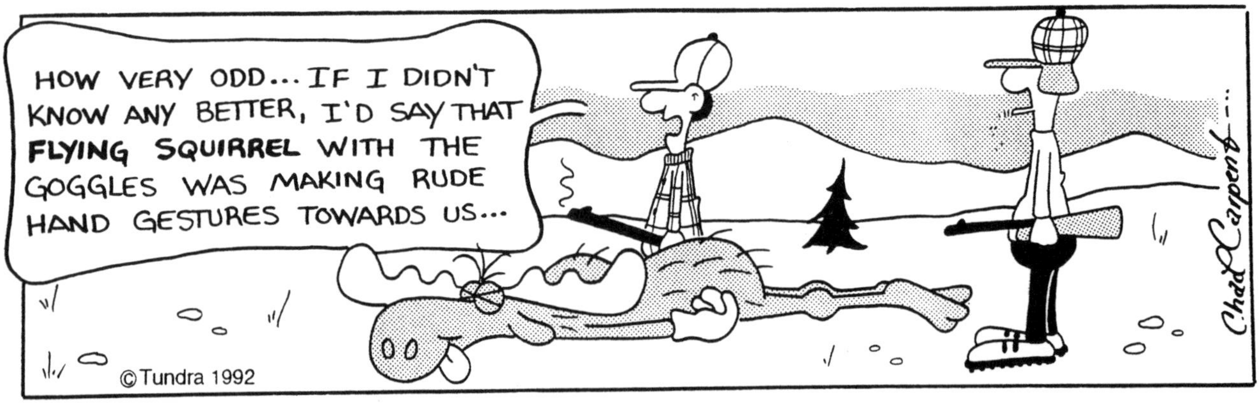
HOW VERY ODD... IF I DIDN'T KNOW ANY BETTER, I'D SAY THAT FLYING SQUIRREL WITH THE GOGGLES WAS MAKING RUDE HAND GESTURES TOWARDS US...
©Tundra 1992

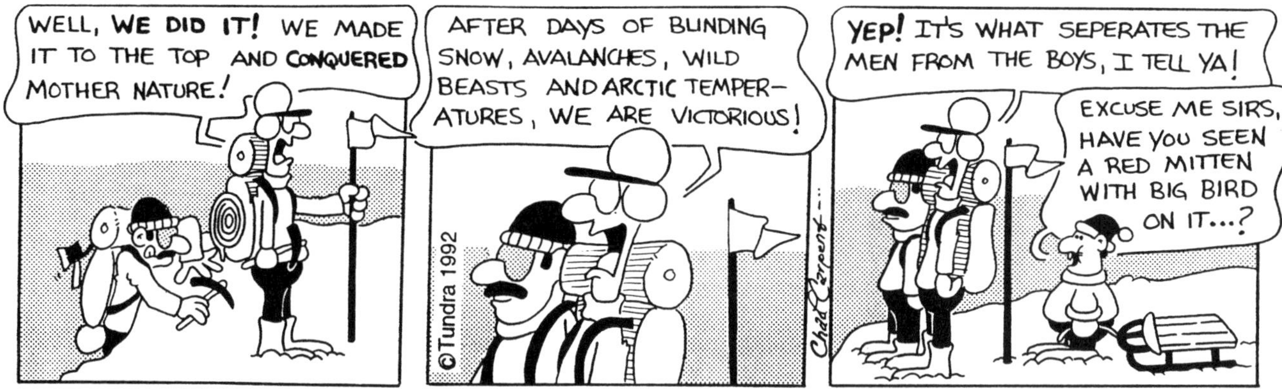
WELL, WE DID IT! WE MADE IT TO THE TOP AND CONQUERED MOTHER NATURE!
AFTER DAYS OF BLINDING SNOW, AVALANCHES, WILD BEASTS AND ARCTIC TEMPER-ATURES, WE ARE VICTORIOUS!
©Tundra 1992
YEP! IT'S WHAT SEPERATES THE MEN FROM THE BOYS, I TELL YA!
EXCUSE ME SIRS, HAVE YOU SEEN A RED MITTEN WITH BIG BIRD ON IT...?

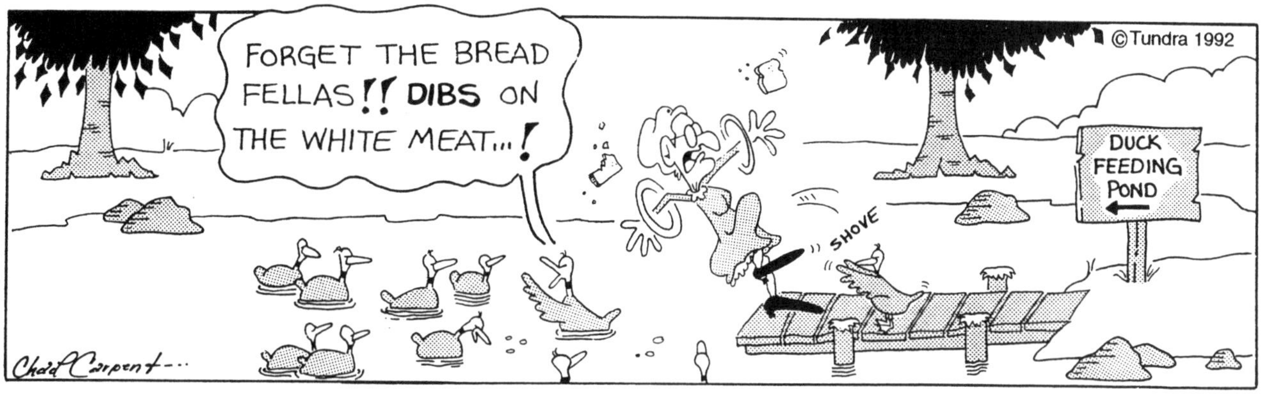
FORGET THE BREAD FELLAS!! DIBS ON THE WHITE MEAT...!
©Tundra 1992
SHOVE
DUCK FEEDING POND

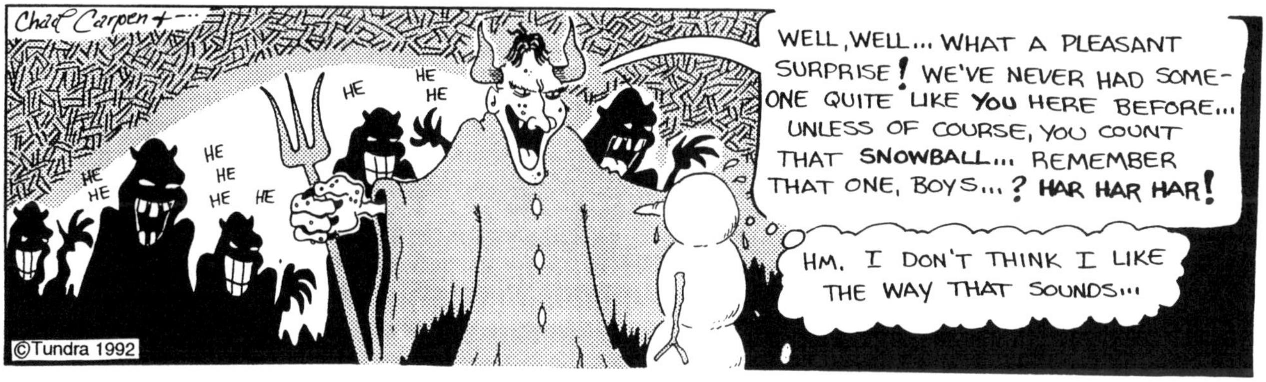
HE HE
HE HE
HE HE
HE HE HE
WELL, WELL... WHAT A PLEASANT SURPRISE! WE'VE NEVER HAD SOME-ONE QUITE LIKE YOU HERE BEFORE... UNLESS OF COURSE, YOU COUNT THAT SNOWBALL... REMEMBER THAT ONE, BOYS...? HAR HAR HAR!
HM. I DON'T THINK I LIKE THE WAY THAT SOUNDS...
©Tundra 1992

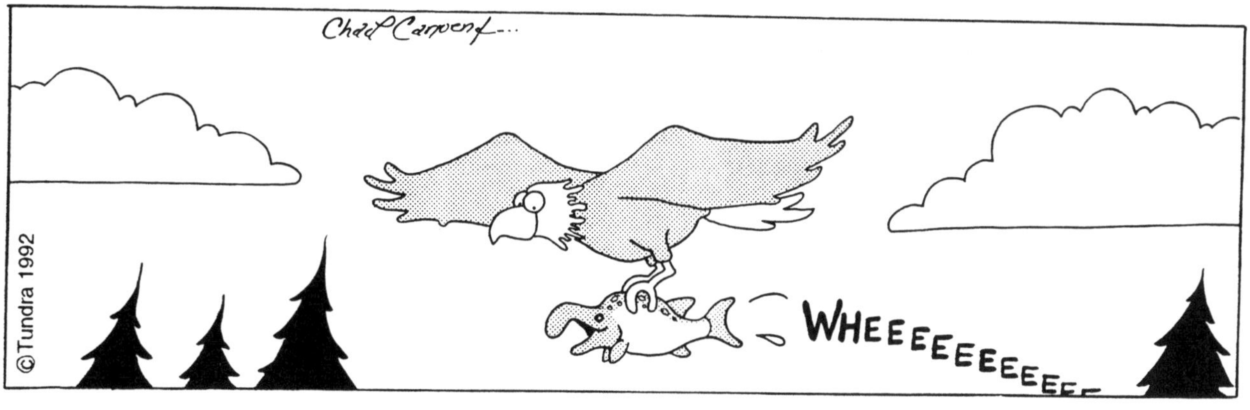
©Tundra 1992
WHEEEEEEEEEE

The MOOSE NUGGETS

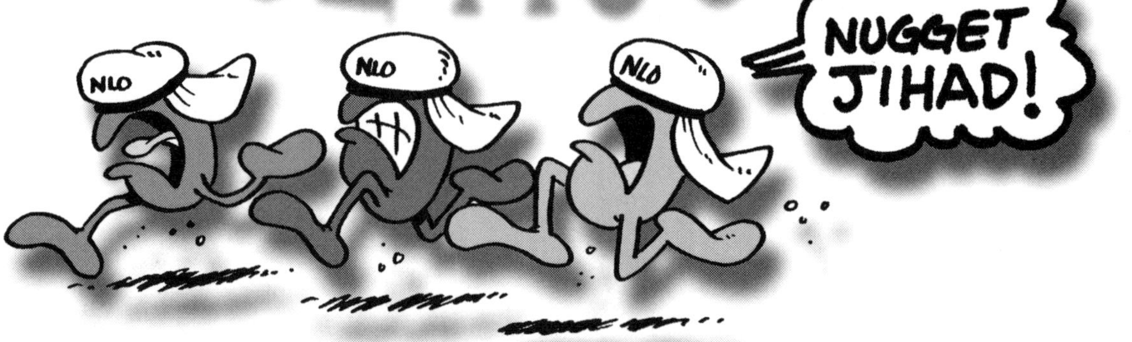
NLO
NLO
NLO
NUGGET JIHAD!

"FIRST CONTACT"

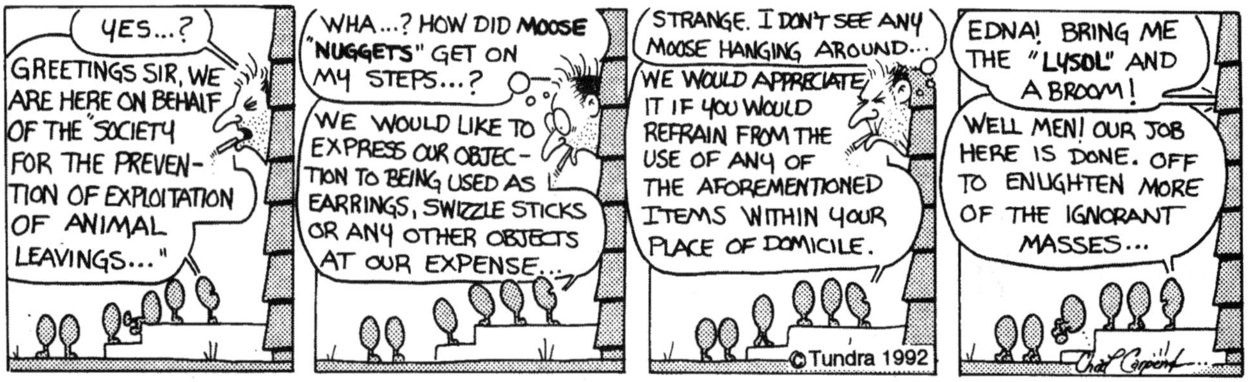
YES...?
GREETINGS SIR, WE ARE HERE ON BEHALF OF THE "SOCIETY FOR THE PREVENTION OF EXPLOITATION OF ANIMAL LEAVINGS..."
WHA...? HOW DID MOOSE "NUGGETS" GET ON MY STEPS...?
WE WOULD LIKE TO EXPRESS OUR OBJECTION TO BEING USED AS EARRINGS, SWIZZLE STICKS OR ANY OTHER OBJECTS AT OUR EXPENSE...
STRANGE. I DON'T SEE ANY MOOSE HANGING AROUND...
WE WOULD APPRECIATE IT IF YOU WOULD REFRAIN FROM THE USE OF ANY OF THE AFOREMENTIONED ITEMS WITHIN YOUR PLACE OF DOMICILE.
©Tundra 1992
EDNA! BRING ME THE "LYSOL" AND A BROOM!
WELL MEN! OUR JOB HERE IS DONE. OFF TO ENLIGHTEN MORE OF THE IGNORANT MASSES...

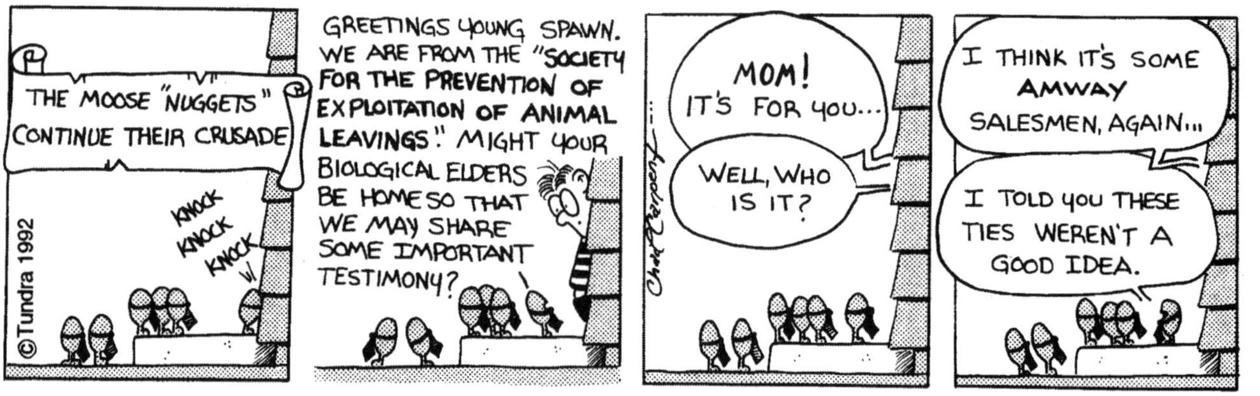
THE MOOSE "NUGGETS" CONTINUE THEIR CRUSADE
KNOCK
KNOCK
KNOCK
©Tundra 1992
GREETINGS YOUNG SPAWN. WE ARE FROM THE "SOCIETY FOR THE PREVENTION OF EXPLOITATION OF ANIMAL LEAVINGS." MIGHT YOUR BIOLOGICAL ELDERS BE HOME SO THAT WE MAY SHARE SOME IMPORTANT TESTIMONY?
MOM! IT'S FOR YOU...
WELL, WHO IS IT?
I THINK IT'S SOME AMWAY SALESMEN, AGAIN...
I TOLD YOU THESE TIES WEREN'T A GOOD IDEA.

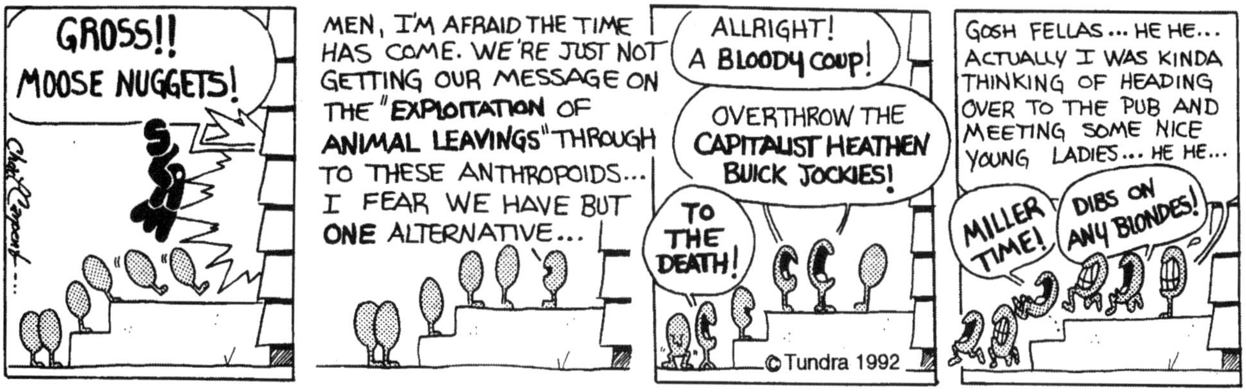
GROSS!! MOOSE NUGGETS!
MEN, I'M AFRAID THE TIME HAS COME. WE'RE JUST NOT GETTING OUR MESSAGE ON THE "EXPLOITATION OF ANIMAL LEAVINGS" THROUGH TO THESE ANTHROPOIDS... I FEAR WE HAVE BUT ONE ALTERNATIVE...
ALLRIGHT! A BLOODY COUP!
OVERTHROW THE CAPITALIST HEATHEN BUICK JOCKIES!
TO THE DEATH!
©Tundra 1992
GOSH FELLAS... HE HE... ACTUALLY I WAS KINDA THINKING OF HEADING OVER TO THE PUB AND MEETING SOME NICE YOUNG LADIES... HE HE...
MILLER TIME!
DIBS ON ANY BLONDES!

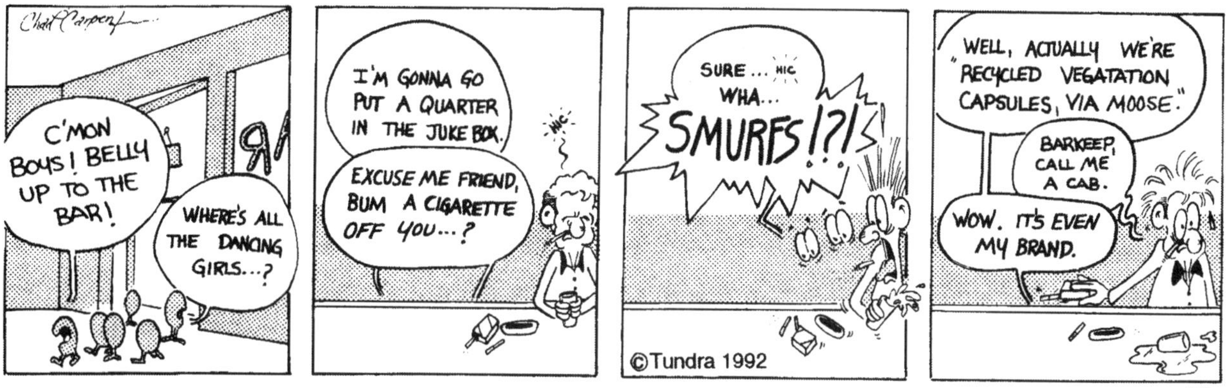
C'MON BOYS! BELLY UP TO THE BAR!
WHERE'S ALL THE DANCING GIRLS...?
I'M GONNA GO PUT A QUARTER IN THE JUKE BOX.
EXCUSE ME FRIEND, BUM A CIGARETTE OFF YOU...?
SURE... HIC WHA...
SMURFS!?!
©Tundra 1992
"WELL, ACTUALLY WE'RE "RECYCLED VEGATATION CAPSULES, VIA MOOSE."
BARKEEP, CALL ME A CAB.
WOW. IT'S EVEN MY BRAND.

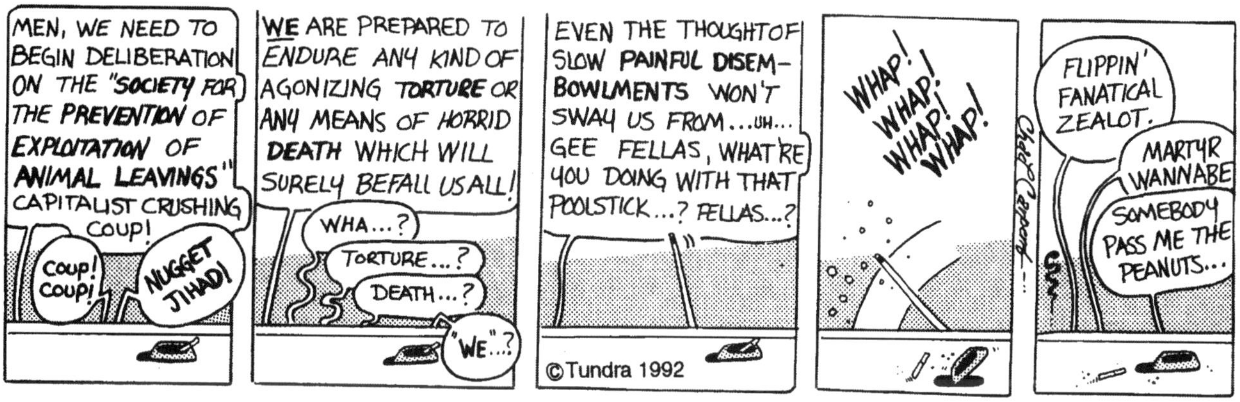
MEN, WE NEED TO BEGIN DELIBERATION ON THE "SOCIETY FOR THE PREVENTION OF EXPLOITATION OF ANIMAL LEAVINGS" CAPITALIST CRUSHING COUP!
COUP! COUP!
NUGGET JIHAD!
WE ARE PREPARED TO ENDURE ANY KIND OF AGONIZING TORTURE OR ANY MEANS OF HORRID DEATH WHICH WILL SURELY BEFALL US ALL!
WHA...?
TORTURE...?
DEATH...?
"WE"...?
EVEN THE THOUGHT OF SLOW PAINFUL DISEM-BOWLMENTS WON'T SWAY US FROM...UH... GEE FELLAS, WHAT'RE YOU DOING WITH THAT POOLSTICK...? FELLAS...?
©Tundra 1992
WHAP! WHAP! WHAP! WHAP!
FLIPPIN' FANATICAL ZEALOT.
MARTYR WANNABE
SOMEBODY PASS ME THE PEANUTS...

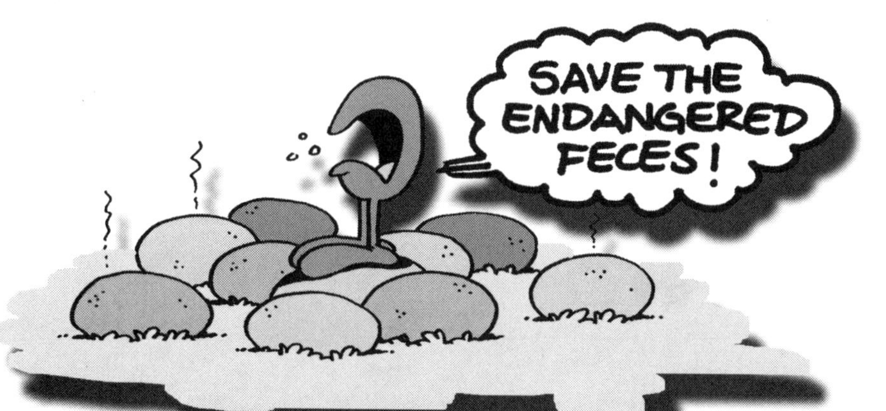
SAVE THE ENDANGERED FECES!

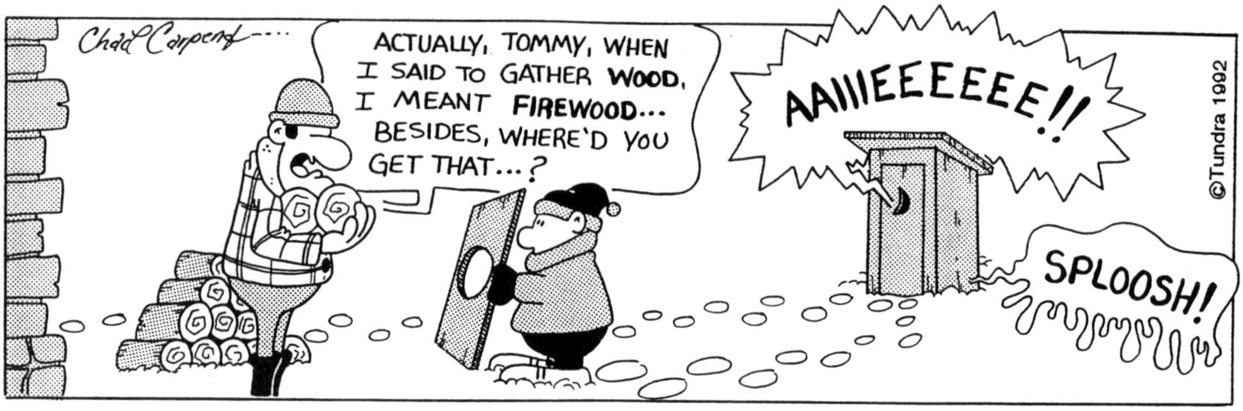

Chad Carpenter
ACTUALLY, TOMMY, WHEN I SAID TO GATHER WOOD, I MEANT FIREWOOD... BESIDES, WHERE'D YOU GET THAT...?
AAIIIEEEEEE!!
SPLOOSH!
©Tundra 1992

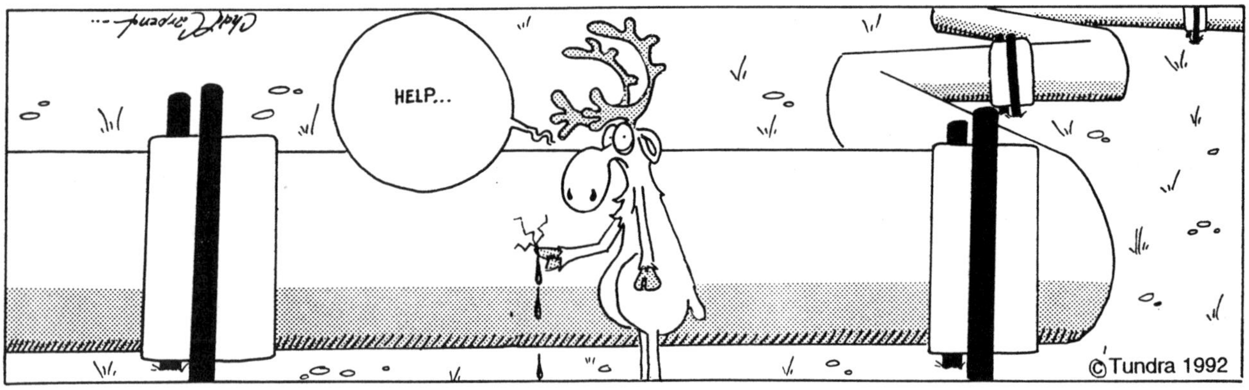

HELP...
©Tundra 1992

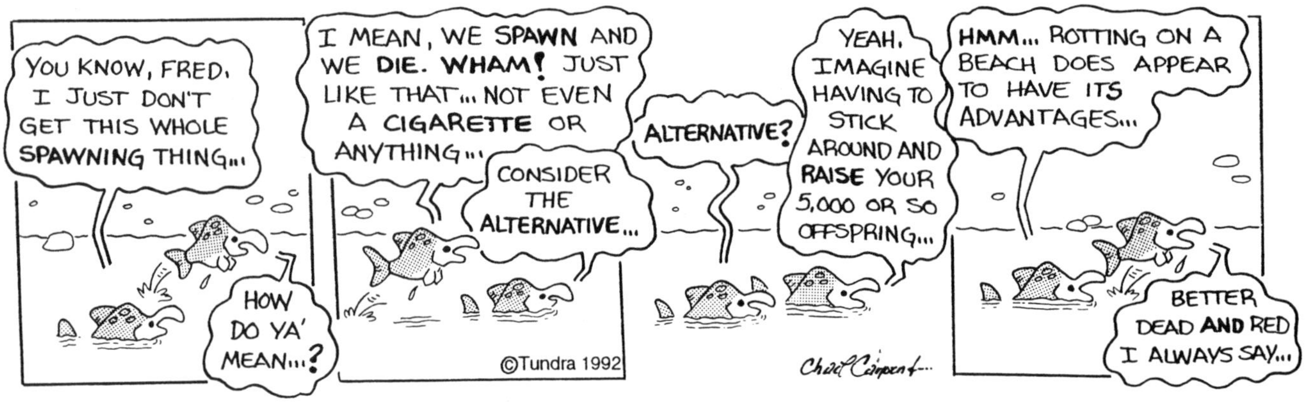

YOU KNOW, FRED, I JUST DON'T GET THIS WHOLE SPAWNING THING...
HOW DO YA' MEAN...?
I MEAN, WE SPAWN AND WE DIE. WHAM! JUST LIKE THAT... NOT EVEN A CIGARETTE OR ANYTHING...
CONSIDER THE ALTERNATIVE...
©Tundra 1992
ALTERNATIVE?
YEAH, IMAGINE HAVING TO STICK AROUND AND RAISE YOUR 5,000 OR SO OFFSPRING...
Chad Carpenter
HMM... ROTTING ON A BEACH DOES APPEAR TO HAVE ITS ADVANTAGES...
BETTER DEAD AND RED I ALWAYS SAY...

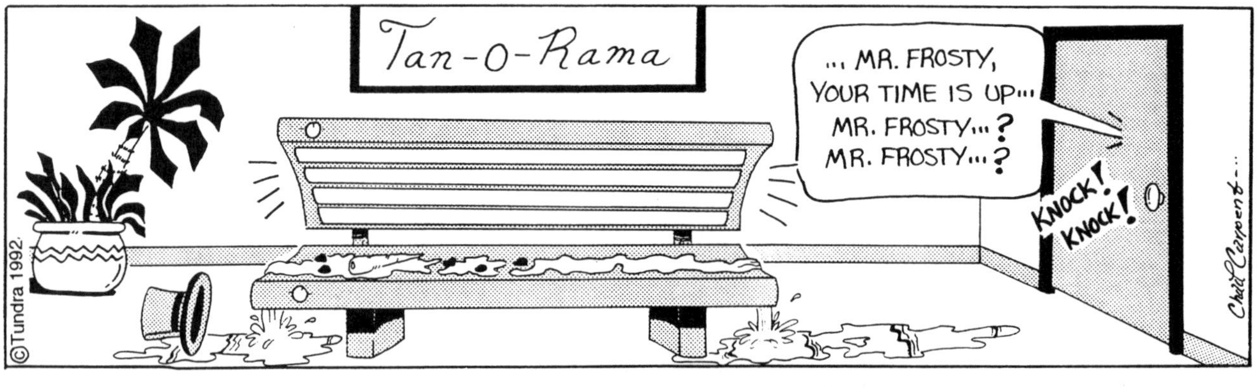

Tan-O-Rama
...MR. FROSTY, YOUR TIME IS UP... MR. FROSTY...? MR. FROSTY...?
KNOCK! KNOCK!
Chad Carpenter
©Tundra 1992

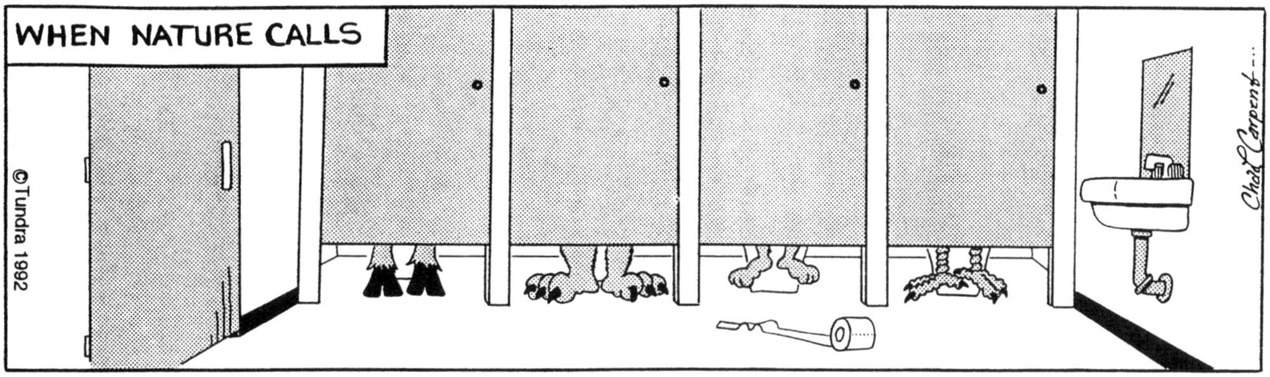
WHEN NATURE CALLS
©Tundra 1992
Chad Carpenter

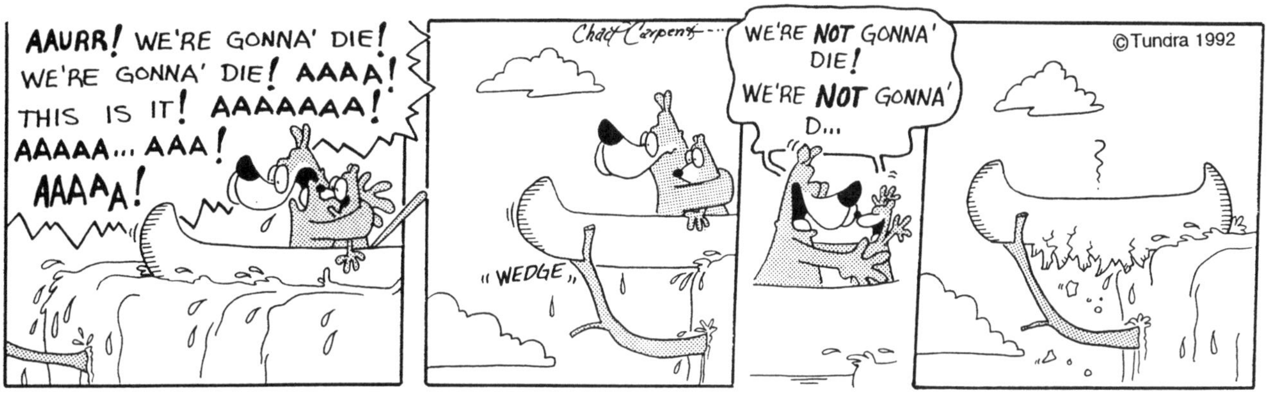
AAURR! WE'RE GONNA' DIE! WE'RE GONNA' DIE! AAAA! THIS IS IT! AAAAAAA! AAAAA... AAA! AAAAA!
"WEDGE"
WE'RE NOT GONNA' DIE! WE'RE NOT GONNA' D...
©Tundra 1992
Chad Carpenter

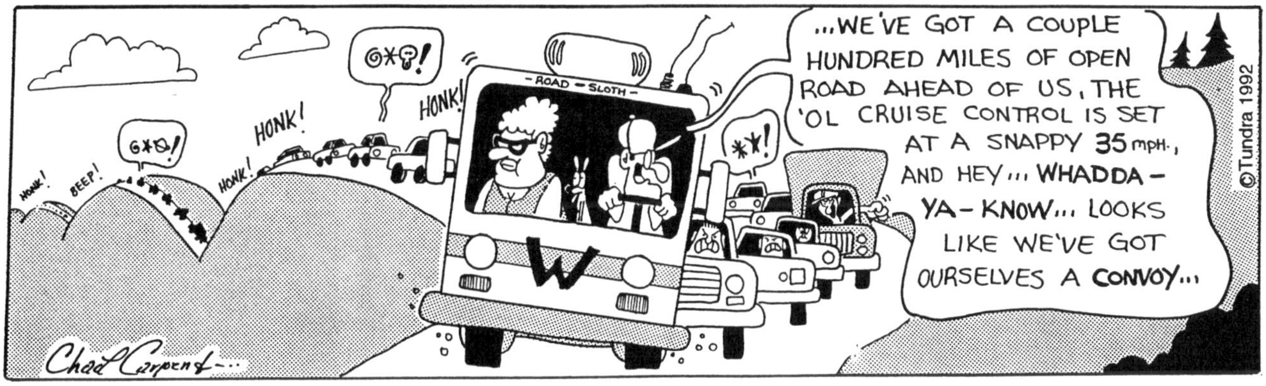
HONK! BEEP! HONK! HONK! HONK!
G*@!
G*@!
ROAD SLOTH
**!
...WE'VE GOT A COUPLE HUNDRED MILES OF OPEN ROAD AHEAD OF US, THE 'OL CRUISE CONTROL IS SET AT A SNAPPY 35 mph., AND HEY... WHADDA-YA-KNOW... LOOKS LIKE WE'VE GOT OURSELVES A CONVOY...
©Tundra 1992
Chad Carpenter

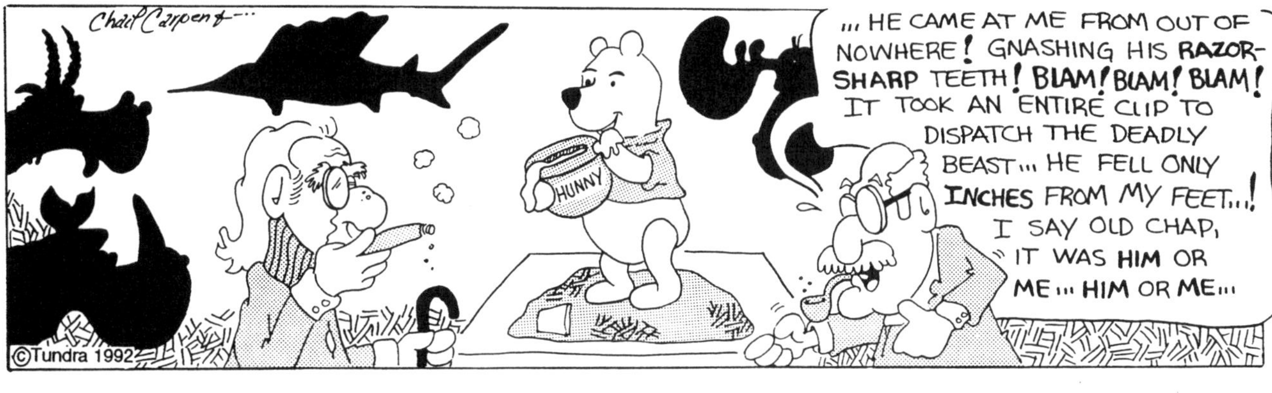
HUNNY
...HE CAME AT ME FROM OUT OF NOWHERE! GNASHING HIS RAZOR-SHARP TEETH! BLAM! BLAM! BLAM! IT TOOK AN ENTIRE CLIP TO DISPATCH THE DEADLY BEAST... HE FELL ONLY INCHES FROM MY FEET...! I SAY OLD CHAP, IT WAS HIM OR ME... HIM OR ME...
©Tundra 1992
Chad Carpenter

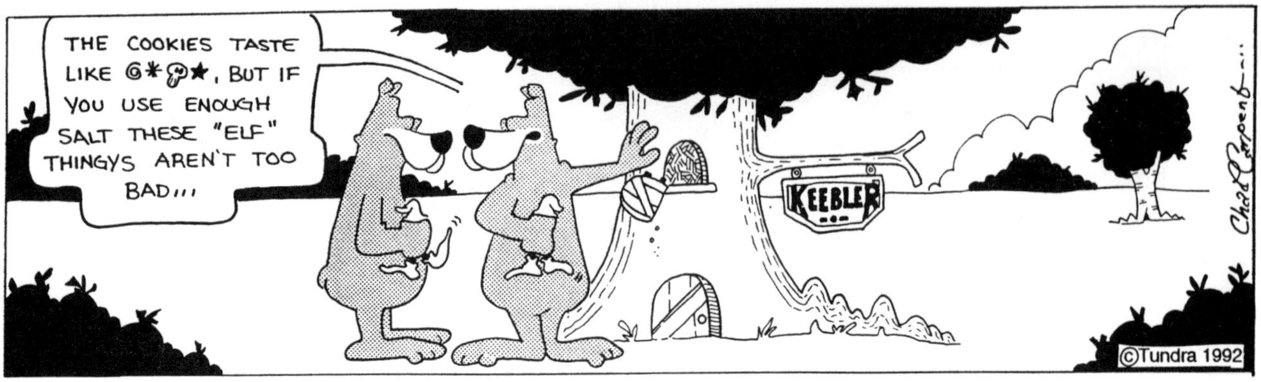
THE COOKIES TASTE LIKE @*?★, BUT IF YOU USE ENOUGH SALT THESE "ELF" THINGYS AREN'T TOO BAD...
KEEBLER
©Tundra 1992

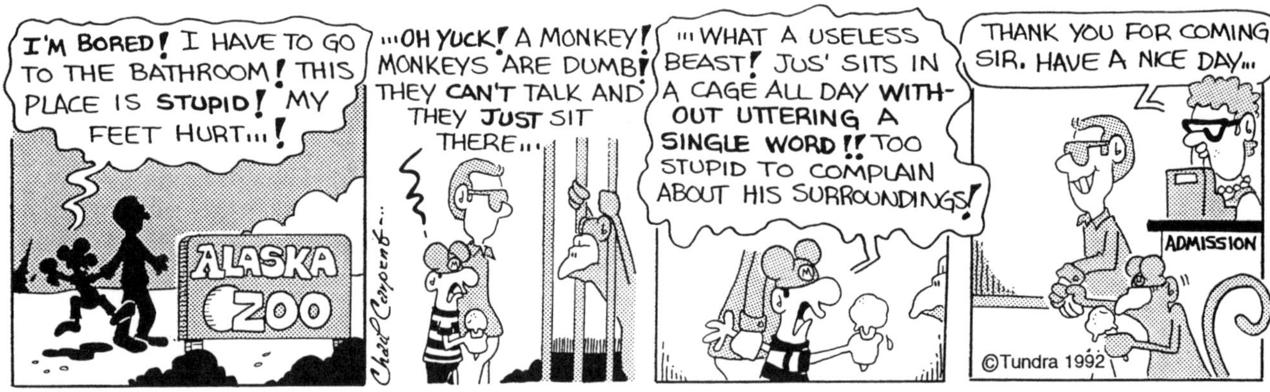
I'M BORED! I HAVE TO GO TO THE BATHROOM! THIS PLACE IS STUPID! MY FEET HURT...!
ALASKA ZOO
...OH YUCK! A MONKEY! MONKEYS ARE DUMB! THEY CAN'T TALK AND THEY JUST SIT THERE...
...WHAT A USELESS BEAST! JUS' SITS IN A CAGE ALL DAY WITHOUT UTTERING A SINGLE WORD!! TOO STUPID TO COMPLAIN ABOUT HIS SURROUNDINGS!
THANK YOU FOR COMING SIR. HAVE A NICE DAY...
ADMISSION
©Tundra 1992

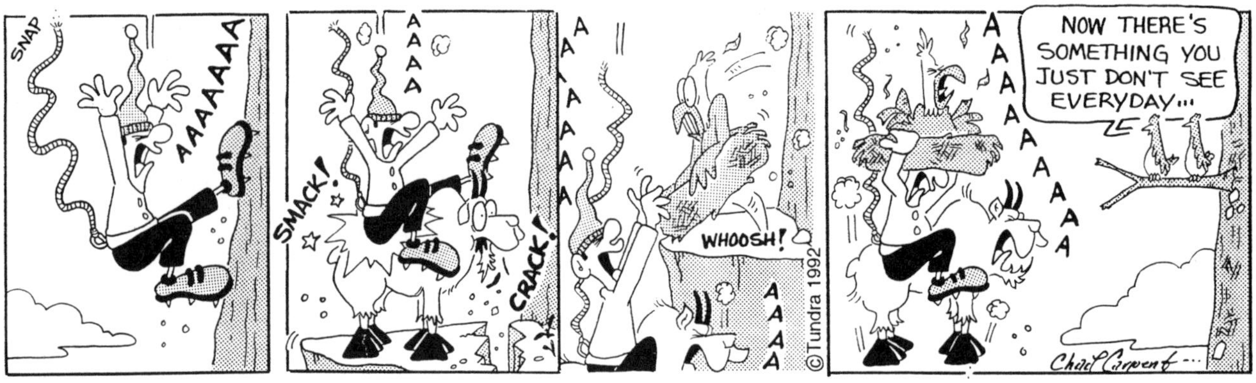
SNAP
AAAAAAA
SMACK!
CRACK!
WHOOSH!
©Tundra 1992
NOW THERE'S SOMETHING YOU JUST DON'T SEE EVERYDAY...

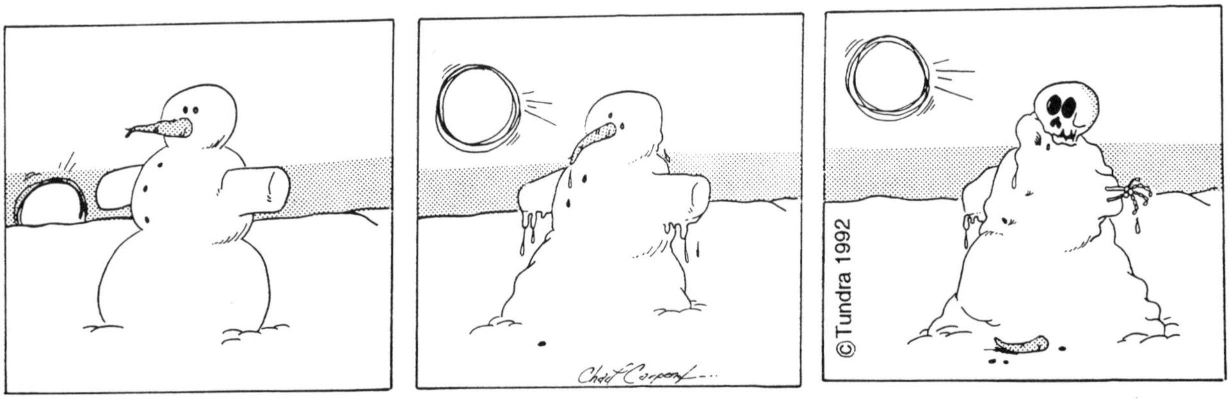
©Tundra 1992

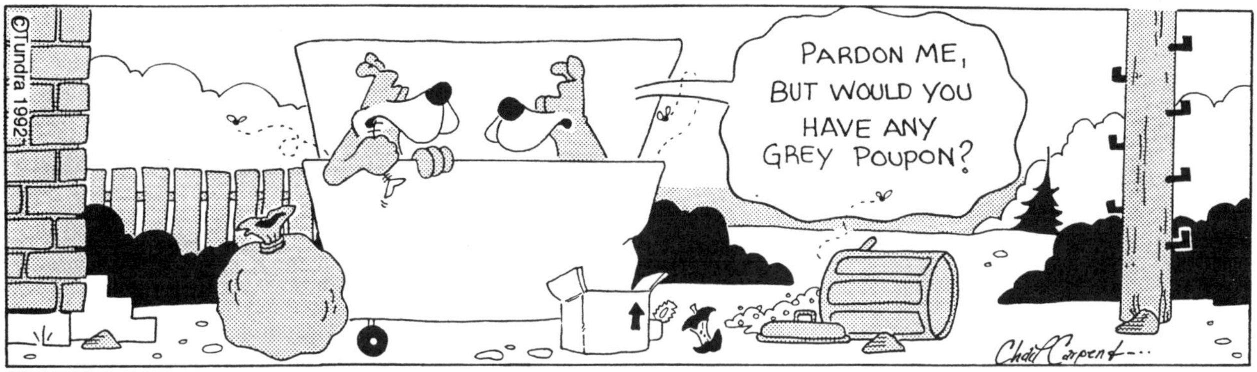
©Tundra 1992
PARDON ME, BUT WOULD YOU HAVE ANY GREY POUPON?
Chad Carpent...

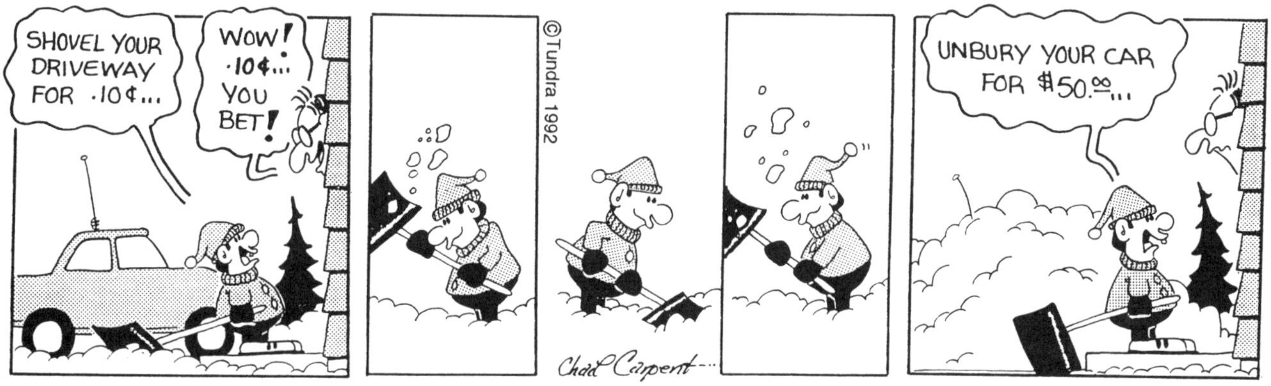
SHOVEL YOUR DRIVEWAY FOR .10¢...
WOW! .10¢... YOU BET!
©Tundra 1992
UNBURY YOUR CAR FOR $50.00...
Chad Carpent...

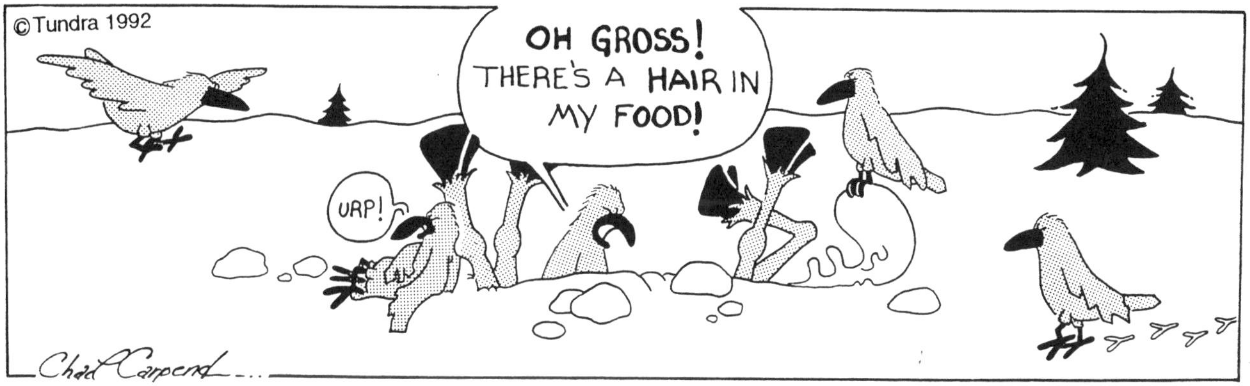
©Tundra 1992
OH GROSS! THERE'S A HAIR IN MY FOOD!
URP!
Chad Carpent...

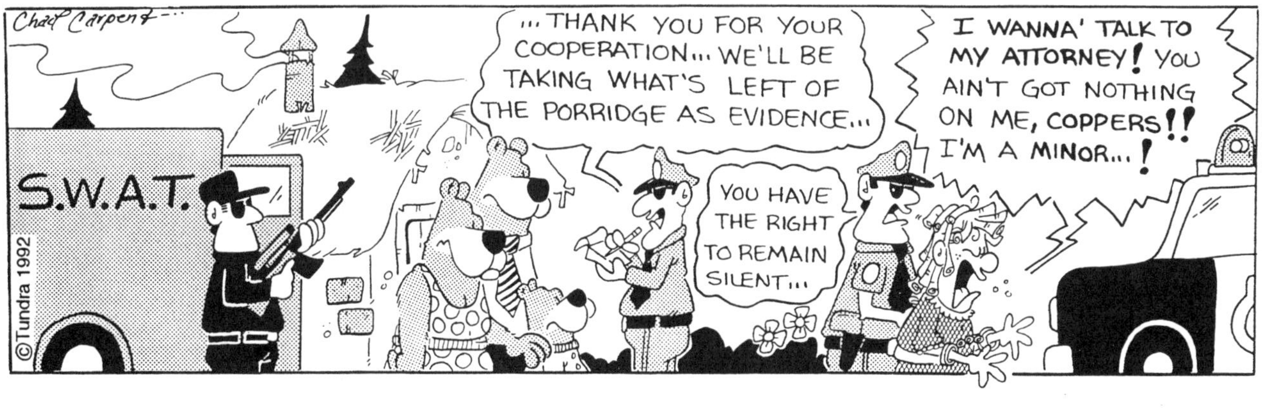
Chad Carpent...
S.W.A.T.
©Tundra 1992
...THANK YOU FOR YOUR COOPERATION... WE'LL BE TAKING WHAT'S LEFT OF THE PORRIDGE AS EVIDENCE...
YOU HAVE THE RIGHT TO REMAIN SILENT...
I WANNA' TALK TO MY ATTORNEY! YOU AIN'T GOT NOTHING ON ME, COPPERS!! I'M A MINOR...!

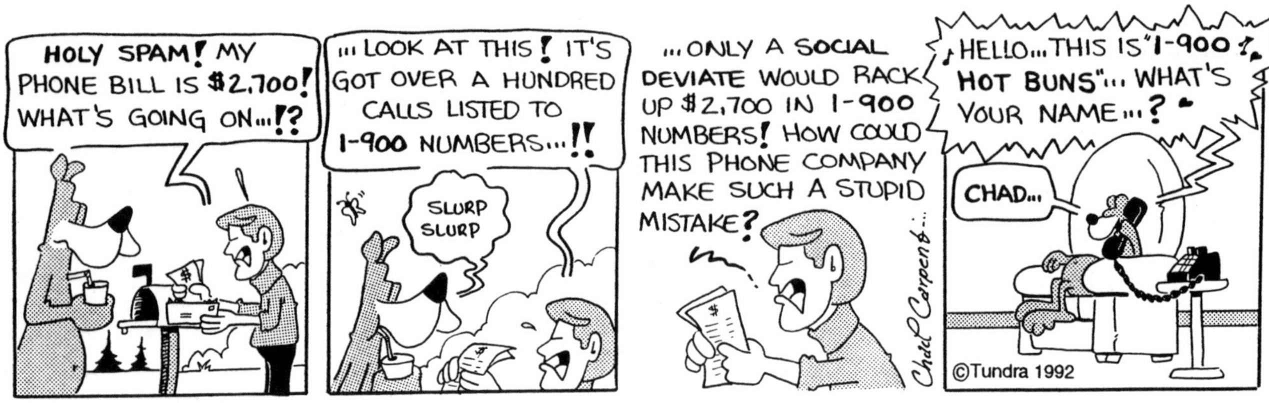
HOLY SPAM! MY PHONE BILL IS $2,700! WHAT'S GOING ON...!?
...LOOK AT THIS! IT'S GOT OVER A HUNDRED CALLS LISTED TO 1-900 NUMBERS...!!
SLURP SLURP
...ONLY A SOCIAL DEVIATE WOULD RACK UP $2,700 IN 1-900 NUMBERS! HOW COULD THIS PHONE COMPANY MAKE SUCH A STUPID MISTAKE?
HELLO...THIS IS "1-900 HOT BUNS"... WHAT'S YOUR NAME...?
CHAD...
©Tundra 1992

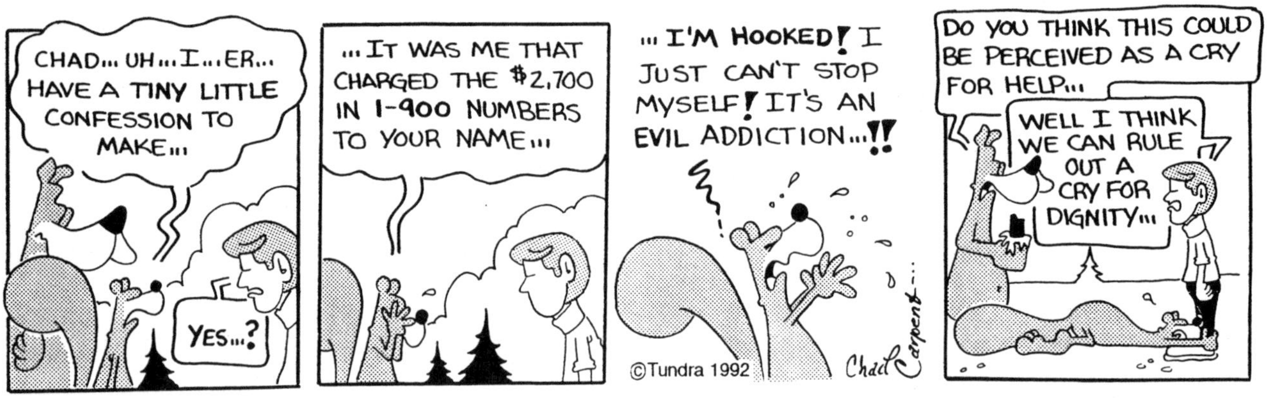
CHAD... UH...I...ER... HAVE A TINY LITTLE CONFESSION TO MAKE...
YES...?
...IT WAS ME THAT CHARGED THE $2,700 IN 1-900 NUMBERS TO YOUR NAME...
...I'M HOOKED! I JUST CAN'T STOP MYSELF! IT'S AN EVIL ADDICTION...!!
©Tundra 1992
DO YOU THINK THIS COULD BE PERCEIVED AS A CRY FOR HELP...
WELL I THINK WE CAN RULE OUT A CRY FOR DIGNITY...

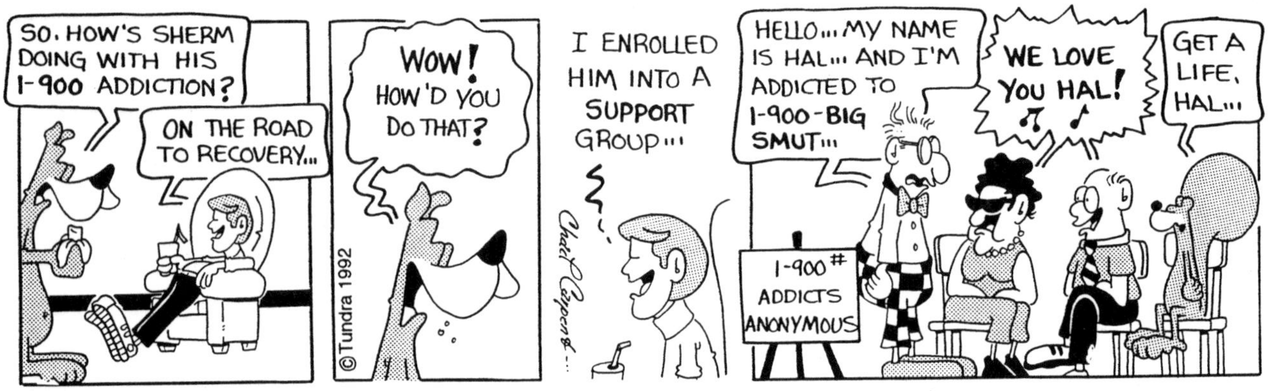
SO, HOW'S SHERM DOING WITH HIS 1-900 ADDICTION?
ON THE ROAD TO RECOVERY...
WOW! HOW'D YOU DO THAT?
©Tundra 1992
I ENROLLED HIM INTO A SUPPORT GROUP...
HELLO... MY NAME IS HAL... AND I'M ADDICTED TO 1-900-BIG SMUT...
WE LOVE YOU HAL!
GET A LIFE, HAL...
1-900 # ADDICTS ANONYMOUS

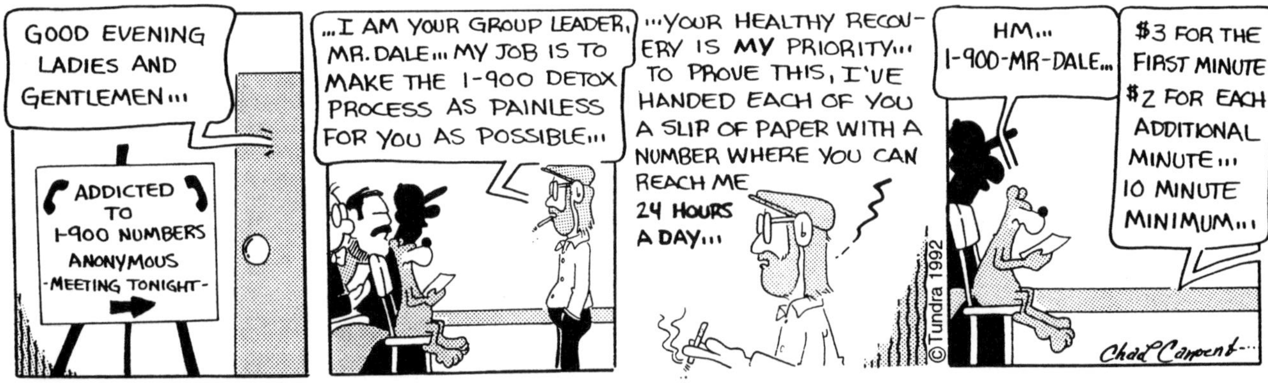
GOOD EVENING LADIES AND GENTLEMEN...
ADDICTED TO 1-900 NUMBERS ANONYMOUS -MEETING TONIGHT-
...I AM YOUR GROUP LEADER, MR. DALE... MY JOB IS TO MAKE THE 1-900 DETOX PROCESS AS PAINLESS FOR YOU AS POSSIBLE...
...YOUR HEALTHY RECOVERY IS MY PRIORITY... TO PROVE THIS, I'VE HANDED EACH OF YOU A SLIP OF PAPER WITH A NUMBER WHERE YOU CAN REACH ME 24 HOURS A DAY...
©Tundra 1992
HM... 1-900-MR-DALE...
$3 FOR THE FIRST MINUTE $2 FOR EACH ADDITIONAL MINUTE... 10 MINUTE MINIMUM...

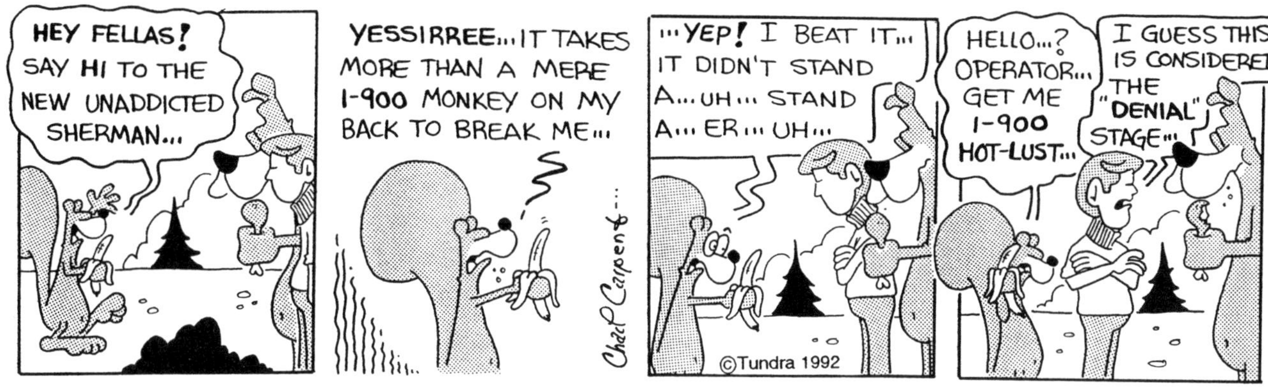
HEY FELLAS! SAY HI TO THE NEW UNADDICTED SHERMAN...
YESSIRREE... IT TAKES MORE THAN A MERE 1-900 MONKEY ON MY BACK TO BREAK ME...
Chad Carpenter...
...YEP! I BEAT IT... IT DIDN'T STAND A... UH... STAND A... ER... UH...
©Tundra 1992
HELLO...? OPERATOR... GET ME 1-900 HOT-LUST...
I GUESS THIS IS CONSIDERED THE "DENIAL" STAGE...

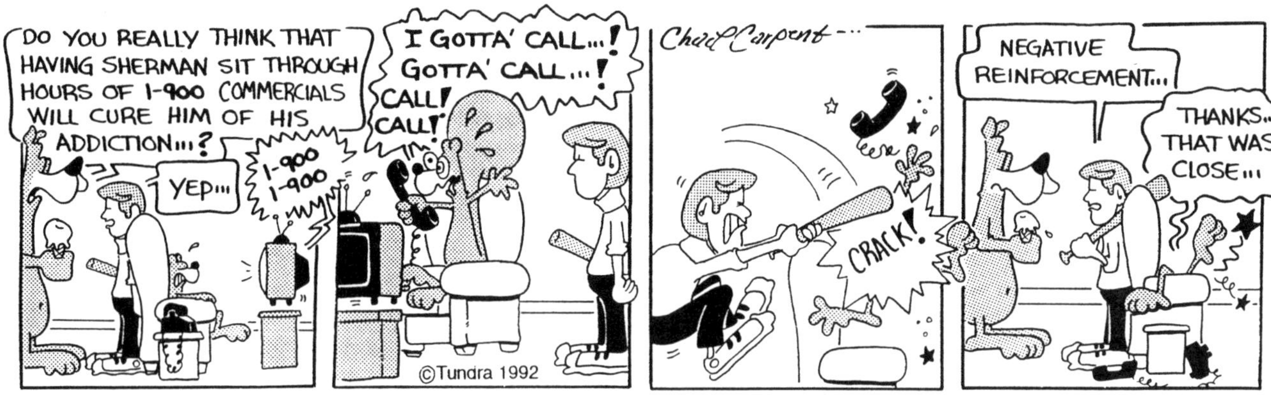
DO YOU REALLY THINK THAT HAVING SHERMAN SIT THROUGH HOURS OF 1-900 COMMERCIALS WILL CURE HIM OF HIS ADDICTION...?
YEP...
1-900 1-900
I GOTTA' CALL...! GOTTA' CALL...!
CALL! CALL!
©Tundra 1992
Chad Carpenter...
CRACK!
NEGATIVE REINFORCEMENT...
THANKS... THAT WAS CLOSE...

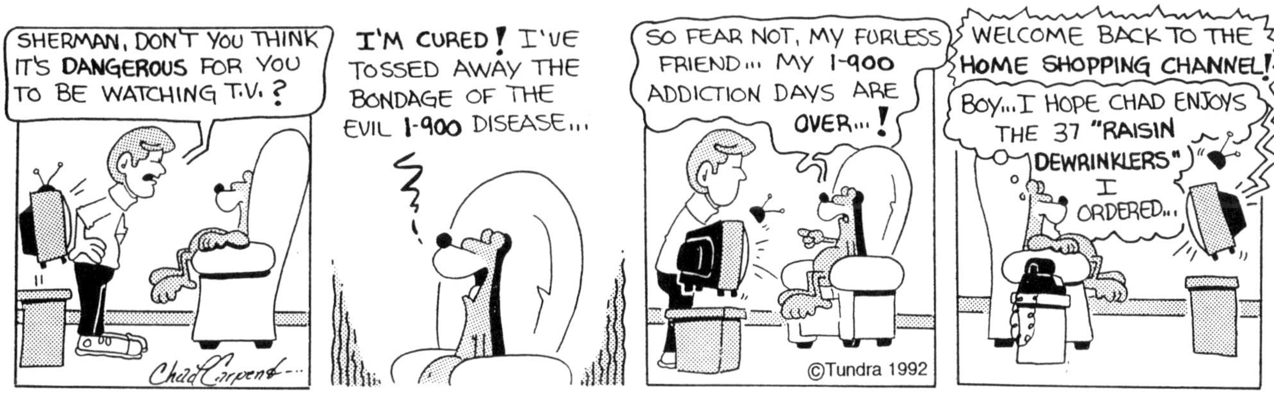
SHERMAN, DON'T YOU THINK IT'S DANGEROUS FOR YOU TO BE WATCHING T.V.?
Chad Carpenter...
I'M CURED! I'VE TOSSED AWAY THE BONDAGE OF THE EVIL 1-900 DISEASE...
SO FEAR NOT, MY FURLESS FRIEND... MY 1-900 ADDICTION DAYS ARE OVER...!
©Tundra 1992
WELCOME BACK TO THE HOME SHOPPING CHANNEL!
BOY... I HOPE CHAD ENJOYS THE 37 "RAISIN DEWRINKLERS" I ORDERED...

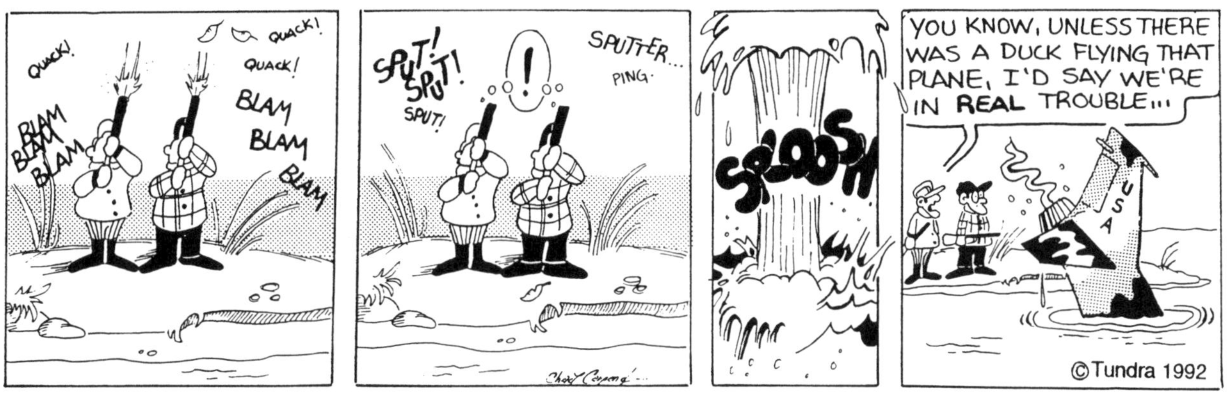
QUACK! QUACK! QUACK!
BLAM BLAM BLAM
BLAM BLAM BLAM
SPUT! SPUT! SPUT!
!
SPUTTER...
PING
Chad Carpenter...
SPLOOSH
YOU KNOW, UNLESS THERE WAS A DUCK FLYING THAT PLANE, I'D SAY WE'RE IN REAL TROUBLE...
USA
©Tundra 1992

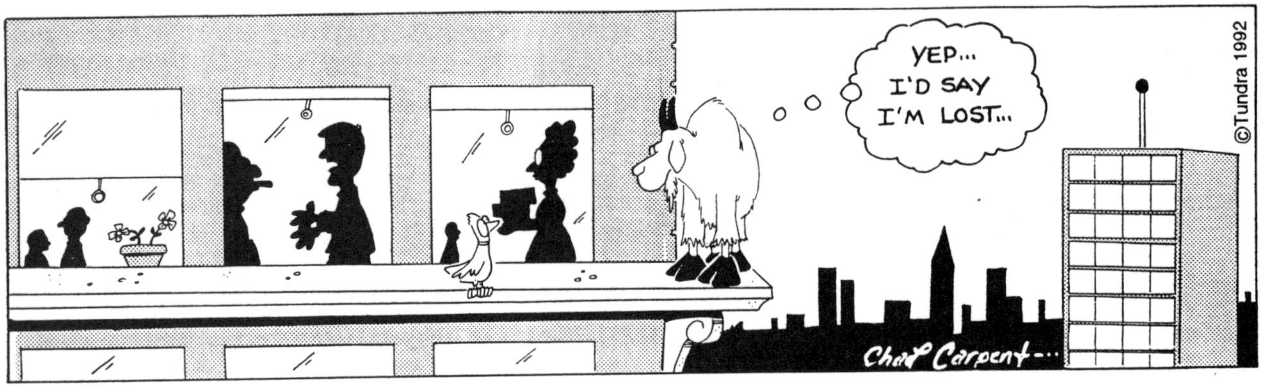
YEP...
I'D SAY
I'M LOST...
©Tundra 1992
Chad Carpent...

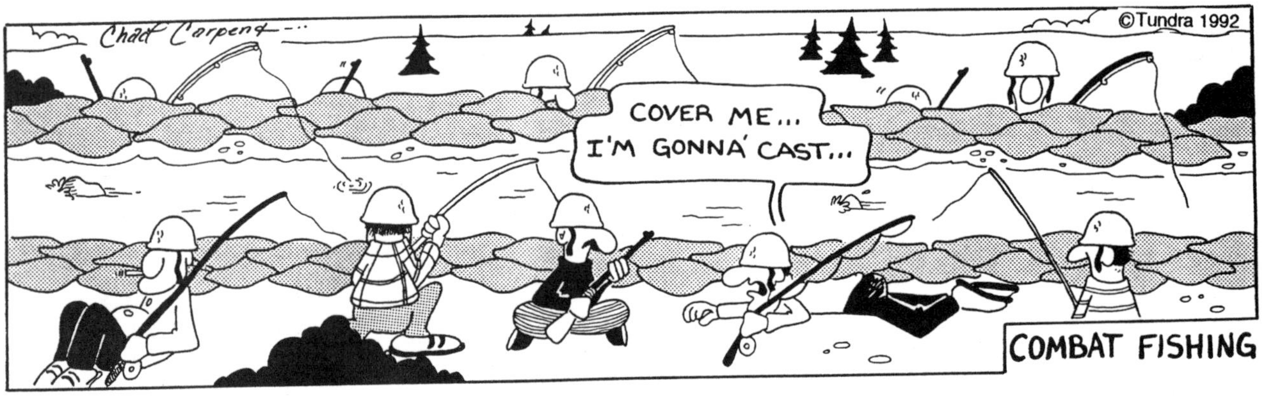
Chad Carpent...
©Tundra 1992
COVER ME...
I'M GONNA' CAST...
COMBAT FISHING

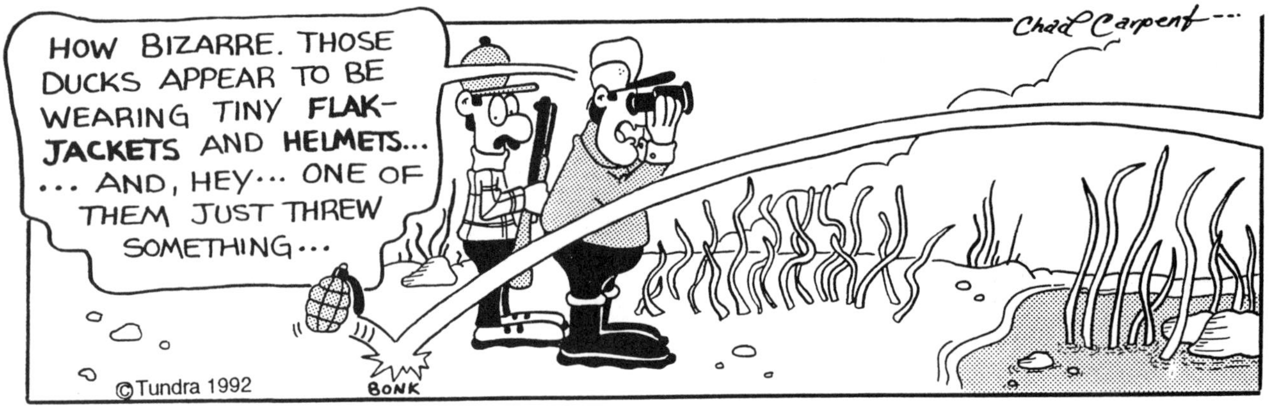
HOW BIZARRE. THOSE DUCKS APPEAR TO BE WEARING TINY FLAK-JACKETS AND HELMETS...
... AND, HEY... ONE OF THEM JUST THREW SOMETHING...
Chad Carpent...
BONK
©Tundra 1992

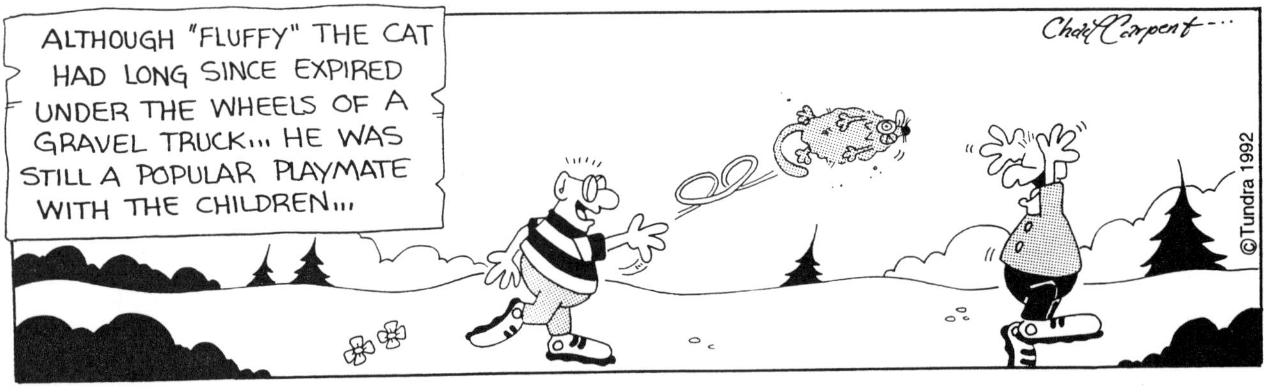
ALTHOUGH "FLUFFY" THE CAT HAD LONG SINCE EXPIRED UNDER THE WHEELS OF A GRAVEL TRUCK... HE WAS STILL A POPULAR PLAYMATE WITH THE CHILDREN...
Chad Carpent...
©Tundra 1992

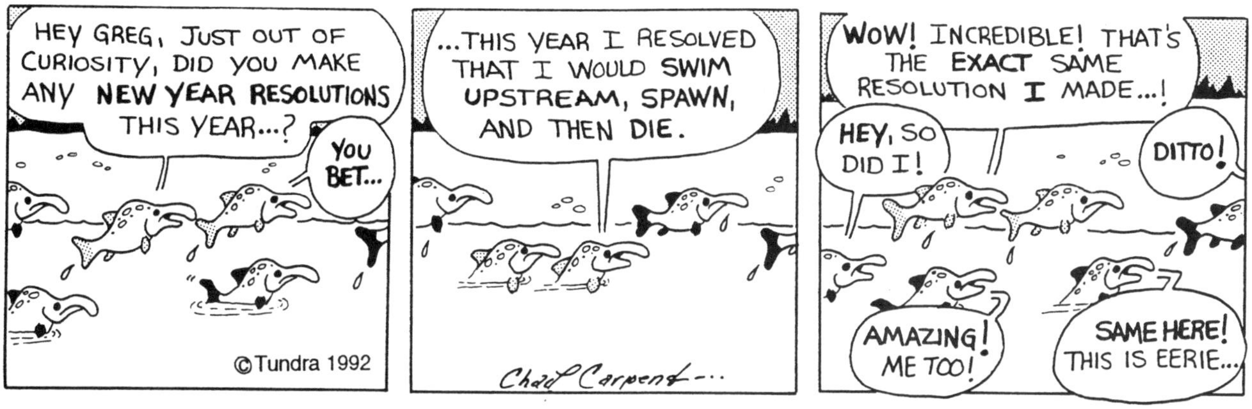
HEY GREG, JUST OUT OF CURIOSITY, DID YOU MAKE ANY NEW YEAR RESOLUTIONS THIS YEAR...?
YOU BET...
...THIS YEAR I RESOLVED THAT I WOULD SWIM UPSTREAM, SPAWN, AND THEN DIE.
WOW! INCREDIBLE! THAT'S THE EXACT SAME RESOLUTION I MADE...!
HEY, SO DID I!
DITTO!
AMAZING! ME TOO!
SAME HERE! THIS IS EERIE...
©Tundra 1992
Chad Carpent-...

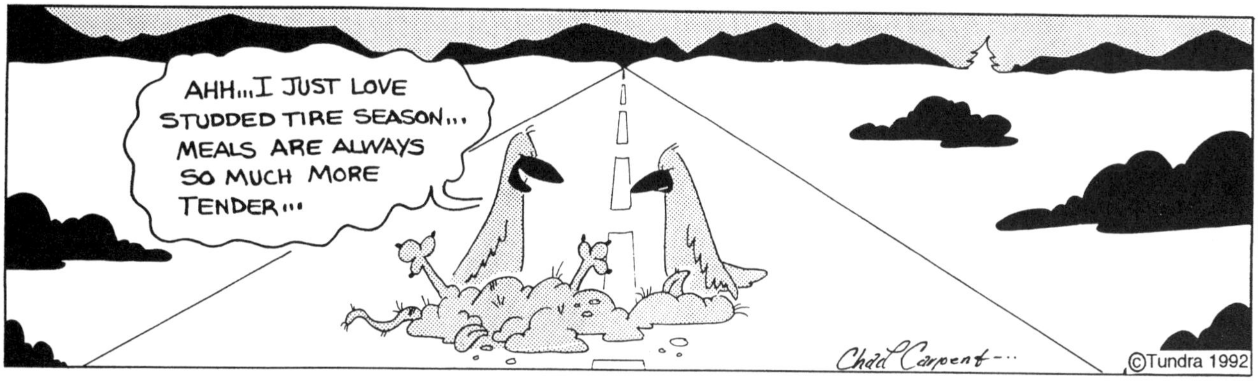
AHH...I JUST LOVE STUDDED TIRE SEASON... MEALS ARE ALWAYS SO MUCH MORE TENDER...
Chad Carpent-...
©Tundra 1992

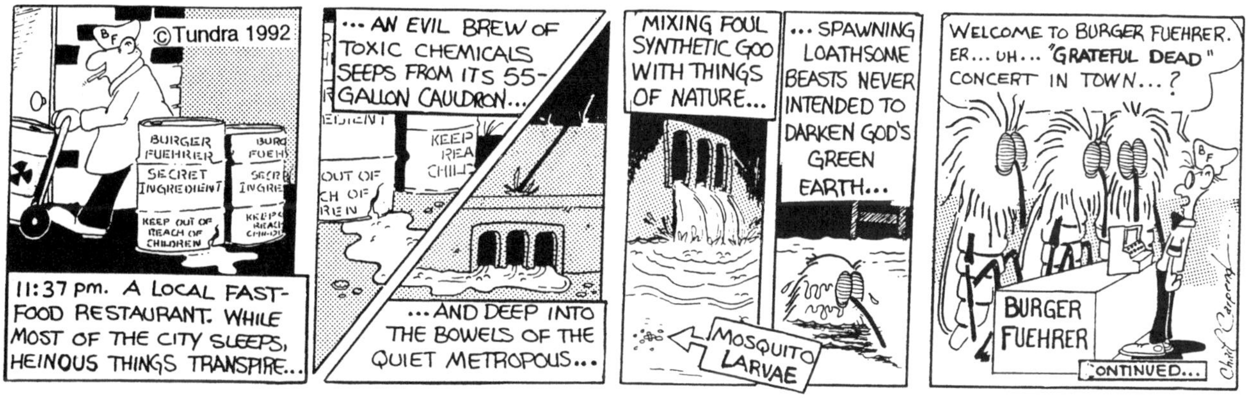
©Tundra 1992
BURGER FUEHRER SECRET INGREDIENT KEEP OUT OF REACH OF CHILDREN
11:37 pm. A LOCAL FAST-FOOD RESTAURANT. WHILE MOST OF THE CITY SLEEPS, HEINOUS THINGS TRANSPIRE...
... AN EVIL BREW OF TOXIC CHEMICALS SEEPS FROM ITS 55-GALLON CAULDRON...
...AND DEEP INTO THE BOWELS OF THE QUIET METROPOLIS...
MIXING FOUL SYNTHETIC GOO WITH THINGS OF NATURE...
... SPAWNING LOATHSOME BEASTS NEVER INTENDED TO DARKEN GOD'S GREEN EARTH...
MOSQUITO LARVAE
WELCOME TO BURGER FUEHRER. ER... UH... "GRATEFUL DEAD" CONCERT IN TOWN...?
BURGER FUEHRER
CONTINUED...

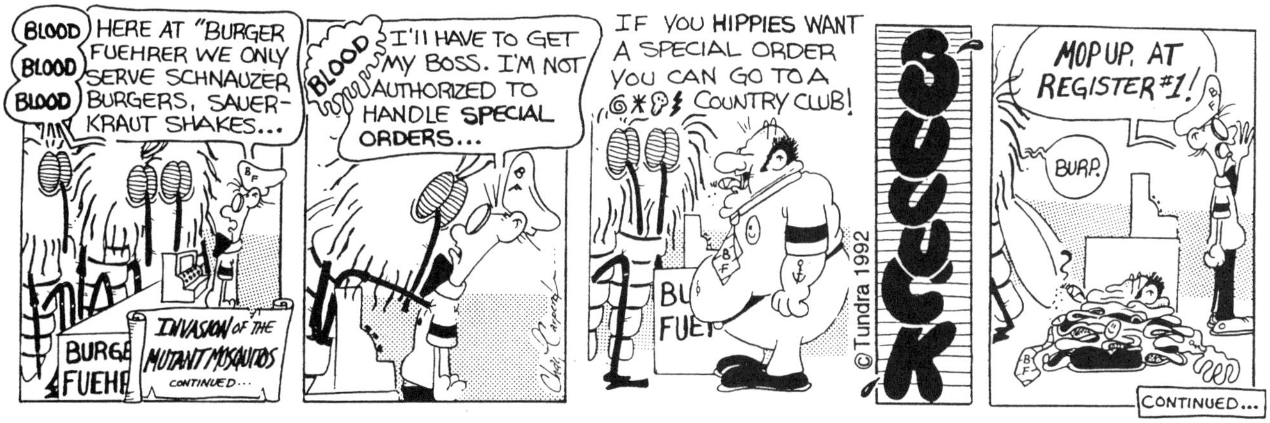
BLOOD
BLOOD
BLOOD
HERE AT "BURGER FUEHRER WE ONLY SERVE SCHNAUZER BURGERS, SAUER-KRAUT SHAKES...
INVASION OF THE MUTANT MOSQUITOS CONTINUED...
BLOOD
I'LL HAVE TO GET MY BOSS. I'M NOT AUTHORIZED TO HANDLE SPECIAL ORDERS...
IF YOU HIPPIES WANT A SPECIAL ORDER YOU CAN GO TO A @*#$ COUNTRY CLUB!
©Tundra 1992
SUCCK
MOP UP, AT REGISTER #1!
BURP.
CONTINUED...

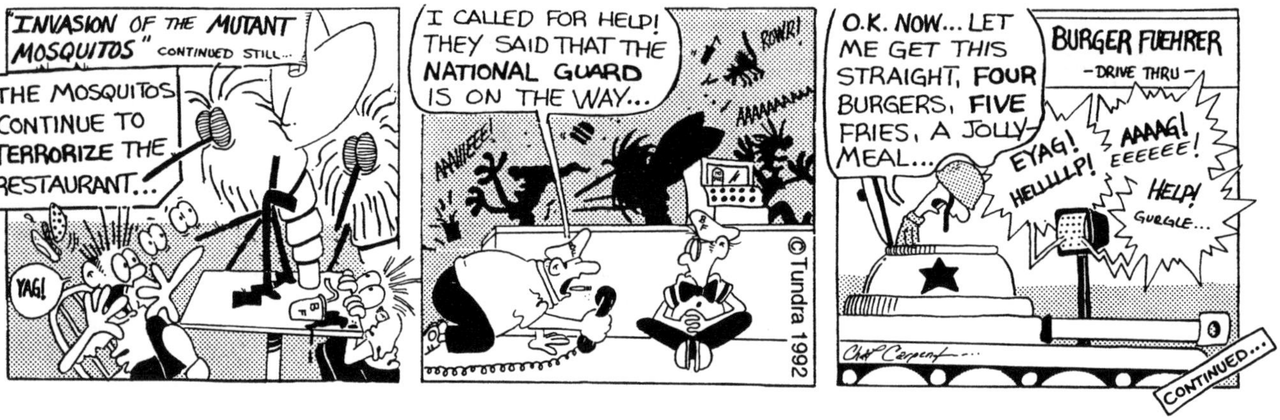
"INVASION OF THE MUTANT MOSQUITOS" CONTINUED STILL...
THE MOSQUITOS CONTINUE TO TERRORIZE THE RESTAURANT...
YAG!
I CALLED FOR HELP! THEY SAID THAT THE NATIONAL GUARD IS ON THE WAY...
© Tundra 1992
O.K. NOW... LET ME GET THIS STRAIGHT, FOUR BURGERS, FIVE FRIES, A JOLLY MEAL...
BURGER FUEHRER
-DRIVE THRU-
EYAG! HELLLLLP! AAAAG! EEEEEE!
HELP! GURGLE...
CONTINUED...

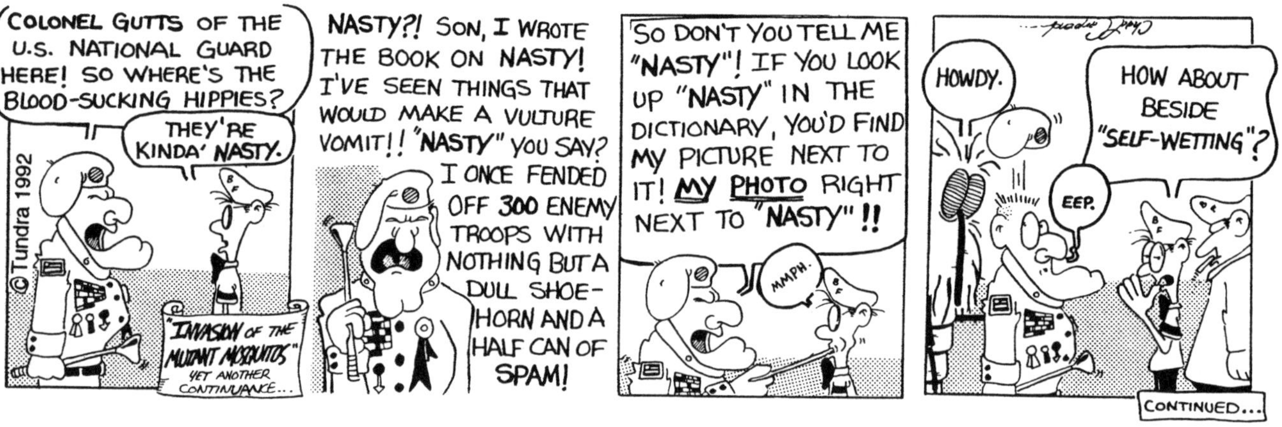
COLONEL GUTTS OF THE U.S. NATIONAL GUARD HERE! SO WHERE'S THE BLOOD-SUCKING HIPPIES?
THEY'RE KINDA' NASTY.
©Tundra 1992
"INVASION OF THE MUTANT MOSQUITOS" YET ANOTHER CONTINUANCE...
NASTY?! SON, I WROTE THE BOOK ON NASTY! I'VE SEEN THINGS THAT WOULD MAKE A VULTURE VOMIT!! "NASTY" YOU SAY? I ONCE FENDED OFF 300 ENEMY TROOPS WITH NOTHING BUT A DULL SHOE-HORN AND A HALF CAN OF SPAM!
SO DON'T YOU TELL ME "NASTY"! IF YOU LOOK UP "NASTY" IN THE DICTIONARY, YOU'D FIND MY PICTURE NEXT TO IT! MY PHOTO RIGHT NEXT TO "NASTY"!!
MMPH.
HOWDY.
HOW ABOUT BESIDE "SELF-WETTING"?
EEP.
CONTINUED...

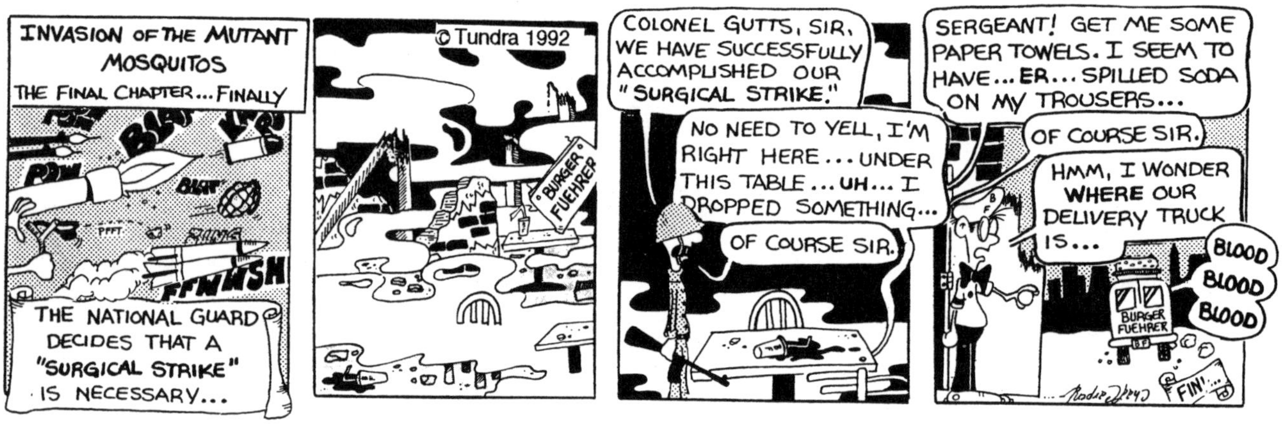
INVASION OF THE MUTANT MOSQUITOS
THE FINAL CHAPTER... FINALLY
THE NATIONAL GUARD DECIDES THAT A "SURGICAL STRIKE" IS NECESSARY...
©Tundra 1992
BURGER FUEHRER
COLONEL GUTTS, SIR, WE HAVE SUCCESSFULLY ACCOMPLISHED OUR "SURGICAL STRIKE."
NO NEED TO YELL, I'M RIGHT HERE... UNDER THIS TABLE... UH... I DROPPED SOMETHING...
OF COURSE SIR.
SERGEANT! GET ME SOME PAPER TOWELS. I SEEM TO HAVE... ER... SPILLED SODA ON MY TROUSERS...
OF COURSE SIR.
HMM, I WONDER WHERE OUR DELIVERY TRUCK IS...
BLOOD
BLOOD
BLOOD
BURGER FUEHRER
FIN!

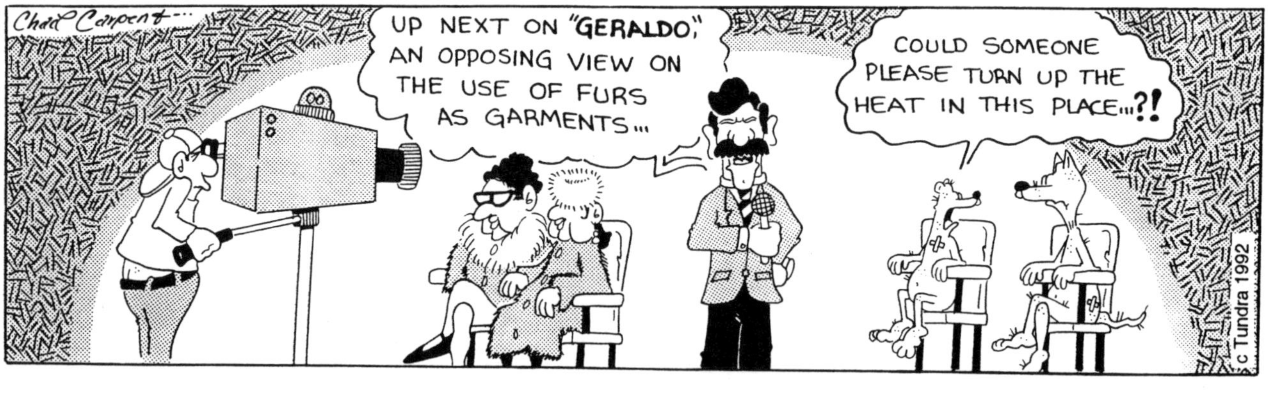
UP NEXT ON "GERALDO," AN OPPOSING VIEW ON THE USE OF FURS AS GARMENTS...
COULD SOMEONE PLEASE TURN UP THE HEAT IN THIS PLACE...?!
c Tundra 1992

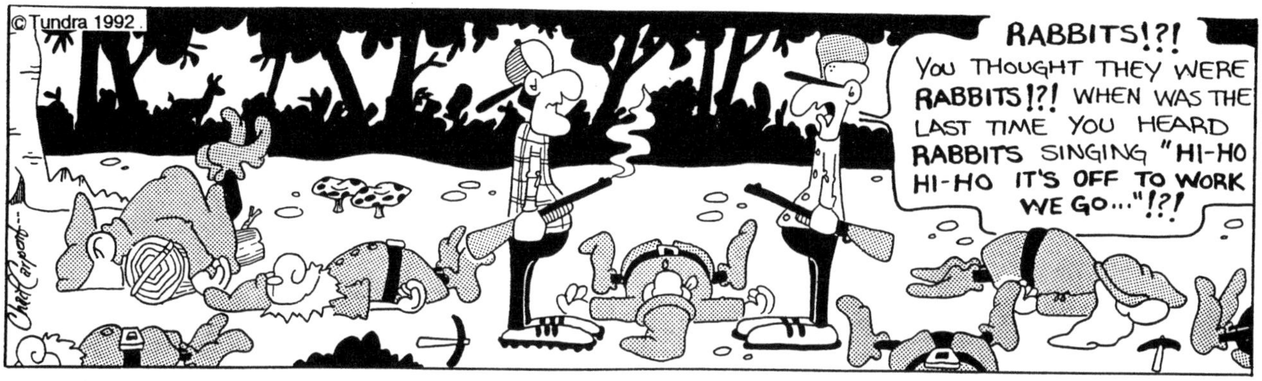
©Tundra 1992
RABBITS!?! YOU THOUGHT THEY WERE RABBITS!?! WHEN WAS THE LAST TIME YOU HEARD RABBITS SINGING "HI-HO HI-HO IT'S OFF TO WORK WE GO..."!?!
Chad Carpent...

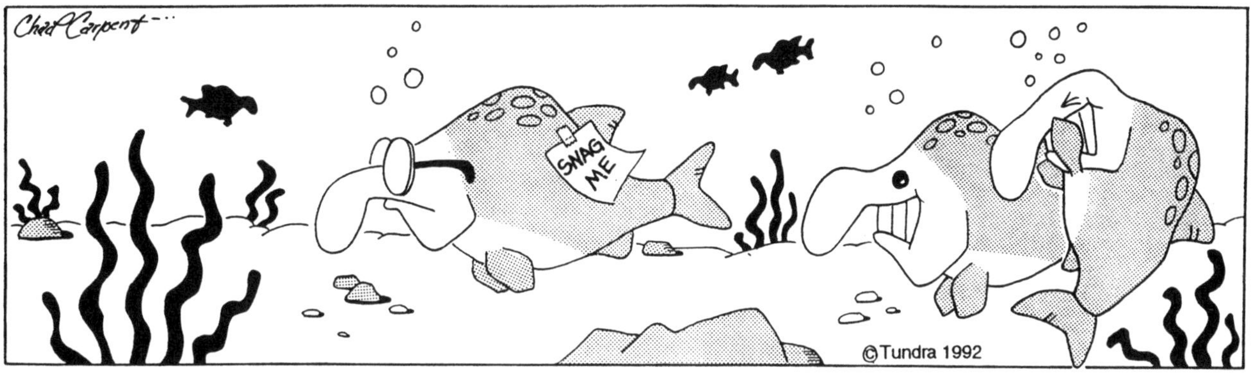
Chad Carpent...
SNAG ME
©Tundra 1992

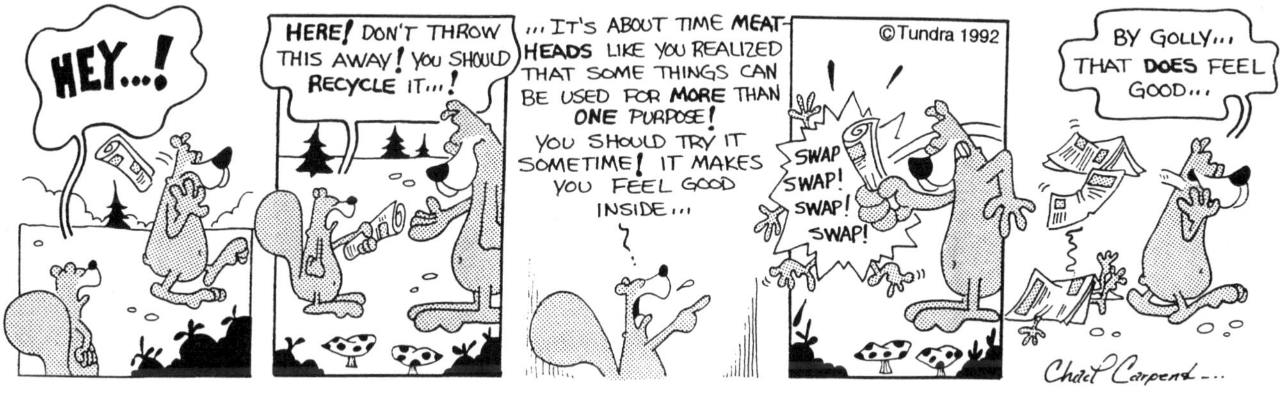
HEY...!
HERE! DON'T THROW THIS AWAY! YOU SHOULD RECYCLE IT...!
...IT'S ABOUT TIME MEAT-HEADS LIKE YOU REALIZED THAT SOME THINGS CAN BE USED FOR MORE THAN ONE PURPOSE! YOU SHOULD TRY IT SOMETIME! IT MAKES YOU FEEL GOOD INSIDE...
©Tundra 1992
SWAP SWAP! SWAP! SWAP!
BY GOLLY... THAT DOES FEEL GOOD...
Chad Carpent...

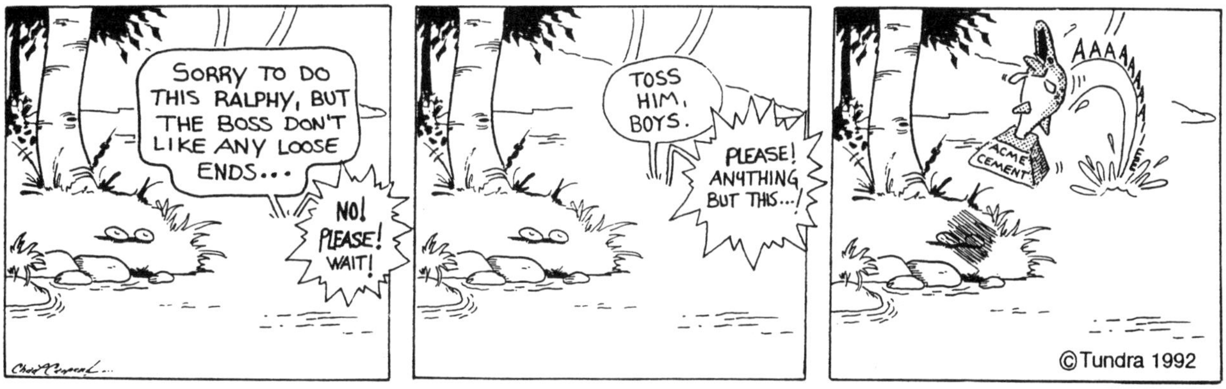
SORRY TO DO THIS RALPHY, BUT THE BOSS DON'T LIKE ANY LOOSE ENDS...
NO! PLEASE! WAIT!
TOSS HIM, BOYS.
PLEASE! ANYTHING BUT THIS...!
AAAAAAA
ACME CEMENT
©Tundra 1992

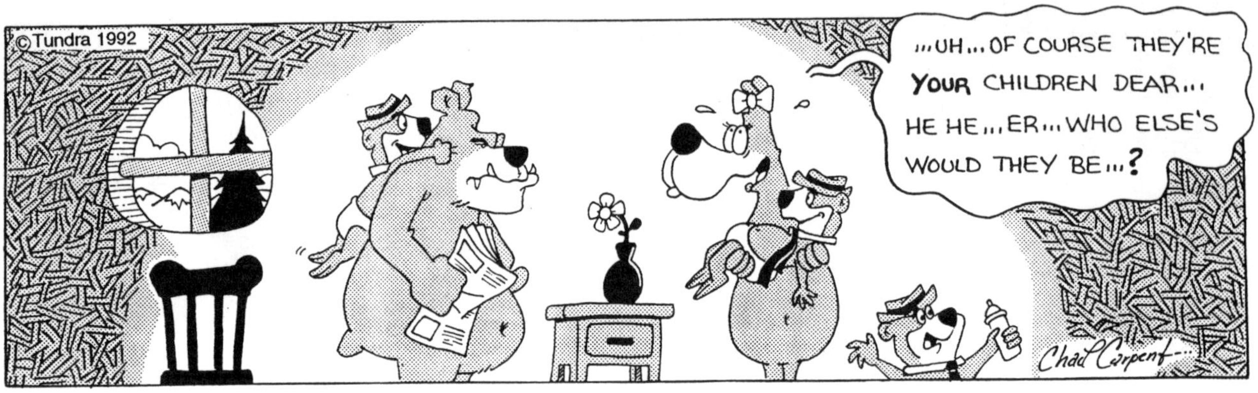
©Tundra 1992
...UH...OF COURSE THEY'RE YOUR CHILDREN DEAR... HE HE...ER...WHO ELSE'S WOULD THEY BE...?
Chad Carpent...

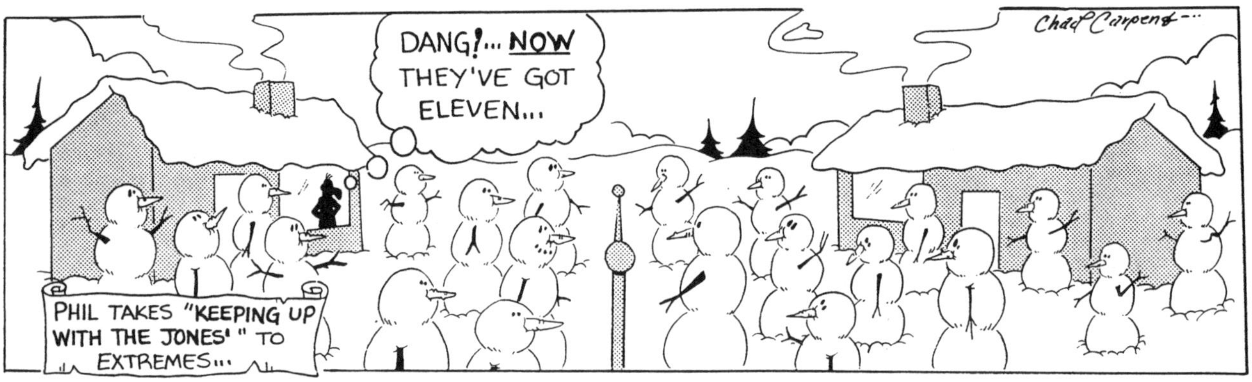
Chad Carpent...
DANG!... NOW THEY'VE GOT ELEVEN...
PHIL TAKES "KEEPING UP WITH THE JONES' " TO EXTREMES...

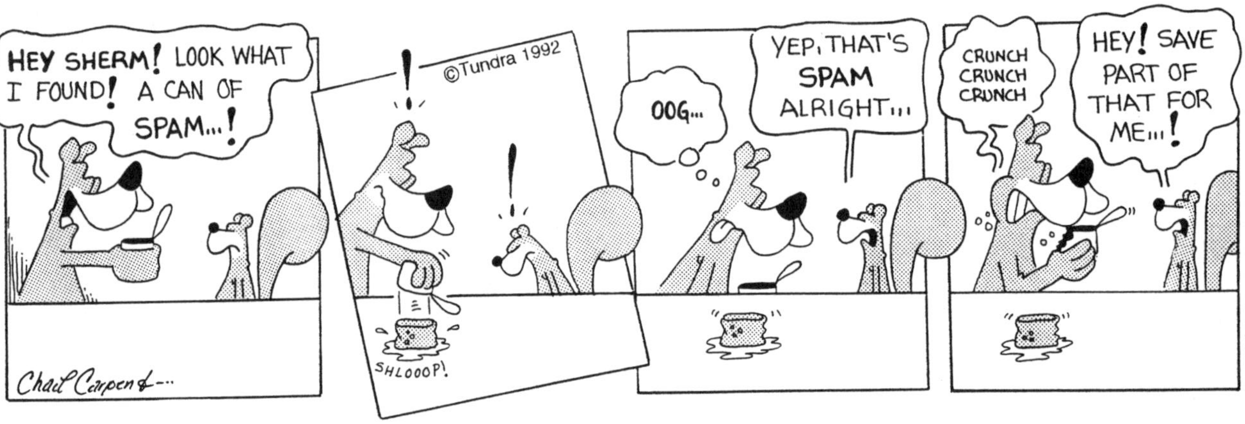
HEY SHERM! LOOK WHAT I FOUND! A CAN OF SPAM...!
Chad Carpent...
©Tundra 1992
!
!
SHLOOOP!
OOG...
YEP, THAT'S SPAM ALRIGHT...
CRUNCH CRUNCH CRUNCH
HEY! SAVE PART OF THAT FOR ME...!

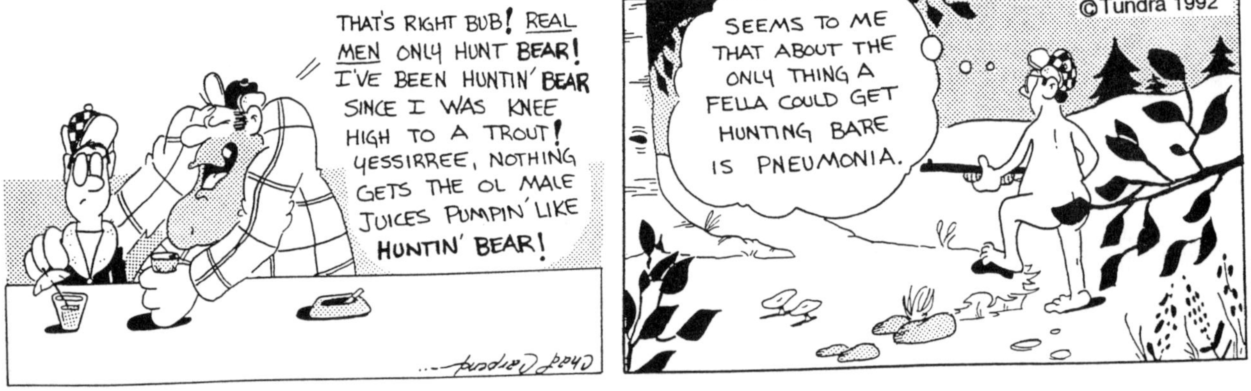
THAT'S RIGHT BUB! REAL MEN ONLY HUNT BEAR! I'VE BEEN HUNTIN' BEAR SINCE I WAS KNEE HIGH TO A TROUT! YESSIRREE, NOTHING GETS THE OL MALE JUICES PUMPIN' LIKE HUNTIN' BEAR!
©Tundra 1992
SEEMS TO ME THAT ABOUT THE ONLY THING A FELLA COULD GET HUNTING BARE IS PNEUMONIA.

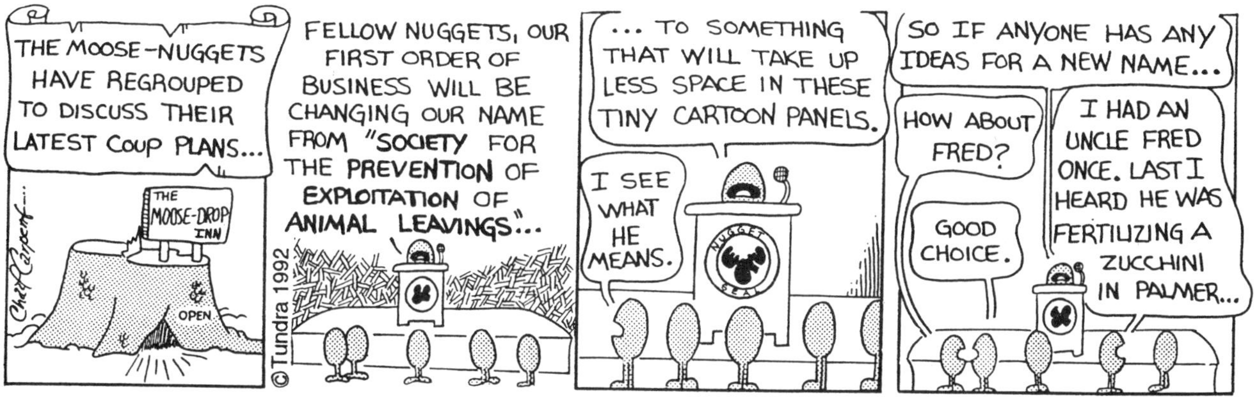
THE MOOSE-NUGGETS HAVE REGROUPED TO DISCUSS THEIR LATEST COUP PLANS...
THE MOOSE-DROP INN
OPEN
Chad Carpenter
©Tundra 1992
FELLOW NUGGETS, OUR FIRST ORDER OF BUSINESS WILL BE CHANGING OUR NAME FROM "SOCIETY FOR THE PREVENTION OF EXPLOITATION OF ANIMAL LEAVINGS"...
... TO SOMETHING THAT WILL TAKE UP LESS SPACE IN THESE TINY CARTOON PANELS.
I SEE WHAT HE MEANS.
NUGGET SEAL
SO IF ANYONE HAS ANY IDEAS FOR A NEW NAME...
HOW ABOUT FRED?
I HAD AN UNCLE FRED ONCE. LAST I HEARD HE WAS FERTILIZING A ZUCCHINI IN PALMER...
GOOD CHOICE.

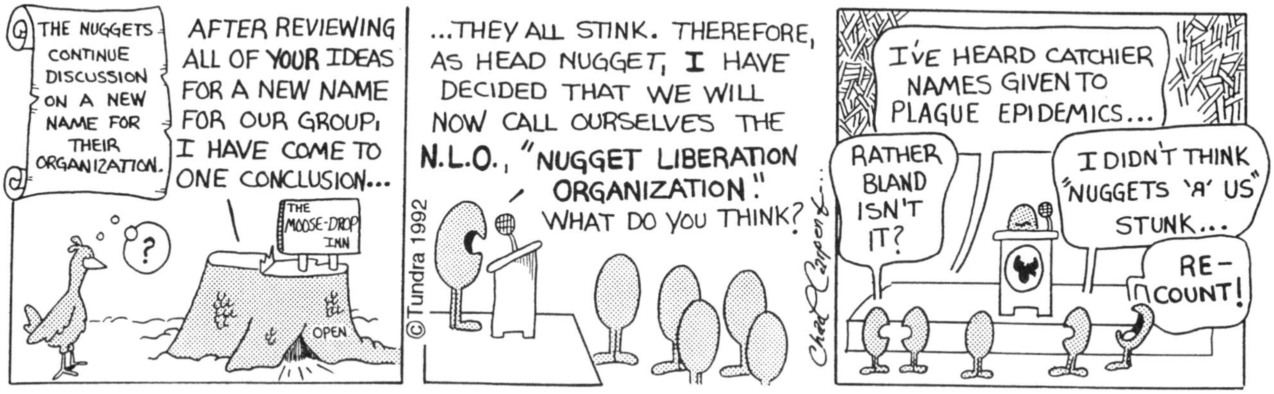
THE NUGGETS CONTINUE DISCUSSION ON A NEW NAME FOR THEIR ORGANIZATION.
AFTER REVIEWING ALL OF YOUR IDEAS FOR A NEW NAME FOR OUR GROUP, I HAVE COME TO ONE CONCLUSION...
?
THE MOOSE-DROP INN
OPEN
©Tundra 1992
...THEY ALL STINK. THEREFORE, AS HEAD NUGGET, I HAVE DECIDED THAT WE WILL NOW CALL OURSELVES THE N.L.O., "NUGGET LIBERATION ORGANIZATION." WHAT DO YOU THINK?
Chad Carpenter
I'VE HEARD CATCHIER NAMES GIVEN TO PLAGUE EPIDEMICS...
RATHER BLAND ISN'T IT?
I DIDN'T THINK "NUGGETS 'A' US" STUNK...
RE-COUNT!

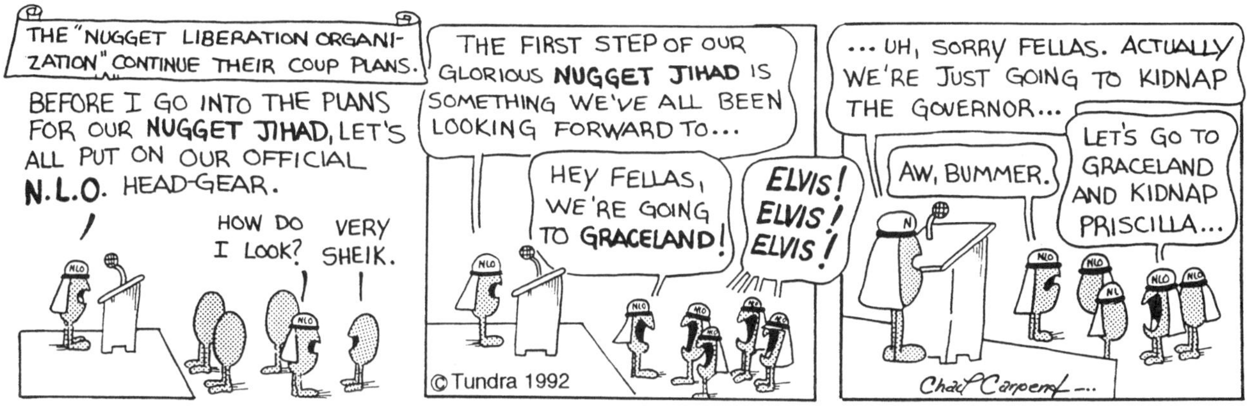
THE "NUGGET LIBERATION ORGANIZATION" CONTINUE THEIR COUP PLANS.
BEFORE I GO INTO THE PLANS FOR OUR NUGGET JIHAD, LET'S ALL PUT ON OUR OFFICIAL N.L.O. HEAD-GEAR.
HOW DO I LOOK?
VERY SHEIK.
THE FIRST STEP OF OUR GLORIOUS NUGGET JIHAD IS SOMETHING WE'VE ALL BEEN LOOKING FORWARD TO...
HEY FELLAS, WE'RE GOING TO GRACELAND!
ELVIS! ELVIS! ELVIS!
©Tundra 1992
... UH, SORRY FELLAS. ACTUALLY WE'RE JUST GOING TO KIDNAP THE GOVERNOR...
AW, BUMMER.
LET'S GO TO GRACELAND AND KIDNAP PRISCILLA...
Chad Carpenter

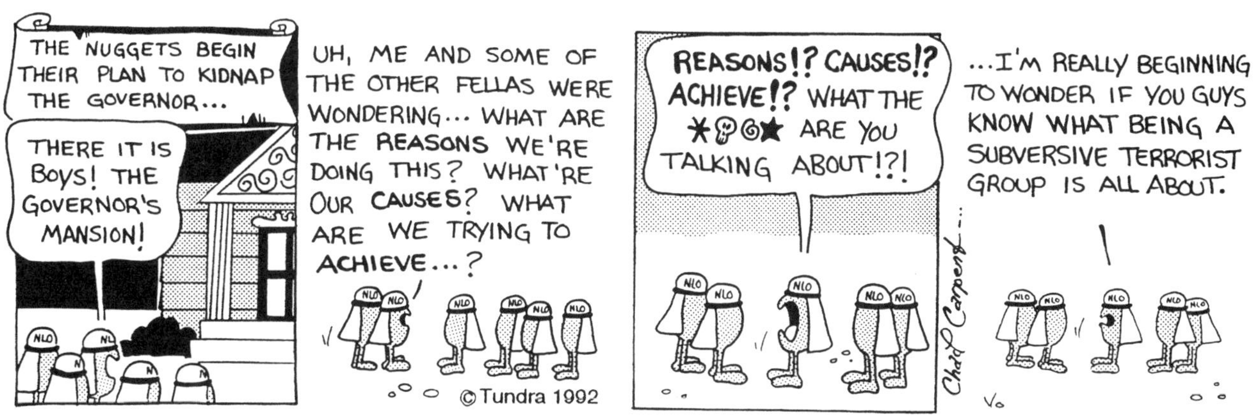
THE NUGGETS BEGIN THEIR PLAN TO KIDNAP THE GOVERNOR...
THERE IT IS BOYS! THE GOVERNOR'S MANSION!
UH, ME AND SOME OF THE OTHER FELLAS WERE WONDERING... WHAT ARE THE REASONS WE'RE DOING THIS? WHAT'RE OUR CAUSES? WHAT ARE WE TRYING TO ACHIEVE...?
©Tundra 1992
REASONS!? CAUSES!? ACHIEVE!? WHAT THE *☠@★ ARE YOU TALKING ABOUT!?!
Chad Carpenter
...I'M REALLY BEGINNING TO WONDER IF YOU GUYS KNOW WHAT BEING A SUBVERSIVE TERRORIST GROUP IS ALL ABOUT.

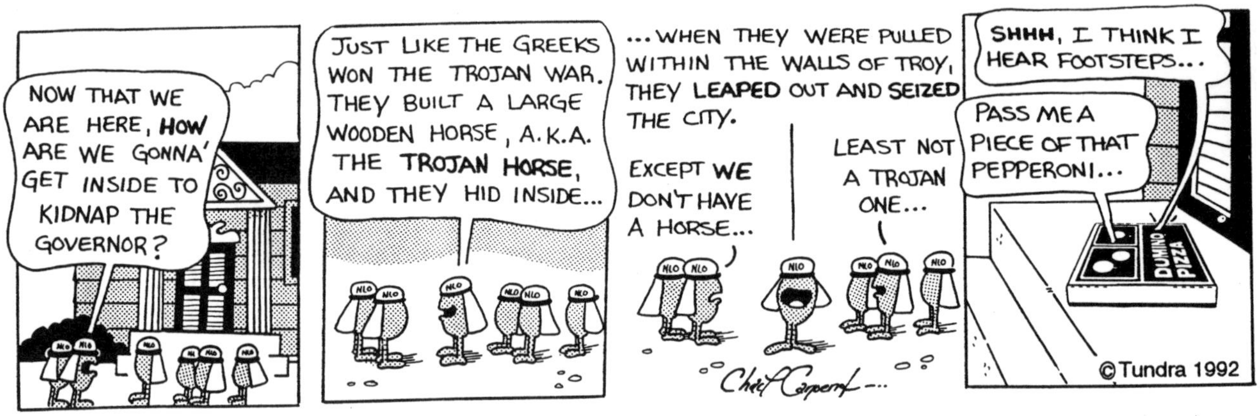
NOW THAT WE ARE HERE, HOW ARE WE GONNA' GET INSIDE TO KIDNAP THE GOVERNOR?
JUST LIKE THE GREEKS WON THE TROJAN WAR. THEY BUILT A LARGE WOODEN HORSE, A.K.A. THE TROJAN HORSE, AND THEY HID INSIDE...
...WHEN THEY WERE PULLED WITHIN THE WALLS OF TROY, THEY LEAPED OUT AND SEIZED THE CITY.
EXCEPT WE DON'T HAVE A HORSE...
LEAST NOT A TROJAN ONE...
SHHH, I THINK I HEAR FOOTSTEPS...
PASS ME A PIECE OF THAT PEPPERONI...
DUMINO PIZZA
©Tundra 1992

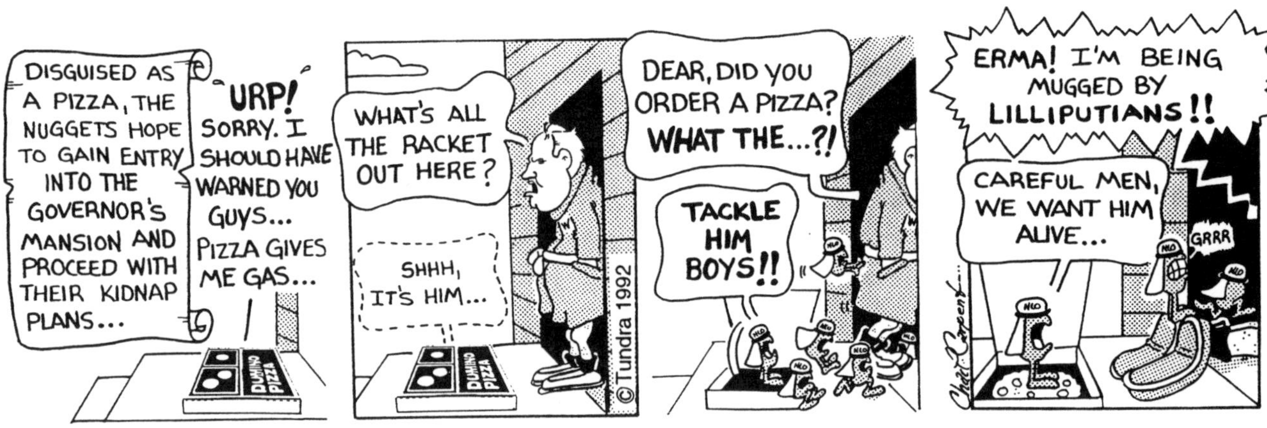
DISGUISED AS A PIZZA, THE NUGGETS HOPE TO GAIN ENTRY INTO THE GOVERNOR'S MANSION AND PROCEED WITH THEIR KIDNAP PLANS...
"URP!" SORRY. I SHOULD HAVE WARNED YOU GUYS... PIZZA GIVES ME GAS...
DUMINO PIZZA
WHAT'S ALL THE RACKET OUT HERE?
SHHH, IT'S HIM...
©Tundra 1992
DEAR, DID YOU ORDER A PIZZA? WHAT THE...?!
TACKLE HIM BOYS!!
ERMA! I'M BEING MUGGED BY LILLIPUTIANS!!
CAREFUL MEN, WE WANT HIM ALIVE...
GRRR

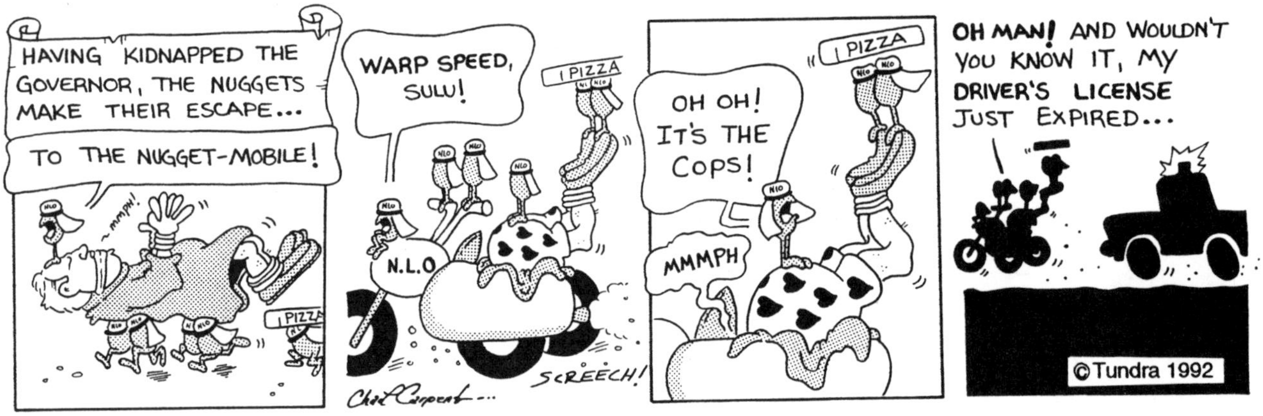
HAVING KIDNAPPED THE GOVERNOR, THE NUGGETS MAKE THEIR ESCAPE...
TO THE NUGGET-MOBILE!
MMPH!
PIZZA
WARP SPEED, SULU!
N.L.O
SCREECH!
OH OH! IT'S THE COPS!
MMMPH
PIZZA
OH MAN! AND WOULDN'T YOU KNOW IT, MY DRIVER'S LICENSE JUST EXPIRED...
©Tundra 1992

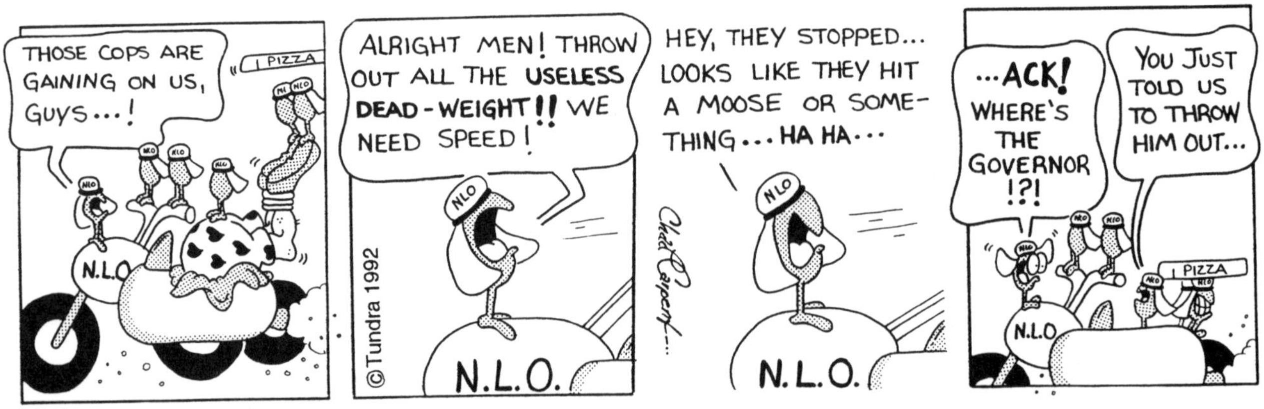
THOSE COPS ARE GAINING ON US, GUYS...!
PIZZA
N.L.O.
ALRIGHT MEN! THROW OUT ALL THE USELESS DEAD-WEIGHT!! WE NEED SPEED!
©Tundra 1992
N.L.O.
HEY, THEY STOPPED... LOOKS LIKE THEY HIT A MOOSE OR SOMETHING... HA HA...
N.L.O.
...ACK! WHERE'S THE GOVERNOR!?!
YOU JUST TOLD US TO THROW HIM OUT...
PIZZA
N.L.O

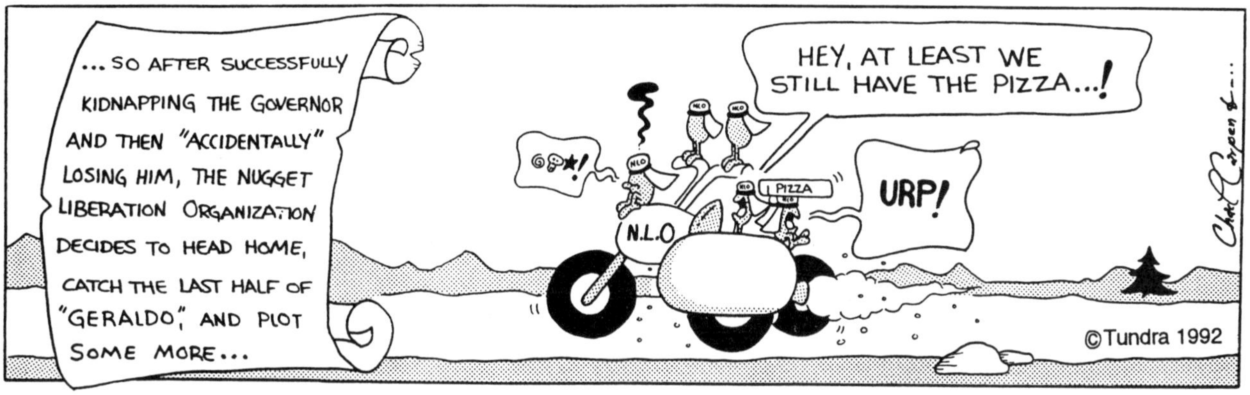
...SO AFTER SUCCESSFULLY KIDNAPPING THE GOVERNOR AND THEN "ACCIDENTALLY" LOSING HIM, THE NUGGET LIBERATION ORGANIZATION DECIDES TO HEAD HOME, CATCH THE LAST HALF OF "GERALDO", AND PLOT SOME MORE...
HEY, AT LEAST WE STILL HAVE THE PIZZA...!
URP!
N.L.O
PIZZA
Chad Carpent...
©Tundra 1992

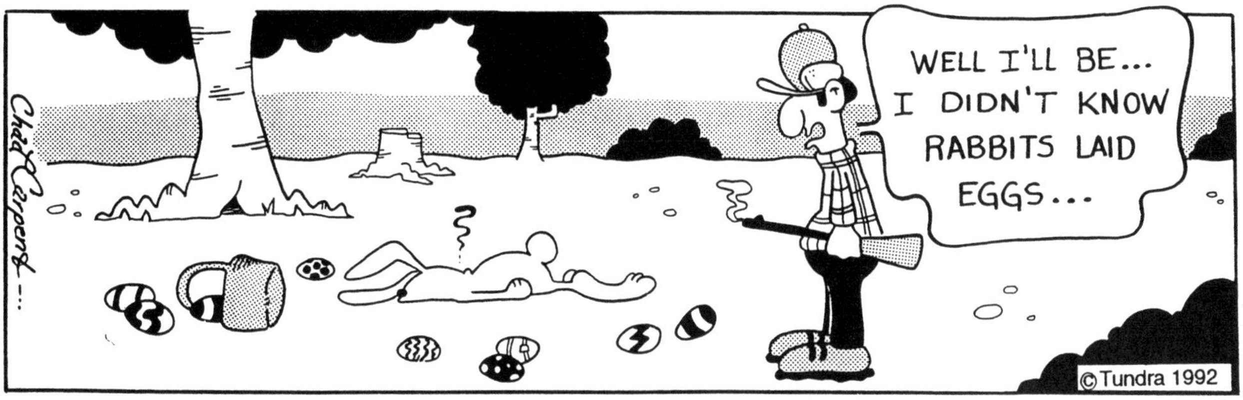
WELL I'LL BE... I DIDN'T KNOW RABBITS LAID EGGS...
Chad Carpent...
©Tundra 1992

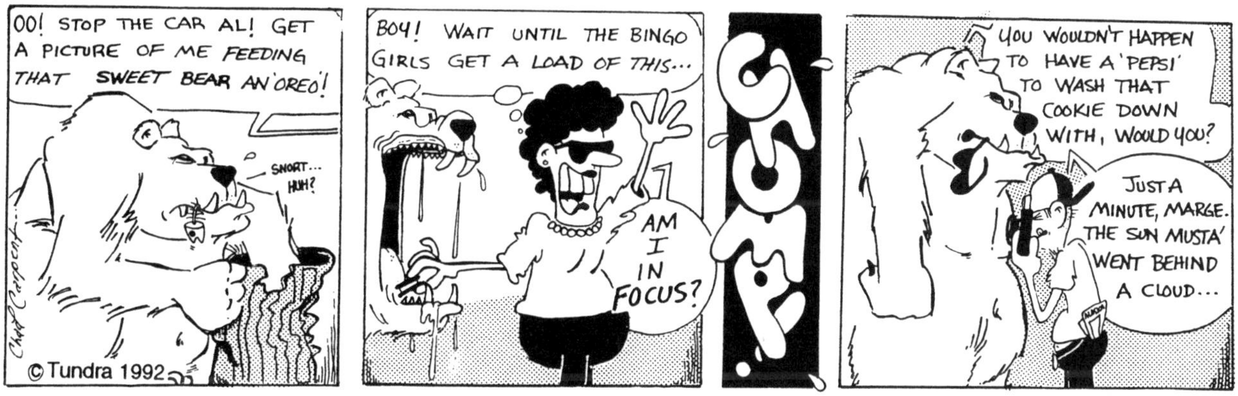
OO! STOP THE CAR AL! GET A PICTURE OF ME FEEDING THAT SWEET BEAR AN OREO!
SNORT... HUH?
©Tundra 1992
BOY! WAIT UNTIL THE BINGO GIRLS GET A LOAD OF THIS...
AM I IN FOCUS?
YOU WOULDN'T HAPPEN TO HAVE A 'PEPSI' TO WASH THAT COOKIE DOWN WITH, WOULD YOU?
JUST A MINUTE, MARGE. THE SUN MUSTA' WENT BEHIND A CLOUD...

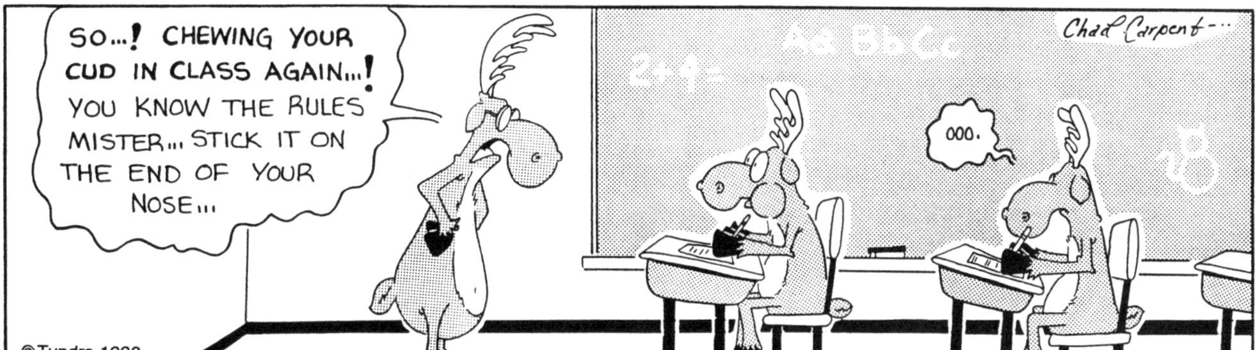
SO...! CHEWING YOUR CUD IN CLASS AGAIN...! YOU KNOW THE RULES MISTER... STICK IT ON THE END OF YOUR NOSE...
Chad Carpent...
Aa Bb Cc
2+4=
OOO.
©Tundra 1992

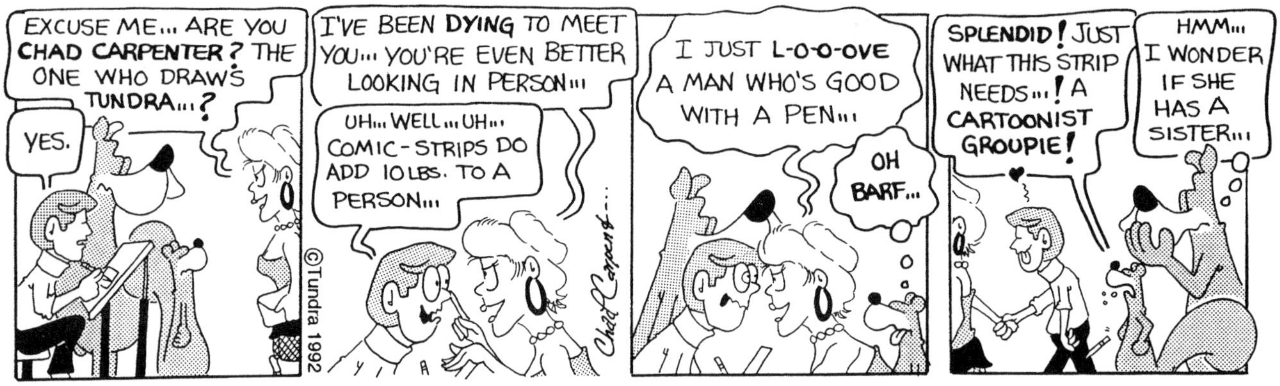
EXCUSE ME... ARE YOU CHAD CARPENTER? THE ONE WHO DRAWS TUNDRA...?
YES.
©Tundra 1992
I'VE BEEN DYING TO MEET YOU... YOU'RE EVEN BETTER LOOKING IN PERSON...
UH... WELL... UH... COMIC-STRIPS DO ADD 10 LBS. TO A PERSON...
Chad Carpenter...
I JUST L-O-O-OVE A MAN WHO'S GOOD WITH A PEN...
OH BARF...
SPLENDID! JUST WHAT THIS STRIP NEEDS...! A CARTOONIST GROUPIE!
HMM... I WONDER IF SHE HAS A SISTER...

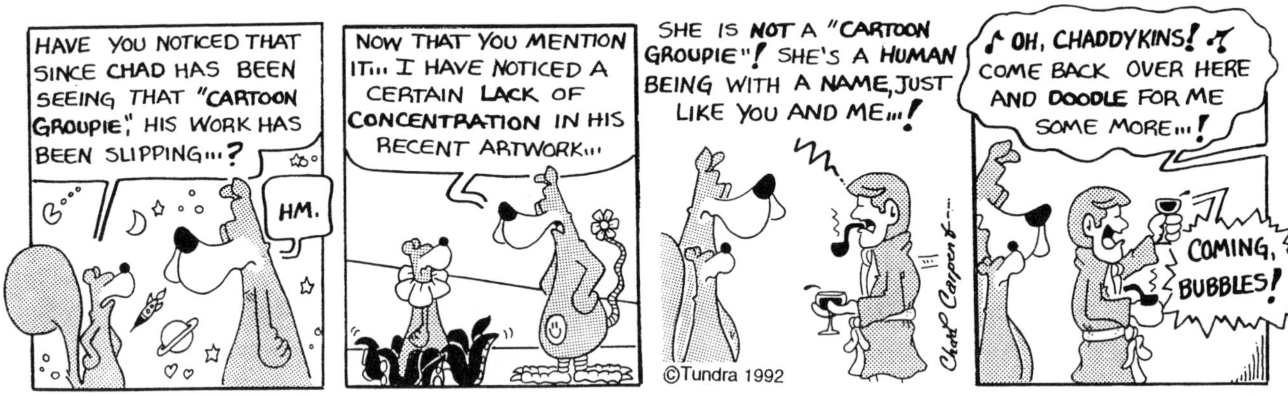
HAVE YOU NOTICED THAT SINCE CHAD HAS BEEN SEEING THAT "CARTOON GROUPIE," HIS WORK HAS BEEN SLIPPING...?
HM.
NOW THAT YOU MENTION IT... I HAVE NOTICED A CERTAIN LACK OF CONCENTRATION IN HIS RECENT ARTWORK...
SHE IS NOT A "CARTOON GROUPIE"! SHE'S A HUMAN BEING WITH A NAME, JUST LIKE YOU AND ME...!
Chad Carpenter...
©Tundra 1992
♪ OH, CHADDYKINS! ♪ COME BACK OVER HERE AND DOODLE FOR ME SOME MORE...!
COMING, BUBBLES!

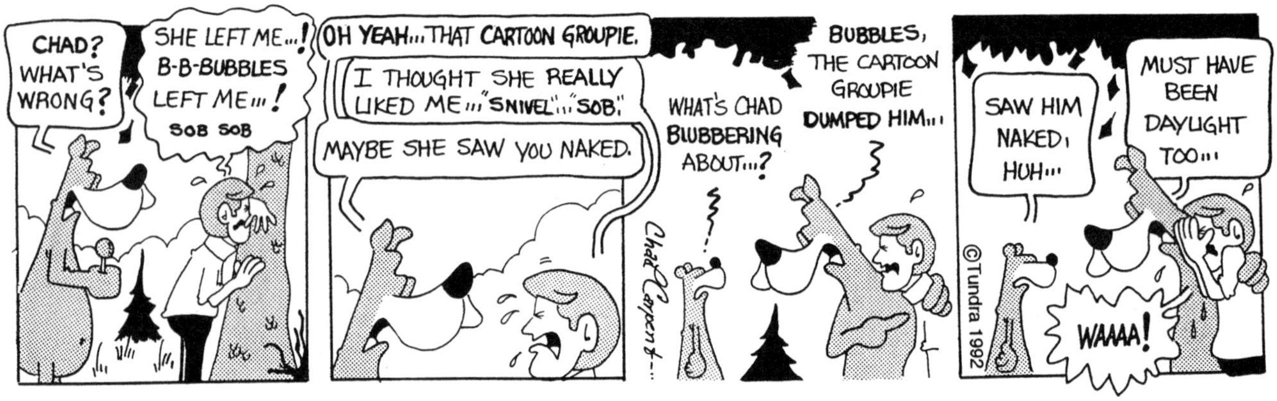
CHAD? WHAT'S WRONG?
SHE LEFT ME...! B-B-BUBBLES LEFT ME...!
SOB SOB
OH YEAH... THAT CARTOON GROUPIE.
I THOUGHT SHE REALLY LIKED ME... "SNIVEL"... "SOB."
MAYBE SHE SAW YOU NAKED.
Chad Carpenter...
WHAT'S CHAD BLUBBERING ABOUT...?
BUBBLES, THE CARTOON GROUPIE DUMPED HIM...
©Tundra 1992
SAW HIM NAKED, HUH...
MUST HAVE BEEN DAYLIGHT TOO...
WAAAA!

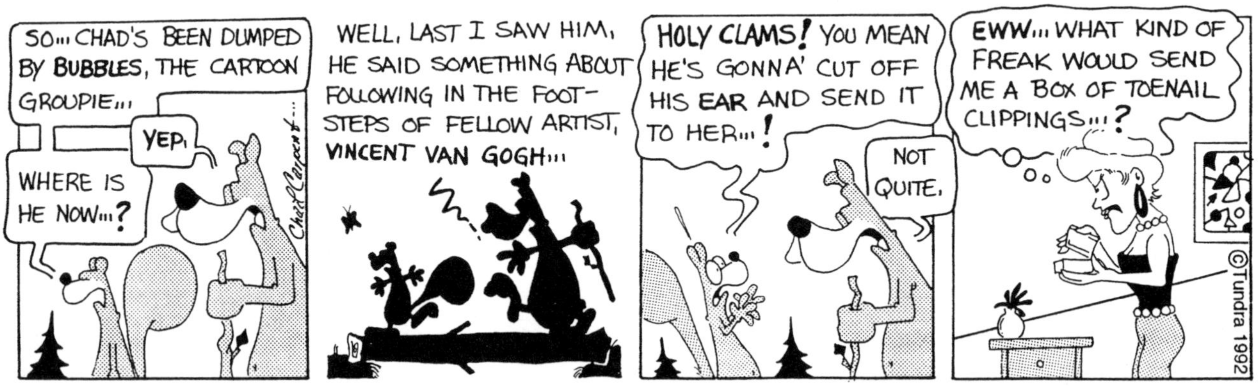
SO... CHAD'S BEEN DUMPED BY BUBBLES, THE CARTOON GROUPIE...
YEP.
WHERE IS HE NOW...?
Chad Carpenter...
WELL, LAST I SAW HIM, HE SAID SOMETHING ABOUT FOLLOWING IN THE FOOT-STEPS OF FELLOW ARTIST, VINCENT VAN GOGH...
HOLY CLAMS! YOU MEAN HE'S GONNA' CUT OFF HIS EAR AND SEND IT TO HER...!
NOT QUITE.
EWW... WHAT KIND OF FREAK WOULD SEND ME A BOX OF TOENAIL CLIPPINGS...?
©Tundra 1992

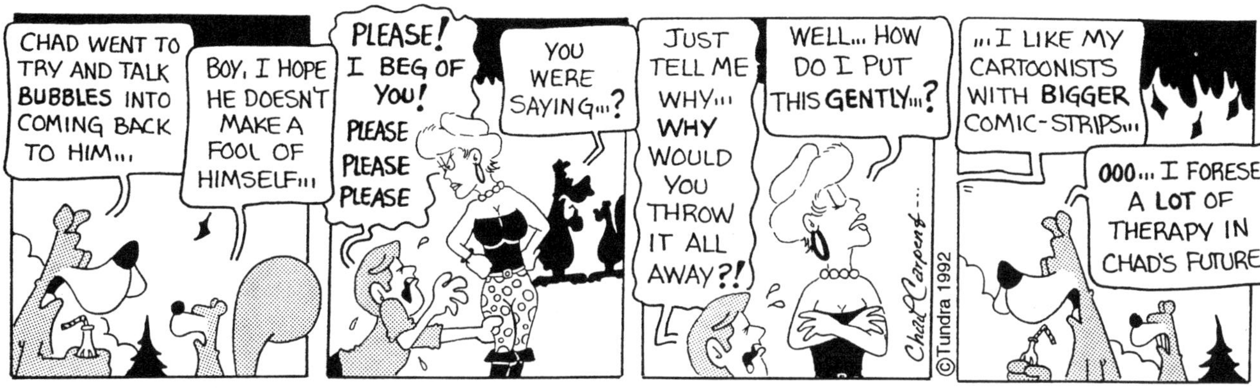
CHAD WENT TO TRY AND TALK BUBBLES INTO COMING BACK TO HIM...
BOY, I HOPE HE DOESN'T MAKE A FOOL OF HIMSELF...
PLEASE! I BEG OF YOU! PLEASE PLEASE PLEASE
YOU WERE SAYING...?
JUST TELL ME WHY... WHY WOULD YOU THROW IT ALL AWAY?!
WELL... HOW DO I PUT THIS GENTLY...?
Chad Carpenter
©Tundra 1992
...I LIKE MY CARTOONISTS WITH BIGGER COMIC-STRIPS...
OOO... I FORESEE A LOT OF THERAPY IN CHAD'S FUTURE...

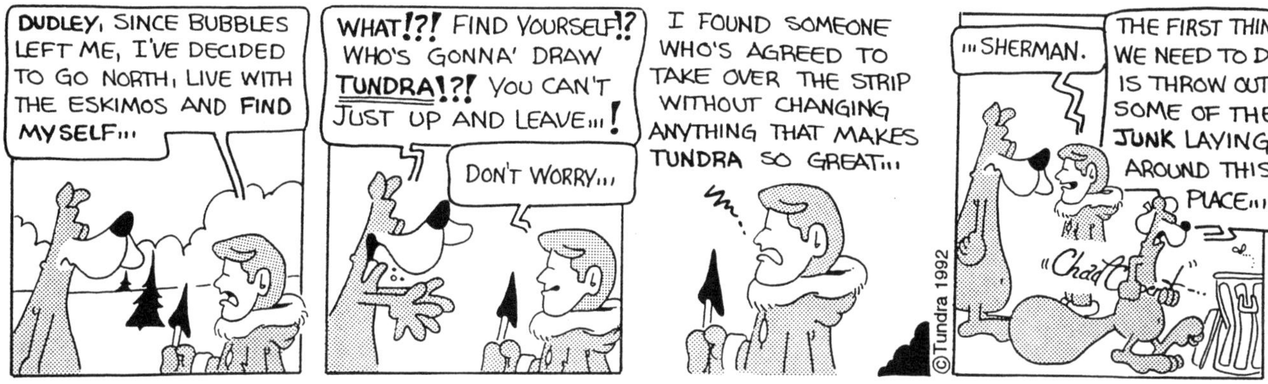
DUDLEY, SINCE BUBBLES LEFT ME, I'VE DECIDED TO GO NORTH, LIVE WITH THE ESKIMOS AND FIND MYSELF...
WHAT!?! FIND YOURSELF!? WHO'S GONNA' DRAW TUNDRA!?! YOU CAN'T JUST UP AND LEAVE...!
DON'T WORRY...
I FOUND SOMEONE WHO'S AGREED TO TAKE OVER THE STRIP WITHOUT CHANGING ANYTHING THAT MAKES TUNDRA SO GREAT...
©Tundra 1992
...SHERMAN.
THE FIRST THING WE NEED TO DO IS THROW OUT SOME OF THE JUNK LAYING AROUND THIS PLACE...
Chad C

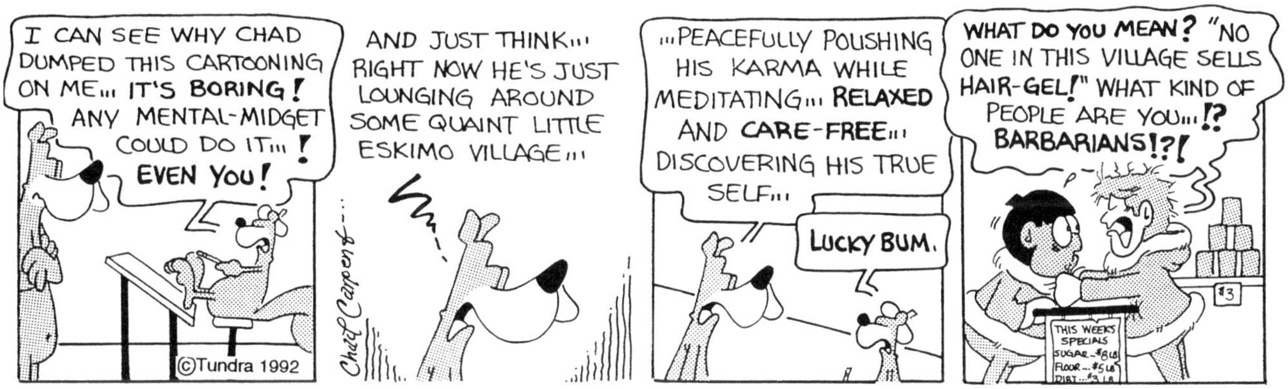
I CAN SEE WHY CHAD DUMPED THIS CARTOONING ON ME... IT'S BORING! ANY MENTAL-MIDGET COULD DO IT...! EVEN YOU!
©Tundra 1992
Chad Carpenter
AND JUST THINK... RIGHT NOW HE'S JUST LOUNGING AROUND SOME QUAINT LITTLE ESKIMO VILLAGE...
...PEACEFULLY POLISHING HIS KARMA WHILE MEDITATING... RELAXED AND CARE-FREE... DISCOVERING HIS TRUE SELF...
LUCKY BUM.
WHAT DO YOU MEAN? "NO ONE IN THIS VILLAGE SELLS HAIR-GEL!" WHAT KIND OF PEOPLE ARE YOU...!? BARBARIANS!?!
THIS WEEKS SPECIALS

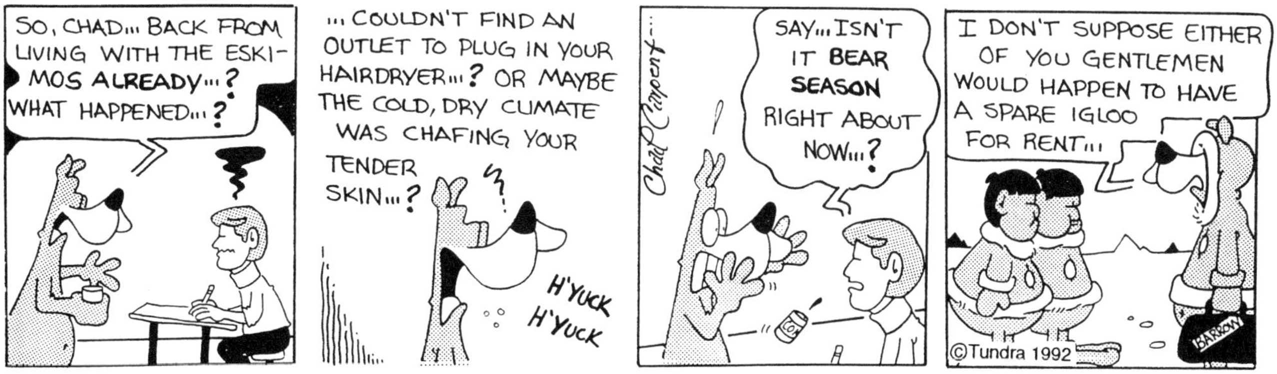
SO, CHAD... BACK FROM LIVING WITH THE ESKI-MOS ALREADY...? WHAT HAPPENED...?
...COULDN'T FIND AN OUTLET TO PLUG IN YOUR HAIRDRYER...? OR MAYBE THE COLD, DRY CLIMATE WAS CHAFING YOUR TENDER SKIN...?
H'YUCK H'YUCK
Chad Carpenter
SAY... ISN'T IT BEAR SEASON RIGHT ABOUT NOW...?
I DON'T SUPPOSE EITHER OF YOU GENTLEMEN WOULD HAPPEN TO HAVE A SPARE IGLOO FOR RENT...
©Tundra 1992

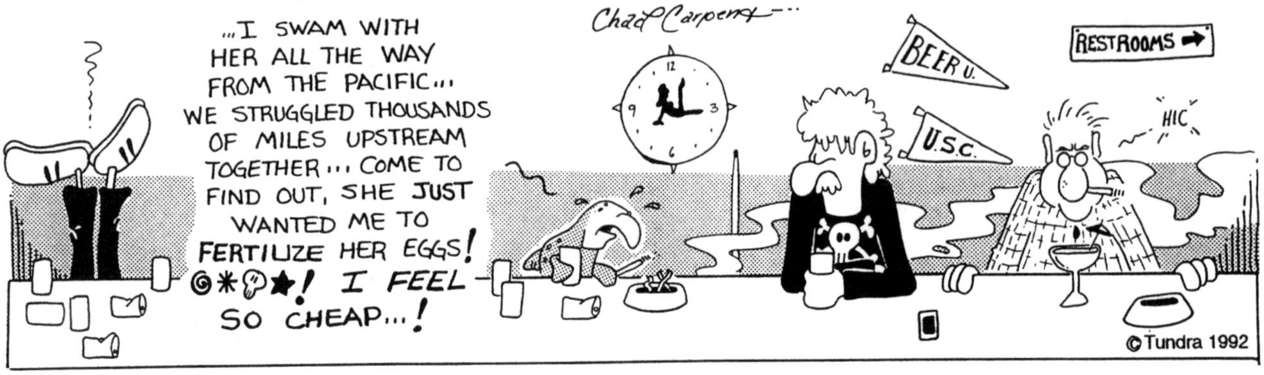
...I SWAM WITH HER ALL THE WAY FROM THE PACIFIC... WE STRUGGLED THOUSANDS OF MILES UPSTREAM TOGETHER... COME TO FIND OUT, SHE JUST WANTED ME TO FERTILIZE HER EGGS! @*?★! I FEEL SO CHEAP...!
BEER U.
U.S.C.
RESTROOMS
HIC
Chad Carpenter
©Tundra 1992

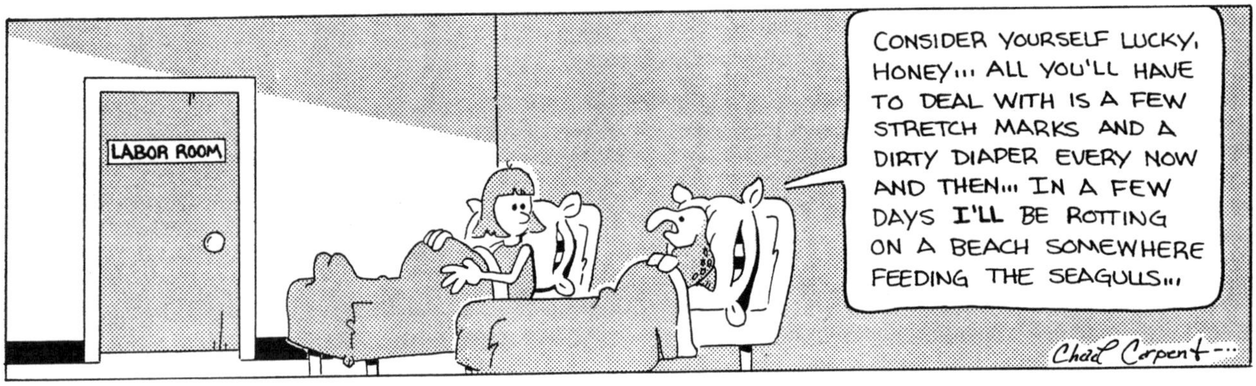
LABOR ROOM
CONSIDER YOURSELF LUCKY, HONEY... ALL YOU'LL HAVE TO DEAL WITH IS A FEW STRETCH MARKS AND A DIRTY DIAPER EVERY NOW AND THEN... IN A FEW DAYS I'LL BE ROTTING ON A BEACH SOMEWHERE FEEDING THE SEAGULLS...
Chad Carpenter

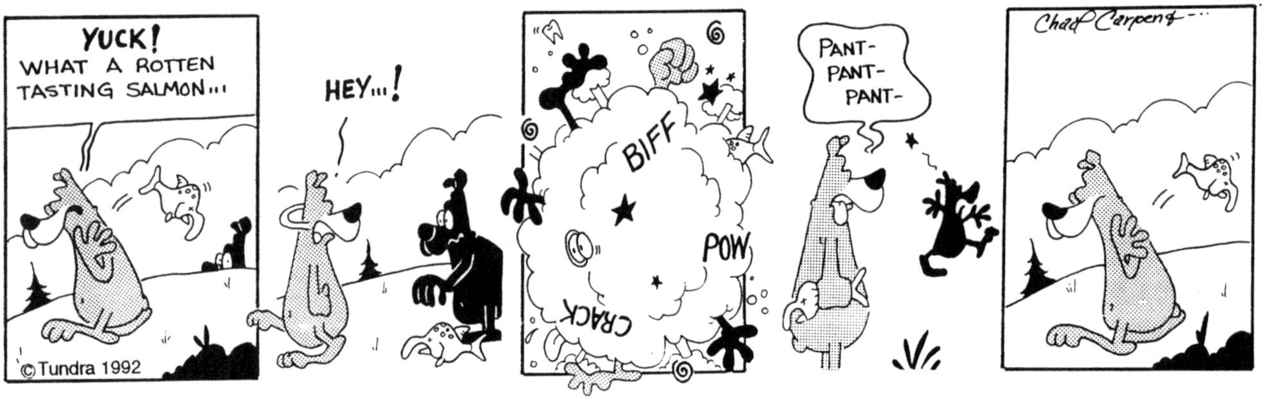
YUCK! WHAT A ROTTEN TASTING SALMON...
©Tundra 1992
HEY...!
BIFF
POW
CRACK
PANT-PANT-PANT-
Chad Carpenter

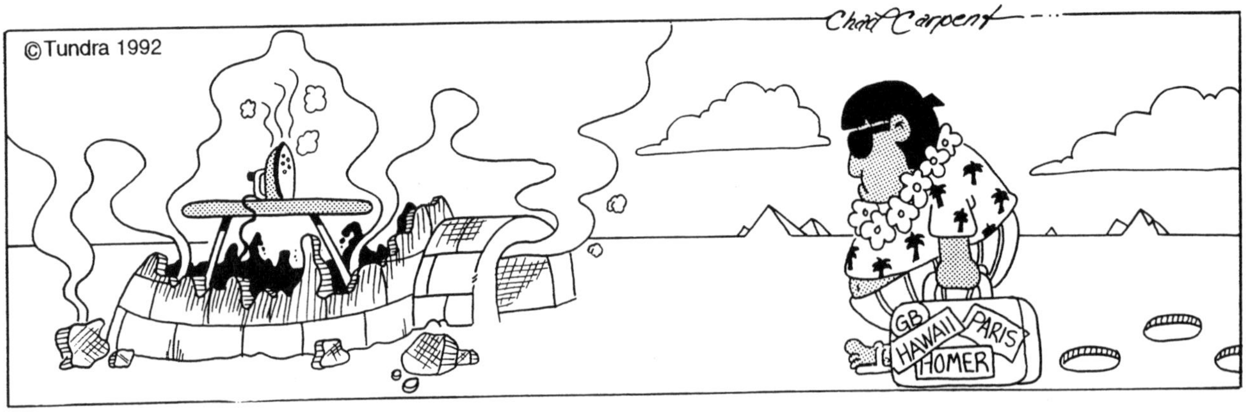
©Tundra 1992
Chad Carpenter
GB
HAWAII
PARIS
HOMER

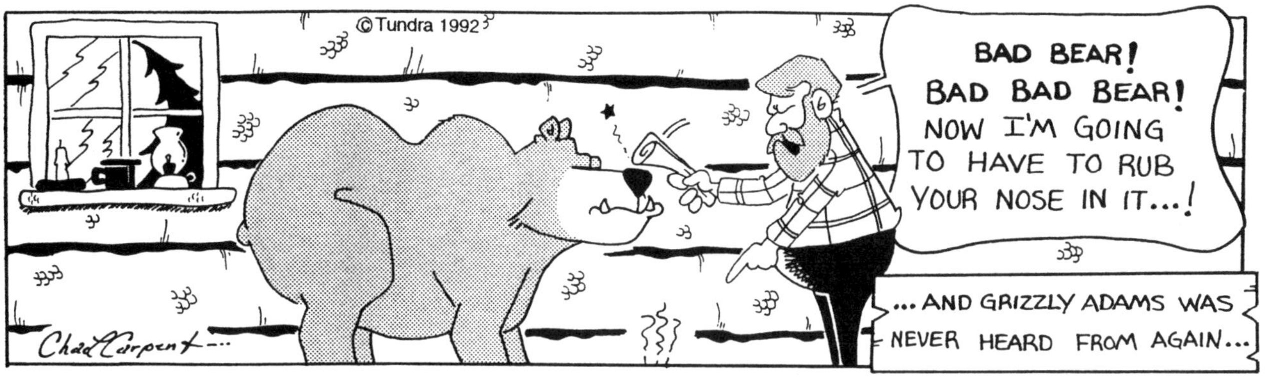
©Tundra 1992
BAD BEAR! BAD BAD BEAR! NOW I'M GOING TO HAVE TO RUB YOUR NOSE IN IT...!
...AND GRIZZLY ADAMS WAS NEVER HEARD FROM AGAIN...

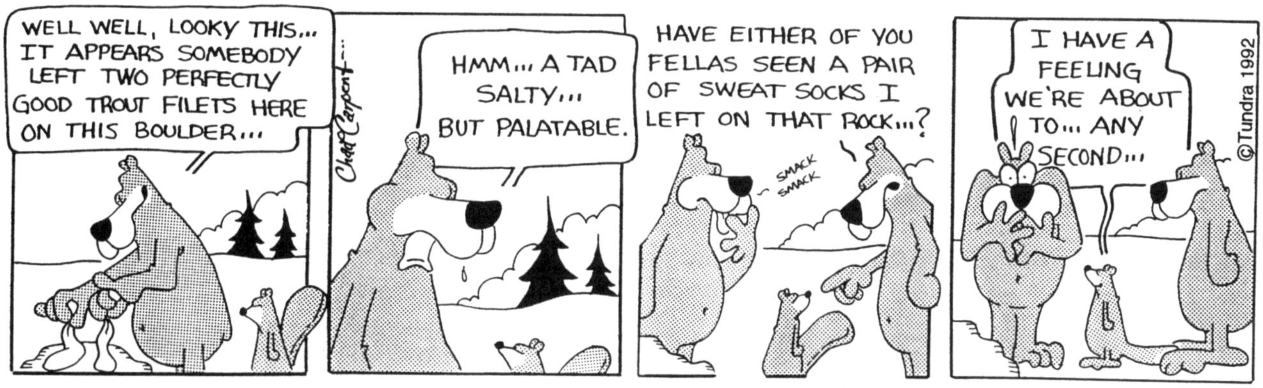
WELL WELL, LOOKY THIS... IT APPEARS SOMEBODY LEFT TWO PERFECTLY GOOD TROUT FILETS HERE ON THIS BOULDER...
HMM... A TAD SALTY... BUT PALATABLE.
HAVE EITHER OF YOU FELLAS SEEN A PAIR OF SWEAT SOCKS I LEFT ON THAT ROCK...?
SMACK SMACK
I HAVE A FEELING WE'RE ABOUT TO... ANY SECOND...
©Tundra 1992

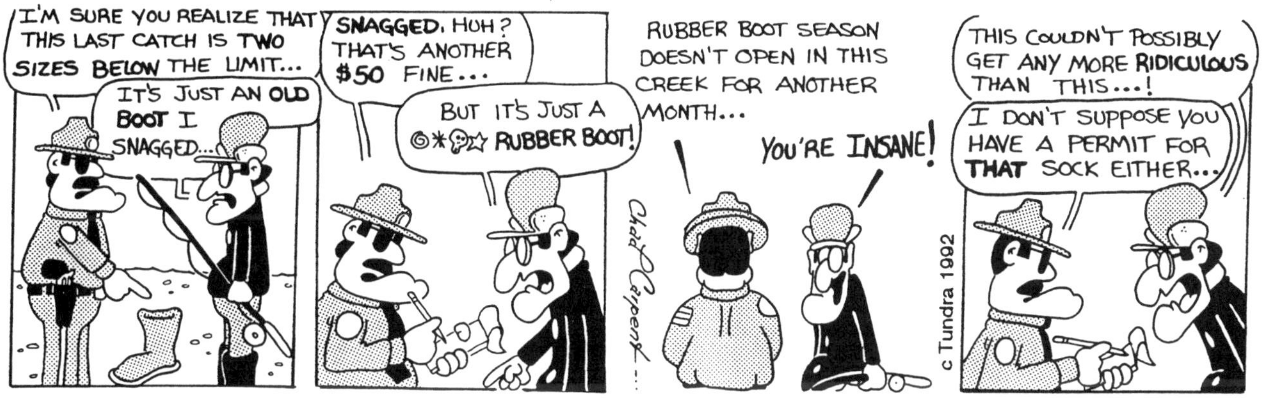
I'M SURE YOU REALIZE THAT THIS LAST CATCH IS TWO SIZES BELOW THE LIMIT...
IT'S JUST AN OLD BOOT I SNAGGED...
SNAGGED, HUH? THAT'S ANOTHER $50 FINE...
BUT IT'S JUST A @*?☆ RUBBER BOOT!
RUBBER BOOT SEASON DOESN'T OPEN IN THIS CREEK FOR ANOTHER MONTH...
YOU'RE INSANE!
c Tundra 1992
THIS COULDN'T POSSIBLY GET ANY MORE RIDICULOUS THAN THIS...!
I DON'T SUPPOSE YOU HAVE A PERMIT FOR THAT SOCK EITHER...

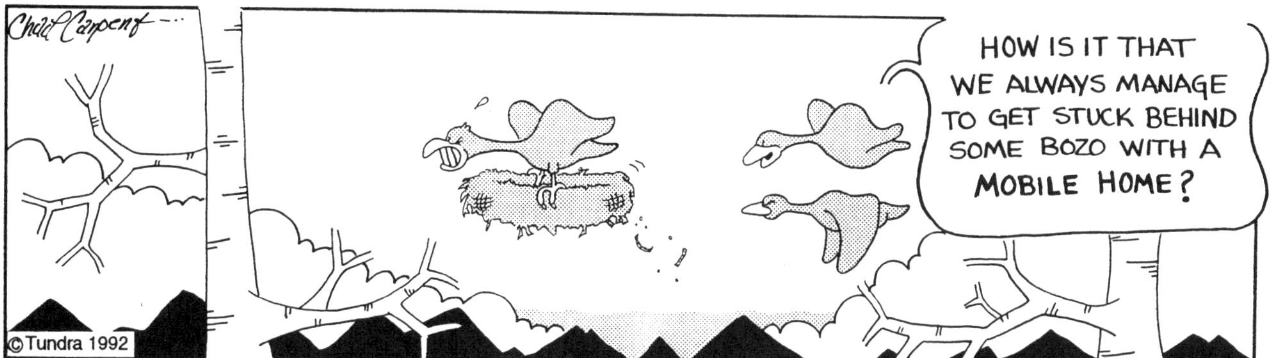
HOW IS IT THAT WE ALWAYS MANAGE TO GET STUCK BEHIND SOME BOZO WITH A MOBILE HOME?
©Tundra 1992

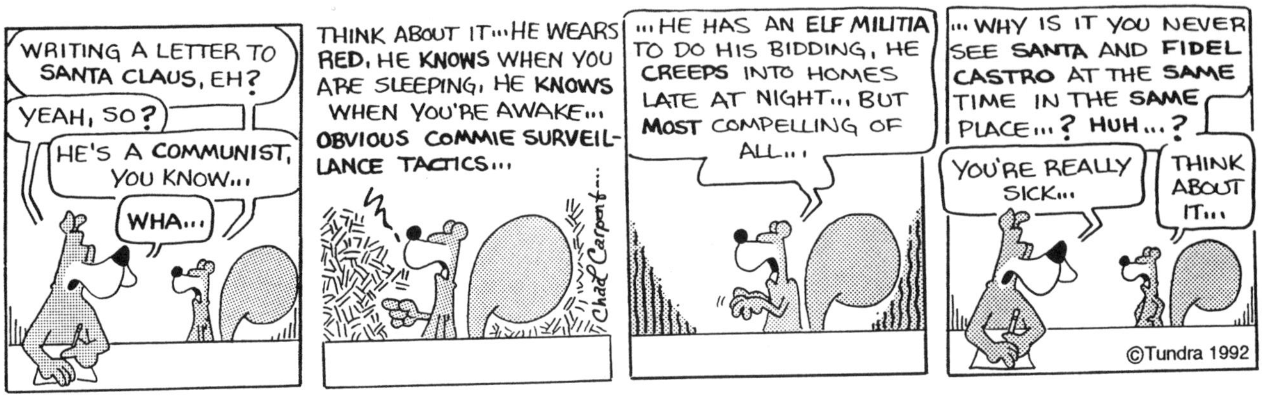
WRITING A LETTER TO SANTA CLAUS, EH?
YEAH, SO?
HE'S A COMMUNIST, YOU KNOW...
WHA...
THINK ABOUT IT... HE WEARS RED, HE KNOWS WHEN YOU ARE SLEEPING, HE KNOWS WHEN YOU'RE AWAKE... OBVIOUS COMMIE SURVEILLANCE TACTICS...
...HE HAS AN ELF MILITIA TO DO HIS BIDDING, HE CREEPS INTO HOMES LATE AT NIGHT... BUT MOST COMPELLING OF ALL...
...WHY IS IT YOU NEVER SEE SANTA AND FIDEL CASTRO AT THE SAME TIME IN THE SAME PLACE...? HUH...?
YOU'RE REALLY SICK...
THINK ABOUT IT...
©Tundra 1992

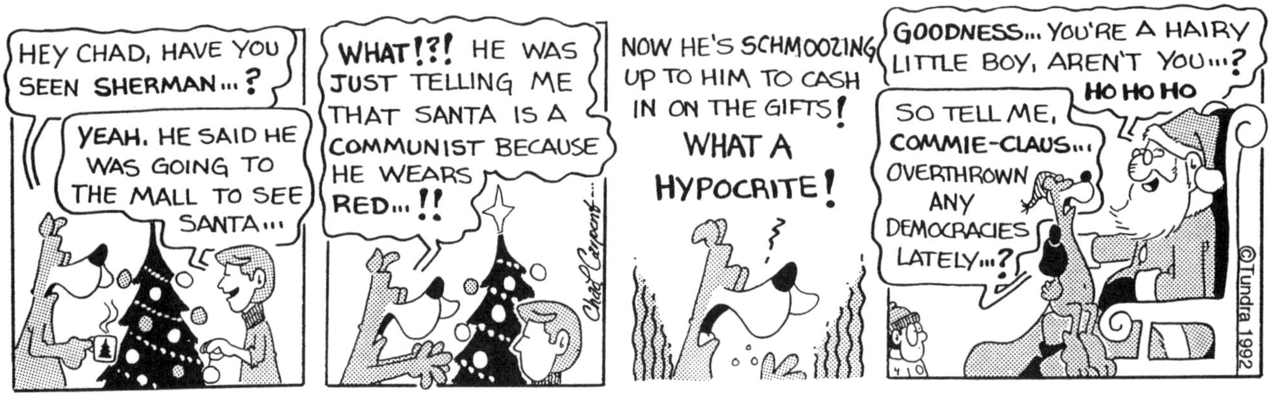
HEY CHAD, HAVE YOU SEEN SHERMAN...?
YEAH. HE SAID HE WAS GOING TO THE MALL TO SEE SANTA...
WHAT!?! HE WAS JUST TELLING ME THAT SANTA IS A COMMUNIST BECAUSE HE WEARS RED...!!
NOW HE'S SCHMOOZING UP TO HIM TO CASH IN ON THE GIFTS! WHAT A HYPOCRITE!
GOODNESS... YOU'RE A HAIRY LITTLE BOY, AREN'T YOU...?
HO HO HO
SO TELL ME, COMMIE-CLAUS... OVERTHROWN ANY DEMOCRACIES LATELY...?
©Tundra 1992

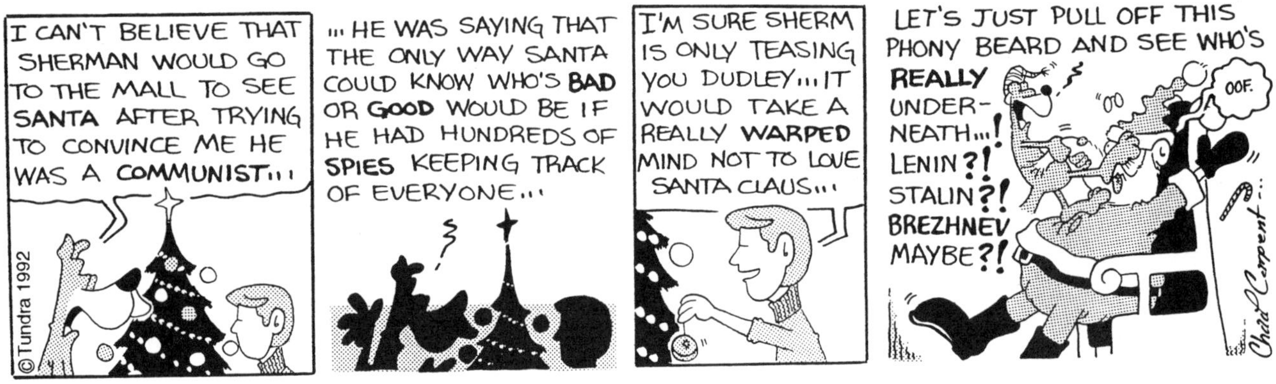
I CAN'T BELIEVE THAT SHERMAN WOULD GO TO THE MALL TO SEE SANTA AFTER TRYING TO CONVINCE ME HE WAS A COMMUNIST...
©Tundra 1992
...HE WAS SAYING THAT THE ONLY WAY SANTA COULD KNOW WHO'S BAD OR GOOD WOULD BE IF HE HAD HUNDREDS OF SPIES KEEPING TRACK OF EVERYONE...
I'M SURE SHERM IS ONLY TEASING YOU DUDLEY... IT WOULD TAKE A REALLY WARPED MIND NOT TO LOVE SANTA CLAUS...
LET'S JUST PULL OFF THIS PHONY BEARD AND SEE WHO'S REALLY UNDERNEATH...! LENIN?! STALIN?! BREZHNEV MAYBE?!
OOF.

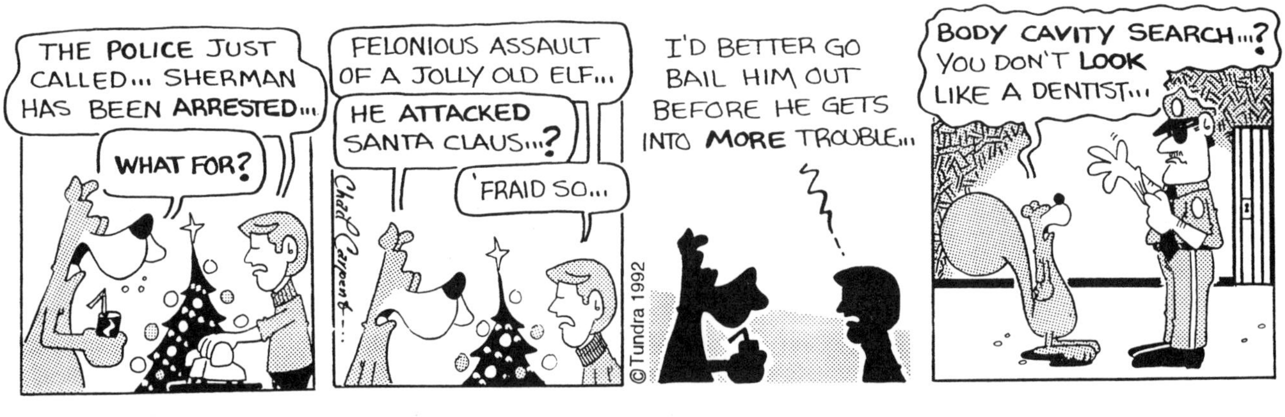
THE POLICE JUST CALLED... SHERMAN HAS BEEN ARRESTED...
WHAT FOR?
FELONIOUS ASSAULT OF A JOLLY OLD ELF...
HE ATTACKED SANTA CLAUS...?
'FRAID SO...
©Tundra 1992
I'D BETTER GO BAIL HIM OUT BEFORE HE GETS INTO MORE TROUBLE...
BODY CAVITY SEARCH...? YOU DON'T LOOK LIKE A DENTIST...

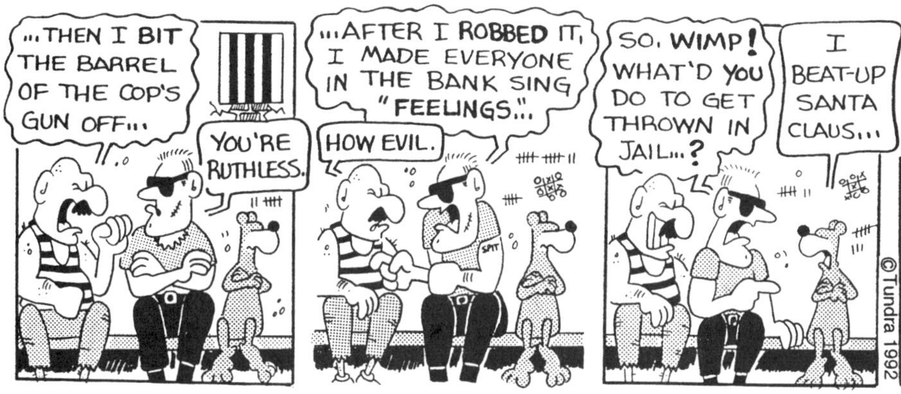
...THEN I BIT THE BARREL OF THE COP'S GUN OFF...
YOU'RE RUTHLESS.
...AFTER I ROBBED IT, I MADE EVERYONE IN THE BANK SING "FEELINGS."...
HOW EVIL.
SO, WIMP! WHAT'D YOU DO TO GET THROWN IN JAIL...?
I BEAT-UP SANTA CLAUS...
MOM
©Tundra 1992
Chad Carpenter...

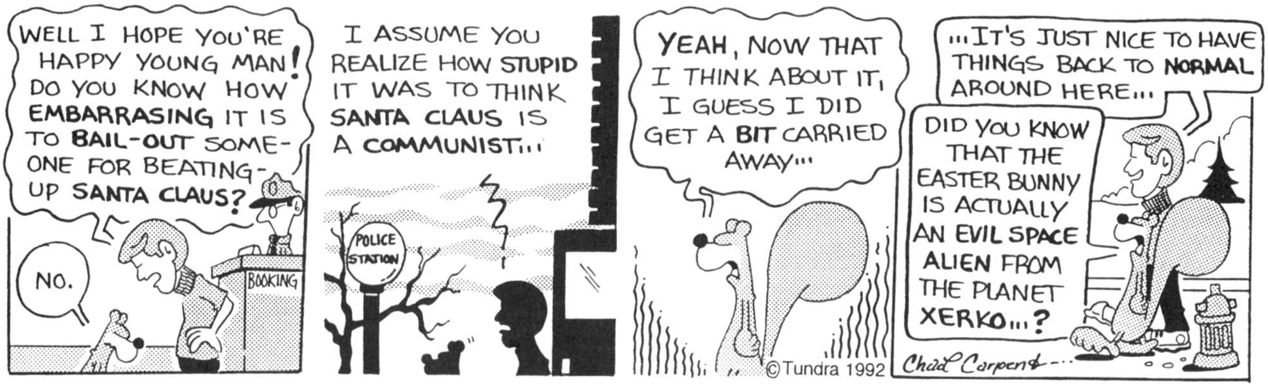
WELL I HOPE YOU'RE HAPPY YOUNG MAN! DO YOU KNOW HOW EMBARRASING IT IS TO BAIL-OUT SOME-ONE FOR BEATING-UP SANTA CLAUS?
NO.
BOOKING
I ASSUME YOU REALIZE HOW STUPID IT WAS TO THINK SANTA CLAUS IS A COMMUNIST...
POLICE STATION
YEAH, NOW THAT I THINK ABOUT IT, I GUESS I DID GET A BIT CARRIED AWAY...
©Tundra 1992
...IT'S JUST NICE TO HAVE THINGS BACK TO NORMAL AROUND HERE...
DID YOU KNOW THAT THE EASTER BUNNY IS ACTUALLY AN EVIL SPACE ALIEN FROM THE PLANET XERKO...?
Chad Carpenter...

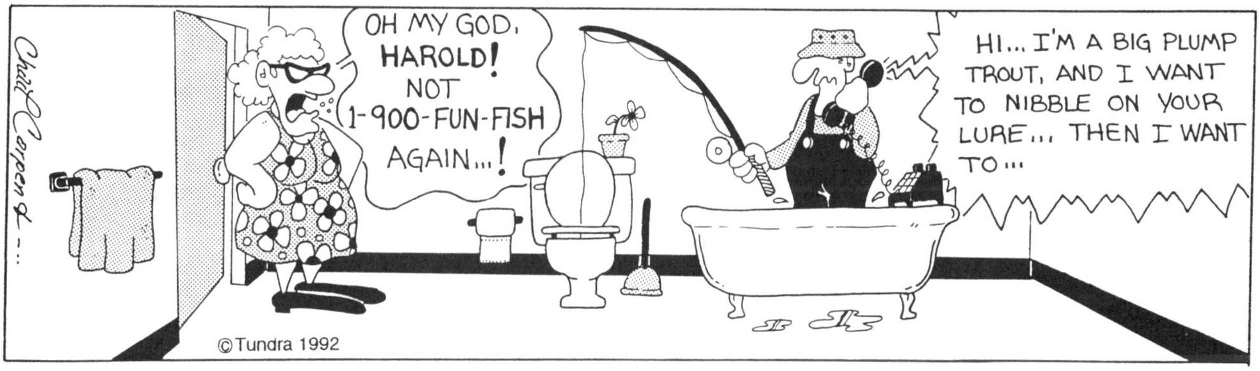
Chad Carpenter...
OH MY GOD, HAROLD! NOT 1-900-FUN-FISH AGAIN...!
HI... I'M A BIG PLUMP TROUT, AND I WANT TO NIBBLE ON YOUR LURE... THEN I WANT TO...
©Tundra 1992

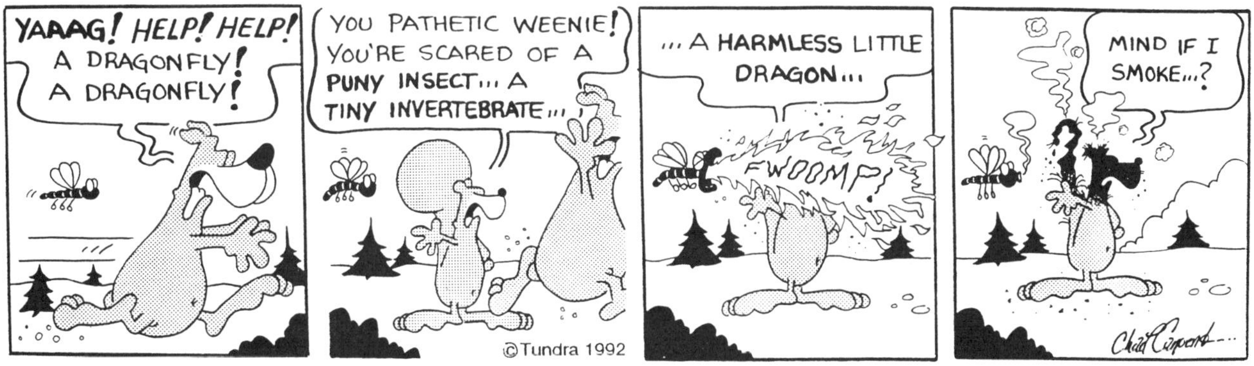
YAAAG! HELP! HELP! A DRAGONFLY! A DRAGONFLY!
YOU PATHETIC WEENIE! YOU'RE SCARED OF A PUNY INSECT... A TINY INVERTEBRATE...
©Tundra 1992
...A HARMLESS LITTLE DRAGON...
FWOOMP!
MIND IF I SMOKE...?
Chad Carpenter...

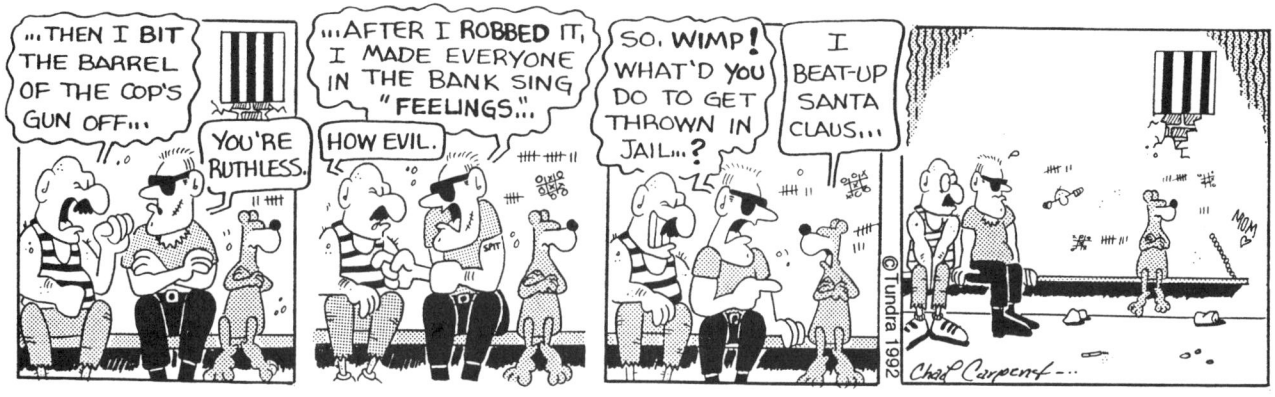

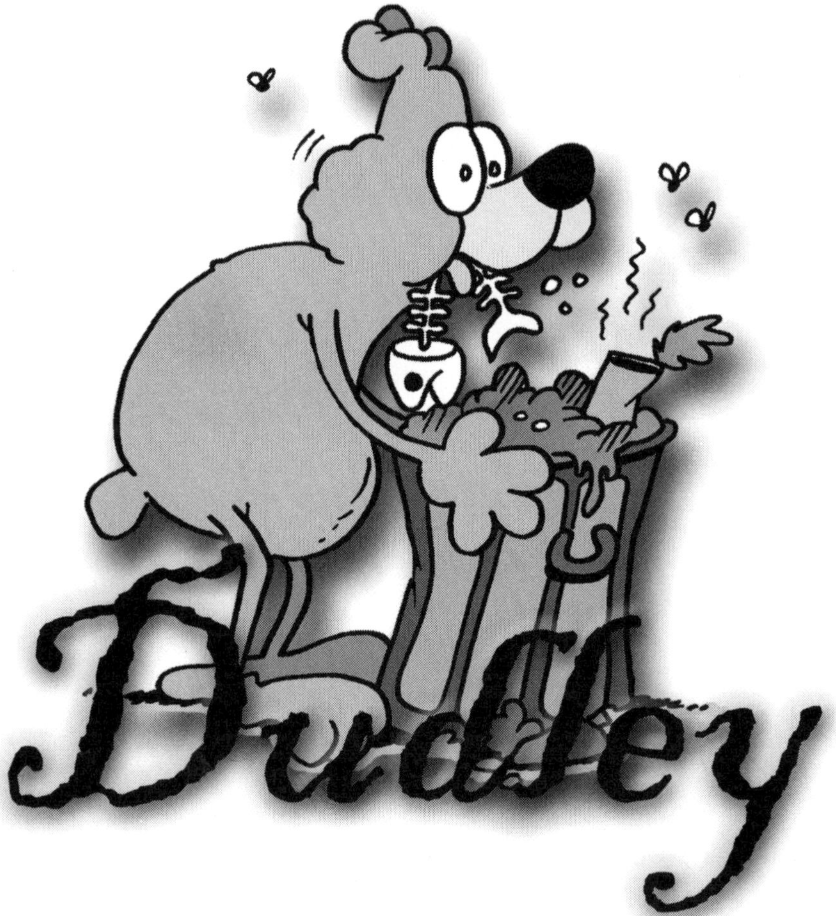
Dudley

Dudley, a well-intentioned but less-than-intelligent bear, appears frequently as the butt of numerous mishaps and jokes within the confines of the Tundra strip.

Dudley was born in the mountainous regions of Northern Kansas to a pair of traveling dancing bears. Dudley spent his early years on the road with his parents and appearing as the bearded lady in the circus.

After setting the unprecedented record of three years in continuous hibernation, he awoke to the startling discovery that he had sleep-walked thousands of miles to the outskirts of beatiful Gangrene Gulch. As the smell of the municipal landfill engulfed his senses, Dudley knew that this was the place that was destined to be his home.

Dudley is a bear of multiple hobbies which include sleeping for long periods of time, turning over logs and collecting priceless works of art.

Chapter Two

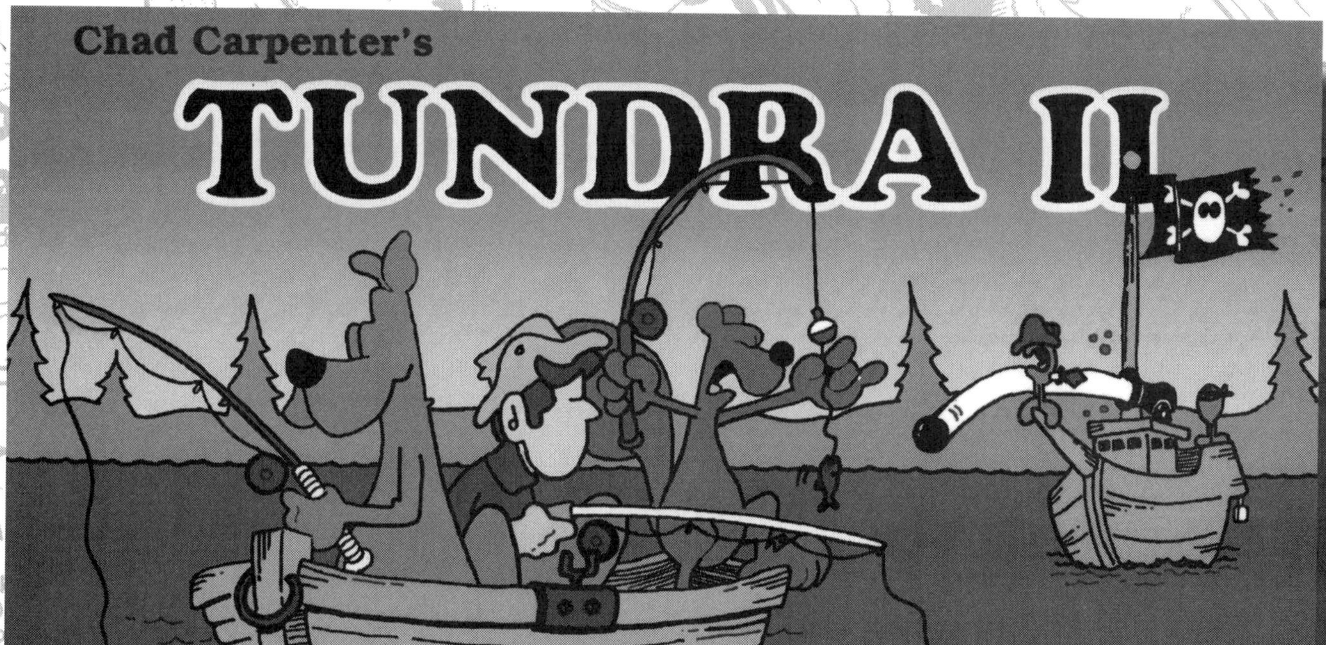
Chad Carpenter's
TUNDRA II
MORE CARTOONS FROM THE LAST FRONTIER

First Printing: April 1994

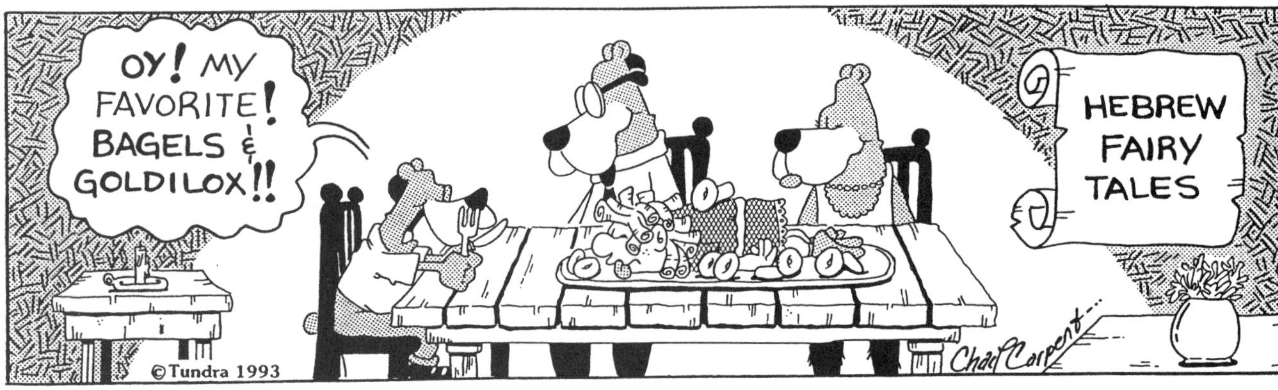
OY! MY FAVORITE! BAGELS & GOLDILOX!!
HEBREW FAIRY TALES
©Tundra 1993
Chad Carpenter

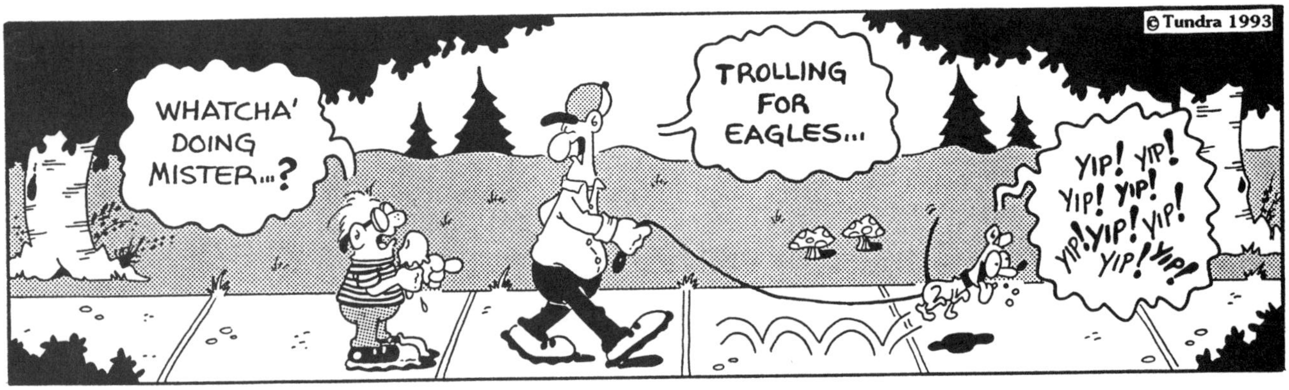
©Tundra 1993
WHATCHA' DOING MISTER...?
TROLLING FOR EAGLES...
YIP! YIP! YIP! YIP! YIP! YIP! YIP! YIP! YIP! YIP!

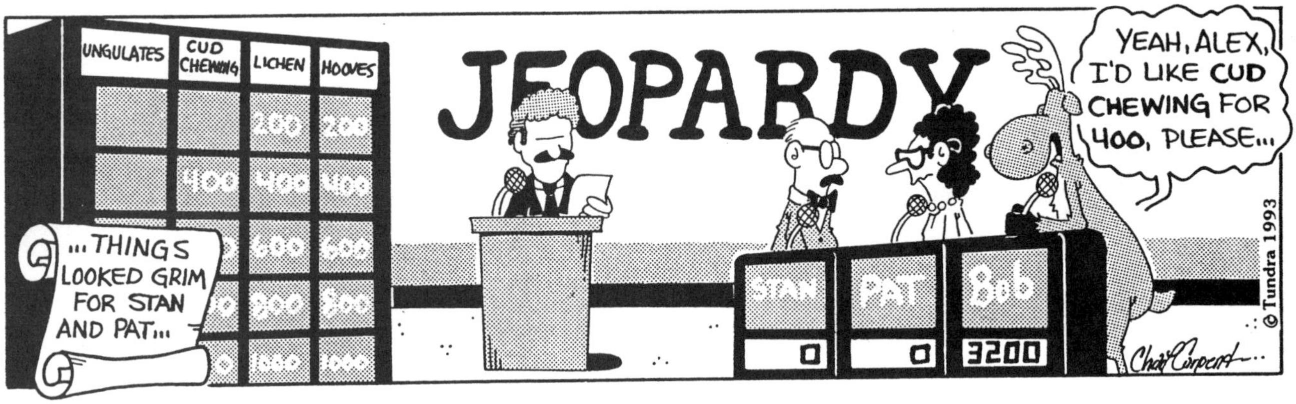
UNGULATES
CUD CHEWING
LICHEN
HOOVES
JEOPARDY
YEAH, ALEX, I'D LIKE CUD CHEWING FOR 400, PLEASE...
...THINGS LOOKED GRIM FOR STAN AND PAT...
STAN
PAT
Bob
0
0
3200
©Tundra 1993
Chad Carpenter

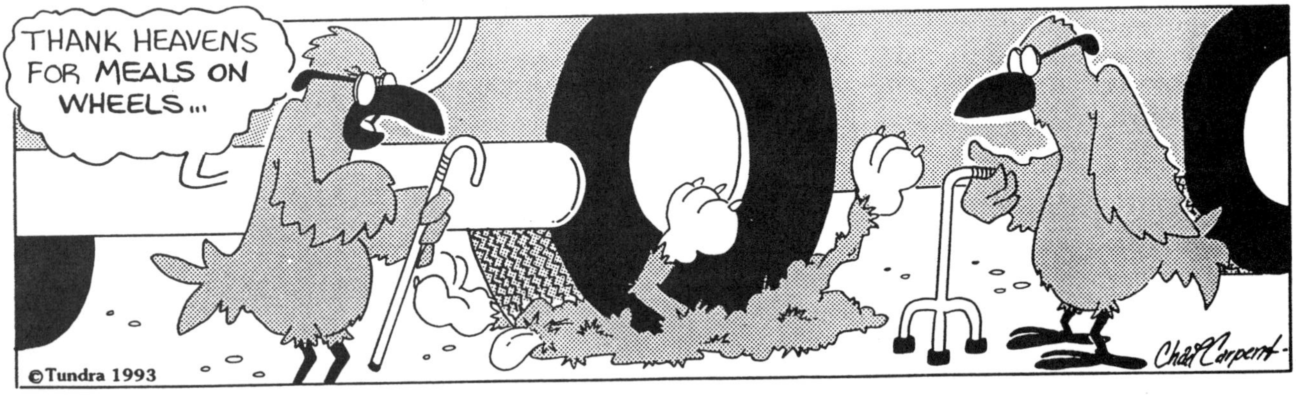
THANK HEAVENS FOR MEALS ON WHEELS...
©Tundra 1993
Chad Carpenter

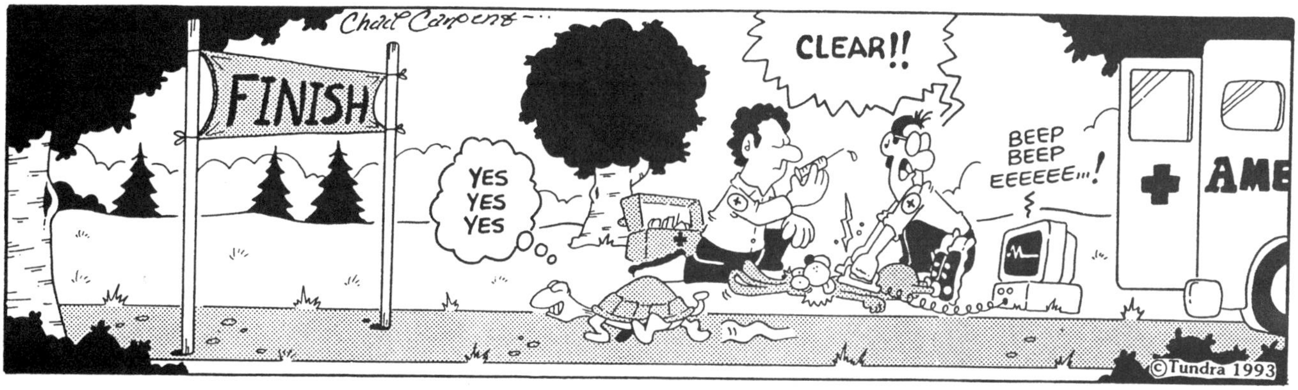
Chad Carpenter
FINISH
YES YES YES
CLEAR!!
BEEP BEEP EEEEEE...!
AME
©Tundra 1993

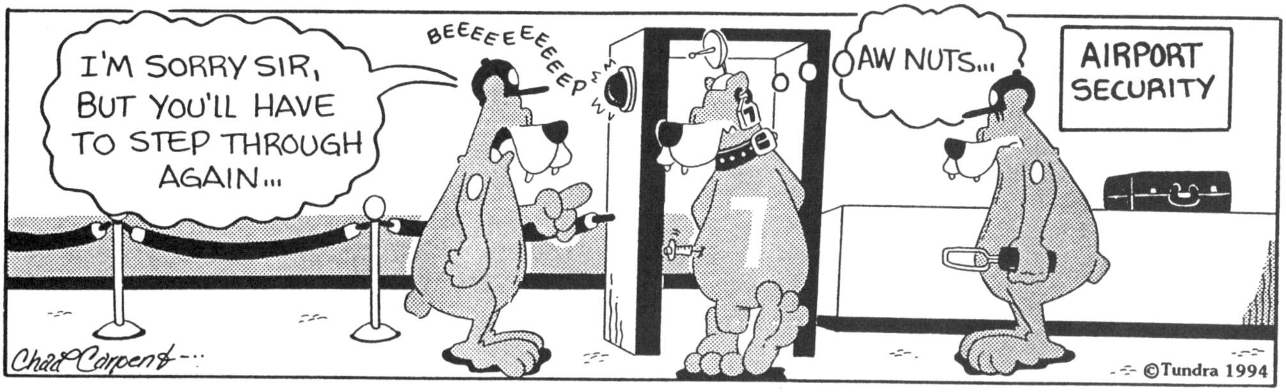
I'M SORRY SIR, BUT YOU'LL HAVE TO STEP THROUGH AGAIN...
BEEEEEEEEEEEEP
AW NUTS...
AIRPORT SECURITY
7
Chad Carpenter
©Tundra 1994

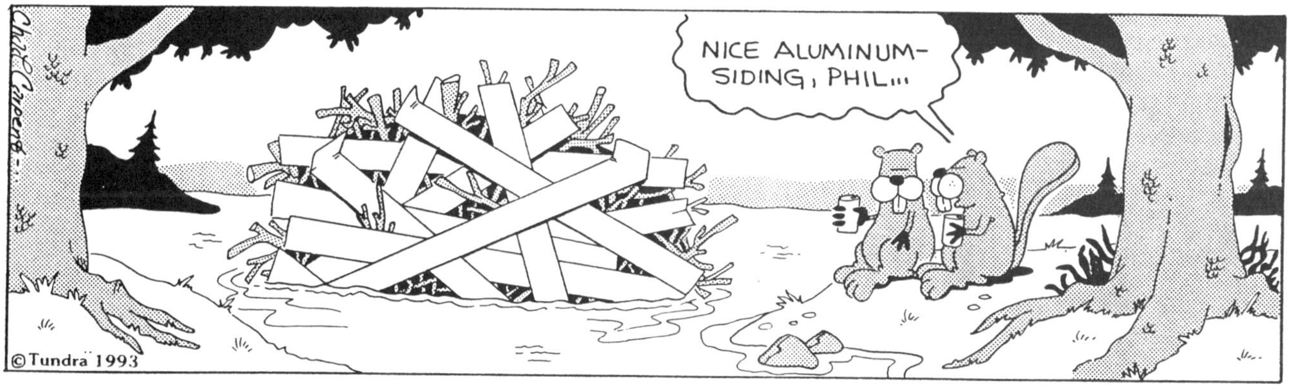
Chad Carpenter
NICE ALUMINUM-SIDING, PHIL...
©Tundra 1993

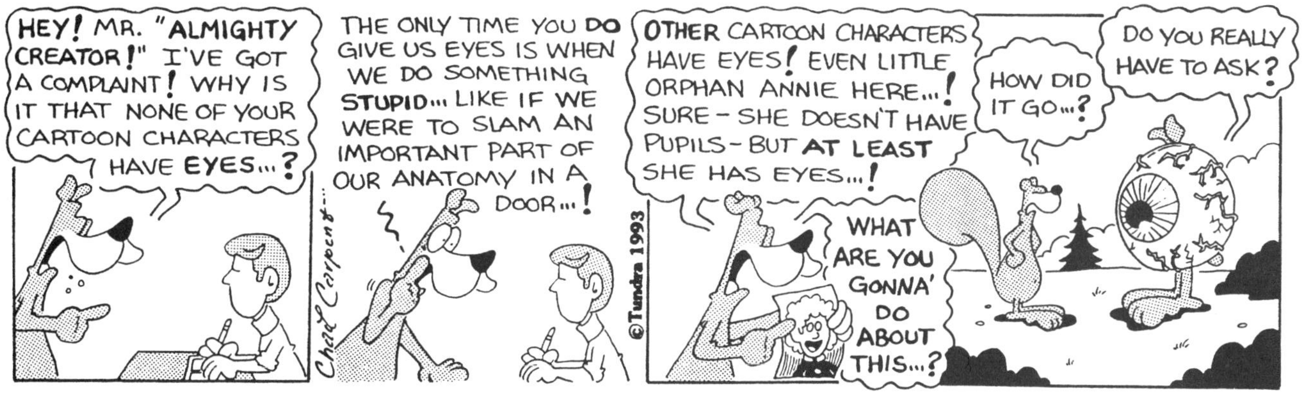
HEY! MR. "ALMIGHTY CREATOR!" I'VE GOT A COMPLAINT! WHY IS IT THAT NONE OF YOUR CARTOON CHARACTERS HAVE EYES...?
THE ONLY TIME YOU DO GIVE US EYES IS WHEN WE DO SOMETHING STUPID... LIKE IF WE WERE TO SLAM AN IMPORTANT PART OF OUR ANATOMY IN A DOOR...!
Chad Carpenter
©Tundra 1993
OTHER CARTOON CHARACTERS HAVE EYES! EVEN LITTLE ORPHAN ANNIE HERE...! SURE - SHE DOESN'T HAVE PUPILS - BUT AT LEAST SHE HAS EYES...!
WHAT ARE YOU GONNA' DO ABOUT THIS...?
HOW DID IT GO...?
DO YOU REALLY HAVE TO ASK?

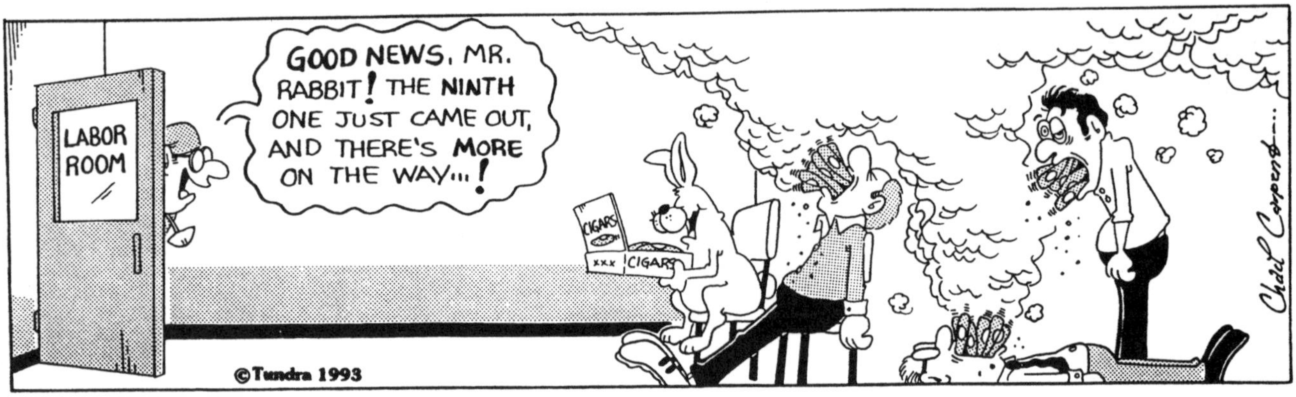
LABOR ROOM
GOOD NEWS, MR. RABBIT! THE NINTH ONE JUST CAME OUT, AND THERE'S MORE ON THE WAY...!
CIGARS
XXX CIGARS
©Tundra 1993

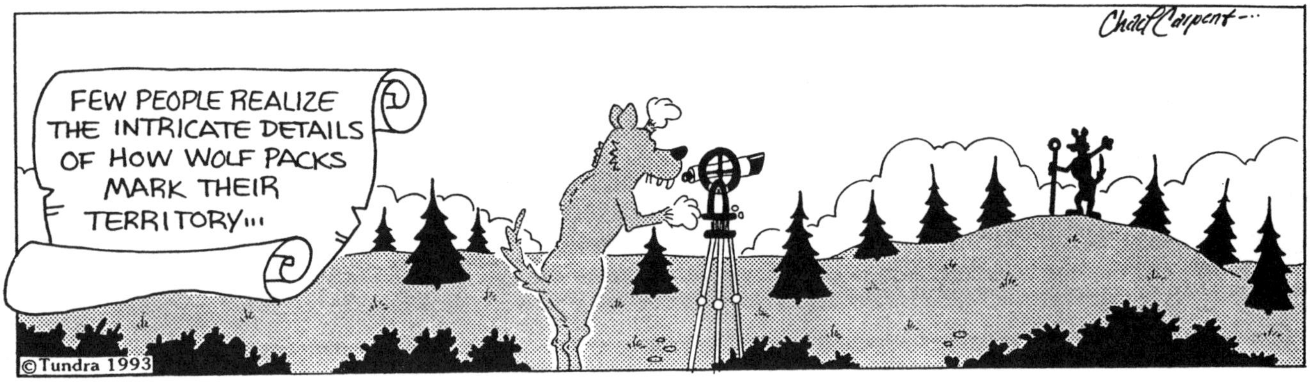
FEW PEOPLE REALIZE THE INTRICATE DETAILS OF HOW WOLF PACKS MARK THEIR TERRITORY...
©Tundra 1993

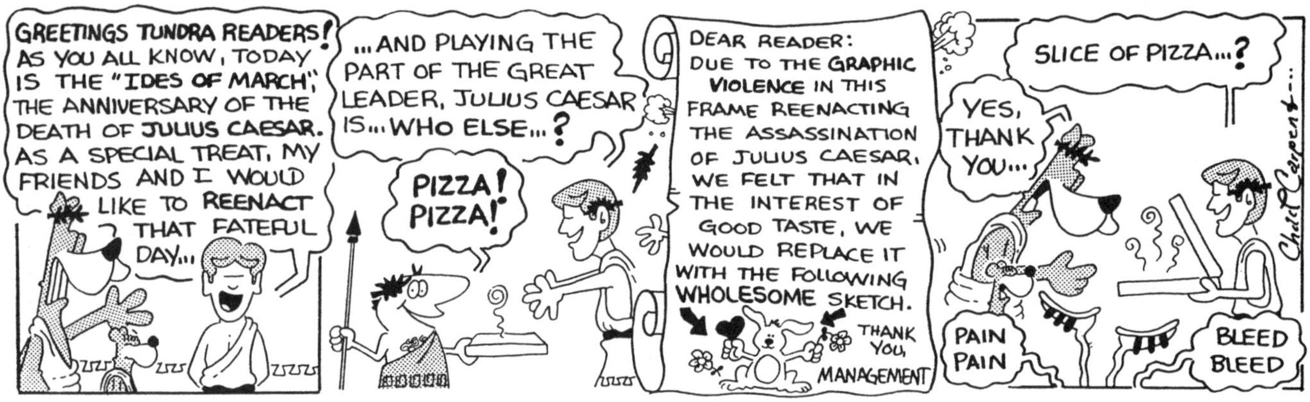
GREETINGS TUNDRA READERS! AS YOU ALL KNOW, TODAY IS THE "IDES OF MARCH", THE ANNIVERSARY OF THE DEATH OF JULIUS CAESAR. AS A SPECIAL TREAT, MY FRIENDS AND I WOULD LIKE TO REENACT THAT FATEFUL DAY...
...AND PLAYING THE PART OF THE GREAT LEADER, JULIUS CAESAR IS... WHO ELSE...?
PIZZA! PIZZA!
DEAR READER: DUE TO THE GRAPHIC VIOLENCE IN THIS FRAME REENACTING THE ASSASSINATION OF JULIUS CAESAR, WE FELT THAT IN THE INTEREST OF GOOD TASTE, WE WOULD REPLACE IT WITH THE FOLLOWING WHOLESOME SKETCH.
THANK YOU, MANAGEMENT
SLICE OF PIZZA...?
YES, THANK YOU...
PAIN PAIN
BLEED BLEED

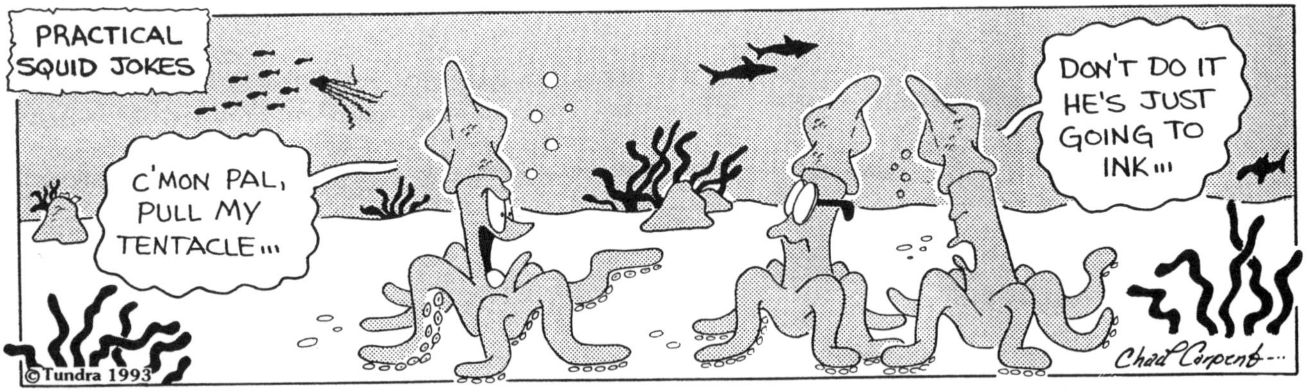
PRACTICAL SQUID JOKES
C'MON PAL, PULL MY TENTACLE...
DON'T DO IT HE'S JUST GOING TO INK...
©Tundra 1993

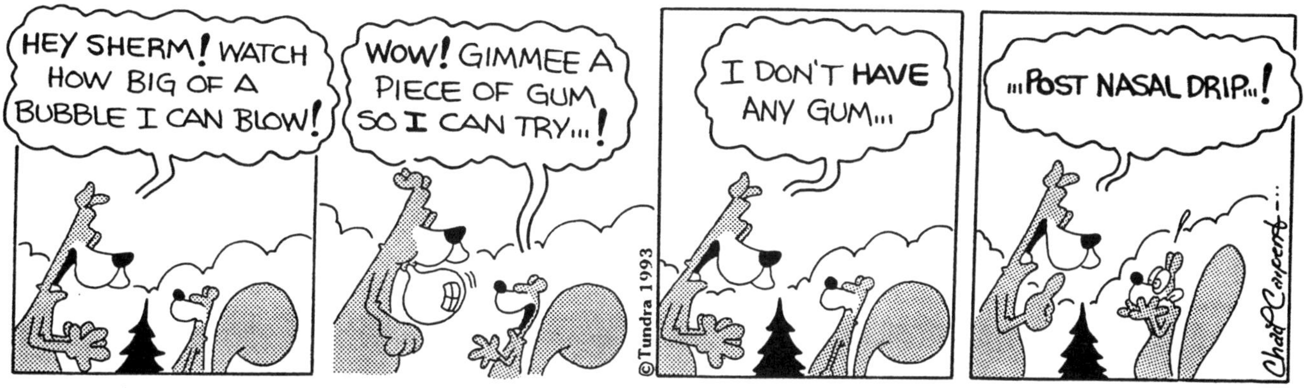
HEY SHERM! WATCH HOW BIG OF A BUBBLE I CAN BLOW!
WOW! GIMMEE A PIECE OF GUM SO I CAN TRY...!
I DON'T HAVE ANY GUM...
...POST NASAL DRIP...!
©Tundra 1993

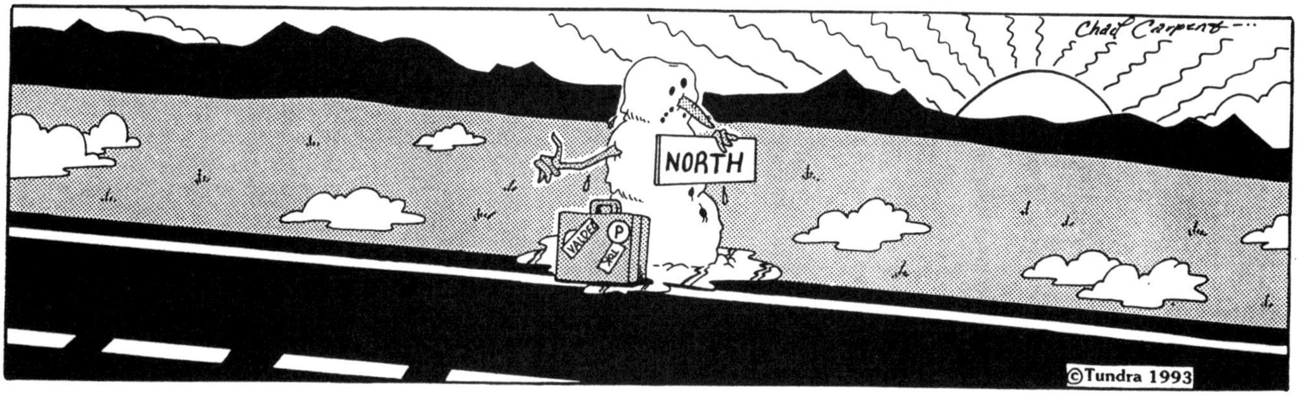
NORTH
VALDEZ
©Tundra 1993

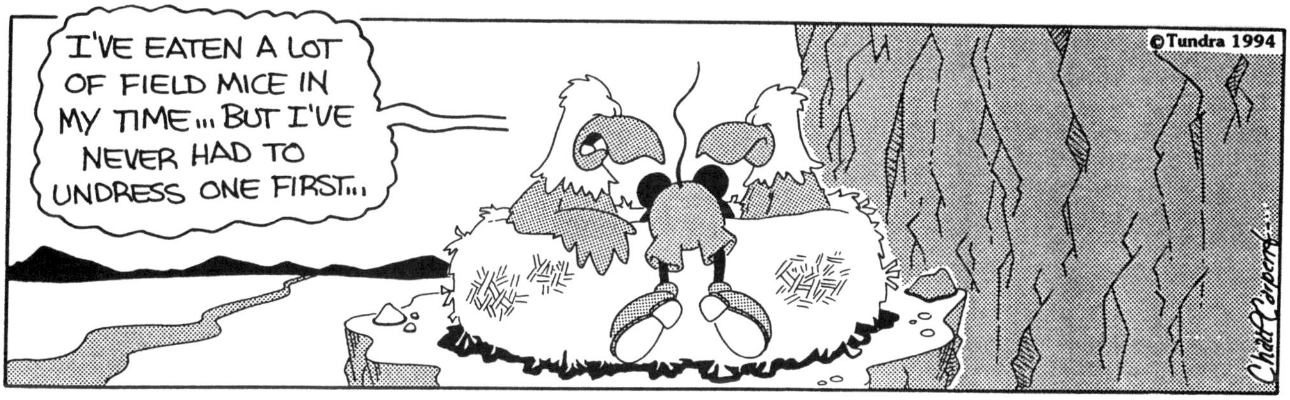
I'VE EATEN A LOT OF FIELD MICE IN MY TIME... BUT I'VE NEVER HAD TO UNDRESS ONE FIRST...
©Tundra 1994

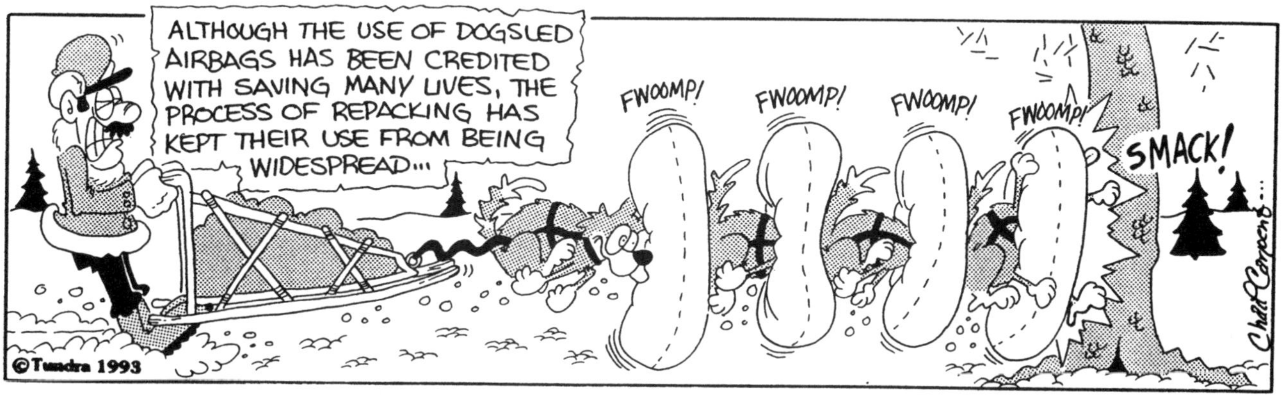
ALTHOUGH THE USE OF DOGSLED AIRBAGS HAS BEEN CREDITED WITH SAVING MANY LIVES, THE PROCESS OF REPACKING HAS KEPT THEIR USE FROM BEING WIDESPREAD...
FWOOMP!
FWOOMP!
FWOOMP!
FWOOMP!
SMACK!
©Tundra 1993

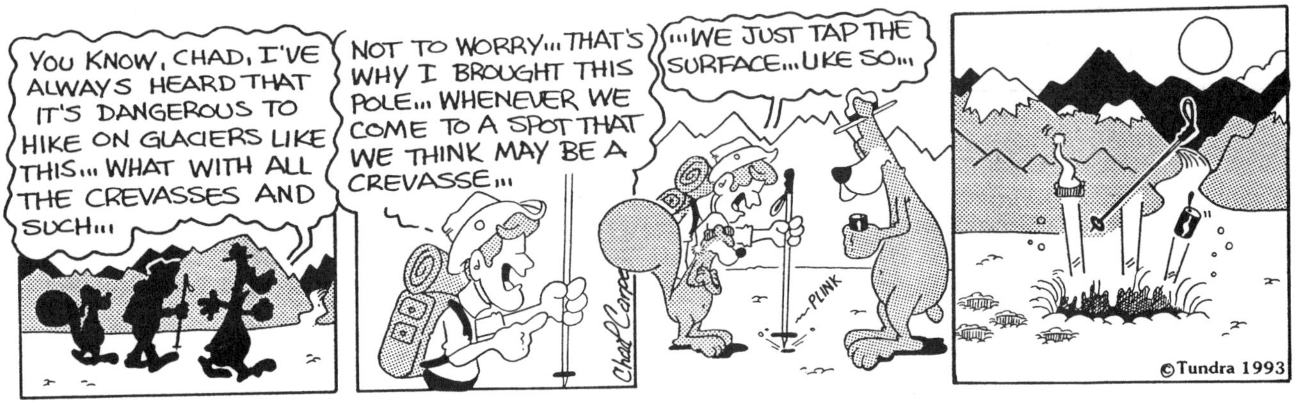
YOU KNOW, CHAD, I'VE ALWAYS HEARD THAT IT'S DANGEROUS TO HIKE ON GLACIERS LIKE THIS... WHAT WITH ALL THE CREVASSES AND SUCH...
NOT TO WORRY... THAT'S WHY I BROUGHT THIS POLE... WHENEVER WE COME TO A SPOT THAT WE THINK MAY BE A CREVASSE...
...WE JUST TAP THE SURFACE... LIKE SO...
PLINK
©Tundra 1993

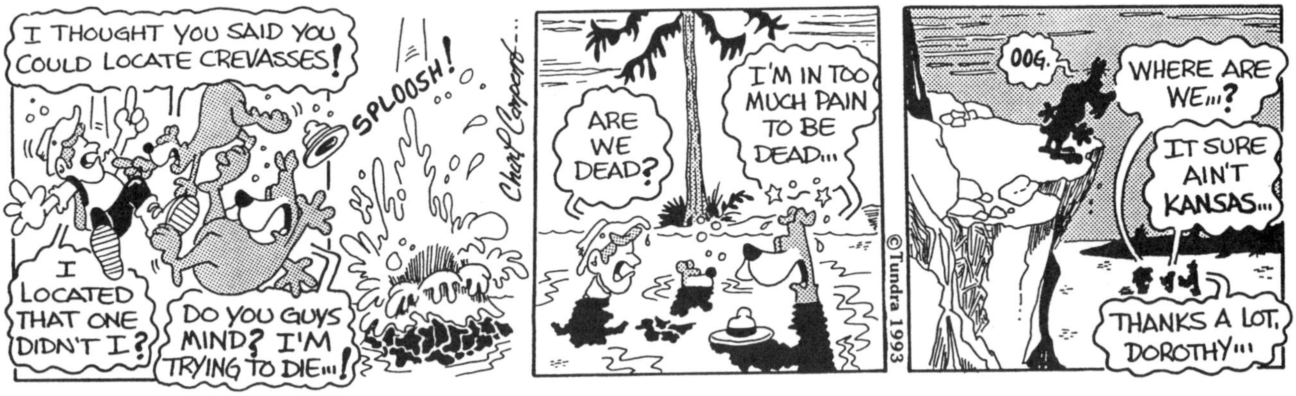
I THOUGHT YOU SAID YOU COULD LOCATE CREVASSES!
I LOCATED THAT ONE DIDN'T I?
DO YOU GUYS MIND? I'M TRYING TO DIE...!
SPLOOSH!
ARE WE DEAD?
I'M IN TOO MUCH PAIN TO BE DEAD...
©Tundra 1993
OOG.
WHERE ARE WE...?
IT SURE AIN'T KANSAS...
THANKS A LOT, DOROTHY...

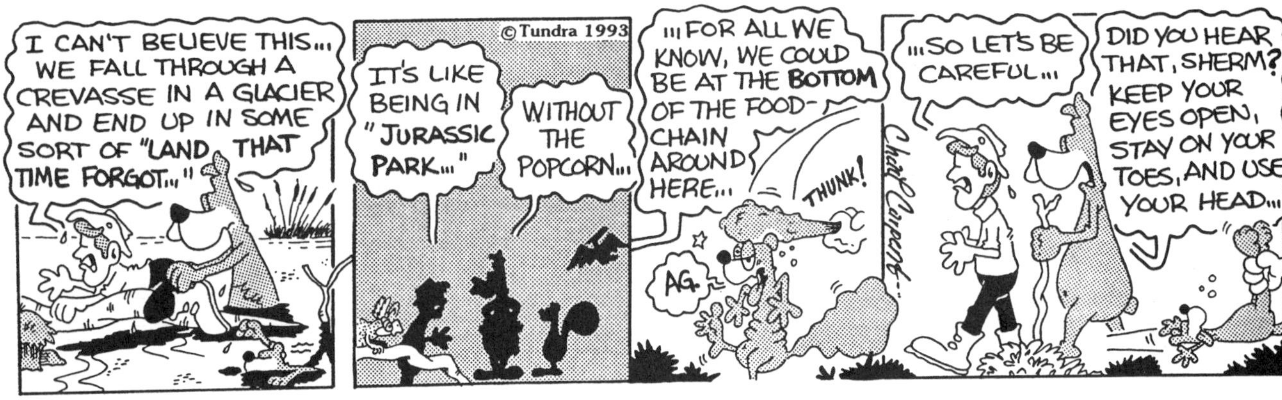
I CAN'T BELIEVE THIS... WE FALL THROUGH A CREVASSE IN A GLACIER AND END UP IN SOME SORT OF "LAND THAT TIME FORGOT..."
©Tundra 1993
IT'S LIKE BEING IN "JURASSIC PARK..."
WITHOUT THE POPCORN...
...FOR ALL WE KNOW, WE COULD BE AT THE BOTTOM OF THE FOOD-CHAIN AROUND HERE...
THUNK!
AG.
...SO LET'S BE CAREFUL...
DID YOU HEAR THAT, SHERM? KEEP YOUR EYES OPEN, STAY ON YOUR TOES, AND USE YOUR HEAD...

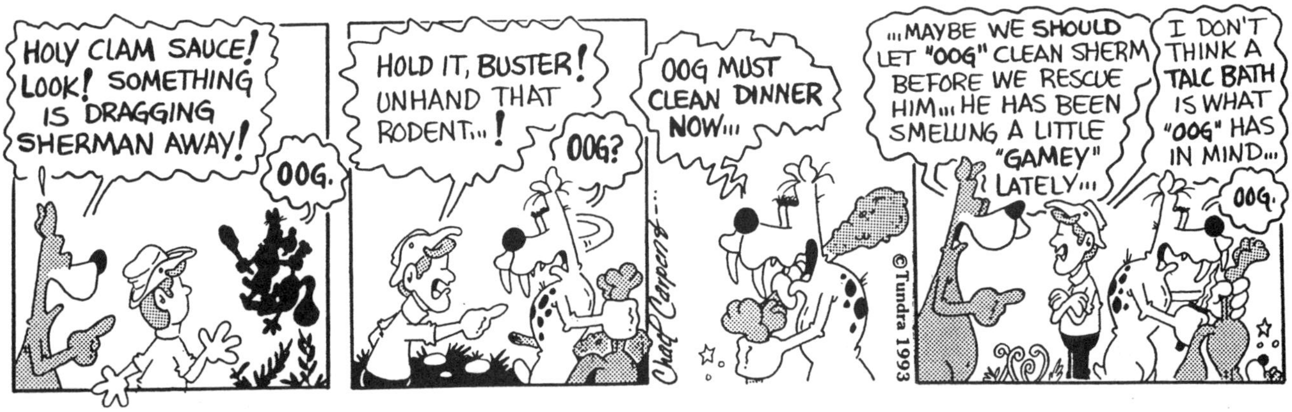
HOLY CLAM SAUCE! LOOK! SOMETHING IS DRAGGING SHERMAN AWAY!
OOG.
HOLD IT, BUSTER! UNHAND THAT RODENT...!
OOG?
OOG MUST CLEAN DINNER NOW...
©Tundra 1993
...MAYBE WE SHOULD LET "OOG" CLEAN SHERM BEFORE WE RESCUE HIM... HE HAS BEEN SMELLING A LITTLE "GAMEY" LATELY...
I DON'T THINK A TALC BATH IS WHAT "OOG" HAS IN MIND...
OOG.

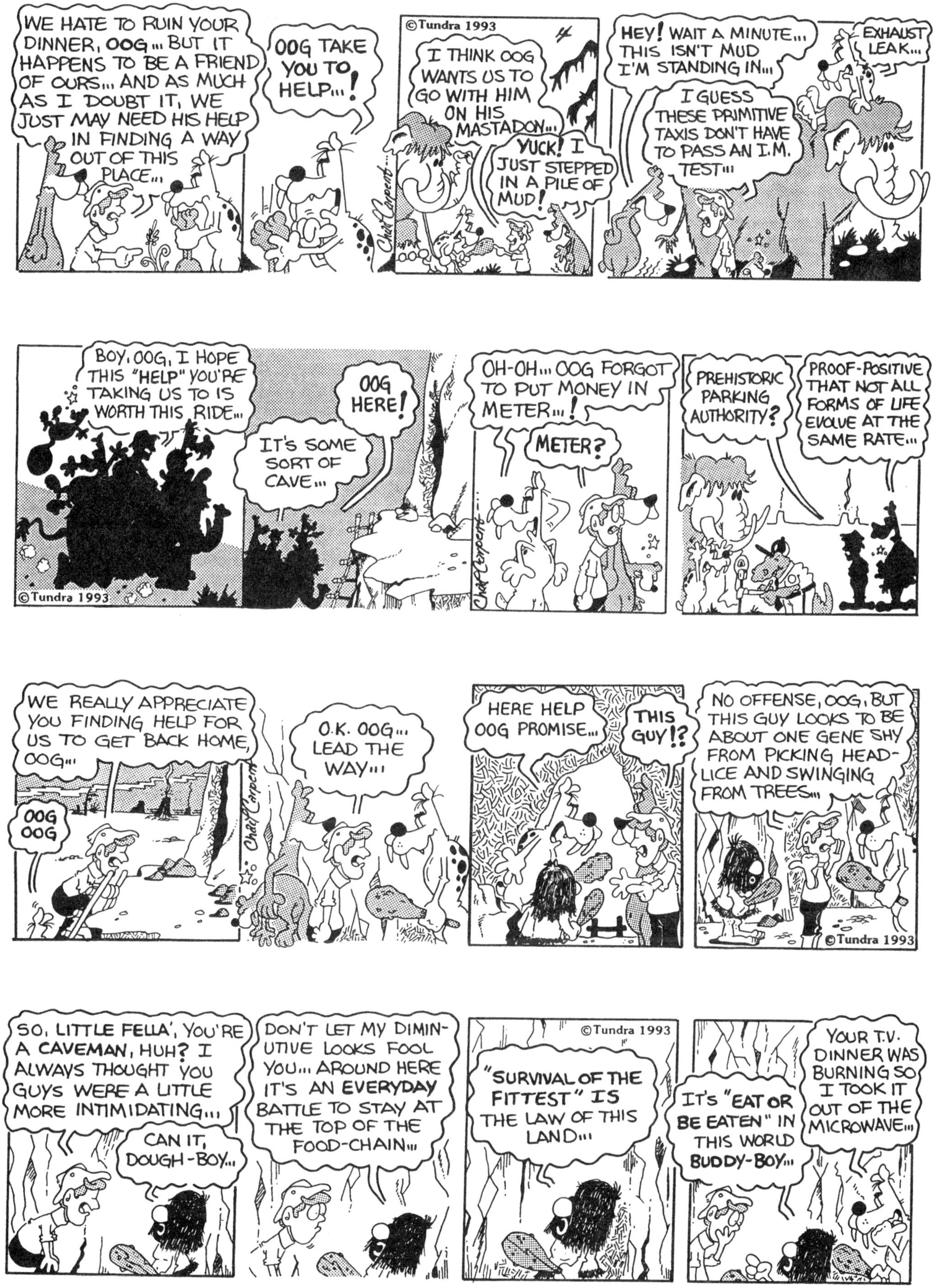
WE HATE TO RUIN YOUR DINNER, OOG... BUT IT HAPPENS TO BE A FRIEND OF OURS... AND AS MUCH AS I DOUBT IT, WE JUST MAY NEED HIS HELP IN FINDING A WAY OUT OF THIS PLACE...
OOG TAKE YOU TO HELP...!
©Tundra 1993
I THINK OOG WANTS US TO GO WITH HIM ON HIS MASTADON...
YUCK! I JUST STEPPED IN A PILE OF MUD!
HEY! WAIT A MINUTE... THIS ISN'T MUD I'M STANDING IN...
EXHAUST LEAK...
I GUESS THESE PRIMITIVE TAXIS DON'T HAVE TO PASS AN I.M. TEST...
BOY, OOG, I HOPE THIS "HELP" YOU'RE TAKING US TO IS WORTH THIS RIDE...
©Tundra 1993
OOG HERE!
IT'S SOME SORT OF CAVE...
OH-OH... OOG FORGOT TO PUT MONEY IN METER...!
METER?
PREHISTORIC PARKING AUTHORITY?
PROOF-POSITIVE THAT NOT ALL FORMS OF LIFE EVOLVE AT THE SAME RATE...
WE REALLY APPRECIATE YOU FINDING HELP FOR US TO GET BACK HOME, OOG...
OOG OOG
O.K. OOG... LEAD THE WAY...
HERE HELP OOG PROMISE...
THIS GUY!?
NO OFFENSE, OOG, BUT THIS GUY LOOKS TO BE ABOUT ONE GENE SHY FROM PICKING HEAD-LICE AND SWINGING FROM TREES...
©Tundra 1993
SO, LITTLE FELLA', YOU'RE A CAVEMAN, HUH? I ALWAYS THOUGHT YOU GUYS WERE A LITTLE MORE INTIMIDATING...
CAN IT, DOUGH-BOY...
DON'T LET MY DIMINUTIVE LOOKS FOOL YOU... AROUND HERE IT'S AN EVERYDAY BATTLE TO STAY AT THE TOP OF THE FOOD-CHAIN...
©Tundra 1993
"SURVIVAL OF THE FITTEST" IS THE LAW OF THIS LAND...
IT'S "EAT OR BE EATEN" IN THIS WORLD BUDDY-BOY...
YOUR T.V. DINNER WAS BURNING SO I TOOK IT OUT OF THE MICROWAVE...

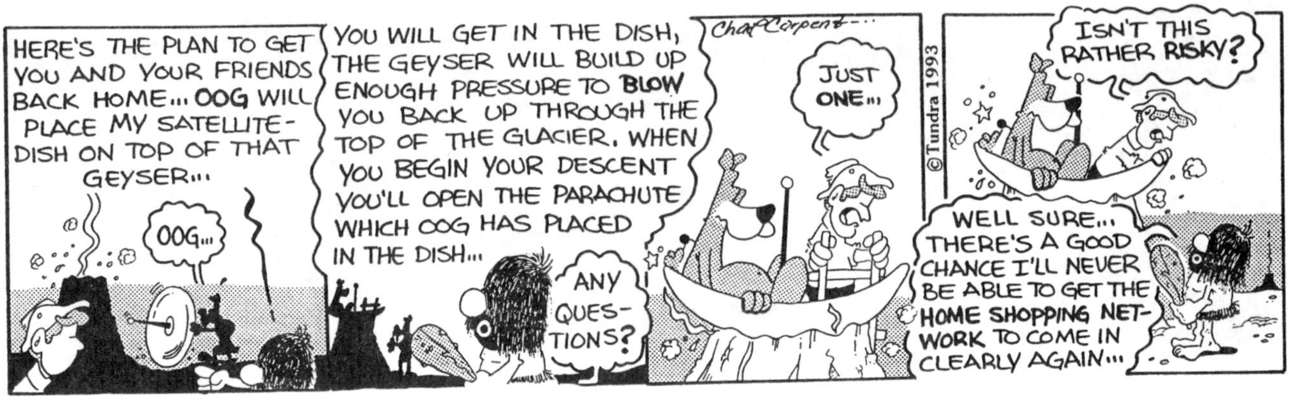
HERE'S THE PLAN TO GET YOU AND YOUR FRIENDS BACK HOME... OOG WILL PLACE MY SATELLITE-DISH ON TOP OF THAT GEYSER...
OOG...
YOU WILL GET IN THE DISH, THE GEYSER WILL BUILD UP ENOUGH PRESSURE TO BLOW YOU BACK UP THROUGH THE TOP OF THE GLACIER. WHEN YOU BEGIN YOUR DESCENT YOU'LL OPEN THE PARACHUTE WHICH OOG HAS PLACED IN THE DISH...
ANY QUES-TIONS?
Chad Carpent...
©Tundra 1993
JUST ONE...
ISN'T THIS RATHER RISKY?
WELL SURE... THERE'S A GOOD CHANCE I'LL NEVER BE ABLE TO GET THE HOME SHOPPING NET-WORK TO COME IN CLEARLY AGAIN...

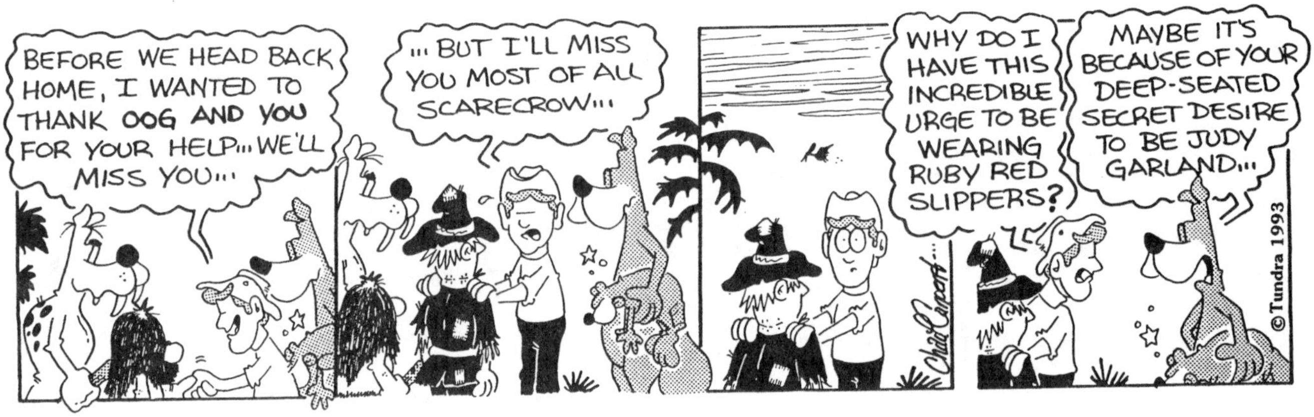
BEFORE WE HEAD BACK HOME, I WANTED TO THANK OOG AND YOU FOR YOUR HELP... WE'LL MISS YOU...
... BUT I'LL MISS YOU MOST OF ALL SCARECROW...
Chad Carpent...
WHY DO I HAVE THIS INCREDIBLE URGE TO BE WEARING RUBY RED SLIPPERS?
MAYBE IT'S BECAUSE OF YOUR DEEP-SEATED SECRET DESIRE TO BE JUDY GARLAND...
©Tundra 1993

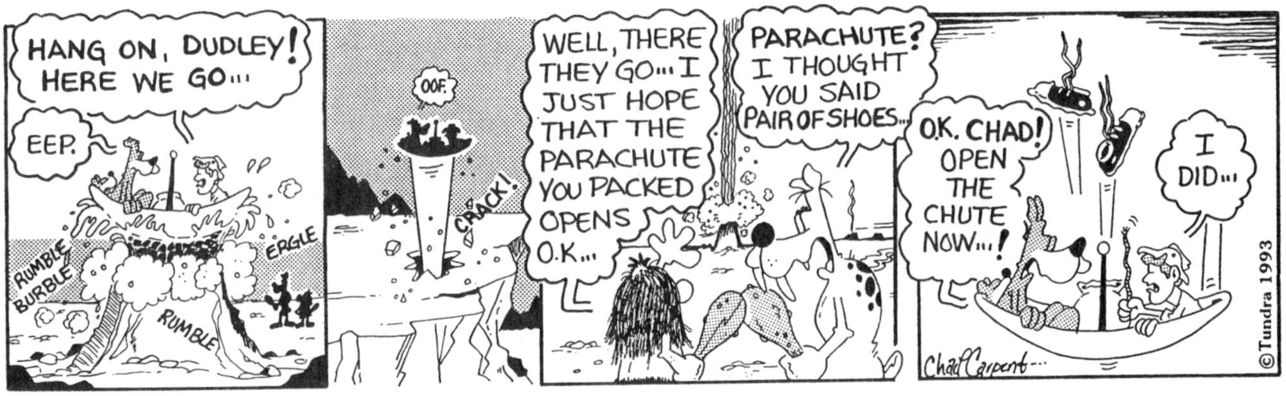
HANG ON, DUDLEY! HERE WE GO...
EEP.
RUMBLE
BURBLE
ERGLE
RUMBLE
OOF.
CRACK!
WELL, THERE THEY GO... I JUST HOPE THAT THE PARACHUTE YOU PACKED OPENS O.K...
PARACHUTE? I THOUGHT YOU SAID PAIR OF SHOES...
O.K. CHAD! OPEN THE CHUTE NOW...!
I DID...
©Tundra 1993
Chad Carpent...

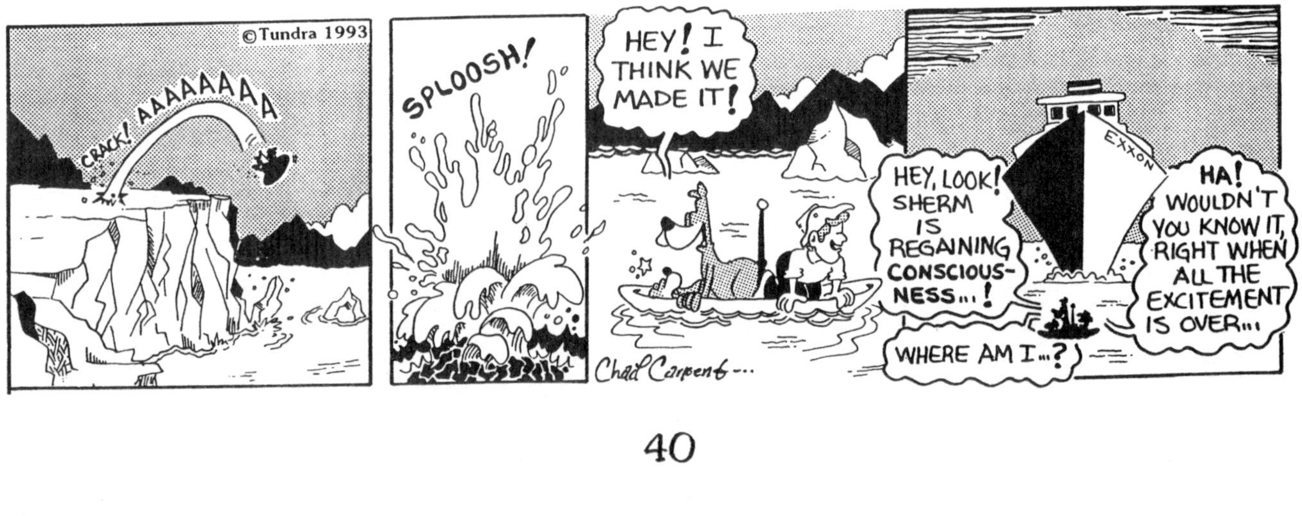
©Tundra 1993
CRACK! AAAAAAAA
SPLOOSH!
Chad Carpent...
HEY! I THINK WE MADE IT!
EXXON
HEY, LOOK! SHERM IS REGAINING CONSCIOUS-NESS...!
WHERE AM I...?
HA! WOULDN'T YOU KNOW IT, RIGHT WHEN ALL THE EXCITEMENT IS OVER...

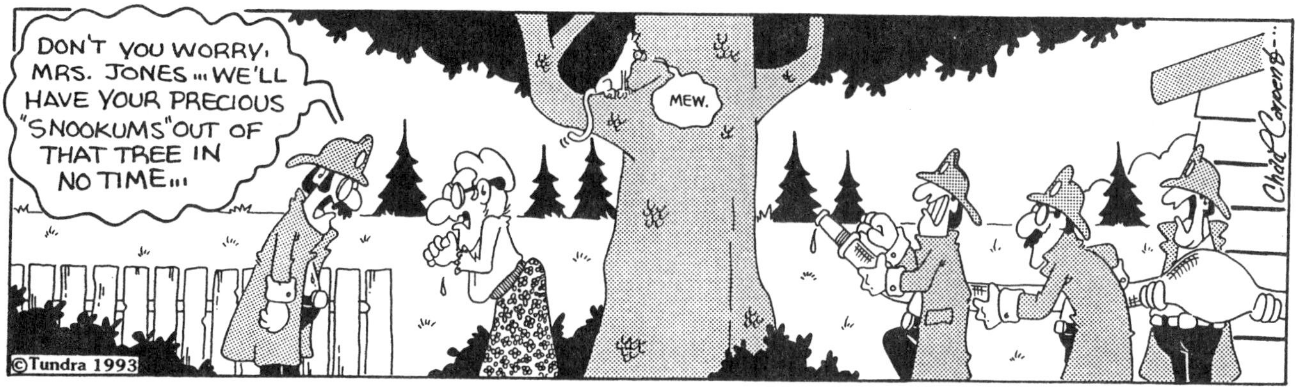
DON'T YOU WORRY, MRS. JONES... WE'LL HAVE YOUR PRECIOUS "SNOOKUMS" OUT OF THAT TREE IN NO TIME...
MEW.
©Tundra 1993

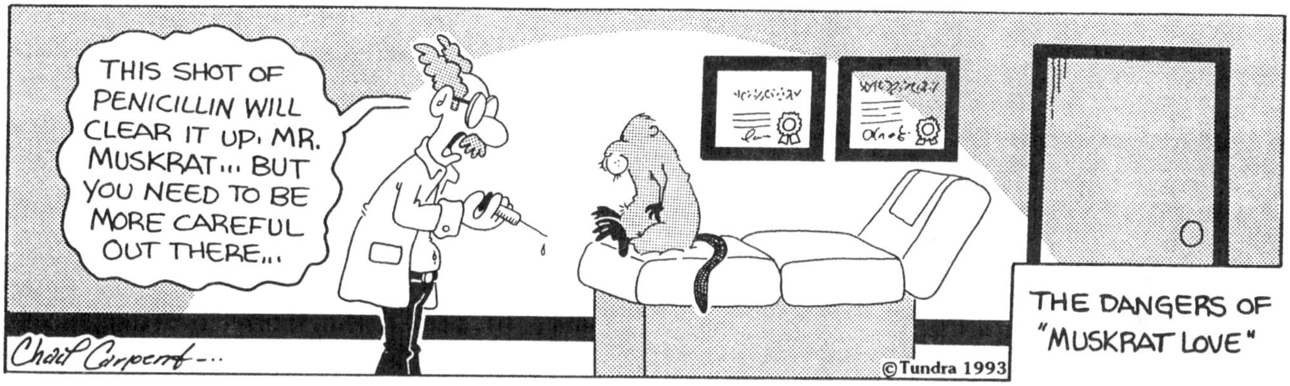
THIS SHOT OF PENICILLIN WILL CLEAR IT UP, MR. MUSKRAT... BUT YOU NEED TO BE MORE CAREFUL OUT THERE...
©Tundra 1993

THE DANGERS OF "MUSKRAT LOVE"

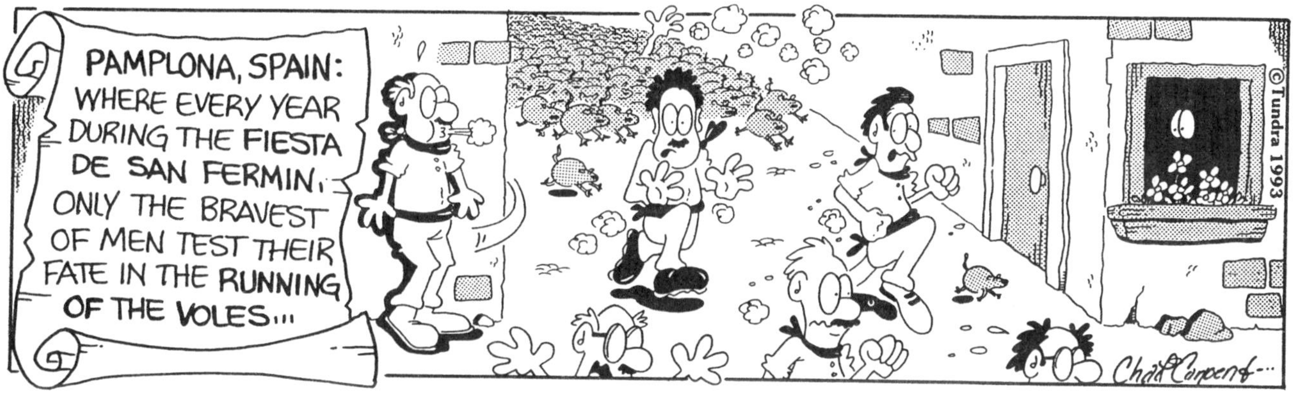
PAMPLONA, SPAIN: WHERE EVERY YEAR DURING THE FIESTA DE SAN FERMIN, ONLY THE BRAVEST OF MEN TEST THEIR FATE IN THE RUNNING OF THE VOLES...
©Tundra 1993

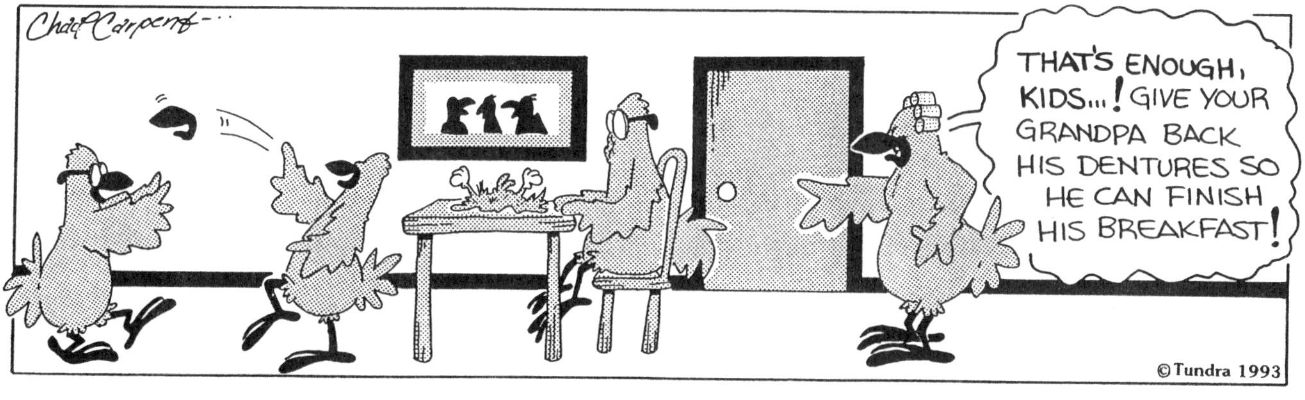
THAT'S ENOUGH, KIDS...! GIVE YOUR GRANDPA BACK HIS DENTURES SO HE CAN FINISH HIS BREAKFAST!
©Tundra 1993

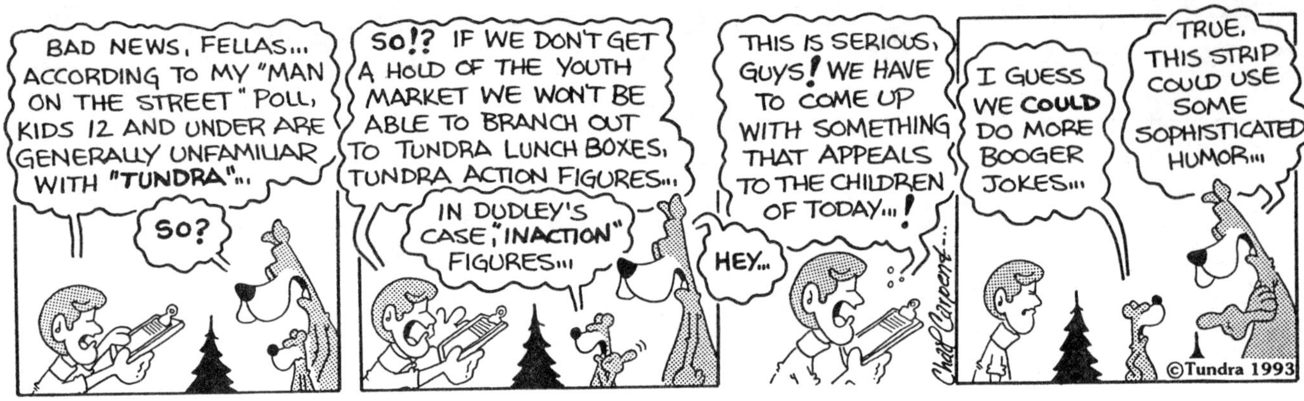
BAD NEWS, FELLAS... ACCORDING TO MY "MAN ON THE STREET" POLL, KIDS 12 AND UNDER ARE GENERALLY UNFAMILIAR WITH "TUNDRA"...
SO?
SO!? IF WE DON'T GET A HOLD OF THE YOUTH MARKET WE WON'T BE ABLE TO BRANCH OUT TO TUNDRA LUNCH BOXES, TUNDRA ACTION FIGURES...
IN DUDLEY'S CASE, "INACTION" FIGURES...
THIS IS SERIOUS, GUYS! WE HAVE TO COME UP WITH SOMETHING THAT APPEALS TO THE CHILDREN OF TODAY...!
HEY...
I GUESS WE COULD DO MORE BOOGER JOKES...
TRUE, THIS STRIP COULD USE SOME SOPHISTICATED HUMOR...
©Tundra 1993

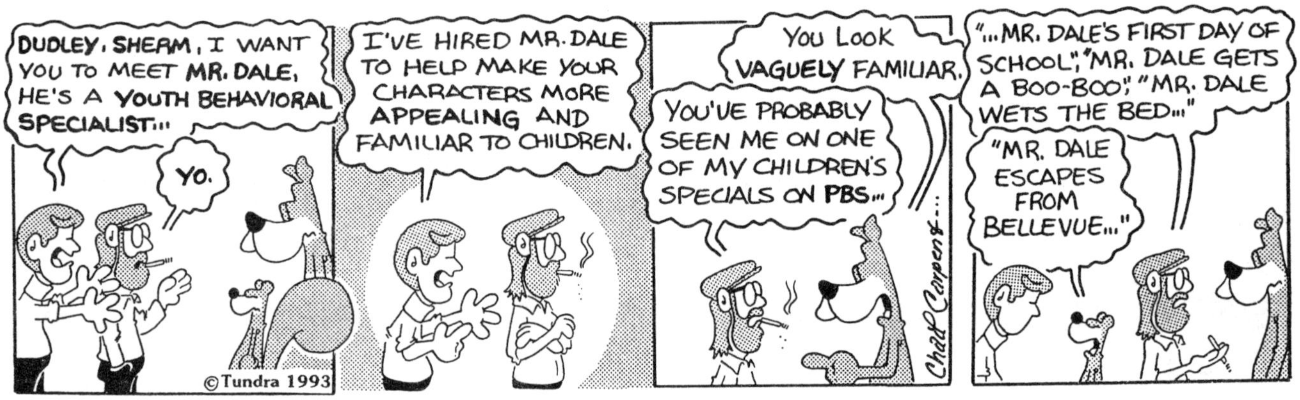
DUDLEY, SHERM, I WANT YOU TO MEET MR. DALE, HE'S A YOUTH BEHAVIORAL SPECIALIST...
YO.
©Tundra 1993
I'VE HIRED MR. DALE TO HELP MAKE YOUR CHARACTERS MORE APPEALING AND FAMILIAR TO CHILDREN.
YOU LOOK VAGUELY FAMILIAR.
YOU'VE PROBABLY SEEN ME ON ONE OF MY CHILDREN'S SPECIALS ON PBS...
"...MR. DALE'S FIRST DAY OF SCHOOL," "MR. DALE GETS A BOO-BOO," "MR. DALE WETS THE BED..."
"MR. DALE ESCAPES FROM BELLEVUE..."

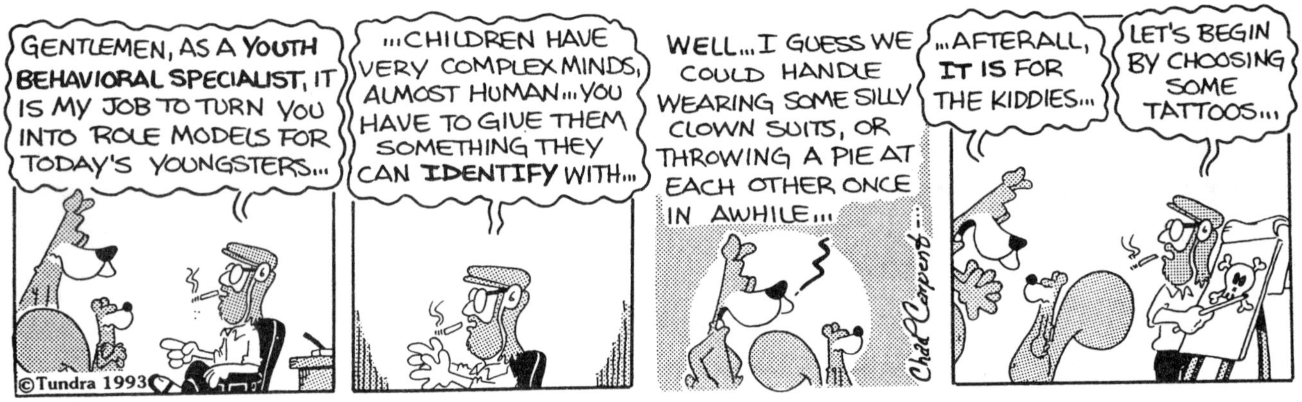
GENTLEMEN, AS A YOUTH BEHAVIORAL SPECIALIST, IT IS MY JOB TO TURN YOU INTO ROLE MODELS FOR TODAY'S YOUNGSTERS...
©Tundra 1993
...CHILDREN HAVE VERY COMPLEX MINDS, ALMOST HUMAN... YOU HAVE TO GIVE THEM SOMETHING THEY CAN IDENTIFY WITH...
WELL... I GUESS WE COULD HANDLE WEARING SOME SILLY CLOWN SUITS, OR THROWING A PIE AT EACH OTHER ONCE IN AWHILE...
...AFTERALL, IT IS FOR THE KIDDIES...
LET'S BEGIN BY CHOOSING SOME TATTOOS...

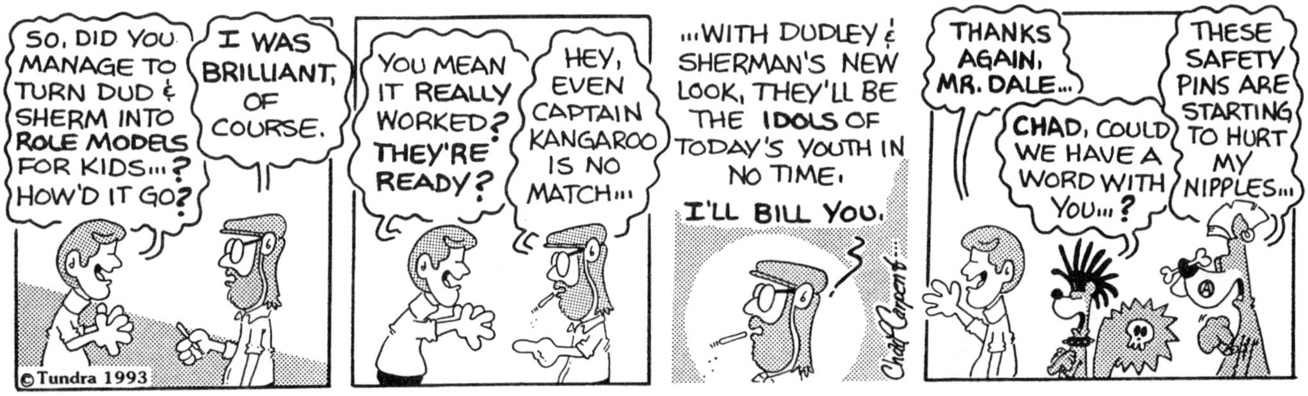
SO, DID YOU MANAGE TO TURN DUD & SHERM INTO ROLE MODELS FOR KIDS...? HOW'D IT GO?
I WAS BRILLIANT, OF COURSE.
©Tundra 1993
YOU MEAN IT REALLY WORKED? THEY'RE READY?
HEY, EVEN CAPTAIN KANGAROO IS NO MATCH...
...WITH DUDLEY & SHERMAN'S NEW LOOK, THEY'LL BE THE IDOLS OF TODAY'S YOUTH IN NO TIME.
I'LL BILL YOU.
THANKS AGAIN, MR. DALE...
CHAD, COULD WE HAVE A WORD WITH YOU...?
THESE SAFETY PINS ARE STARTING TO HURT MY NIPPLES...

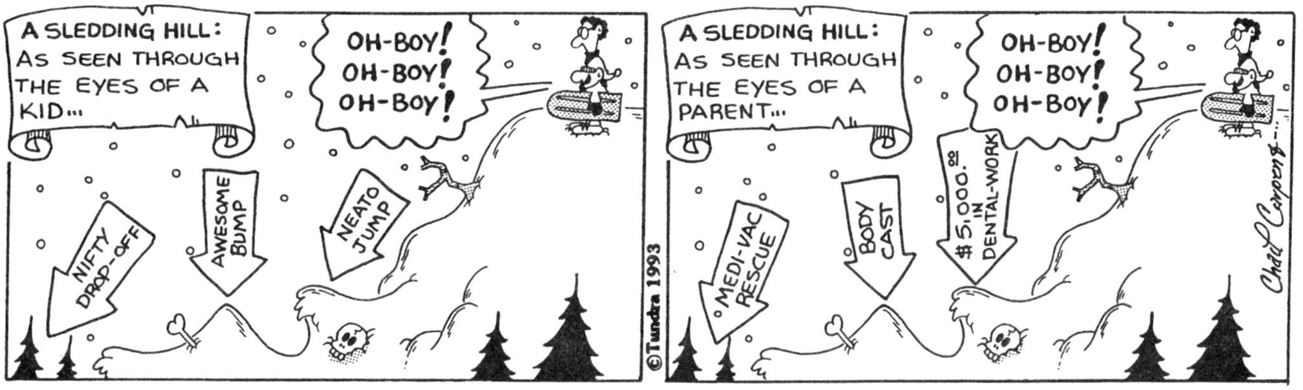
A SLEDDING HILL: AS SEEN THROUGH THE EYES OF A KID...
OH-BOY! OH-BOY! OH-BOY!
NIFTY DROP-OFF
AWESOME BUMP
NEATO JUMP
©Tundra 1993
A SLEDDING HILL: AS SEEN THROUGH THE EYES OF A PARENT...
OH-BOY! OH-BOY! OH-BOY!
MEDI-VAC RESCUE
BODY CAST
$5,000.00 IN DENTAL-WORK

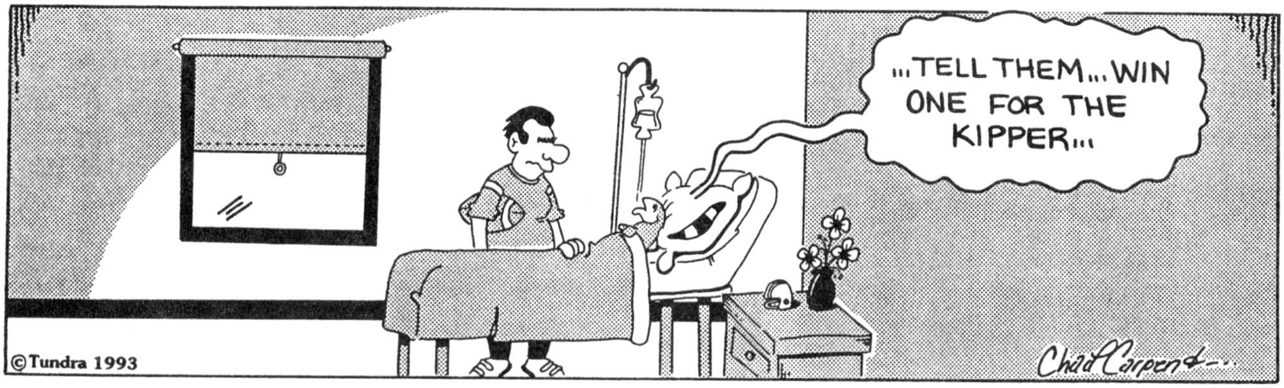
...TELL THEM... WIN ONE FOR THE KIPPER...
©Tundra 1993

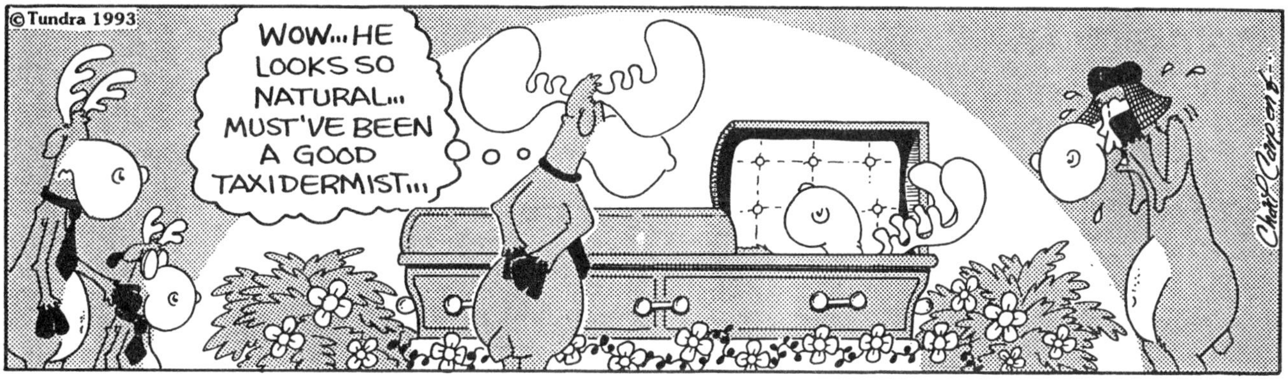
©Tundra 1993
WOW... HE LOOKS SO NATURAL... MUST'VE BEEN A GOOD TAXIDERMIST...

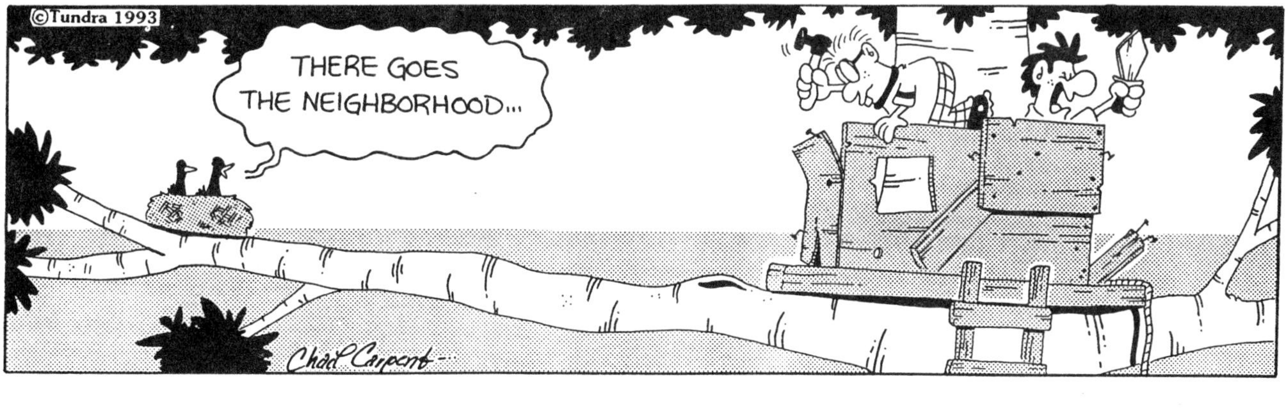
©Tundra 1993
THERE GOES THE NEIGHBORHOOD...

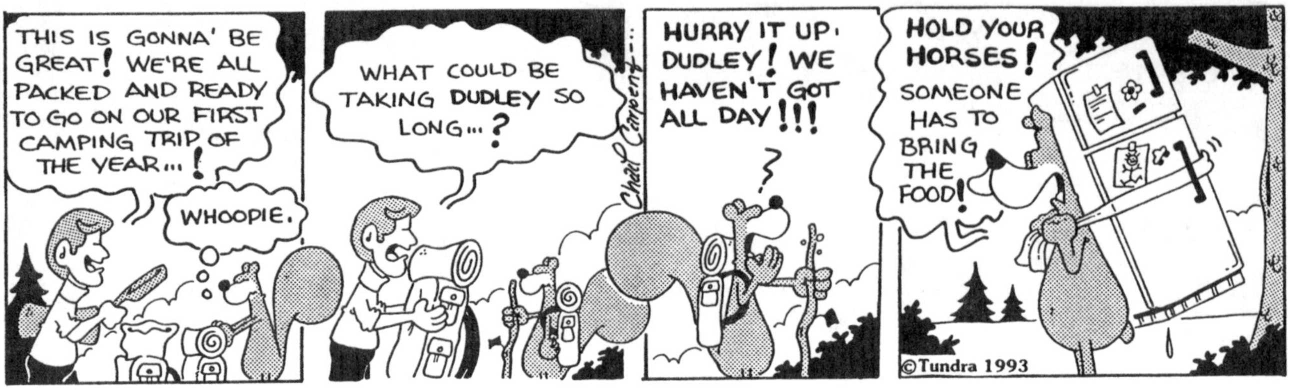
THIS IS GONNA' BE GREAT! WE'RE ALL PACKED AND READY TO GO ON OUR FIRST CAMPING TRIP OF THE YEAR...!
WHOOPIE.
WHAT COULD BE TAKING DUDLEY SO LONG...?
Chad Carpent...
HURRY IT UP, DUDLEY! WE HAVEN'T GOT ALL DAY!!!
?
HOLD YOUR HORSES! SOMEONE HAS TO BRING THE FOOD!
©Tundra 1993

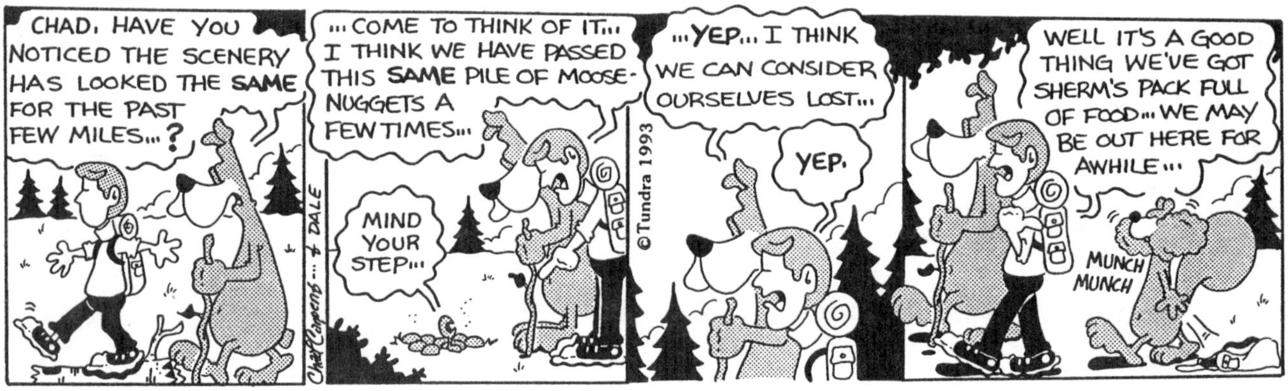
CHAD, HAVE YOU NOTICED THE SCENERY HAS LOOKED THE SAME FOR THE PAST FEW MILES...?
Chad Carpent... & DALE
...COME TO THINK OF IT... I THINK WE HAVE PASSED THIS SAME PILE OF MOOSE-NUGGETS A FEW TIMES...
MIND YOUR STEP...
©Tundra 1993
...YEP... I THINK WE CAN CONSIDER OURSELVES LOST...
YEP.
WELL IT'S A GOOD THING WE'VE GOT SHERM'S PACK FULL OF FOOD... WE MAY BE OUT HERE FOR AWHILE...
MUNCH MUNCH

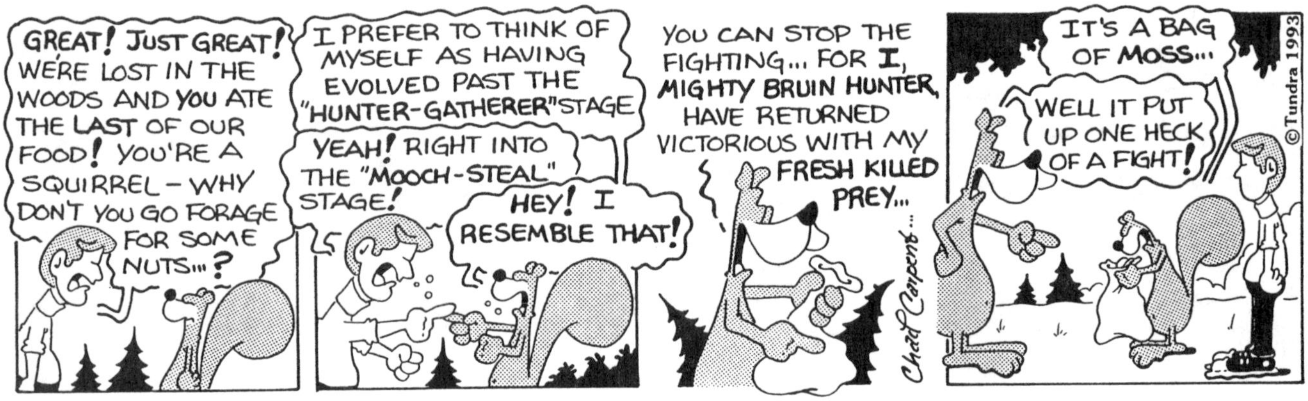
GREAT! JUST GREAT! WE'RE LOST IN THE WOODS AND YOU ATE THE LAST OF OUR FOOD! YOU'RE A SQUIRREL - WHY DON'T YOU GO FORAGE FOR SOME NUTS...?
I PREFER TO THINK OF MYSELF AS HAVING EVOLVED PAST THE "HUNTER-GATHERER" STAGE.
YEAH! RIGHT INTO THE "MOOCH-STEAL" STAGE!
HEY! I RESEMBLE THAT!
YOU CAN STOP THE FIGHTING... FOR I, MIGHTY BRUIN HUNTER, HAVE RETURNED VICTORIOUS WITH MY FRESH KILLED PREY...
Chad Carpent...
IT'S A BAG OF MOSS...
WELL IT PUT UP ONE HECK OF A FIGHT!
©Tundra 1993

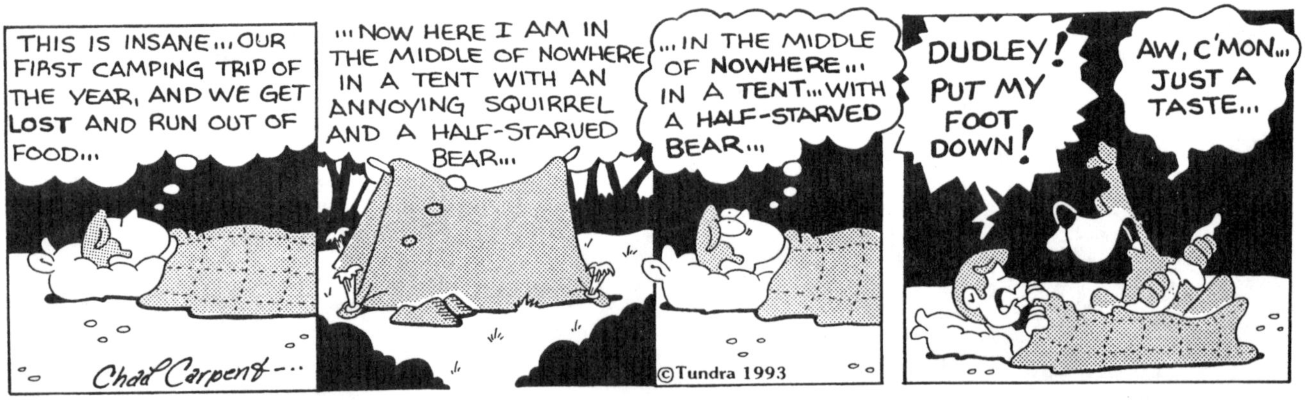
THIS IS INSANE... OUR FIRST CAMPING TRIP OF THE YEAR, AND WE GET LOST AND RUN OUT OF FOOD...
Chad Carpent...
...NOW HERE I AM IN THE MIDDLE OF NOWHERE IN A TENT WITH AN ANNOYING SQUIRREL AND A HALF-STARVED BEAR...
...IN THE MIDDLE OF NOWHERE... IN A TENT... WITH A HALF-STARVED BEAR...
©Tundra 1993
DUDLEY! PUT MY FOOT DOWN!
AW, C'MON... JUST A TASTE...

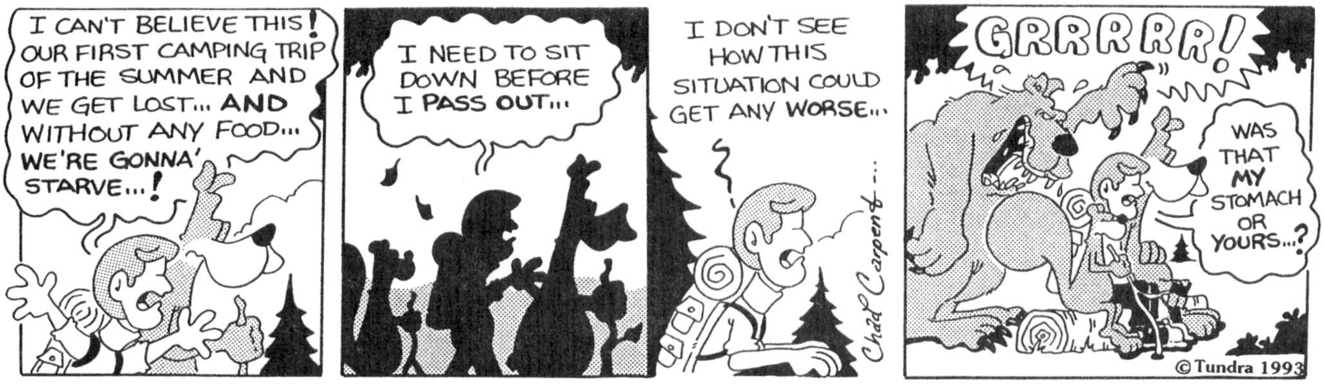
I CAN'T BELIEVE THIS! OUR FIRST CAMPING TRIP OF THE SUMMER AND WE GET LOST... AND WITHOUT ANY FOOD... WE'RE GONNA' STARVE...!
I NEED TO SIT DOWN BEFORE I PASS OUT...
I DON'T SEE HOW THIS SITUATION COULD GET ANY WORSE...
GRRRRRR!
WAS THAT MY STOMACH OR YOURS...?
©Tundra 1993

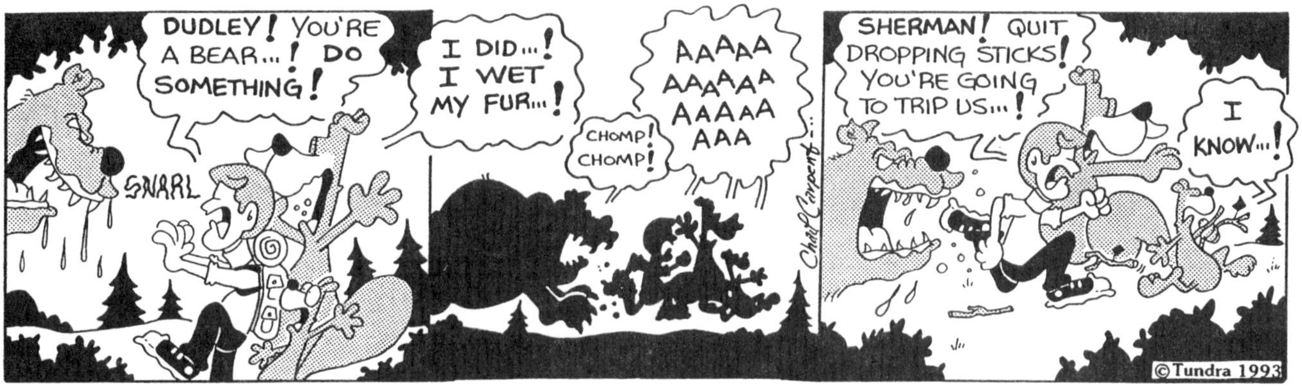
DUDLEY! YOU'RE A BEAR...! DO SOMETHING!
SNARL
I DID...! I WET MY FUR...!
CHOMP! CHOMP!
AAAAA AAAAAA AAAAA AAA
SHERMAN! QUIT DROPPING STICKS! YOU'RE GOING TO TRIP US...!
I KNOW...!
©Tundra 1993

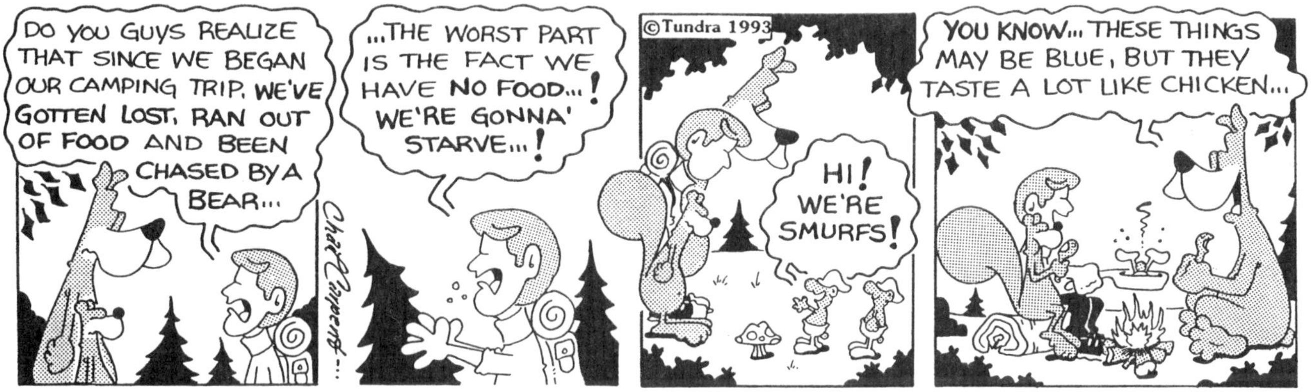
DO YOU GUYS REALIZE THAT SINCE WE BEGAN OUR CAMPING TRIP, WE'VE GOTTEN LOST, RAN OUT OF FOOD AND BEEN CHASED BY A BEAR...
...THE WORST PART IS THE FACT WE HAVE NO FOOD...! WE'RE GONNA' STARVE...!
©Tundra 1993
HI! WE'RE SMURFS!
YOU KNOW... THESE THINGS MAY BE BLUE, BUT THEY TASTE A LOT LIKE CHICKEN...

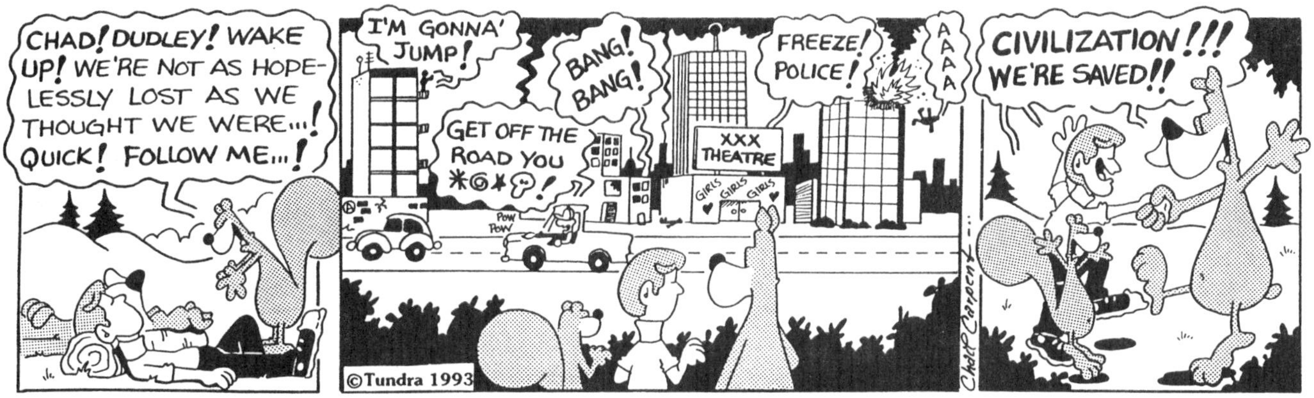
CHAD! DUDLEY! WAKE UP! WE'RE NOT AS HOPE-LESSLY LOST AS WE THOUGHT WE WERE...! QUICK! FOLLOW ME...!
I'M GONNA' JUMP!
BANG! BANG!
GET OFF THE ROAD YOU
POW POW
XXX THEATRE
GIRLS GIRLS GIRLS
FREEZE! POLICE!
AAAA
©Tundra 1993
CIVILIZATION!!! WE'RE SAVED!!

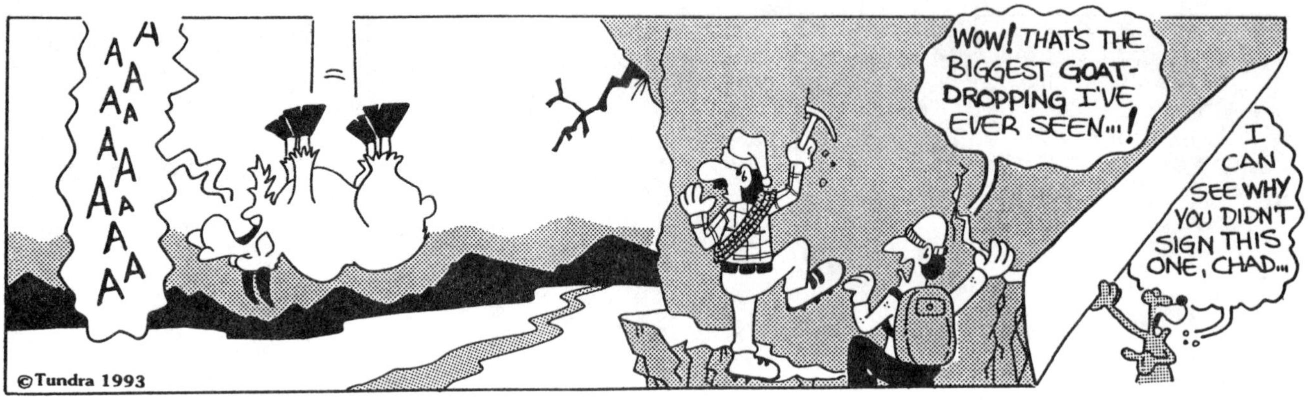
AAAAAAAAAAAAAAA
WOW! THAT'S THE BIGGEST GOAT-DROPPING I'VE EVER SEEN...!
I CAN SEE WHY YOU DIDN'T SIGN THIS ONE, CHAD...
©Tundra 1993

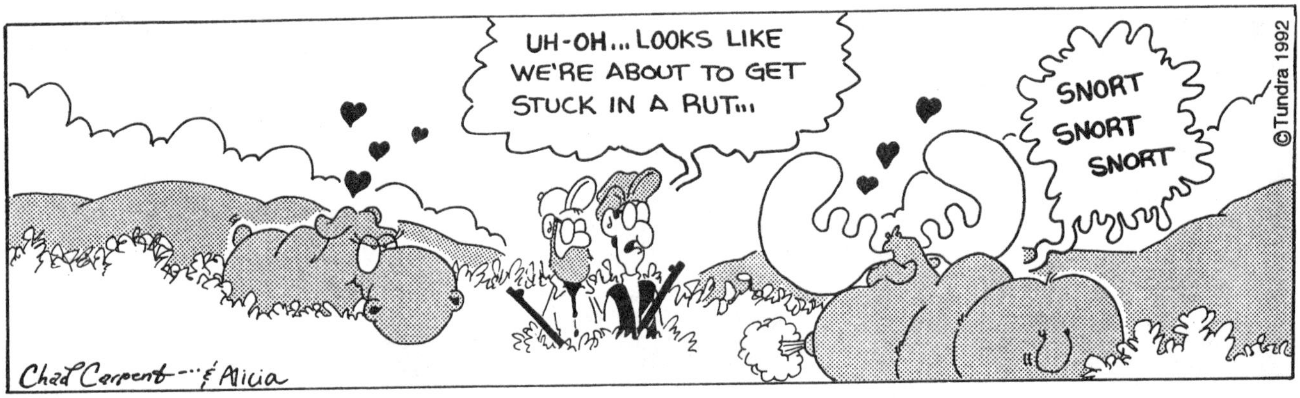
UH-OH... LOOKS LIKE WE'RE ABOUT TO GET STUCK IN A RUT...
SNORT SNORT SNORT
©Tundra 1992
Chad Carpent-... & Alicia

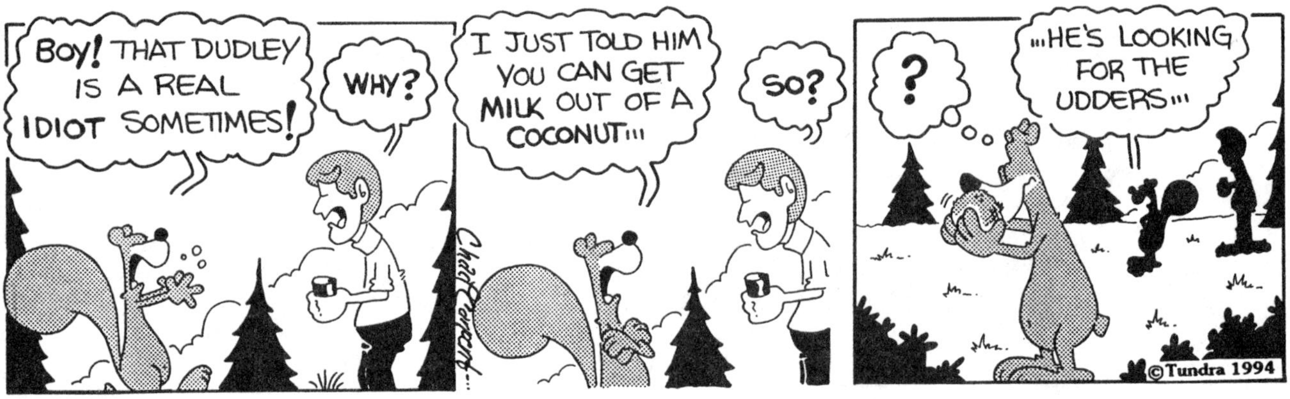
BOY! THAT DUDLEY IS A REAL IDIOT SOMETIMES!
WHY?
I JUST TOLD HIM YOU CAN GET MILK OUT OF A COCONUT...
SO?
?
...HE'S LOOKING FOR THE UDDERS...
Chad Carpent-...
©Tundra 1994

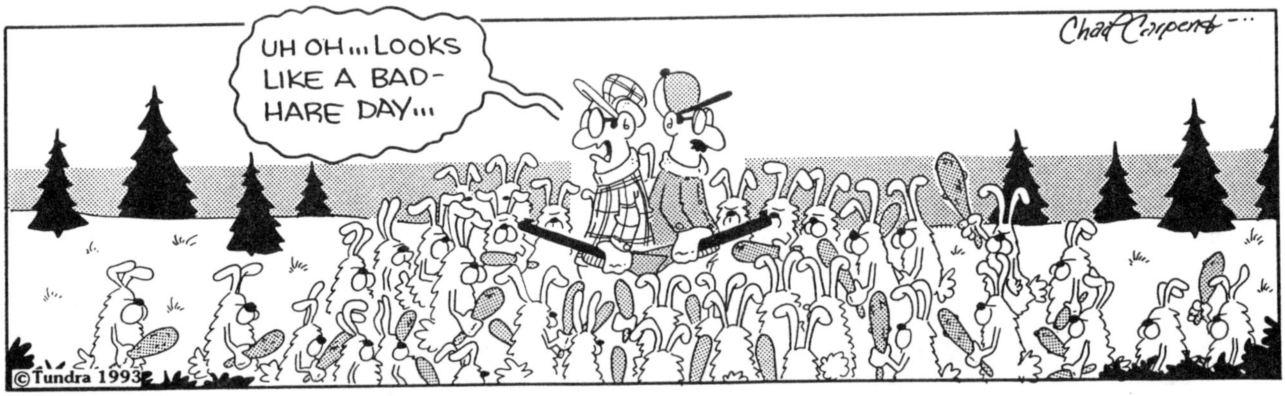
UH OH... LOOKS LIKE A BAD-HARE DAY...
Chad Carpent-...
©Tundra 1993

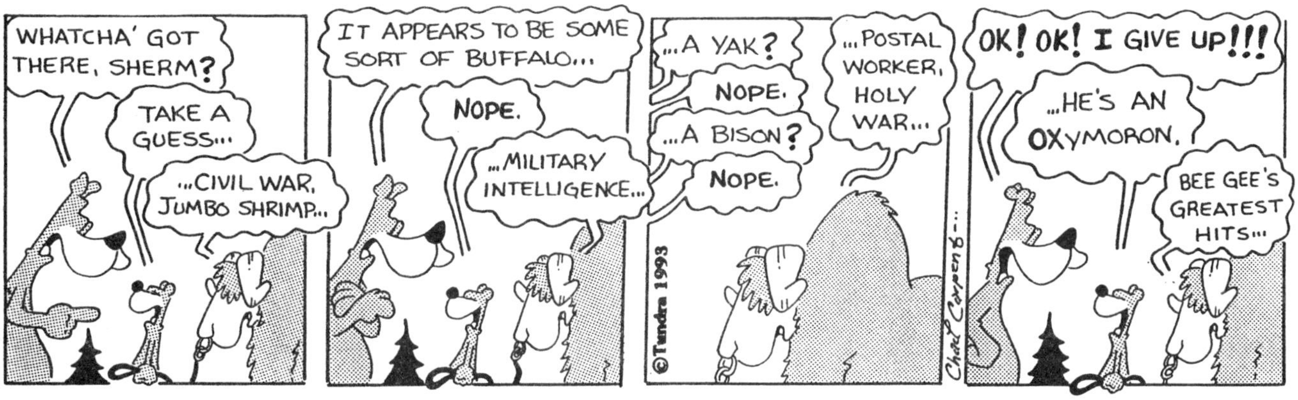
WHATCHA' GOT THERE, SHERM?
TAKE A GUESS...
...CIVIL WAR, JUMBO SHRIMP...
IT APPEARS TO BE SOME SORT OF BUFFALO...
NOPE.
...MILITARY INTELLIGENCE...
...A YAK?
NOPE.
...A BISON?
NOPE.
...POSTAL WORKER, HOLY WAR...
OK! OK! I GIVE UP!!!
...HE'S AN OXYMORON.
BEE GEE'S GREATEST HITS...
©Tundra 1993

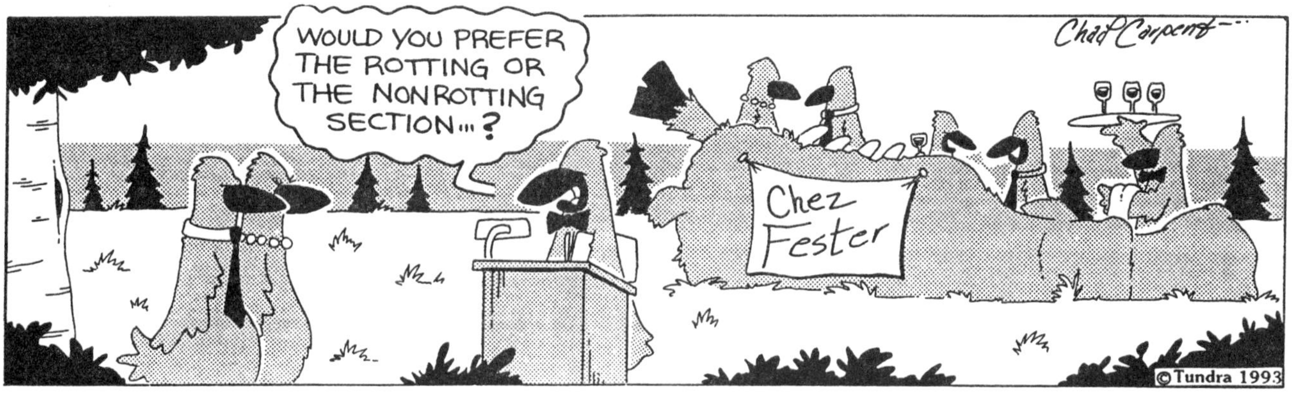
WOULD YOU PREFER THE ROTTING OR THE NONROTTING SECTION...?
Chez Fester
©Tundra 1993

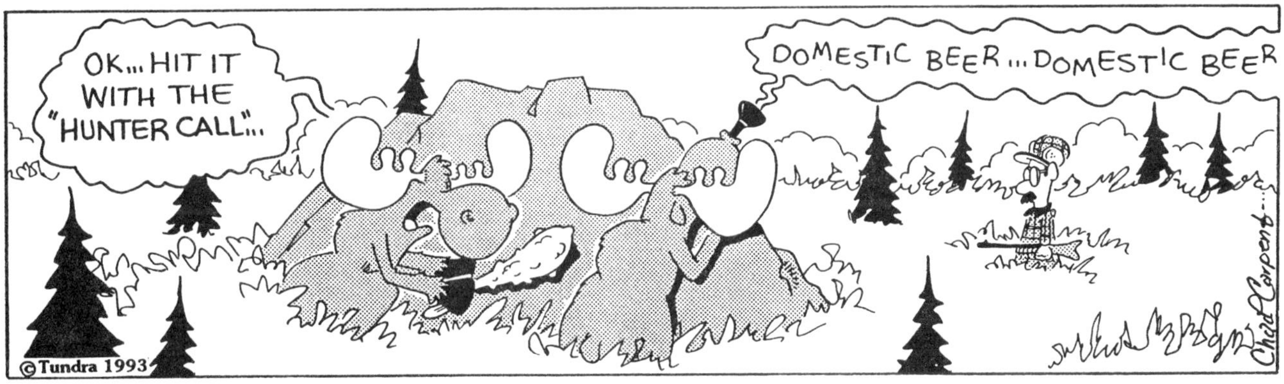
OK... HIT IT WITH THE "HUNTER CALL"...
DOMESTIC BEER... DOMESTIC BEER
©Tundra 1993

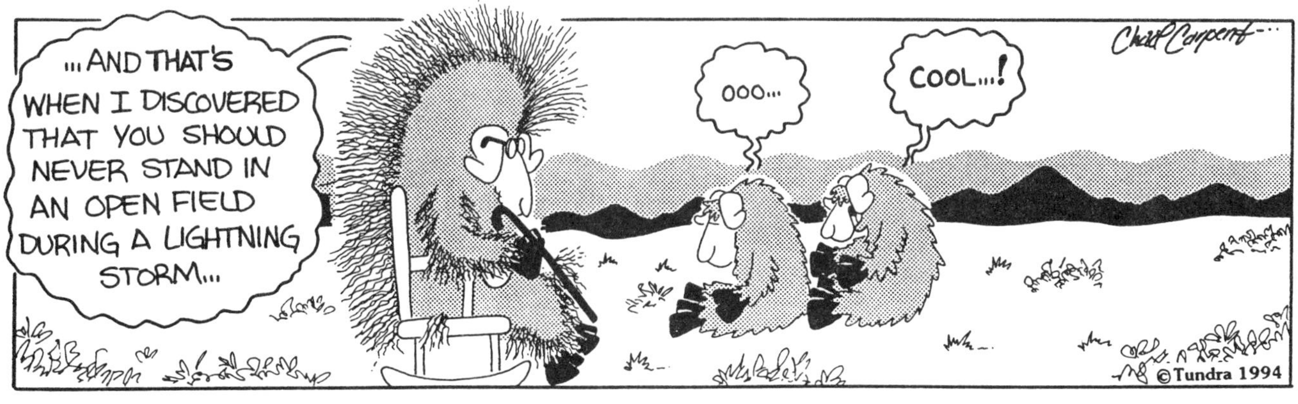
...AND THAT'S WHEN I DISCOVERED THAT YOU SHOULD NEVER STAND IN AN OPEN FIELD DURING A LIGHTNING STORM...
OOO...
COOL...!
©Tundra 1994

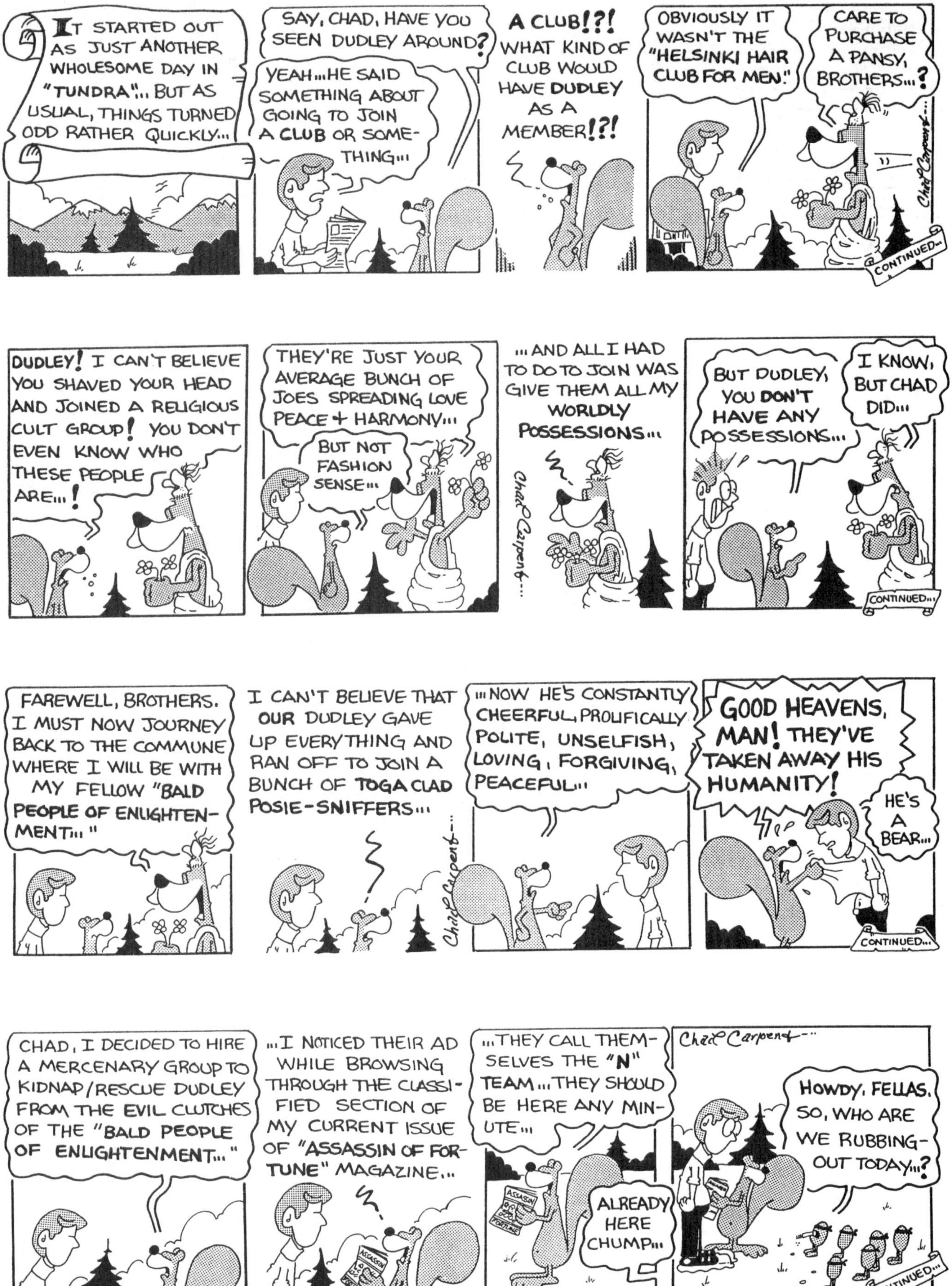
IT STARTED OUT AS JUST ANOTHER WHOLESOME DAY IN "TUNDRA"... BUT AS USUAL, THINGS TURNED ODD RATHER QUICKLY...
SAY, CHAD, HAVE YOU SEEN DUDLEY AROUND?
YEAH... HE SAID SOMETHING ABOUT GOING TO JOIN A CLUB OR SOME-THING...
A CLUB!?! WHAT KIND OF CLUB WOULD HAVE DUDLEY AS A MEMBER!?!
OBVIOUSLY IT WASN'T THE "HELSINKI HAIR CLUB FOR MEN."
CARE TO PURCHASE A PANSY, BROTHERS...?
CONTINUED...
DUDLEY! I CAN'T BELIEVE YOU SHAVED YOUR HEAD AND JOINED A RELIGIOUS CULT GROUP! YOU DON'T EVEN KNOW WHO THESE PEOPLE ARE...!
THEY'RE JUST YOUR AVERAGE BUNCH OF JOES SPREADING LOVE PEACE + HARMONY...
BUT NOT FASHION SENSE...
...AND ALL I HAD TO DO TO JOIN WAS GIVE THEM ALL MY WORLDLY POSSESSIONS...
BUT DUDLEY, YOU DON'T HAVE ANY POSSESSIONS...
I KNOW, BUT CHAD DID...
CONTINUED...
FAREWELL, BROTHERS. I MUST NOW JOURNEY BACK TO THE COMMUNE WHERE I WILL BE WITH MY FELLOW "BALD PEOPLE OF ENLIGHTEN-MENT..."
I CAN'T BELIEVE THAT OUR DUDLEY GAVE UP EVERYTHING AND RAN OFF TO JOIN A BUNCH OF TOGA CLAD POSIE-SNIFFERS...
...NOW HE'S CONSTANTLY CHEERFUL, PROLIFICALLY POLITE, UNSELFISH, LOVING, FORGIVING, PEACEFUL...
GOOD HEAVENS, MAN! THEY'VE TAKEN AWAY HIS HUMANITY!
HE'S A BEAR...
CONTINUED...
CHAD, I DECIDED TO HIRE A MERCENARY GROUP TO KIDNAP/RESCUE DUDLEY FROM THE EVIL CLUTCHES OF THE "BALD PEOPLE OF ENLIGHTENMENT..."
...I NOTICED THEIR AD WHILE BROWSING THROUGH THE CLASSI-FIED SECTION OF MY CURRENT ISSUE OF "ASSASSIN OF FOR-TUNE" MAGAZINE...
...THEY CALL THEM-SELVES THE "N" TEAM... THEY SHOULD BE HERE ANY MIN-UTE...
ALREADY HERE CHUMP...
HOWDY, FELLAS. SO, WHO ARE WE RUBBING-OUT TODAY...?
CONTINUED...

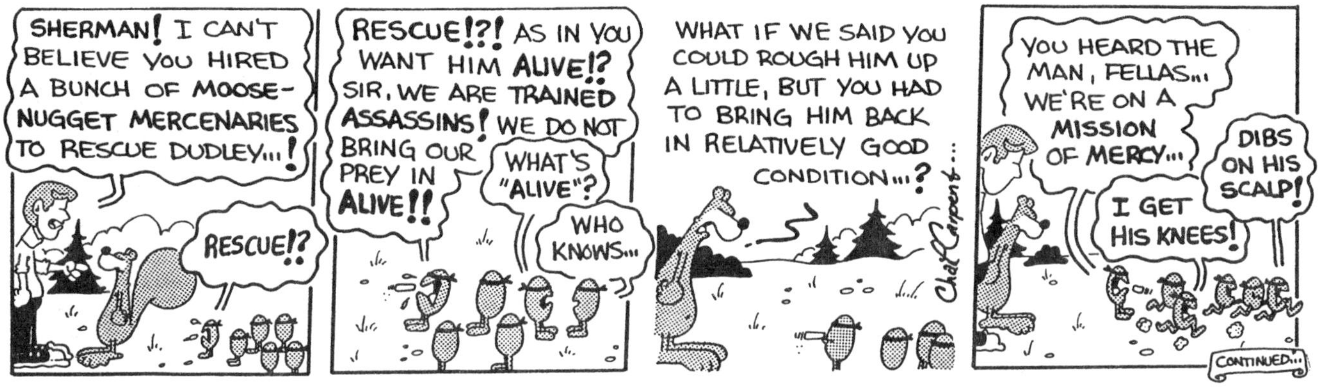
SHERMAN! I CAN'T BELIEVE YOU HIRED A BUNCH OF MOOSE-NUGGET MERCENARIES TO RESCUE DUDLEY...!
RESCUE!?
RESCUE!?! AS IN YOU WANT HIM ALIVE!? SIR, WE ARE TRAINED ASSASSINS! WE DO NOT BRING OUR PREY IN ALIVE!!
WHAT'S "ALIVE"?
WHO KNOWS...
WHAT IF WE SAID YOU COULD ROUGH HIM UP A LITTLE, BUT YOU HAD TO BRING HIM BACK IN RELATIVELY GOOD CONDITION...?
YOU HEARD THE MAN, FELLAS... WE'RE ON A MISSION OF MERCY...
DIBS ON HIS SCALP!
I GET HIS KNEES!
CONTINUED...

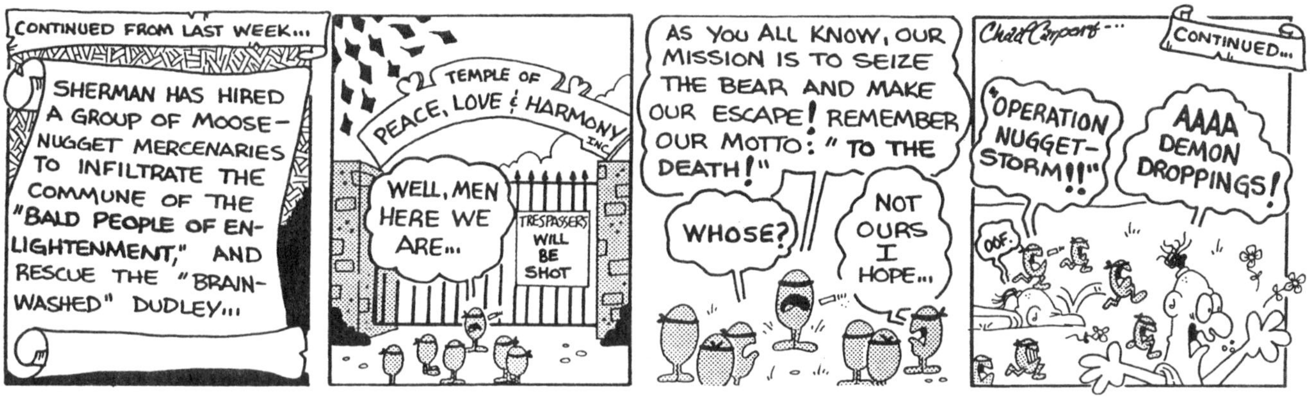
CONTINUED FROM LAST WEEK...
SHERMAN HAS HIRED A GROUP OF MOOSE-NUGGET MERCENARIES TO INFILTRATE THE COMMUNE OF THE "BALD PEOPLE OF ENLIGHTENMENT," AND RESCUE THE "BRAIN-WASHED" DUDLEY...
TEMPLE OF PEACE, LOVE & HARMONY INC.
WELL, MEN HERE WE ARE...
TRESPASSERS WILL BE SHOT
AS YOU ALL KNOW, OUR MISSION IS TO SEIZE THE BEAR AND MAKE OUR ESCAPE! REMEMBER OUR MOTTO: "TO THE DEATH!"
WHOSE?
NOT OURS I HOPE...
CONTINUED...
"OPERATION NUGGET-STORM!!"
AAAA DEMON DROPPINGS!
OOF.

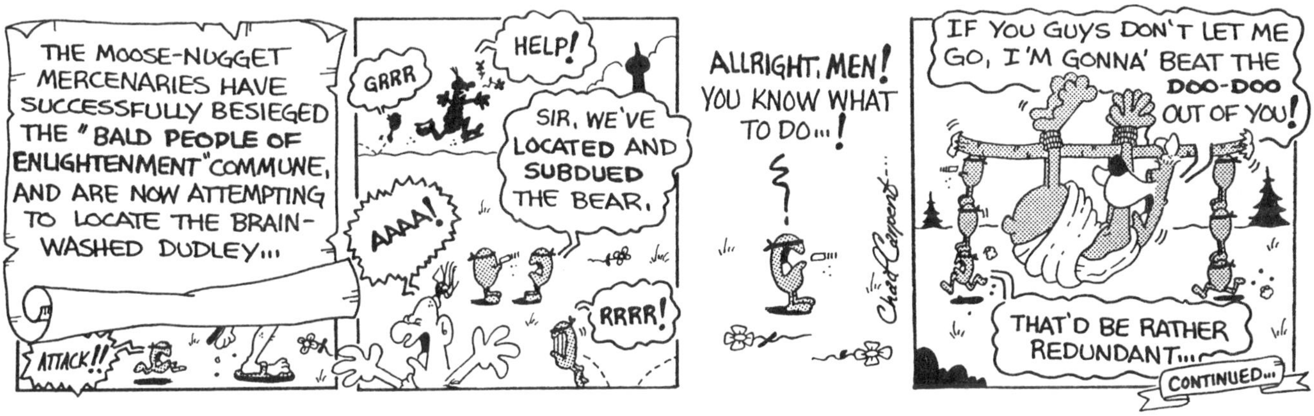
THE MOOSE-NUGGET MERCENARIES HAVE SUCCESSFULLY BESIEGED THE "BALD PEOPLE OF ENLIGHTENMENT" COMMUNE, AND ARE NOW ATTEMPTING TO LOCATE THE BRAIN-WASHED DUDLEY...
ATTACK!!
GRRR
HELP!
SIR, WE'VE LOCATED AND SUBDUED THE BEAR.
AAAA!
RRRR!
ALLRIGHT, MEN! YOU KNOW WHAT TO DO...!
IF YOU GUYS DON'T LET ME GO, I'M GONNA' BEAT THE DOO-DOO OUT OF YOU!
THAT'D BE RATHER REDUNDANT...
CONTINUED...

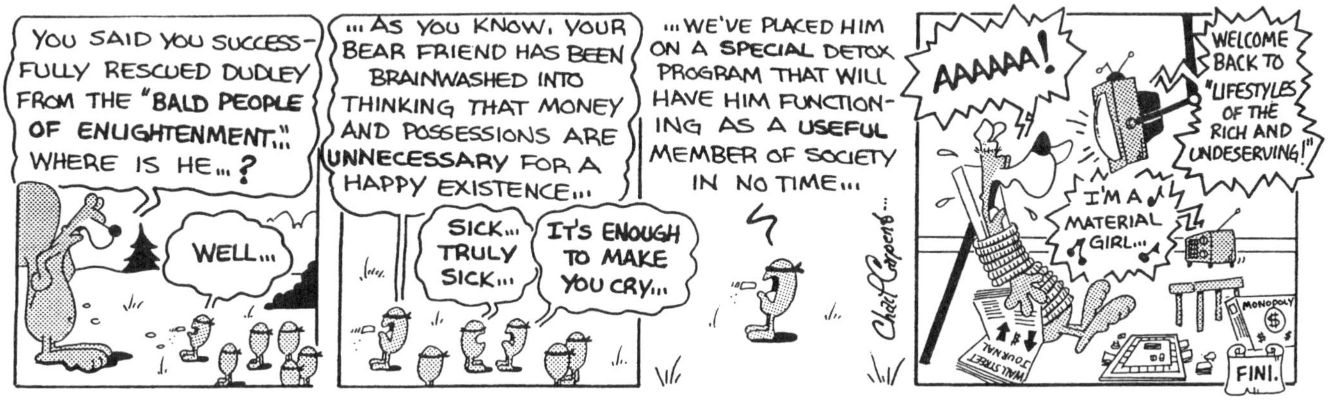
YOU SAID YOU SUCCESSFULLY RESCUED DUDLEY FROM THE "BALD PEOPLE OF ENLIGHTENMENT," WHERE IS HE...?
WELL...
...AS YOU KNOW, YOUR BEAR FRIEND HAS BEEN BRAINWASHED INTO THINKING THAT MONEY AND POSSESSIONS ARE UNNECESSARY FOR A HAPPY EXISTENCE...
SICK... TRULY SICK...
IT'S ENOUGH TO MAKE YOU CRY...
...WE'VE PLACED HIM ON A SPECIAL DETOX PROGRAM THAT WILL HAVE HIM FUNCTIONING AS A USEFUL MEMBER OF SOCIETY IN NO TIME...
AAAAAA!
WELCOME BACK TO "LIFESTYLES OF THE RICH AND UNDESERVING!"
I'M A MATERIAL GIRL...
WALL STREET JOURNAL
MONOPOLY
FINI.

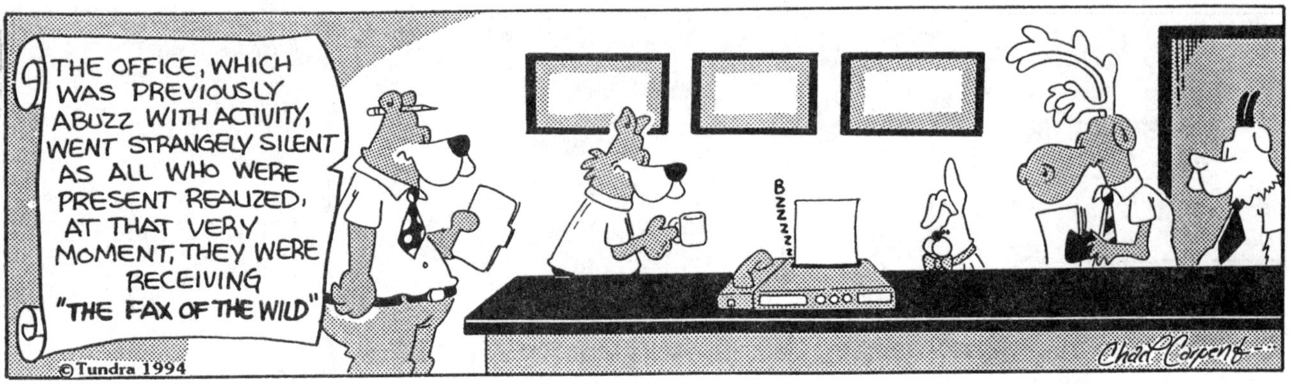
THE OFFICE, WHICH WAS PREVIOUSLY ABUZZ WITH ACTIVITY, WENT STRANGELY SILENT AS ALL WHO WERE PRESENT REALIZED, AT THAT VERY MOMENT, THEY WERE RECEIVING "THE FAX OF THE WILD"
BZZZZZ
©Tundra 1994

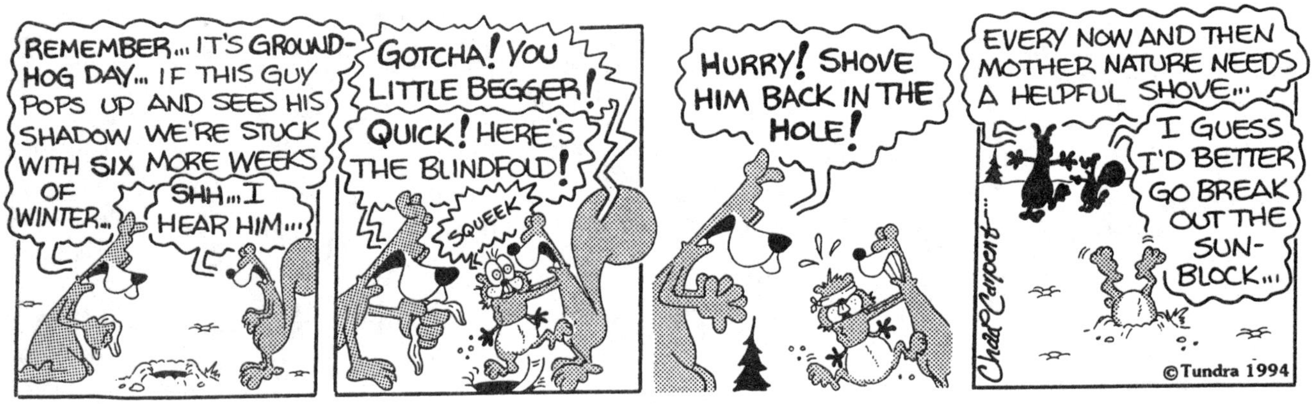
REMEMBER... IT'S GROUND-HOG DAY... IF THIS GUY POPS UP AND SEES HIS SHADOW WE'RE STUCK WITH SIX MORE WEEKS OF WINTER...
SHH... I HEAR HIM...
GOTCHA! YOU LITTLE BEGGER!
QUICK! HERE'S THE BLINDFOLD!
SQUEEK
HURRY! SHOVE HIM BACK IN THE HOLE!
EVERY NOW AND THEN MOTHER NATURE NEEDS A HELPFUL SHOVE...
I GUESS I'D BETTER GO BREAK OUT THE SUN-BLOCK...
©Tundra 1994

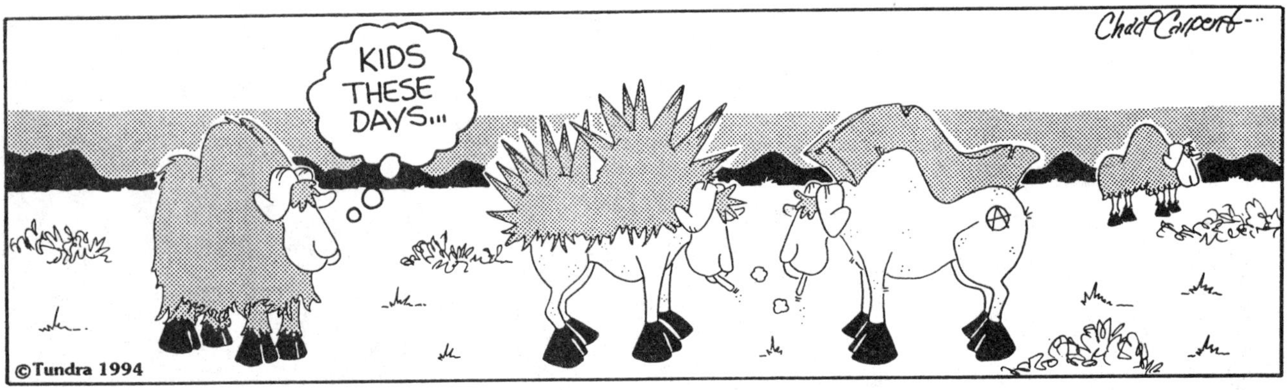
KIDS THESE DAYS...
©Tundra 1994

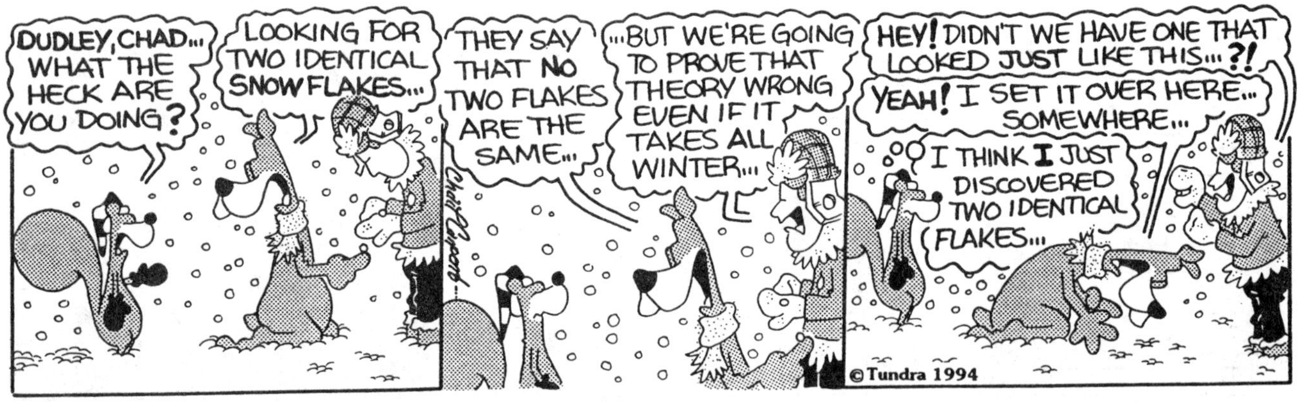
DUDLEY, CHAD... WHAT THE HECK ARE YOU DOING?
LOOKING FOR TWO IDENTICAL SNOWFLAKES...
THEY SAY THAT NO TWO FLAKES ARE THE SAME...
...BUT WE'RE GOING TO PROVE THAT THEORY WRONG EVEN IF IT TAKES ALL WINTER...
HEY! DIDN'T WE HAVE ONE THAT LOOKED JUST LIKE THIS...?!
YEAH! I SET IT OVER HERE... SOMEWHERE...
I THINK I JUST DISCOVERED TWO IDENTICAL FLAKES...
©Tundra 1994

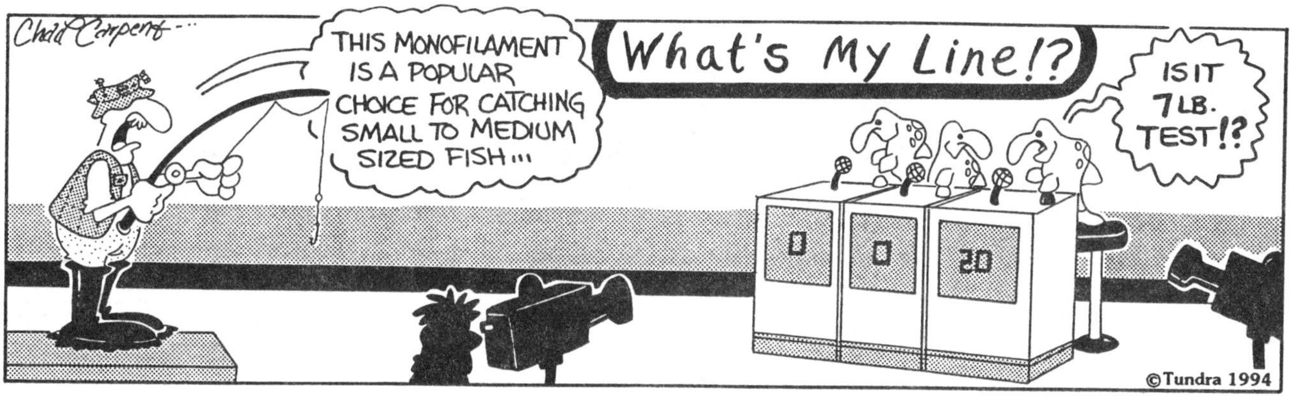
Chad Carpenter...
THIS MONOFILAMENT IS A POPULAR CHOICE FOR CATCHING SMALL TO MEDIUM SIZED FISH...
What's My Line!?
IS IT 7LB. TEST!?
0
0
20
©Tundra 1994

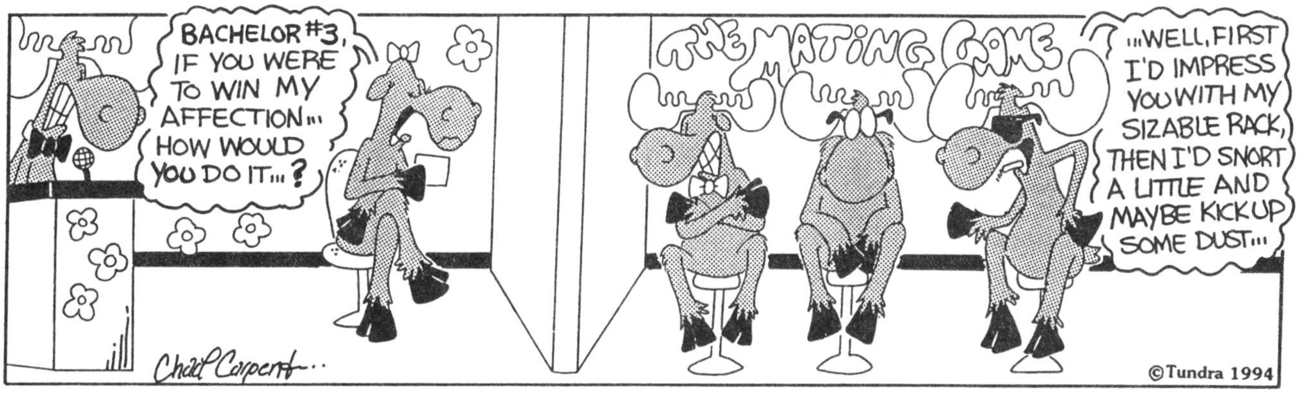
BACHELOR #3, IF YOU WERE TO WIN MY AFFECTION... HOW WOULD YOU DO IT...?
THE MATING GAME
...WELL, FIRST I'D IMPRESS YOU WITH MY SIZABLE RACK, THEN I'D SNORT A LITTLE AND MAYBE KICK UP SOME DUST...
Chad Carpenter...
©Tundra 1994

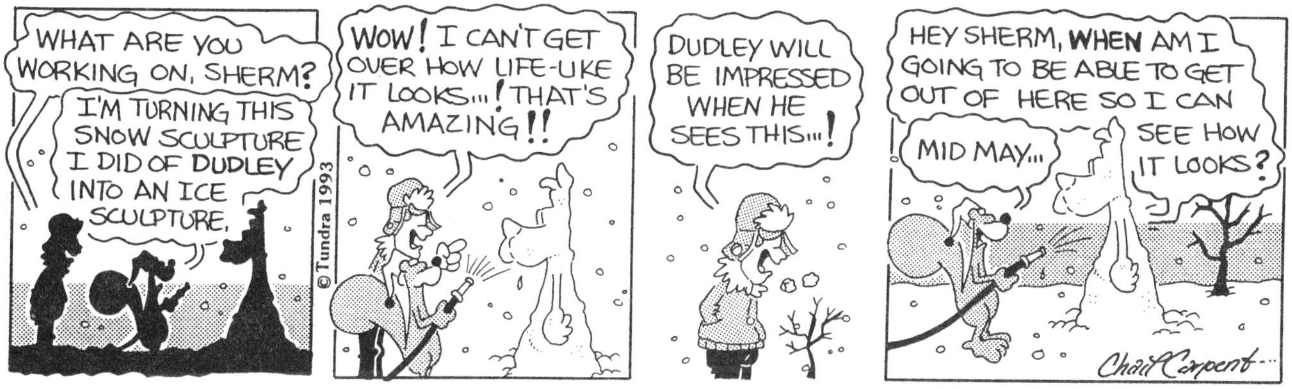
WHAT ARE YOU WORKING ON, SHERM?
I'M TURNING THIS SNOW SCULPTURE I DID OF DUDLEY INTO AN ICE SCULPTURE.
©Tundra 1993
WOW! I CAN'T GET OVER HOW LIFE-LIKE IT LOOKS...! THAT'S AMAZING!!
DUDLEY WILL BE IMPRESSED WHEN HE SEES THIS...!
HEY SHERM, WHEN AM I GOING TO BE ABLE TO GET OUT OF HERE SO I CAN SEE HOW IT LOOKS?
MID MAY...
Chad Carpenter...

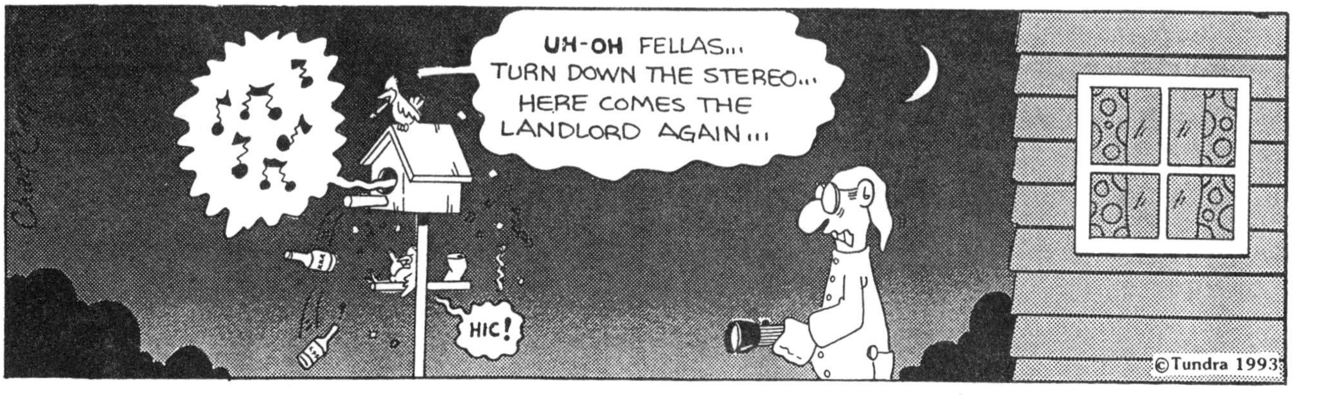
UH-OH FELLAS... TURN DOWN THE STEREO... HERE COMES THE LANDLORD AGAIN...
HIC!
©Tundra 1993

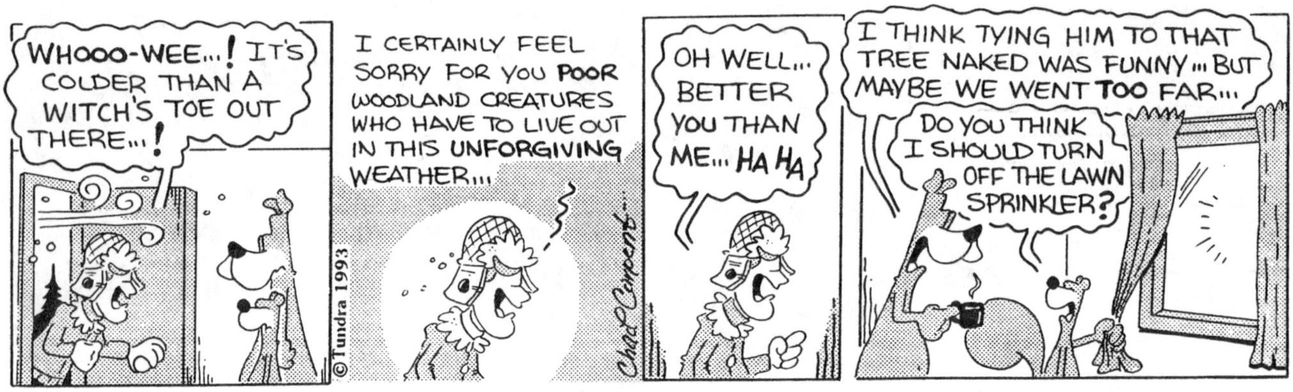
WHOOO-WEE...! IT'S COLDER THAN A WITCH'S TOE OUT THERE...!
I CERTAINLY FEEL SORRY FOR YOU POOR WOODLAND CREATURES WHO HAVE TO LIVE OUT IN THIS UNFORGIVING WEATHER...
OH WELL... BETTER YOU THAN ME... HA HA
I THINK TYING HIM TO THAT TREE NAKED WAS FUNNY... BUT MAYBE WE WENT TOO FAR...
DO YOU THINK I SHOULD TURN OFF THE LAWN SPRINKLER?
©Tundra 1993
Chad Carpenter

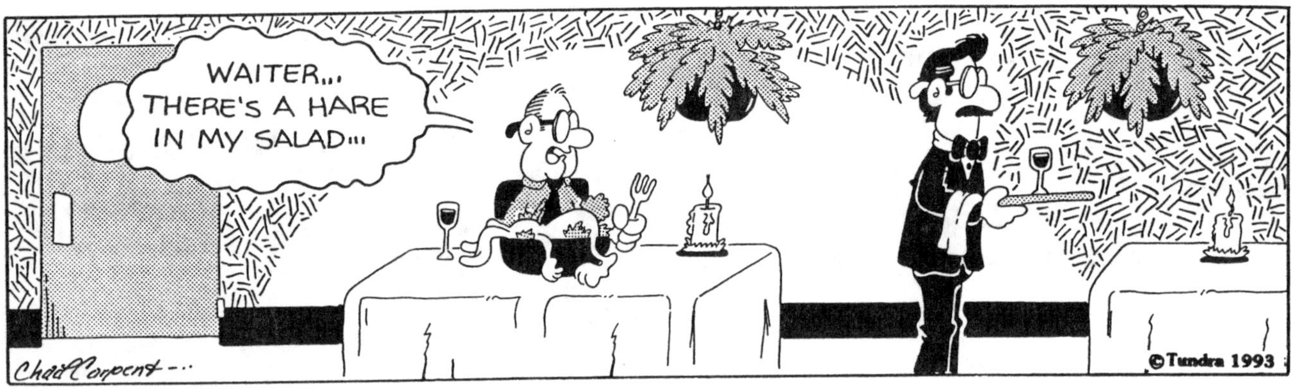
WAITER... THERE'S A HARE IN MY SALAD...
Chad Carpenter
©Tundra 1993

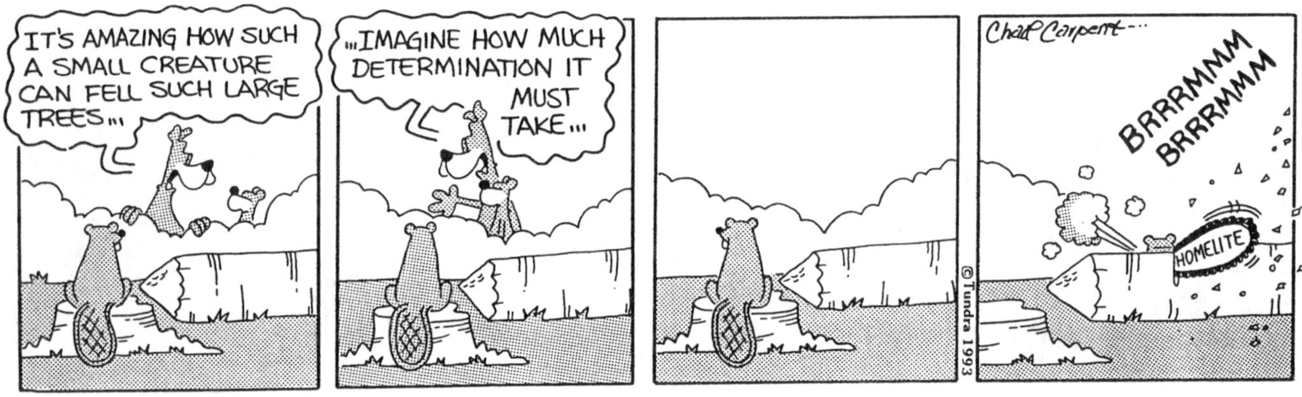
IT'S AMAZING HOW SUCH A SMALL CREATURE CAN FELL SUCH LARGE TREES...
...IMAGINE HOW MUCH DETERMINATION IT MUST TAKE...
©Tundra 1993
Chad Carpenter
BRRRMMM BRRRMMM
HOMELITE

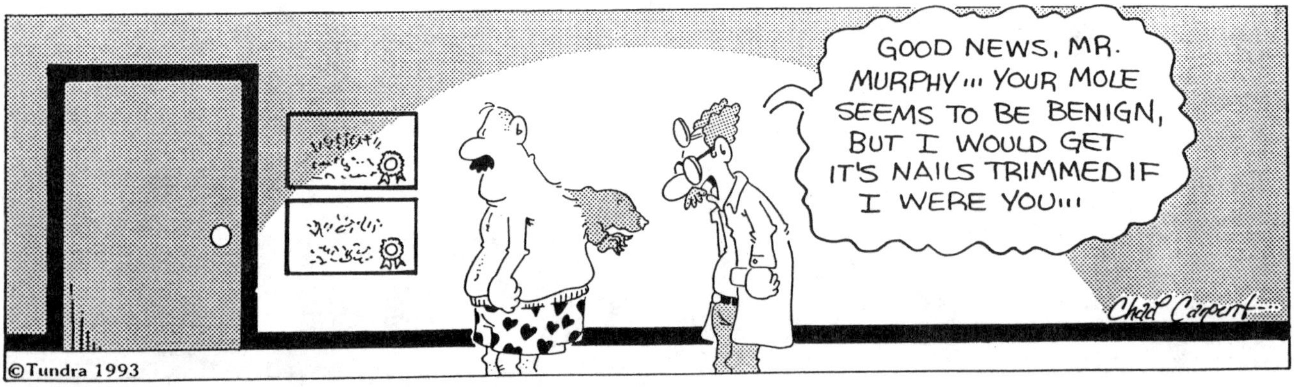
GOOD NEWS, MR. MURPHY... YOUR MOLE SEEMS TO BE BENIGN, BUT I WOULD GET IT'S NAILS TRIMMED IF I WERE YOU...
Chad Carpenter
©Tundra 1993

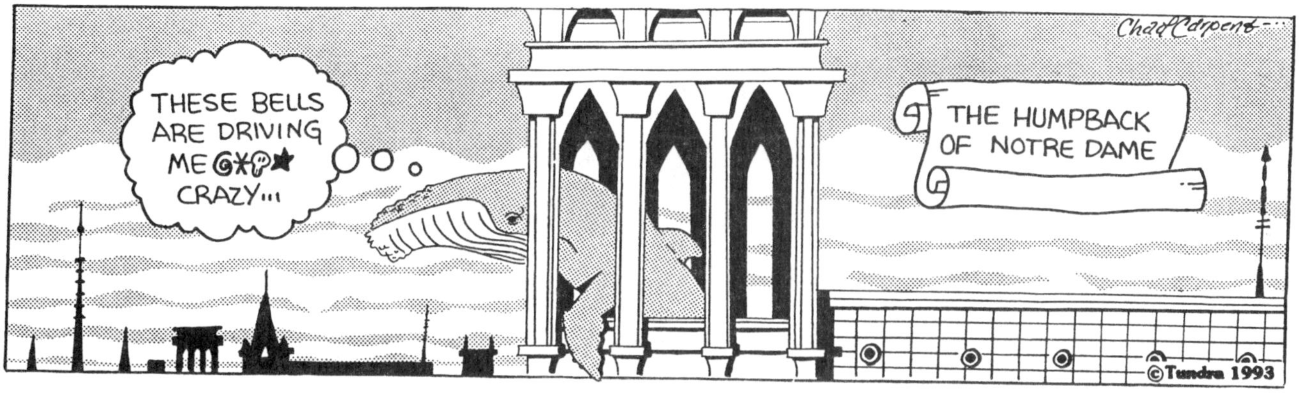
Chad Carpenter
THESE BELLS ARE DRIVING ME @*!★ CRAZY...
THE HUMPBACK OF NOTRE DAME
©Tundra 1993

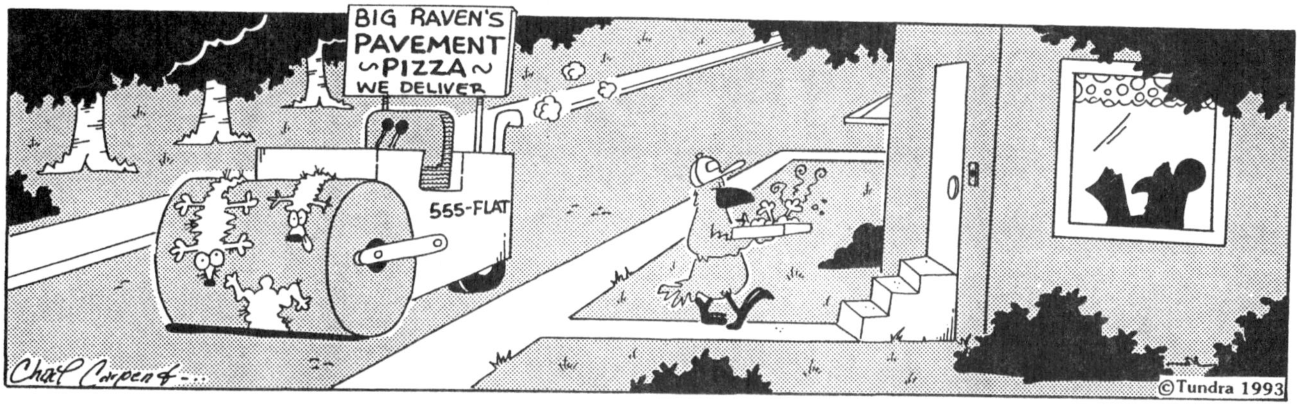
BIG RAVEN'S PAVEMENT PIZZA WE DELIVER
555-FLAT
Chad Carpenter
©Tundra 1993

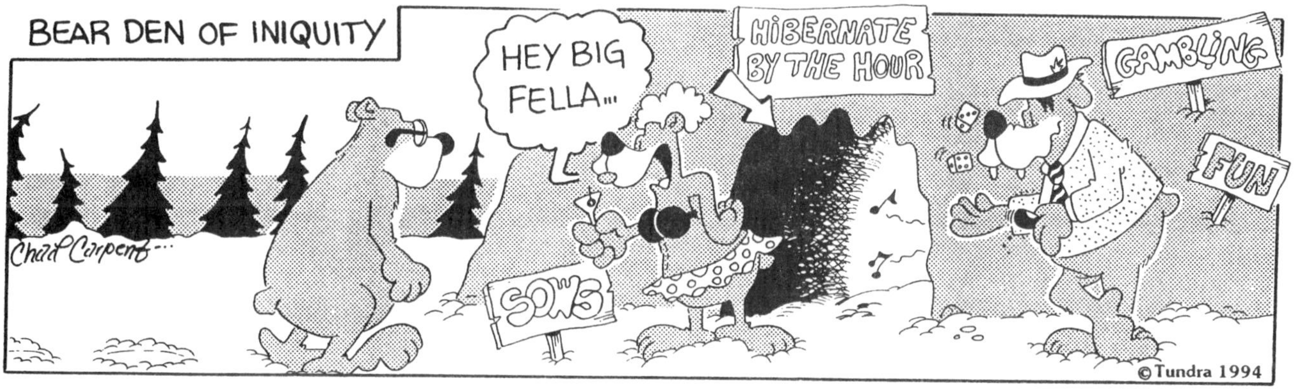
BEAR DEN OF INIQUITY
HEY BIG FELLA...
HIBERNATE BY THE HOUR
GAMBLING
FUN
SOWS
Chad Carpenter
©Tundra 1994

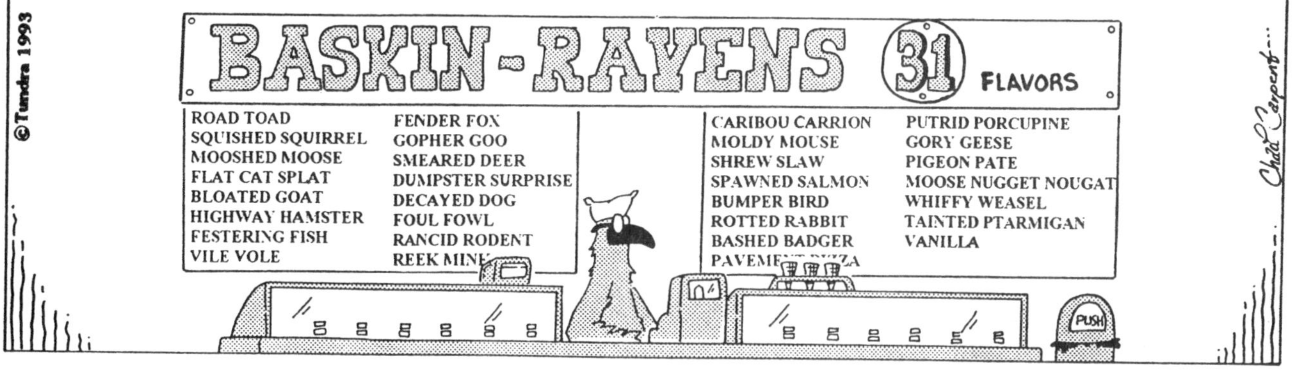
©Tundra 1993
BASKIN-RAVENS 31 FLAVORS
ROAD TOAD
SQUISHED SQUIRREL
MOOSHED MOOSE
FLAT CAT SPLAT
BLOATED GOAT
HIGHWAY HAMSTER
FESTERING FISH
VILE VOLE
FENDER FOX
GOPHER GOO
SMEARED DEER
DUMPSTER SURPRISE
DECAYED DOG
FOUL FOWL
RANCID RODENT
REEK MIN
CARIBOU CARRION
MOLDY MOUSE
SHREW SLAW
SPAWNED SALMON
BUMPER BIRD
ROTTED RABBIT
BASHED BADGER
PAVEME
PUTRID PORCUPINE
GORY GEESE
PIGEON PATE
MOOSE NUGGET NOUGAT
WHIFFY WEASEL
TAINTED PTARMIGAN
VANILLA
PUSH
Chad Carpenter

Sherman

Sherman the Squirrel fulfills the role of the antagonist in the strip. Never one to lapse in his performance, Sherman is the self-serving instigator of the schemes that act as the catalyst for chaos.

Most information about Sherman's life is scarce due to sealed court records. However, files released to the press recently show an extensive trail of credit card fraud, stolen vehicles and dozens of failed pyramid schemes. After several unsuccessful attempts at anti-assertiveness training, it was deemed necessary to send Sherman to a secluded rehabilitation center in Gangrene Gulch to complete his 200,000 hours of community service.

Sherman's ideal date would consist of taking out the most beautiful female in town, talk about himself all night, have her pay for dinner and then close a deal with her for 1,200 acres of prime Nevada nuclear testing site commercial property.

Chapter Three

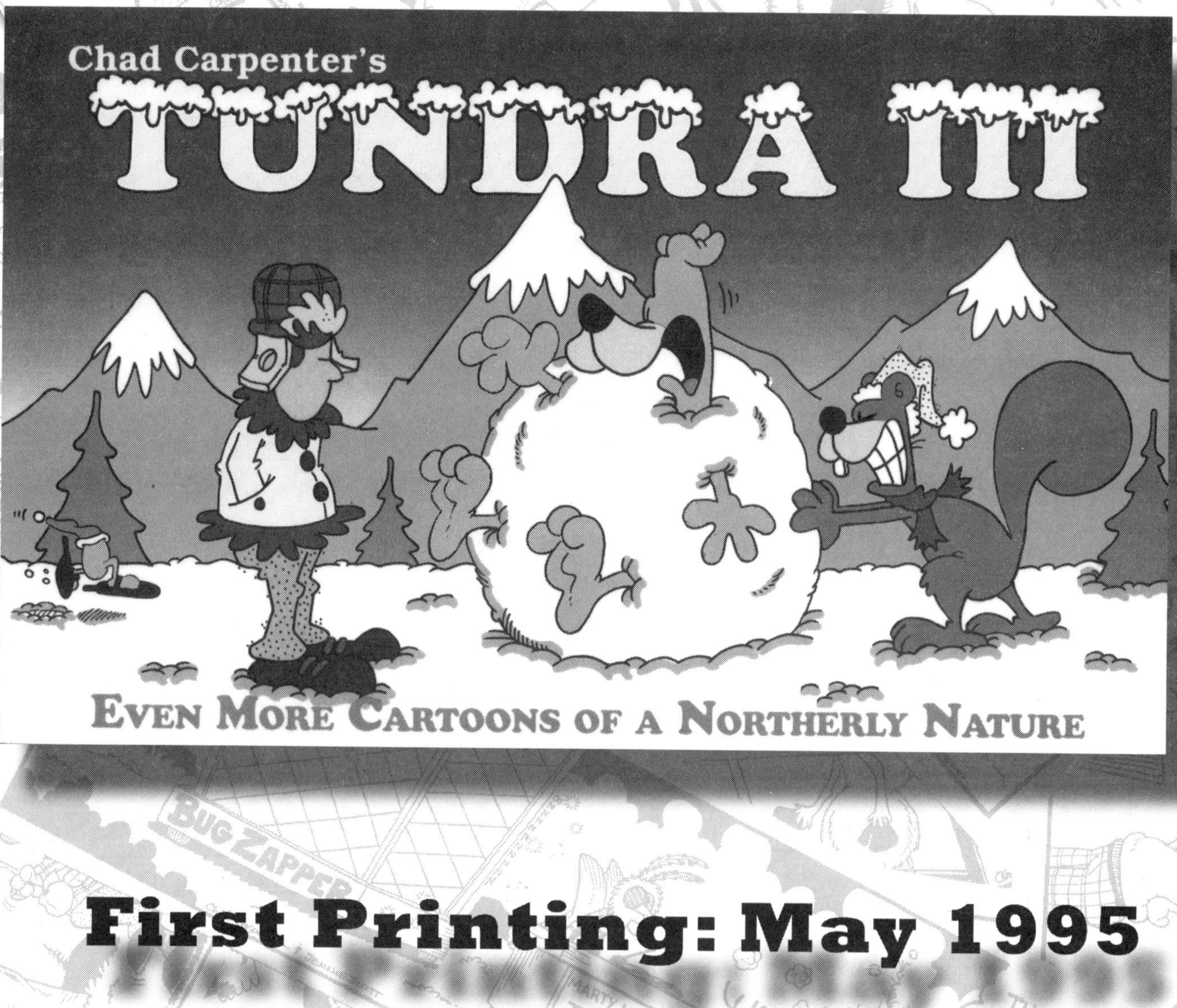
Chad Carpenter's
TUNDRA III
EVEN MORE CARTOONS OF A NORTHERLY NATURE

First Printing: May 1995

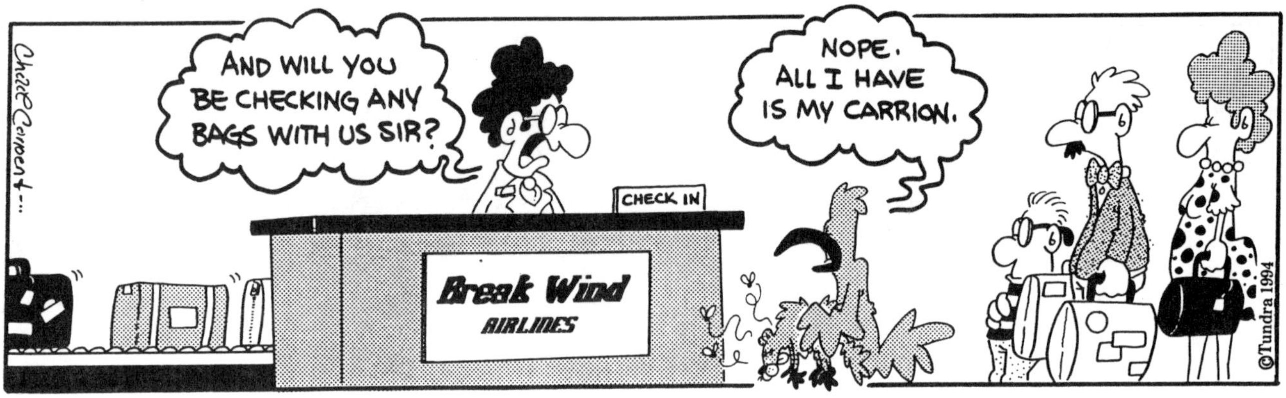
AND WILL YOU BE CHECKING ANY BAGS WITH US SIR?
NOPE. ALL I HAVE IS MY CARRION.
CHECK IN
Break Wind AIRLINES
©Tundra 1994

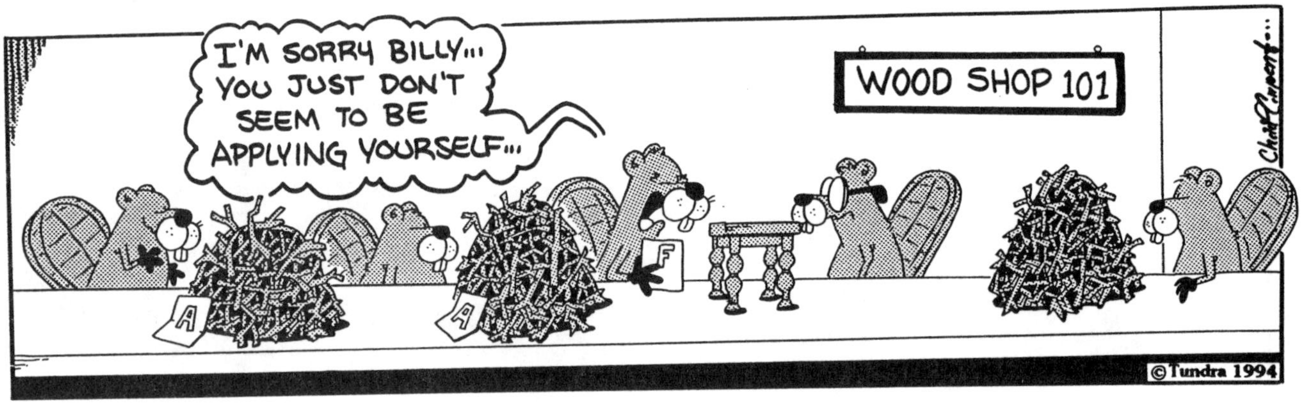
I'M SORRY BILLY... YOU JUST DON'T SEEM TO BE APPLYING YOURSELF...
WOOD SHOP 101
A
A
F
©Tundra 1994

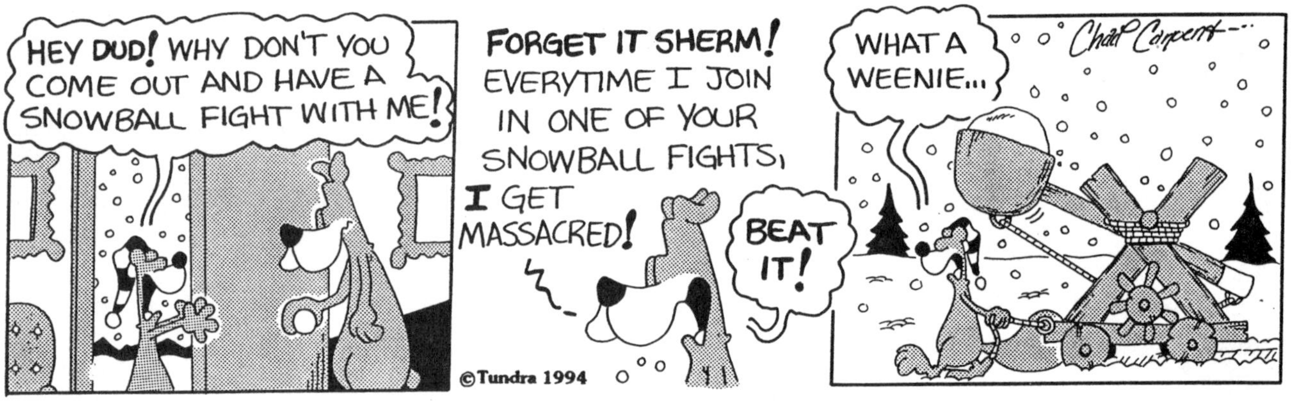
HEY DUD! WHY DON'T YOU COME OUT AND HAVE A SNOWBALL FIGHT WITH ME!
FORGET IT SHERM! EVERYTIME I JOIN IN ONE OF YOUR SNOWBALL FIGHTS, I GET MASSACRED!
BEAT IT!
WHAT A WEENIE...
©Tundra 1994

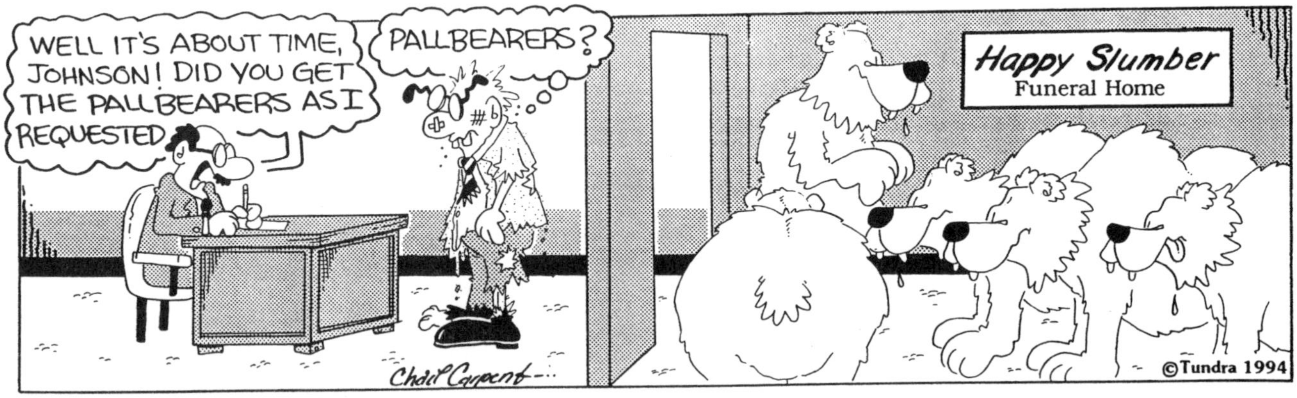
WELL IT'S ABOUT TIME, JOHNSON! DID YOU GET THE PALLBEARERS AS I REQUESTED
PALLBEARERS?
Happy Slumber Funeral Home
©Tundra 1994

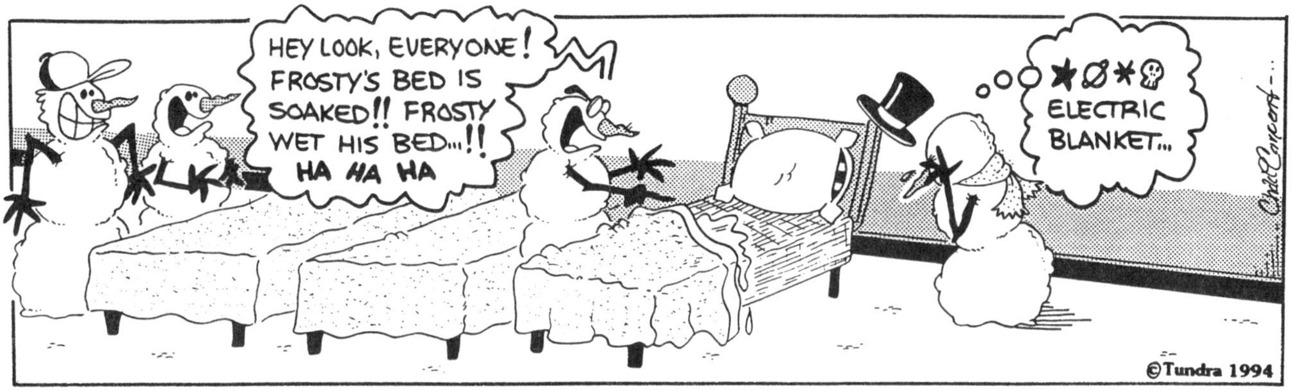
HEY LOOK, EVERYONE! FROSTY'S BED IS SOAKED!! FROSTY WET HIS BED...!! HA HA HA
Ø
ELECTRIC BLANKET...
Chad Carpenter
©Tundra 1994

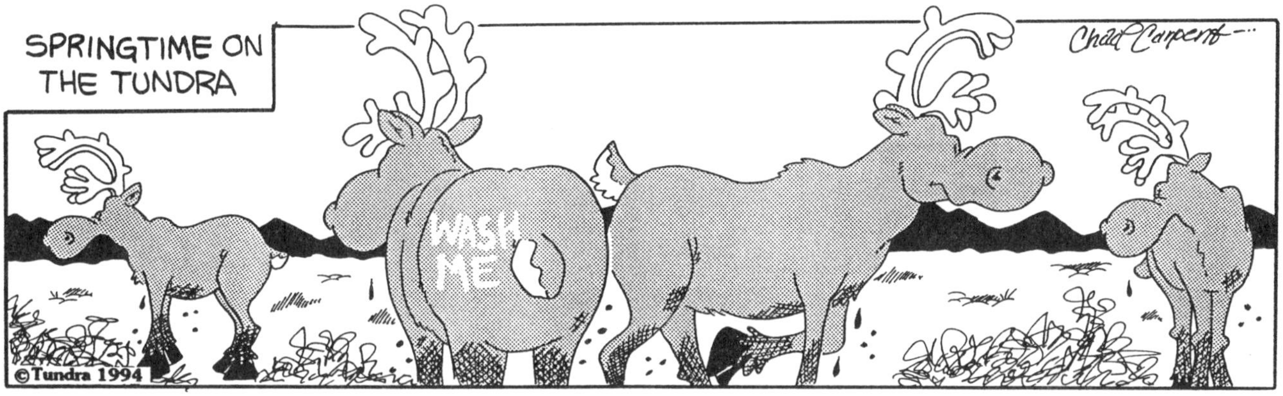
SPRINGTIME ON THE TUNDRA
Chad Carpenter
WASH ME
©Tundra 1994

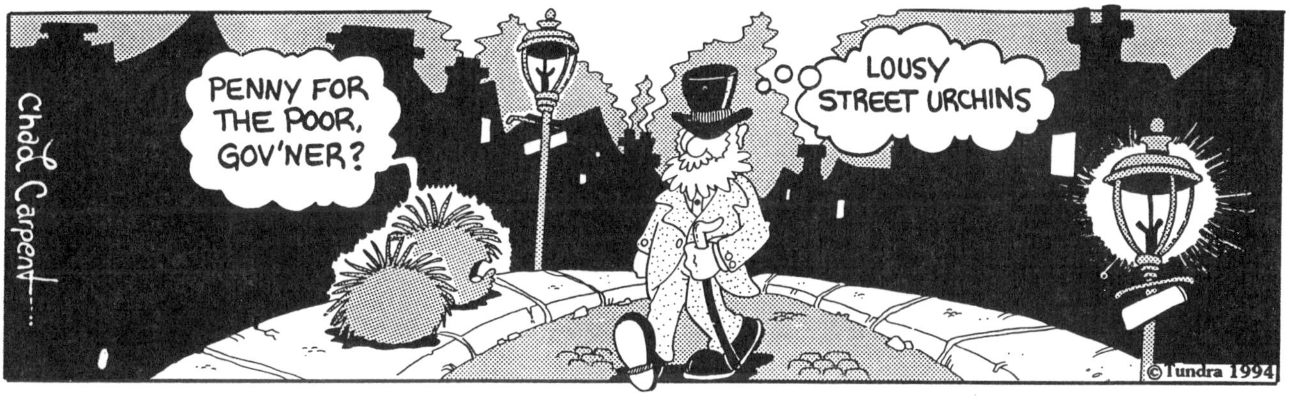
Chad Carpenter
PENNY FOR THE POOR, GOV'NER?
LOUSY STREET URCHINS
©Tundra 1994

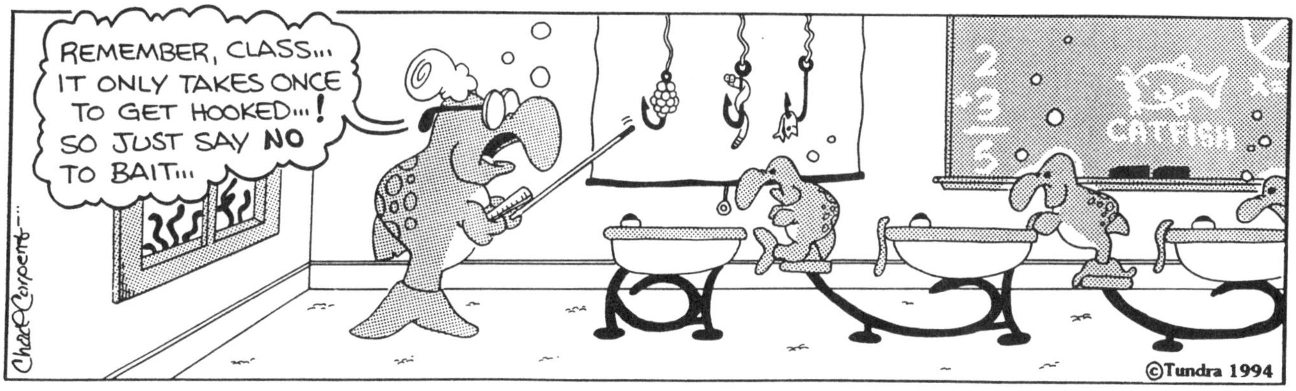
REMEMBER, CLASS... IT ONLY TAKES ONCE TO GET HOOKED...! SO JUST SAY NO TO BAIT...
CATFISH
Chad Carpenter
©Tundra 1994

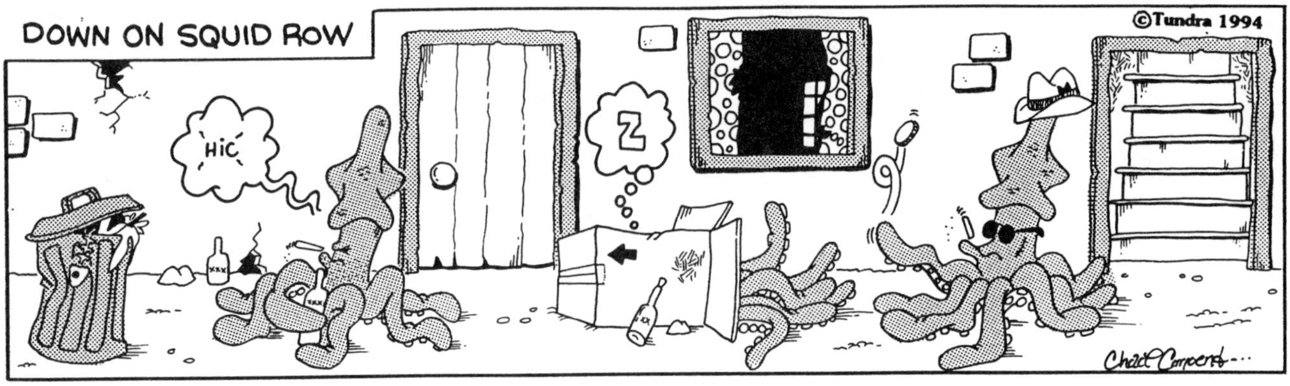
DOWN ON SQUID ROW
©Tundra 1994
HIC
Z

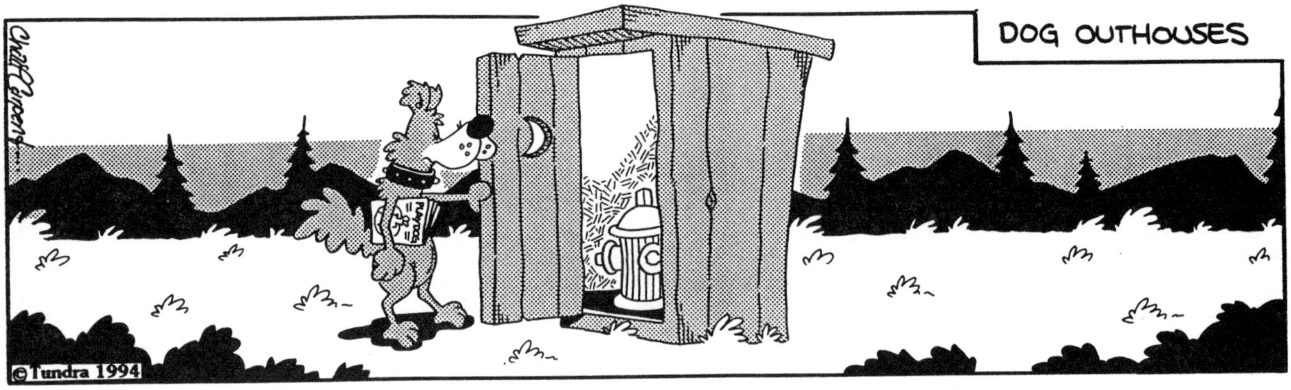
DOG OUTHOUSES
©Tundra 1994

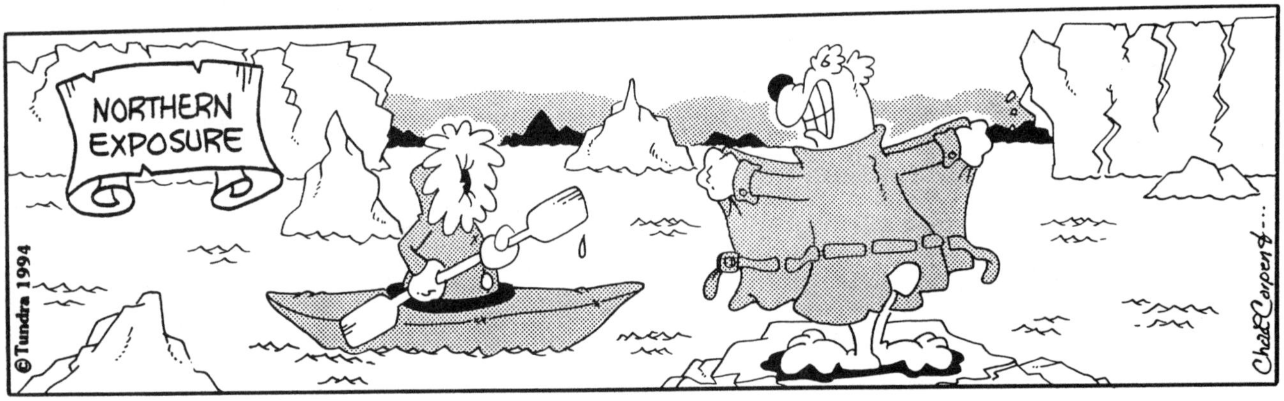
NORTHERN EXPOSURE
©Tundra 1994

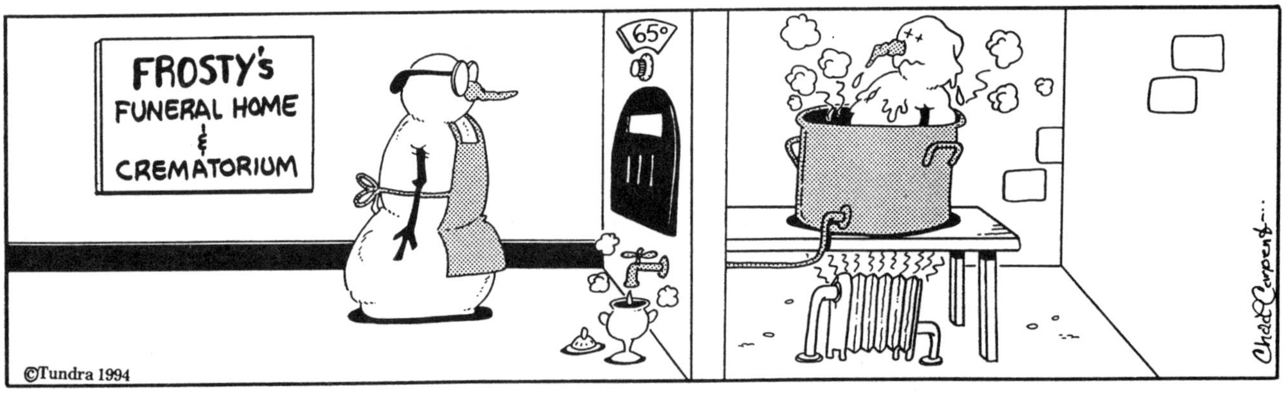
FROSTY's FUNERAL HOME & CREMATORIUM
65°
©Tundra 1994

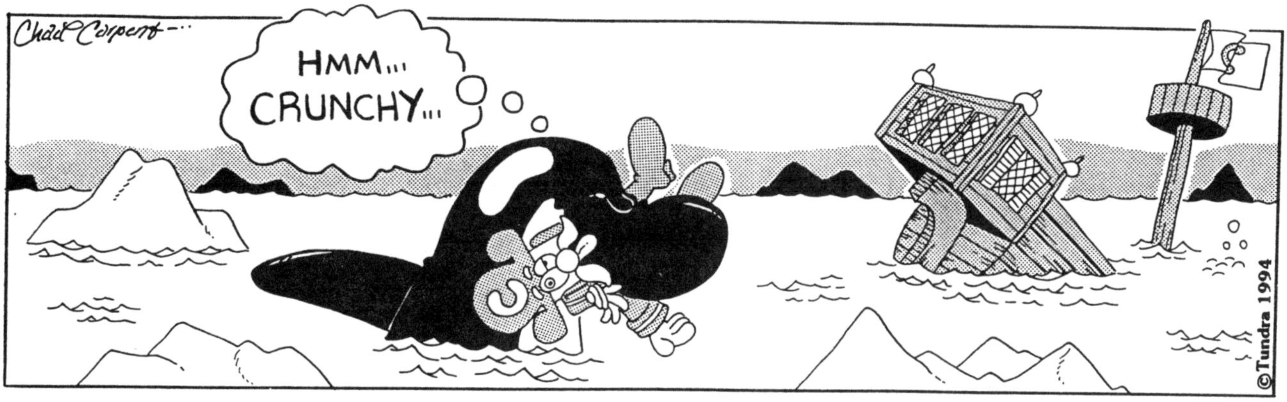
HMM...
CRUNCHY...
©Tundra 1994

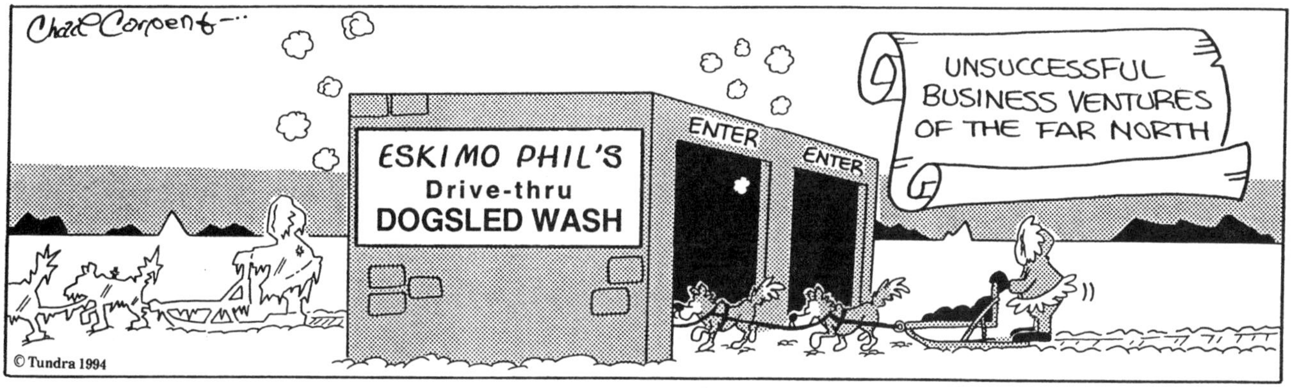
UNSUCCESSFUL BUSINESS VENTURES OF THE FAR NORTH
ESKIMO PHIL'S
Drive-thru
DOGSLED WASH
ENTER
ENTER
© Tundra 1994

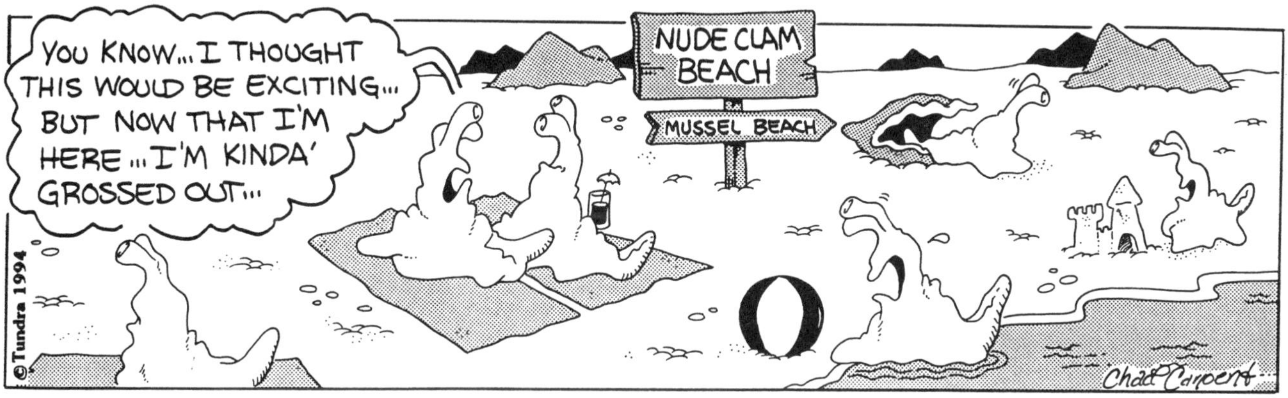
YOU KNOW... I THOUGHT THIS WOULD BE EXCITING... BUT NOW THAT I'M HERE... I'M KINDA' GROSSED OUT...
NUDE CLAM BEACH
MUSSEL BEACH
©Tundra 1994

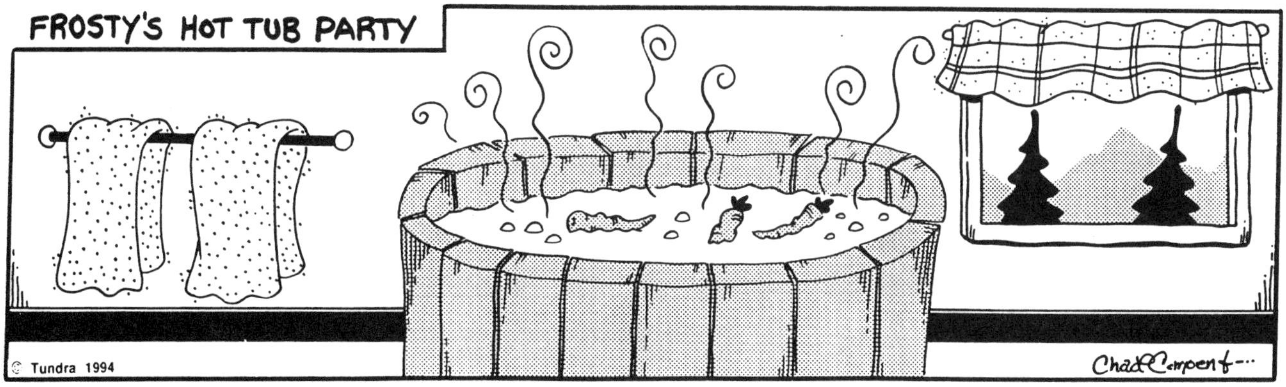
FROSTY'S HOT TUB PARTY
© Tundra 1994

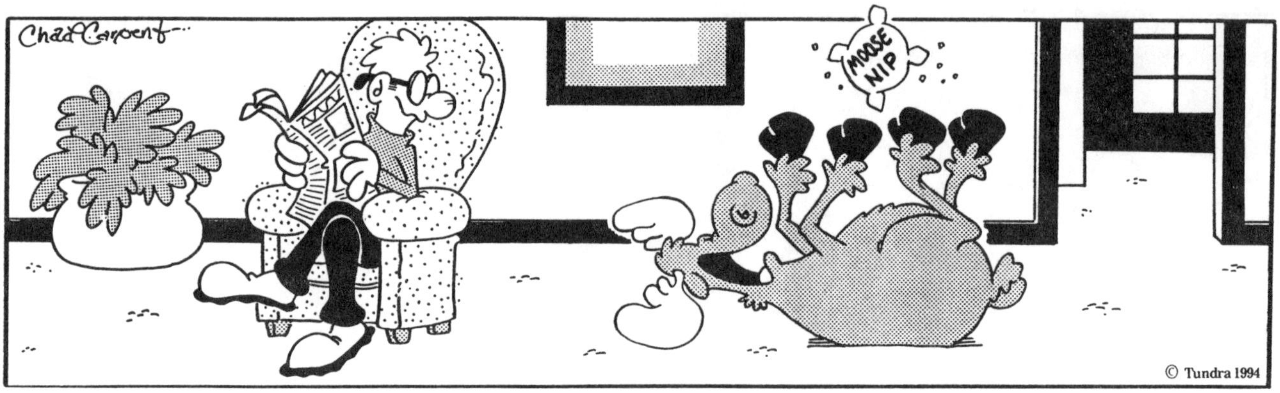
MOOSE NIP
© Tundra 1994

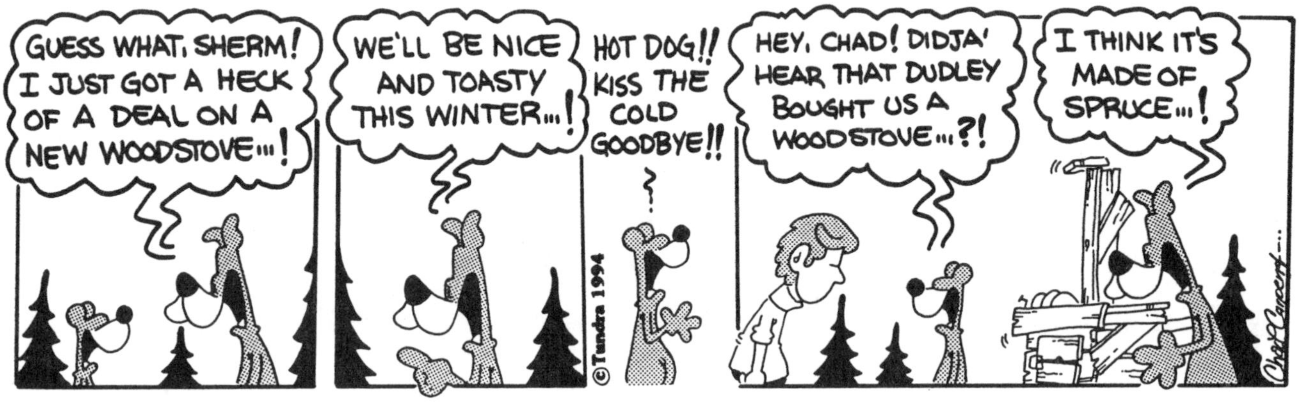
GUESS WHAT, SHERM! I JUST GOT A HECK OF A DEAL ON A NEW WOODSTOVE...!
WE'LL BE NICE AND TOASTY THIS WINTER...!
HOT DOG!! KISS THE COLD GOODBYE!!
©Tundra 1994
HEY, CHAD! DIDJA' HEAR THAT DUDLEY BOUGHT US A WOODSTOVE...?!
I THINK IT'S MADE OF SPRUCE...!

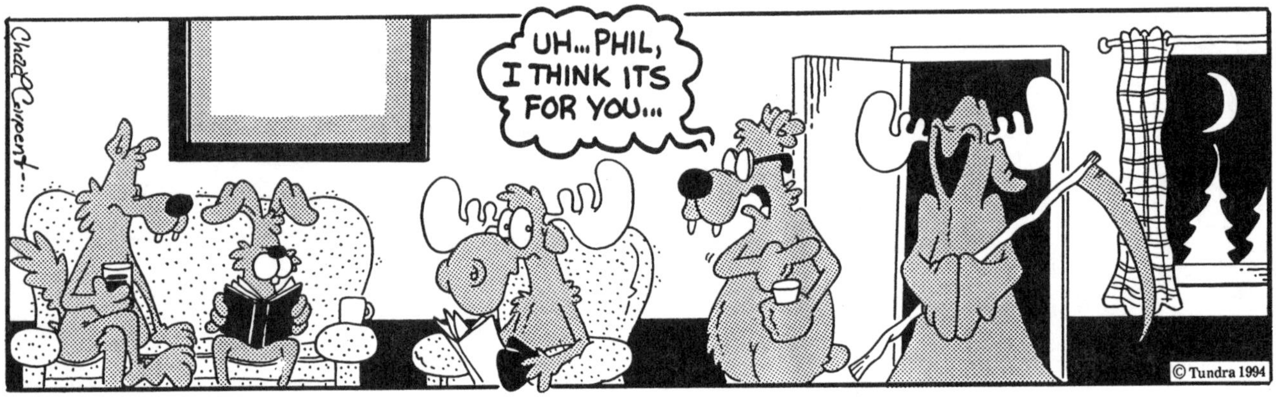
UH...PHIL, I THINK ITS FOR YOU...
© Tundra 1994

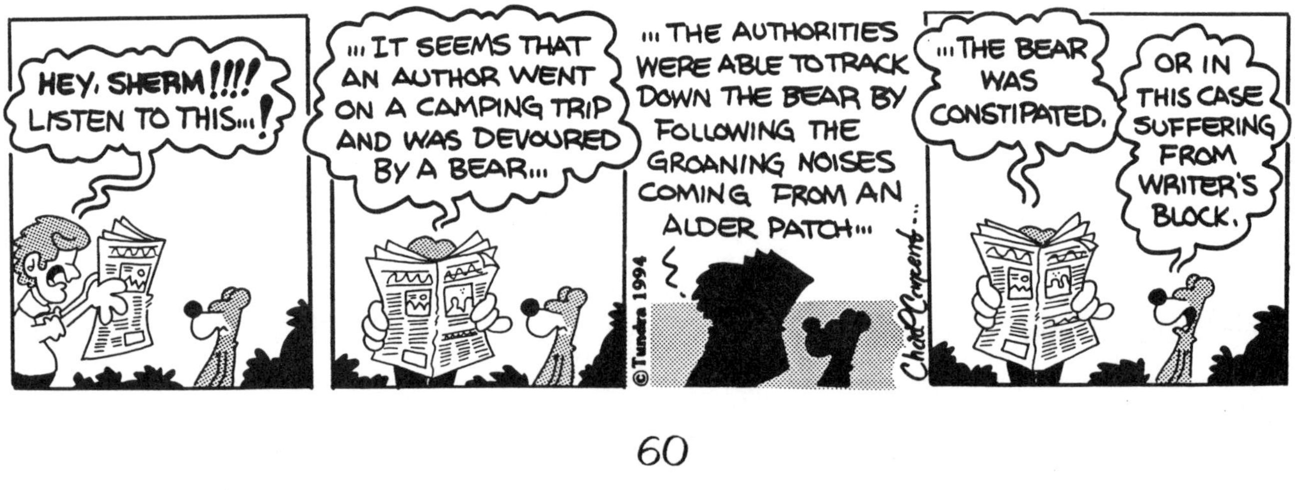
HEY, SHERM!!!! LISTEN TO THIS...!
...IT SEEMS THAT AN AUTHOR WENT ON A CAMPING TRIP AND WAS DEVOURED BY A BEAR...
...THE AUTHORITIES WERE ABLE TO TRACK DOWN THE BEAR BY FOLLOWING THE GROANING NOISES COMING FROM AN ALDER PATCH...
©Tundra 1994
...THE BEAR WAS CONSTIPATED.
OR IN THIS CASE SUFFERING FROM WRITER'S BLOCK.

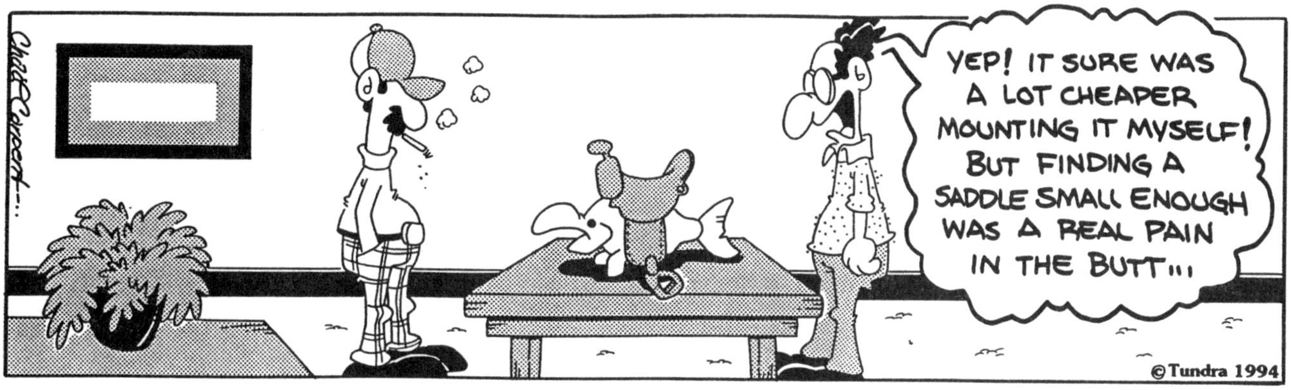
YEP! IT SURE WAS A LOT CHEAPER MOUNTING IT MYSELF! BUT FINDING A SADDLE SMALL ENOUGH WAS A REAL PAIN IN THE BUTT...
©Tundra 1994

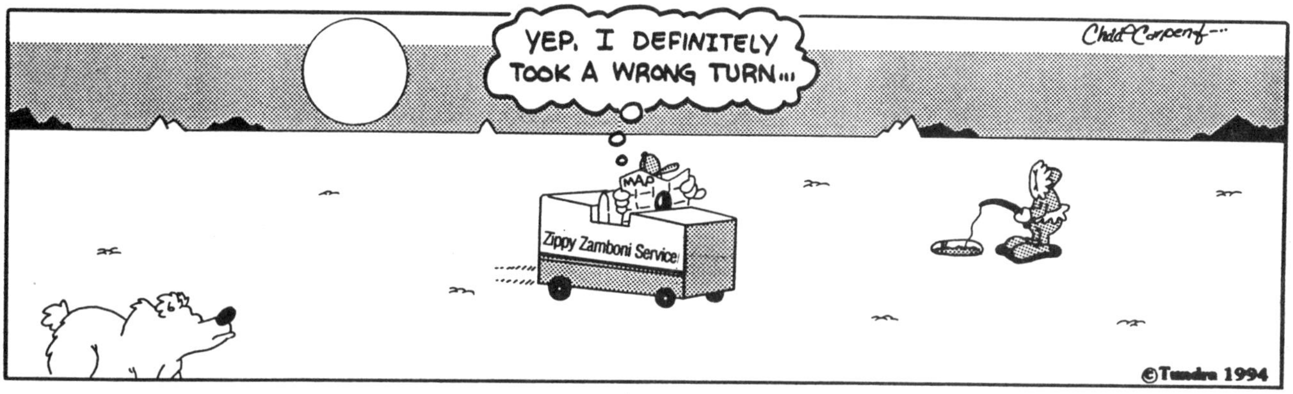
YEP. I DEFINITELY TOOK A WRONG TURN...
MAP
Zippy Zamboni Service
©Tundra 1994

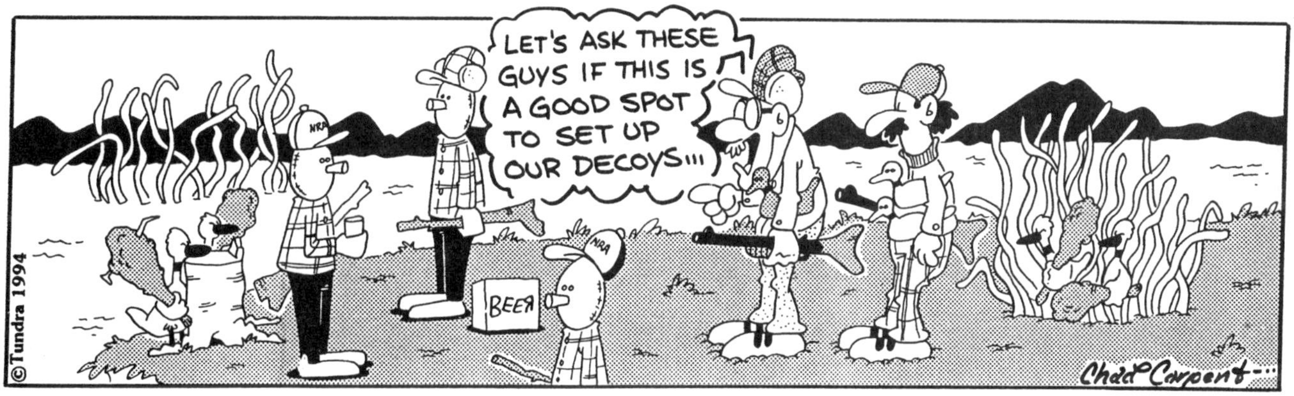
LET'S ASK THESE GUYS IF THIS IS A GOOD SPOT TO SET UP OUR DECOYS...
NRA
BEER
©Tundra 1994

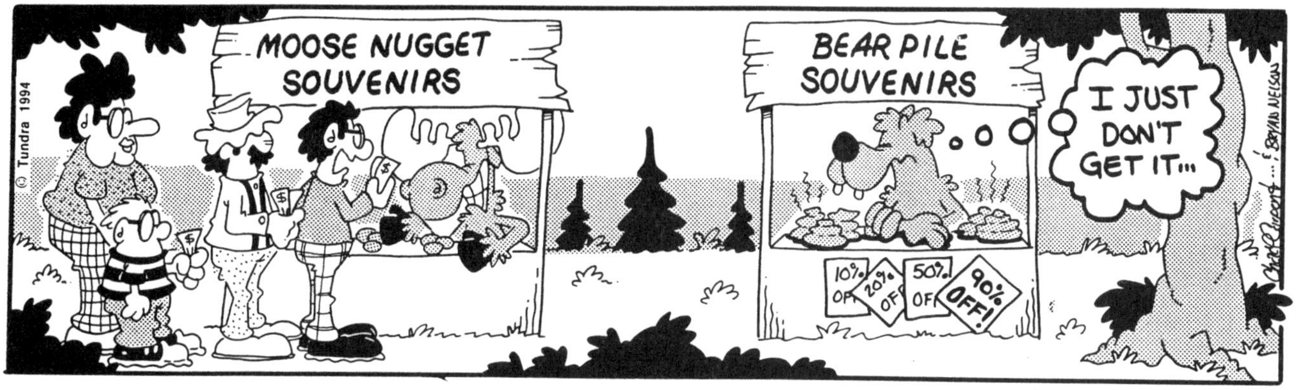
MOOSE NUGGET SOUVENIRS
BEAR PILE SOUVENIRS
I JUST DON'T GET IT...
10% OFF
20% OFF
50% OFF
90% OFF!
© Tundra 1994

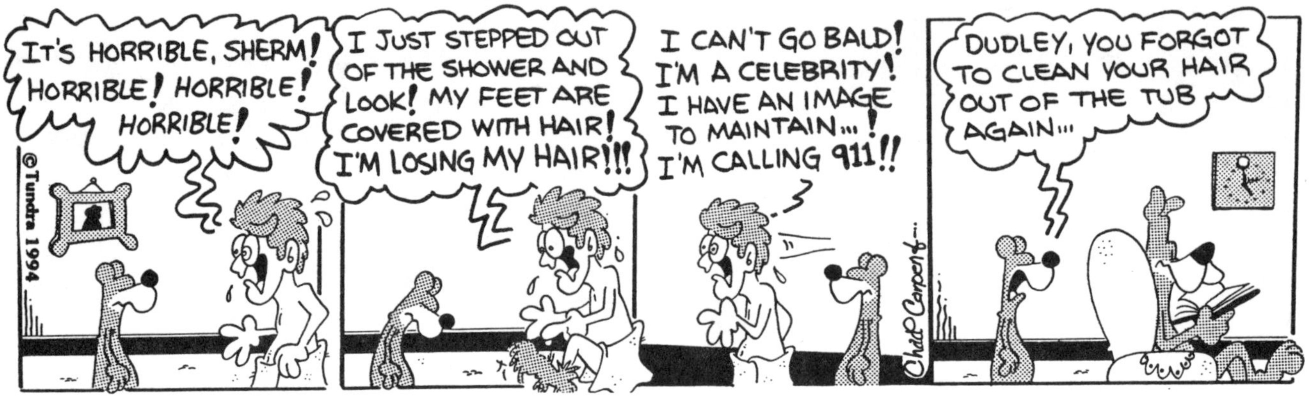
IT'S HORRIBLE, SHERM! HORRIBLE! HORRIBLE! HORRIBLE!
©Tundra 1994
I JUST STEPPED OUT OF THE SHOWER AND LOOK! MY FEET ARE COVERED WITH HAIR! I'M LOSING MY HAIR!!!
I CAN'T GO BALD! I'M A CELEBRITY! I HAVE AN IMAGE TO MAINTAIN...! I'M CALLING 911!!
DUDLEY, YOU FORGOT TO CLEAN YOUR HAIR OUT OF THE TUB AGAIN...

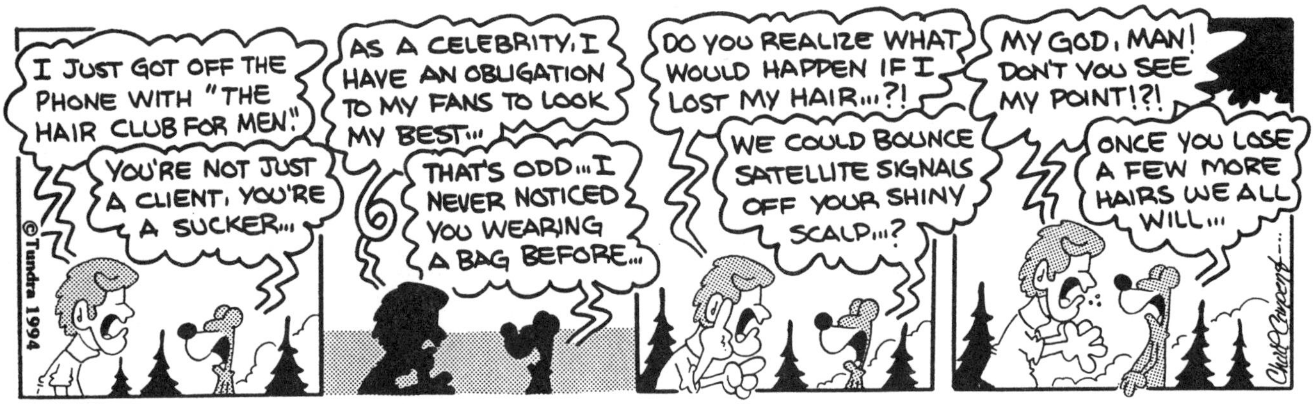
I JUST GOT OFF THE PHONE WITH "THE HAIR CLUB FOR MEN."
YOU'RE NOT JUST A CLIENT, YOU'RE A SUCKER...
©Tundra 1994
AS A CELEBRITY, I HAVE AN OBLIGATION TO MY FANS TO LOOK MY BEST...
THAT'S ODD... I NEVER NOTICED YOU WEARING A BAG BEFORE...
DO YOU REALIZE WHAT WOULD HAPPEN IF I LOST MY HAIR...?!
WE COULD BOUNCE SATELLITE SIGNALS OFF YOUR SHINY SCALP...?
MY GOD, MAN! DON'T YOU SEE MY POINT!?!
ONCE YOU LOSE A FEW MORE HAIRS WE ALL WILL...

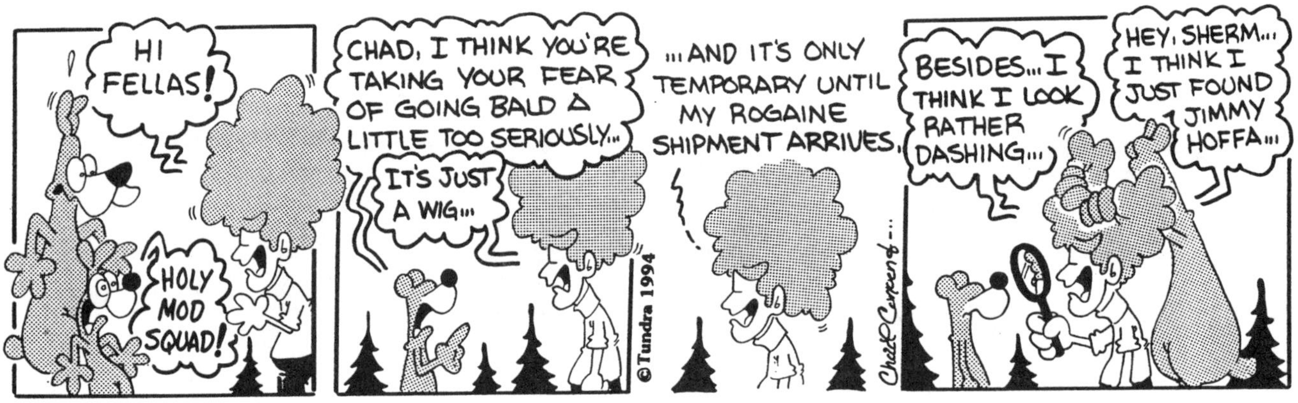
HI FELLAS!
HOLY MOD SQUAD!
CHAD, I THINK YOU'RE TAKING YOUR FEAR OF GOING BALD A LITTLE TOO SERIOUSLY...
IT'S JUST A WIG...
©Tundra 1994
...AND IT'S ONLY TEMPORARY UNTIL MY ROGAINE SHIPMENT ARRIVES.
BESIDES... I THINK I LOOK RATHER DASHING...
HEY, SHERM... I THINK I JUST FOUND JIMMY HOFFA...

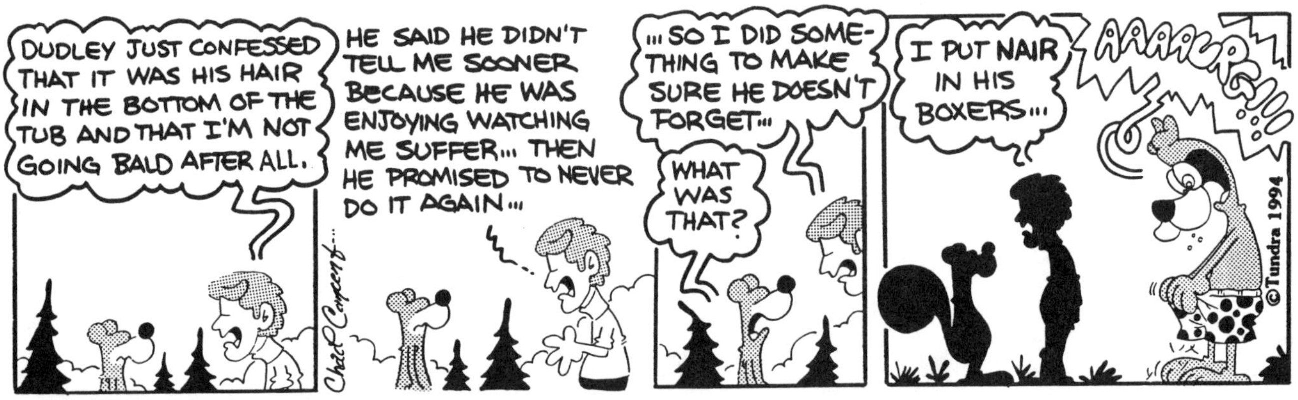
DUDLEY JUST CONFESSED THAT IT WAS HIS HAIR IN THE BOTTOM OF THE TUB AND THAT I'M NOT GOING BALD AFTER ALL.
HE SAID HE DIDN'T TELL ME SOONER BECAUSE HE WAS ENJOYING WATCHING ME SUFFER... THEN HE PROMISED TO NEVER DO IT AGAIN...
...SO I DID SOMETHING TO MAKE SURE HE DOESN'T FORGET...
WHAT WAS THAT?
I PUT NAIR IN HIS BOXERS...
AAAARGH!!!
©Tundra 1994

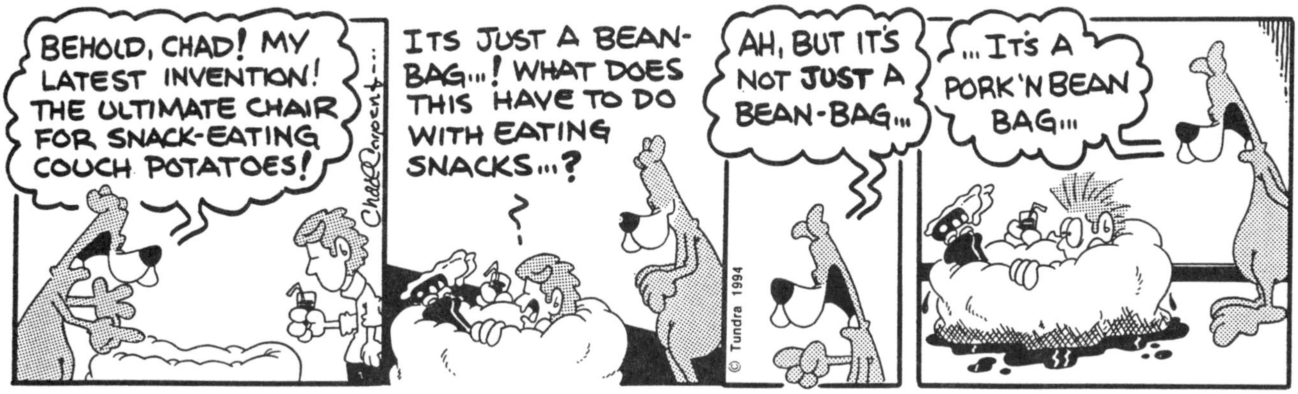
BEHOLD, CHAD! MY LATEST INVENTION! THE ULTIMATE CHAIR FOR SNACK-EATING COUCH POTATOES!
ITS JUST A BEAN-BAG...! WHAT DOES THIS HAVE TO DO WITH EATING SNACKS...?
?
AH, BUT IT'S NOT JUST A BEAN-BAG...
... IT'S A PORK'N BEAN BAG...
© Tundra 1994

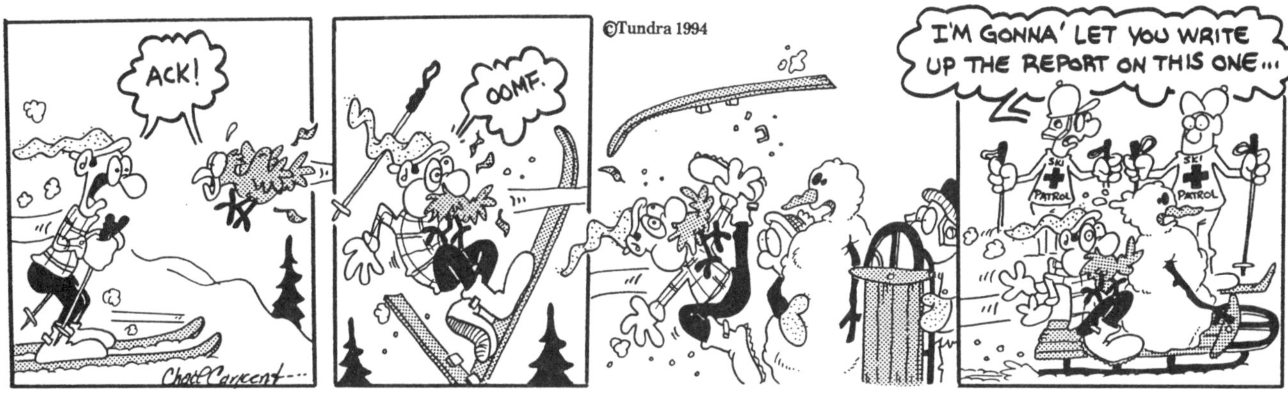
ACK!
OOMF.
©Tundra 1994
I'M GONNA' LET YOU WRITE UP THE REPORT ON THIS ONE...
SKI PATROL
SKI PATROL

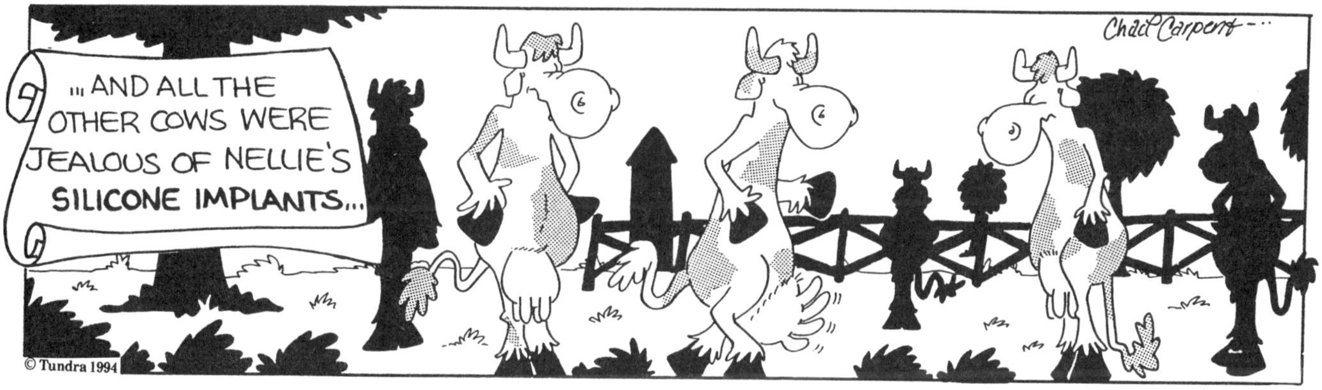
...AND ALL THE OTHER COWS WERE JEALOUS OF NELLIE'S SILICONE IMPLANTS...
© Tundra 1994

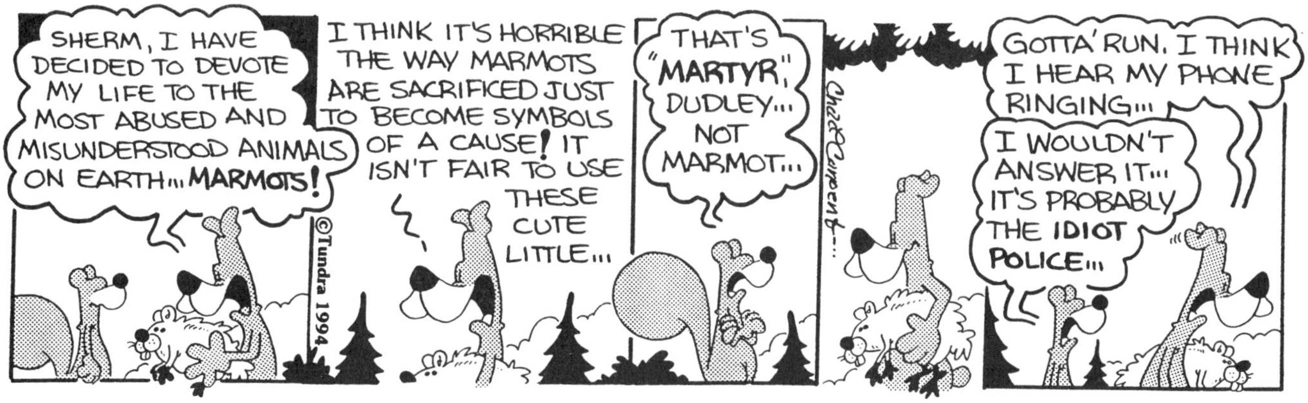
SHERM, I HAVE DECIDED TO DEVOTE MY LIFE TO THE MOST ABUSED AND MISUNDERSTOOD ANIMALS ON EARTH... MARMOTS!
©Tundra 1994
I THINK IT'S HORRIBLE THE WAY MARMOTS ARE SACRIFICED JUST TO BECOME SYMBOLS OF A CAUSE! IT ISN'T FAIR TO USE THESE CUTE LITTLE...
THAT'S "MARTYR", DUDLEY... NOT MARMOT...
GOTTA' RUN. I THINK I HEAR MY PHONE RINGING...
I WOULDN'T ANSWER IT... IT'S PROBABLY THE IDIOT POLICE...

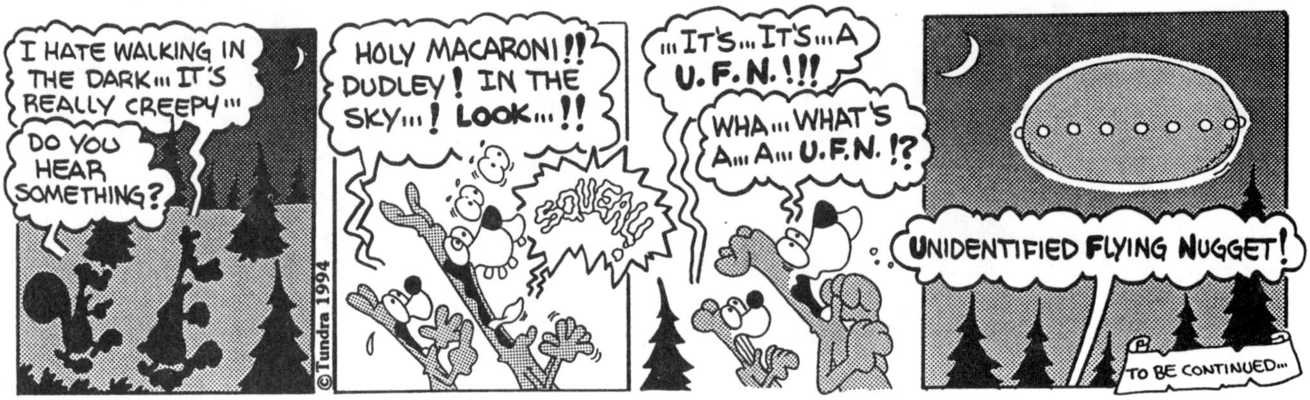
I HATE WALKING IN THE DARK... IT'S REALLY CREEPY...
DO YOU HEAR SOMETHING?
©Tundra 1994
HOLY MACARONI!! DUDLEY! IN THE SKY...! LOOK...!!
...IT'S...IT'S...A U.F.N.!!!
WHA... WHAT'S A... A... U.F.N.!?
UNIDENTIFIED FLYING NUGGET!
TO BE CONTINUED...

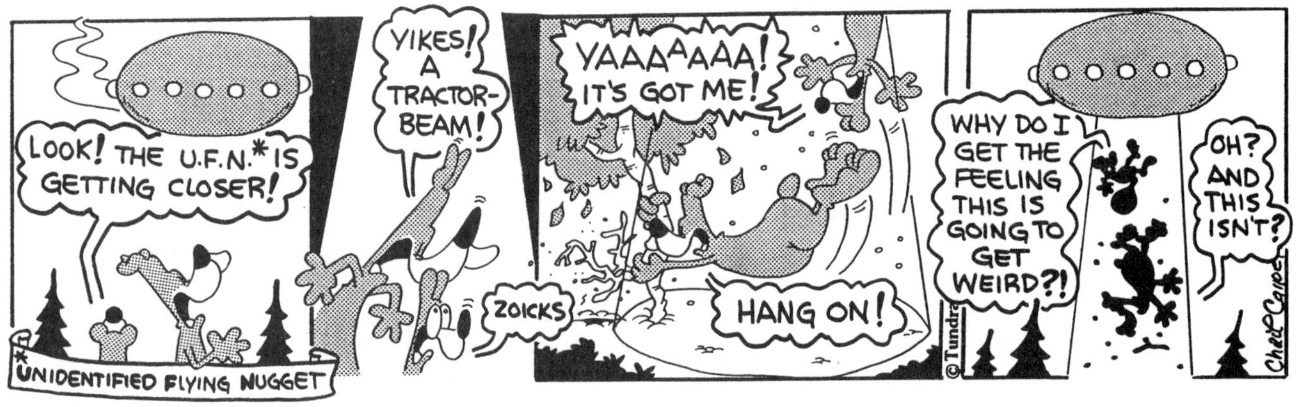
LOOK! THE U.F.N.* IS GETTING CLOSER!
*UNIDENTIFIED FLYING NUGGET
YIKES! A TRACTOR-BEAM!
ZOICKS
YAAAAAAA! IT'S GOT ME!
HANG ON!
©Tundra
WHY DO I GET THE FEELING THIS IS GOING TO GET WEIRD?!
OH? AND THIS ISN'T?

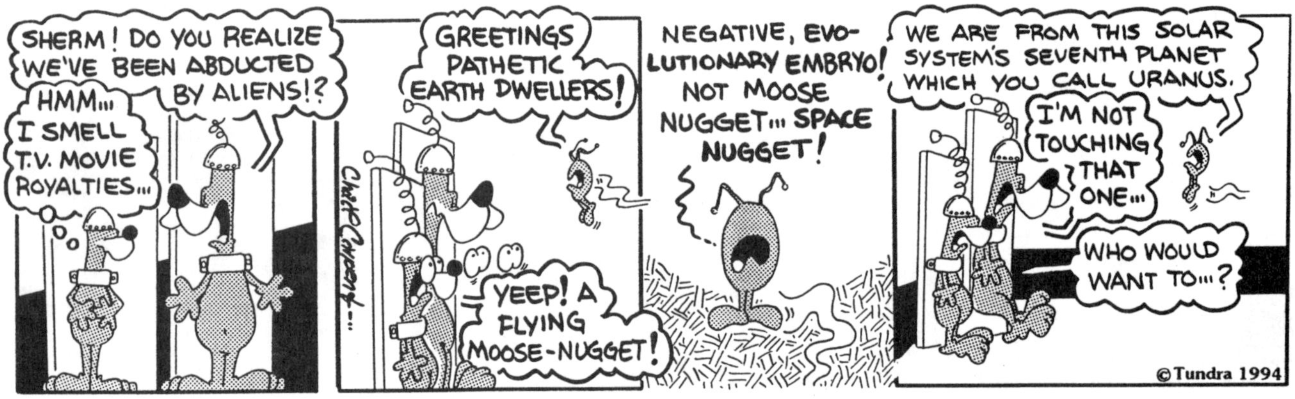
SHERM! DO YOU REALIZE WE'VE BEEN ABDUCTED BY ALIENS!?
HMM... I SMELL T.V. MOVIE ROYALTIES...
GREETINGS PATHETIC EARTH DWELLERS!
YEEP! A FLYING MOOSE-NUGGET!
NEGATIVE, EVO-LUTIONARY EMBRYO! NOT MOOSE NUGGET... SPACE NUGGET!
WE ARE FROM THIS SOLAR SYSTEM'S SEVENTH PLANET WHICH YOU CALL URANUS.
I'M NOT TOUCHING THAT ONE...
WHO WOULD WANT TO...?
©Tundra 1994

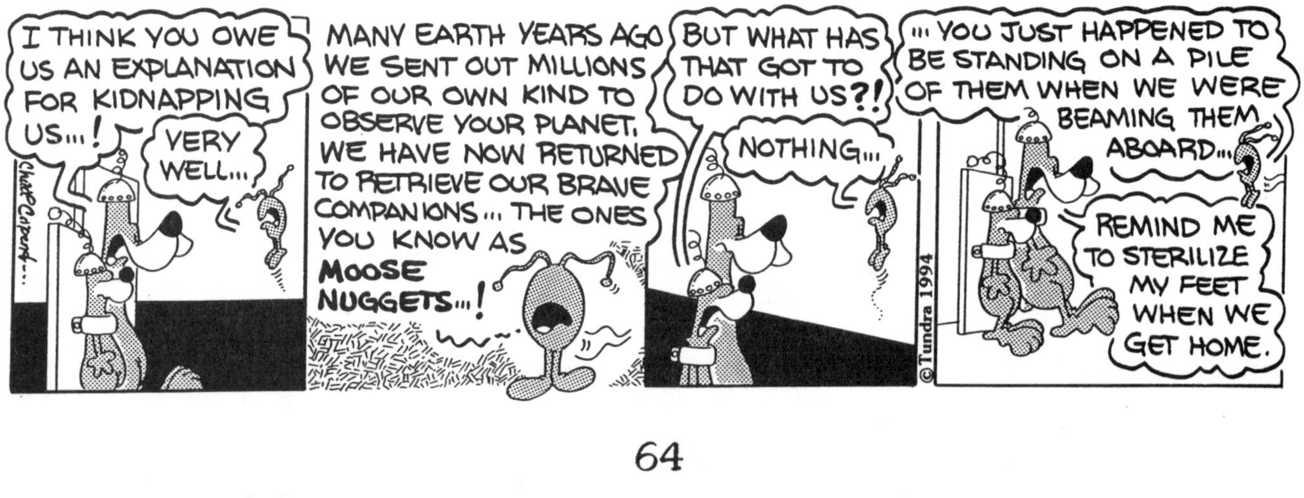
I THINK YOU OWE US AN EXPLANATION FOR KIDNAPPING US...!
VERY WELL...
MANY EARTH YEARS AGO WE SENT OUT MILLIONS OF OUR OWN KIND TO OBSERVE YOUR PLANET. WE HAVE NOW RETURNED TO RETRIEVE OUR BRAVE COMPANIONS... THE ONES YOU KNOW AS MOOSE NUGGETS...!
BUT WHAT HAS THAT GOT TO DO WITH US?!
NOTHING...
©Tundra 1994
...YOU JUST HAPPENED TO BE STANDING ON A PILE OF THEM WHEN WE WERE BEAMING THEM ABOARD...
REMIND ME TO STERILIZE MY FEET WHEN WE GET HOME.

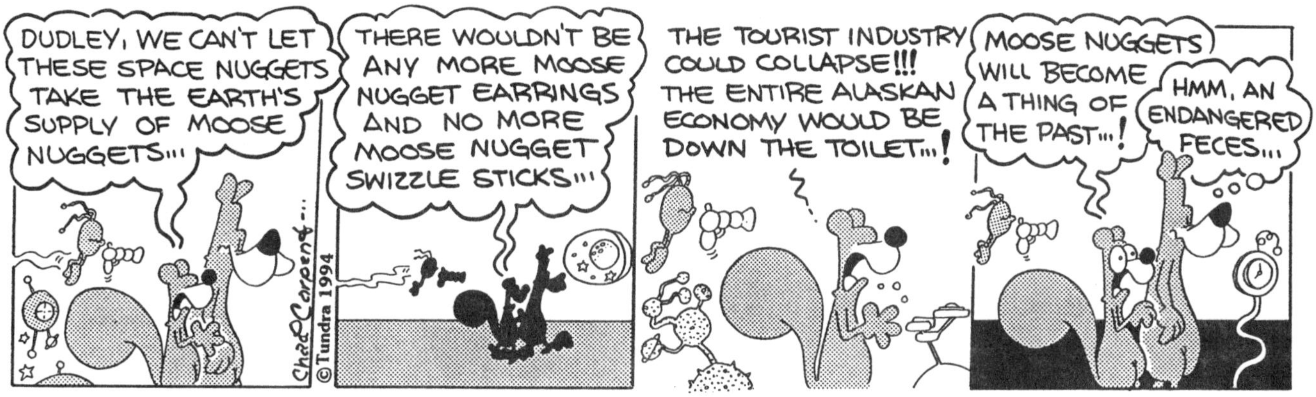
DUDLEY, WE CAN'T LET THESE SPACE NUGGETS TAKE THE EARTH'S SUPPLY OF MOOSE NUGGETS...
THERE WOULDN'T BE ANY MORE MOOSE NUGGET EARRINGS AND NO MORE MOOSE NUGGET SWIZZLE STICKS...
THE TOURIST INDUSTRY COULD COLLAPSE!!! THE ENTIRE ALASKAN ECONOMY WOULD BE DOWN THE TOILET...!
MOOSE NUGGETS WILL BECOME A THING OF THE PAST...!
HMM, AN ENDANGERED FECES...
Chad Carpenter
©Tundra 1994

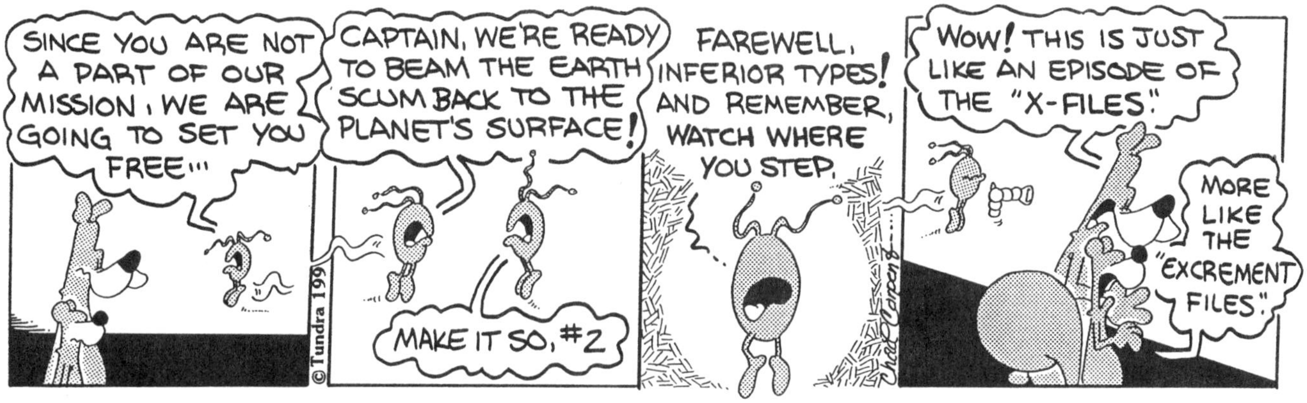
SINCE YOU ARE NOT A PART OF OUR MISSION, WE ARE GOING TO SET YOU FREE...
CAPTAIN, WE'RE READY TO BEAM THE EARTH SCUM BACK TO THE PLANET'S SURFACE!
MAKE IT SO, #2
FAREWELL, INFERIOR TYPES! AND REMEMBER, WATCH WHERE YOU STEP.
WOW! THIS IS JUST LIKE AN EPISODE OF THE "X-FILES".
MORE LIKE THE "EXCREMENT FILES".
©Tundra 1994
Chad Carpenter

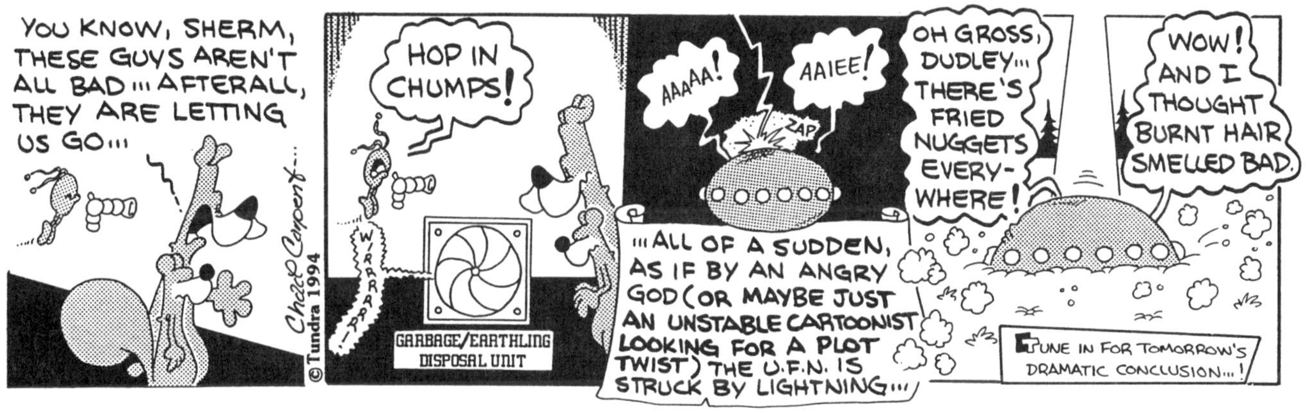
YOU KNOW, SHERM, THESE GUYS AREN'T ALL BAD... AFTERALL, THEY ARE LETTING US GO...
Chad Carpenter
©Tundra 1994
HOP IN CHUMPS!
WIRRRAPP!
GARBAGE/EARTHLING DISPOSAL UNIT
AAAAA!
AAIEE!
ZAP
...ALL OF A SUDDEN, AS IF BY AN ANGRY GOD (OR MAYBE JUST AN UNSTABLE CARTOONIST LOOKING FOR A PLOT TWIST) THE U.F.N. IS STRUCK BY LIGHTNING...
OH GROSS, DUDLEY... THERE'S FRIED NUGGETS EVERYWHERE!
WOW! AND I THOUGHT BURNT HAIR SMELLED BAD.
TUNE IN FOR TOMORROW'S DRAMATIC CONCLUSION...!

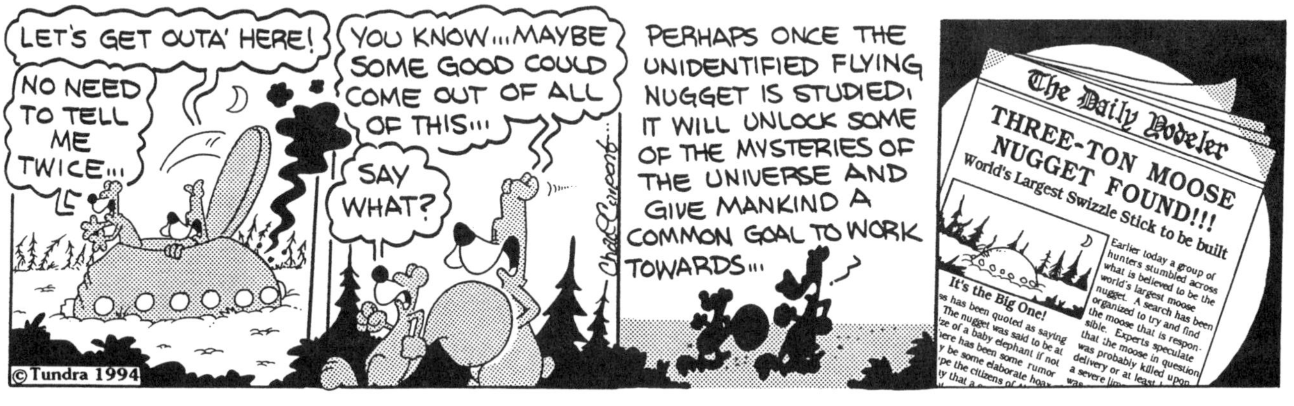
LET'S GET OUTA' HERE!
NO NEED TO TELL ME TWICE...
YOU KNOW... MAYBE SOME GOOD COULD COME OUT OF ALL OF THIS...
SAY WHAT?
Chad Carpenter
PERHAPS ONCE THE UNIDENTIFIED FLYING NUGGET IS STUDIED, IT WILL UNLOCK SOME OF THE MYSTERIES OF THE UNIVERSE AND GIVE MANKIND A COMMON GOAL TO WORK TOWARDS...
The Daily Yodeler
THREE-TON MOOSE NUGGET FOUND!!!
World's Largest Swizzle Stick to be built
It's the Big One!
©Tundra 1994

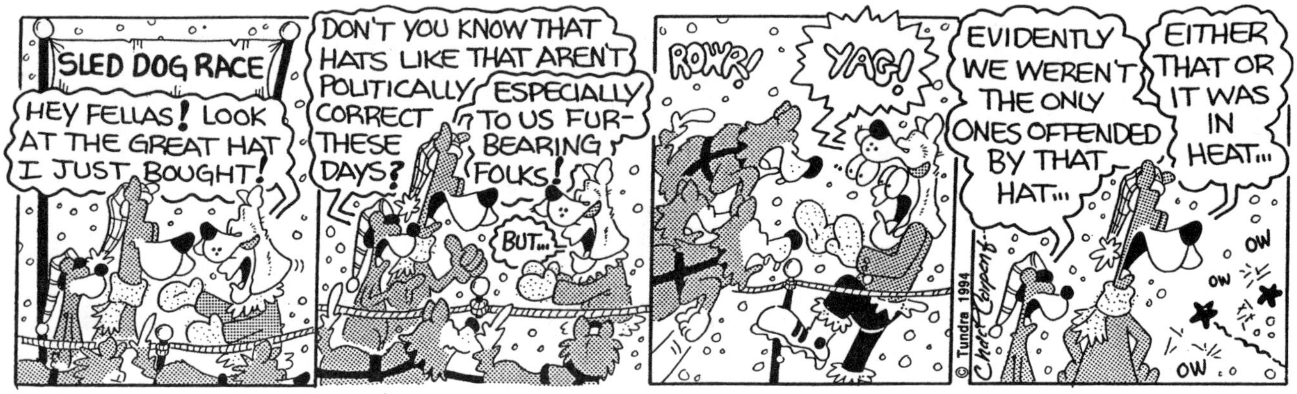
SLED DOG RACE
HEY FELLAS! LOOK AT THE GREAT HAT I JUST BOUGHT!
DON'T YOU KNOW THAT HATS LIKE THAT AREN'T POLITICALLY CORRECT THESE DAYS?
ESPECIALLY TO US FUR-BEARING FOLKS!
BUT...
ROWR!
YAG!
EVIDENTLY WE WEREN'T THE ONLY ONES OFFENDED BY THAT HAT...
EITHER THAT OR IT WAS IN HEAT...
OW
OW
OW
© Tundra 1994
Chad Carpenter

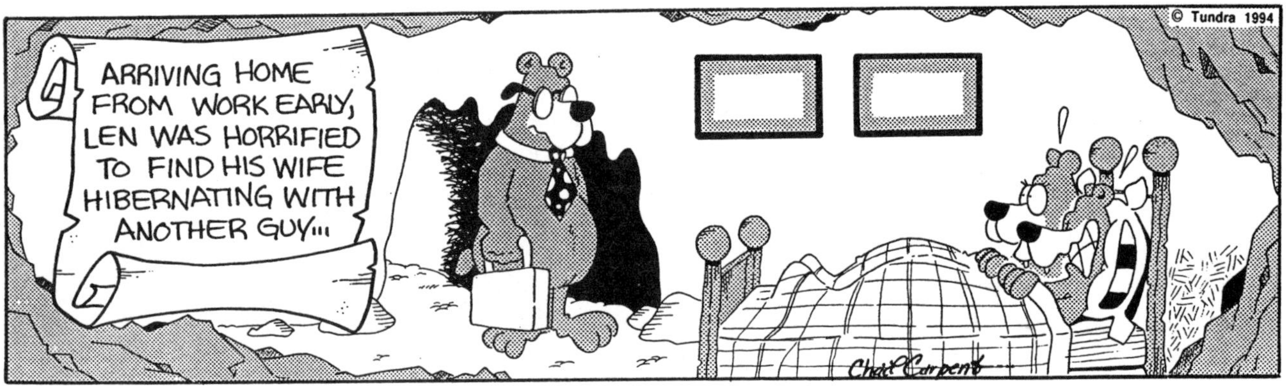
© Tundra 1994
ARRIVING HOME FROM WORK EARLY, LEN WAS HORRIFIED TO FIND HIS WIFE HIBERNATING WITH ANOTHER GUY...
Chad Carpenter

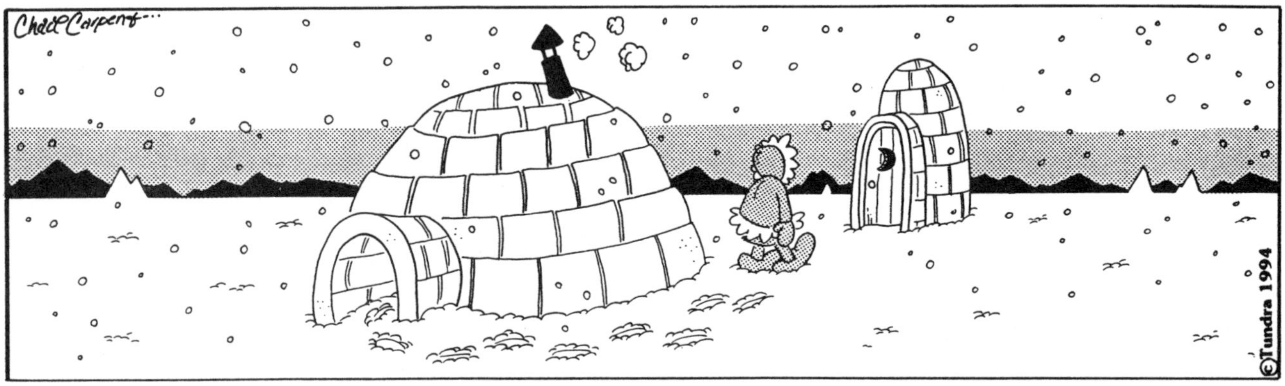
Chad Carpenter...
©Tundra 1994

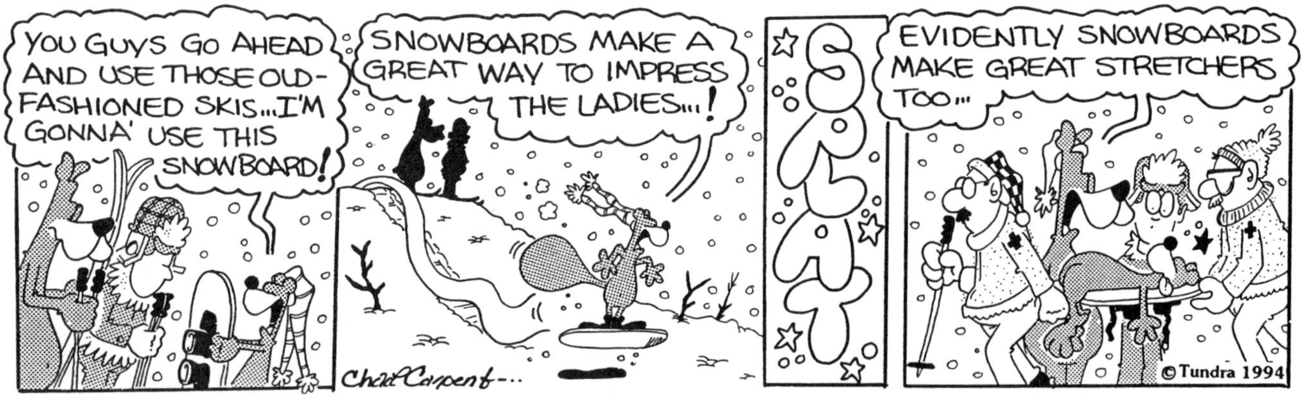
YOU GUYS GO AHEAD AND USE THOSE OLD-FASHIONED SKIS...I'M GONNA' USE THIS SNOWBOARD!
SNOWBOARDS MAKE A GREAT WAY TO IMPRESS THE LADIES...!
Chad Carpenter...
SPLAT
EVIDENTLY SNOWBOARDS MAKE GREAT STRETCHERS TOO...
©Tundra 1994

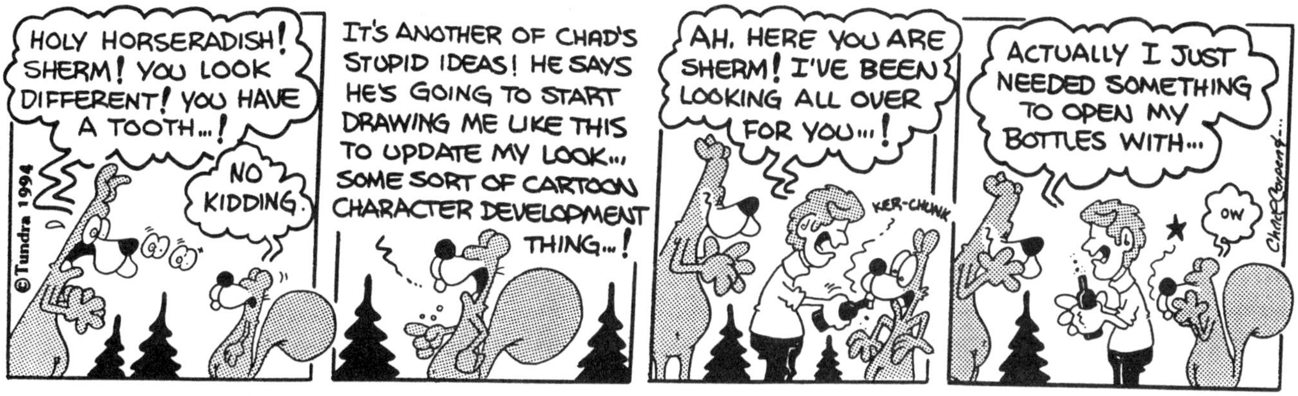
HOLY HORSERADISH! SHERM! YOU LOOK DIFFERENT! YOU HAVE A TOOTH...!
NO KIDDING.
©Tundra 1994
IT'S ANOTHER OF CHAD'S STUPID IDEAS! HE SAYS HE'S GOING TO START DRAWING ME LIKE THIS TO UPDATE MY LOOK..., SOME SORT OF CARTOON CHARACTER DEVELOPMENT THING...!
AH, HERE YOU ARE SHERM! I'VE BEEN LOOKING ALL OVER FOR YOU...!
KER-CHUNK
ACTUALLY I JUST NEEDED SOMETHING TO OPEN MY BOTTLES WITH...
OW

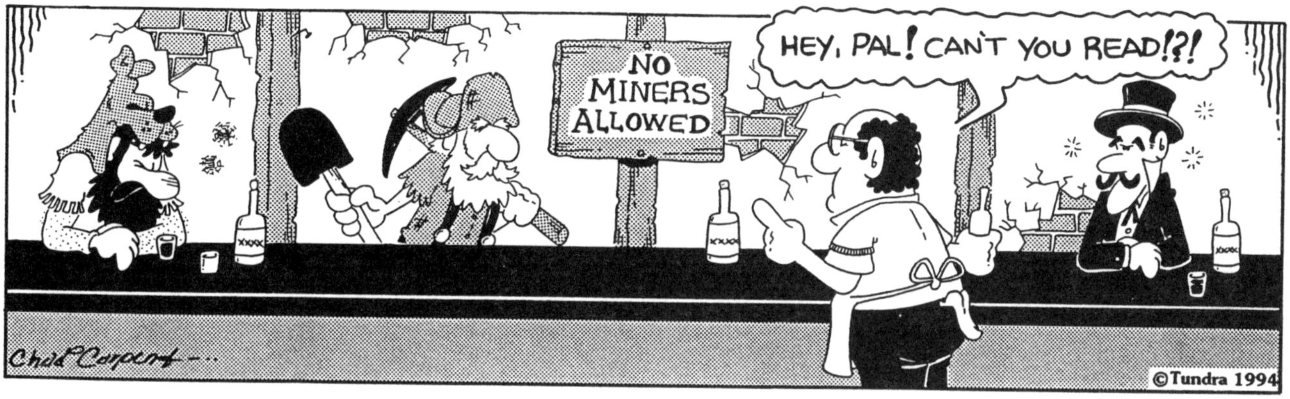
NO MINERS ALLOWED
HEY, PAL! CAN'T YOU READ!?!
©Tundra 1994

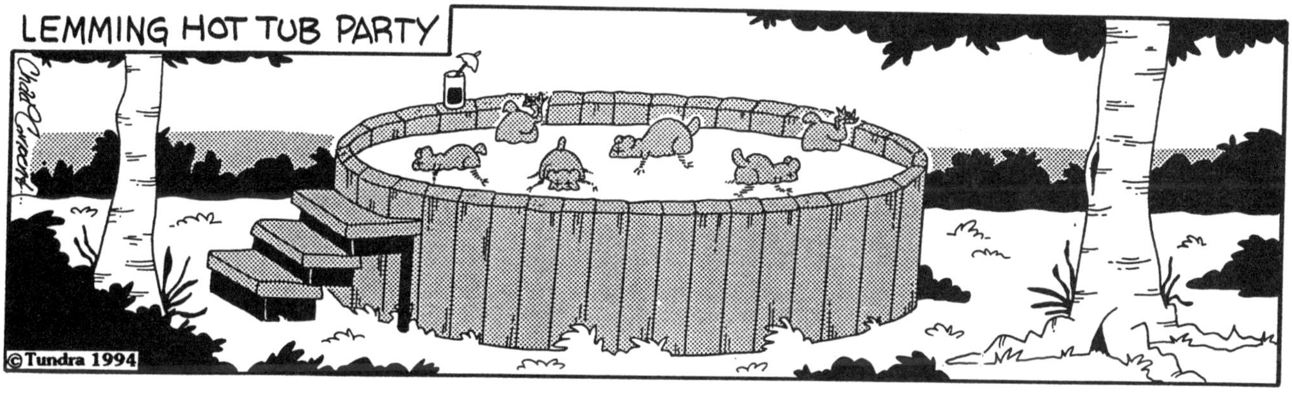
LEMMING HOT TUB PARTY
©Tundra 1994

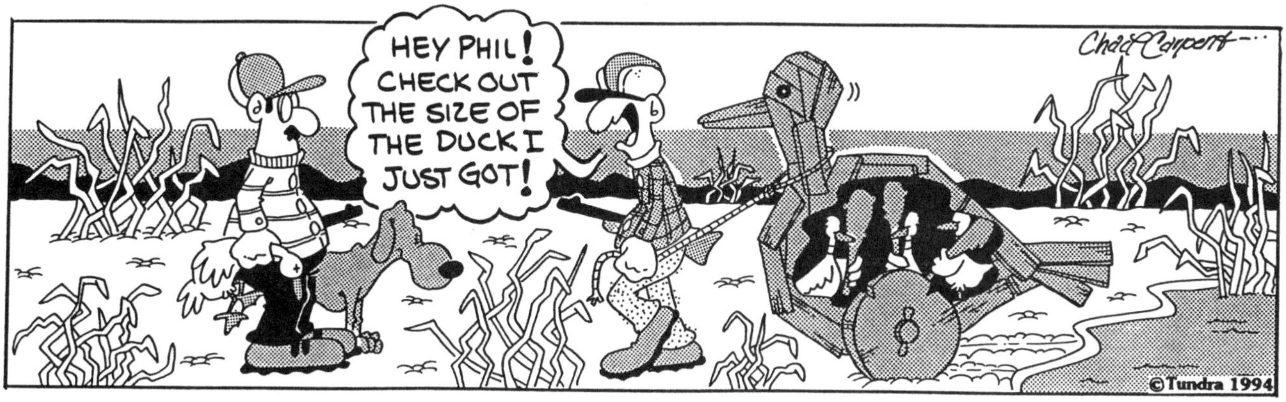
HEY PHIL! CHECK OUT THE SIZE OF THE DUCK I JUST GOT!
©Tundra 1994

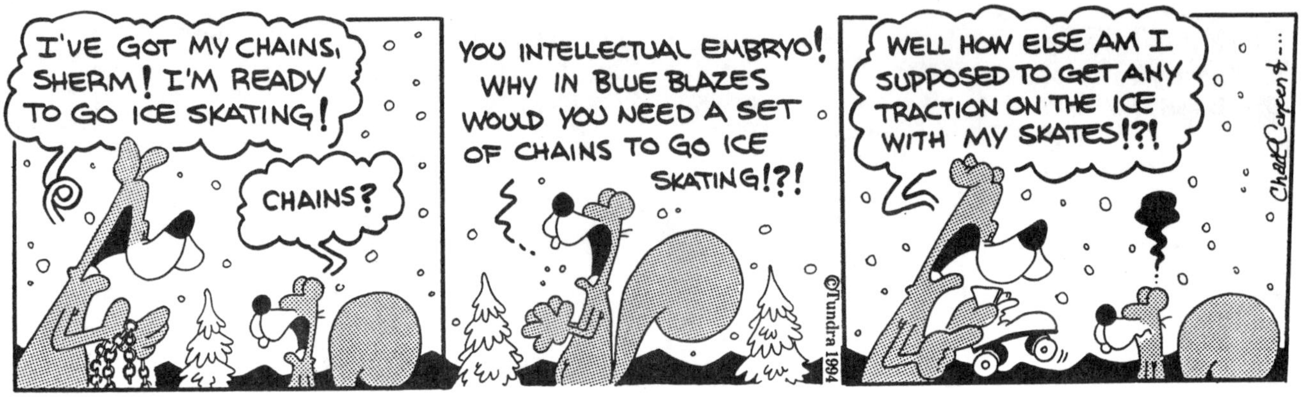
I'VE GOT MY CHAINS, SHERM! I'M READY TO GO ICE SKATING!
CHAINS?
YOU INTELLECTUAL EMBRYO! WHY IN BLUE BLAZES WOULD YOU NEED A SET OF CHAINS TO GO ICE SKATING!?!
©Tundra 1994
WELL HOW ELSE AM I SUPPOSED TO GET ANY TRACTION ON THE ICE WITH MY SKATES!?!

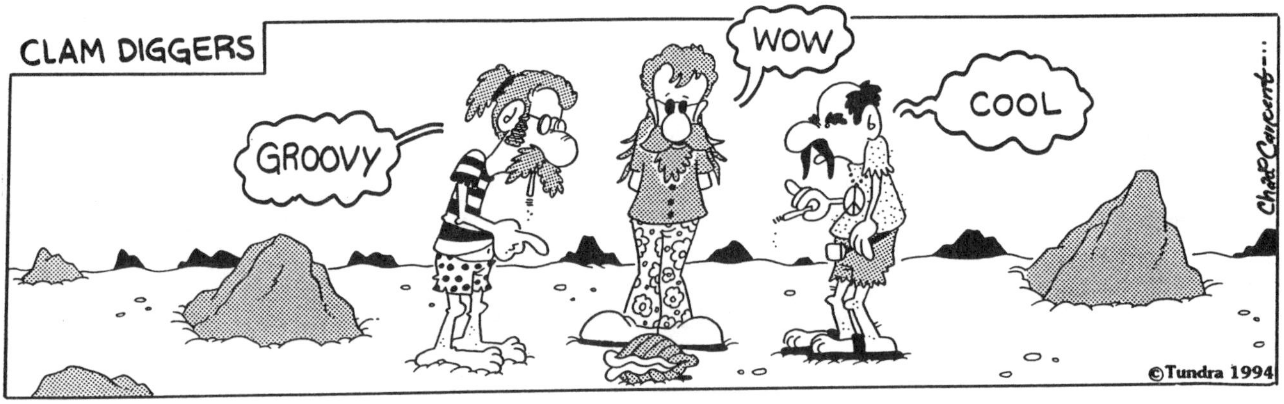
CLAM DIGGERS
GROOVY
WOW
COOL
©Tundra 1994

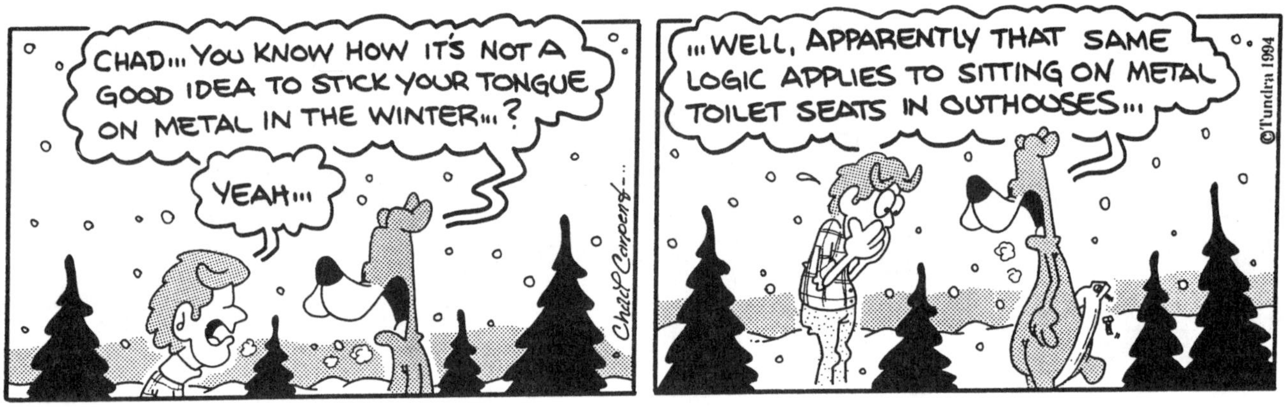
CHAD... YOU KNOW HOW IT'S NOT A GOOD IDEA TO STICK YOUR TONGUE ON METAL IN THE WINTER...?
YEAH...
...WELL, APPARENTLY THAT SAME LOGIC APPLIES TO SITTING ON METAL TOILET SEATS IN OUTHOUSES...
©Tundra 1994

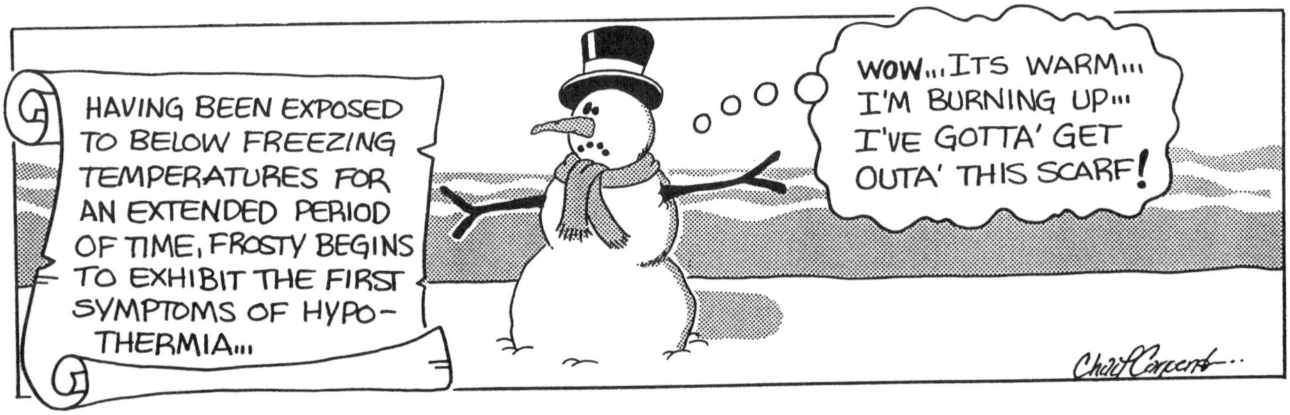
HAVING BEEN EXPOSED TO BELOW FREEZING TEMPERATURES FOR AN EXTENDED PERIOD OF TIME, FROSTY BEGINS TO EXHIBIT THE FIRST SYMPTOMS OF HYPO-THERMIA...
WOW... ITS WARM... I'M BURNING UP... I'VE GOTTA' GET OUTA' THIS SCARF!

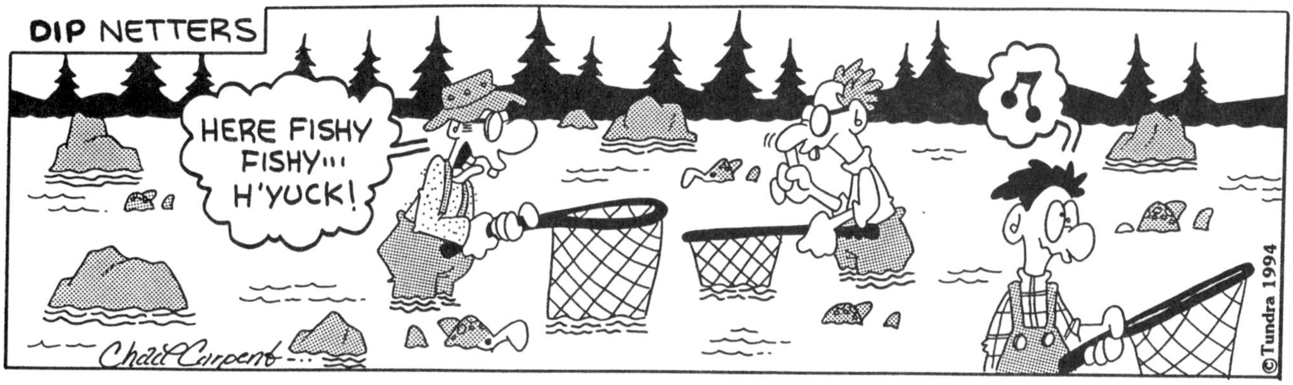
DIP NETTERS
HERE FISHY FISHY... H'YUCK!
©Tundra 1994

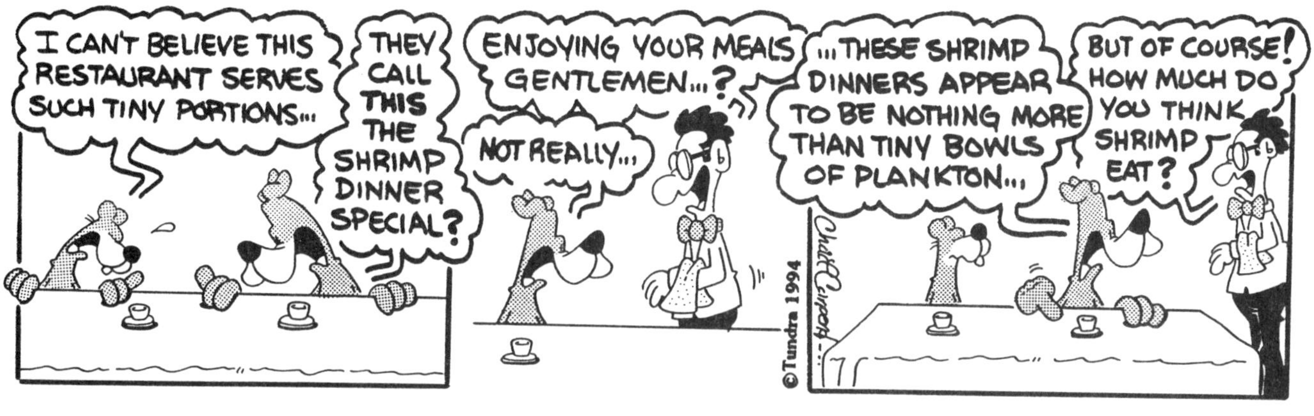
I CAN'T BELIEVE THIS RESTAURANT SERVES SUCH TINY PORTIONS...
THEY CALL THIS THE SHRIMP DINNER SPECIAL?
ENJOYING YOUR MEALS GENTLEMEN...?
NOT REALLY...
...THESE SHRIMP DINNERS APPEAR TO BE NOTHING MORE THAN TINY BOWLS OF PLANKTON...
BUT OF COURSE! HOW MUCH DO YOU THINK SHRIMP EAT?
©Tundra 1994

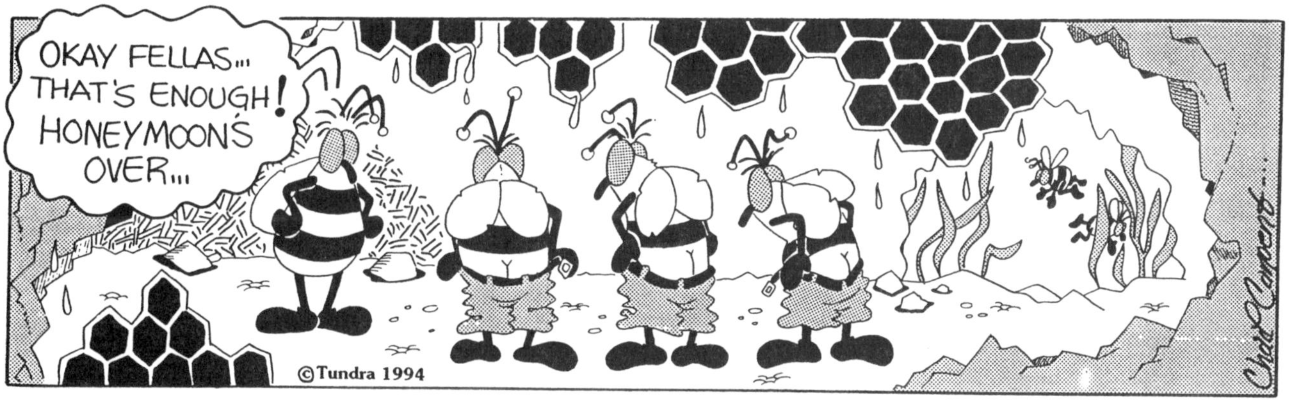
OKAY FELLAS... THAT'S ENOUGH! HONEYMOON'S OVER...
©Tundra 1994

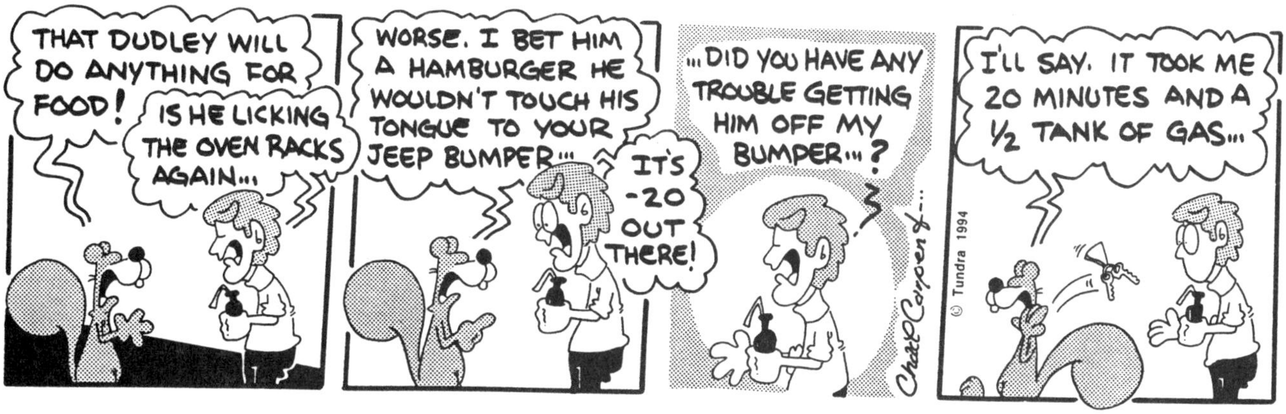
THAT DUDLEY WILL DO ANYTHING FOR FOOD!
IS HE LICKING THE OVEN RACKS AGAIN...
WORSE. I BET HIM A HAMBURGER HE WOULDN'T TOUCH HIS TONGUE TO YOUR JEEP BUMPER...
IT'S -20 OUT THERE!
...DID YOU HAVE ANY TROUBLE GETTING HIM OFF MY BUMPER...?
I'LL SAY. IT TOOK ME 20 MINUTES AND A 1/2 TANK OF GAS...
© Tundra 1994

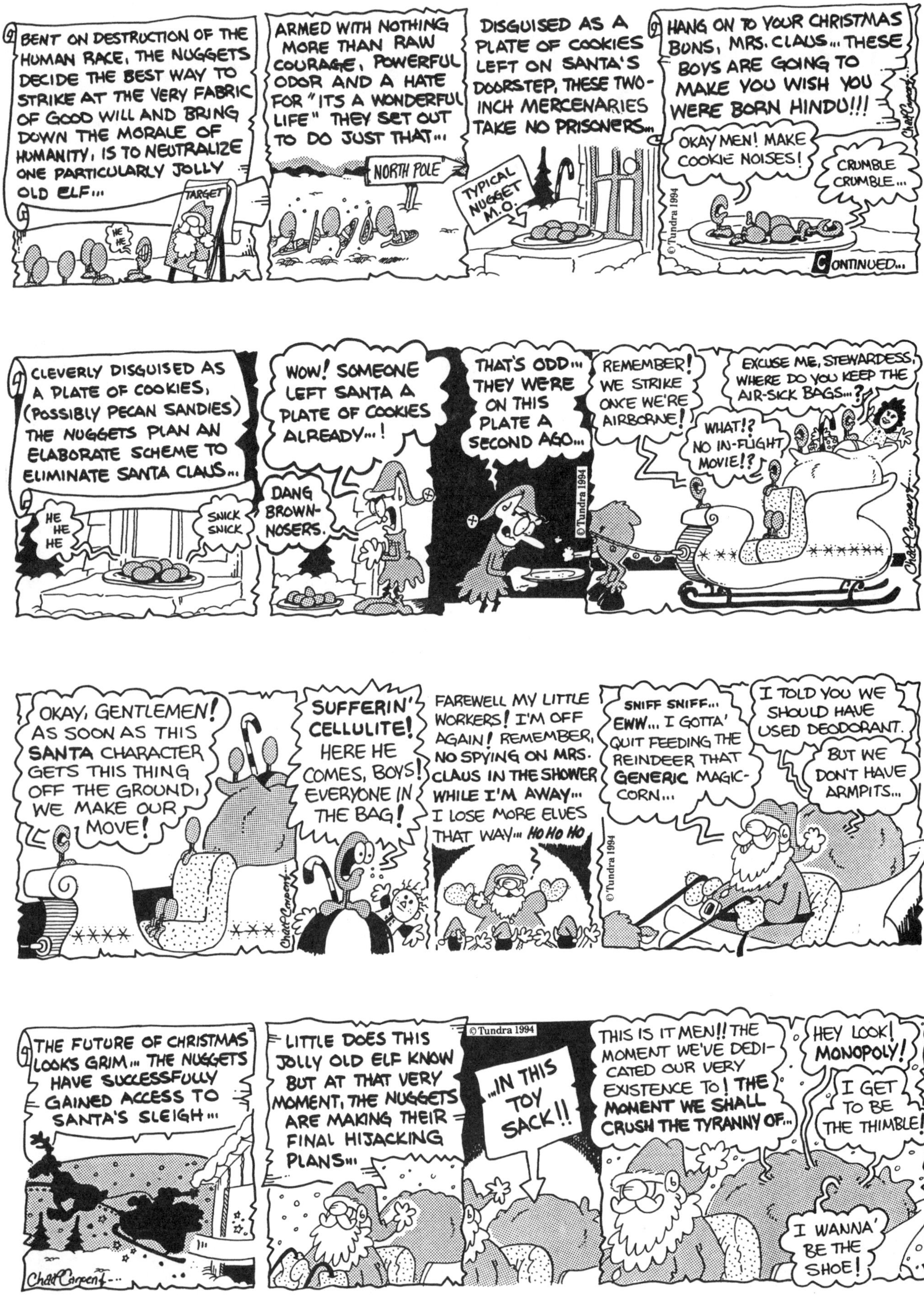
BENT ON DESTRUCTION OF THE HUMAN RACE, THE NUGGETS DECIDE THE BEST WAY TO STRIKE AT THE VERY FABRIC OF GOOD WILL AND BRING DOWN THE MORALE OF HUMANITY, IS TO NEUTRALIZE ONE PARTICULARLY JOLLY OLD ELF...
TARGET
HE HE
ARMED WITH NOTHING MORE THAN RAW COURAGE, POWERFUL ODOR AND A HATE FOR "ITS A WONDERFUL LIFE" THEY SET OUT TO DO JUST THAT...
NORTH POLE
DISGUISED AS A PLATE OF COOKIES LEFT ON SANTA'S DOORSTEP, THESE TWO-INCH MERCENARIES TAKE NO PRISONERS...
TYPICAL NUGGET M.O.
© Tundra 1994
HANG ON TO YOUR CHRISTMAS BUNS, MRS. CLAUS... THESE BOYS ARE GOING TO MAKE YOU WISH YOU WERE BORN HINDU!!!
OKAY MEN! MAKE COOKIE NOISES!
CRUMBLE CRUMBLE...
CONTINUED...
CLEVERLY DISGUISED AS A PLATE OF COOKIES, (POSSIBLY PECAN SANDIES) THE NUGGETS PLAN AN ELABORATE SCHEME TO ELIMINATE SANTA CLAUS...
HE HE HE
SNICK SNICK
WOW! SOMEONE LEFT SANTA A PLATE OF COOKIES ALREADY...!
DANG BROWN-NOSERS.
THAT'S ODD... THEY WERE ON THIS PLATE A SECOND AGO...
© Tundra 1994
REMEMBER! WE STRIKE ONCE WE'RE AIRBORNE!
EXCUSE ME, STEWARDESS, WHERE DO YOU KEEP THE AIR-SICK BAGS...?
WHAT!? NO IN-FLIGHT MOVIE!?
OKAY, GENTLEMEN! AS SOON AS THIS SANTA CHARACTER GETS THIS THING OFF THE GROUND, WE MAKE OUR MOVE!
SUFFERIN' CELLULITE! HERE HE COMES, BOYS! EVERYONE IN THE BAG!
FAREWELL MY LITTLE WORKERS! I'M OFF AGAIN! REMEMBER, NO SPYING ON MRS. CLAUS IN THE SHOWER WHILE I'M AWAY... I LOSE MORE ELVES THAT WAY... HO HO HO
© Tundra 1994
SNIFF SNIFF... EWW... I GOTTA' QUIT FEEDING THE REINDEER THAT GENERIC MAGIC-CORN...
I TOLD YOU WE SHOULD HAVE USED DEODORANT.
BUT WE DON'T HAVE ARMPITS...
THE FUTURE OF CHRISTMAS LOOKS GRIM... THE NUGGETS HAVE SUCCESSFULLY GAINED ACCESS TO SANTA'S SLEIGH...
LITTLE DOES THIS JOLLY OLD ELF KNOW BUT AT THAT VERY MOMENT, THE NUGGETS ARE MAKING THEIR FINAL HIJACKING PLANS...
© Tundra 1994
...IN THIS TOY SACK!!
THIS IS IT MEN!! THE MOMENT WE'VE DEDICATED OUR VERY EXISTENCE TO! THE MOMENT WE SHALL CRUSH THE TYRANNY OF...
HEY LOOK! MONOPOLY!
I GET TO BE THE THIMBLE!
I WANNA' BE THE SHOE!

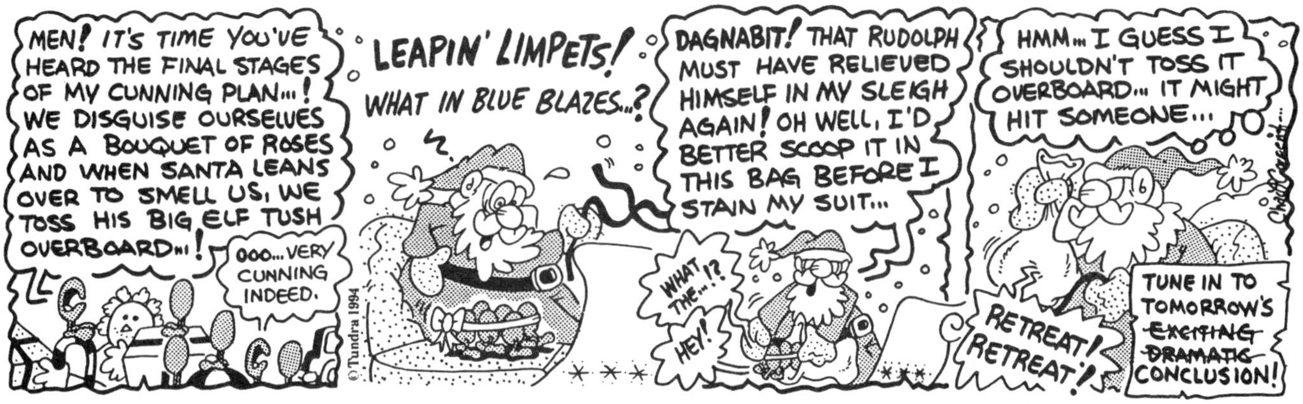
MEN! IT'S TIME YOU'VE HEARD THE FINAL STAGES OF MY CUNNING PLAN...! WE DISGUISE OURSELVES AS A BOUQUET OF ROSES AND WHEN SANTA LEANS OVER TO SMELL US, WE TOSS HIS BIG ELF TUSH OVERBOARD...!
OOO... VERY CUNNING INDEED.
LEAPIN' LIMPETS!
WHAT IN BLUE BLAZES...?
© Tundra 1994
DAGNABIT! THAT RUDOLPH MUST HAVE RELIEVED HIMSELF IN MY SLEIGH AGAIN! OH WELL, I'D BETTER SCOOP IT IN THIS BAG BEFORE I STAIN MY SUIT...
WHAT THE...!?
HEY!
HMM... I GUESS I SHOULDN'T TOSS IT OVERBOARD... IT MIGHT HIT SOMEONE...
RETREAT! RETREAT!
TUNE IN TO TOMORROW'S ~~EXCITING~~ ~~DRAMATIC~~ CONCLUSION!

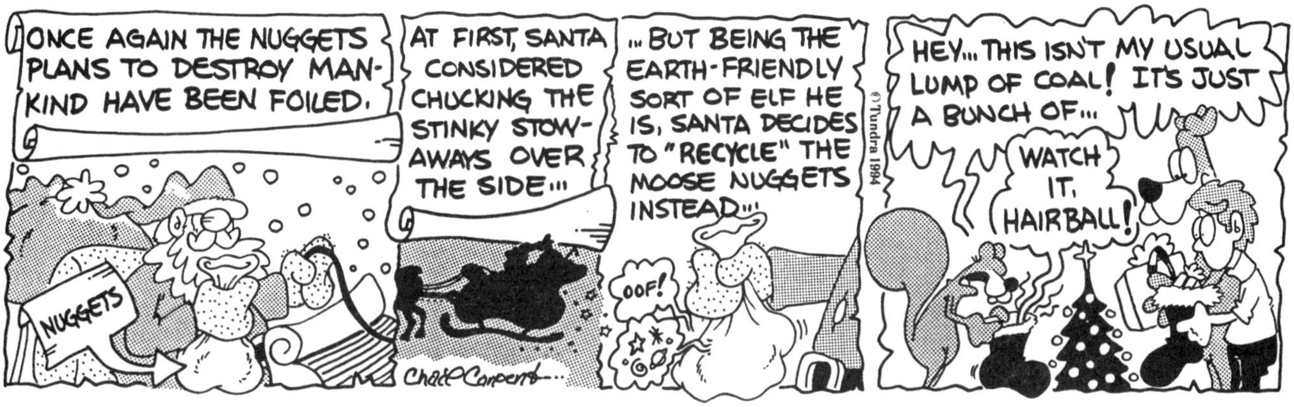
ONCE AGAIN THE NUGGETS PLANS TO DESTROY MANKIND HAVE BEEN FOILED.
NUGGETS
AT FIRST, SANTA CONSIDERED CHUCKING THE STINKY STOWAWAYS OVER THE SIDE...
...BUT BEING THE EARTH-FRIENDLY SORT OF ELF HE IS, SANTA DECIDES TO "RECYCLE" THE MOOSE NUGGETS INSTEAD...
OOF!
© Tundra 1994
HEY... THIS ISN'T MY USUAL LUMP OF COAL! IT'S JUST A BUNCH OF...
WATCH IT, HAIRBALL!

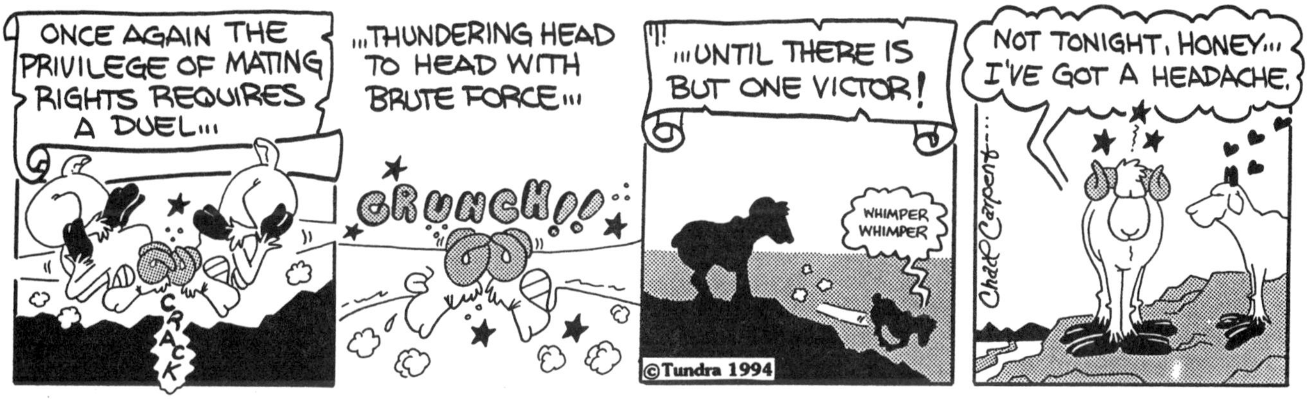
ONCE AGAIN THE PRIVILEGE OF MATING RIGHTS REQUIRES A DUEL...
CRACK
...THUNDERING HEAD TO HEAD WITH BRUTE FORCE...
CRUNCH!!
...UNTIL THERE IS BUT ONE VICTOR!
WHIMPER WHIMPER
©Tundra 1994
NOT TONIGHT, HONEY... I'VE GOT A HEADACHE.

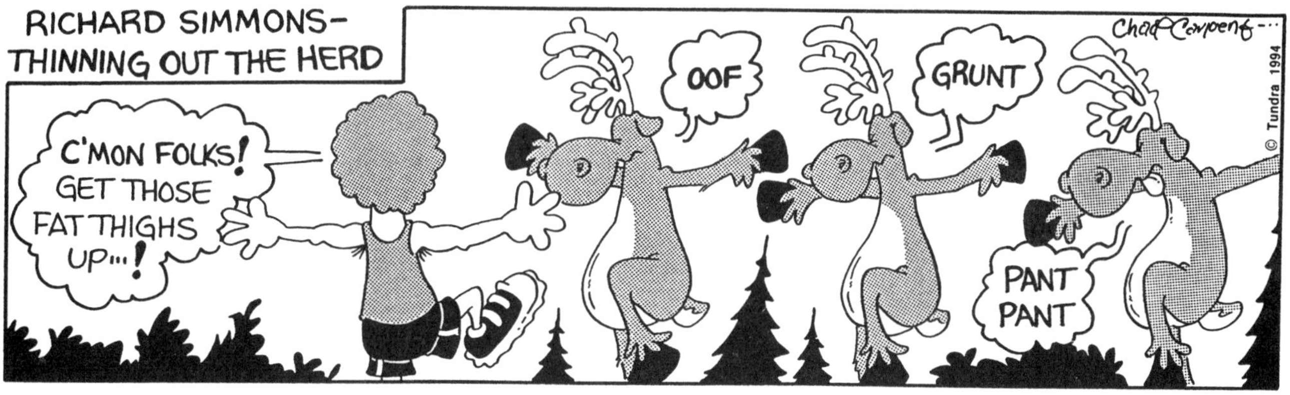
RICHARD SIMMONS-
THINNING OUT THE HERD
C'MON FOLKS! GET THOSE FAT THIGHS UP...!
OOF
GRUNT
PANT PANT
© Tundra 1994

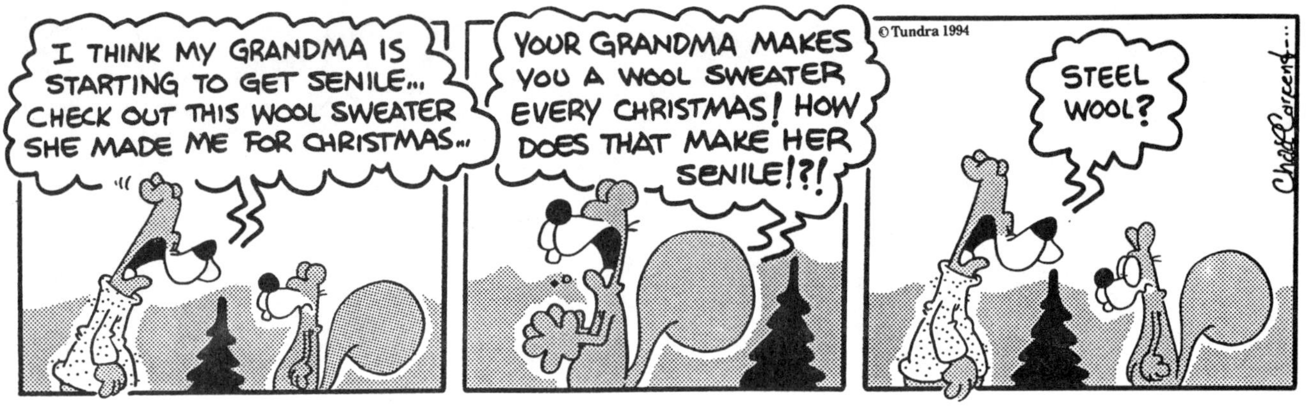
I THINK MY GRANDMA IS STARTING TO GET SENILE... CHECK OUT THIS WOOL SWEATER SHE MADE ME FOR CHRISTMAS...
YOUR GRANDMA MAKES YOU A WOOL SWEATER EVERY CHRISTMAS! HOW DOES THAT MAKE HER SENILE!?!
©Tundra 1994
STEEL WOOL?
Chad Carpenter

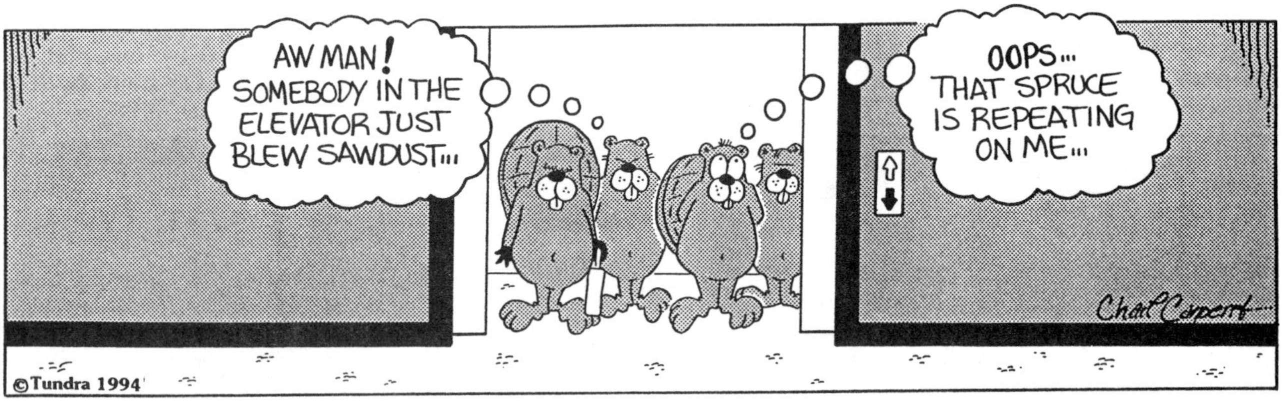
AW MAN! SOMEBODY IN THE ELEVATOR JUST BLEW SAWDUST...
OOPS... THAT SPRUCE IS REPEATING ON ME...
Chad Carpenter
©Tundra 1994

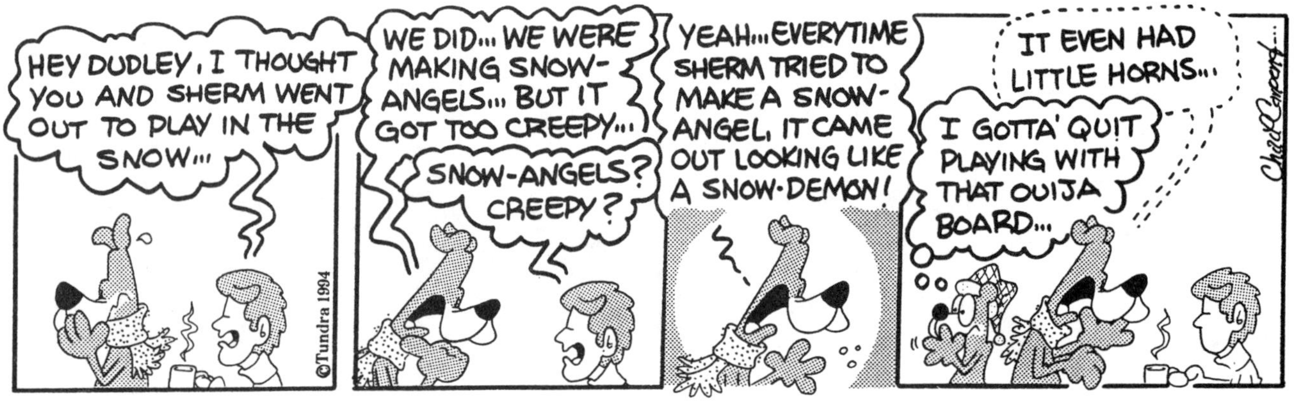
HEY DUDLEY, I THOUGHT YOU AND SHERM WENT OUT TO PLAY IN THE SNOW...
©Tundra 1994
WE DID... WE WERE MAKING SNOW-ANGELS... BUT IT GOT TOO CREEPY...
SNOW-ANGELS? CREEPY?
YEAH... EVERYTIME SHERM TRIED TO MAKE A SNOW-ANGEL, IT CAME OUT LOOKING LIKE A SNOW-DEMON!
IT EVEN HAD LITTLE HORNS...
I GOTTA' QUIT PLAYING WITH THAT OUIJA BOARD...
Chad Carpenter

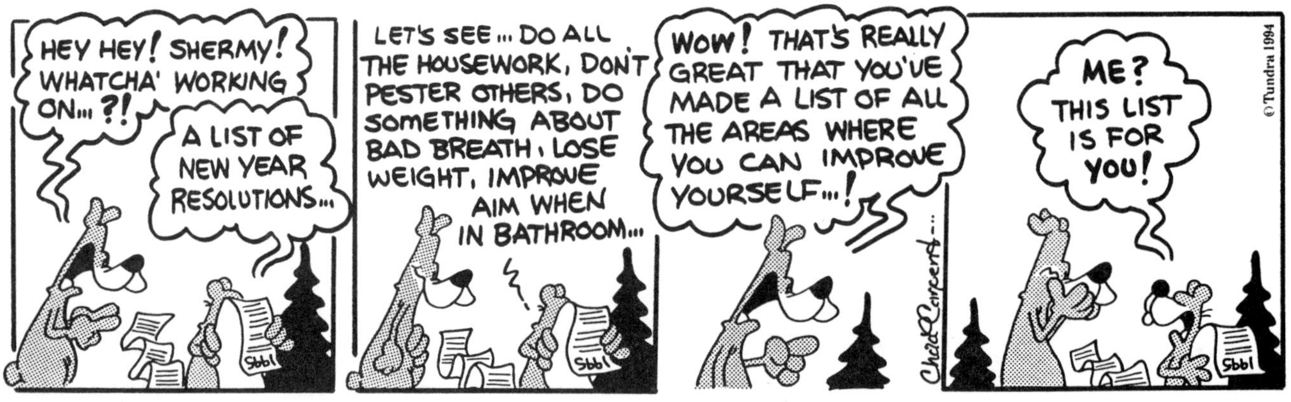
HEY HEY! SHERMY! WHATCHA' WORKING ON...?!
A LIST OF NEW YEAR RESOLUTIONS...
LET'S SEE... DO ALL THE HOUSEWORK, DON'T PESTER OTHERS, DO SOMETHING ABOUT BAD BREATH, LOSE WEIGHT, IMPROVE AIM WHEN IN BATHROOM...
WOW! THAT'S REALLY GREAT THAT YOU'VE MADE A LIST OF ALL THE AREAS WHERE YOU CAN IMPROVE YOURSELF...!
Chad Carpenter
ME? THIS LIST IS FOR YOU!
©Tundra 1994

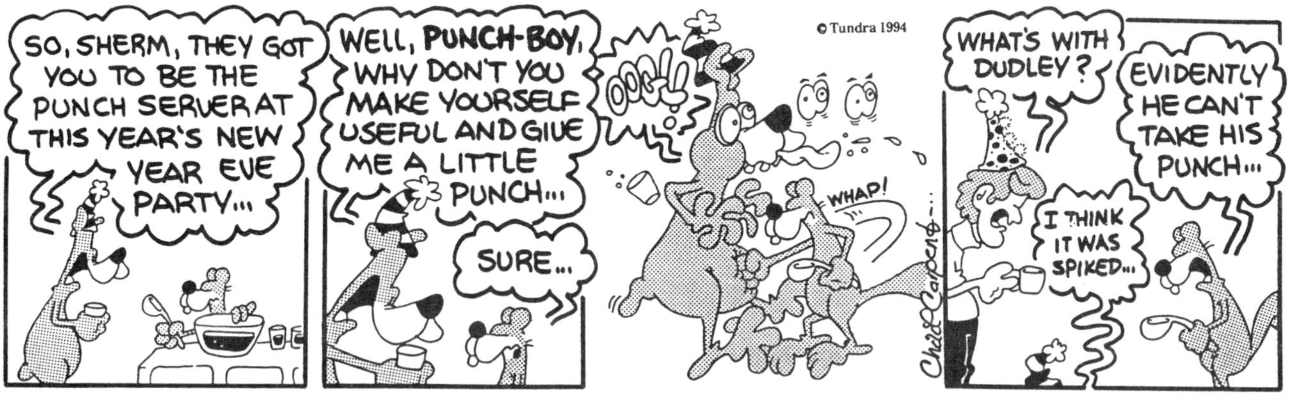
SO, SHERM, THEY GOT YOU TO BE THE PUNCH SERVER AT THIS YEAR'S NEW YEAR EVE PARTY...
WELL, PUNCH-BOY, WHY DON'T YOU MAKE YOURSELF USEFUL AND GIVE ME A LITTLE PUNCH...
SURE...
© Tundra 1994
OOF!!
WHAP!
WHAT'S WITH DUDLEY?
EVIDENTLY HE CAN'T TAKE HIS PUNCH...
I THINK IT WAS SPIKED...

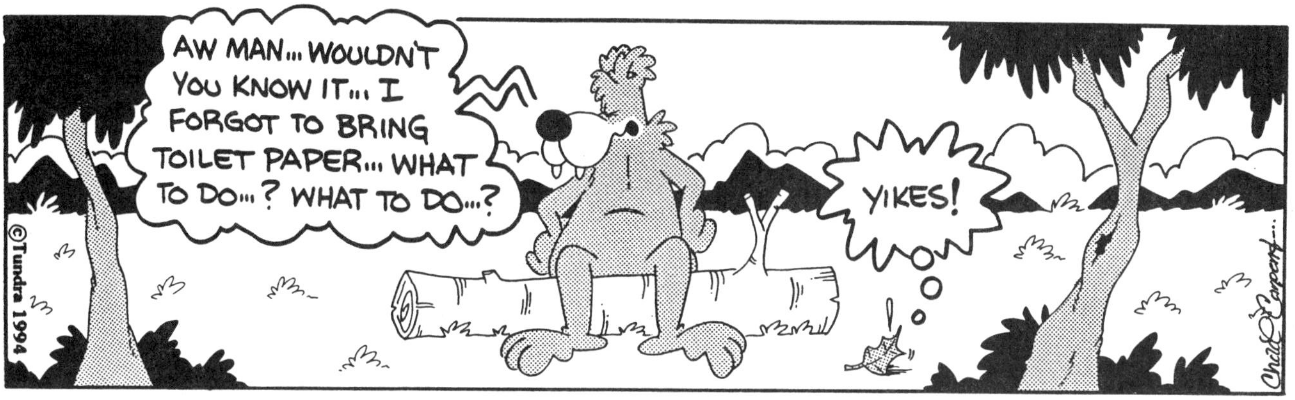
AW MAN... WOULDN'T YOU KNOW IT... I FORGOT TO BRING TOILET PAPER... WHAT TO DO...? WHAT TO DO...?
YIKES!
!
©Tundra 1994

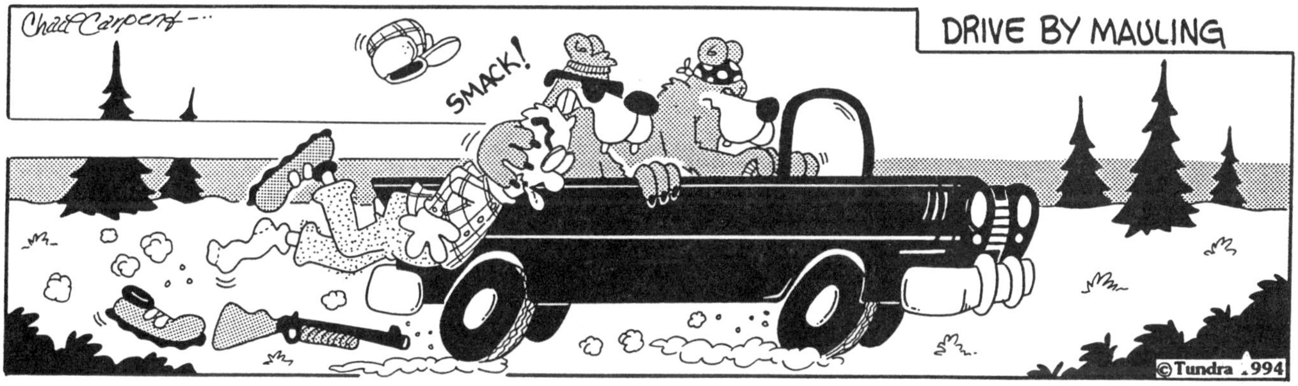
DRIVE BY MAULING
SMACK!
©Tundra 1994

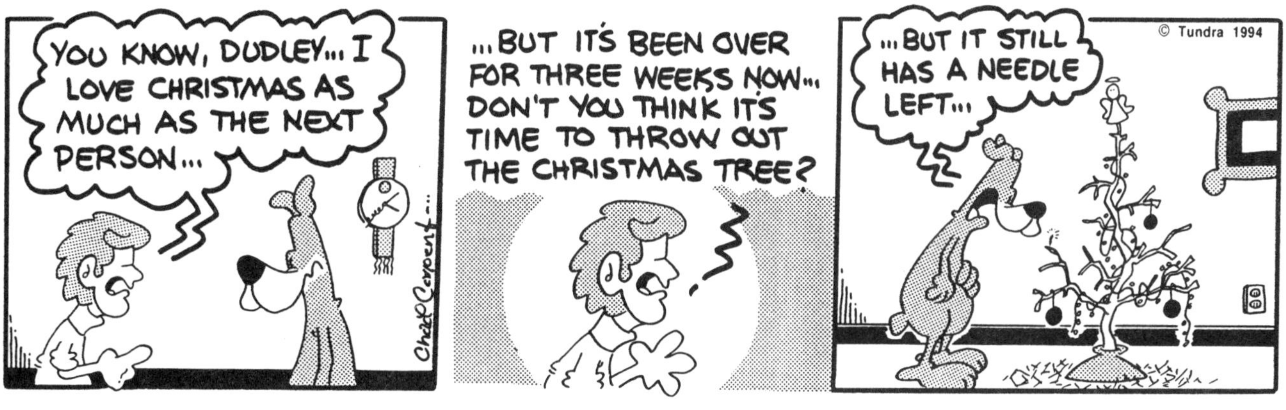
YOU KNOW, DUDLEY... I LOVE CHRISTMAS AS MUCH AS THE NEXT PERSON...
...BUT IT'S BEEN OVER FOR THREE WEEKS NOW... DON'T YOU THINK IT'S TIME TO THROW OUT THE CHRISTMAS TREE?
...BUT IT STILL HAS A NEEDLE LEFT...
© Tundra 1994

Andy

Every comic strip has its need for humor and cuteness, and here to fill this position is the newest addition to our comic strip family, Andy the Lemming. Andy is our ever-effervescent supplier of snappy comebacks and quick wit.

Born high in the Himalayan mountains of Tibet, Andy's parents realized early on that he was different from the other lemmings when they found him weaving a climbing harness out of goat droppings and hair clippings. Realizing the potential for disaster, Andy's parents whisked him off to the Acapulco School of Cliff Diving. It was there that they hoped he would be indoctrinated with the necessary lemming instincts - it didn't work.

On his way to a scheduled family reunion in the ocean, Andy "accidentally" missed his bus transfer. It was through this twist of fate that Andy arrived in his ideal town. A small picturesque community located on the edge of a deep chasm - Gangrene Gulch.

Chapter Four

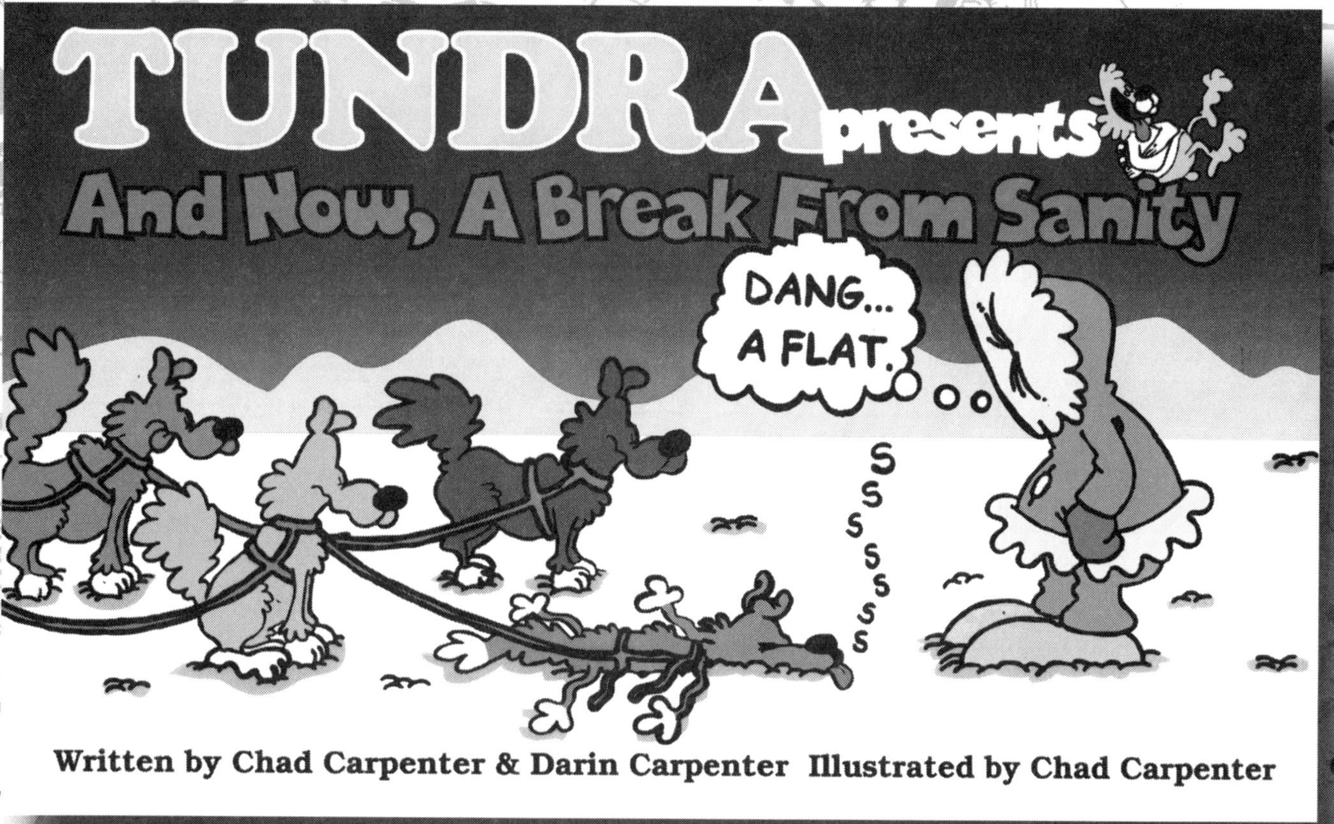
TUNDRA presents
And Now, A Break From Sanity
DANG... A FLAT.
SSSSSSS
Written by Chad Carpenter & Darin Carpenter Illustrated by Chad Carpenter

First Printing: August 1996

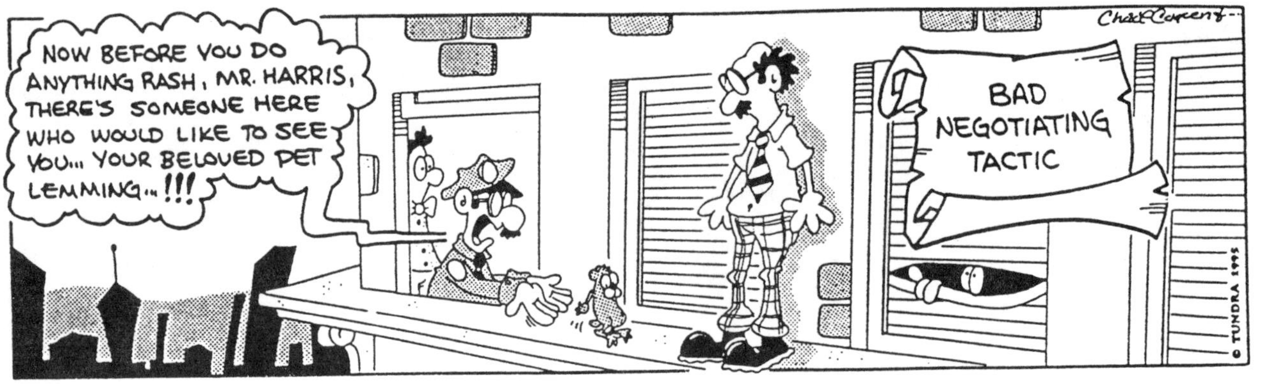
NOW BEFORE YOU DO ANYTHING RASH, MR. HARRIS, THERE'S SOMEONE HERE WHO WOULD LIKE TO SEE YOU... YOUR BELOVED PET LEMMING...!!!
BAD NEGOTIATING TACTIC
© TUNDRA 1995

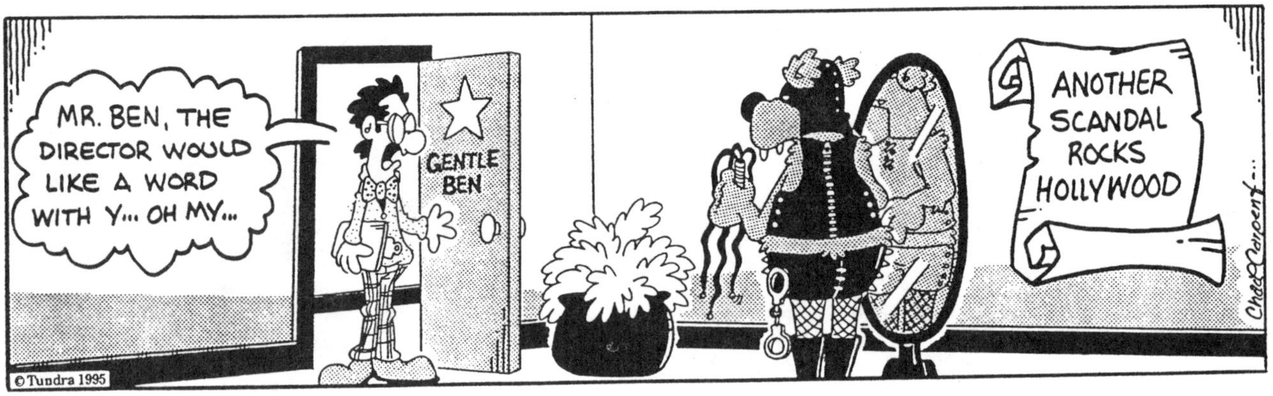
MR. BEN, THE DIRECTOR WOULD LIKE A WORD WITH Y... OH MY...
GENTLE BEN
ANOTHER SCANDAL ROCKS HOLLYWOOD
© Tundra 1995

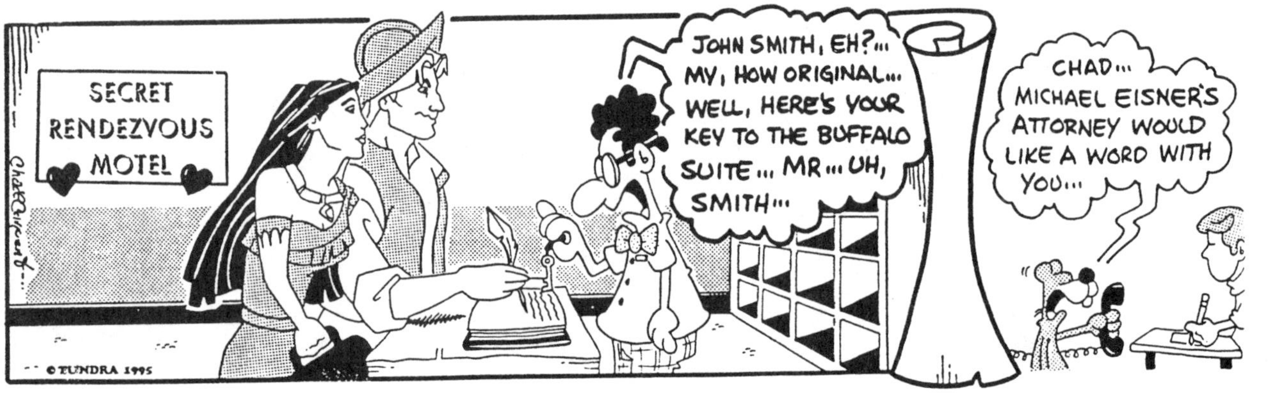
SECRET RENDEZVOUS MOTEL
JOHN SMITH, EH?... MY, HOW ORIGINAL... WELL, HERE'S YOUR KEY TO THE BUFFALO SUITE... MR... UH, SMITH...
CHAD... MICHAEL EISNER'S ATTORNEY WOULD LIKE A WORD WITH YOU...
© TUNDRA 1995

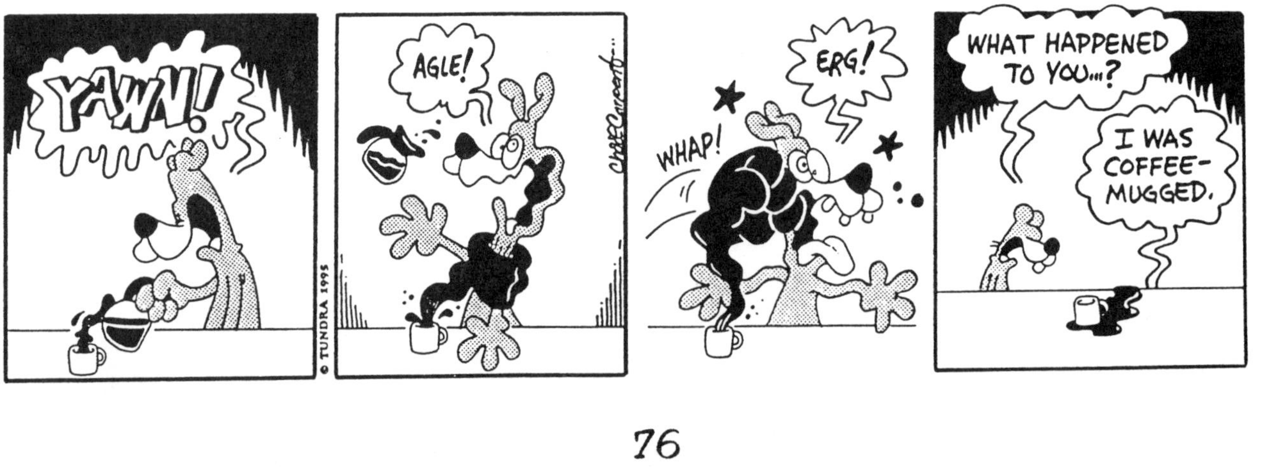
YAWN!
AGLE!
© TUNDRA 1995
WHAP!
ERG!
WHAT HAPPENED TO YOU...?
I WAS COFFEE-MUGGED.

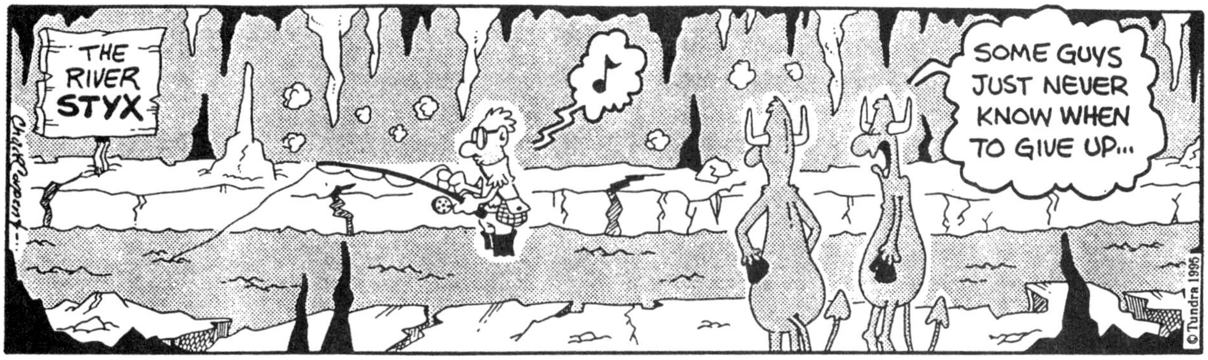
THE RIVER STYX
SOME GUYS JUST NEVER KNOW WHEN TO GIVE UP...

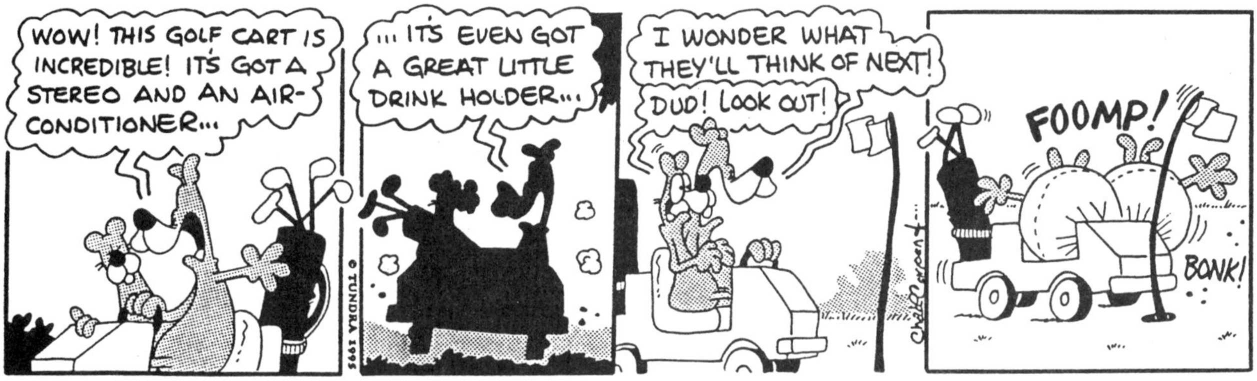
WOW! THIS GOLF CART IS INCREDIBLE! IT'S GOT A STEREO AND AN AIR-CONDITIONER...
...IT'S EVEN GOT A GREAT LITTLE DRINK HOLDER...
I WONDER WHAT THEY'LL THINK OF NEXT!
DUD! LOOK OUT!
FOOMP!
BONK!

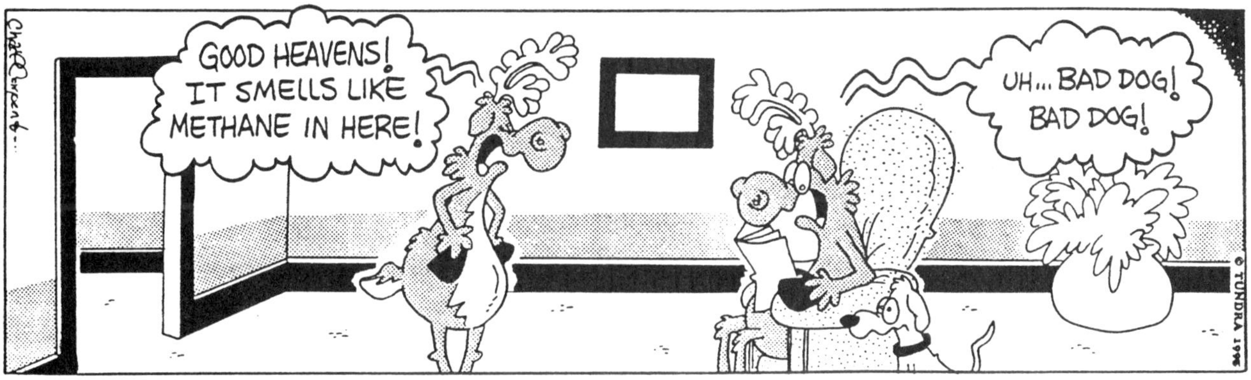
GOOD HEAVENS! IT SMELLS LIKE METHANE IN HERE!
UH... BAD DOG! BAD DOG!

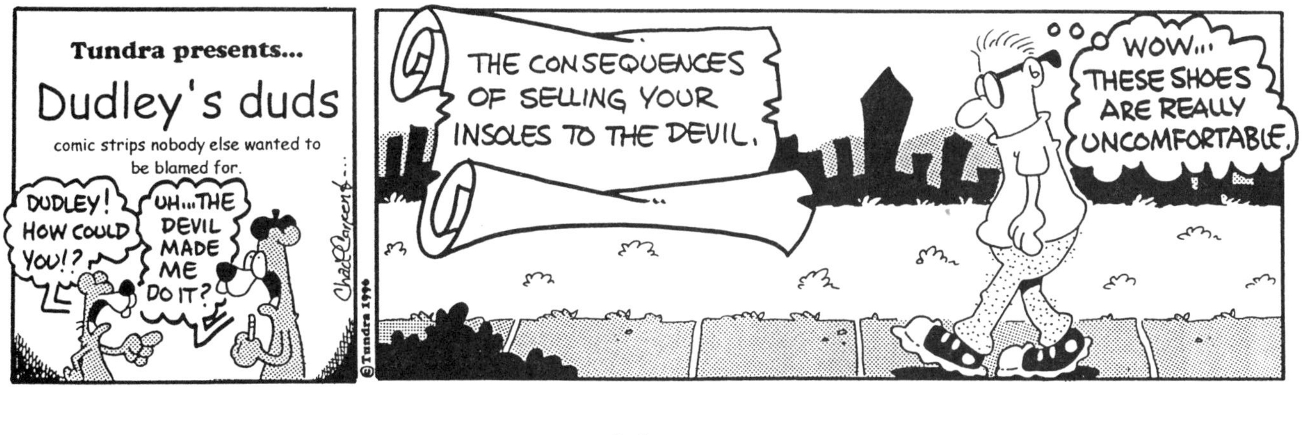
Tundra presents...
Dudley's duds
comic strips nobody else wanted to be blamed for.
DUDLEY! HOW COULD YOU!?
UH...THE DEVIL MADE ME DO IT?
THE CONSEQUENCES OF SELLING YOUR INSOLES TO THE DEVIL.
WOW... THESE SHOES ARE REALLY UNCOMFORTABLE.

THE BARKING WALL SPIDERS

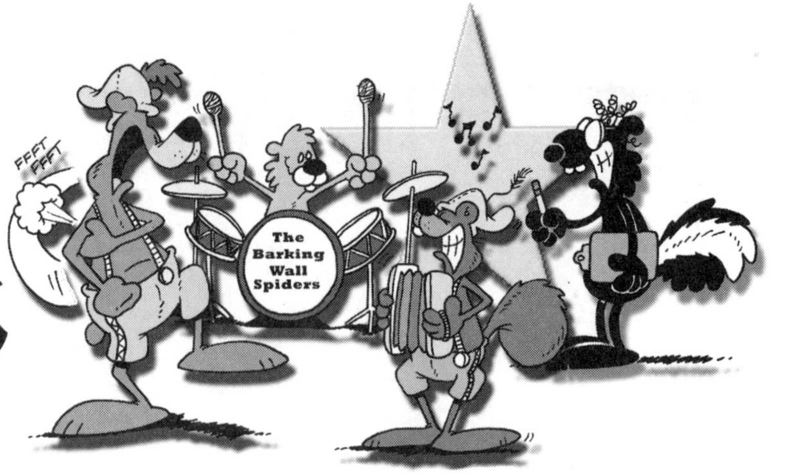

FFFT
FFFT
The Barking Wall Spiders

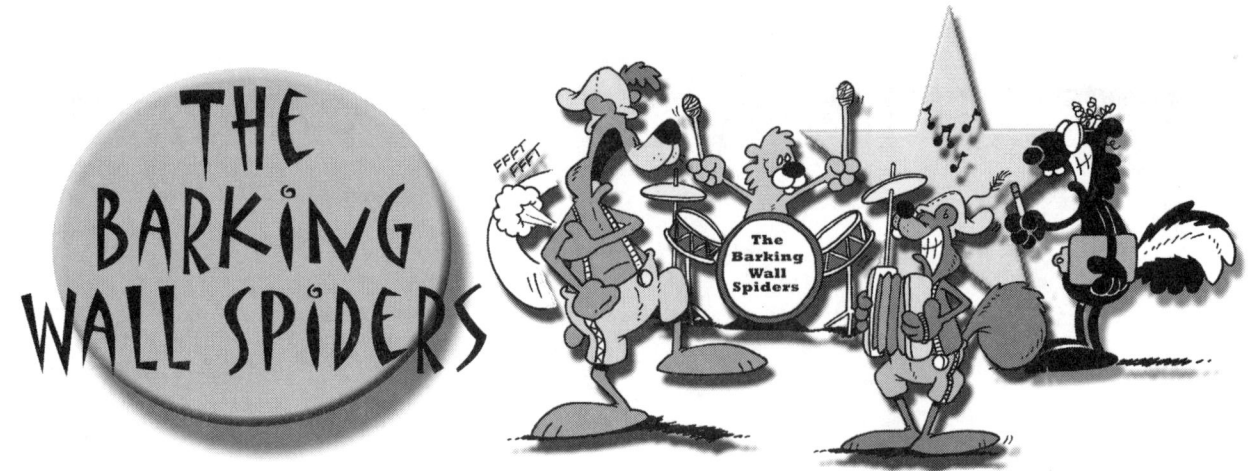

*The first appearances of Andy the Lemming & Whiff the Skunk!

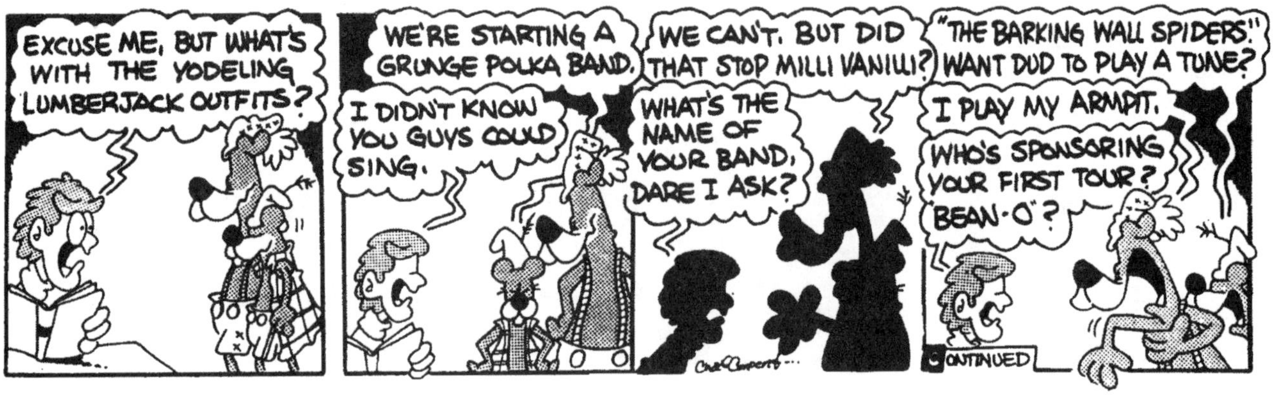

EXCUSE ME, BUT WHAT'S WITH THE YODELING LUMBERJACK OUTFITS?
WE'RE STARTING A GRUNGE POLKA BAND.
I DIDN'T KNOW YOU GUYS COULD SING.
WE CAN'T. BUT DID THAT STOP MILLI VANILLI?
WHAT'S THE NAME OF YOUR BAND, DARE I ASK?
"THE BARKING WALL SPIDERS." WANT DUD TO PLAY A TUNE?
I PLAY MY ARMPIT.
WHO'S SPONSORING YOUR FIRST TOUR? 'BEAN-O'?
CONTINUED

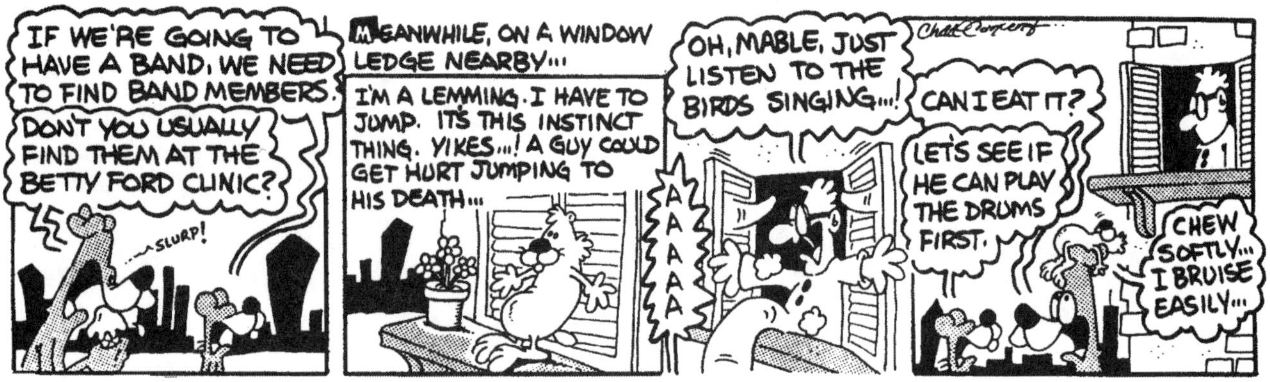

IF WE'RE GOING TO HAVE A BAND, WE NEED TO FIND BAND MEMBERS.
DON'T YOU USUALLY FIND THEM AT THE BETTY FORD CLINIC?
SLURP!
MEANWHILE, ON A WINDOW LEDGE NEARBY...
I'M A LEMMING. I HAVE TO JUMP. IT'S THIS INSTINCT THING. YIKES...! A GUY COULD GET HURT JUMPING TO HIS DEATH...
OH, MABLE, JUST LISTEN TO THE BIRDS SINGING...!
AAAAAA
CAN I EAT IT?
LET'S SEE IF HE CAN PLAY THE DRUMS FIRST.
CHEW SOFTLY... I BRUISE EASILY...

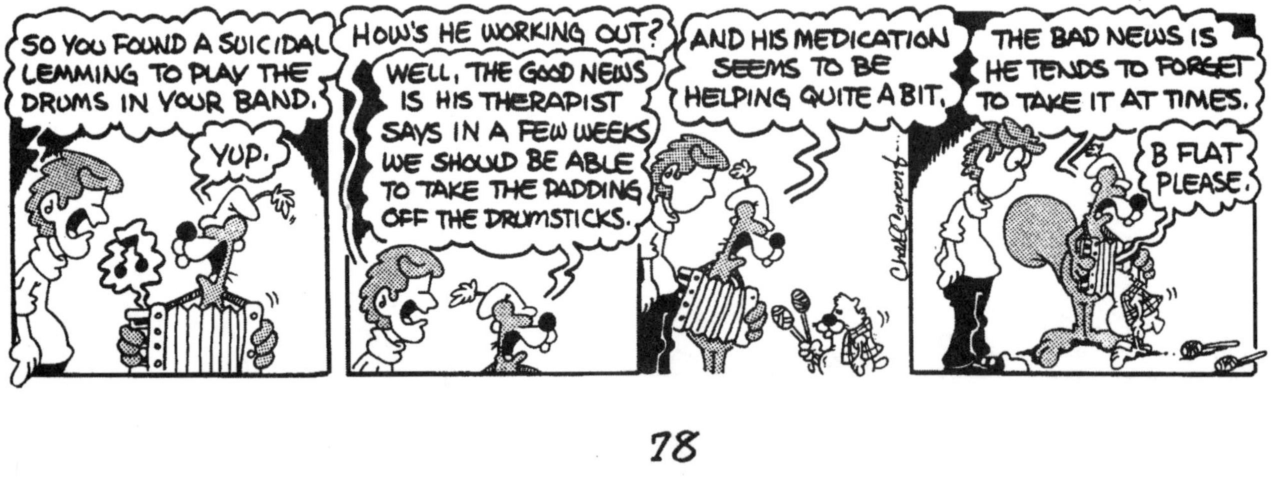

SO YOU FOUND A SUICIDAL LEMMING TO PLAY THE DRUMS IN YOUR BAND.
YUP.
HOW'S HE WORKING OUT?
WELL, THE GOOD NEWS IS HIS THERAPIST SAYS IN A FEW WEEKS WE SHOULD BE ABLE TO TAKE THE PADDING OFF THE DRUMSTICKS.
AND HIS MEDICATION SEEMS TO BE HELPING QUITE A BIT.
THE BAD NEWS IS HE TENDS TO FORGET TO TAKE IT AT TIMES.
B FLAT PLEASE.

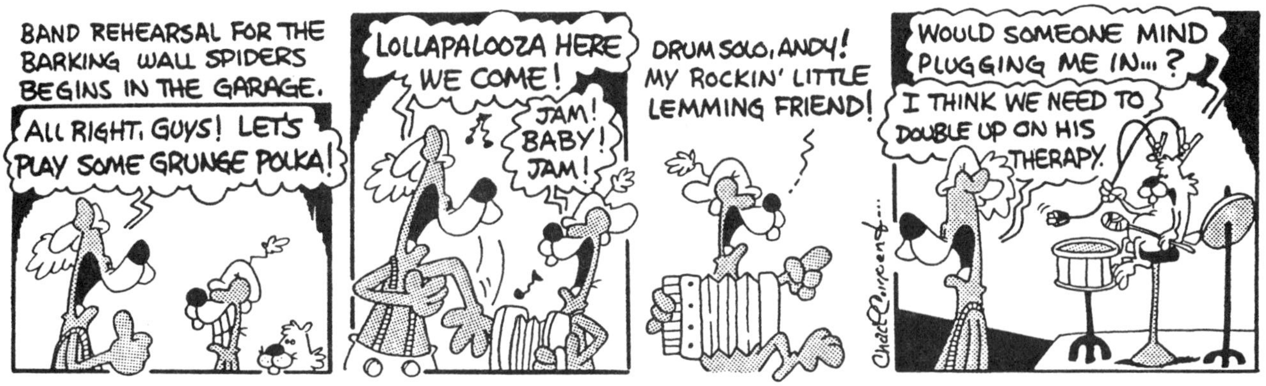
BAND REHEARSAL FOR THE BARKING WALL SPIDERS BEGINS IN THE GARAGE.
ALL RIGHT, GUYS! LET'S PLAY SOME GRUNGE POLKA!
LOLLAPALOOZA HERE WE COME!
JAM! BABY! JAM!
DRUM SOLO, ANDY! MY ROCKIN' LITTLE LEMMING FRIEND!
WOULD SOMEONE MIND PLUGGING ME IN...?
I THINK WE NEED TO DOUBLE UP ON HIS THERAPY.

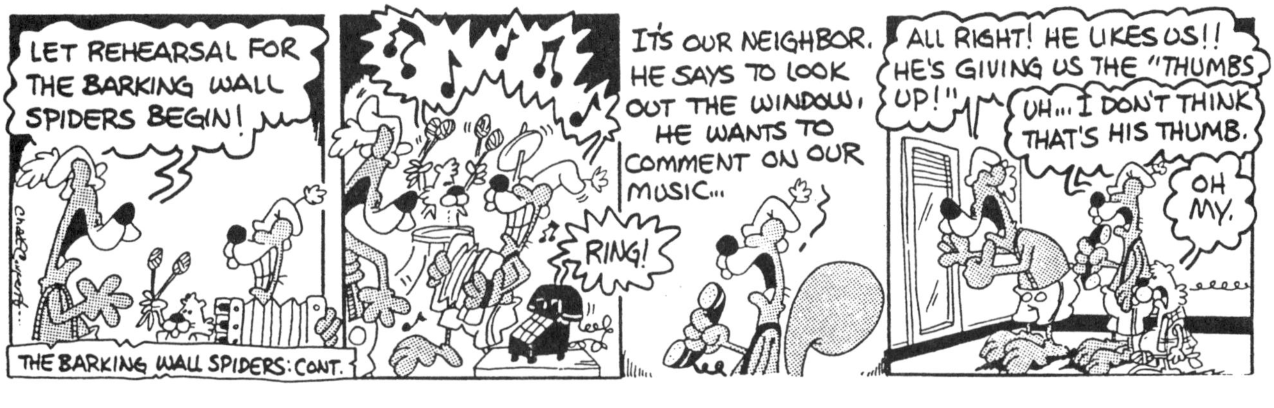
LET REHEARSAL FOR THE BARKING WALL SPIDERS BEGIN!
THE BARKING WALL SPIDERS: CONT.
RING!
IT'S OUR NEIGHBOR. HE SAYS TO LOOK OUT THE WINDOW, HE WANTS TO COMMENT ON OUR MUSIC...
ALL RIGHT! HE LIKES US!! HE'S GIVING US THE "THUMBS UP!"
UH... I DON'T THINK THAT'S HIS THUMB.
OH MY.

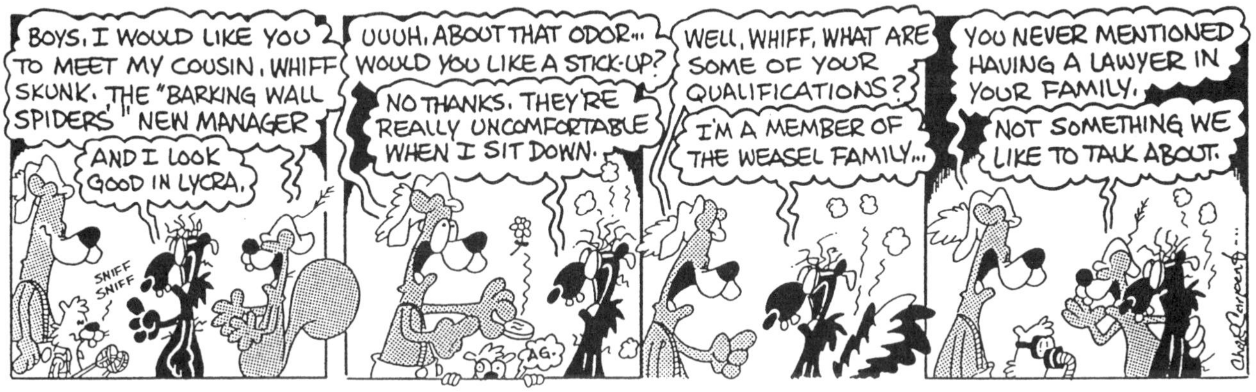
BOYS, I WOULD LIKE YOU TO MEET MY COUSIN, WHIFF SKUNK, THE "BARKING WALL SPIDERS'" NEW MANAGER
AND I LOOK GOOD IN LYCRA.
SNIFF SNIFF
UUUH, ABOUT THAT ODOR... WOULD YOU LIKE A STICK-UP?
NO THANKS, THEY'RE REALLY UNCOMFORTABLE WHEN I SIT DOWN.
AG.
WELL, WHIFF, WHAT ARE SOME OF YOUR QUALIFICATIONS?
I'M A MEMBER OF THE WEASEL FAMILY...
YOU NEVER MENTIONED HAVING A LAWYER IN YOUR FAMILY.
NOT SOMETHING WE LIKE TO TALK ABOUT.

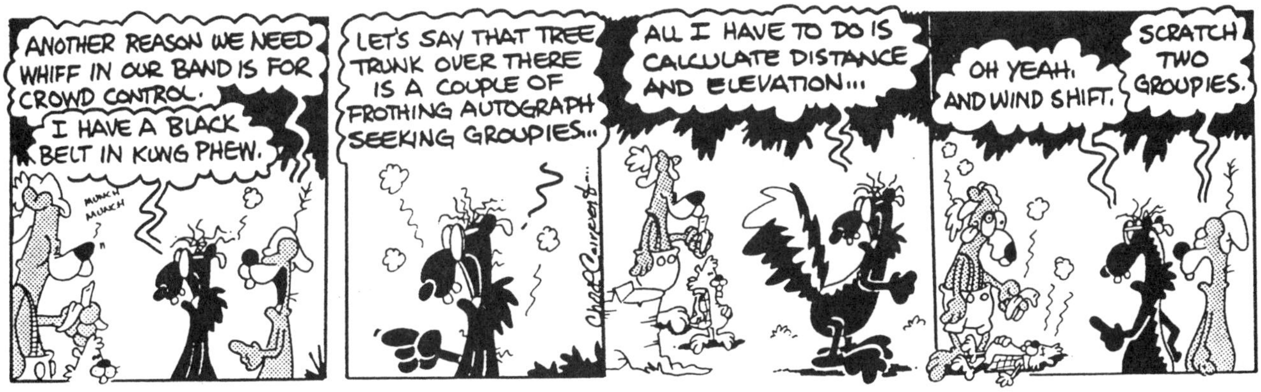
ANOTHER REASON WE NEED WHIFF IN OUR BAND IS FOR CROWD CONTROL.
I HAVE A BLACK BELT IN KUNG PHEW.
MUNCH MUNCH
LET'S SAY THAT TREE TRUNK OVER THERE IS A COUPLE OF FROTHING AUTOGRAPH SEEKING GROUPIES...
ALL I HAVE TO DO IS CALCULATE DISTANCE AND ELEVATION...
OH YEAH, AND WIND SHIFT.
SCRATCH TWO GROUPIES.

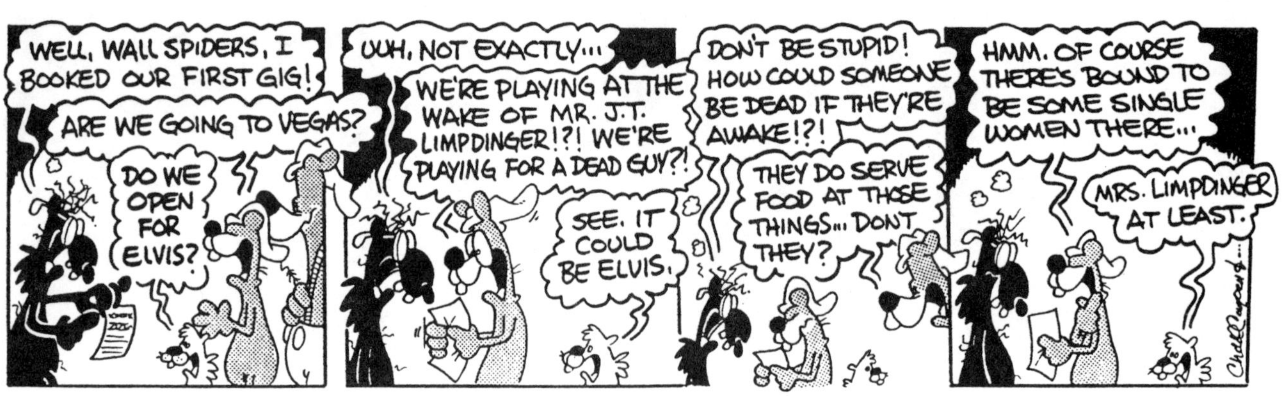
WELL, WALL SPIDERS, I BOOKED OUR FIRST GIG!
ARE WE GOING TO VEGAS?
DO WE OPEN FOR ELVIS?
UUH, NOT EXACTLY...
WE'RE PLAYING AT THE WAKE OF MR. J.T. LIMPDINGER!?! WE'RE PLAYING FOR A DEAD GUY?!
SEE, IT COULD BE ELVIS.
DON'T BE STUPID! HOW COULD SOMEONE BE DEAD IF THEY'RE AWAKE!?!
THEY DO SERVE FOOD AT THOSE THINGS... DONT THEY?
HMM. OF COURSE THERE'S BOUND TO BE SOME SINGLE WOMEN THERE...
MRS. LIMPDINGER AT LEAST.

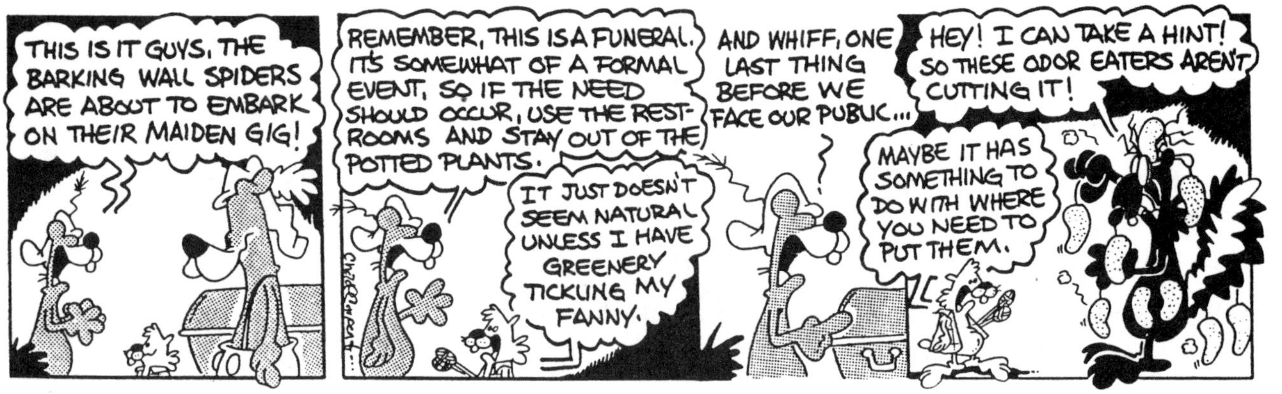
THIS IS IT GUYS, THE BARKING WALL SPIDERS ARE ABOUT TO EMBARK ON THEIR MAIDEN GIG!
REMEMBER, THIS IS A FUNERAL. IT'S SOMEWHAT OF A FORMAL EVENT, SO IF THE NEED SHOULD OCCUR, USE THE REST-ROOMS AND STAY OUT OF THE POTTED PLANTS.
IT JUST DOESN'T SEEM NATURAL UNLESS I HAVE GREENERY TICKLING MY FANNY.
AND WHIFF, ONE LAST THING BEFORE WE FACE OUR PUBLIC...
HEY! I CAN TAKE A HINT! SO THESE ODOR EATERS AREN'T CUTTING IT!
MAYBE IT HAS SOMETHING TO DO WITH WHERE YOU NEED TO PUT THEM.

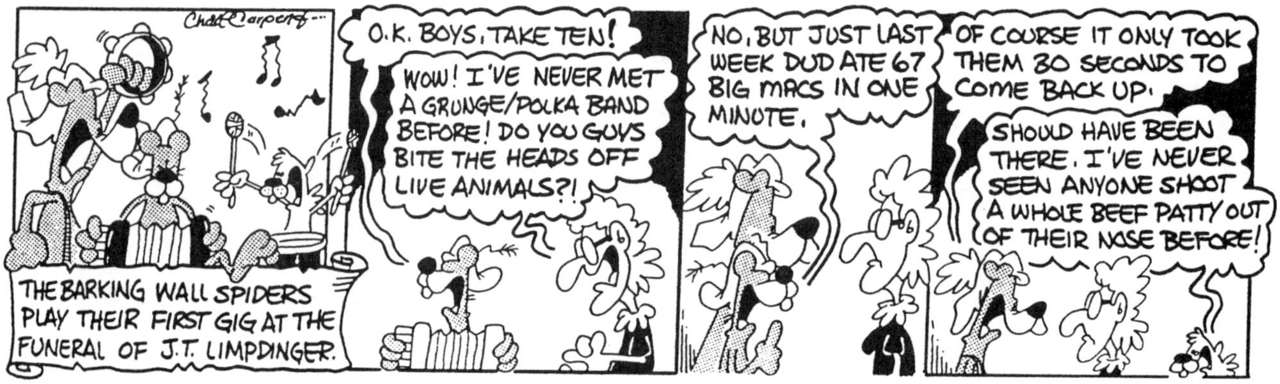
THE BARKING WALL SPIDERS PLAY THEIR FIRST GIG AT THE FUNERAL OF J.T. LIMPDINGER.
O.K. BOYS, TAKE TEN!
WOW! I'VE NEVER MET A GRUNGE/POLKA BAND BEFORE! DO YOU GUYS BITE THE HEADS OFF LIVE ANIMALS?!
NO, BUT JUST LAST WEEK DUD ATE 67 BIG MACS IN ONE MINUTE.
OF COURSE IT ONLY TOOK THEM 30 SECONDS TO COME BACK UP.
SHOULD HAVE BEEN THERE. I'VE NEVER SEEN ANYONE SHOOT A WHOLE BEEF PATTY OUT OF THEIR NOSE BEFORE!

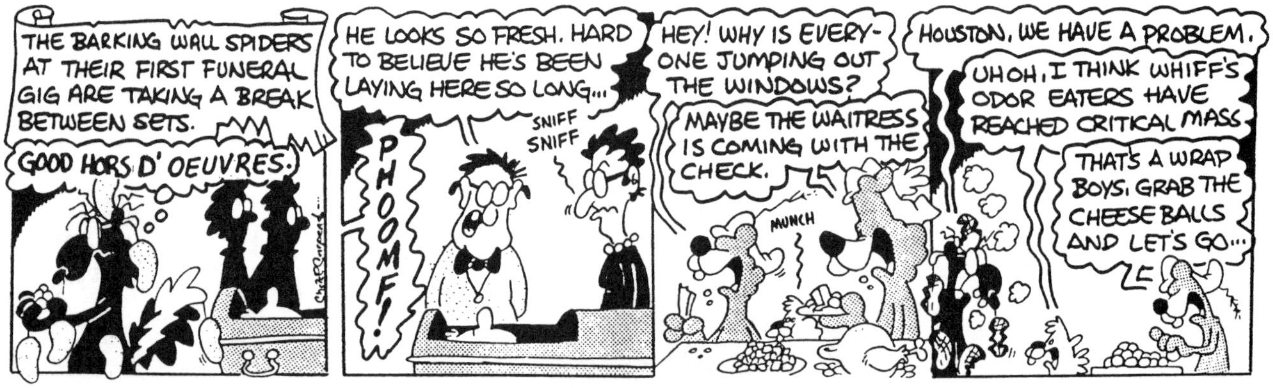
THE BARKING WALL SPIDERS AT THEIR FIRST FUNERAL GIG ARE TAKING A BREAK BETWEEN SETS.
GOOD HORS D' OEUVRES.
HE LOOKS SO FRESH. HARD TO BELIEVE HE'S BEEN LAYING HERE SO LONG...
SNIFF SNIFF
PHOOMF!
HEY! WHY IS EVERY-ONE JUMPING OUT THE WINDOWS?
MAYBE THE WAITRESS IS COMING WITH THE CHECK.
MUNCH
HOUSTON, WE HAVE A PROBLEM.
UH OH, I THINK WHIFF'S ODOR EATERS HAVE REACHED CRITICAL MASS.
THAT'S A WRAP BOYS, GRAB THE CHEESE BALLS AND LET'S GO...

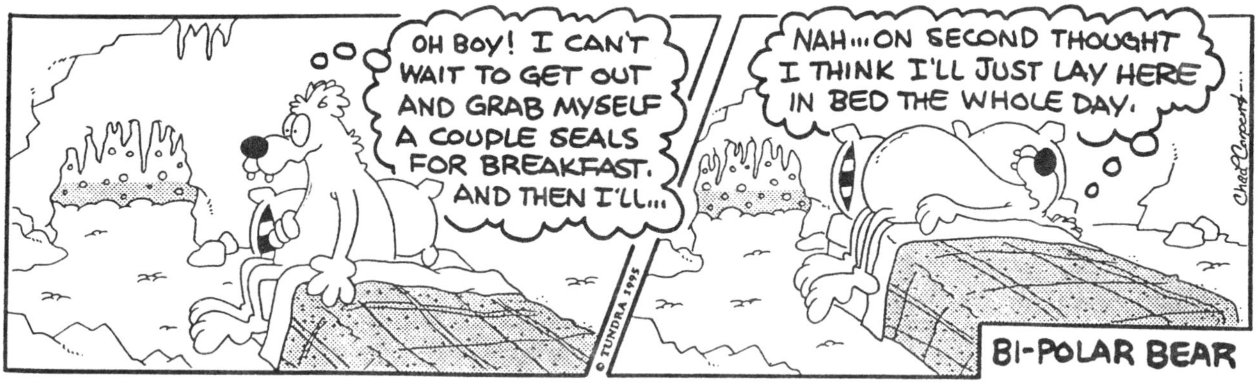
OH BOY! I CAN'T WAIT TO GET OUT AND GRAB MYSELF A COUPLE SEALS FOR BREAKFAST. AND THEN I'LL...
NAH... ON SECOND THOUGHT I THINK I'LL JUST LAY HERE IN BED THE WHOLE DAY.
© TUNDRA 1995
BI-POLAR BEAR

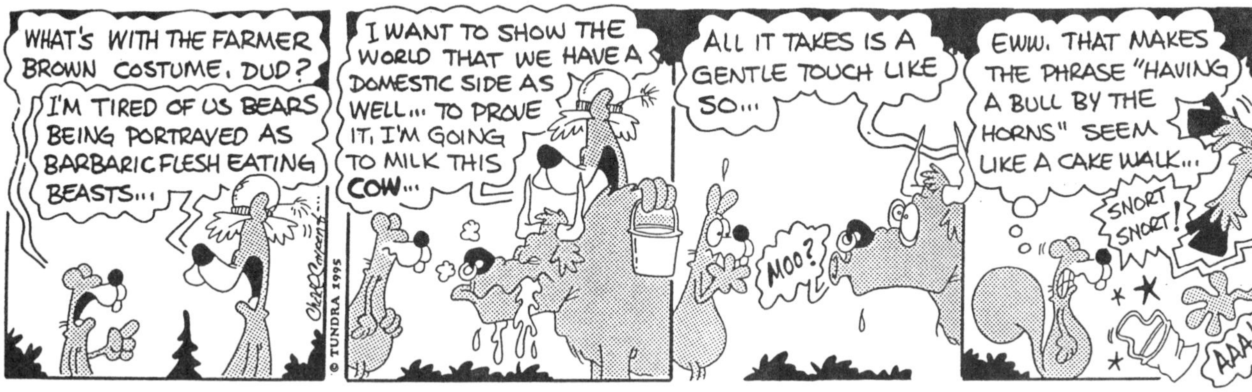
WHAT'S WITH THE FARMER BROWN COSTUME, DUD?
I'M TIRED OF US BEARS BEING PORTRAYED AS BARBARIC FLESH EATING BEASTS...
© TUNDRA 1995
I WANT TO SHOW THE WORLD THAT WE HAVE A DOMESTIC SIDE AS WELL... TO PROVE IT, I'M GOING TO MILK THIS COW...
ALL IT TAKES IS A GENTLE TOUCH LIKE SO...
MOO?
EWW. THAT MAKES THE PHRASE "HAVING A BULL BY THE HORNS" SEEM LIKE A CAKE WALK...
SNORT SNORT!
AAA!

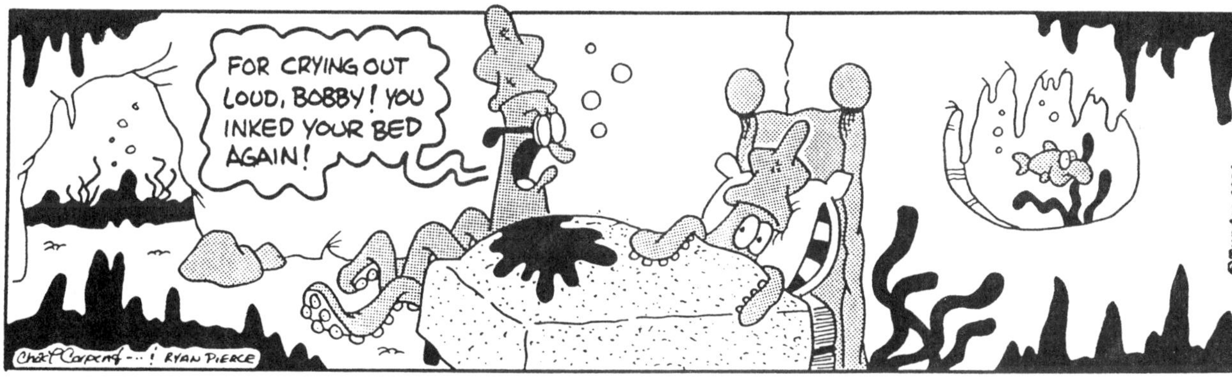
FOR CRYING OUT LOUD, BOBBY! YOU INKED YOUR BED AGAIN!
©Tundra 1996
RYAN PIERCE

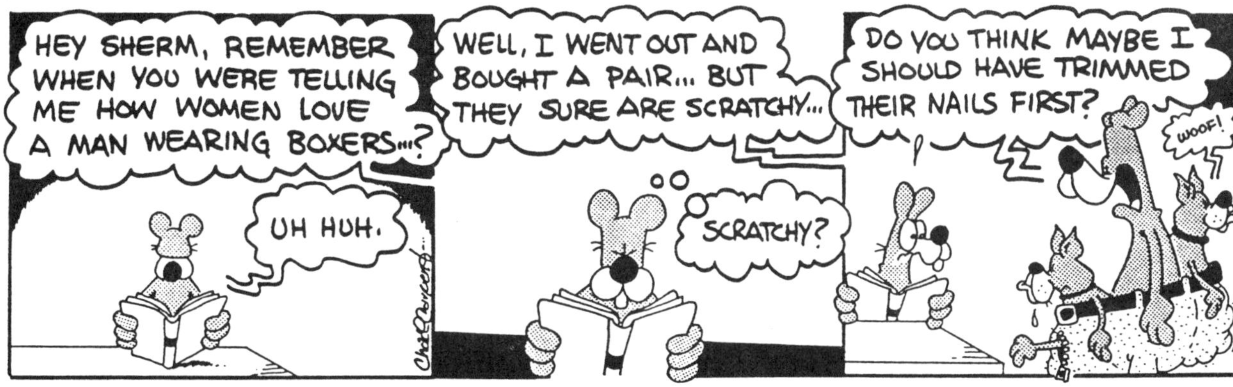
HEY SHERM, REMEMBER WHEN YOU WERE TELLING ME HOW WOMEN LOVE A MAN WEARING BOXERS...?
UH HUH.
WELL, I WENT OUT AND BOUGHT A PAIR... BUT THEY SURE ARE SCRATCHY...
SCRATCHY?
DO YOU THINK MAYBE I SHOULD HAVE TRIMMED THEIR NAILS FIRST?
WOOF!

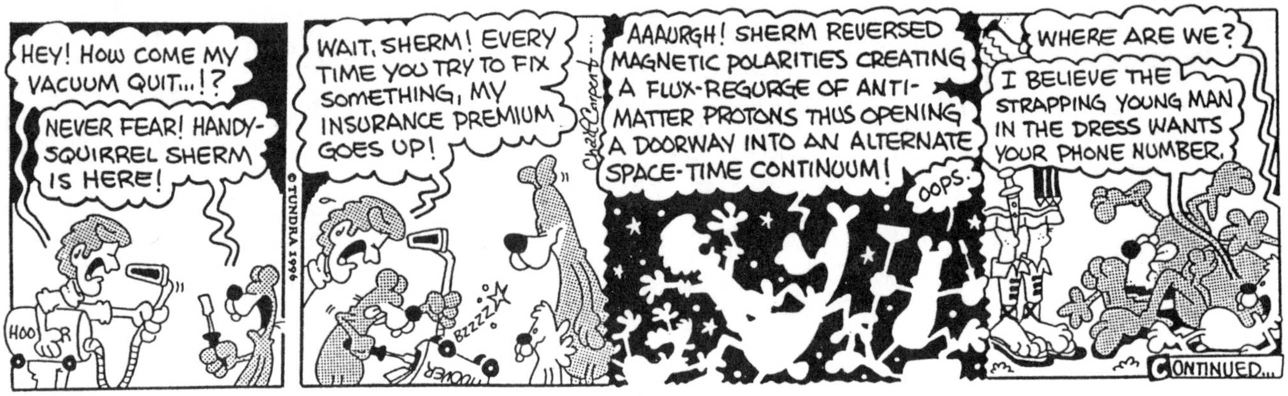
HEY! HOW COME MY VACUUM QUIT...!?
NEVER FEAR! HANDY-SQUIRREL SHERM IS HERE!
© TUNDRA 1996
WAIT, SHERM! EVERY TIME YOU TRY TO FIX SOMETHING, MY INSURANCE PREMIUM GOES UP!
BZZZZ
AAAURGH! SHERM REVERSED MAGNETIC POLARITIES CREATING A FLUX-REGURGE OF ANTI-MATTER PROTONS THUS OPENING A DOORWAY INTO AN ALTERNATE SPACE-TIME CONTINUUM!
OOPS.
WHERE ARE WE?
I BELIEVE THE STRAPPING YOUNG MAN IN THE DRESS WANTS YOUR PHONE NUMBER.
CONTINUED...

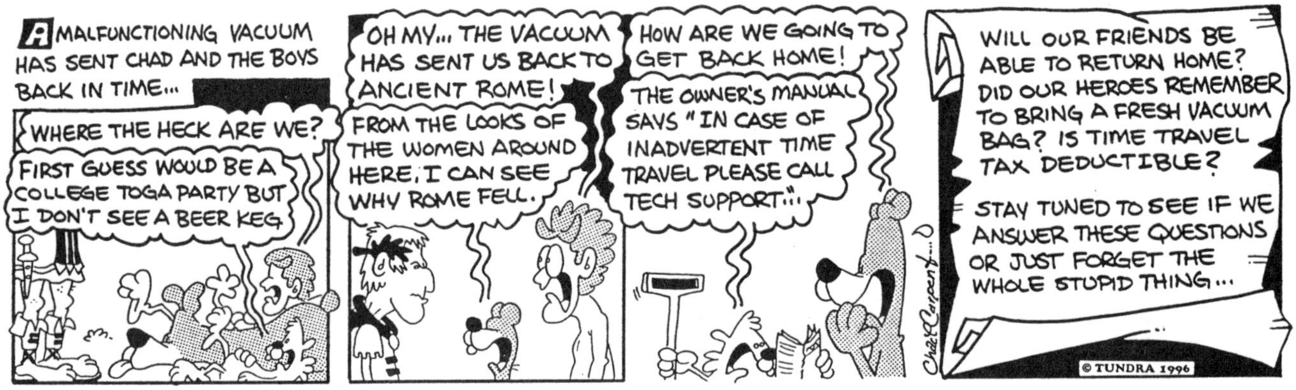
A MALFUNCTIONING VACUUM HAS SENT CHAD AND THE BOYS BACK IN TIME...
WHERE THE HECK ARE WE?
FIRST GUESS WOULD BE A COLLEGE TOGA PARTY BUT I DON'T SEE A BEER KEG.
OH MY... THE VACUUM HAS SENT US BACK TO ANCIENT ROME!
FROM THE LOOKS OF THE WOMEN AROUND HERE, I CAN SEE WHY ROME FELL.
HOW ARE WE GOING TO GET BACK HOME!
THE OWNER'S MANUAL SAYS "IN CASE OF INADVERTENT TIME TRAVEL PLEASE CALL TECH SUPPORT."...
WILL OUR FRIENDS BE ABLE TO RETURN HOME? DID OUR HEROES REMEMBER TO BRING A FRESH VACUUM BAG? IS TIME TRAVEL TAX DEDUCTIBLE?
STAY TUNED TO SEE IF WE ANSWER THESE QUESTIONS OR JUST FORGET THE WHOLE STUPID THING...
© TUNDRA 1996

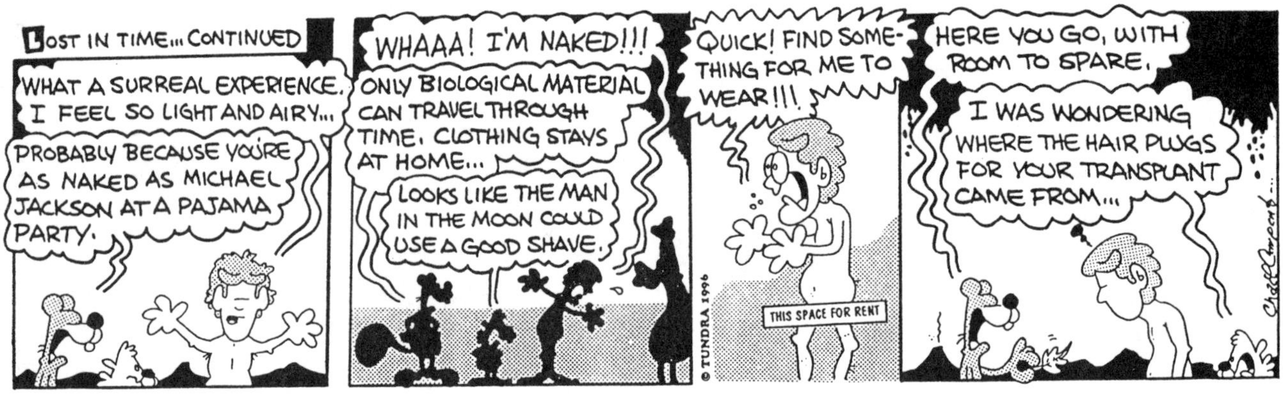
LOST IN TIME... CONTINUED
WHAT A SURREAL EXPERIENCE. I FEEL SO LIGHT AND AIRY...
PROBABLY BECAUSE YOU'RE AS NAKED AS MICHAEL JACKSON AT A PAJAMA PARTY.
WHAAA! I'M NAKED!!!
ONLY BIOLOGICAL MATERIAL CAN TRAVEL THROUGH TIME. CLOTHING STAYS AT HOME...
LOOKS LIKE THE MAN IN THE MOON COULD USE A GOOD SHAVE.
© TUNDRA 1996
QUICK! FIND SOMETHING FOR ME TO WEAR!!!
THIS SPACE FOR RENT
HERE YOU GO, WITH ROOM TO SPARE.
I WAS WONDERING WHERE THE HAIR PLUGS FOR YOUR TRANSPLANT CAME FROM...

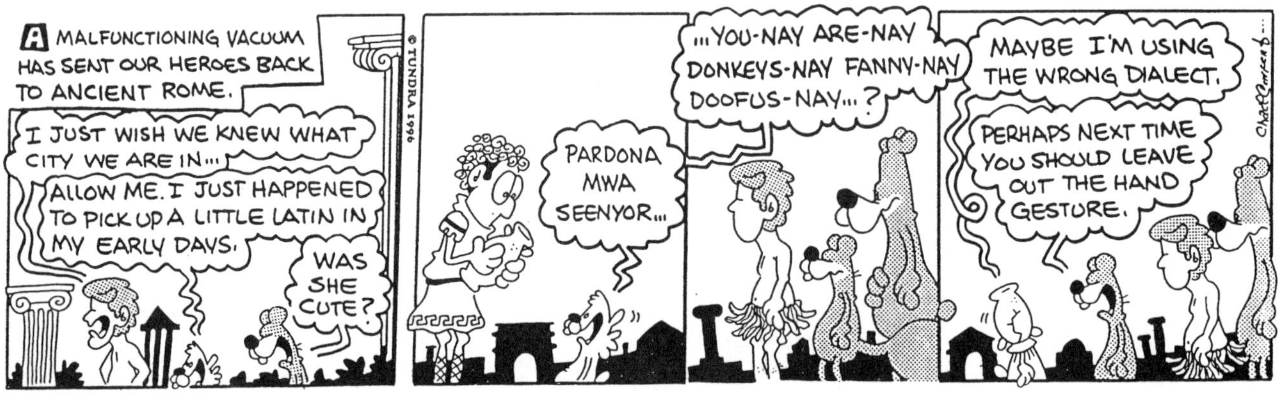
A MALFUNCTIONING VACUUM HAS SENT OUR HEROES BACK TO ANCIENT ROME.
I JUST WISH WE KNEW WHAT CITY WE ARE IN...
ALLOW ME. I JUST HAPPENED TO PICK UP A LITTLE LATIN IN MY EARLY DAYS.
WAS SHE CUTE?
© TUNDRA 1996
PARDONA MWA SEENYOR...
...YOU-NAY ARE-NAY DONKEYS-NAY FANNY-NAY DOOFUS-NAY...?
MAYBE I'M USING THE WRONG DIALECT.
PERHAPS NEXT TIME YOU SHOULD LEAVE OUT THE HAND GESTURE.

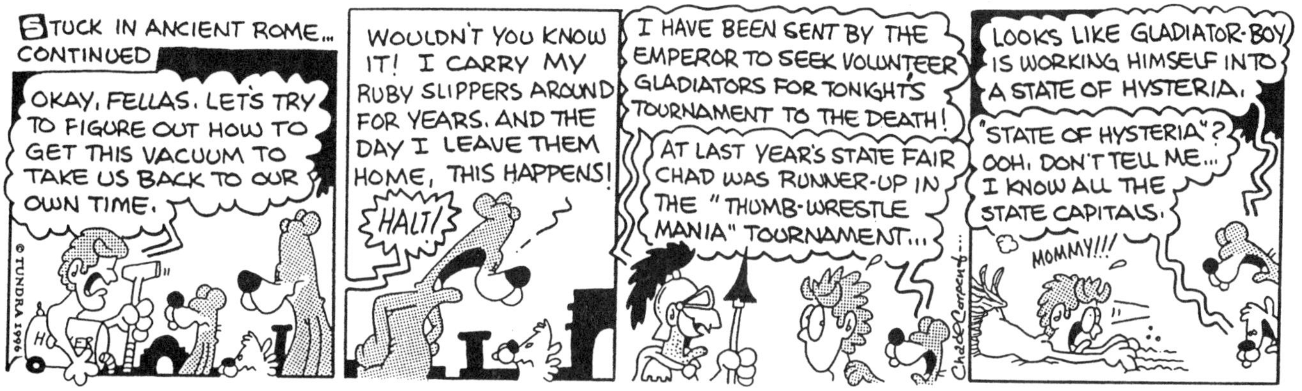
STUCK IN ANCIENT ROME... CONTINUED
OKAY, FELLAS. LET'S TRY TO FIGURE OUT HOW TO GET THIS VACUUM TO TAKE US BACK TO OUR OWN TIME.
© TUNDRA 1996
WOULDN'T YOU KNOW IT! I CARRY MY RUBY SLIPPERS AROUND FOR YEARS, AND THE DAY I LEAVE THEM HOME, THIS HAPPENS!
HALT!
I HAVE BEEN SENT BY THE EMPEROR TO SEEK VOLUNTEER GLADIATORS FOR TONIGHT'S TOURNAMENT TO THE DEATH!
AT LAST YEAR'S STATE FAIR CHAD WAS RUNNER-UP IN THE "THUMB-WRESTLE MANIA" TOURNAMENT...
LOOKS LIKE GLADIATOR-BOY IS WORKING HIMSELF INTO A STATE OF HYSTERIA.
"STATE OF HYSTERIA"? OOH, DON'T TELL ME... I KNOW ALL THE STATE CAPITALS.
MOMMY!!!

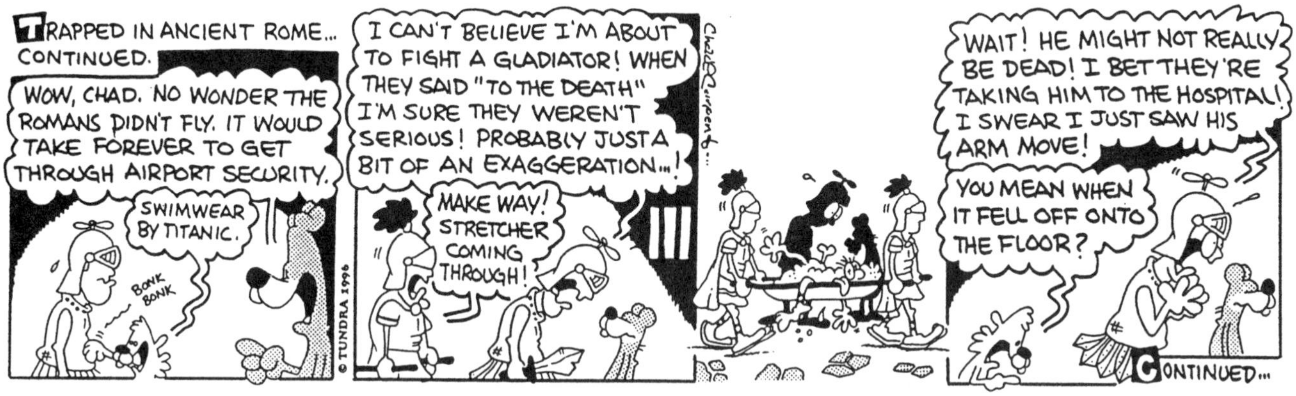
TRAPPED IN ANCIENT ROME... CONTINUED.
WOW, CHAD. NO WONDER THE ROMANS DIDN'T FLY. IT WOULD TAKE FOREVER TO GET THROUGH AIRPORT SECURITY.
SWIMWEAR BY TITANIC.
BONK BONK
© TUNDRA 1996
I CAN'T BELIEVE I'M ABOUT TO FIGHT A GLADIATOR! WHEN THEY SAID "TO THE DEATH" I'M SURE THEY WEREN'T SERIOUS! PROBABLY JUST A BIT OF AN EXAGGERATION...!
MAKE WAY! STRETCHER COMING THROUGH!
WAIT! HE MIGHT NOT REALLY BE DEAD! I BET THEY'RE TAKING HIM TO THE HOSPITAL! I SWEAR I JUST SAW HIS ARM MOVE!
YOU MEAN WHEN IT FELL OFF ONTO THE FLOOR?
CONTINUED...

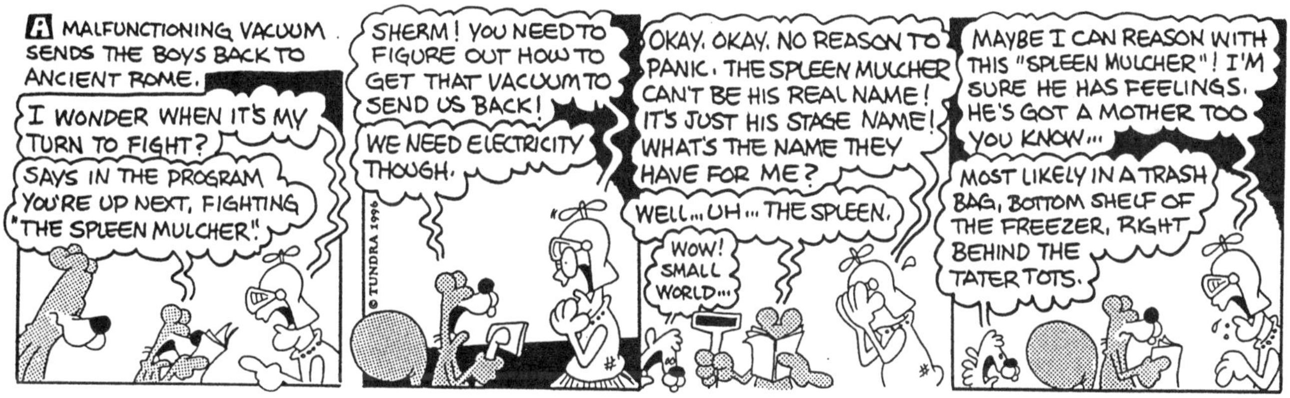
A MALFUNCTIONING VACUUM SENDS THE BOYS BACK TO ANCIENT ROME.
I WONDER WHEN IT'S MY TURN TO FIGHT?
SAYS IN THE PROGRAM YOU'RE UP NEXT, FIGHTING "THE SPLEEN MULCHER".
SHERM! YOU NEED TO FIGURE OUT HOW TO GET THAT VACUUM TO SEND US BACK!
WE NEED ELECTRICITY THOUGH.
© TUNDRA 1996
OKAY, OKAY, NO REASON TO PANIC. THE SPLEEN MULCHER CAN'T BE HIS REAL NAME! IT'S JUST HIS STAGE NAME! WHAT'S THE NAME THEY HAVE FOR ME?
WELL... UH... THE SPLEEN.
WOW! SMALL WORLD...
MAYBE I CAN REASON WITH THIS "SPLEEN MULCHER"! I'M SURE HE HAS FEELINGS. HE'S GOT A MOTHER TOO YOU KNOW...
MOST LIKELY IN A TRASH BAG, BOTTOM SHELF OF THE FREEZER, RIGHT BEHIND THE TATER TOTS.

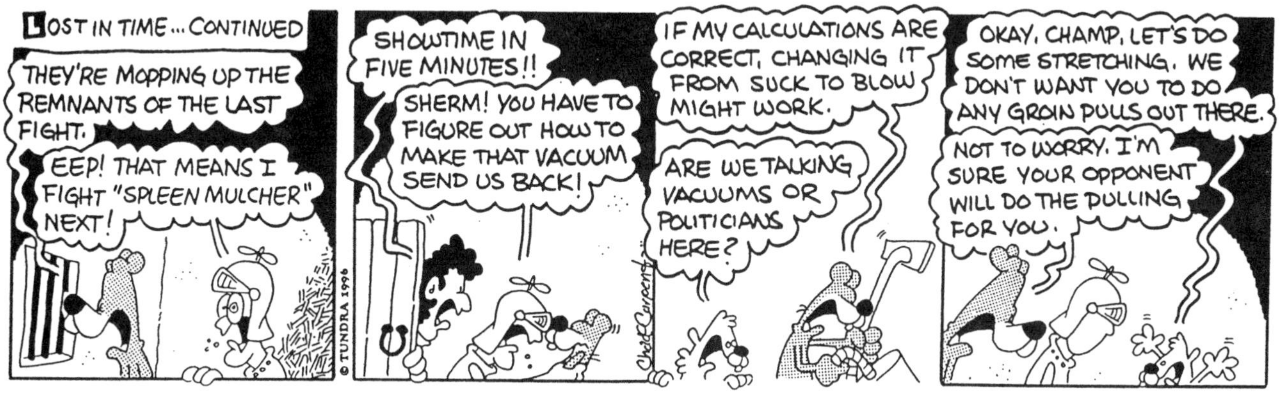
LOST IN TIME... CONTINUED
THEY'RE MOPPING UP THE REMNANTS OF THE LAST FIGHT.
EEP! THAT MEANS I FIGHT "SPLEEN MULCHER" NEXT!
© TUNDRA 1996
SHOWTIME IN FIVE MINUTES!!
SHERM! YOU HAVE TO FIGURE OUT HOW TO MAKE THAT VACUUM SEND US BACK!
IF MY CALCULATIONS ARE CORRECT, CHANGING IT FROM SUCK TO BLOW MIGHT WORK.
ARE WE TALKING VACUUMS OR POLITICIANS HERE?
OKAY, CHAMP, LET'S DO SOME STRETCHING. WE DON'T WANT YOU TO DO ANY GROIN PULLS OUT THERE.
NOT TO WORRY. I'M SURE YOUR OPPONENT WILL DO THE PULLING FOR YOU.

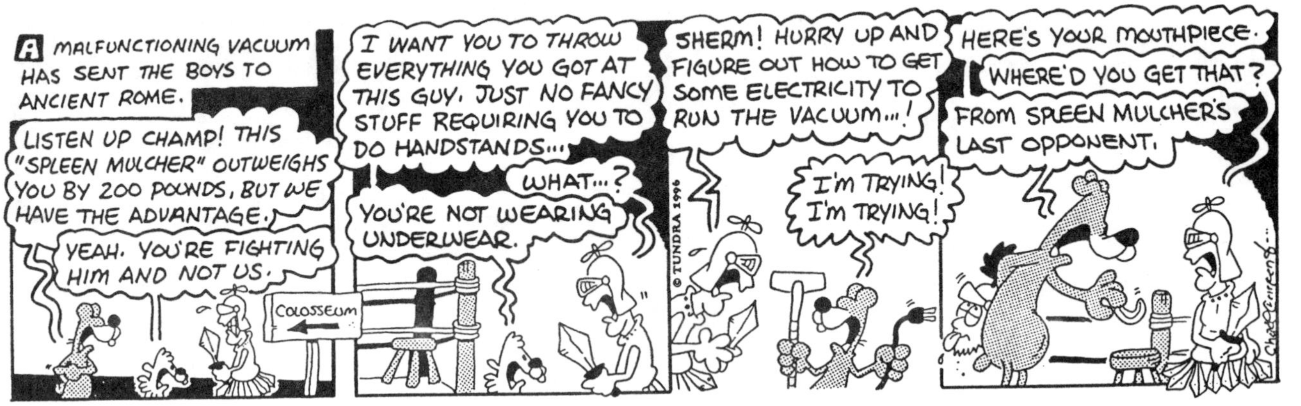
A MALFUNCTIONING VACUUM HAS SENT THE BOYS TO ANCIENT ROME.
LISTEN UP CHAMP! THIS "SPLEEN MULCHER" OUTWEIGHS YOU BY 200 POUNDS, BUT WE HAVE THE ADVANTAGE.
YEAH. YOU'RE FIGHTING HIM AND NOT US.
COLOSSEUM
I WANT YOU TO THROW EVERYTHING YOU GOT AT THIS GUY. JUST NO FANCY STUFF REQUIRING YOU TO DO HANDSTANDS...
WHAT...?
YOU'RE NOT WEARING UNDERWEAR.
SHERM! HURRY UP AND FIGURE OUT HOW TO GET SOME ELECTRICITY TO RUN THE VACUUM...!
I'M TRYING! I'M TRYING!
© TUNDRA 1996
HERE'S YOUR MOUTHPIECE.
WHERE'D YOU GET THAT?
FROM SPLEEN MULCHER'S LAST OPPONENT.

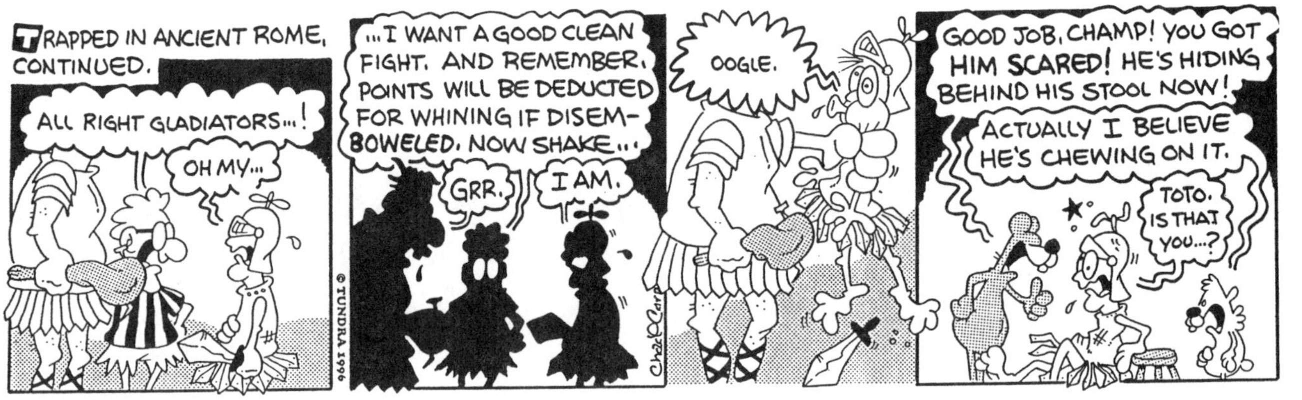
TRAPPED IN ANCIENT ROME, CONTINUED.
ALL RIGHT GLADIATORS...!
OH MY...
© TUNDRA 1996
...I WANT A GOOD CLEAN FIGHT. AND REMEMBER, POINTS WILL BE DEDUCTED FOR WHINING IF DISEMBOWELED. NOW SHAKE...
GRR.
I AM.
OOGLE.
GOOD JOB, CHAMP! YOU GOT HIM SCARED! HE'S HIDING BEHIND HIS STOOL NOW!
ACTUALLY I BELIEVE HE'S CHEWING ON IT.
TOTO. IS THAT YOU...?

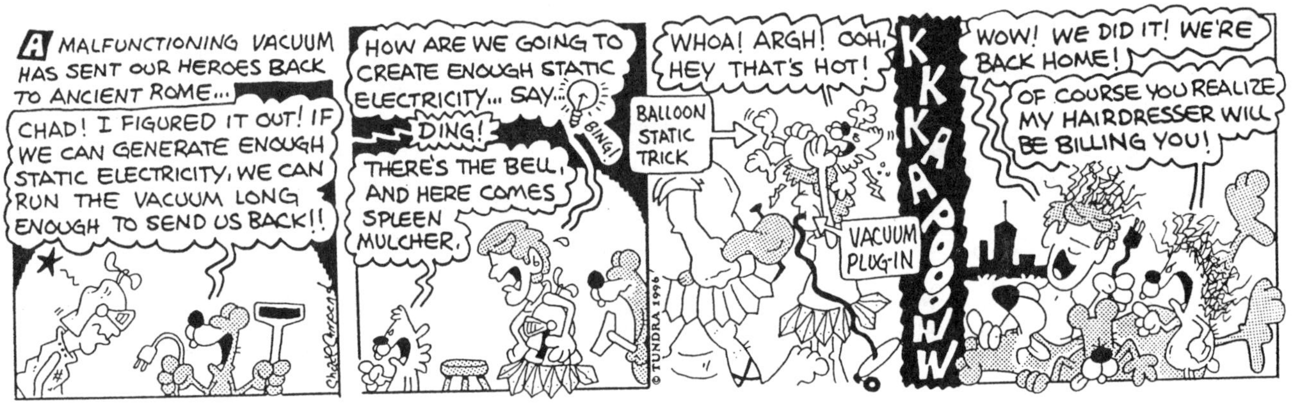
A MALFUNCTIONING VACUUM HAS SENT OUR HEROES BACK TO ANCIENT ROME...
CHAD! I FIGURED IT OUT! IF WE CAN GENERATE ENOUGH STATIC ELECTRICITY, WE CAN RUN THE VACUUM LONG ENOUGH TO SEND US BACK!!
HOW ARE WE GOING TO CREATE ENOUGH STATIC ELECTRICITY... SAY...
DING!
BING!
THERE'S THE BELL, AND HERE COMES SPLEEN MULCHER.
© TUNDRA 1996
WHOA! ARGH! OOH, HEY THAT'S HOT!
BALLOON STATIC TRICK
VACUUM PLUG-IN
KKAPOOOWW
WOW! WE DID IT! WE'RE BACK HOME!
OF COURSE YOU REALIZE MY HAIRDRESSER WILL BE BILLING YOU!

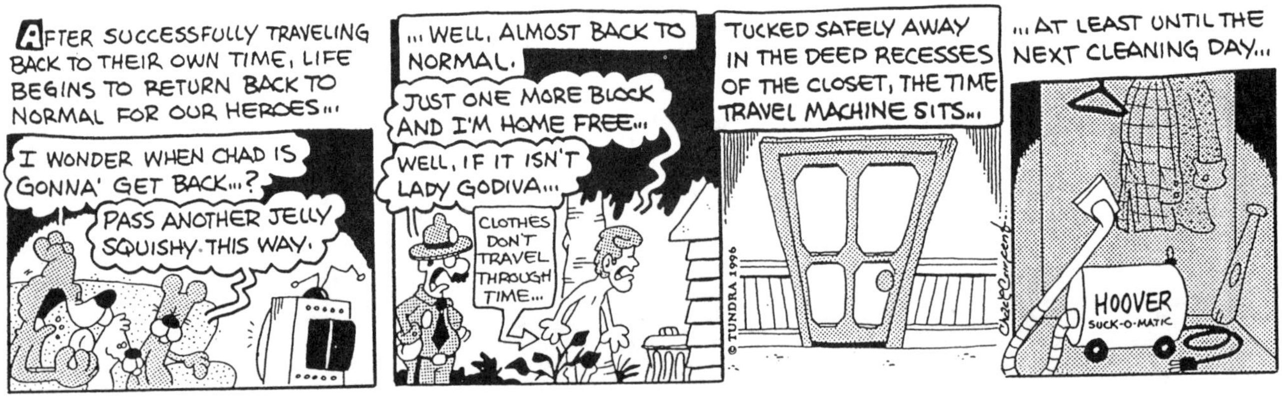
AFTER SUCCESSFULLY TRAVELING BACK TO THEIR OWN TIME, LIFE BEGINS TO RETURN BACK TO NORMAL FOR OUR HEROES...
I WONDER WHEN CHAD IS GONNA' GET BACK...?
PASS ANOTHER JELLY SQUISHY THIS WAY.
...WELL, ALMOST BACK TO NORMAL.
JUST ONE MORE BLOCK AND I'M HOME FREE...
WELL, IF IT ISN'T LADY GODIVA...
CLOTHES DON'T TRAVEL THROUGH TIME...
© TUNDRA 1996
TUCKED SAFELY AWAY IN THE DEEP RECESSES OF THE CLOSET, THE TIME TRAVEL MACHINE SITS...
...AT LEAST UNTIL THE NEXT CLEANING DAY...
HOOVER
SUCK-O-MATIC

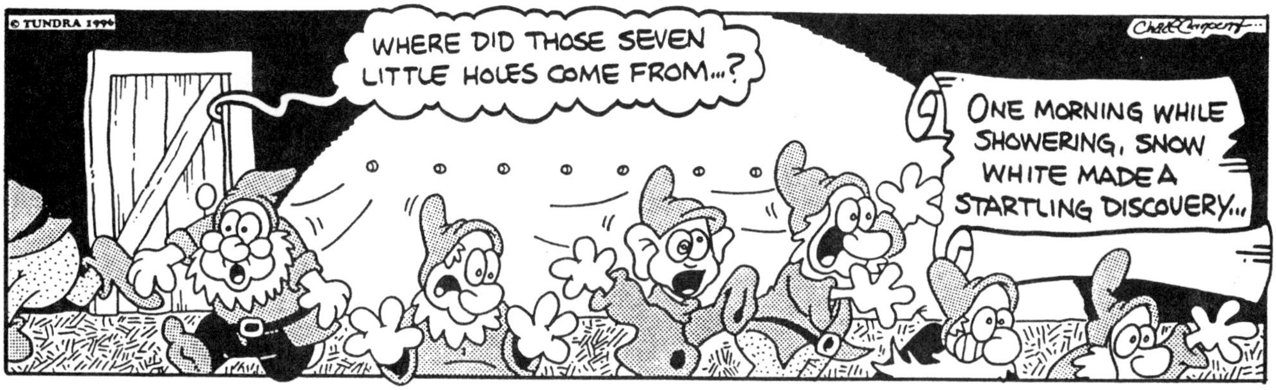
© TUNDRA 1994
WHERE DID THOSE SEVEN LITTLE HOLES COME FROM...?
ONE MORNING WHILE SHOWERING, SNOW WHITE MADE A STARTLING DISCOVERY...

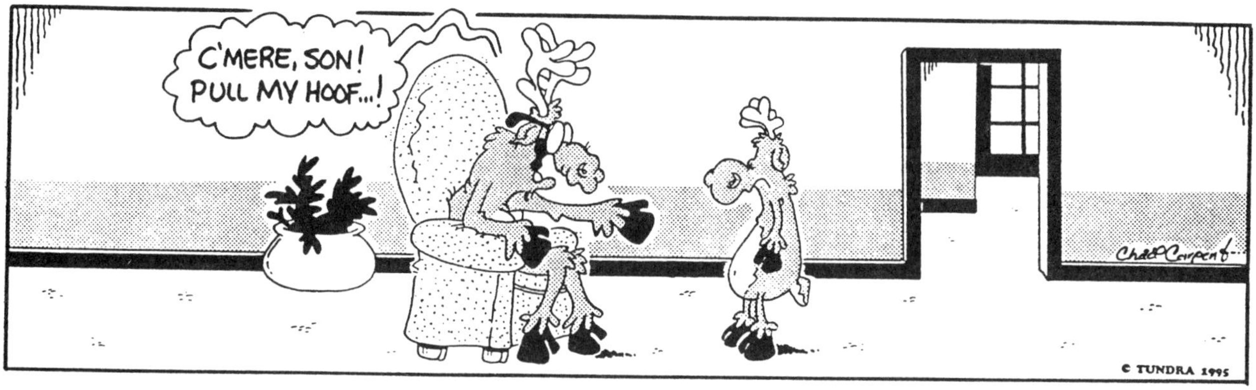
C'MERE, SON! PULL MY HOOF...!
© TUNDRA 1995

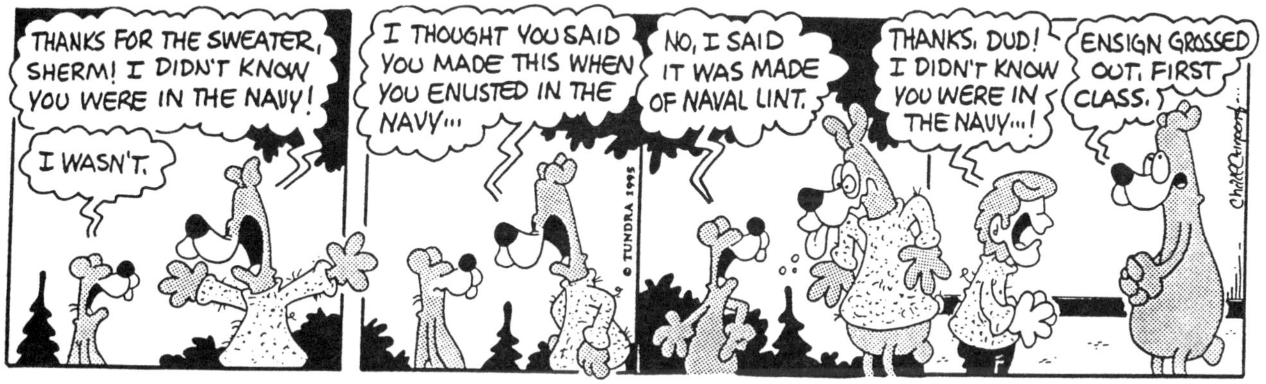
THANKS FOR THE SWEATER, SHERM! I DIDN'T KNOW YOU WERE IN THE NAVY!
I WASN'T.
I THOUGHT YOU SAID YOU MADE THIS WHEN YOU ENLISTED IN THE NAVY...
© TUNDRA 1995
NO, I SAID IT WAS MADE OF NAVAL LINT.
THANKS, DUD! I DIDN'T KNOW YOU WERE IN THE NAVY...!
ENSIGN GROSSED OUT, FIRST CLASS.

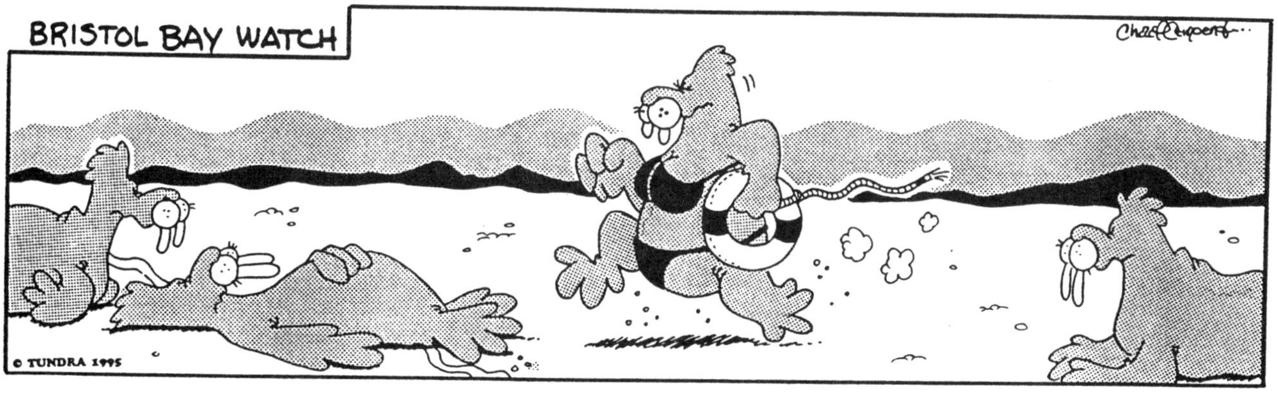
BRISTOL BAY WATCH
© TUNDRA 1995

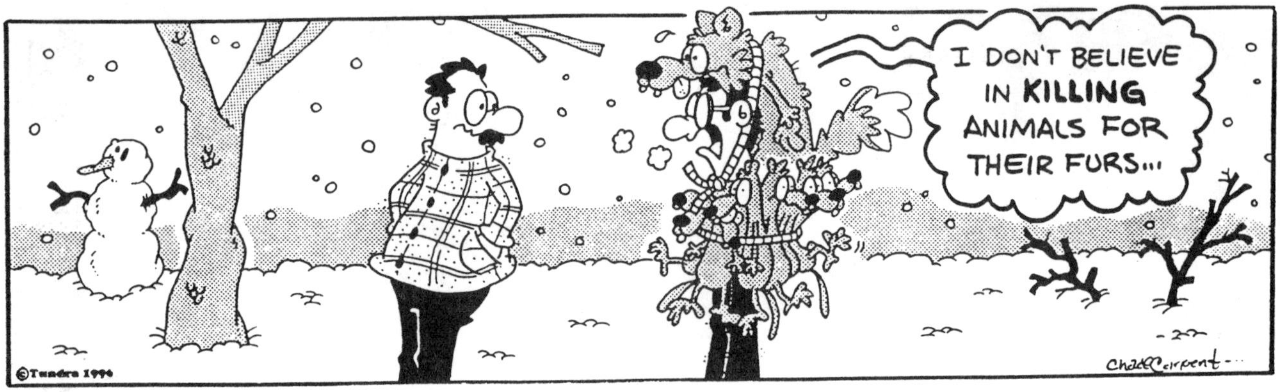
I DON'T BELIEVE IN KILLING ANIMALS FOR THEIR FURS...
©Tundra 1994

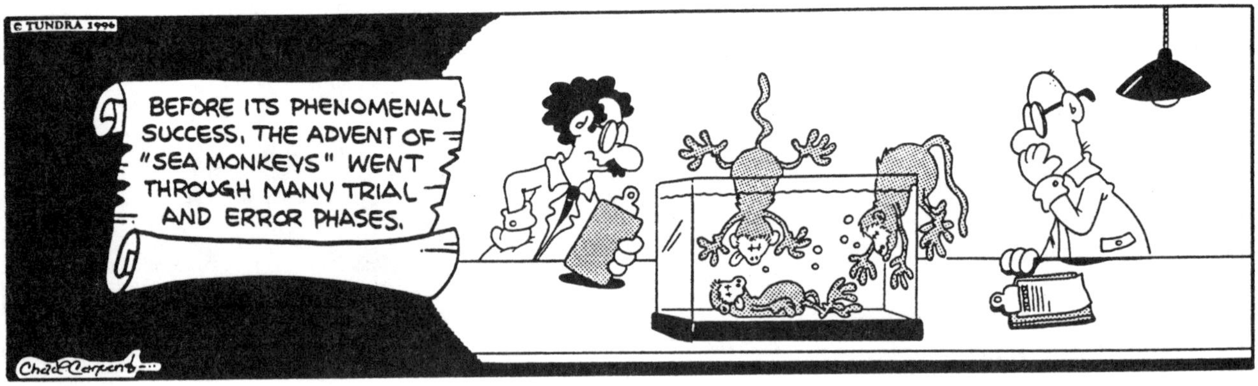
© TUNDRA 1994
BEFORE ITS PHENOMENAL SUCCESS, THE ADVENT OF "SEA MONKEYS" WENT THROUGH MANY TRIAL AND ERROR PHASES.

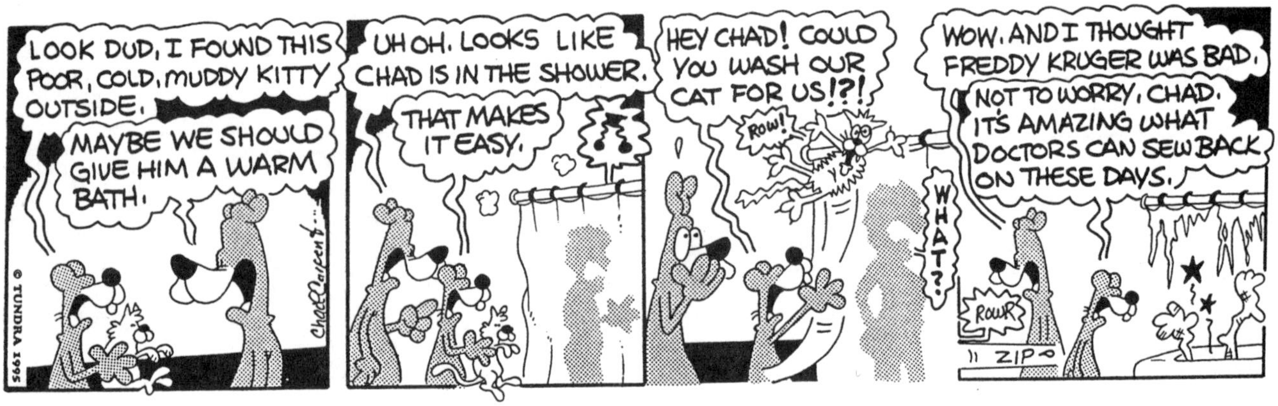
LOOK DUD, I FOUND THIS POOR, COLD, MUDDY KITTY OUTSIDE.
MAYBE WE SHOULD GIVE HIM A WARM BATH.
© TUNDRA 1995
UH OH. LOOKS LIKE CHAD IS IN THE SHOWER.
THAT MAKES IT EASY.
HEY CHAD! COULD YOU WASH OUR CAT FOR US!?!
ROW!
WHAT?
WOW. AND I THOUGHT FREDDY KRUGER WAS BAD.
NOT TO WORRY, CHAD. IT'S AMAZING WHAT DOCTORS CAN SEW BACK ON THESE DAYS.
ROWR
ZIP

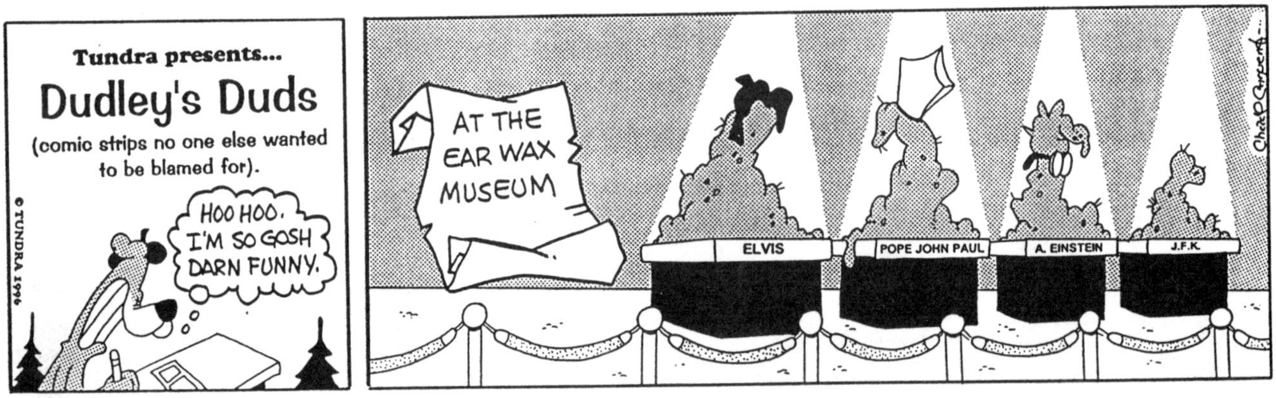
Tundra presents...
Dudley's Duds
(comic strips no one else wanted to be blamed for).
HOO HOO. I'M SO GOSH DARN FUNNY.
© TUNDRA 1996
AT THE EAR WAX MUSEUM
ELVIS
POPE JOHN PAUL
A. EINSTEIN
J.F.K.

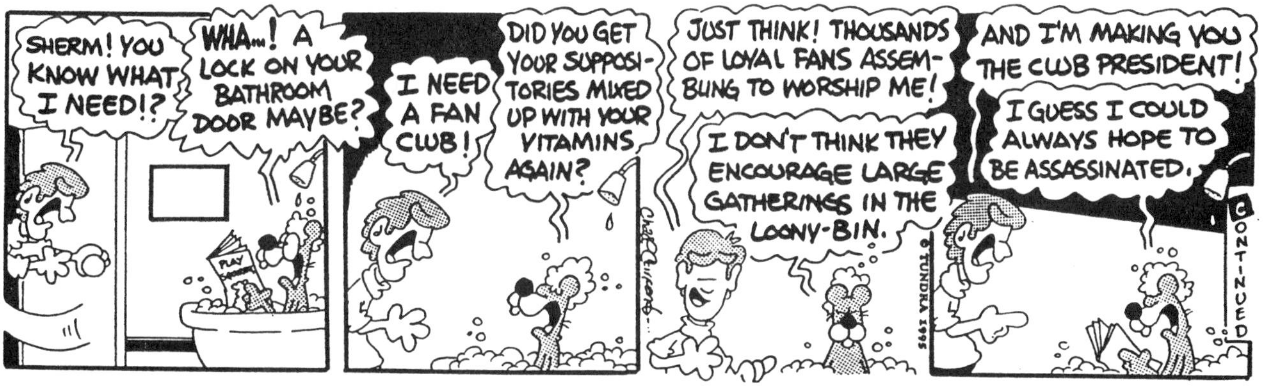
SHERM! YOU KNOW WHAT I NEED!?
WHA...! A LOCK ON YOUR BATHROOM DOOR MAYBE?
I NEED A FAN CLUB!
DID YOU GET YOUR SUPPOSITORIES MIXED UP WITH YOUR VITAMINS AGAIN?
JUST THINK! THOUSANDS OF LOYAL FANS ASSEMBLING TO WORSHIP ME!
I DON'T THINK THEY ENCOURAGE LARGE GATHERINGS IN THE LOONY-BIN.
AND I'M MAKING YOU THE CLUB PRESIDENT!
I GUESS I COULD ALWAYS HOPE TO BE ASSASSINATED.
CONTINUED
© TUNDRA 1995

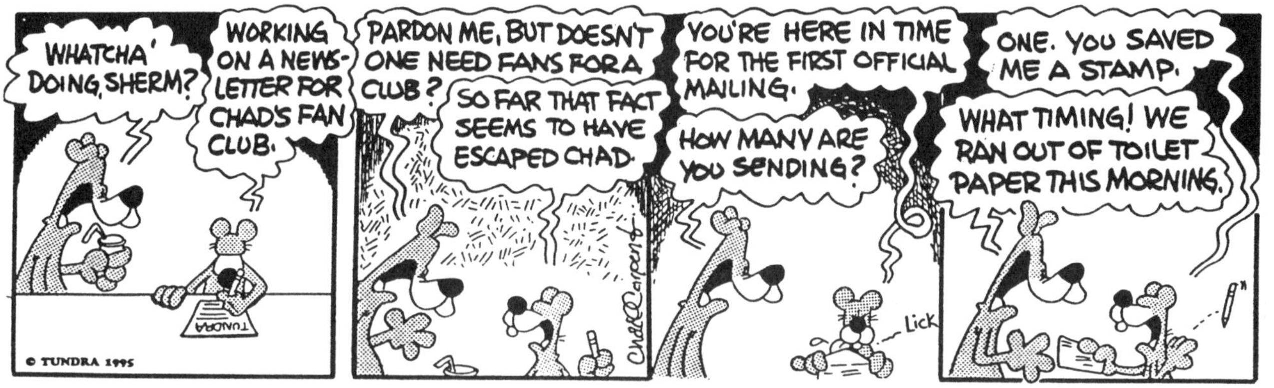
WHATCHA' DOING, SHERM?
WORKING ON A NEWSLETTER FOR CHAD'S FAN CLUB.
TUNDRA
© TUNDRA 1995
PARDON ME, BUT DOESN'T ONE NEED FANS FOR A CLUB?
SO FAR THAT FACT SEEMS TO HAVE ESCAPED CHAD.
YOU'RE HERE IN TIME FOR THE FIRST OFFICIAL MAILING.
HOW MANY ARE YOU SENDING?
LICK
ONE. YOU SAVED ME A STAMP.
WHAT TIMING! WE RAN OUT OF TOILET PAPER THIS MORNING.

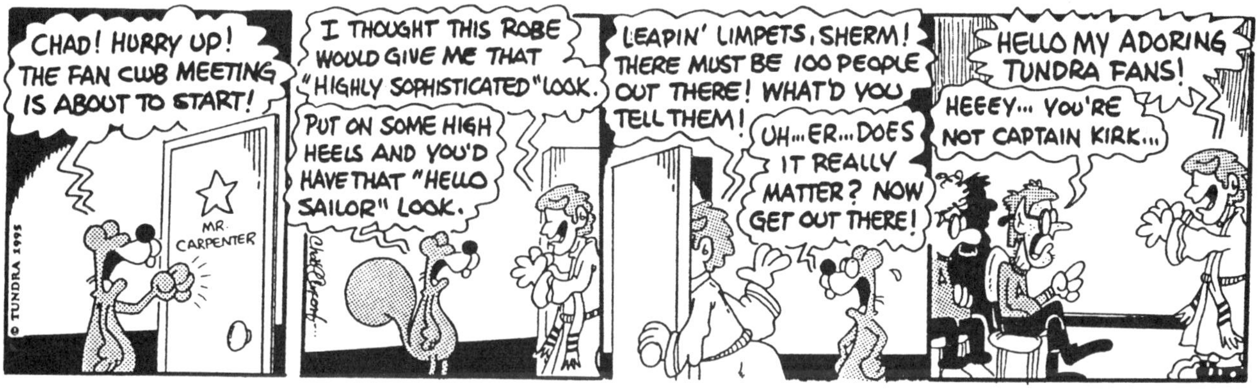
CHAD! HURRY UP! THE FAN CLUB MEETING IS ABOUT TO START!
MR. CARPENTER
© TUNDRA 1995
I THOUGHT THIS ROBE WOULD GIVE ME THAT "HIGHLY SOPHISTICATED" LOOK.
PUT ON SOME HIGH HEELS AND YOU'D HAVE THAT "HELLO SAILOR" LOOK.
LEAPIN' LIMPETS, SHERM! THERE MUST BE 100 PEOPLE OUT THERE! WHAT'D YOU TELL THEM!
UH...ER...DOES IT REALLY MATTER? NOW GET OUT THERE!
HELLO MY ADORING TUNDRA FANS!
HEEEY... YOU'RE NOT CAPTAIN KIRK...

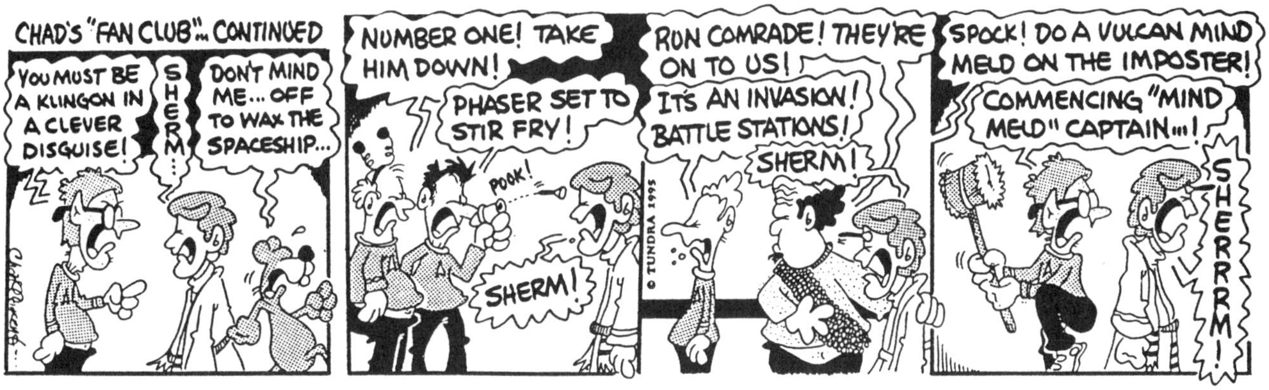
CHAD'S "FAN CLUB"... CONTINUED
YOU MUST BE A KLINGON IN A CLEVER DISGUISE!
SHERM...
DON'T MIND ME... OFF TO WAX THE SPACESHIP...
NUMBER ONE! TAKE HIM DOWN!
PHASER SET TO STIR FRY!
POOK!
SHERM!
RUN COMRADE! THEY'RE ON TO US!
IT'S AN INVASION! BATTLE STATIONS!
SHERM!
© TUNDRA 1995
SPOCK! DO A VULCAN MIND MELD ON THE IMPOSTER!
COMMENCING "MIND MELD" CAPTAIN...!
SHERRRM!

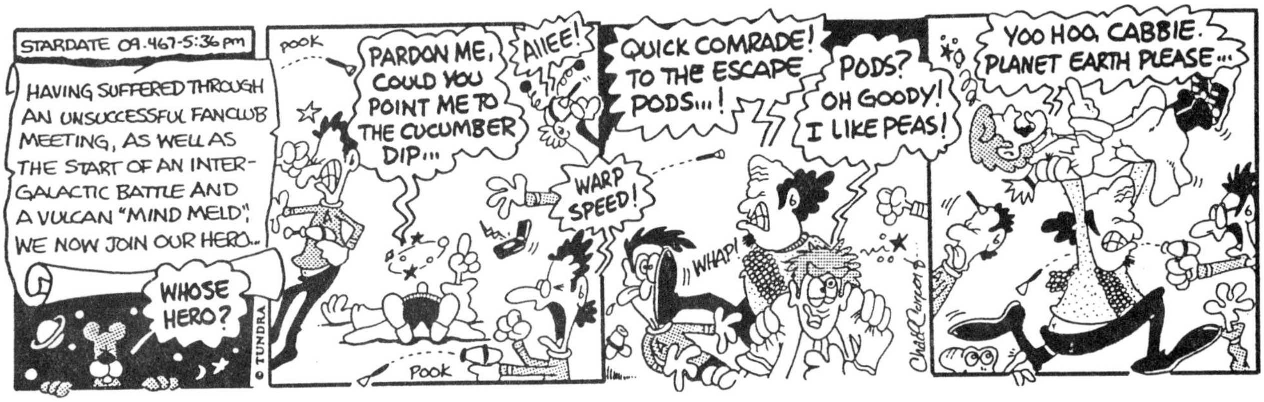
STARDATE 09.467-5:36 pm
HAVING SUFFERED THROUGH AN UNSUCCESSFUL FANCLUB MEETING, AS WELL AS THE START OF AN INTER-GALACTIC BATTLE AND A VULCAN "MIND MELD", WE NOW JOIN OUR HERO...
WHOSE HERO?
© TUNDRA
POOK
PARDON ME, COULD YOU POINT ME TO THE CUCUMBER DIP...
AIIEE!
WARP SPEED!
POOK
QUICK COMRADE! TO THE ESCAPE PODS...!
PODS? OH GOODY! I LIKE PEAS!
WHAP!
YOO HOO, CABBIE. PLANET EARTH PLEASE...

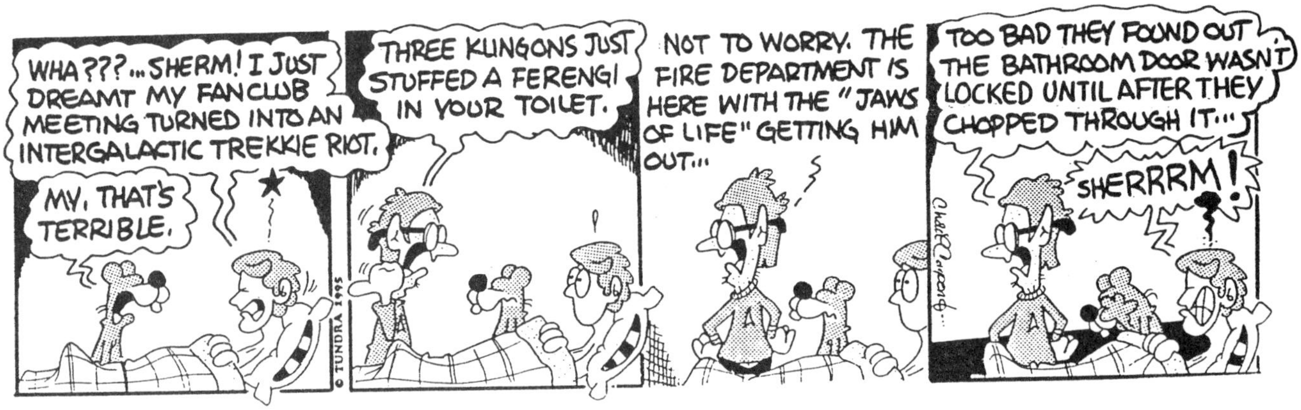
WHA??? ...SHERM! I JUST DREAMT MY FANCLUB MEETING TURNED INTO AN INTERGALACTIC TREKKIE RIOT.
MY, THAT'S TERRIBLE.
THREE KLINGONS JUST STUFFED A FERENGI IN YOUR TOILET.
© TUNDRA 1995
NOT TO WORRY. THE FIRE DEPARTMENT IS HERE WITH THE "JAWS OF LIFE" GETTING HIM OUT...
TOO BAD THEY FOUND OUT THE BATHROOM DOOR WASN'T LOCKED UNTIL AFTER THEY CHOPPED THROUGH IT...
SHERRRM!

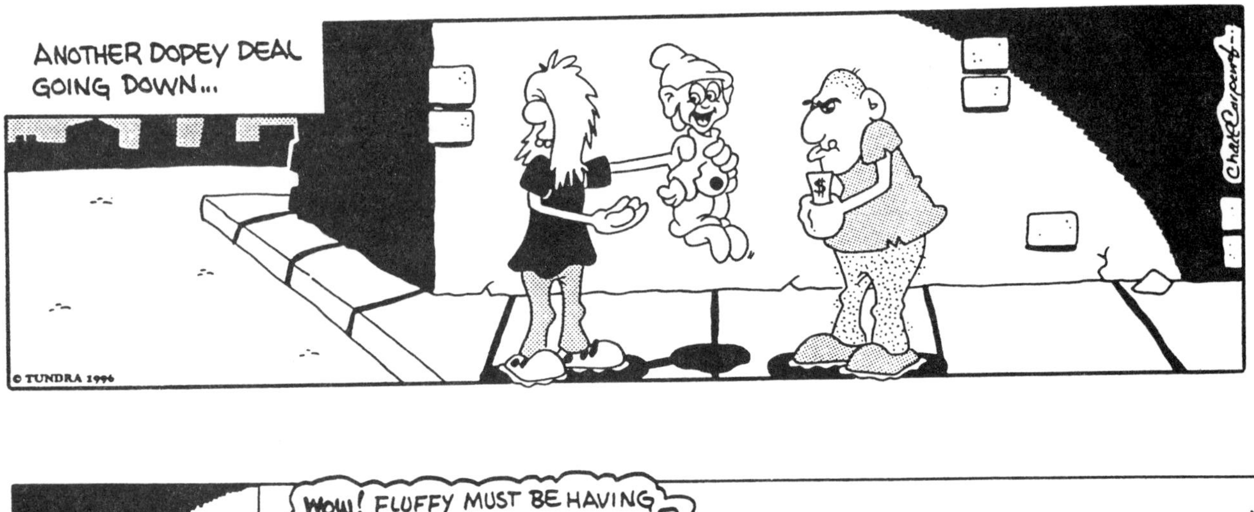
ANOTHER DOPEY DEAL GOING DOWN...
© TUNDRA 1996

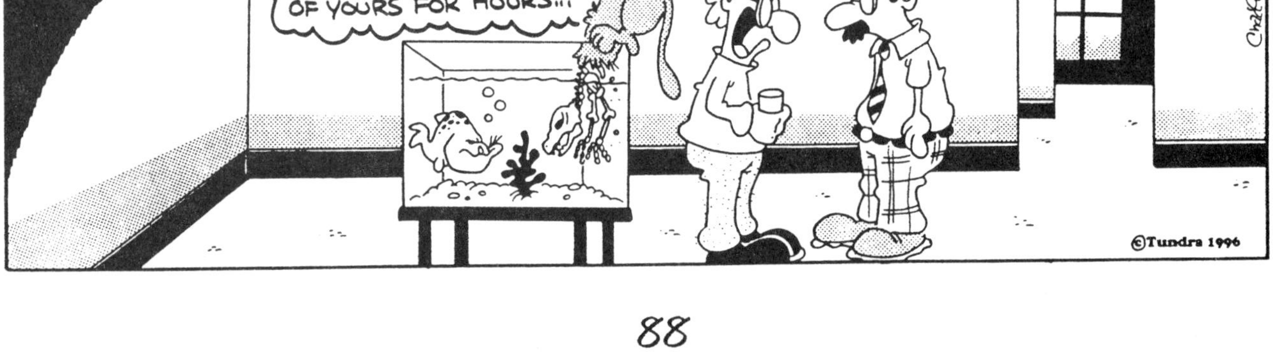
WOW! FLUFFY MUST BE HAVING A GOOD TIME! HE'S BEEN PLAYING WITH THAT FISH OF YOURS FOR HOURS...
©Tundra 1996

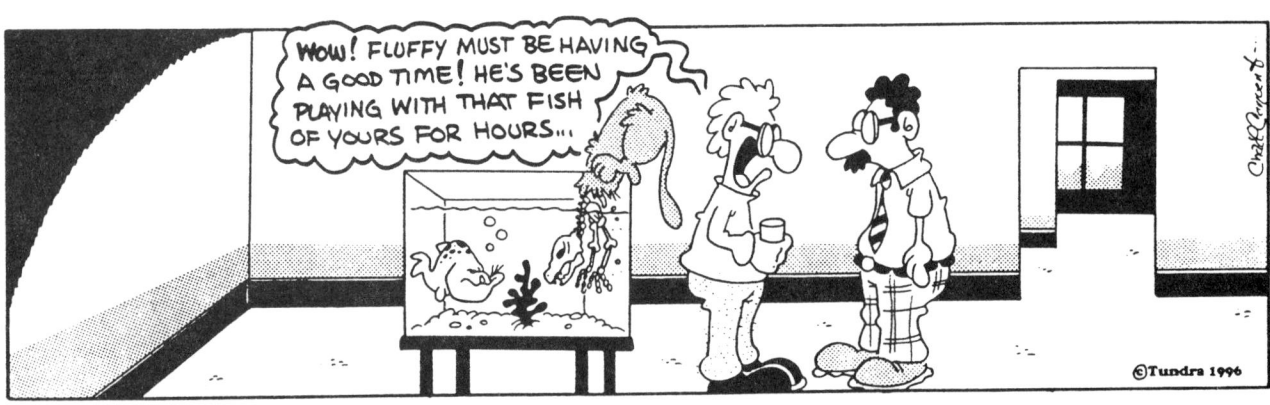

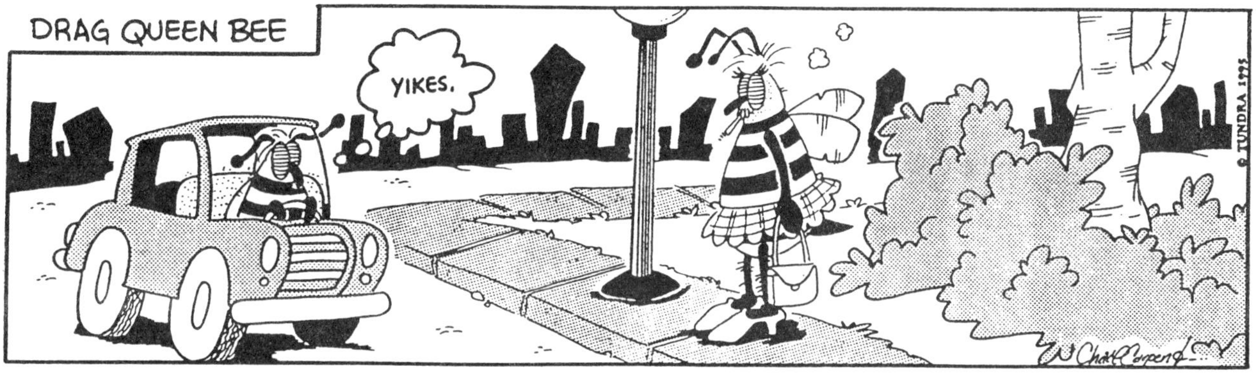
DRAG QUEEN BEE
YIKES.
© TUNDRA 1995

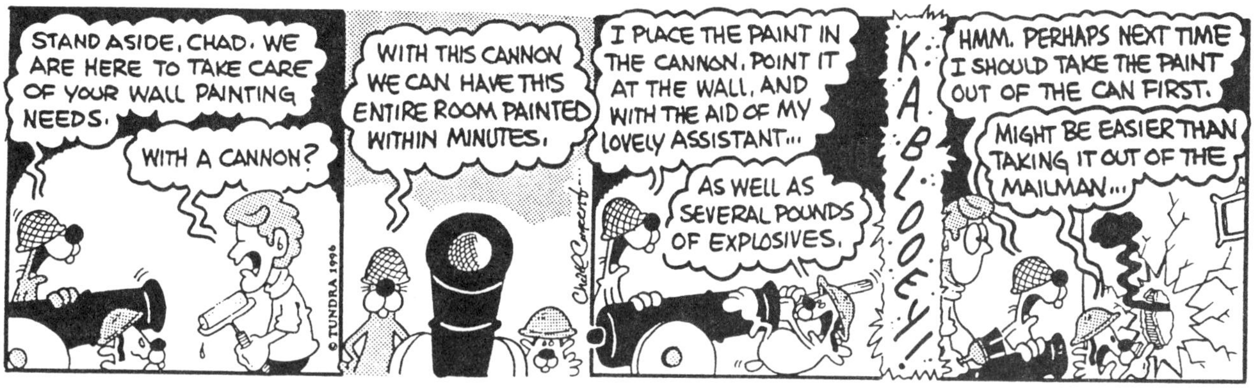
STAND ASIDE, CHAD. WE ARE HERE TO TAKE CARE OF YOUR WALL PAINTING NEEDS.
WITH A CANNON?
© TUNDRA 1996
WITH THIS CANNON WE CAN HAVE THIS ENTIRE ROOM PAINTED WITHIN MINUTES.
I PLACE THE PAINT IN THE CANNON, POINT IT AT THE WALL, AND WITH THE AID OF MY LOVELY ASSISTANT...
AS WELL AS SEVERAL POUNDS OF EXPLOSIVES.
KABLOOEY!
HMM. PERHAPS NEXT TIME I SHOULD TAKE THE PAINT OUT OF THE CAN FIRST.
MIGHT BE EASIER THAN TAKING IT OUT OF THE MAILMAN...

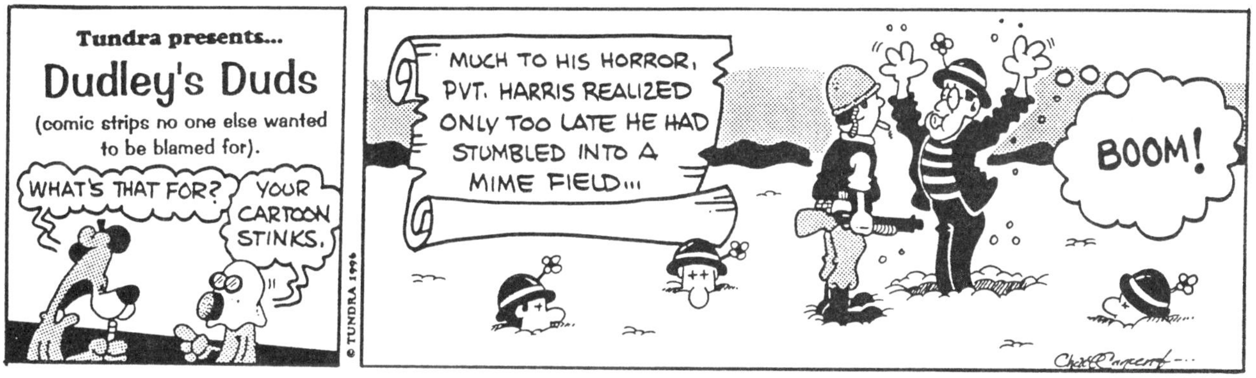
Tundra presents...
Dudley's Duds
(comic strips no one else wanted to be blamed for).
WHAT'S THAT FOR?
YOUR CARTOON STINKS.
© TUNDRA 1996
MUCH TO HIS HORROR, PVT. HARRIS REALIZED ONLY TOO LATE HE HAD STUMBLED INTO A MIME FIELD...
BOOM!

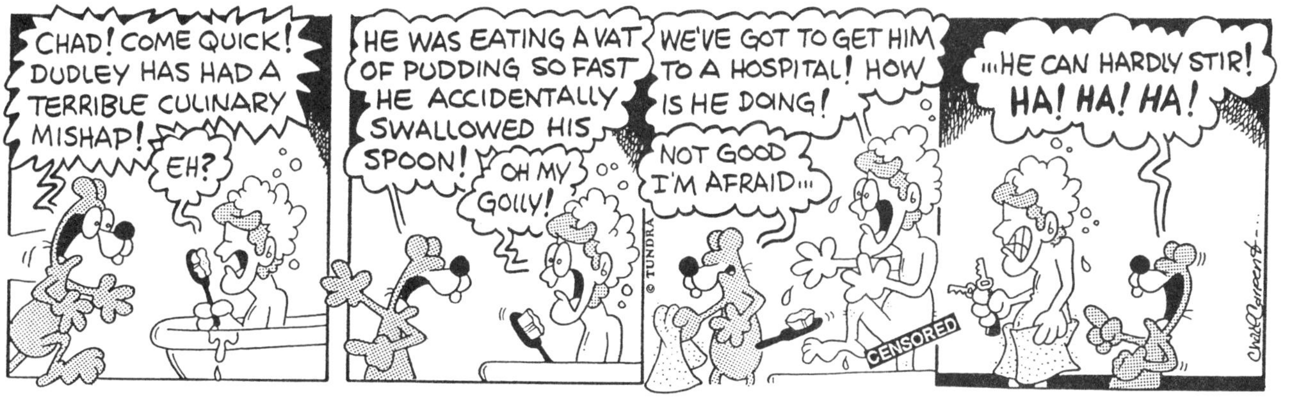
CHAD! COME QUICK! DUDLEY HAS HAD A TERRIBLE CULINARY MISHAP!
EH?
HE WAS EATING A VAT OF PUDDING SO FAST HE ACCIDENTALLY SWALLOWED HIS SPOON!
OH MY GOLLY!
© TUNDRA
WE'VE GOT TO GET HIM TO A HOSPITAL! HOW IS HE DOING!
NOT GOOD I'M AFRAID...
CENSORED
...HE CAN HARDLY STIR! HA! HA! HA!

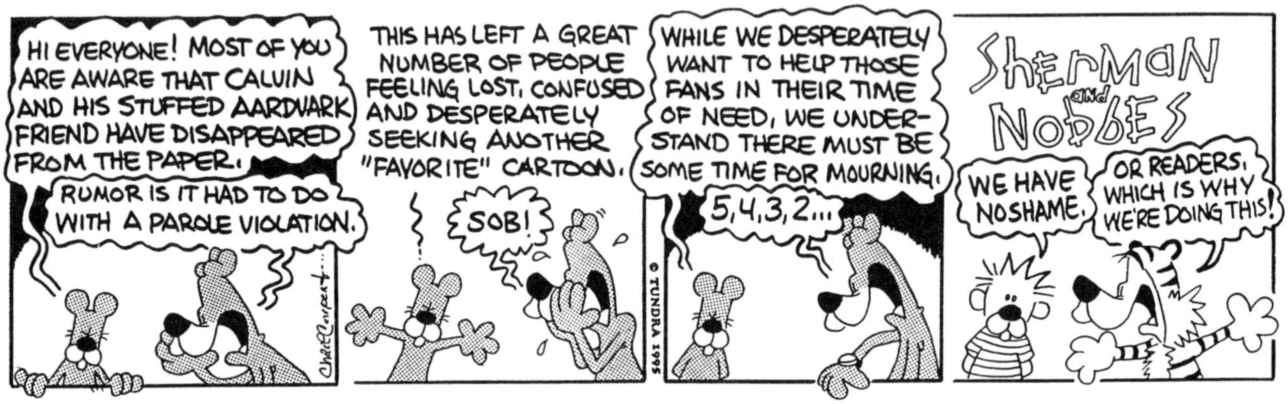
HI EVERYONE! MOST OF YOU ARE AWARE THAT CALVIN AND HIS STUFFED AARDVARK FRIEND HAVE DISAPPEARED FROM THE PAPER.
RUMOR IS IT HAD TO DO WITH A PAROLE VIOLATION.
THIS HAS LEFT A GREAT NUMBER OF PEOPLE FEELING LOST, CONFUSED AND DESPERATELY SEEKING ANOTHER "FAVORITE" CARTOON.
SOB!
© TUNDRA 1995
WHILE WE DESPERATELY WANT TO HELP THOSE FANS IN THEIR TIME OF NEED, WE UNDERSTAND THERE MUST BE SOME TIME FOR MOURNING.
5,4,3,2...
Sherman and Nobbes
WE HAVE NO SHAME.
OR READERS, WHICH IS WHY WE'RE DOING THIS!

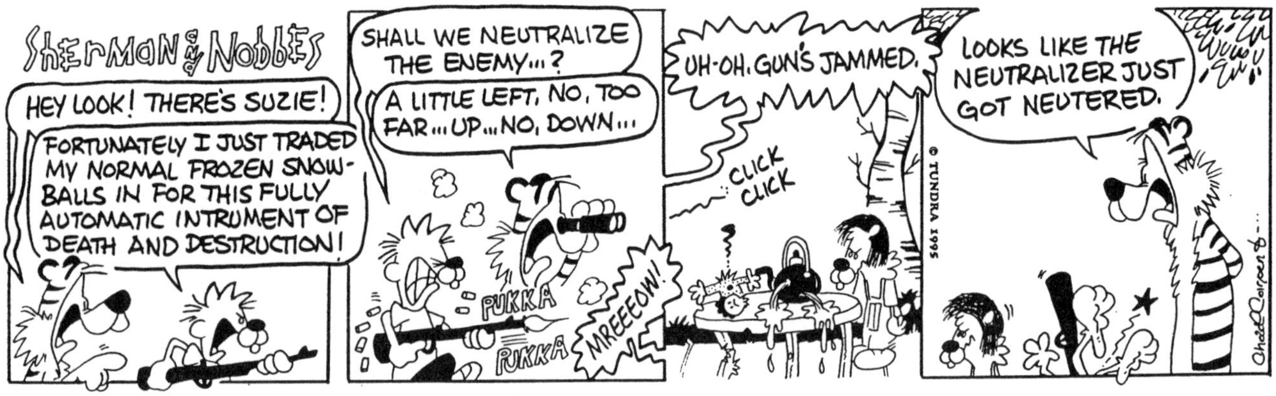
Sherman and Nobbes
HEY LOOK! THERE'S SUZIE!
FORTUNATELY I JUST TRADED MY NORMAL FROZEN SNOWBALLS IN FOR THIS FULLY AUTOMATIC INTRUMENT OF DEATH AND DESTRUCTION!
SHALL WE NEUTRALIZE THE ENEMY...?
A LITTLE LEFT, NO, TOO FAR...UP...NO, DOWN...
PUKKA
PUKKA
MREEEOW!
UH-OH, GUN'S JAMMED.
CLICK
CLICK
© TUNDRA 1995
LOOKS LIKE THE NEUTRALIZER JUST GOT NEUTERED.

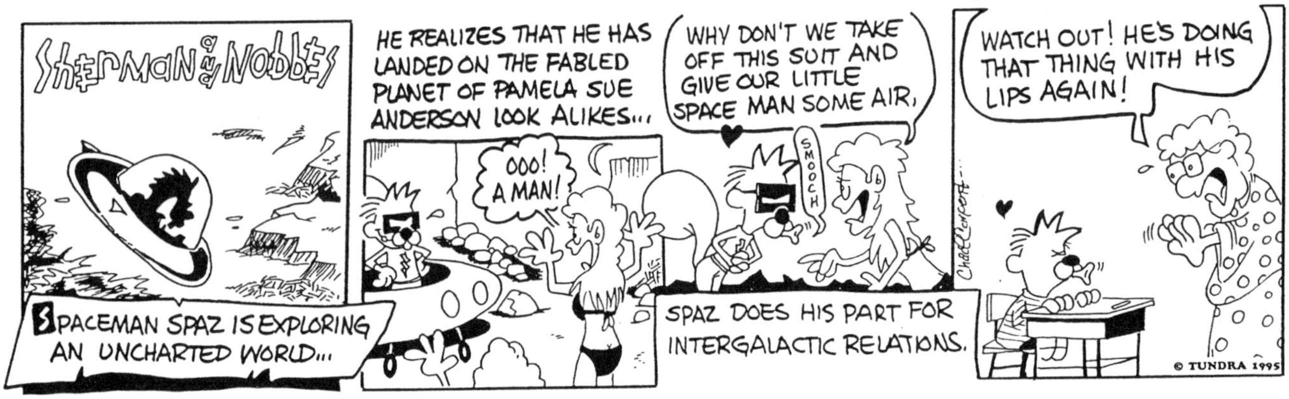
Sherman and Nobbes
SPACEMAN SPAZ IS EXPLORING AN UNCHARTED WORLD...
HE REALIZES THAT HE HAS LANDED ON THE FABLED PLANET OF PAMELA SUE ANDERSON LOOK ALIKES...
OOO! A MAN!
WHY DON'T WE TAKE OFF THIS SUIT AND GIVE OUR LITTLE SPACE MAN SOME AIR.
SMOOCH
SPAZ DOES HIS PART FOR INTERGALACTIC RELATIONS.
WATCH OUT! HE'S DOING THAT THING WITH HIS LIPS AGAIN!
© TUNDRA 1995

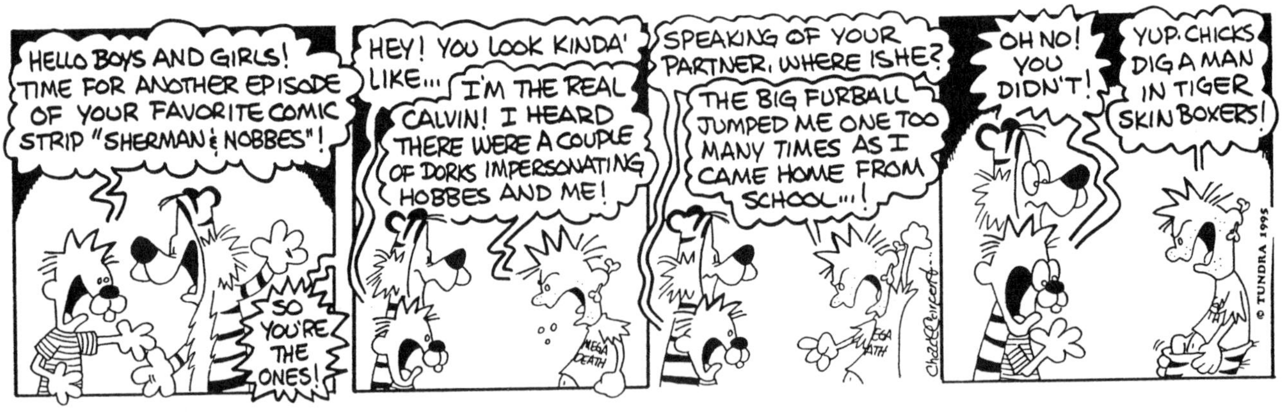
HELLO BOYS AND GIRLS! TIME FOR ANOTHER EPISODE OF YOUR FAVORITE COMIC STRIP "SHERMAN & NOBBES"!
SO YOU'RE THE ONES!
HEY! YOU LOOK KINDA' LIKE...
I'M THE REAL CALVIN! I HEARD THERE WERE A COUPLE OF DORKS IMPERSONATING HOBBES AND ME!
SPEAKING OF YOUR PARTNER, WHERE IS HE?
THE BIG FURBALL JUMPED ME ONE TOO MANY TIMES AS I CAME HOME FROM SCHOOL...!
OH NO! YOU DIDN'T!
YUP. CHICKS DIG A MAN IN TIGER SKIN BOXERS!
© TUNDRA 1995

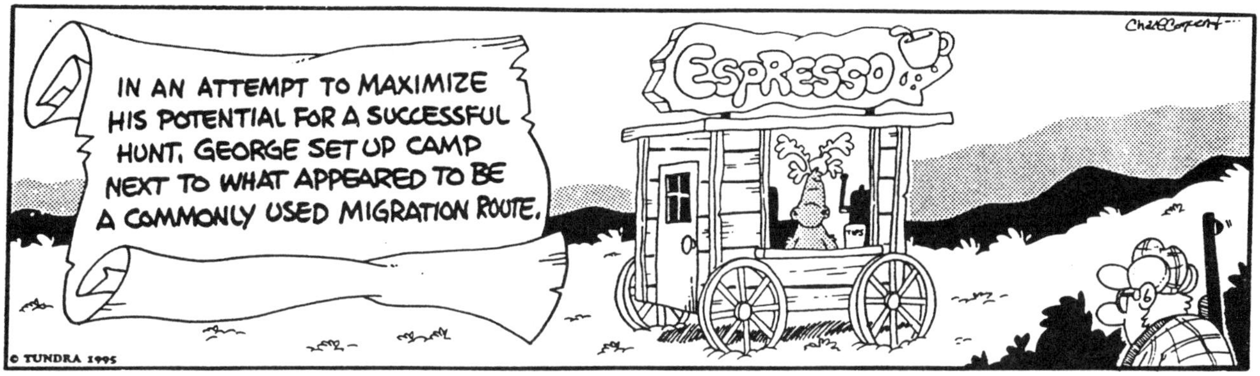
IN AN ATTEMPT TO MAXIMIZE HIS POTENTIAL FOR A SUCCESSFUL HUNT, GEORGE SET UP CAMP NEXT TO WHAT APPEARED TO BE A COMMONLY USED MIGRATION ROUTE.
ESPRESSO
TIPS
© TUNDRA 1995

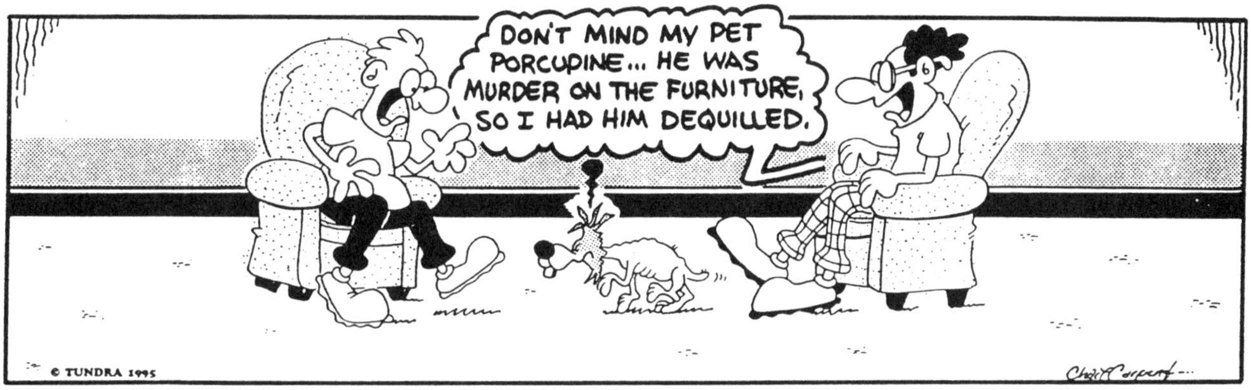
DON'T MIND MY PET PORCUPINE... HE WAS MURDER ON THE FURNITURE, SO I HAD HIM DEQUILLED.
© TUNDRA 1995

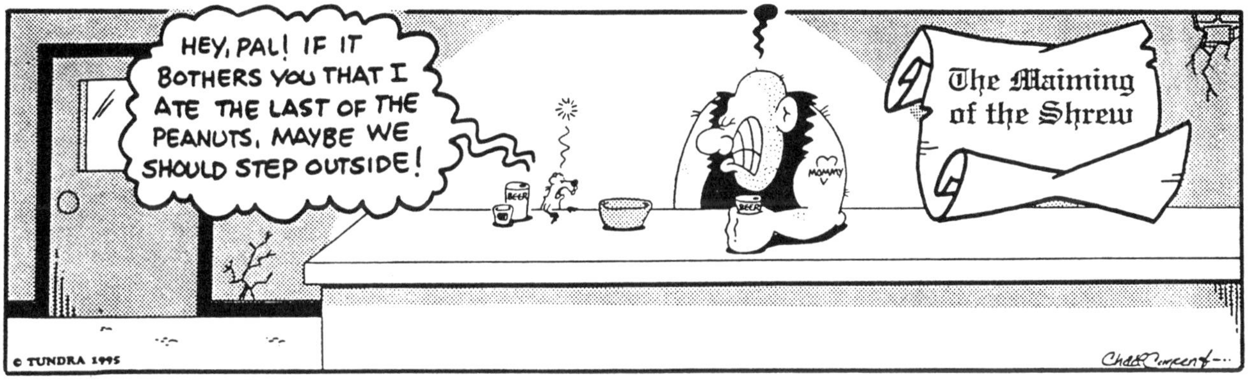
HEY, PAL! IF IT BOTHERS YOU THAT I ATE THE LAST OF THE PEANUTS, MAYBE WE SHOULD STEP OUTSIDE!
BEER
MOMMY
The Maiming of the Shrew
© TUNDRA 1995

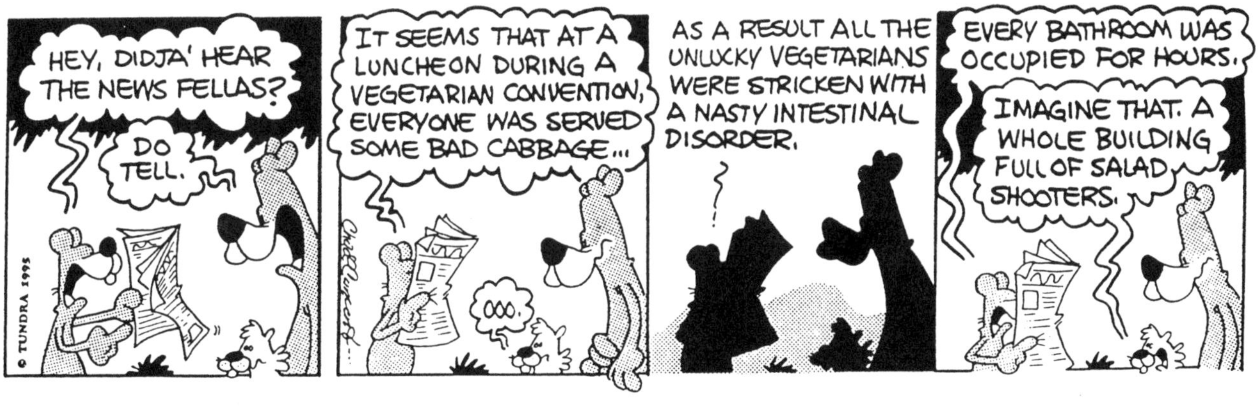
HEY, DIDJA' HEAR THE NEWS FELLAS?
DO TELL.
IT SEEMS THAT AT A LUNCHEON DURING A VEGETARIAN CONVENTION, EVERYONE WAS SERVED SOME BAD CABBAGE...
OOO.
AS A RESULT ALL THE UNLUCKY VEGETARIANS WERE STRICKEN WITH A NASTY INTESTINAL DISORDER.
EVERY BATHROOM WAS OCCUPIED FOR HOURS.
IMAGINE THAT. A WHOLE BUILDING FULL OF SALAD SHOOTERS.
© TUNDRA 1995

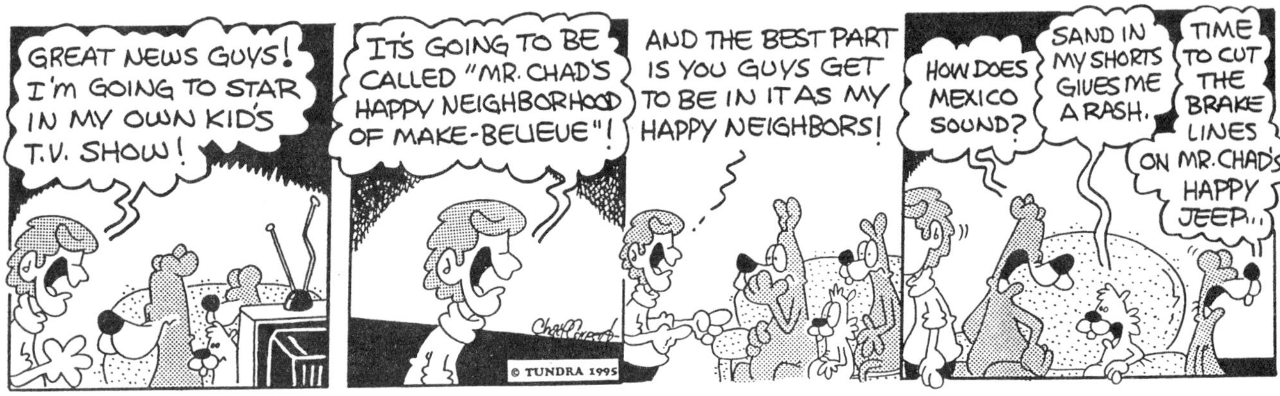
GREAT NEWS GUYS! I'M GOING TO STAR IN MY OWN KID'S T.V. SHOW!
IT'S GOING TO BE CALLED "MR. CHAD'S HAPPY NEIGHBORHOOD OF MAKE-BELIEVE"!
© TUNDRA 1995
AND THE BEST PART IS YOU GUYS GET TO BE IN IT AS MY HAPPY NEIGHBORS!
HOW DOES MEXICO SOUND?
SAND IN MY SHORTS GIVES ME A RASH.
TIME TO CUT THE BRAKE LINES ON MR. CHAD'S HAPPY JEEP...

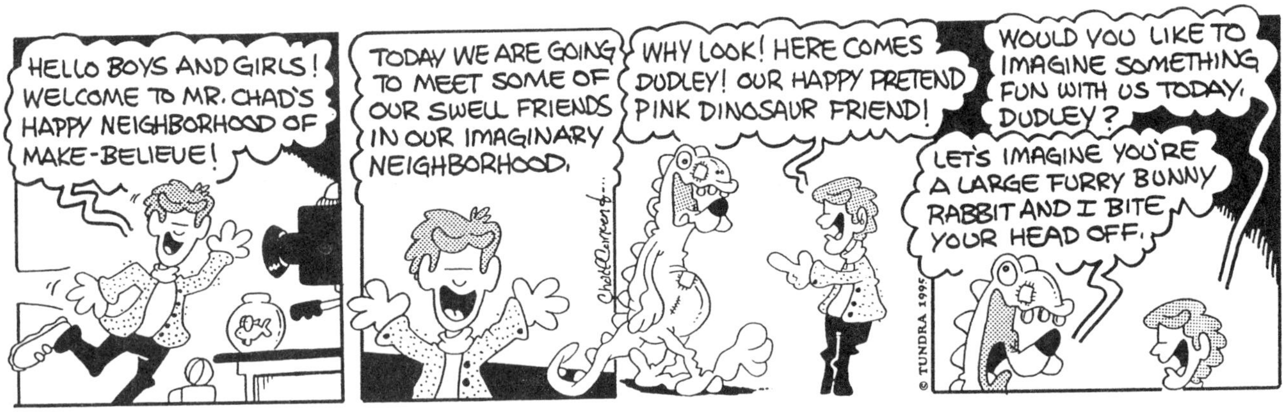
HELLO BOYS AND GIRLS! WELCOME TO MR. CHAD'S HAPPY NEIGHBORHOOD OF MAKE-BELIEVE!
TODAY WE ARE GOING TO MEET SOME OF OUR SWELL FRIENDS IN OUR IMAGINARY NEIGHBORHOOD.
WHY LOOK! HERE COMES DUDLEY! OUR HAPPY PRETEND PINK DINOSAUR FRIEND!
WOULD YOU LIKE TO IMAGINE SOMETHING FUN WITH US TODAY, DUDLEY?
LET'S IMAGINE YOU'RE A LARGE FURRY BUNNY RABBIT AND I BITE YOUR HEAD OFF.
© TUNDRA 1995

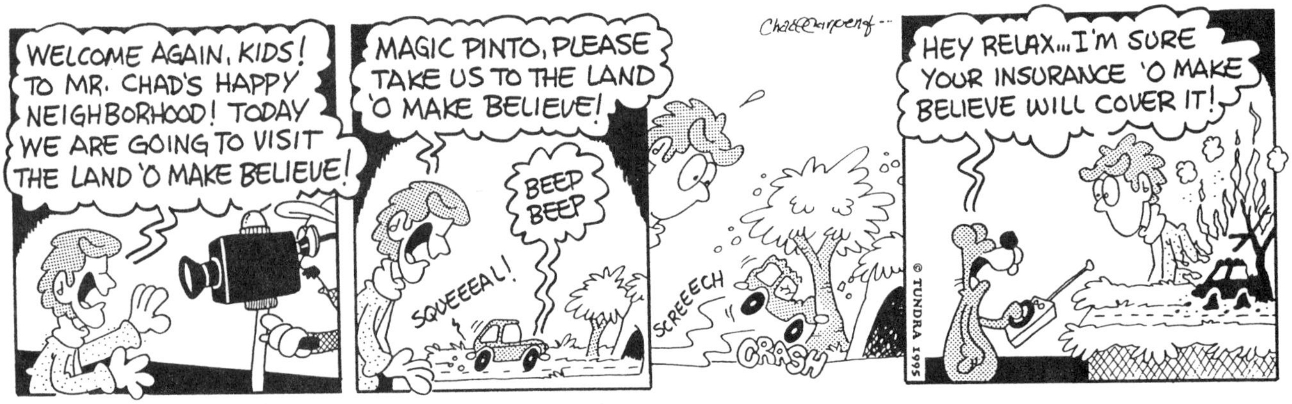
WELCOME AGAIN, KIDS! TO MR. CHAD'S HAPPY NEIGHBORHOOD! TODAY WE ARE GOING TO VISIT THE LAND 'O MAKE BELIEVE!
MAGIC PINTO, PLEASE TAKE US TO THE LAND 'O MAKE BELIEVE!
BEEP BEEP
SQUEEEAL!
SCREEECH
CRASH
HEY RELAX... I'M SURE YOUR INSURANCE 'O MAKE BELIEVE WILL COVER IT!
© TUNDRA 1995

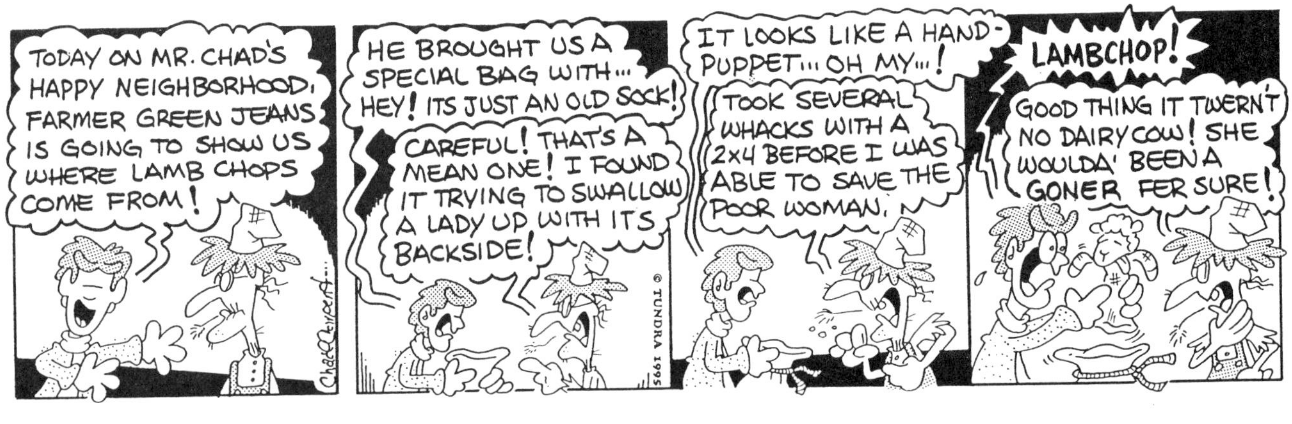
TODAY ON MR. CHAD'S HAPPY NEIGHBORHOOD, FARMER GREEN JEANS IS GOING TO SHOW US WHERE LAMB CHOPS COME FROM!
HE BROUGHT US A SPECIAL BAG WITH... HEY! ITS JUST AN OLD SOCK!
CAREFUL! THAT'S A MEAN ONE! I FOUND IT TRYING TO SWALLOW A LADY UP WITH ITS BACKSIDE!
© TUNDRA 1995
IT LOOKS LIKE A HAND-PUPPET... OH MY...!
TOOK SEVERAL WHACKS WITH A 2x4 BEFORE I WAS ABLE TO SAVE THE POOR WOMAN.
LAMBCHOP!
GOOD THING IT TWERN'T NO DAIRY COW! SHE WOULDA' BEEN A GONER FER SURE!

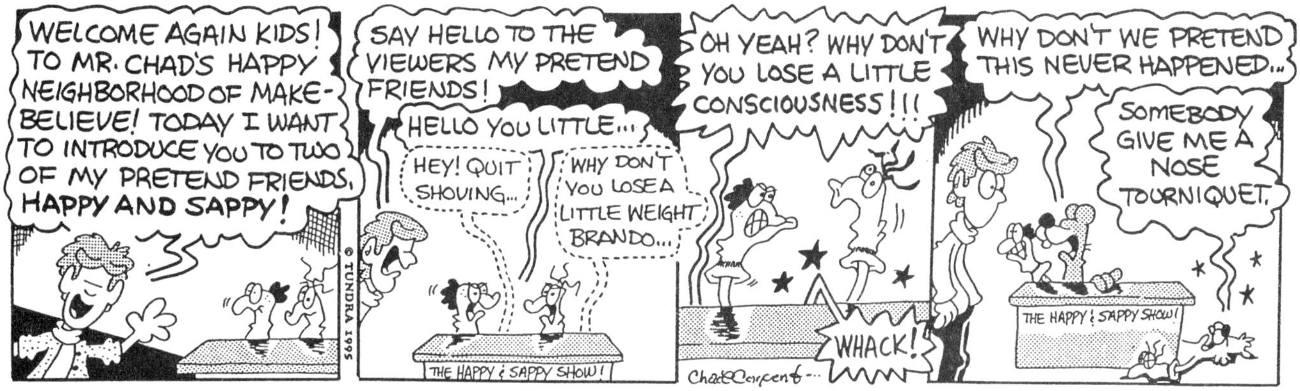
WELCOME AGAIN KIDS! TO MR. CHAD'S HAPPY NEIGHBORHOOD OF MAKE-BELIEVE! TODAY I WANT TO INTRODUCE YOU TO TWO OF MY PRETEND FRIENDS, HAPPY AND SAPPY!
© TUNDRA 1995
SAY HELLO TO THE VIEWERS MY PRETEND FRIENDS!
HELLO YOU LITTLE...
HEY! QUIT SHOVING...
WHY DON'T YOU LOSE A LITTLE WEIGHT BRANDO...
THE HAPPY & SAPPY SHOW!
OH YEAH? WHY DON'T YOU LOSE A LITTLE CONSCIOUSNESS!!!
WHACK!
WHY DON'T WE PRETEND THIS NEVER HAPPENED...
SOMEBODY GIVE ME A NOSE TOURNIQUET.
THE HAPPY & SAPPY SHOW!

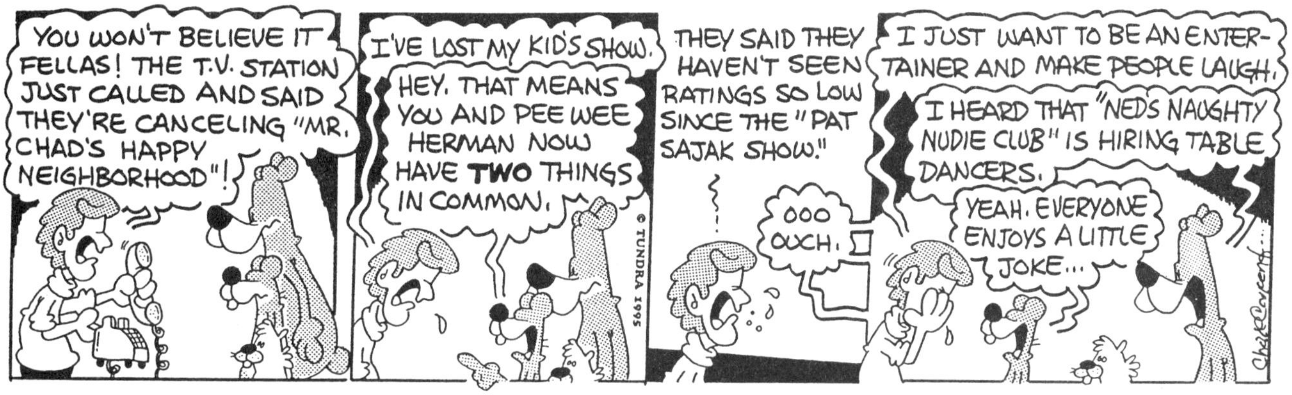
YOU WON'T BELIEVE IT FELLAS! THE T.V. STATION JUST CALLED AND SAID THEY'RE CANCELING "MR. CHAD'S HAPPY NEIGHBORHOOD"!
I'VE LOST MY KID'S SHOW.
HEY. THAT MEANS YOU AND PEE WEE HERMAN NOW HAVE TWO THINGS IN COMMON.
© TUNDRA 1995
THEY SAID THEY HAVEN'T SEEN RATINGS SO LOW SINCE THE "PAT SAJAK SHOW."
OOO OUCH.
I JUST WANT TO BE AN ENTERTAINER AND MAKE PEOPLE LAUGH.
I HEARD THAT "NED'S NAUGHTY NUDIE CLUB" IS HIRING TABLE DANCERS.
YEAH. EVERYONE ENJOYS A LITTLE JOKE...

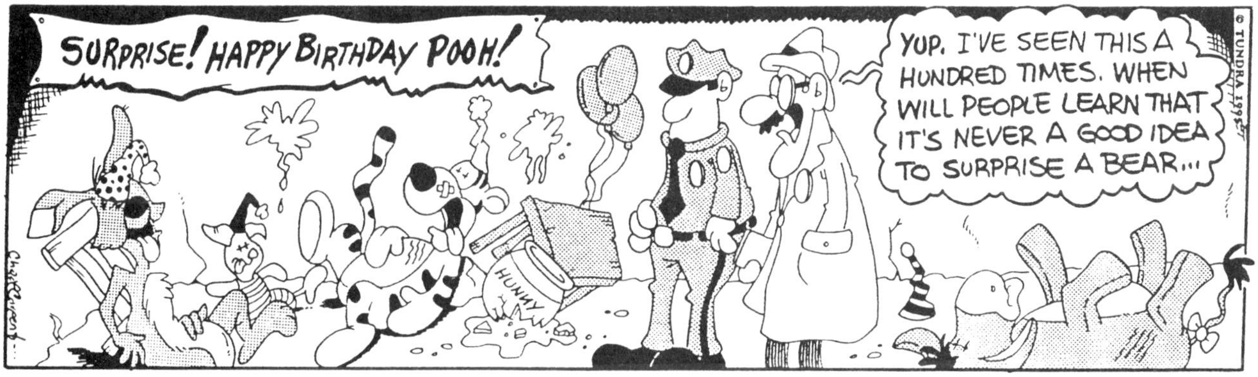
SURPRISE! HAPPY BIRTHDAY POOH!
YUP. I'VE SEEN THIS A HUNDRED TIMES. WHEN WILL PEOPLE LEARN THAT IT'S NEVER A GOOD IDEA TO SURPRISE A BEAR...
HUNNY
© TUNDRA 1995

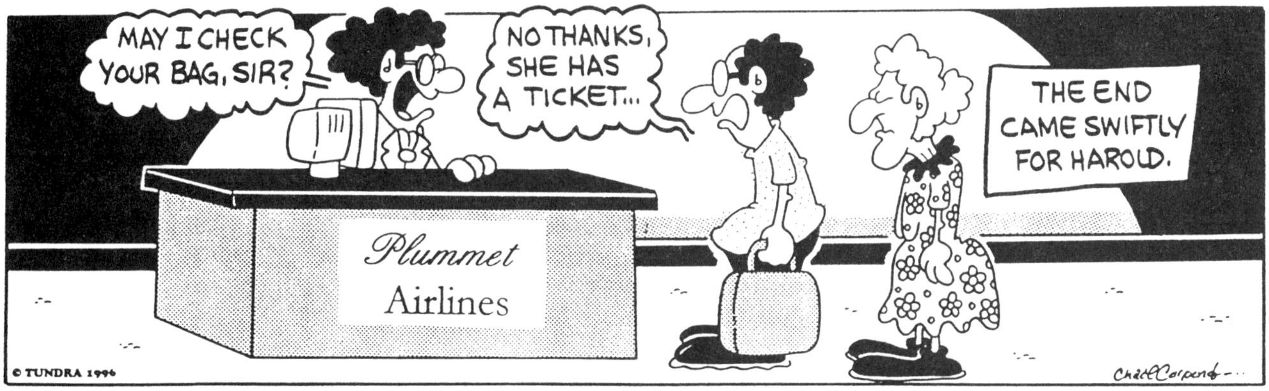
MAY I CHECK YOUR BAG, SIR?
NO THANKS, SHE HAS A TICKET...
THE END CAME SWIFTLY FOR HAROLD.
Plummet Airlines
© TUNDRA 1994

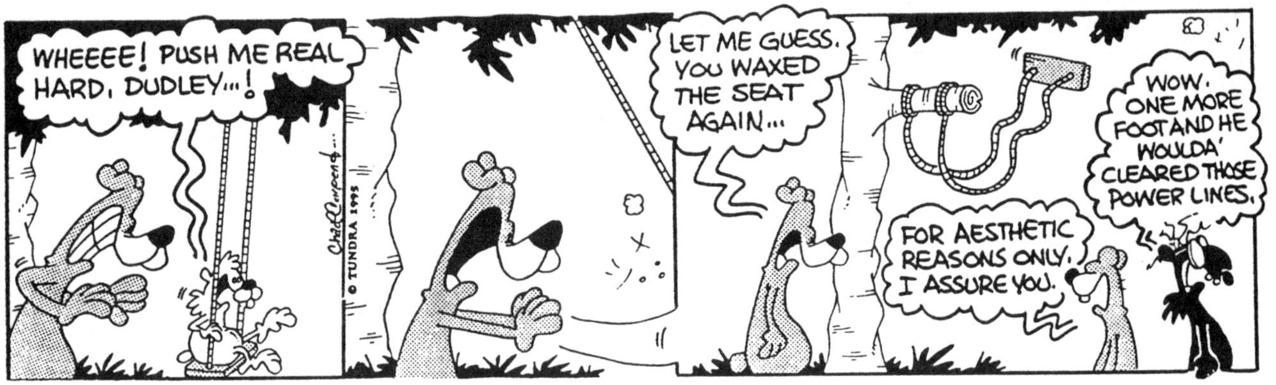
WHEEEE! PUSH ME REAL HARD, DUDLEY...!
© TUNDRA 1995
LET ME GUESS. YOU WAXED THE SEAT AGAIN...
WOW. ONE MORE FOOT AND HE WOULDA' CLEARED THOSE POWER LINES.
FOR AESTHETIC REASONS ONLY, I ASSURE YOU.

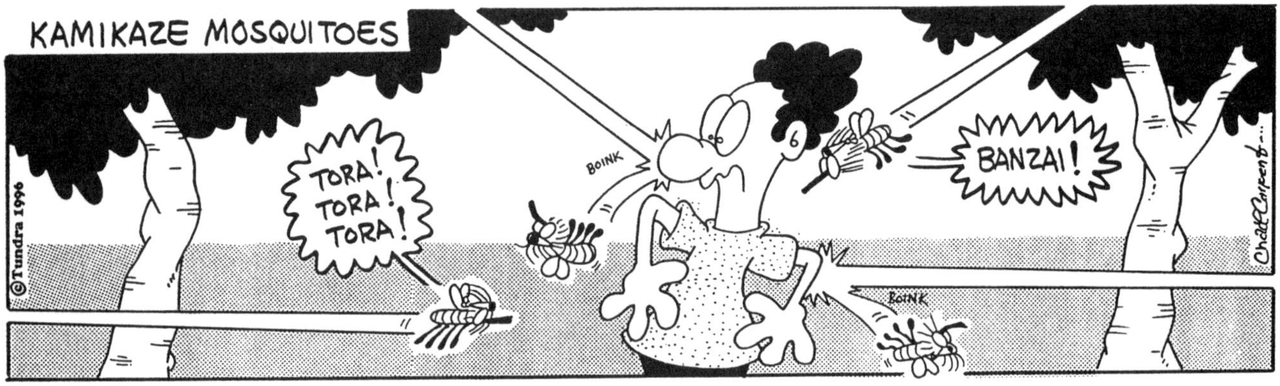
KAMIKAZE MOSQUITOES
©Tundra 1996
TORA! TORA! TORA!
BOINK
BANZAI!
BOINK

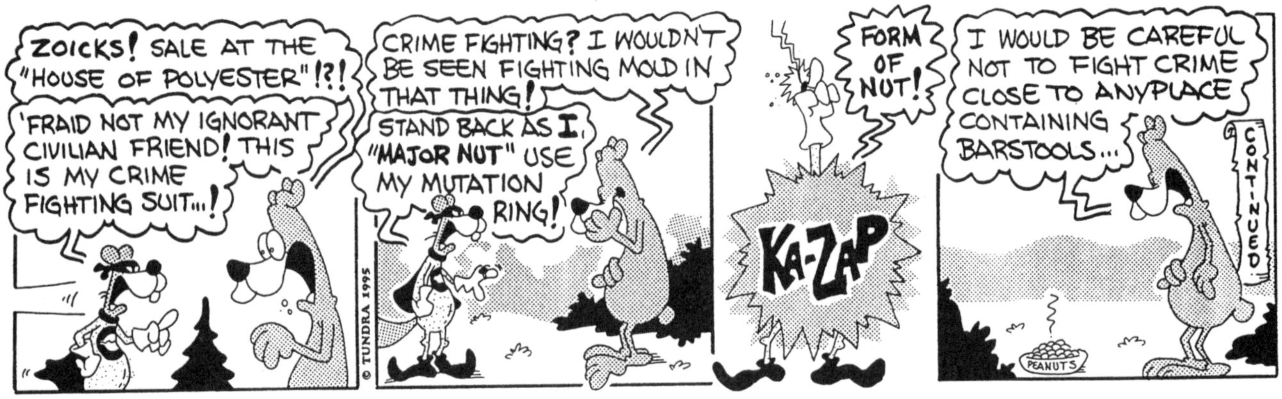
ZOICKS! SALE AT THE "HOUSE OF POLYESTER"!?!
'FRAID NOT MY IGNORANT CIVILIAN FRIEND! THIS IS MY CRIME FIGHTING SUIT...!
CRIME FIGHTING? I WOULDN'T BE SEEN FIGHTING MOLD IN THAT THING!
STAND BACK AS I, "MAJOR NUT" USE MY MUTATION RING!
© TUNDRA 1995
FORM OF NUT!
KA-ZAP
I WOULD BE CAREFUL NOT TO FIGHT CRIME CLOSE TO ANYPLACE CONTAINING BARSTOOLS...
PEANUTS
CONTINUED

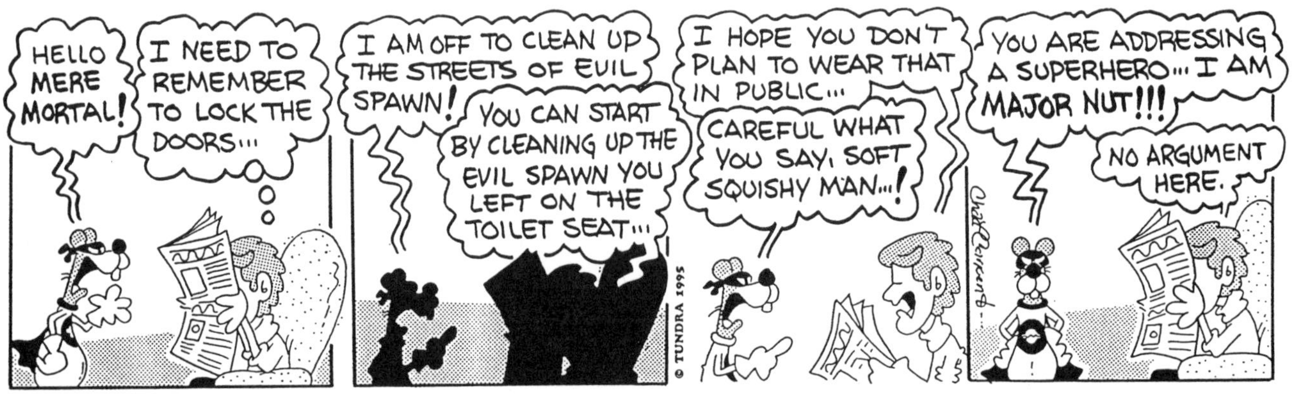
HELLO MERE MORTAL!
I NEED TO REMEMBER TO LOCK THE DOORS...
I AM OFF TO CLEAN UP THE STREETS OF EVIL SPAWN!
YOU CAN START BY CLEANING UP THE EVIL SPAWN YOU LEFT ON THE TOILET SEAT...
© TUNDRA 1995
I HOPE YOU DON'T PLAN TO WEAR THAT IN PUBLIC...
CAREFUL WHAT YOU SAY, SOFT SQUISHY MAN...!
YOU ARE ADDRESSING A SUPERHERO... I AM MAJOR NUT!!!
NO ARGUMENT HERE.

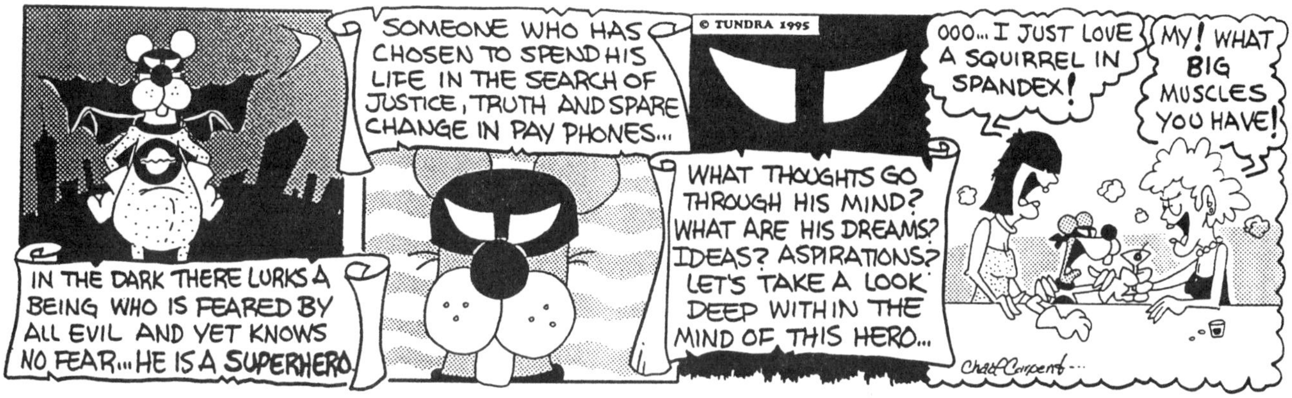
IN THE DARK THERE LURKS A BEING WHO IS FEARED BY ALL EVIL AND YET KNOWS NO FEAR... HE IS A SUPERHERO
SOMEONE WHO HAS CHOSEN TO SPEND HIS LIFE IN THE SEARCH OF JUSTICE, TRUTH AND SPARE CHANGE IN PAY PHONES...
© TUNDRA 1995
WHAT THOUGHTS GO THROUGH HIS MIND? WHAT ARE HIS DREAMS? IDEAS? ASPIRATIONS? LET'S TAKE A LOOK DEEP WITHIN THE MIND OF THIS HERO...
OOO... I JUST LOVE A SQUIRREL IN SPANDEX!
MY! WHAT BIG MUSCLES YOU HAVE!

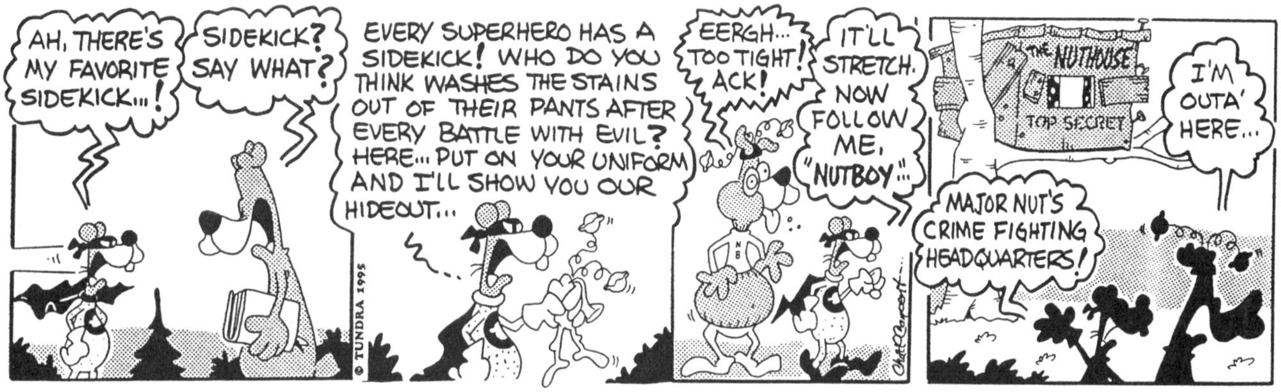
AH, THERE'S MY FAVORITE SIDEKICK...!
SIDEKICK? SAY WHAT?
EVERY SUPERHERO HAS A SIDEKICK! WHO DO YOU THINK WASHES THE STAINS OUT OF THEIR PANTS AFTER EVERY BATTLE WITH EVIL? HERE... PUT ON YOUR UNIFORM AND I'LL SHOW YOU OUR HIDEOUT...
© TUNDRA 1995
EERGH... TOO TIGHT! ACK!
IT'LL STRETCH. NOW FOLLOW ME, "NUTBOY"...
THE NUTHOUSE
TOP SECRET
I'M OUTA' HERE...
MAJOR NUT'S CRIME FIGHTING HEADQUARTERS!

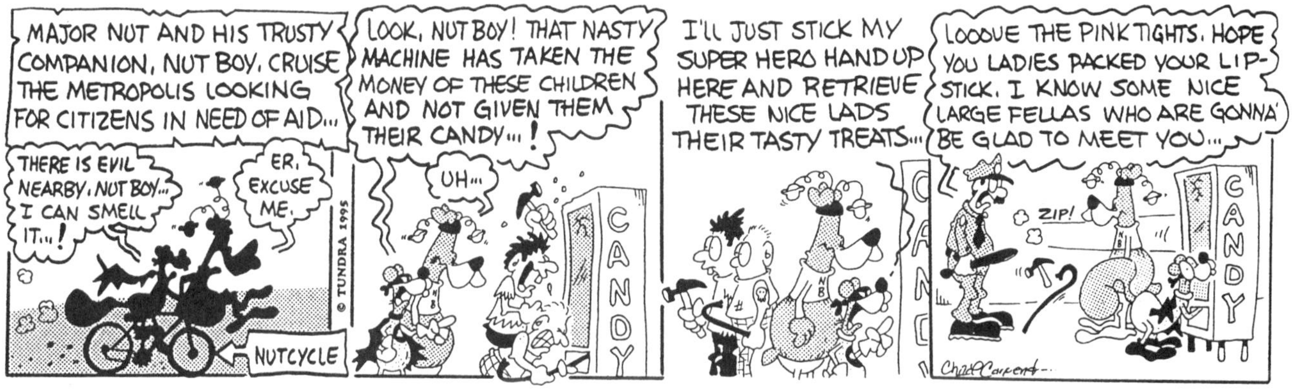
MAJOR NUT AND HIS TRUSTY COMPANION, NUT BOY, CRUISE THE METROPOLIS LOOKING FOR CITIZENS IN NEED OF AID...
THERE IS EVIL NEARBY, NUT BOY... I CAN SMELL IT...!
ER, EXCUSE ME.
NUTCYCLE
© TUNDRA 1995
LOOK, NUT BOY! THAT NASTY MACHINE HAS TAKEN THE MONEY OF THESE CHILDREN AND NOT GIVEN THEM THEIR CANDY...!
UH...
CANDY
I'LL JUST STICK MY SUPER HERO HAND UP HERE AND RETRIEVE THESE NICE LADS THEIR TASTY TREATS...
LOOOVE THE PINK TIGHTS. HOPE YOU LADIES PACKED YOUR LIPSTICK. I KNOW SOME NICE LARGE FELLAS WHO ARE GONNA' BE GLAD TO MEET YOU...
ZIP!
CANDY

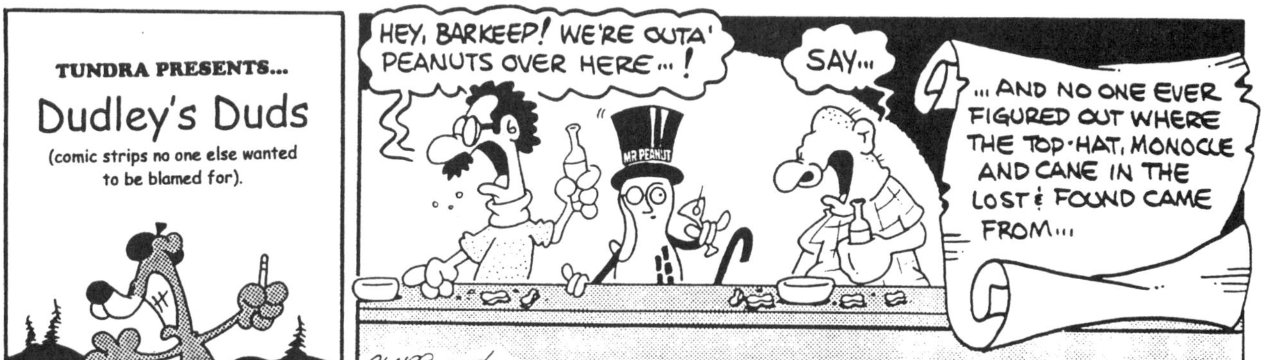
TUNDRA PRESENTS...
Dudley's Duds
(comic strips no one else wanted to be blamed for).
HEY, BARKEEP! WE'RE OUTA' PEANUTS OVER HERE...!
SAY...
MR PEANUT
... AND NO ONE EVER FIGURED OUT WHERE THE TOP-HAT, MONOCLE AND CANE IN THE LOST & FOUND CAME FROM...
©Tundra 1996

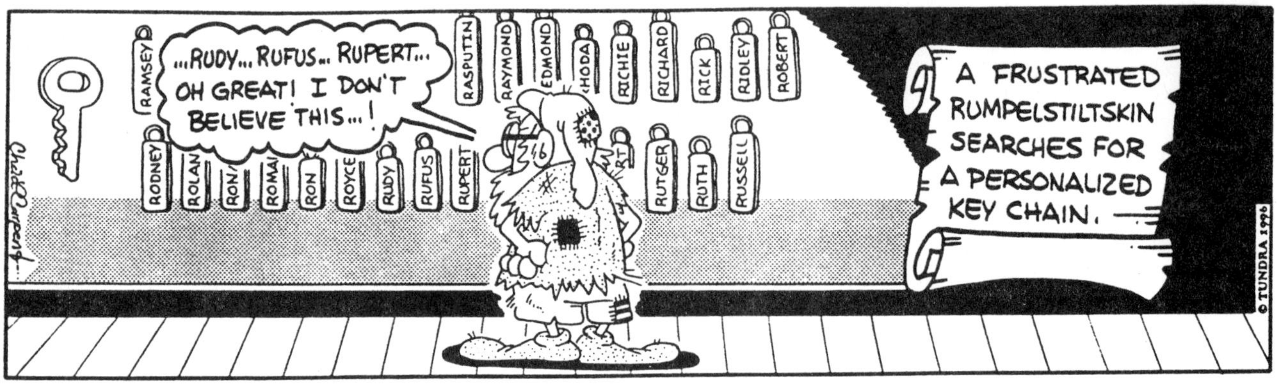
A FRUSTRATED RUMPELSTILTSKIN SEARCHES FOR A PERSONALIZED KEY CHAIN.
...RUDY... RUFUS... RUPERT... OH GREAT! I DON'T BELIEVE THIS...!
RAMSEY
RASPUTIN
RAYMOND
EDMOND
HODA
RICHIE
RICHARD
RICK
RIDLEY
ROBERT
RODNEY
RON
ROYCE
RUDY
RUFUS
RUPERT
RUTGER
RUTH
RUSSELL
© TUNDRA 1996

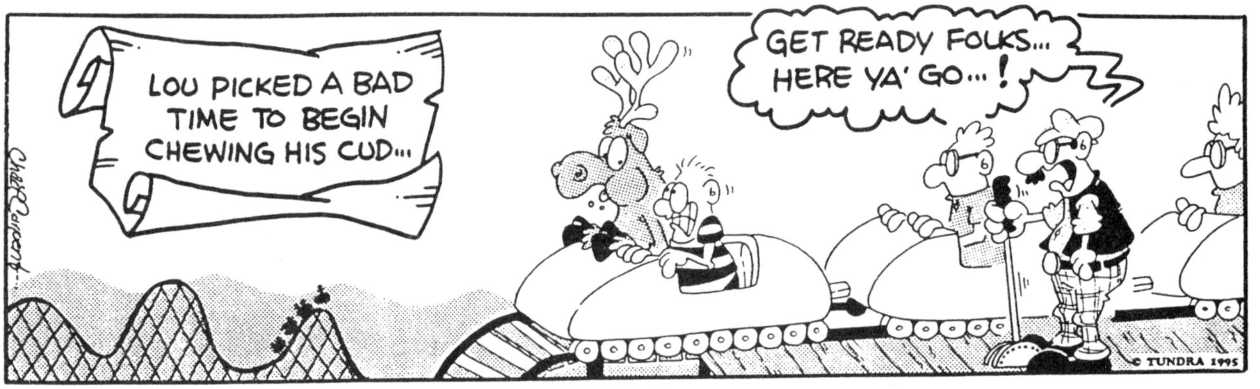
LOU PICKED A BAD TIME TO BEGIN CHEWING HIS CUD...
GET READY FOLKS... HERE YA' GO...!
© TUNDRA 1995

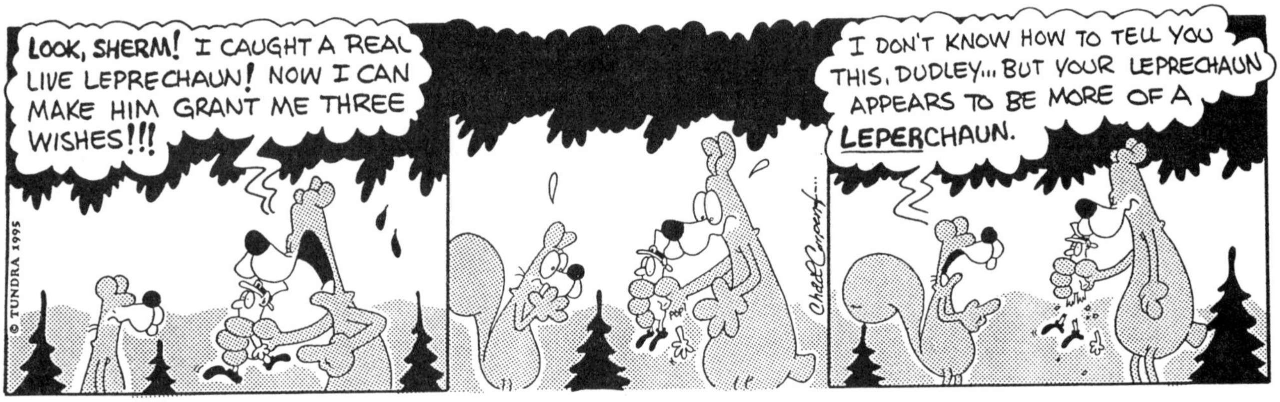
LOOK, SHERM! I CAUGHT A REAL LIVE LEPRECHAUN! NOW I CAN MAKE HIM GRANT ME THREE WISHES!!!
I DON'T KNOW HOW TO TELL YOU THIS, DUDLEY... BUT YOUR LEPRECHAUN APPEARS TO BE MORE OF A LEPERCHAUN.
© TUNDRA 1995

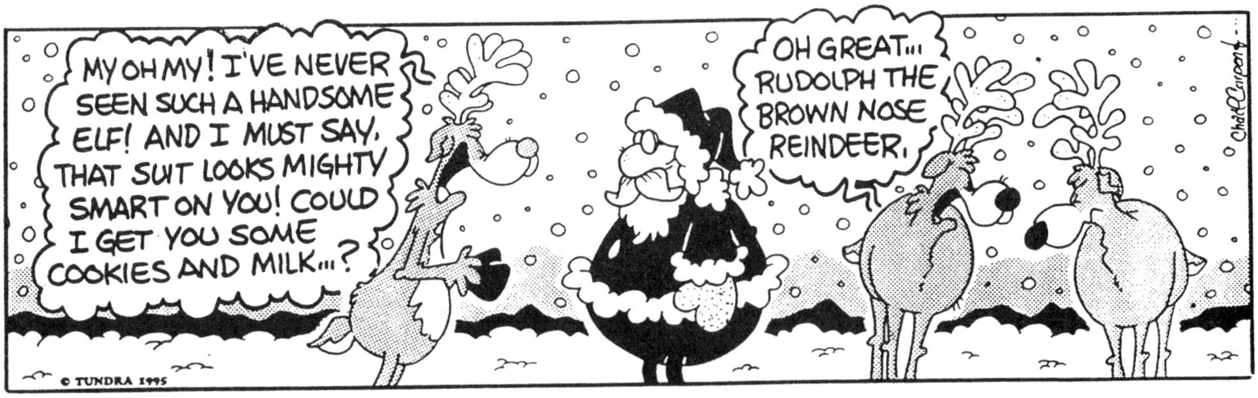
MY OH MY! I'VE NEVER SEEN SUCH A HANDSOME ELF! AND I MUST SAY, THAT SUIT LOOKS MIGHTY SMART ON YOU! COULD I GET YOU SOME COOKIES AND MILK...?
OH GREAT... RUDOLPH THE BROWN NOSE REINDEER.
© TUNDRA 1995

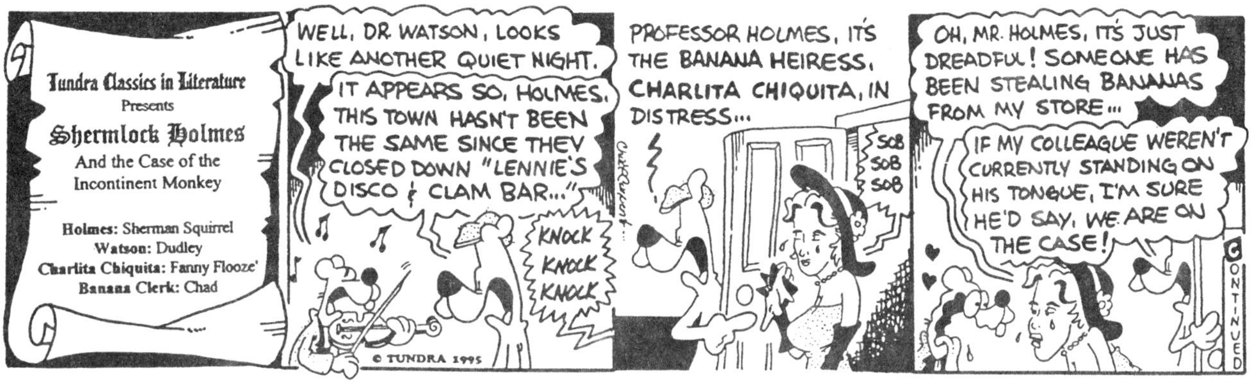

Tundra Classics in Literature
Presents
Shermlock Holmes
And the Case of the
Incontinent Monkey
Holmes: Sherman Squirrel
Watson: Dudley
Charlita Chiquita: Fanny Flooze'
Banana Clerk: Chad
WELL, DR. WATSON, LOOKS LIKE ANOTHER QUIET NIGHT.
IT APPEARS SO, HOLMES. THIS TOWN HASN'T BEEN THE SAME SINCE THEY CLOSED DOWN "LENNIE'S DISCO & CLAM BAR..."
KNOCK KNOCK KNOCK
© TUNDRA 1995
PROFESSOR HOLMES, IT'S THE BANANA HEIRESS, CHARLITA CHIQUITA, IN DISTRESS...
SOB SOB SOB
OH, MR. HOLMES, IT'S JUST DREADFUL! SOMEONE HAS BEEN STEALING BANANAS FROM MY STORE...
IF MY COLLEAGUE WEREN'T CURRENTLY STANDING ON HIS TONGUE, I'M SURE HE'D SAY, WE ARE ON THE CASE!
CONTINUED

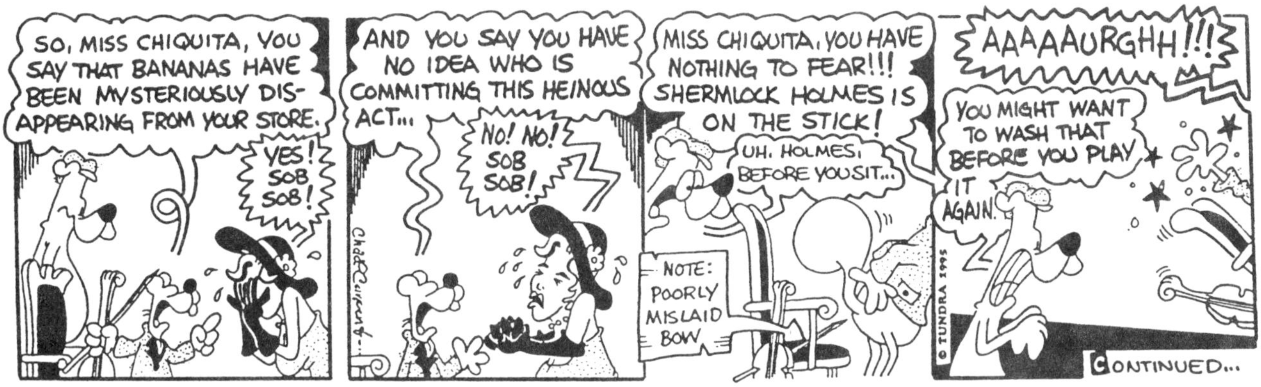

SO, MISS CHIQUITA, YOU SAY THAT BANANAS HAVE BEEN MYSTERIOUSLY DIS-APPEARING FROM YOUR STORE.
YES! SOB SOB!
AND YOU SAY YOU HAVE NO IDEA WHO IS COMMITTING THIS HEINOUS ACT...
NO! NO! SOB SOB!
MISS CHIQUITA, YOU HAVE NOTHING TO FEAR!!! SHERMLOCK HOLMES IS ON THE STICK!
UH, HOLMES, BEFORE YOU SIT...
NOTE: POORLY MISLAID BOW
© TUNDRA 1995
AAAAAURGHH!!!
YOU MIGHT WANT TO WASH THAT BEFORE YOU PLAY IT AGAIN.
CONTINUED...

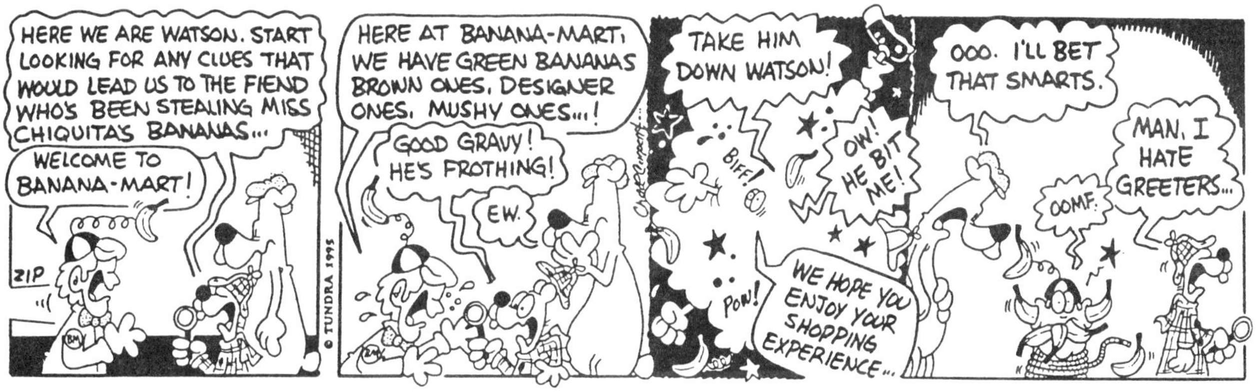

HERE WE ARE WATSON. START LOOKING FOR ANY CLUES THAT WOULD LEAD US TO THE FIEND WHO'S BEEN STEALING MISS CHIQUITA'S BANANAS...
WELCOME TO BANANA-MART!
ZIP
© TUNDRA 1995
HERE AT BANANA-MART, WE HAVE GREEN BANANAS BROWN ONES, DESIGNER ONES, MUSHY ONES...!
GOOD GRAVY! HE'S FROTHING!
EW.
TAKE HIM DOWN WATSON!
BIFF!
OW! HE BIT ME!
POW!
WE HOPE YOU ENJOY YOUR SHOPPING EXPERIENCE...
OOO. I'LL BET THAT SMARTS.
OOMF.
MAN, I HATE GREETERS...

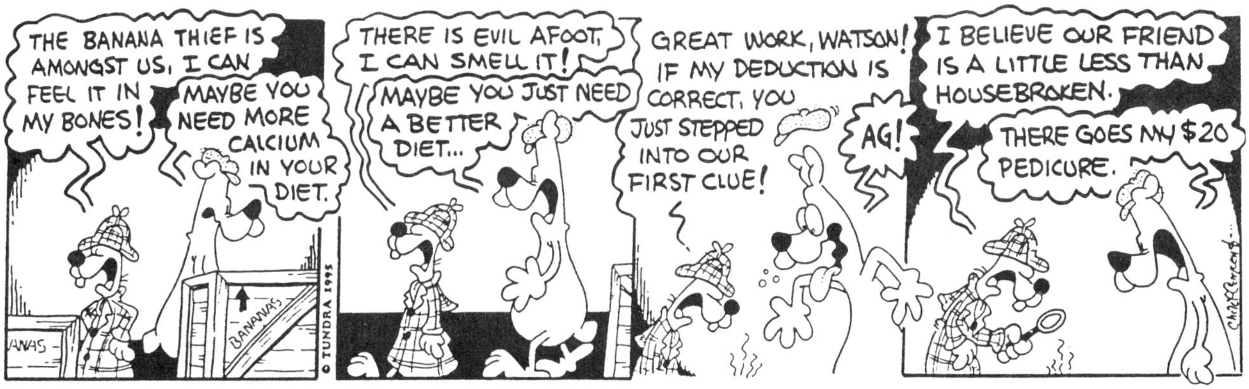

THE BANANA THIEF IS AMONGST US, I CAN FEEL IT IN MY BONES!
MAYBE YOU NEED MORE CALCIUM IN YOUR DIET.
BANANAS
© TUNDRA 1995
THERE IS EVIL AFOOT, I CAN SMELL IT!
MAYBE YOU JUST NEED A BETTER DIET...
GREAT WORK, WATSON! IF MY DEDUCTION IS CORRECT, YOU JUST STEPPED INTO OUR FIRST CLUE!
AG!
I BELIEVE OUR FRIEND IS A LITTLE LESS THAN HOUSEBROKEN.
THERE GOES MY $20 PEDICURE.

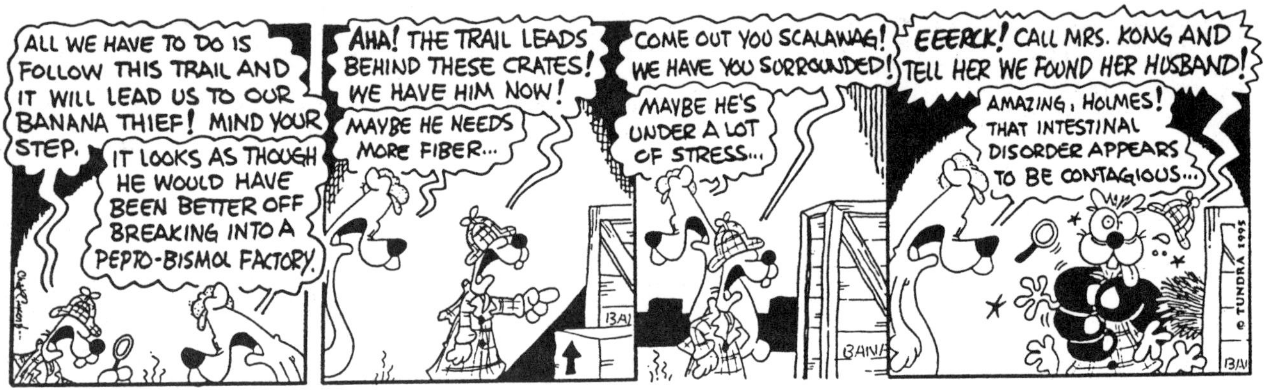
ALL WE HAVE TO DO IS FOLLOW THIS TRAIL AND IT WILL LEAD US TO OUR BANANA THIEF! MIND YOUR STEP.
IT LOOKS AS THOUGH HE WOULD HAVE BEEN BETTER OFF BREAKING INTO A PEPTO-BISMOL FACTORY.
AHA! THE TRAIL LEADS BEHIND THESE CRATES! WE HAVE HIM NOW!
MAYBE HE NEEDS MORE FIBER...
COME OUT YOU SCALAWAG! WE HAVE YOU SURROUNDED!
MAYBE HE'S UNDER A LOT OF STRESS...
EEERCK! CALL MRS. KONG AND TELL HER WE FOUND HER HUSBAND!
AMAZING, HOLMES! THAT INTESTINAL DISORDER APPEARS TO BE CONTAGIOUS...
© TUNDRA 1995

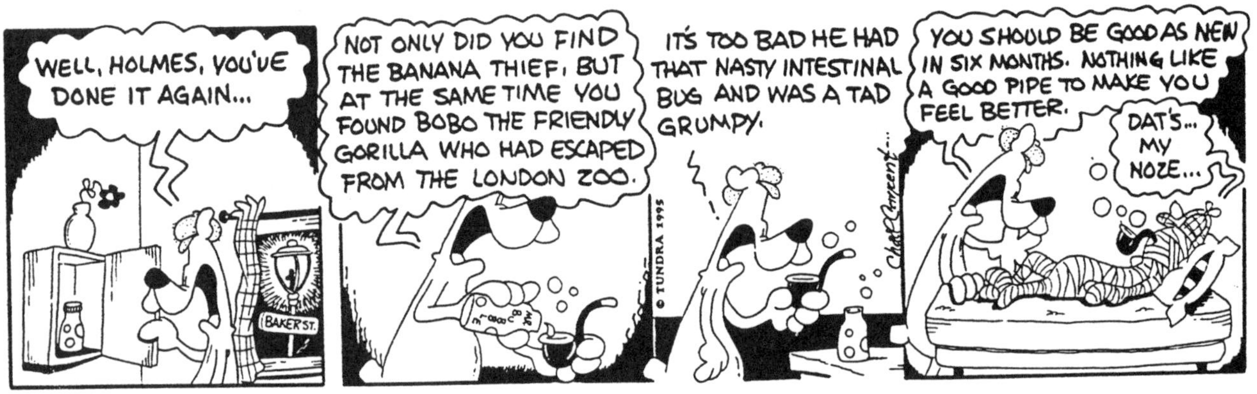
WELL, HOLMES, YOU'VE DONE IT AGAIN...
BAKER ST.
NOT ONLY DID YOU FIND THE BANANA THIEF, BUT AT THE SAME TIME YOU FOUND BOBO THE FRIENDLY GORILLA WHO HAD ESCAPED FROM THE LONDON ZOO.
© TUNDRA 1995
IT'S TOO BAD HE HAD THAT NASTY INTESTINAL BUG AND WAS A TAD GRUMPY.
YOU SHOULD BE GOOD AS NEW IN SIX MONTHS. NOTHING LIKE A GOOD PIPE TO MAKE YOU FEEL BETTER.
DAT'S... MY NOZE...

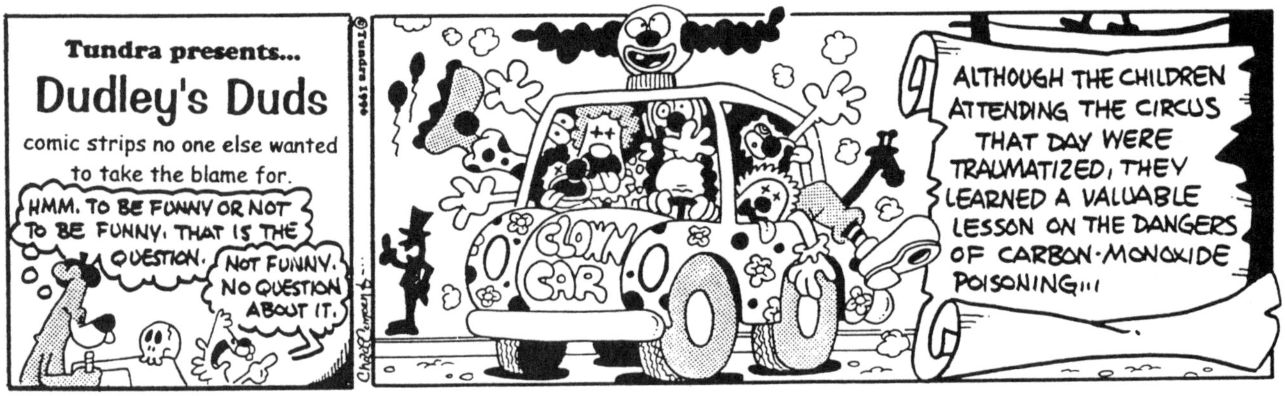
Tundra presents...
Dudley's Duds
comic strips no one else wanted to take the blame for.
HMM. TO BE FUNNY OR NOT TO BE FUNNY. THAT IS THE QUESTION.
NOT FUNNY. NO QUESTION ABOUT IT.
© Tundra 1996
CLOWN CAR
ALTHOUGH THE CHILDREN ATTENDING THE CIRCUS THAT DAY WERE TRAUMATIZED, THEY LEARNED A VALUABLE LESSON ON THE DANGERS OF CARBON-MONOXIDE POISONING...

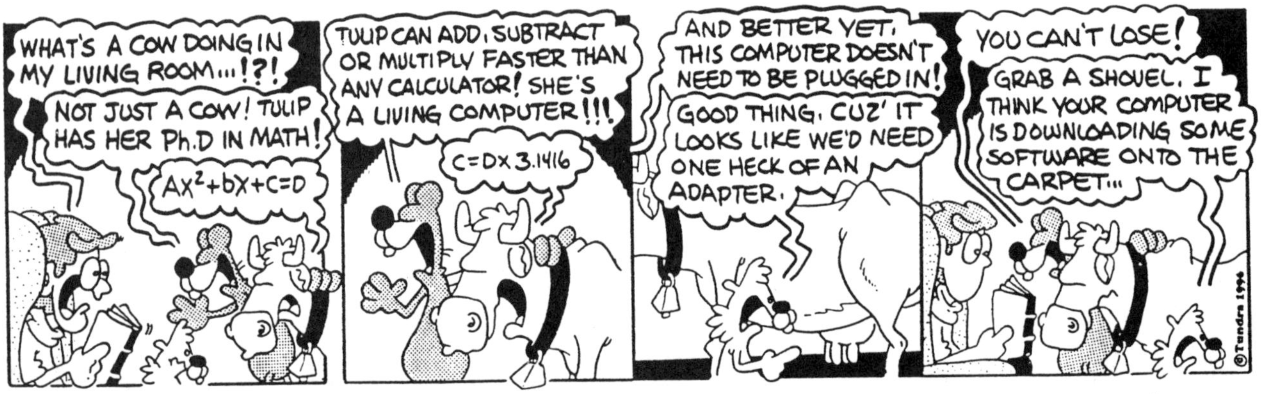
WHAT'S A COW DOING IN MY LIVING ROOM...!?!
NOT JUST A COW! TULIP HAS HER Ph.D IN MATH!
AX²+BX+C=D
TULIP CAN ADD, SUBTRACT OR MULTIPLY FASTER THAN ANY CALCULATOR! SHE'S A LIVING COMPUTER!!!
C=DX 3.1416
AND BETTER YET, THIS COMPUTER DOESN'T NEED TO BE PLUGGED IN!
GOOD THING, CUZ' IT LOOKS LIKE WE'D NEED ONE HECK OF AN ADAPTER.
YOU CAN'T LOSE!
GRAB A SHOVEL. I THINK YOUR COMPUTER IS DOWNLOADING SOME SOFTWARE ONTO THE CARPET...
© Tundra 1996

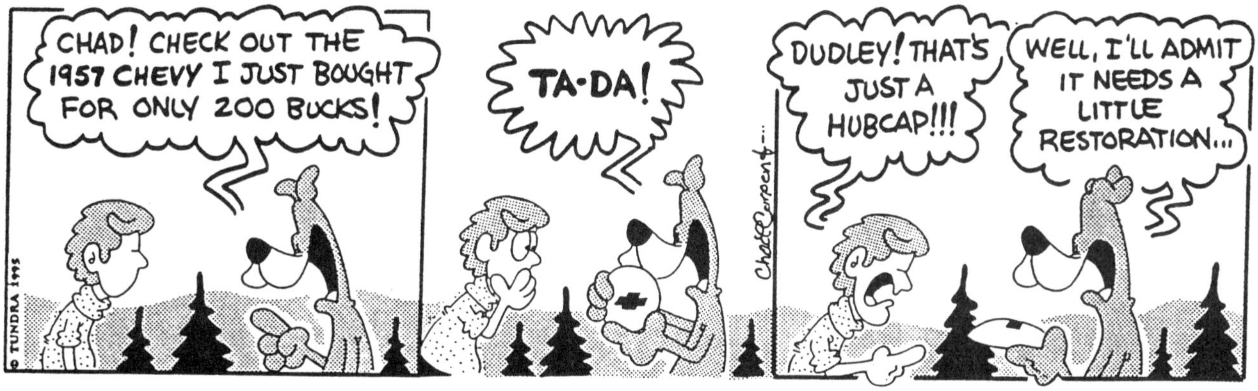
CHAD! CHECK OUT THE 1957 CHEVY I JUST BOUGHT FOR ONLY 200 BUCKS!
TA-DA!
DUDLEY! THAT'S JUST A HUBCAP!!!
WELL, I'LL ADMIT IT NEEDS A LITTLE RESTORATION...
© TUNDRA 1995

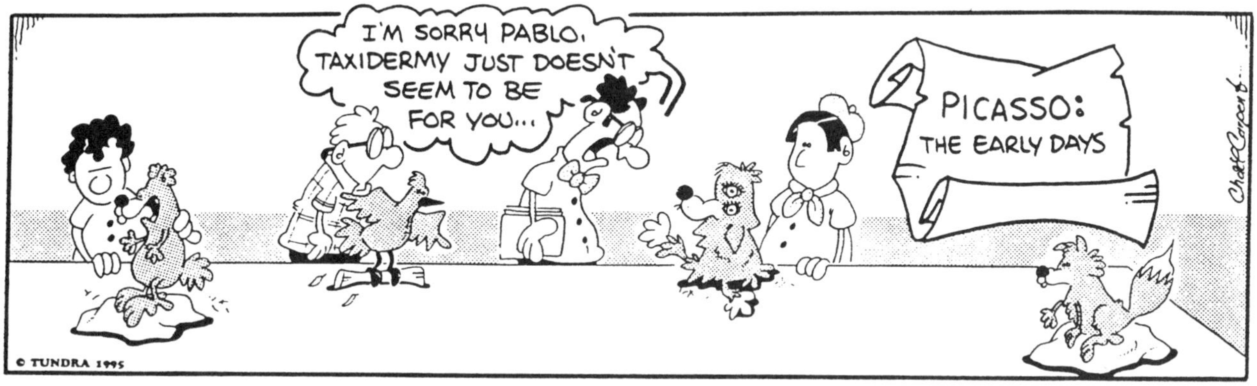
I'M SORRY PABLO, TAXIDERMY JUST DOESN'T SEEM TO BE FOR YOU...
PICASSO: THE EARLY DAYS
© TUNDRA 1995

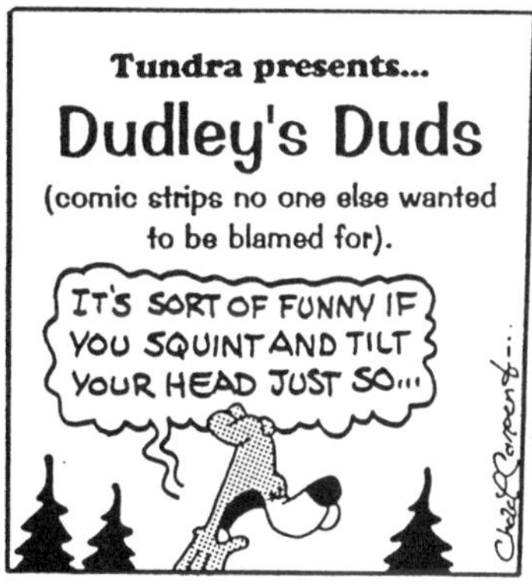
Tundra presents...
Dudley's Duds
(comic strips no one else wanted to be blamed for).
IT'S SORT OF FUNNY IF YOU SQUINT AND TILT YOUR HEAD JUST SO...

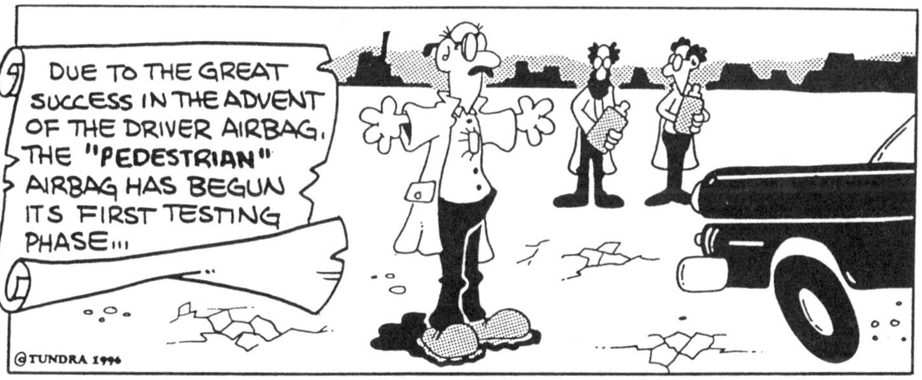
DUE TO THE GREAT SUCCESS IN THE ADVENT OF THE DRIVER AIRBAG, THE "PEDESTRIAN" AIRBAG HAS BEGUN ITS FIRST TESTING PHASE...
©TUNDRA 1996

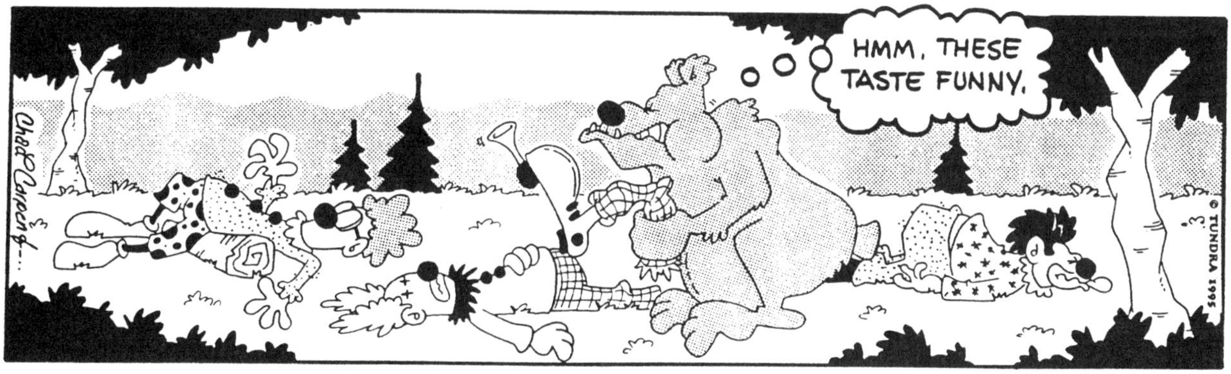
HMM, THESE TASTE FUNNY.
© TUNDRA 1995

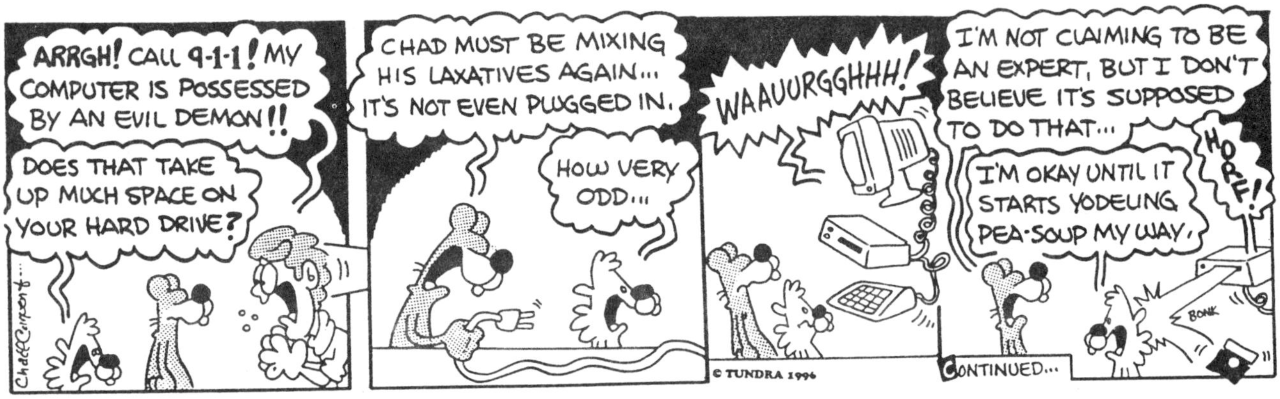
ARRGH! CALL 9-1-1! MY COMPUTER IS POSSESSED BY AN EVIL DEMON!!
DOES THAT TAKE UP MUCH SPACE ON YOUR HARD DRIVE?
CHAD MUST BE MIXING HIS LAXATIVES AGAIN... IT'S NOT EVEN PLUGGED IN.
HOW VERY ODD...
WAAUURGGHHH!
© TUNDRA 1996
I'M NOT CLAIMING TO BE AN EXPERT, BUT I DON'T BELIEVE IT'S SUPPOSED TO DO THAT...
I'M OKAY UNTIL IT STARTS YODELING PEA-SOUP MY WAY.
HORF!
BONK
CONTINUED...

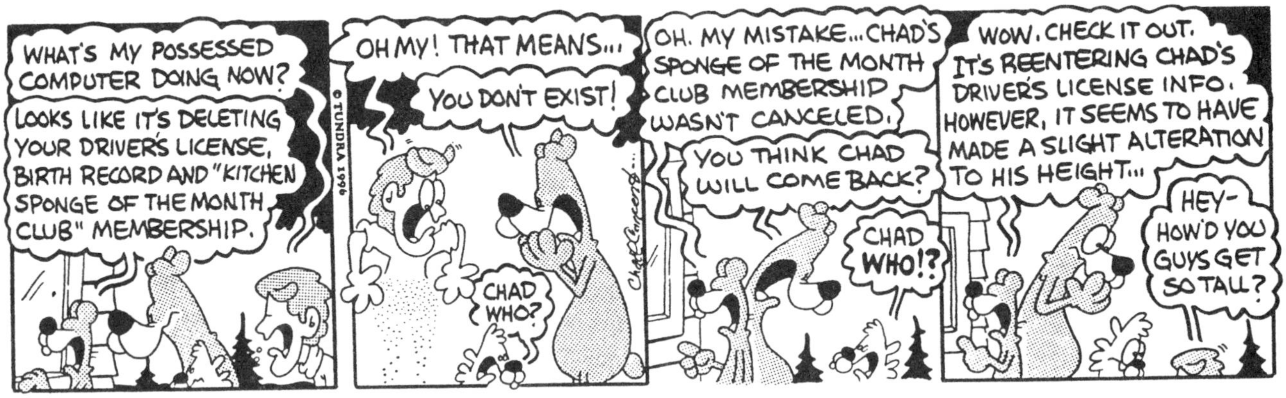
WHAT'S MY POSSESSED COMPUTER DOING NOW?
LOOKS LIKE IT'S DELETING YOUR DRIVER'S LICENSE, BIRTH RECORD AND "KITCHEN SPONGE OF THE MONTH CLUB" MEMBERSHIP.
© TUNDRA 1996
OH MY! THAT MEANS...
YOU DON'T EXIST!
CHAD WHO?
OH. MY MISTAKE...CHAD'S SPONGE OF THE MONTH CLUB MEMBERSHIP WASN'T CANCELED.
YOU THINK CHAD WILL COME BACK?
CHAD WHO!?
WOW. CHECK IT OUT. IT'S REENTERING CHAD'S DRIVER'S LICENSE INFO. HOWEVER, IT SEEMS TO HAVE MADE A SLIGHT ALTERATION TO HIS HEIGHT...
HEY- HOW'D YOU GUYS GET SO TALL?

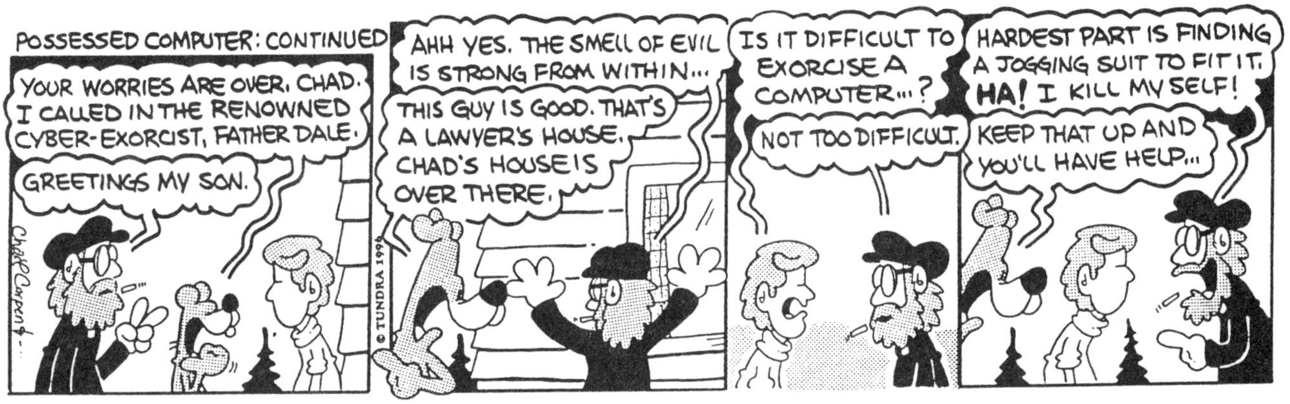
POSSESSED COMPUTER: CONTINUED
YOUR WORRIES ARE OVER, CHAD. I CALLED IN THE RENOWNED CYBER-EXORCIST, FATHER DALE.
GREETINGS MY SON.
AHH YES. THE SMELL OF EVIL IS STRONG FROM WITHIN...
THIS GUY IS GOOD. THAT'S A LAWYER'S HOUSE. CHAD'S HOUSE IS OVER THERE.
© TUNDRA 1996
IS IT DIFFICULT TO EXORCISE A COMPUTER...?
NOT TOO DIFFICULT.
HARDEST PART IS FINDING A JOGGING SUIT TO FIT IT. HA! I KILL MYSELF!
KEEP THAT UP AND YOU'LL HAVE HELP...

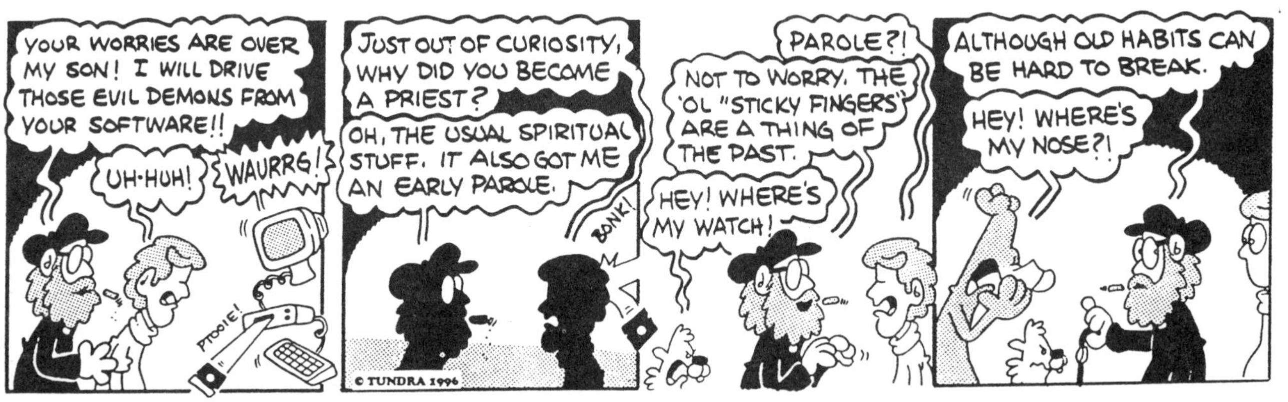
YOUR WORRIES ARE OVER MY SON! I WILL DRIVE THOSE EVIL DEMONS FROM YOUR SOFTWARE!!
UH-HUH!
WAURRG!
PTOOIE!
JUST OUT OF CURIOSITY, WHY DID YOU BECOME A PRIEST?
OH, THE USUAL SPIRITUAL STUFF. IT ALSO GOT ME AN EARLY PAROLE.
BONK!
© TUNDRA 1996
PAROLE?!
NOT TO WORRY. THE 'OL "STICKY FINGERS" ARE A THING OF THE PAST.
HEY! WHERE'S MY WATCH!
ALTHOUGH OLD HABITS CAN BE HARD TO BREAK.
HEY! WHERE'S MY NOSE?!

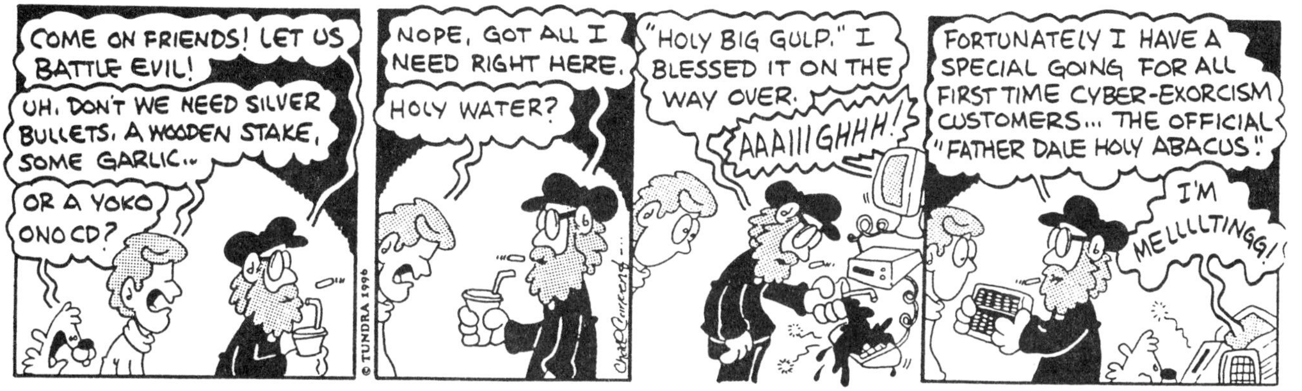
COME ON FRIENDS! LET US BATTLE EVIL!
UH, DON'T WE NEED SILVER BULLETS, A WOODEN STAKE, SOME GARLIC..
OR A YOKO ONO CD?
© TUNDRA 1996
NOPE, GOT ALL I NEED RIGHT HERE.
HOLY WATER?
"HOLY BIG GULP." I BLESSED IT ON THE WAY OVER.
AAAIIIGHHH!
FORTUNATELY I HAVE A SPECIAL GOING FOR ALL FIRST TIME CYBER-EXORCISM CUSTOMERS... THE OFFICIAL "FATHER DALE HOLY ABACUS."
I'M MELLLLTINGG!

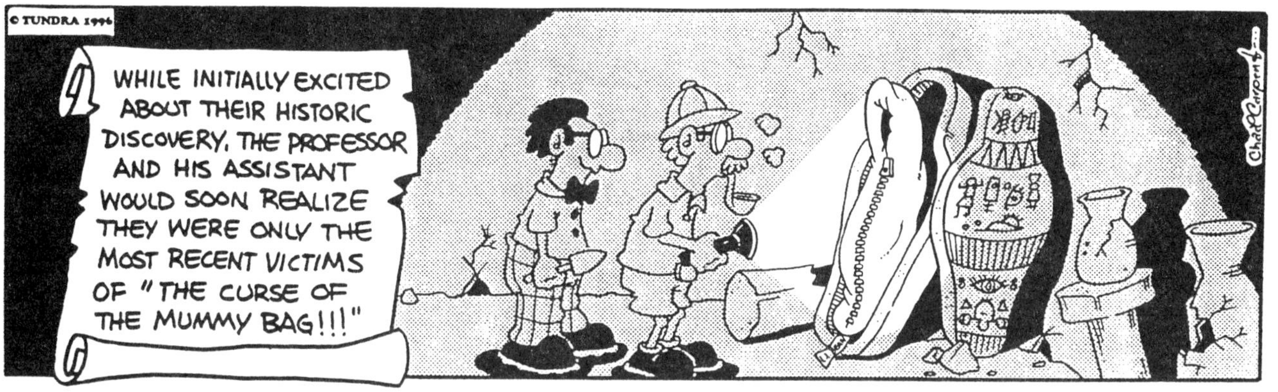
© TUNDRA 1996
WHILE INITIALLY EXCITED ABOUT THEIR HISTORIC DISCOVERY, THE PROFESSOR AND HIS ASSISTANT WOULD SOON REALIZE THEY WERE ONLY THE MOST RECENT VICTIMS OF "THE CURSE OF THE MUMMY BAG!!!"

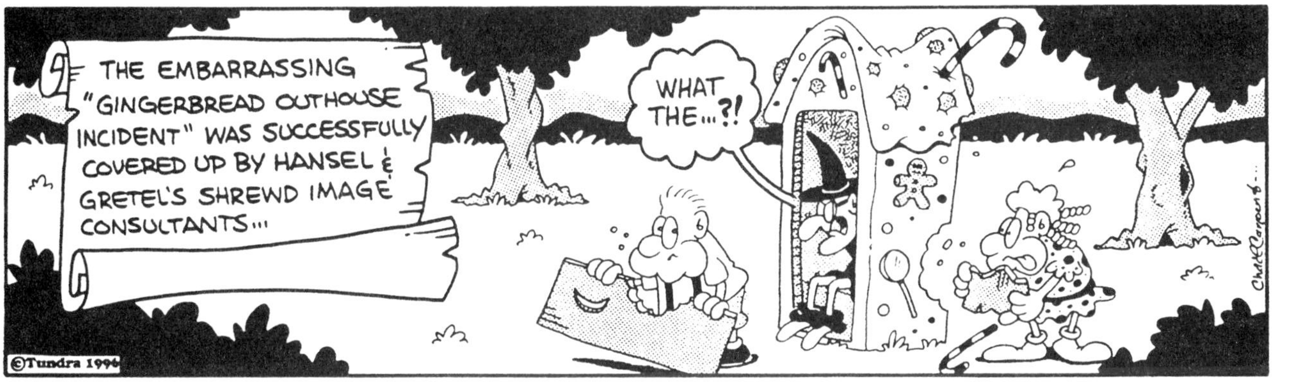
THE EMBARRASSING "GINGERBREAD OUTHOUSE INCIDENT" WAS SUCCESSFULLY COVERED UP BY HANSEL & GRETEL'S SHREWD IMAGE CONSULTANTS...
WHAT THE...?!
©Tundra 1996

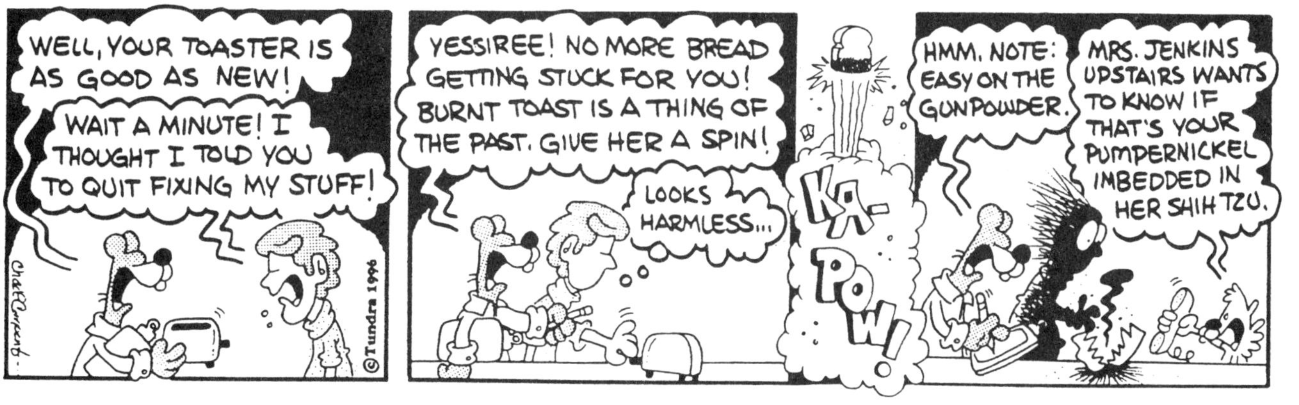
WELL, YOUR TOASTER IS AS GOOD AS NEW!
WAIT A MINUTE! I THOUGHT I TOLD YOU TO QUIT FIXING MY STUFF!
©Tundra 1996
YESSIREE! NO MORE BREAD GETTING STUCK FOR YOU! BURNT TOAST IS A THING OF THE PAST. GIVE HER A SPIN!
LOOKS HARMLESS...
KA-POW!
HMM. NOTE: EASY ON THE GUNPOWDER.
MRS. JENKINS UPSTAIRS WANTS TO KNOW IF THAT'S YOUR PUMPERNICKEL IMBEDDED IN HER SHIH TZU.

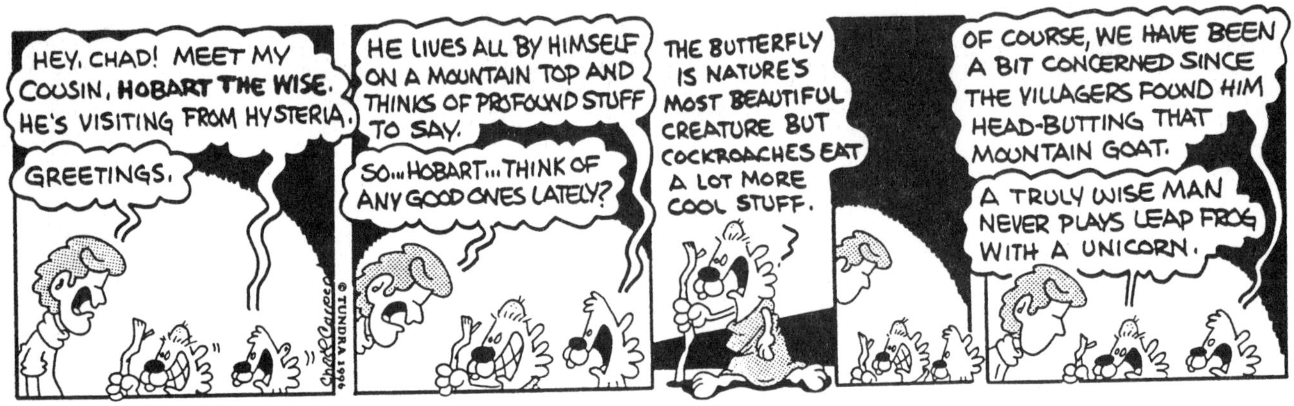
HEY, CHAD! MEET MY COUSIN, HOBART THE WISE. HE'S VISITING FROM HYSTERIA.
GREETINGS.
© TUNDRA 1996
HE LIVES ALL BY HIMSELF ON A MOUNTAIN TOP AND THINKS OF PROFOUND STUFF TO SAY.
SO... HOBART... THINK OF ANY GOOD ONES LATELY?
THE BUTTERFLY IS NATURE'S MOST BEAUTIFUL CREATURE BUT COCKROACHES EAT A LOT MORE COOL STUFF.
OF COURSE, WE HAVE BEEN A BIT CONCERNED SINCE THE VILLAGERS FOUND HIM HEAD-BUTTING THAT MOUNTAIN GOAT.
A TRULY WISE MAN NEVER PLAYS LEAP FROG WITH A UNICORN.

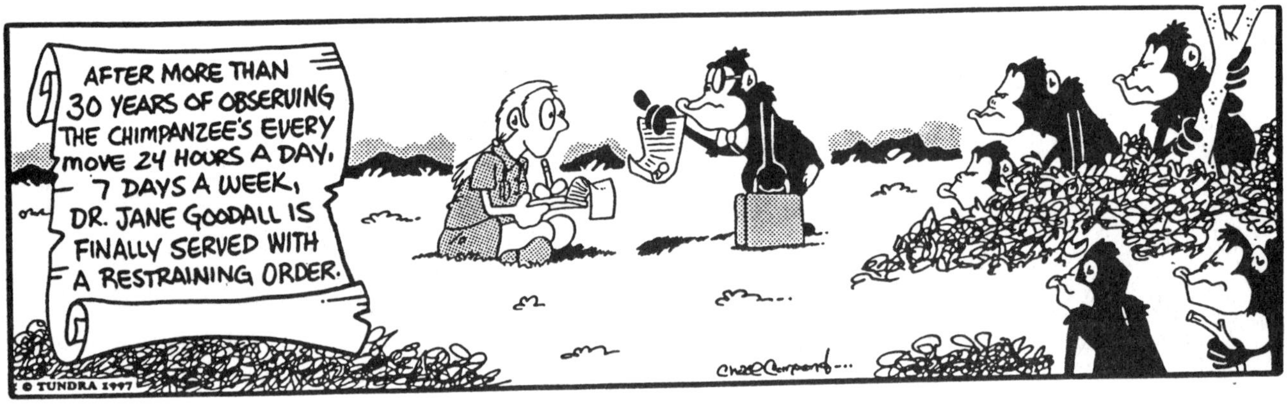
AFTER MORE THAN 30 YEARS OF OBSERVING THE CHIMPANZEE'S EVERY MOVE 24 HOURS A DAY, 7 DAYS A WEEK, DR. JANE GOODALL IS FINALLY SERVED WITH A RESTRAINING ORDER.
© TUNDRA 1997

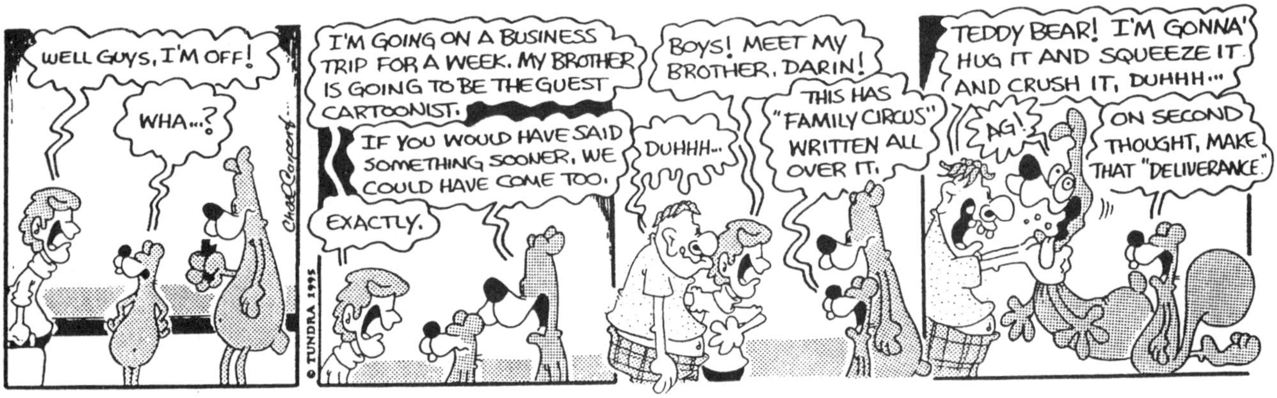
WELL GUYS, I'M OFF!
WHA...?
I'M GOING ON A BUSINESS TRIP FOR A WEEK. MY BROTHER IS GOING TO BE THE GUEST CARTOONIST.
IF YOU WOULD HAVE SAID SOMETHING SOONER, WE COULD HAVE COME TOO.
EXACTLY.
© TUNDRA 1995
BOYS! MEET MY BROTHER, DARIN!
DUHHH...
THIS HAS "FAMILY CIRCUS" WRITTEN ALL OVER IT.
TEDDY BEAR! I'M GONNA' HUG IT AND SQUEEZE IT AND CRUSH IT, DUHHH...
AG!
ON SECOND THOUGHT, MAKE THAT "DELIVERANCE".

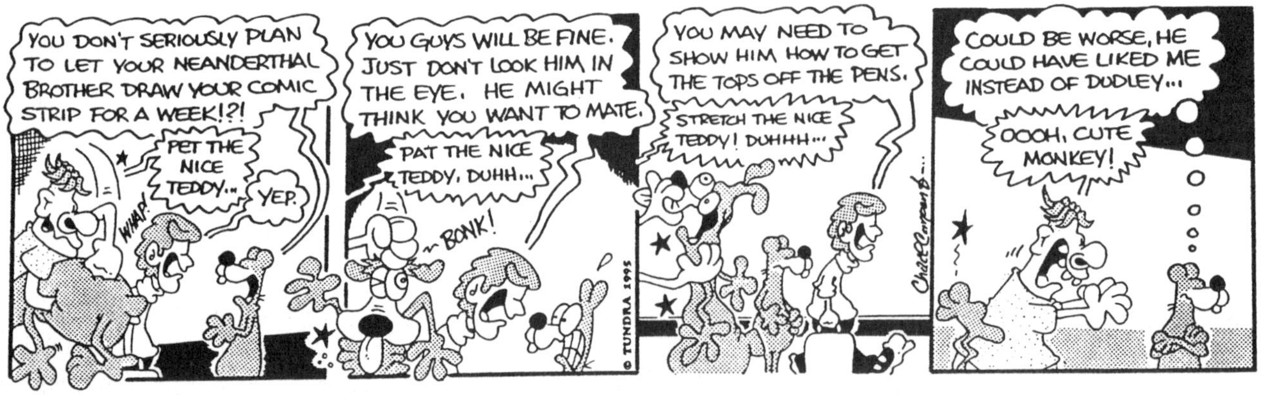
YOU DON'T SERIOUSLY PLAN TO LET YOUR NEANDERTHAL BROTHER DRAW YOUR COMIC STRIP FOR A WEEK!?!
PET THE NICE TEDDY...
YEP.
WHAP!
YOU GUYS WILL BE FINE. JUST DON'T LOOK HIM IN THE EYE. HE MIGHT THINK YOU WANT TO MATE.
PAT THE NICE TEDDY, DUHH...
BONK!
© TUNDRA 1995
YOU MAY NEED TO SHOW HIM HOW TO GET THE TOPS OFF THE PENS.
STRETCH THE NICE TEDDY! DUHHH...
COULD BE WORSE, HE COULD HAVE LIKED ME INSTEAD OF DUDLEY...
OOOH, CUTE MONKEY!

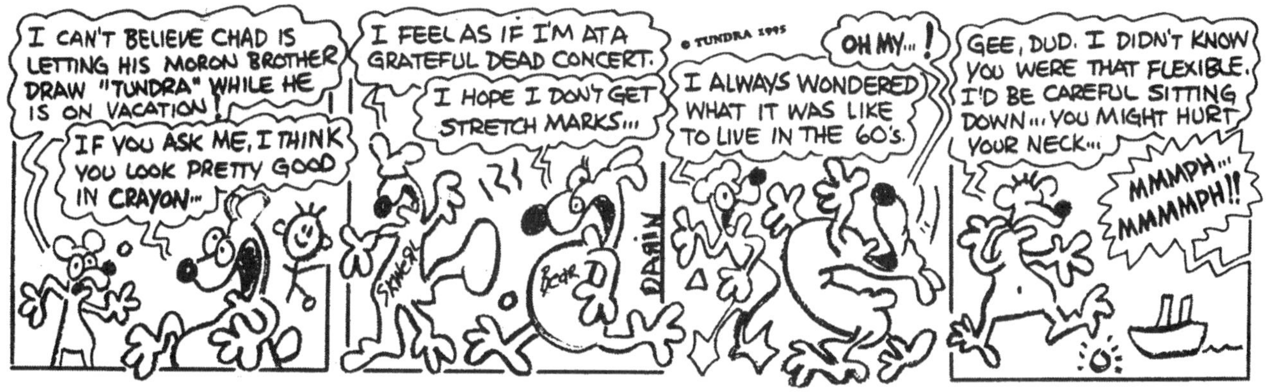
I CAN'T BELIEVE CHAD IS LETTING HIS MORON BROTHER DRAW "TUNDRA" WHILE HE IS ON VACATION!
IF YOU ASK ME, I THINK YOU LOOK PRETTY GOOD IN CRAYON...
I FEEL AS IF I'M AT A GRATEFUL DEAD CONCERT.
I HOPE I DON'T GET STRETCH MARKS...
DARIN
© TUNDRA 1995
OH MY...!
I ALWAYS WONDERED WHAT IT WAS LIKE TO LIVE IN THE 60's.
GEE, DUD. I DIDN'T KNOW YOU WERE THAT FLEXIBLE. I'D BE CAREFUL SITTING DOWN... YOU MIGHT HURT YOUR NECK...
MMMPH... MMMMPH!!

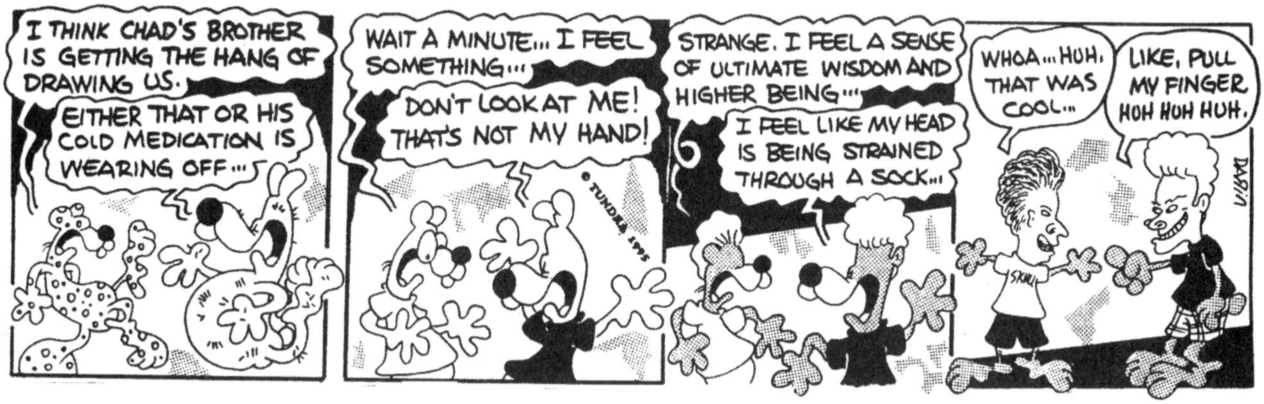
I THINK CHAD'S BROTHER IS GETTING THE HANG OF DRAWING US.
EITHER THAT OR HIS COLD MEDICATION IS WEARING OFF...
WAIT A MINUTE... I FEEL SOMETHING...
DON'T LOOK AT ME! THAT'S NOT MY HAND!
© TUNDRA 1995
STRANGE. I FEEL A SENSE OF ULTIMATE WISDOM AND HIGHER BEING...
I FEEL LIKE MY HEAD IS BEING STRAINED THROUGH A SOCK...
WHOA... HUH. THAT WAS COOL...
LIKE, PULL MY FINGER. HUH HUH HUH.

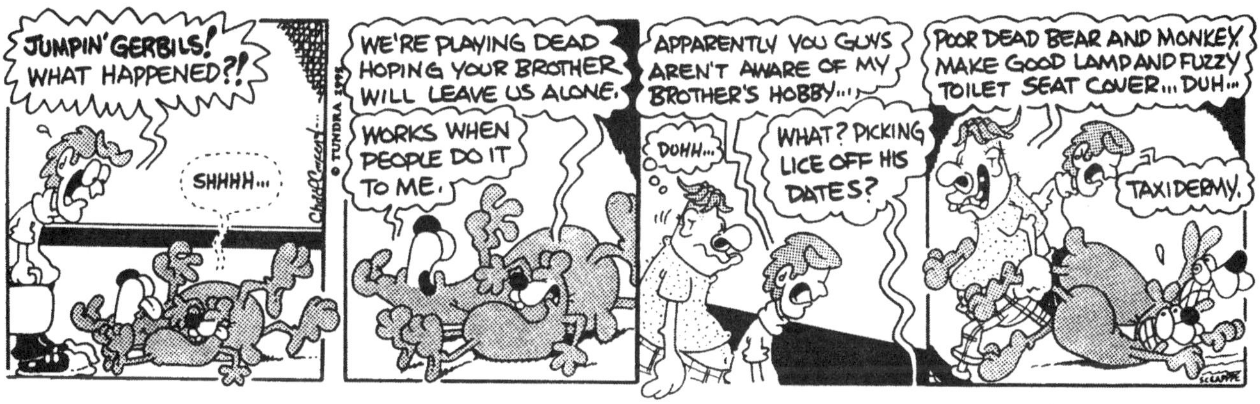
JUMPIN' GERBILS! WHAT HAPPENED?!
SHHHH...
© TUNDRA 1995
WE'RE PLAYING DEAD HOPING YOUR BROTHER WILL LEAVE US ALONE.
WORKS WHEN PEOPLE DO IT TO ME.
APPARENTLY YOU GUYS AREN'T AWARE OF MY BROTHER'S HOBBY...
DOHH...
WHAT? PICKING LICE OFF HIS DATES?
POOR DEAD BEAR AND MONKEY MAKE GOOD LAMP AND FUZZY TOILET SEAT COVER... DUH...
TAXIDERMY.

Cartoonist's note:

When the above series appeared in the newspapers, my mother was shocked that I would portray my big brother in such an unflattering manner. She felt that people would think that my caricature of him was accurate. So, in a sincere effort to show my dear mother that I have nothing but the highest respect for my elder brother, and to wash away any misconceptions folks may have about him, I have decided to print the following photo of Darin in one of his more contemplative moments...

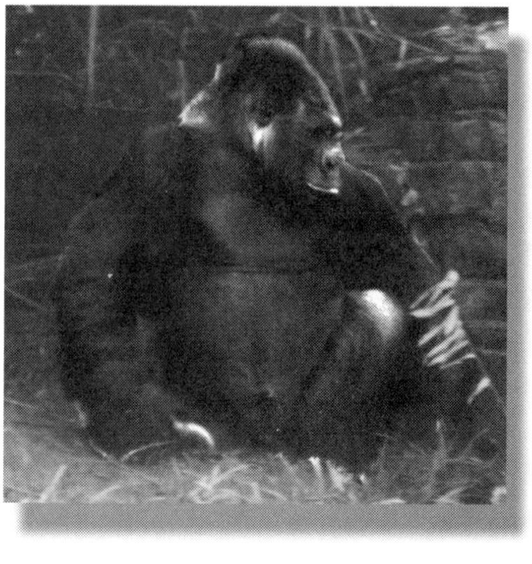

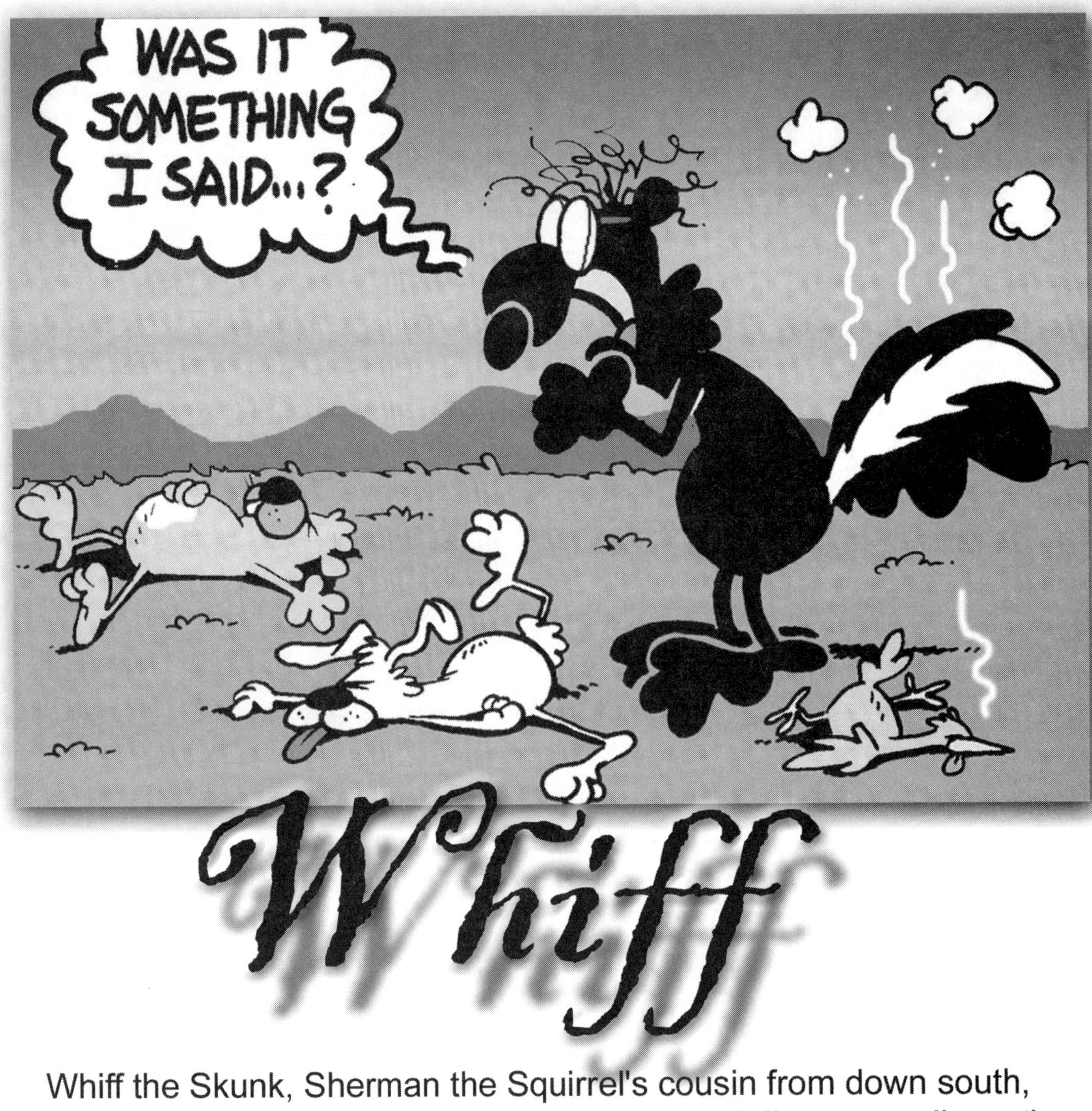
WAS IT SOMETHING I SAID...?

Whiff

Whiff the Skunk, Sherman the Squirrel's cousin from down south, first blew onto the Tundra scene as the token "vile, gross, disgusting guy." Once he arrived at the little town of Gangrene Gulch, he knew he was home. Not only because of Gangrene Gulch's world-famous "Refried Beans & Cabbage Festival," but also for the hundreds of new noses he could share his "Pull My Finger" routine with. Since his addition to the Tundra family, Whiff has proven to be a breath of fresh air - if mustard gas and rotting fish entrails is your idea of fresh air...

Chapter Five

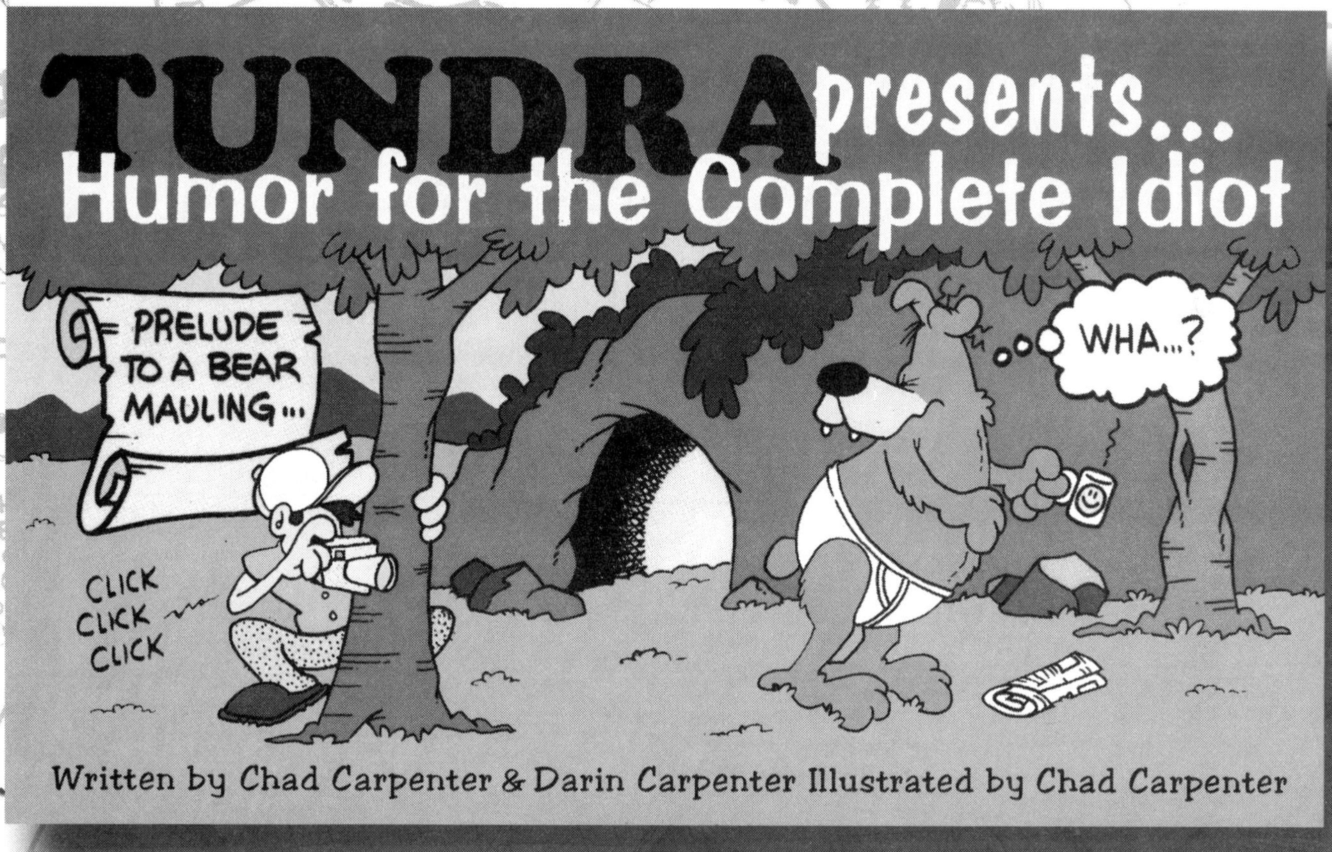
TUNDRA presents...
Humor for the Complete Idiot
PRELUDE TO A BEAR MAULING...
WHA...?
CLICK CLICK CLICK
Written by Chad Carpenter & Darin Carpenter Illustrated by Chad Carpenter

First Printing: June 1998

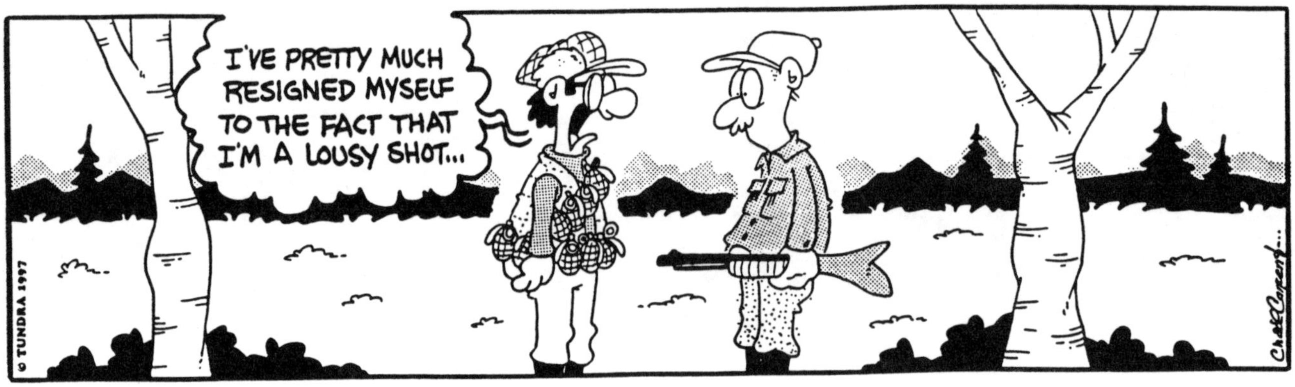
I'VE PRETTY MUCH RESIGNED MYSELF TO THE FACT THAT I'M A LOUSY SHOT...
© TUNDRA 1997

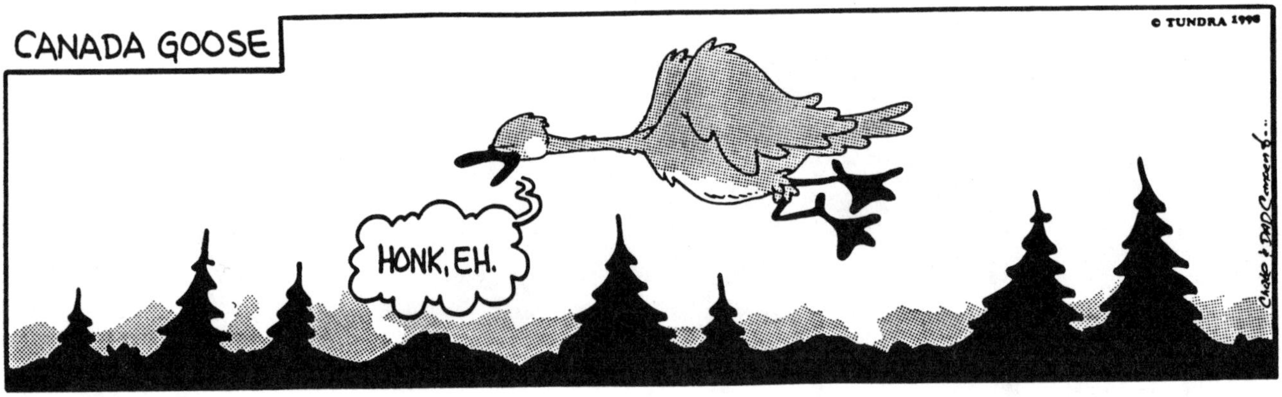
CANADA GOOSE
© TUNDRA 1998
HONK, EH.

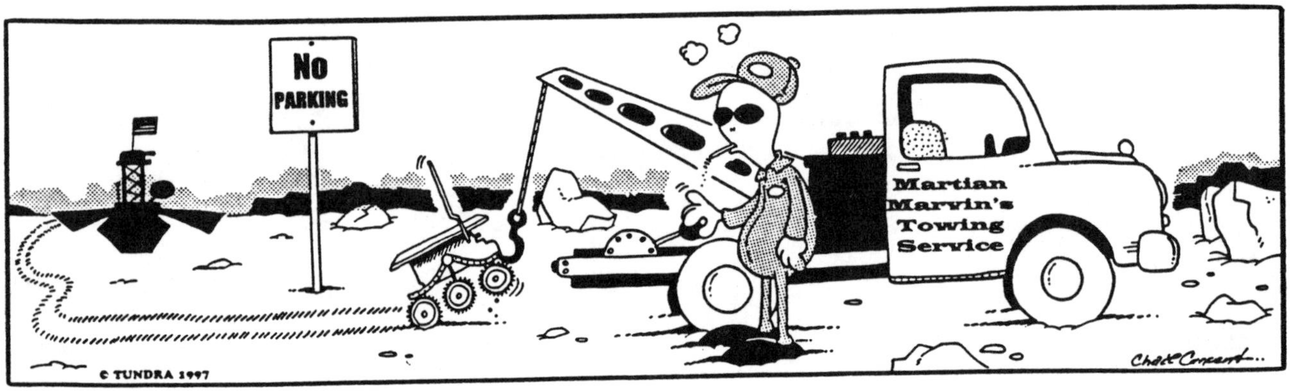
No PARKING
Martian Marvin's Towing Service
© TUNDRA 1997

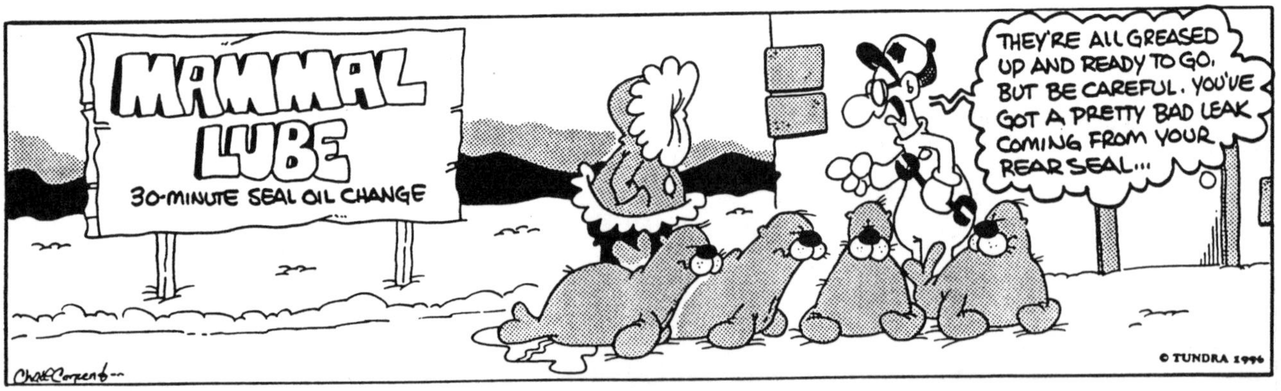
MAMMAL LUBE
30-MINUTE SEAL OIL CHANGE
THEY'RE ALL GREASED UP AND READY TO GO. BUT BE CAREFUL. YOU'VE GOT A PRETTY BAD LEAK COMING FROM YOUR REAR SEAL...
© TUNDRA 1996

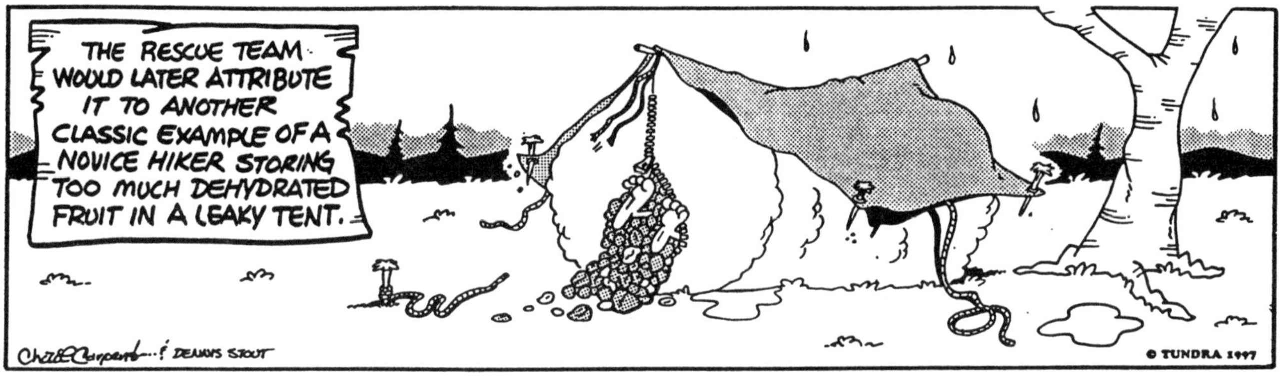
THE RESCUE TEAM WOULD LATER ATTRIBUTE IT TO ANOTHER CLASSIC EXAMPLE OF A NOVICE HIKER STORING TOO MUCH DEHYDRATED FRUIT IN A LEAKY TENT.
© TUNDRA 1997

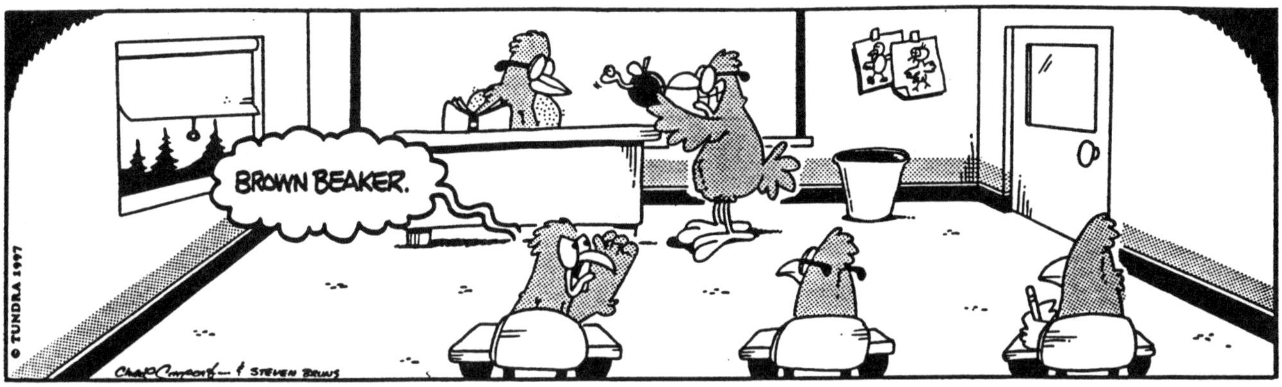
BROWN BEAKER.
© TUNDRA 1997

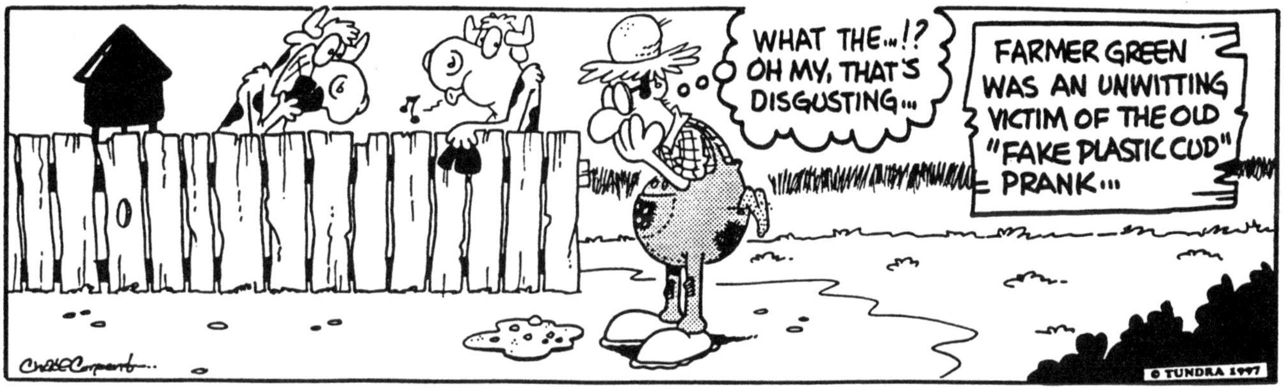
WHAT THE...!? OH MY, THAT'S DISGUSTING...
FARMER GREEN WAS AN UNWITTING VICTIM OF THE OLD "FAKE PLASTIC CUD" PRANK...
© TUNDRA 1997

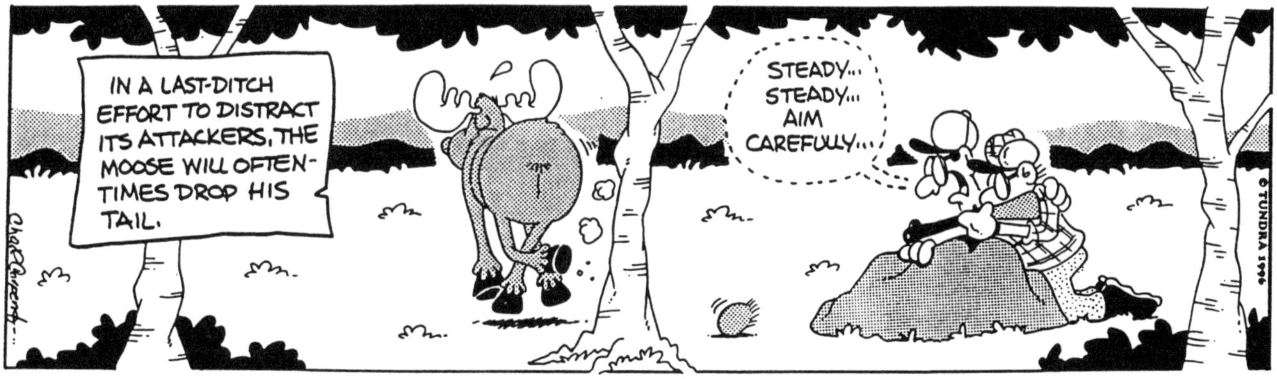
IN A LAST-DITCH EFFORT TO DISTRACT ITS ATTACKERS, THE MOOSE WILL OFTEN-TIMES DROP HIS TAIL.
STEADY... STEADY... AIM CAREFULLY...
© TUNDRA 1996

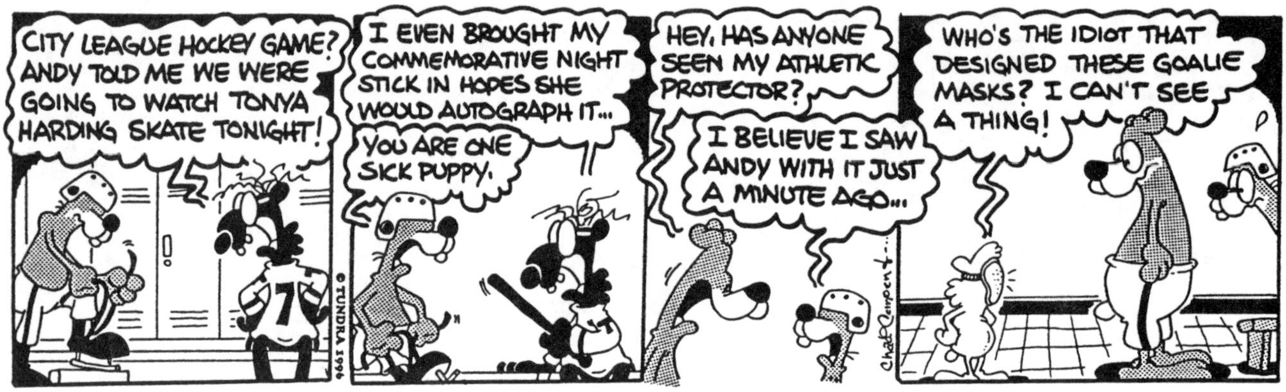
CITY LEAGUE HOCKEY GAME? ANDY TOLD ME WE WERE GOING TO WATCH TONYA HARDING SKATE TONIGHT!
© TUNDRA 1996
I EVEN BROUGHT MY COMMEMORATIVE NIGHT STICK IN HOPES SHE WOULD AUTOGRAPH IT...
YOU ARE ONE SICK PUPPY.
HEY, HAS ANYONE SEEN MY ATHLETIC PROTECTOR?
I BELIEVE I SAW ANDY WITH IT JUST A MINUTE AGO...
WHO'S THE IDIOT THAT DESIGNED THESE GOALIE MASKS? I CAN'T SEE A THING!

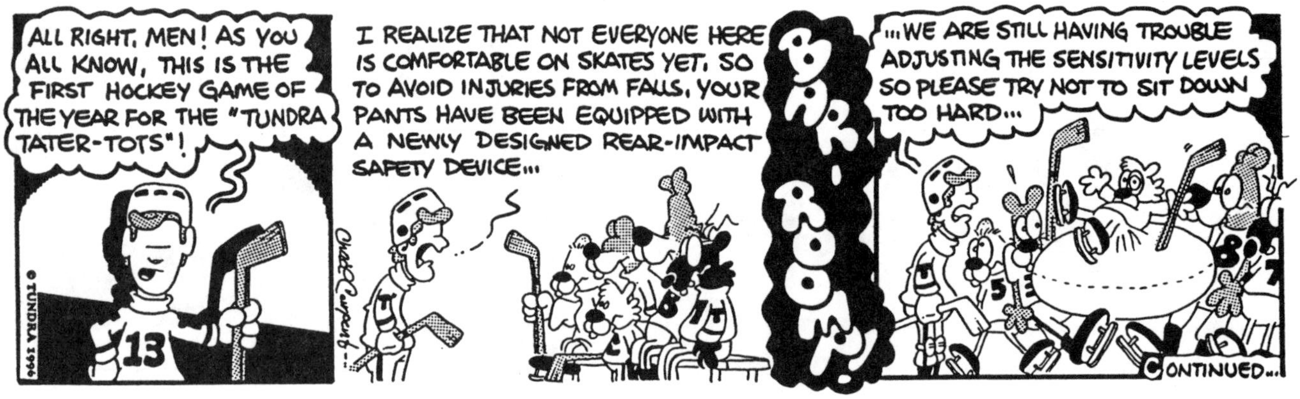
ALL RIGHT, MEN! AS YOU ALL KNOW, THIS IS THE FIRST HOCKEY GAME OF THE YEAR FOR THE "TUNDRA TATER-TOTS"!
© TUNDRA 1996
I REALIZE THAT NOT EVERYONE HERE IS COMFORTABLE ON SKATES YET, SO TO AVOID INJURIES FROM FALLS, YOUR PANTS HAVE BEEN EQUIPPED WITH A NEWLY DESIGNED REAR-IMPACT SAFETY DEVICE...
BAR-ROOM!
...WE ARE STILL HAVING TROUBLE ADJUSTING THE SENSITIVITY LEVELS SO PLEASE TRY NOT TO SIT DOWN TOO HARD...
CONTINUED...

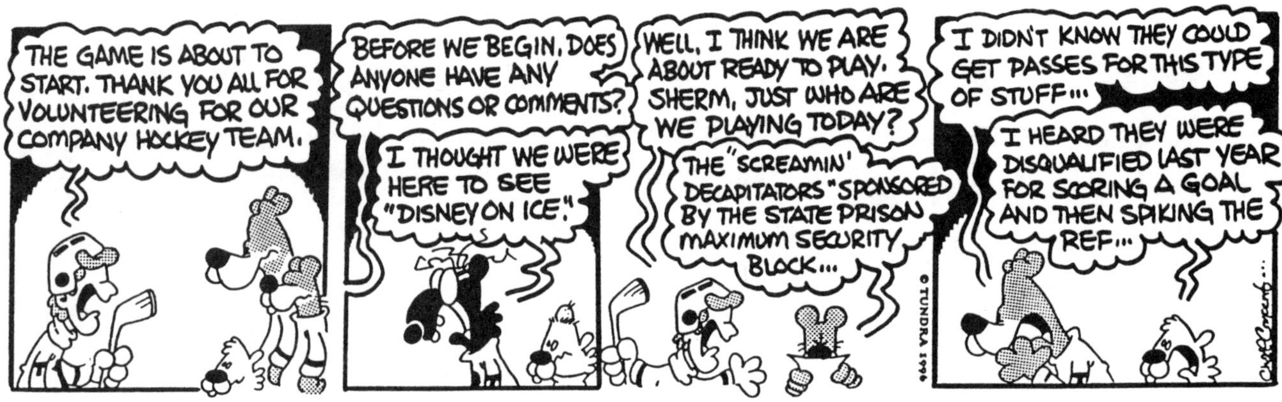
THE GAME IS ABOUT TO START. THANK YOU ALL FOR VOLUNTEERING FOR OUR COMPANY HOCKEY TEAM.
BEFORE WE BEGIN, DOES ANYONE HAVE ANY QUESTIONS OR COMMENTS?
I THOUGHT WE WERE HERE TO SEE "DISNEY ON ICE."
WELL, I THINK WE ARE ABOUT READY TO PLAY. SHERM, JUST WHO ARE WE PLAYING TODAY?
THE "SCREAMIN' DECAPITATORS" SPONSORED BY THE STATE PRISON MAXIMUM SECURITY BLOCK...
© TUNDRA 1996
I DIDN'T KNOW THEY COULD GET PASSES FOR THIS TYPE OF STUFF...
I HEARD THEY WERE DISQUALIFIED LAST YEAR FOR SCORING A GOAL AND THEN SPIKING THE REF...

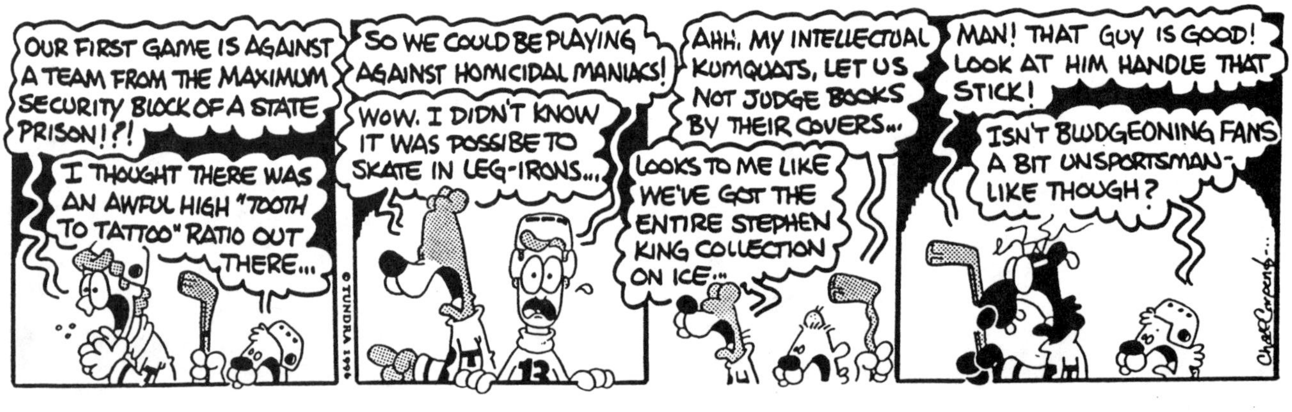
OUR FIRST GAME IS AGAINST A TEAM FROM THE MAXIMUM SECURITY BLOCK OF A STATE PRISON!?!
I THOUGHT THERE WAS AN AWFUL HIGH "TOOTH TO TATTOO" RATIO OUT THERE...
© TUNDRA 1996
SO WE COULD BE PLAYING AGAINST HOMICIDAL MANIACS!
WOW. I DIDN'T KNOW IT WAS POSSIBE TO SKATE IN LEG-IRONS...
AHH, MY INTELLECTUAL KUMQUATS, LET US NOT JUDGE BOOKS BY THEIR COVERS...
LOOKS TO ME LIKE WE'VE GOT THE ENTIRE STEPHEN KING COLLECTION ON ICE...
MAN! THAT GUY IS GOOD! LOOK AT HIM HANDLE THAT STICK!
ISN'T BLUDGEONING FANS A BIT UNSPORTSMAN-LIKE THOUGH?

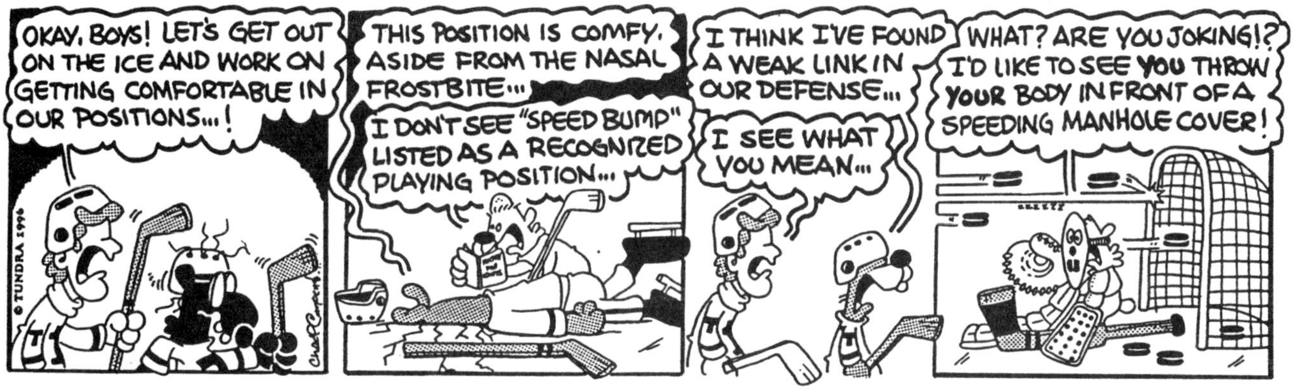
OKAY, BOYS! LET'S GET OUT ON THE ICE AND WORK ON GETTING COMFORTABLE IN OUR POSITIONS...!
© TUNDRA 1996
THIS POSITION IS COMFY, ASIDE FROM THE NASAL FROSTBITE...
I DON'T SEE "SPEED BUMP" LISTED AS A RECOGNIZED PLAYING POSITION...
I THINK I'VE FOUND A WEAK LINK IN OUR DEFENSE...
I SEE WHAT YOU MEAN...
WHAT? ARE YOU JOKING!? I'D LIKE TO SEE YOU THROW YOUR BODY IN FRONT OF A SPEEDING MANHOLE COVER!

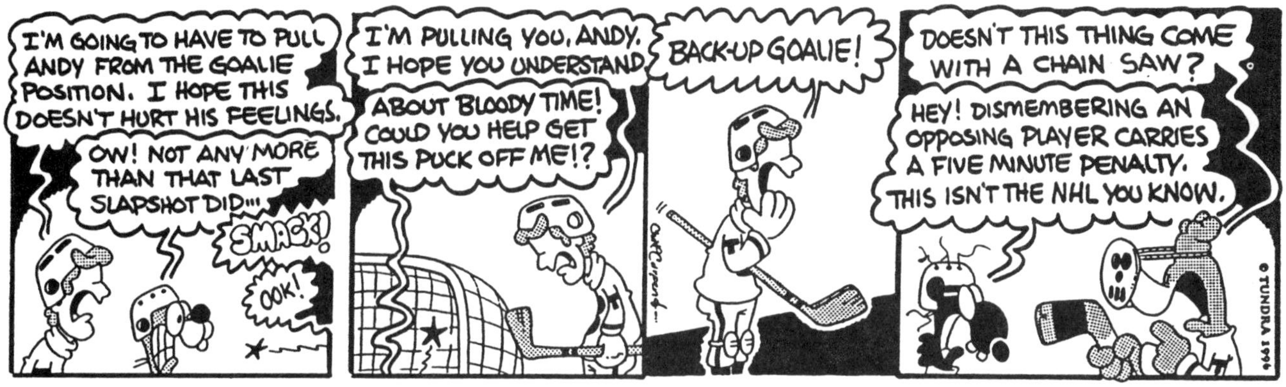
I'M GOING TO HAVE TO PULL ANDY FROM THE GOALIE POSITION. I HOPE THIS DOESN'T HURT HIS FEELINGS.
OW! NOT ANY MORE THAN THAT LAST SLAPSHOT DID...
SMACK!
OOK!
I'M PULLING YOU, ANDY. I HOPE YOU UNDERSTAND.
ABOUT BLOODY TIME! COULD YOU HELP GET THIS PUCK OFF ME!?
BACK-UP GOALIE!
DOESN'T THIS THING COME WITH A CHAIN SAW?
HEY! DISMEMBERING AN OPPOSING PLAYER CARRIES A FIVE MINUTE PENALTY. THIS ISN'T THE NHL YOU KNOW.
© TUNDRA 1996

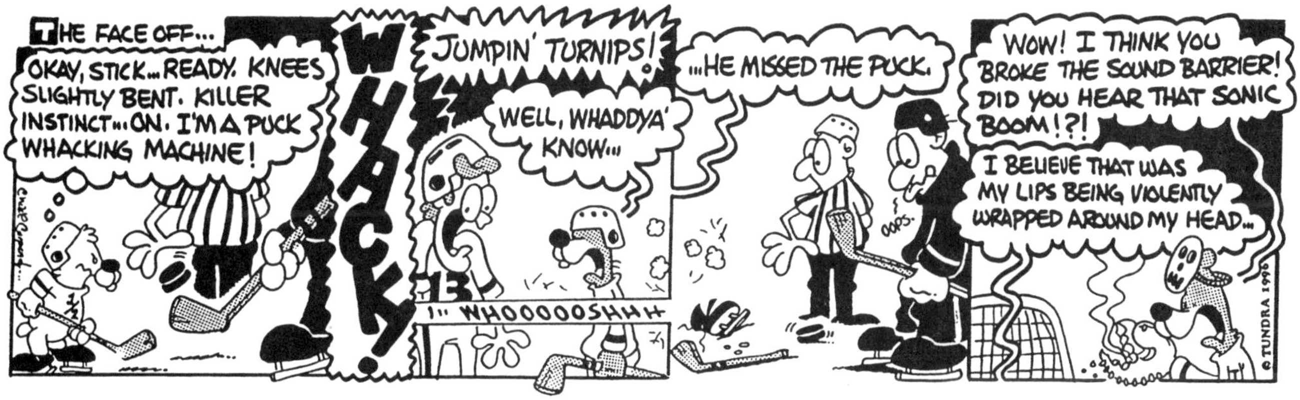
THE FACE OFF...
OKAY, STICK... READY. KNEES SLIGHTLY BENT. KILLER INSTINCT... ON. I'M A PUCK WHACKING MACHINE!
WHACK!
JUMPIN' TURNIPS!
WELL, WHADDYA' KNOW...
13
WHOOOOOSHHH
...HE MISSED THE PUCK.
OOPS.
WOW! I THINK YOU BROKE THE SOUND BARRIER! DID YOU HEAR THAT SONIC BOOM!?!
I BELIEVE THAT WAS MY LIPS BEING VIOLENTLY WRAPPED AROUND MY HEAD...
© TUNDRA 1996

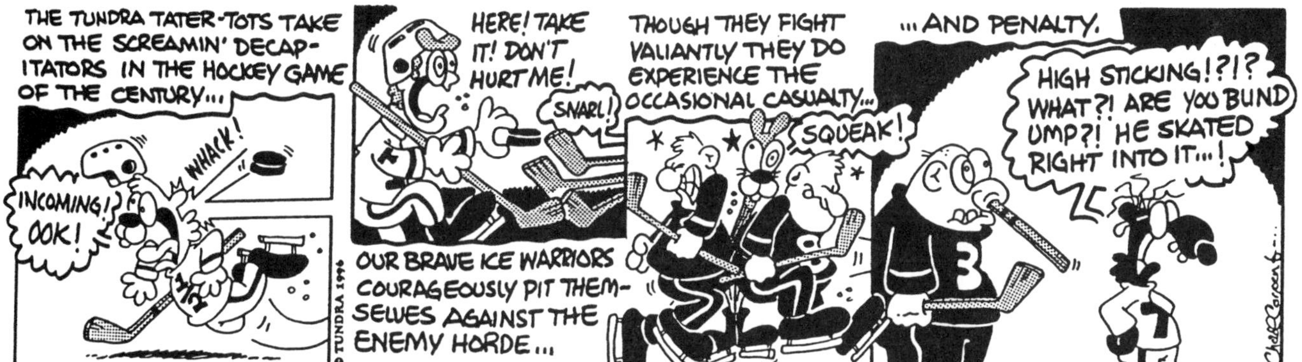
THE TUNDRA TATER-TOTS TAKE ON THE SCREAMIN' DECAPITATORS IN THE HOCKEY GAME OF THE CENTURY...
WHACK!
INCOMING! OOK!
© TUNDRA 1996
HERE! TAKE IT! DON'T HURT ME!
SNARL!
OUR BRAVE ICE WARRIORS COURAGEOUSLY PIT THEMSELVES AGAINST THE ENEMY HORDE...
THOUGH THEY FIGHT VALIANTLY THEY DO EXPERIENCE THE OCCASIONAL CASUALTY...
SQUEAK!
...AND PENALTY.
HIGH STICKING!?!? WHAT?! ARE YOU BLIND UMP?! HE SKATED RIGHT INTO IT...!
3
7

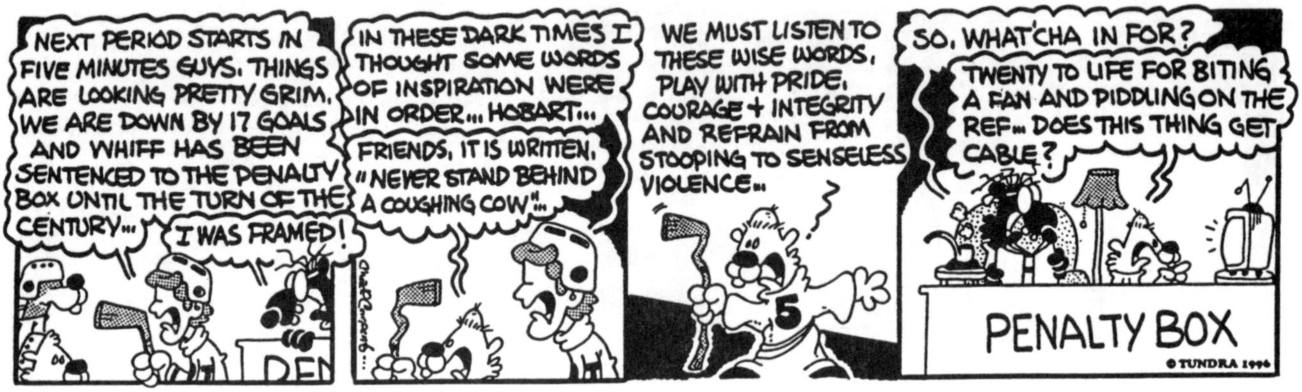
NEXT PERIOD STARTS IN FIVE MINUTES GUYS. THINGS ARE LOOKING PRETTY GRIM. WE ARE DOWN BY 17 GOALS AND WHIFF HAS BEEN SENTENCED TO THE PENALTY BOX UNTIL THE TURN OF THE CENTURY...
I WAS FRAMED!
IN THESE DARK TIMES I THOUGHT SOME WORDS OF INSPIRATION WERE IN ORDER... HOBART...
FRIENDS, IT IS WRITTEN, "NEVER STAND BEHIND A COUGHING COW"...
WE MUST LISTEN TO THESE WISE WORDS. PLAY WITH PRIDE, COURAGE + INTEGRITY AND REFRAIN FROM STOOPING TO SENSELESS VIOLENCE...
SO, WHAT'CHA IN FOR?
TWENTY TO LIFE FOR BITING A FAN AND PIDDLING ON THE REF... DOES THIS THING GET CABLE?
PENALTY BOX
© TUNDRA 1996

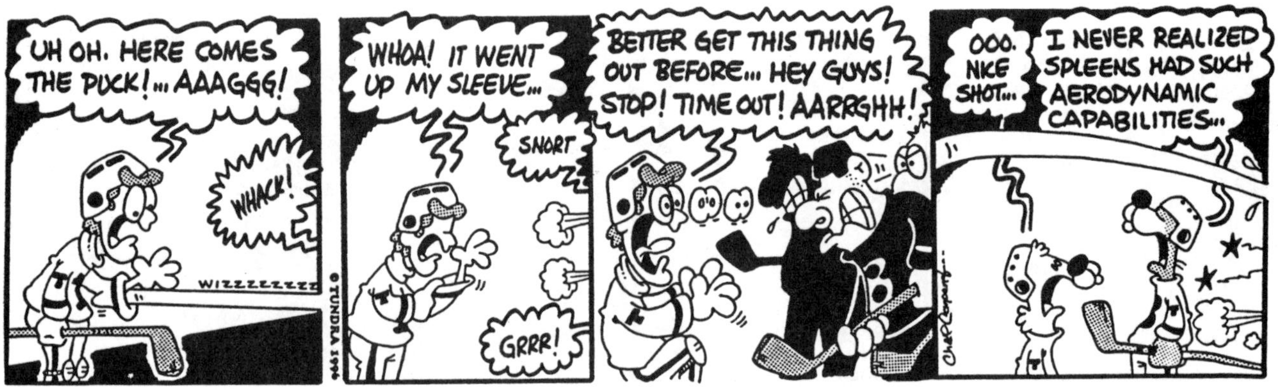
UH OH. HERE COMES THE PUCK!... AAAGGG!
WHACK!
WIZZZZZZZZ
WHOA! IT WENT UP MY SLEEVE...
SNORT
GRRR!
BETTER GET THIS THING OUT BEFORE... HEY GUYS! STOP! TIME OUT! AARRGHH!
OOO. NICE SHOT...
I NEVER REALIZED SPLEENS HAD SUCH AERODYNAMIC CAPABILITIES...

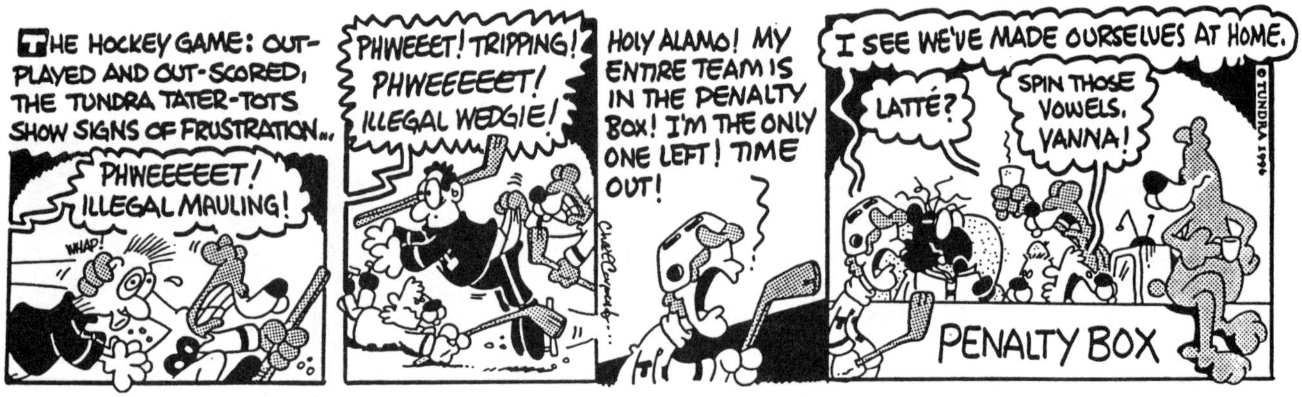
THE HOCKEY GAME: OUT-PLAYED AND OUT-SCORED, THE TUNDRA TATER-TOTS SHOW SIGNS OF FRUSTRATION...
PHWEEEEET! ILLEGAL MAULING!
WHAP!
PHWEEET! TRIPPING! PHWEEEEEET! ILLEGAL WEDGIE!
HOLY ALAMO! MY ENTIRE TEAM IS IN THE PENALTY BOX! I'M THE ONLY ONE LEFT! TIME OUT!
I SEE WE'VE MADE OURSELVES AT HOME.
LATTÉ?
SPIN THOSE VOWELS, VANNA!
PENALTY BOX

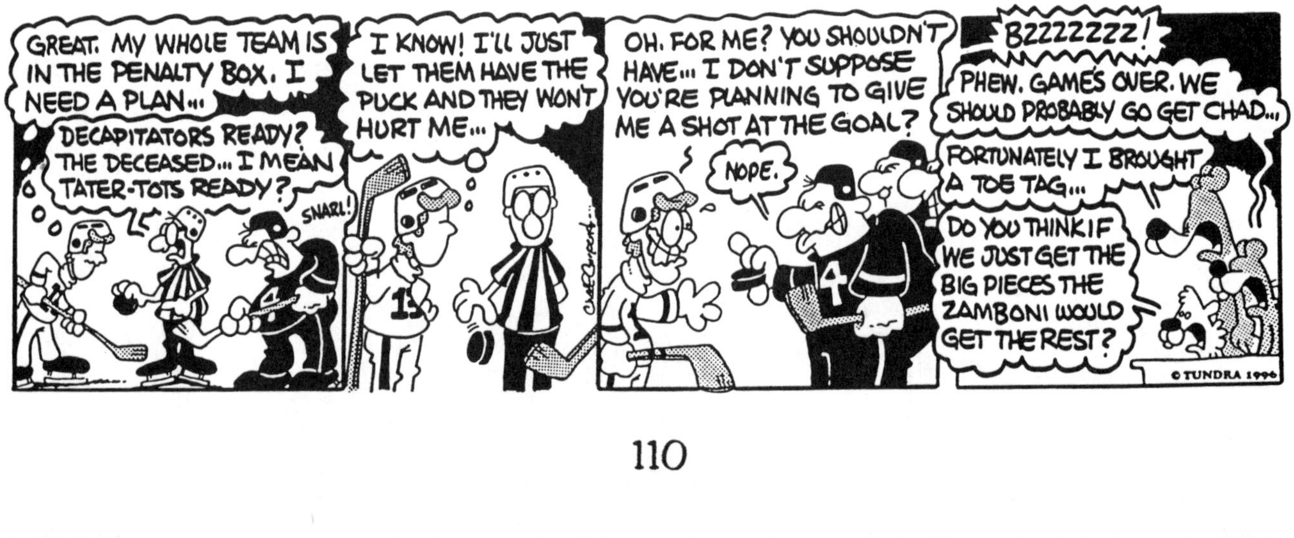
GREAT. MY WHOLE TEAM IS IN THE PENALTY BOX. I NEED A PLAN...
DECAPITATORS READY? THE DECEASED... I MEAN TATER-TOTS READY?
SNARL!
I KNOW! I'LL JUST LET THEM HAVE THE PUCK AND THEY WON'T HURT ME...
OH. FOR ME? YOU SHOULDN'T HAVE... I DON'T SUPPOSE YOU'RE PLANNING TO GIVE ME A SHOT AT THE GOAL?
NOPE.
BZZZZZZZ!
PHEW. GAME'S OVER. WE SHOULD PROBABLY GO GET CHAD...
FORTUNATELY I BROUGHT A TOE TAG...
DO YOU THINK IF WE JUST GET THE BIG PIECES THE ZAMBONI WOULD GET THE REST?
© TUNDRA 1996

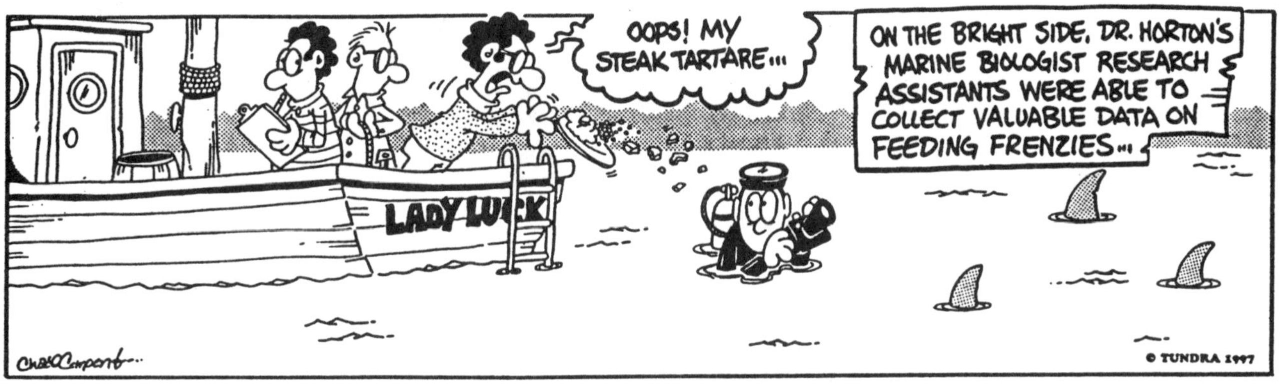
OOPS! MY STEAK TARTARE...
ON THE BRIGHT SIDE, DR. HORTON'S MARINE BIOLOGIST RESEARCH ASSISTANTS WERE ABLE TO COLLECT VALUABLE DATA ON FEEDING FRENZIES...
LADY LUCK
© TUNDRA 1997

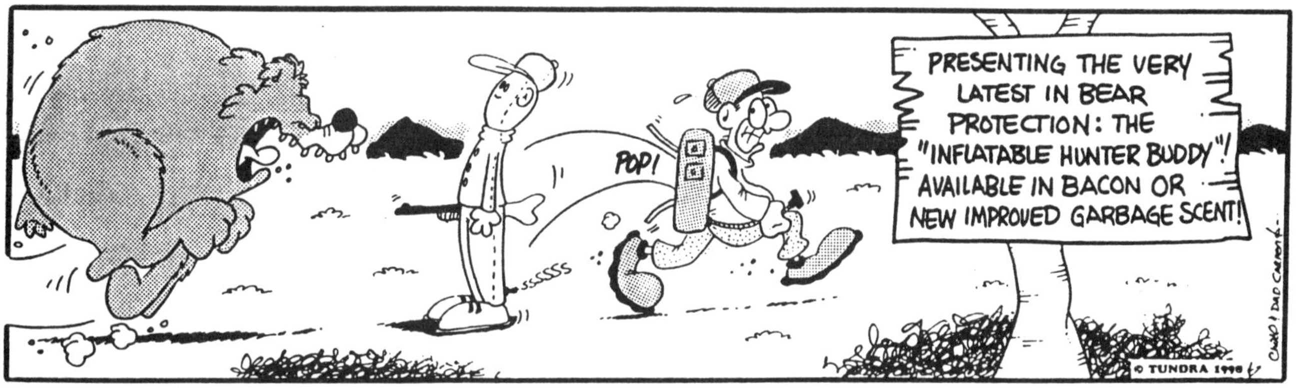
PRESENTING THE VERY LATEST IN BEAR PROTECTION: THE "INFLATABLE HUNTER BUDDY"! AVAILABLE IN BACON OR NEW IMPROVED GARBAGE SCENT!
POP!
SSSSSS
© TUNDRA 1998

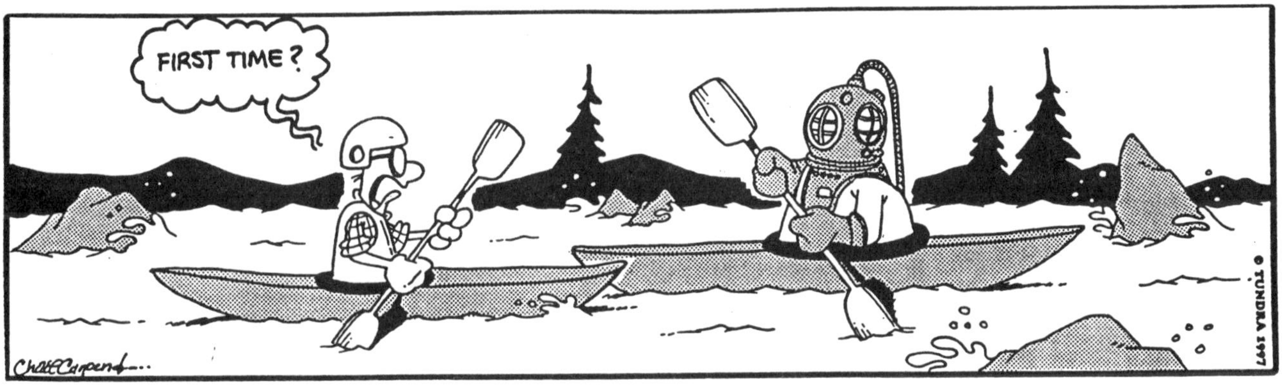
FIRST TIME?
© TUNDRA 1997

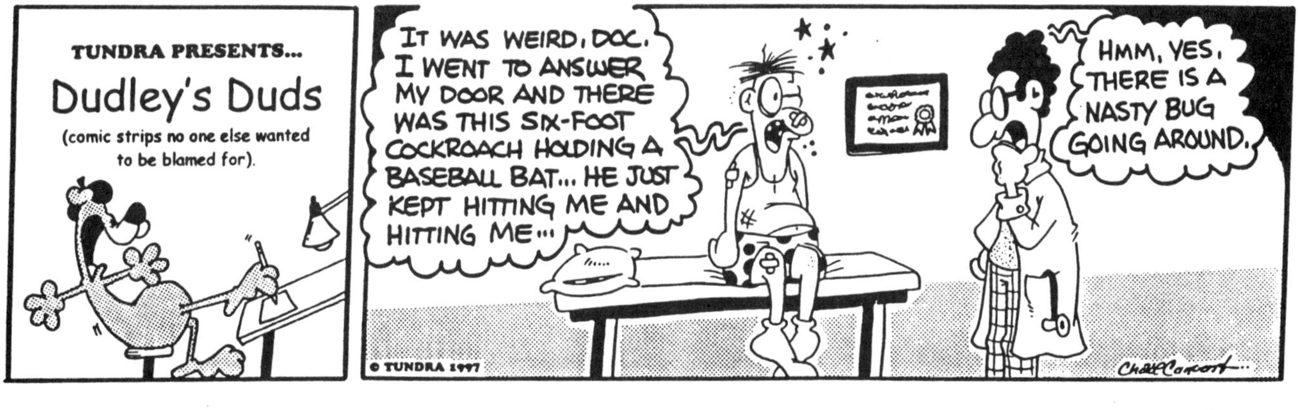
TUNDRA PRESENTS...
Dudley's Duds
(comic strips no one else wanted to be blamed for).
IT WAS WEIRD, DOC. I WENT TO ANSWER MY DOOR AND THERE WAS THIS SIX-FOOT COCKROACH HOLDING A BASEBALL BAT... HE JUST KEPT HITTING ME AND HITTING ME...
HMM, YES. THERE IS A NASTY BUG GOING AROUND.
© TUNDRA 1997

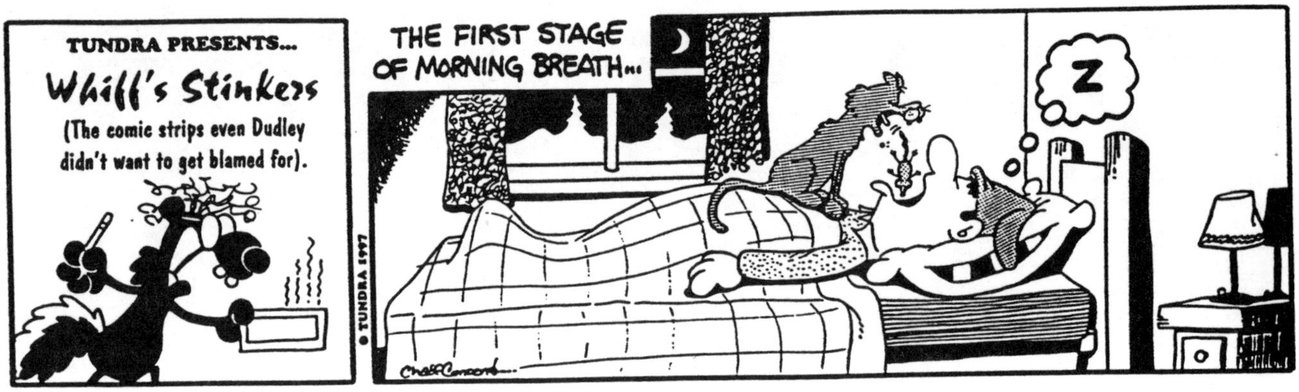
TUNDRA PRESENTS...
Whiff's Stinkers
(The comic strips even Dudley didn't want to get blamed for).
THE FIRST STAGE OF MORNING BREATH...
Z
© TUNDRA 1997

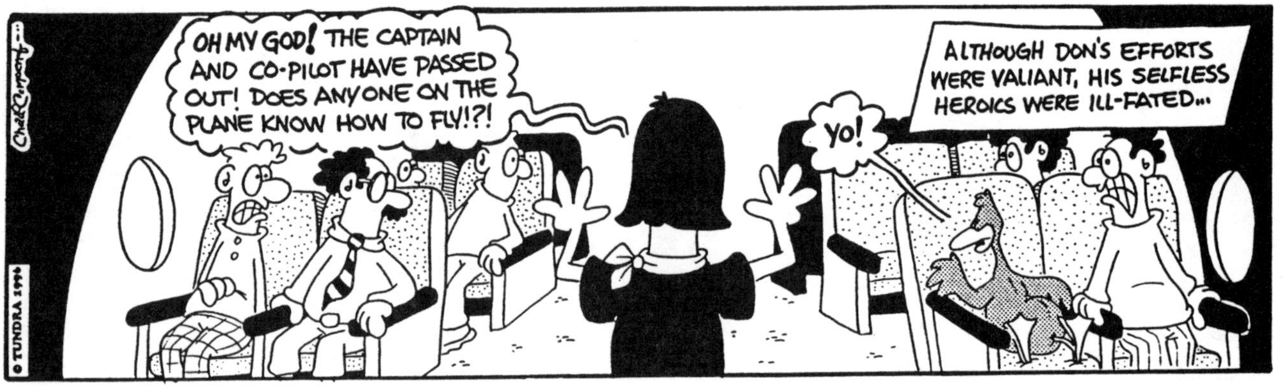
OH MY GOD! THE CAPTAIN AND CO-PILOT HAVE PASSED OUT! DOES ANYONE ON THE PLANE KNOW HOW TO FLY!?!
YO!
ALTHOUGH DON'S EFFORTS WERE VALIANT, HIS SELFLESS HEROICS WERE ILL-FATED...
© TUNDRA 1996

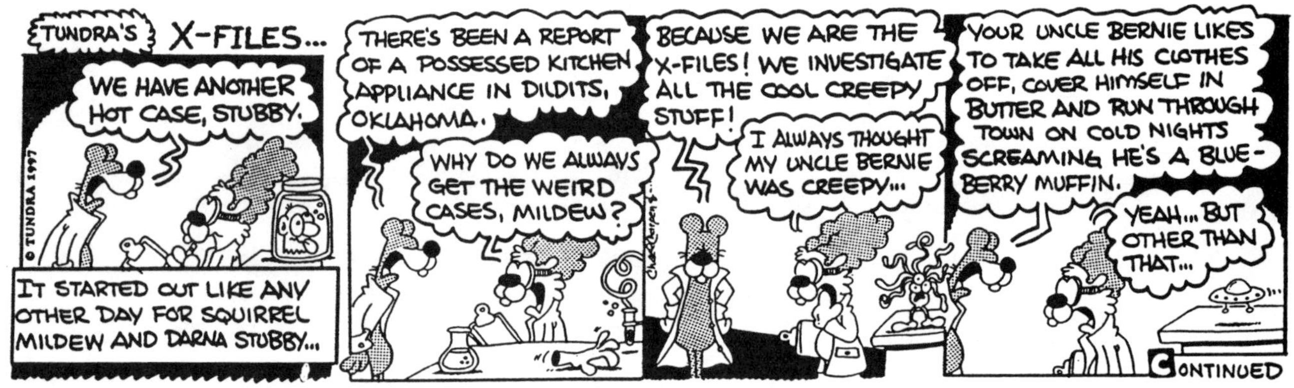
TUNDRA'S X-FILES...
WE HAVE ANOTHER HOT CASE, STUBBY.
IT STARTED OUT LIKE ANY OTHER DAY FOR SQUIRREL MILDEW AND DARNA STUBBY...
THERE'S BEEN A REPORT OF A POSSESSED KITCHEN APPLIANCE IN DILDITS, OKLAHOMA.
WHY DO WE ALWAYS GET THE WEIRD CASES, MILDEW?
BECAUSE WE ARE THE X-FILES! WE INVESTIGATE ALL THE COOL CREEPY STUFF!
I ALWAYS THOUGHT MY UNCLE BERNIE WAS CREEPY...
YOUR UNCLE BERNIE LIKES TO TAKE ALL HIS CLOTHES OFF, COVER HIMSELF IN BUTTER AND RUN THROUGH TOWN ON COLD NIGHTS SCREAMING HE'S A BLUE-BERRY MUFFIN.
YEAH... BUT OTHER THAN THAT...
CONTINUED
© TUNDRA 1997

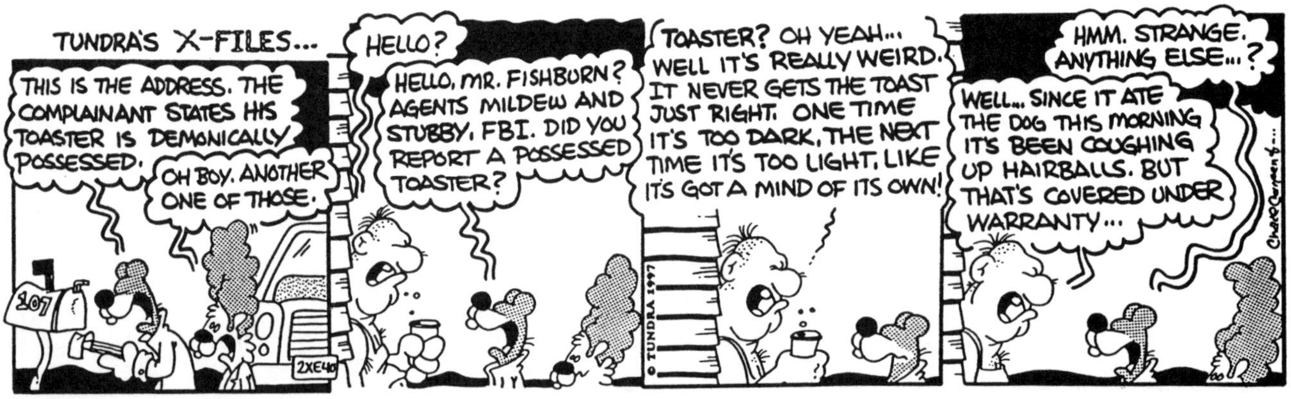
TUNDRA'S X-FILES...
THIS IS THE ADDRESS. THE COMPLAINANT STATES HIS TOASTER IS DEMONICALLY POSSESSED.
OH BOY. ANOTHER ONE OF THOSE.
107
2XE40
HELLO?
HELLO, MR. FISHBURN? AGENTS MILDEW AND STUBBY, FBI. DID YOU REPORT A POSSESSED TOASTER?
TOASTER? OH YEAH... WELL IT'S REALLY WEIRD. IT NEVER GETS THE TOAST JUST RIGHT. ONE TIME IT'S TOO DARK, THE NEXT TIME IT'S TOO LIGHT, LIKE ITS GOT A MIND OF ITS OWN!
HMM. STRANGE. ANYTHING ELSE...?
WELL... SINCE IT ATE THE DOG THIS MORNING ITS BEEN COUGHING UP HAIRBALLS. BUT THAT'S COVERED UNDER WARRANTY...
© TUNDRA 1997

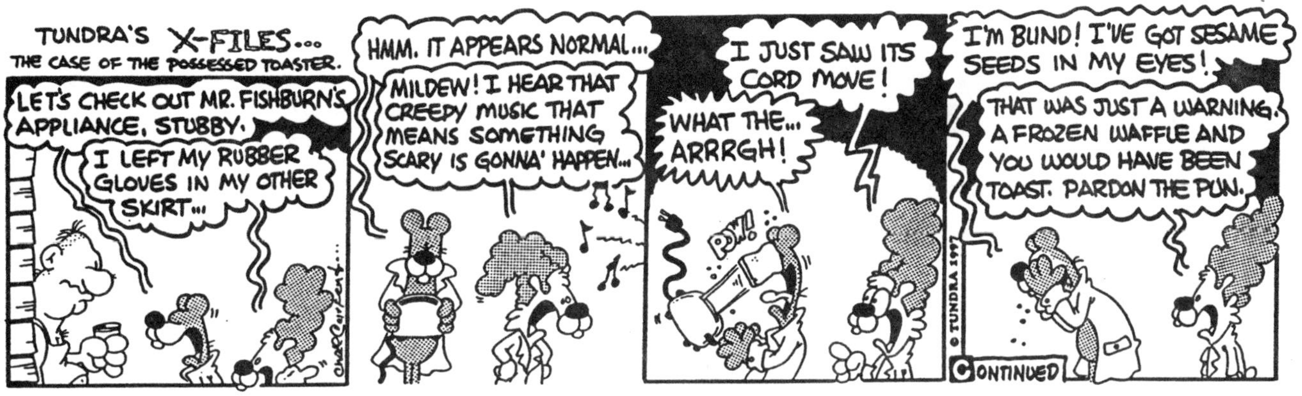
TUNDRA'S X-FILES...
THE CASE OF THE POSSESSED TOASTER.
LET'S CHECK OUT MR. FISHBURN'S APPLIANCE, STUBBY.
I LEFT MY RUBBER GLOVES IN MY OTHER SKIRT...
HMM. IT APPEARS NORMAL...
MILDEW! I HEAR THAT CREEPY MUSIC THAT MEANS SOMETHING SCARY IS GONNA' HAPPEN...
I JUST SAW ITS CORD MOVE!
WHAT THE... ARRRGH!
POW!
I'M BLIND! I'VE GOT SESAME SEEDS IN MY EYES!
THAT WAS JUST A WARNING. A FROZEN WAFFLE AND YOU WOULD HAVE BEEN TOAST. PARDON THE PUN.
© TUNDRA 1997
CONTINUED

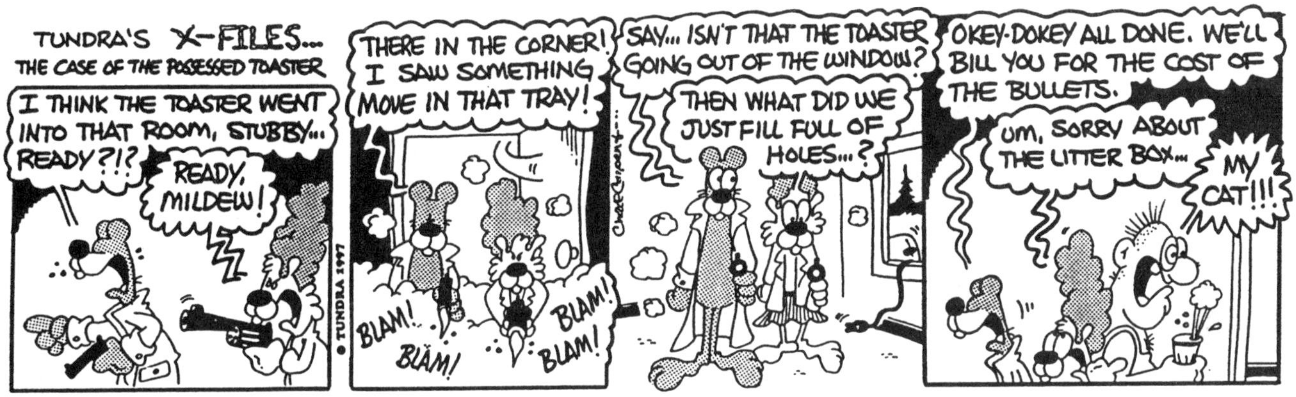
TUNDRA'S X-FILES...
THE CASE OF THE POSSESSED TOASTER
I THINK THE TOASTER WENT INTO THAT ROOM, STUBBY... READY?!?
READY, MILDEW!
© TUNDRA 1997
THERE IN THE CORNER! I SAW SOMETHING MOVE IN THAT TRAY!
BLAM!
BLÄM!
BLAM!
BLAM!
SAY... ISN'T THAT THE TOASTER GOING OUT OF THE WINDOW?
THEN WHAT DID WE JUST FILL FULL OF HOLES...?
OKEY-DOKEY ALL DONE. WE'LL BILL YOU FOR THE COST OF THE BULLETS.
UM, SORRY ABOUT THE LITTER BOX...
MY CAT!!!

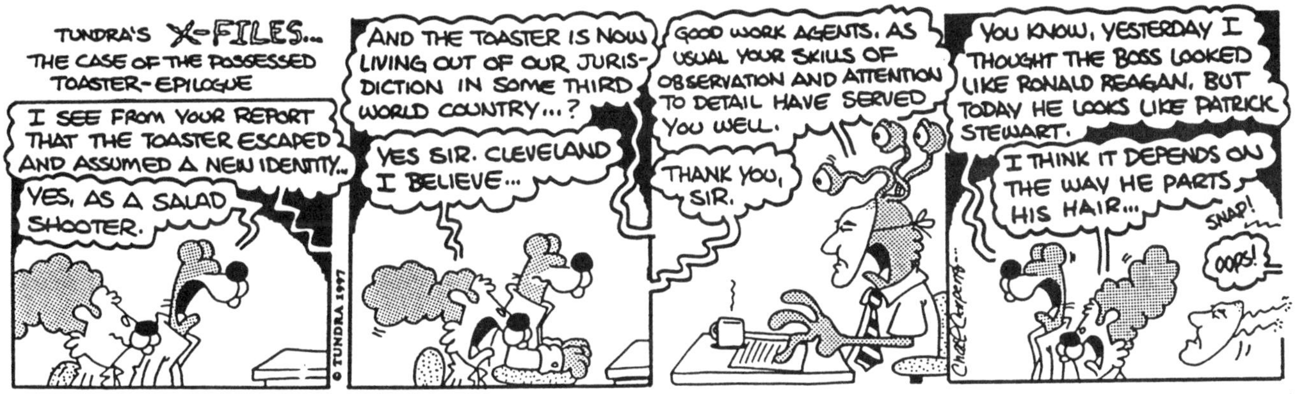
TUNDRA'S X-FILES...
THE CASE OF THE POSSESSED TOASTER- EPILOGUE
I SEE FROM YOUR REPORT THAT THE TOASTER ESCAPED AND ASSUMED A NEW IDENTITY...
YES, AS A SALAD SHOOTER.
© TUNDRA 1997
AND THE TOASTER IS NOW LIVING OUT OF OUR JURISDICTION IN SOME THIRD WORLD COUNTRY...?
YES SIR. CLEVELAND I BELIEVE...
GOOD WORK AGENTS. AS USUAL YOUR SKILLS OF OBSERVATION AND ATTENTION TO DETAIL HAVE SERVED YOU WELL.
THANK YOU, SIR.
YOU KNOW, YESTERDAY I THOUGHT THE BOSS LOOKED LIKE RONALD REAGAN. BUT TODAY HE LOOKS LIKE PATRICK STEWART.
I THINK IT DEPENDS ON THE WAY HE PARTS HIS HAIR...
SNAP!
OOPS!

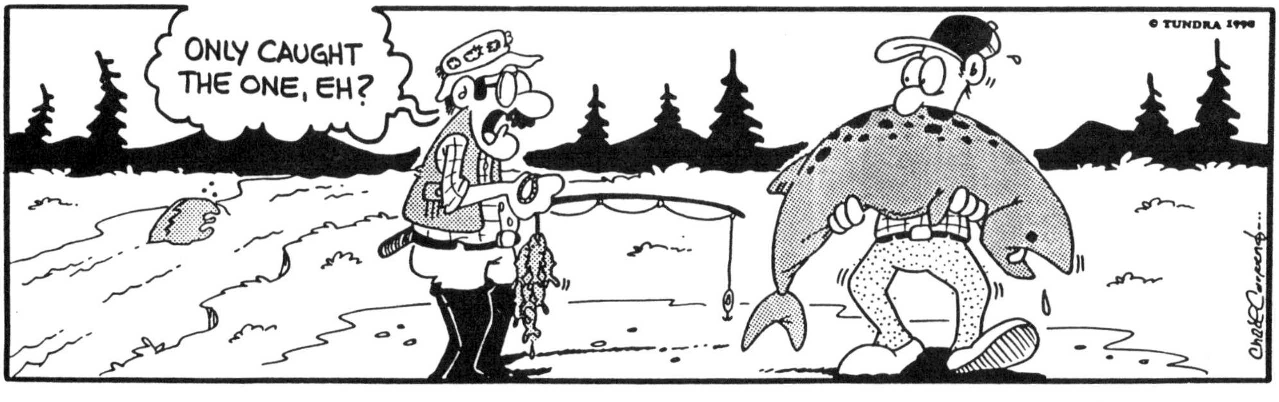
ONLY CAUGHT THE ONE, EH?
© TUNDRA 1998

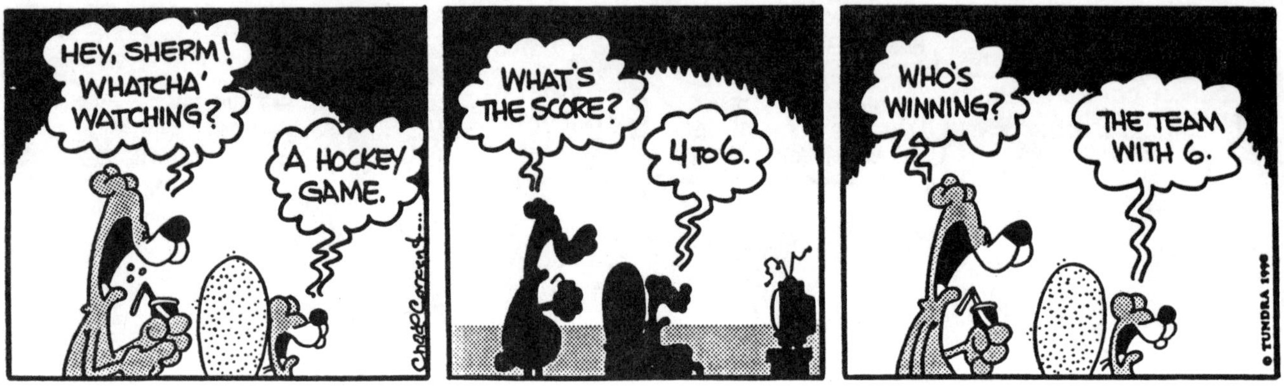
HEY, SHERM! WHATCHA' WATCHING?
A HOCKEY GAME.
WHAT'S THE SCORE?
4 TO 6.
WHO'S WINNING?
THE TEAM WITH 6.
© TUNDRA 1998

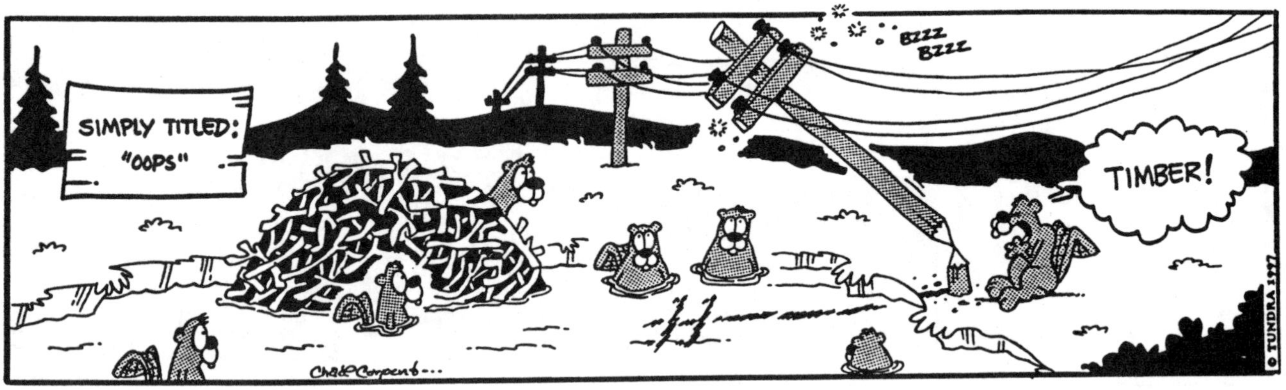
SIMPLY TITLED: "OOPS"
BZZZ BZZZ
TIMBER!
© TUNDRA 1997

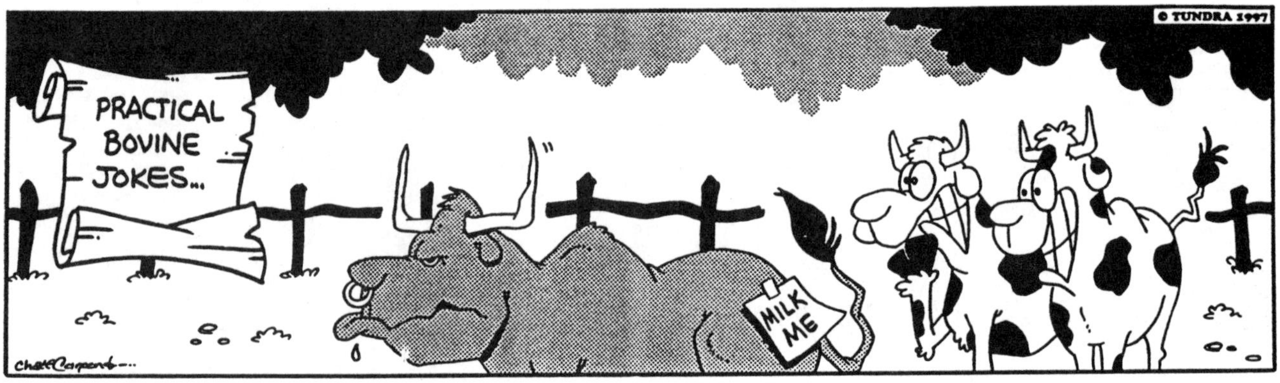
© TUNDRA 1997
PRACTICAL BOVINE JOKES...
MILK ME

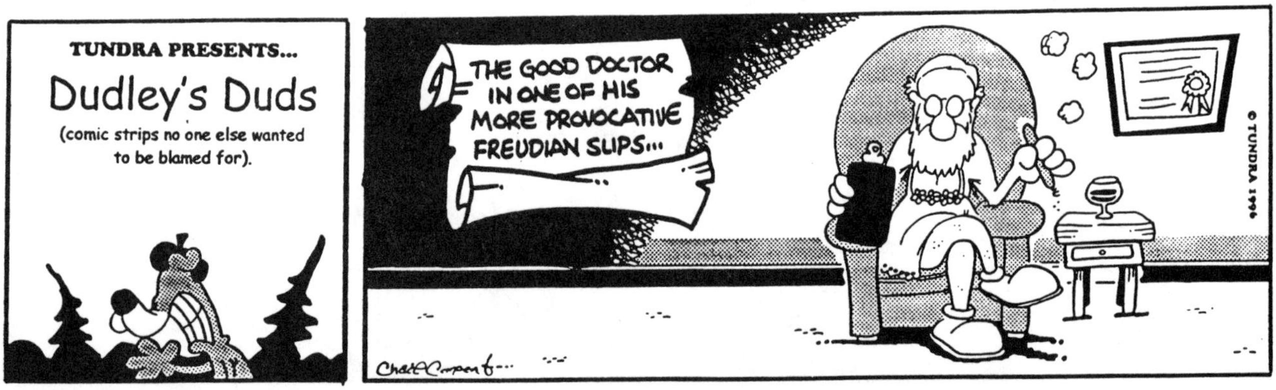
TUNDRA PRESENTS...
Dudley's Duds
(comic strips no one else wanted to be blamed for).
THE GOOD DOCTOR IN ONE OF HIS MORE PROVOCATIVE FREUDIAN SLIPS...
© TUNDRA 1996

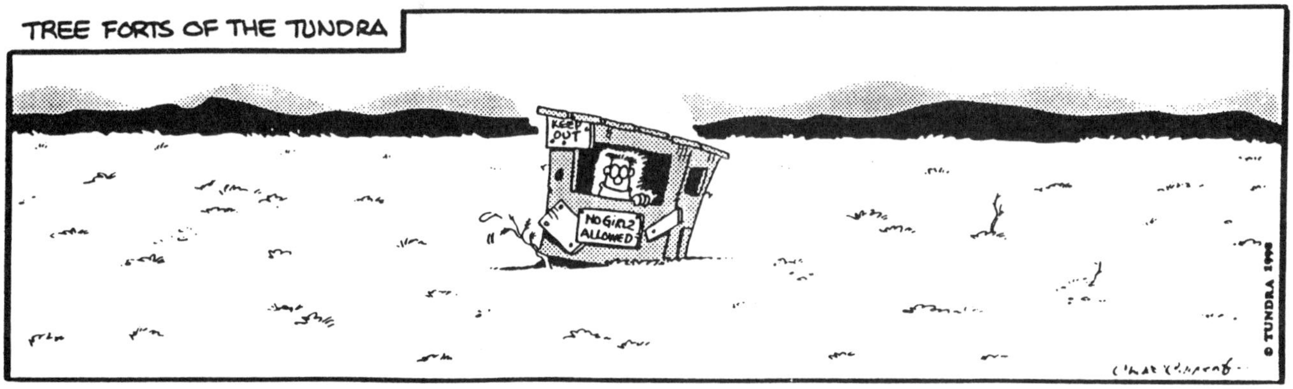
TREE FORTS OF THE TUNDRA
KEEP OUT
NO GIRLZ ALLOWED
© TUNDRA 1998

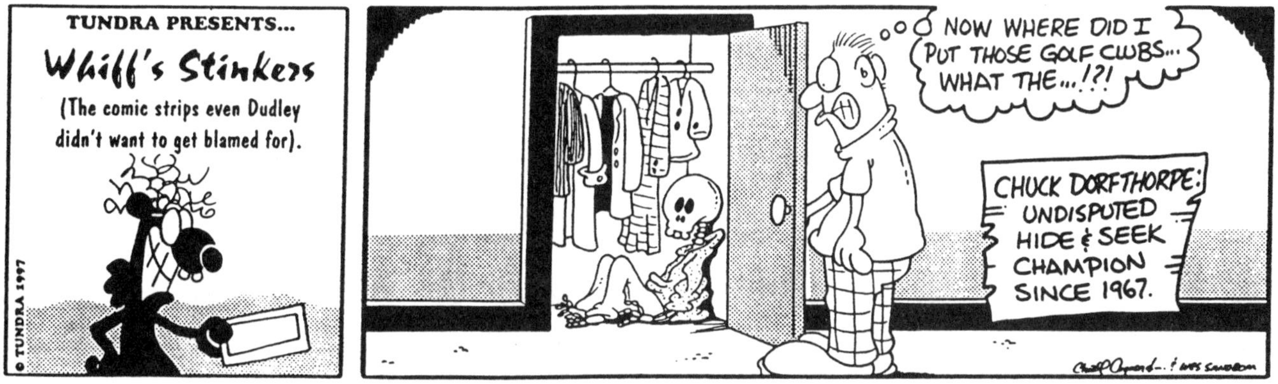
TUNDRA PRESENTS...
Whiff's Stinkers
(The comic strips even Dudley didn't want to get blamed for).
© TUNDRA 1997
NOW WHERE DID I PUT THOSE GOLF CLUBS... WHAT THE...!?!
CHUCK DORFTHORPE: UNDISPUTED HIDE & SEEK CHAMPION SINCE 1967.

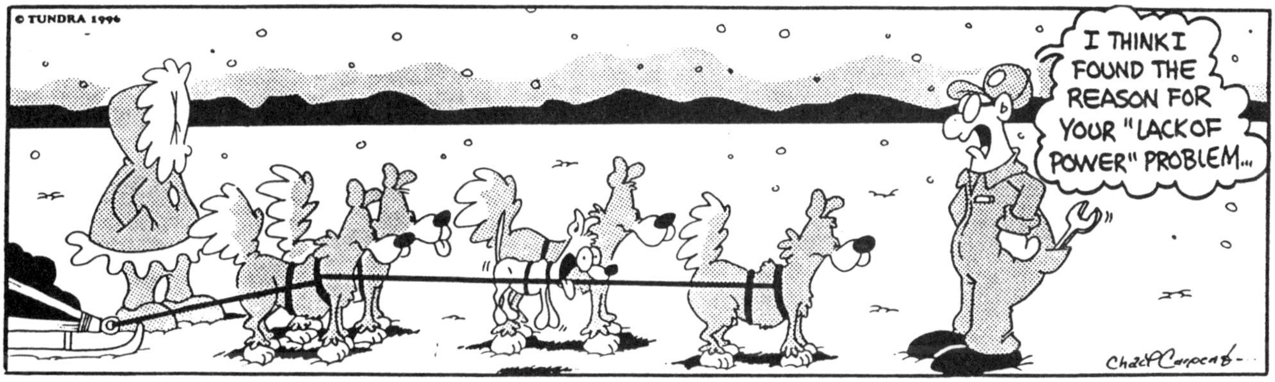
© TUNDRA 1996
I THINK I FOUND THE REASON FOR YOUR "LACK OF POWER" PROBLEM...

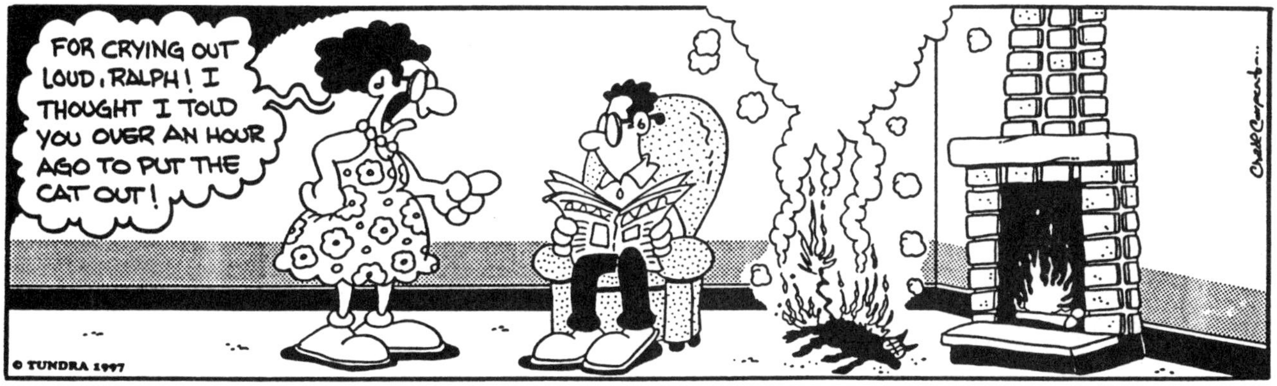
FOR CRYING OUT LOUD, RALPH! I THOUGHT I TOLD YOU OVER AN HOUR AGO TO PUT THE CAT OUT!
© TUNDRA 1997

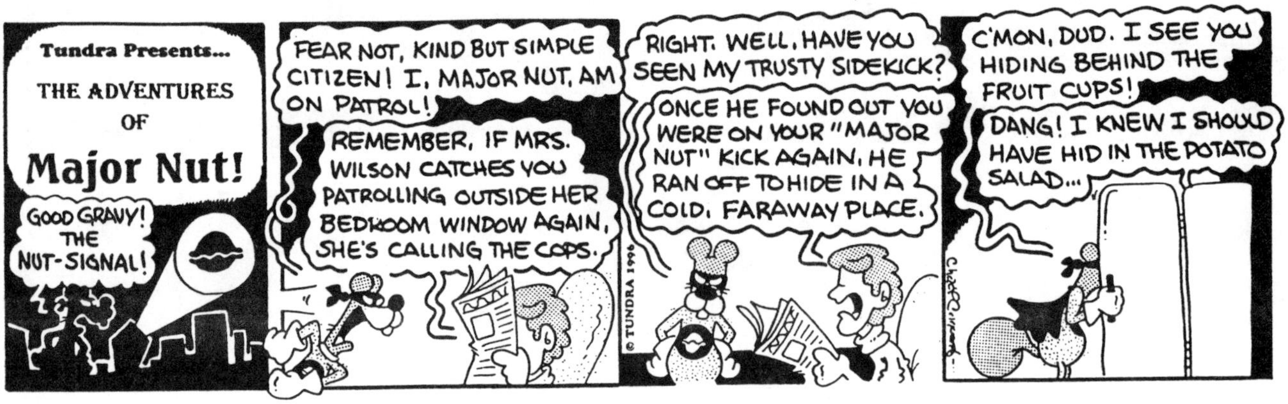
Tundra Presents...
THE ADVENTURES OF
Major Nut!
GOOD GRAVY! THE NUT-SIGNAL!
FEAR NOT, KIND BUT SIMPLE CITIZEN! I, MAJOR NUT, AM ON PATROL!
REMEMBER, IF MRS. WILSON CATCHES YOU PATROLLING OUTSIDE HER BEDROOM WINDOW AGAIN, SHE'S CALLING THE COPS.
© TUNDRA 1996
RIGHT. WELL, HAVE YOU SEEN MY TRUSTY SIDEKICK?
ONCE HE FOUND OUT YOU WERE ON YOUR "MAJOR NUT" KICK AGAIN, HE RAN OFF TO HIDE IN A COLD, FARAWAY PLACE.
C'MON, DUD. I SEE YOU HIDING BEHIND THE FRUIT CUPS!
DANG! I KNEW I SHOULD HAVE HID IN THE POTATO SALAD...

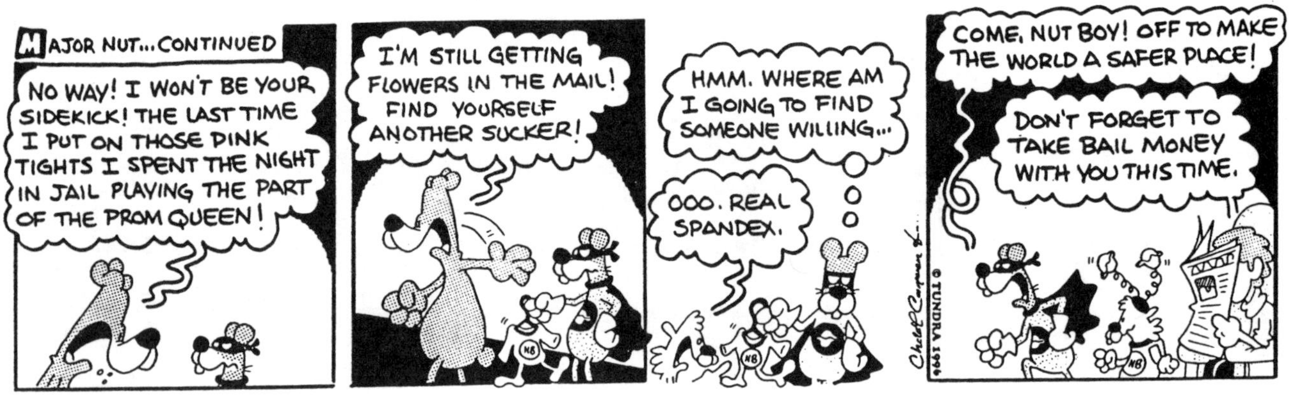
MAJOR NUT... CONTINUED
NO WAY! I WON'T BE YOUR SIDEKICK! THE LAST TIME I PUT ON THOSE PINK TIGHTS I SPENT THE NIGHT IN JAIL PLAYING THE PART OF THE PROM QUEEN!
I'M STILL GETTING FLOWERS IN THE MAIL! FIND YOURSELF ANOTHER SUCKER!
HMM. WHERE AM I GOING TO FIND SOMEONE WILLING...
OOO. REAL SPANDEX.
© TUNDRA 1996
COME, NUT BOY! OFF TO MAKE THE WORLD A SAFER PLACE!
DON'T FORGET TO TAKE BAIL MONEY WITH YOU THIS TIME.

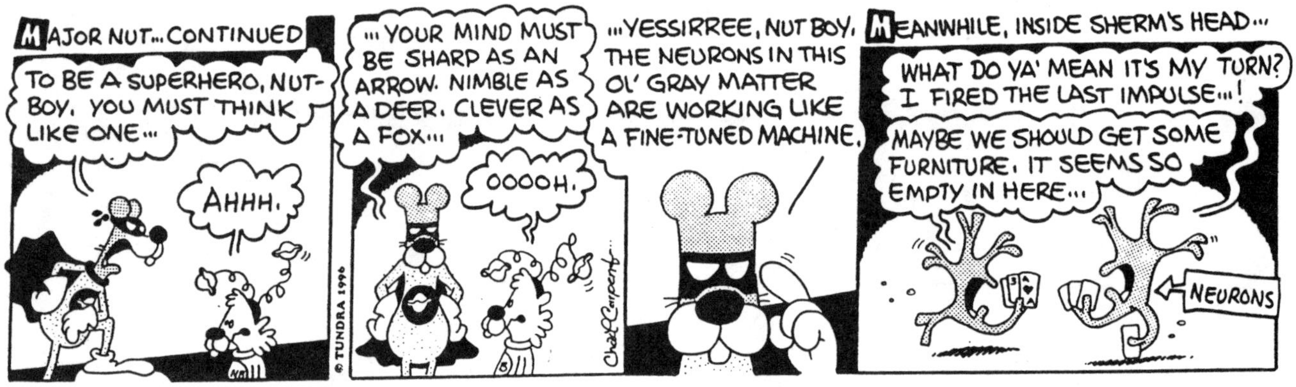
MAJOR NUT... CONTINUED
TO BE A SUPERHERO, NUT-BOY, YOU MUST THINK LIKE ONE...
AHHH.
© TUNDRA 1996
...YOUR MIND MUST BE SHARP AS AN ARROW. NIMBLE AS A DEER. CLEVER AS A FOX...
OOOOH.
...YESSIRREE, NUT BOY. THE NEURONS IN THIS OL' GRAY MATTER ARE WORKING LIKE A FINE-TUNED MACHINE.
MEANWHILE, INSIDE SHERM'S HEAD...
WHAT DO YA' MEAN IT'S MY TURN? I FIRED THE LAST IMPULSE...!
MAYBE WE SHOULD GET SOME FURNITURE. IT SEEMS SO EMPTY IN HERE...
NEURONS

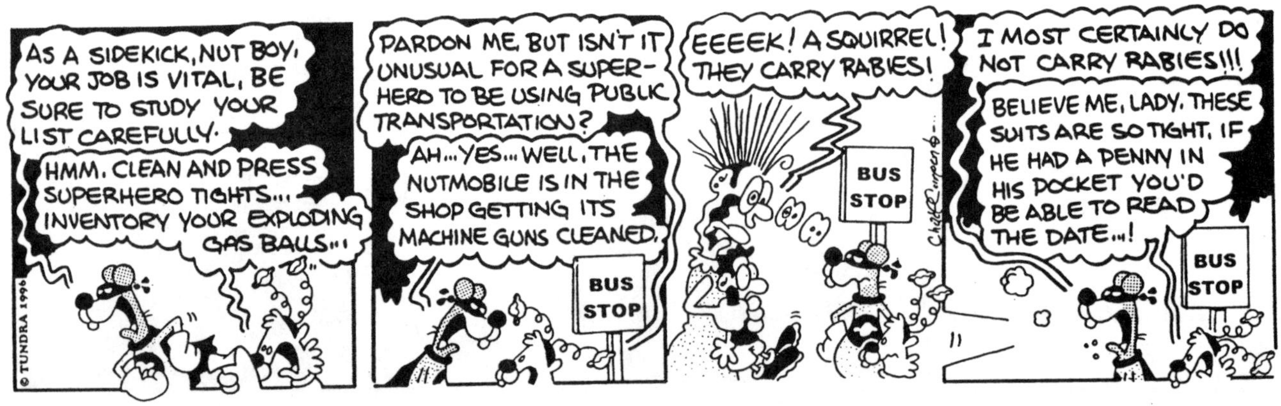
AS A SIDEKICK, NUT BOY, YOUR JOB IS VITAL. BE SURE TO STUDY YOUR LIST CAREFULLY.
HMM. CLEAN AND PRESS SUPERHERO TIGHTS... INVENTORY YOUR EXPLODING GAS BALLS...!
© TUNDRA 1996
PARDON ME, BUT ISN'T IT UNUSUAL FOR A SUPER-HERO TO BE USING PUBLIC TRANSPORTATION?
AH... YES... WELL, THE NUTMOBILE IS IN THE SHOP GETTING ITS MACHINE GUNS CLEANED.
BUS STOP
EEEEK! A SQUIRREL! THEY CARRY RABIES!
BUS STOP
I MOST CERTAINLY DO NOT CARRY RABIES!!!
BELIEVE ME, LADY. THESE SUITS ARE SO TIGHT, IF HE HAD A PENNY IN HIS POCKET YOU'D BE ABLE TO READ THE DATE...!
BUS STOP

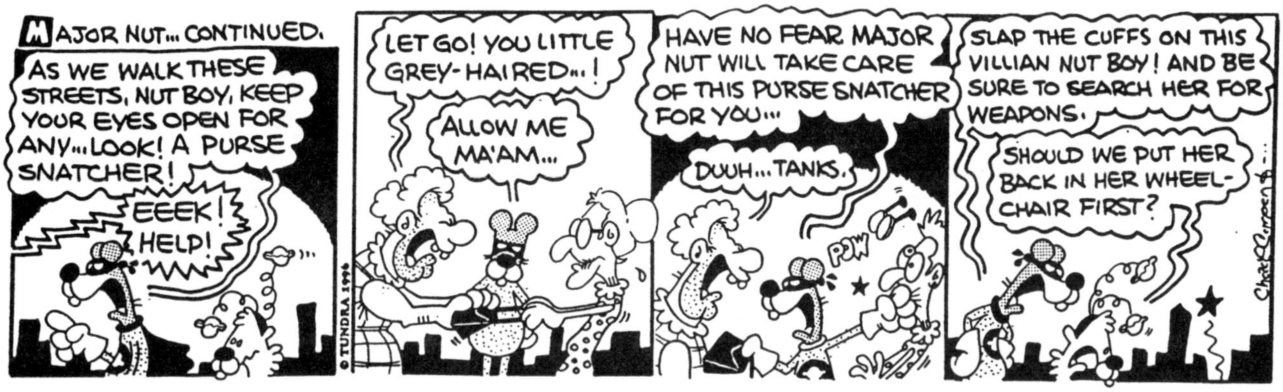
MAJOR NUT... CONTINUED.
AS WE WALK THESE STREETS, NUT BOY, KEEP YOUR EYES OPEN FOR ANY... LOOK! A PURSE SNATCHER!
EEEK! HELP!
© TUNDRA 1996
LET GO! YOU LITTLE GREY-HAIRED...!
ALLOW ME MA'AM...
HAVE NO FEAR MAJOR NUT WILL TAKE CARE OF THIS PURSE SNATCHER FOR YOU...
DUUH... TANKS.
POW
SLAP THE CUFFS ON THIS VILLIAN NUT BOY! AND BE SURE TO SEARCH HER FOR WEAPONS.
SHOULD WE PUT HER BACK IN HER WHEEL-CHAIR FIRST?

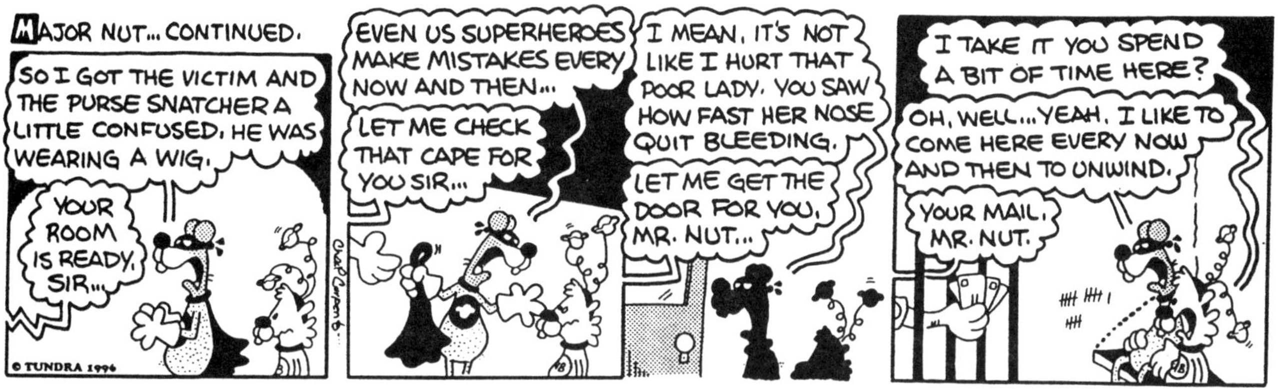
MAJOR NUT... CONTINUED.
SO I GOT THE VICTIM AND THE PURSE SNATCHER A LITTLE CONFUSED. HE WAS WEARING A WIG.
YOUR ROOM IS READY, SIR...
© TUNDRA 1996
EVEN US SUPERHEROES MAKE MISTAKES EVERY NOW AND THEN...
LET ME CHECK THAT CAPE FOR YOU SIR...
I MEAN, IT'S NOT LIKE I HURT THAT POOR LADY. YOU SAW HOW FAST HER NOSE QUIT BLEEDING.
LET ME GET THE DOOR FOR YOU, MR. NUT...
I TAKE IT YOU SPEND A BIT OF TIME HERE?
OH, WELL... YEAH. I LIKE TO COME HERE EVERY NOW AND THEN TO UNWIND.
YOUR MAIL, MR. NUT.

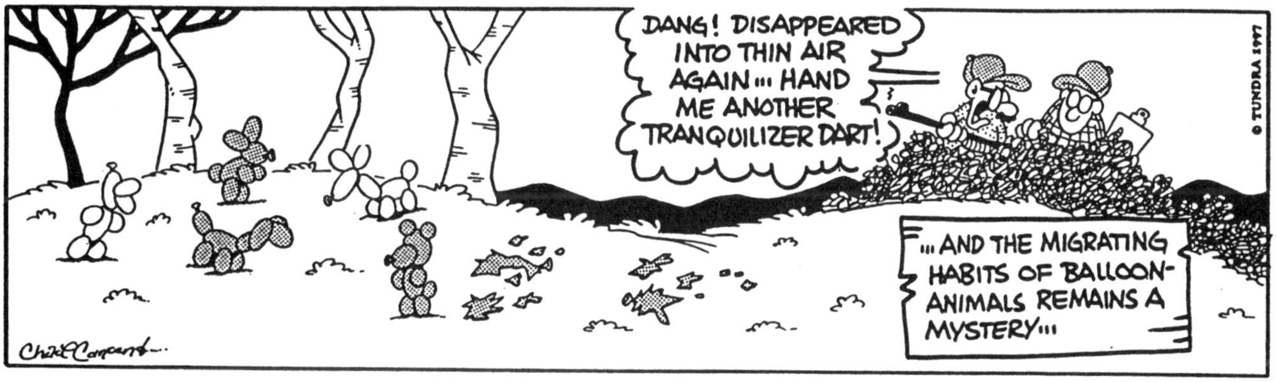
DANG! DISAPPEARED INTO THIN AIR AGAIN... HAND ME ANOTHER TRANQUILIZER DART!
...AND THE MIGRATING HABITS OF BALLOON-ANIMALS REMAINS A MYSTERY...
© TUNDRA 1997

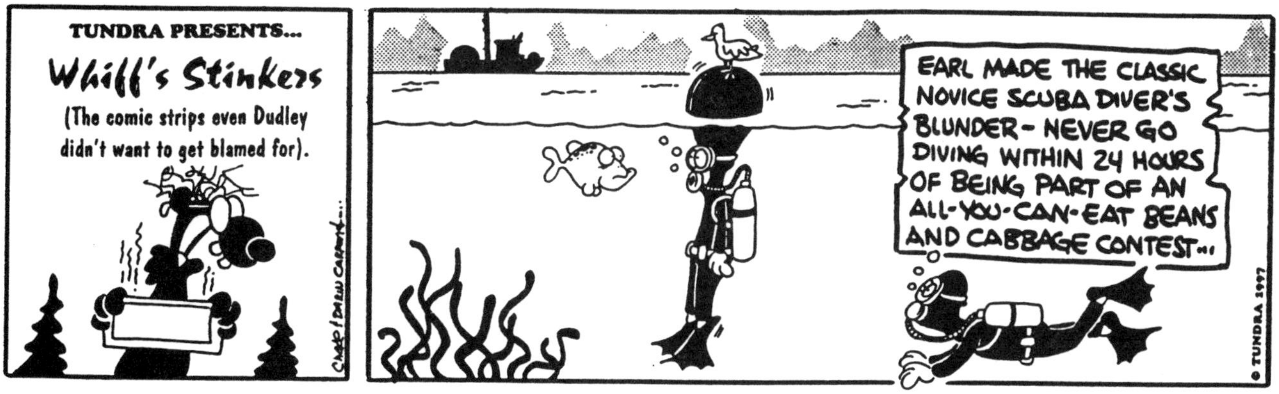
TUNDRA PRESENTS...
Whiff's Stinkers
(The comic strips even Dudley didn't want to get blamed for).
EARL MADE THE CLASSIC NOVICE SCUBA DIVER'S BLUNDER - NEVER GO DIVING WITHIN 24 HOURS OF BEING PART OF AN ALL-YOU-CAN-EAT BEANS AND CABBAGE CONTEST...
© TUNDRA 1997

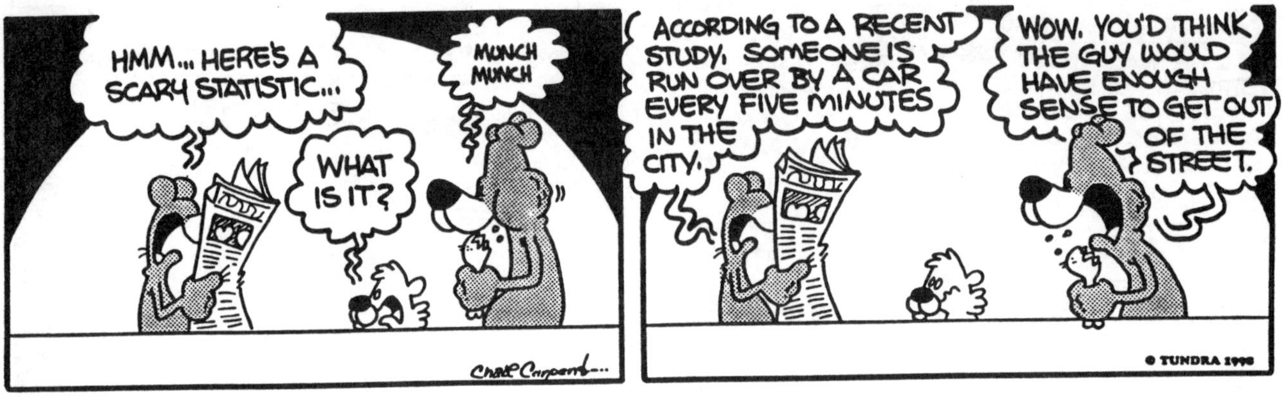
HMM... HERE'S A SCARY STATISTIC...
WHAT IS IT?
MUNCH MUNCH
ACCORDING TO A RECENT STUDY, SOMEONE IS RUN OVER BY A CAR EVERY FIVE MINUTES IN THE CITY.
WOW. YOU'D THINK THE GUY WOULD HAVE ENOUGH SENSE TO GET OUT OF THE STREET.
© TUNDRA 1998

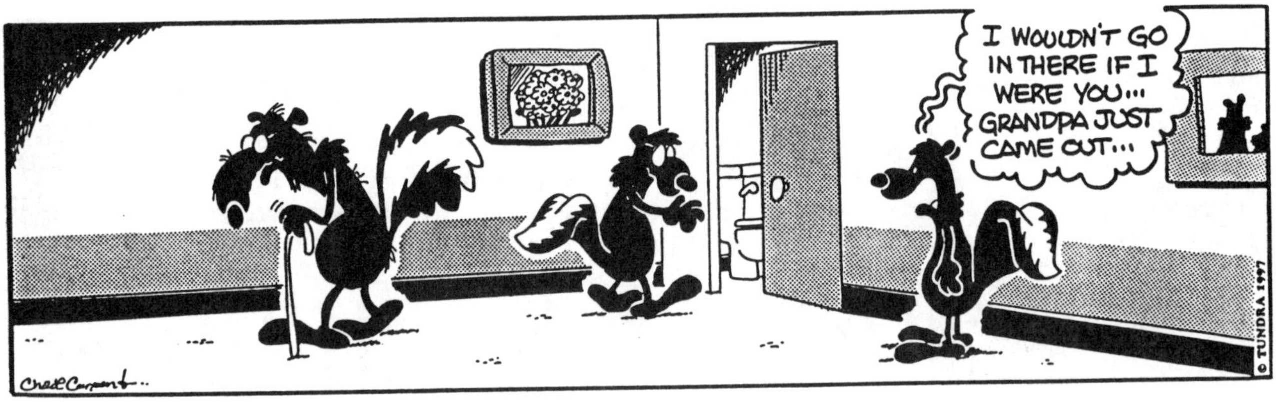
I WOULDN'T GO IN THERE IF I WERE YOU... GRANDPA JUST CAME OUT...
© TUNDRA 1997

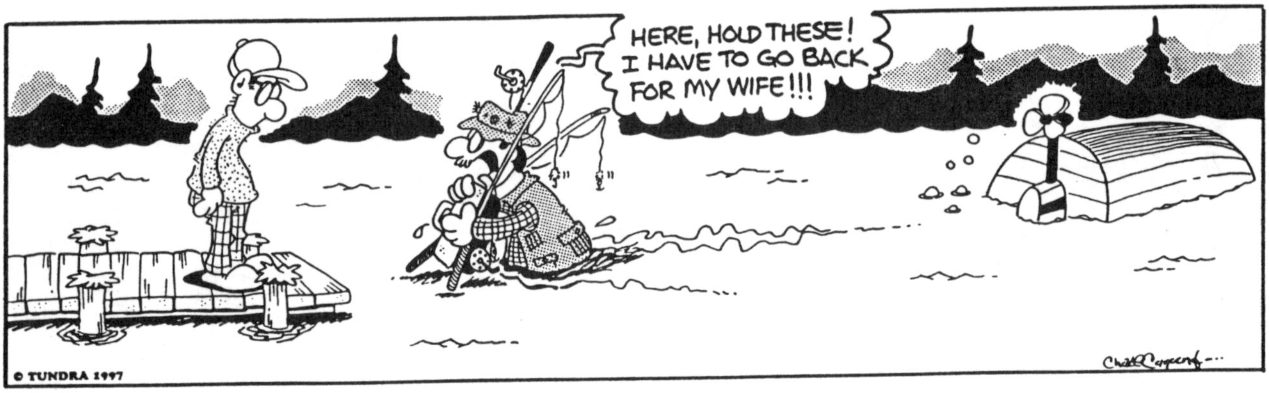
HERE, HOLD THESE! I HAVE TO GO BACK FOR MY WIFE!!!
© TUNDRA 1997

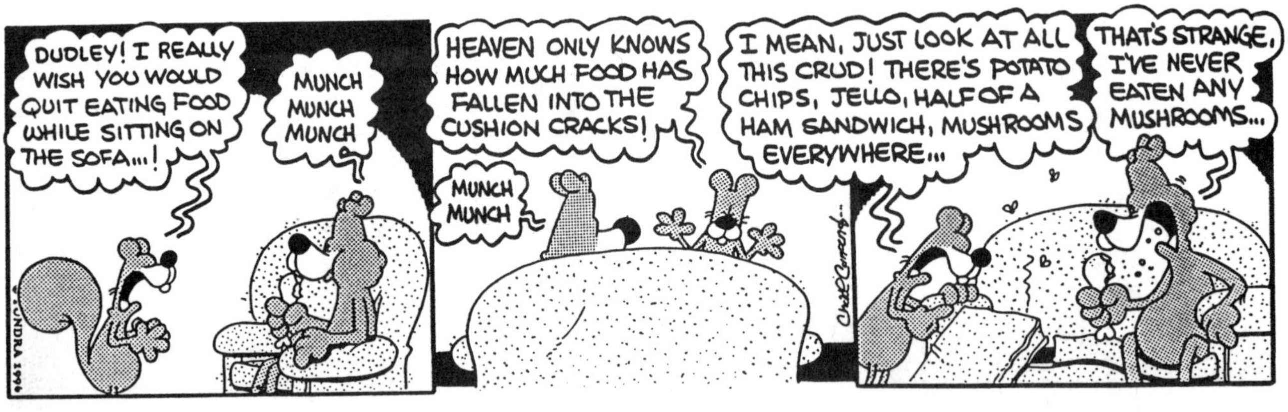
DUDLEY! I REALLY WISH YOU WOULD QUIT EATING FOOD WHILE SITTING ON THE SOFA...!
MUNCH MUNCH MUNCH
HEAVEN ONLY KNOWS HOW MUCH FOOD HAS FALLEN INTO THE CUSHION CRACKS!
MUNCH MUNCH
I MEAN, JUST LOOK AT ALL THIS CRUD! THERE'S POTATO CHIPS, JELLO, HALF OF A HAM SANDWICH, MUSHROOMS EVERYWHERE...
THAT'S STRANGE, I'VE NEVER EATEN ANY MUSHROOMS...
© TUNDRA 1996

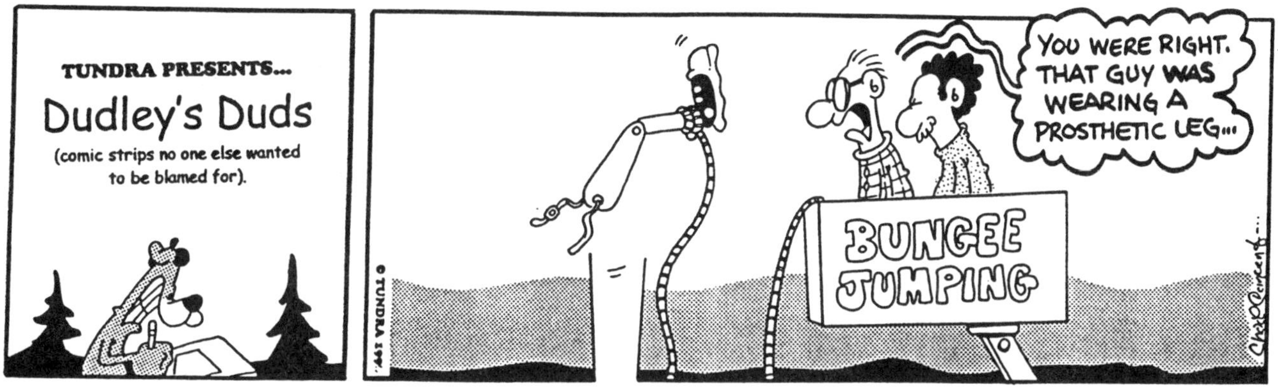
TUNDRA PRESENTS...
Dudley's Duds
(comic strips no one else wanted to be blamed for).
YOU WERE RIGHT. THAT GUY WAS WEARING A PROSTHETIC LEG...
BUNGEE JUMPING

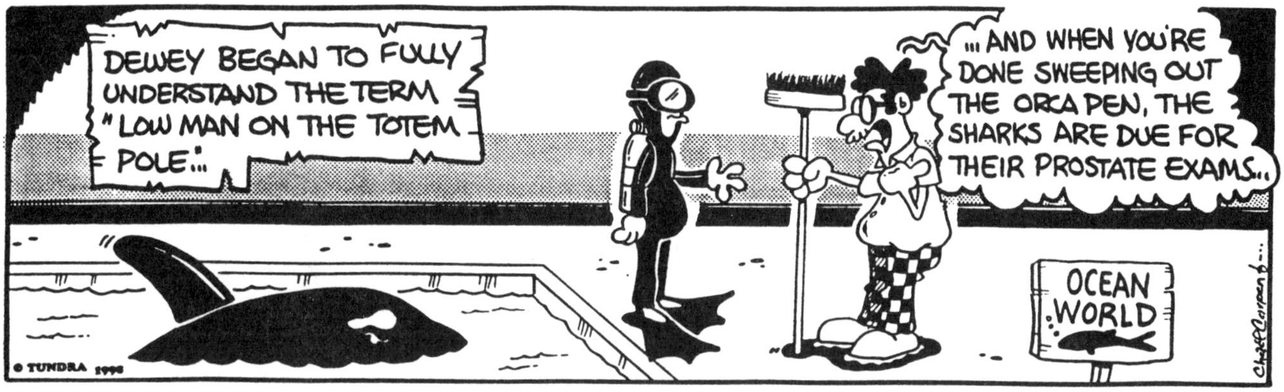
DEWEY BEGAN TO FULLY UNDERSTAND THE TERM "LOW MAN ON THE TOTEM POLE."...
...AND WHEN YOU'RE DONE SWEEPING OUT THE ORCA PEN, THE SHARKS ARE DUE FOR THEIR PROSTATE EXAMS...
OCEAN WORLD
© TUNDRA

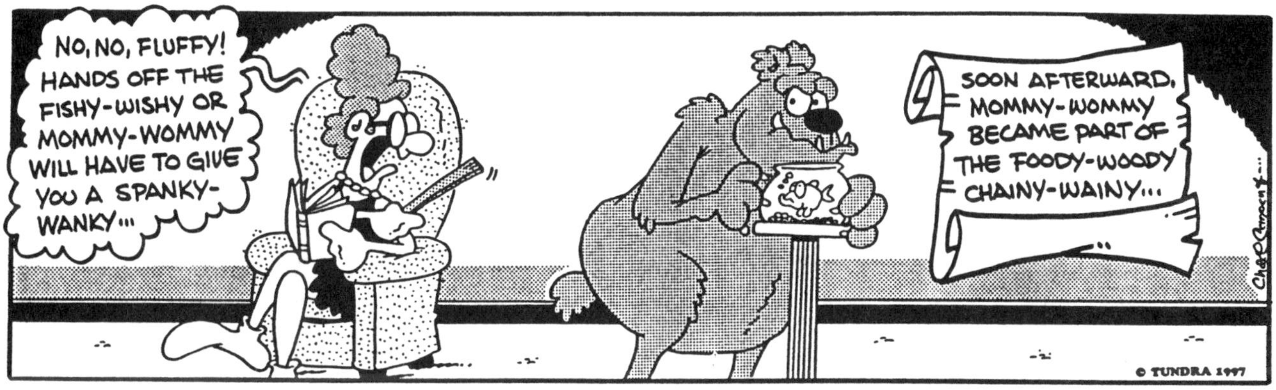
NO, NO, FLUFFY! HANDS OFF THE FISHY-WISHY OR MOMMY-WOMMY WILL HAVE TO GIVE YOU A SPANKY-WANKY...
SOON AFTERWARD, MOMMY-WOMMY BECAME PART OF THE FOODY-WOODY CHAINY-WAINY...
© TUNDRA 1997

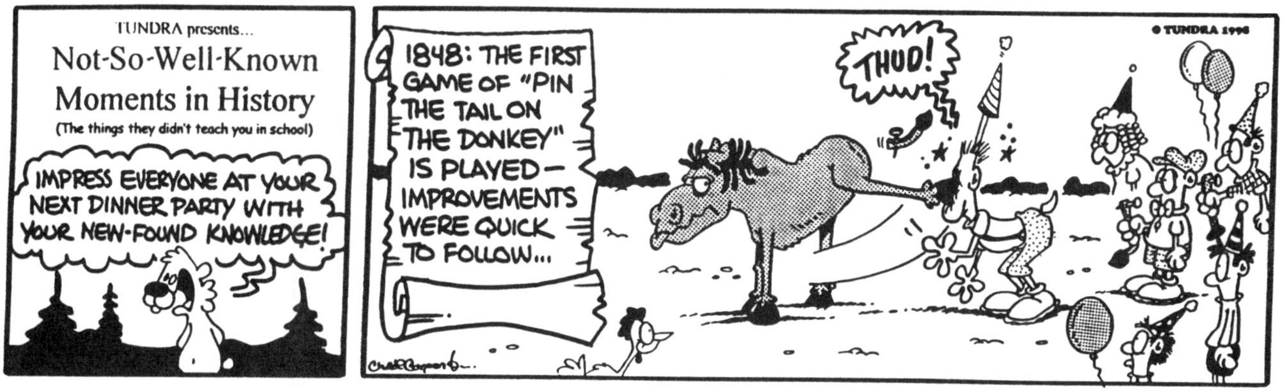
TUNDRA presents...
Not-So-Well-Known Moments in History
(The things they didn't teach you in school)
IMPRESS EVERYONE AT YOUR NEXT DINNER PARTY WITH YOUR NEW-FOUND KNOWLEDGE!
1848: THE FIRST GAME OF "PIN THE TAIL ON THE DONKEY" IS PLAYED— IMPROVEMENTS WERE QUICK TO FOLLOW...
THUD!
© TUNDRA

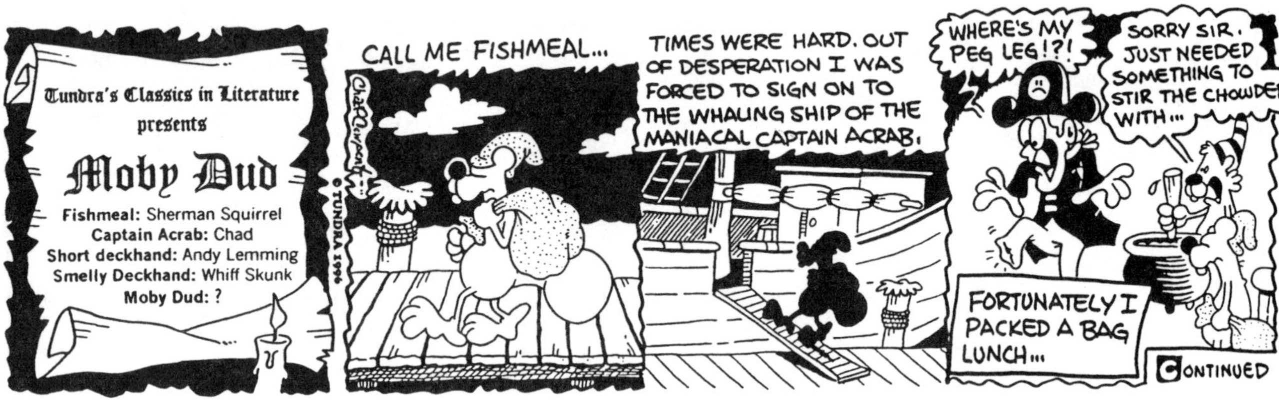
Tundra's Classics in Literature
presents
Moby Dud
Fishmeal: Sherman Squirrel
Captain Acrab: Chad
Short deckhand: Andy Lemming
Smelly Deckhand: Whiff Skunk
Moby Dud: ?
CALL ME FISHMEAL...
© TUNDRA 1996
TIMES WERE HARD. OUT OF DESPERATION I WAS FORCED TO SIGN ON TO THE WHALING SHIP OF THE MANIACAL CAPTAIN ACRAB.
WHERE'S MY PEG LEG!?!
SORRY SIR. JUST NEEDED SOMETHING TO STIR THE CHOWDER WITH...
FORTUNATELY I PACKED A BAG LUNCH...
CONTINUED

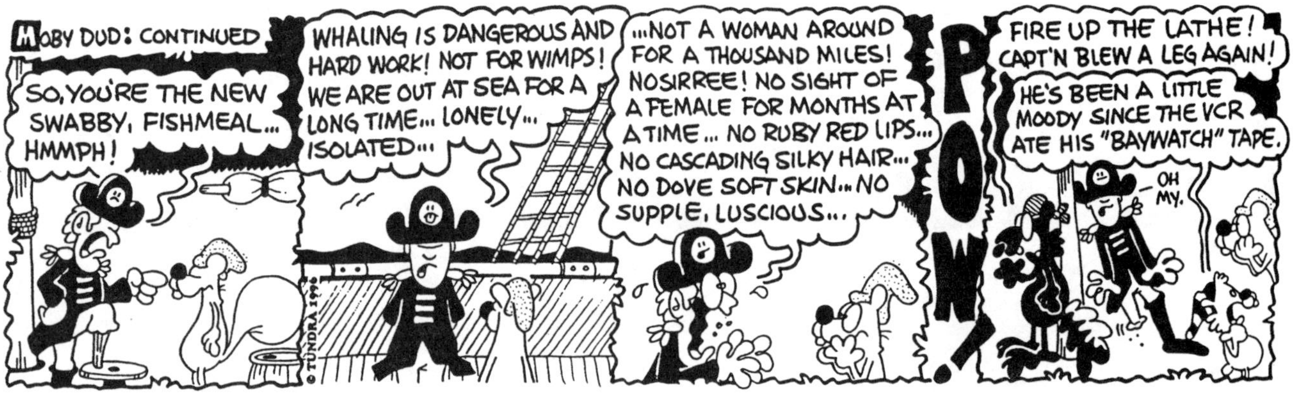
MOBY DUD: CONTINUED
SO, YOU'RE THE NEW SWABBY, FISHMEAL... HMMPH!
WHALING IS DANGEROUS AND HARD WORK! NOT FOR WIMPS! WE ARE OUT AT SEA FOR A LONG TIME... LONELY... ISOLATED...
© TUNDRA 1996
...NOT A WOMAN AROUND FOR A THOUSAND MILES! NOSIRREE! NO SIGHT OF A FEMALE FOR MONTHS AT A TIME... NO RUBY RED LIPS... NO CASCADING SILKY HAIR... NO DOVE SOFT SKIN... NO SUPPLE, LUSCIOUS...
POW!
FIRE UP THE LATHE! CAPT'N BLEW A LEG AGAIN!
HE'S BEEN A LITTLE MOODY SINCE THE VCR ATE HIS "BAYWATCH" TAPE.
OH MY.

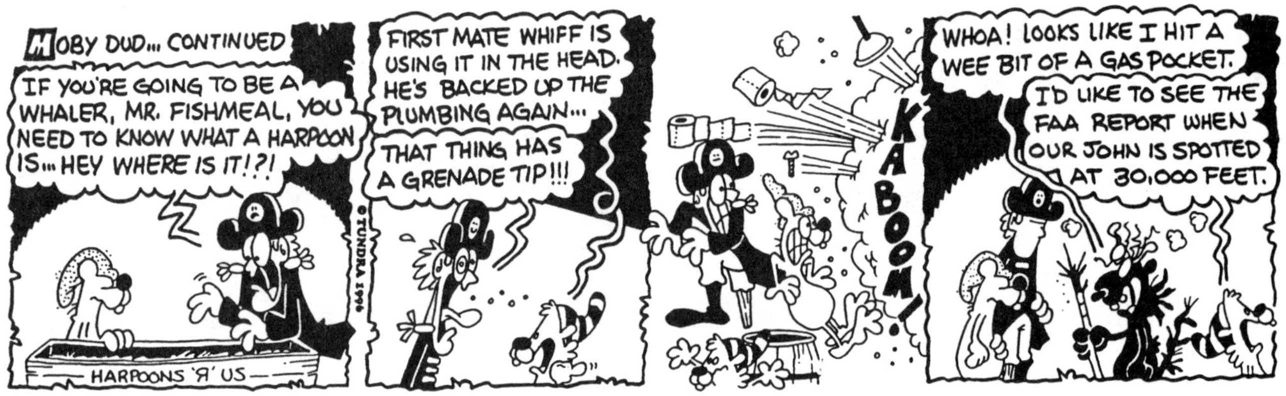
MOBY DUD... CONTINUED
IF YOU'RE GOING TO BE A WHALER, MR. FISHMEAL, YOU NEED TO KNOW WHAT A HARPOON IS... HEY WHERE IS IT!?!
HARPOONS 'R' US
FIRST MATE WHIFF IS USING IT IN THE HEAD. HE'S BACKED UP THE PLUMBING AGAIN...
THAT THING HAS A GRENADE TIP!!!
© TUNDRA 1996
KABOOM!
WHOA! LOOKS LIKE I HIT A WEE BIT OF A GAS POCKET.
I'D LIKE TO SEE THE FAA REPORT WHEN OUR JOHN IS SPOTTED AT 30,000 FEET.

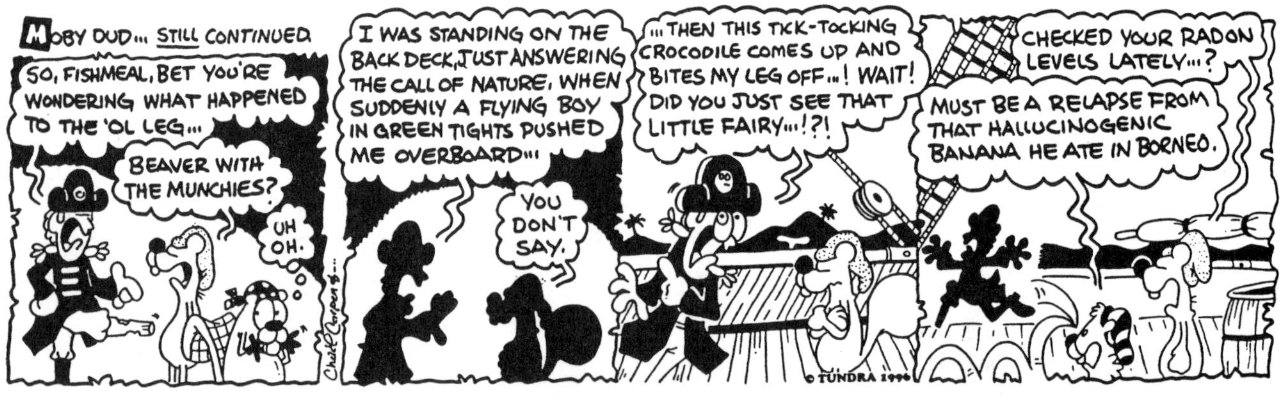
MOBY DUD... STILL CONTINUED
SO, FISHMEAL, BET YOU'RE WONDERING WHAT HAPPENED TO THE 'OL LEG...
BEAVER WITH THE MUNCHIES?
UH OH.
I WAS STANDING ON THE BACK DECK, JUST ANSWERING THE CALL OF NATURE, WHEN SUDDENLY A FLYING BOY IN GREEN TIGHTS PUSHED ME OVERBOARD...
YOU DON'T SAY.
...THEN THIS TICK-TOCKING CROCODILE COMES UP AND BITES MY LEG OFF...! WAIT! DID YOU JUST SEE THAT LITTLE FAIRY...!?!
© TUNDRA 1996
CHECKED YOUR RADON LEVELS LATELY...?
MUST BE A RELAPSE FROM THAT HALLUCINOGENIC BANANA HE ATE IN BORNEO.

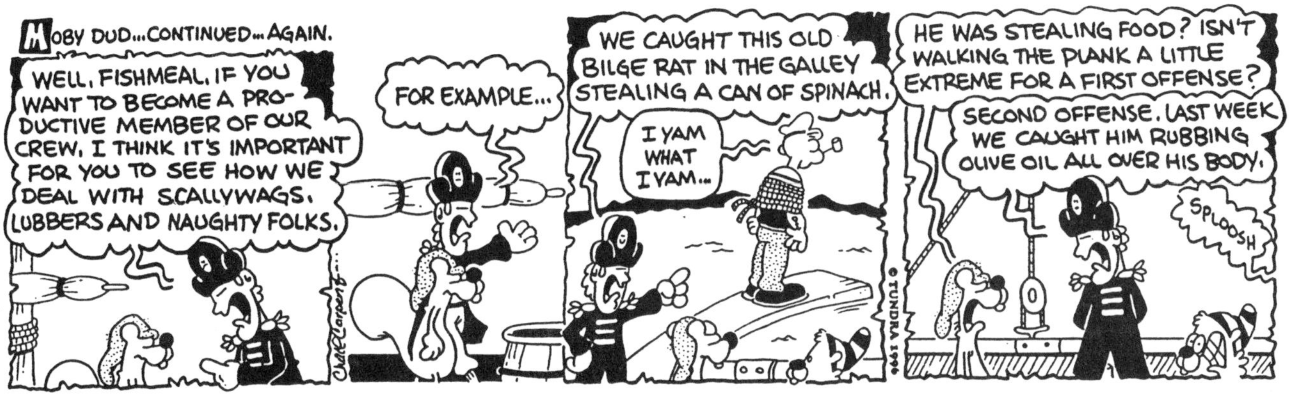
MOBY DUD... CONTINUED... AGAIN.
WELL, FISHMEAL, IF YOU WANT TO BECOME A PRODUCTIVE MEMBER OF OUR CREW, I THINK IT'S IMPORTANT FOR YOU TO SEE HOW WE DEAL WITH SCALLYWAGS, LUBBERS AND NAUGHTY FOLKS.
FOR EXAMPLE...
WE CAUGHT THIS OLD BILGE RAT IN THE GALLEY STEALING A CAN OF SPINACH.
I YAM WHAT I YAM...
© TUNDRA 1996
HE WAS STEALING FOOD? ISN'T WALKING THE PLANK A LITTLE EXTREME FOR A FIRST OFFENSE?
SECOND OFFENSE. LAST WEEK WE CAUGHT HIM RUBBING OLIVE OIL ALL OVER HIS BODY.
SPLOOSH

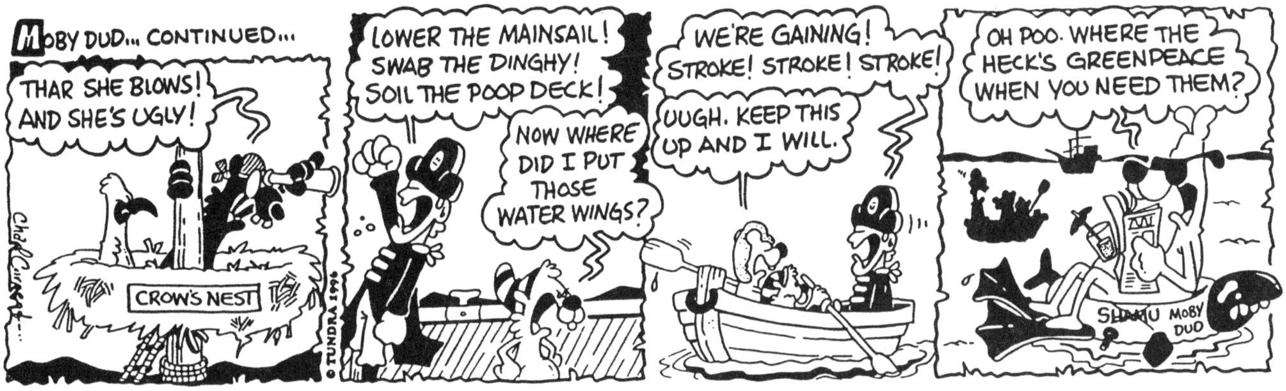
MOBY DUD... CONTINUED...
THAR SHE BLOWS! AND SHE'S UGLY!
CROW'S NEST
© TUNDRA 1996
LOWER THE MAINSAIL! SWAB THE DINGHY! SOIL THE POOP DECK!
NOW WHERE DID I PUT THOSE WATER WINGS?
WE'RE GAINING! STROKE! STROKE! STROKE!
UUGH. KEEP THIS UP AND I WILL.
OH POO. WHERE THE HECK'S GREENPEACE WHEN YOU NEED THEM?
MOBY DUD

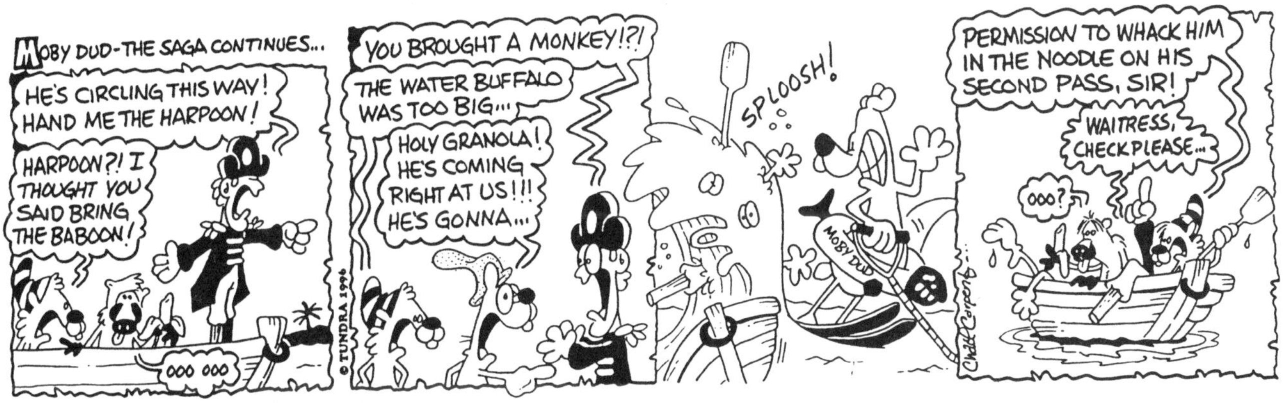
MOBY DUD - THE SAGA CONTINUES...
HE'S CIRCLING THIS WAY! HAND ME THE HARPOON!
HARPOON?! I THOUGHT YOU SAID BRING THE BABOON!
OOO OOO
© TUNDRA 1996
YOU BROUGHT A MONKEY!?!
THE WATER BUFFALO WAS TOO BIG...
HOLY GRANOLA! HE'S COMING RIGHT AT US!!! HE'S GONNA...
SPLOOSH!
MOBY DUD
PERMISSION TO WHACK HIM IN THE NOODLE ON HIS SECOND PASS, SIR!
WAITRESS, CHECK PLEASE...
OOO?

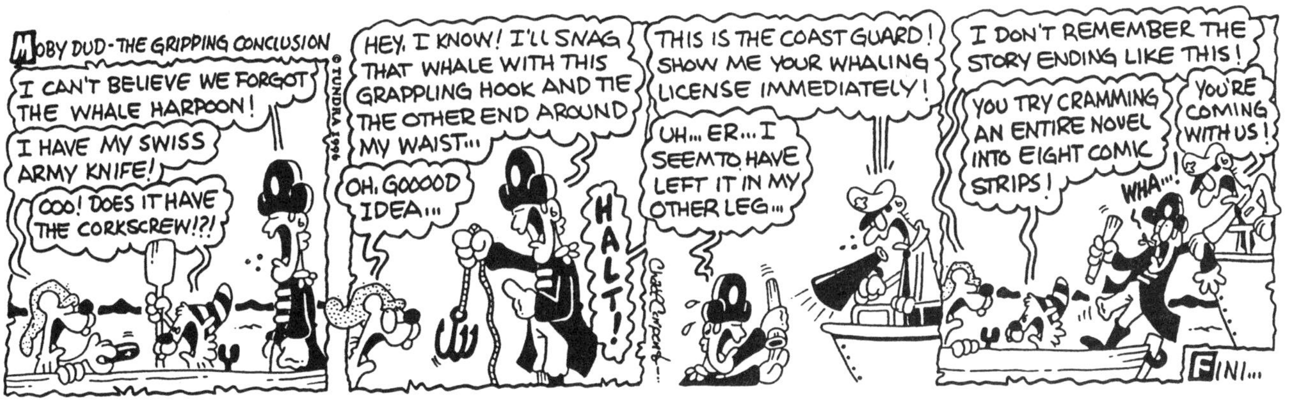
MOBY DUD - THE GRIPPING CONCLUSION
I CAN'T BELIEVE WE FORGOT THE WHALE HARPOON!
I HAVE MY SWISS ARMY KNIFE!
OOO! DOES IT HAVE THE CORKSCREW!?!
© TUNDRA 1996
HEY, I KNOW! I'LL SNAG THAT WHALE WITH THIS GRAPPLING HOOK AND TIE THE OTHER END AROUND MY WAIST...
OH, GOOOOD IDEA...
HALT!
THIS IS THE COAST GUARD! SHOW ME YOUR WHALING LICENSE IMMEDIATELY!
UH... ER... I SEEM TO HAVE LEFT IT IN MY OTHER LEG...
I DON'T REMEMBER THE STORY ENDING LIKE THIS!
YOU TRY CRAMMING AN ENTIRE NOVEL INTO EIGHT COMIC STRIPS!
YOU'RE COMING WITH US!
WHA...!
FINI...

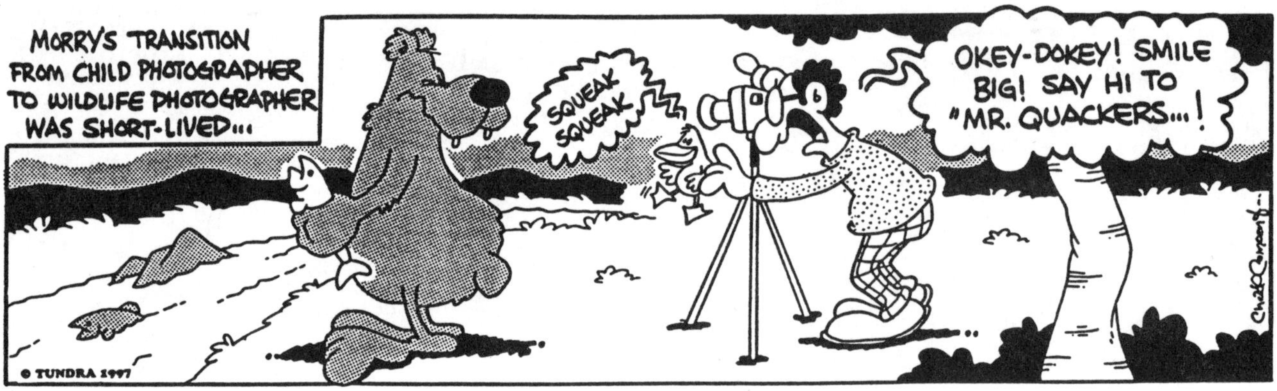
MORRY'S TRANSITION FROM CHILD PHOTOGRAPHER TO WILDLIFE PHOTOGRAPHER WAS SHORT-LIVED...
SQUEAK SQUEAK
OKEY-DOKEY! SMILE BIG! SAY HI TO "MR. QUACKERS...!
© TUNDRA 1997

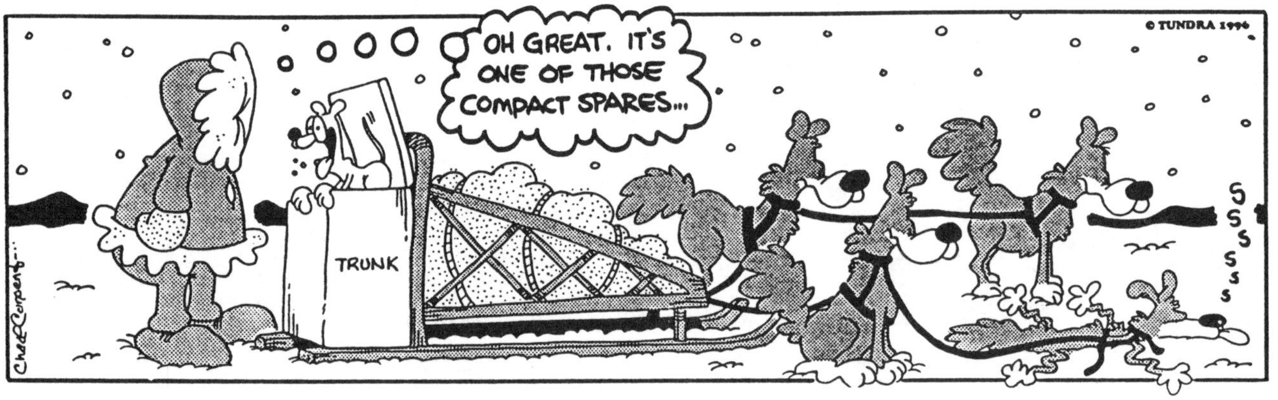
OH GREAT. IT'S ONE OF THOSE COMPACT SPARES...
TRUNK
SSSSSS
© TUNDRA 1996

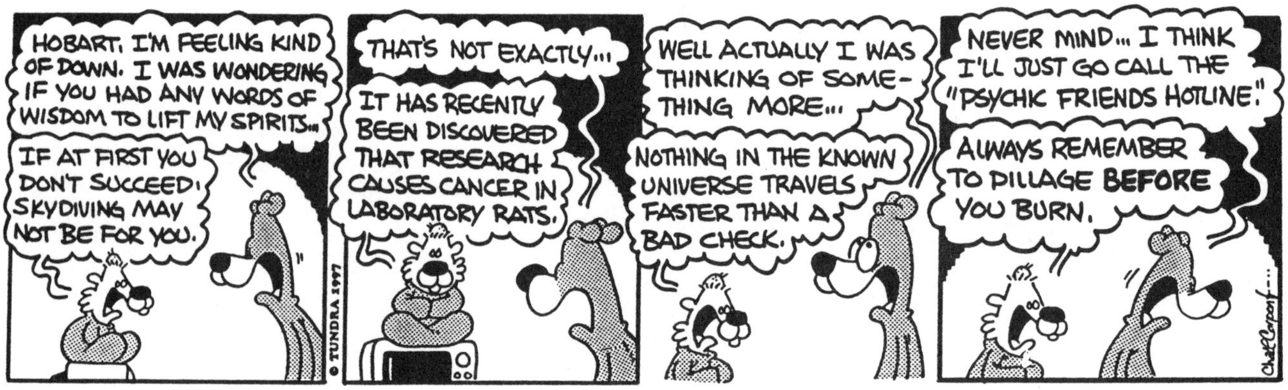
HOBART, I'M FEELING KIND OF DOWN. I WAS WONDERING IF YOU HAD ANY WORDS OF WISDOM TO LIFT MY SPIRITS...
IF AT FIRST YOU DON'T SUCCEED, SKYDIVING MAY NOT BE FOR YOU.
THAT'S NOT EXACTLY...
IT HAS RECENTLY BEEN DISCOVERED THAT RESEARCH CAUSES CANCER IN LABORATORY RATS.
WELL ACTUALLY I WAS THINKING OF SOMETHING MORE...
NOTHING IN THE KNOWN UNIVERSE TRAVELS FASTER THAN A BAD CHECK.
NEVER MIND... I THINK I'LL JUST GO CALL THE "PSYCHIC FRIENDS HOTLINE."
ALWAYS REMEMBER TO PILLAGE BEFORE YOU BURN.
© TUNDRA 1997

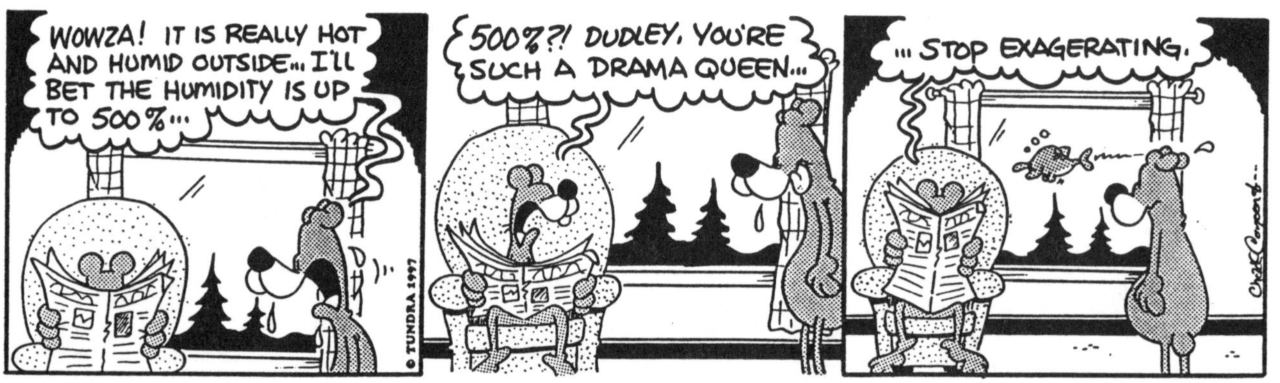
WOWZA! IT IS REALLY HOT AND HUMID OUTSIDE... I'LL BET THE HUMIDITY IS UP TO 500%...
500%?! DUDLEY, YOU'RE SUCH A DRAMA QUEEN...
...STOP EXAGERATING.
© TUNDRA 1997

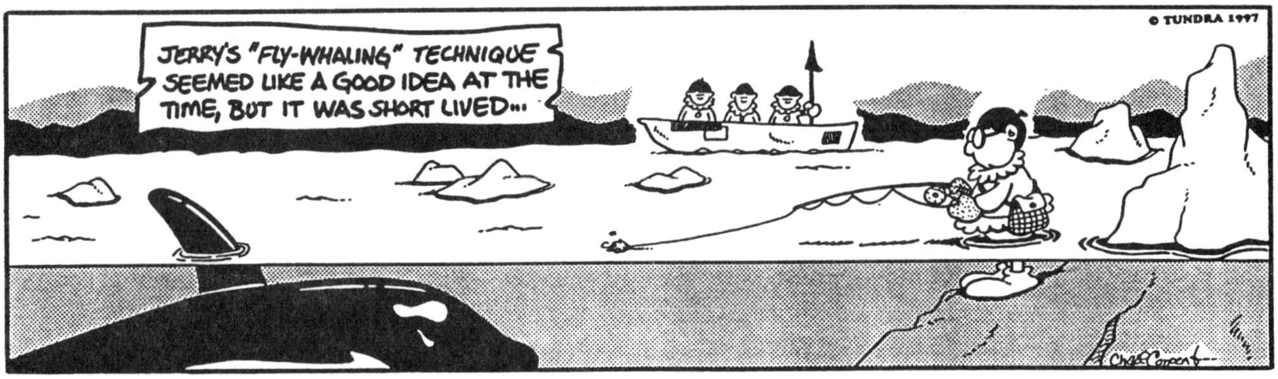
© TUNDRA 1997
JERRY'S "FLY-WHALING" TECHNIQUE SEEMED LIKE A GOOD IDEA AT THE TIME, BUT IT WAS SHORT LIVED...

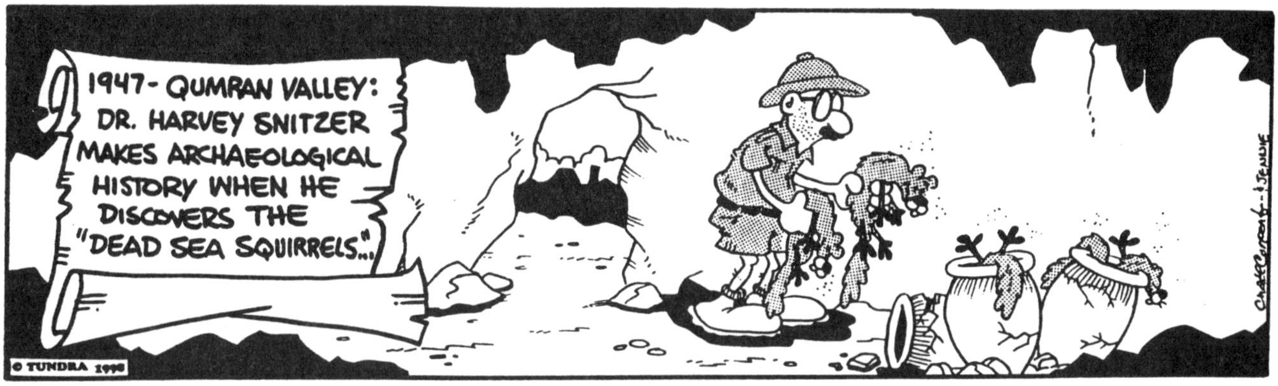
1947 - QUMRAN VALLEY: DR. HARVEY SNITZER MAKES ARCHAEOLOGICAL HISTORY WHEN HE DISCOVERS THE "DEAD SEA SQUIRRELS."
© TUNDRA 1998

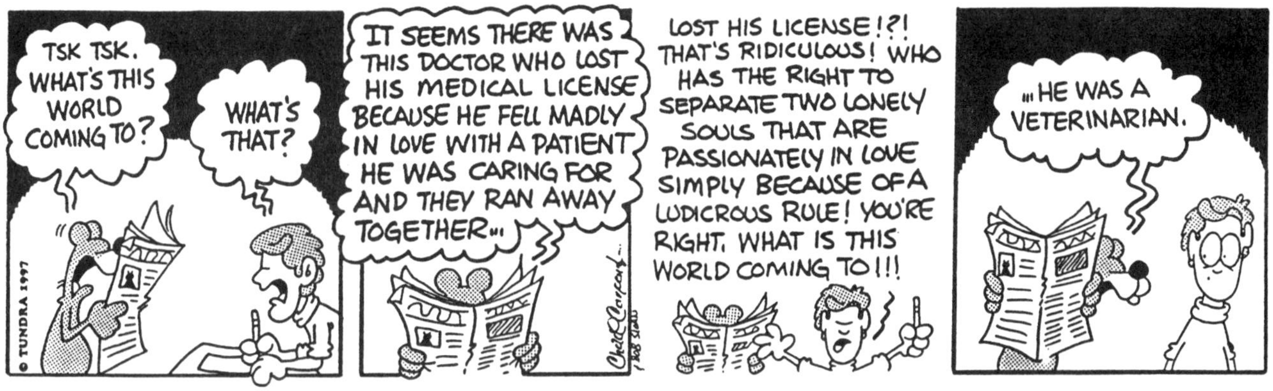
TSK TSK. WHAT'S THIS WORLD COMING TO?
WHAT'S THAT?
© TUNDRA 1997
IT SEEMS THERE WAS THIS DOCTOR WHO LOST HIS MEDICAL LICENSE BECAUSE HE FELL MADLY IN LOVE WITH A PATIENT HE WAS CARING FOR AND THEY RAN AWAY TOGETHER...
LOST HIS LICENSE!?! THAT'S RIDICULOUS! WHO HAS THE RIGHT TO SEPARATE TWO LONELY SOULS THAT ARE PASSIONATELY IN LOVE SIMPLY BECAUSE OF A LUDICROUS RULE! YOU'RE RIGHT. WHAT IS THIS WORLD COMING TO!!!
...HE WAS A VETERINARIAN.

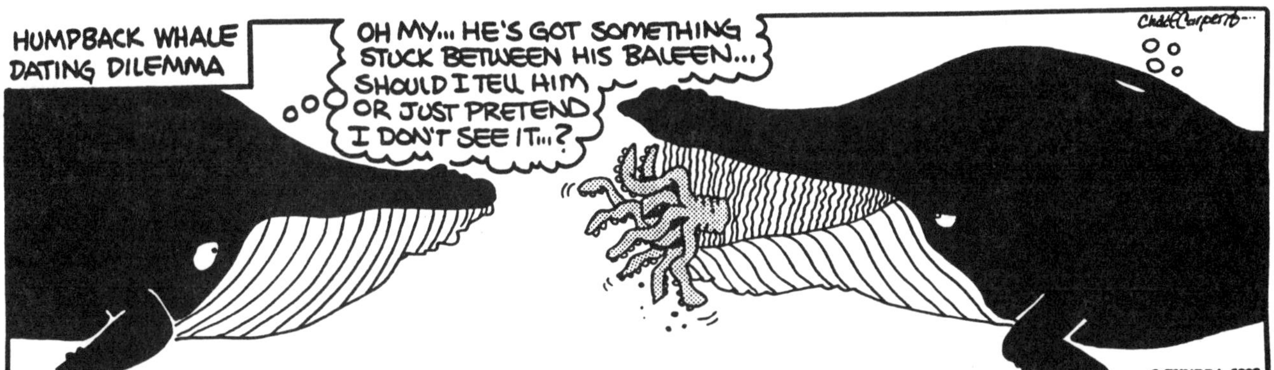
HUMPBACK WHALE DATING DILEMMA
OH MY... HE'S GOT SOMETHING STUCK BETWEEN HIS BALEEN... SHOULD I TELL HIM OR JUST PRETEND I DON'T SEE IT...?
© TUNDRA 1998

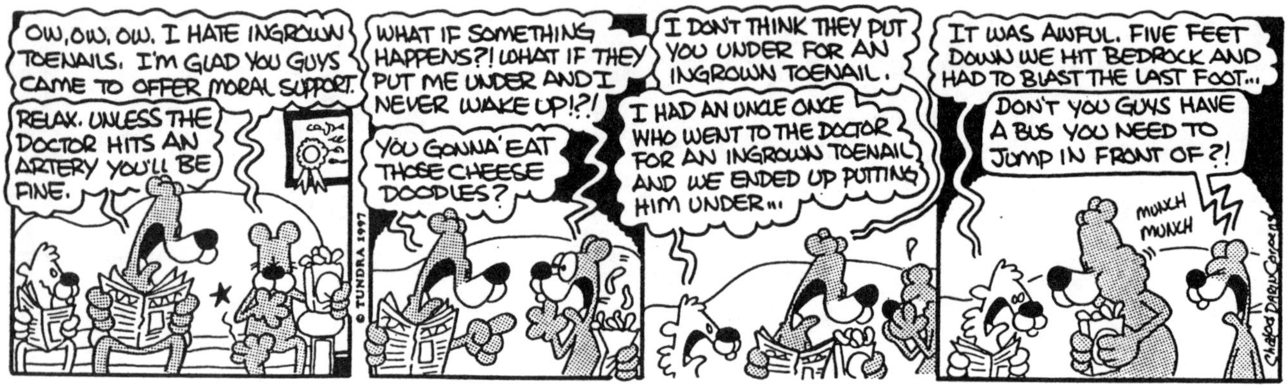
OW, OW, OW. I HATE INGROWN TOENAILS. I'M GLAD YOU GUYS CAME TO OFFER MORAL SUPPORT.
RELAX. UNLESS THE DOCTOR HITS AN ARTERY YOU'LL BE FINE.
© TUNDRA 1997
WHAT IF SOMETHING HAPPENS?! WHAT IF THEY PUT ME UNDER AND I NEVER WAKE UP!?!
YOU GONNA' EAT THOSE CHEESE DOODLES?
I DON'T THINK THEY PUT YOU UNDER FOR AN INGROWN TOENAIL.
I HAD AN UNCLE ONCE WHO WENT TO THE DOCTOR FOR AN INGROWN TOENAIL AND WE ENDED UP PUTTING HIM UNDER...
IT WAS AWFUL. FIVE FEET DOWN WE HIT BEDROCK AND HAD TO BLAST THE LAST FOOT...
DON'T YOU GUYS HAVE A BUS YOU NEED TO JUMP IN FRONT OF?!
MUNCH MUNCH

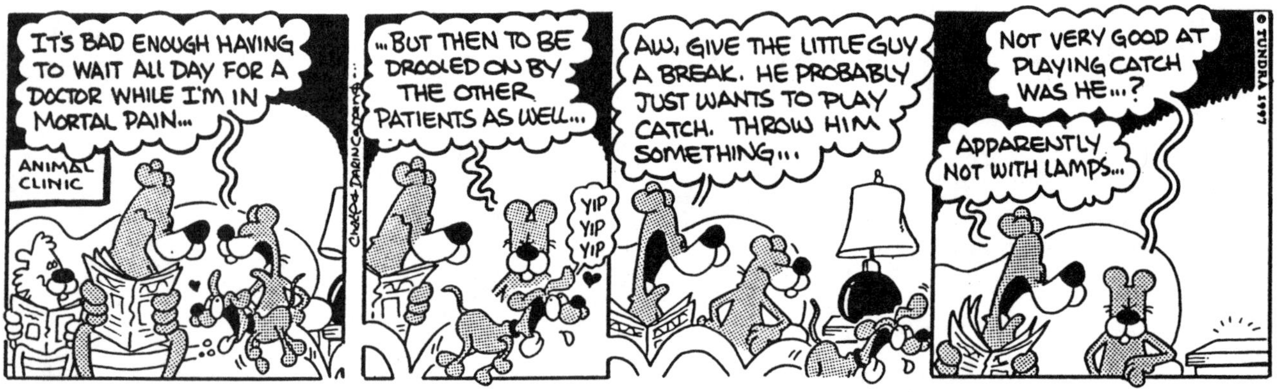
IT'S BAD ENOUGH HAVING TO WAIT ALL DAY FOR A DOCTOR WHILE I'M IN MORTAL PAIN...
ANIMAL CLINIC
...BUT THEN TO BE DROOLED ON BY THE OTHER PATIENTS AS WELL...
YIP YIP YIP
AW, GIVE THE LITTLE GUY A BREAK. HE PROBABLY JUST WANTS TO PLAY CATCH. THROW HIM SOMETHING...
NOT VERY GOOD AT PLAYING CATCH WAS HE...?
APPARENTLY NOT WITH LAMPS...
© TUNDRA 1997

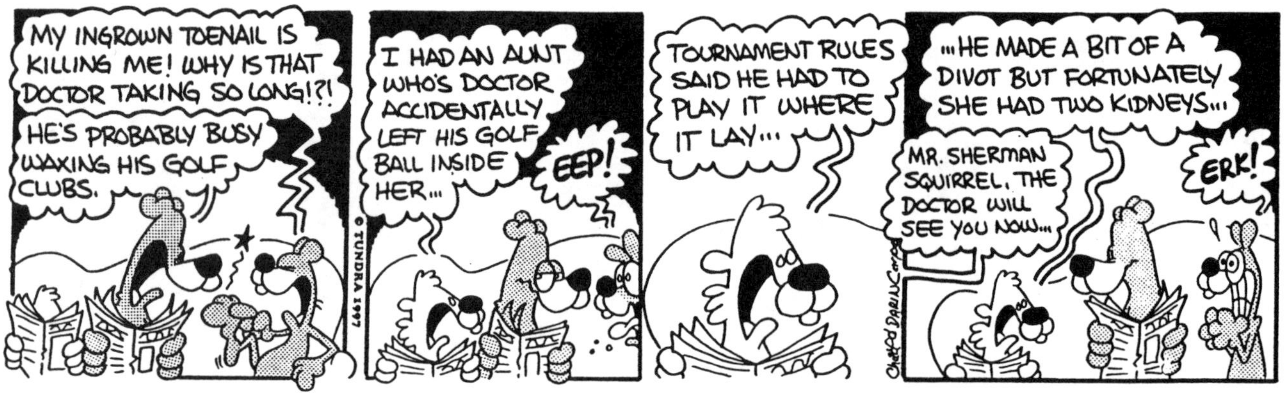
MY INGROWN TOENAIL IS KILLING ME! WHY IS THAT DOCTOR TAKING SO LONG!?!
HE'S PROBABLY BUSY WAXING HIS GOLF CLUBS.
I HAD AN AUNT WHO'S DOCTOR ACCIDENTALLY LEFT HIS GOLF BALL INSIDE HER...
EEP!
© TUNDRA 1997
TOURNAMENT RULES SAID HE HAD TO PLAY IT WHERE IT LAY...
...HE MADE A BIT OF A DIVOT BUT FORTUNATELY SHE HAD TWO KIDNEYS...
MR. SHERMAN SQUIRREL, THE DOCTOR WILL SEE YOU NOW...
ERK!

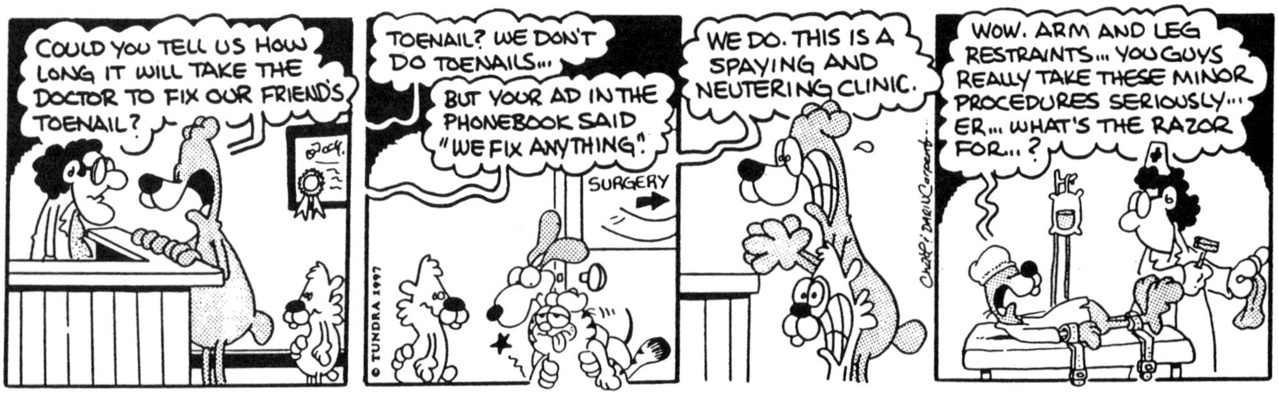
COULD YOU TELL US HOW LONG IT WILL TAKE THE DOCTOR TO FIX OUR FRIEND'S TOENAIL?
TOENAIL? WE DON'T DO TOENAILS...
BUT YOUR AD IN THE PHONEBOOK SAID "WE FIX ANYTHING".
SURGERY
© TUNDRA 1997
WE DO. THIS IS A SPAYING AND NEUTERING CLINIC.
WOW. ARM AND LEG RESTRAINTS... YOU GUYS REALLY TAKE THESE MINOR PROCEDURES SERIOUSLY... ER... WHAT'S THE RAZOR FOR...?

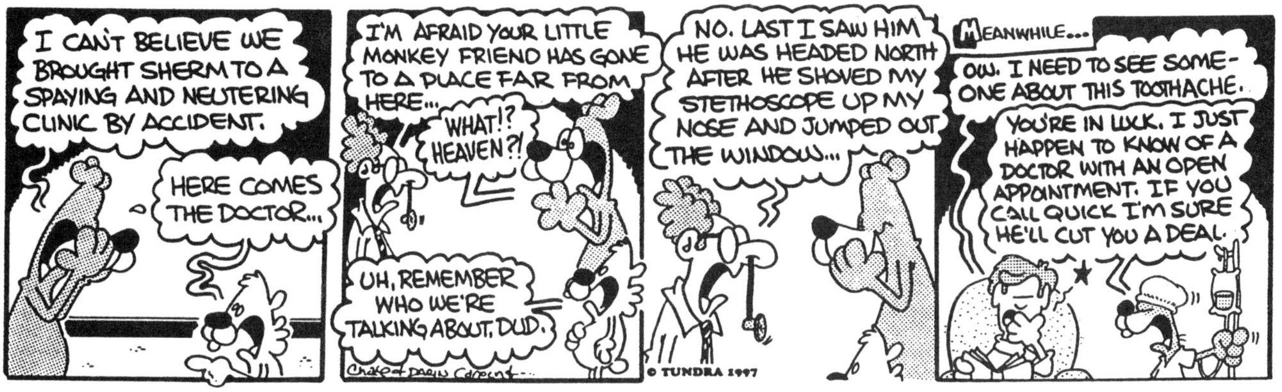
I CAN'T BELIEVE WE BROUGHT SHERM TO A SPAYING AND NEUTERING CLINIC BY ACCIDENT.
HERE COMES THE DOCTOR...
I'M AFRAID YOUR LITTLE MONKEY FRIEND HAS GONE TO A PLACE FAR FROM HERE...
WHAT!? HEAVEN?!
UH, REMEMBER WHO WE'RE TALKING ABOUT, DUD.
NO. LAST I SAW HIM HE WAS HEADED NORTH AFTER HE SHOVED MY STETHOSCOPE UP MY NOSE AND JUMPED OUT THE WINDOW...
© TUNDRA 1997
MEANWHILE...
OW. I NEED TO SEE SOME-ONE ABOUT THIS TOOTHACHE.
YOU'RE IN LUCK. I JUST HAPPEN TO KNOW OF A DOCTOR WITH AN OPEN APPOINTMENT. IF YOU CALL QUICK I'M SURE HE'LL CUT YOU A DEAL.

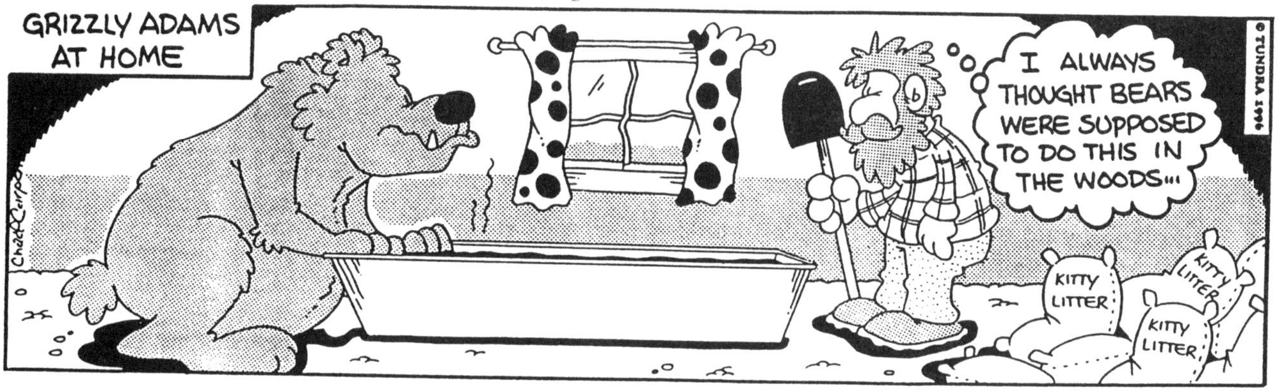
GRIZZLY ADAMS AT HOME
I ALWAYS THOUGHT BEARS WERE SUPPOSED TO DO THIS IN THE WOODS...
KITTY LITTER
KITTY LITTER
KITTY LITTER
© TUNDRA 1996

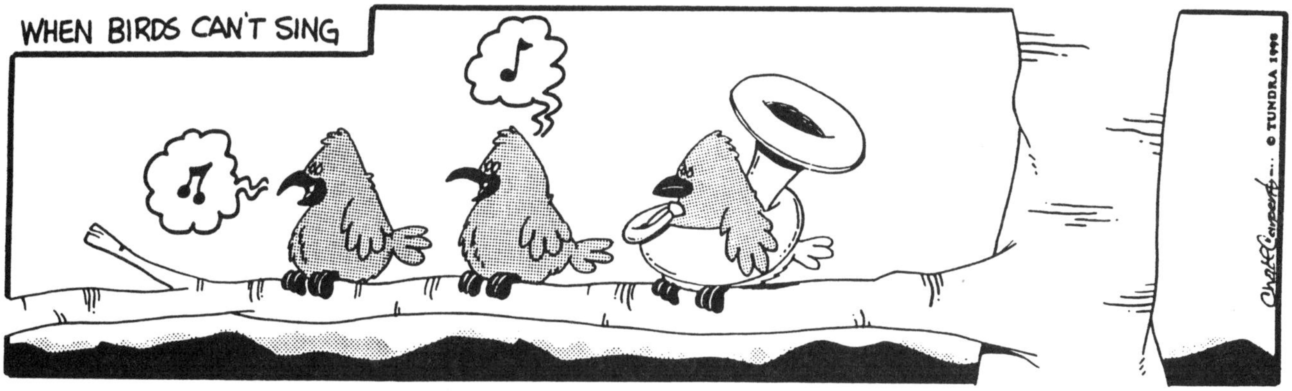
WHEN BIRDS CAN'T SING
© TUNDRA 1998

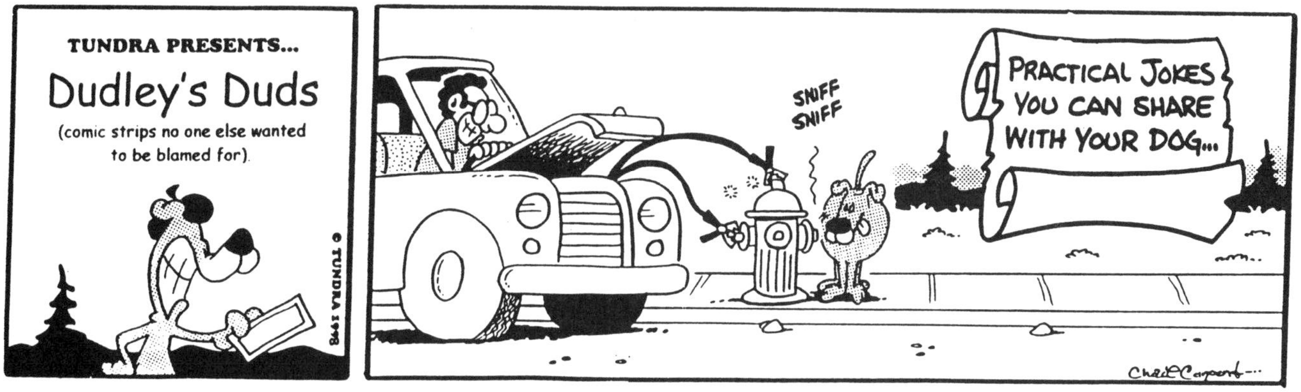
TUNDRA PRESENTS...
Dudley's Duds
(comic strips no one else wanted to be blamed for).
© TUNDRA 1998
SNIFF SNIFF
PRACTICAL JOKES YOU CAN SHARE WITH YOUR DOG...

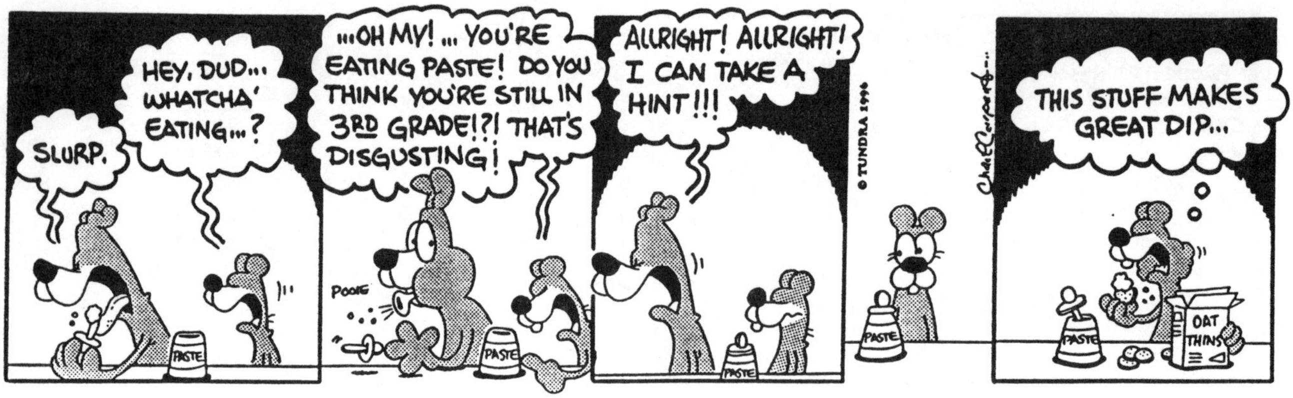
SLURP.
HEY, DUD... WHATCHA' EATING...?
PASTE
...OH MY! ... YOU'RE EATING PASTE! DO YOU THINK YOU'RE STILL IN 3RD GRADE!?! THAT'S DISGUSTING!
POOIE
PASTE
ALLRIGHT! ALLRIGHT! I CAN TAKE A HINT!!!
PASTE
© TUNDRA 1996
PASTE
THIS STUFF MAKES GREAT DIP...
PASTE
OAT THINS

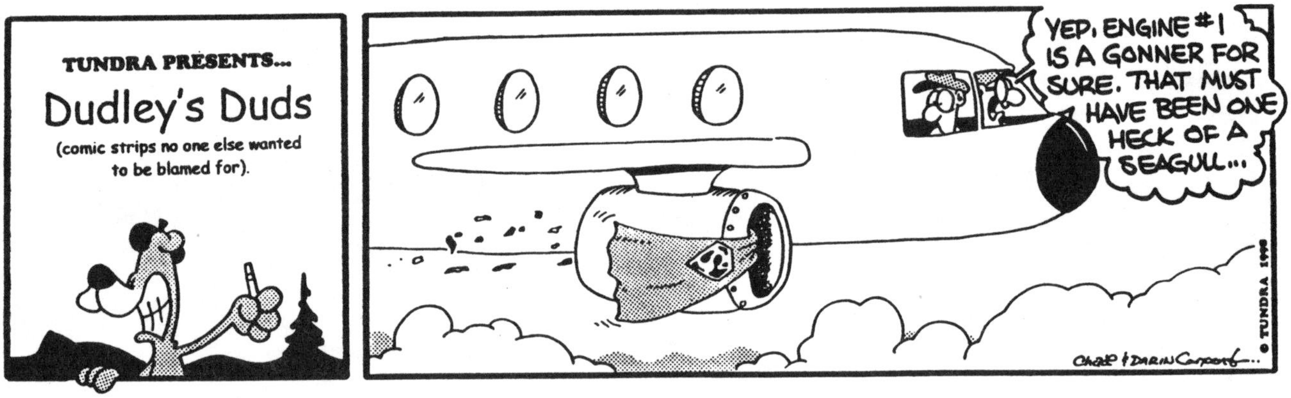
TUNDRA PRESENTS...
Dudley's Duds
(comic strips no one else wanted to be blamed for).
YEP, ENGINE #1 IS A GONNER FOR SURE. THAT MUST HAVE BEEN ONE HECK OF A SEAGULL...

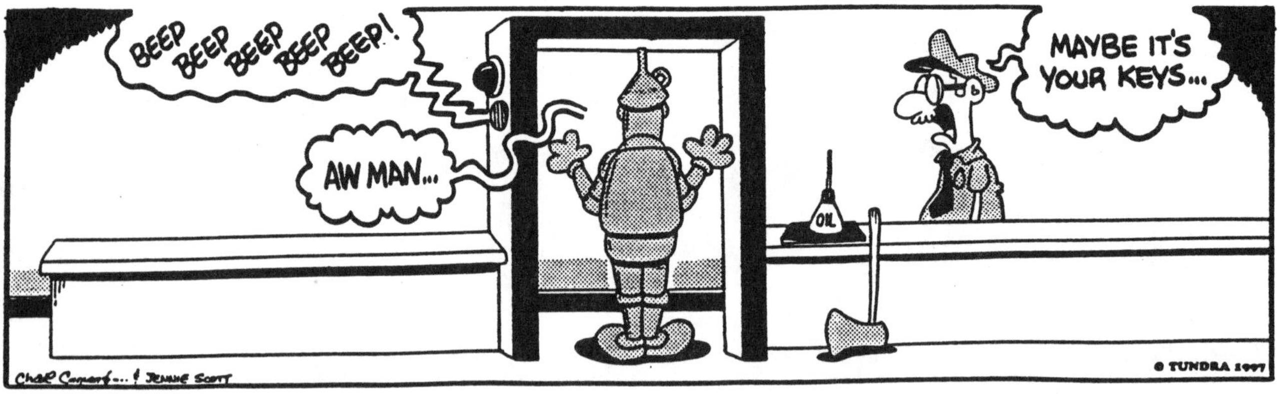
BEEP BEEP BEEP BEEP BEEP!
AW MAN...
MAYBE IT'S YOUR KEYS...
OIL
© TUNDRA 1997

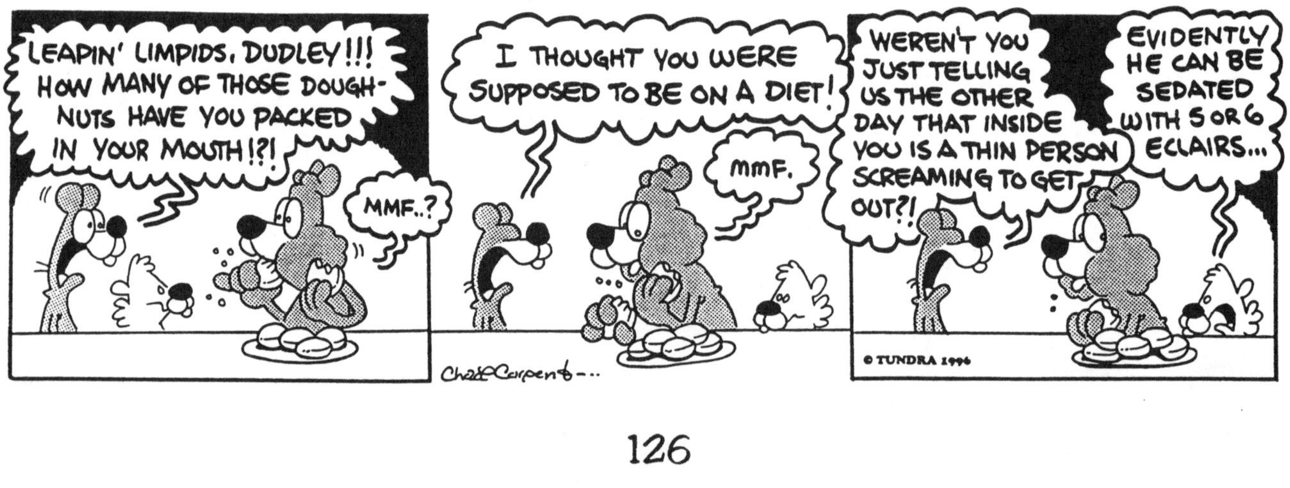
LEAPIN' LIMPIDS, DUDLEY!!! HOW MANY OF THOSE DOUGH-NUTS HAVE YOU PACKED IN YOUR MOUTH!?!
MMF..?
I THOUGHT YOU WERE SUPPOSED TO BE ON A DIET!
mmF.
WEREN'T YOU JUST TELLING US THE OTHER DAY THAT INSIDE YOU IS A THIN PERSON SCREAMING TO GET OUT?!
EVIDENTLY HE CAN BE SEDATED WITH 5 OR 6 ECLAIRS...
© TUNDRA 1996

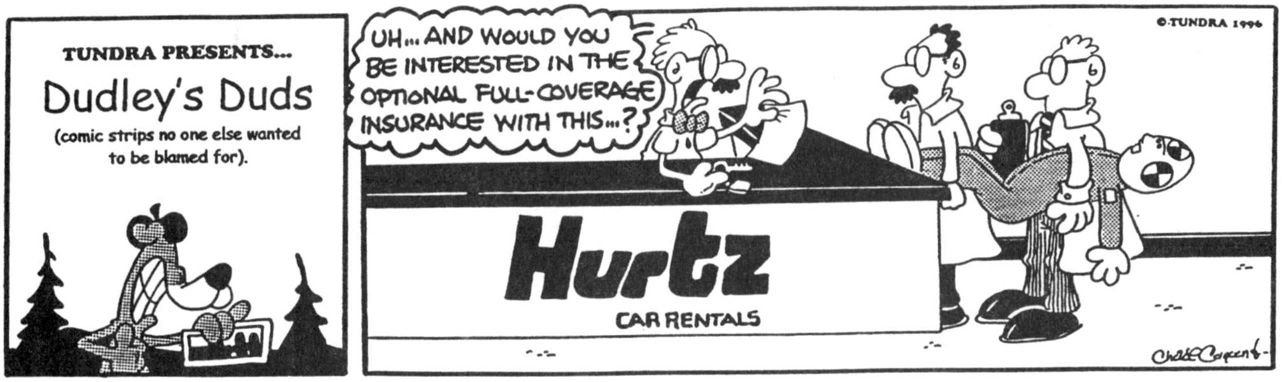
TUNDRA PRESENTS...
Dudley's Duds
(comic strips no one else wanted to be blamed for).
UH... AND WOULD YOU BE INTERESTED IN THE OPTIONAL FULL-COVERAGE INSURANCE WITH THIS...?
© TUNDRA 1996
Hurtz
CAR RENTALS

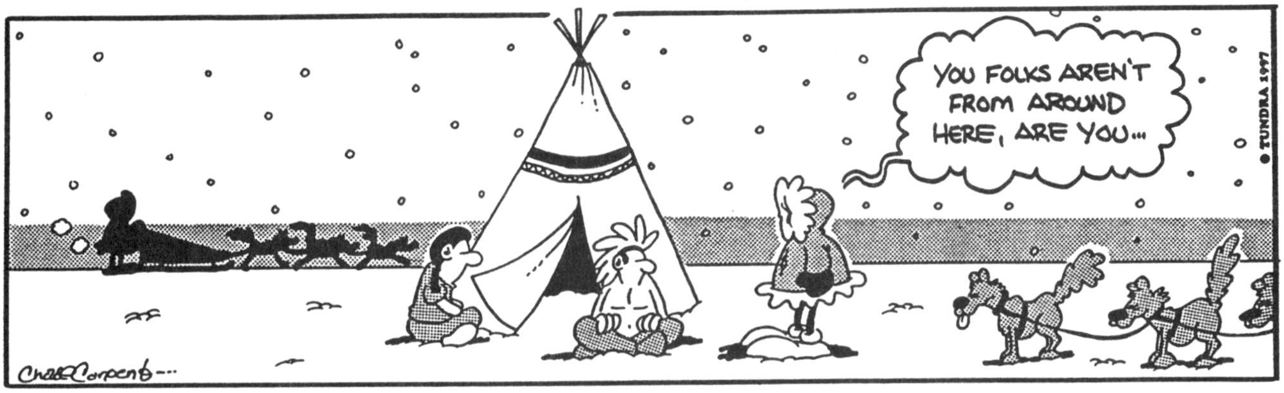
YOU FOLKS AREN'T FROM AROUND HERE, ARE YOU...
© TUNDRA 1997

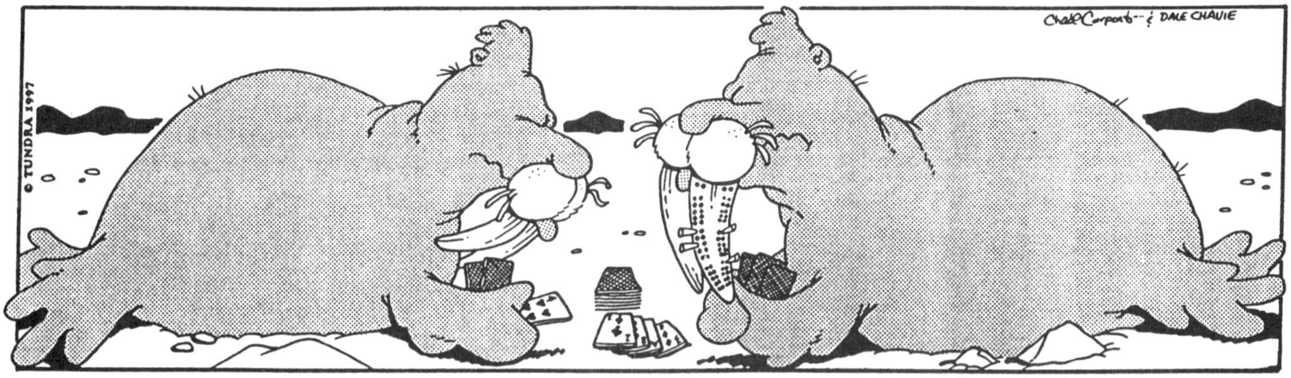
© TUNDRA 1997

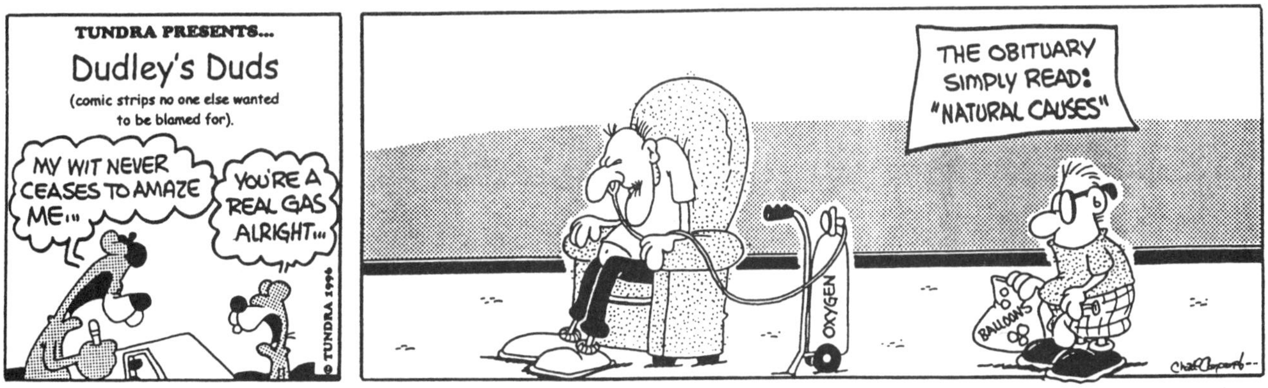
TUNDRA PRESENTS...
Dudley's Duds
(comic strips no one else wanted to be blamed for).
MY WIT NEVER CEASES TO AMAZE ME...
YOU'RE A REAL GAS ALRIGHT...
© TUNDRA 1996
THE OBITUARY SIMPLY READ: "NATURAL CAUSES"
OXYGEN
BALLOONS

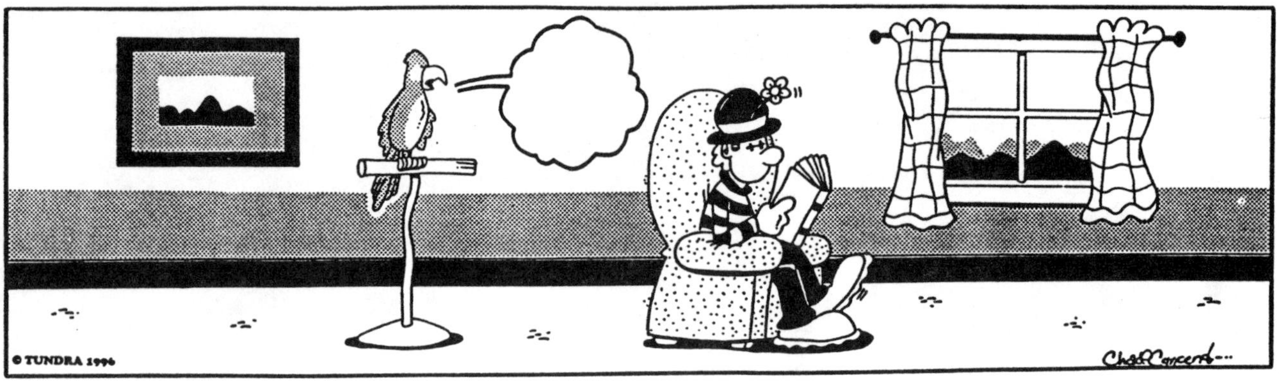
© TUNDRA 1996

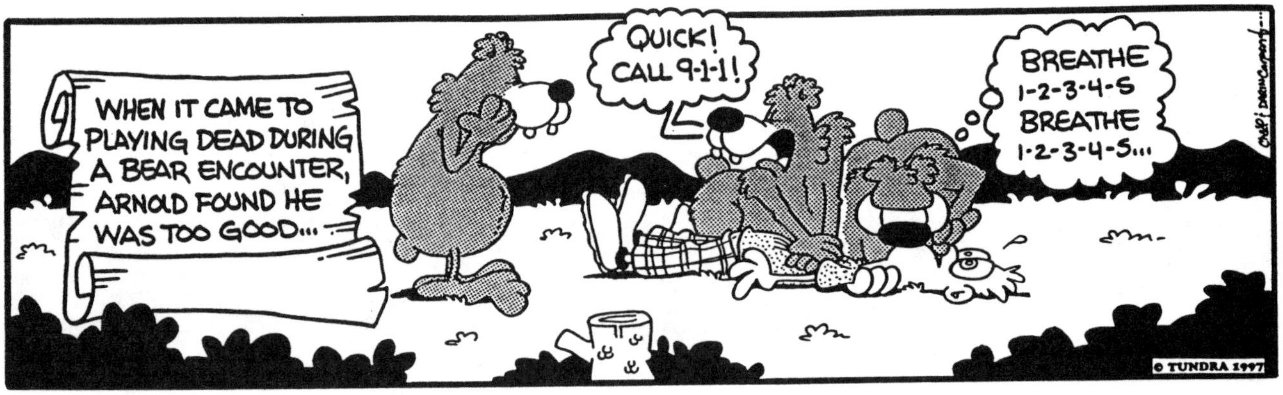
WHEN IT CAME TO PLAYING DEAD DURING A BEAR ENCOUNTER, ARNOLD FOUND HE WAS TOO GOOD...
QUICK! CALL 9-1-1!
BREATHE 1-2-3-4-5 BREATHE 1-2-3-4-5...
© TUNDRA 1997

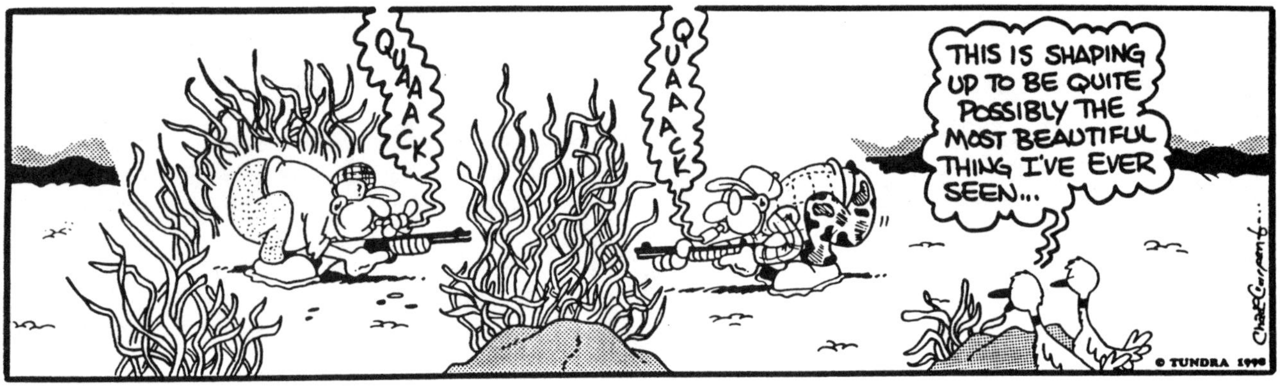
QUAAACK
QUAAACK
THIS IS SHAPING UP TO BE QUITE POSSIBLY THE MOST BEAUTIFUL THING I'VE EVER SEEN...
© TUNDRA 1998

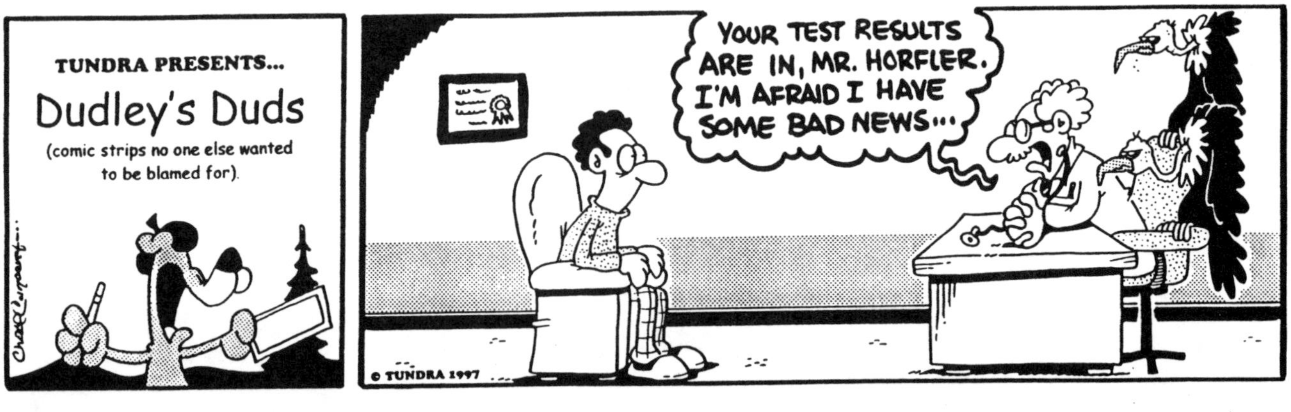
TUNDRA PRESENTS...
Dudley's Duds
(comic strips no one else wanted to be blamed for).
YOUR TEST RESULTS ARE IN, MR. HORFLER. I'M AFRAID I HAVE SOME BAD NEWS...
© TUNDRA 1997

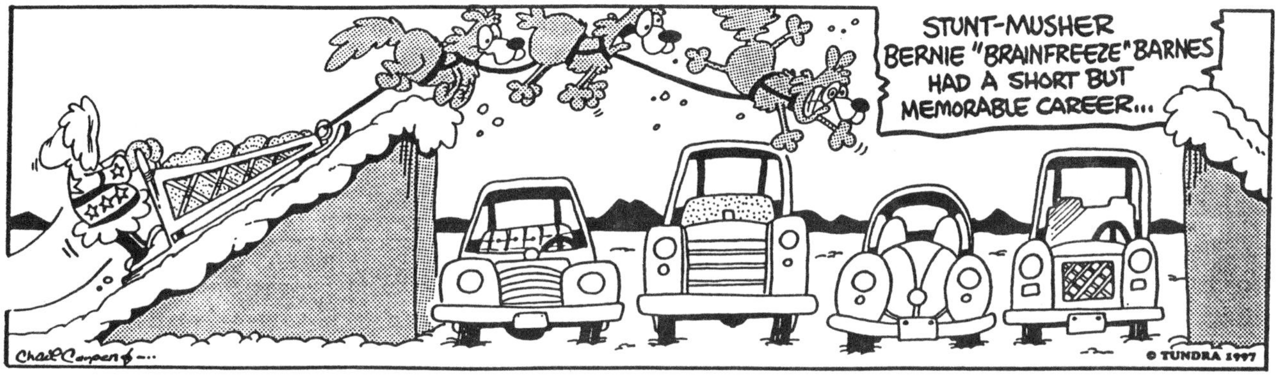
STUNT-MUSHER BERNIE "BRAINFREEZE" BARNES HAD A SHORT BUT MEMORABLE CAREER...
© TUNDRA 1997

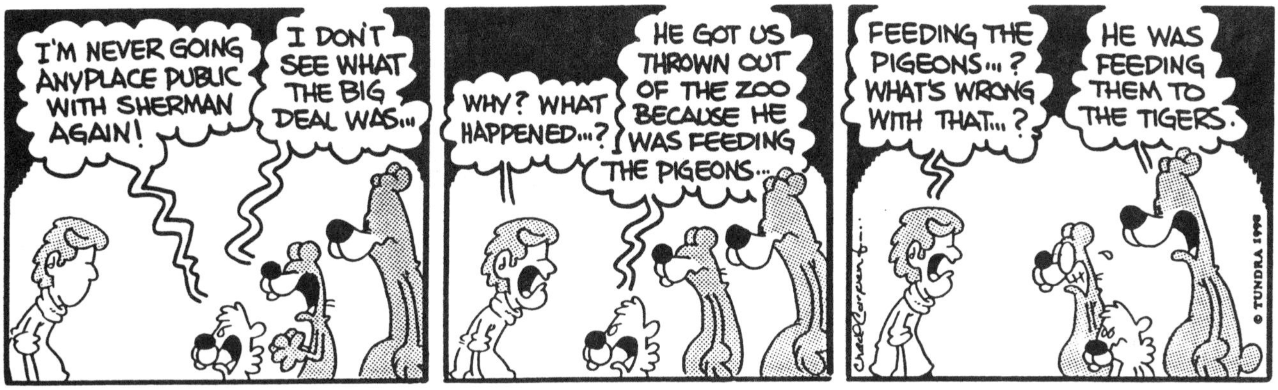
I'M NEVER GOING ANYPLACE PUBLIC WITH SHERMAN AGAIN!
I DON'T SEE WHAT THE BIG DEAL WAS...
WHY? WHAT HAPPENED...?
HE GOT US THROWN OUT OF THE ZOO BECAUSE HE WAS FEEDING THE PIGEONS...
FEEDING THE PIGEONS...? WHAT'S WRONG WITH THAT...?
HE WAS FEEDING THEM TO THE TIGERS.
© TUNDRA 1998

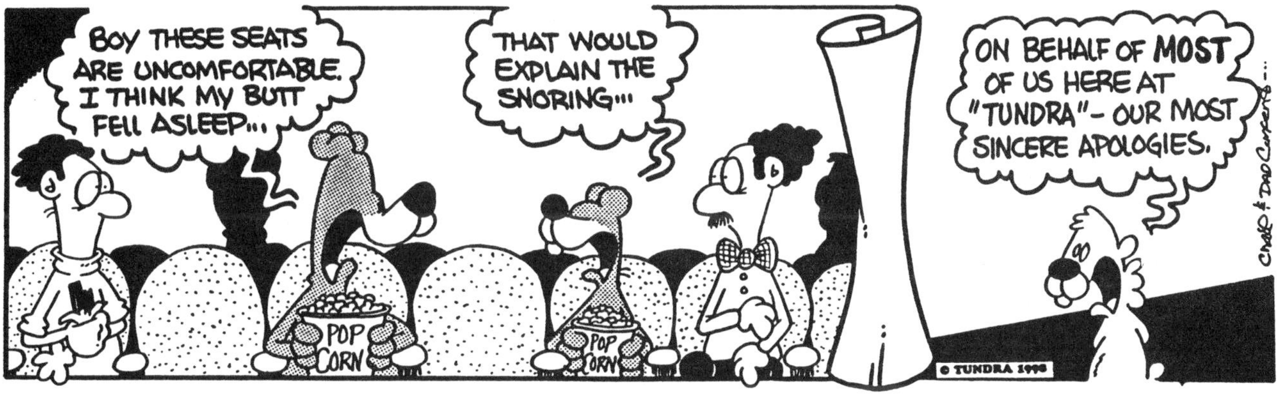
BOY THESE SEATS ARE UNCOMFORTABLE. I THINK MY BUTT FELL ASLEEP...
THAT WOULD EXPLAIN THE SNORING...
ON BEHALF OF MOST OF US HERE AT "TUNDRA"- OUR MOST SINCERE APOLOGIES.
POP CORN
POP CORN
© TUNDRA 1998

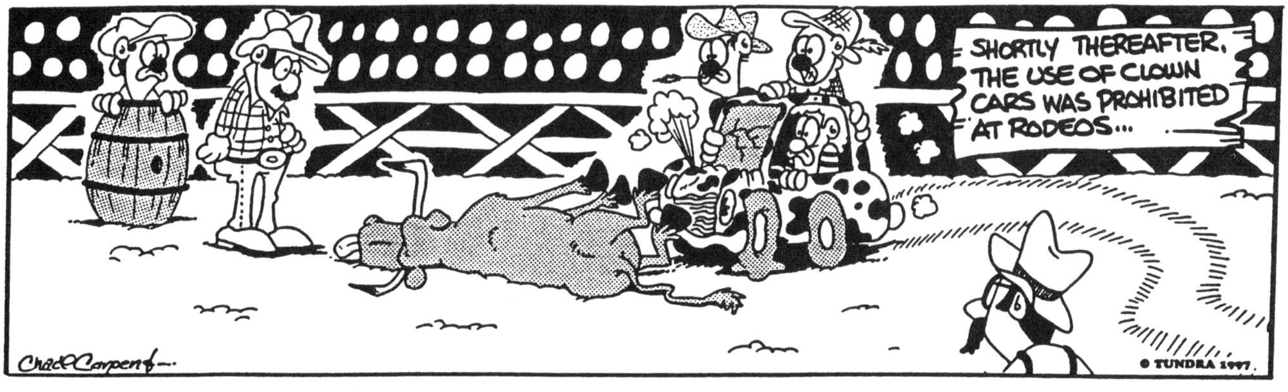
SHORTLY THEREAFTER, THE USE OF CLOWN CARS WAS PROHIBITED AT RODEOS...
© TUNDRA 1997.

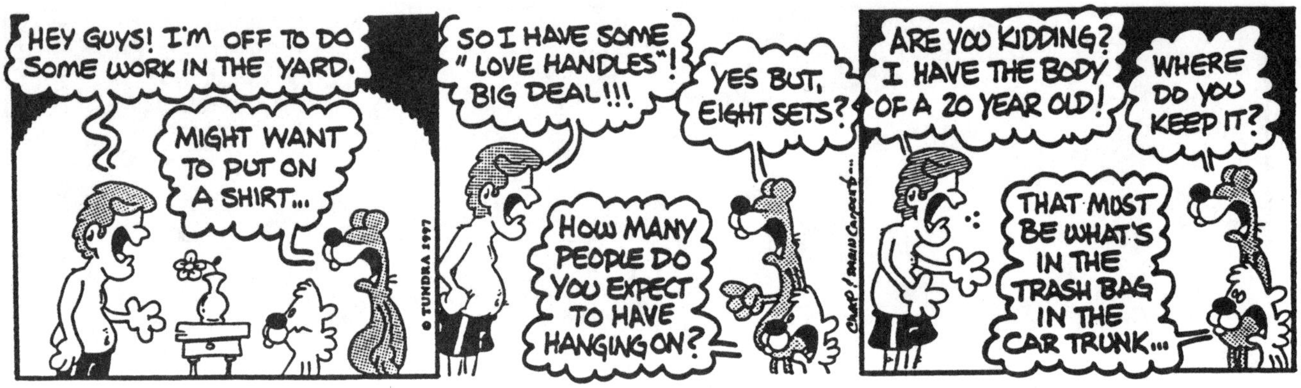
HEY GUYS! I'M OFF TO DO SOME WORK IN THE YARD.
MIGHT WANT TO PUT ON A SHIRT...
© TUNDRA 1997
SO I HAVE SOME "LOVE HANDLES"! BIG DEAL!!!
YES BUT, EIGHT SETS?
HOW MANY PEOPLE DO YOU EXPECT TO HAVE HANGING ON?
ARE YOU KIDDING? I HAVE THE BODY OF A 20 YEAR OLD!
WHERE DO YOU KEEP IT?
THAT MUST BE WHAT'S IN THE TRASH BAG IN THE CAR TRUNK...

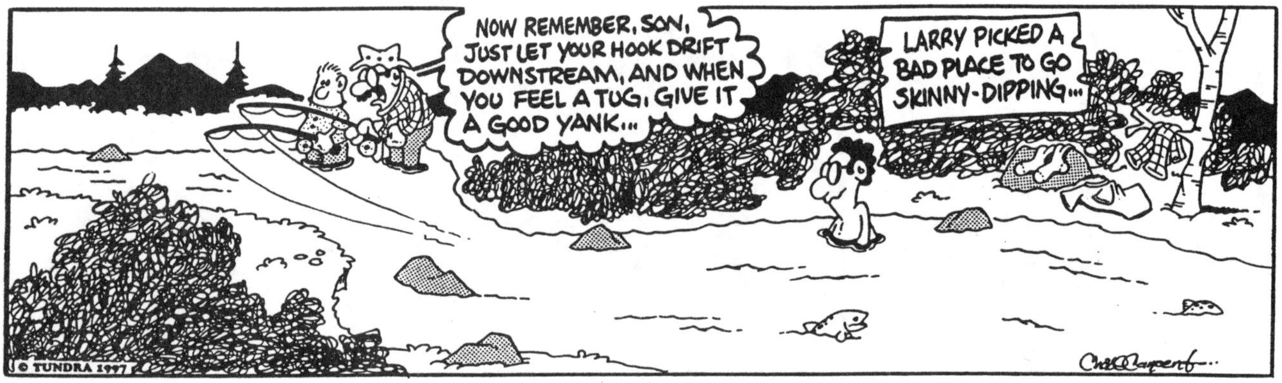
NOW REMEMBER, SON, JUST LET YOUR HOOK DRIFT DOWNSTREAM, AND WHEN YOU FEEL A TUG, GIVE IT A GOOD YANK...
LARRY PICKED A BAD PLACE TO GO SKINNY-DIPPING...
© TUNDRA 1997

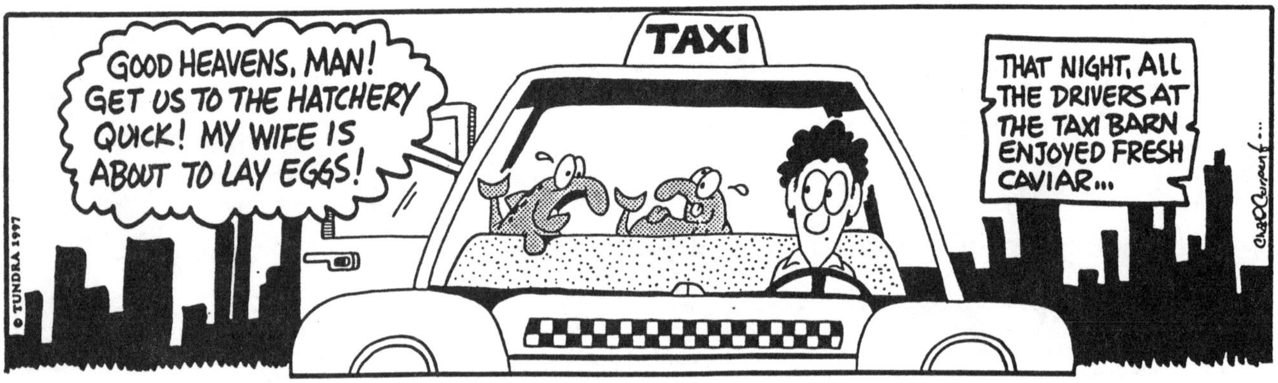
TAXI
GOOD HEAVENS, MAN! GET US TO THE HATCHERY QUICK! MY WIFE IS ABOUT TO LAY EGGS!
THAT NIGHT, ALL THE DRIVERS AT THE TAXI BARN ENJOYED FRESH CAVIAR...
© TUNDRA 1997

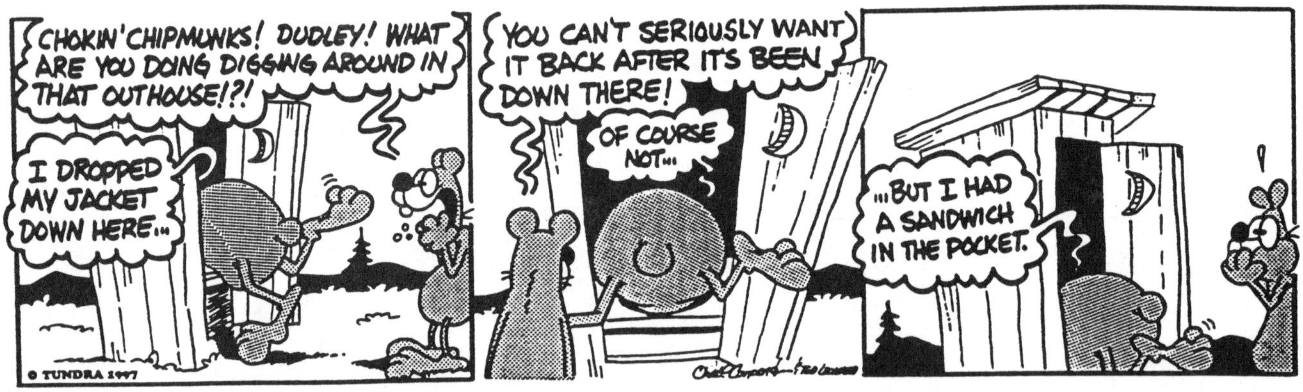
CHOKIN' CHIPMUNKS! DUDLEY! WHAT ARE YOU DOING DIGGING AROUND IN THAT OUTHOUSE!?!
I DROPPED MY JACKET DOWN HERE...
© TUNDRA 1997
YOU CAN'T SERIOUSLY WANT IT BACK AFTER IT'S BEEN DOWN THERE!
OF COURSE NOT...
...BUT I HAD A SANDWICH IN THE POCKET.

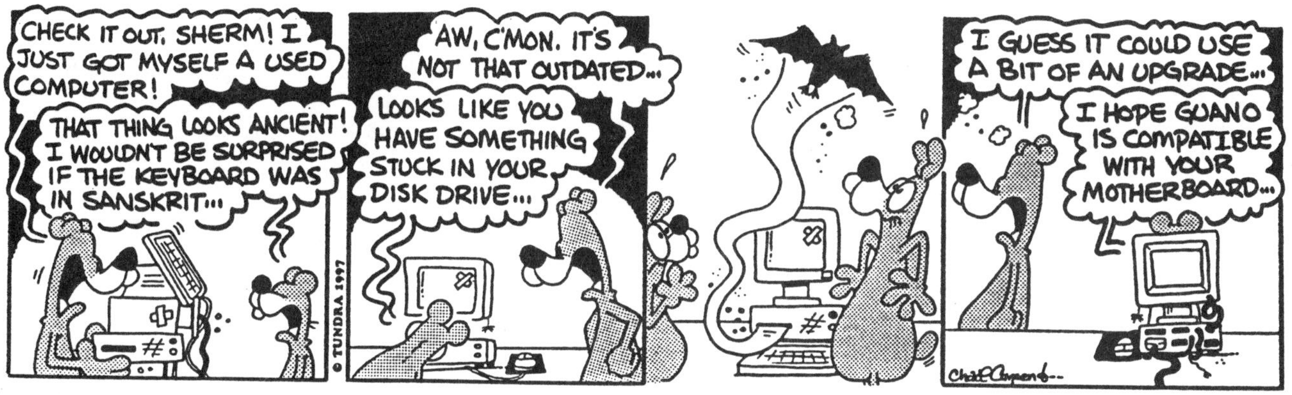
CHECK IT OUT, SHERM! I JUST GOT MYSELF A USED COMPUTER!
THAT THING LOOKS ANCIENT! I WOULDN'T BE SURPRISED IF THE KEYBOARD WAS IN SANSKRIT...
© TUNDRA 1997
AW, C'MON. IT'S NOT THAT OUTDATED...
LOOKS LIKE YOU HAVE SOMETHING STUCK IN YOUR DISK DRIVE...
I GUESS IT COULD USE A BIT OF AN UPGRADE...
I HOPE GUANO IS COMPATIBLE WITH YOUR MOTHERBOARD...

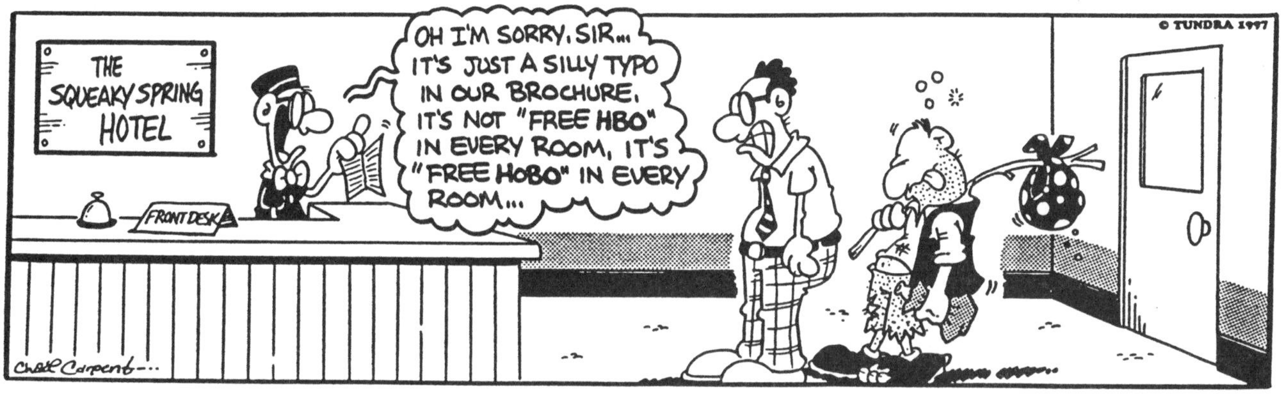
© TUNDRA 1997
THE SQUEAKY SPRING HOTEL
FRONT DESK
OH I'M SORRY, SIR... IT'S JUST A SILLY TYPO IN OUR BROCHURE. IT'S NOT "FREE HBO" IN EVERY ROOM, IT'S "FREE HOBO" IN EVERY ROOM...

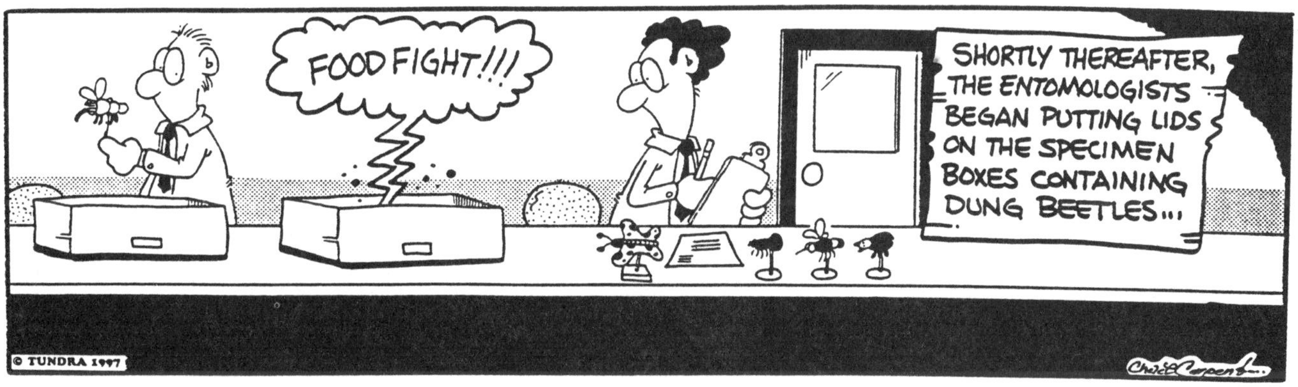
FOOD FIGHT!!!
SHORTLY THEREAFTER, THE ENTOMOLOGISTS BEGAN PUTTING LIDS ON THE SPECIMEN BOXES CONTAINING DUNG BEETLES...
© TUNDRA 1997

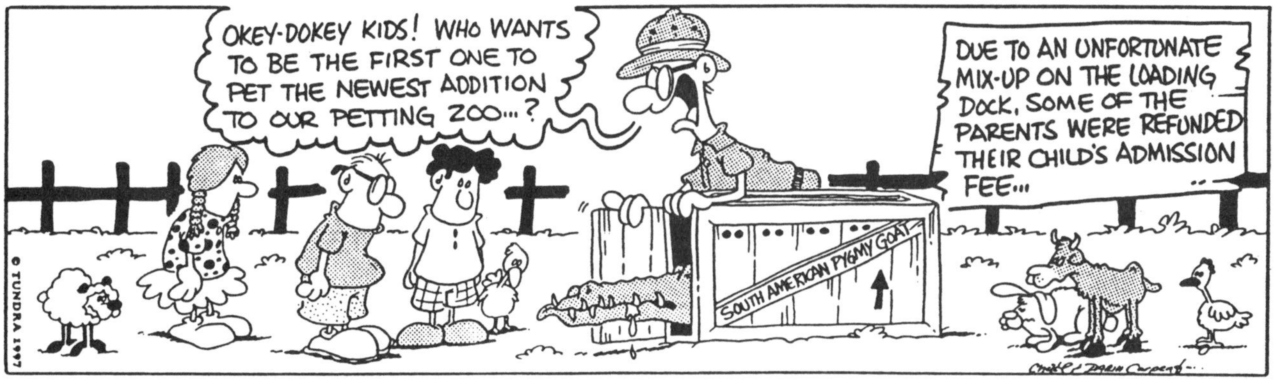
OKEY-DOKEY KIDS! WHO WANTS TO BE THE FIRST ONE TO PET THE NEWEST ADDITION TO OUR PETTING ZOO...?
DUE TO AN UNFORTUNATE MIX-UP ON THE LOADING DOCK, SOME OF THE PARENTS WERE REFUNDED THEIR CHILD'S ADMISSION FEE...
SOUTH AMERICAN PYGMY GOAT
© TUNDRA 1997

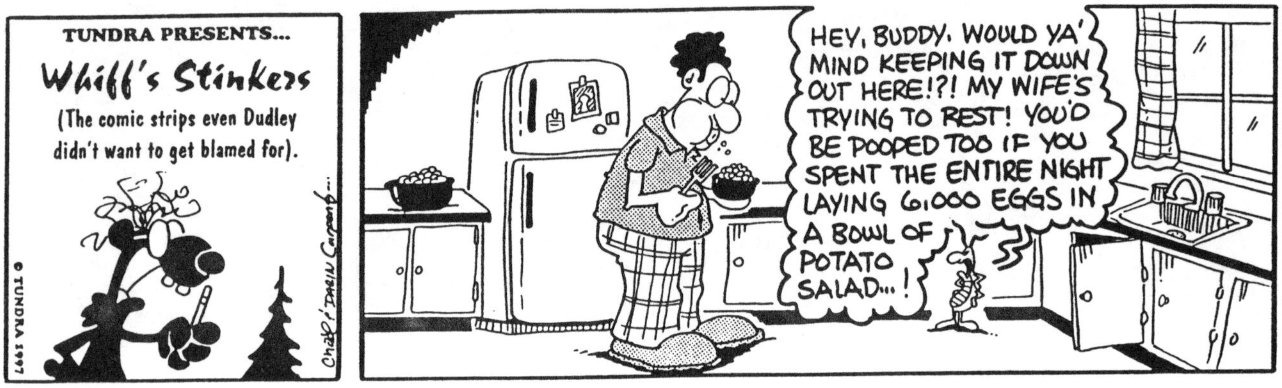
TUNDRA PRESENTS...
Whiff's Stinkers
(The comic strips even Dudley didn't want to get blamed for).
© TUNDRA 1997
HEY, BUDDY, WOULD YA' MIND KEEPING IT DOWN OUT HERE!?! MY WIFE'S TRYING TO REST! YOU'D BE POOPED TOO IF YOU SPENT THE ENTIRE NIGHT LAYING 61,000 EGGS IN A BOWL OF POTATO SALAD... !

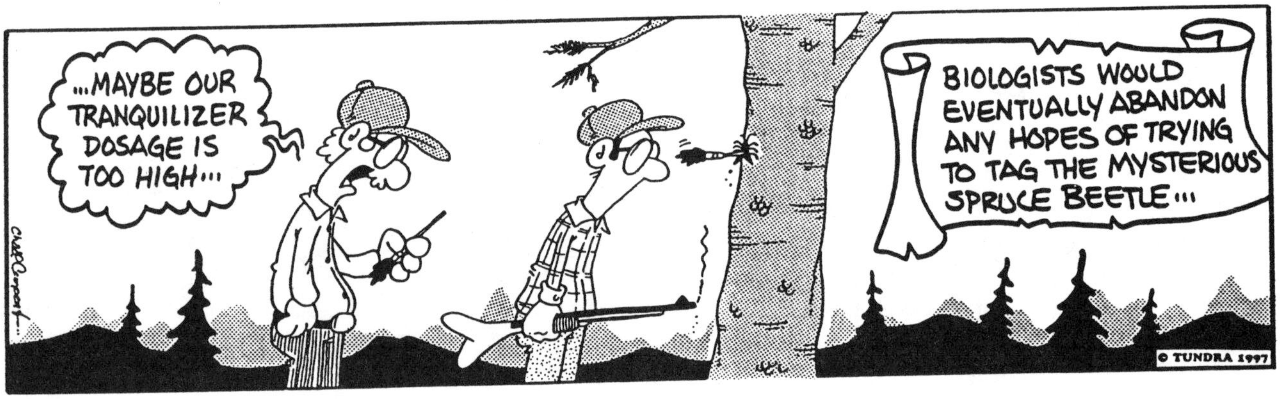
...MAYBE OUR TRANQUILIZER DOSAGE IS TOO HIGH...
BIOLOGISTS WOULD EVENTUALLY ABANDON ANY HOPES OF TRYING TO TAG THE MYSTERIOUS SPRUCE BEETLE...
© TUNDRA 1997

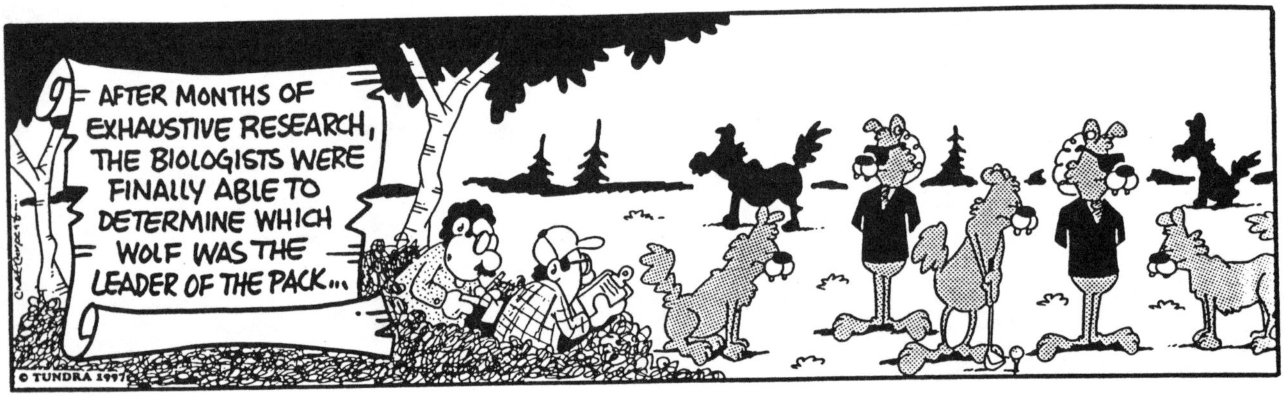
AFTER MONTHS OF EXHAUSTIVE RESEARCH, THE BIOLOGISTS WERE FINALLY ABLE TO DETERMINE WHICH WOLF WAS THE LEADER OF THE PACK...
© TUNDRA 1997

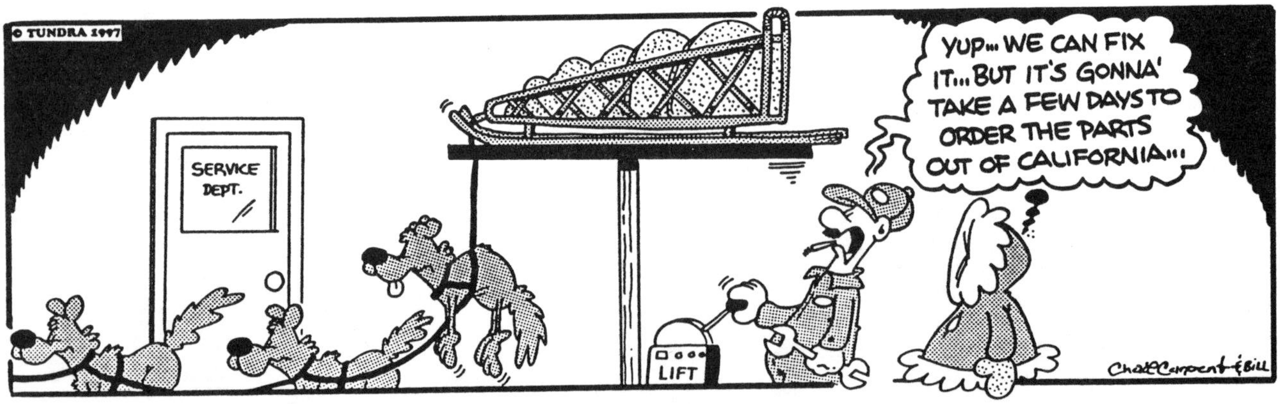
© TUNDRA 1997
SERVICE DEPT.
YUP... WE CAN FIX IT... BUT IT'S GONNA' TAKE A FEW DAYS TO ORDER THE PARTS OUT OF CALIFORNIA...
LIFT

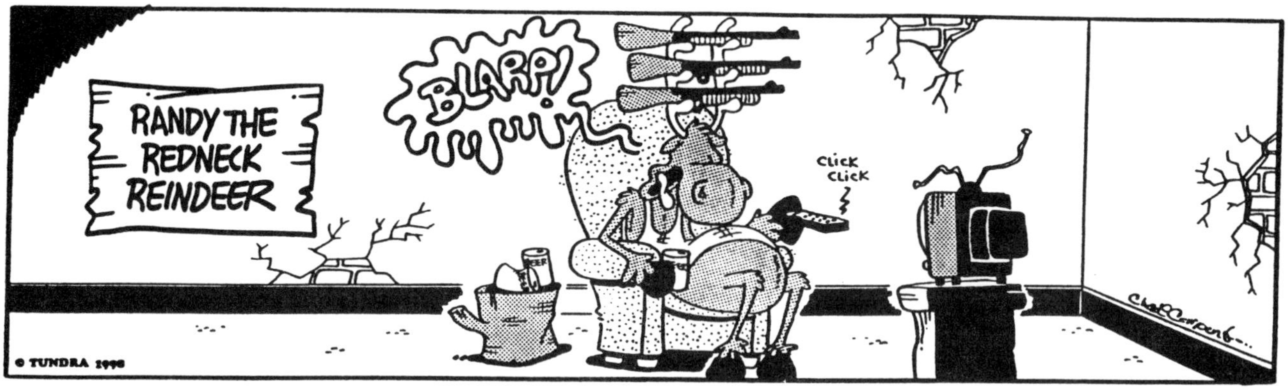
RANDY THE REDNECK REINDEER
BLARP!
CLICK CLICK
© TUNDRA 1998

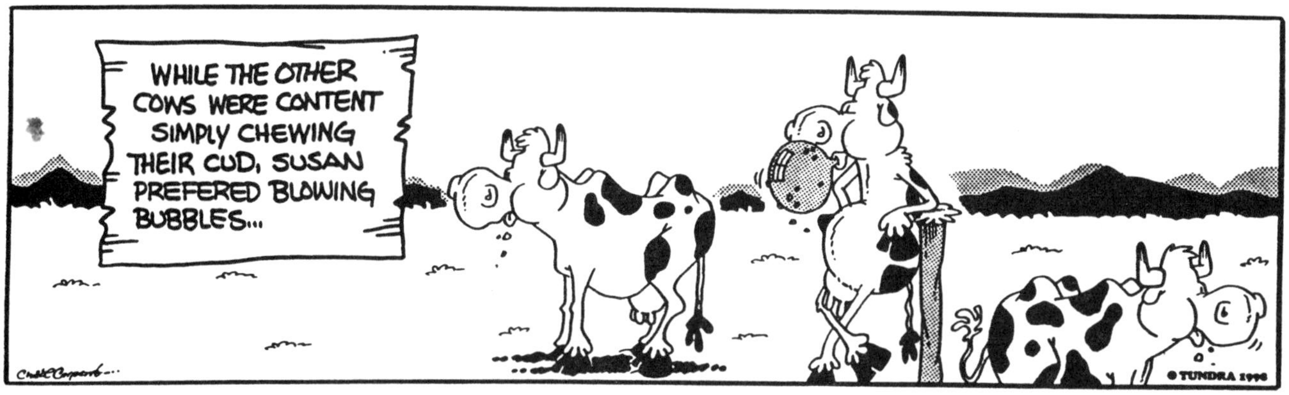
WHILE THE OTHER COWS WERE CONTENT SIMPLY CHEWING THEIR CUD, SUSAN PREFERED BLOWING BUBBLES...
© TUNDRA 1998

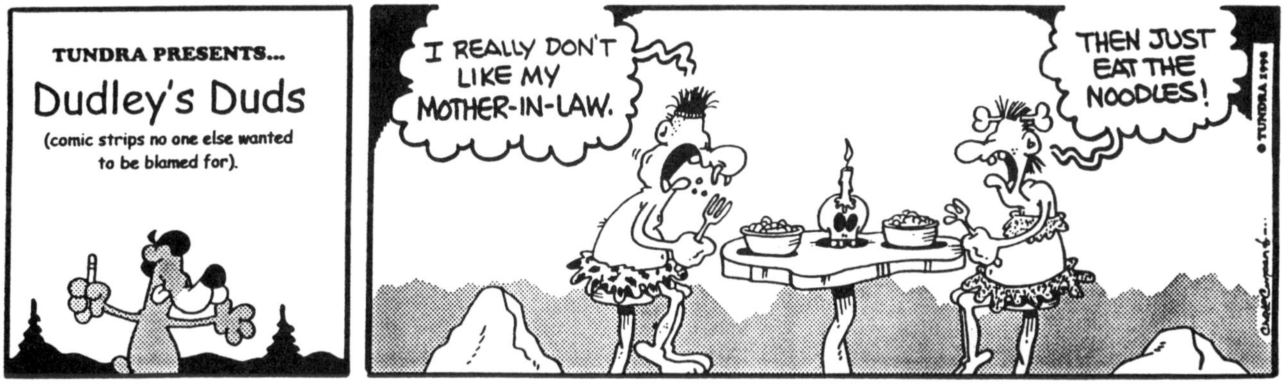
TUNDRA PRESENTS...
Dudley's Duds
(comic strips no one else wanted to be blamed for).
I REALLY DON'T LIKE MY MOTHER-IN-LAW.
THEN JUST EAT THE NOODLES!
© TUNDRA 1998

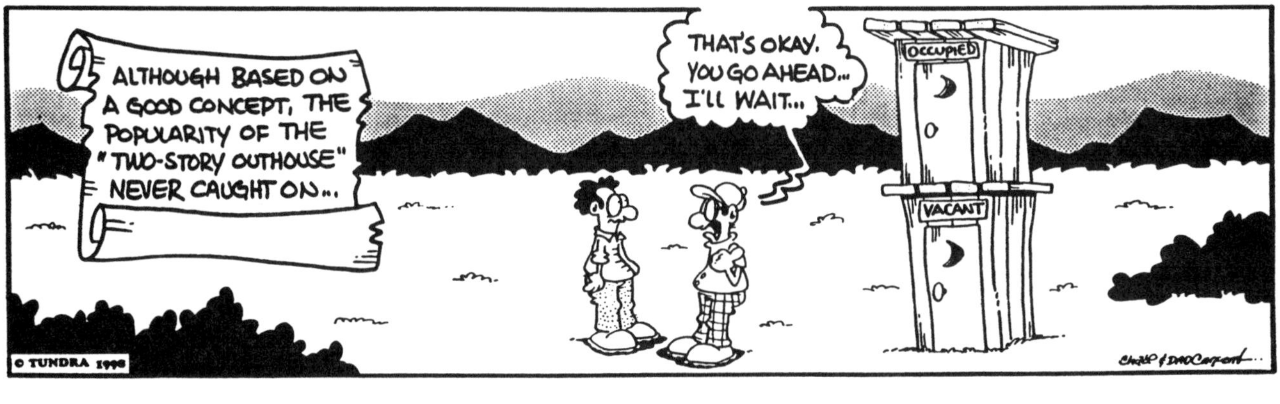
ALTHOUGH BASED ON A GOOD CONCEPT, THE POPULARITY OF THE "TWO-STORY OUTHOUSE" NEVER CAUGHT ON...
THAT'S OKAY. YOU GO AHEAD... I'LL WAIT...
OCCUPIED
VACANT
© TUNDRA 1998

STAR TREK
The Next Degeneration

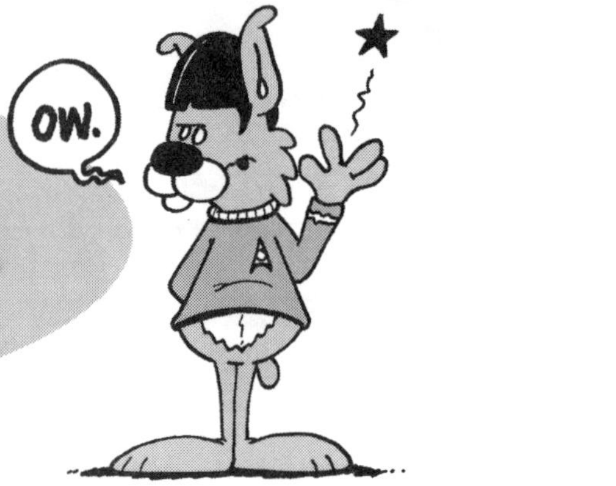

OW.

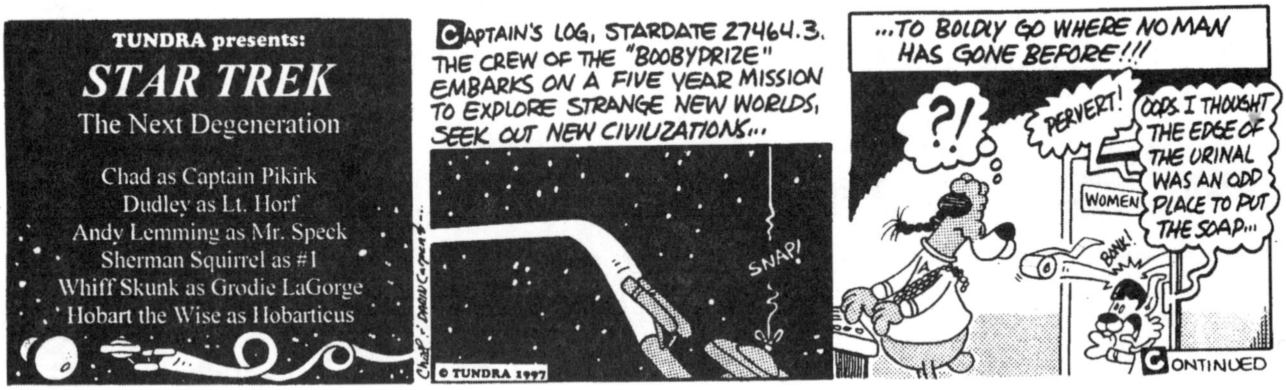

TUNDRA presents:
STAR TREK
The Next Degeneration
Chad as Captain Pikirk
Dudley as Lt. Horf
Andy Lemming as Mr. Speck
Sherman Squirrel as #1
Whiff Skunk as Grodie LaGorge
Hobart the Wise as Hobarticus
CAPTAIN'S LOG, STARDATE 27464.3. THE CREW OF THE "BOOBYPRIZE" EMBARKS ON A FIVE YEAR MISSION TO EXPLORE STRANGE NEW WORLDS, SEEK OUT NEW CIVILIZATIONS...
SNAP!
© TUNDRA 1997
...TO BOLDLY GO WHERE NO MAN HAS GONE BEFORE!!!
?!
PERVERT!
OOPS. I THOUGHT THE EDGE OF THE URINAL WAS AN ODD PLACE TO PUT THE SOAP...
WOMEN
BONK!
CONTINUED

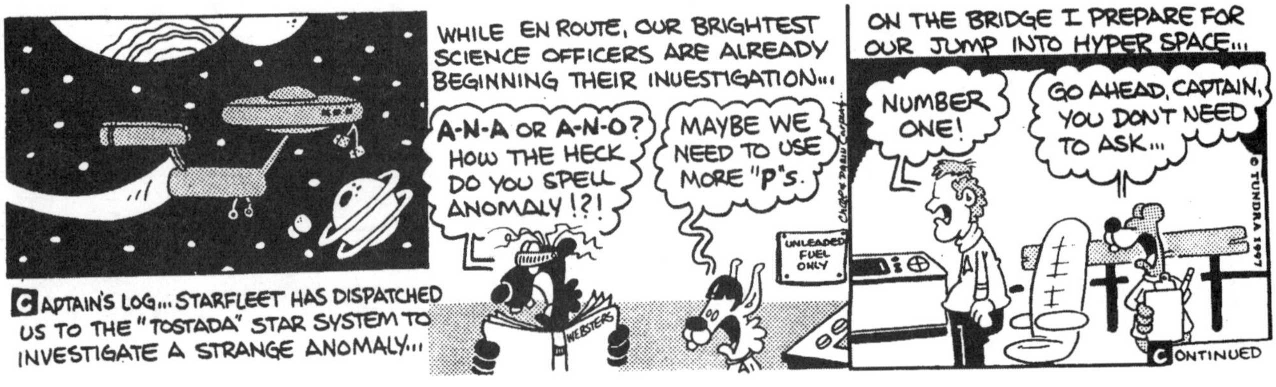

CAPTAIN'S LOG... STARFLEET HAS DISPATCHED US TO THE "TOSTADA" STAR SYSTEM TO INVESTIGATE A STRANGE ANOMALY...
WHILE EN ROUTE, OUR BRIGHTEST SCIENCE OFFICERS ARE ALREADY BEGINNING THEIR INVESTIGATION...
A-N-A OR A-N-O? HOW THE HECK DO YOU SPELL ANOMALY!?!
MAYBE WE NEED TO USE MORE "P"S.
UNLEADED FUEL ONLY
WEBSTERS
ON THE BRIDGE I PREPARE FOR OUR JUMP INTO HYPER SPACE...
NUMBER ONE!
GO AHEAD, CAPTAIN, YOU DON'T NEED TO ASK...
© TUNDRA 1997
CONTINUED

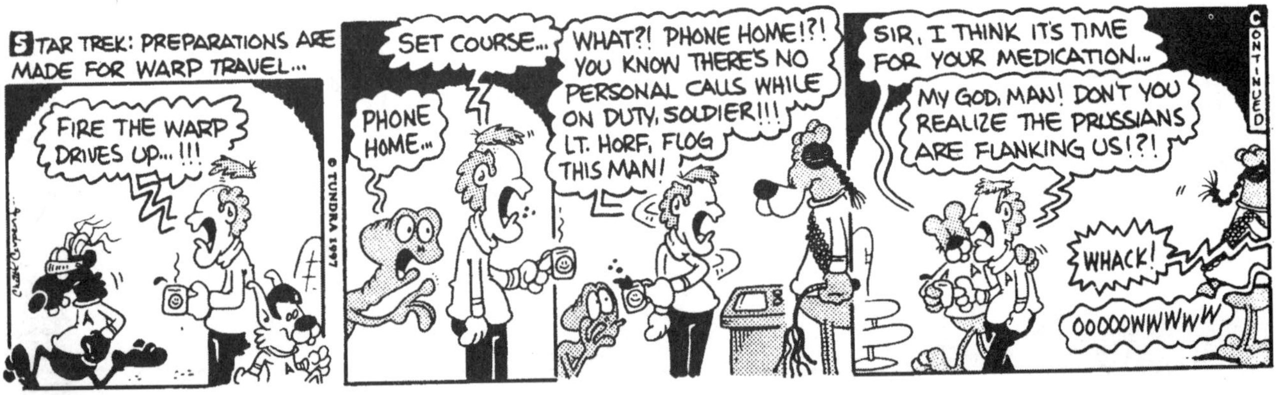

STAR TREK: PREPARATIONS ARE MADE FOR WARP TRAVEL...
FIRE THE WARP DRIVES UP...!!!
© TUNDRA 1997
SET COURSE...
PHONE HOME...
WHAT?! PHONE HOME!?! YOU KNOW THERE'S NO PERSONAL CALLS WHILE ON DUTY, SOLDIER!!! LT. HORF, FLOG THIS MAN!
SIR, I THINK IT'S TIME FOR YOUR MEDICATION...
MY GOD, MAN! DON'T YOU REALIZE THE PRUSSIANS ARE FLANKING US!?!
WHACK!
OOOOOWWWWW
CONTINUED

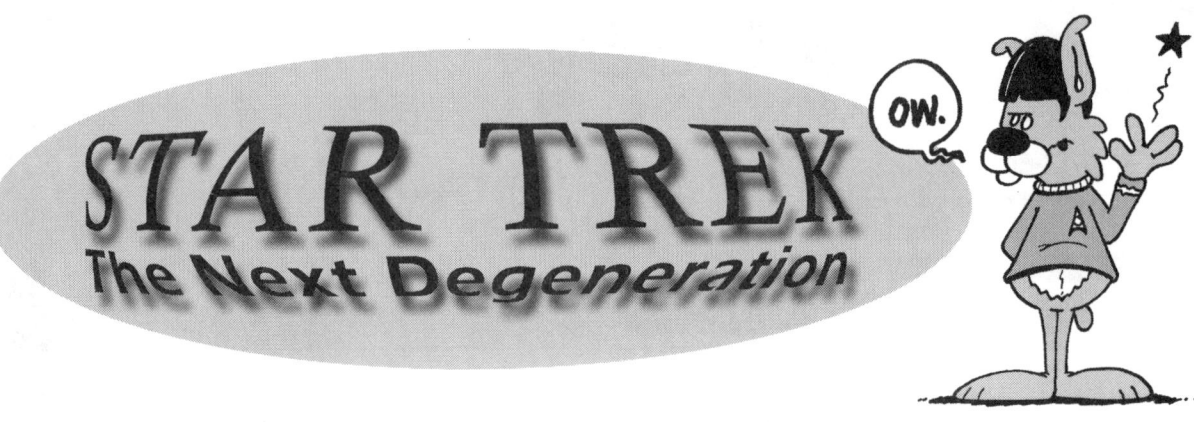

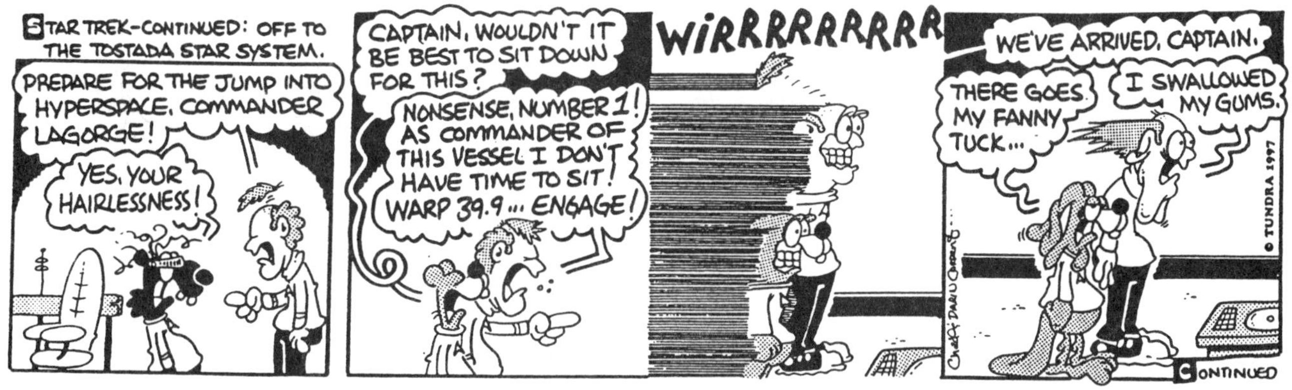
STAR TREK-CONTINUED: OFF TO THE TOSTADA STAR SYSTEM.
PREPARE FOR THE JUMP INTO HYPERSPACE, COMMANDER LAGORGE!
YES, YOUR HAIRLESSNESS!
CAPTAIN, WOULDN'T IT BE BEST TO SIT DOWN FOR THIS?
NONSENSE, NUMBER 1! AS COMMANDER OF THIS VESSEL I DON'T HAVE TIME TO SIT! WARP 39.9... ENGAGE!
WIRRRRRRRRRR
WE'VE ARRIVED, CAPTAIN.
THERE GOES MY FANNY TUCK...
I SWALLOWED MY GUMS.
© TUNDRA 1997
CONTINUED

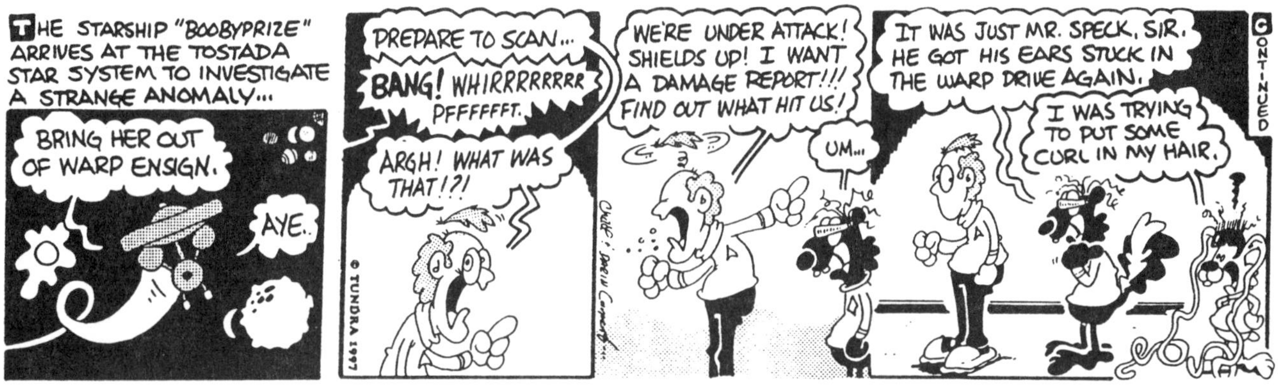
THE STARSHIP "BOOBYPRIZE" ARRIVES AT THE TOSTADA STAR SYSTEM TO INVESTIGATE A STRANGE ANOMALY...
BRING HER OUT OF WARP ENSIGN.
AYE.
PREPARE TO SCAN...
BANG! WHIRRRRRRRR PFFFFFFT.
ARGH! WHAT WAS THAT!?!
© TUNDRA 1997
WE'RE UNDER ATTACK! SHIELDS UP! I WANT A DAMAGE REPORT!!! FIND OUT WHAT HIT US!
UM...
IT WAS JUST MR. SPECK, SIR. HE GOT HIS EARS STUCK IN THE WARP DRIVE AGAIN.
I WAS TRYING TO PUT SOME CURL IN MY HAIR.
CONTINUED

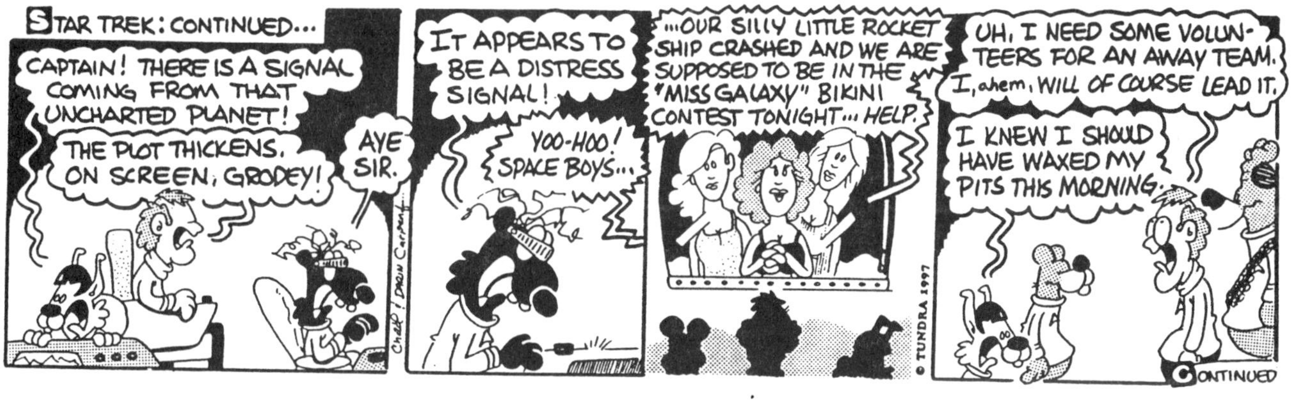
STAR TREK: CONTINUED...
CAPTAIN! THERE IS A SIGNAL COMING FROM THAT UNCHARTED PLANET!
THE PLOT THICKENS. ON SCREEN, GRODEY!
AYE SIR.
IT APPEARS TO BE A DISTRESS SIGNAL!
YOO-HOO! SPACE BOYS...
...OUR SILLY LITTLE ROCKET SHIP CRASHED AND WE ARE SUPPOSED TO BE IN THE "MISS GALAXY" BIKINI CONTEST TONIGHT... HELP.
© TUNDRA 1997
UH, I NEED SOME VOLUNTEERS FOR AN AWAY TEAM. I, ahem, WILL OF COURSE LEAD IT.
I KNEW I SHOULD HAVE WAXED MY PITS THIS MORNING.
CONTINUED

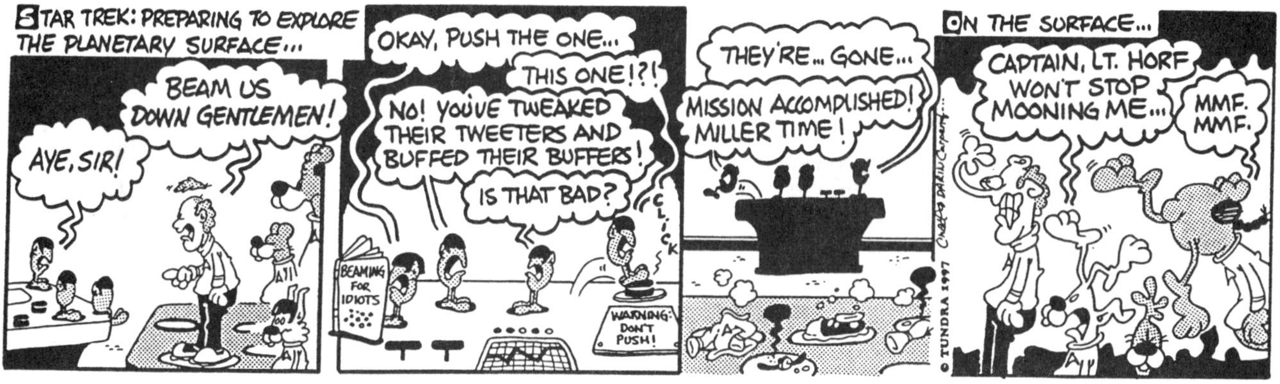
STAR TREK: PREPARING TO EXPLORE THE PLANETARY SURFACE...
BEAM US DOWN GENTLEMEN!
AYE, SIR!
AYE!
OKAY, PUSH THE ONE...
THIS ONE!?!
NO! YOU'VE TWEAKED THEIR TWEETERS AND BUFFED THEIR BUFFERS!
IS THAT BAD?
CLICK
BEAMING FOR IDIOTS
WARNING: DON'T PUSH!
THEY'RE... GONE...
MISSION ACCOMPLISHED! MILLER TIME!
© TUNDRA 1997
ON THE SURFACE...
CAPTAIN, LT. HORF WON'T STOP MOONING ME...
MMF. MMF.

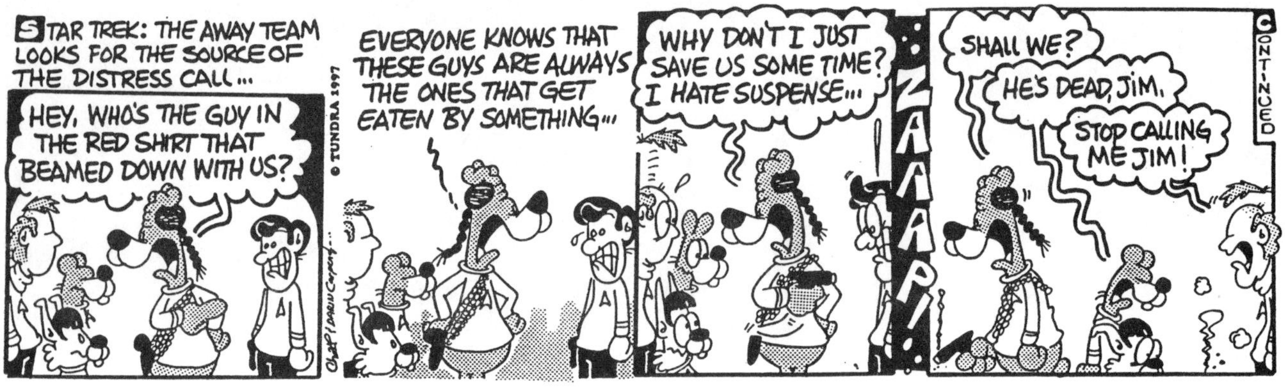
STAR TREK: THE AWAY TEAM LOOKS FOR THE SOURCE OF THE DISTRESS CALL...
HEY, WHO'S THE GUY IN THE RED SHIRT THAT BEAMED DOWN WITH US?
© TUNDRA 1997
EVERYONE KNOWS THAT THESE GUYS ARE ALWAYS THE ONES THAT GET EATEN BY SOMETHING...
WHY DON'T I JUST SAVE US SOME TIME? I HATE SUSPENSE...
ZAAAP!
SHALL WE?
HE'S DEAD, JIM.
STOP CALLING ME JIM!
CONTINUED

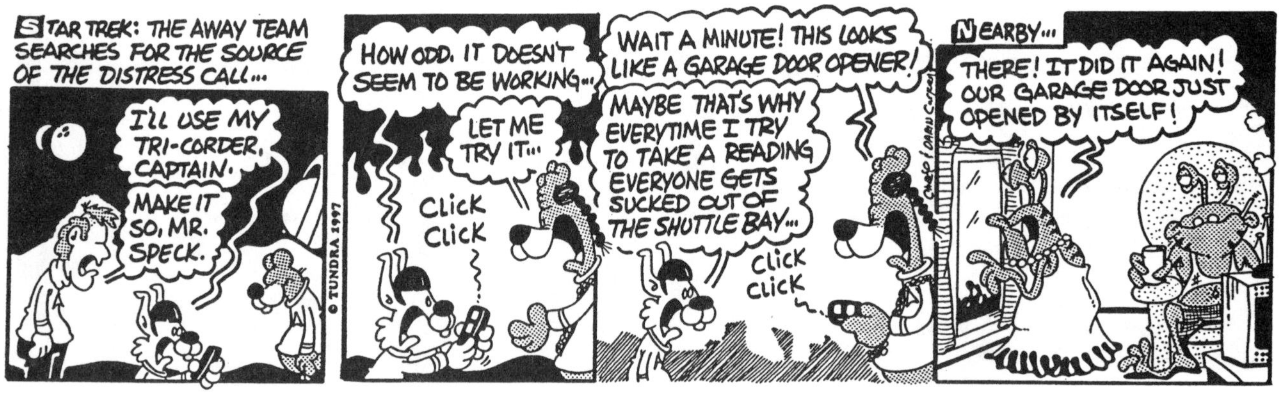
STAR TREK: THE AWAY TEAM SEARCHES FOR THE SOURCE OF THE DISTRESS CALL...
I'LL USE MY TRI-CORDER, CAPTAIN.
MAKE IT SO, MR. SPECK.
© TUNDRA 1997
HOW ODD. IT DOESN'T SEEM TO BE WORKING...
LET ME TRY IT...
CLICK CLICK
WAIT A MINUTE! THIS LOOKS LIKE A GARAGE DOOR OPENER!
MAYBE THAT'S WHY EVERYTIME I TRY TO TAKE A READING EVERYONE GETS SUCKED OUT OF THE SHUTTLE BAY...
CLICK CLICK
NEARBY...
THERE! IT DID IT AGAIN! OUR GARAGE DOOR JUST OPENED BY ITSELF!

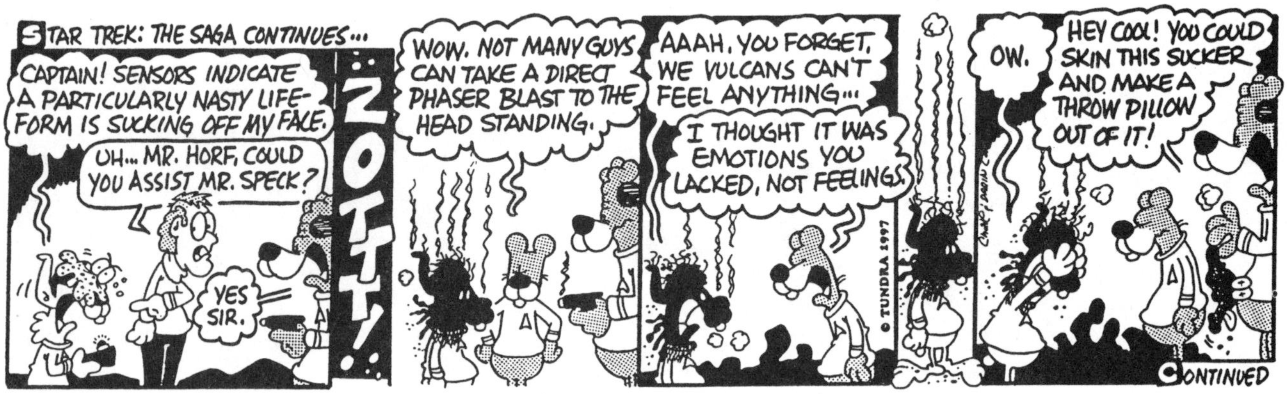
STAR TREK: THE SAGA CONTINUES...
CAPTAIN! SENSORS INDICATE A PARTICULARLY NASTY LIFE-FORM IS SUCKING OFF MY FACE.
UH... MR. HORF, COULD YOU ASSIST MR. SPECK?
YES SIR.
ZOTTT!
WOW. NOT MANY GUYS CAN TAKE A DIRECT PHASER BLAST TO THE HEAD STANDING.
AAAH, YOU FORGET, WE VULCANS CAN'T FEEL ANYTHING...
I THOUGHT IT WAS EMOTIONS YOU LACKED, NOT FEELINGS.
© TUNDRA 1997
OW.
HEY COOL! YOU COULD SKIN THIS SUCKER AND MAKE A THROW PILLOW OUT OF IT!
CONTINUED

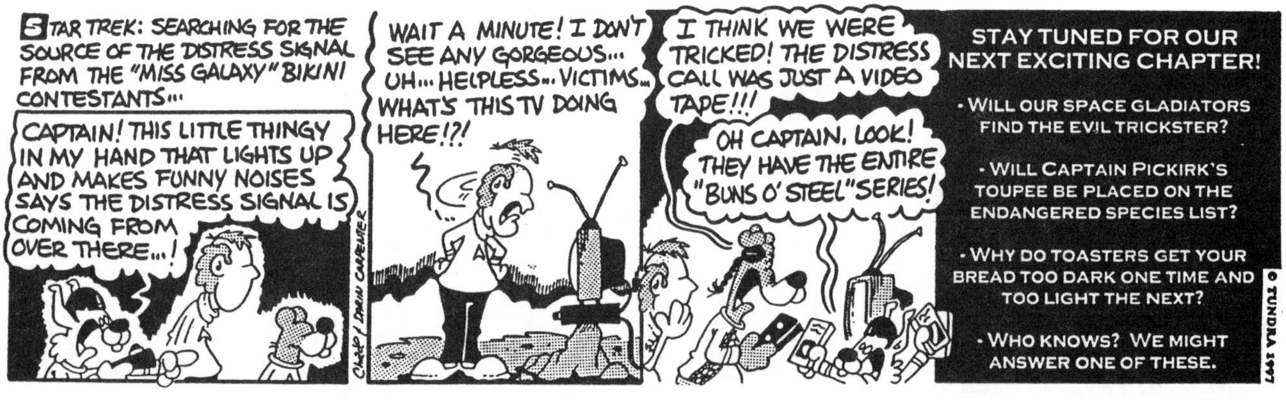
STAR TREK: SEARCHING FOR THE SOURCE OF THE DISTRESS SIGNAL FROM THE "MISS GALAXY" BIKINI CONTESTANTS...
CAPTAIN! THIS LITTLE THINGY IN MY HAND THAT LIGHTS UP AND MAKES FUNNY NOISES SAYS THE DISTRESS SIGNAL IS COMING FROM OVER THERE...!
WAIT A MINUTE! I DON'T SEE ANY GORGEOUS... UH... HELPLESS... VICTIMS... WHAT'S THIS TV DOING HERE!?!
I THINK WE WERE TRICKED! THE DISTRESS CALL WAS JUST A VIDEO TAPE!!!
OH CAPTAIN, LOOK! THEY HAVE THE ENTIRE "BUNS O' STEEL" SERIES!
STAY TUNED FOR OUR NEXT EXCITING CHAPTER!
• WILL OUR SPACE GLADIATORS FIND THE EVIL TRICKSTER?
• WILL CAPTAIN PICKIRK'S TOUPEE BE PLACED ON THE ENDANGERED SPECIES LIST?
• WHY DO TOASTERS GET YOUR BREAD TOO DARK ONE TIME AND TOO LIGHT THE NEXT?
• WHO KNOWS? WE MIGHT ANSWER ONE OF THESE.
© TUNDRA 1997

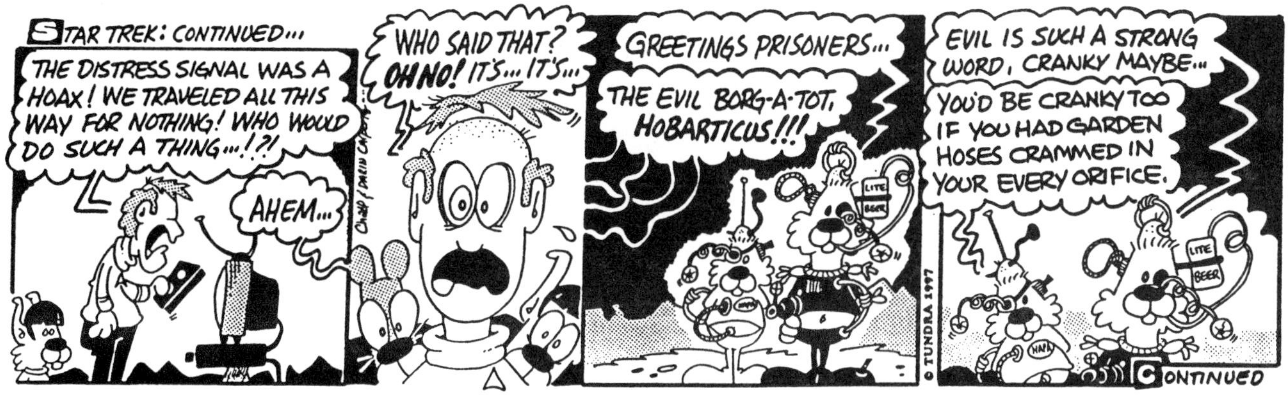
STAR TREK: CONTINUED...
THE DISTRESS SIGNAL WAS A HOAX! WE TRAVELED ALL THIS WAY FOR NOTHING! WHO WOULD DO SUCH A THING...!?!
AHEM...
WHO SAID THAT? OH NO! IT'S... IT'S...
GREETINGS PRISONERS...
THE EVIL BORG-A-TOT, HOBARTICUS!!!
© TUNDRA 1997
EVIL IS SUCH A STRONG WORD, CRANKY MAYBE...
YOU'D BE CRANKY TOO IF YOU HAD GARDEN HOSES CRAMMED IN YOUR EVERY ORIFICE.
CONTINUED

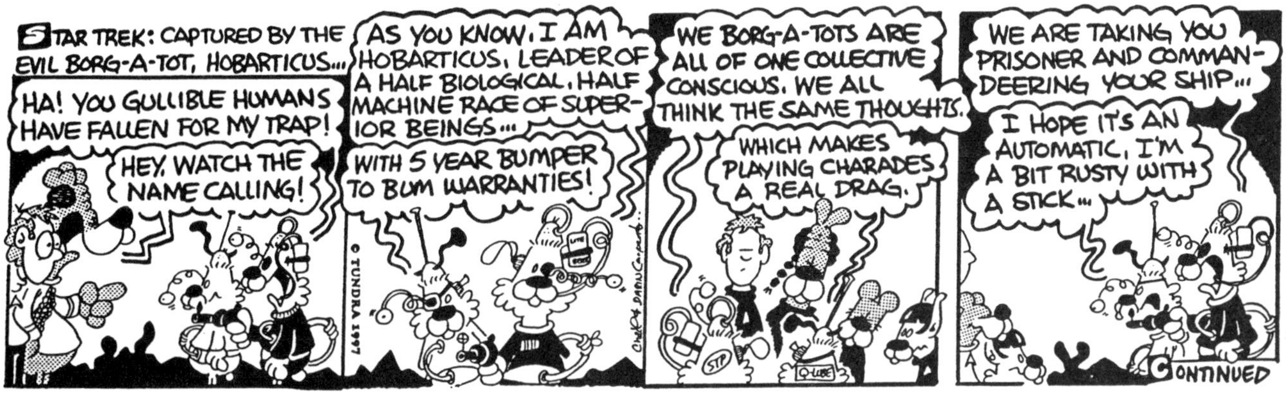
STAR TREK: CAPTURED BY THE EVIL BORG-A-TOT, HOBARTICUS...
HA! YOU GULLIBLE HUMANS HAVE FALLEN FOR MY TRAP!
HEY, WATCH THE NAME CALLING!
AS YOU KNOW, I AM HOBARTICUS, LEADER OF A HALF BIOLOGICAL, HALF MACHINE RACE OF SUPERIOR BEINGS...
WITH 5 YEAR BUMPER TO BUM WARRANTIES!
© TUNDRA 1997
WE BORG-A-TOTS ARE ALL OF ONE COLLECTIVE CONSCIOUS. WE ALL THINK THE SAME THOUGHTS.
WHICH MAKES PLAYING CHARADES A REAL DRAG.
WE ARE TAKING YOU PRISONER AND COMMANDEERING YOUR SHIP...
I HOPE IT'S AN AUTOMATIC, I'M A BIT RUSTY WITH A STICK...
CONTINUED

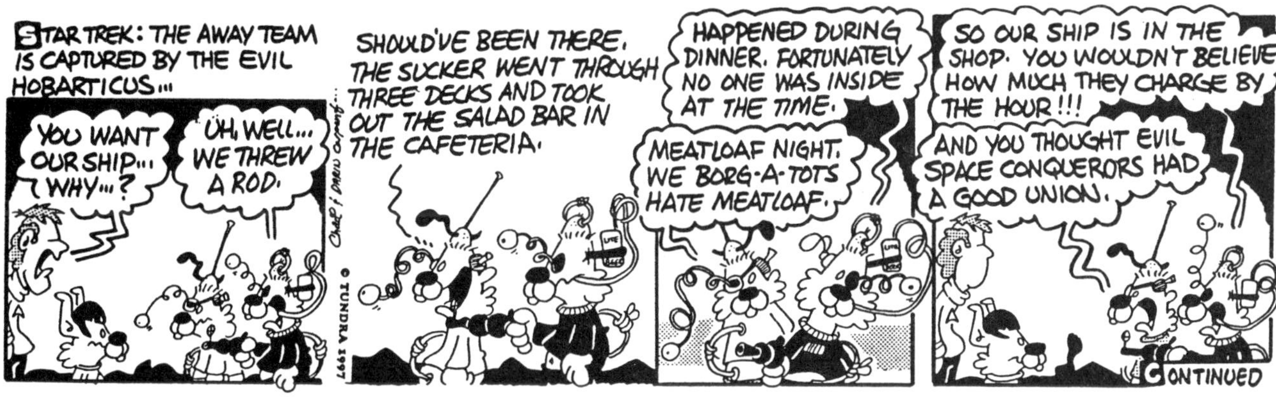
STAR TREK: THE AWAY TEAM IS CAPTURED BY THE EVIL HOBARTICUS...
YOU WANT OUR SHIP... WHY...?
UH, WELL... WE THREW A ROD.
© TUNDRA 1997
SHOULD'VE BEEN THERE. THE SUCKER WENT THROUGH THREE DECKS AND TOOK OUT THE SALAD BAR IN THE CAFETERIA.
HAPPENED DURING DINNER. FORTUNATELY NO ONE WAS INSIDE AT THE TIME.
MEATLOAF NIGHT. WE BORG-A-TOTS HATE MEATLOAF.
SO OUR SHIP IS IN THE SHOP. YOU WOULDN'T BELIEVE HOW MUCH THEY CHARGE BY THE HOUR!!!
AND YOU THOUGHT EVIL SPACE CONQUERORS HAD A GOOD UNION.
CONTINUED

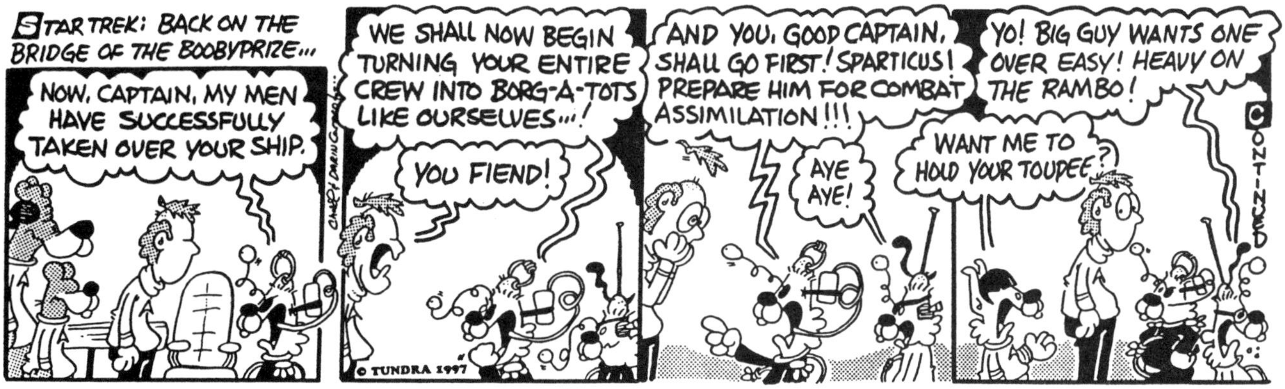
STAR TREK: BACK ON THE BRIDGE OF THE BOOBYPRIZE...
NOW, CAPTAIN, MY MEN HAVE SUCCESSFULLY TAKEN OVER YOUR SHIP.
WE SHALL NOW BEGIN TURNING YOUR ENTIRE CREW INTO BORG-A-TOTS LIKE OURSELVES...!
YOU FIEND!
© TUNDRA 1997
AND YOU, GOOD CAPTAIN, SHALL GO FIRST! SPARTICUS! PREPARE HIM FOR COMBAT ASSIMILATION!!!
AYE AYE!
YO! BIG GUY WANTS ONE OVER EASY! HEAVY ON THE RAMBO!
WANT ME TO HOLD YOUR TOUPEE?
CONTINUED

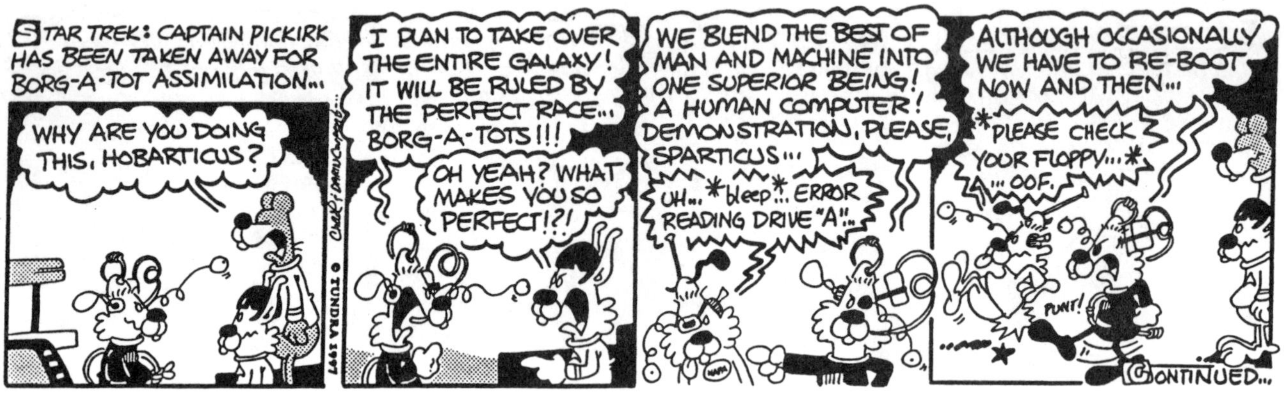
STAR TREK: CAPTAIN PICKIRK HAS BEEN TAKEN AWAY FOR BORG-A-TOT ASSIMILATION...
WHY ARE YOU DOING THIS, HOBARTICUS?
© TUNDRA 1997
I PLAN TO TAKE OVER THE ENTIRE GALAXY! IT WILL BE RULED BY THE PERFECT RACE... BORG-A-TOTS!!!
OH YEAH? WHAT MAKES YOU SO PERFECT!?!
WE BLEND THE BEST OF MAN AND MACHINE INTO ONE SUPERIOR BEING! A HUMAN COMPUTER! DEMONSTRATION, PLEASE, SPARTICUS...
UH... *bleep*... ERROR READING DRIVE "A"...
ALTHOUGH OCCASIONALLY WE HAVE TO RE-BOOT NOW AND THEN...
PLEASE CHECK YOUR FLOPPY...
...OOF.
PUNT!
CONTINUED...

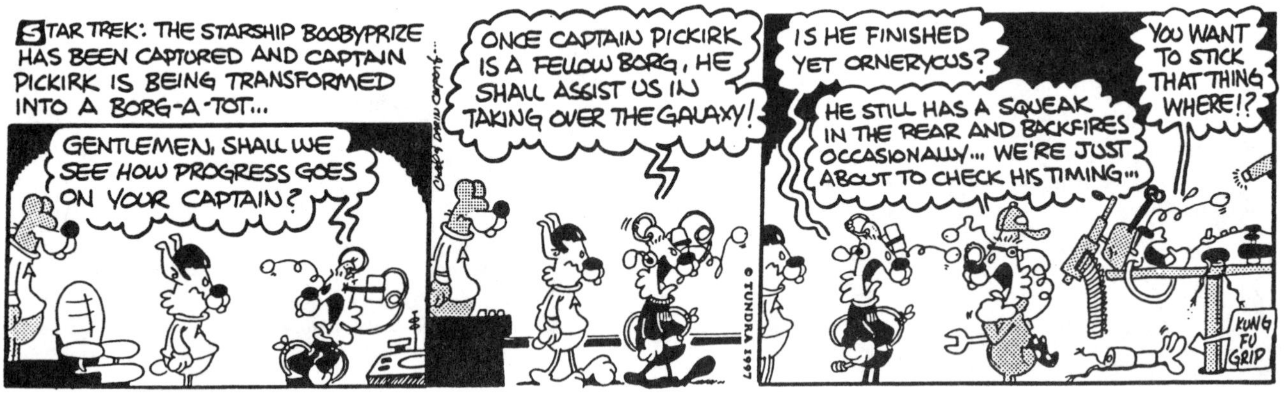
STAR TREK: THE STARSHIP BOOBYPRIZE HAS BEEN CAPTURED AND CAPTAIN PICKIRK IS BEING TRANSFORMED INTO A BORG-A-TOT...
GENTLEMEN, SHALL WE SEE HOW PROGRESS GOES ON YOUR CAPTAIN?
ONCE CAPTAIN PICKIRK IS A FELLOW BORG, HE SHALL ASSIST US IN TAKING OVER THE GALAXY!
© TUNDRA 1997
IS HE FINISHED YET ORNERYCUS?
HE STILL HAS A SQUEAK IN THE REAR AND BACKFIRES OCCASIONALLY... WE'RE JUST ABOUT TO CHECK HIS TIMING...
YOU WANT TO STICK THAT THING WHERE!?
KUNG FU GRIP

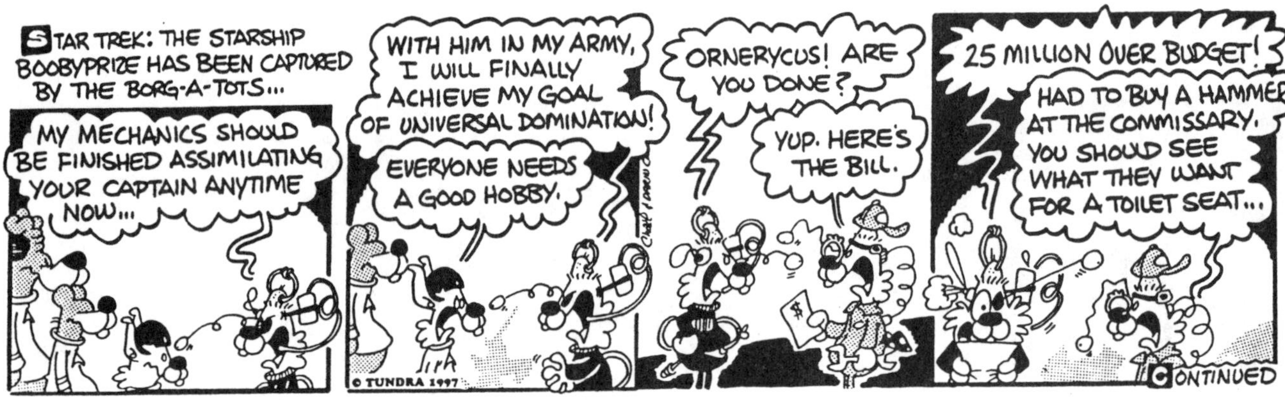
STAR TREK: THE STARSHIP BOOBYPRIZE HAS BEEN CAPTURED BY THE BORG-A-TOTS...
MY MECHANICS SHOULD BE FINISHED ASSIMILATING YOUR CAPTAIN ANYTIME NOW...
© TUNDRA 1997
WITH HIM IN MY ARMY, I WILL FINALLY ACHIEVE MY GOAL OF UNIVERSAL DOMINATION!
EVERYONE NEEDS A GOOD HOBBY.
ORNERYCUS! ARE YOU DONE?
YUP. HERE'S THE BILL.
25 MILLION OVER BUDGET!
HAD TO BUY A HAMMER AT THE COMMISSARY. YOU SHOULD SEE WHAT THEY WANT FOR A TOILET SEAT...
CONTINUED

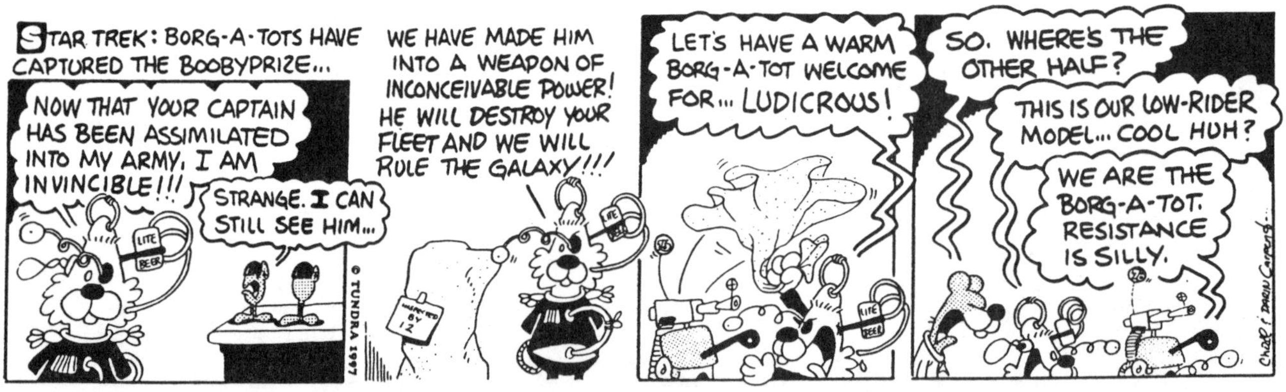
STAR TREK: BORG-A-TOTS HAVE CAPTURED THE BOOBYPRIZE...
NOW THAT YOUR CAPTAIN HAS BEEN ASSIMILATED INTO MY ARMY, I AM INVINCIBLE!!!
STRANGE. I CAN STILL SEE HIM...
LITE BEER
© TUNDRA 1997
WE HAVE MADE HIM INTO A WEAPON OF INCONCEIVABLE POWER! HE WILL DESTROY YOUR FLEET AND WE WILL RULE THE GALAXY!!!
LET'S HAVE A WARM BORG-A-TOT WELCOME FOR... LUDICROUS!
SO. WHERE'S THE OTHER HALF?
THIS IS OUR LOW-RIDER MODEL... COOL HUH?
WE ARE THE BORG-A-TOT. RESISTANCE IS SILLY.

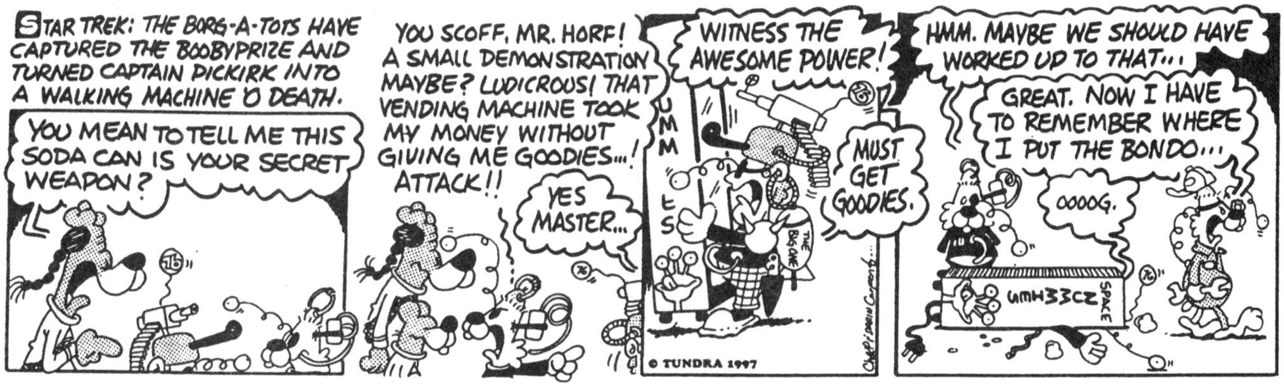
STAR TREK: THE BORG-A-TOTS HAVE CAPTURED THE BOOBYPRIZE AND TURNED CAPTAIN PICKIRK INTO A WALKING MACHINE O' DEATH.
YOU MEAN TO TELL ME THIS SODA CAN IS YOUR SECRET WEAPON?
YOU SCOFF, MR. HORF! A SMALL DEMONSTRATION MAYBE? LUDICROUS! THAT VENDING MACHINE TOOK MY MONEY WITHOUT GIVING ME GOODIES...! ATTACK!!
YES MASTER...
WITNESS THE AWESOME POWER!
UMM
MUST GET GOODIES.
THE BIG ONE
© TUNDRA 1997
HMM. MAYBE WE SHOULD HAVE WORKED UP TO THAT...
GREAT. NOW I HAVE TO REMEMBER WHERE I PUT THE BONDO...
OOOOG.
UMH33CZ
SPACE

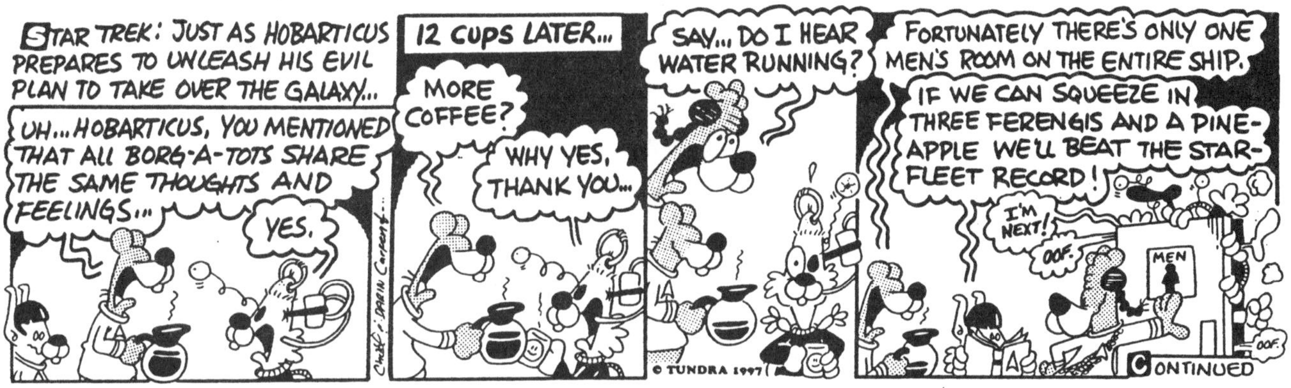
STAR TREK: JUST AS HOBARTICUS PREPARES TO UNLEASH HIS EVIL PLAN TO TAKE OVER THE GALAXY...
UH... HOBARTICUS, YOU MENTIONED THAT ALL BORG-A-TOTS SHARE THE SAME THOUGHTS AND FEELINGS...
YES.
12 CUPS LATER...
MORE COFFEE?
WHY YES, THANK YOU...
SAY... DO I HEAR WATER RUNNING?
© TUNDRA 1997
FORTUNATELY THERE'S ONLY ONE MEN'S ROOM ON THE ENTIRE SHIP.
IF WE CAN SQUEEZE IN THREE FERENGIS AND A PINE-APPLE WE'LL BEAT THE STAR-FLEET RECORD!
I'M NEXT!
OOF.
MEN
OOF.
CONTINUED

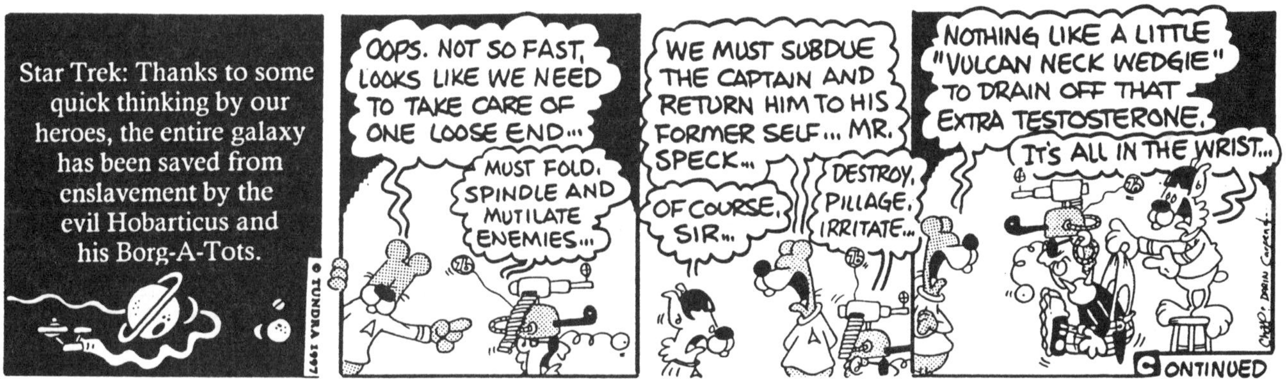
Star Trek: Thanks to some quick thinking by our heroes, the entire galaxy has been saved from enslavement by the evil Hobarticus and his Borg-A-Tots.
© TUNDRA 1997
OOPS. NOT SO FAST, LOOKS LIKE WE NEED TO TAKE CARE OF ONE LOOSE END...
MUST FOLD, SPINDLE AND MUTILATE ENEMIES...
WE MUST SUBDUE THE CAPTAIN AND RETURN HIM TO HIS FORMER SELF... MR. SPECK...
OF COURSE, SIR...
DESTROY, PILLAGE, IRRITATE...
NOTHING LIKE A LITTLE "VULCAN NECK WEDGIE" TO DRAIN OFF THAT EXTRA TESTOSTERONE.
IT'S ALL IN THE WRIST...
CONTINUED

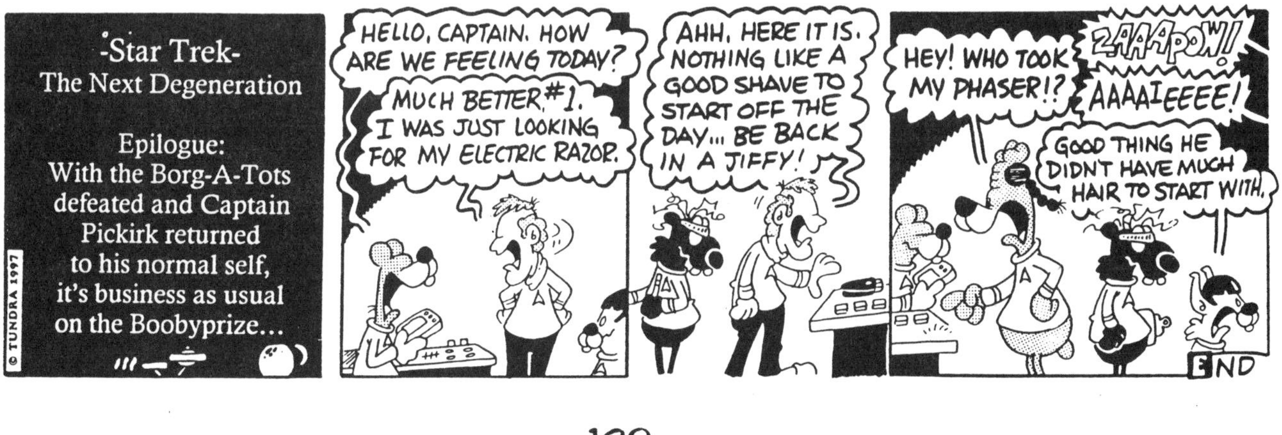
-Star Trek-
The Next Degeneration
Epilogue:
With the Borg-A-Tots defeated and Captain Pickirk returned to his normal self, it's business as usual on the Boobyprize...
© TUNDRA 1997
HELLO, CAPTAIN. HOW ARE WE FEELING TODAY?
MUCH BETTER, #1. I WAS JUST LOOKING FOR MY ELECTRIC RAZOR.
AHH, HERE IT IS. NOTHING LIKE A GOOD SHAVE TO START OFF THE DAY... BE BACK IN A JIFFY!
HEY! WHO TOOK MY PHASER!?
ZAAAPOW!!
AAAAIEEEE!
GOOD THING HE DIDN'T HAVE MUCH HAIR TO START WITH.
END

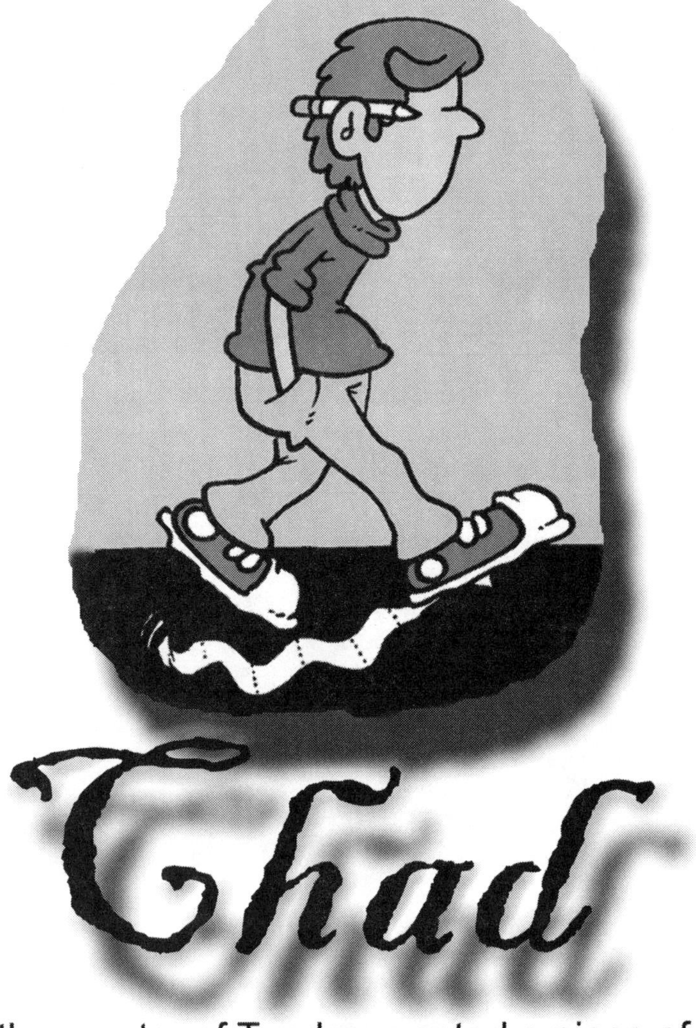

Chad

Chad Carpenter, the creator of Tundra, wanted a piece of himself in his comic strip. However, due to the fact that he was unwilling to relinquish any body parts, he opted to pen a character in his own image. This character, aptly named Chad the Cartoonist, ironically plays the role of a struggling cartoonist. Chad is the constant victim of the other Tundra characters' exploits and cruel practical jokes - e.g., switching his toothpaste with hemorrhoid cream & slipping an open tube of Super-Glue in his pillow.

Chad embarked on his career as a cartoonist when he realized it was the job that requires the least amount of physical labor within the human and/or plant kingdom.

Chad's current project is trying to locate his long-lost parents. After living with them for over 30 years, his folks mysteriously disappeared into the night leaving no clues save a couple of missing suitcases and a note telling Chad that he was adopted.

Chapter Six

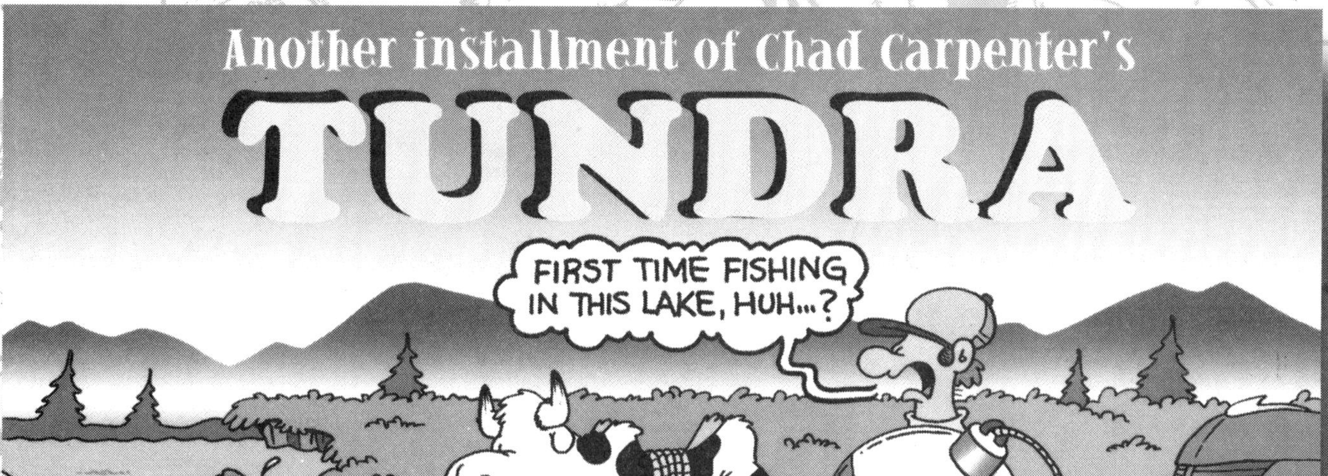
Another installment of Chad Carpenter's
TUNDRA
FIRST TIME FISHING IN THIS LAKE, HUH...?
Le Fish Tube
NATURE'S FINEST COMIC STRIP - PACKED IN ITS OWN JUICES!

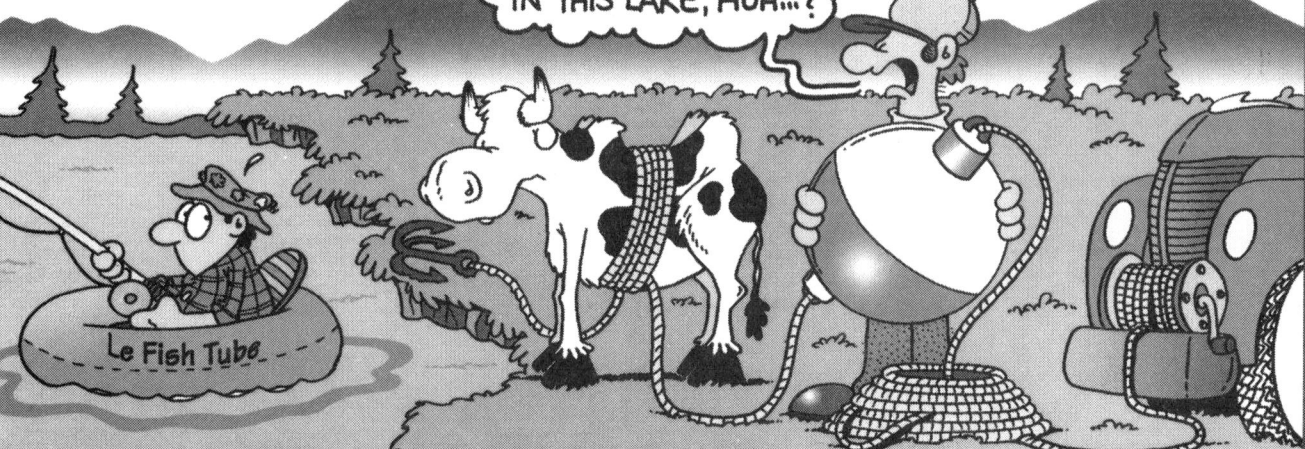

First Printing: May 2000

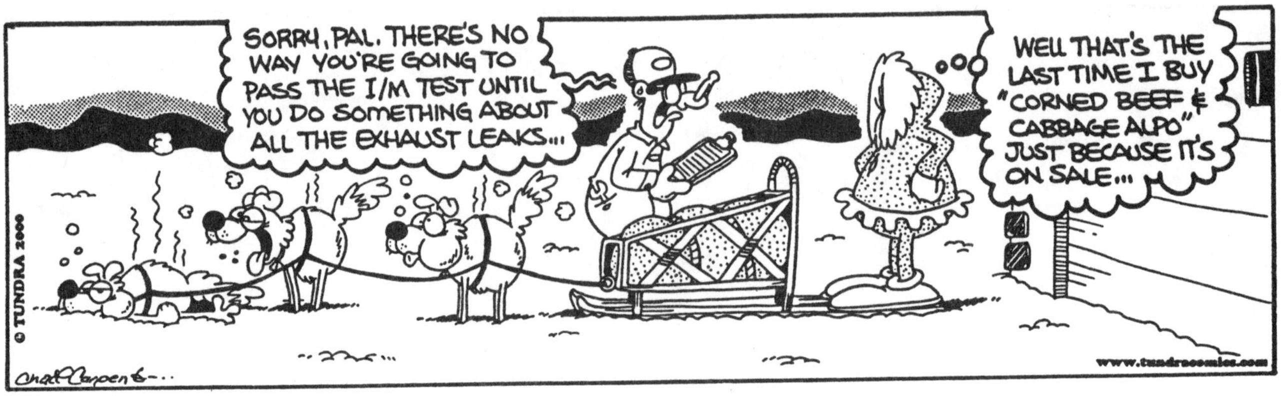
SORRY, PAL. THERE'S NO WAY YOU'RE GOING TO PASS THE I/M TEST UNTIL YOU DO SOMETHING ABOUT ALL THE EXHAUST LEAKS...
WELL THAT'S THE LAST TIME I BUY "CORNED BEEF & CABBAGE ALPO" JUST BECAUSE IT'S ON SALE...
© TUNDRA 2000
www.tundracomics.com

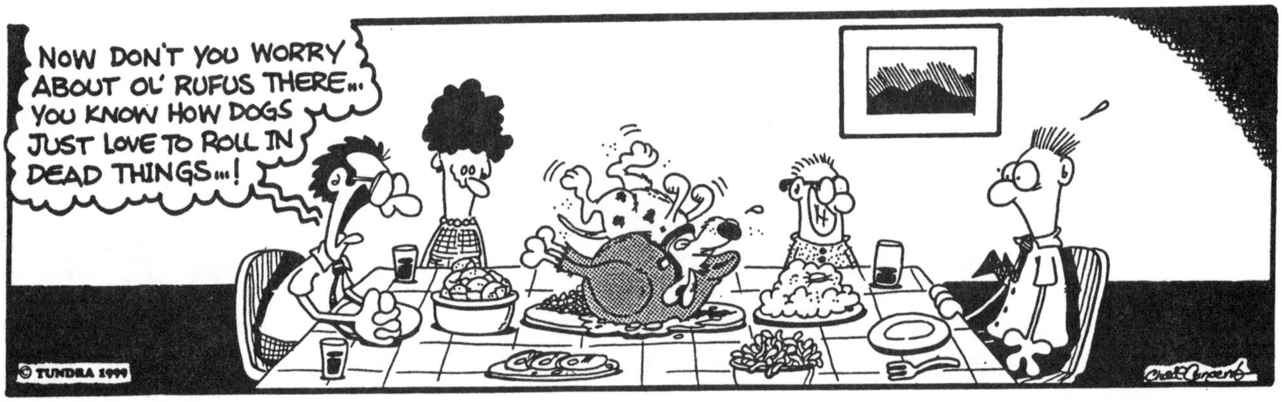
NOW DON'T YOU WORRY ABOUT OL' RUFUS THERE... YOU KNOW HOW DOGS JUST LOVE TO ROLL IN DEAD THINGS...!
© TUNDRA 1999

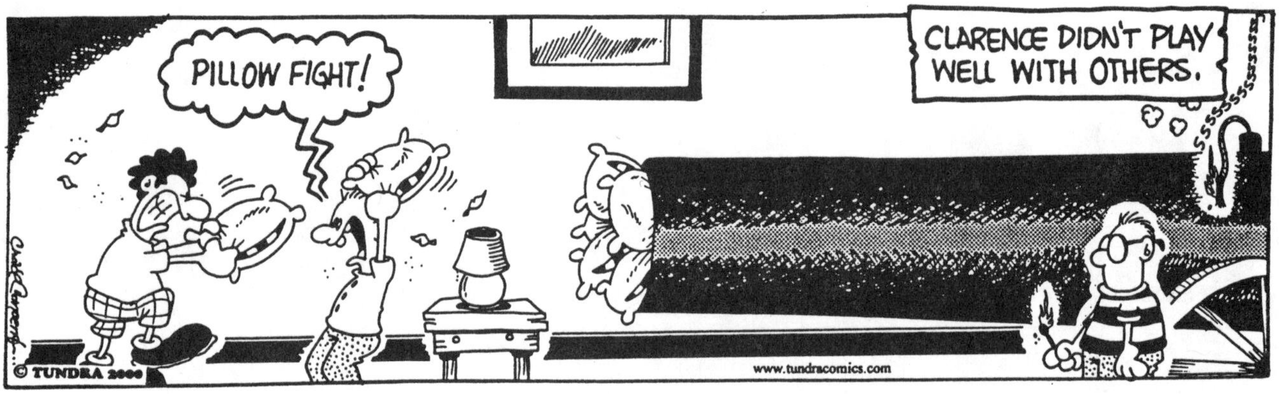
PILLOW FIGHT!
CLARENCE DIDN'T PLAY WELL WITH OTHERS.
© TUNDRA 2000
www.tundracomics.com

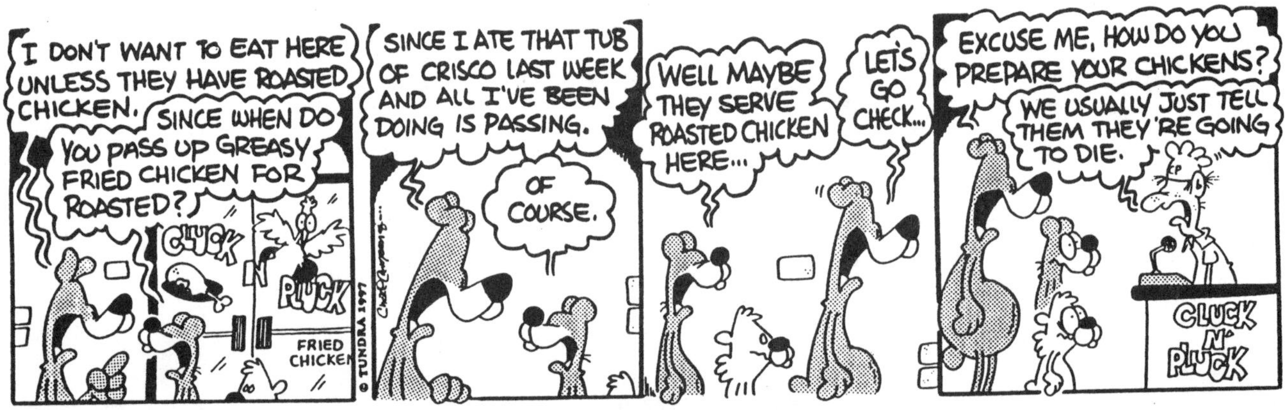
I DON'T WANT TO EAT HERE UNLESS THEY HAVE ROASTED CHICKEN.
SINCE WHEN DO YOU PASS UP GREASY FRIED CHICKEN FOR ROASTED?
CLUCK N PLUCK
FRIED
SINCE I ATE THAT TUB OF CRISCO LAST WEEK AND ALL I'VE BEEN DOING IS PASSING.
OF COURSE.
© TUNDRA 1997
WELL MAYBE THEY SERVE ROASTED CHICKEN HERE...
LET'S GO CHECK...
EXCUSE ME, HOW DO YOU PREPARE YOUR CHICKENS?
WE USUALLY JUST TELL THEM THEY'RE GOING TO DIE.
CLUCK N' PLUCK

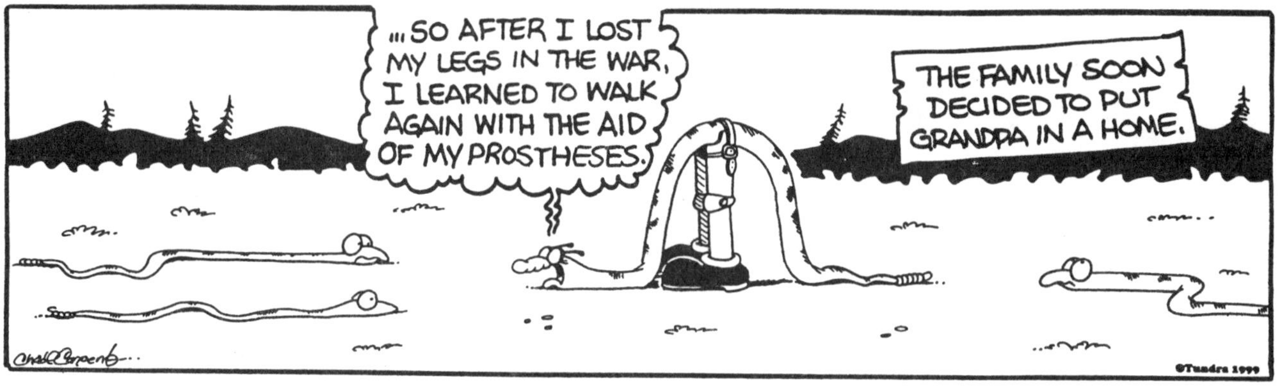
...SO AFTER I LOST MY LEGS IN THE WAR, I LEARNED TO WALK AGAIN WITH THE AID OF MY PROSTHESES.
THE FAMILY SOON DECIDED TO PUT GRANDPA IN A HOME.
©Tundra 1999

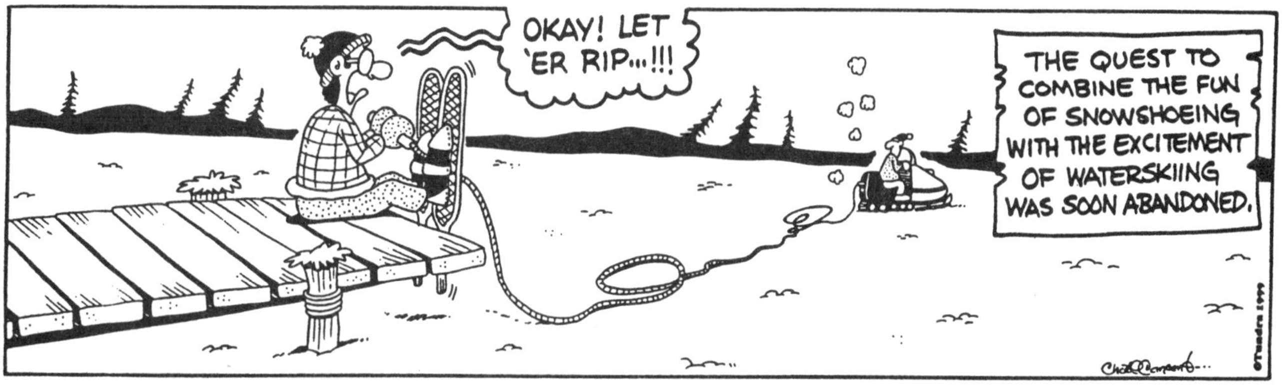
OKAY! LET 'ER RIP...!!!
THE QUEST TO COMBINE THE FUN OF SNOWSHOEING WITH THE EXCITEMENT OF WATERSKIING WAS SOON ABANDONED.
©Tundra 1999

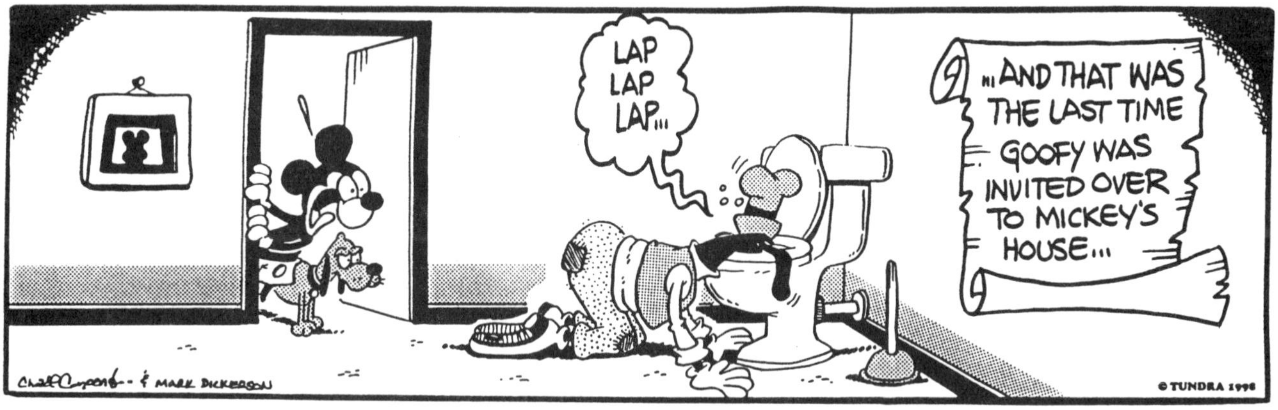
LAP LAP LAP...
...AND THAT WAS THE LAST TIME GOOFY WAS INVITED OVER TO MICKEY'S HOUSE...
& MARK DICKERSON
©TUNDRA 1998

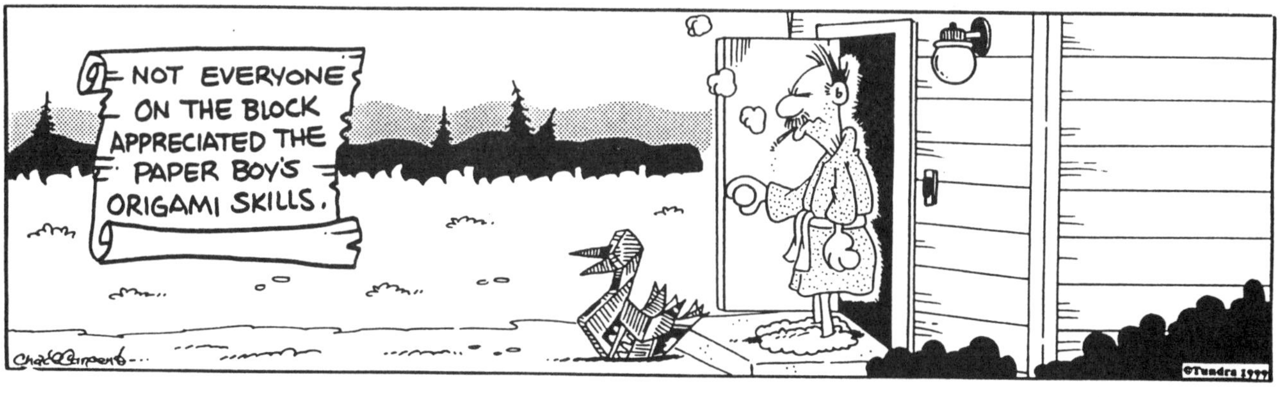
NOT EVERYONE ON THE BLOCK APPRECIATED THE PAPER BOY'S ORIGAMI SKILLS.
©Tundra 1999

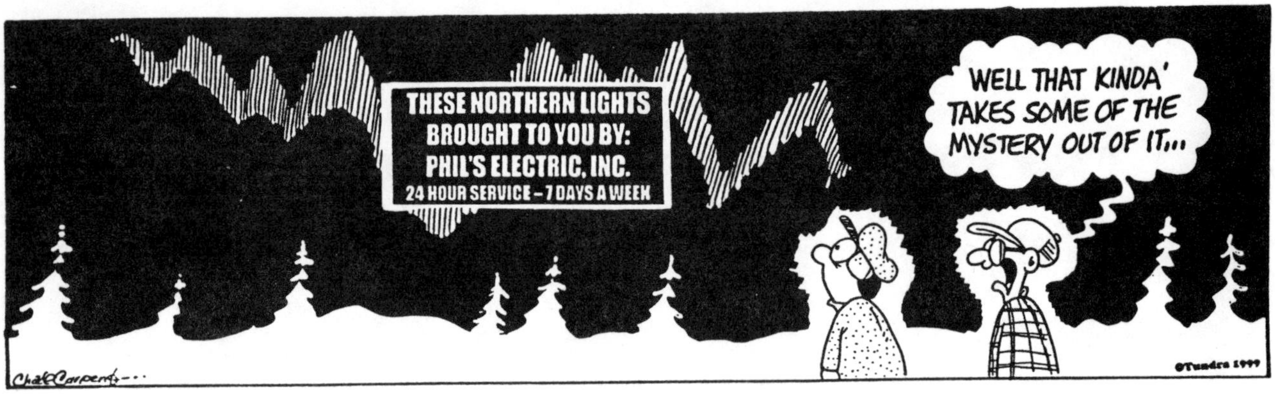

THESE NORTHERN LIGHTS BROUGHT TO YOU BY: PHIL'S ELECTRIC, INC. 24 HOUR SERVICE – 7 DAYS A WEEK
WELL THAT KINDA' TAKES SOME OF THE MYSTERY OUT OF IT...
©Tundra 1999

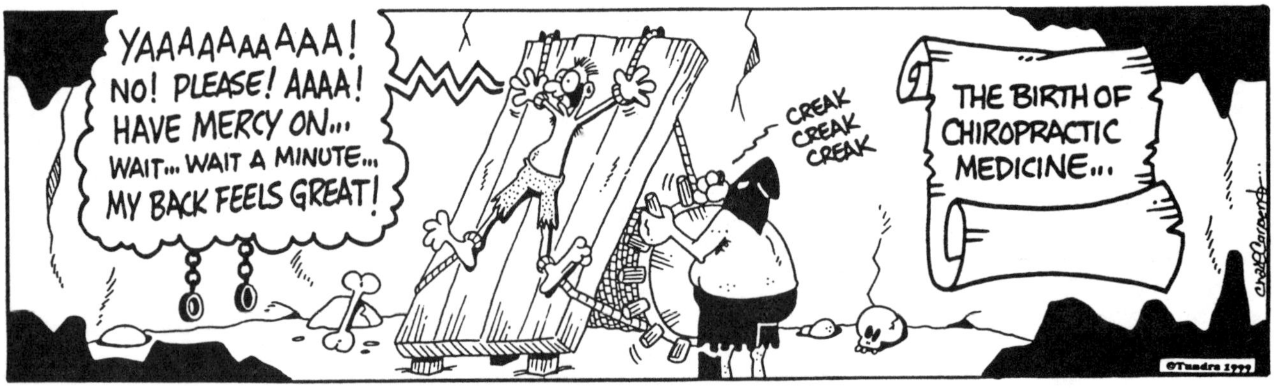

YAAAAAAAAAA! NO! PLEASE! AAAA! HAVE MERCY ON... WAIT... WAIT A MINUTE... MY BACK FEELS GREAT!
CREAK CREAK CREAK
THE BIRTH OF CHIROPRACTIC MEDICINE...
©Tundra 1999

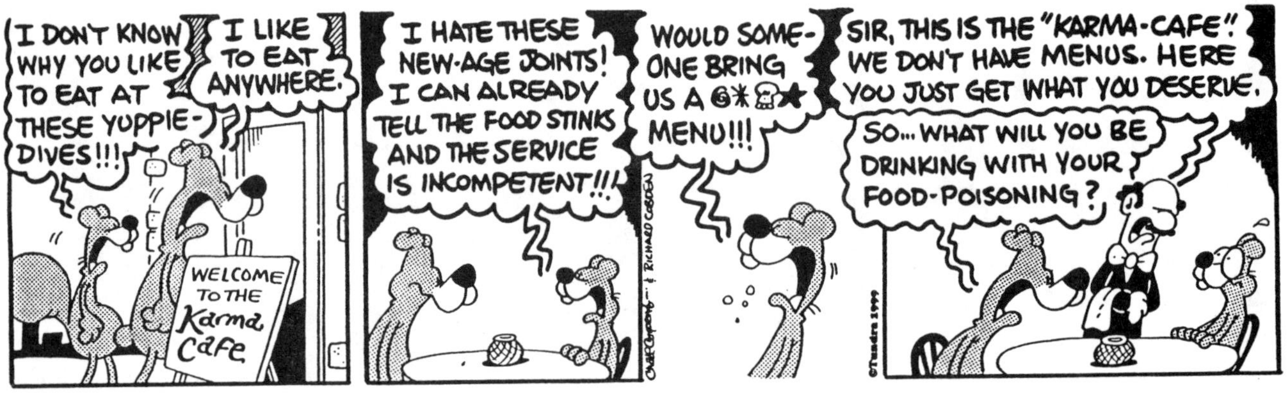

I DON'T KNOW WHY YOU LIKE TO EAT AT THESE YUPPIE-DIVES!!!
I LIKE TO EAT ANYWHERE.
WELCOME TO THE Karma Cafe
I HATE THESE NEW-AGE JOINTS! I CAN ALREADY TELL THE FOOD STINKS AND THE SERVICE IS INCOMPETENT!!!
WOULD SOME-ONE BRING US A @*!★ MENU!!!
SIR, THIS IS THE "KARMA-CAFE". WE DON'T HAVE MENUS. HERE YOU JUST GET WHAT YOU DESERVE.
SO... WHAT WILL YOU BE DRINKING WITH YOUR FOOD-POISONING?
©Tundra 1999

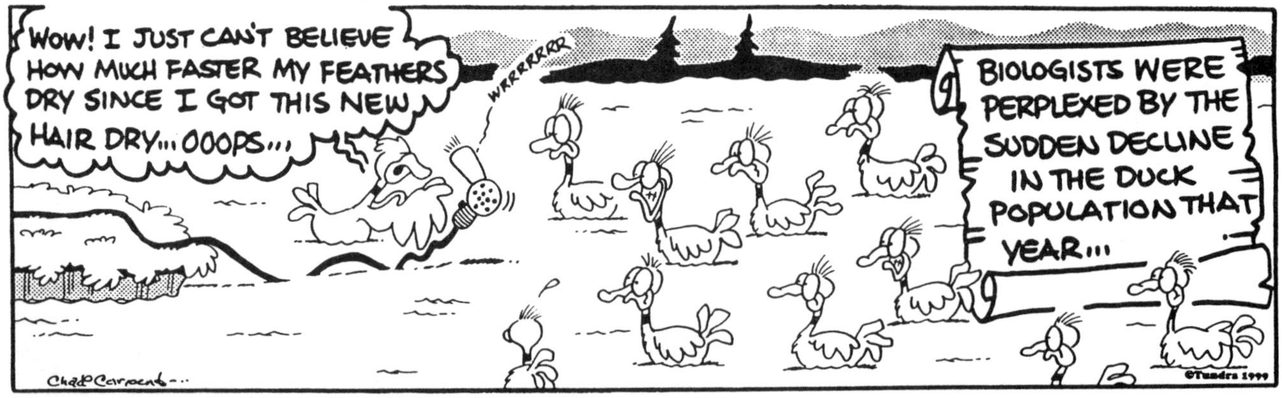

WOW! I JUST CAN'T BELIEVE HOW MUCH FASTER MY FEATHERS DRY SINCE I GOT THIS NEW HAIR DRY... OOOPS...
WARRRRRR
BIOLOGISTS WERE PERPLEXED BY THE SUDDEN DECLINE IN THE DUCK POPULATION THAT YEAR...
©Tundra 1999

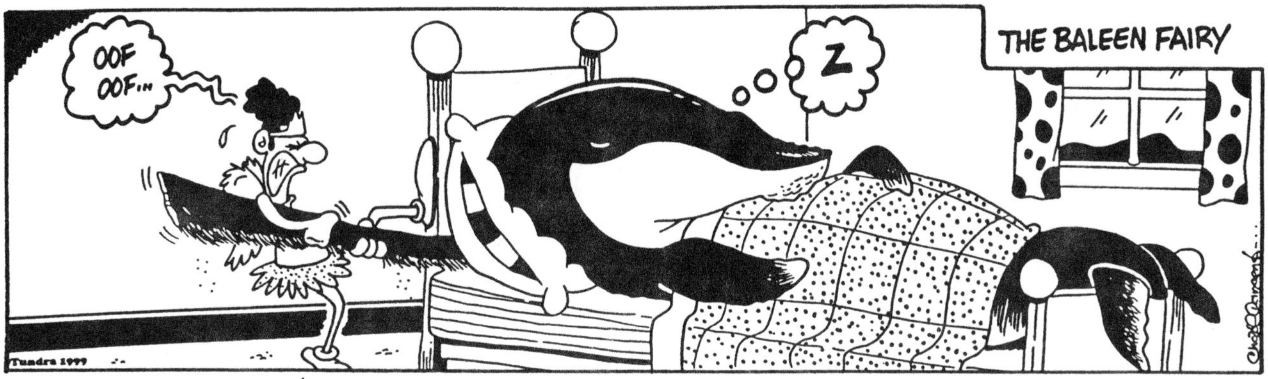
THE BALEEN FAIRY
OOF OOF...
Z
Tundra 1999

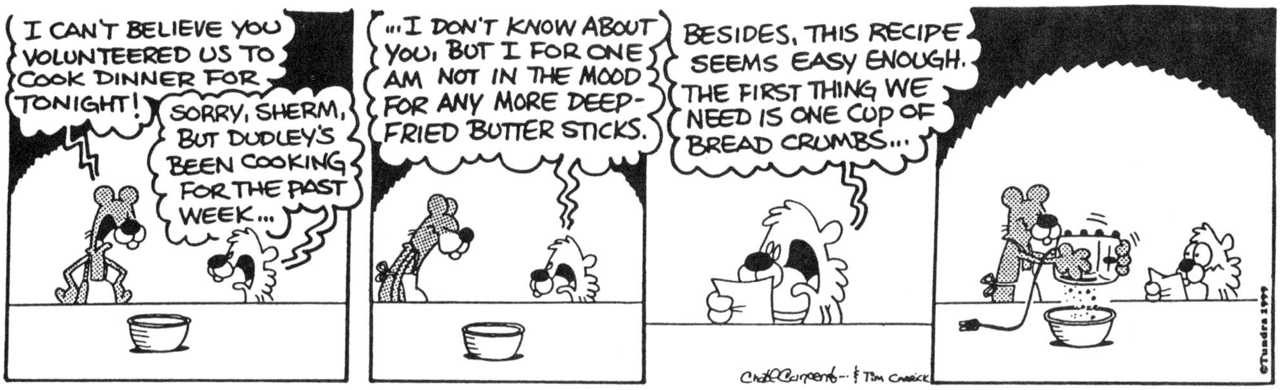
I CAN'T BELIEVE YOU VOLUNTEERED US TO COOK DINNER FOR TONIGHT!
SORRY, SHERM, BUT DUDLEY'S BEEN COOKING FOR THE PAST WEEK...
...I DON'T KNOW ABOUT YOU, BUT I FOR ONE AM NOT IN THE MOOD FOR ANY MORE DEEP-FRIED BUTTER STICKS.
BESIDES, THIS RECIPE SEEMS EASY ENOUGH. THE FIRST THING WE NEED IS ONE CUP OF BREAD CRUMBS...
©Tundra 1999

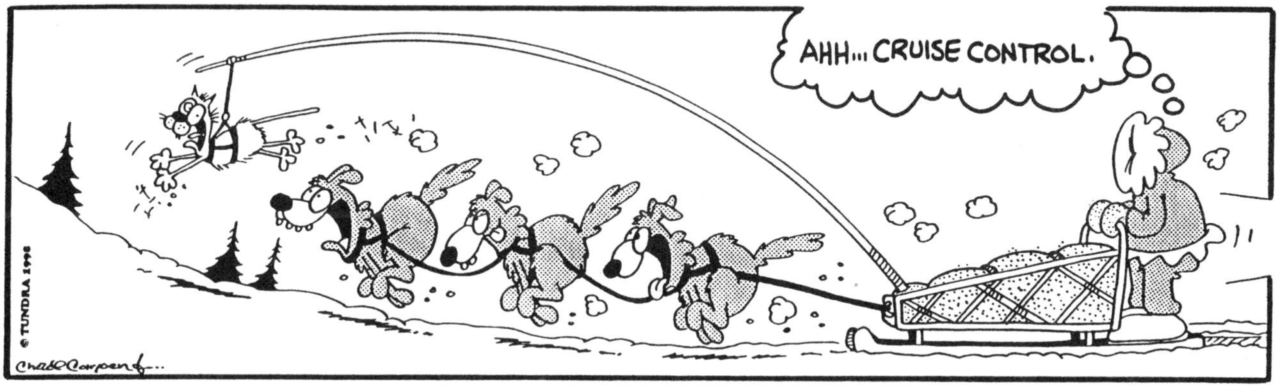
AHH... CRUISE CONTROL.
© TUNDRA 1998

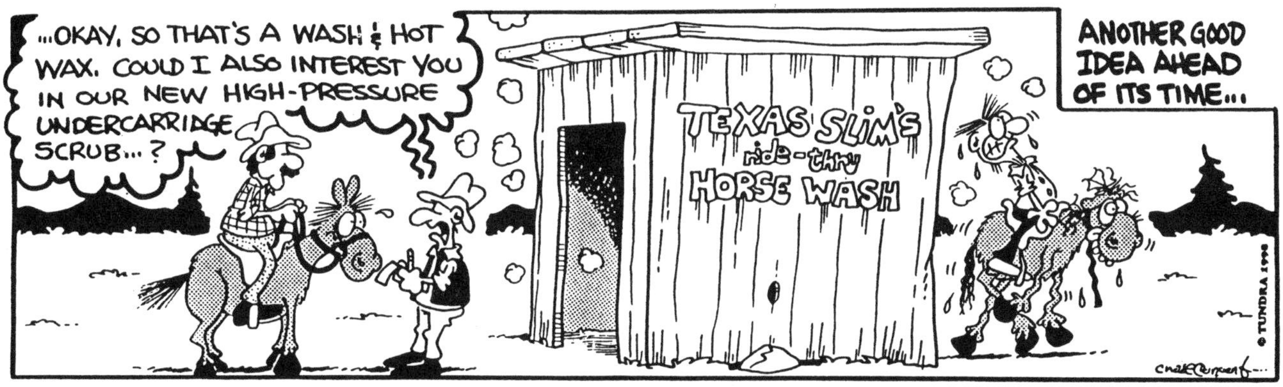
...OKAY, SO THAT'S A WASH & HOT WAX. COULD I ALSO INTEREST YOU IN OUR NEW HIGH-PRESSURE UNDERCARRIAGE SCRUB...?
TEXAS SLIM'S ride-thru HORSE WASH
ANOTHER GOOD IDEA AHEAD OF ITS TIME...
© TUNDRA 1998

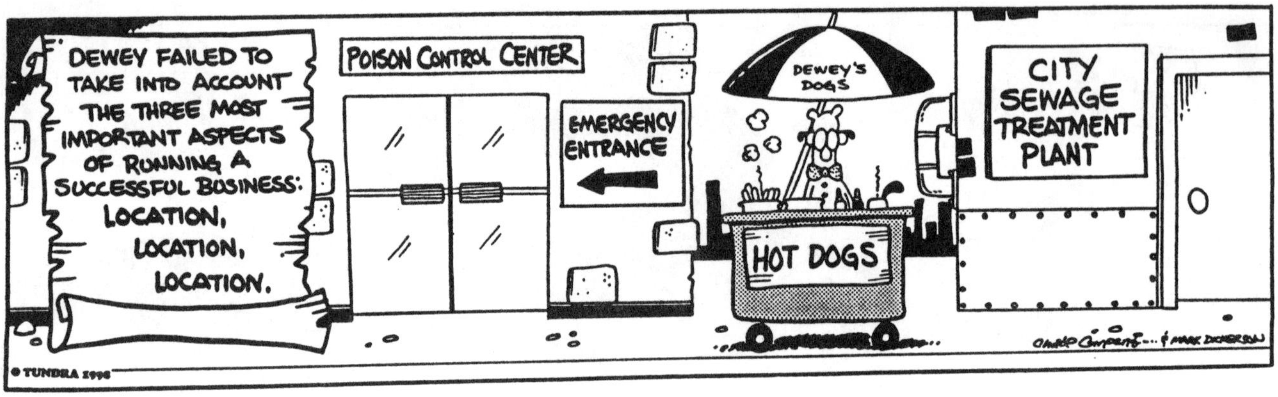
DEWEY FAILED TO TAKE INTO ACCOUNT THE THREE MOST IMPORTANT ASPECTS OF RUNNING A SUCCESSFUL BUSINESS: LOCATION, LOCATION, LOCATION.
POISON CONTROL CENTER
EMERGENCY ENTRANCE
DEWEY'S DOGS
HOT DOGS
CITY SEWAGE TREATMENT PLANT
© TUNDRA 1998

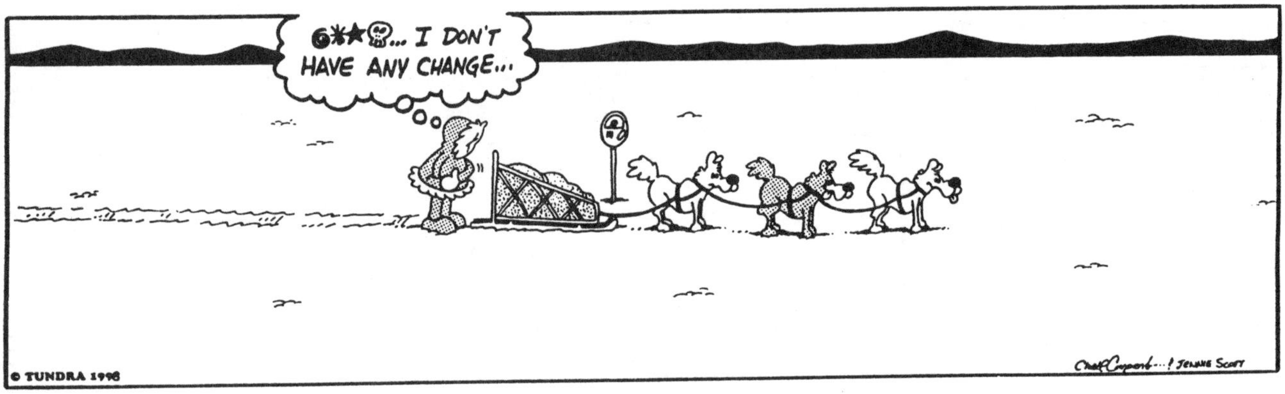
... I DON'T HAVE ANY CHANGE...
© TUNDRA 1998

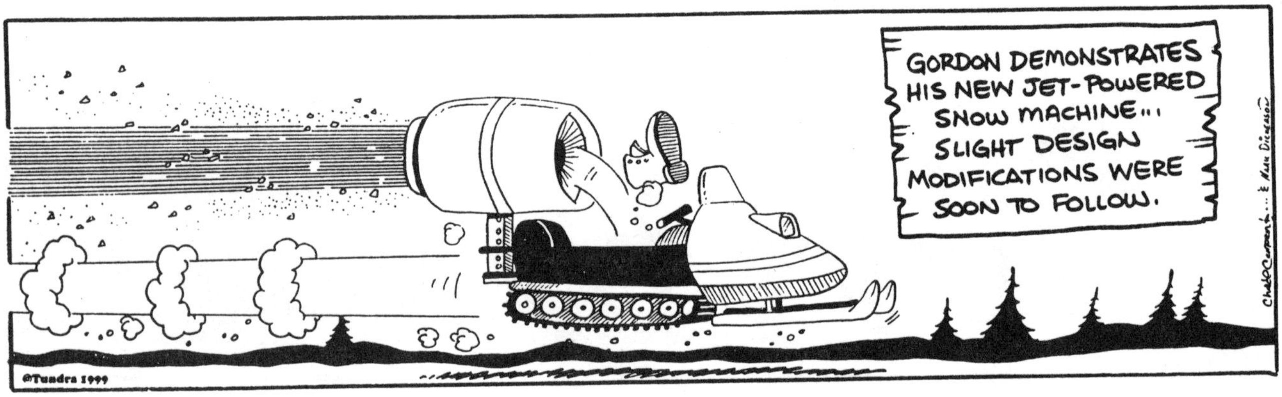
GORDON DEMONSTRATES HIS NEW JET-POWERED SNOW MACHINE... SLIGHT DESIGN MODIFICATIONS WERE SOON TO FOLLOW.
©Tundra 1999

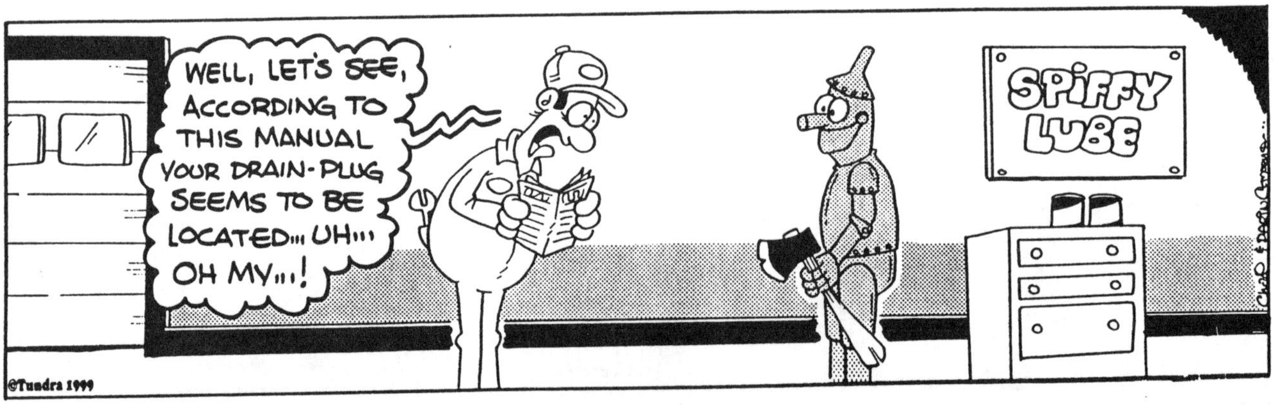
WELL, LET'S SEE, ACCORDING TO THIS MANUAL YOUR DRAIN-PLUG SEEMS TO BE LOCATED... UH... OH MY...!
SPIFFY LUBE
©Tundra 1999

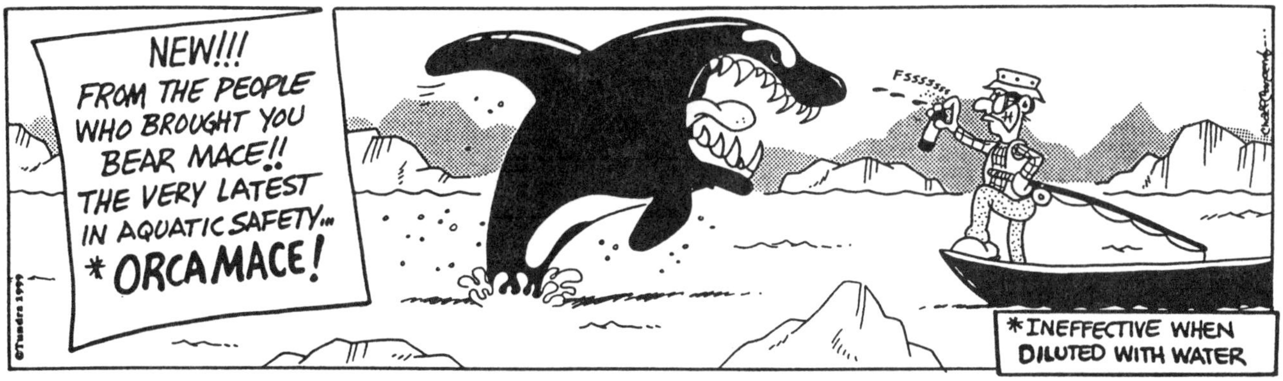
NEW!!! FROM THE PEOPLE WHO BROUGHT YOU BEAR MACE!! THE VERY LATEST IN AQUATIC SAFETY... * ORCAMACE!
FSSSSSSS
*INEFFECTIVE WHEN DILUTED WITH WATER
©Tundra 1999

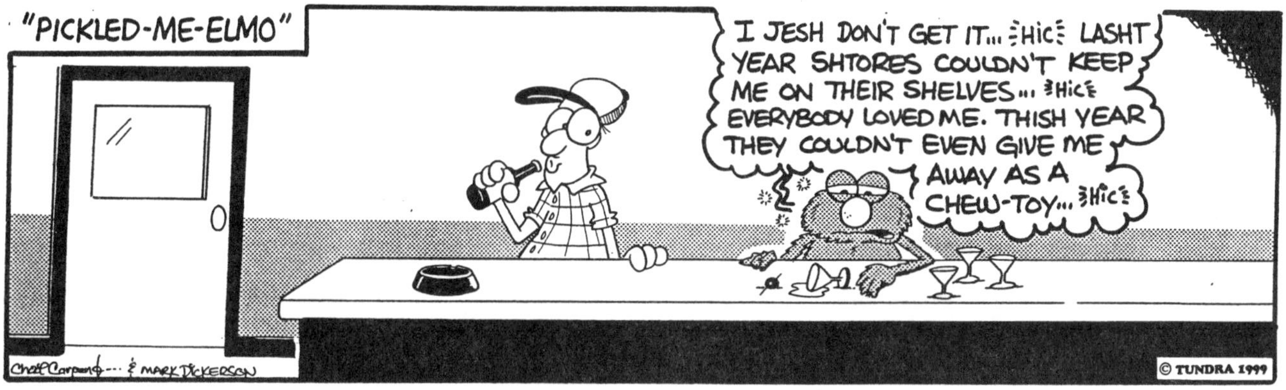
"PICKLED-ME-ELMO"
I JESH DON'T GET IT... HIC LASHT YEAR SHTORES COULDN'T KEEP ME ON THEIR SHELVES... HIC EVERYBODY LOVED ME. THISH YEAR THEY COULDN'T EVEN GIVE ME AWAY AS A CHEW-TOY... HIC
MARK DICKERSON
© TUNDRA 1999

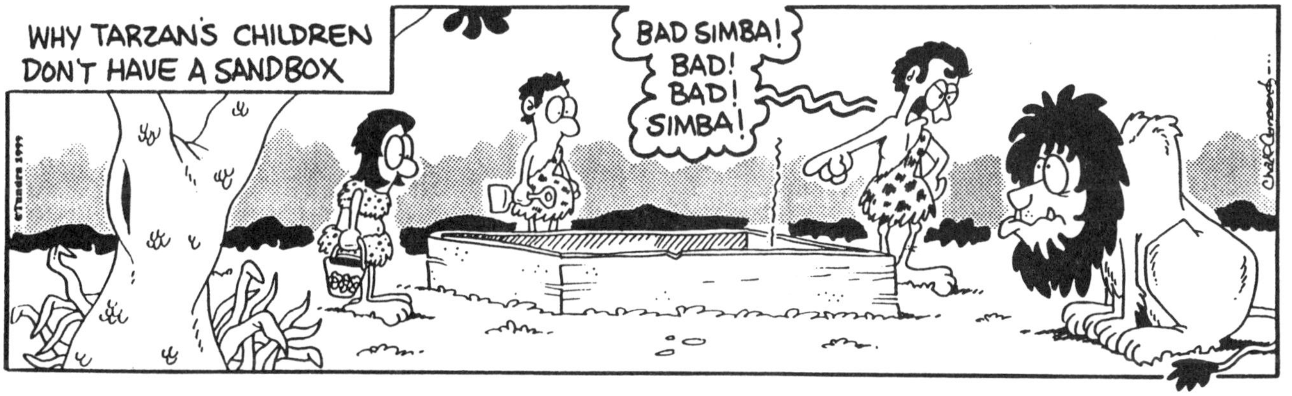
WHY TARZAN'S CHILDREN DON'T HAVE A SANDBOX
BAD SIMBA! BAD! BAD! SIMBA!
©Tundra 1999

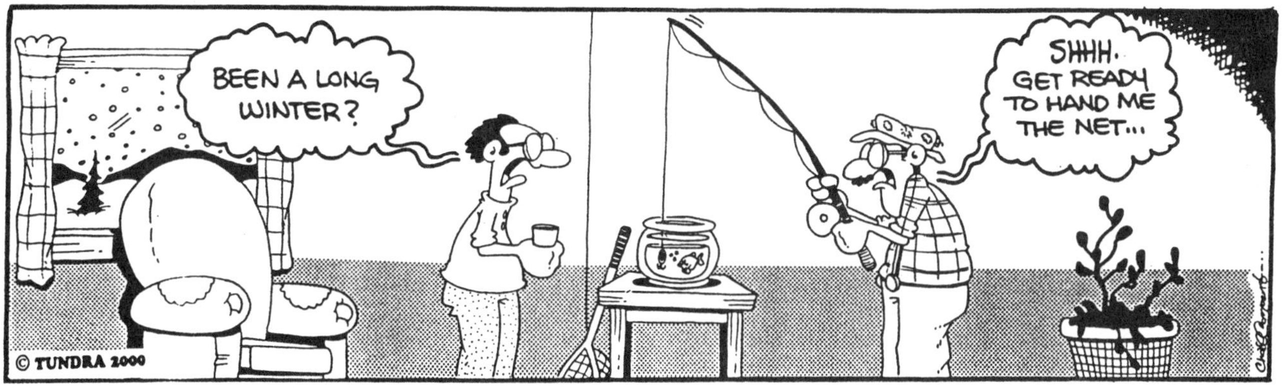
BEEN A LONG WINTER?
SHHH. GET READY TO HAND ME THE NET...
© TUNDRA 2000

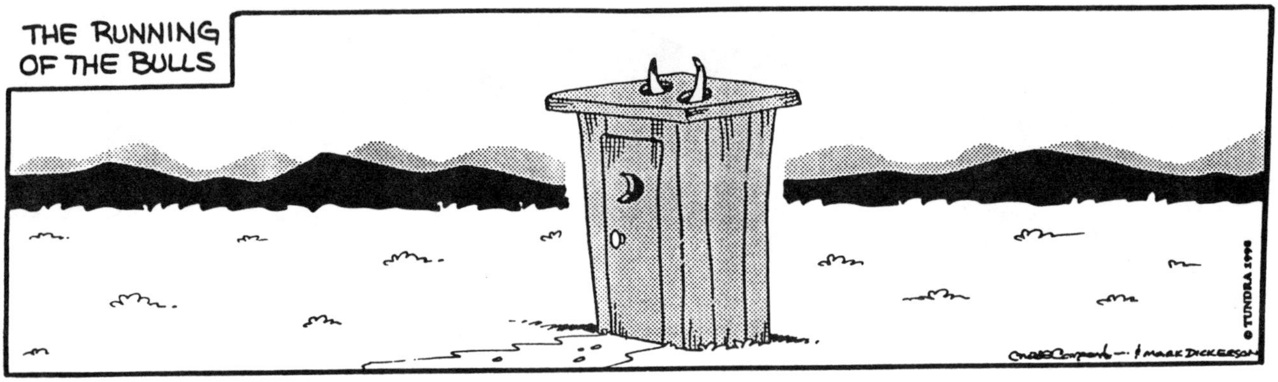
THE RUNNING OF THE BULLS
© TUNDRA 1999

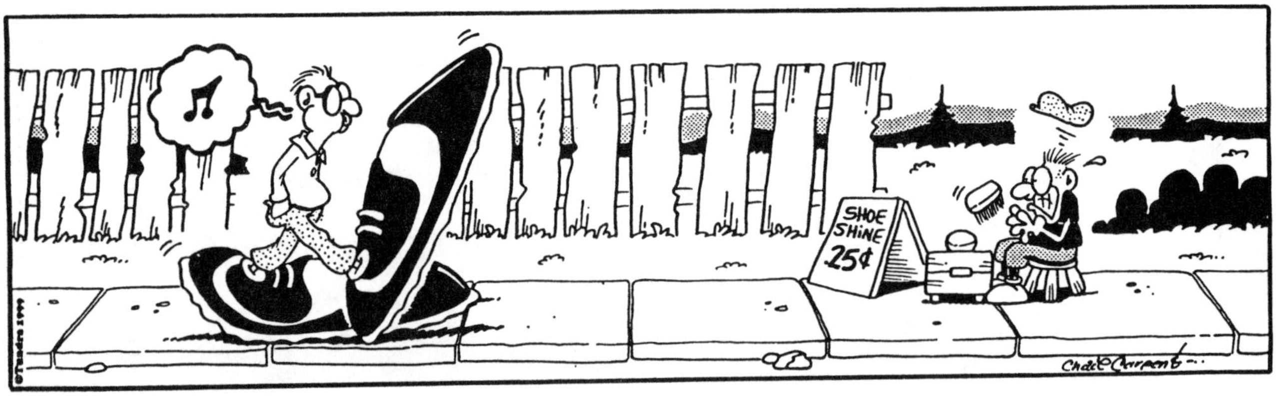
SHOE SHINE 25¢

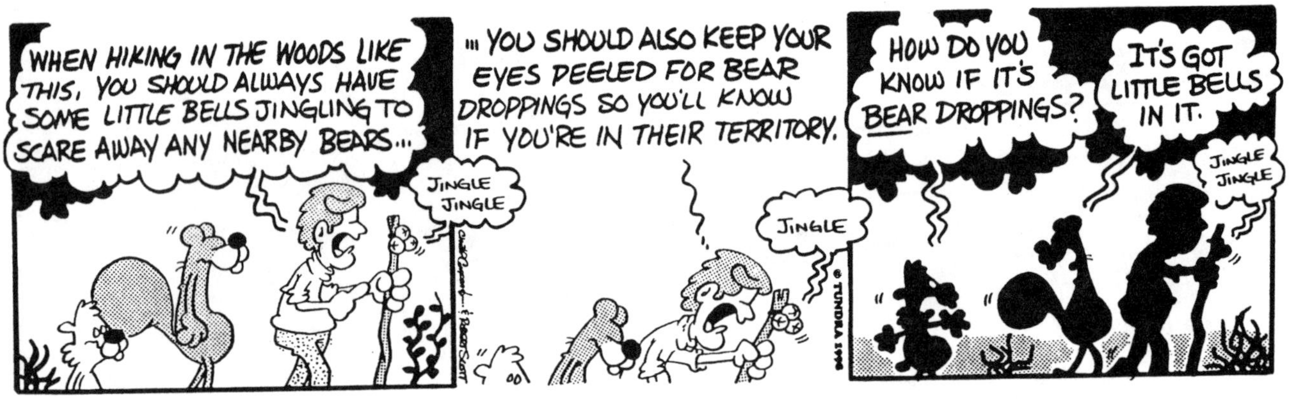
WHEN HIKING IN THE WOODS LIKE THIS, YOU SHOULD ALWAYS HAVE SOME LITTLE BELLS JINGLING TO SCARE AWAY ANY NEARBY BEARS...
JINGLE JINGLE
...YOU SHOULD ALSO KEEP YOUR EYES PEELED FOR BEAR DROPPINGS SO YOU'LL KNOW IF YOU'RE IN THEIR TERRITORY.
JINGLE
© TUNDRA 1998
HOW DO YOU KNOW IF IT'S BEAR DROPPINGS?
IT'S GOT LITTLE BELLS IN IT.
JINGLE JINGLE

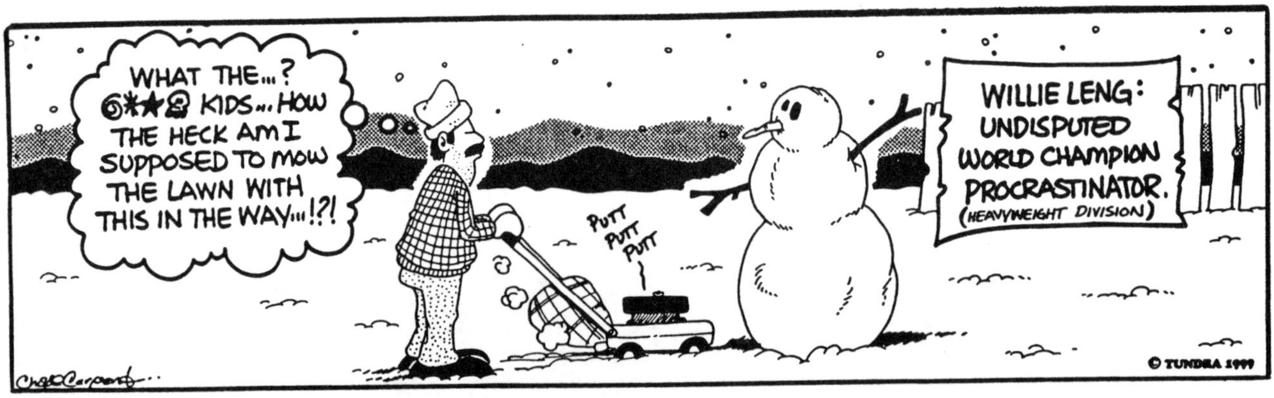
WHAT THE...? @*★@ KIDS... HOW THE HECK AM I SUPPOSED TO MOW THE LAWN WITH THIS IN THE WAY...!?!
PUTT PUTT PUTT
WILLIE LENG: UNDISPUTED WORLD CHAMPION PROCRASTINATOR. (HEAVYWEIGHT DIVISION)
© TUNDRA 1999

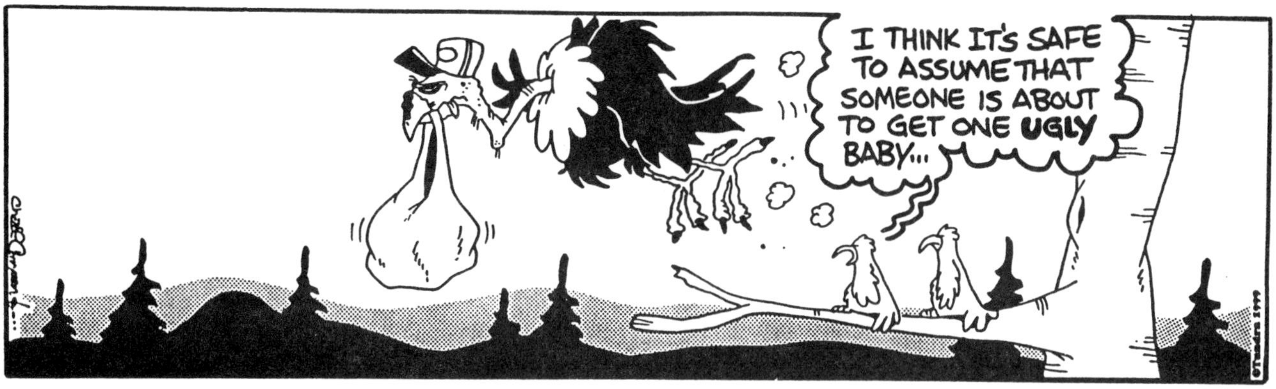
I THINK IT'S SAFE TO ASSUME THAT SOMEONE IS ABOUT TO GET ONE **UGLY** BABY...

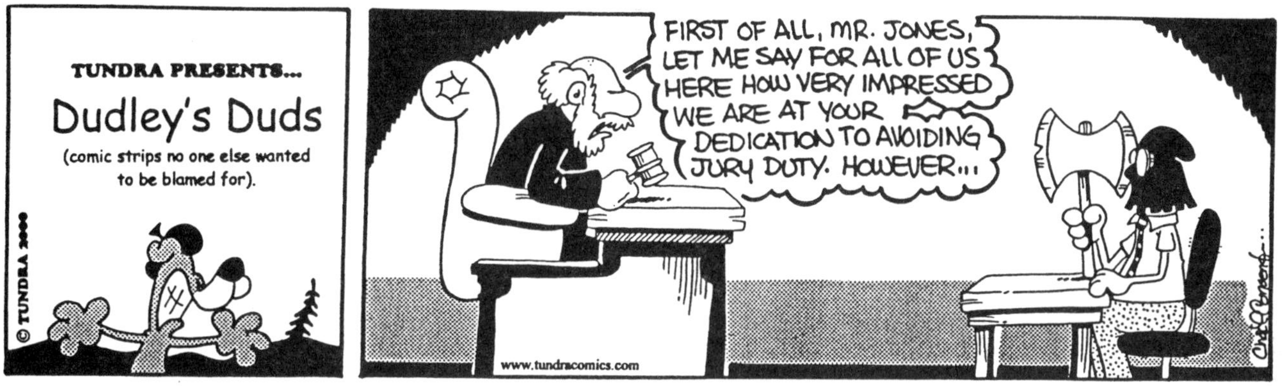
TUNDRA PRESENTS...
Dudley's Duds
(comic strips no one else wanted to be blamed for).
© TUNDRA 2000
FIRST OF ALL, MR. JONES, LET ME SAY FOR ALL OF US HERE HOW VERY IMPRESSED WE ARE AT YOUR DEDICATION TO AVOIDING JURY DUTY. HOWEVER...
www.tundracomics.com

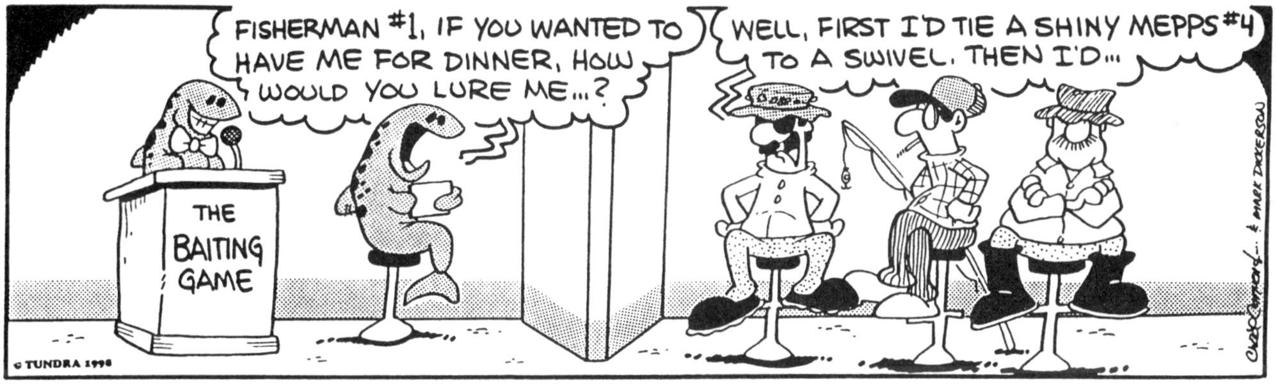
FISHERMAN #1, IF YOU WANTED TO HAVE ME FOR DINNER, HOW WOULD YOU LURE ME...?
WELL, FIRST I'D TIE A SHINY MEPPS #4 TO A SWIVEL. THEN I'D...
THE BAITING GAME
© TUNDRA 1998

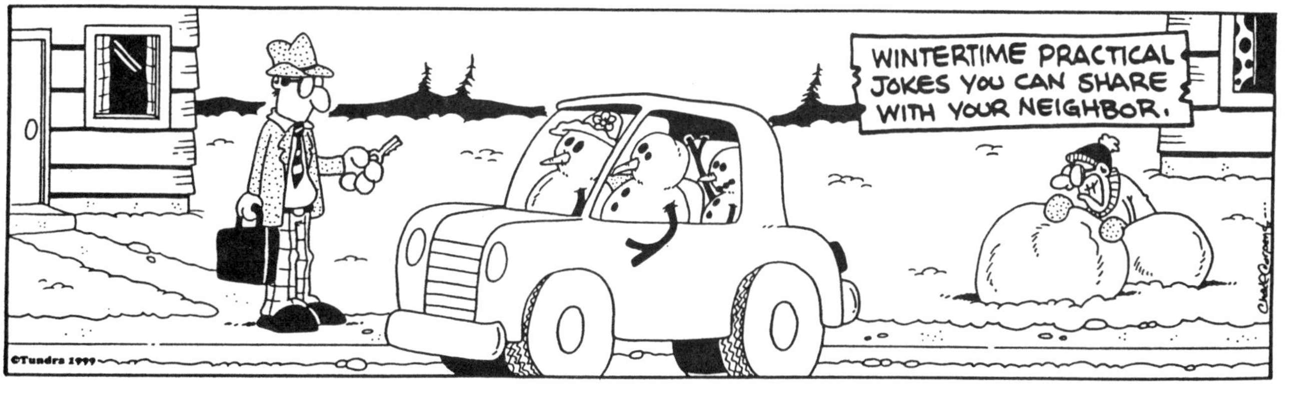
WINTERTIME PRACTICAL JOKES YOU CAN SHARE WITH YOUR NEIGHBOR.
©Tundra 1999

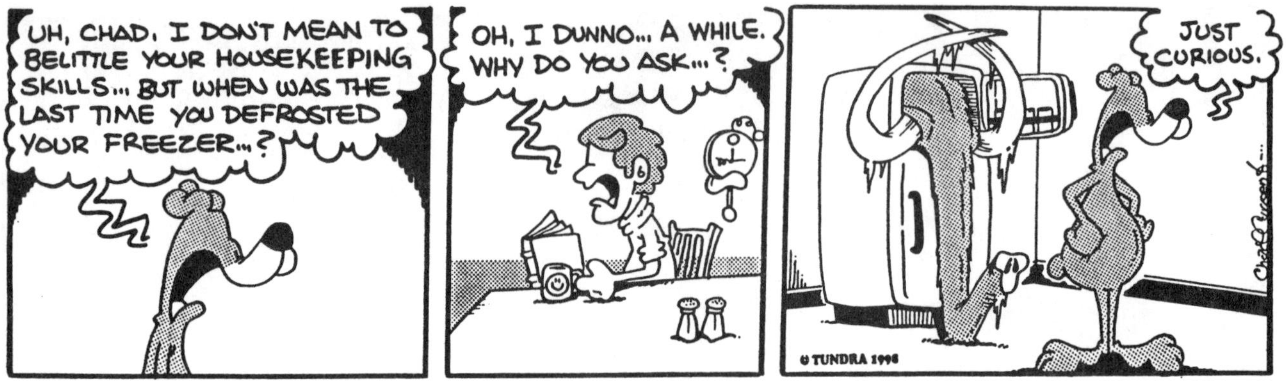
UH, CHAD. I DON'T MEAN TO BELITTLE YOUR HOUSEKEEPING SKILLS... BUT WHEN WAS THE LAST TIME YOU DEFROSTED YOUR FREEZER...?
OH, I DUNNO... A WHILE. WHY DO YOU ASK...?
JUST CURIOUS.
© TUNDRA 1998

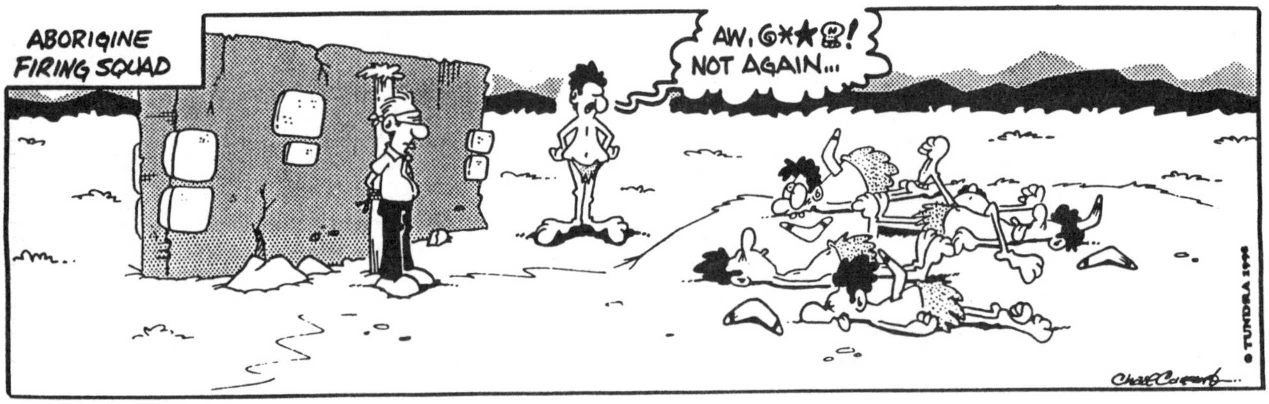
ABORIGINE FIRING SQUAD
AW, @*★☠! NOT AGAIN...
© TUNDRA 1998

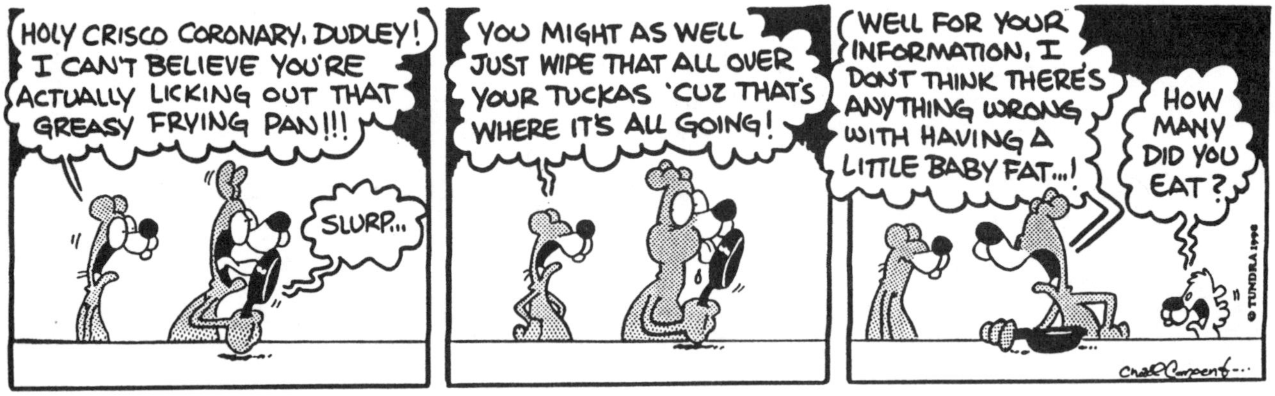
HOLY CRISCO CORONARY, DUDLEY! I CAN'T BELIEVE YOU'RE ACTUALLY LICKING OUT THAT GREASY FRYING PAN!!!
SLURP...
YOU MIGHT AS WELL JUST WIPE THAT ALL OVER YOUR TUCKAS 'CUZ THAT'S WHERE IT'S ALL GOING!
WELL FOR YOUR INFORMATION, I DON'T THINK THERE'S ANYTHING WRONG WITH HAVING A LITTLE BABY FAT...!
HOW MANY DID YOU EAT?
© TUNDRA 1998

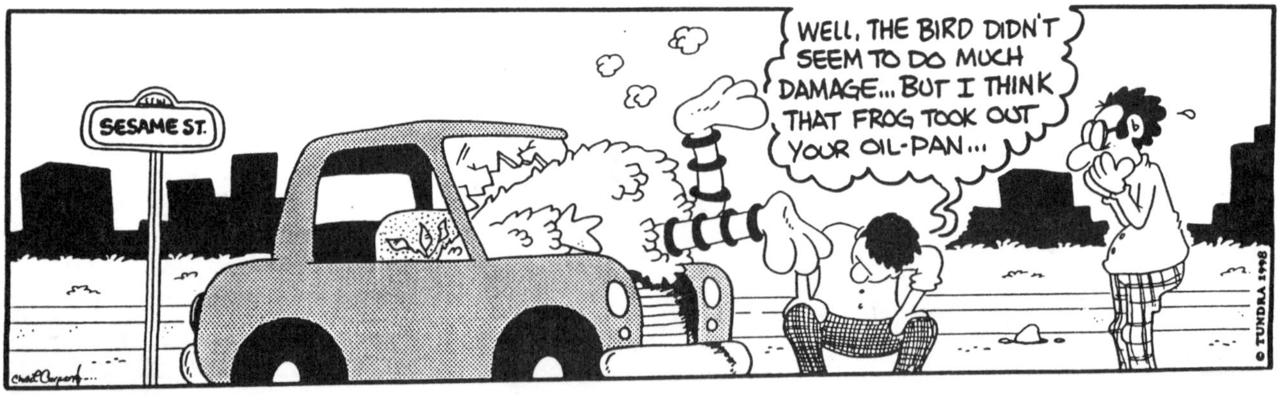
SESAME ST.
WELL, THE BIRD DIDN'T SEEM TO DO MUCH DAMAGE... BUT I THINK THAT FROG TOOK OUT YOUR OIL-PAN...
© TUNDRA 1998

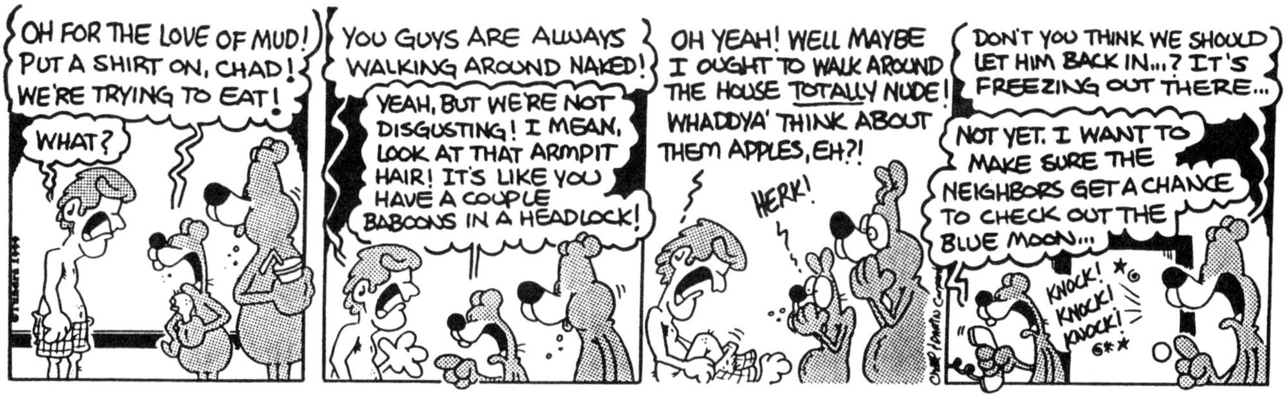
OH FOR THE LOVE OF MUD! PUT A SHIRT ON, CHAD! WE'RE TRYING TO EAT!
WHAT?
YOU GUYS ARE ALWAYS WALKING AROUND NAKED!
YEAH, BUT WE'RE NOT DISGUSTING! I MEAN, LOOK AT THAT ARMPIT HAIR! IT'S LIKE YOU HAVE A COUPLE BABOONS IN A HEADLOCK!
OH YEAH! WELL MAYBE I OUGHT TO WALK AROUND THE HOUSE TOTALLY NUDE! WHADDYA' THINK ABOUT THEM APPLES, EH?!
HERK!
DON'T YOU THINK WE SHOULD LET HIM BACK IN...? IT'S FREEZING OUT THERE...
NOT YET. I WANT TO MAKE SURE THE NEIGHBORS GET A CHANCE TO CHECK OUT THE BLUE MOON...
KNOCK! KNOCK! KNOCK!

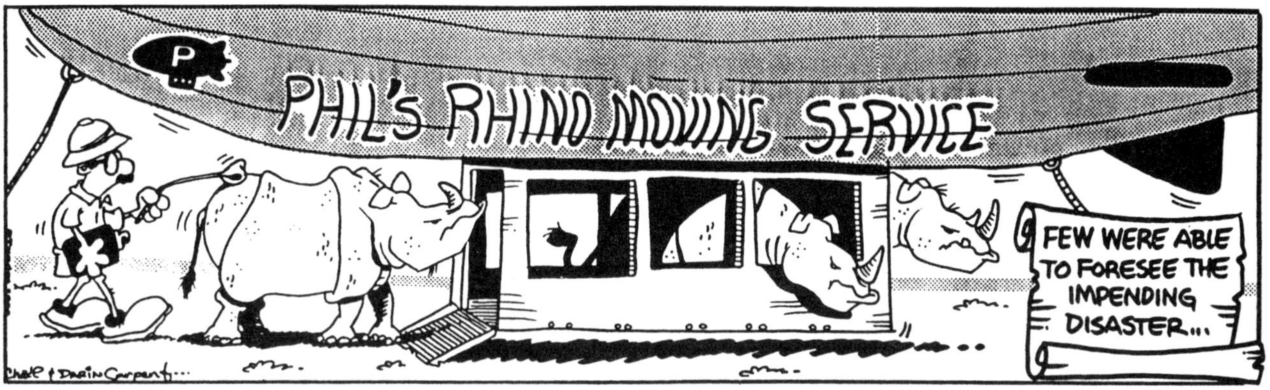
P
PHIL'S RHINO MOVING SERVICE
FEW WERE ABLE TO FORESEE THE IMPENDING DISASTER...
Chad & Darin Carpenter...

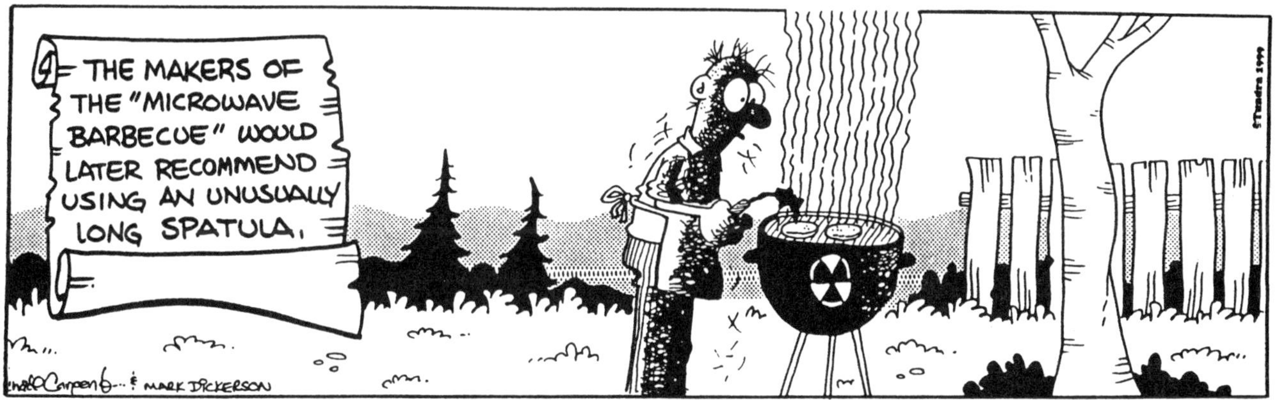
THE MAKERS OF THE "MICROWAVE BARBECUE" WOULD LATER RECOMMEND USING AN UNUSUALLY LONG SPATULA.
©Tundra 1999
Chad Carpenter... & MARK DICKERSON

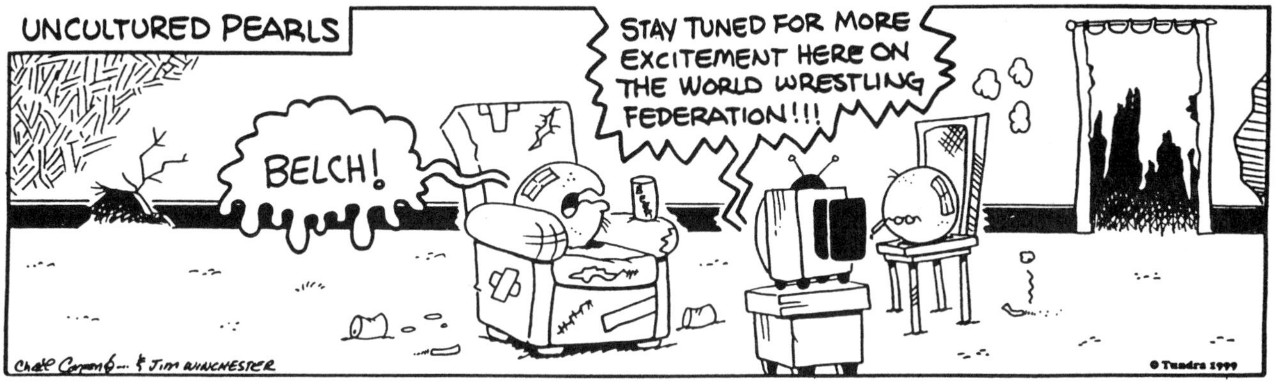
UNCULTURED PEARLS
BELCH!
STAY TUNED FOR MORE EXCITEMENT HERE ON THE WORLD WRESTLING FEDERATION!!!
Chad Carpenter... & JIM WINCHESTER
© Tundra 1999

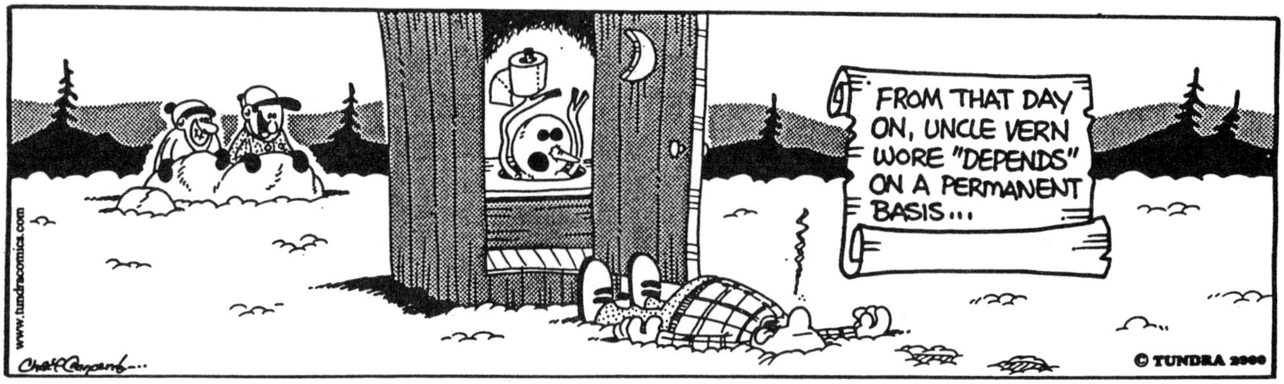
FROM THAT DAY ON, UNCLE VERN WORE "DEPENDS" ON A PERMANENT BASIS...
www.tundracomics.com
© TUNDRA 2000

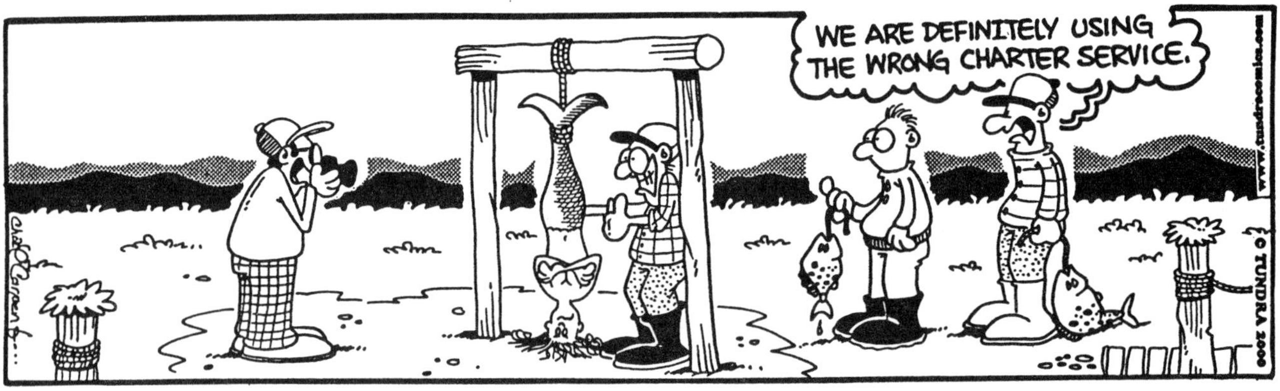
WE ARE DEFINITELY USING THE WRONG CHARTER SERVICE.
www.tundracomics.com
© TUNDRA 2000

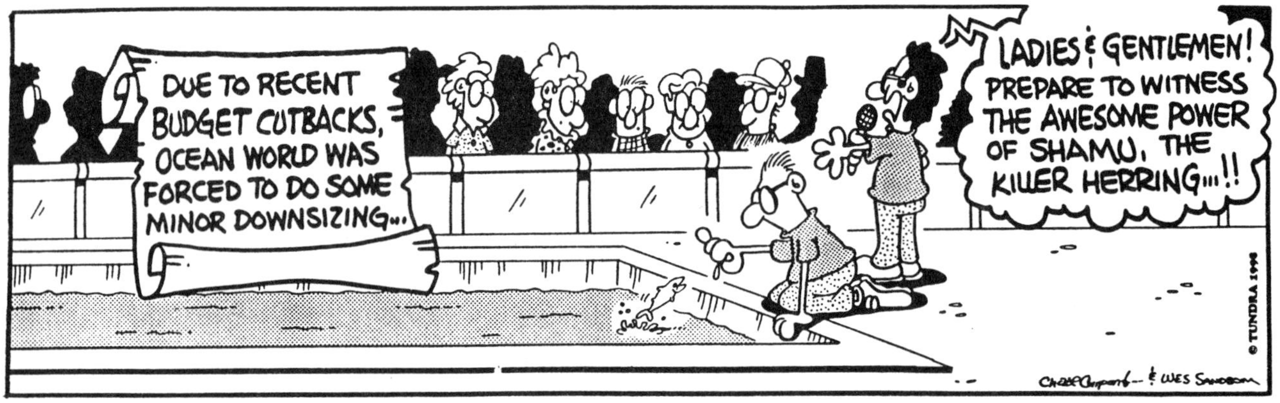
DUE TO RECENT BUDGET CUTBACKS, OCEAN WORLD WAS FORCED TO DO SOME MINOR DOWNSIZING...
LADIES & GENTLEMEN! PREPARE TO WITNESS THE AWESOME POWER OF SHAMU, THE KILLER HERRING...!!
© TUNDRA 1998
& WES SANDSON

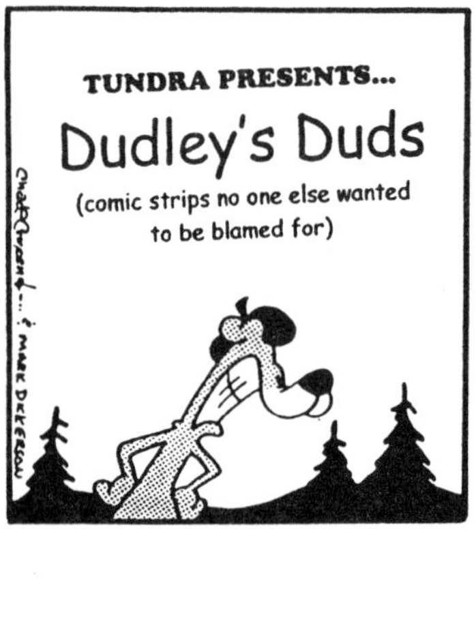
TUNDRA PRESENTS...
Dudley's Duds
(comic strips no one else wanted to be blamed for)
& MARK DICKERSON

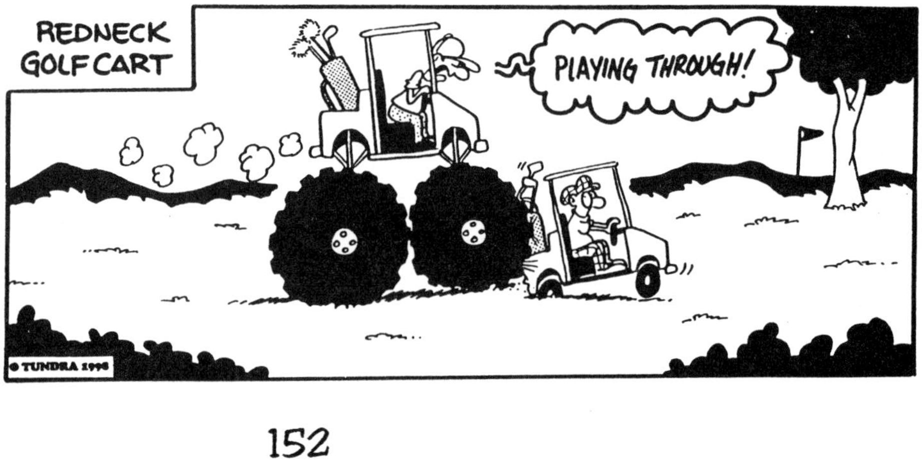
REDNECK GOLF CART
PLAYING THROUGH!
© TUNDRA 1998

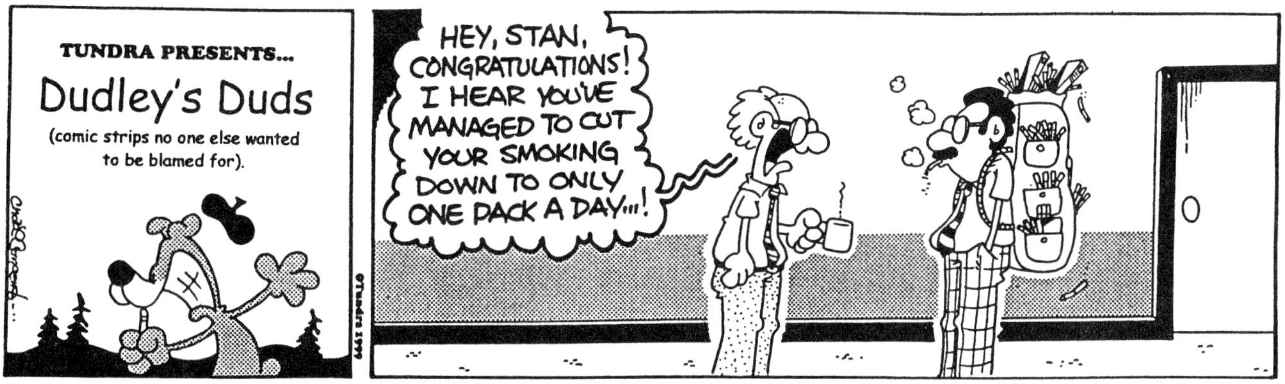
TUNDRA PRESENTS...
Dudley's Duds
(comic strips no one else wanted to be blamed for).
HEY, STAN, CONGRATULATIONS! I HEAR YOU'VE MANAGED TO CUT YOUR SMOKING DOWN TO ONLY ONE PACK A DAY...!

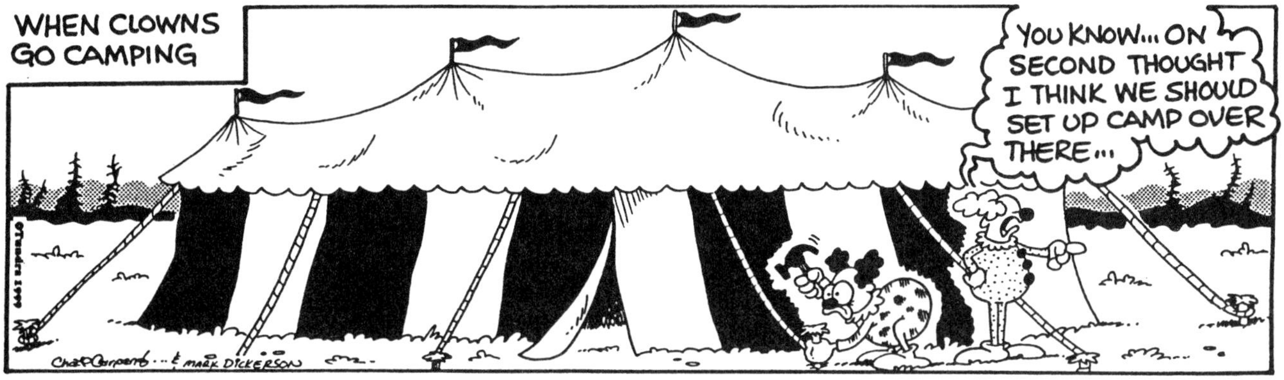
WHEN CLOWNS GO CAMPING
YOU KNOW... ON SECOND THOUGHT I THINK WE SHOULD SET UP CAMP OVER THERE...

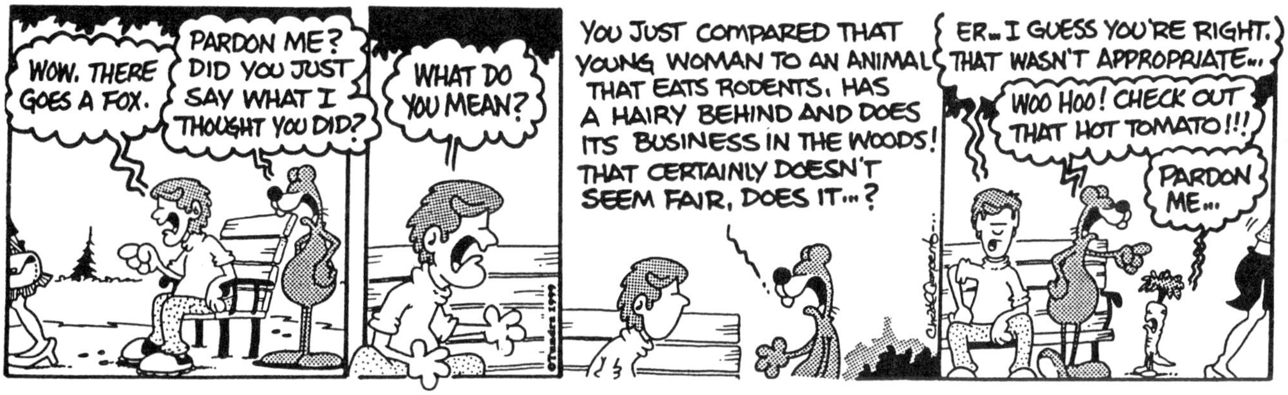
WOW. THERE GOES A FOX.
PARDON ME? DID YOU JUST SAY WHAT I THOUGHT YOU DID?
WHAT DO YOU MEAN?
YOU JUST COMPARED THAT YOUNG WOMAN TO AN ANIMAL THAT EATS RODENTS, HAS A HAIRY BEHIND AND DOES ITS BUSINESS IN THE WOODS! THAT CERTAINLY DOESN'T SEEM FAIR, DOES IT...?
ER... I GUESS YOU'RE RIGHT. THAT WASN'T APPROPRIATE...
WOO HOO! CHECK OUT THAT HOT TOMATO!!!
PARDON ME...

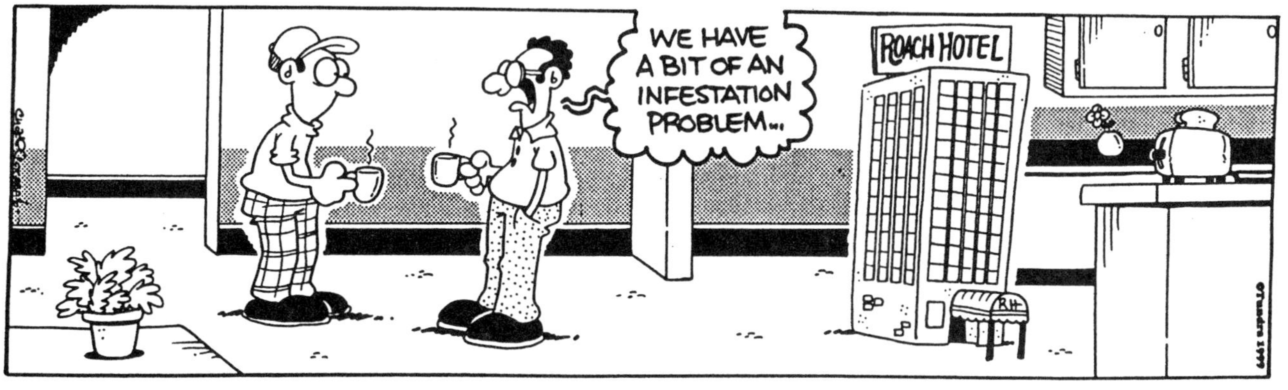
WE HAVE A BIT OF AN INFESTATION PROBLEM...
ROACH HOTEL

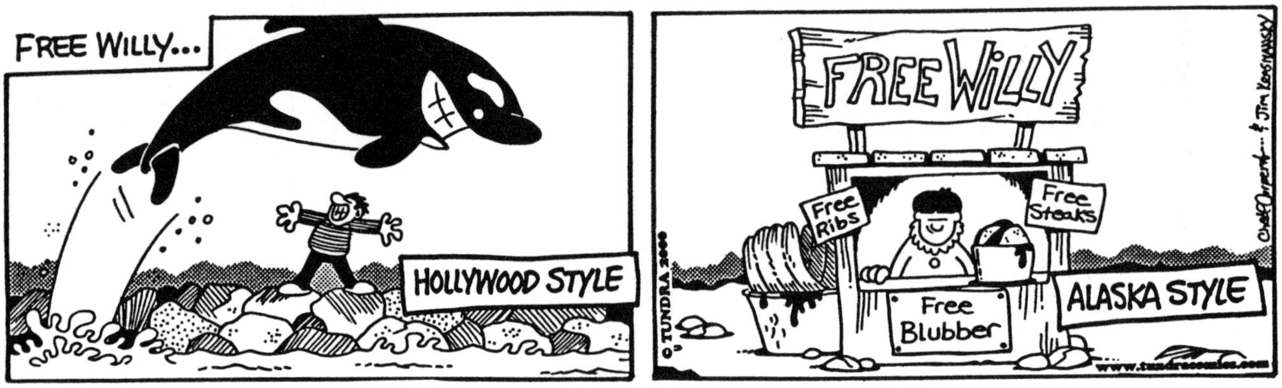
FREE WILLY...
HOLLYWOOD STYLE
FREE WILLY
Free Ribs
Free Steaks
Free Blubber
ALASKA STYLE
© TUNDRA 2000
www.tundracomics.com

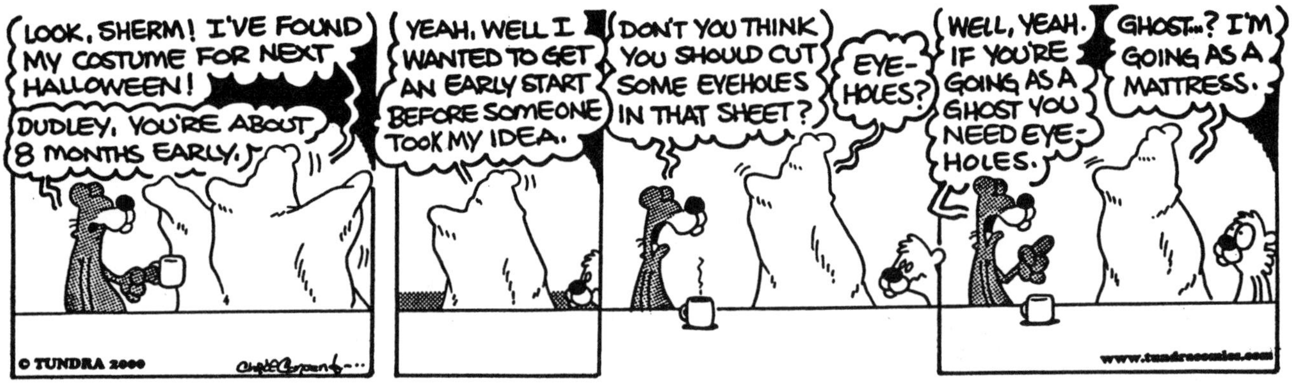
LOOK, SHERM! I'VE FOUND MY COSTUME FOR NEXT HALLOWEEN!
DUDLEY, YOU'RE ABOUT 8 MONTHS EARLY.
YEAH, WELL I WANTED TO GET AN EARLY START BEFORE SOMEONE TOOK MY IDEA.
DON'T YOU THINK YOU SHOULD CUT SOME EYEHOLES IN THAT SHEET?
EYE-HOLES?
WELL, YEAH. IF YOU'RE GOING AS A GHOST YOU NEED EYE-HOLES.
GHOST...? I'M GOING AS A MATTRESS.
© TUNDRA 2000
www.tundracomics.com

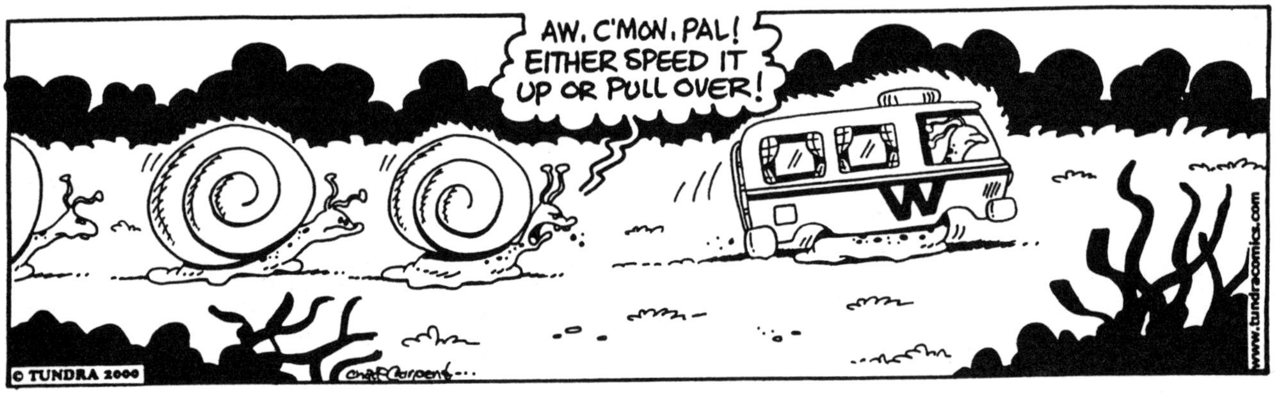
AW, C'MON, PAL! EITHER SPEED IT UP OR PULL OVER!
W
© TUNDRA 2000
www.tundracomics.com

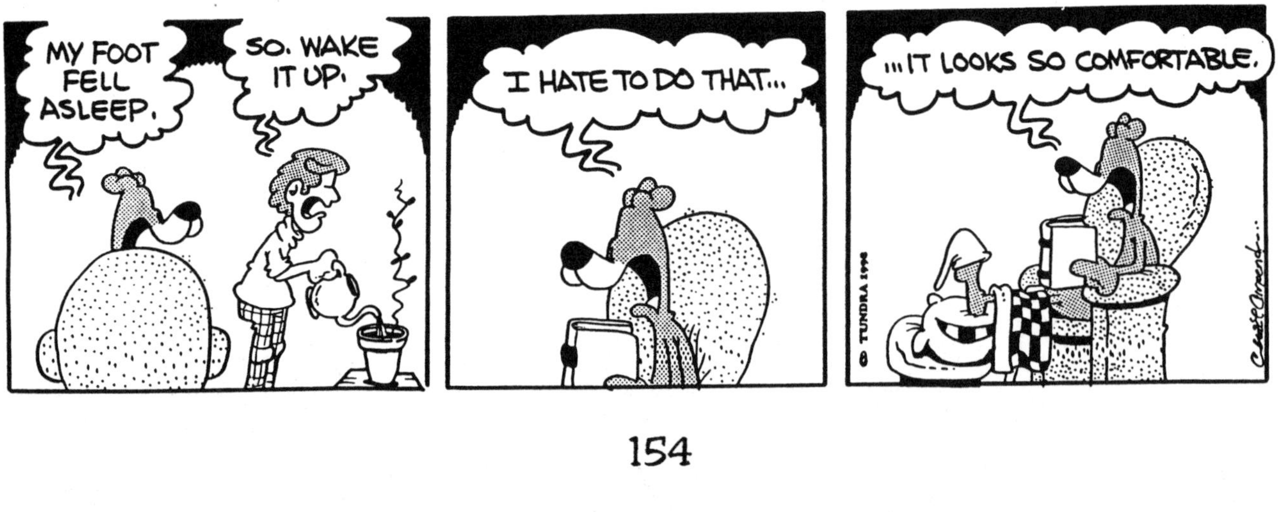
MY FOOT FELL ASLEEP.
SO, WAKE IT UP.
I HATE TO DO THAT...
...IT LOOKS SO COMFORTABLE.

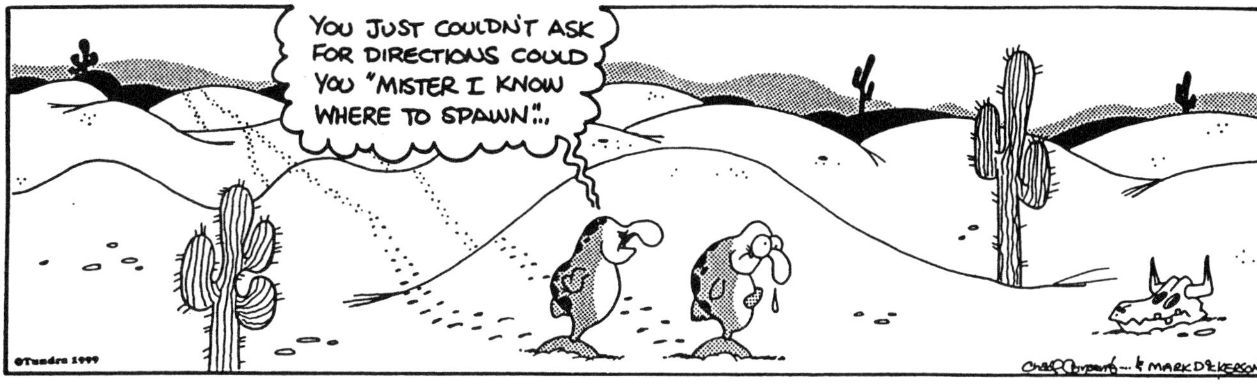
YOU JUST COULDN'T ASK FOR DIRECTIONS COULD YOU "MISTER I KNOW WHERE TO SPAWN"...
©Tundra 1999
CHAD CARPENTER ... & MARK DICKERSON

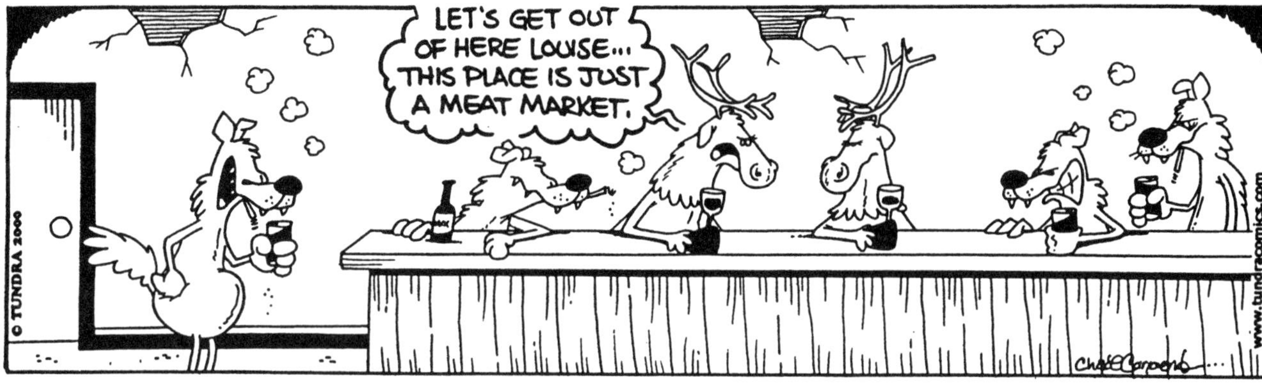
LET'S GET OUT OF HERE LOUISE... THIS PLACE IS JUST A MEAT MARKET.
© TUNDRA 2000
www.tundracomics.com

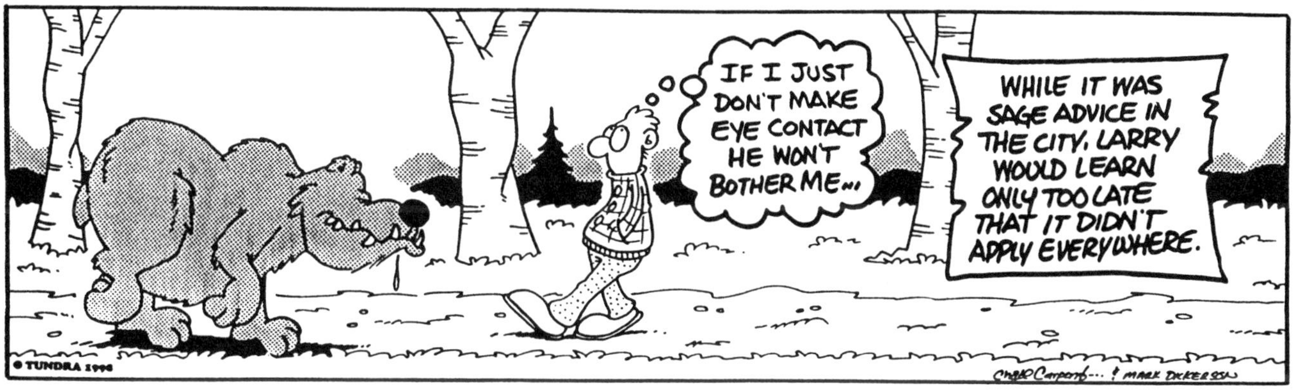
IF I JUST DON'T MAKE EYE CONTACT HE WON'T BOTHER ME...
WHILE IT WAS SAGE ADVICE IN THE CITY, LARRY WOULD LEARN ONLY TOO LATE THAT IT DIDN'T APPLY EVERYWHERE.
© TUNDRA 1998

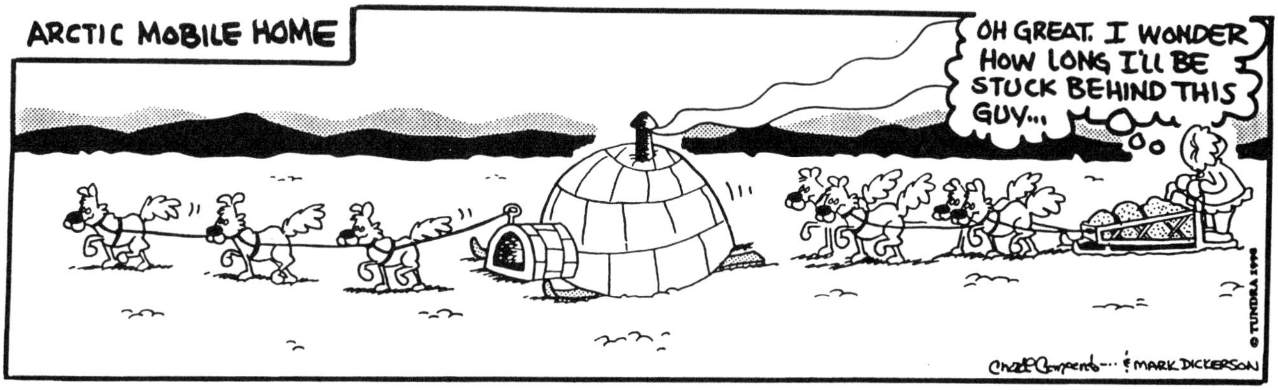
ARCTIC MOBILE HOME
OH GREAT. I WONDER HOW LONG I'LL BE STUCK BEHIND THIS GUY...
MARK DICKERSON

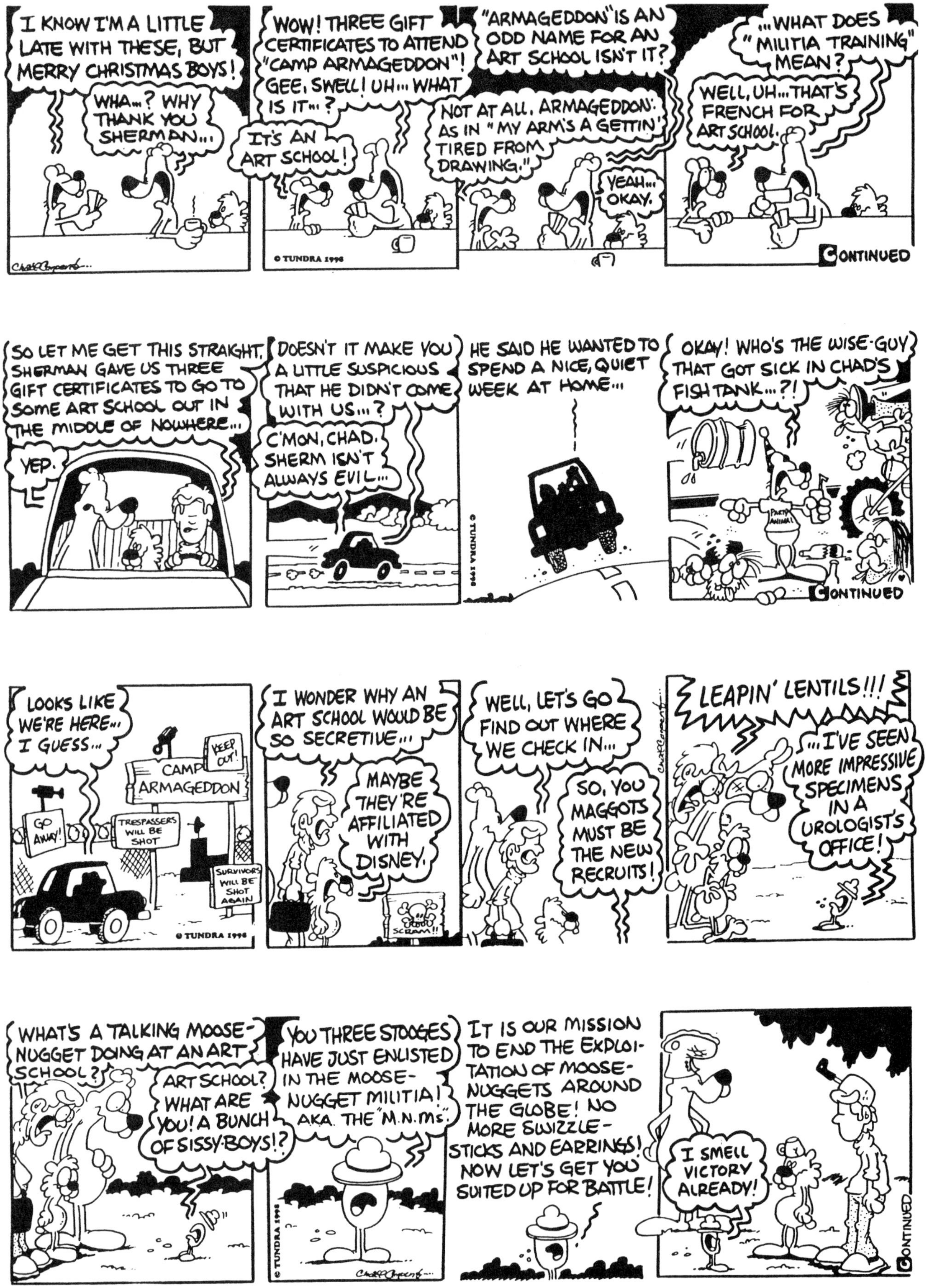

I KNOW I'M A LITTLE LATE WITH THESE, BUT MERRY CHRISTMAS BOYS!
WHA...? WHY THANK YOU SHERMAN...
WOW! THREE GIFT CERTIFICATES TO ATTEND "CAMP ARMAGEDDON"! GEE, SWELL! UH... WHAT IS IT...?
IT'S AN ART SCHOOL!
© TUNDRA 1998
"ARMAGEDDON" IS AN ODD NAME FOR AN ART SCHOOL ISN'T IT?
NOT AT ALL. ARMAGEDDON: AS IN "MY ARM'S A GETTIN' TIRED FROM DRAWING."
YEAH... OKAY.
...WHAT DOES "MILITIA TRAINING" MEAN?
WELL, UH... THAT'S FRENCH FOR ART SCHOOL.
CONTINUED
SO LET ME GET THIS STRAIGHT, SHERMAN GAVE US THREE GIFT CERTIFICATES TO GO TO SOME ART SCHOOL OUT IN THE MIDDLE OF NOWHERE...
YEP.
DOESN'T IT MAKE YOU A LITTLE SUSPICIOUS THAT HE DIDN'T COME WITH US...?
C'MON, CHAD, SHERM ISN'T ALWAYS EVIL...
HE SAID HE WANTED TO SPEND A NICE, QUIET WEEK AT HOME...
© TUNDRA 1998
OKAY! WHO'S THE WISE-GUY THAT GOT SICK IN CHAD'S FISH TANK...?!
PARTY ANIMAL
CONTINUED
LOOKS LIKE WE'RE HERE... I GUESS...
KEEP OUT!
CAMP ARMAGEDDON
GO AWAY!
TRESPASSERS WILL BE SHOT
SURVIVORS WILL BE SHOT AGAIN
© TUNDRA 1998
I WONDER WHY AN ART SCHOOL WOULD BE SO SECRETIVE...
MAYBE THEY'RE AFFILIATED WITH DISNEY.
SCRAM!!
WELL, LET'S GO FIND OUT WHERE WE CHECK IN...
SO, YOU MAGGOTS MUST BE THE NEW RECRUITS!
LEAPIN' LENTILS!!!
...I'VE SEEN MORE IMPRESSIVE SPECIMENS IN A UROLOGIST'S OFFICE!
WHAT'S A TALKING MOOSE-NUGGET DOING AT AN ART SCHOOL?
ART SCHOOL? WHAT ARE YOU! A BUNCH OF SISSY-BOYS!?
YOU THREE STOOGES HAVE JUST ENLISTED IN THE MOOSE-NUGGET MILITIA! AKA THE "M.N.MS."
© TUNDRA 1998
IT IS OUR MISSION TO END THE EXPLOITATION OF MOOSE-NUGGETS AROUND THE GLOBE! NO MORE SWIZZLE-STICKS AND EARRINGS! NOW LET'S GET YOU SUITED UP FOR BATTLE!
I SMELL VICTORY ALREADY!
CONTINUED

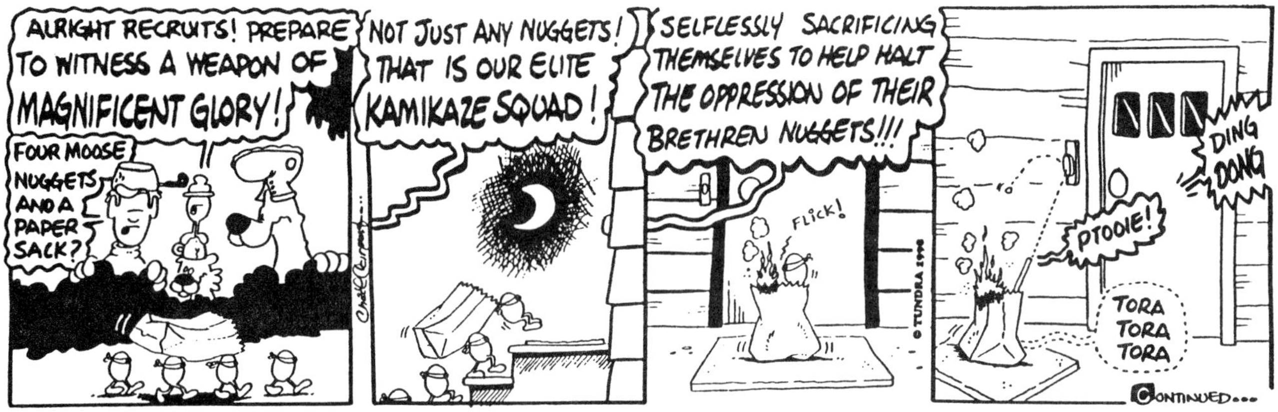
ALRIGHT RECRUITS! PREPARE TO WITNESS A WEAPON OF MAGNIFICENT GLORY!
FOUR MOOSE NUGGETS AND A PAPER SACK?
NOT JUST ANY NUGGETS! THAT IS OUR ELITE KAMIKAZE SQUAD!
SELFLESSLY SACRIFICING THEMSELVES TO HELP HALT THE OPPRESSION OF THEIR BRETHREN NUGGETS!!!
FLICK!
© TUNDRA 1996
DING DONG
PTOOIE!
TORA TORA TORA
CONTINUED...

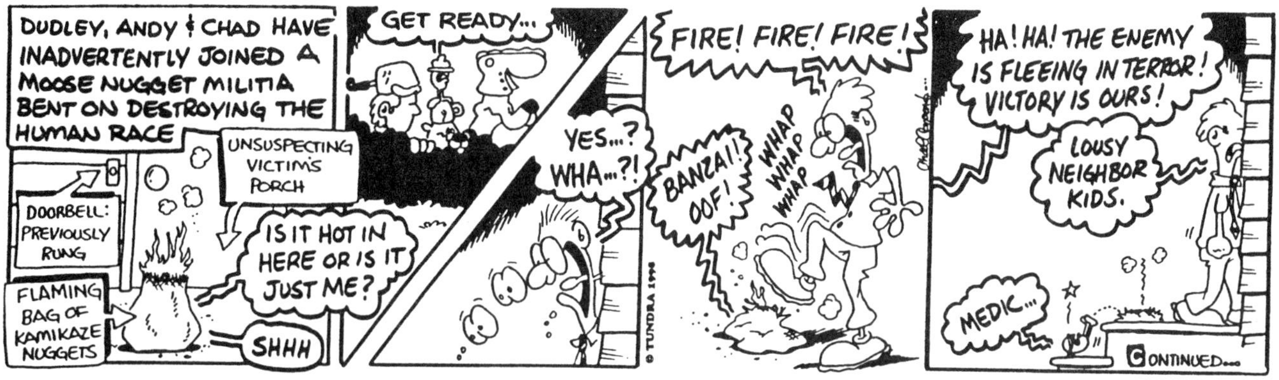
DUDLEY, ANDY & CHAD HAVE INADVERTENTLY JOINED A MOOSE NUGGET MILITIA BENT ON DESTROYING THE HUMAN RACE
UNSUSPECTING VICTIM'S PORCH
DOORBELL: PREVIOUSLY RUNG
IS IT HOT IN HERE OR IS IT JUST ME?
FLAMING BAG OF KAMIKAZE NUGGETS
SHHH
GET READY...
YES...? WHA...?!
© TUNDRA 1996
FIRE! FIRE! FIRE!
BANZAI! OOF!
WHAP WHAP WHAP
HA! HA! THE ENEMY IS FLEEING IN TERROR! VICTORY IS OURS!
LOUSY NEIGHBOR KIDS.
MEDIC...
CONTINUED...

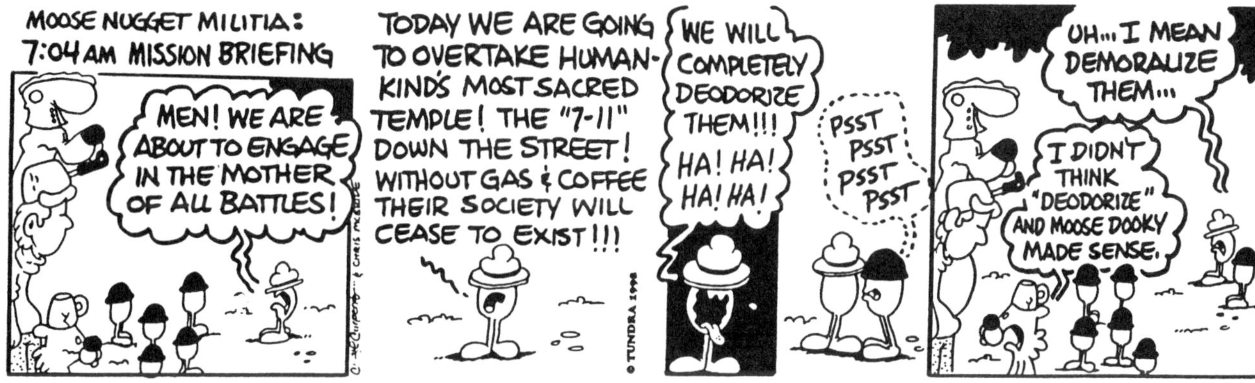
MOOSE NUGGET MILITIA: 7:04 AM MISSION BRIEFING
MEN! WE ARE ABOUT TO ENGAGE IN THE MOTHER OF ALL BATTLES!
TODAY WE ARE GOING TO OVERTAKE HUMAN-KIND'S MOST SACRED TEMPLE! THE "7-11" DOWN THE STREET! WITHOUT GAS & COFFEE THEIR SOCIETY WILL CEASE TO EXIST!!!
© TUNDRA 1996
WE WILL COMPLETELY DEODORIZE THEM!!!
HA! HA! HA! HA!
PSST PSST PSST PSST
UH... I MEAN DEMORALIZE THEM...
I DIDN'T THINK "DEODORIZE" AND MOOSE DOOKY MADE SENSE.

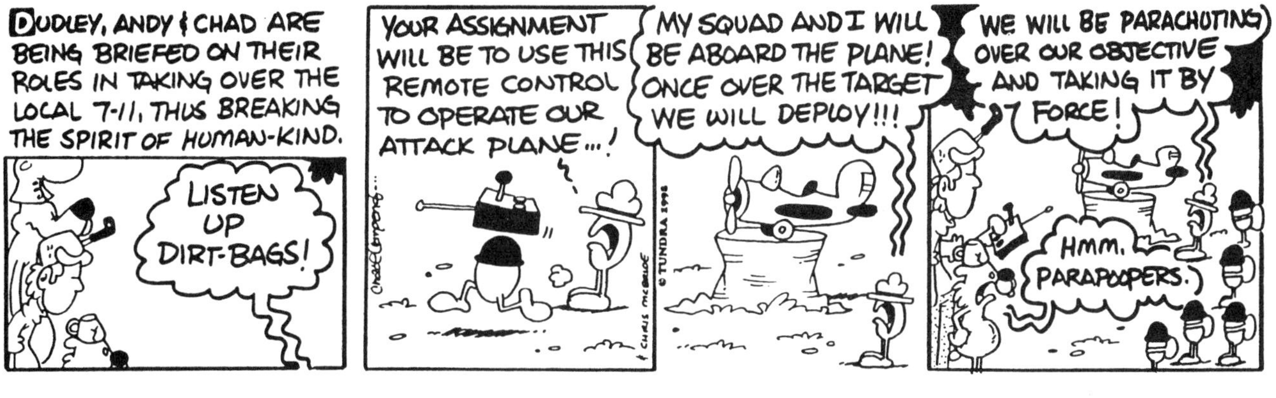
DUDLEY, ANDY & CHAD ARE BEING BRIEFED ON THEIR ROLES IN TAKING OVER THE LOCAL 7-11, THUS BREAKING THE SPIRIT OF HUMAN-KIND.
LISTEN UP DIRT-BAGS!
YOUR ASSIGNMENT WILL BE TO USE THIS REMOTE CONTROL TO OPERATE OUR ATTACK PLANE...!
© TUNDRA 1996
MY SQUAD AND I WILL BE ABOARD THE PLANE! ONCE OVER THE TARGET WE WILL DEPLOY!!!
WE WILL BE PARACHUTING OVER OUR OBJECTIVE AND TAKING IT BY FORCE!
HMM. PARAPOOPERS.

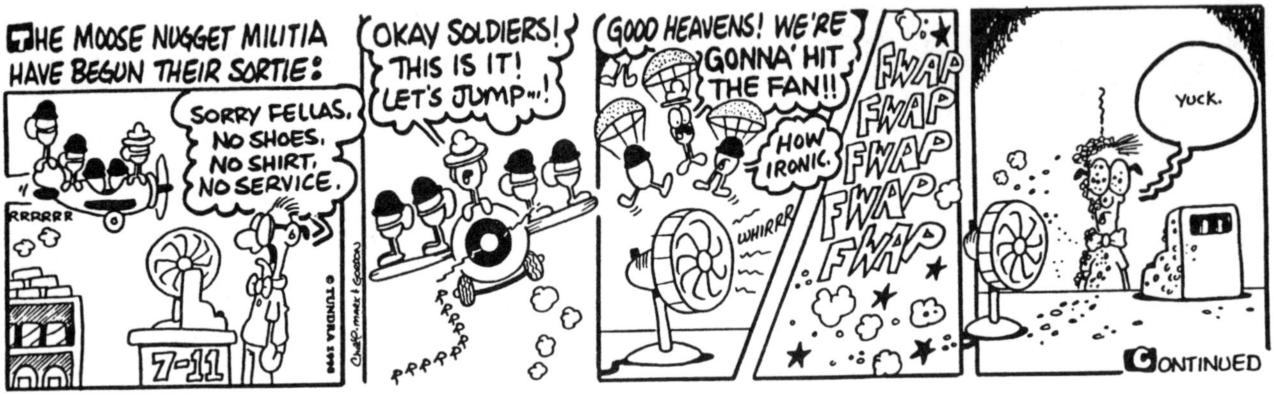
THE MOOSE NUGGET MILITIA HAVE BEGUN THEIR SORTIE:
SORRY FELLAS. NO SHOES. NO SHIRT. NO SERVICE.
RRRRRR
7-11
OKAY SOLDIERS! THIS IS IT! LET'S JUMP...!
RRRRR
PPPPPPP
GOOD HEAVENS! WE'RE GONNA' HIT THE FAN!!
HOW IRONIC.
WHIRRR
FWAP FWAP FWAP FWAP FWAP
YUCK.
CONTINUED

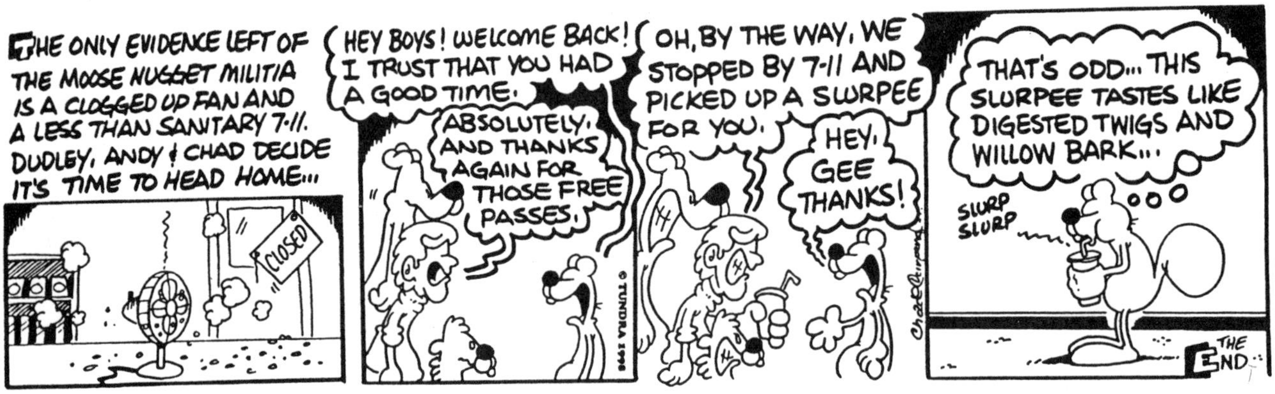
THE ONLY EVIDENCE LEFT OF THE MOOSE NUGGET MILITIA IS A CLOGGED UP FAN AND A LESS THAN SANITARY 7-11. DUDLEY, ANDY & CHAD DECIDE IT'S TIME TO HEAD HOME...
CLOSED
HEY BOYS! WELCOME BACK! I TRUST THAT YOU HAD A GOOD TIME.
ABSOLUTELY. AND THANKS AGAIN FOR THOSE FREE PASSES.
OH, BY THE WAY, WE STOPPED BY 7-11 AND PICKED UP A SLURPEE FOR YOU.
HEY, GEE THANKS!
THAT'S ODD... THIS SLURPEE TASTES LIKE DIGESTED TWIGS AND WILLOW BARK...
SLURP SLURP
THE END

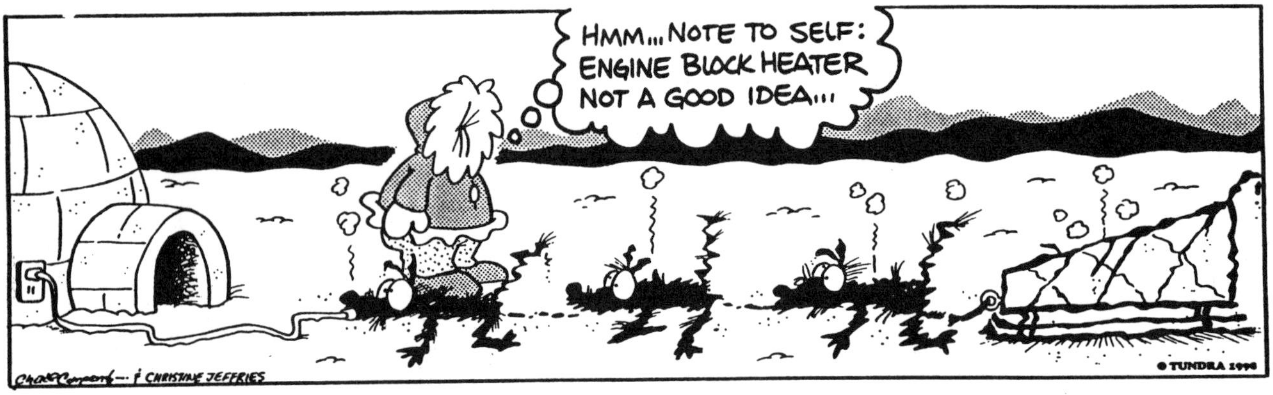
HMM... NOTE TO SELF: ENGINE BLOCK HEATER NOT A GOOD IDEA...

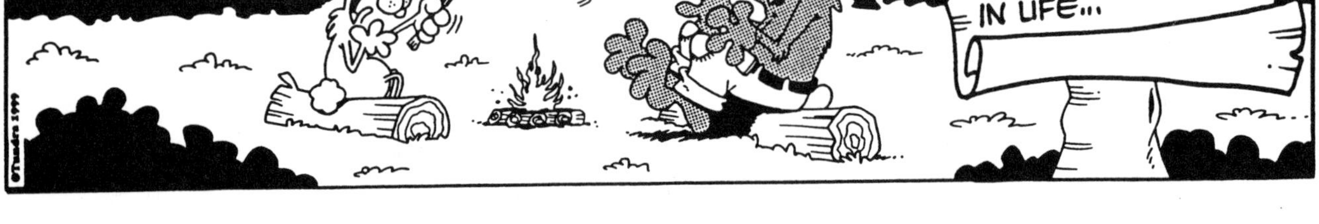
OH POO! MY MARSHMALLOW CAUGHT ON FIRE! I'LL JUST... OOPS.
ALTHOUGH YOUNG SMOKEY WAS EMOTIONALLY SCARRED, HE WAS ABLE TO PUT A POSITIVE SPIN ON IT LATER IN LIFE...

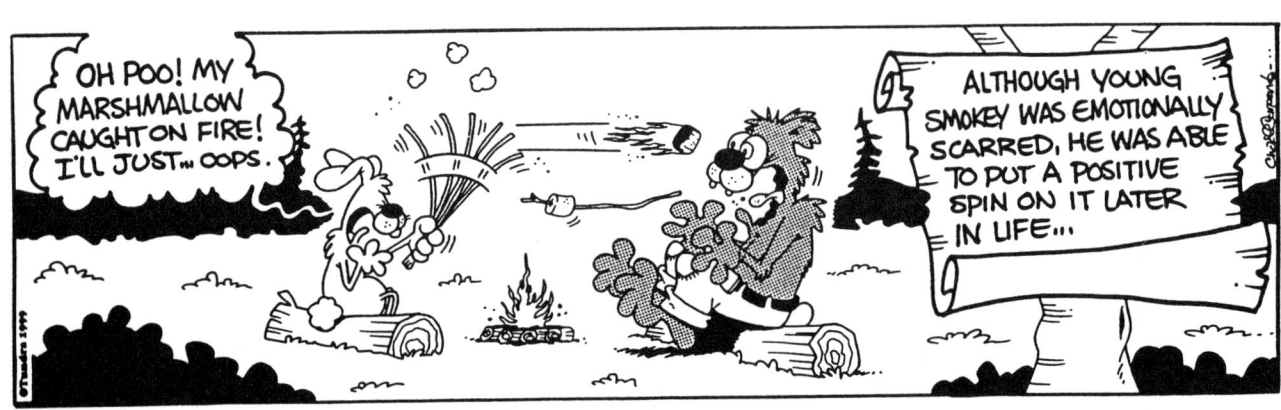

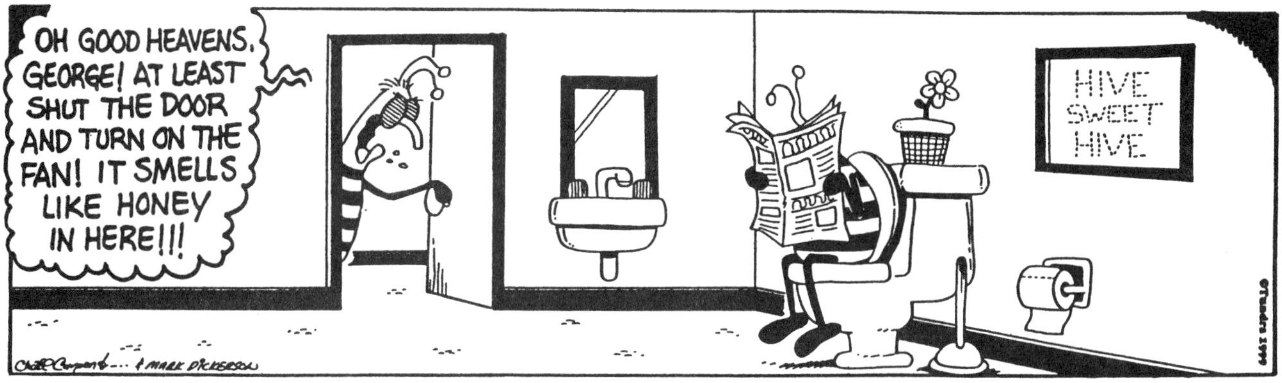
OH GOOD HEAVENS, GEORGE! AT LEAST SHUT THE DOOR AND TURN ON THE FAN! IT SMELLS LIKE HONEY IN HERE!!!
HIVE SWEET HIVE

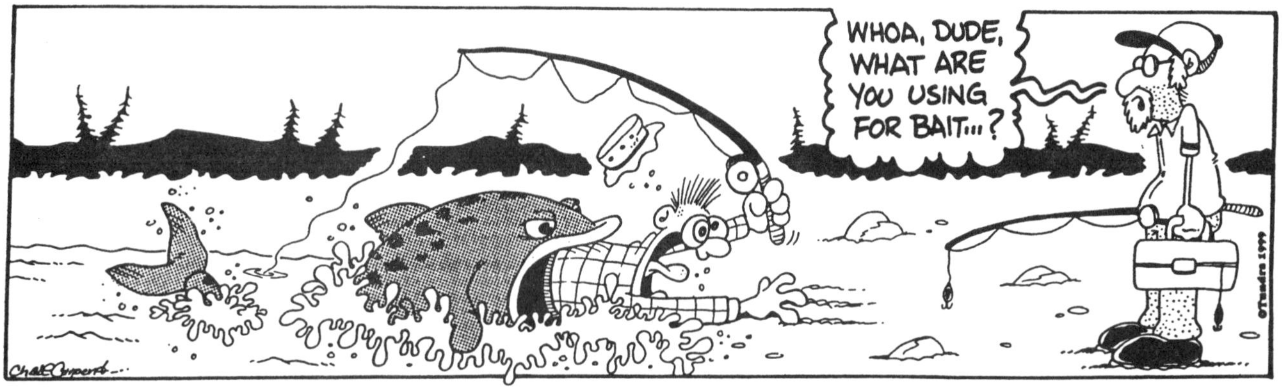
WHOA, DUDE, WHAT ARE YOU USING FOR BAIT...?

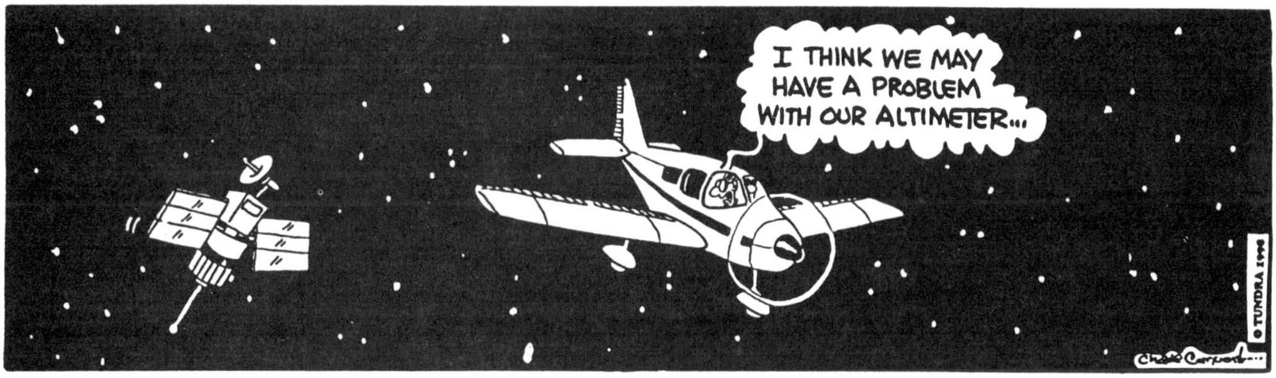
I THINK WE MAY HAVE A PROBLEM WITH OUR ALTIMETER...
© TUNDRA 1998

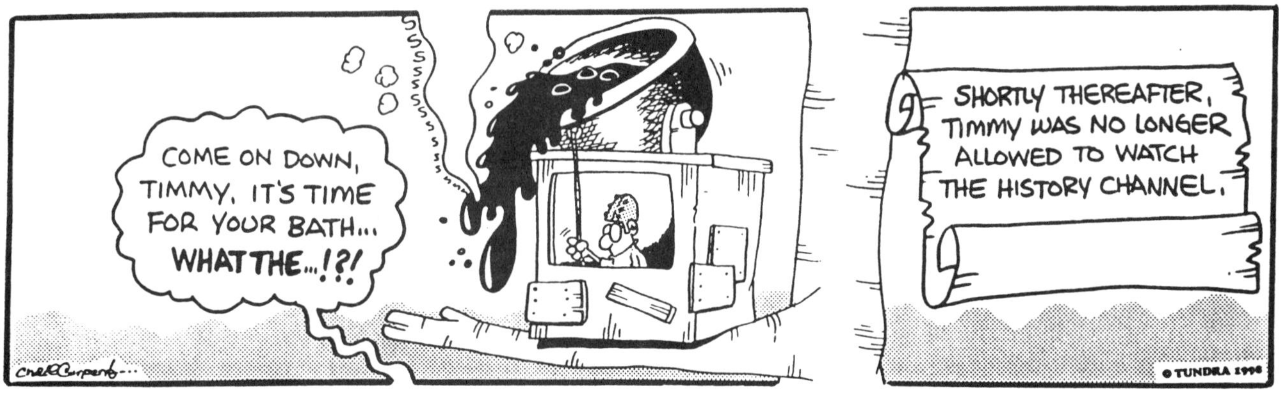
COME ON DOWN, TIMMY, IT'S TIME FOR YOUR BATH... WHAT THE...!?!
SHORTLY THEREAFTER, TIMMY WAS NO LONGER ALLOWED TO WATCH THE HISTORY CHANNEL.
© TUNDRA 1998

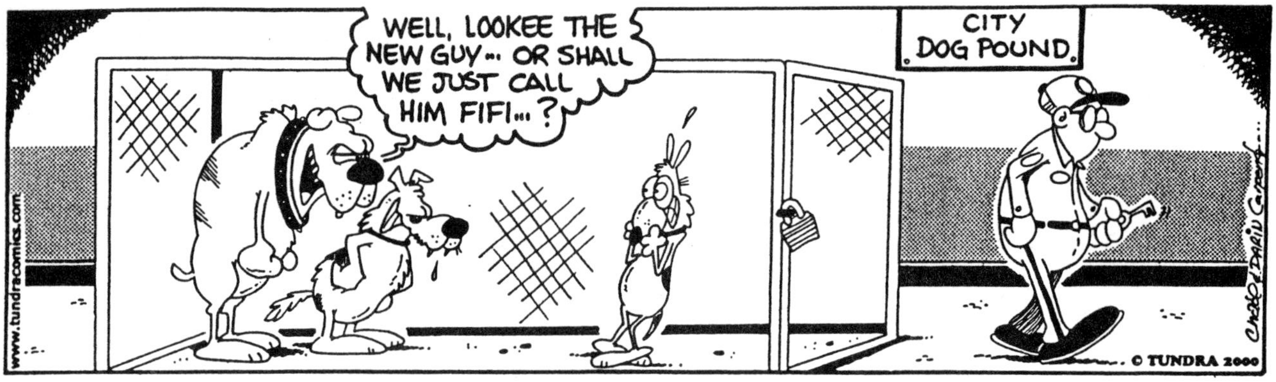
WELL, LOOKEE THE NEW GUY... OR SHALL WE JUST CALL HIM FIFI...?
CITY DOG POUND
www.tundracomics.com
© TUNDRA 2000

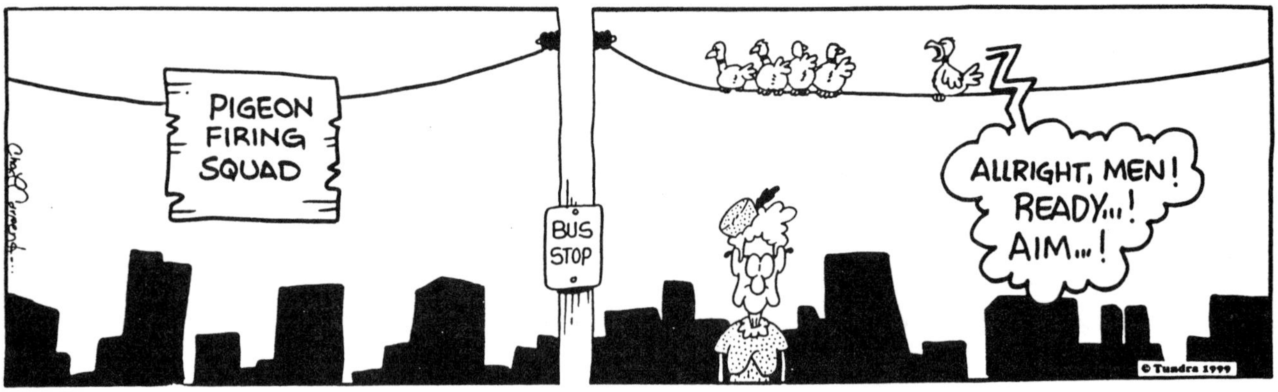
PIGEON FIRING SQUAD
BUS STOP
ALLRIGHT, MEN! READY...! AIM...!
© Tundra 1999

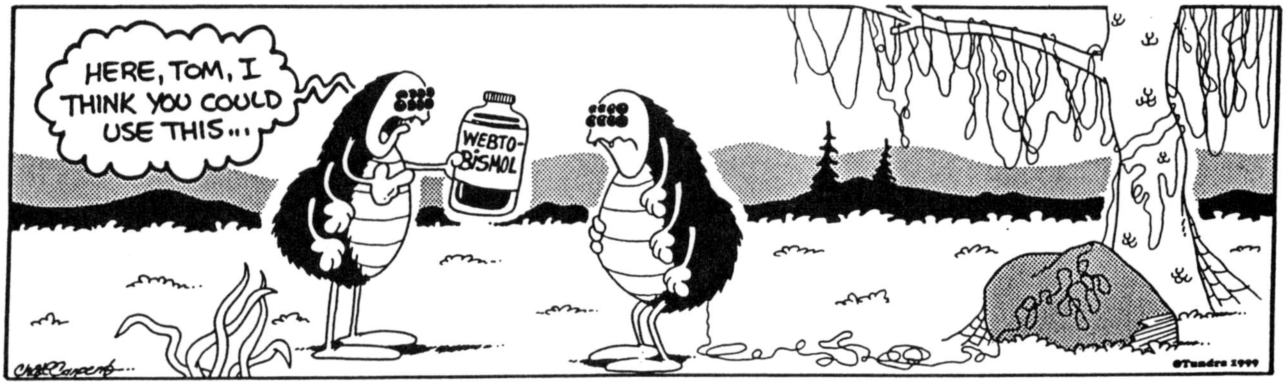
HERE, TOM, I THINK YOU COULD USE THIS...
WEBTO-BISMOL
©Tundra 1999

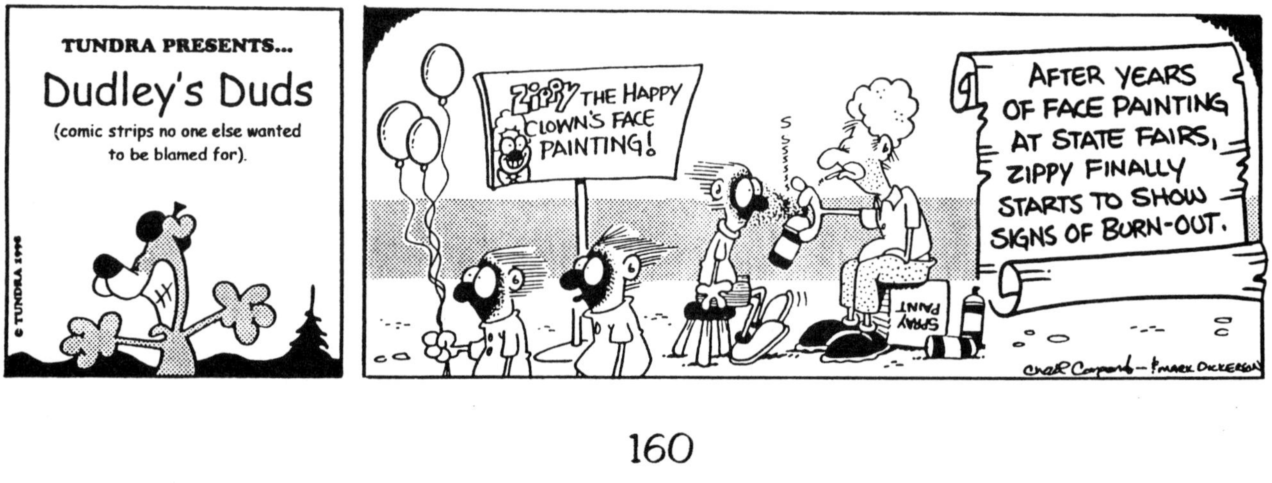
TUNDRA PRESENTS...
Dudley's Duds
(comic strips no one else wanted to be blamed for).
ZIPPY THE HAPPY CLOWN'S FACE PAINTING!
AFTER YEARS OF FACE PAINTING AT STATE FAIRS, ZIPPY FINALLY STARTS TO SHOW SIGNS OF BURN-OUT.
SPRAY PAINT

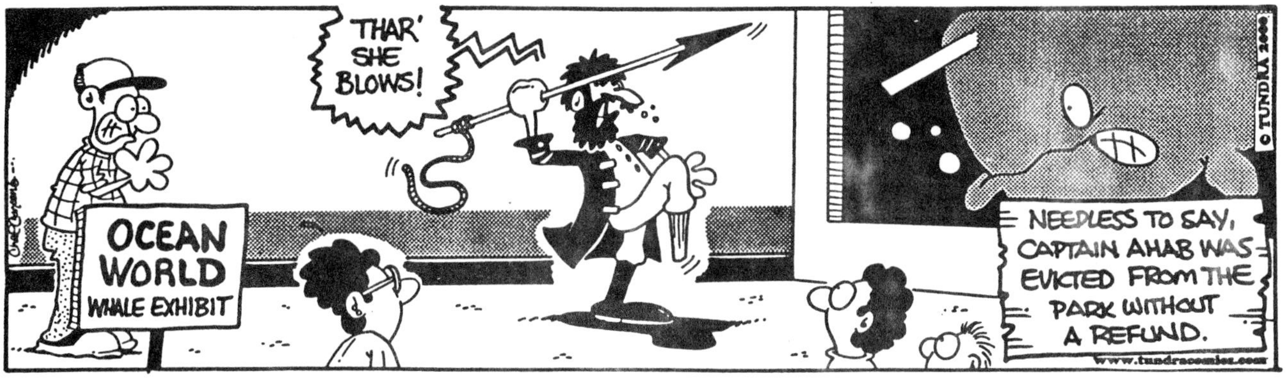
OCEAN WORLD WHALE EXHIBIT
THAR' SHE BLOWS!
NEEDLESS TO SAY, CAPTAIN AHAB WAS EVICTED FROM THE PARK WITHOUT A REFUND.
© TUNDRA 2000
www.tundracomics.com

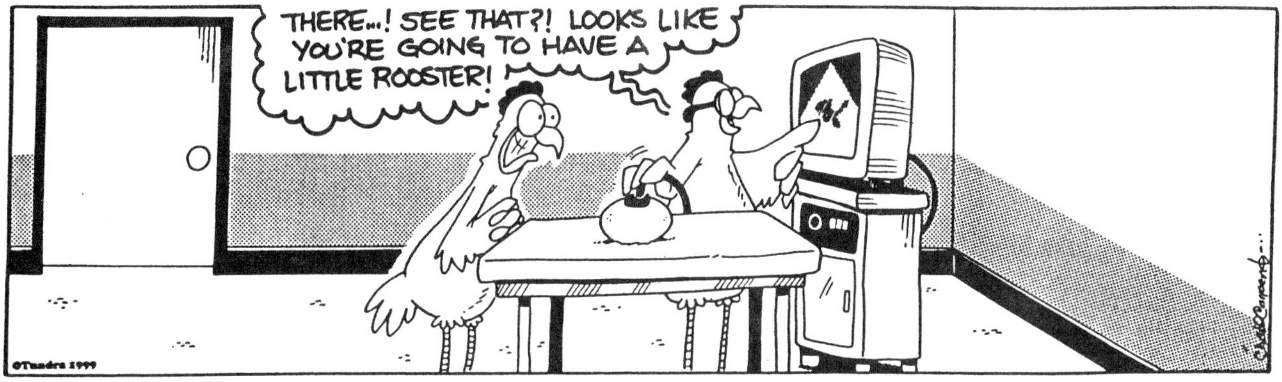
THERE...! SEE THAT?! LOOKS LIKE YOU'RE GOING TO HAVE A LITTLE ROOSTER!
©Tundra 1999

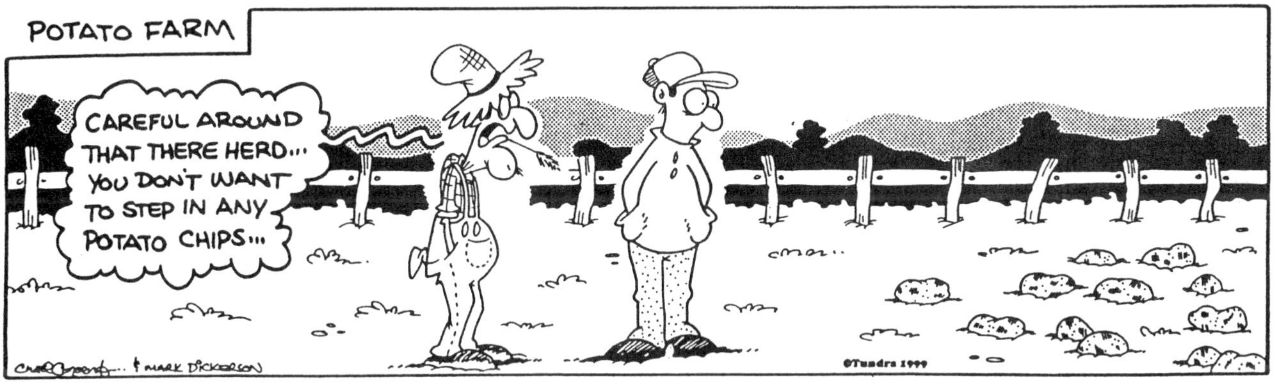
POTATO FARM
CAREFUL AROUND THAT THERE HERD... YOU DON'T WANT TO STEP IN ANY POTATO CHIPS...
& MARK DICKERSON
©Tundra 1999

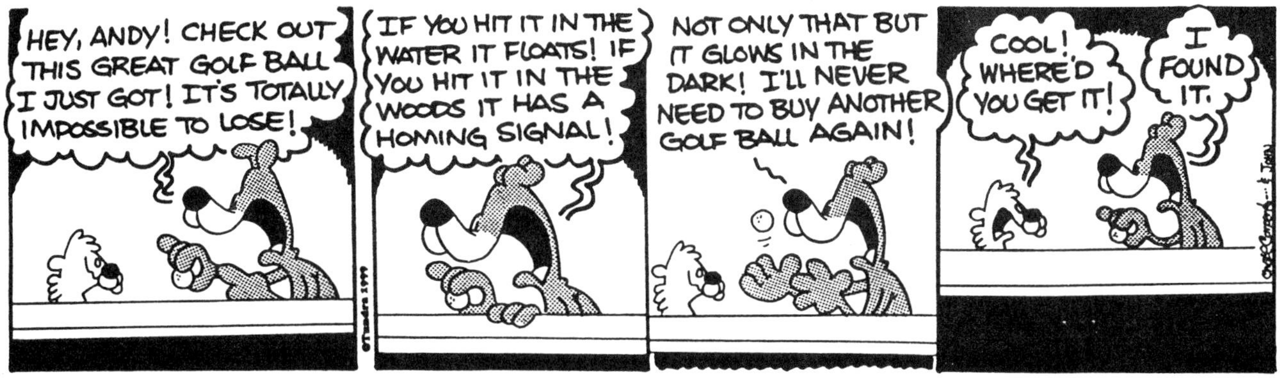
HEY, ANDY! CHECK OUT THIS GREAT GOLF BALL I JUST GOT! IT'S TOTALLY IMPOSSIBLE TO LOSE!
IF YOU HIT IT IN THE WATER IT FLOATS! IF YOU HIT IT IN THE WOODS IT HAS A HOMING SIGNAL!
NOT ONLY THAT BUT IT GLOWS IN THE DARK! I'LL NEVER NEED TO BUY ANOTHER GOLF BALL AGAIN!
COOL! WHERE'D YOU GET IT!
I FOUND IT.
©Tundra 1999

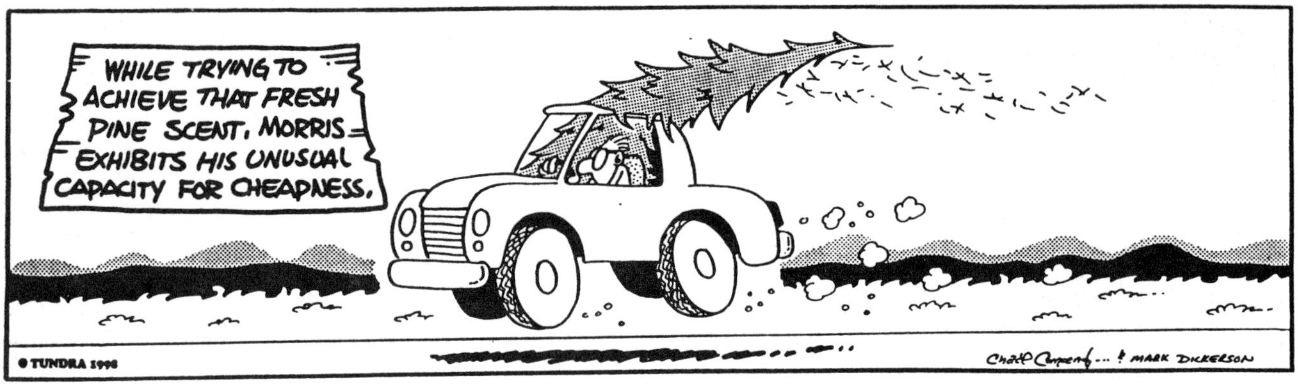
WHILE TRYING TO ACHIEVE THAT FRESH PINE SCENT, MORRIS EXHIBITS HIS UNUSUAL CAPACITY FOR CHEAPNESS.

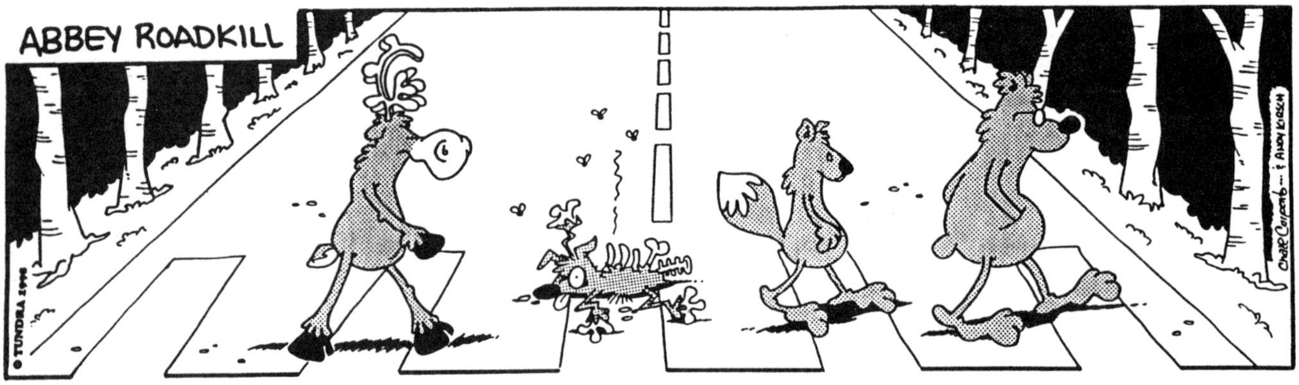
ABBEY ROADKILL

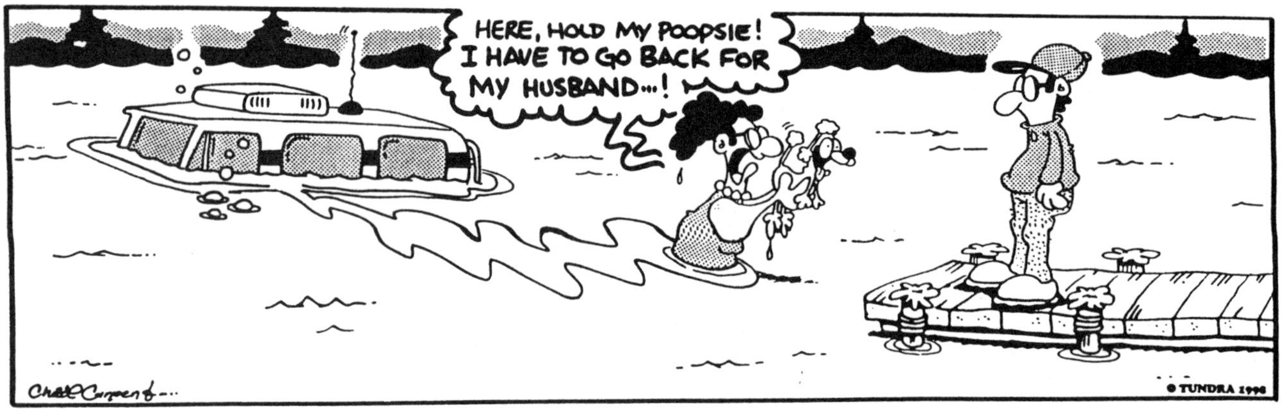
HERE, HOLD MY POOPSIE! I HAVE TO GO BACK FOR MY HUSBAND...!

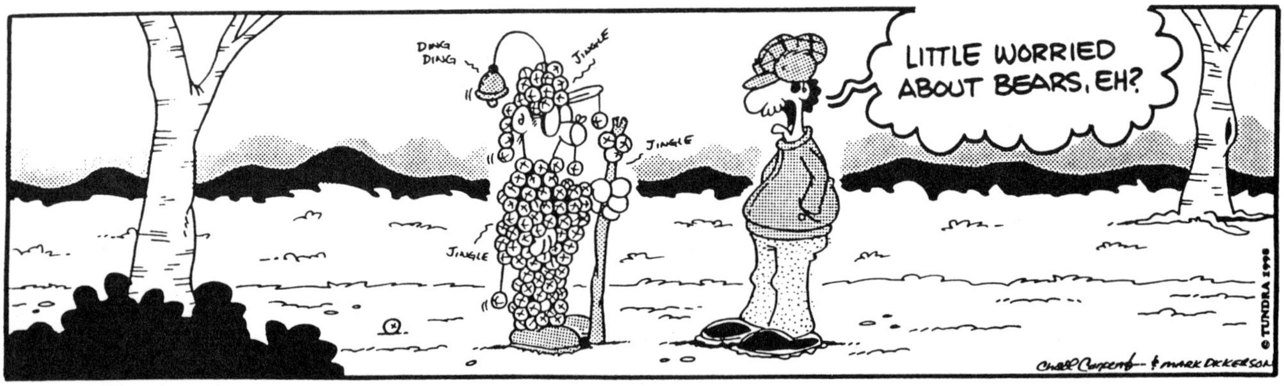
LITTLE WORRIED ABOUT BEARS, EH?

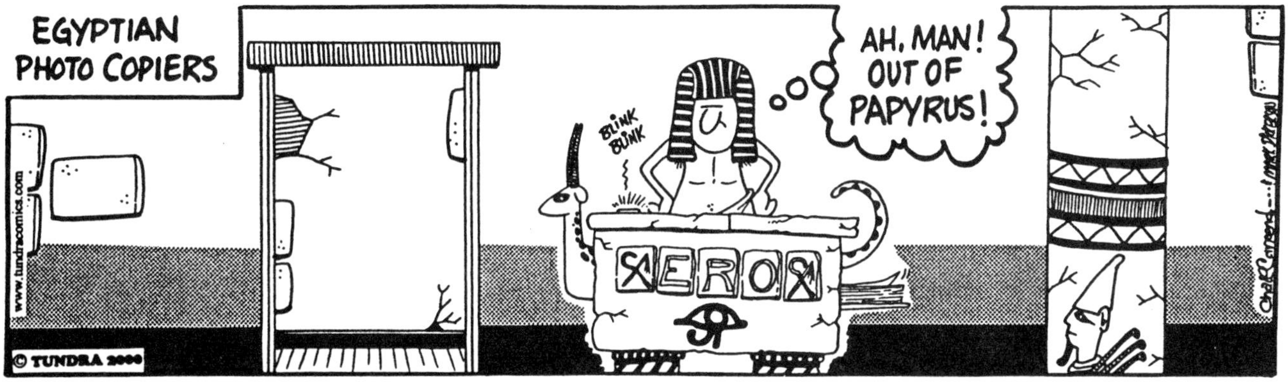
EGYPTIAN PHOTO COPIERS
AH, MAN! OUT OF PAPYRUS!
BLINK BLINK
© TUNDRA 2000

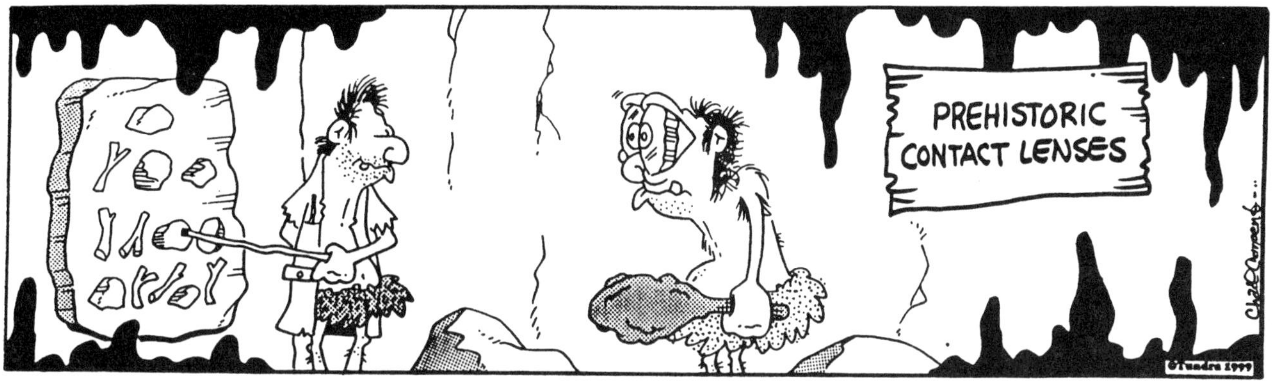
PREHISTORIC CONTACT LENSES
©Tundra 1999

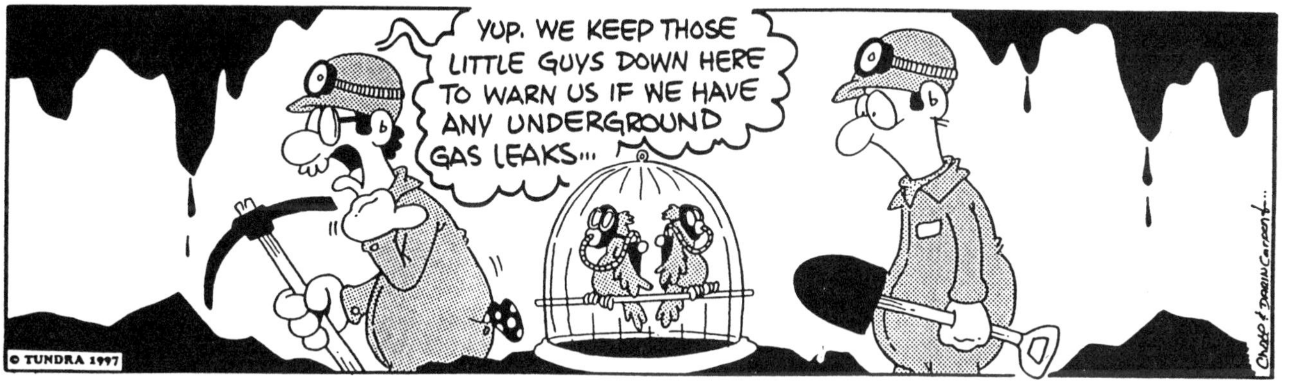
YUP. WE KEEP THOSE LITTLE GUYS DOWN HERE TO WARN US IF WE HAVE ANY UNDERGROUND GAS LEAKS...
© TUNDRA 1997

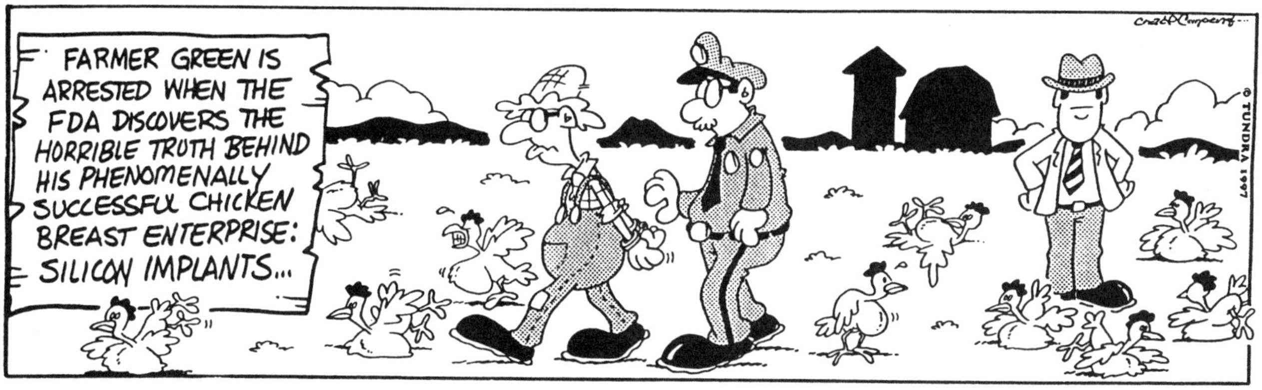
FARMER GREEN IS ARRESTED WHEN THE FDA DISCOVERS THE HORRIBLE TRUTH BEHIND HIS PHENOMENALLY SUCCESSFUL CHICKEN BREAST ENTERPRISE: SILICON IMPLANTS...

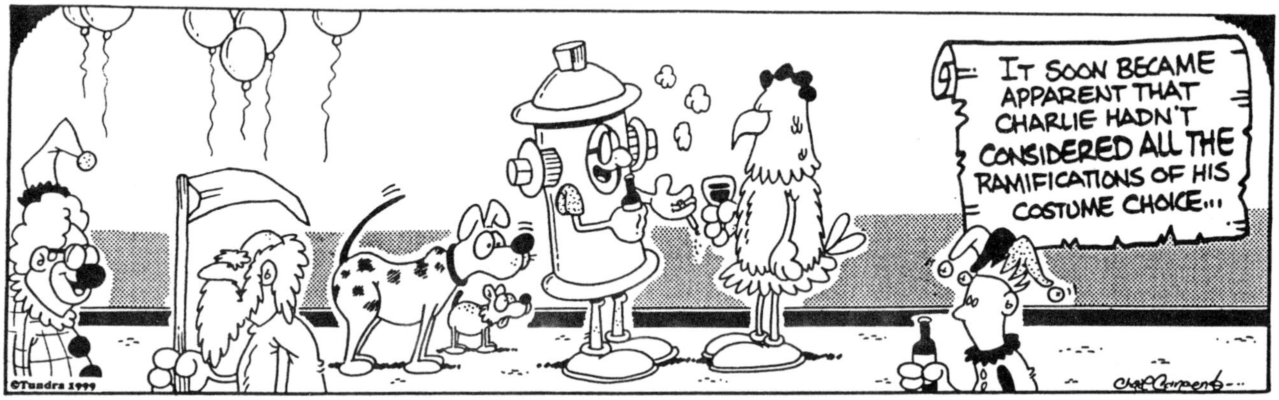
IT SOON BECAME APPARENT THAT CHARLIE HADN'T CONSIDERED ALL THE RAMIFICATIONS OF HIS COSTUME CHOICE...
©Tundra 1999

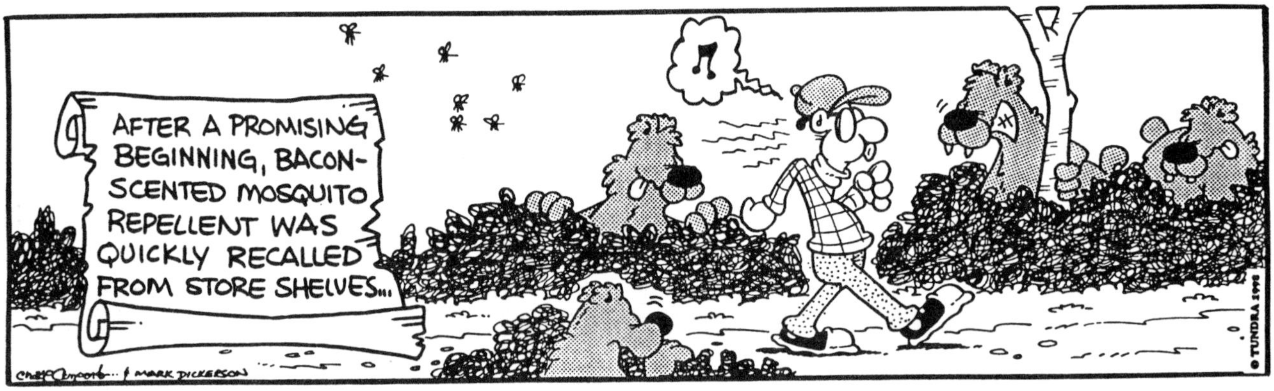
AFTER A PROMISING BEGINNING, BACON-SCENTED MOSQUITO REPELLENT WAS QUICKLY RECALLED FROM STORE SHELVES...
& MARK DICKERSON

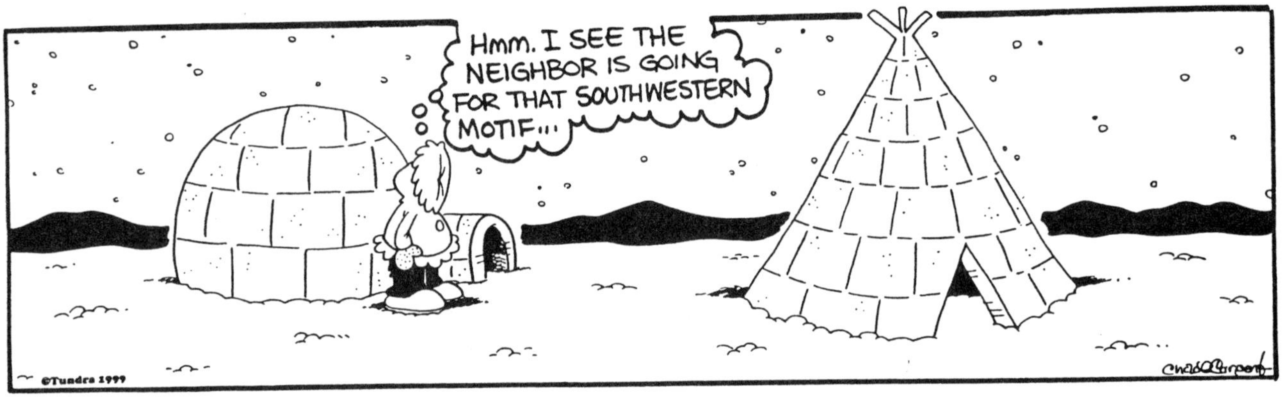
HMM. I SEE THE NEIGHBOR IS GOING FOR THAT SOUTHWESTERN MOTIF...
©Tundra 1999

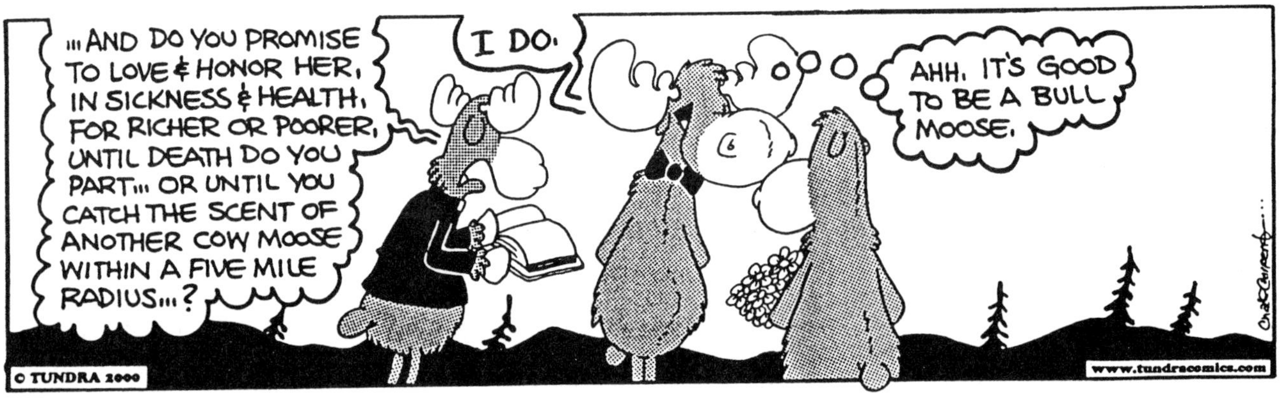
...AND DO YOU PROMISE TO LOVE & HONOR HER, IN SICKNESS & HEALTH, FOR RICHER OR POORER, UNTIL DEATH DO YOU PART... OR UNTIL YOU CATCH THE SCENT OF ANOTHER COW MOOSE WITHIN A FIVE MILE RADIUS...?
I DO.
AHH. IT'S GOOD TO BE A BULL MOOSE.
© TUNDRA 2000
www.tundracomics.com

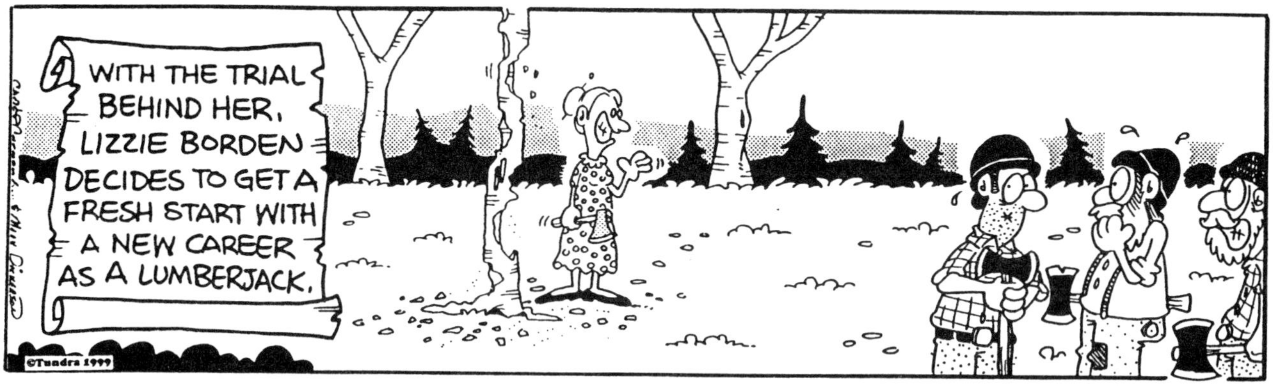
WITH THE TRIAL BEHIND HER, LIZZIE BORDEN DECIDES TO GET A FRESH START WITH A NEW CAREER AS A LUMBERJACK.
©Tundra 1999

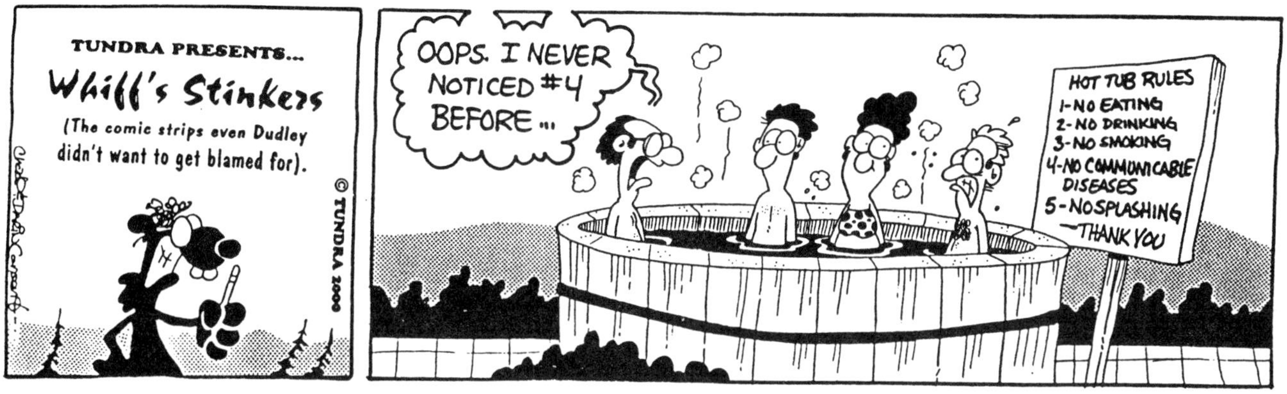
TUNDRA PRESENTS...
Whiff's Stinkers
(The comic strips even Dudley didn't want to get blamed for).
© TUNDRA 2000
OOPS. I NEVER NOTICED #4 BEFORE...
HOT TUB RULES
1-NO EATING
2-NO DRINKING
3-NO SMOKING
4-NO COMMUNICABLE DISEASES
5-NO SPLASHING
—THANK YOU

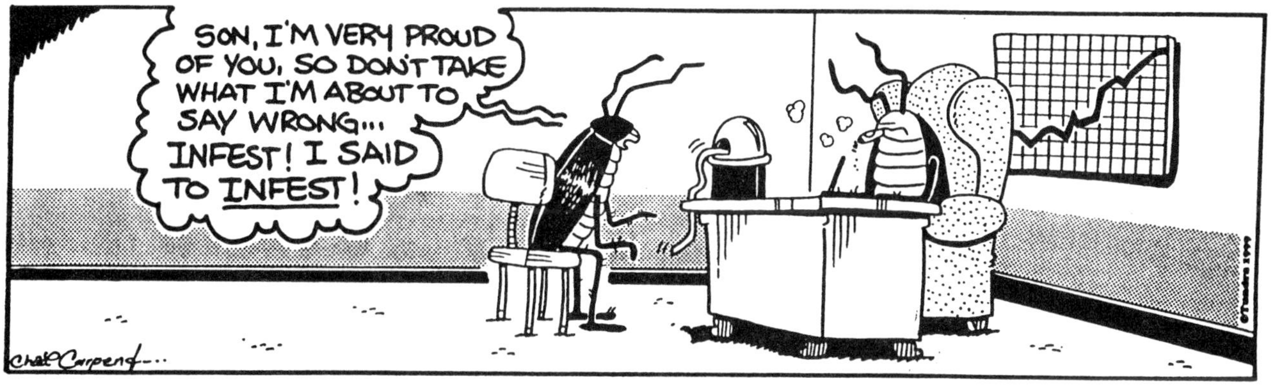
SON, I'M VERY PROUD OF YOU, SO DON'T TAKE WHAT I'M ABOUT TO SAY WRONG... INFEST! I SAID TO INFEST!
©Tundra 1999

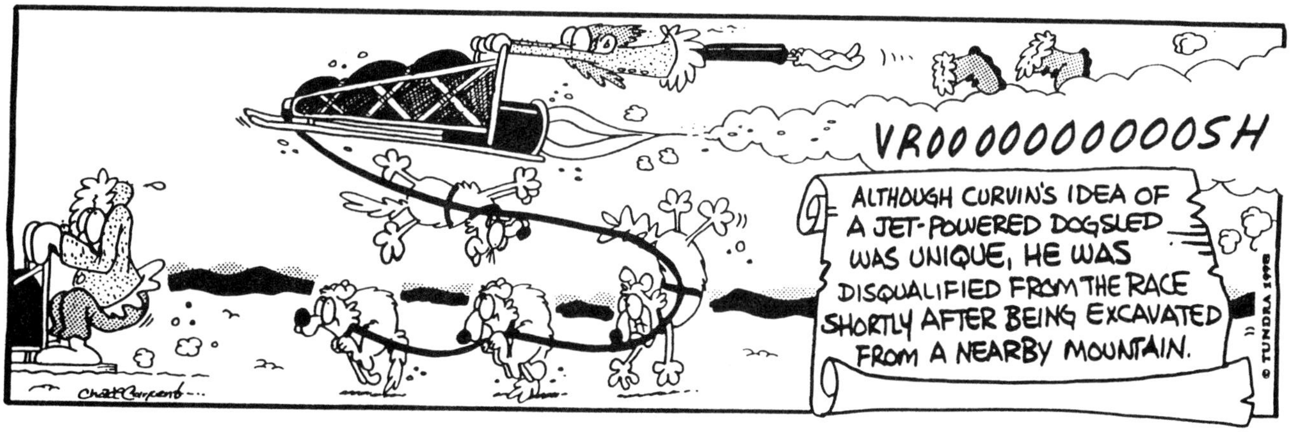
VROOOOOOOOOOOSH
ALTHOUGH CURVIN'S IDEA OF A JET-POWERED DOGSLED WAS UNIQUE, HE WAS DISQUALIFIED FROM THE RACE SHORTLY AFTER BEING EXCAVATED FROM A NEARBY MOUNTAIN.
© TUNDRA 1998

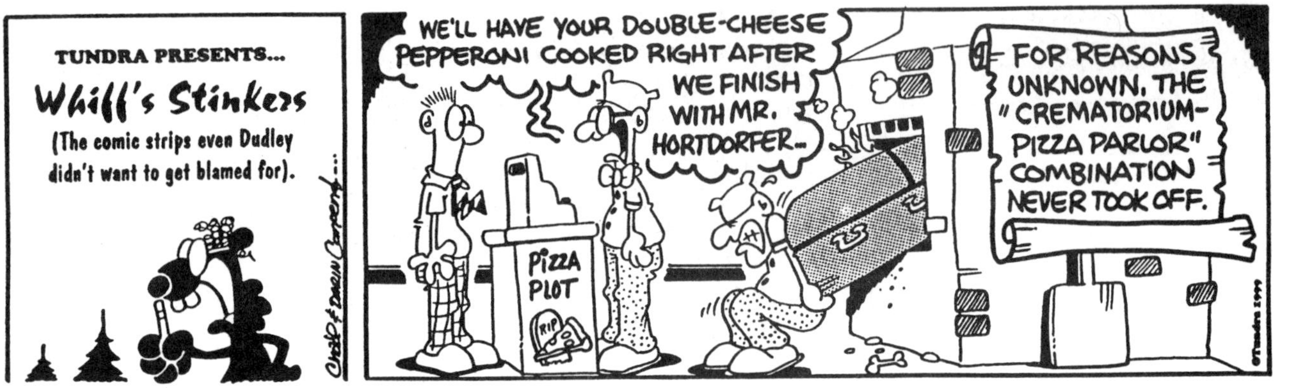
TUNDRA PRESENTS...
Whiff's Stinkers
(The comic strips even Dudley didn't want to get blamed for).
WE'LL HAVE YOUR DOUBLE-CHEESE PEPPERONI COOKED RIGHT AFTER WE FINISH WITH MR. HORTDORFER...
PIZZA PLOT
RIP
FOR REASONS UNKNOWN, THE "CREMATORIUM-PIZZA PARLOR" COMBINATION NEVER TOOK OFF.

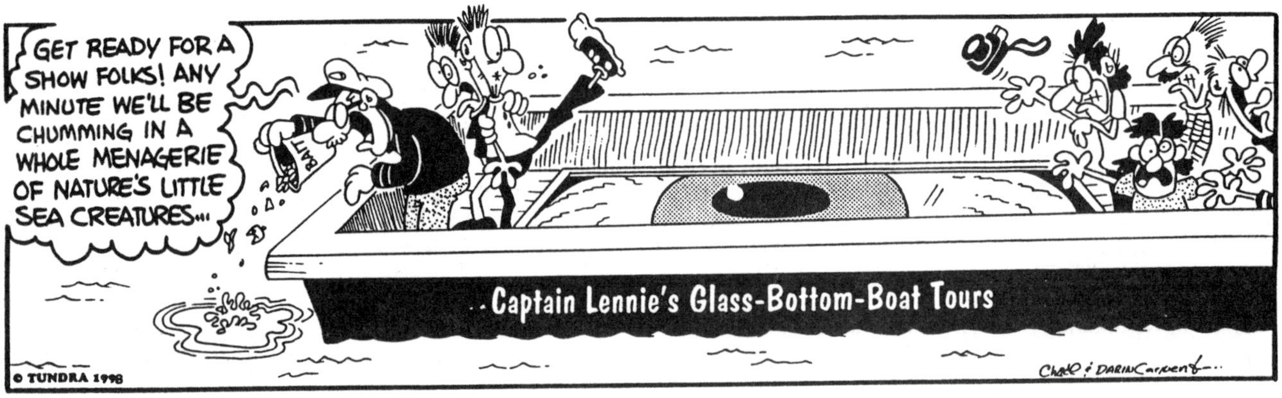
GET READY FOR A SHOW FOLKS! ANY MINUTE WE'LL BE CHUMMING IN A WHOLE MENAGERIE OF NATURE'S LITTLE SEA CREATURES...
BAIT
..Captain Lennie's Glass-Bottom-Boat Tours
© TUNDRA 1998

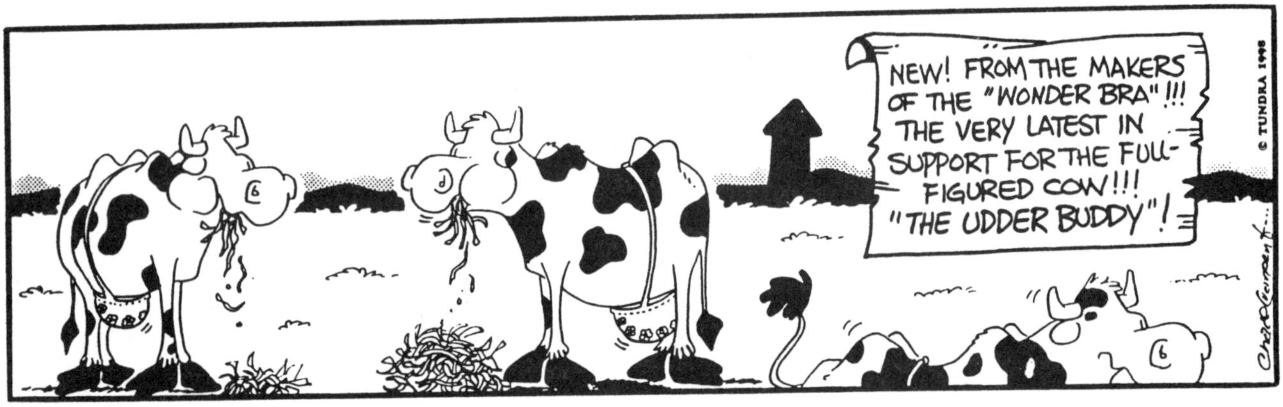
NEW! FROM THE MAKERS OF THE "WONDER BRA"!!! THE VERY LATEST IN SUPPORT FOR THE FULL-FIGURED COW!!! "THE UDDER BUDDY"!
© TUNDRA 1998

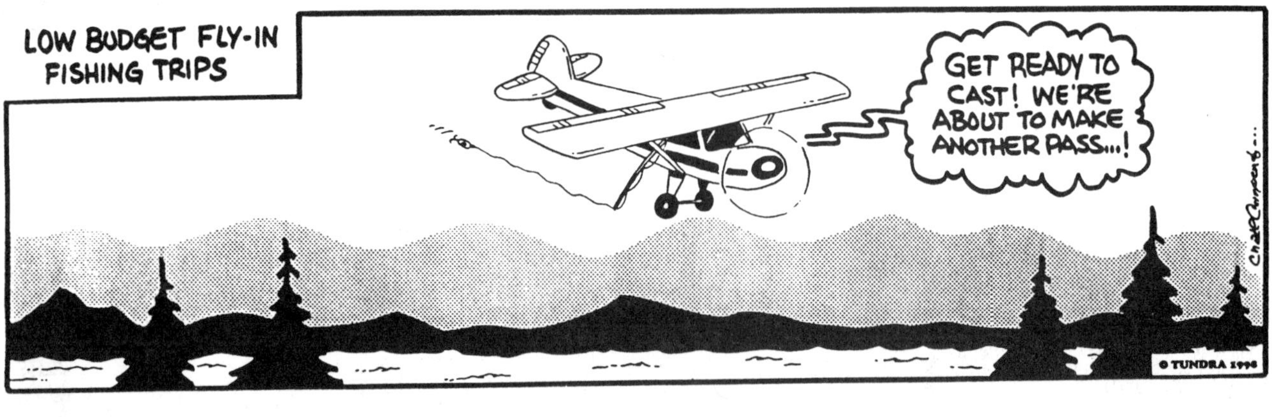
LOW BUDGET FLY-IN FISHING TRIPS
GET READY TO CAST! WE'RE ABOUT TO MAKE ANOTHER PASS...!
© TUNDRA 1998

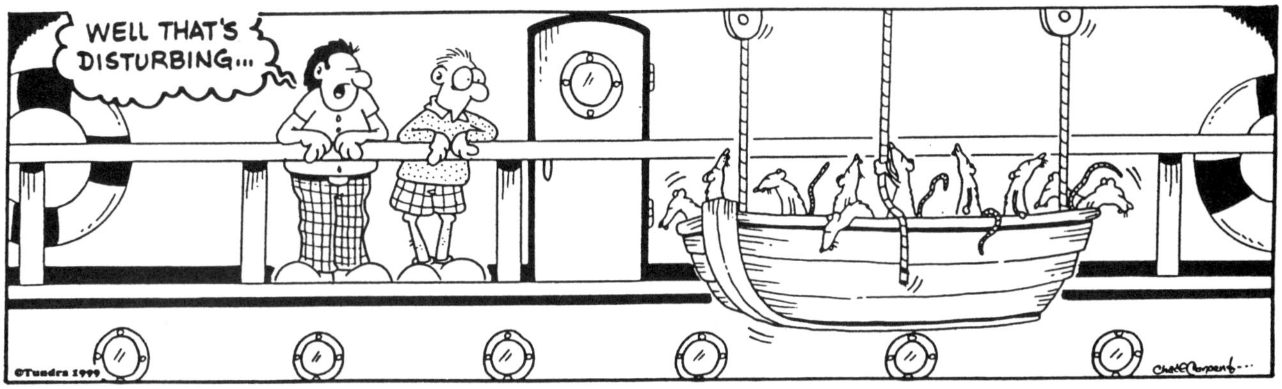
WELL THAT'S DISTURBING...
©Tundra 1999

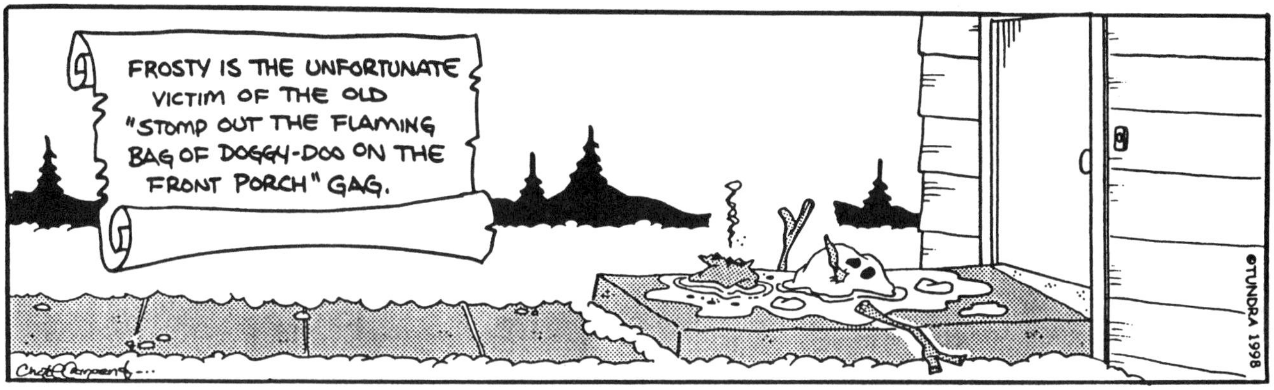
FROSTY IS THE UNFORTUNATE VICTIM OF THE OLD "STOMP OUT THE FLAMING BAG OF DOGGY-DOO ON THE FRONT PORCH" GAG.
©TUNDRA 1998

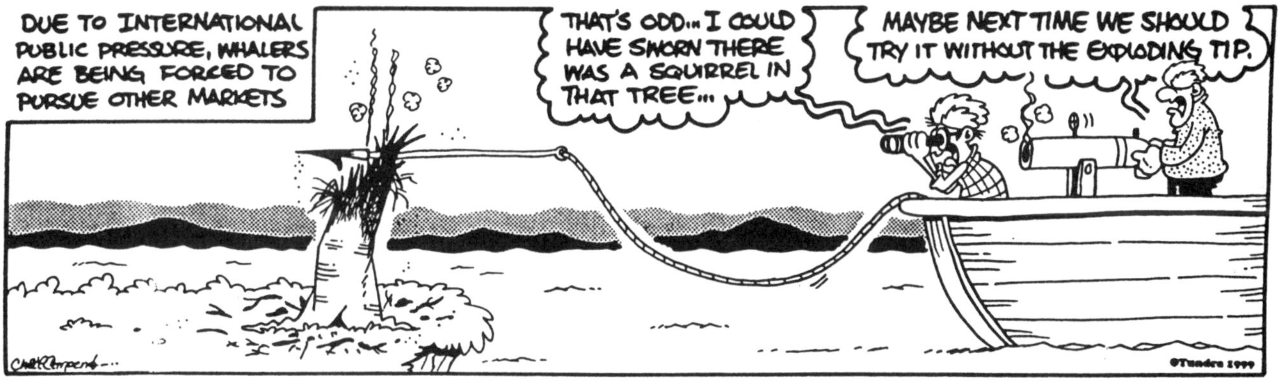
DUE TO INTERNATIONAL PUBLIC PRESSURE, WHALERS ARE BEING FORCED TO PURSUE OTHER MARKETS
THAT'S ODD... I COULD HAVE SWORN THERE WAS A SQUIRREL IN THAT TREE...
MAYBE NEXT TIME WE SHOULD TRY IT WITHOUT THE EXPLODING TIP.
©Tundra 1999

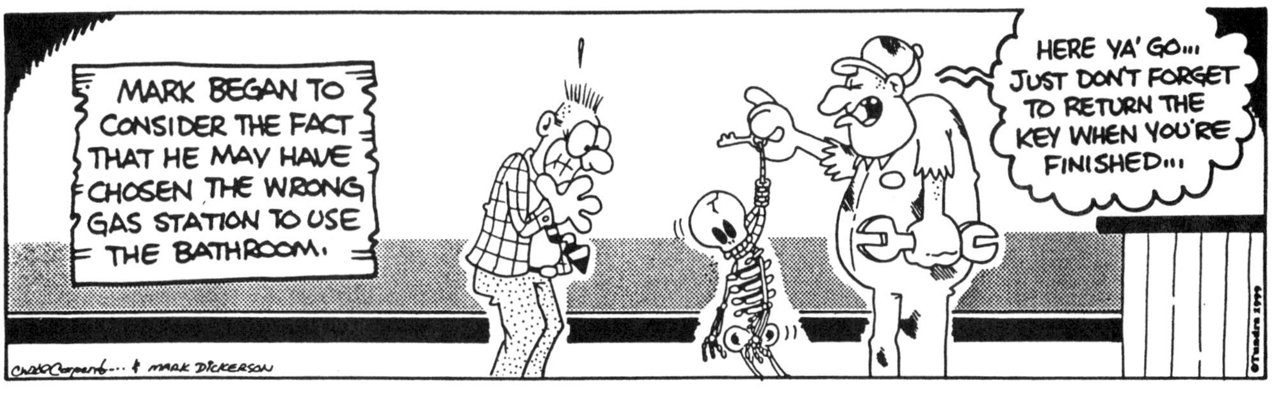
MARK BEGAN TO CONSIDER THE FACT THAT HE MAY HAVE CHOSEN THE WRONG GAS STATION TO USE THE BATHROOM.
!
HERE YA' GO... JUST DON'T FORGET TO RETURN THE KEY WHEN YOU'RE FINISHED...
& MARK DICKERSON
©Tundra 1999

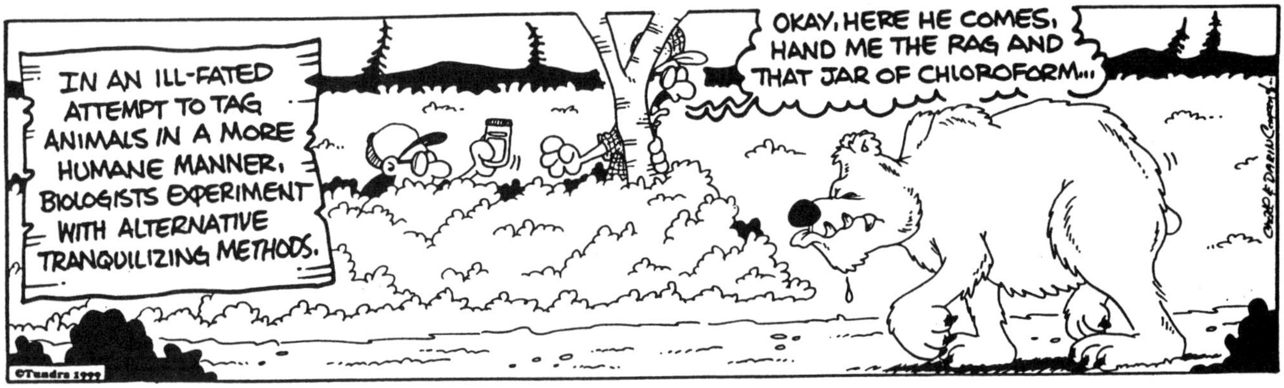
IN AN ILL-FATED ATTEMPT TO TAG ANIMALS IN A MORE HUMANE MANNER, BIOLOGISTS EXPERIMENT WITH ALTERNATIVE TRANQUILIZING METHODS.
OKAY, HERE HE COMES, HAND ME THE RAG AND THAT JAR OF CHLOROFORM...
©Tundra 1999

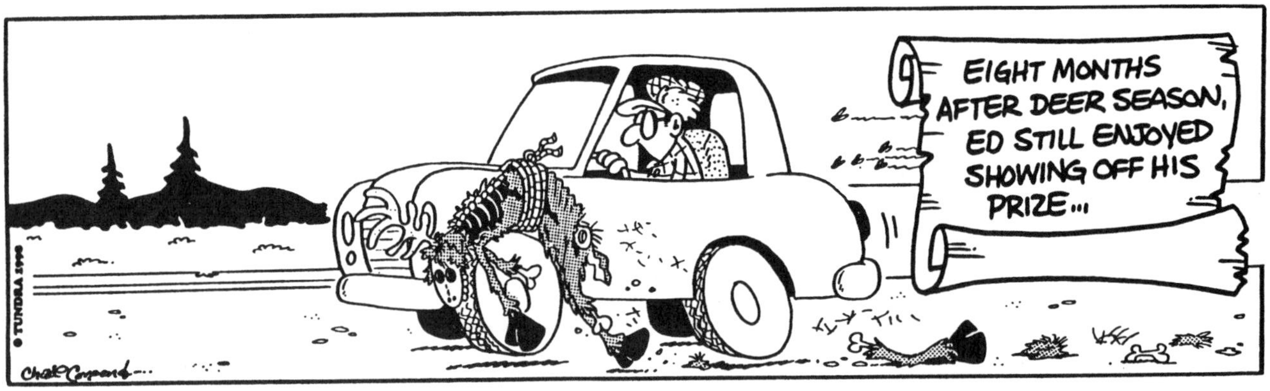
EIGHT MONTHS AFTER DEER SEASON, ED STILL ENJOYED SHOWING OFF HIS PRIZE...
© TUNDRA 1999

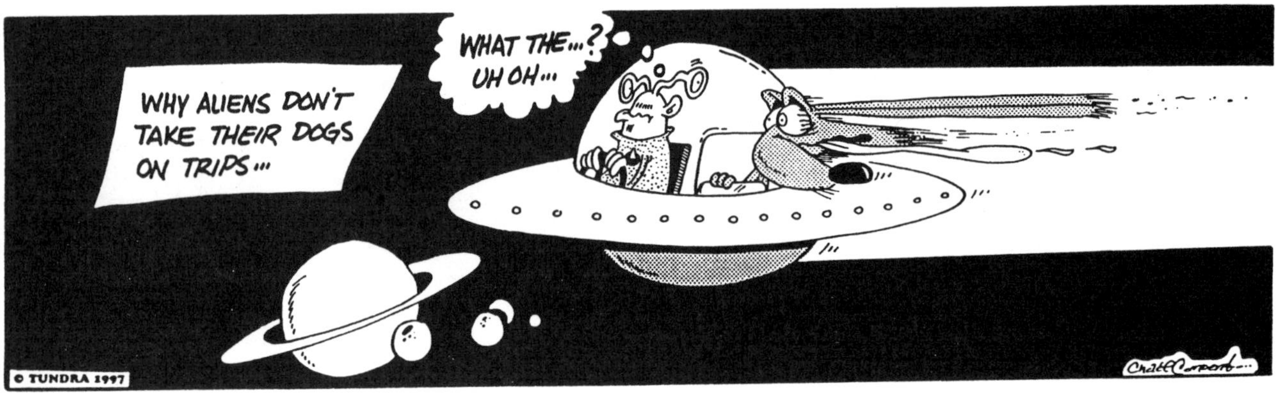
WHY ALIENS DON'T TAKE THEIR DOGS ON TRIPS...
WHAT THE...? UH OH...
© TUNDRA 1997

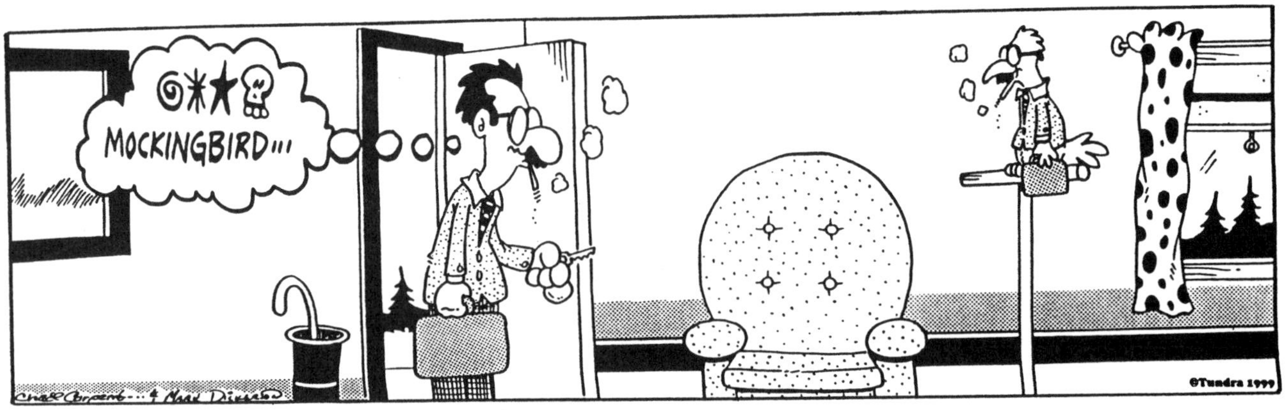
MOCKINGBIRD...
©Tundra 1999

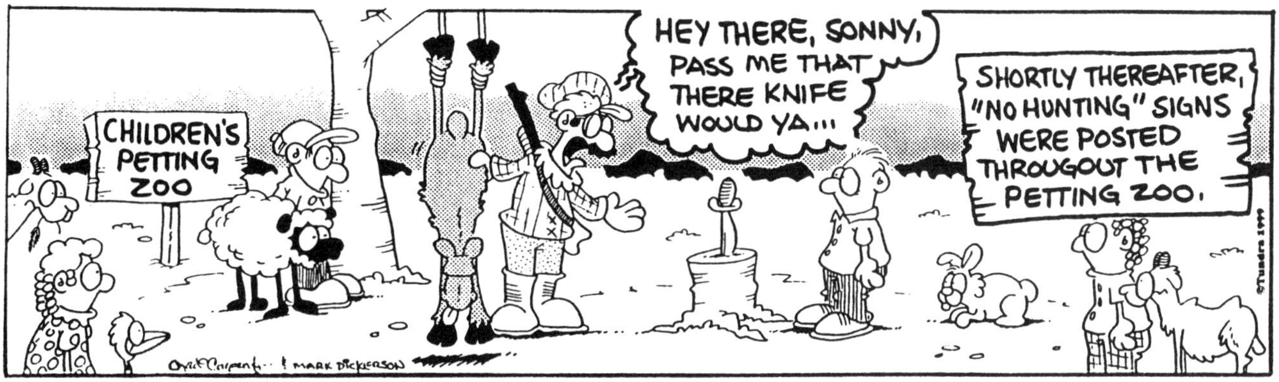
CHILDREN'S PETTING ZOO
HEY THERE, SONNY, PASS ME THAT THERE KNIFE WOULD YA...
SHORTLY THEREAFTER, "NO HUNTING" SIGNS WERE POSTED THROUGOUT THE PETTING ZOO.
MARK DICKERSON

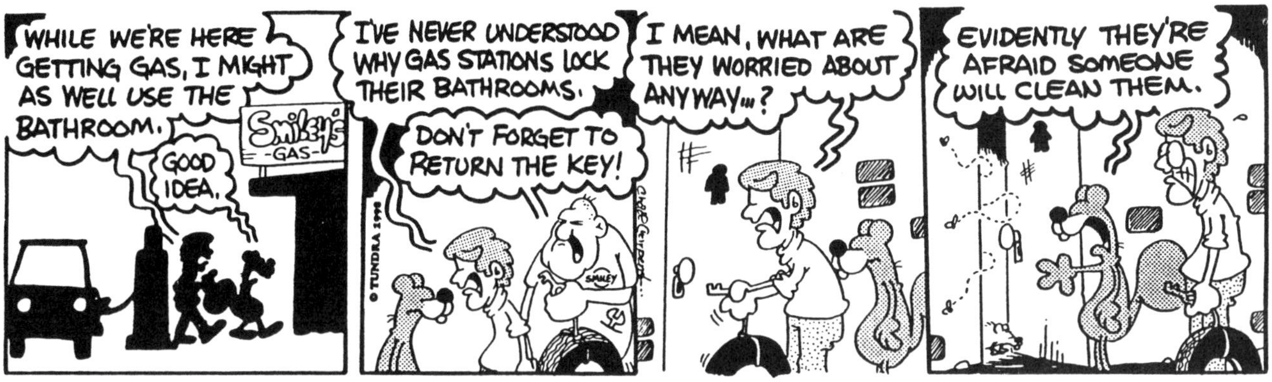
WHILE WE'RE HERE GETTING GAS, I MIGHT AS WELL USE THE BATHROOM.
Smiley's -GAS-
GOOD IDEA.
I'VE NEVER UNDERSTOOD WHY GAS STATIONS LOCK THEIR BATHROOMS.
DON'T FORGET TO RETURN THE KEY!
© TUNDRA 1999
I MEAN, WHAT ARE THEY WORRIED ABOUT ANYWAY...?
EVIDENTLY THEY'RE AFRAID SOMEONE WILL CLEAN THEM.

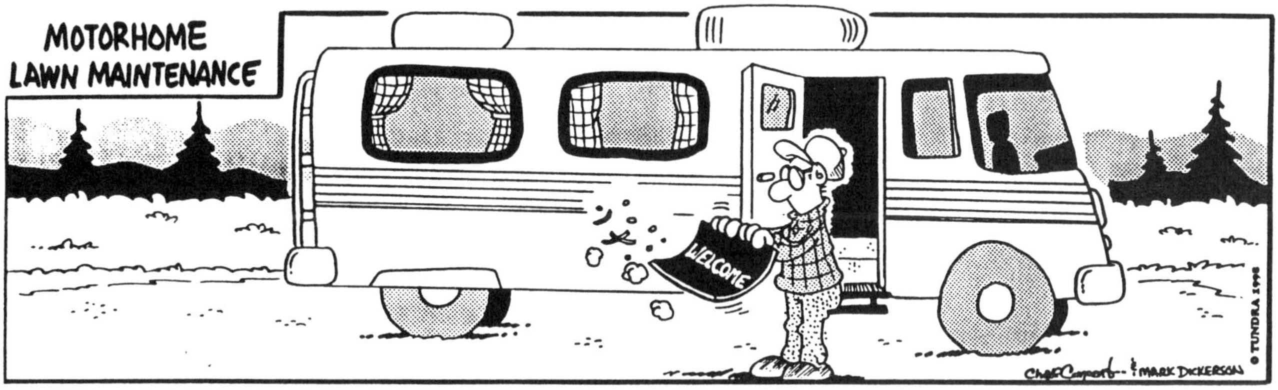
MOTORHOME LAWN MAINTENANCE
WELCOME
© TUNDRA 1999
MARK DICKERSON

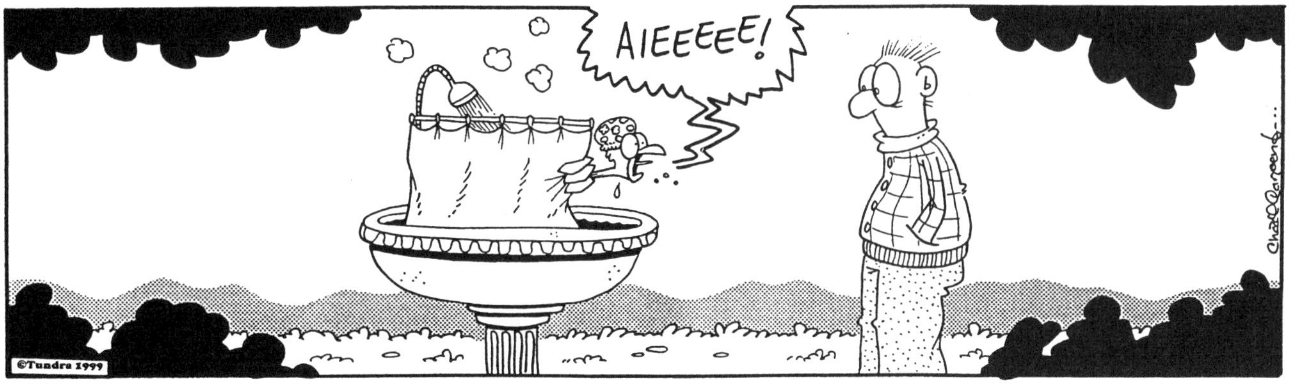
AIEEEEE!
©Tundra 1999

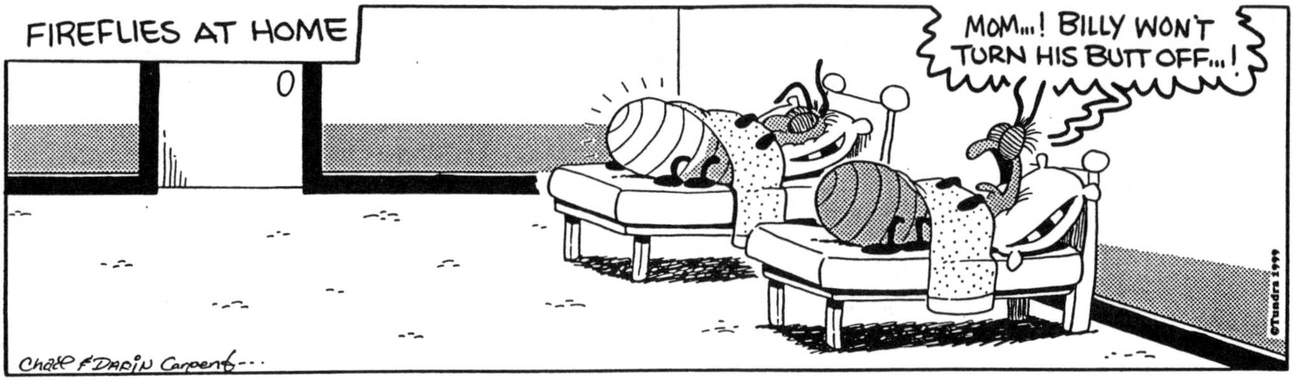
FIREFLIES AT HOME
MOM...! BILLY WON'T TURN HIS BUTT OFF...!
©Tundra 1999

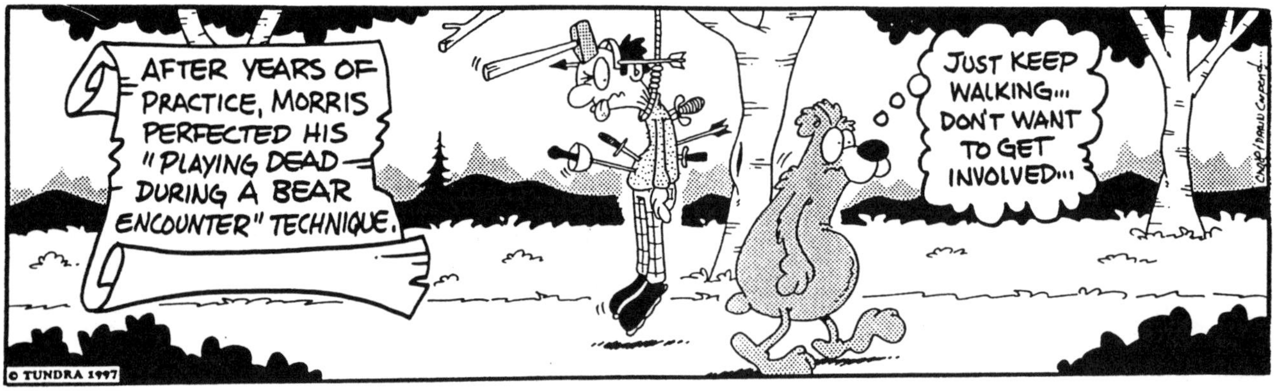
AFTER YEARS OF PRACTICE, MORRIS PERFECTED HIS "PLAYING DEAD DURING A BEAR ENCOUNTER" TECHNIQUE.
JUST KEEP WALKING... DON'T WANT TO GET INVOLVED...
© TUNDRA 1997

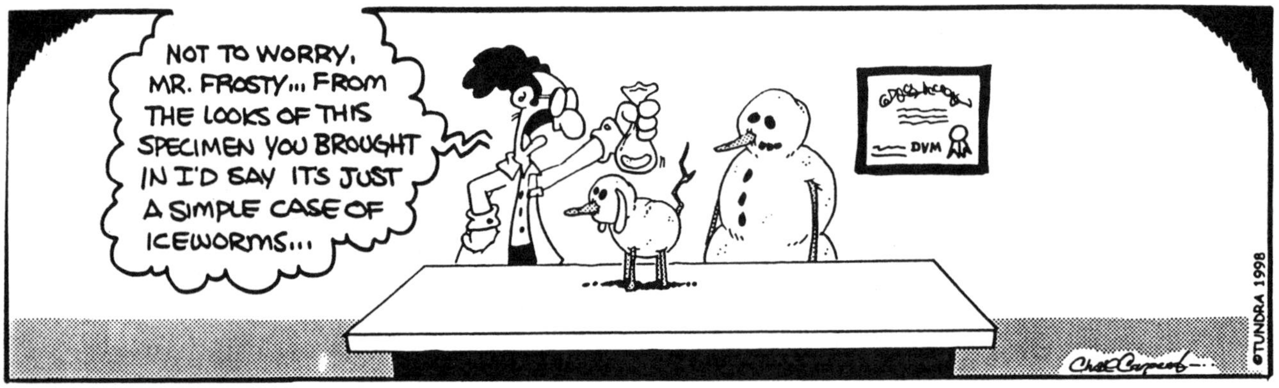
NOT TO WORRY, MR. FROSTY... FROM THE LOOKS OF THIS SPECIMEN YOU BROUGHT IN I'D SAY ITS JUST A SIMPLE CASE OF ICEWORMS...
DVM
©TUNDRA 1998

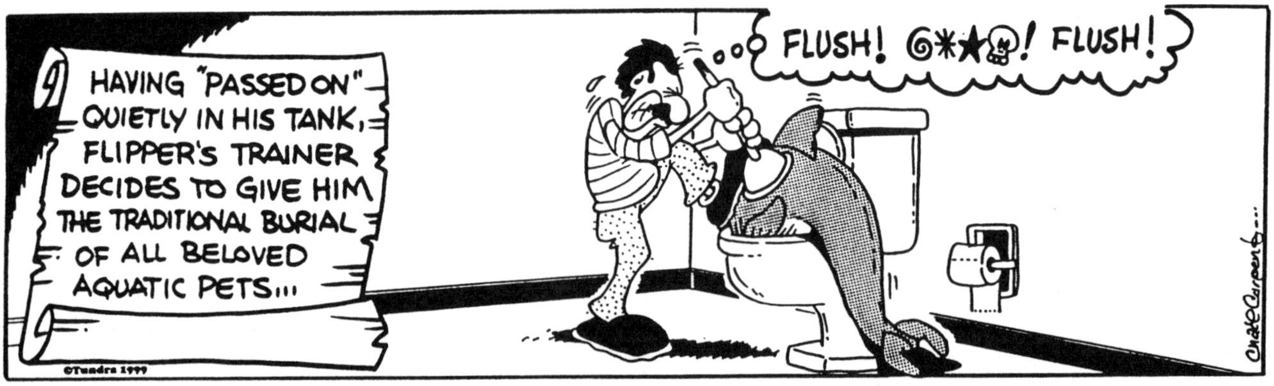
HAVING "PASSED ON" QUIETLY IN HIS TANK, FLIPPER'S TRAINER DECIDES TO GIVE HIM THE TRADITIONAL BURIAL OF ALL BELOVED AQUATIC PETS...
FLUSH! @*★☠! FLUSH!
©Tundra 1999

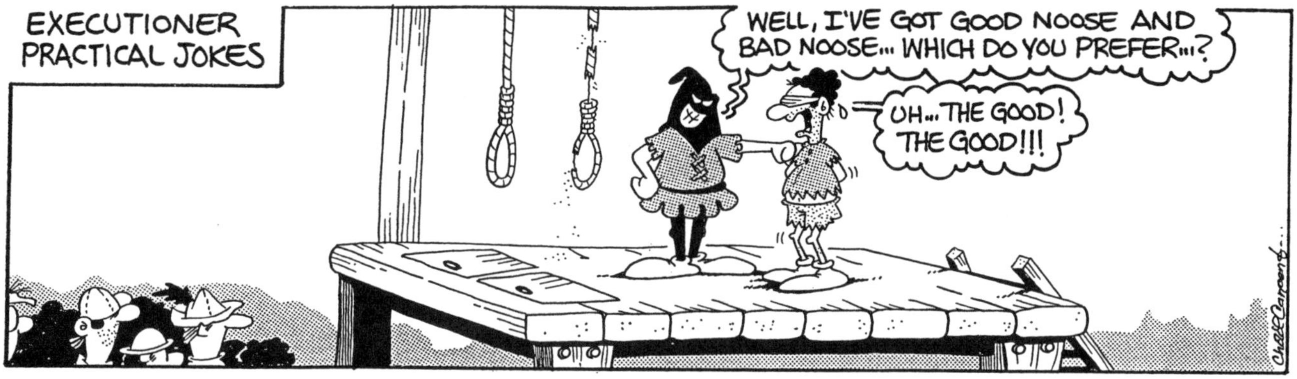
EXECUTIONER PRACTICAL JOKES
WELL, I'VE GOT GOOD NOOSE AND BAD NOOSE... WHICH DO YOU PREFER...?
UH... THE GOOD! THE GOOD!!!

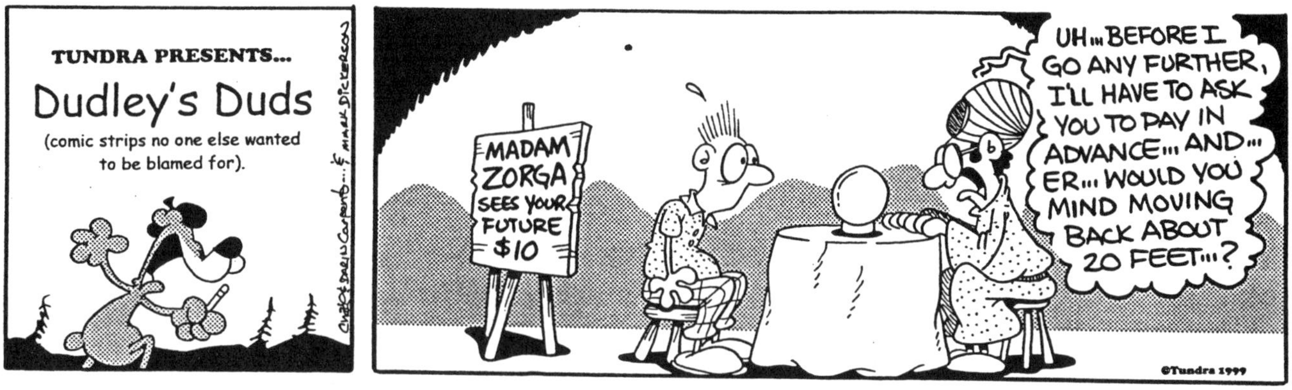
TUNDRA PRESENTS...
Dudley's Duds
(comic strips no one else wanted to be blamed for).
MADAM ZORGA SEES YOUR FUTURE $10
UH... BEFORE I GO ANY FURTHER, I'LL HAVE TO ASK YOU TO PAY IN ADVANCE... AND... ER... WOULD YOU MIND MOVING BACK ABOUT 20 FEET...?
©Tundra 1999

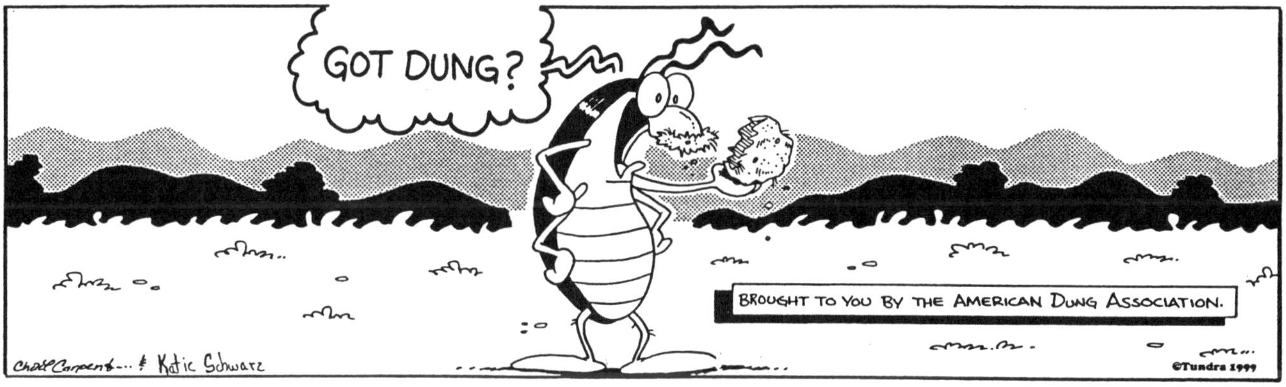
GOT DUNG?
BROUGHT TO YOU BY THE AMERICAN DUNG ASSOCIATION.
©Tundra 1999

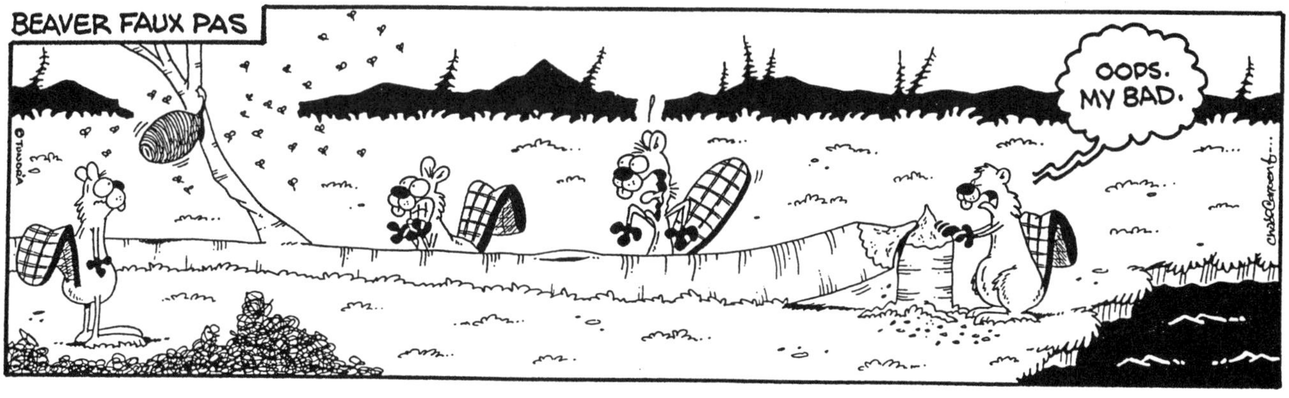
BEAVER FAUX PAS
OOPS. MY BAD.

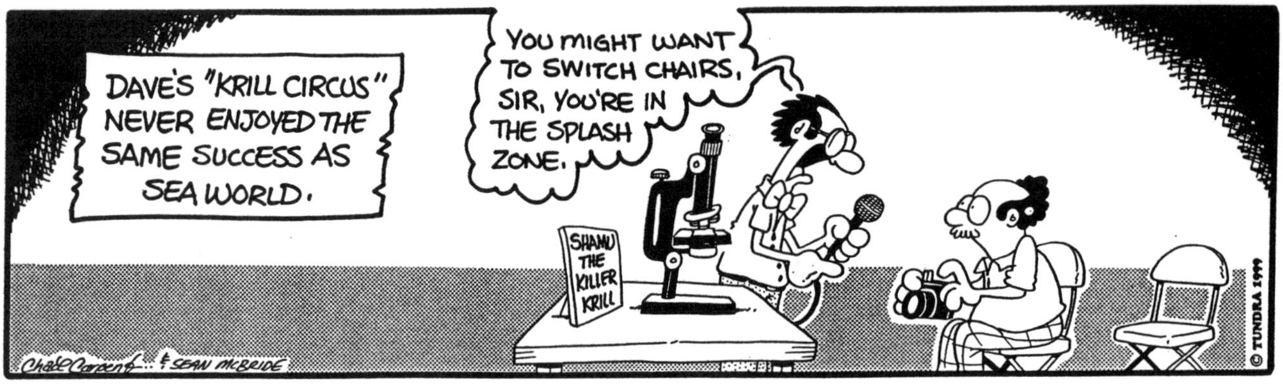
DAVE'S "KRILL CIRCUS" NEVER ENJOYED THE SAME SUCCESS AS SEA WORLD.
YOU MIGHT WANT TO SWITCH CHAIRS, SIR, YOU'RE IN THE SPLASH ZONE.
SHAMU THE KILLER KRILL
© TUNDRA 1999

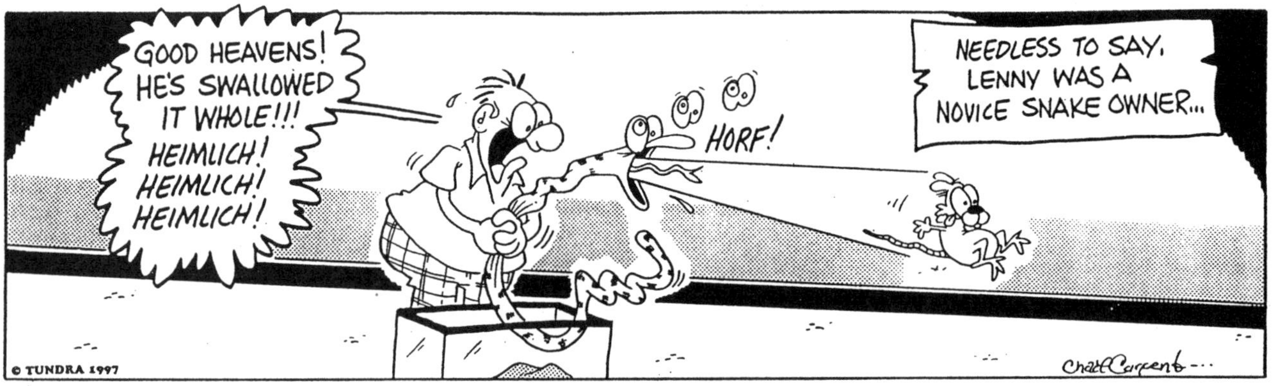
GOOD HEAVENS! HE'S SWALLOWED IT WHOLE!!! HEIMLICH! HEIMLICH! HEIMLICH!
HORF!
NEEDLESS TO SAY, LENNY WAS A NOVICE SNAKE OWNER...
© TUNDRA 1997

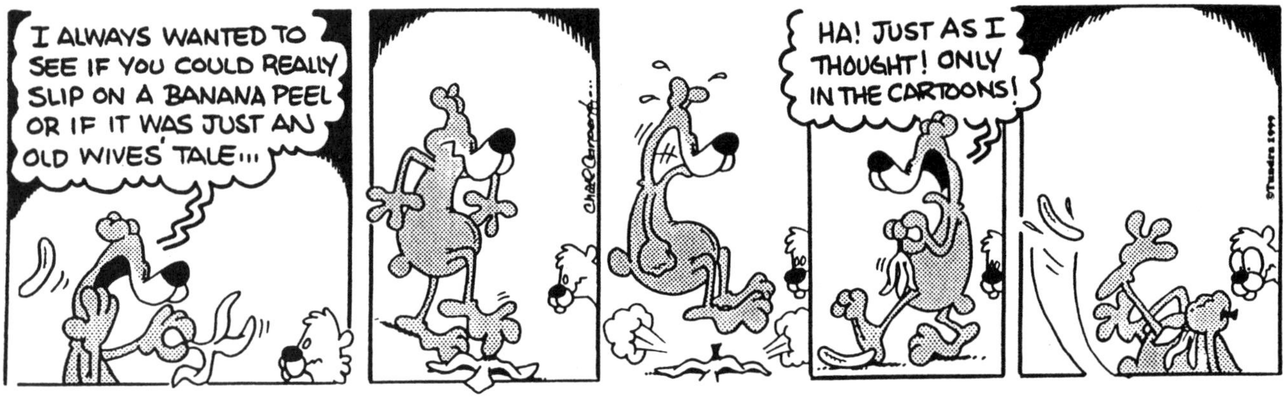
I ALWAYS WANTED TO SEE IF YOU COULD REALLY SLIP ON A BANANA PEEL OR IF IT WAS JUST AN OLD WIVES' TALE...
HA! JUST AS I THOUGHT! ONLY IN THE CARTOONS!

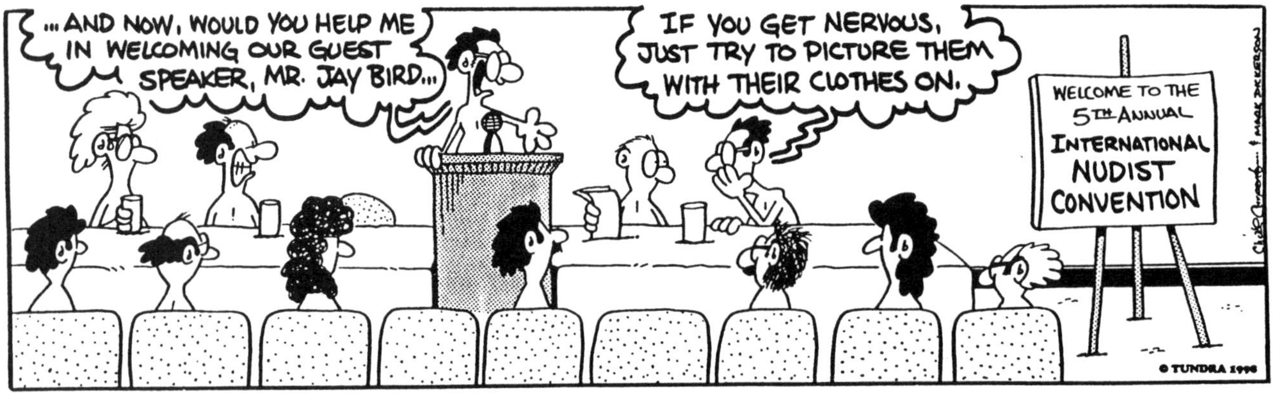
...AND NOW, WOULD YOU HELP ME IN WELCOMING OUR GUEST SPEAKER, MR. JAY BIRD...
IF YOU GET NERVOUS, JUST TRY TO PICTURE THEM WITH THEIR CLOTHES ON.
WELCOME TO THE 5TH ANNUAL INTERNATIONAL NUDIST CONVENTION
© TUNDRA 1998

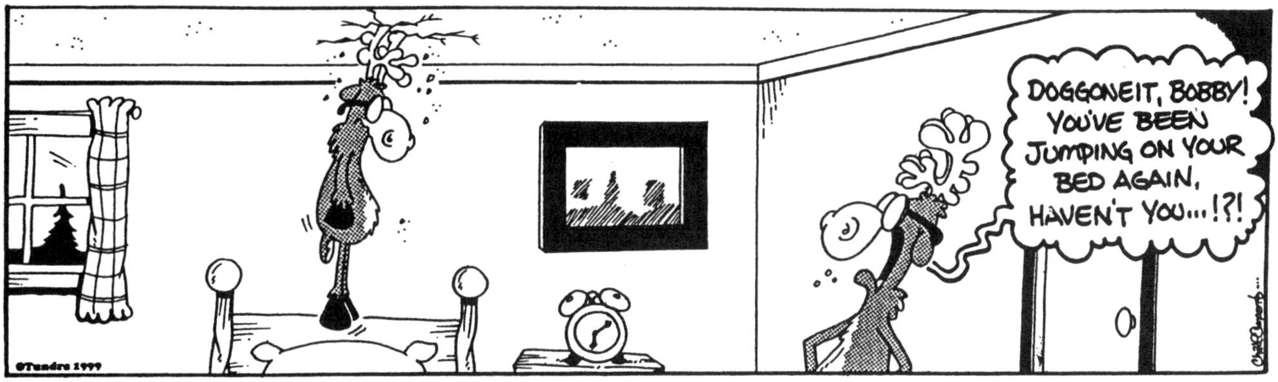
DOGGONEIT, BOBBY! YOU'VE BEEN JUMPING ON YOUR BED AGAIN, HAVEN'T YOU...!?!
©Tundra 1999

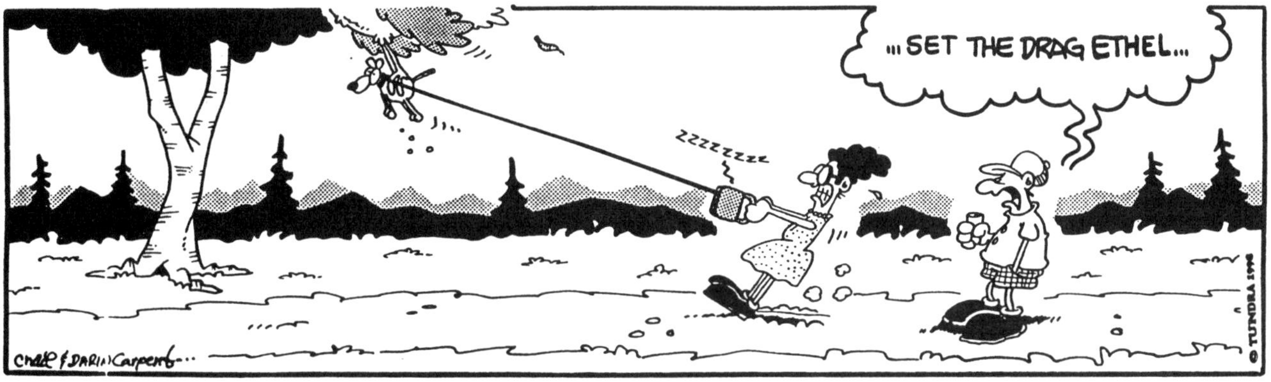
...SET THE DRAG ETHEL...
ZZZZZZZZ
© TUNDRA 1998

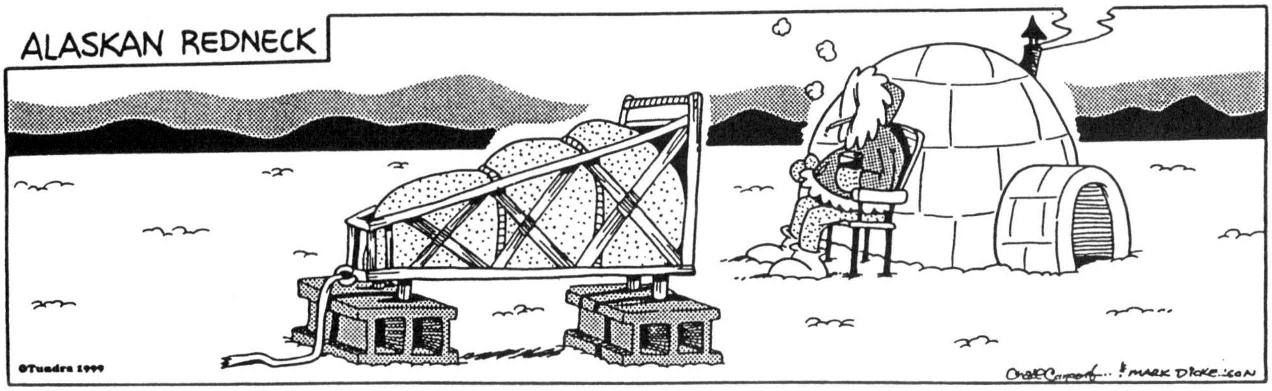
ALASKAN REDNECK
©Tundra 1999

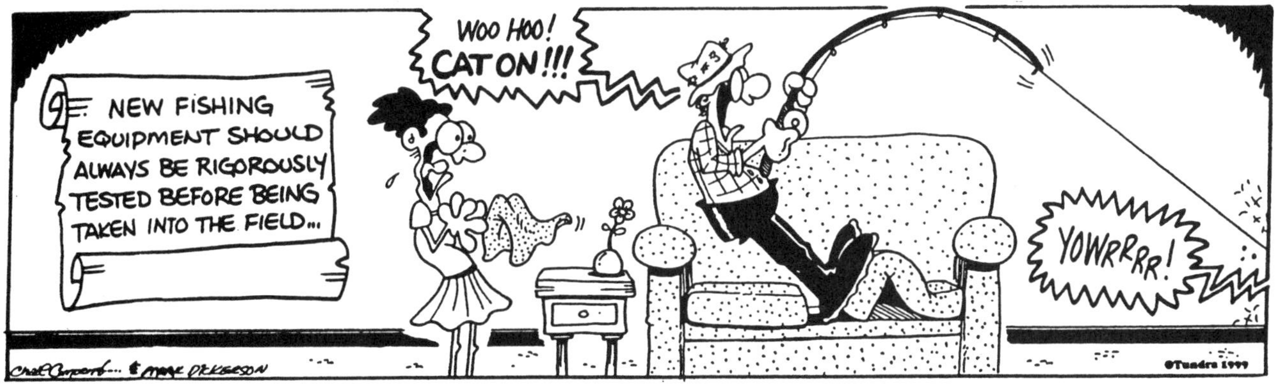
NEW FISHING EQUIPMENT SHOULD ALWAYS BE RIGOROUSLY TESTED BEFORE BEING TAKEN INTO THE FIELD...
WOO HOO! CAT ON!!!
YOWRRRR!
©Tundra 1999

Hobart

Serving as guru to the Tundra staff is Hobart. Hobart hails from the mountains of a tiny country in Northern Europe by the name of Hysteria. After what was intended to be a two-week vacation to visit his cousin Andy in Gangrene Gulch, Hobart decided to become a permanent resident. His official reasoning for this drastic move was to help enlighten the ignorant masses. However, there have been rumors of large gambling debts and indecent exposure charges back in his homeland. When questioned about these strange reports, Hobart will simply say "*Only the mountain can square dance with the forest,*" and then feign an attack of narcolepsy.

Mr. Dale

Filling in as the comic strip's friendly neighborhood snake-oil salesman is Mr. Dale. Anytime an opportunity arises to liberate somebody from some or all of their cash, Mr. Dale is there to help... himself. With all the charm of an unlanced boil, Mr. Dale spends 23 hours a day coming up with new & imaginative ways to get rich quick at the expense of others. The remaining hour of the day he spends making prank phone calls. While some describe him as the lowest, greediest, foulest, most slimy creature on the planet, others don't like him quite that much.

Chapter Seven

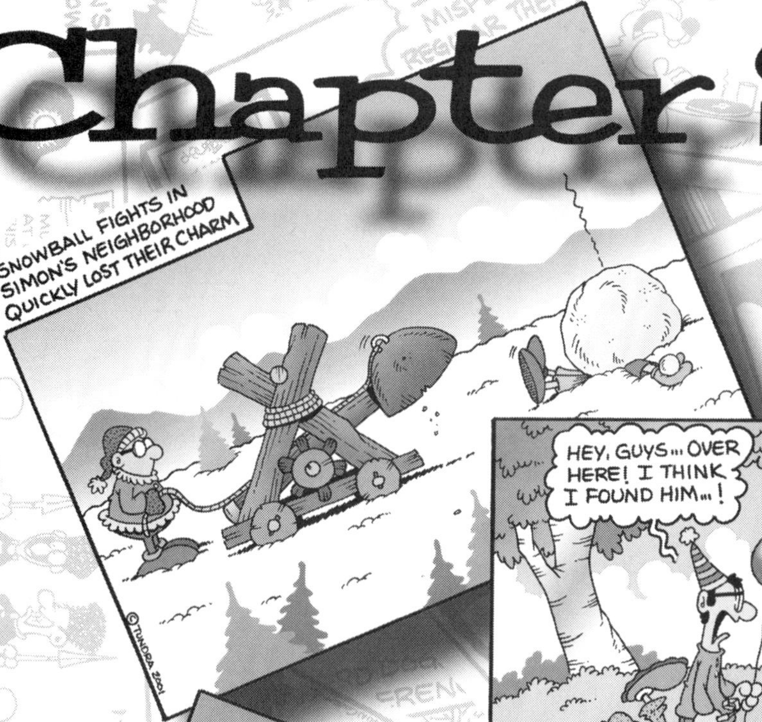

SNOWBALL FIGHTS IN SIMON'S NEIGHBORHOOD QUICKLY LOST THEIR CHARM
©TUNDRA 2001

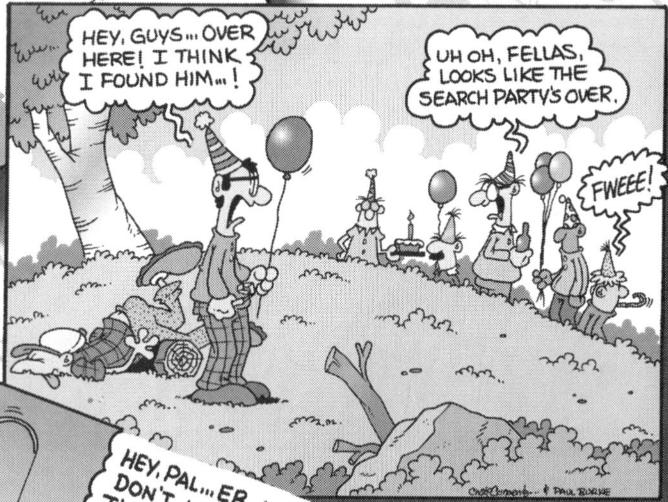

HEY, GUYS... OVER HERE! I THINK I FOUND HIM...!
UH OH, FELLAS, LOOKS LIKE THE SEARCH PARTY'S OVER.
FWEEE!

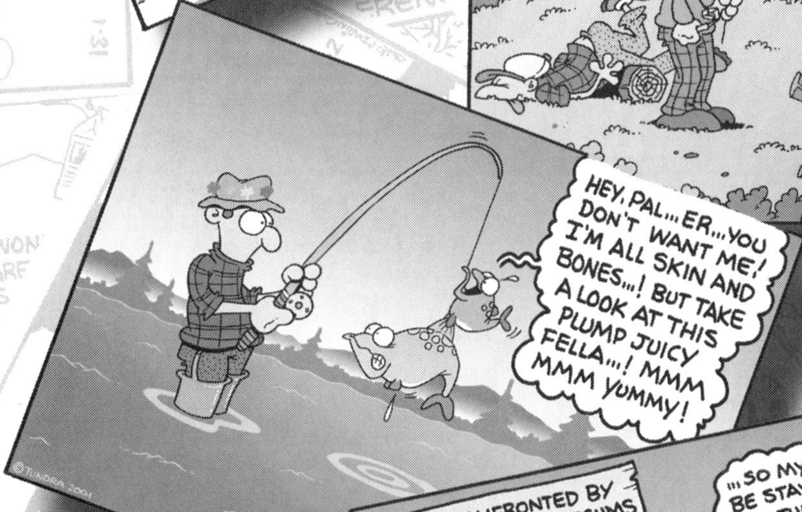

HEY, PAL... ER... YOU DON'T WANT ME! I'M ALL SKIN AND BONES...! BUT TAKE A LOOK AT THIS PLUMP JUICY FELLA...! MMM MMM YUMMY!
©TUNDRA 2001

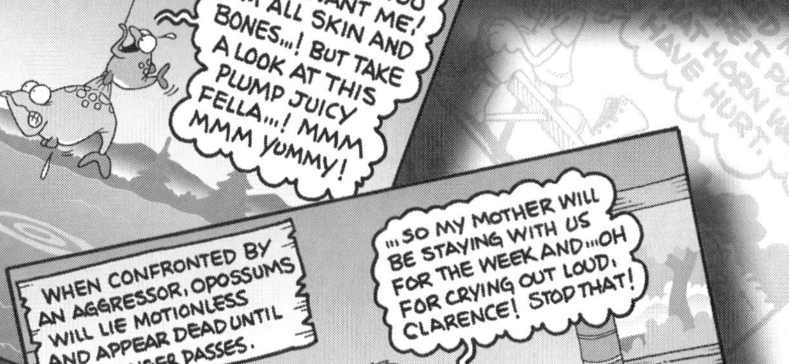

WHEN CONFRONTED BY AN AGGRESSOR, OPOSSUMS WILL LIE MOTIONLESS AND APPEAR DEAD UNTIL THE DANGER PASSES.
...SO MY MOTHER WILL BE STAYING WITH US FOR THE WEEK AND...OH FOR CRYING OUT LOUD, CLARENCE! STOP THAT!
© TUNDRA 2001

The New Stuff...

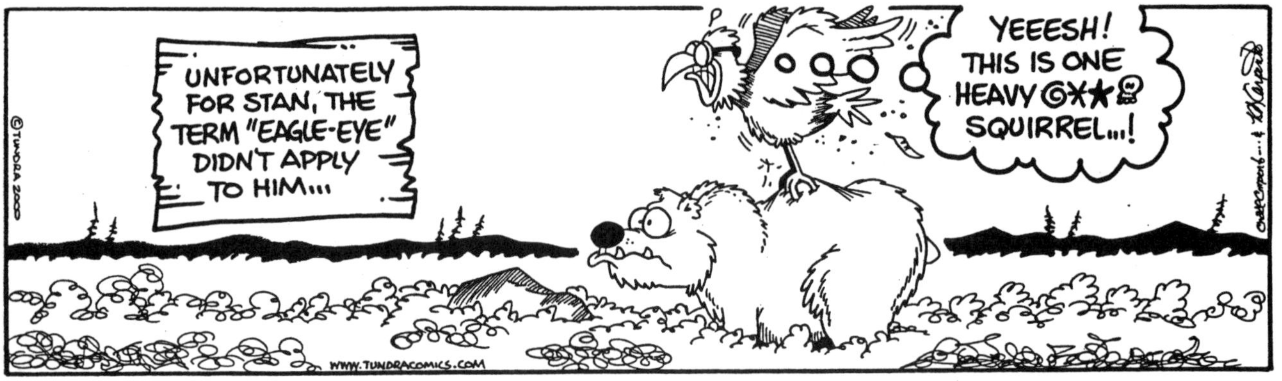
UNFORTUNATELY FOR STAN, THE TERM "EAGLE-EYE" DIDN'T APPLY TO HIM...
YEEESH! THIS IS ONE HEAVY @X★☠ SQUIRREL...!
©TUNDRA 2000
WWW.TUNDRACOMICS.COM

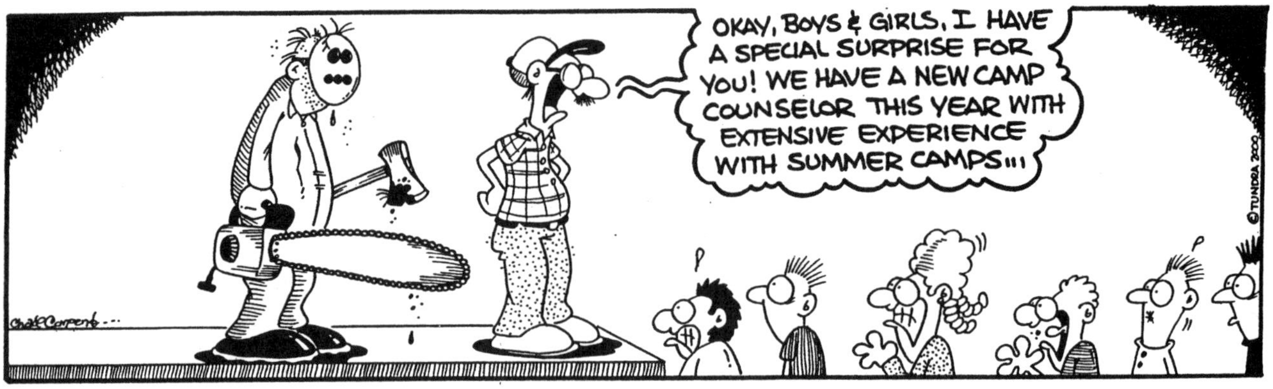
OKAY, BOYS & GIRLS, I HAVE A SPECIAL SURPRISE FOR YOU! WE HAVE A NEW CAMP COUNSELOR THIS YEAR WITH EXTENSIVE EXPERIENCE WITH SUMMER CAMPS...
©TUNDRA 2000

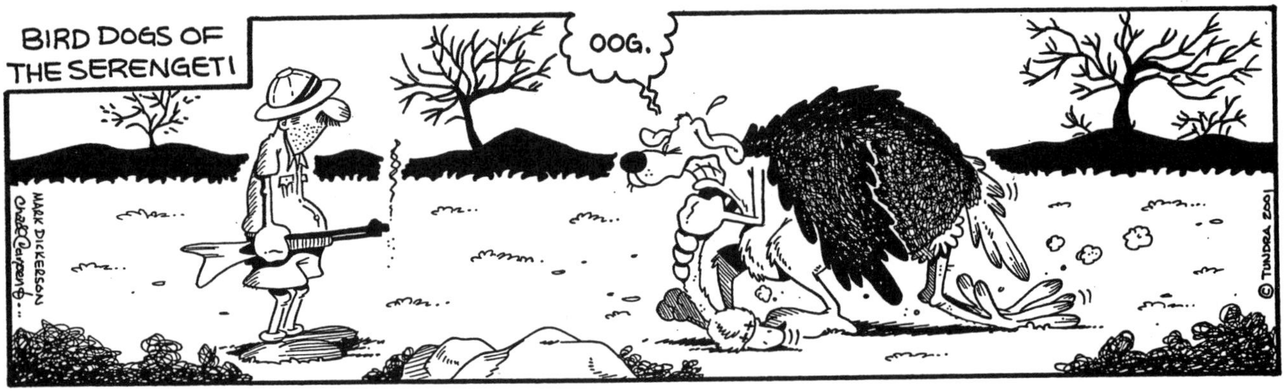
BIRD DOGS OF THE SERENGETI
OOG.
MARK DICKERSON
©TUNDRA 2001

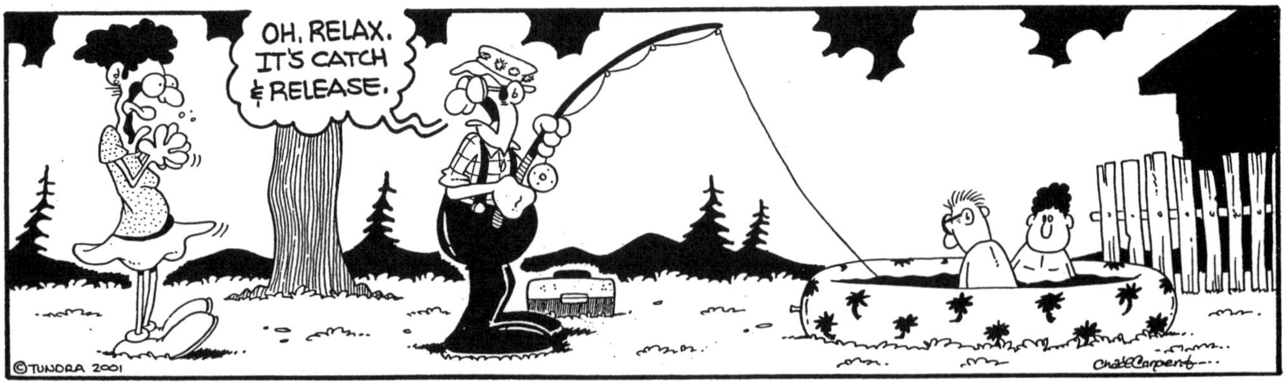
OH, RELAX. IT'S CATCH & RELEASE.
©TUNDRA 2001

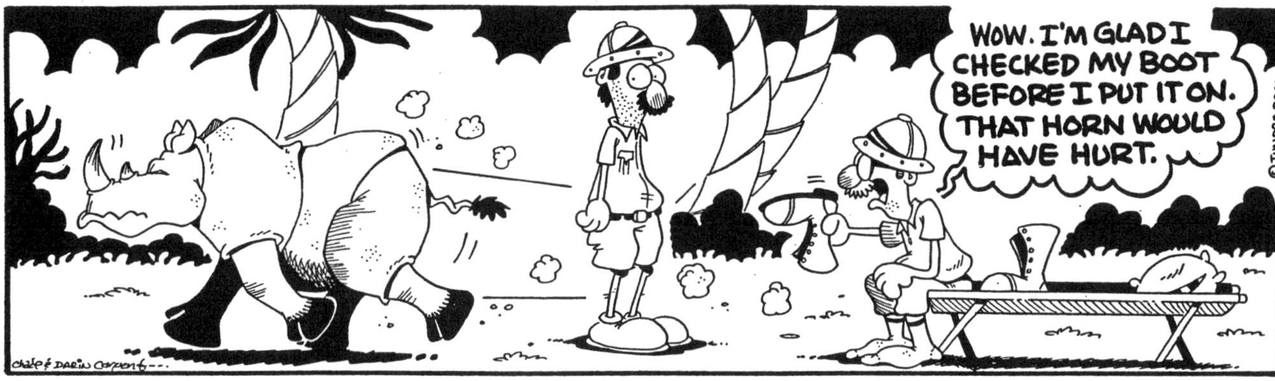
WOW. I'M GLAD I CHECKED MY BOOT BEFORE I PUT IT ON. THAT HORN WOULD HAVE HURT.
© TUNDRA 2001
Chad & Darin Carpenter...

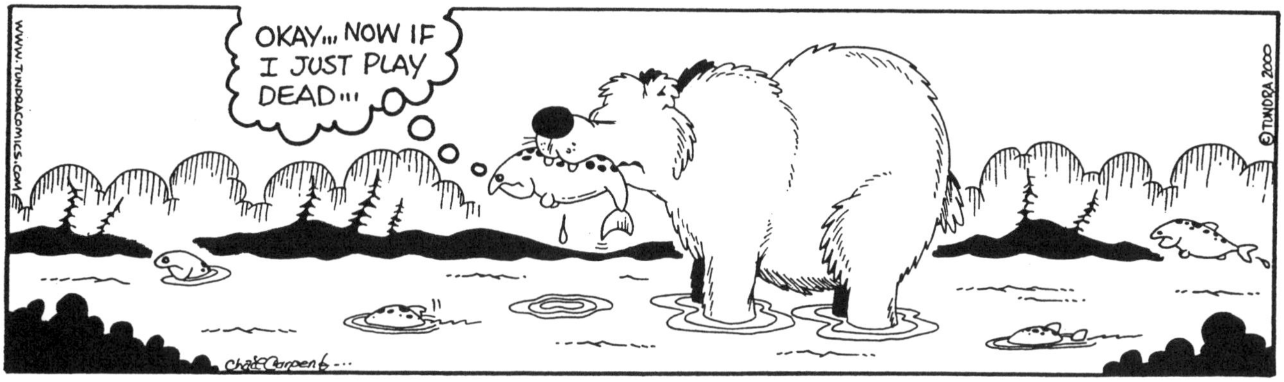
OKAY... NOW IF I JUST PLAY DEAD...
WWW.TUNDRACOMICS.COM
© TUNDRA 2000
Chad Carpenter...

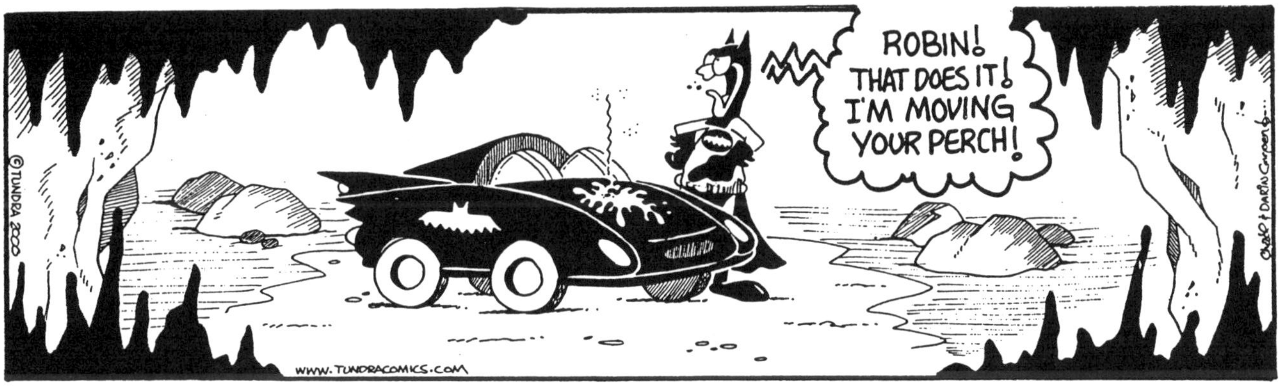
ROBIN! THAT DOES IT! I'M MOVING YOUR PERCH!
© TUNDRA 2000
Chad & Darin Carpenter...
WWW.TUNDRACOMICS.COM

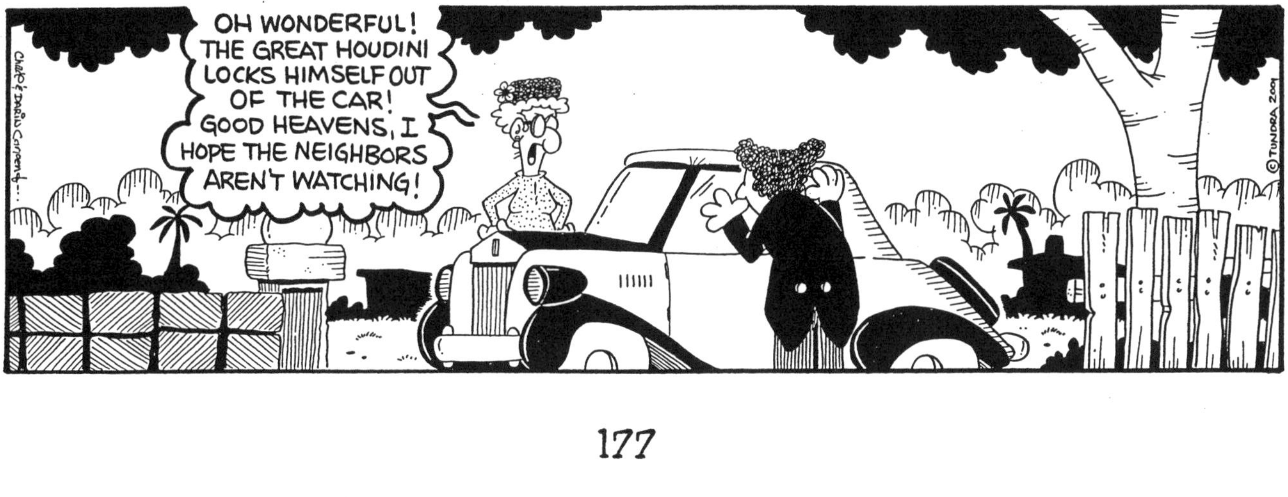
OH WONDERFUL! THE GREAT HOUDINI LOCKS HIMSELF OUT OF THE CAR! GOOD HEAVENS, I HOPE THE NEIGHBORS AREN'T WATCHING!
Chad & Darin Carpenter...
© TUNDRA 2001

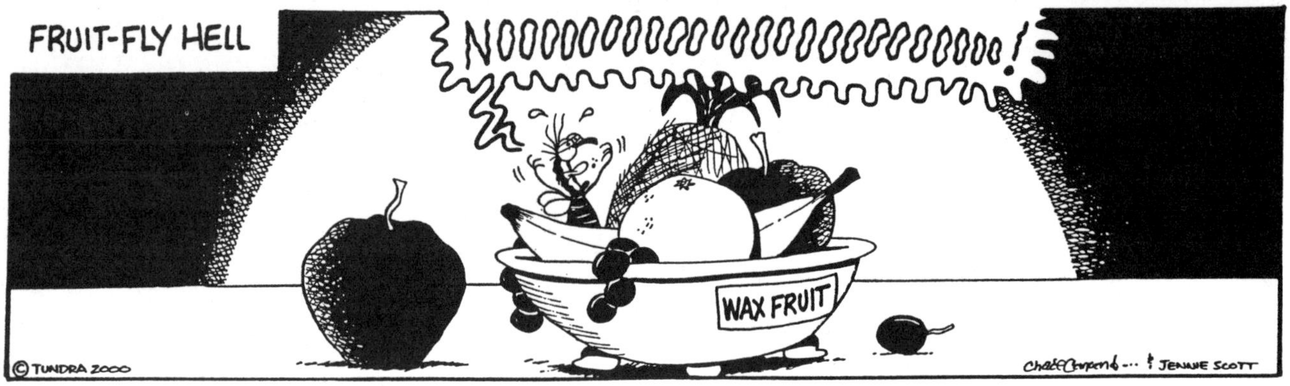
FRUIT-FLY HELL
NOOOOOOOOOOOOOOOOOOOOOOOOOOOO!
WAX FRUIT
© TUNDRA 2000
Chad Carpenter... & JENNIE SCOTT

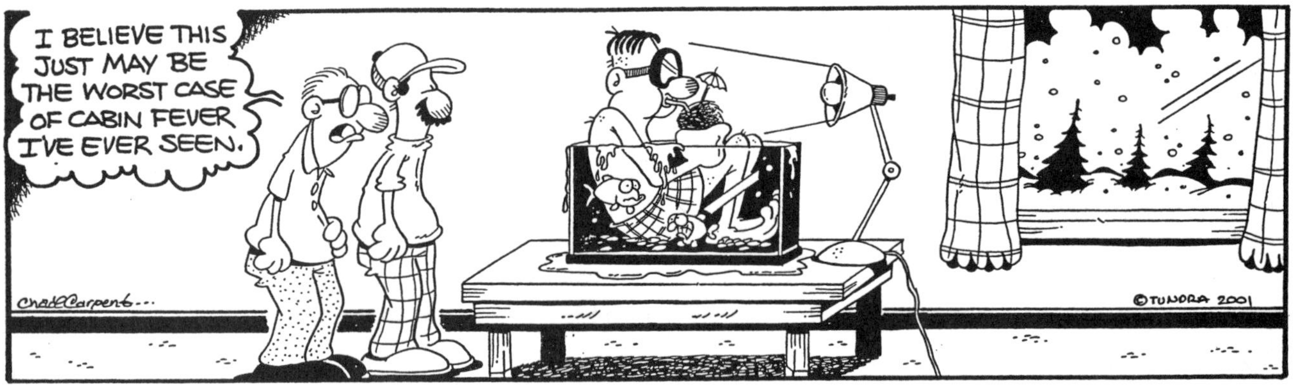
I BELIEVE THIS JUST MAY BE THE WORST CASE OF CABIN FEVER I'VE EVER SEEN.
Chad Carpenter...
© TUNDRA 2001

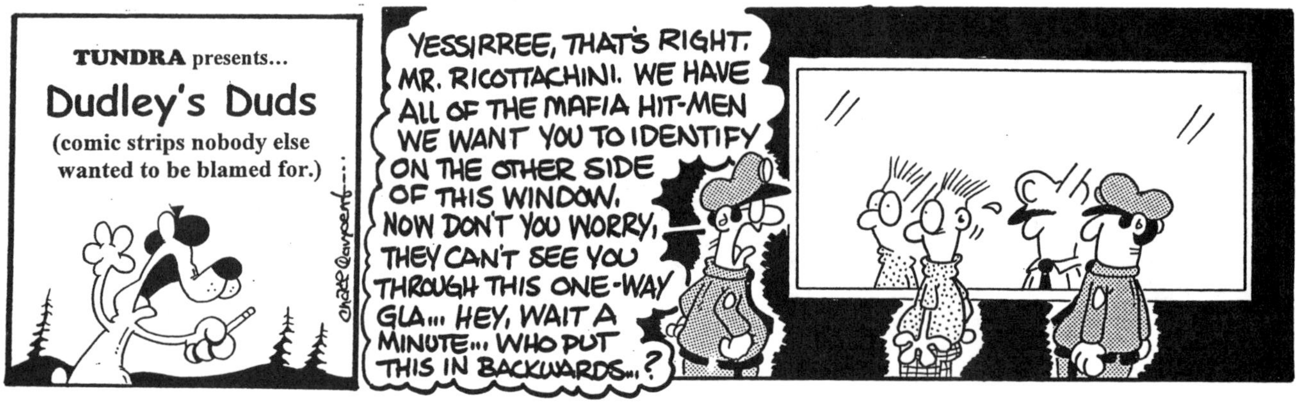
TUNDRA presents...
Dudley's Duds
(comic strips nobody else wanted to be blamed for.)
Chad Carpenter...
YESSIRREE, THAT'S RIGHT, MR. RICOTTACHINI. WE HAVE ALL OF THE MAFIA HIT-MEN WE WANT YOU TO IDENTIFY ON THE OTHER SIDE OF THIS WINDOW. NOW DON'T YOU WORRY, THEY CAN'T SEE YOU THROUGH THIS ONE-WAY GLA... HEY, WAIT A MINUTE... WHO PUT THIS IN BACKWARDS...?

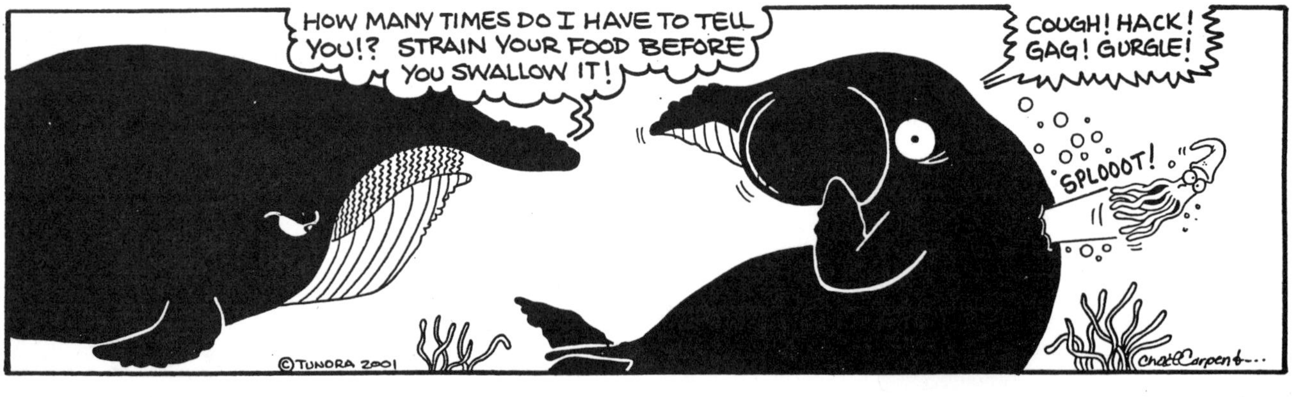
HOW MANY TIMES DO I HAVE TO TELL YOU!? STRAIN YOUR FOOD BEFORE YOU SWALLOW IT!
COUGH! HACK! GAG! GURGLE!
SPLOOOT!
© TUNDRA 2001
Chad Carpenter...

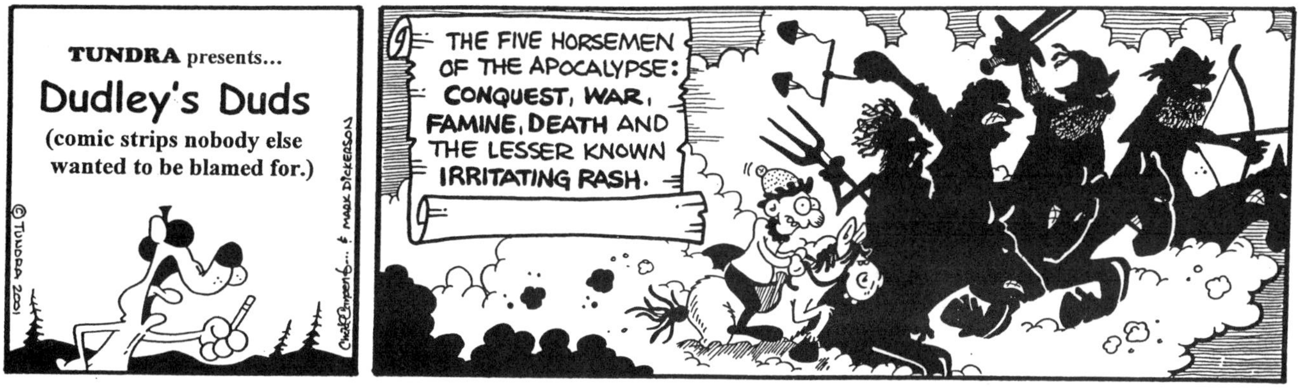
TUNDRA presents...
Dudley's Duds
(comic strips nobody else wanted to be blamed for.)
© TUNDRA 2001
THE FIVE HORSEMEN OF THE APOCALYPSE: CONQUEST, WAR, FAMINE, DEATH AND THE LESSER KNOWN IRRITATING RASH.

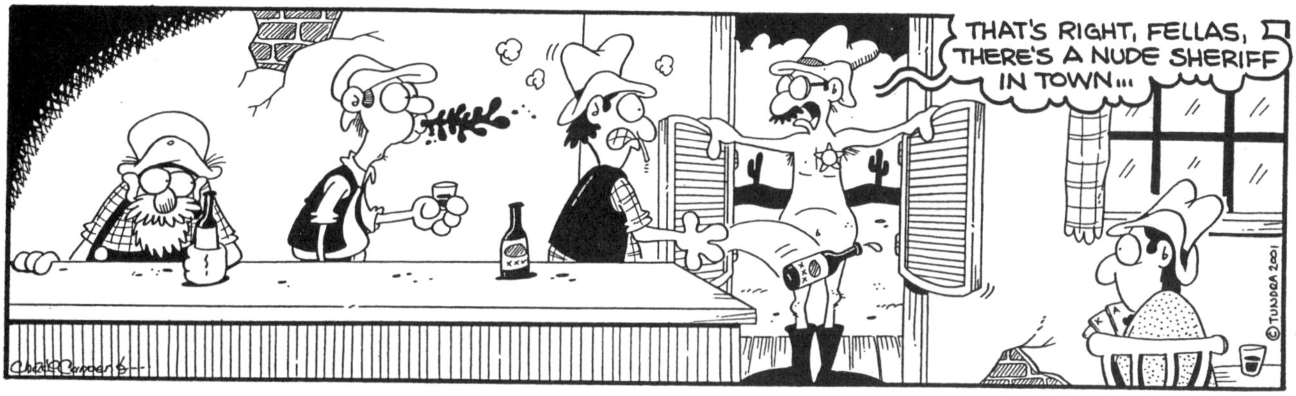
THAT'S RIGHT, FELLAS, THERE'S A NUDE SHERIFF IN TOWN...
© TUNDRA 2001

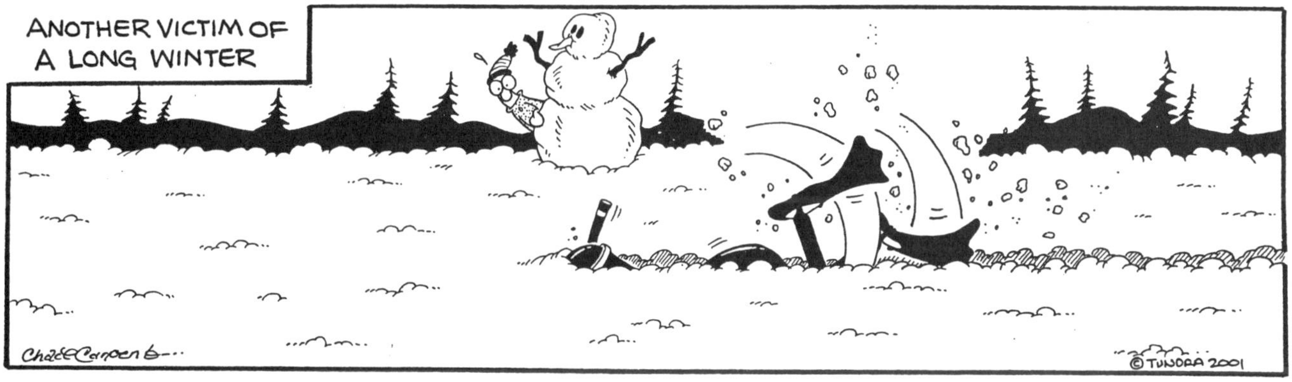
ANOTHER VICTIM OF A LONG WINTER
© TUNDRA 2001

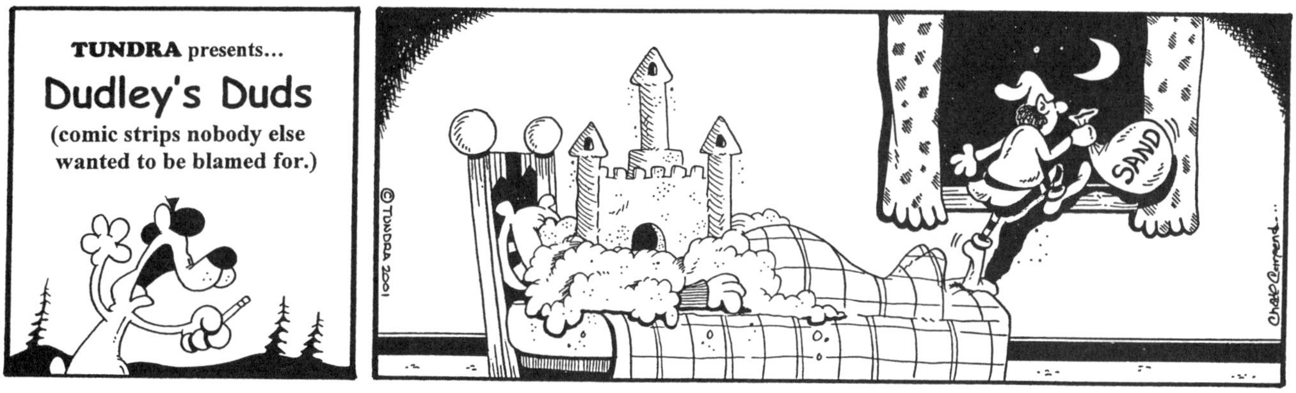
TUNDRA presents...
Dudley's Duds
(comic strips nobody else wanted to be blamed for.)
© TUNDRA 2001
SAND

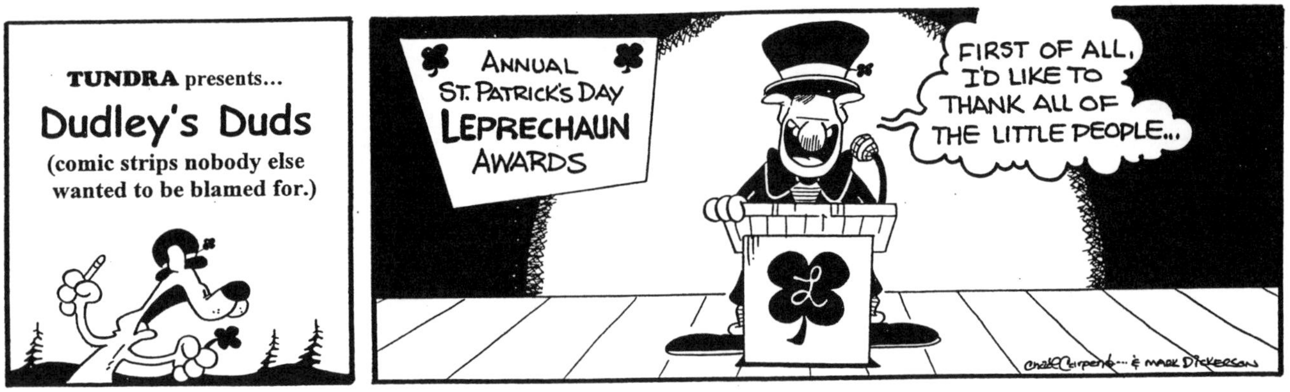
TUNDRA presents...
Dudley's Duds
(comic strips nobody else wanted to be blamed for.)
ANNUAL ST. PATRICK'S DAY LEPRECHAUN AWARDS
FIRST OF ALL, I'D LIKE TO THANK ALL OF THE LITTLE PEOPLE...
Chad Carpenter... & MARK DICKERSON

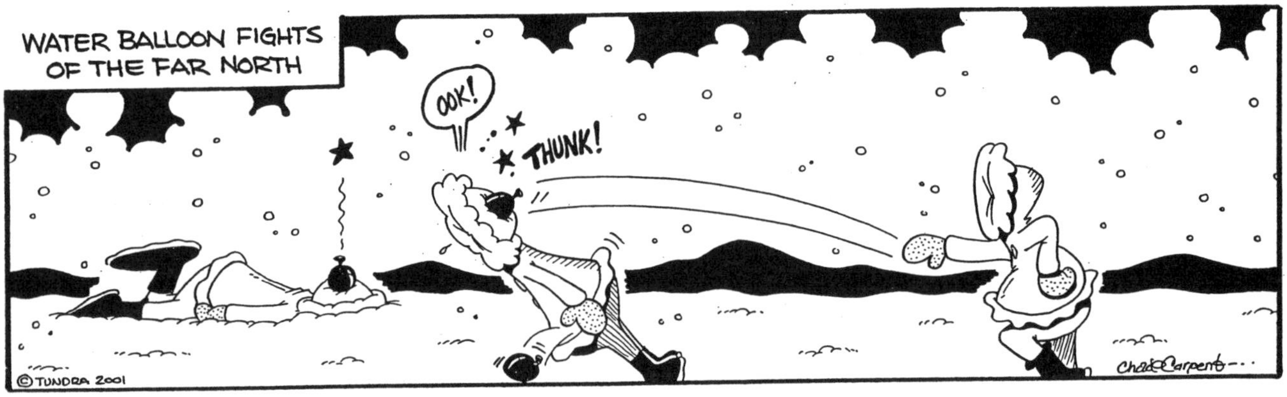
WATER BALLOON FIGHTS OF THE FAR NORTH
OOK!
THUNK!
© TUNDRA 2001
Chad Carpenter...

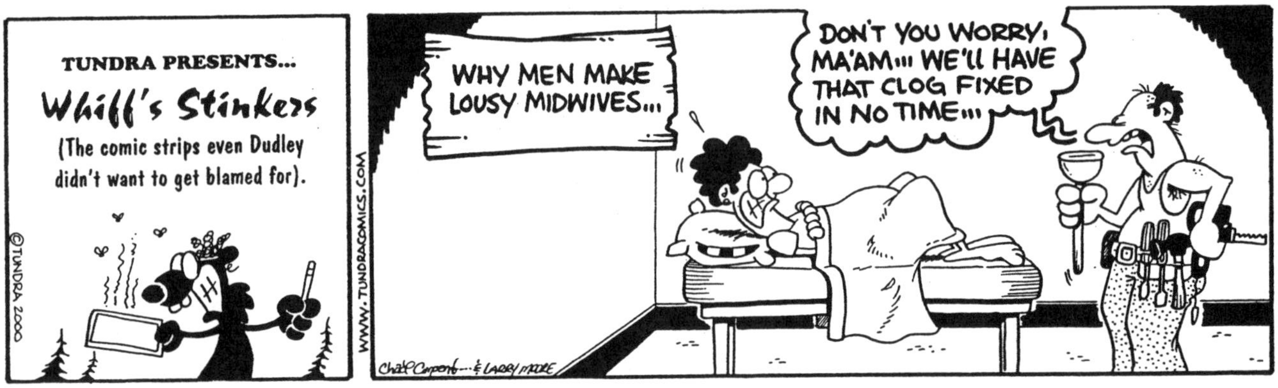
TUNDRA PRESENTS...
Whiff's Stinkers
(The comic strips even Dudley didn't want to get blamed for).
© TUNDRA 2000
WWW.TUNDRACOMICS.COM
WHY MEN MAKE LOUSY MIDWIVES...
DON'T YOU WORRY, MA'AM... WE'LL HAVE THAT CLOG FIXED IN NO TIME...
Chad Carpenter... & LARRY MOORE

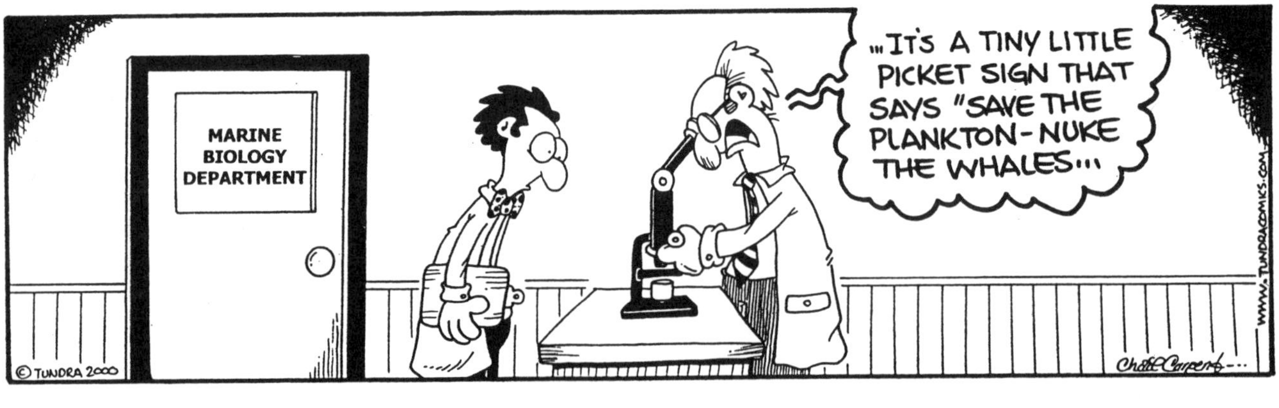
MARINE BIOLOGY DEPARTMENT
...IT'S A TINY LITTLE PICKET SIGN THAT SAYS "SAVE THE PLANKTON-NUKE THE WHALES"...
WWW.TUNDRACOMICS.COM
© TUNDRA 2000
Chad Carpenter...

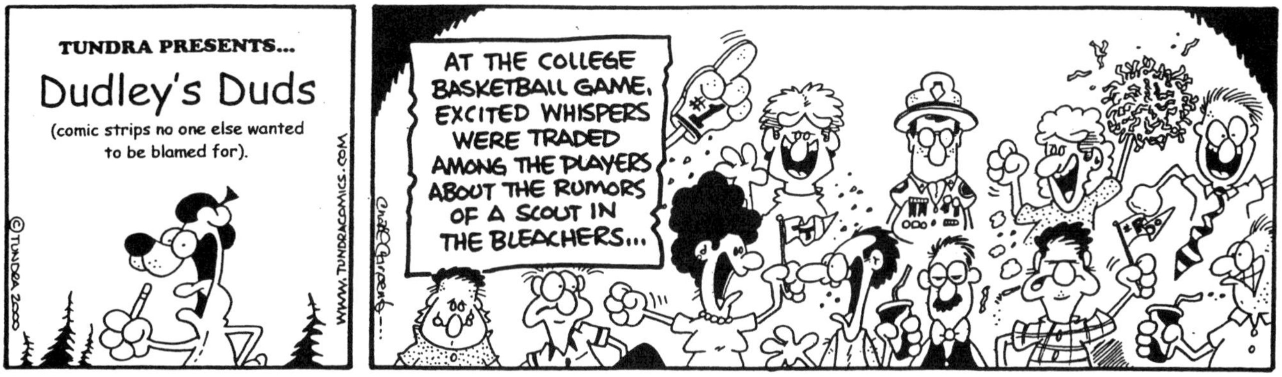
TUNDRA PRESENTS...
Dudley's Duds
(comic strips no one else wanted to be blamed for).
© TUNDRA 2000
WWW.TUNDRACOMICS.COM
AT THE COLLEGE BASKETBALL GAME, EXCITED WHISPERS WERE TRADED AMONG THE PLAYERS ABOUT THE RUMORS OF A SCOUT IN THE BLEACHERS...
#1

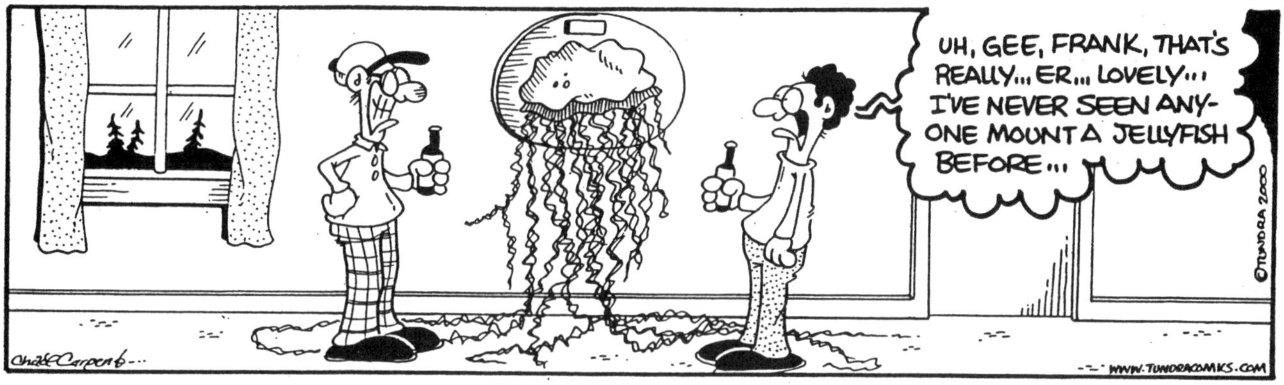
UH, GEE, FRANK, THAT'S REALLY... ER... LOVELY... I'VE NEVER SEEN ANY-ONE MOUNT A JELLYFISH BEFORE...
© TUNDRA 2000
WWW.TUNDRACOMICS.COM

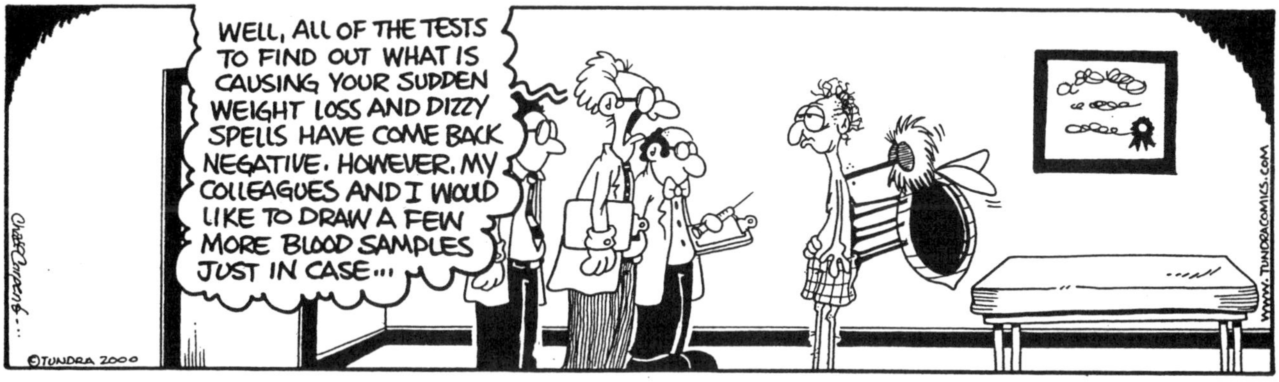
WELL, ALL OF THE TESTS TO FIND OUT WHAT IS CAUSING YOUR SUDDEN WEIGHT LOSS AND DIZZY SPELLS HAVE COME BACK NEGATIVE. HOWEVER, MY COLLEAGUES AND I WOULD LIKE TO DRAW A FEW MORE BLOOD SAMPLES JUST IN CASE...
© TUNDRA 2000
WWW.TUNDRACOMICS.COM

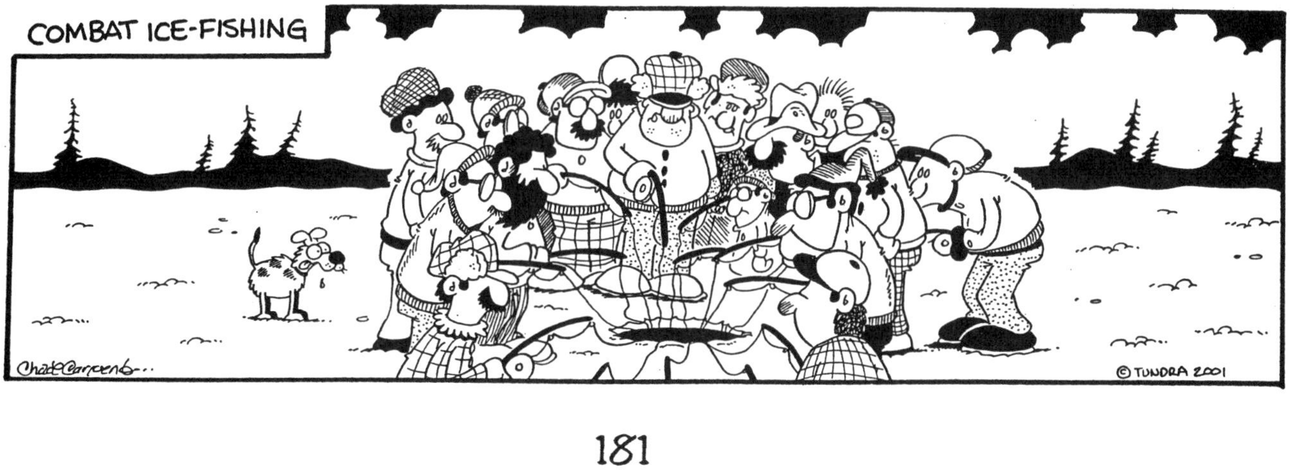
COMBAT ICE-FISHING
© TUNDRA 2001

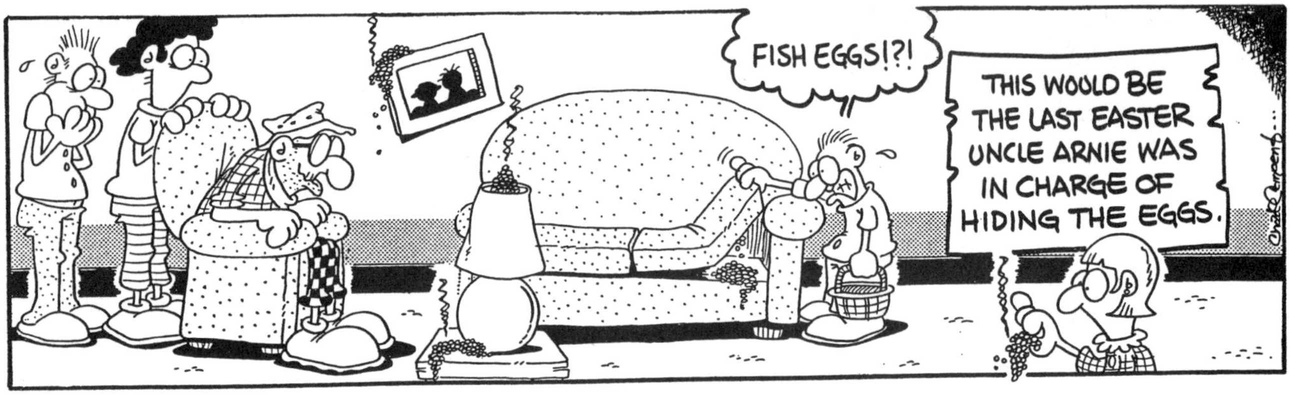
FISH EGGS!?!
THIS WOULD BE THE LAST EASTER UNCLE ARNIE WAS IN CHARGE OF HIDING THE EGGS.

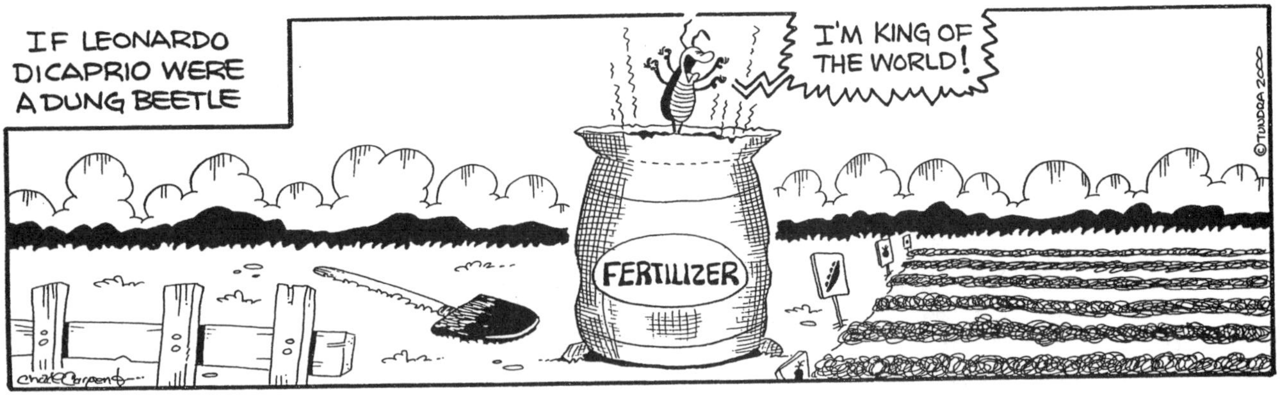
IF LEONARDO DICAPRIO WERE A DUNG BEETLE
I'M KING OF THE WORLD!
FERTILIZER
©TUNDRA 2000

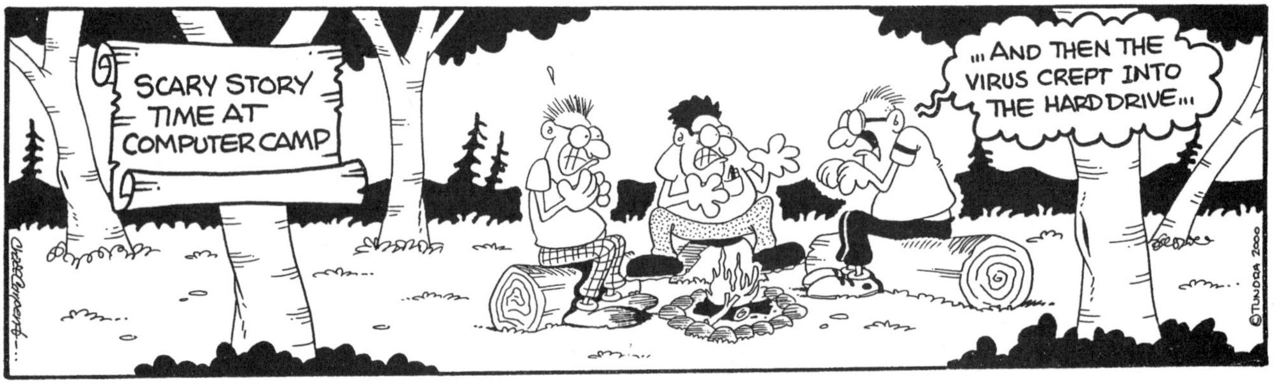
SCARY STORY TIME AT COMPUTER CAMP
...AND THEN THE VIRUS CREPT INTO THE HARD DRIVE...
©TUNDRA 2000

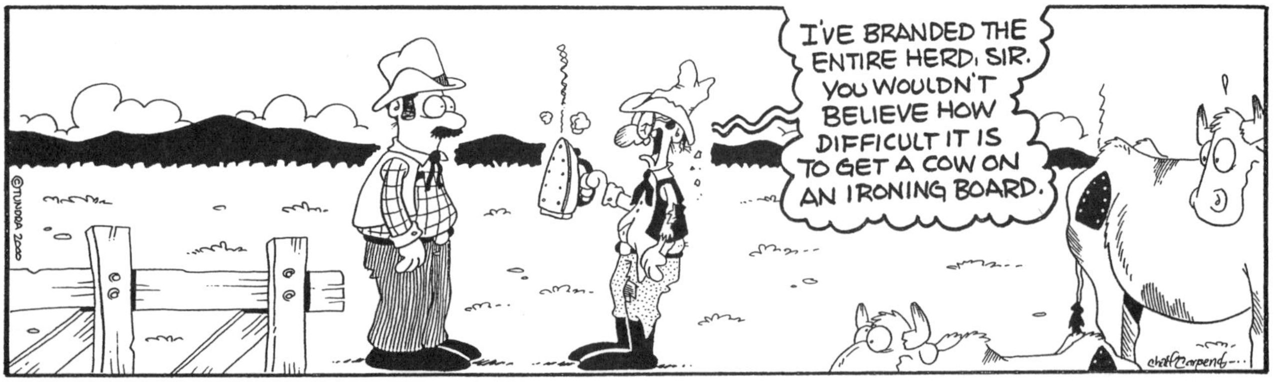
I'VE BRANDED THE ENTIRE HERD, SIR. YOU WOULDN'T BELIEVE HOW DIFFICULT IT IS TO GET A COW ON AN IRONING BOARD.
©TUNDRA 2000

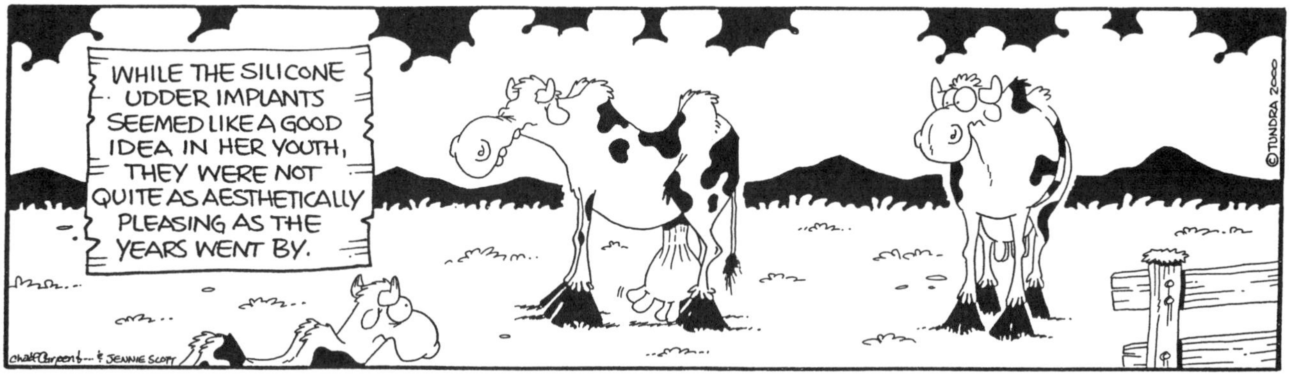
WHILE THE SILICONE UDDER IMPLANTS SEEMED LIKE A GOOD IDEA IN HER YOUTH, THEY WERE NOT QUITE AS AESTHETICALLY PLEASING AS THE YEARS WENT BY.
©TUNDRA 2000

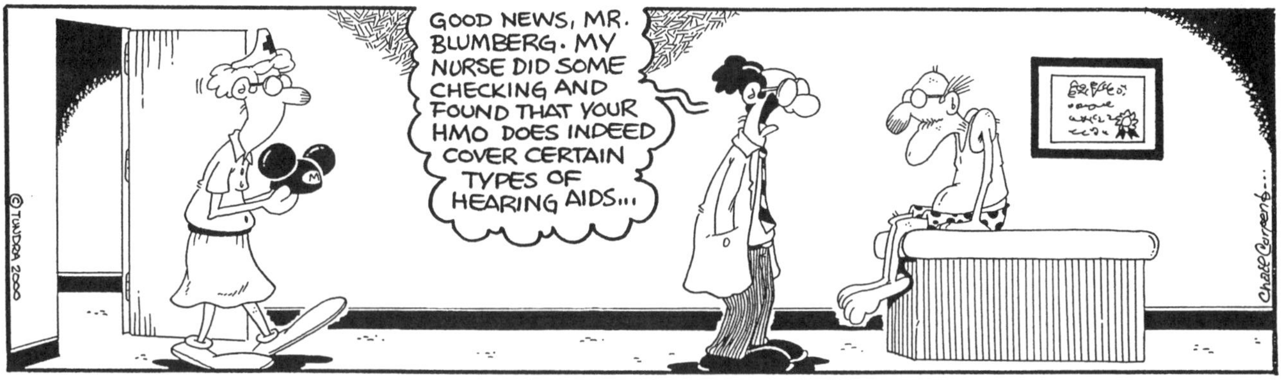
GOOD NEWS, MR. BLUMBERG. MY NURSE DID SOME CHECKING AND FOUND THAT YOUR HMO DOES INDEED COVER CERTAIN TYPES OF HEARING AIDS...
©TUNDRA 2000

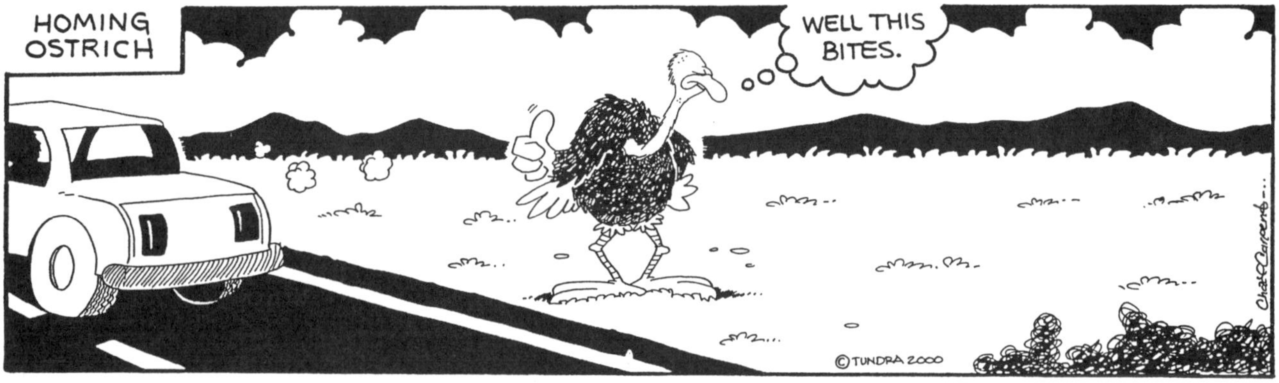
HOMING OSTRICH
WELL THIS BITES.
©TUNDRA 2000

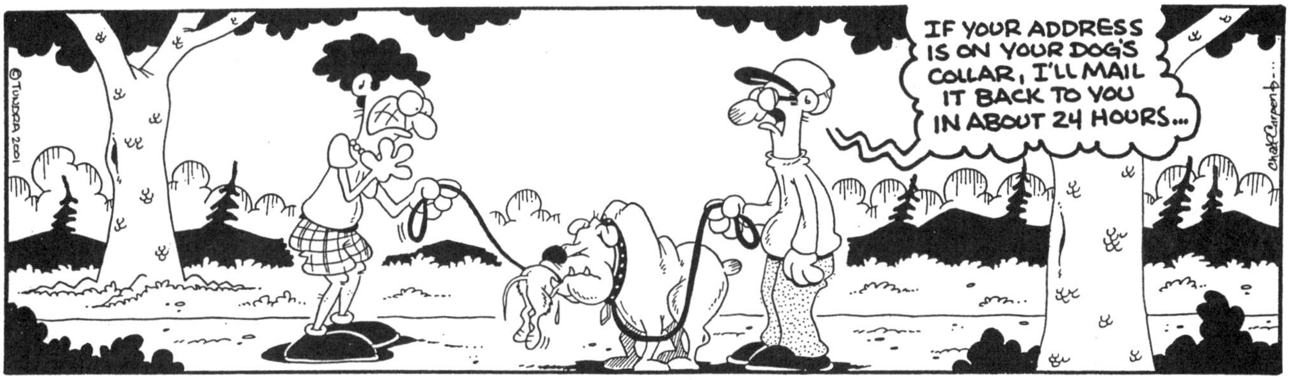
IF YOUR ADDRESS IS ON YOUR DOG'S COLLAR, I'LL MAIL IT BACK TO YOU IN ABOUT 24 HOURS...
©TUNDRA 2001

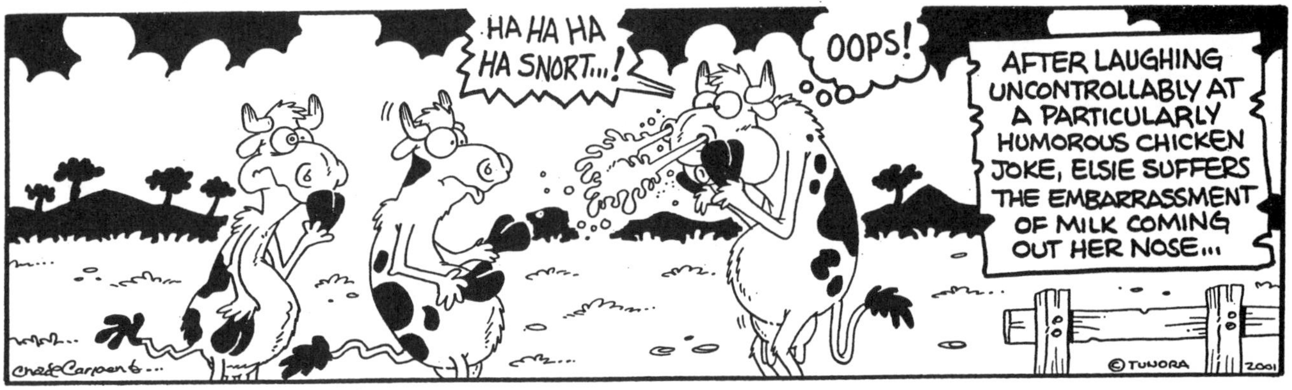
HA HA HA HA SNORT...!
OOPS!
AFTER LAUGHING UNCONTROLLABLY AT A PARTICULARLY HUMOROUS CHICKEN JOKE, ELSIE SUFFERS THE EMBARRASSMENT OF MILK COMING OUT HER NOSE...
©TUNDRA 2001

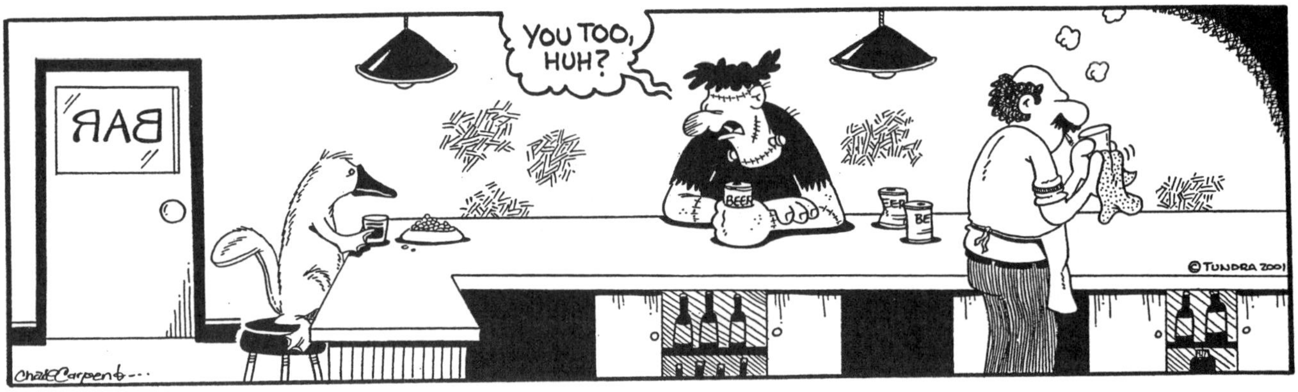
YOU TOO, HUH?
BAR
BEEF
©TUNDRA 2001

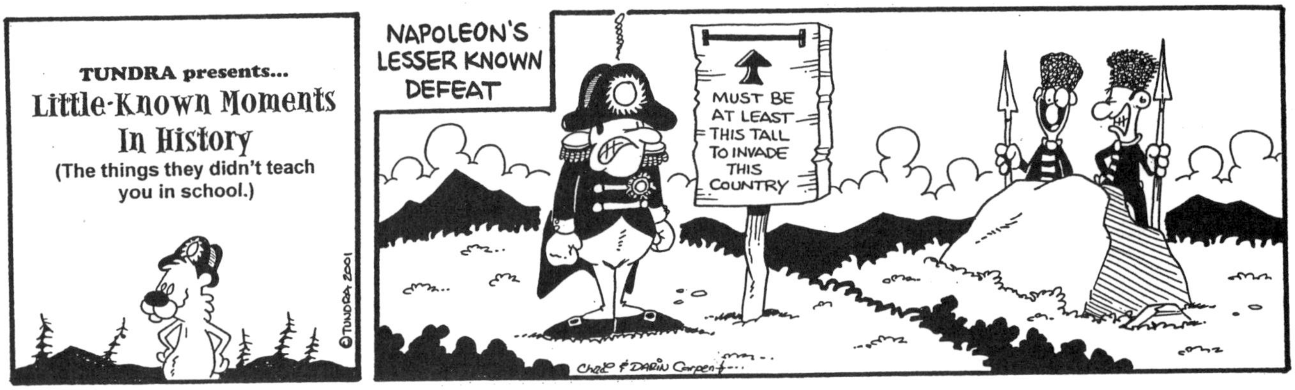
TUNDRA presents...
Little-Known Moments In History
(The things they didn't teach you in school.)
©TUNDRA 2001
NAPOLEON'S LESSER KNOWN DEFEAT
MUST BE AT LEAST THIS TALL TO INVADE THIS COUNTRY

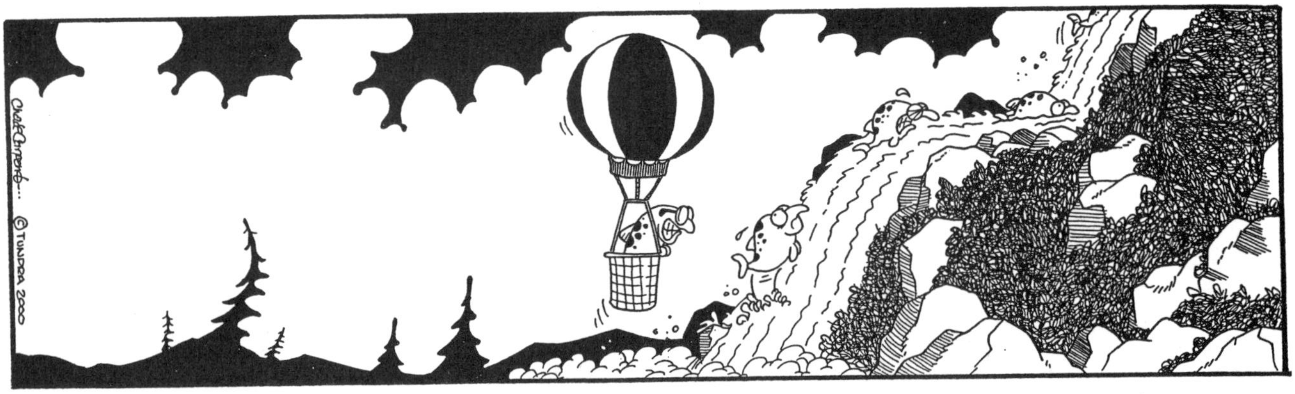
©TUNDRA 2000

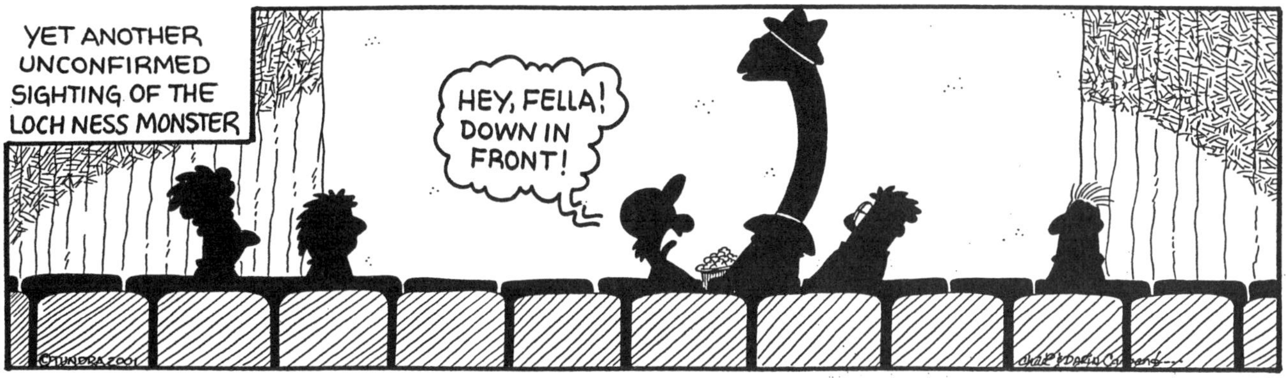

YET ANOTHER UNCONFIRMED SIGHTING OF THE LOCH NESS MONSTER
HEY, FELLA! DOWN IN FRONT!
©TUNDRA 2001

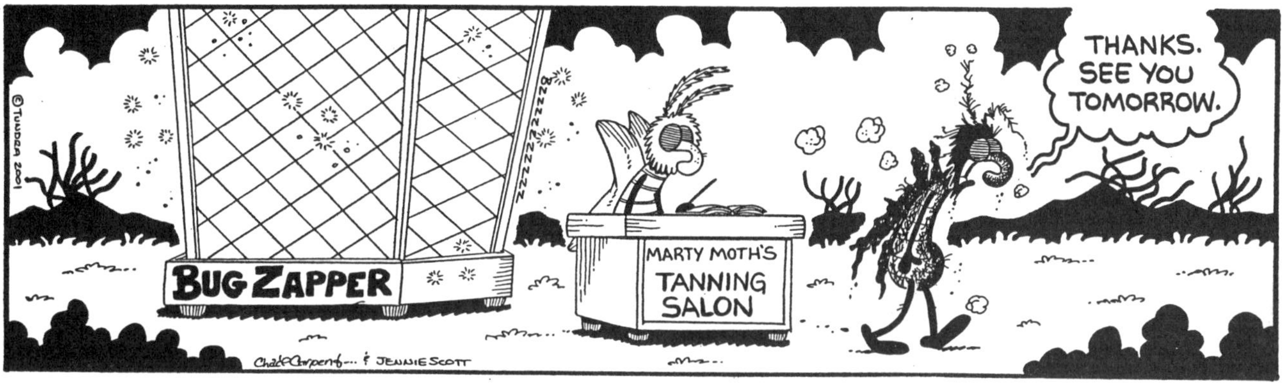

BUG ZAPPER
MARTY MOTH'S TANNING SALON
THANKS. SEE YOU TOMORROW.
©TUNDRA 2001

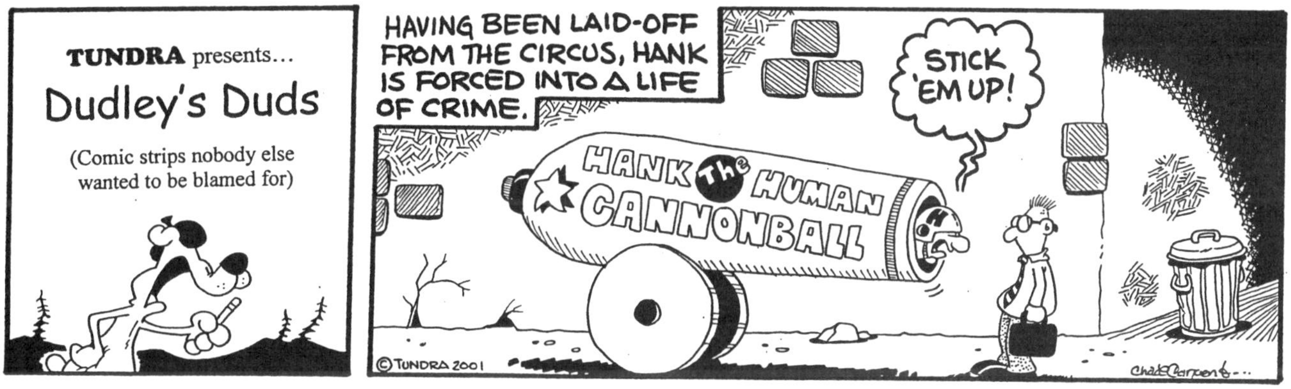

TUNDRA presents...
Dudley's Duds
(Comic strips nobody else wanted to be blamed for)
HAVING BEEN LAID-OFF FROM THE CIRCUS, HANK IS FORCED INTO A LIFE OF CRIME.
STICK 'EM UP!
HANK The HUMAN CANNONBALL
©TUNDRA 2001

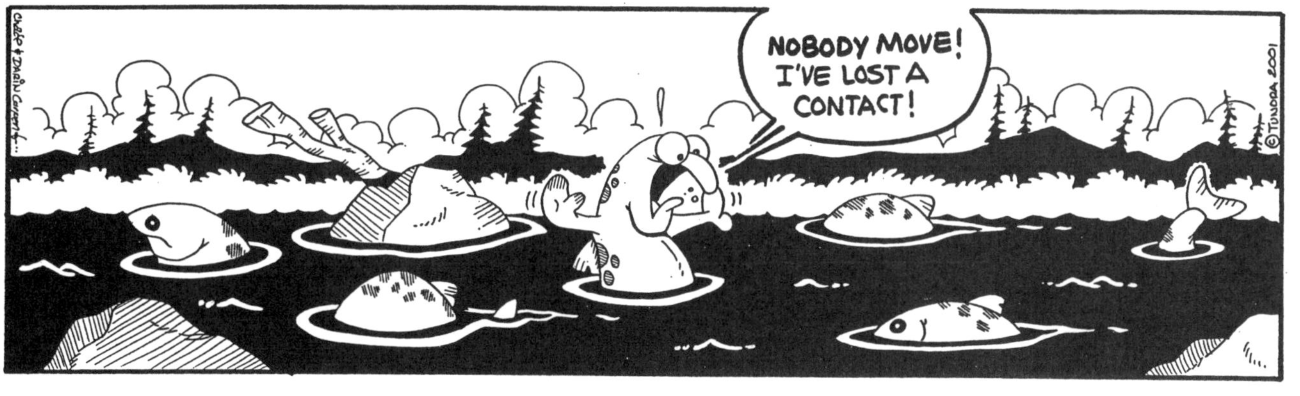

NOBODY MOVE! I'VE LOST A CONTACT!
©TUNDRA 2001

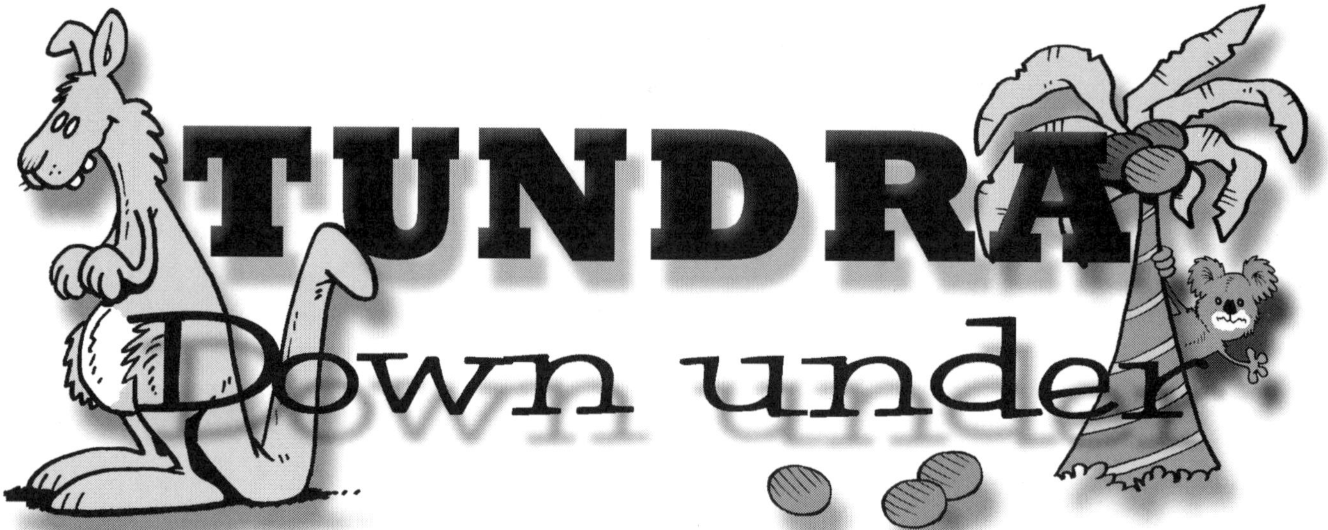
TUNDRA
Down under

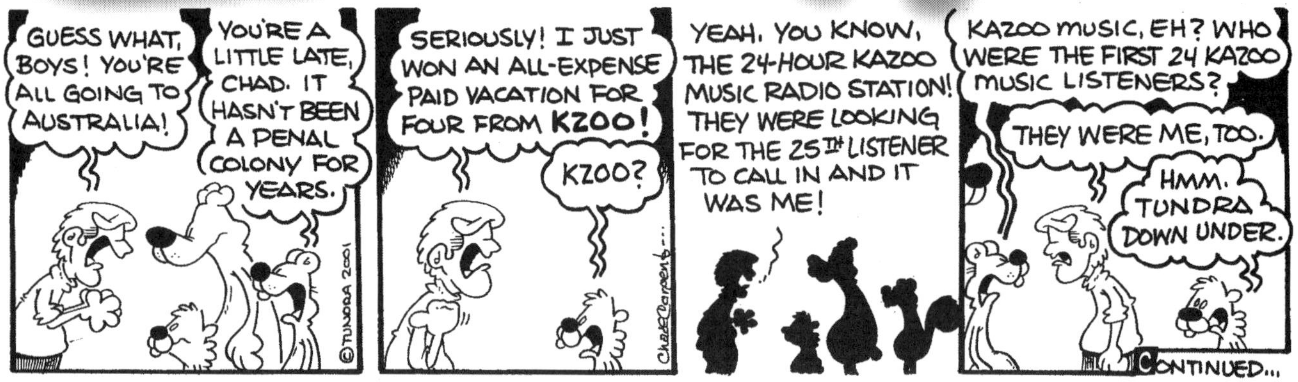
GUESS WHAT, BOYS! YOU'RE ALL GOING TO AUSTRALIA!
YOU'RE A LITTLE LATE, CHAD. IT HASN'T BEEN A PENAL COLONY FOR YEARS.
©TUNDRA 2001
SERIOUSLY! I JUST WON AN ALL-EXPENSE PAID VACATION FOR FOUR FROM KZOO!
KZOO?
YEAH. YOU KNOW, THE 24-HOUR KAZOO MUSIC RADIO STATION! THEY WERE LOOKING FOR THE 25TH LISTENER TO CALL IN AND IT WAS ME!
KAZOO MUSIC, EH? WHO WERE THE FIRST 24 KAZOO MUSIC LISTENERS?
THEY WERE ME, TOO.
HMM. TUNDRA DOWN UNDER.
CONTINUED...

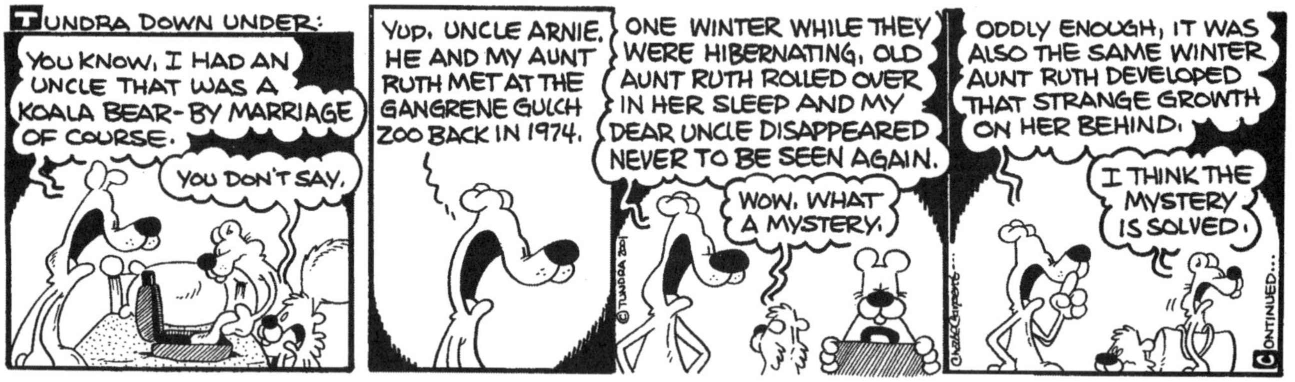
TUNDRA DOWN UNDER:
YOU KNOW, I HAD AN UNCLE THAT WAS A KOALA BEAR- BY MARRIAGE OF COURSE.
YOU DON'T SAY.
YUP. UNCLE ARNIE. HE AND MY AUNT RUTH MET AT THE GANGRENE GULCH ZOO BACK IN 1974.
ONE WINTER WHILE THEY WERE HIBERNATING, OLD AUNT RUTH ROLLED OVER IN HER SLEEP AND MY DEAR UNCLE DISAPPEARED NEVER TO BE SEEN AGAIN.
WOW. WHAT A MYSTERY.
©TUNDRA 2001
ODDLY ENOUGH, IT WAS ALSO THE SAME WINTER AUNT RUTH DEVELOPED THAT STRANGE GROWTH ON HER BEHIND.
I THINK THE MYSTERY IS SOLVED.
CONTINUED...

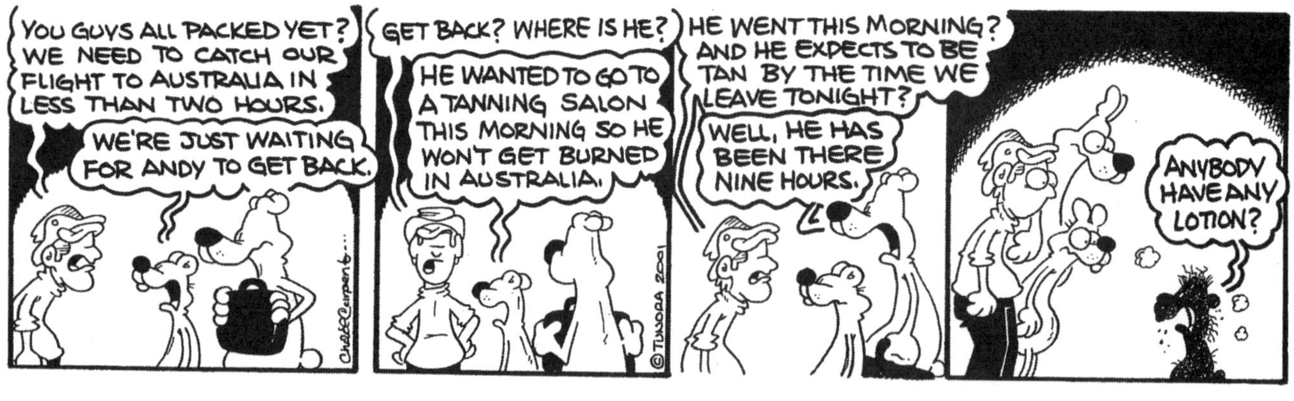
YOU GUYS ALL PACKED YET? WE NEED TO CATCH OUR FLIGHT TO AUSTRALIA IN LESS THAN TWO HOURS.
WE'RE JUST WAITING FOR ANDY TO GET BACK.
GET BACK? WHERE IS HE?
HE WANTED TO GO TO A TANNING SALON THIS MORNING SO HE WON'T GET BURNED IN AUSTRALIA.
©TUNDRA 2001
HE WENT THIS MORNING? AND HE EXPECTS TO BE TAN BY THE TIME WE LEAVE TONIGHT?
WELL, HE HAS BEEN THERE NINE HOURS.
ANYBODY HAVE ANY LOTION?

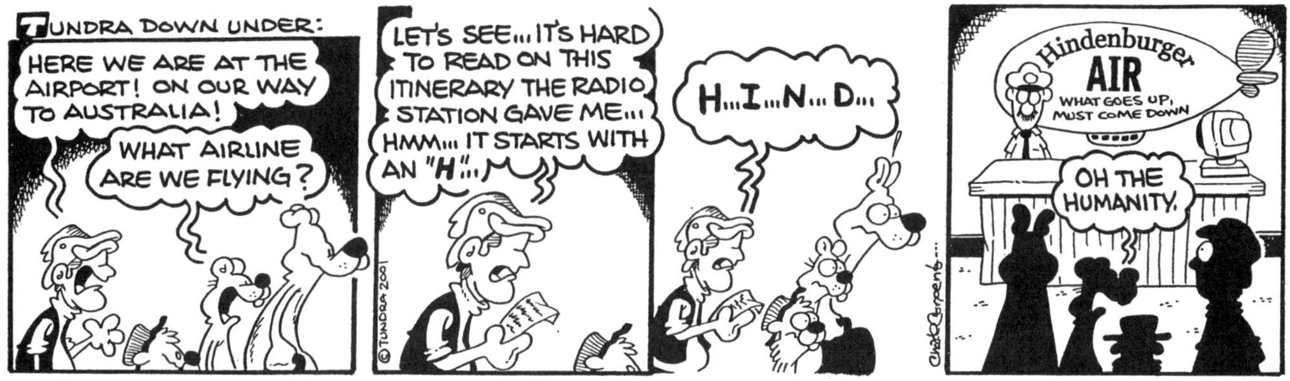
TUNDRA DOWN UNDER:
HERE WE ARE AT THE AIRPORT! ON OUR WAY TO AUSTRALIA!
WHAT AIRLINE ARE WE FLYING?
LET'S SEE... IT'S HARD TO READ ON THIS ITINERARY THE RADIO STATION GAVE ME... HMM... IT STARTS WITH AN "H"...
H...I...N...D...
Hindenburger AIR
WHAT GOES UP, MUST COME DOWN
OH THE HUMANITY.
© TUNDRA 2001

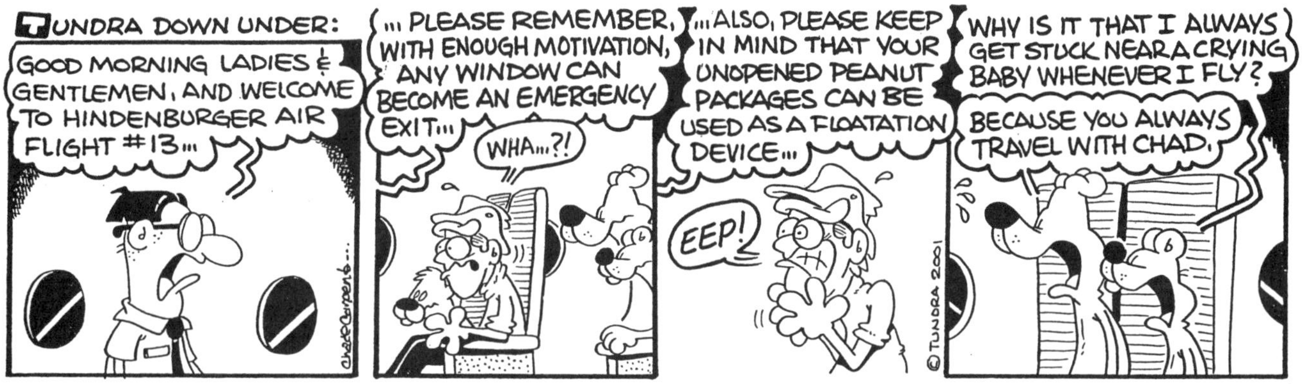
TUNDRA DOWN UNDER:
GOOD MORNING LADIES & GENTLEMEN, AND WELCOME TO HINDENBURGER AIR FLIGHT #13...
... PLEASE REMEMBER, WITH ENOUGH MOTIVATION, ANY WINDOW CAN BECOME AN EMERGENCY EXIT...
WHA...?!
...ALSO, PLEASE KEEP IN MIND THAT YOUR UNOPENED PEANUT PACKAGES CAN BE USED AS A FLOATATION DEVICE...
EEP!
WHY IS IT THAT I ALWAYS GET STUCK NEAR A CRYING BABY WHENEVER I FLY?
BECAUSE YOU ALWAYS TRAVEL WITH CHAD.
© TUNDRA 2001

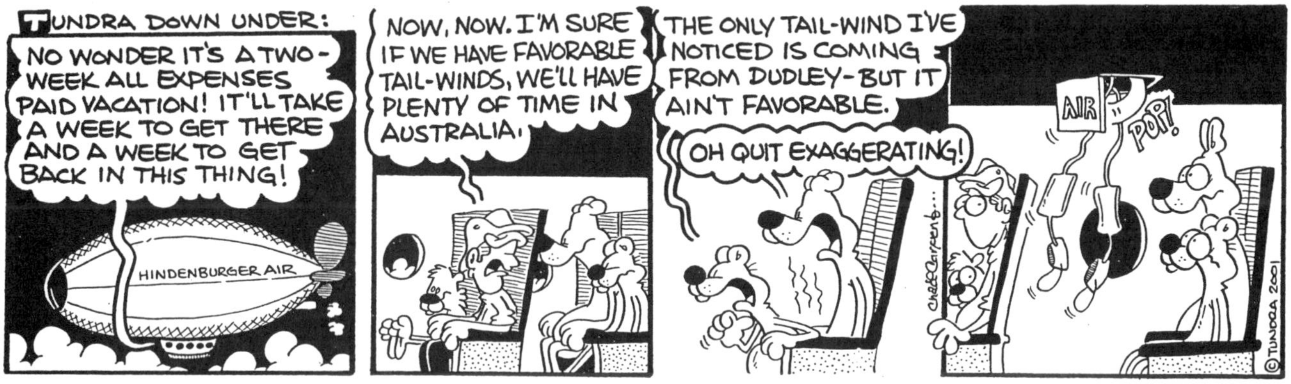
TUNDRA DOWN UNDER:
NO WONDER IT'S A TWO-WEEK ALL EXPENSES PAID VACATION! IT'LL TAKE A WEEK TO GET THERE AND A WEEK TO GET BACK IN THIS THING!
HINDENBURGER AIR
NOW, NOW. I'M SURE IF WE HAVE FAVORABLE TAIL-WINDS, WE'LL HAVE PLENTY OF TIME IN AUSTRALIA.
THE ONLY TAIL-WIND I'VE NOTICED IS COMING FROM DUDLEY - BUT IT AIN'T FAVORABLE.
OH QUIT EXAGGERATING!
AIR
POP!
© TUNDRA 2001

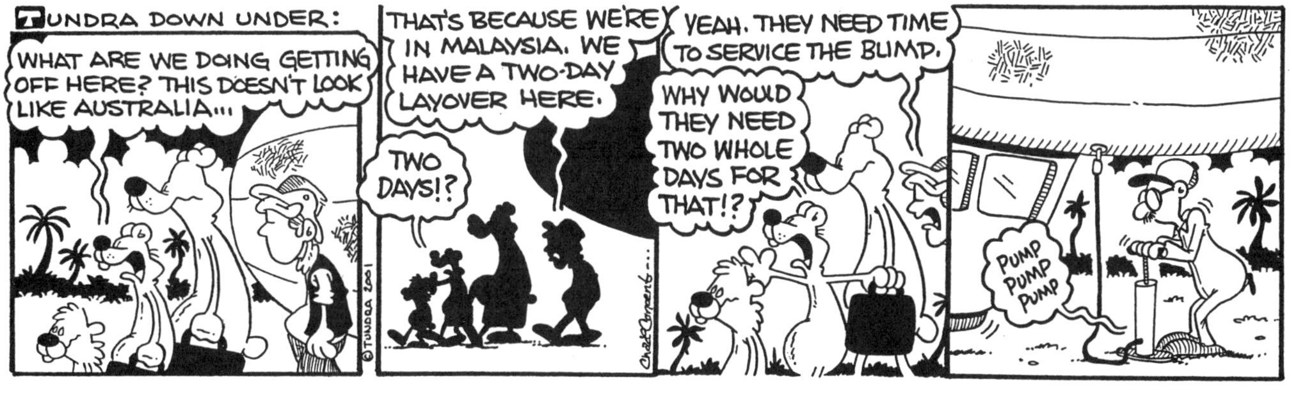
TUNDRA DOWN UNDER:
WHAT ARE WE DOING GETTING OFF HERE? THIS DOESN'T LOOK LIKE AUSTRALIA...
THAT'S BECAUSE WE'RE IN MALAYSIA. WE HAVE A TWO-DAY LAYOVER HERE.
TWO DAYS!?
YEAH. THEY NEED TIME TO SERVICE THE BLIMP.
WHY WOULD THEY NEED TWO WHOLE DAYS FOR THAT!?
PUMP PUMP PUMP
© TUNDRA 2001

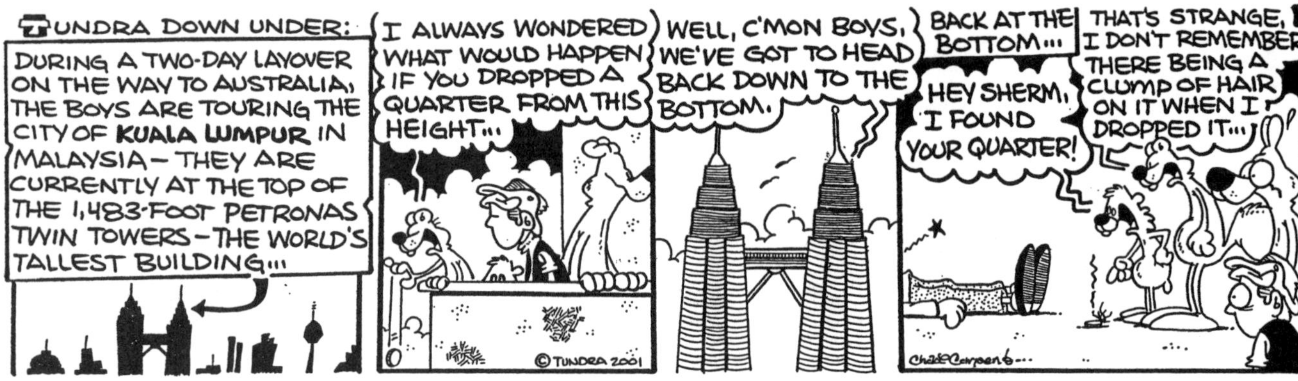
TUNDRA DOWN UNDER:
DURING A TWO-DAY LAYOVER ON THE WAY TO AUSTRALIA, THE BOYS ARE TOURING THE CITY OF KUALA LUMPUR IN MALAYSIA – THEY ARE CURRENTLY AT THE TOP OF THE 1,483-FOOT PETRONAS TWIN TOWERS – THE WORLD'S TALLEST BUILDING...
I ALWAYS WONDERED WHAT WOULD HAPPEN IF YOU DROPPED A QUARTER FROM THIS HEIGHT...
© TUNDRA 2001
WELL, C'MON BOYS, WE'VE GOT TO HEAD BACK DOWN TO THE BOTTOM.
BACK AT THE BOTTOM...
HEY SHERM, I FOUND YOUR QUARTER!
THAT'S STRANGE, I DON'T REMEMBER THERE BEING A CLUMP OF HAIR ON IT WHEN I DROPPED IT...

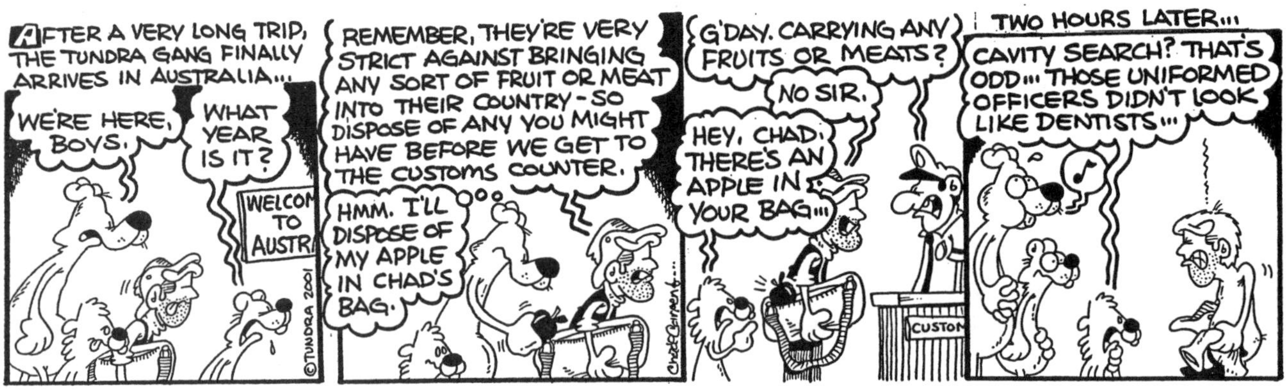
AFTER A VERY LONG TRIP, THE TUNDRA GANG FINALLY ARRIVES IN AUSTRALIA...
WE'RE HERE, BOYS.
WHAT YEAR IS IT?
WELCOM TO AUSTR
©TUNDRA 2001
REMEMBER, THEY'RE VERY STRICT AGAINST BRINGING ANY SORT OF FRUIT OR MEAT INTO THEIR COUNTRY - SO DISPOSE OF ANY YOU MIGHT HAVE BEFORE WE GET TO THE CUSTOMS COUNTER.
HMM. I'LL DISPOSE OF MY APPLE IN CHAD'S BAG.
G'DAY. CARRYING ANY FRUITS OR MEATS?
NO SIR.
HEY, CHAD. THERE'S AN APPLE IN YOUR BAG...
CUSTOM
TWO HOURS LATER...
CAVITY SEARCH? THAT'S ODD... THOSE UNIFORMED OFFICERS DIDN'T LOOK LIKE DENTISTS...

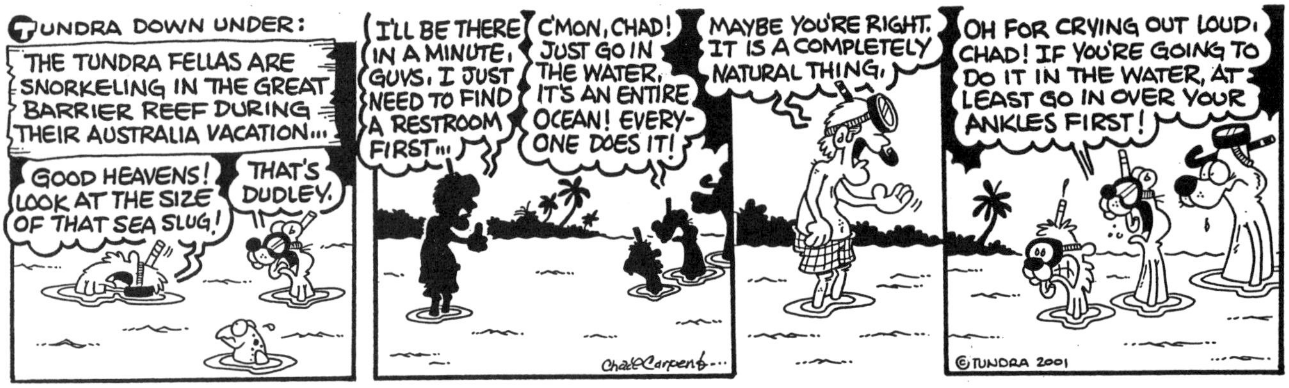
TUNDRA DOWN UNDER:
THE TUNDRA FELLAS ARE SNORKELING IN THE GREAT BARRIER REEF DURING THEIR AUSTRALIA VACATION...
GOOD HEAVENS! LOOK AT THE SIZE OF THAT SEA SLUG!
THAT'S DUDLEY.
I'LL BE THERE IN A MINUTE, GUYS. I JUST NEED TO FIND A RESTROOM FIRST...
C'MON, CHAD! JUST GO IN THE WATER, IT'S AN ENTIRE OCEAN! EVERY-ONE DOES IT!
MAYBE YOU'RE RIGHT. IT IS A COMPLETELY NATURAL THING.
OH FOR CRYING OUT LOUD, CHAD! IF YOU'RE GOING TO DO IT IN THE WATER, AT LEAST GO IN OVER YOUR ANKLES FIRST!
©TUNDRA 2001

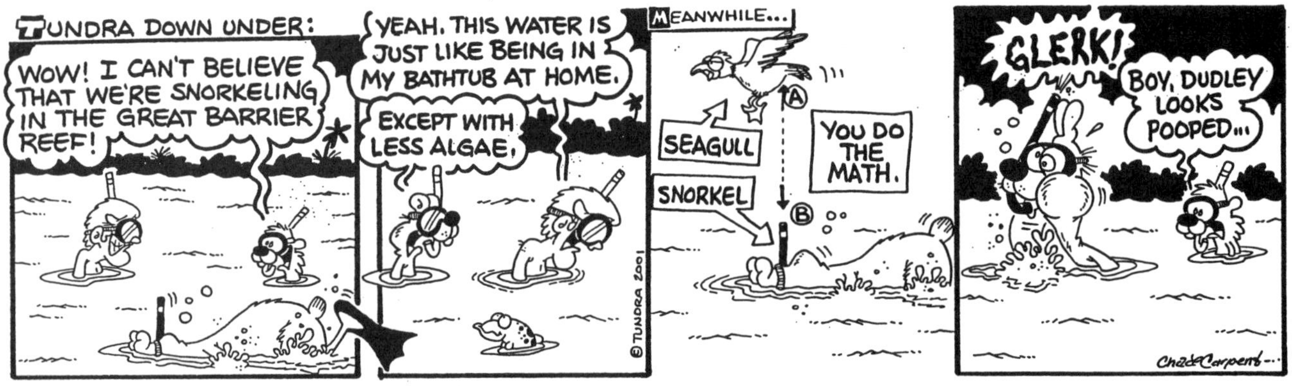
TUNDRA DOWN UNDER:
WOW! I CAN'T BELIEVE THAT WE'RE SNORKELING IN THE GREAT BARRIER REEF!
YEAH. THIS WATER IS JUST LIKE BEING IN MY BATHTUB AT HOME.
EXCEPT WITH LESS ALGAE.
©TUNDRA 2001
MEANWHILE...
SEAGULL
A
YOU DO THE MATH.
SNORKEL
B
GLERK!
BOY, DUDLEY LOOKS POOPED...

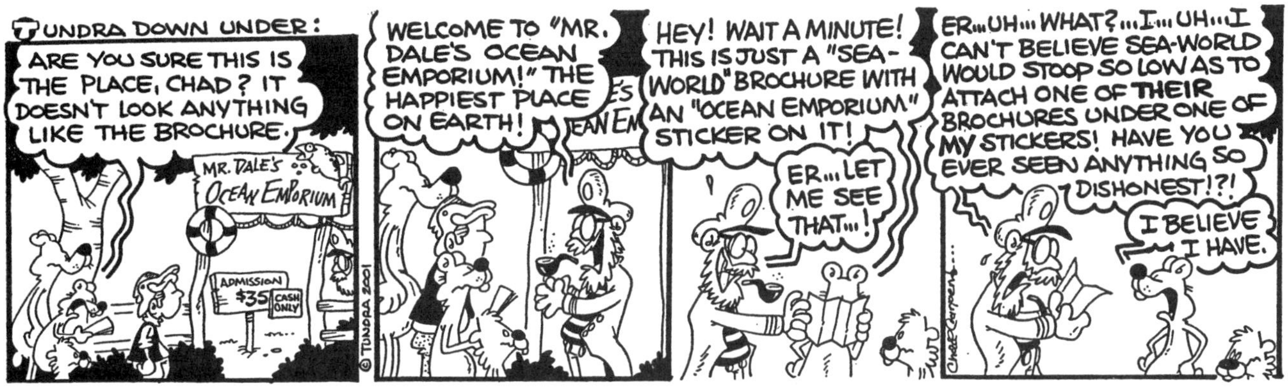
TUNDRA DOWN UNDER:
ARE YOU SURE THIS IS THE PLACE, CHAD? IT DOESN'T LOOK ANYTHING LIKE THE BROCHURE.
MR. DALE'S OCEAN EMPORIUM
ADMISSION $35
CASH ONLY
WELCOME TO "MR. DALE'S OCEAN EMPORIUM!" THE HAPPIEST PLACE ON EARTH!
© TUNDRA 2001
HEY! WAIT A MINUTE! THIS IS JUST A "SEA-WORLD" BROCHURE WITH AN "OCEAN EMPORIUM" STICKER ON IT!
ER... LET ME SEE THAT...!
ER... UH... WHAT?... I... UH... I CAN'T BELIEVE SEA-WORLD WOULD STOOP SO LOW AS TO ATTACH ONE OF THEIR BROCHURES UNDER ONE OF MY STICKERS! HAVE YOU EVER SEEN ANYTHING SO DISHONEST!?!
I BELIEVE I HAVE.

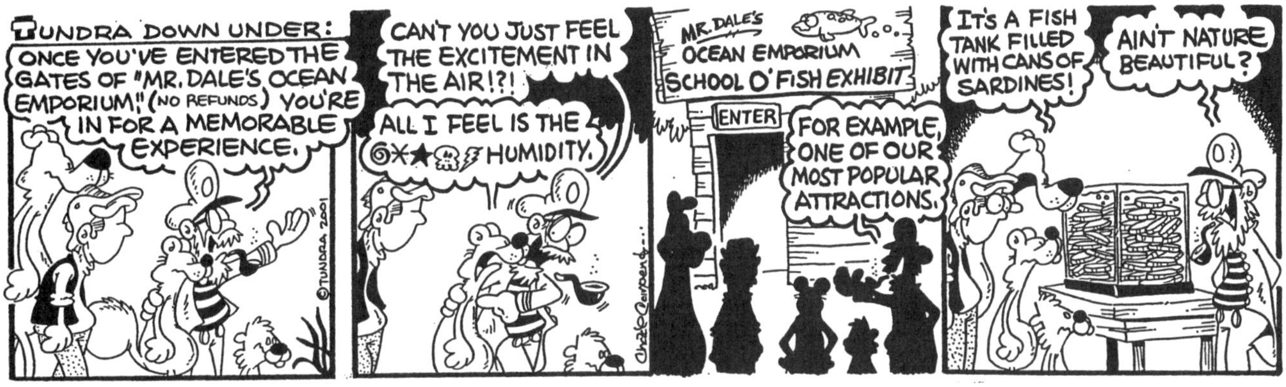
TUNDRA DOWN UNDER:
ONCE YOU'VE ENTERED THE GATES OF "MR. DALE'S OCEAN EMPORIUM!" (NO REFUNDS) YOU'RE IN FOR A MEMORABLE EXPERIENCE.
© TUNDRA 2001
CAN'T YOU JUST FEEL THE EXCITEMENT IN THE AIR!?!
ALL I FEEL IS THE @X★☠⚡ HUMIDITY.
MR. DALE'S OCEAN EMPORIUM
SCHOOL O' FISH EXHIBIT
ENTER
FOR EXAMPLE, ONE OF OUR MOST POPULAR ATTRACTIONS.
IT'S A FISH TANK FILLED WITH CANS OF SARDINES!
AIN'T NATURE BEAUTIFUL?

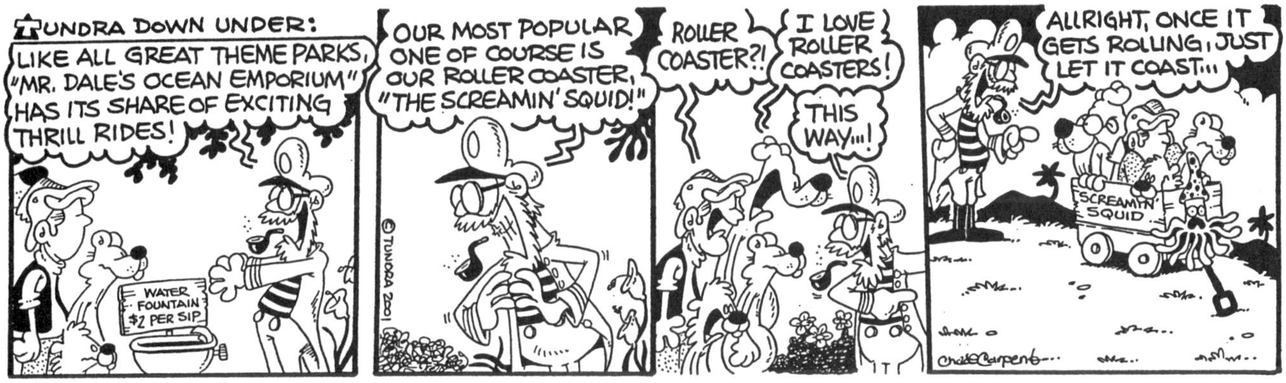
TUNDRA DOWN UNDER:
LIKE ALL GREAT THEME PARKS, "MR. DALE'S OCEAN EMPORIUM" HAS ITS SHARE OF EXCITING THRILL RIDES!
WATER FOUNTAIN $2 PER SIP
OUR MOST POPULAR ONE OF COURSE IS OUR ROLLER COASTER, "THE SCREAMIN' SQUID!"
© TUNDRA 2001
ROLLER COASTER?!
I LOVE ROLLER COASTERS!
THIS WAY...!
ALLRIGHT, ONCE IT GETS ROLLING, JUST LET IT COAST...
SCREAMIN' SQUID

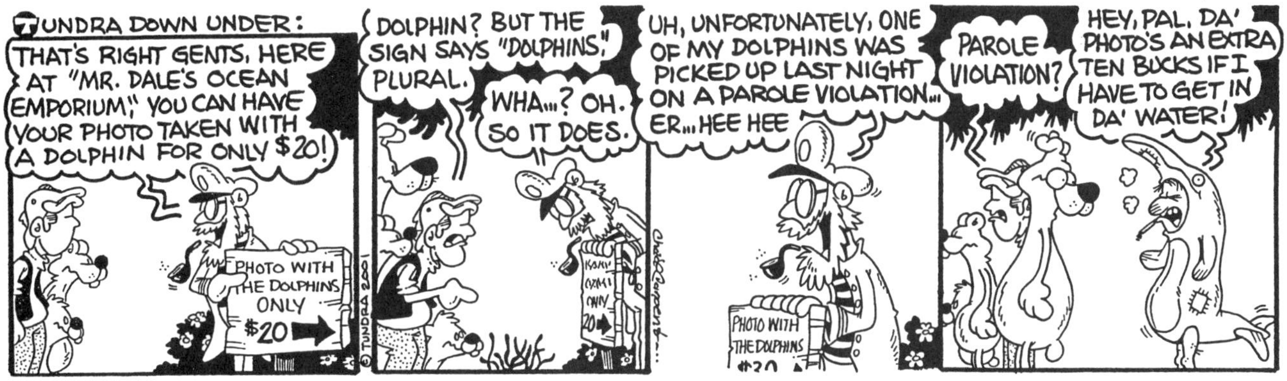
TUNDRA DOWN UNDER:
THAT'S RIGHT GENTS, HERE AT "MR. DALE'S OCEAN EMPORIUM," YOU CAN HAVE YOUR PHOTO TAKEN WITH A DOLPHIN FOR ONLY $20!
PHOTO WITH THE DOLPHINS ONLY $20
© TUNDRA 2001
DOLPHIN? BUT THE SIGN SAYS "DOLPHINS," PLURAL.
WHA...? OH. SO IT DOES.
UH, UNFORTUNATELY, ONE OF MY DOLPHINS WAS PICKED UP LAST NIGHT ON A PAROLE VIOLATION... ER... HEE HEE
PHOTO WITH THE DOLPHINS
PAROLE VIOLATION?
HEY, PAL, DA' PHOTO'S AN EXTRA TEN BUCKS IF I HAVE TO GET IN DA' WATER!

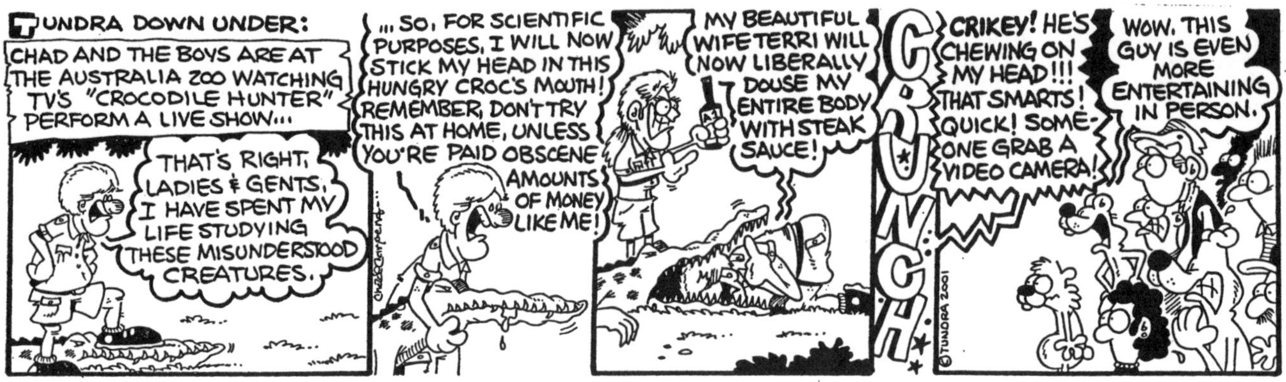
TUNDRA DOWN UNDER:
CHAD AND THE BOYS ARE AT THE AUSTRALIA ZOO WATCHING TV'S "CROCODILE HUNTER" PERFORM A LIVE SHOW...
THAT'S RIGHT, LADIES & GENTS, I HAVE SPENT MY LIFE STUDYING THESE MISUNDERSTOOD CREATURES.
... SO, FOR SCIENTIFIC PURPOSES, I WILL NOW STICK MY HEAD IN THIS HUNGRY CROC'S MOUTH! REMEMBER, DON'T TRY THIS AT HOME, UNLESS YOU'RE PAID OBSCENE AMOUNTS OF MONEY LIKE ME!
MY BEAUTIFUL WIFE TERRI WILL NOW LIBERALLY DOUSE MY ENTIRE BODY WITH STEAK SAUCE!
CRUNCH
CRIKEY! HE'S CHEWING ON MY HEAD!!! THAT SMARTS! QUICK! SOME-ONE GRAB A VIDEO CAMERA!
WOW. THIS GUY IS EVEN MORE ENTERTAINING IN PERSON.
© TUNDRA 2001

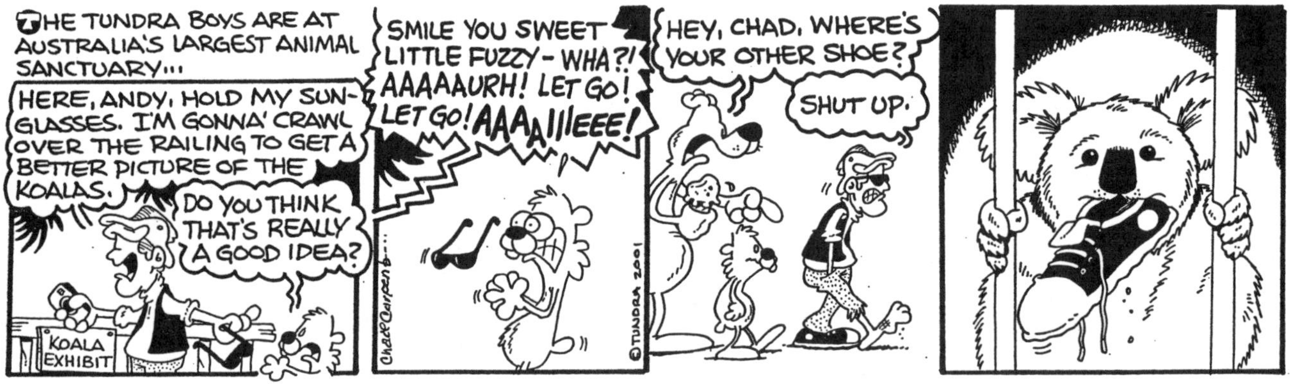
THE TUNDRA BOYS ARE AT AUSTRALIA'S LARGEST ANIMAL SANCTUARY...
HERE, ANDY, HOLD MY SUN-GLASSES. I'M GONNA' CRAWL OVER THE RAILING TO GET A BETTER PICTURE OF THE KOALAS.
DO YOU THINK THAT'S REALLY A GOOD IDEA?
KOALA EXHIBIT
SMILE YOU SWEET LITTLE FUZZY - WHA?! AAAAAURH! LET GO! LET GO! AAAAIIIEEE!
© TUNDRA 2001
HEY, CHAD, WHERE'S YOUR OTHER SHOE?
SHUT UP.

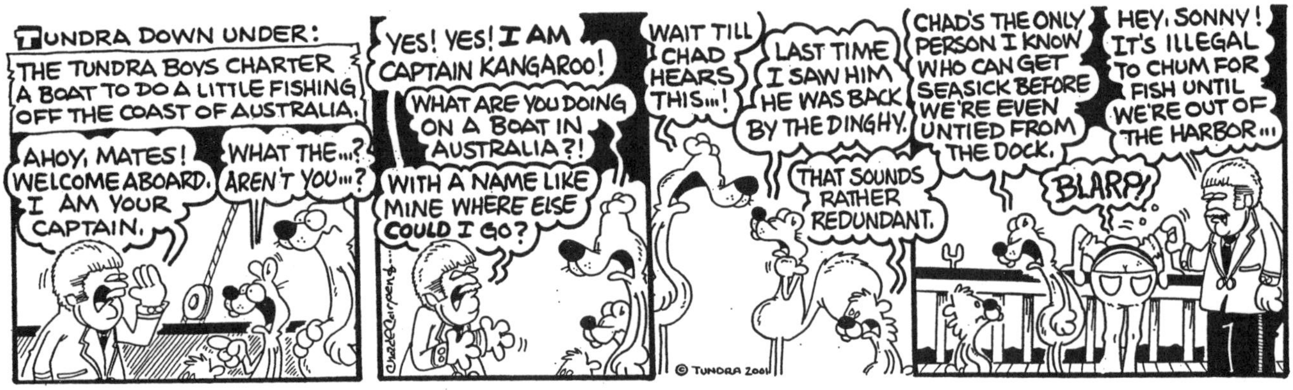
TUNDRA DOWN UNDER:
THE TUNDRA BOYS CHARTER A BOAT TO DO A LITTLE FISHING OFF THE COAST OF AUSTRALIA.
AHOY, MATES! WELCOME ABOARD. I AM YOUR CAPTAIN.
WHAT THE...? AREN'T YOU...?
YES! YES! I AM CAPTAIN KANGAROO!
WHAT ARE YOU DOING ON A BOAT IN AUSTRALIA?!
WITH A NAME LIKE MINE WHERE ELSE COULD I GO?
WAIT TILL CHAD HEARS THIS...!
LAST TIME I SAW HIM HE WAS BACK BY THE DINGHY.
THAT SOUNDS RATHER REDUNDANT.
© TUNDRA 2001
CHAD'S THE ONLY PERSON I KNOW WHO CAN GET SEASICK BEFORE WE'RE EVEN UNTIED FROM THE DOCK.
HEY, SONNY! IT'S ILLEGAL TO CHUM FOR FISH UNTIL WE'RE OUT OF THE HARBOR...
BLARP!

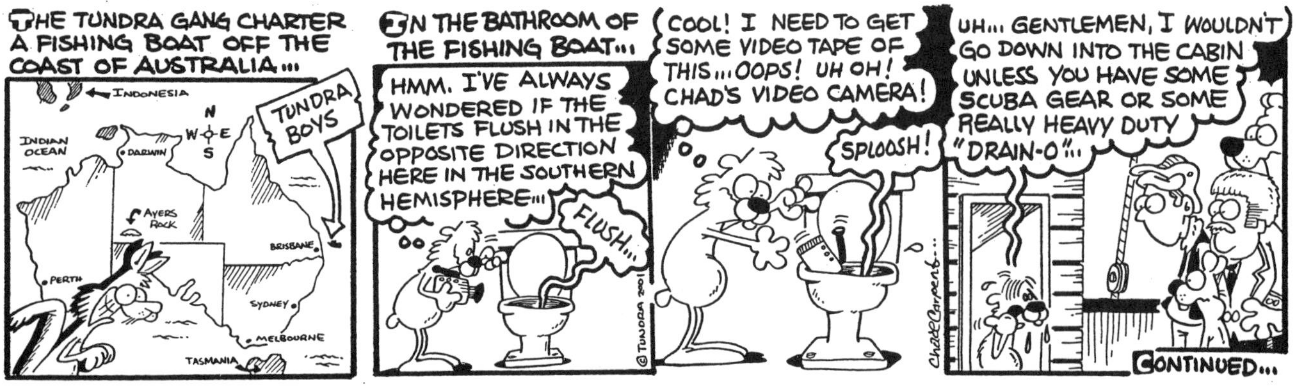
THE TUNDRA GANG CHARTER A FISHING BOAT OFF THE COAST OF AUSTRALIA...
INDONESIA
INDIAN OCEAN
DARWIN
N
W
E
S
AYERS ROCK
BRISBANE
PERTH
SYDNEY
MELBOURNE
TASMANIA
TUNDRA BOYS
IN THE BATHROOM OF THE FISHING BOAT...
HMM. I'VE ALWAYS WONDERED IF THE TOILETS FLUSH IN THE OPPOSITE DIRECTION HERE IN THE SOUTHERN HEMISPHERE...
FLUSH...
© TUNDRA 2001
COOL! I NEED TO GET SOME VIDEO TAPE OF THIS... OOPS! UH OH! CHAD'S VIDEO CAMERA!
SPLOOSH!
UH... GENTLEMEN, I WOULDN'T GO DOWN INTO THE CABIN UNLESS YOU HAVE SOME SCUBA GEAR OR SOME REALLY HEAVY DUTY "DRAIN-O"!
CONTINUED...

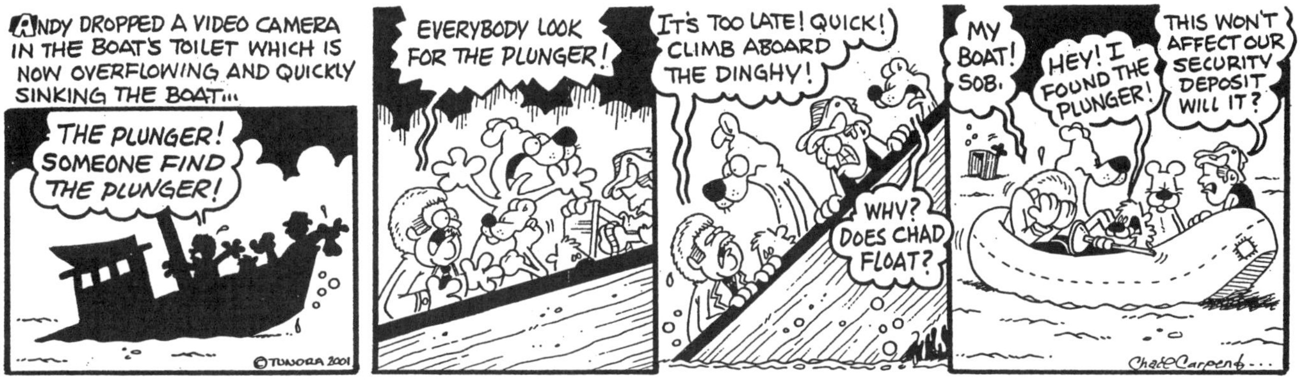
ANDY DROPPED A VIDEO CAMERA IN THE BOAT'S TOILET WHICH IS NOW OVERFLOWING AND QUICKLY SINKING THE BOAT...
THE PLUNGER! SOMEONE FIND THE PLUNGER!
©TUNDRA 2001
EVERYBODY LOOK FOR THE PLUNGER!
IT'S TOO LATE! QUICK! CLIMB ABOARD THE DINGHY!
WHY? DOES CHAD FLOAT?
MY BOAT! SOB.
HEY! I FOUND THE PLUNGER!
THIS WON'T AFFECT OUR SECURITY DEPOSIT WILL IT?

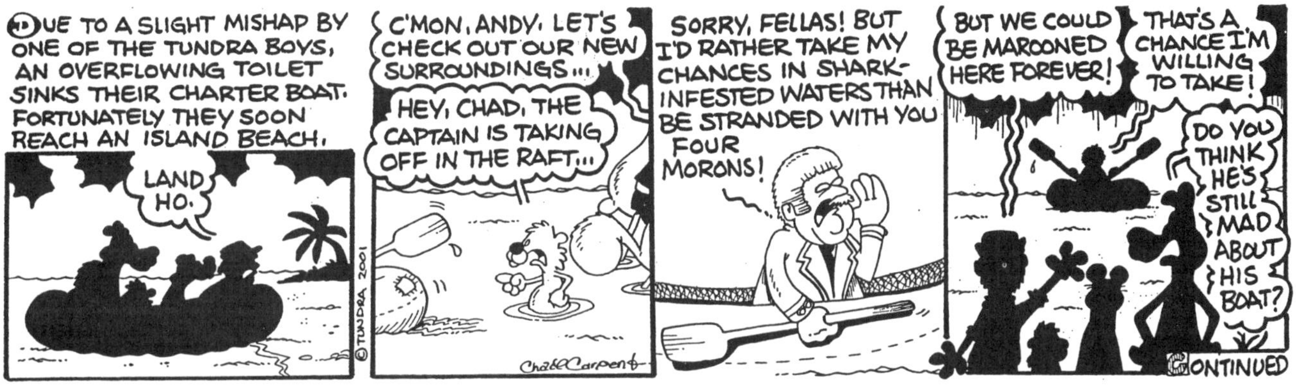
DUE TO A SLIGHT MISHAP BY ONE OF THE TUNDRA BOYS, AN OVERFLOWING TOILET SINKS THEIR CHARTER BOAT. FORTUNATELY THEY SOON REACH AN ISLAND BEACH.
LAND HO.
©TUNDRA 2001
C'MON, ANDY. LET'S CHECK OUT OUR NEW SURROUNDINGS...
HEY, CHAD, THE CAPTAIN IS TAKING OFF IN THE RAFT...
SORRY, FELLAS! BUT I'D RATHER TAKE MY CHANCES IN SHARK-INFESTED WATERS THAN BE STRANDED WITH YOU FOUR MORONS!
BUT WE COULD BE MAROONED HERE FOREVER!
THAT'S A CHANCE I'M WILLING TO TAKE!
DO YOU THINK HE'S STILL MAD ABOUT HIS BOAT?
CONTINUED

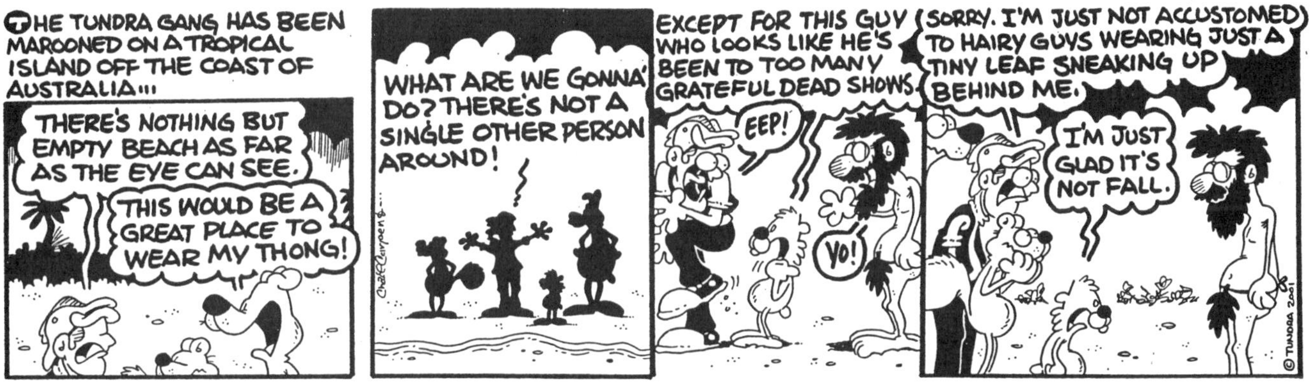
THE TUNDRA GANG HAS BEEN MAROONED ON A TROPICAL ISLAND OFF THE COAST OF AUSTRALIA...
THERE'S NOTHING BUT EMPTY BEACH AS FAR AS THE EYE CAN SEE.
THIS WOULD BE A GREAT PLACE TO WEAR MY THONG!
WHAT ARE WE GONNA' DO? THERE'S NOT A SINGLE OTHER PERSON AROUND!
EXCEPT FOR THIS GUY WHO LOOKS LIKE HE'S BEEN TO TOO MANY GRATEFUL DEAD SHOWS.
EEP!
YO!
SORRY. I'M JUST NOT ACCUSTOMED TO HAIRY GUYS WEARING JUST A TINY LEAF SNEAKING UP BEHIND ME.
I'M JUST GLAD IT'S NOT FALL.
©TUNDRA 2001

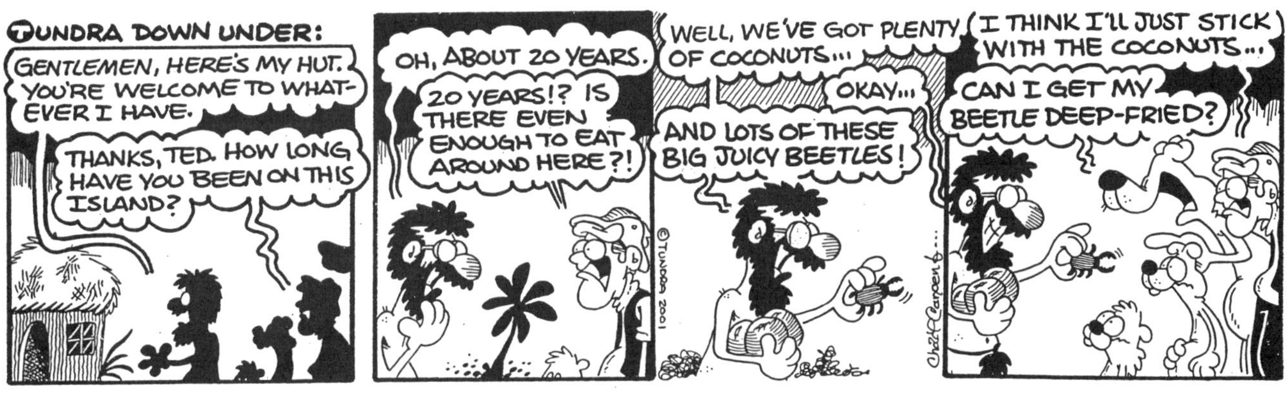
TUNDRA DOWN UNDER:
GENTLEMEN, HERE'S MY HUT. YOU'RE WELCOME TO WHAT-EVER I HAVE.
THANKS, TED. HOW LONG HAVE YOU BEEN ON THIS ISLAND?
OH, ABOUT 20 YEARS.
20 YEARS!? IS THERE EVEN ENOUGH TO EAT AROUND HERE?!
©TUNDRA 2001
WELL, WE'VE GOT PLENTY OF COCONUTS...
OKAY...
AND LOTS OF THESE BIG JUICY BEETLES!
I THINK I'LL JUST STICK WITH THE COCONUTS...
CAN I GET MY BEETLE DEEP-FRIED?

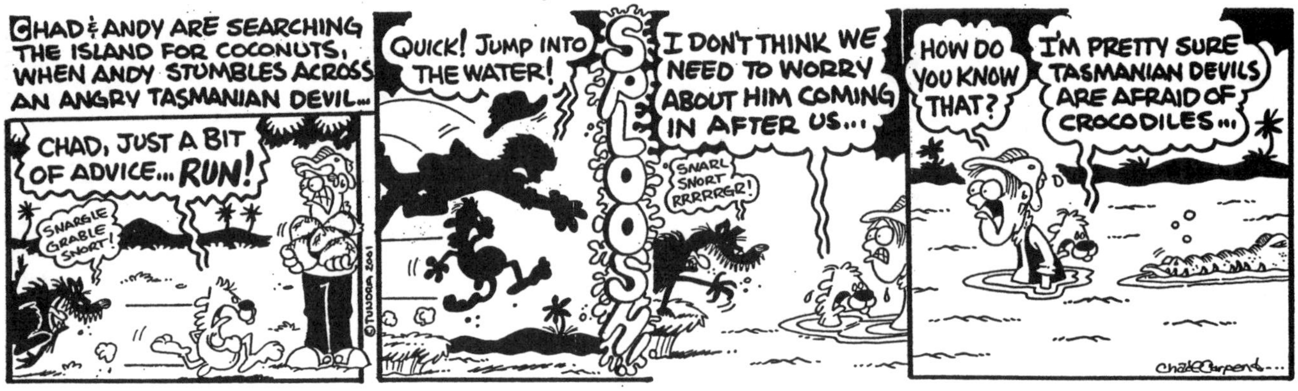
CHAD & ANDY ARE SEARCHING THE ISLAND FOR COCONUTS, WHEN ANDY STUMBLES ACROSS AN ANGRY TASMANIAN DEVIL...
CHAD, JUST A BIT OF ADVICE... RUN!
SNARGLE GRABLE SNORT!
© TUNDRA 2001
QUICK! JUMP INTO THE WATER!
SPLOOSH
I DON'T THINK WE NEED TO WORRY ABOUT HIM COMING IN AFTER US...
SNARL SNORT RRRRRGR!
HOW DO YOU KNOW THAT?
I'M PRETTY SURE TASMANIAN DEVILS ARE AFRAID OF CROCODILES...

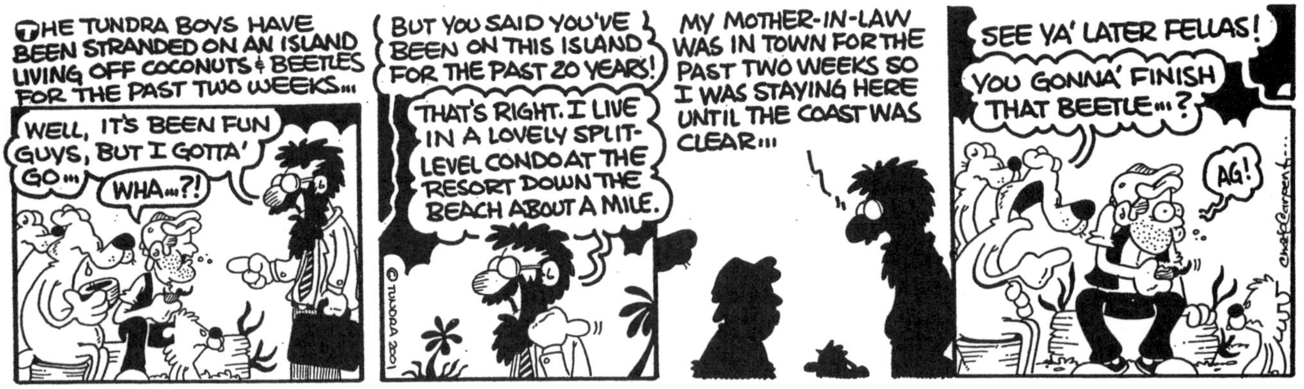
THE TUNDRA BOYS HAVE BEEN STRANDED ON AN ISLAND LIVING OFF COCONUTS & BEETLES FOR THE PAST TWO WEEKS...
WELL, IT'S BEEN FUN GUYS, BUT I GOTTA' GO...
WHA...?!
BUT YOU SAID YOU'VE BEEN ON THIS ISLAND FOR THE PAST 20 YEARS!
THAT'S RIGHT. I LIVE IN A LOVELY SPLIT-LEVEL CONDO AT THE RESORT DOWN THE BEACH ABOUT A MILE.
© TUNDRA 2001
MY MOTHER-IN-LAW WAS IN TOWN FOR THE PAST TWO WEEKS SO I WAS STAYING HERE UNTIL THE COAST WAS CLEAR...
SEE YA' LATER FELLAS!
YOU GONNA' FINISH THAT BEETLE...?
AG!

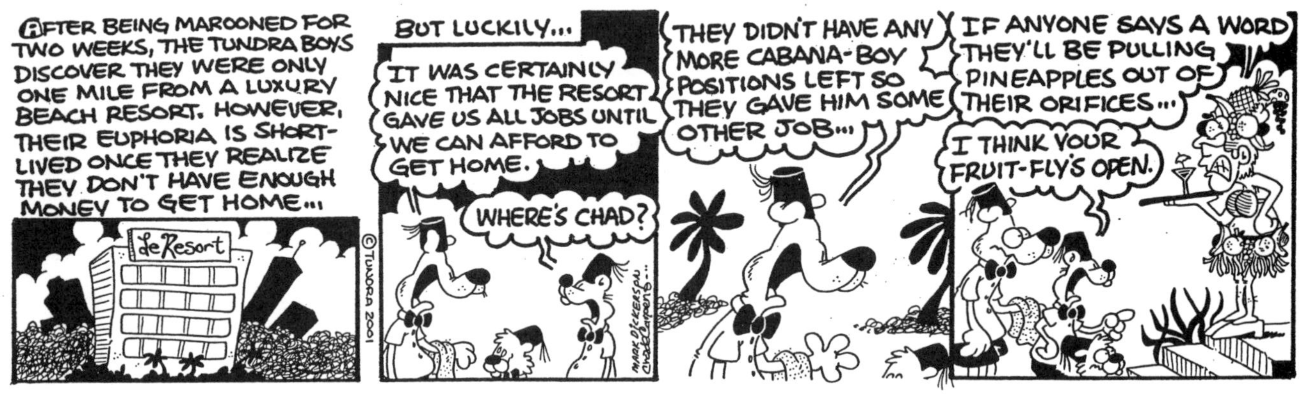
AFTER BEING MAROONED FOR TWO WEEKS, THE TUNDRA BOYS DISCOVER THEY WERE ONLY ONE MILE FROM A LUXURY BEACH RESORT. HOWEVER, THEIR EUPHORIA IS SHORT-LIVED ONCE THEY REALIZE THEY DON'T HAVE ENOUGH MONEY TO GET HOME...
Le Resort
© TUNDRA 2001
BUT LUCKILY...
IT WAS CERTAINLY NICE THAT THE RESORT GAVE US ALL JOBS UNTIL WE CAN AFFORD TO GET HOME.
WHERE'S CHAD?
THEY DIDN'T HAVE ANY MORE CABANA-BOY POSITIONS LEFT SO THEY GAVE HIM SOME OTHER JOB...
IF ANYONE SAYS A WORD THEY'LL BE PULLING PINEAPPLES OUT OF THEIR ORIFICES...
I THINK YOUR FRUIT-FLY'S OPEN.

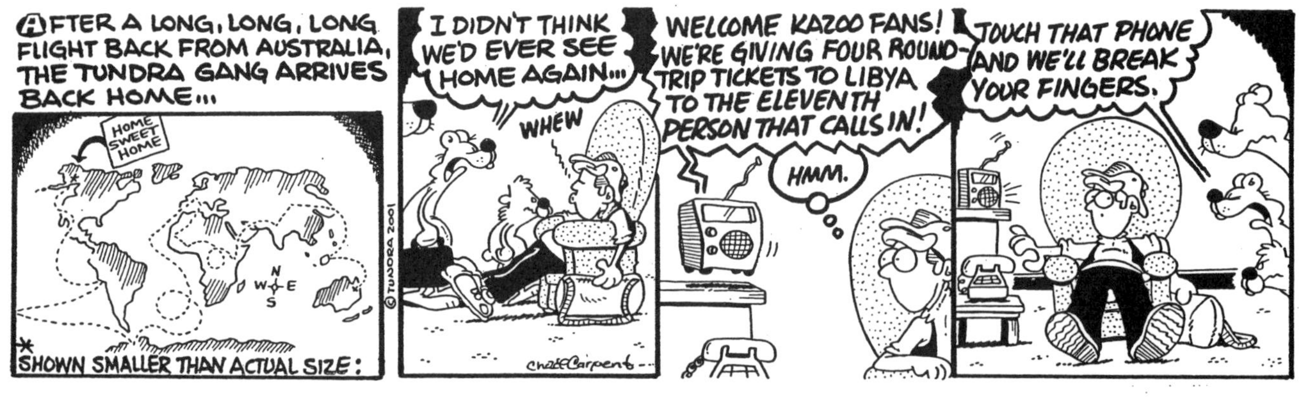
AFTER A LONG, LONG, LONG FLIGHT BACK FROM AUSTRALIA, THE TUNDRA GANG ARRIVES BACK HOME...
HOME SWEET HOME
N
W E
S
* SHOWN SMALLER THAN ACTUAL SIZE:
© TUNDRA 2001
I DIDN'T THINK WE'D EVER SEE HOME AGAIN...
WHEW
WELCOME KAZOO FANS! WE'RE GIVING FOUR ROUND-TRIP TICKETS TO LIBYA TO THE ELEVENTH PERSON THAT CALLS IN!
HMM.
TOUCH THAT PHONE AND WE'LL BREAK YOUR FINGERS.

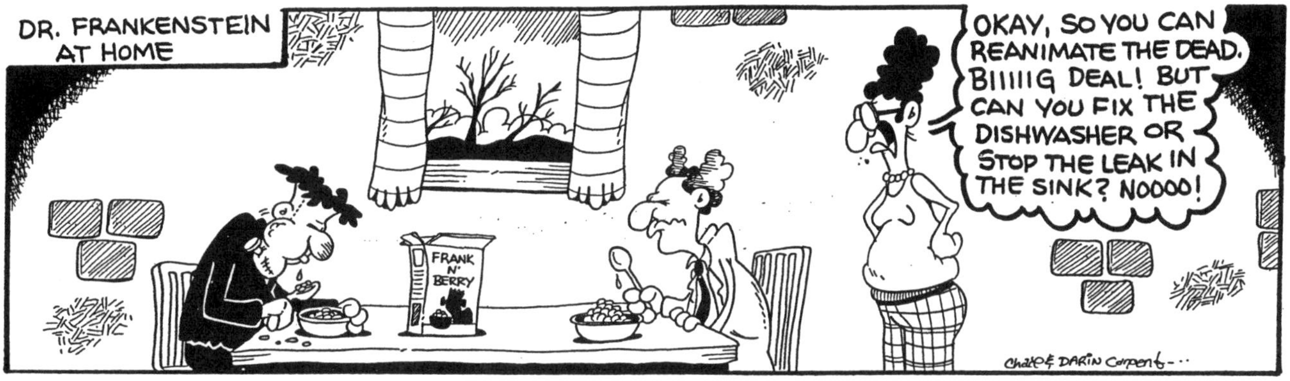
DR. FRANKENSTEIN AT HOME
FRANK N' BERRY
OKAY, SO YOU CAN REANIMATE THE DEAD. BIIIIIG DEAL! BUT CAN YOU FIX THE DISHWASHER OR STOP THE LEAK IN THE SINK? NOOOO!

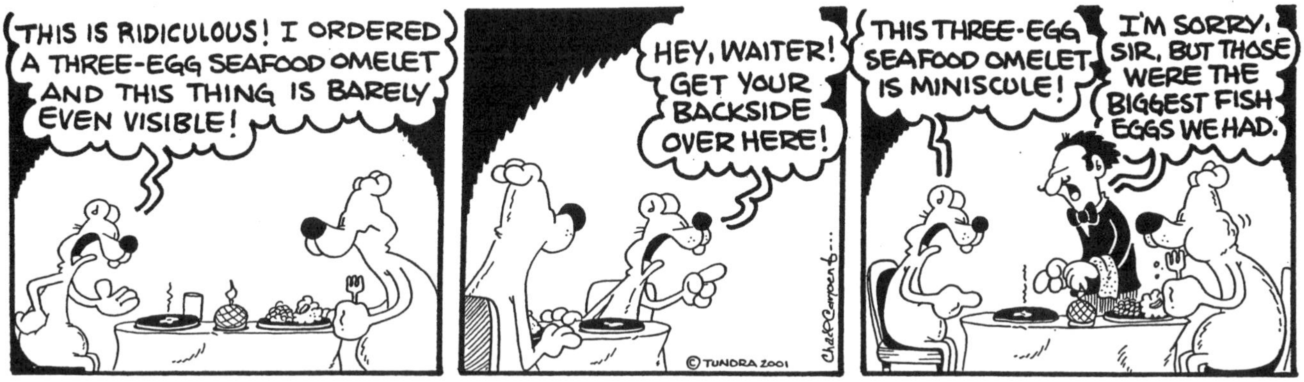
THIS IS RIDICULOUS! I ORDERED A THREE-EGG SEAFOOD OMELET AND THIS THING IS BARELY EVEN VISIBLE!
HEY, WAITER! GET YOUR BACKSIDE OVER HERE!
© TUNDRA 2001
THIS THREE-EGG SEAFOOD OMELET IS MINISCULE!
I'M SORRY, SIR, BUT THOSE WERE THE BIGGEST FISH EGGS WE HAD.

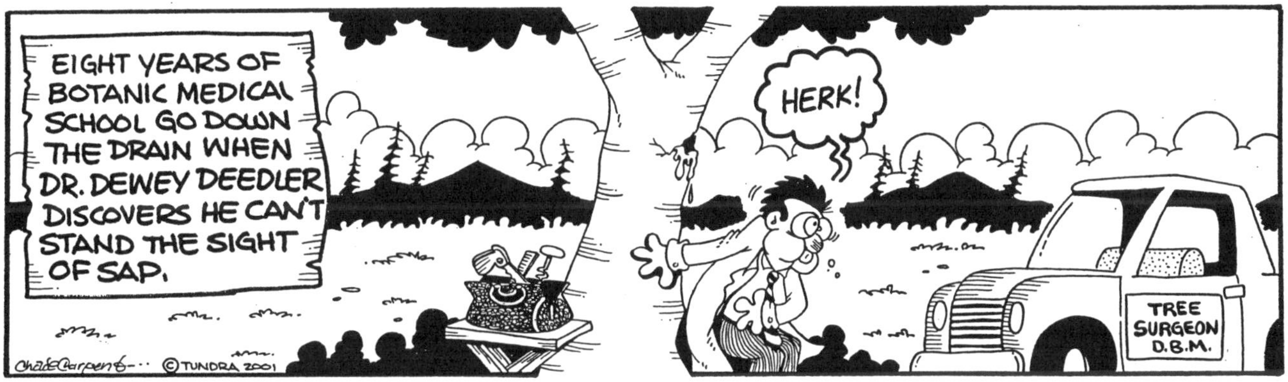
EIGHT YEARS OF BOTANIC MEDICAL SCHOOL GO DOWN THE DRAIN WHEN DR. DEWEY DEEDLER DISCOVERS HE CAN'T STAND THE SIGHT OF SAP.
© TUNDRA 2001
HERK!
TREE SURGEON D.B.M.

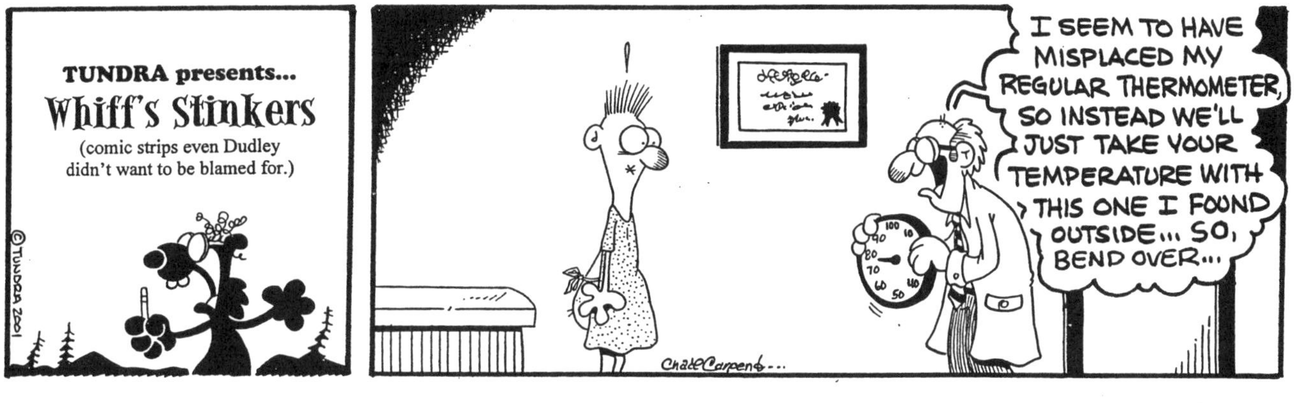
TUNDRA presents...
Whiff's Stinkers
(comic strips even Dudley didn't want to be blamed for.)
© TUNDRA 2001
I SEEM TO HAVE MISPLACED MY REGULAR THERMOMETER, SO INSTEAD WE'LL JUST TAKE YOUR TEMPERATURE WITH THIS ONE I FOUND OUTSIDE... SO, BEND OVER...

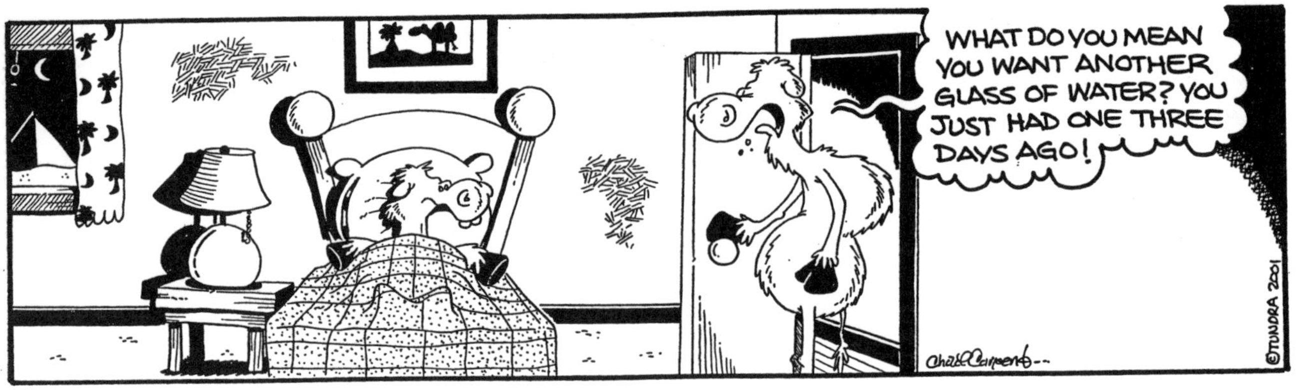
WHAT DO YOU MEAN YOU WANT ANOTHER GLASS OF WATER? YOU JUST HAD ONE THREE DAYS AGO!
©TUNDRA 2001

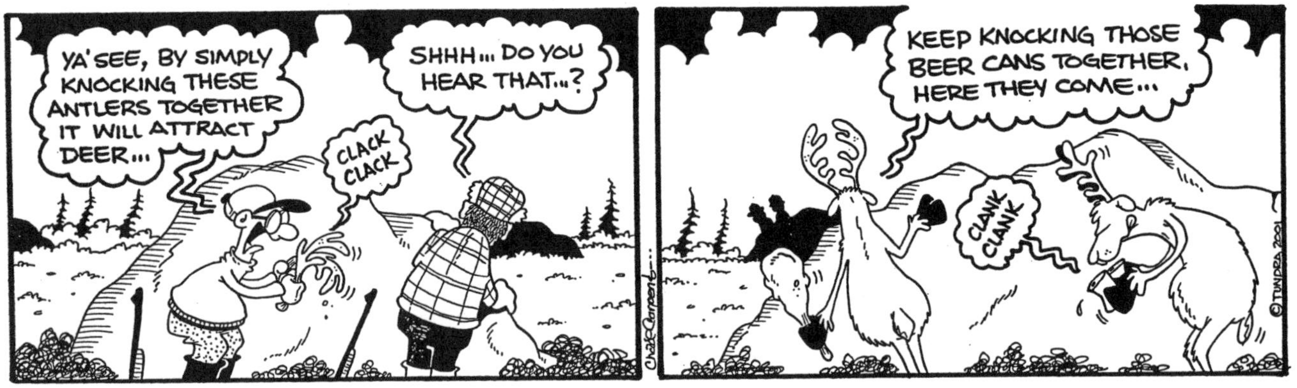
YA' SEE, BY SIMPLY KNOCKING THESE ANTLERS TOGETHER IT WILL ATTRACT DEER...
CLACK CLACK
SHHH... DO YOU HEAR THAT...?
KEEP KNOCKING THOSE BEER CANS TOGETHER. HERE THEY COME...
CLANK CLANK
©TUNDRA 2001

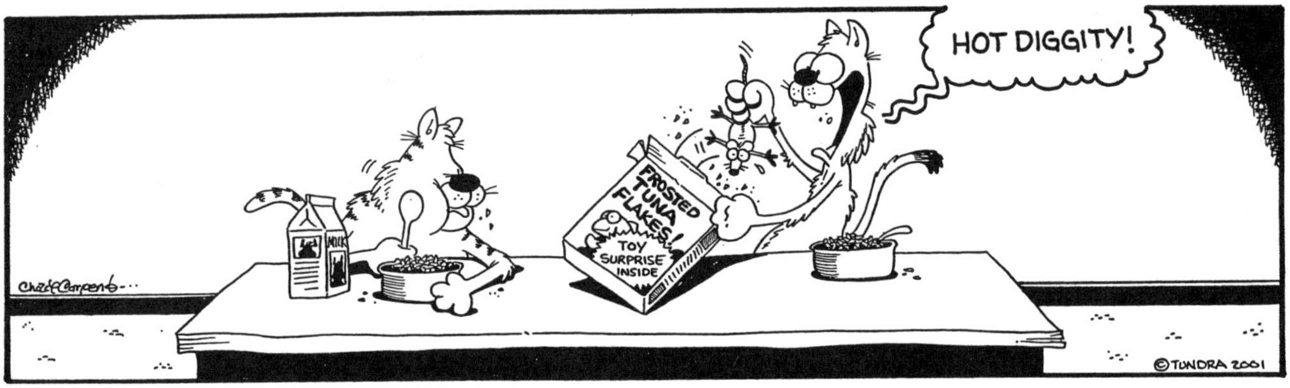
HOT DIGGITY!
MILK
FROSTED TUNA FLAKES!
TOY SURPRISE INSIDE
©TUNDRA 2001

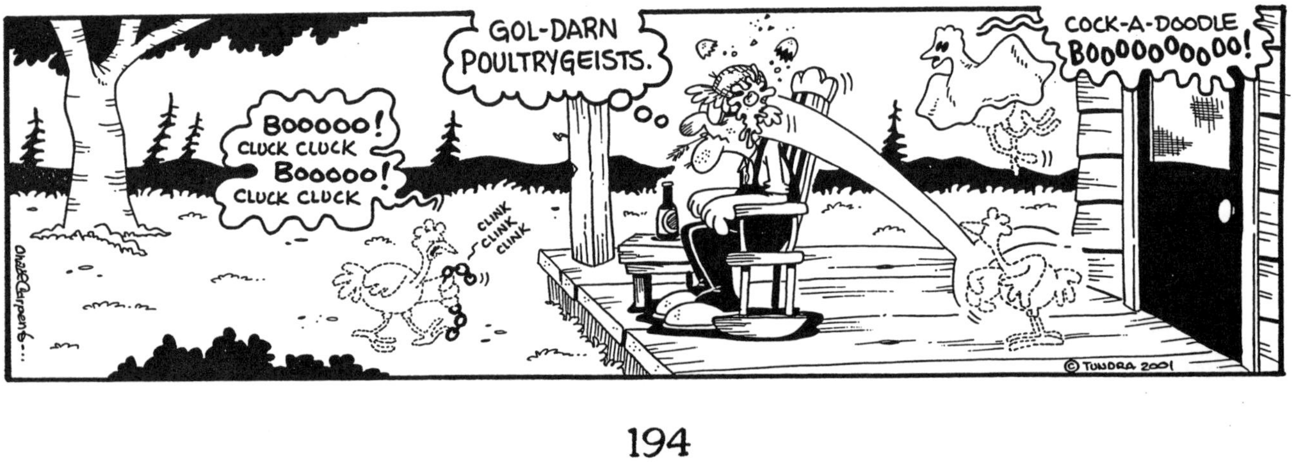
GOL-DARN POULTRYGEISTS.
COCK-A-DOODLE BOOOOOOOOOO!
BOOOOO! CLUCK CLUCK BOOOOO! CLUCK CLUCK
CLINK CLINK CLINK
©TUNDRA 2001

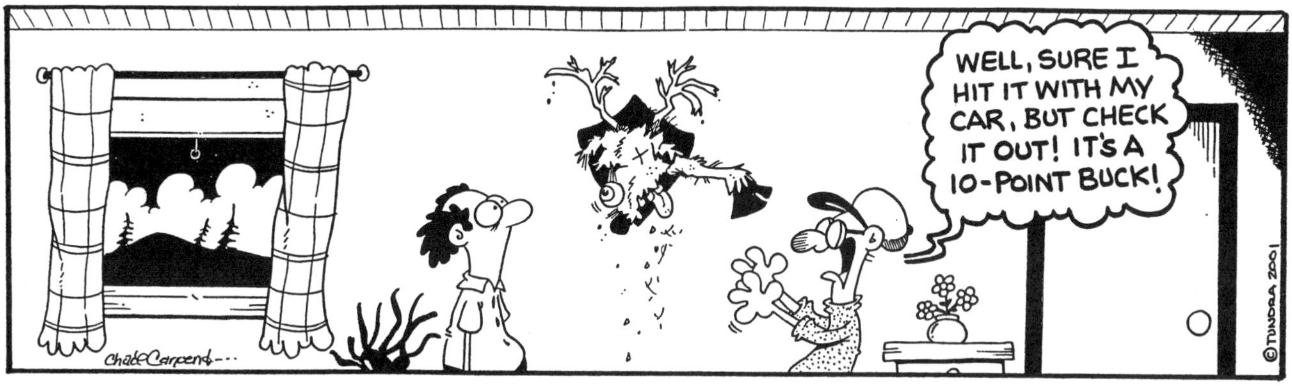
WELL, SURE I HIT IT WITH MY CAR, BUT CHECK IT OUT! IT'S A 10-POINT BUCK!
©TUNDRA 2001

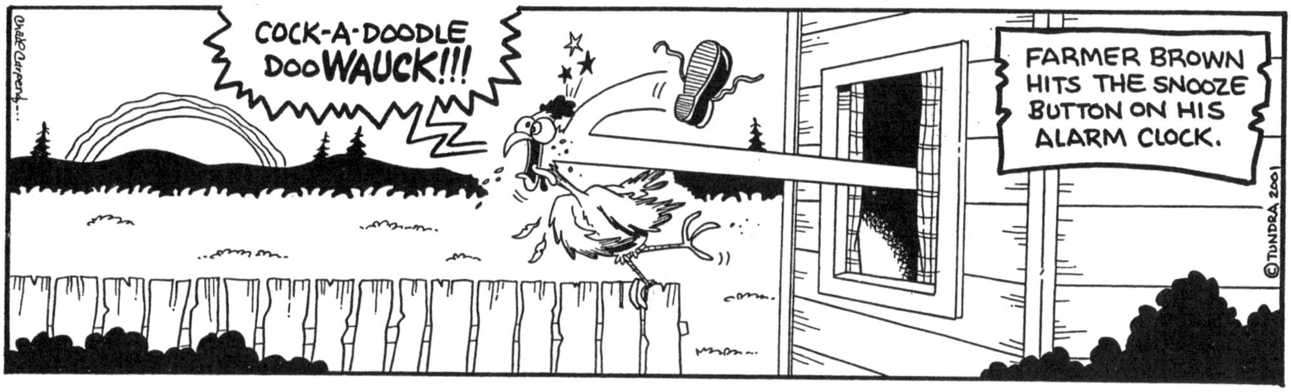
COCK-A-DOODLE DOOWAUCK!!!
FARMER BROWN HITS THE SNOOZE BUTTON ON HIS ALARM CLOCK.
©TUNDRA 2001

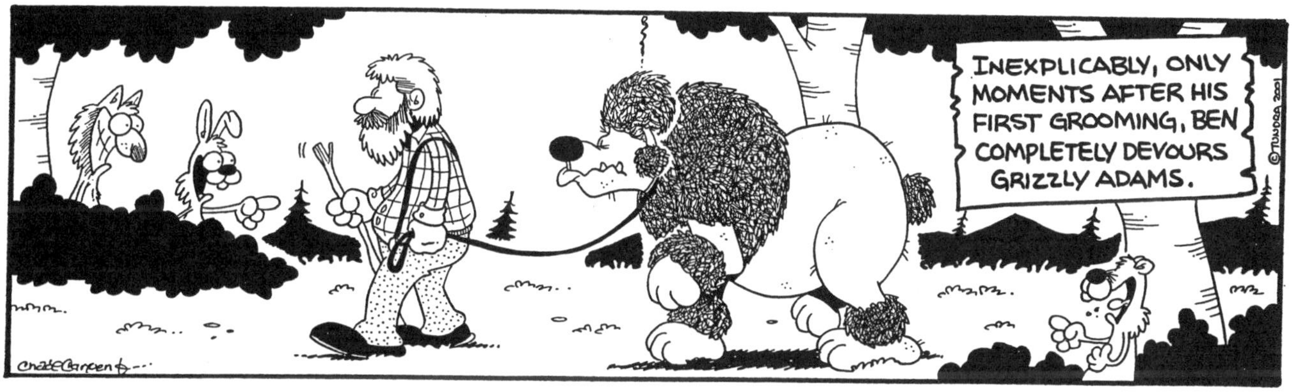
INEXPLICABLY, ONLY MOMENTS AFTER HIS FIRST GROOMING, BEN COMPLETELY DEVOURS GRIZZLY ADAMS.

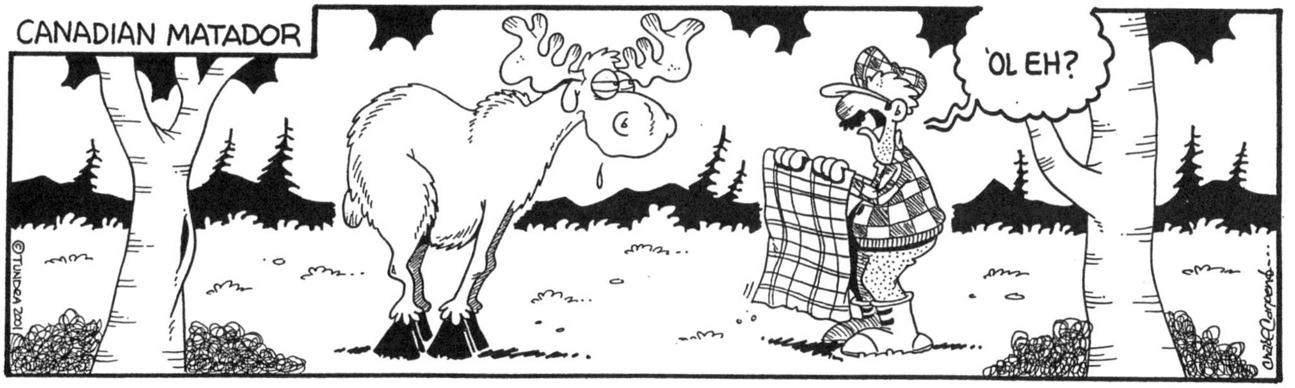
CANADIAN MATADOR
'OL EH?
©TUNDRA 2001

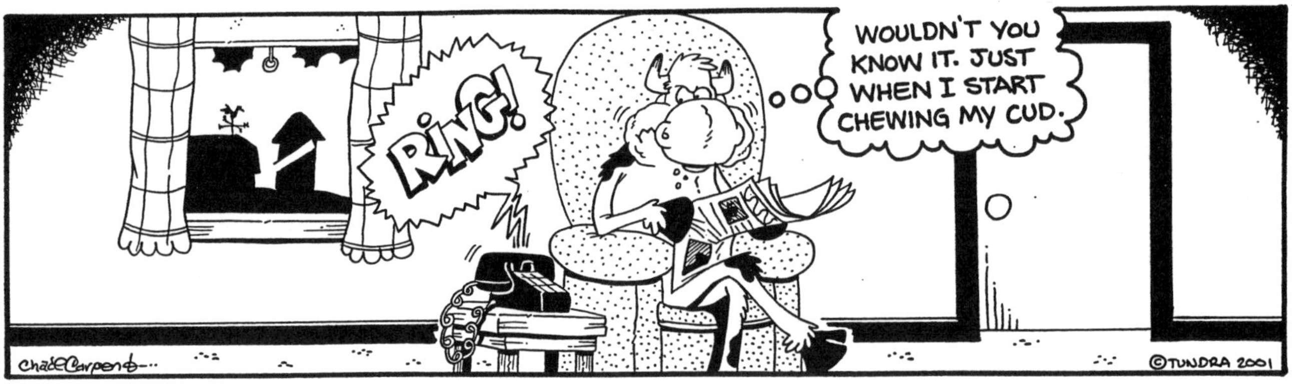
RING!
WOULDN'T YOU KNOW IT. JUST WHEN I START CHEWING MY CUD.
©TUNDRA 2001

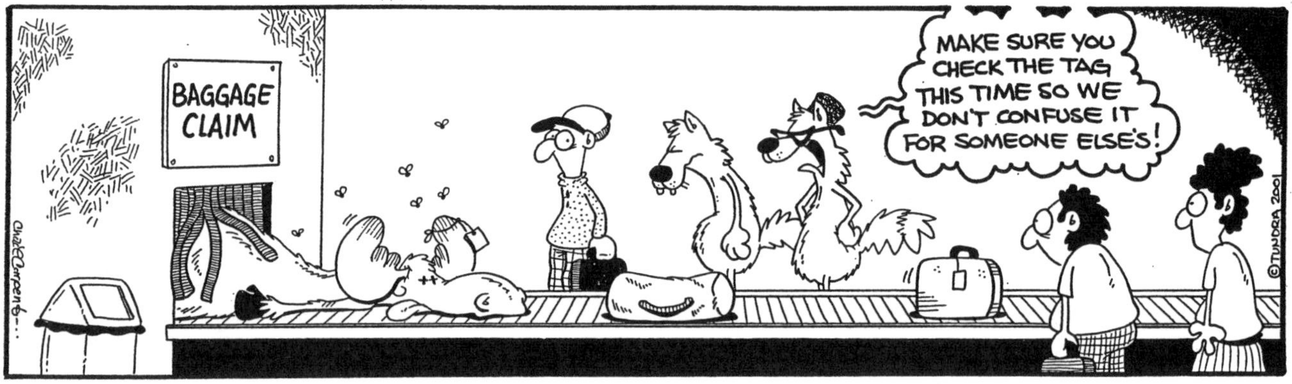
BAGGAGE CLAIM
MAKE SURE YOU CHECK THE TAG THIS TIME SO WE DON'T CONFUSE IT FOR SOMEONE ELSE'S!
©TUNDRA 2001

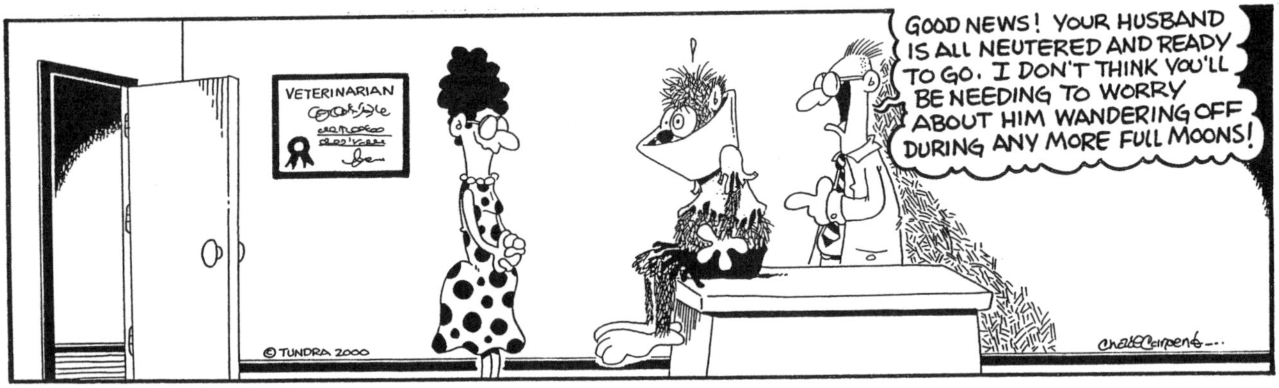
VETERINARIAN
GOOD NEWS! YOUR HUSBAND IS ALL NEUTERED AND READY TO GO. I DON'T THINK YOU'LL BE NEEDING TO WORRY ABOUT HIM WANDERING OFF DURING ANY MORE FULL MOONS!
© TUNDRA 2000

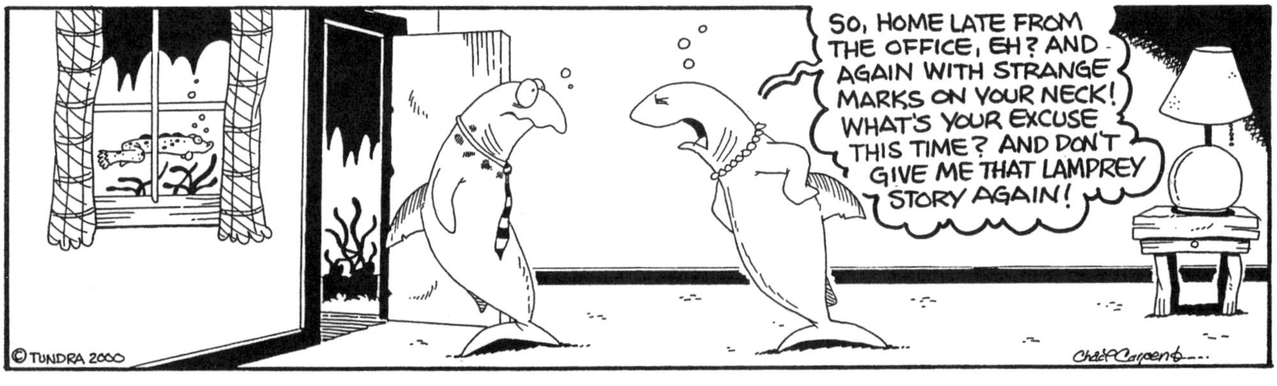
SO, HOME LATE FROM THE OFFICE, EH? AND AGAIN WITH STRANGE MARKS ON YOUR NECK! WHAT'S YOUR EXCUSE THIS TIME? AND DON'T GIVE ME THAT LAMPREY STORY AGAIN!
© TUNDRA 2000

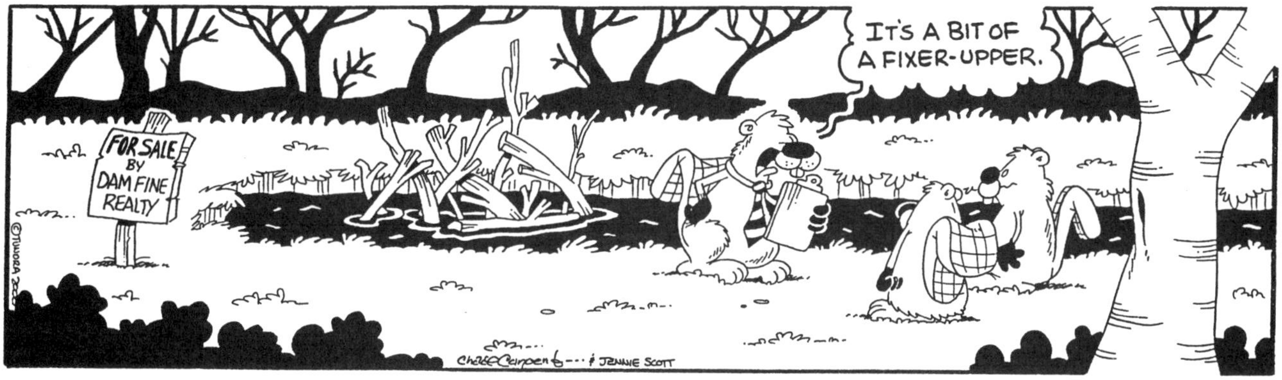
IT'S A BIT OF A FIXER-UPPER.
FOR SALE BY DAM FINE REALTY
©TUNDRA 2000
JENNIE SCOTT

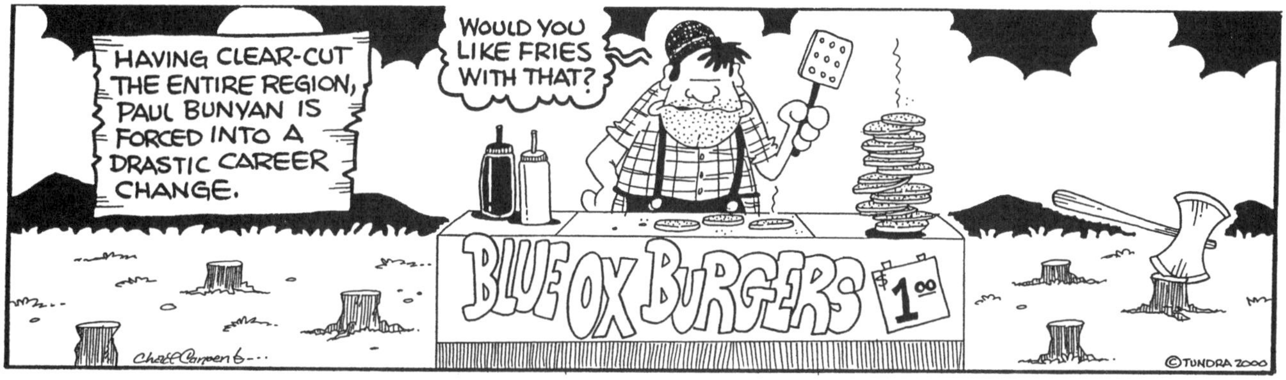
HAVING CLEAR-CUT THE ENTIRE REGION, PAUL BUNYAN IS FORCED INTO A DRASTIC CAREER CHANGE.
WOULD YOU LIKE FRIES WITH THAT?
BLUE OX BURGERS
$1.00
©TUNDRA 2000

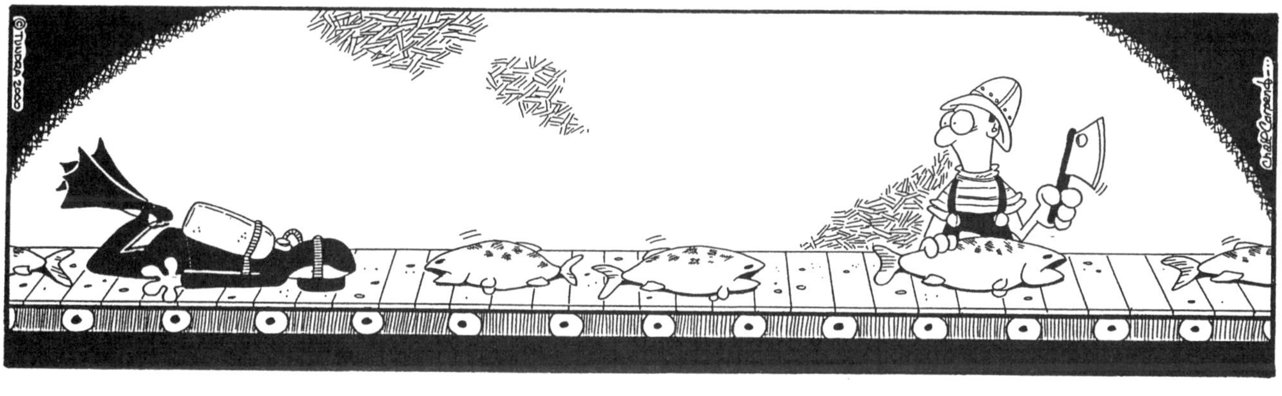
©TUNDRA 2000

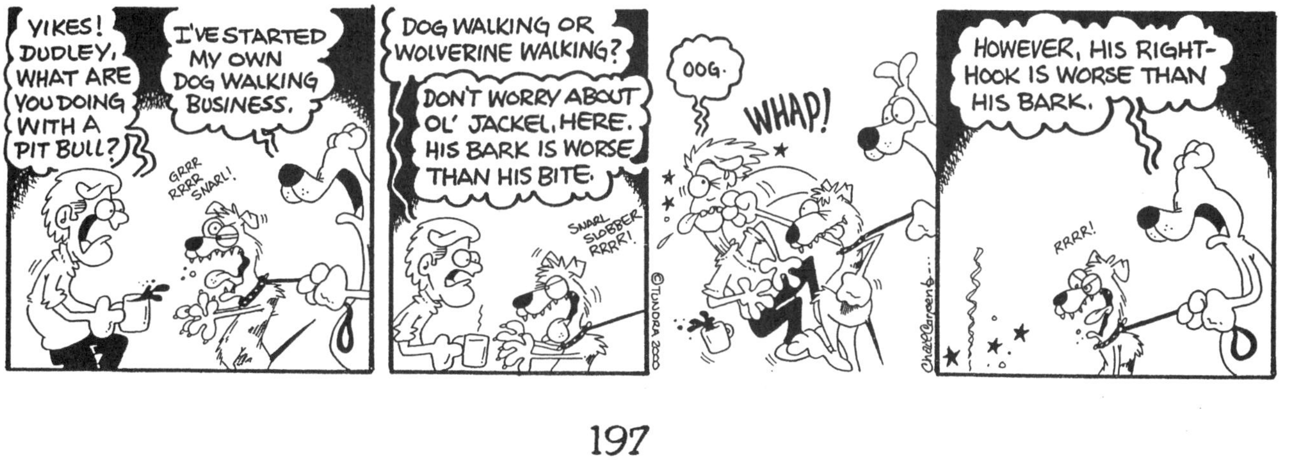
YIKES! DUDLEY, WHAT ARE YOU DOING WITH A PIT BULL?
I'VE STARTED MY OWN DOG WALKING BUSINESS.
GRRR RRRR SNARL!
DOG WALKING OR WOLVERINE WALKING?
DON'T WORRY ABOUT OL' JACKEL, HERE. HIS BARK IS WORSE THAN HIS BITE.
SNARL SLOBBER RRRR!
OOG.
WHAP!
©TUNDRA 2000
HOWEVER, HIS RIGHT-HOOK IS WORSE THAN HIS BARK.
RRRR!

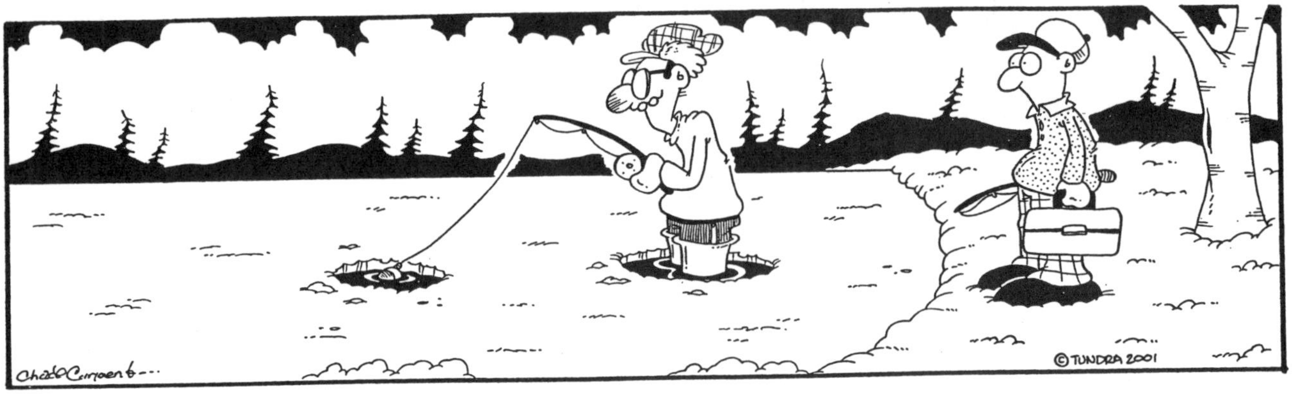
© TUNDRA 2001

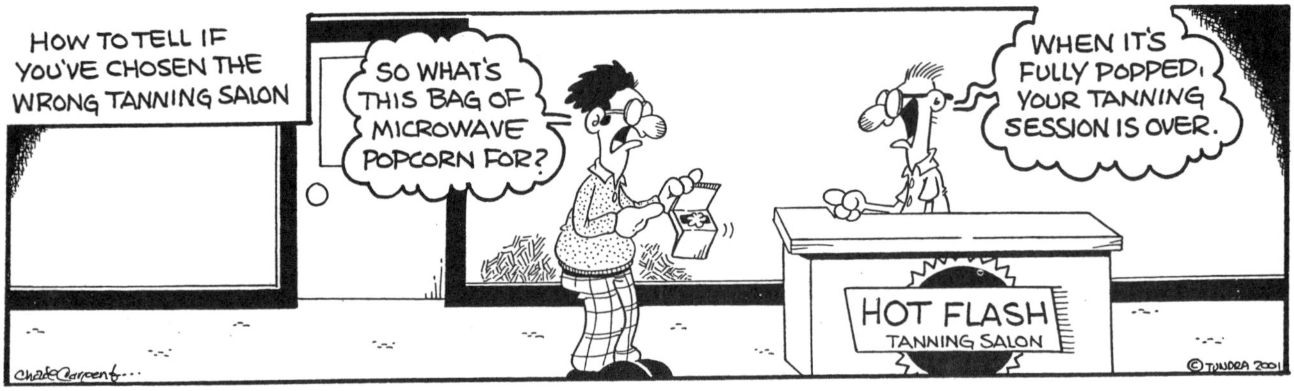
HOW TO TELL IF YOU'VE CHOSEN THE WRONG TANNING SALON
SO WHAT'S THIS BAG OF MICROWAVE POPCORN FOR?
WHEN IT'S FULLY POPPED, YOUR TANNING SESSION IS OVER.
HOT FLASH
TANNING SALON
© TUNDRA 2001

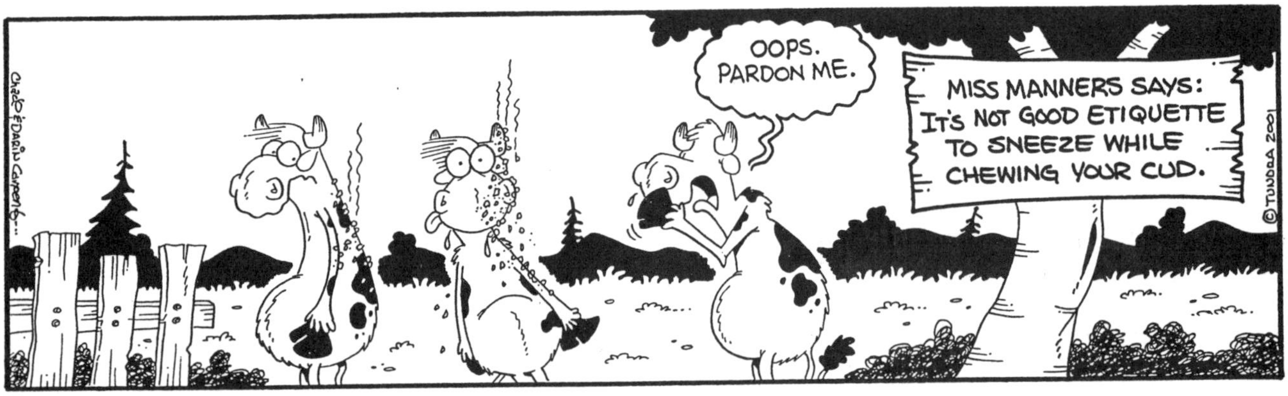
OOPS. PARDON ME.
MISS MANNERS SAYS: IT'S NOT GOOD ETIQUETTE TO SNEEZE WHILE CHEWING YOUR CUD.
© TUNDRA 2001

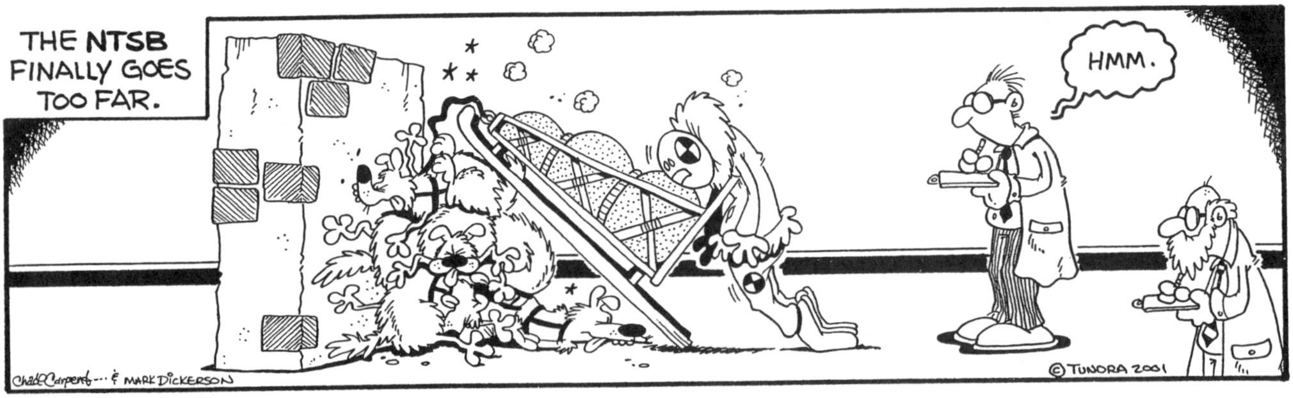
THE NTSB FINALLY GOES TOO FAR.
HMM.
MARK DICKERSON
© TUNDRA 2001

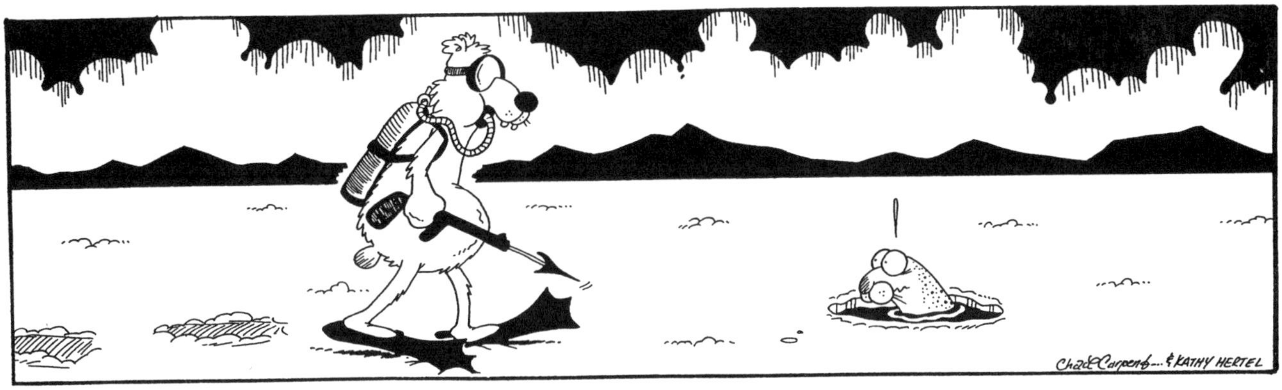
!
& KATHY HERTEL

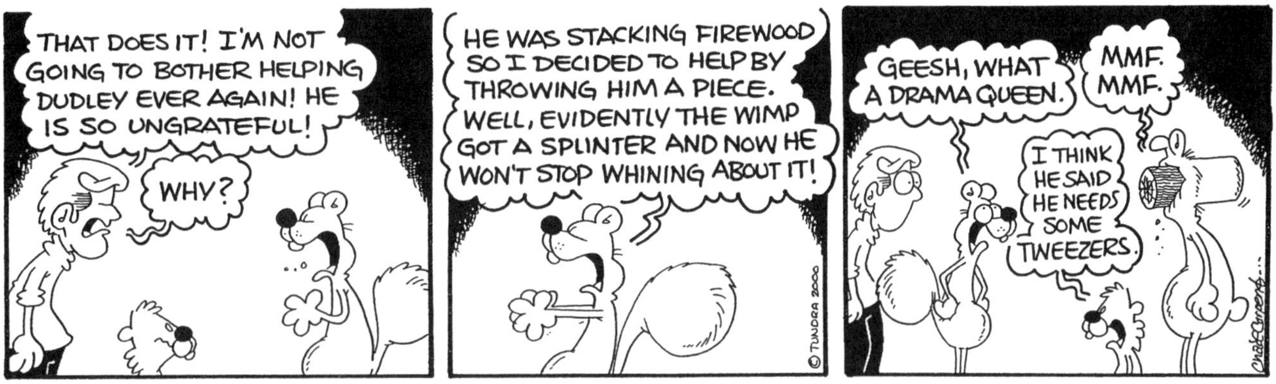
THAT DOES IT! I'M NOT GOING TO BOTHER HELPING DUDLEY EVER AGAIN! HE IS SO UNGRATEFUL!
WHY?
HE WAS STACKING FIREWOOD SO I DECIDED TO HELP BY THROWING HIM A PIECE. WELL, EVIDENTLY THE WIMP GOT A SPLINTER AND NOW HE WON'T STOP WHINING ABOUT IT!
© TUNDRA 2000
GEESH, WHAT A DRAMA QUEEN.
MMF. MMF.
I THINK HE SAID HE NEEDS SOME TWEEZERS.

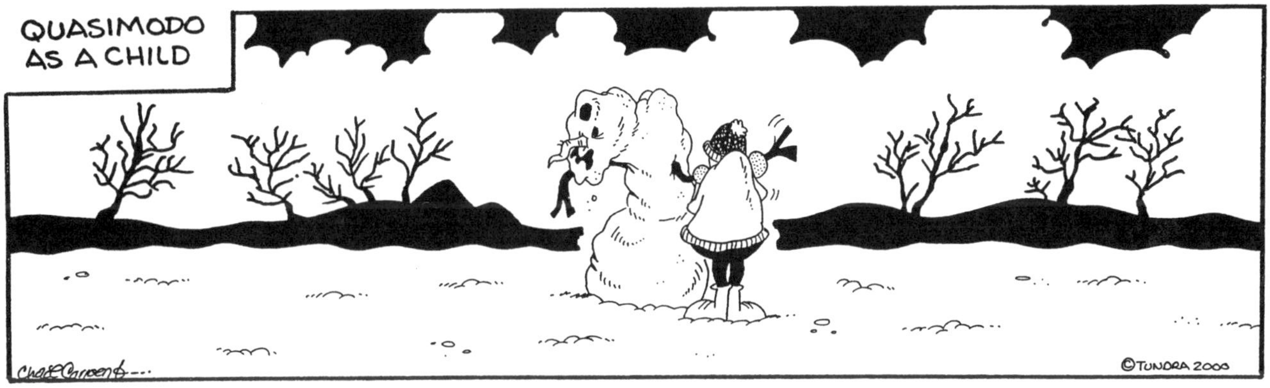
QUASIMODO AS A CHILD
©TUNDRA 2000

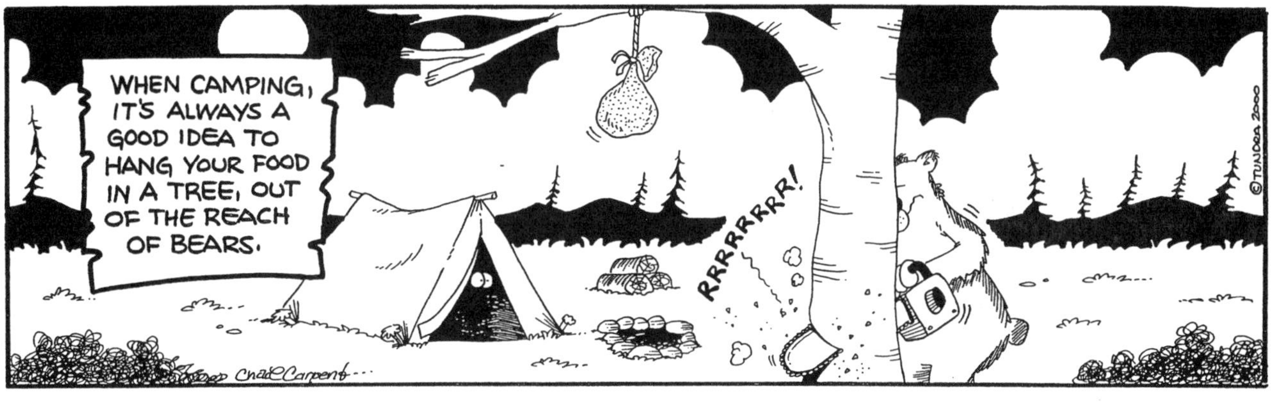
WHEN CAMPING, IT'S ALWAYS A GOOD IDEA TO HANG YOUR FOOD IN A TREE, OUT OF THE REACH OF BEARS.
RRRRRRRR!
©TUNDRA 2000

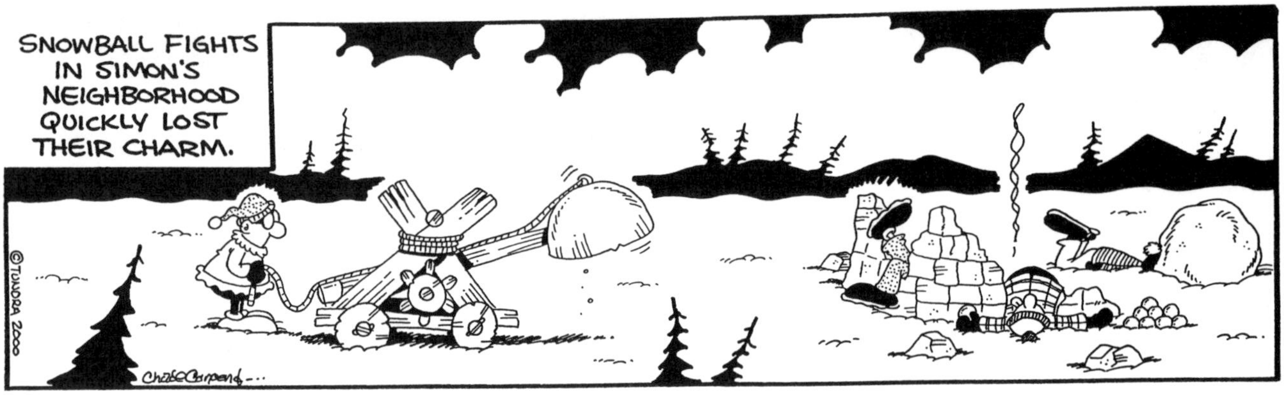

SNOWBALL FIGHTS IN SIMON'S NEIGHBORHOOD QUICKLY LOST THEIR CHARM.
©TUNDRA 2000

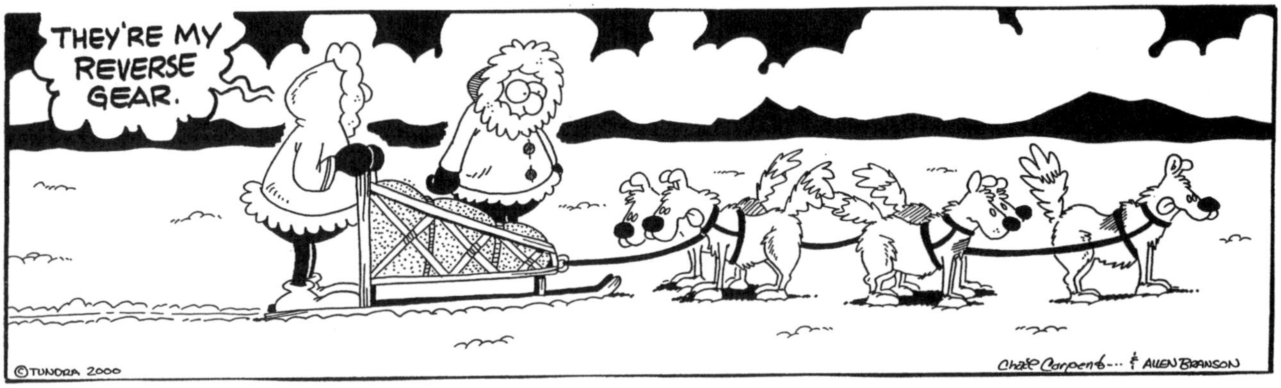

THEY'RE MY REVERSE GEAR.
©TUNDRA 2000
ALLEN BRANSON

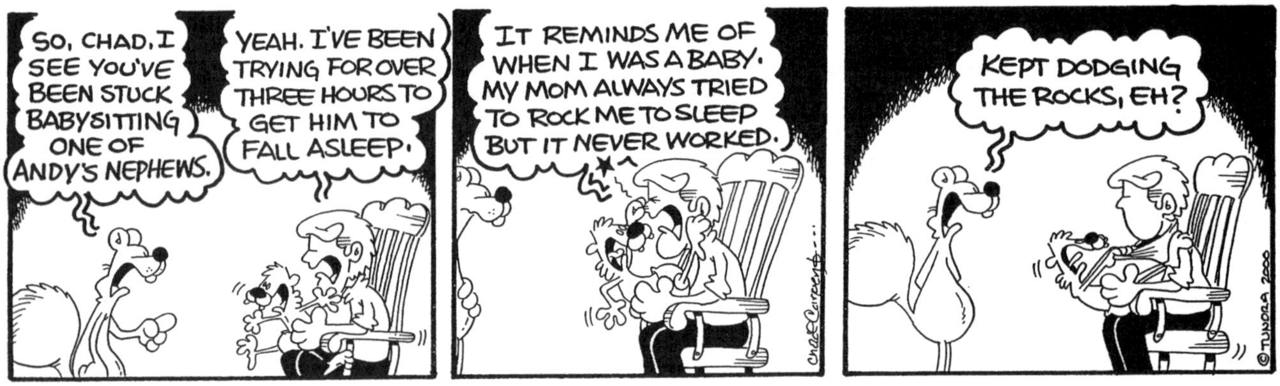

SO, CHAD, I SEE YOU'VE BEEN STUCK BABYSITTING ONE OF ANDY'S NEPHEWS.
YEAH. I'VE BEEN TRYING FOR OVER THREE HOURS TO GET HIM TO FALL ASLEEP.
IT REMINDS ME OF WHEN I WAS A BABY. MY MOM ALWAYS TRIED TO ROCK ME TO SLEEP BUT IT NEVER WORKED.
KEPT DODGING THE ROCKS, EH?
©TUNDRA 2000

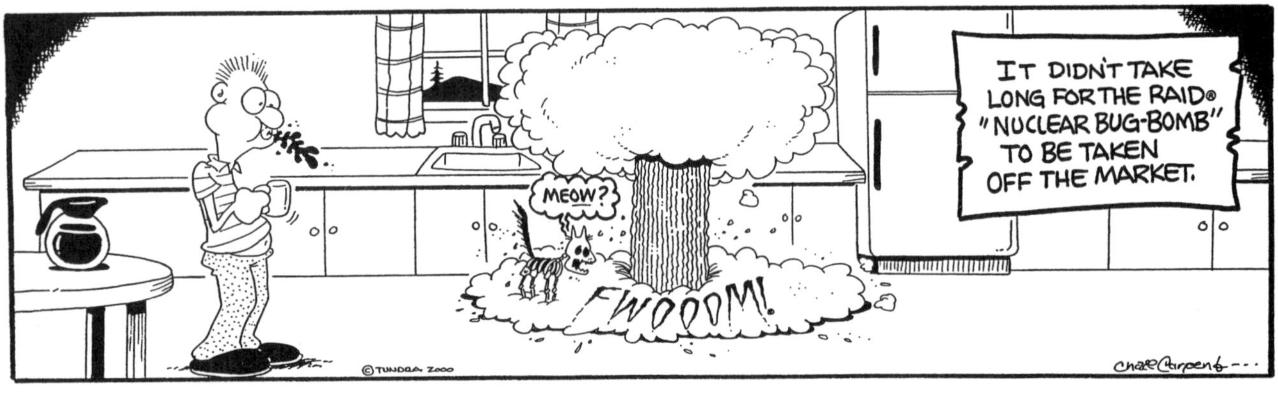

IT DIDN'T TAKE LONG FOR THE RAID® "NUCLEAR BUG-BOMB" TO BE TAKEN OFF THE MARKET.
MEOW?
FWOOOM!
©TUNDRA 2000

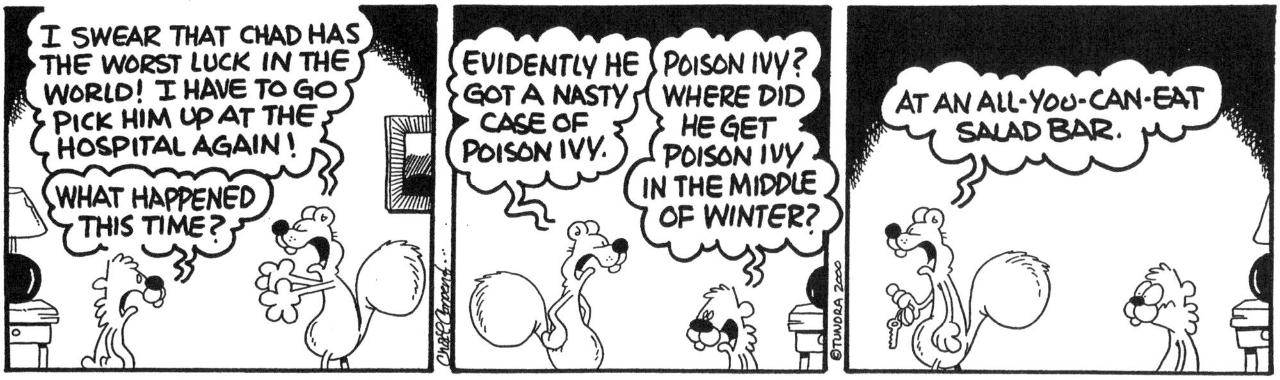
I SWEAR THAT CHAD HAS THE WORST LUCK IN THE WORLD! I HAVE TO GO PICK HIM UP AT THE HOSPITAL AGAIN!
WHAT HAPPENED THIS TIME?
EVIDENTLY HE GOT A NASTY CASE OF POISON IVY.
POISON IVY? WHERE DID HE GET POISON IVY IN THE MIDDLE OF WINTER?
AT AN ALL-YOU-CAN-EAT SALAD BAR.
©TUNDRA 2000

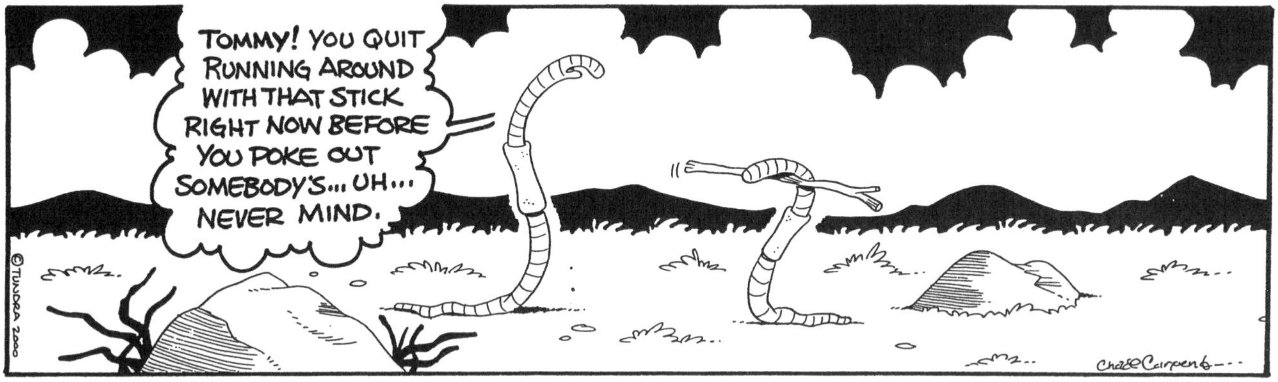
TOMMY! YOU QUIT RUNNING AROUND WITH THAT STICK RIGHT NOW BEFORE YOU POKE OUT SOMEBODY'S... UH... NEVER MIND.
© TUNDRA 2000

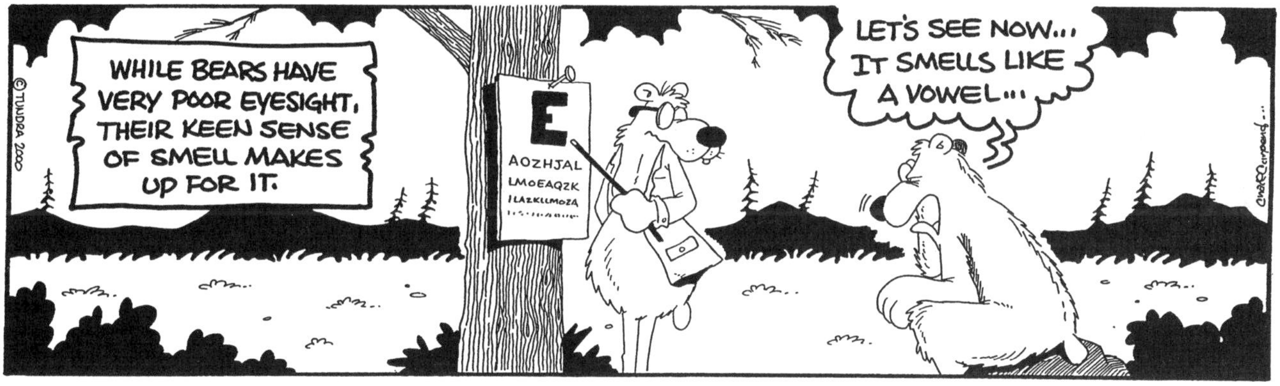
WHILE BEARS HAVE VERY POOR EYESIGHT, THEIR KEEN SENSE OF SMELL MAKES UP FOR IT.
E
AOZHJAL
LET'S SEE NOW... IT SMELLS LIKE A VOWEL...
© TUNDRA 2000

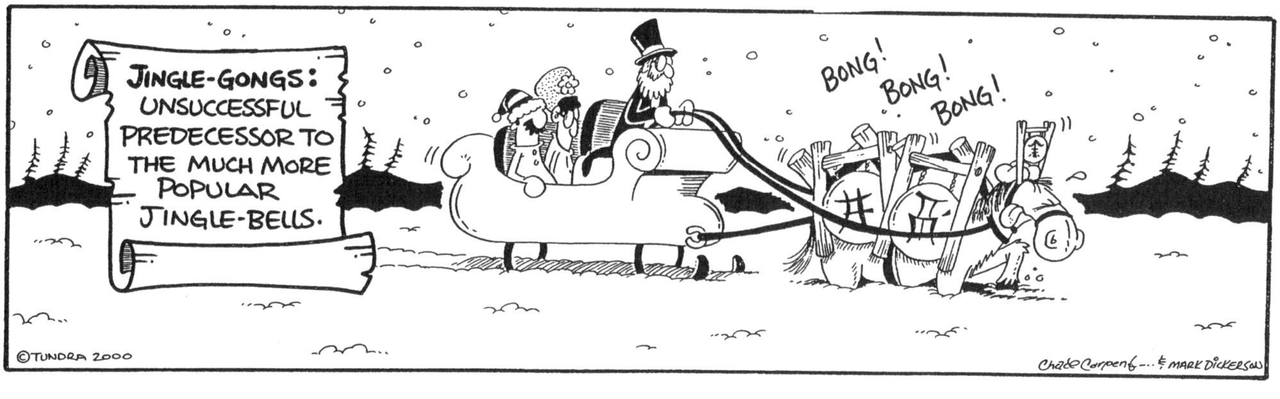
JINGLE-GONGS: UNSUCCESSFUL PREDECESSOR TO THE MUCH MORE POPULAR JINGLE-BELLS.
BONG! BONG! BONG!
©TUNDRA 2000
& MARK DICKERSON

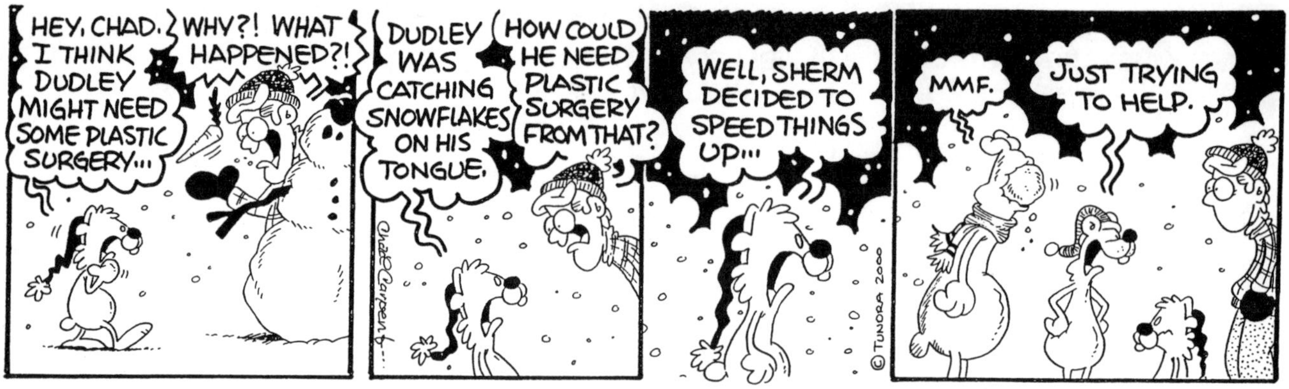
HEY, CHAD. I THINK DUDLEY MIGHT NEED SOME PLASTIC SURGERY...
WHY?! WHAT HAPPENED?!
DUDLEY WAS CATCHING SNOWFLAKES ON HIS TONGUE.
HOW COULD HE NEED PLASTIC SURGERY FROM THAT?
WELL, SHERM DECIDED TO SPEED THINGS UP...
© TUNDRA 2000
MMF.
JUST TRYING TO HELP.

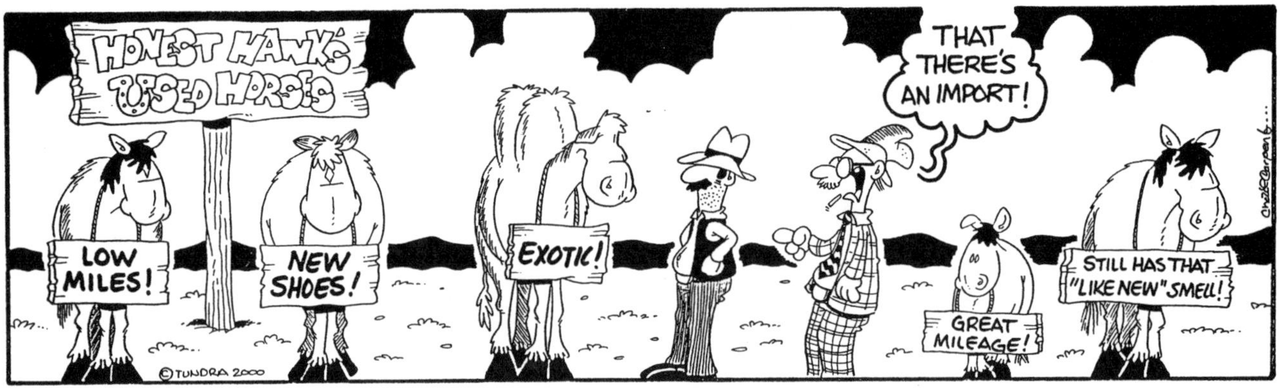
HONEST HANK'S USED HORSES
LOW MILES!
NEW SHOES!
EXOTIC!
THAT THERE'S AN IMPORT!
GREAT MILEAGE!
STILL HAS THAT "LIKE NEW" SMELL!
© TUNDRA 2000

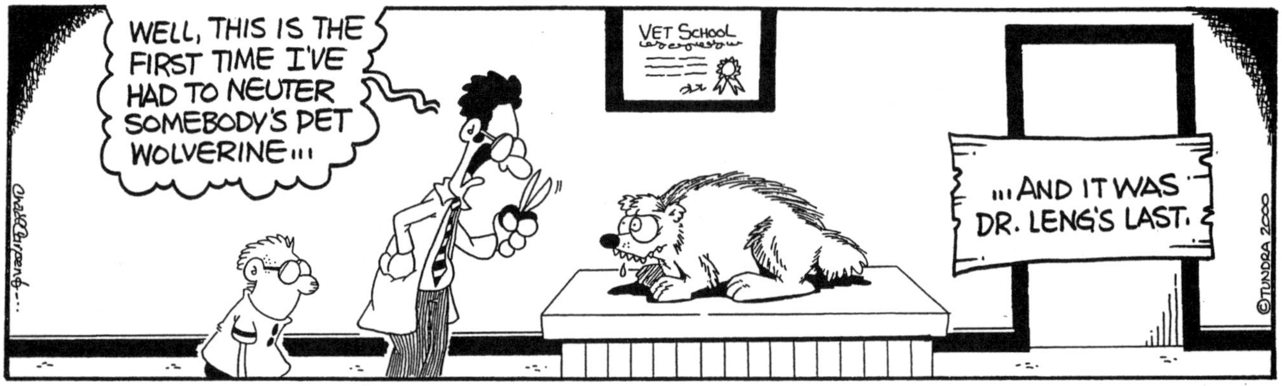
WELL, THIS IS THE FIRST TIME I'VE HAD TO NEUTER SOMEBODY'S PET WOLVERINE...
VET SCHOOL
...AND IT WAS DR. LENG'S LAST.
© TUNDRA 2000

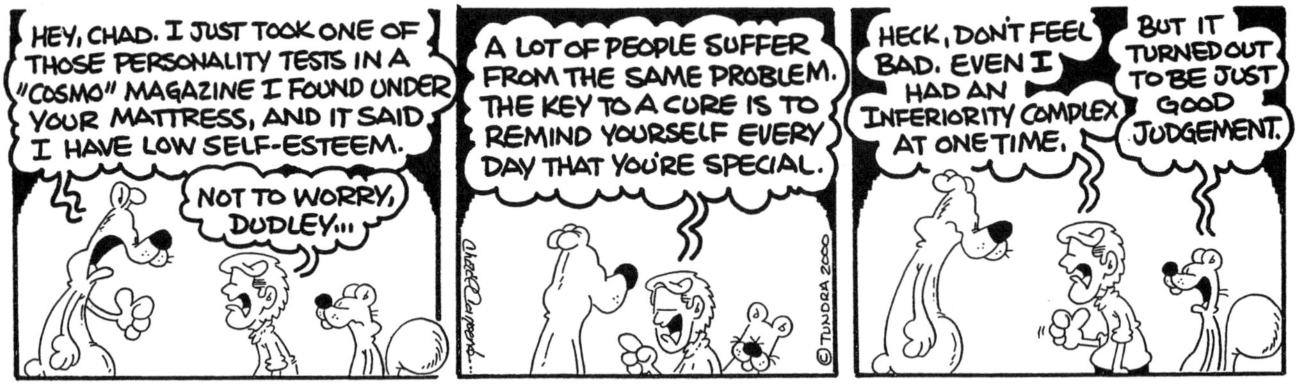
HEY, CHAD. I JUST TOOK ONE OF THOSE PERSONALITY TESTS IN A "COSMO" MAGAZINE I FOUND UNDER YOUR MATTRESS, AND IT SAID I HAVE LOW SELF-ESTEEM.
NOT TO WORRY, DUDLEY...
A LOT OF PEOPLE SUFFER FROM THE SAME PROBLEM. THE KEY TO A CURE IS TO REMIND YOURSELF EVERY DAY THAT YOU'RE SPECIAL.
© TUNDRA 2000
HECK, DON'T FEEL BAD. EVEN I HAD AN INFERIORITY COMPLEX AT ONE TIME.
BUT IT TURNED OUT TO BE JUST GOOD JUDGEMENT.

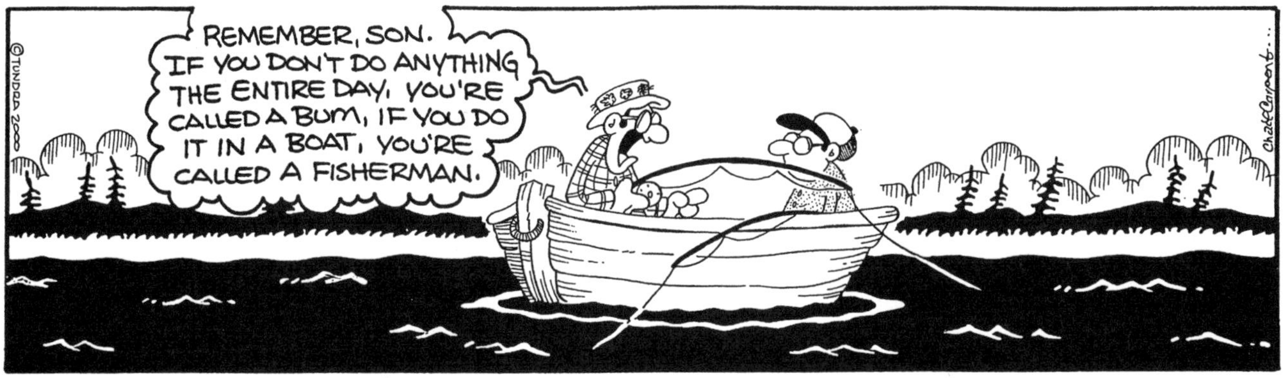
REMEMBER, SON. IF YOU DON'T DO ANYTHING THE ENTIRE DAY, YOU'RE CALLED A BUM, IF YOU DO IT IN A BOAT, YOU'RE CALLED A FISHERMAN.
©TUNDRA 2000

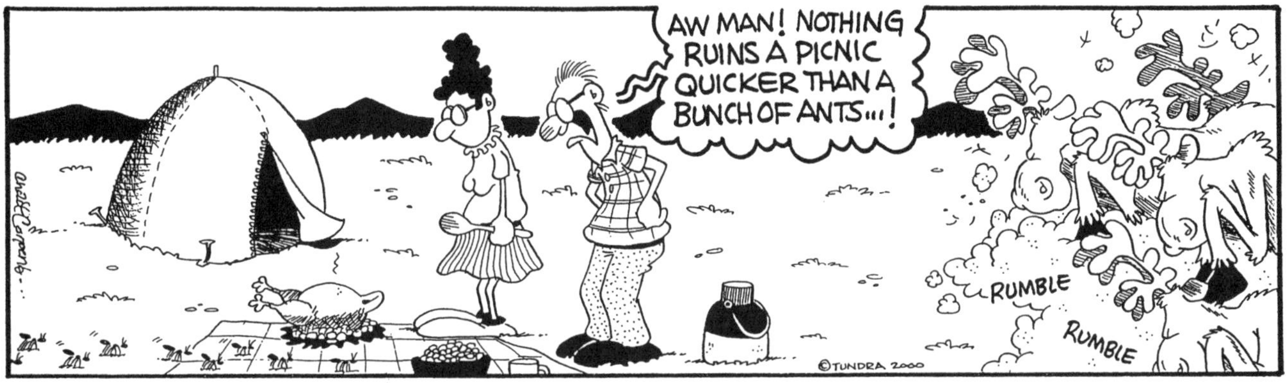
AW MAN! NOTHING RUINS A PICNIC QUICKER THAN A BUNCH OF ANTS...!
RUMBLE
RUMBLE
©TUNDRA 2000

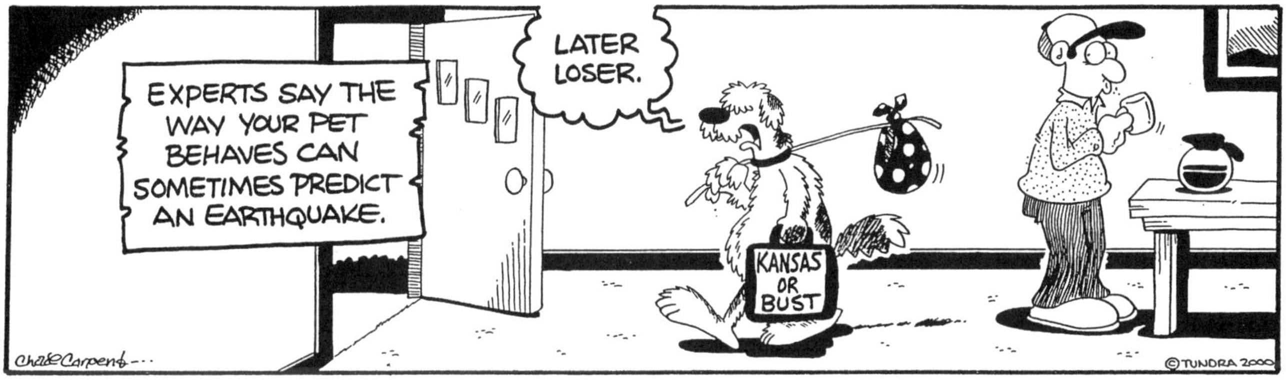
EXPERTS SAY THE WAY YOUR PET BEHAVES CAN SOMETIMES PREDICT AN EARTHQUAKE.
LATER LOSER.
KANSAS OR BUST
©TUNDRA 2000

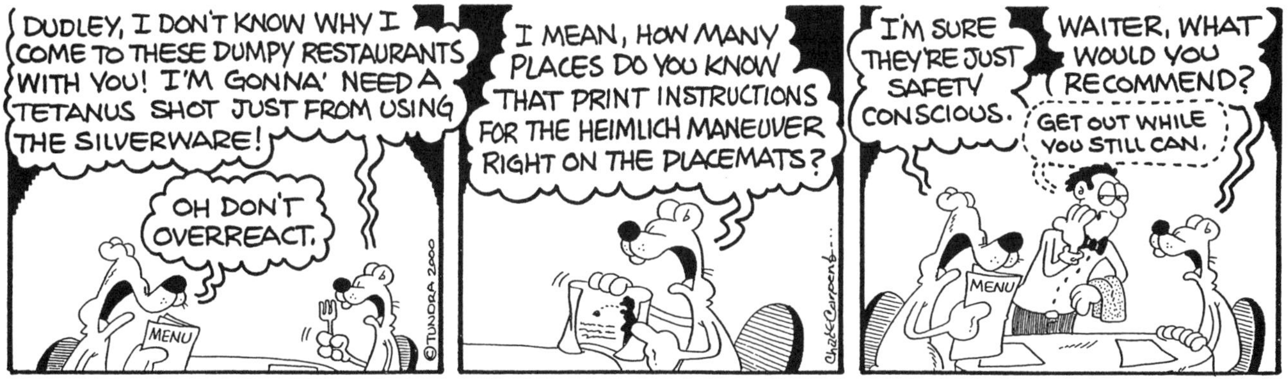
DUDLEY, I DON'T KNOW WHY I COME TO THESE DUMPY RESTAURANTS WITH YOU! I'M GONNA' NEED A TETANUS SHOT JUST FROM USING THE SILVERWARE!
OH DON'T OVERREACT.
MENU
©TUNDRA 2000
I MEAN, HOW MANY PLACES DO YOU KNOW THAT PRINT INSTRUCTIONS FOR THE HEIMLICH MANEUVER RIGHT ON THE PLACEMATS?
I'M SURE THEY'RE JUST SAFETY CONSCIOUS.
WAITER, WHAT WOULD YOU RECOMMEND?
GET OUT WHILE YOU STILL CAN.
MENU

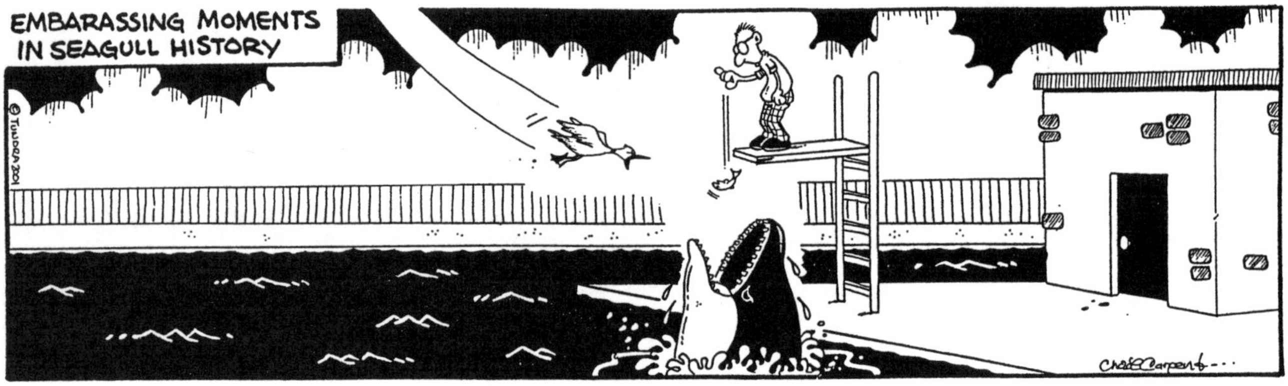
EMBARASSING MOMENTS IN SEAGULL HISTORY

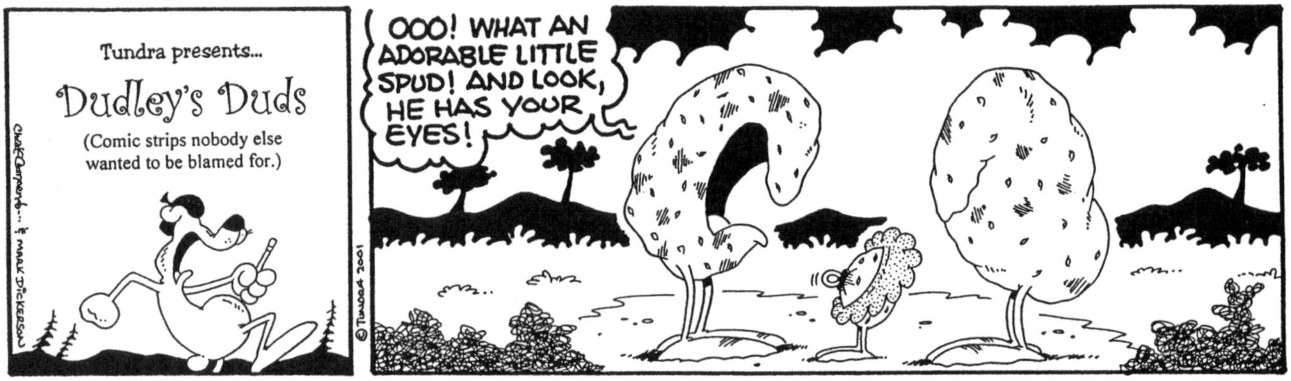
Tundra presents...
Dudley's Duds
(Comic strips nobody else wanted to be blamed for.)
OOO! WHAT AN ADORABLE LITTLE SPUD! AND LOOK, HE HAS YOUR EYES!

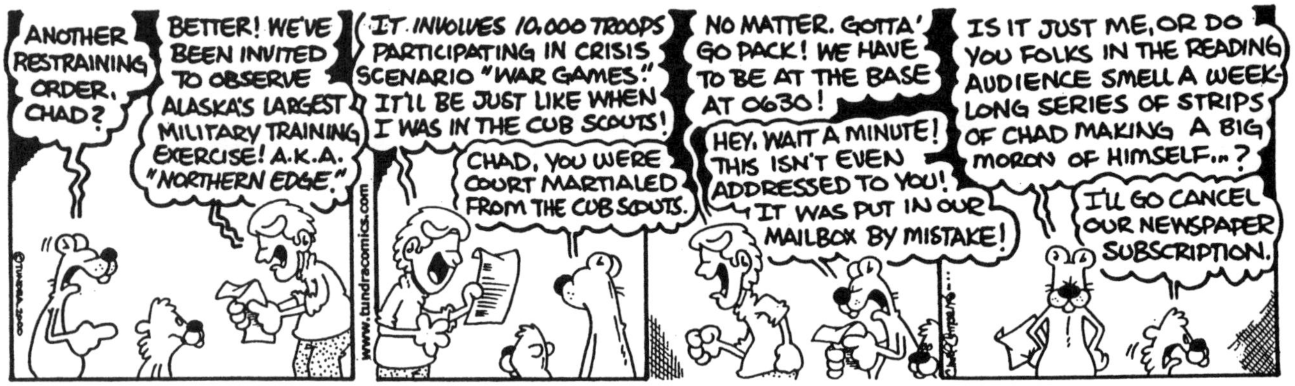
ANOTHER RESTRAINING ORDER, CHAD?
BETTER! WE'VE BEEN INVITED TO OBSERVE ALASKA'S LARGEST MILITARY TRAINING EXERCISE! A.K.A. "NORTHERN EDGE."
IT INVOLVES 10,000 TROOPS PARTICIPATING IN CRISIS SCENARIO "WAR GAMES." IT'LL BE JUST LIKE WHEN I WAS IN THE CUB SCOUTS!
CHAD, YOU WERE COURT MARTIALED FROM THE CUB SCOUTS.
www.tundracomics.com
NO MATTER. GOTTA' GO PACK! WE HAVE TO BE AT THE BASE AT 0630!
HEY, WAIT A MINUTE! THIS ISN'T EVEN ADDRESSED TO YOU! IT WAS PUT IN OUR MAILBOX BY MISTAKE!
IS IT JUST ME, OR DO YOU FOLKS IN THE READING AUDIENCE SMELL A WEEK-LONG SERIES OF STRIPS OF CHAD MAKING A BIG MORON OF HIMSELF...?
I'LL GO CANCEL OUR NEWSPAPER SUBSCRIPTION.

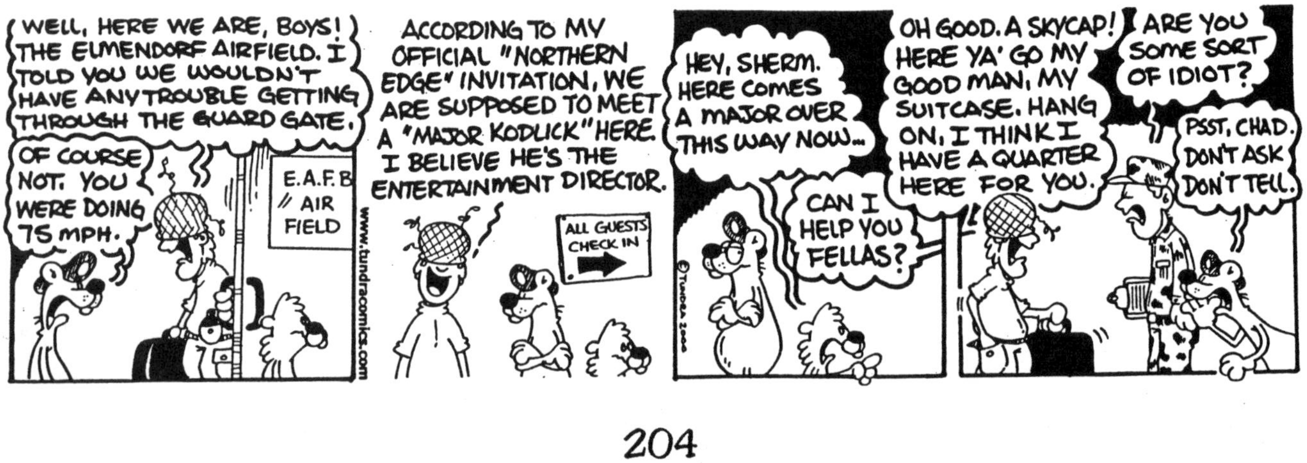
WELL, HERE WE ARE, BOYS! THE ELMENDORF AIRFIELD. I TOLD YOU WE WOULDN'T HAVE ANY TROUBLE GETTING THROUGH THE GUARD GATE.
OF COURSE NOT. YOU WERE DOING 75 MPH.
E.A.F.B AIR FIELD
ACCORDING TO MY OFFICIAL "NORTHERN EDGE" INVITATION, WE ARE SUPPOSED TO MEET A "MAJOR KODLICK" HERE. I BELIEVE HE'S THE ENTERTAINMENT DIRECTOR.
ALL GUESTS CHECK IN
www.tundracomics.com
HEY, SHERM. HERE COMES A MAJOR OVER THIS WAY NOW...
CAN I HELP YOU FELLAS?
OH GOOD. A SKYCAP! HERE YA' GO MY GOOD MAN, MY SUITCASE. HANG ON, I THINK I HAVE A QUARTER HERE FOR YOU.
ARE YOU SOME SORT OF IDIOT?
PSST, CHAD. DON'T ASK DON'T TELL.

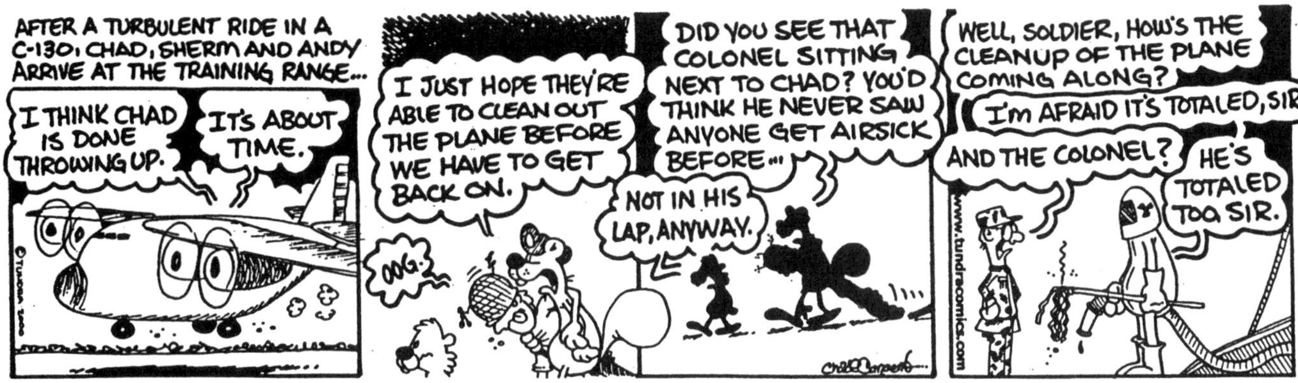
AFTER A TURBULENT RIDE IN A C-130, CHAD, SHERM AND ANDY ARRIVE AT THE TRAINING RANGE...
I THINK CHAD IS DONE THROWING UP.
IT'S ABOUT TIME.
I JUST HOPE THEY'RE ABLE TO CLEAN OUT THE PLANE BEFORE WE HAVE TO GET BACK ON.
OOG.
DID YOU SEE THAT COLONEL SITTING NEXT TO CHAD? YOU'D THINK HE NEVER SAW ANYONE GET AIRSICK BEFORE...
NOT IN HIS LAP, ANYWAY.
WELL, SOLDIER, HOW'S THE CLEANUP OF THE PLANE COMING ALONG?
I'M AFRAID IT'S TOTALED, SIR.
AND THE COLONEL?
HE'S TOTALED TOO, SIR.
www.tundracomics.com

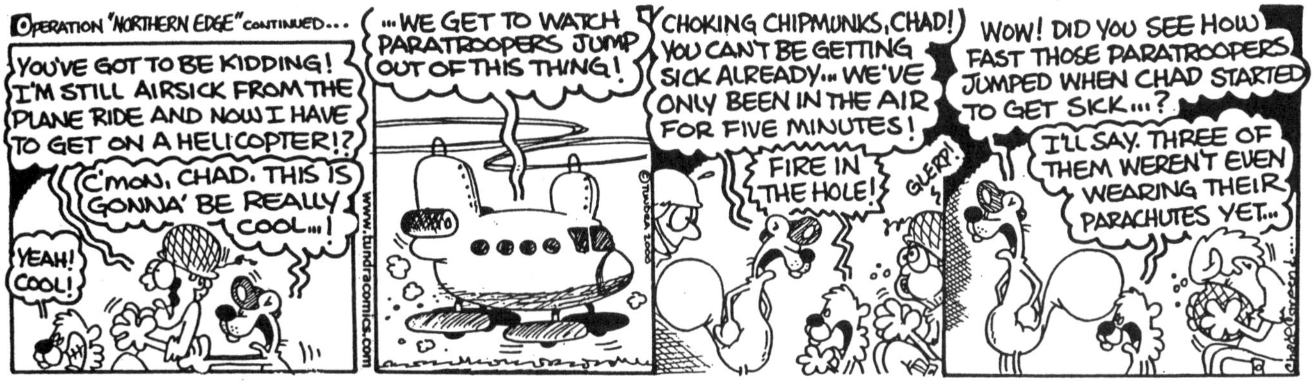
OPERATION "NORTHERN EDGE" CONTINUED...
YOU'VE GOT TO BE KIDDING! I'M STILL AIRSICK FROM THE PLANE RIDE AND NOW I HAVE TO GET ON A HELICOPTER!?
C'MON, CHAD. THIS IS GONNA' BE REALLY COOL...!
YEAH! COOL!
www.tundracomics.com
...WE GET TO WATCH PARATROOPERS JUMP OUT OF THIS THING!
CHOKING CHIPMUNKS, CHAD! YOU CAN'T BE GETTING SICK ALREADY... WE'VE ONLY BEEN IN THE AIR FOR FIVE MINUTES!
FIRE IN THE HOLE!
GLERP!
WOW! DID YOU SEE HOW FAST THOSE PARATROOPERS JUMPED WHEN CHAD STARTED TO GET SICK...?
I'LL SAY. THREE OF THEM WEREN'T EVEN WEARING THEIR PARACHUTES YET...

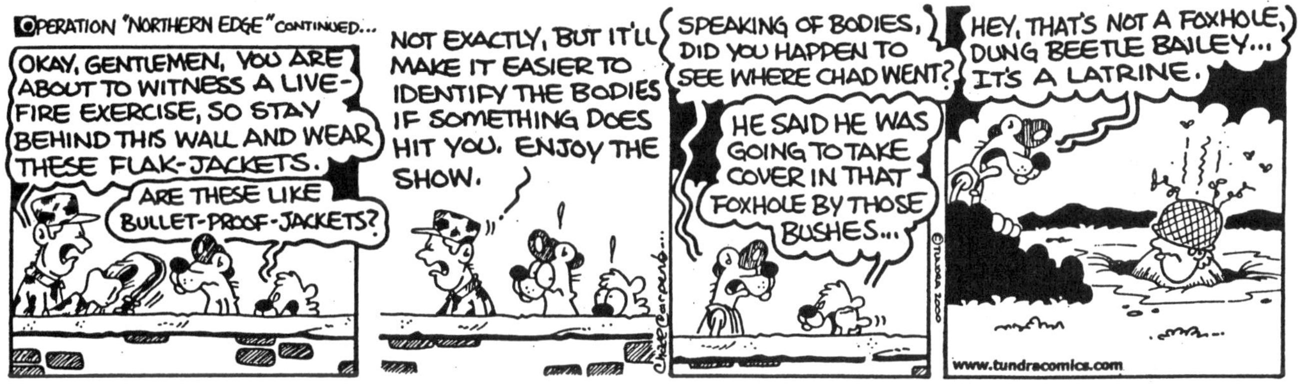
OPERATION "NORTHERN EDGE" CONTINUED...
OKAY, GENTLEMEN, YOU ARE ABOUT TO WITNESS A LIVE-FIRE EXERCISE, SO STAY BEHIND THIS WALL AND WEAR THESE FLAK-JACKETS.
ARE THESE LIKE BULLET-PROOF-JACKETS?
NOT EXACTLY, BUT IT'LL MAKE IT EASIER TO IDENTIFY THE BODIES IF SOMETHING DOES HIT YOU. ENJOY THE SHOW.
SPEAKING OF BODIES, DID YOU HAPPEN TO SEE WHERE CHAD WENT?
HE SAID HE WAS GOING TO TAKE COVER IN THAT FOXHOLE BY THOSE BUSHES...
HEY, THAT'S NOT A FOXHOLE, DUNG BEETLE BAILEY... IT'S A LATRINE.
www.tundracomics.com

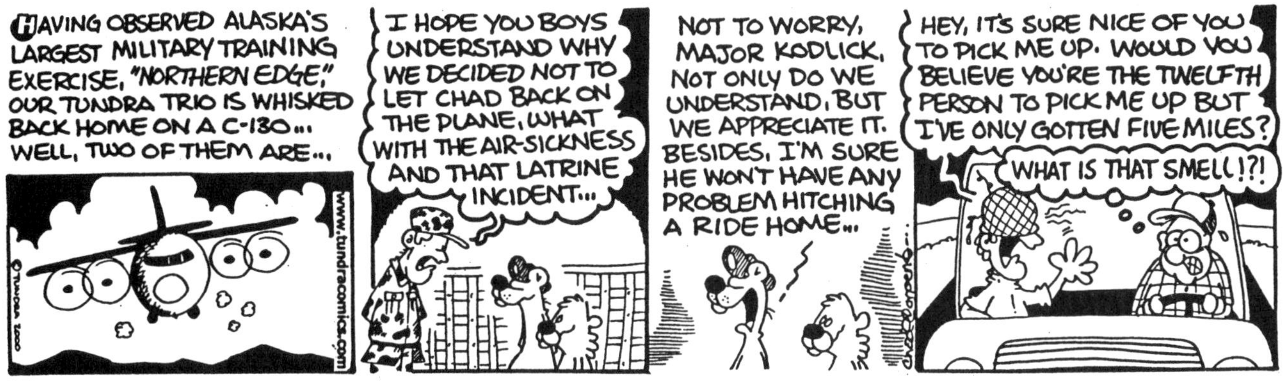
HAVING OBSERVED ALASKA'S LARGEST MILITARY TRAINING EXERCISE, "NORTHERN EDGE," OUR TUNDRA TRIO IS WHISKED BACK HOME ON A C-130... WELL, TWO OF THEM ARE...
www.tundracomics.com
I HOPE YOU BOYS UNDERSTAND WHY WE DECIDED NOT TO LET CHAD BACK ON THE PLANE, WHAT WITH THE AIR-SICKNESS AND THAT LATRINE INCIDENT...
NOT TO WORRY, MAJOR KODLICK, NOT ONLY DO WE UNDERSTAND, BUT WE APPRECIATE IT. BESIDES, I'M SURE HE WON'T HAVE ANY PROBLEM HITCHING A RIDE HOME...
HEY, IT'S SURE NICE OF YOU TO PICK ME UP. WOULD YOU BELIEVE YOU'RE THE TWELFTH PERSON TO PICK ME UP BUT I'VE ONLY GOTTEN FIVE MILES?
WHAT IS THAT SMELL!?!

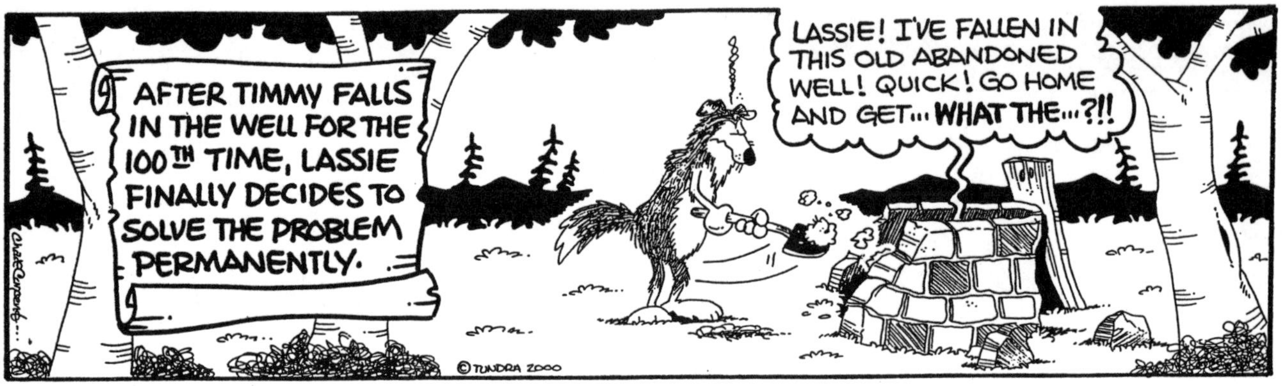
AFTER TIMMY FALLS IN THE WELL FOR THE 100TH TIME, LASSIE FINALLY DECIDES TO SOLVE THE PROBLEM PERMANENTLY.
LASSIE! I'VE FALLEN IN THIS OLD ABANDONED WELL! QUICK! GO HOME AND GET... WHAT THE...?!!
©TUNDRA 2000

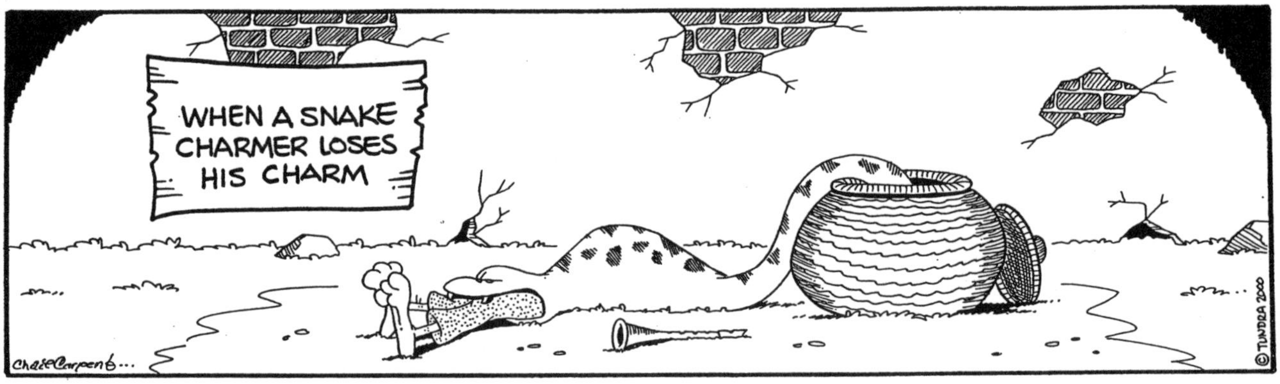
WHEN A SNAKE CHARMER LOSES HIS CHARM
©TUNDRA 2000

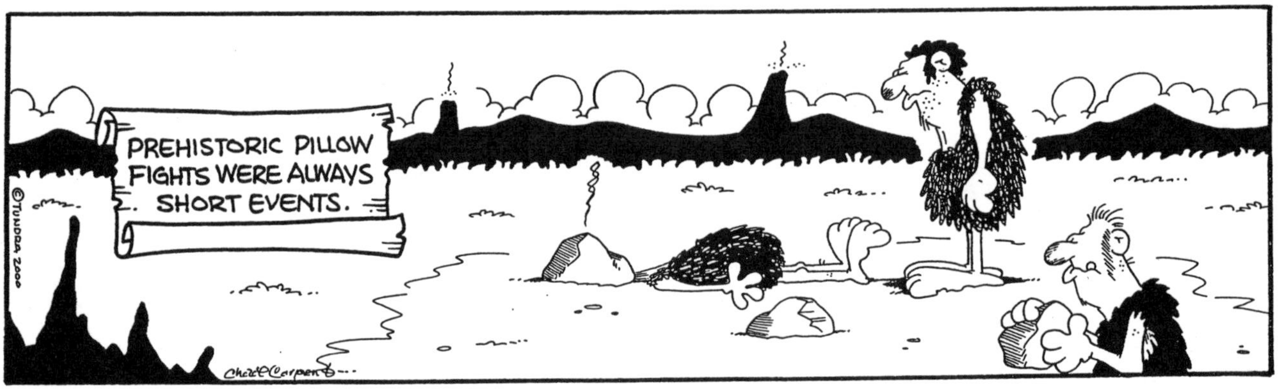
PREHISTORIC PILLOW FIGHTS WERE ALWAYS SHORT EVENTS.
©TUNDRA 2000

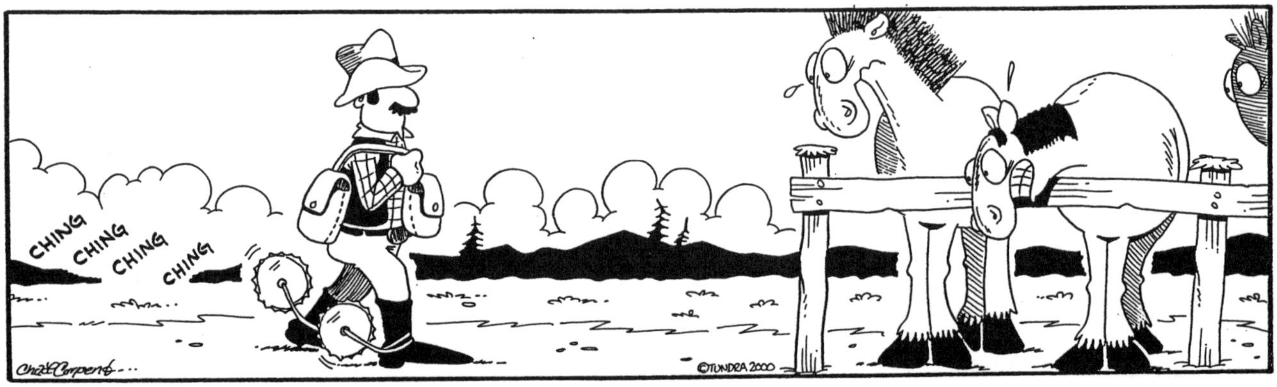
CHING
CHING
CHING
CHING
©TUNDRA 2000

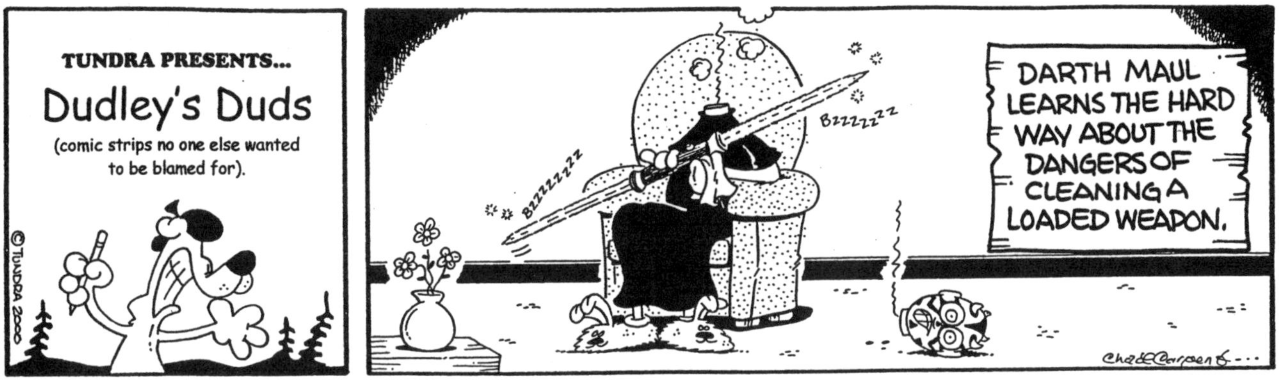
TUNDRA PRESENTS...
Dudley's Duds
(comic strips no one else wanted to be blamed for).
© TUNDRA 2000
Bzzzzzzz
Bzzzzzz
DARTH MAUL LEARNS THE HARD WAY ABOUT THE DANGERS OF CLEANING A LOADED WEAPON.

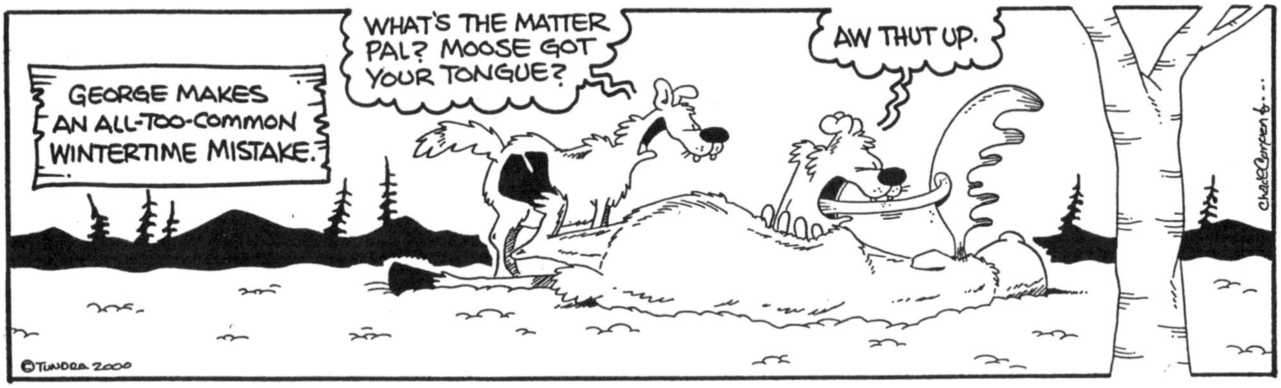
GEORGE MAKES AN ALL-TOO-COMMON WINTERTIME MISTAKE.
WHAT'S THE MATTER PAL? MOOSE GOT YOUR TONGUE?
AW THUT UP.
©TUNDRA 2000

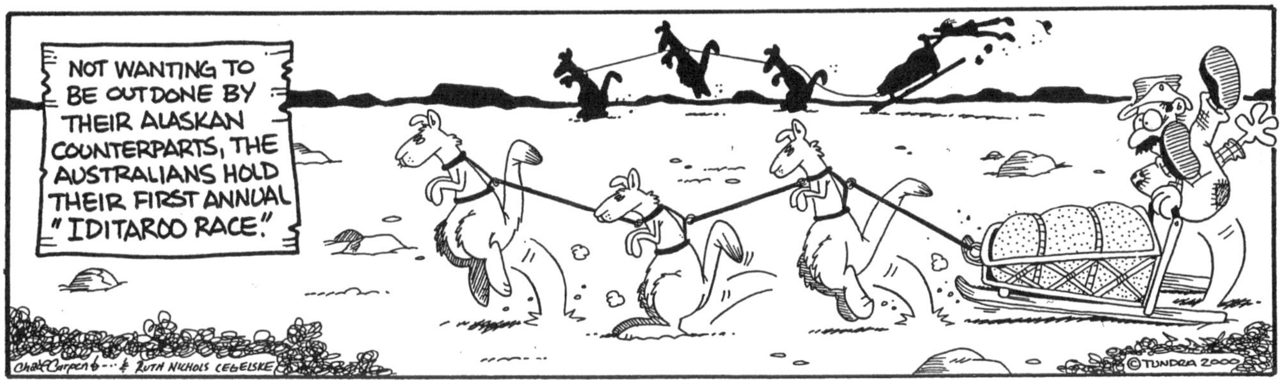
NOT WANTING TO BE OUTDONE BY THEIR ALASKAN COUNTERPARTS, THE AUSTRALIANS HOLD THEIR FIRST ANNUAL "IDITAROO RACE."
& RUTH NICHOLS CEGELSKE
©TUNDRA 2000

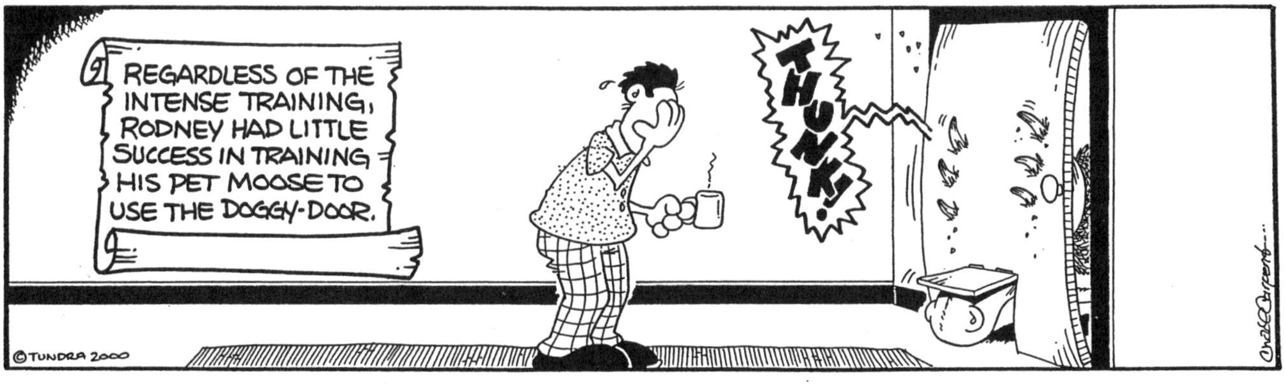
REGARDLESS OF THE INTENSE TRAINING, RODNEY HAD LITTLE SUCCESS IN TRAINING HIS PET MOOSE TO USE THE DOGGY-DOOR.
THUNK!
©TUNDRA 2000

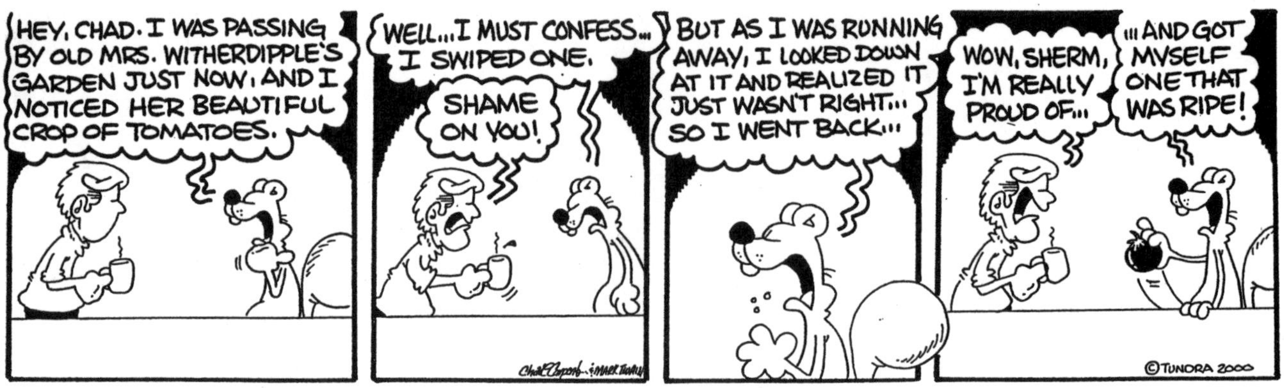
HEY, CHAD. I WAS PASSING BY OLD MRS. WITHERDIPPLE'S GARDEN JUST NOW, AND I NOTICED HER BEAUTIFUL CROP OF TOMATOES.
WELL... I MUST CONFESS... I SWIPED ONE.
SHAME ON YOU!
BUT AS I WAS RUNNING AWAY, I LOOKED DOWN AT IT AND REALIZED IT JUST WASN'T RIGHT... SO I WENT BACK...
WOW, SHERM, I'M REALLY PROUD OF...
...AND GOT MYSELF ONE THAT WAS RIPE!
©TUNDRA 2000

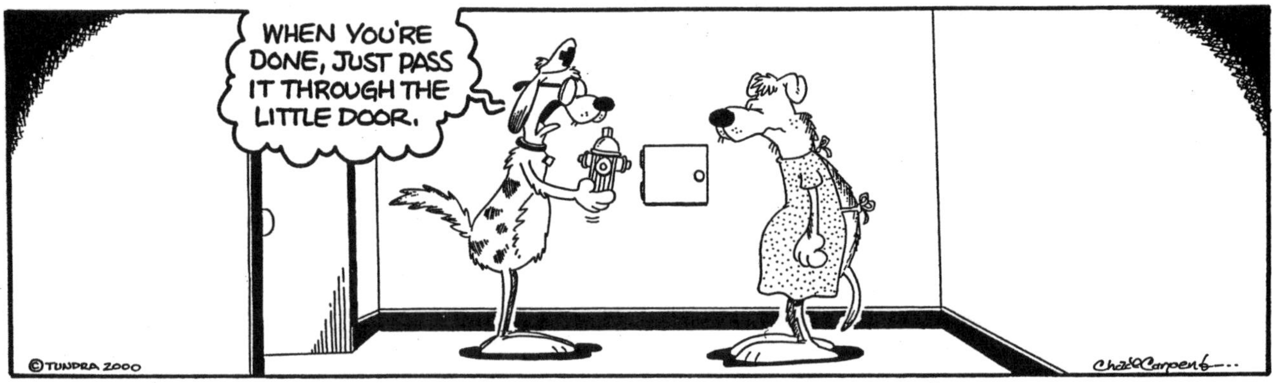
WHEN YOU'RE DONE, JUST PASS IT THROUGH THE LITTLE DOOR.
©TUNDRA 2000

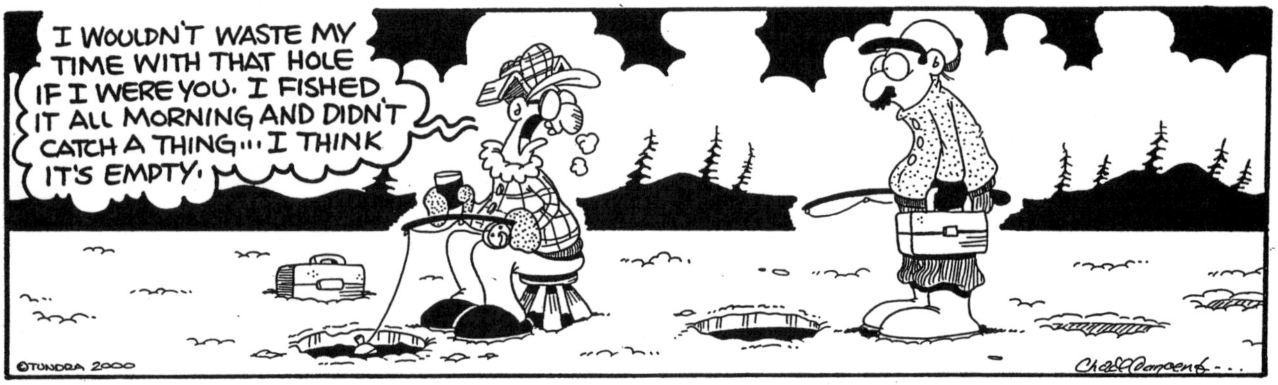
I WOULDN'T WASTE MY TIME WITH THAT HOLE IF I WERE YOU. I FISHED IT ALL MORNING AND DIDN'T CATCH A THING... I THINK IT'S EMPTY.
©TUNDRA 2000

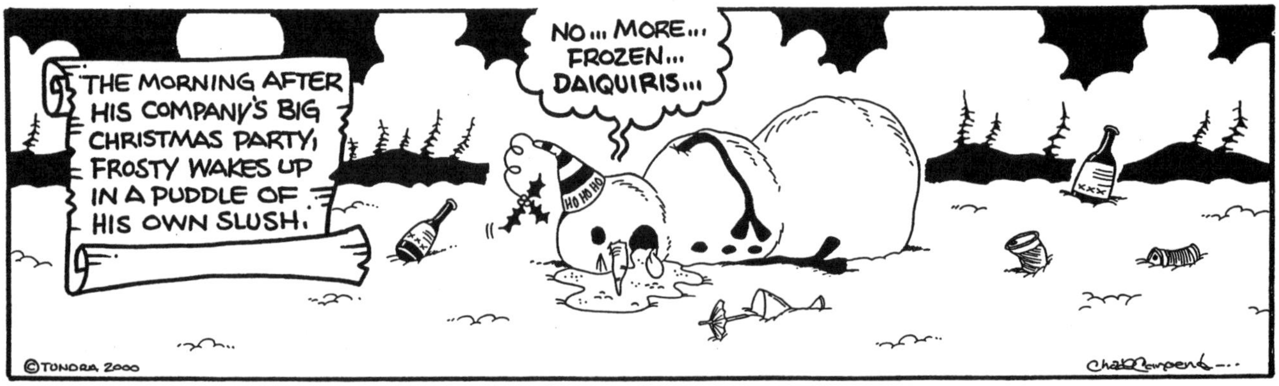
THE MORNING AFTER HIS COMPANY'S BIG CHRISTMAS PARTY, FROSTY WAKES UP IN A PUDDLE OF HIS OWN SLUSH.
NO... MORE... FROZEN... DAIQUIRIS...
HO HO HO
©TUNDRA 2000

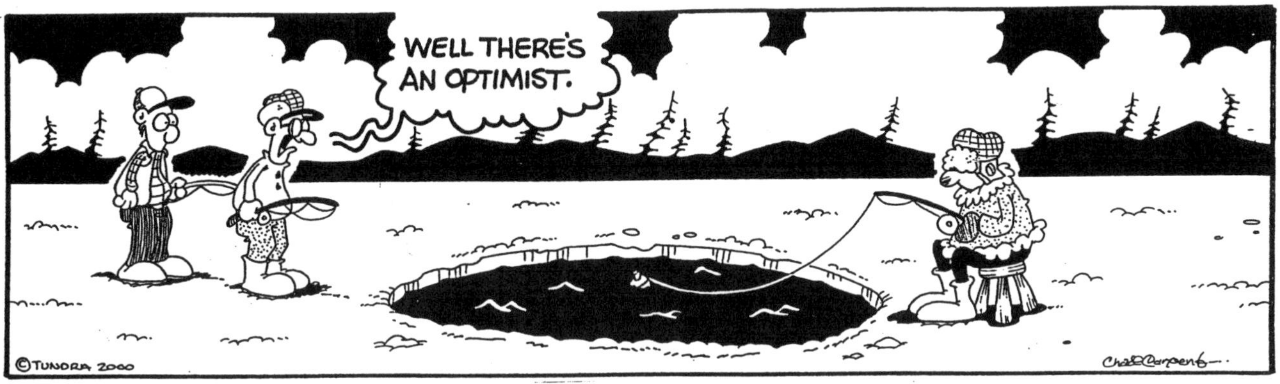
WELL THERE'S AN OPTIMIST.
©TUNDRA 2000

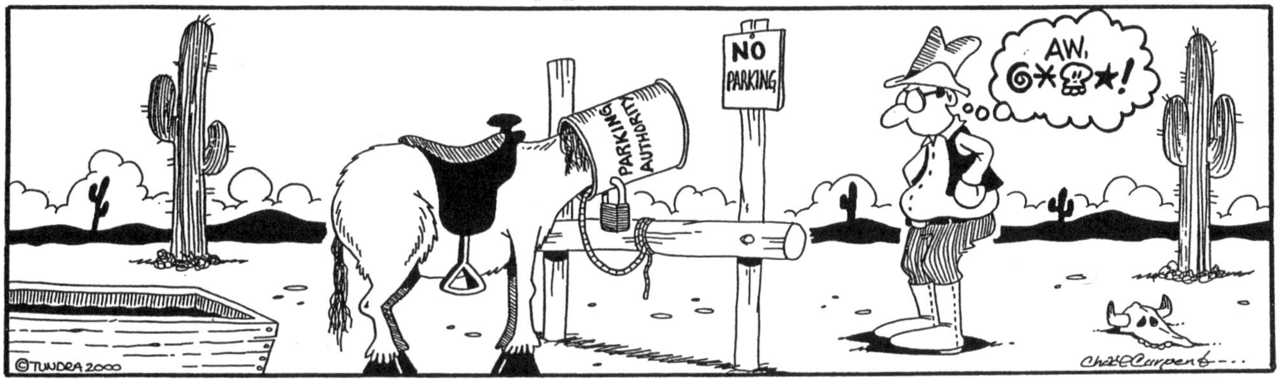
NO PARKING
PARKING AUTHORITY
AW,
©TUNDRA 2000

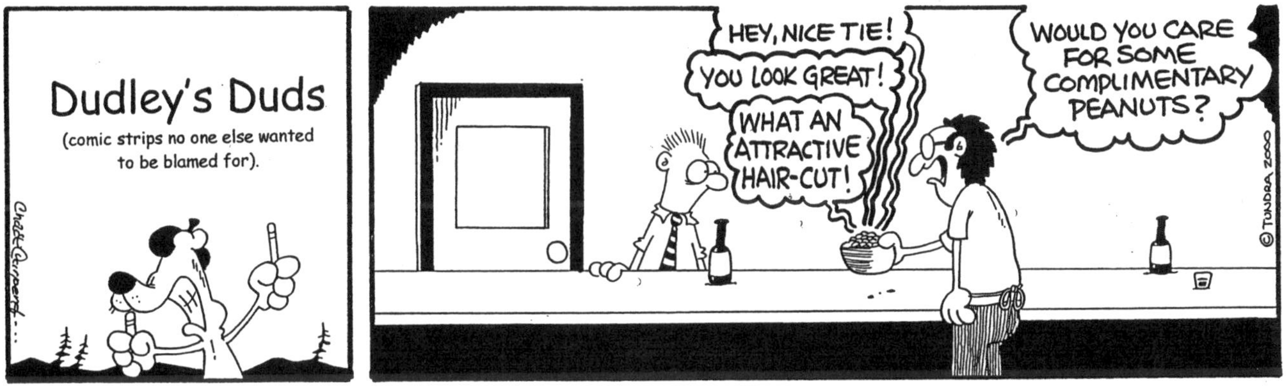
Dudley's Duds
(comic strips no one else wanted to be blamed for).
HEY, NICE TIE!
YOU LOOK GREAT!
WHAT AN ATTRACTIVE HAIR-CUT!
WOULD YOU CARE FOR SOME COMPLIMENTARY PEANUTS?
©TUNDRA 2000

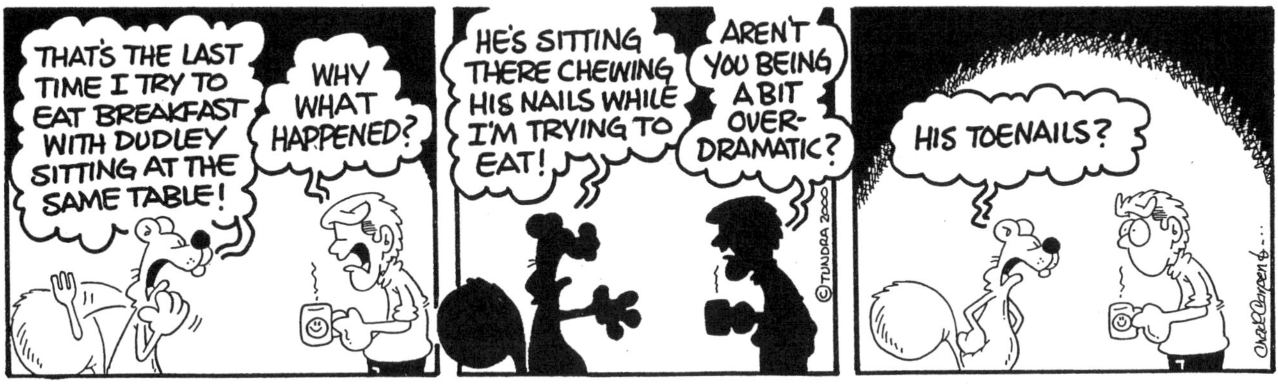
THAT'S THE LAST TIME I TRY TO EAT BREAKFAST WITH DUDLEY SITTING AT THE SAME TABLE!
WHY WHAT HAPPENED?
HE'S SITTING THERE CHEWING HIS NAILS WHILE I'M TRYING TO EAT!
AREN'T YOU BEING A BIT OVER-DRAMATIC?
©TUNDRA 2000
HIS TOENAILS?

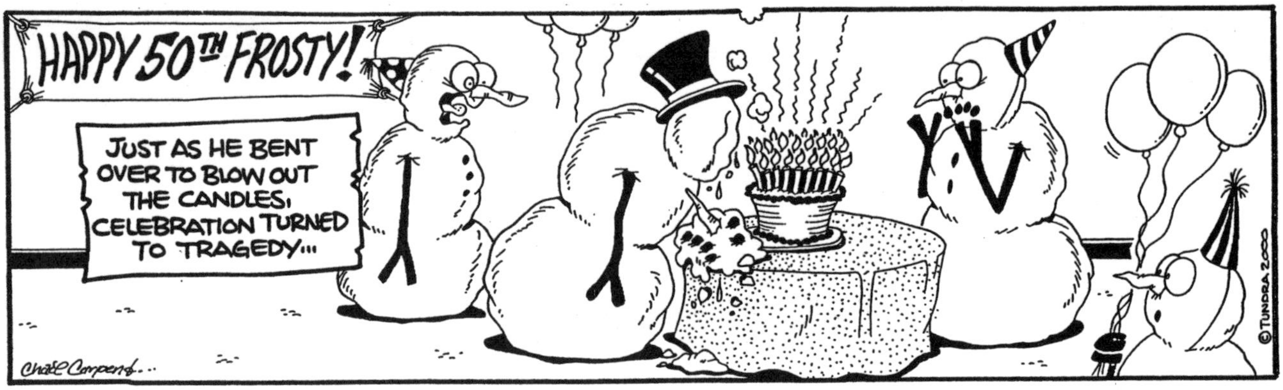
HAPPY 50TH FROSTY!
JUST AS HE BENT OVER TO BLOW OUT THE CANDLES, CELEBRATION TURNED TO TRAGEDY...
© TUNDRA 2000

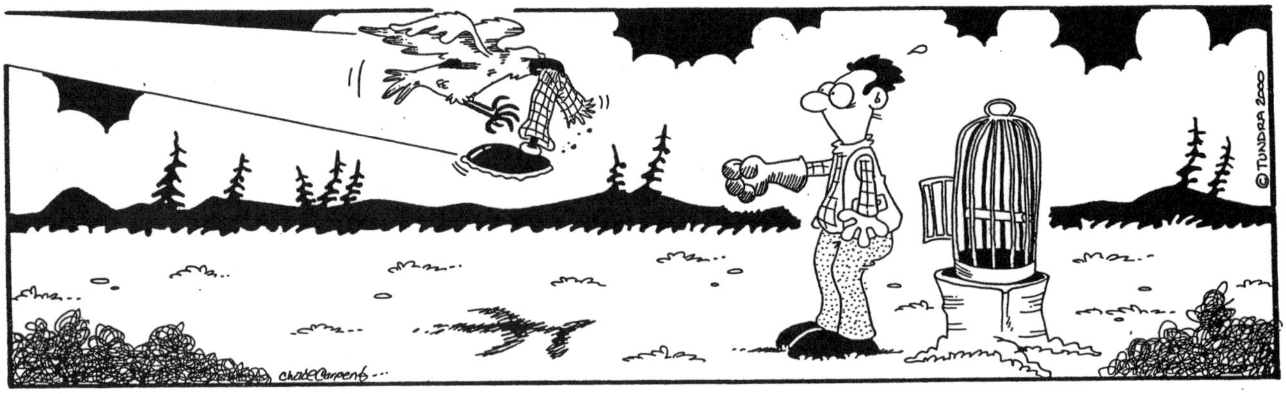
© TUNDRA 2000

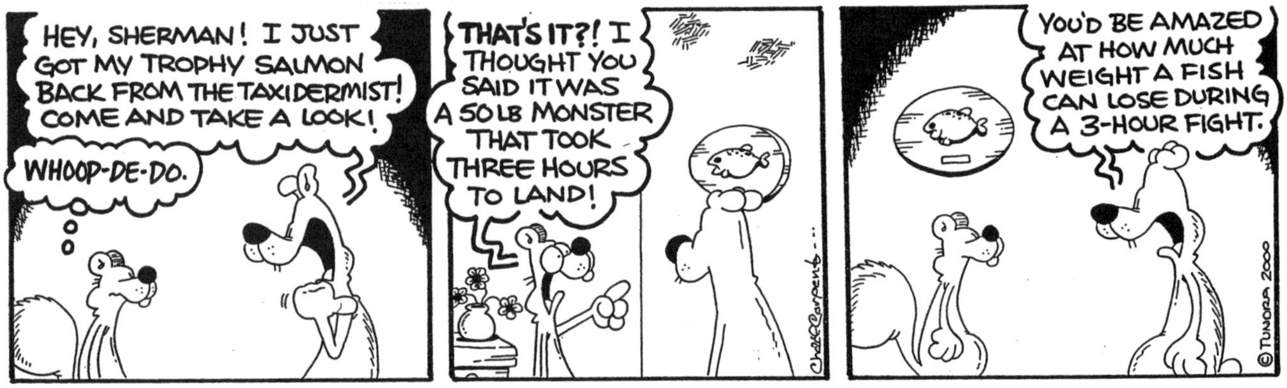
HEY, SHERMAN! I JUST GOT MY TROPHY SALMON BACK FROM THE TAXIDERMIST! COME AND TAKE A LOOK!
WHOOP-DE-DO.
THAT'S IT?! I THOUGHT YOU SAID IT WAS A 50 LB MONSTER THAT TOOK THREE HOURS TO LAND!
YOU'D BE AMAZED AT HOW MUCH WEIGHT A FISH CAN LOSE DURING A 3-HOUR FIGHT.
© TUNDRA 2000

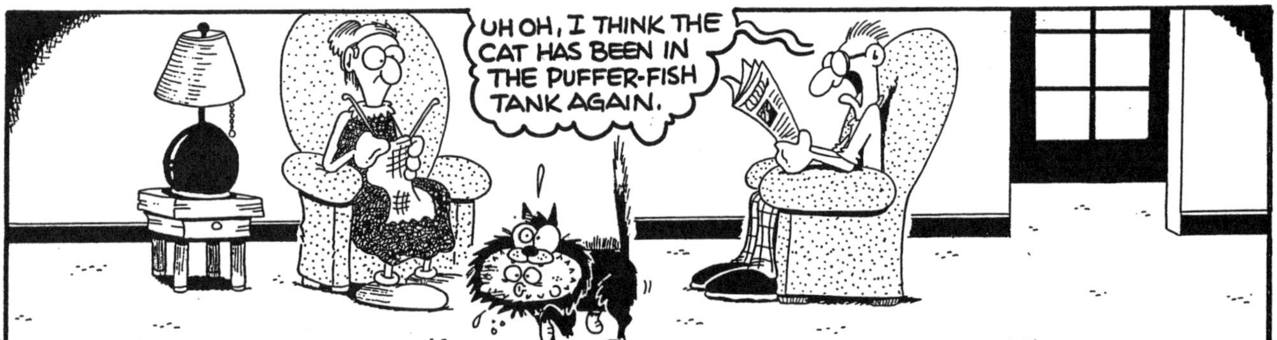
UH OH, I THINK THE CAT HAS BEEN IN THE PUFFER-FISH TANK AGAIN.
© TUNDRA 2000

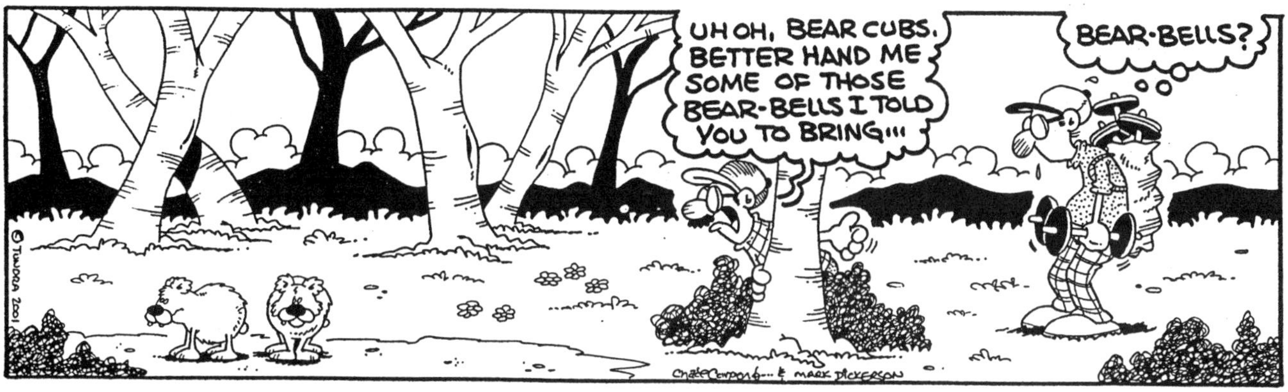
UH OH, BEAR CUBS. BETTER HAND ME SOME OF THOSE BEAR-BELLS I TOLD YOU TO BRING!!!
BEAR-BELLS?
© TUNDRA 2001

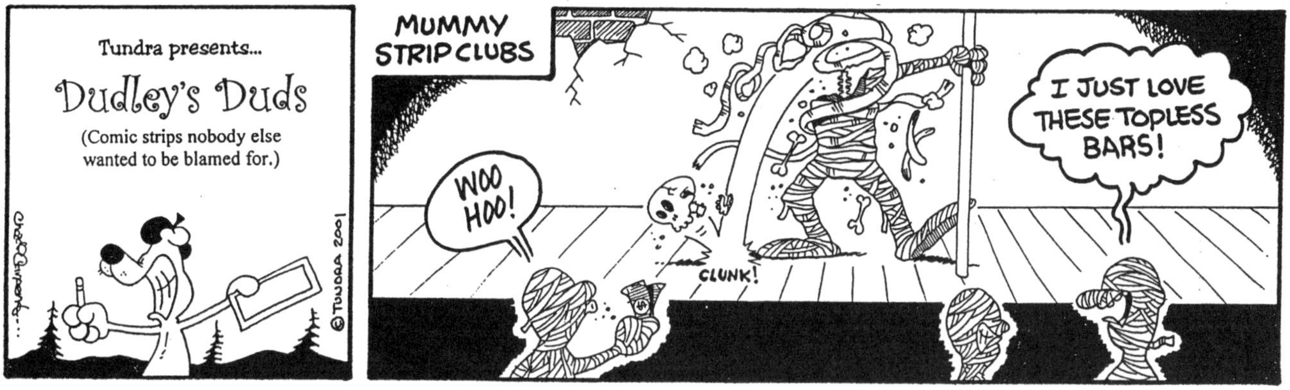
Tundra presents...
Dudley's Duds
(Comic strips nobody else wanted to be blamed for.)
© TUNDRA 2001
MUMMY STRIP CLUBS
WOO HOO!
CLUNK!
I JUST LOVE THESE TOPLESS BARS!

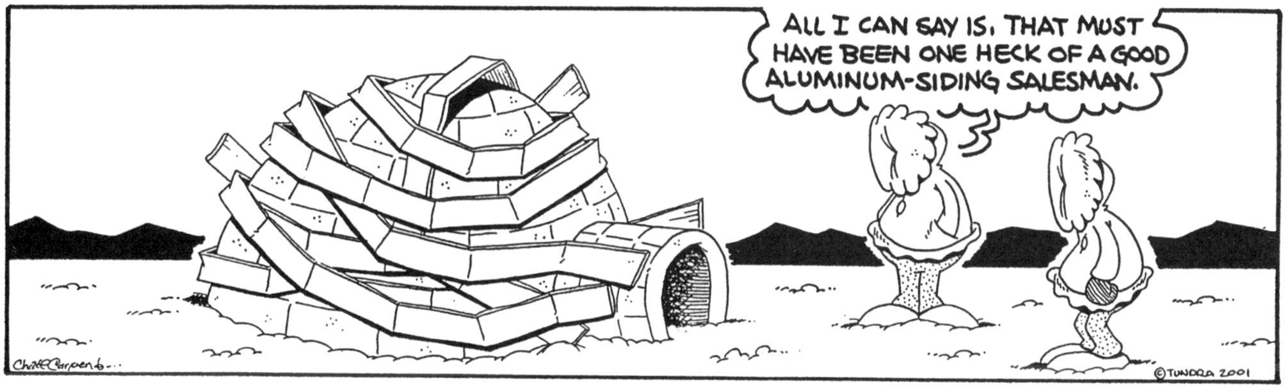
ALL I CAN SAY IS, THAT MUST HAVE BEEN ONE HECK OF A GOOD ALUMINUM-SIDING SALESMAN.
© TUNDRA 2001

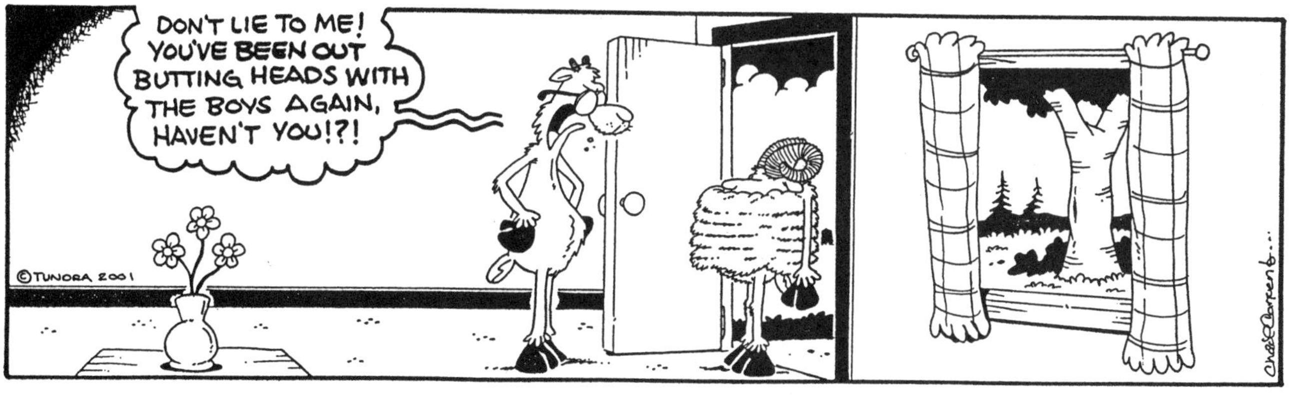
DON'T LIE TO ME! YOU'VE BEEN OUT BUTTING HEADS WITH THE BOYS AGAIN, HAVEN'T YOU!?!
© TUNDRA 2001

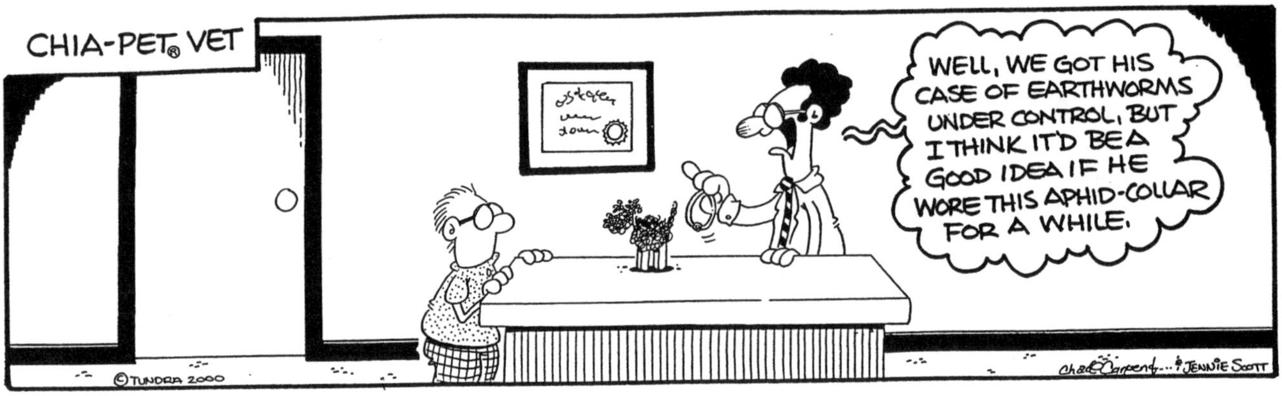
CHIA-PET® VET
WELL, WE GOT HIS CASE OF EARTHWORMS UNDER CONTROL, BUT I THINK IT'D BE A GOOD IDEA IF HE WORE THIS APHID-COLLAR FOR A WHILE.
©TUNDRA 2000
JENNIE SCOTT

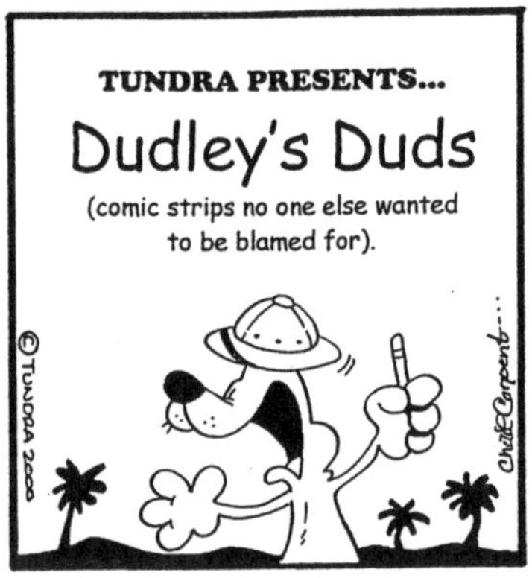
TUNDRA PRESENTS...
Dudley's Duds
(comic strips no one else wanted to be blamed for).
©TUNDRA 2000

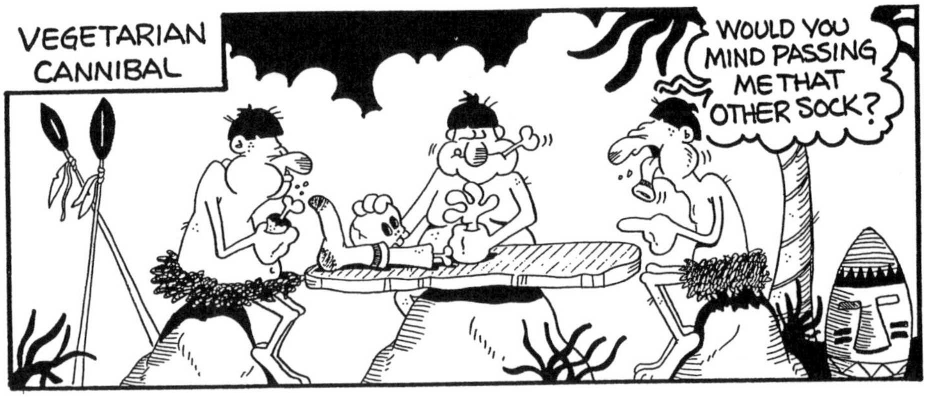
VEGETARIAN CANNIBAL
WOULD YOU MIND PASSING ME THAT OTHER SOCK?

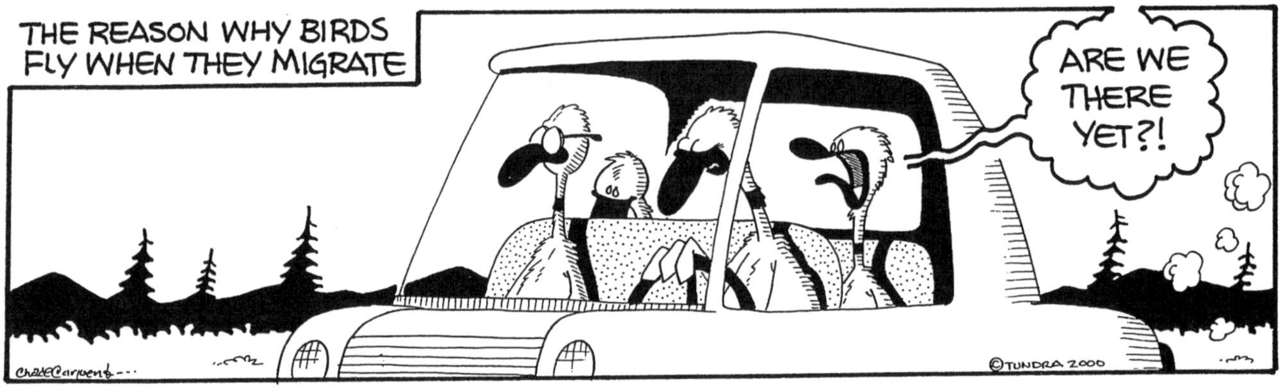
THE REASON WHY BIRDS FLY WHEN THEY MIGRATE
ARE WE THERE YET?!
©TUNDRA 2000

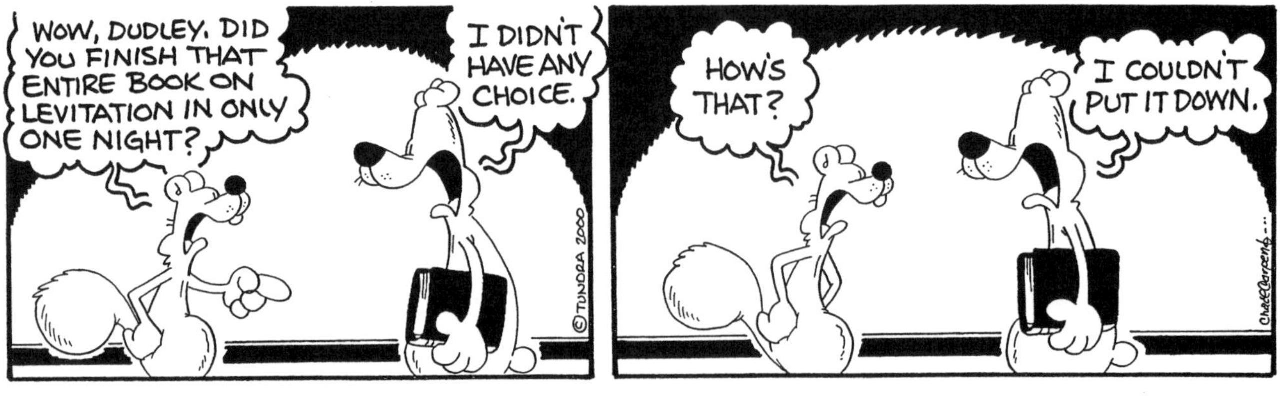
WOW, DUDLEY. DID YOU FINISH THAT ENTIRE BOOK ON LEVITATION IN ONLY ONE NIGHT?
I DIDN'T HAVE ANY CHOICE.
©TUNDRA 2000
HOW'S THAT?
I COULDN'T PUT IT DOWN.

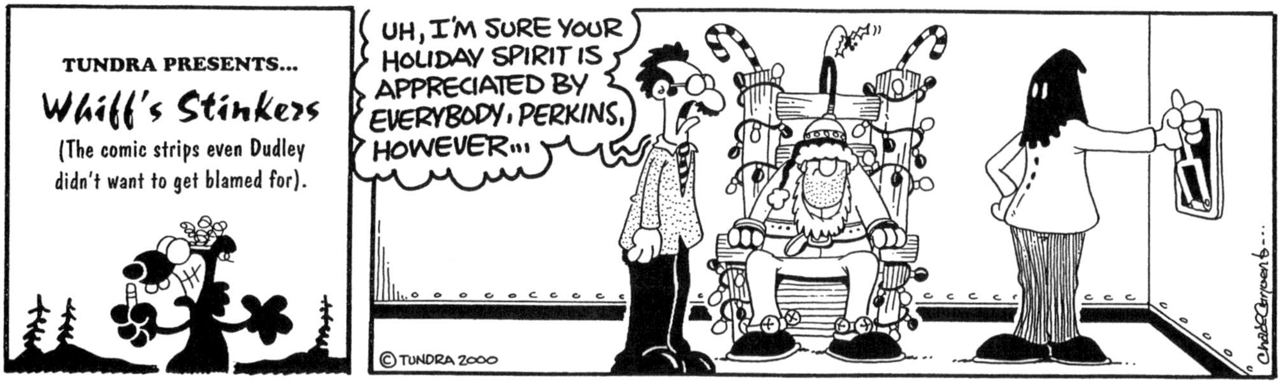
TUNDRA PRESENTS...
Whiff's Stinkers
(The comic strips even Dudley didn't want to get blamed for).
UH, I'M SURE YOUR HOLIDAY SPIRIT IS APPRECIATED BY EVERYBODY, PERKINS, HOWEVER...
© TUNDRA 2000

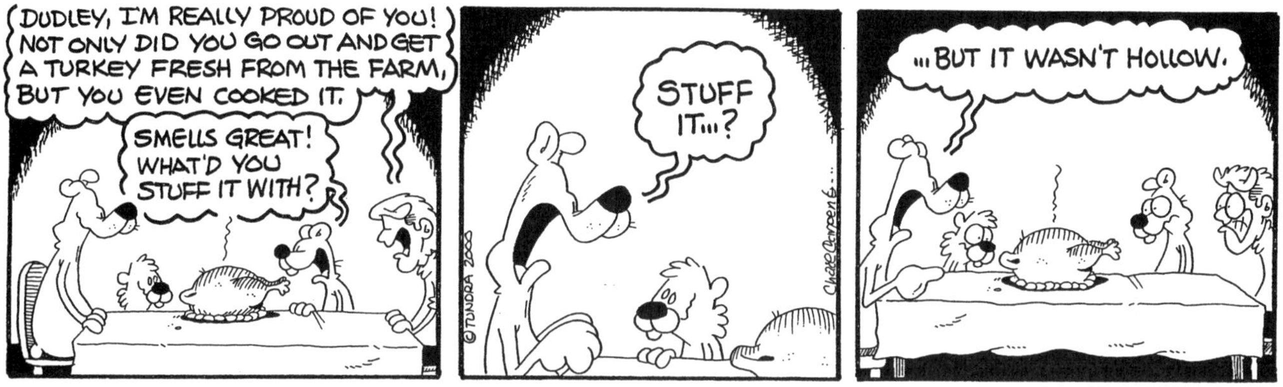
DUDLEY, I'M REALLY PROUD OF YOU! NOT ONLY DID YOU GO OUT AND GET A TURKEY FRESH FROM THE FARM, BUT YOU EVEN COOKED IT.
SMELLS GREAT! WHAT'D YOU STUFF IT WITH?
STUFF IT...?
©TUNDRA 2000
...BUT IT WASN'T HOLLOW.

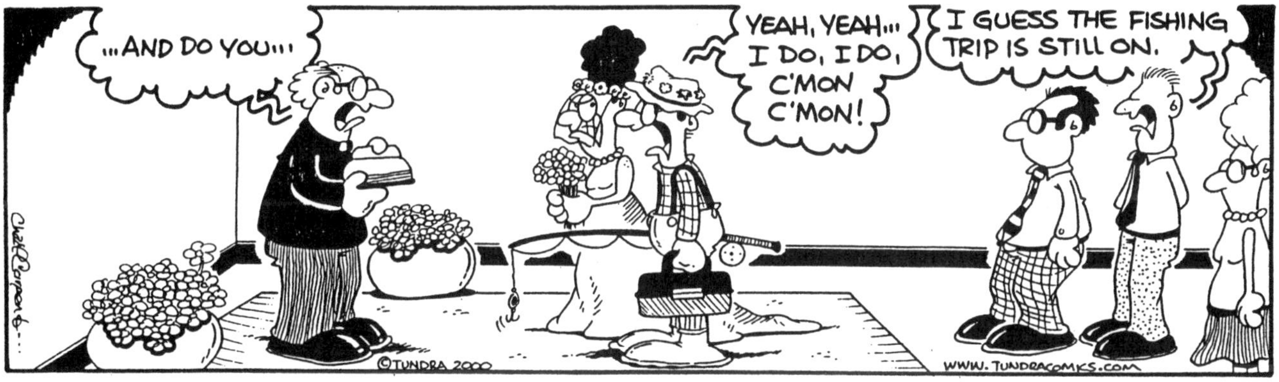
...AND DO YOU...
YEAH, YEAH... I DO, I DO, C'MON C'MON!
I GUESS THE FISHING TRIP IS STILL ON.
©TUNDRA 2000
WWW.TUNDRACOMKS.COM

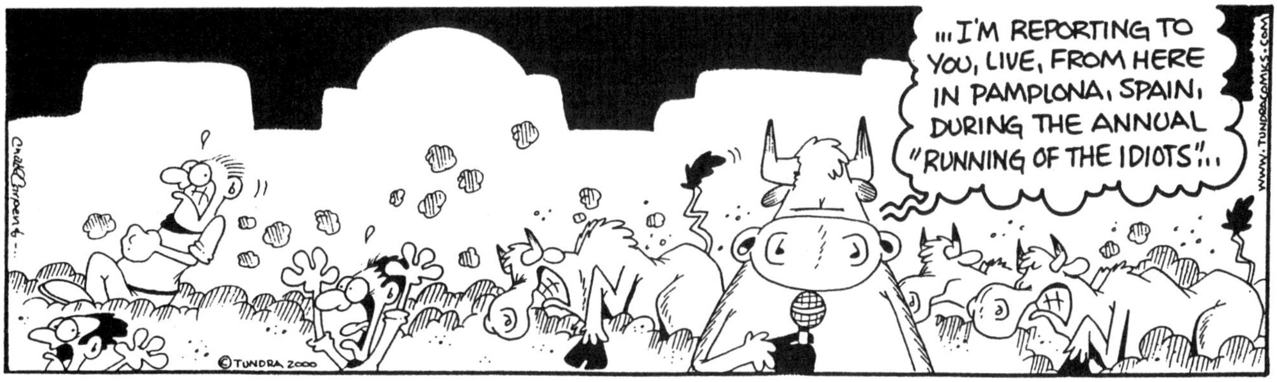
...I'M REPORTING TO YOU, LIVE, FROM HERE IN PAMPLONA, SPAIN, DURING THE ANNUAL "RUNNING OF THE IDIOTS"...
©TUNDRA 2000
WWW.TUNDRACOMKS.COM

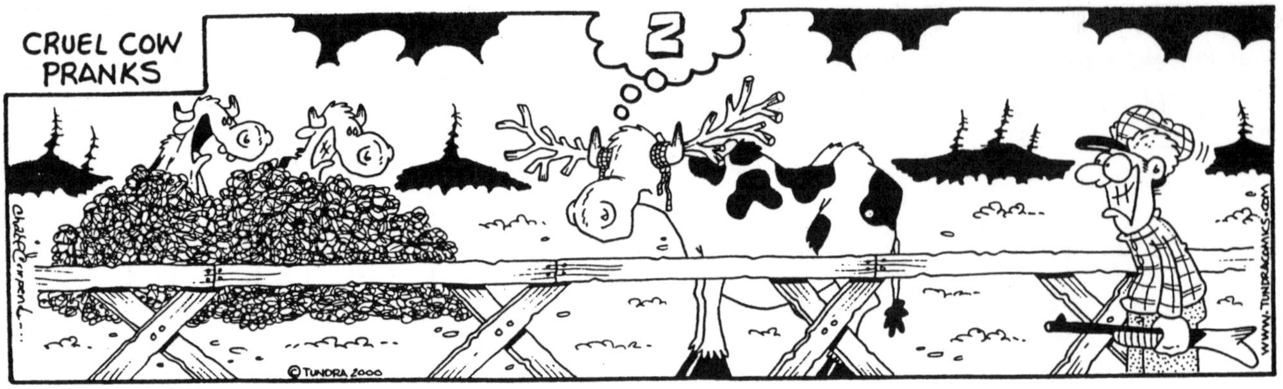
CRUEL COW PRANKS
Z
© TUNDRA 2000
WWW.TUNDRACOMICS.COM

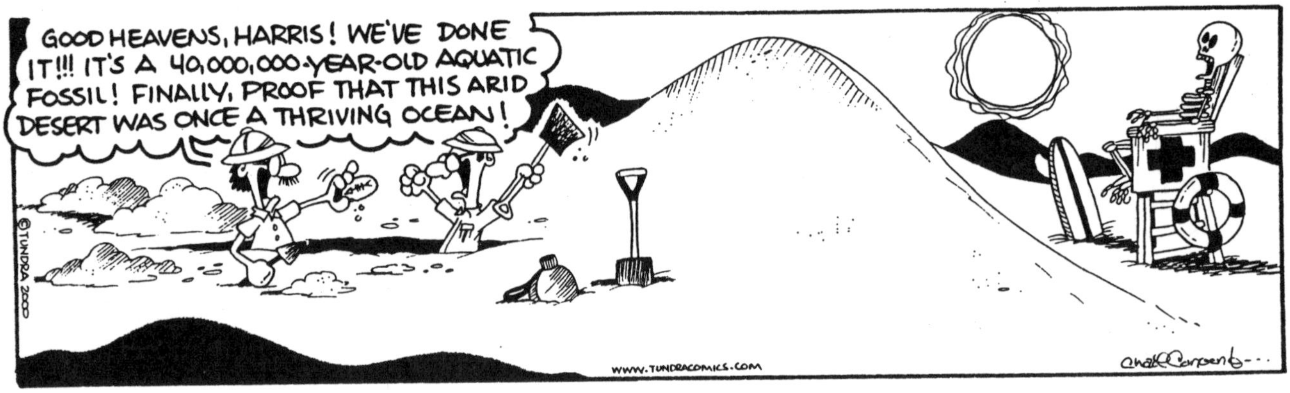
GOOD HEAVENS, HARRIS! WE'VE DONE IT!!! IT'S A 40,000,000-YEAR-OLD AQUATIC FOSSIL! FINALLY, PROOF THAT THIS ARID DESERT WAS ONCE A THRIVING OCEAN!
© TUNDRA 2000
WWW.TUNDRACOMICS.COM

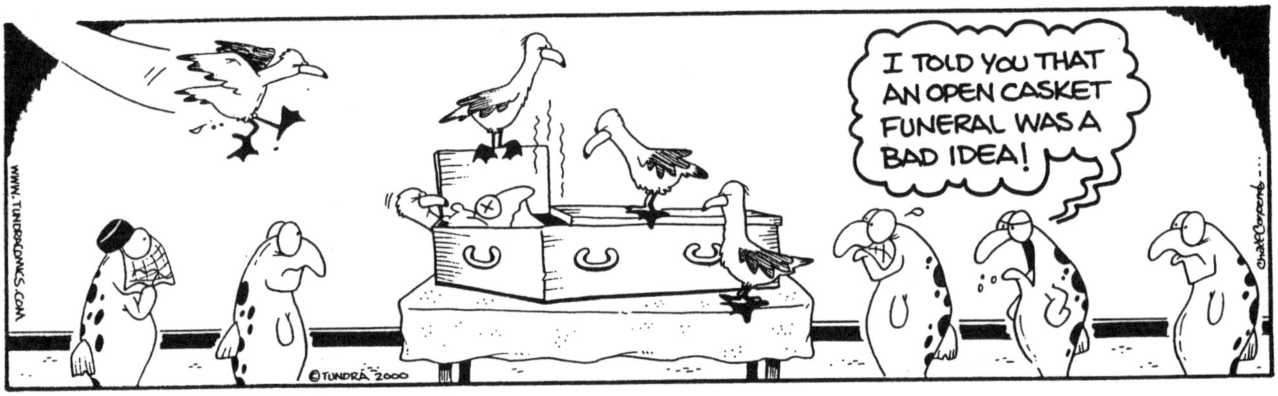
I TOLD YOU THAT AN OPEN CASKET FUNERAL WAS A BAD IDEA!
WWW.TUNDRACOMICS.COM
© TUNDRA 2000

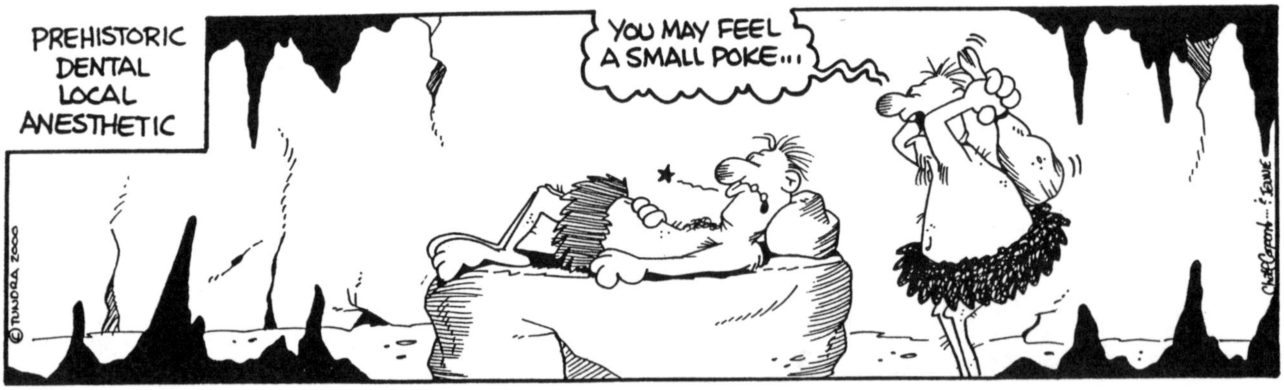
PREHISTORIC DENTAL LOCAL ANESTHETIC
YOU MAY FEEL A SMALL POKE...
© TUNDRA 2000

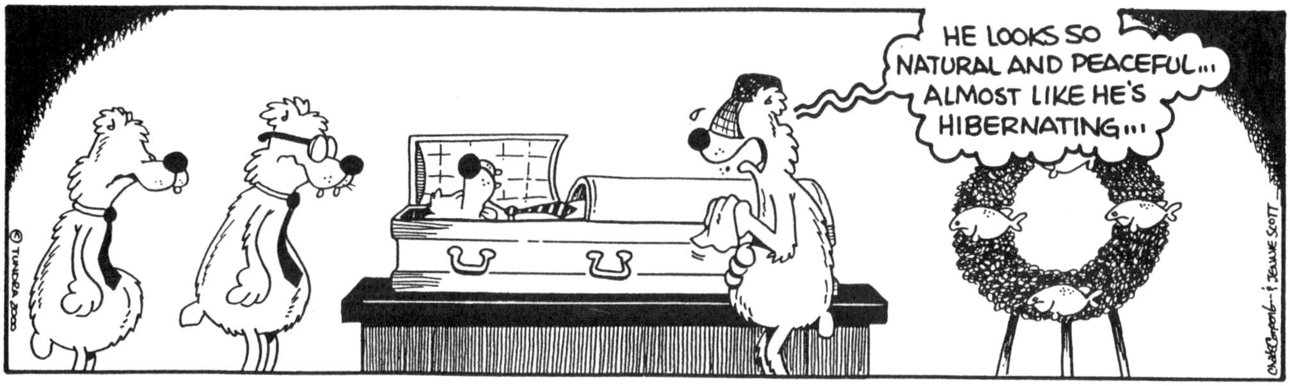
HE LOOKS SO NATURAL AND PEACEFUL... ALMOST LIKE HE'S HIBERNATING...
© TUNDRA 2000

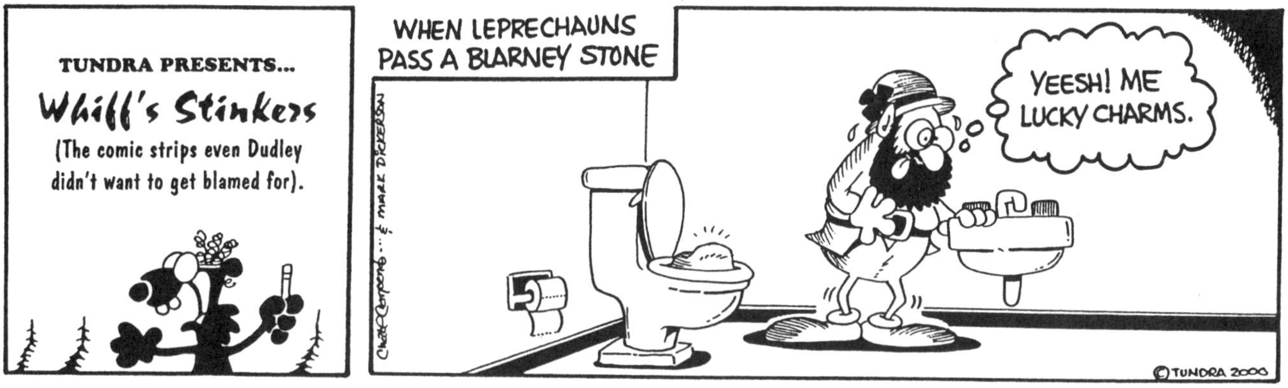
TUNDRA PRESENTS...
Whiff's Stinkers
(The comic strips even Dudley didn't want to get blamed for).
WHEN LEPRECHAUNS PASS A BLARNEY STONE
YEESH! ME LUCKY CHARMS.
© TUNDRA 2000

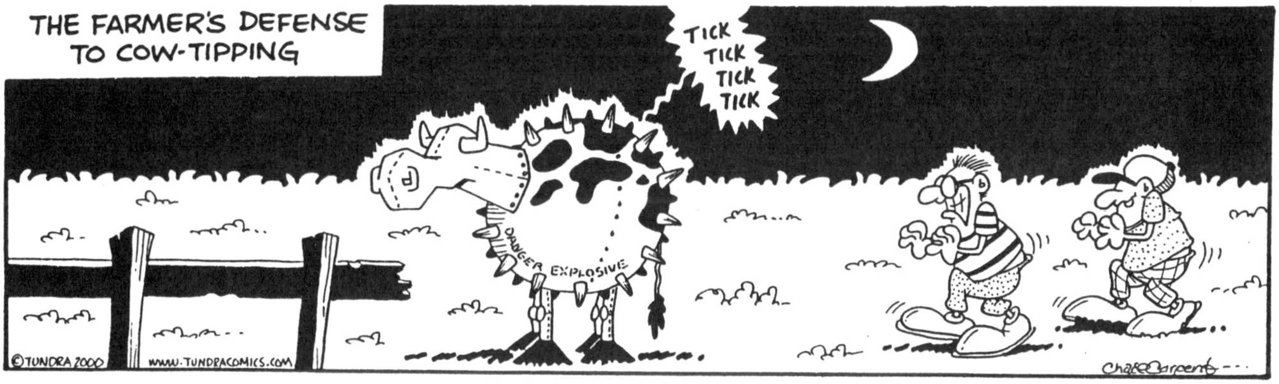
THE FARMER'S DEFENSE TO COW-TIPPING
TICK TICK TICK TICK
DANGER EXPLOSIVE
© TUNDRA 2000
WWW.TUNDRACOMICS.COM

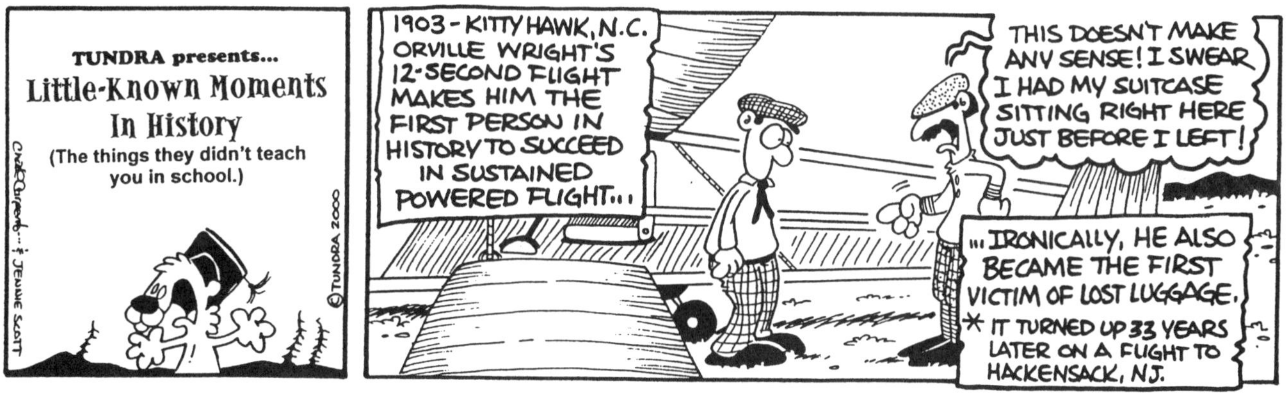
TUNDRA presents...
Little-Known Moments In History
(The things they didn't teach you in school.)
© TUNDRA 2000
1903 - KITTY HAWK, N.C. ORVILLE WRIGHT'S 12-SECOND FLIGHT MAKES HIM THE FIRST PERSON IN HISTORY TO SUCCEED IN SUSTAINED POWERED FLIGHT...
THIS DOESN'T MAKE ANY SENSE! I SWEAR I HAD MY SUITCASE SITTING RIGHT HERE JUST BEFORE I LEFT!
...IRONICALLY, HE ALSO BECAME THE FIRST VICTIM OF LOST LUGGAGE.
* IT TURNED UP 33 YEARS LATER ON A FLIGHT TO HACKENSACK, NJ.

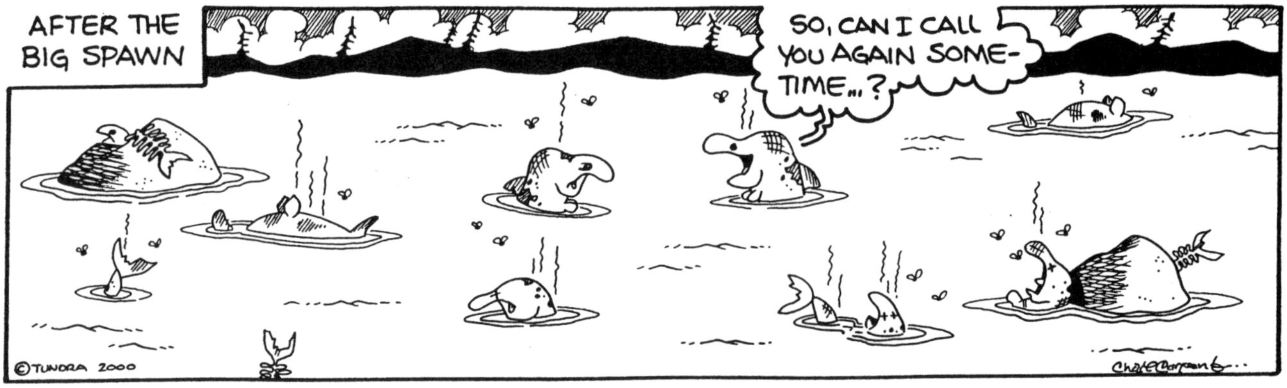
AFTER THE BIG SPAWN
SO, CAN I CALL YOU AGAIN SOME-TIME...?
©TUNDRA 2000

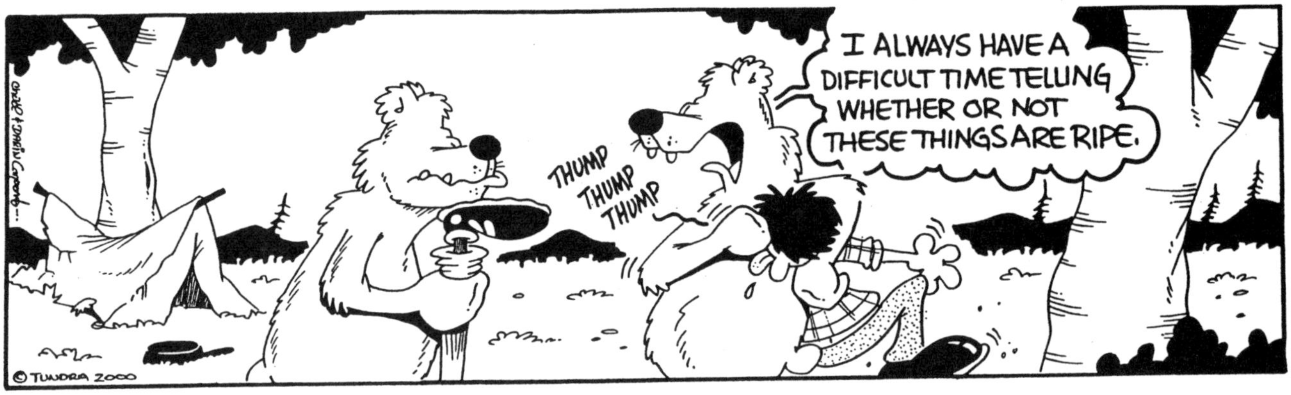
I ALWAYS HAVE A DIFFICULT TIME TELLING WHETHER OR NOT THESE THINGS ARE RIPE.
THUMP THUMP THUMP
©TUNDRA 2000

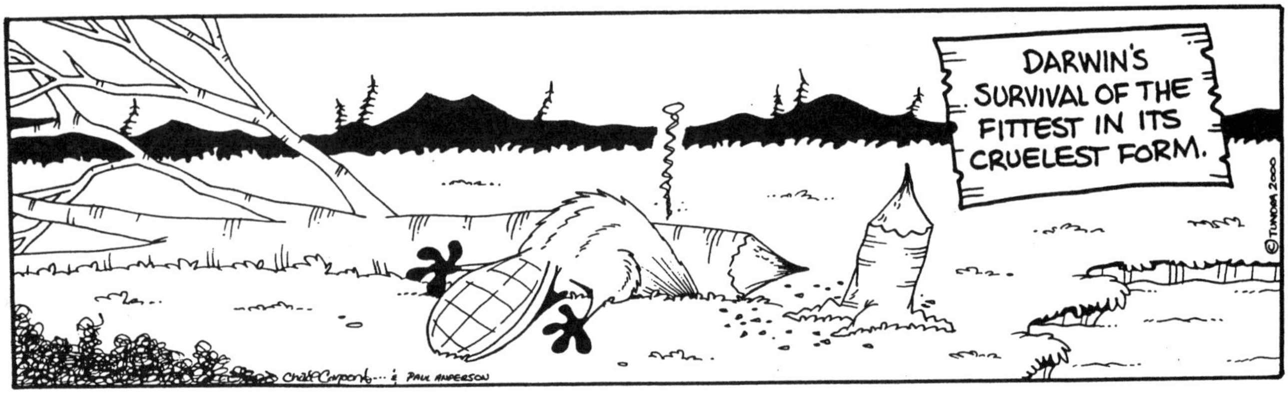
DARWIN'S SURVIVAL OF THE FITTEST IN ITS CRUELEST FORM.
©TUNDRA 2000

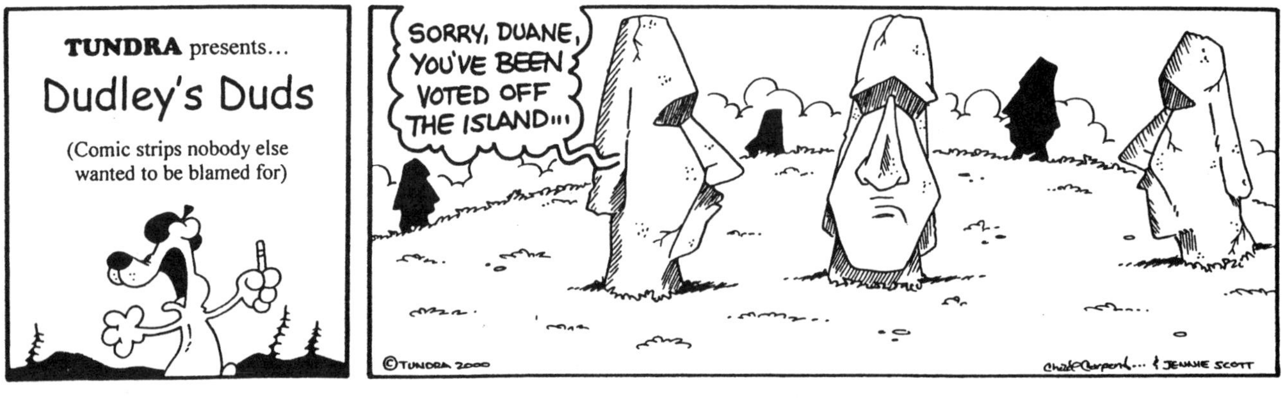
TUNDRA presents...
Dudley's Duds
(Comic strips nobody else wanted to be blamed for)
SORRY, DUANE, YOU'VE BEEN VOTED OFF THE ISLAND...
©TUNDRA 2000

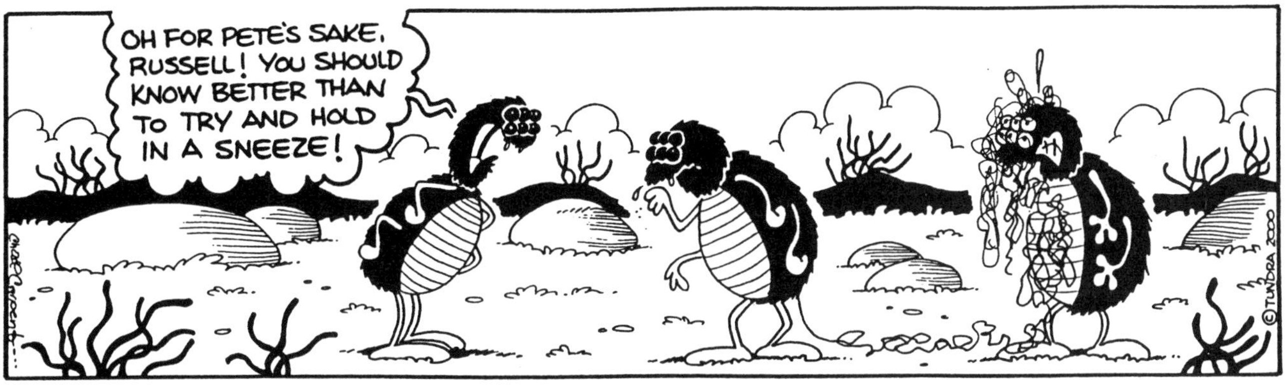
OH FOR PETE'S SAKE, RUSSELL! YOU SHOULD KNOW BETTER THAN TO TRY AND HOLD IN A SNEEZE!

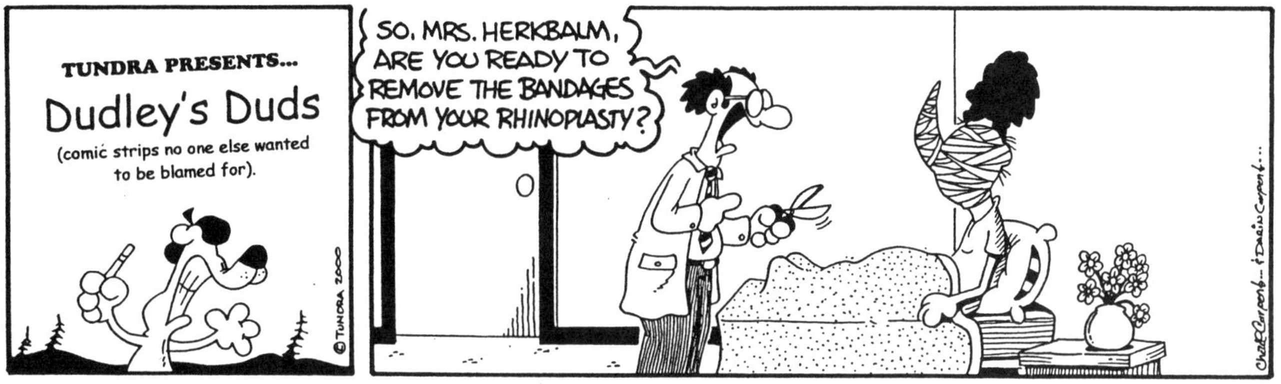
TUNDRA PRESENTS...
Dudley's Duds
(comic strips no one else wanted to be blamed for).
SO, MRS. HERKBALM, ARE YOU READY TO REMOVE THE BANDAGES FROM YOUR RHINOPLASTY?

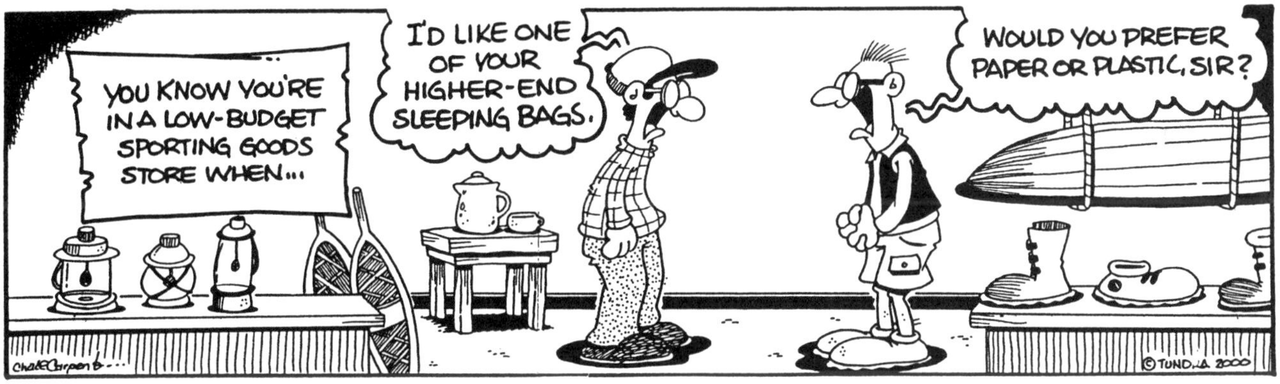
YOU KNOW YOU'RE IN A LOW-BUDGET SPORTING GOODS STORE WHEN...
I'D LIKE ONE OF YOUR HIGHER-END SLEEPING BAGS.
WOULD YOU PREFER PAPER OR PLASTIC, SIR?

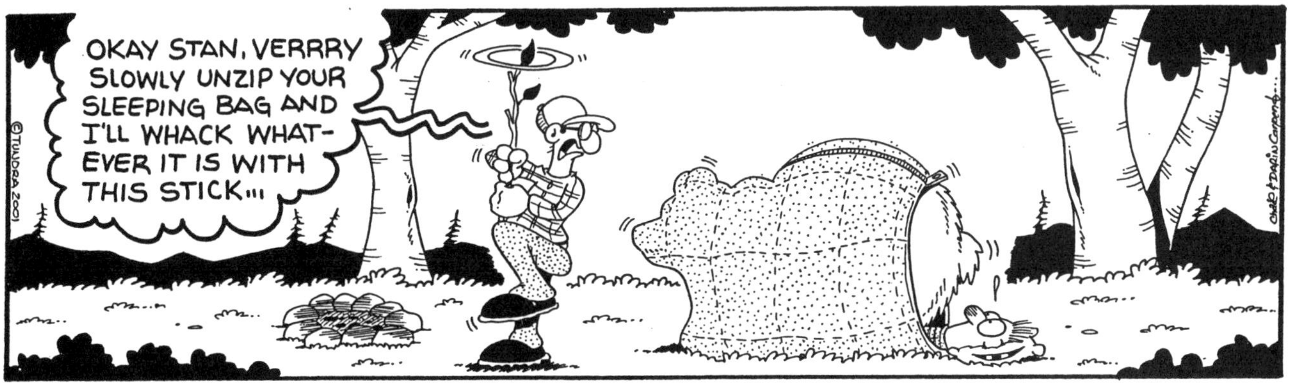
OKAY STAN, VERRRY SLOWLY UNZIP YOUR SLEEPING BAG AND I'LL WHACK WHATEVER IT IS WITH THIS STICK...

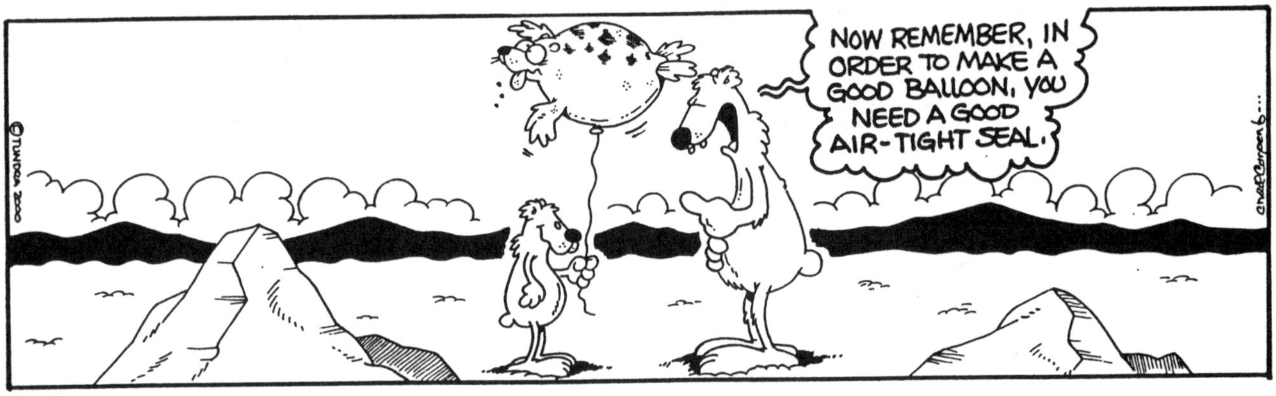
NOW REMEMBER, IN ORDER TO MAKE A GOOD BALLOON, YOU NEED A GOOD AIR-TIGHT SEAL.
© TUNDRA 2000
Chad Carpenter

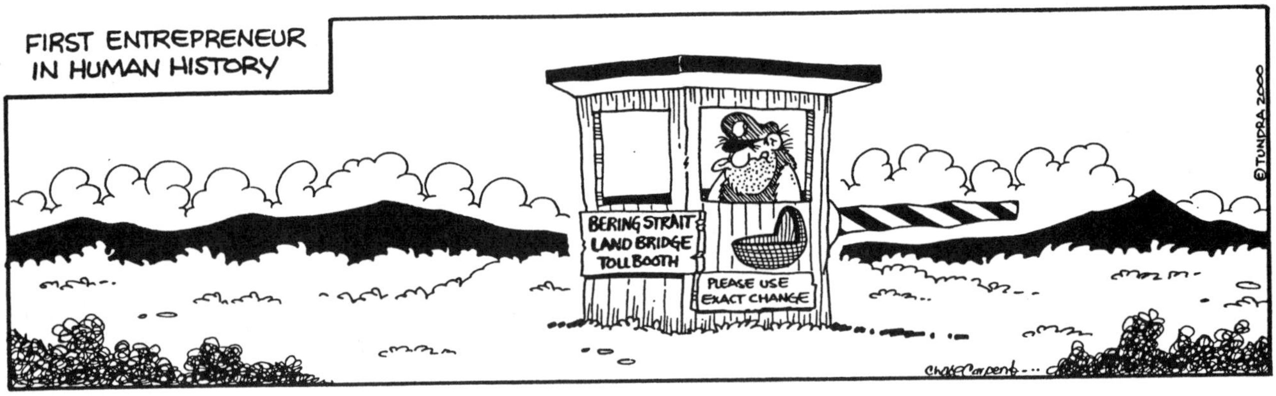
FIRST ENTREPRENEUR IN HUMAN HISTORY
BERING STRAIT LAND BRIDGE TOLL BOOTH
PLEASE USE EXACT CHANGE
© TUNDRA 2000
Chad Carpenter

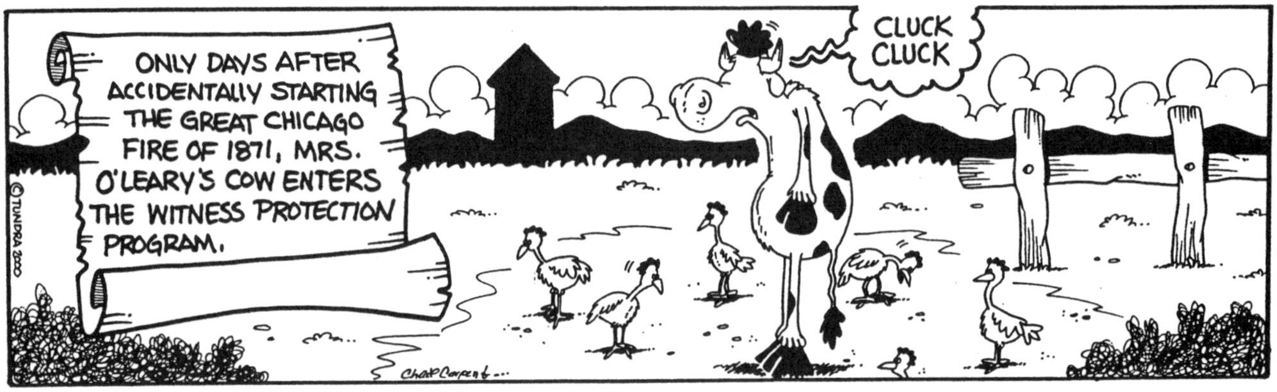
ONLY DAYS AFTER ACCIDENTALLY STARTING THE GREAT CHICAGO FIRE OF 1871, MRS. O'LEARY'S COW ENTERS THE WITNESS PROTECTION PROGRAM.
CLUCK CLUCK
© TUNDRA 2000
Chad Carpenter

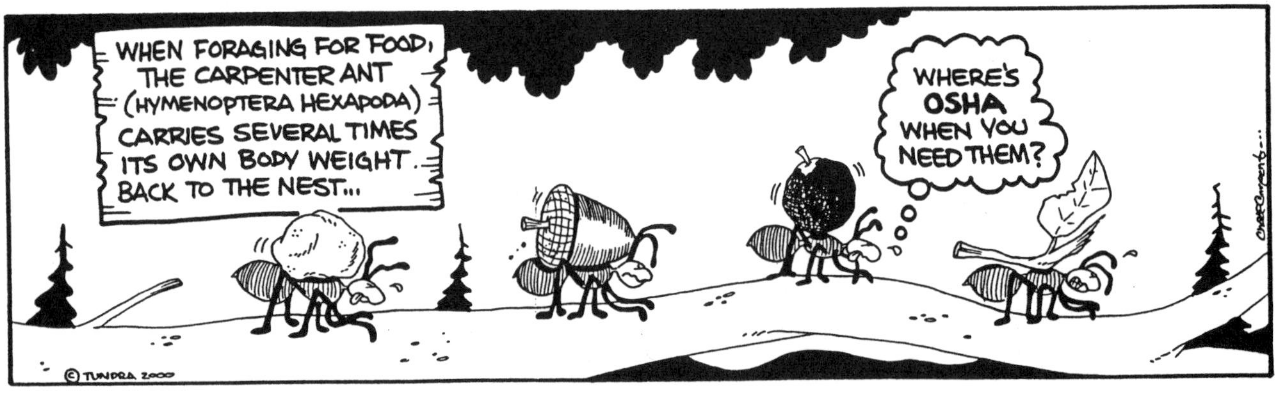
WHEN FORAGING FOR FOOD, THE CARPENTER ANT (HYMENOPTERA HEXAPODA) CARRIES SEVERAL TIMES ITS OWN BODY WEIGHT BACK TO THE NEST...
WHERE'S OSHA WHEN YOU NEED THEM?
© TUNDRA 2000
Chad Carpenter

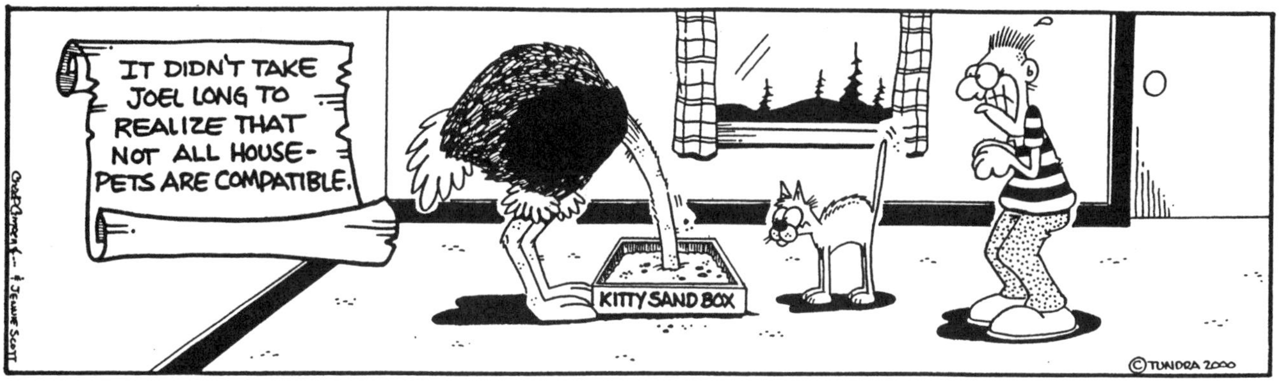
IT DIDN'T TAKE JOEL LONG TO REALIZE THAT NOT ALL HOUSE-PETS ARE COMPATIBLE.
KITTY SAND BOX
©TUNDRA 2000

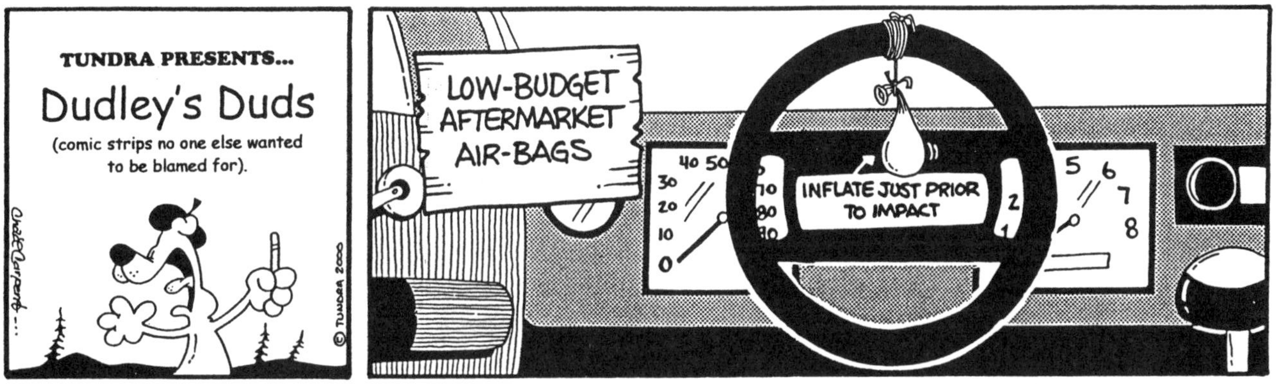
TUNDRA PRESENTS...
Dudley's Duds
(comic strips no one else wanted to be blamed for).
© TUNDRA 2000
LOW-BUDGET AFTERMARKET AIR-BAGS
INFLATE JUST PRIOR TO IMPACT

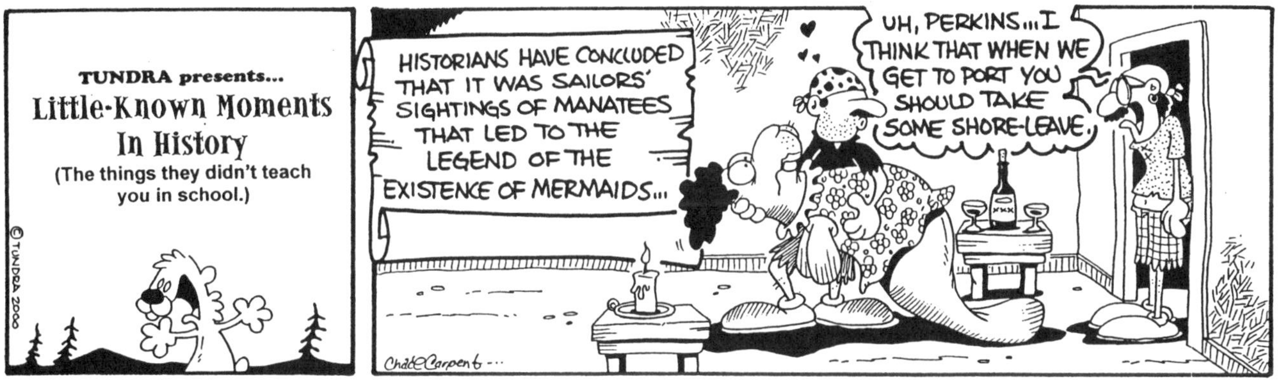
TUNDRA presents...
Little-Known Moments In History
(The things they didn't teach you in school.)
© TUNDRA 2000
HISTORIANS HAVE CONCLUDED THAT IT WAS SAILORS' SIGHTINGS OF MANATEES THAT LED TO THE LEGEND OF THE EXISTENCE OF MERMAIDS...
UH, PERKINS... I THINK THAT WHEN WE GET TO PORT YOU SHOULD TAKE SOME SHORE-LEAVE.

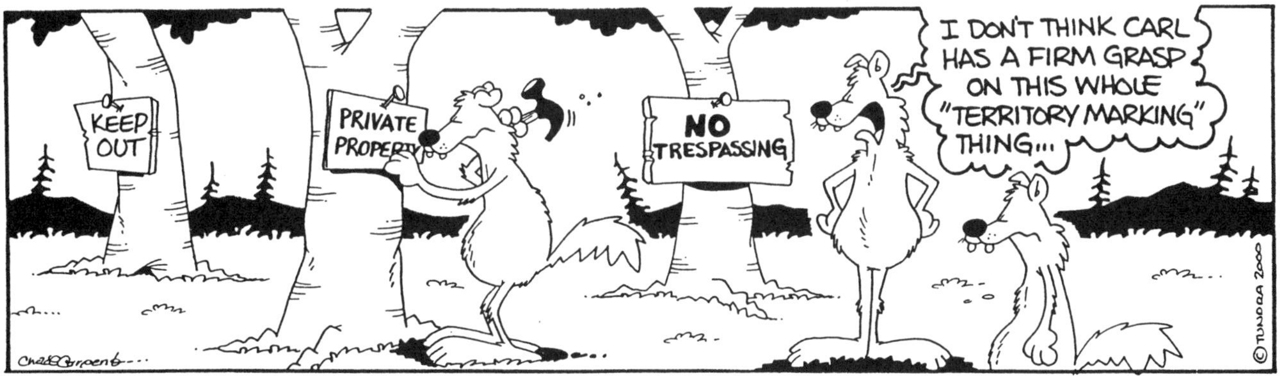
KEEP OUT
PRIVATE PROPERTY
NO TRESPASSING
I DON'T THINK CARL HAS A FIRM GRASP ON THIS WHOLE "TERRITORY MARKING" THING...
© TUNDRA 2000

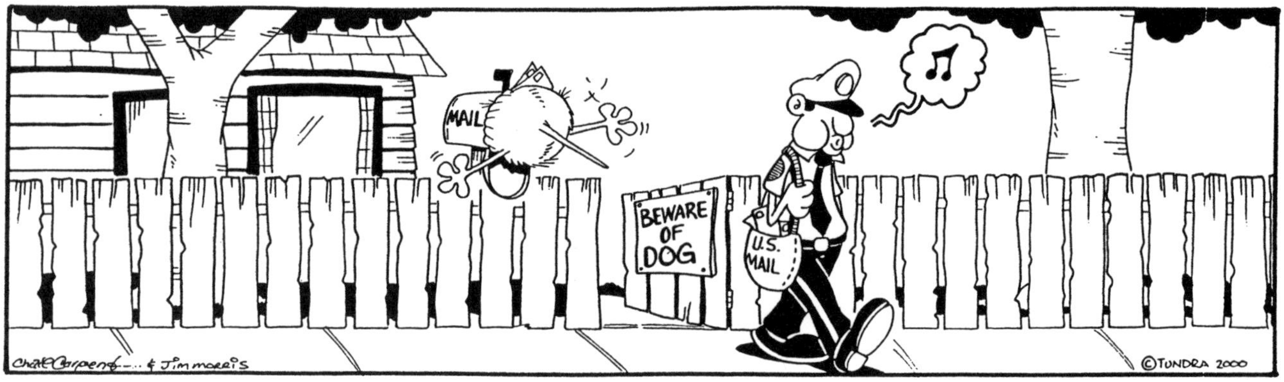
MAIL
BEWARE OF DOG
U.S. MAIL
©TUNDRA 2000

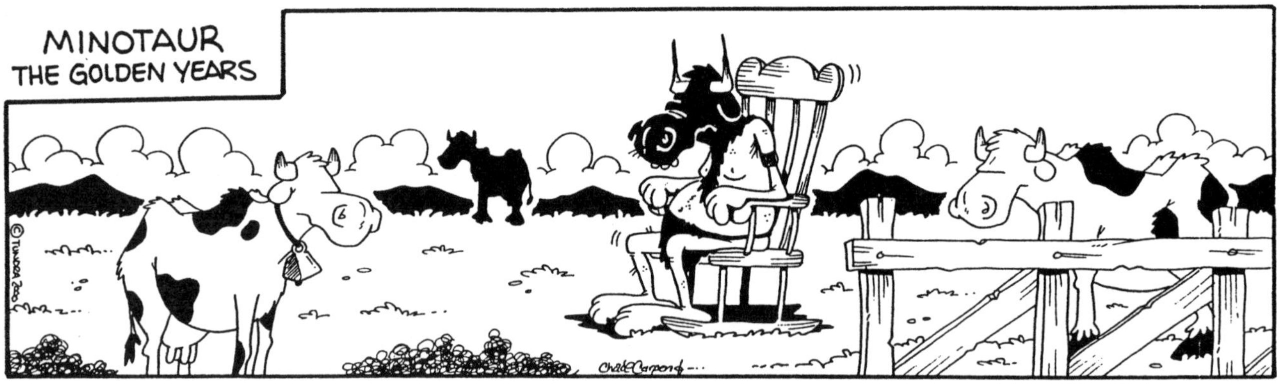
MINOTAUR
THE GOLDEN YEARS

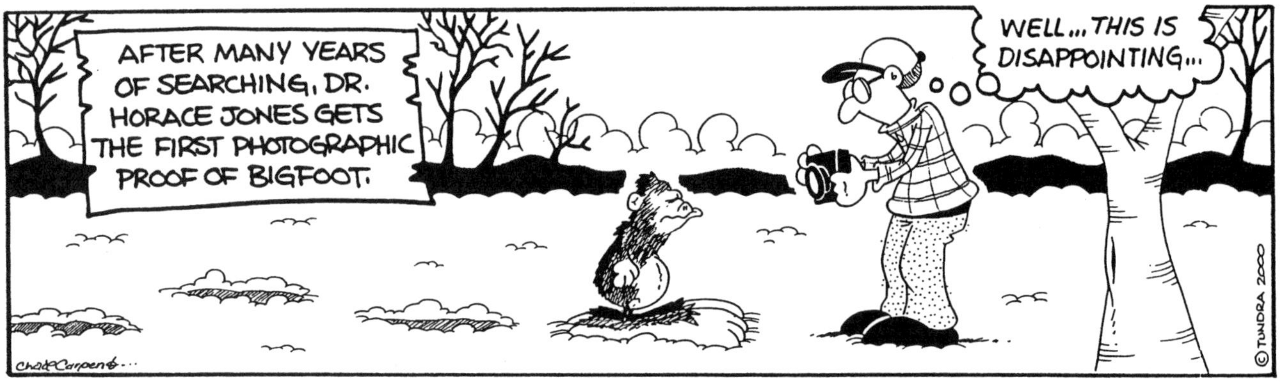
AFTER MANY YEARS OF SEARCHING, DR. HORACE JONES GETS THE FIRST PHOTOGRAPHIC PROOF OF BIGFOOT.
WELL... THIS IS DISAPPOINTING...
©TUNDRA 2000

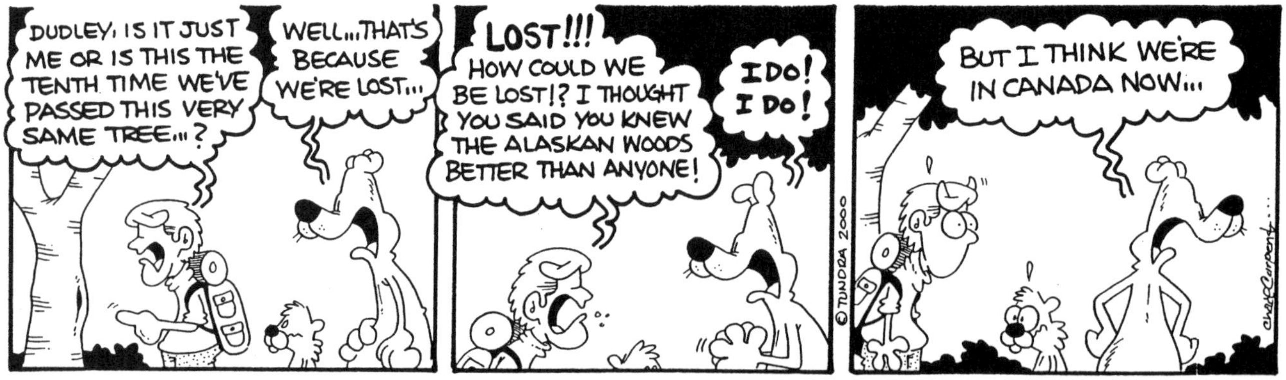
DUDLEY, IS IT JUST ME OR IS THIS THE TENTH TIME WE'VE PASSED THIS VERY SAME TREE...?
WELL... THAT'S BECAUSE WE'RE LOST...
LOST!!! HOW COULD WE BE LOST!? I THOUGHT YOU SAID YOU KNEW THE ALASKAN WOODS BETTER THAN ANYONE!
I DO! I DO!
©TUNDRA 2000
BUT I THINK WE'RE IN CANADA NOW...

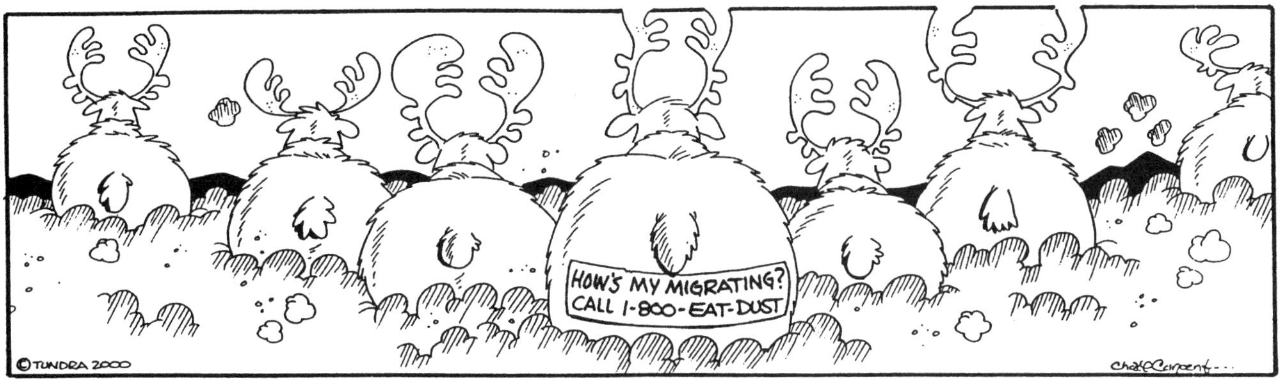
HOW'S MY MIGRATING?
CALL 1-800-EAT-DUST
©TUNDRA 2000

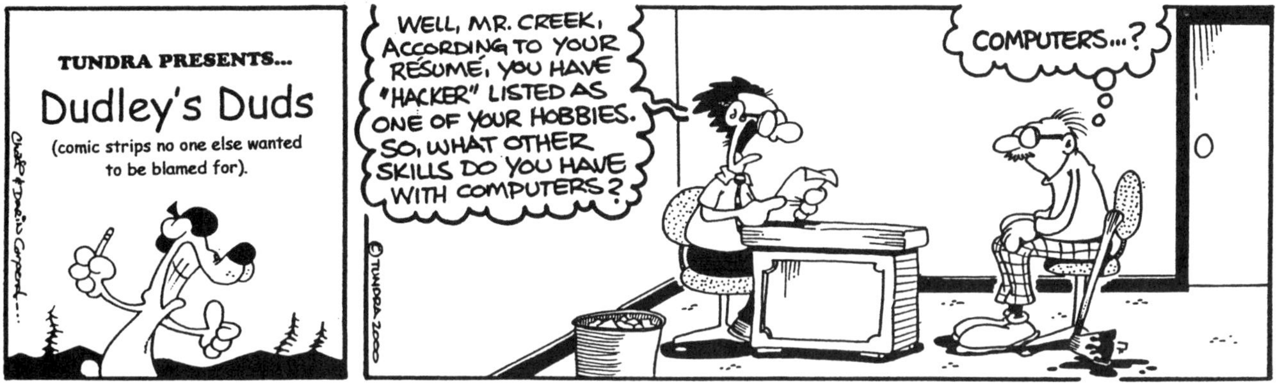
TUNDRA PRESENTS...
Dudley's Duds
(comic strips no one else wanted to be blamed for).
WELL, MR. CREEK, ACCORDING TO YOUR RÉSUMÉ, YOU HAVE "HACKER" LISTED AS ONE OF YOUR HOBBIES. SO, WHAT OTHER SKILLS DO YOU HAVE WITH COMPUTERS?
COMPUTERS...?
© TUNDRA 2000

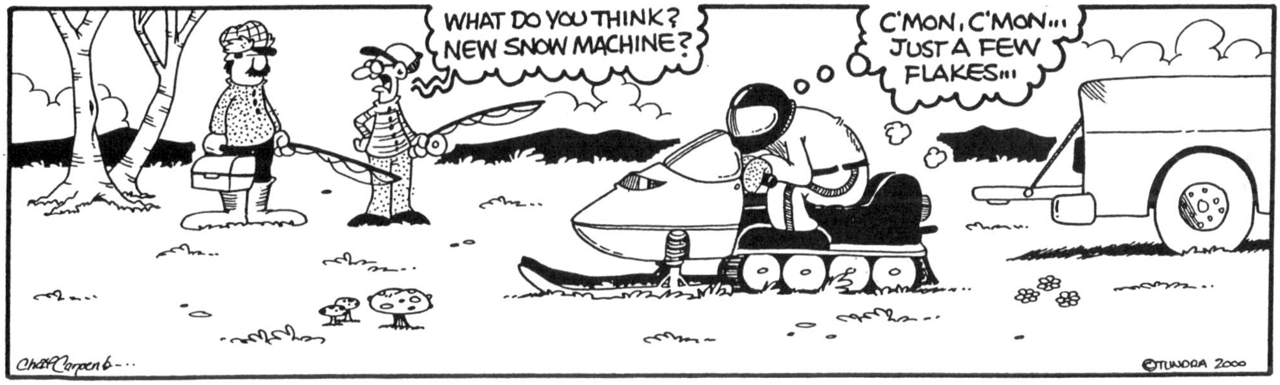
WHAT DO YOU THINK? NEW SNOW MACHINE?
C'MON, C'MON... JUST A FEW FLAKES...
©TUNDRA 2000

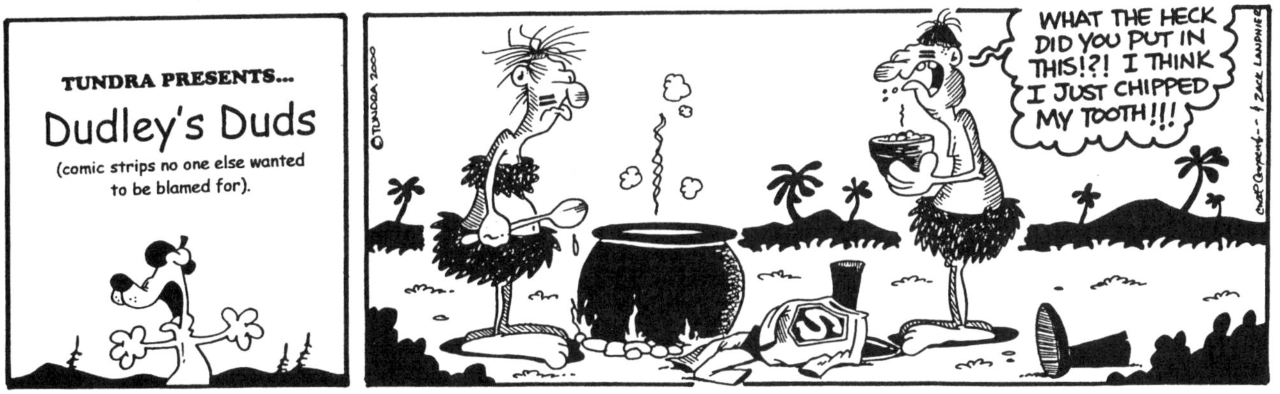
TUNDRA PRESENTS...
Dudley's Duds
(comic strips no one else wanted to be blamed for).
© TUNDRA 2000
WHAT THE HECK DID YOU PUT IN THIS!?! I THINK I JUST CHIPPED MY TOOTH!!!

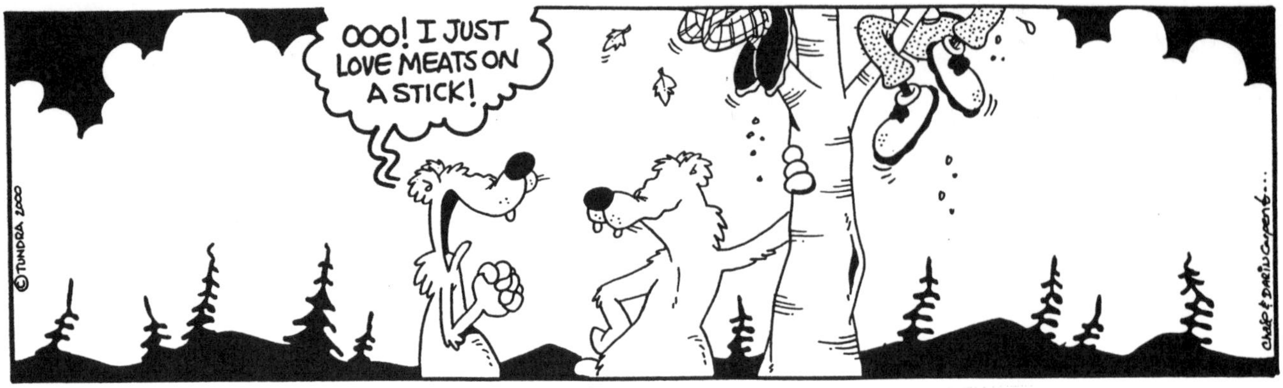
OOO! I JUST LOVE MEATS ON A STICK!
© TUNDRA 2000

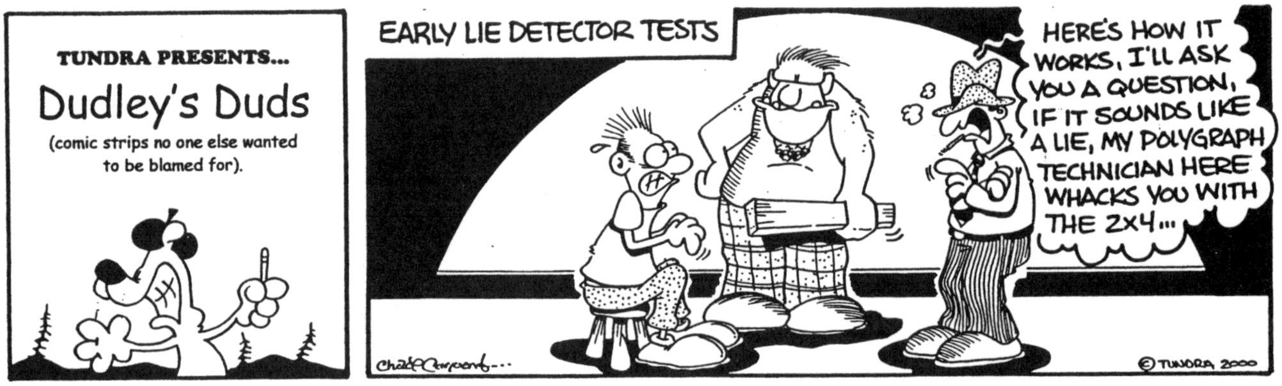
TUNDRA PRESENTS...
Dudley's Duds
(comic strips no one else wanted to be blamed for).
EARLY LIE DETECTOR TESTS
HERE'S HOW IT WORKS, I'LL ASK YOU A QUESTION, IF IT SOUNDS LIKE A LIE, MY POLYGRAPH TECHNICIAN HERE WHACKS YOU WITH THE 2x4...
© TUNDRA 2000

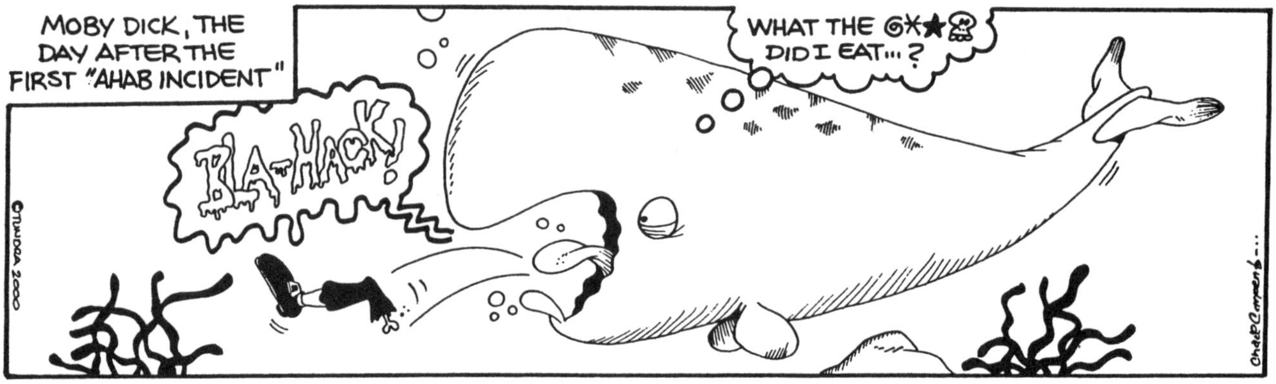
MOBY DICK, THE DAY AFTER THE FIRST "AHAB INCIDENT"
WHAT THE @*★☠ DID I EAT...?
BLA-HACK!
© TUNDRA 2000

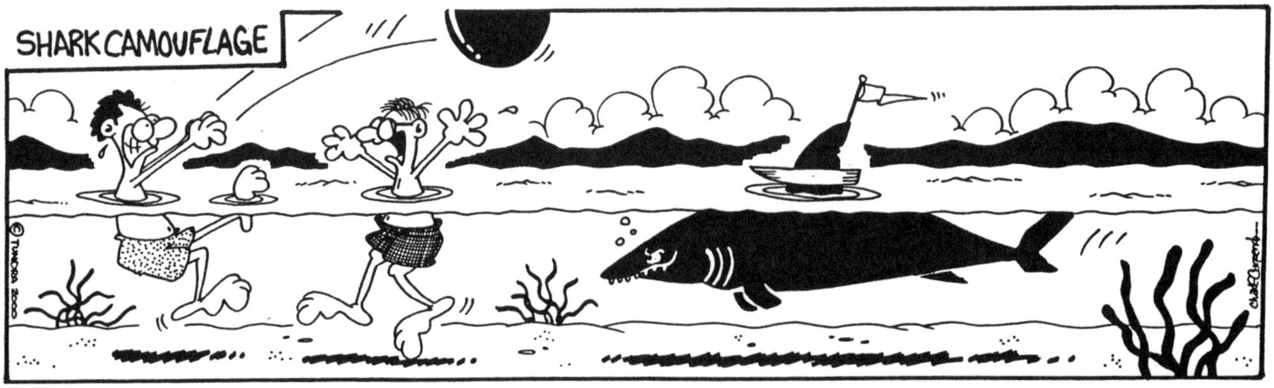
SHARK CAMOUFLAGE
© TUNDRA 2000

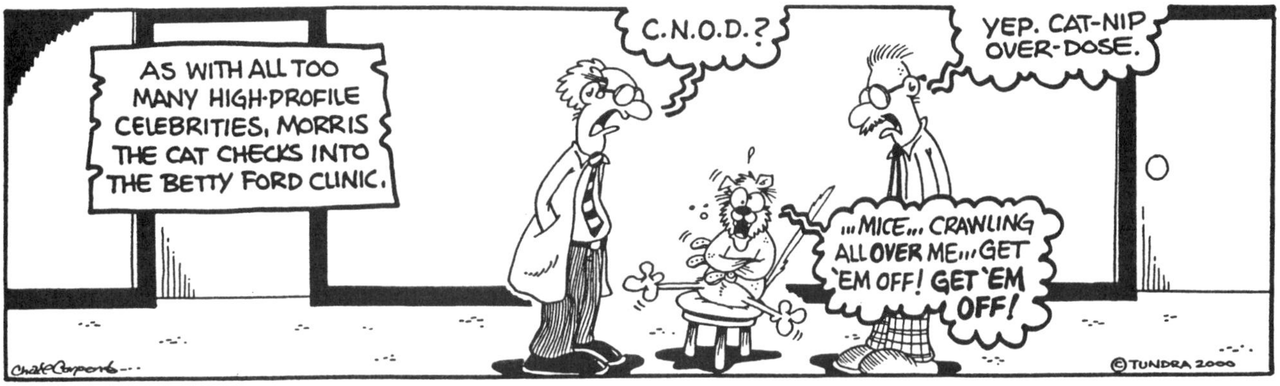
AS WITH ALL TOO MANY HIGH-PROFILE CELEBRITIES, MORRIS THE CAT CHECKS INTO THE BETTY FORD CLINIC.
C.N.O.D.?
YEP. CAT-NIP OVER-DOSE.
...MICE... CRAWLING ALL OVER ME... GET 'EM OFF! GET 'EM OFF!
©TUNDRA 2000

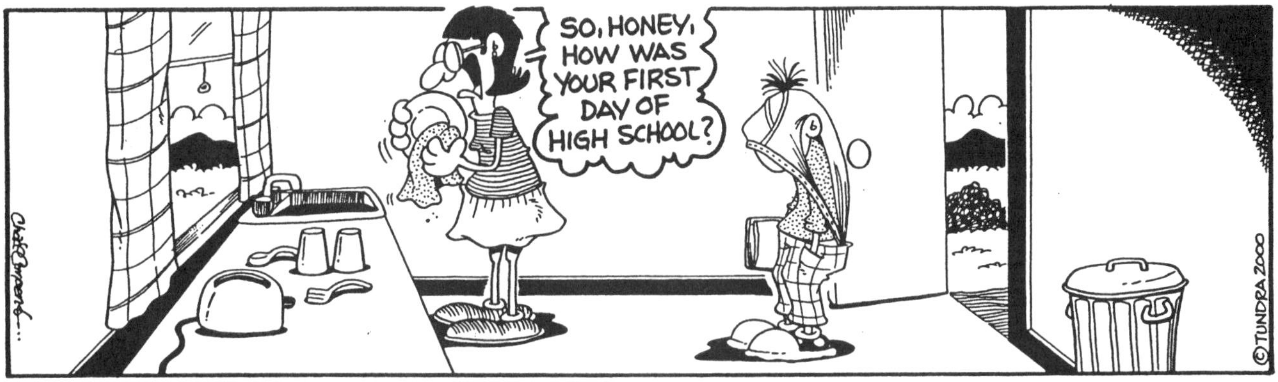
SO, HONEY, HOW WAS YOUR FIRST DAY OF HIGH SCHOOL?
©TUNDRA 2000

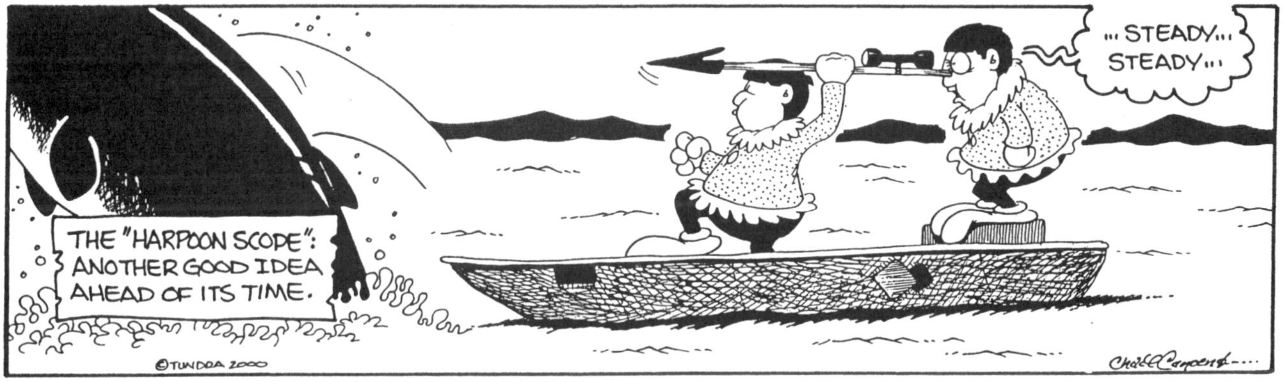
...STEADY... STEADY...
THE "HARPOON SCOPE": ANOTHER GOOD IDEA AHEAD OF ITS TIME.
©TUNDRA 2000

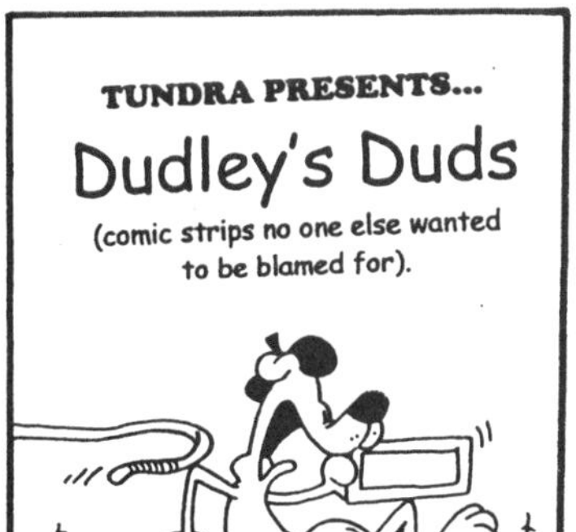
TUNDRA PRESENTS...
Dudley's Duds
(comic strips no one else wanted to be blamed for).

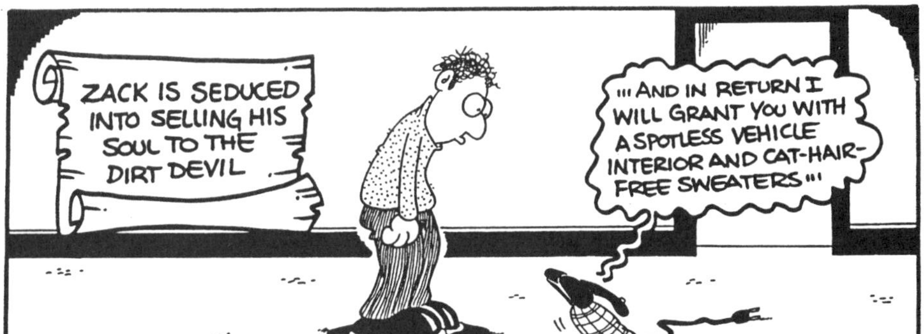
ZACK IS SEDUCED INTO SELLING HIS SOUL TO THE DIRT DEVIL
...AND IN RETURN I WILL GRANT YOU WITH A SPOTLESS VEHICLE INTERIOR AND CAT-HAIR-FREE SWEATERS...
©TUNDRA 2000

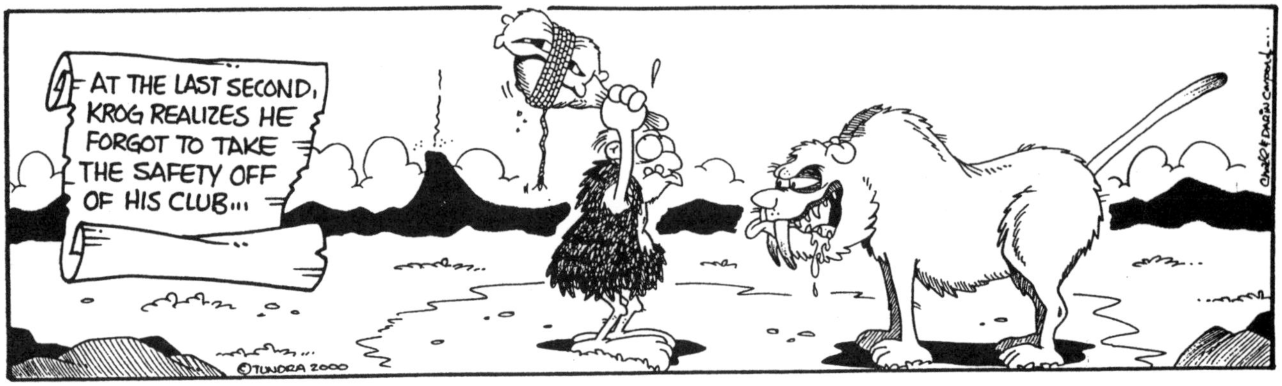
AT THE LAST SECOND, KROG REALIZES HE FORGOT TO TAKE THE SAFETY OFF OF HIS CLUB...
©TUNDRA 2000

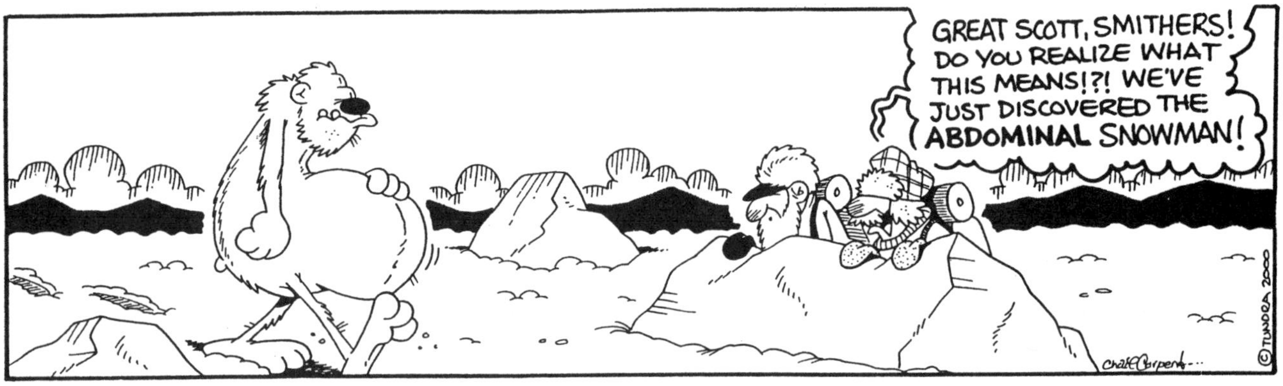
GREAT SCOTT, SMITHERS! DO YOU REALIZE WHAT THIS MEANS!?! WE'VE JUST DISCOVERED THE **ABDOMINAL** SNOWMAN!
©TUNDRA 2000

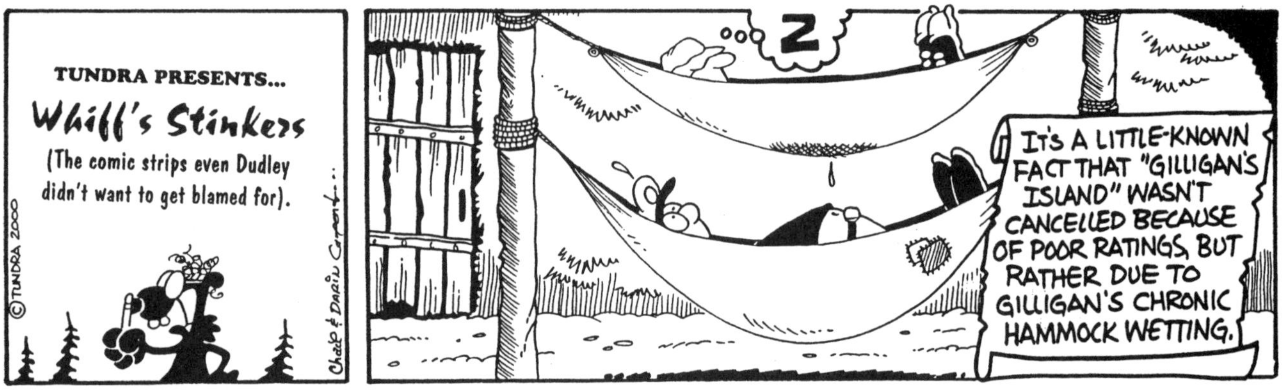
TUNDRA PRESENTS...
Whiff's Stinkers
(The comic strips even Dudley didn't want to get blamed for).
©TUNDRA 2000
Z
IT'S A LITTLE-KNOWN FACT THAT "GILLIGAN'S ISLAND" WASN'T CANCELLED BECAUSE OF POOR RATINGS, BUT RATHER DUE TO GILLIGAN'S CHRONIC HAMMOCK WETTING.

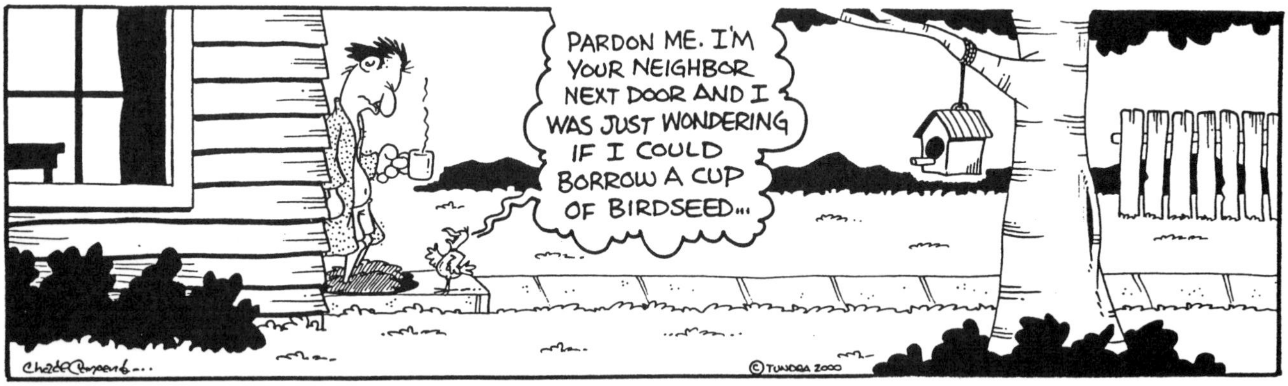
PARDON ME. I'M YOUR NEIGHBOR NEXT DOOR AND I WAS JUST WONDERING IF I COULD BORROW A CUP OF BIRDSEED...
©TUNDRA 2000

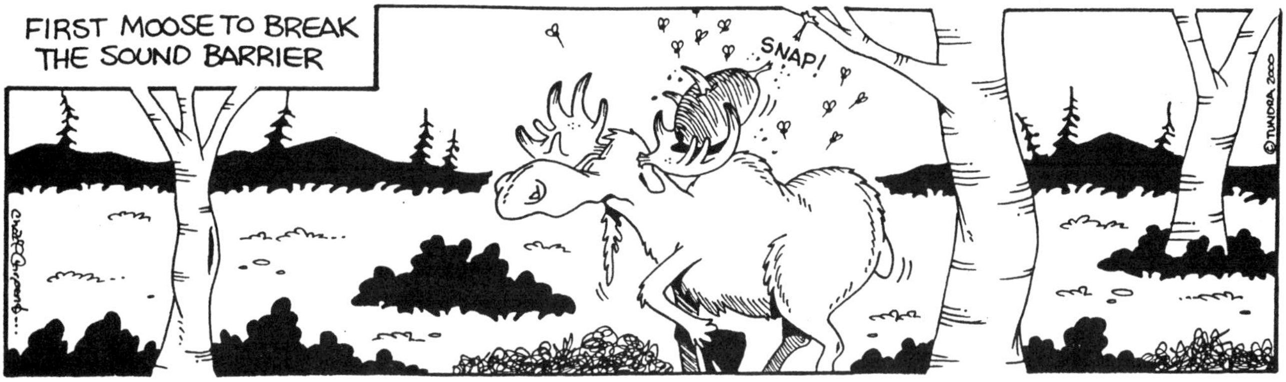
FIRST MOOSE TO BREAK THE SOUND BARRIER
SNAP!
© TUNDRA 2000

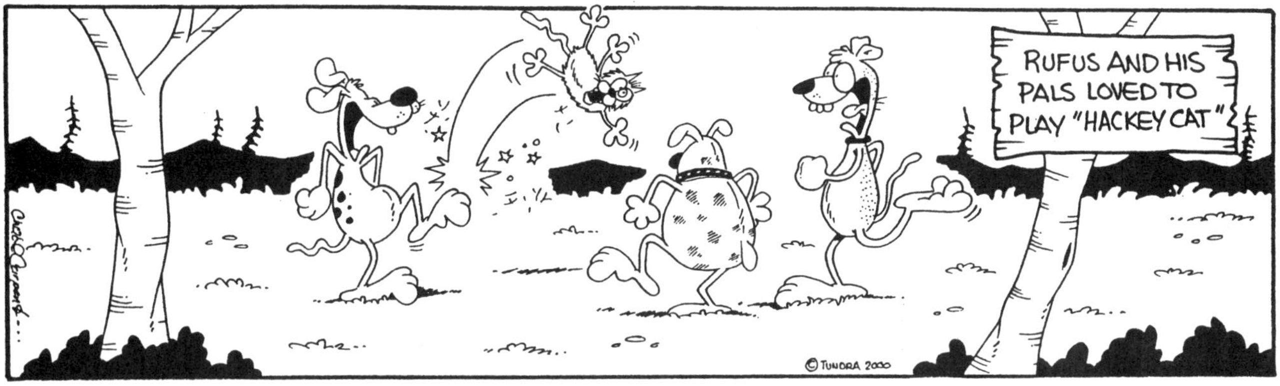
RUFUS AND HIS PALS LOVED TO PLAY "HACKEY CAT"
© TUNDRA 2000

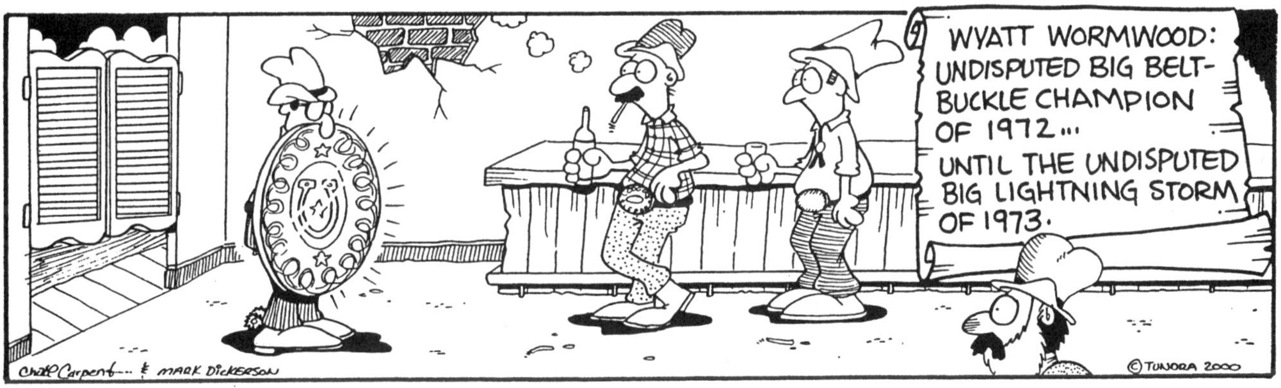
WYATT WORMWOOD: UNDISPUTED BIG BELT-BUCKLE CHAMPION OF 1972...
UNTIL THE UNDISPUTED BIG LIGHTNING STORM OF 1973.
MARK DICKERSON
© TUNDRA 2000

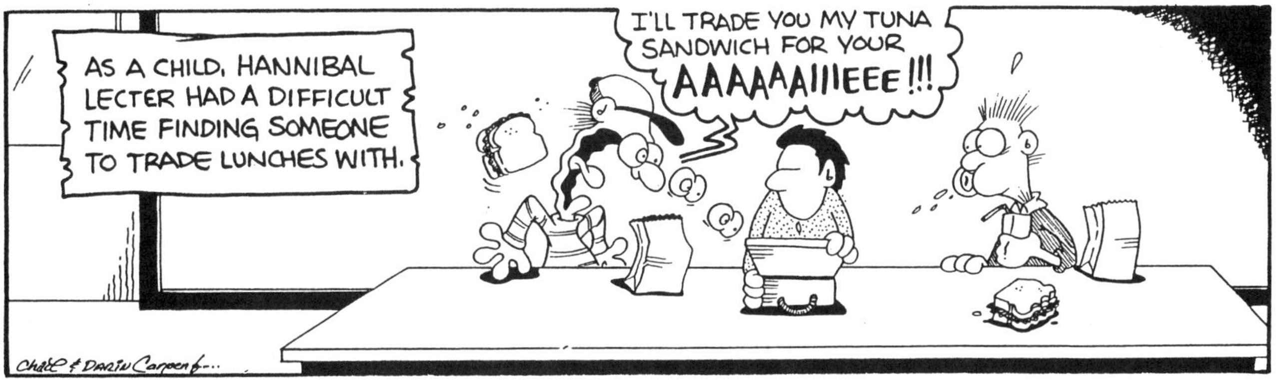
AS A CHILD, HANNIBAL LECTER HAD A DIFFICULT TIME FINDING SOMEONE TO TRADE LUNCHES WITH.
I'LL TRADE YOU MY TUNA SANDWICH FOR YOUR
AAAAAAIIIEEE!!!

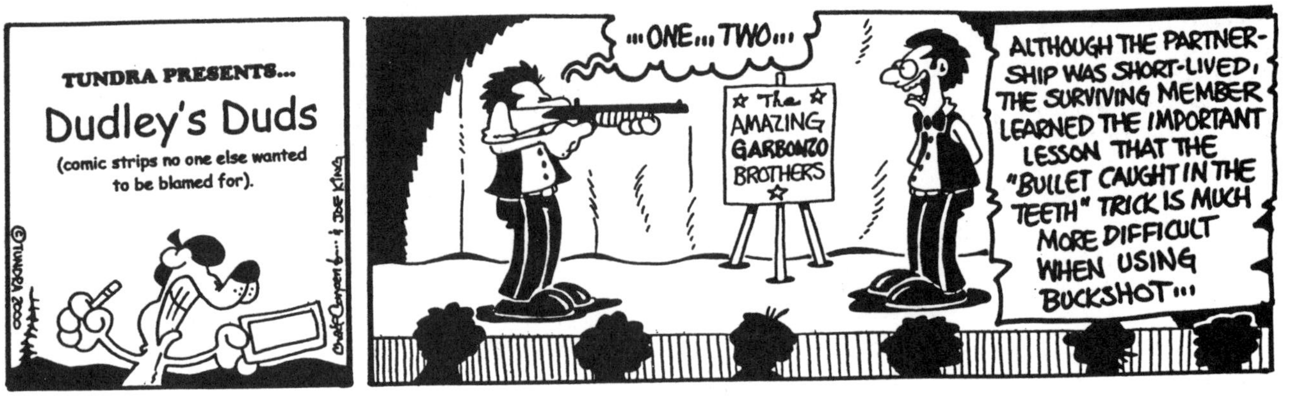
TUNDRA PRESENTS...
Dudley's Duds
(comic strips no one else wanted to be blamed for).
©TUNDRA 2000
...ONE...TWO...
The AMAZING GARBONZO BROTHERS
ALTHOUGH THE PARTNERSHIP WAS SHORT-LIVED, THE SURVIVING MEMBER LEARNED THE IMPORTANT LESSON THAT THE "BULLET CAUGHT IN THE TEETH" TRICK IS MUCH MORE DIFFICULT WHEN USING BUCKSHOT...

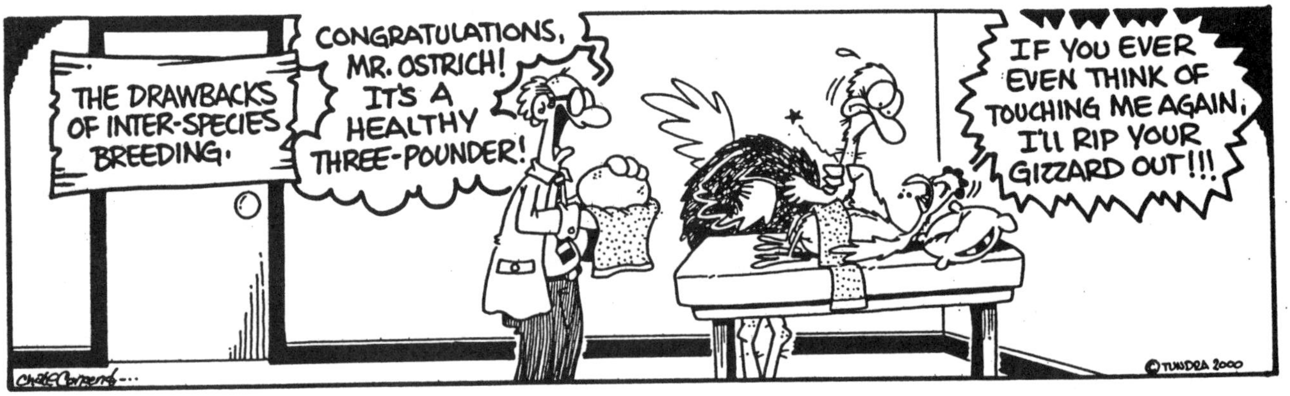
THE DRAWBACKS OF INTER-SPECIES BREEDING.
CONGRATULATIONS, MR. OSTRICH! IT'S A HEALTHY THREE-POUNDER!
IF YOU EVER EVEN THINK OF TOUCHING ME AGAIN, I'LL RIP YOUR GIZZARD OUT!!!
©TUNDRA 2000

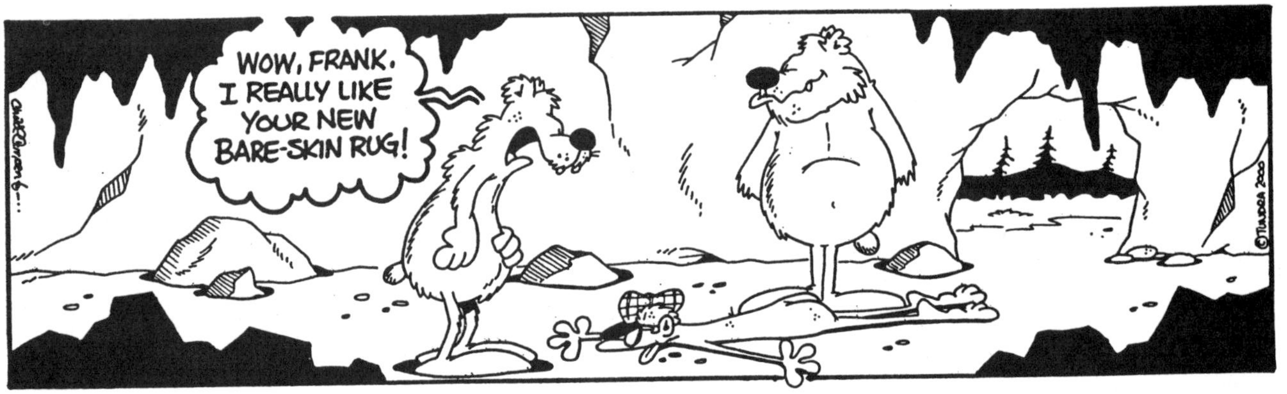
WOW, FRANK. I REALLY LIKE YOUR NEW BARE-SKIN RUG!
©TUNDRA 2000

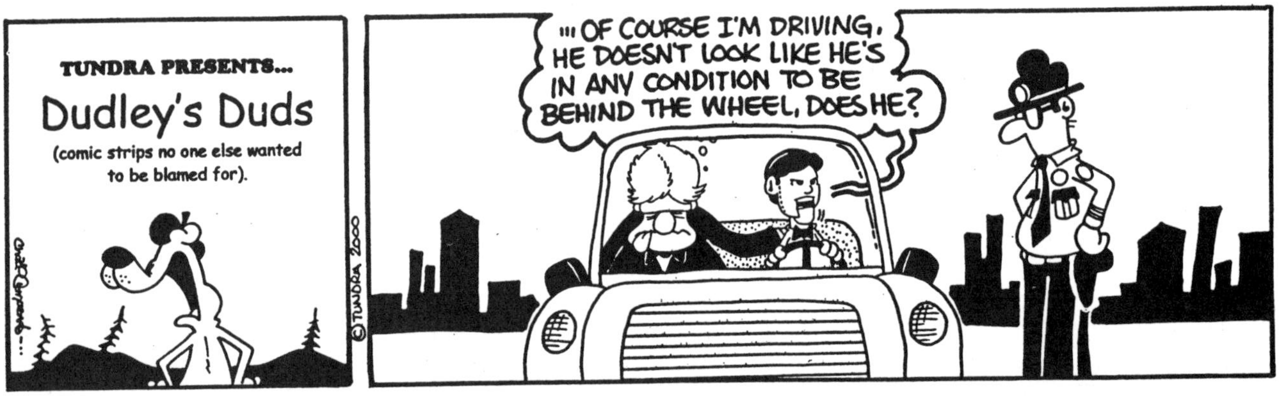
TUNDRA PRESENTS...
Dudley's Duds
(comic strips no one else wanted to be blamed for).
©TUNDRA 2000
...OF COURSE I'M DRIVING. HE DOESN'T LOOK LIKE HE'S IN ANY CONDITION TO BE BEHIND THE WHEEL, DOES HE?

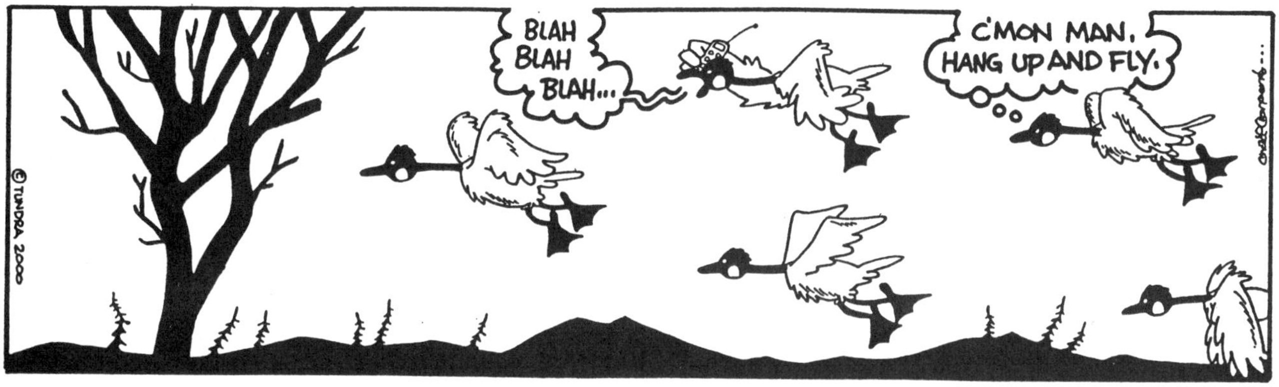
BLAH BLAH BLAH...
C'MON MAN, HANG UP AND FLY.
© TUNDRA 2000

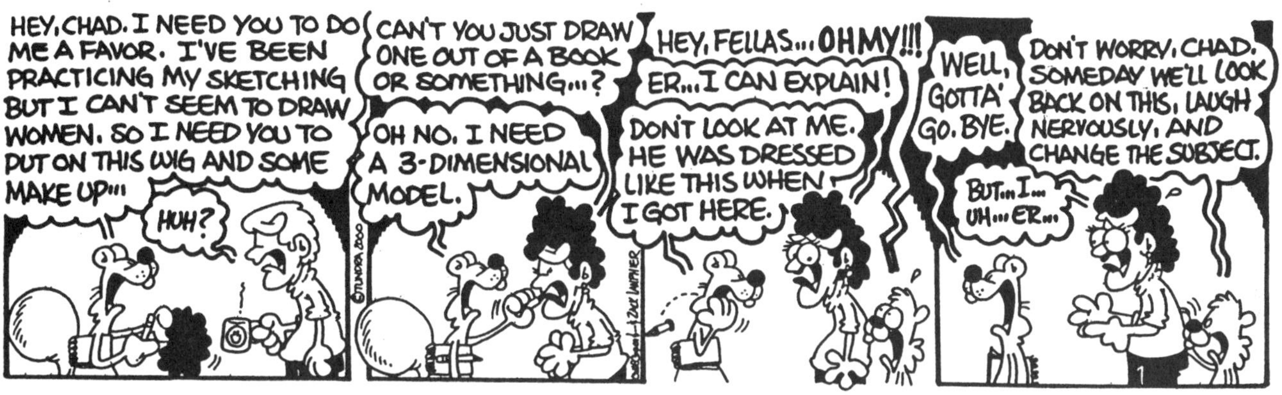
HEY, CHAD. I NEED YOU TO DO ME A FAVOR. I'VE BEEN PRACTICING MY SKETCHING BUT I CAN'T SEEM TO DRAW WOMEN. SO I NEED YOU TO PUT ON THIS WIG AND SOME MAKE UP...
HUH?
CAN'T YOU JUST DRAW ONE OUT OF A BOOK OR SOMETHING...?
OH NO. I NEED A 3-DIMENSIONAL MODEL.
©TUNDRA 2000
HEY, FELLAS... OH MY!!!
ER...I CAN EXPLAIN!
DON'T LOOK AT ME. HE WAS DRESSED LIKE THIS WHEN I GOT HERE.
WELL, GOTTA' GO. BYE.
DON'T WORRY, CHAD. SOMEDAY WE'LL LOOK BACK ON THIS, LAUGH NERVOUSLY, AND CHANGE THE SUBJECT.
BUT...I... UH...ER...

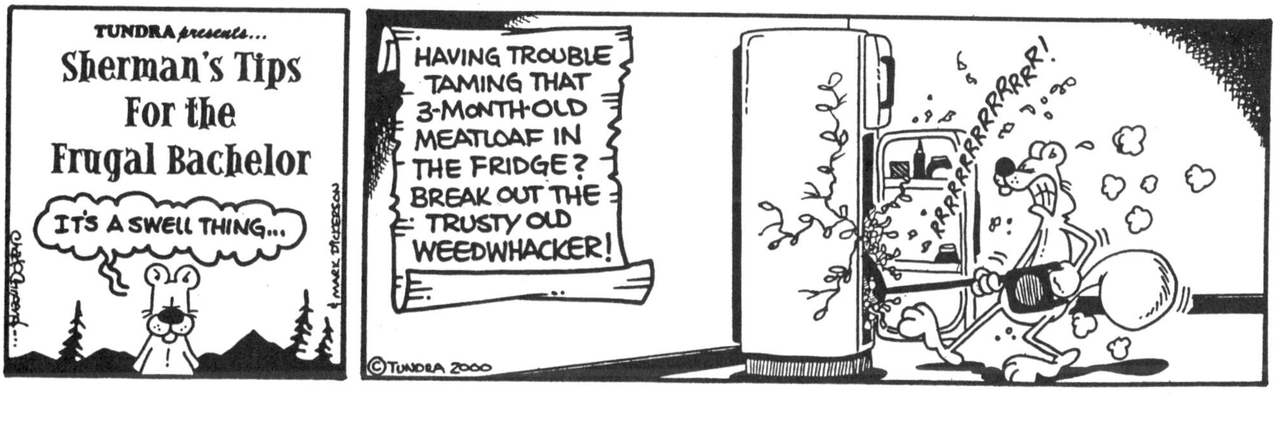
TUNDRA presents...
Sherman's Tips For the Frugal Bachelor
IT'S A SWELL THING...
MARK DICKERSON
HAVING TROUBLE TAMING THAT 3-MONTH-OLD MEATLOAF IN THE FRIDGE? BREAK OUT THE TRUSTY OLD WEEDWHACKER!
RRRRRRRRRRRRRR!
©TUNDRA 2000

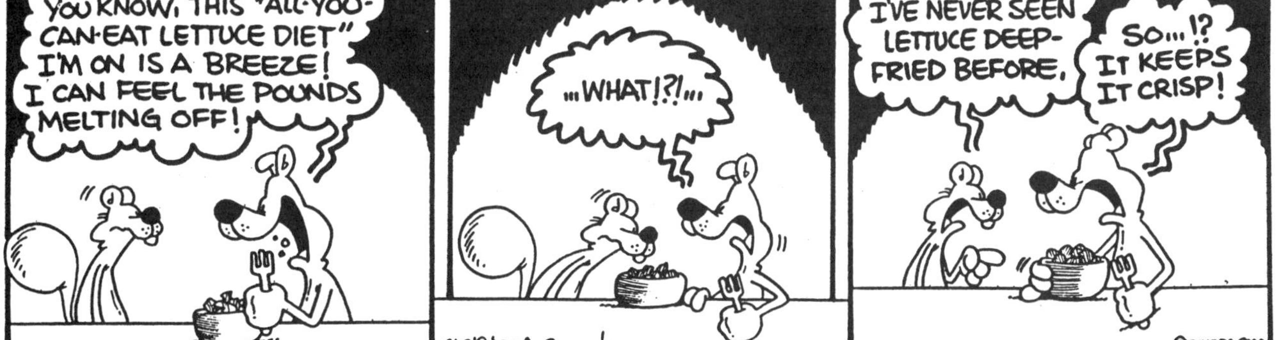
YOU KNOW, THIS "ALL-YOU-CAN-EAT LETTUCE DIET" I'M ON IS A BREEZE! I CAN FEEL THE POUNDS MELTING OFF!
...WHAT!?!...
I'VE NEVER SEEN LETTUCE DEEP-FRIED BEFORE.
SO...!? IT KEEPS IT CRISP!
©TUNDRA 2000

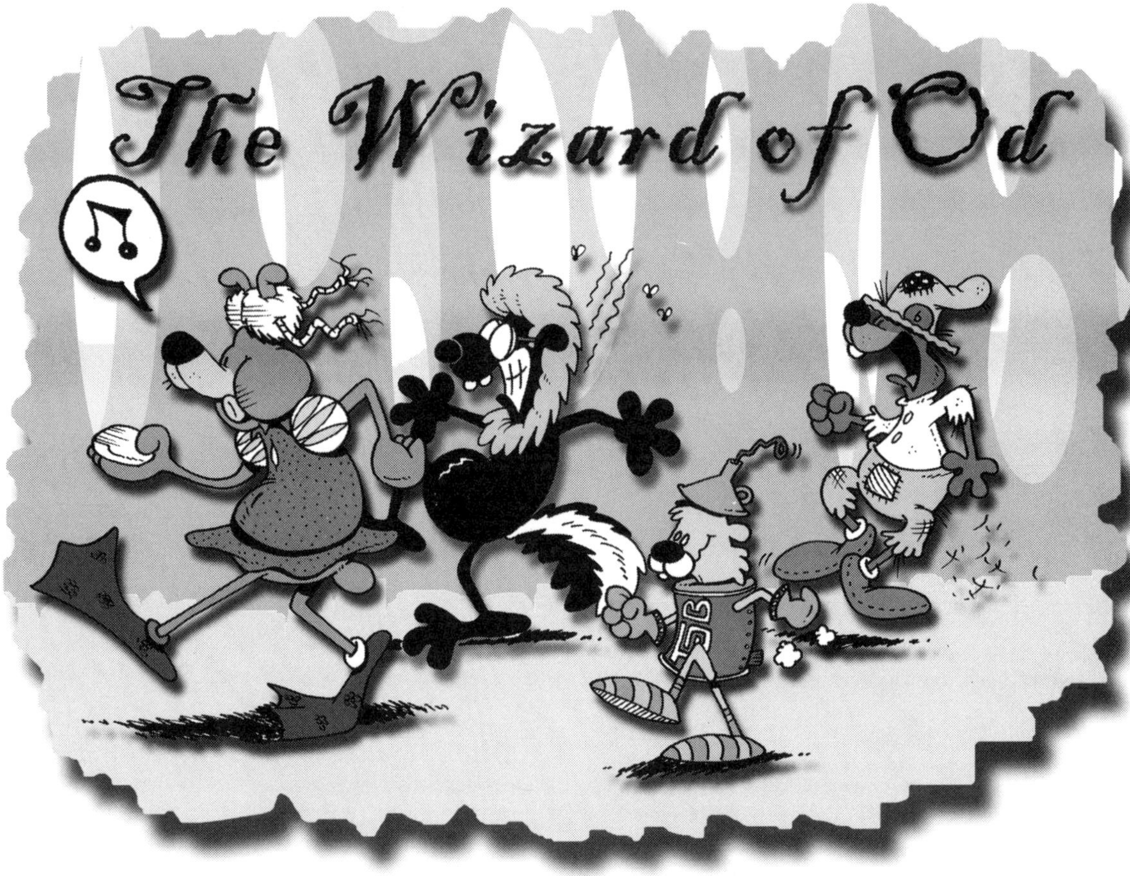
The Wizard of Od

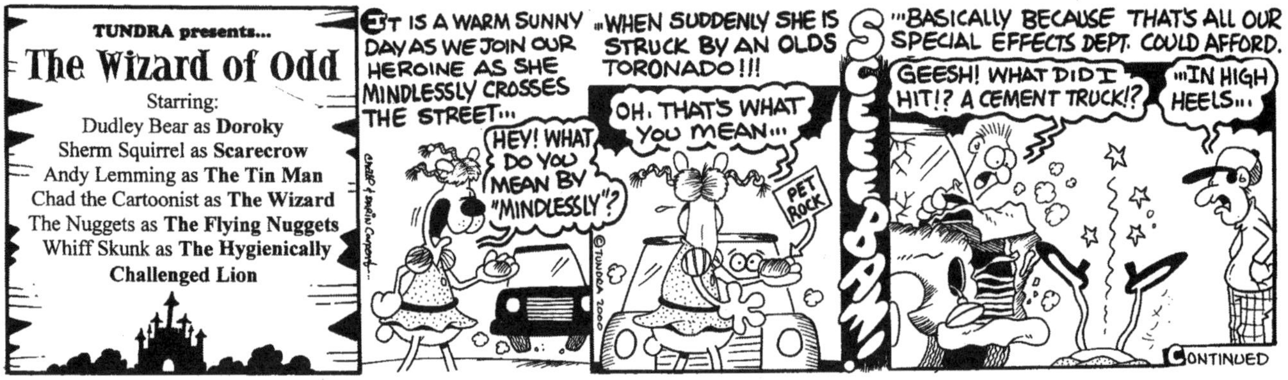
TUNDRA presents...
The Wizard of Odd
Starring:
Dudley Bear as Doroky
Sherm Squirrel as Scarecrow
Andy Lemming as The Tin Man
Chad the Cartoonist as The Wizard
The Nuggets as The Flying Nuggets
Whiff Skunk as The Hygienically Challenged Lion
IT IS A WARM SUNNY DAY AS WE JOIN OUR HEROINE AS SHE MINDLESSLY CROSSES THE STREET...
HEY! WHAT DO YOU MEAN BY "MINDLESSLY"?
© TUNDRA 2000
...WHEN SUDDENLY SHE IS STRUCK BY AN OLDS TORONADO!!!
OH, THAT'S WHAT YOU MEAN...
PET ROCK
...BASICALLY BECAUSE THAT'S ALL OUR SPECIAL EFFECTS DEPT. COULD AFFORD.
GEESH! WHAT DID I HIT!? A CEMENT TRUCK!?
...IN HIGH HEELS...
CONTINUED

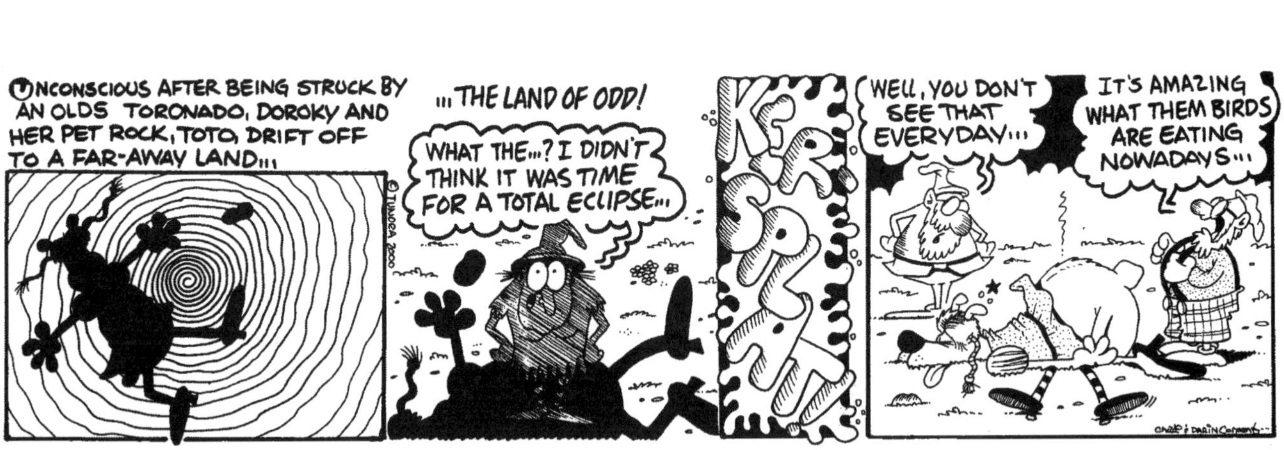
UNCONSCIOUS AFTER BEING STRUCK BY AN OLDS TORONADO, DOROKY AND HER PET ROCK, TOTO, DRIFT OFF TO A FAR-AWAY LAND...
© TUNDRA 2000
...THE LAND OF ODD!
WHAT THE...? I DIDN'T THINK IT WAS TIME FOR A TOTAL ECLIPSE...
WELL, YOU DON'T SEE THAT EVERYDAY...
IT'S AMAZING WHAT THEM BIRDS ARE EATING NOWADAYS...

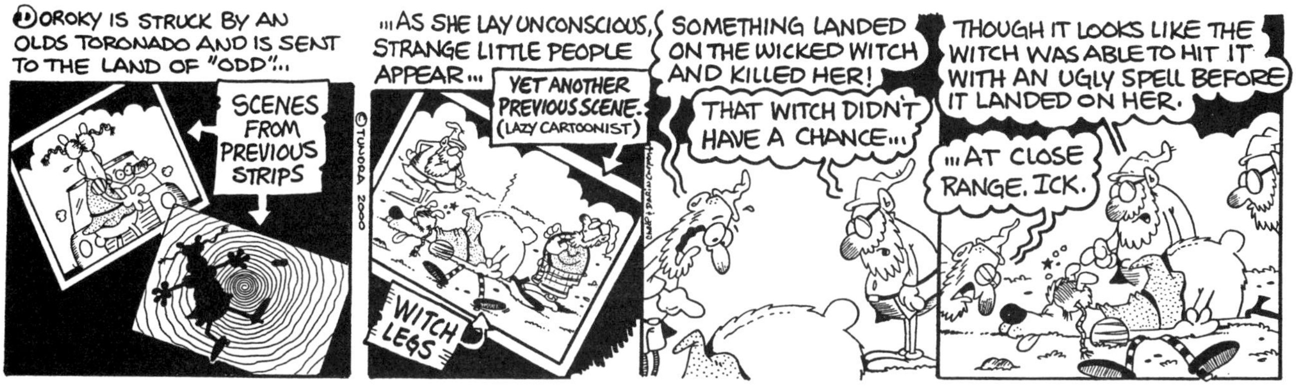
DOROKY IS STRUCK BY AN OLDS TORONADO AND IS SENT TO THE LAND OF "ODD"...
SCENES FROM PREVIOUS STRIPS
...AS SHE LAY UNCONSCIOUS, STRANGE LITTLE PEOPLE APPEAR...
YET ANOTHER PREVIOUS SCENE. (LAZY CARTOONIST)
© TUNDRA 2000
WITCH LEGS
SOMETHING LANDED ON THE WICKED WITCH AND KILLED HER!
THAT WITCH DIDN'T HAVE A CHANCE...
THOUGH IT LOOKS LIKE THE WITCH WAS ABLE TO HIT IT WITH AN UGLY SPELL BEFORE IT LANDED ON HER.
...AT CLOSE RANGE. ICK.

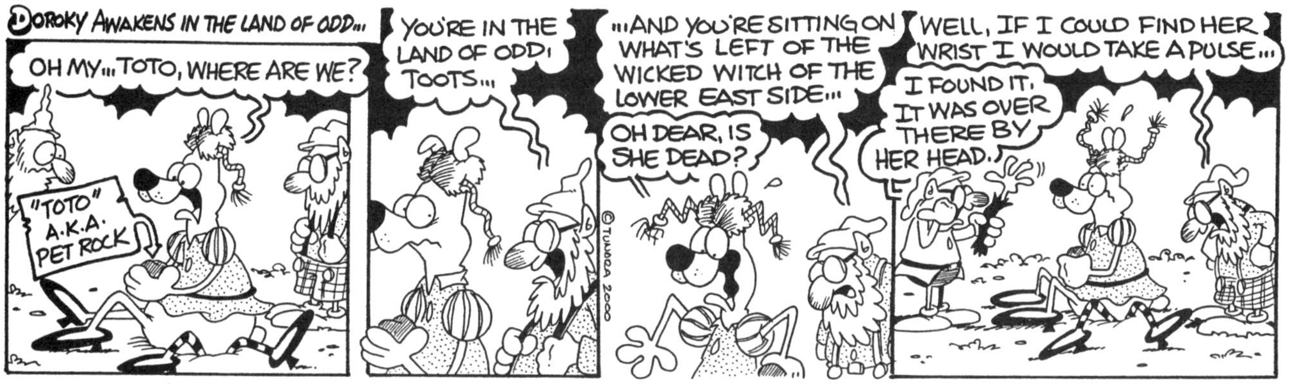
DOROKY AWAKENS IN THE LAND OF ODD...
OH MY... TOTO, WHERE ARE WE?
"TOTO" A.K.A. PET ROCK
YOU'RE IN THE LAND OF ODD, TOOTS...
© TUNDRA 2000
...AND YOU'RE SITTING ON WHAT'S LEFT OF THE WICKED WITCH OF THE LOWER EAST SIDE...
OH DEAR, IS SHE DEAD?
WELL, IF I COULD FIND HER WRIST I WOULD TAKE A PULSE...
I FOUND IT. IT WAS OVER THERE BY HER HEAD.

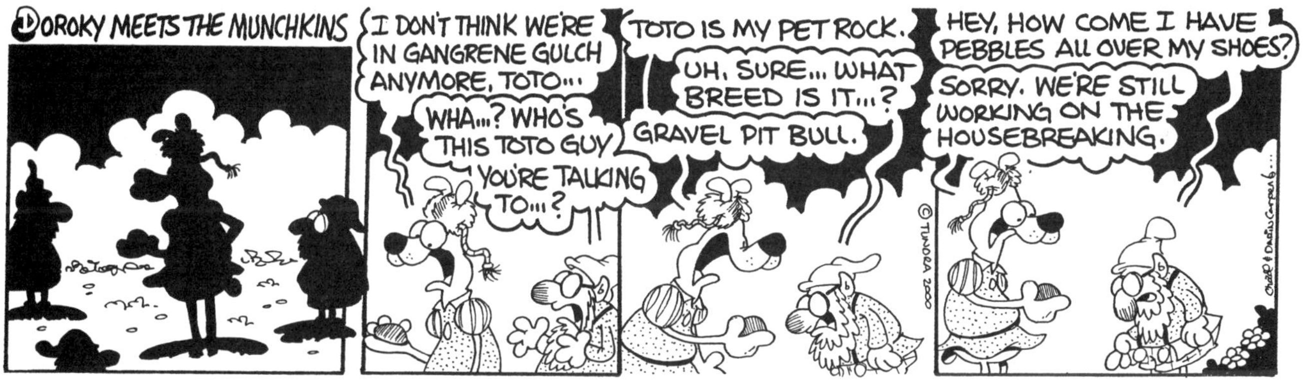
DOROKY MEETS THE MUNCHKINS
I DON'T THINK WE'RE IN GANGRENE GULCH ANYMORE, TOTO...
WHA...? WHO'S THIS TOTO GUY YOU'RE TALKING TO...?
TOTO IS MY PET ROCK.
UH, SURE... WHAT BREED IS IT...?
GRAVEL PIT BULL.
© TUNDRA 2000
HEY, HOW COME I HAVE PEBBLES ALL OVER MY SHOES?
SORRY. WE'RE STILL WORKING ON THE HOUSEBREAKING.

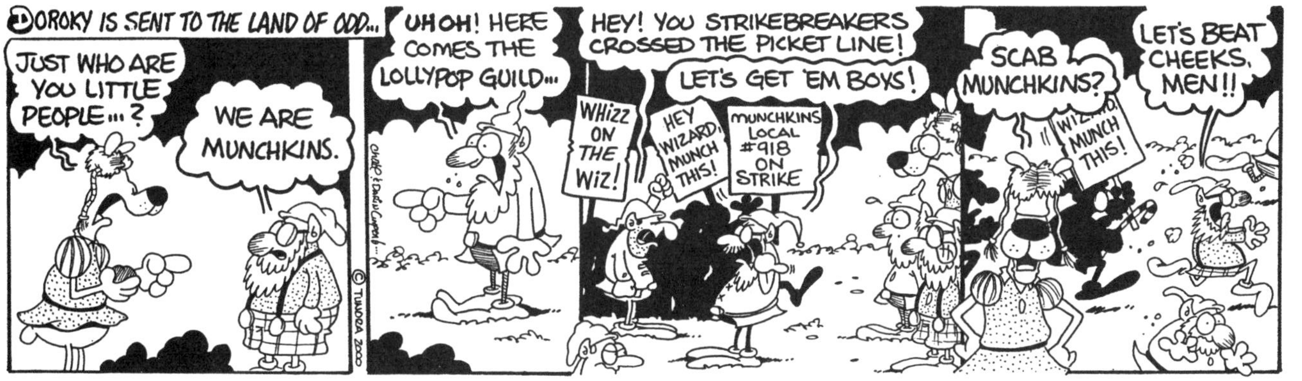
DOROKY IS SENT TO THE LAND OF ODD...
JUST WHO ARE YOU LITTLE PEOPLE...?
WE ARE MUNCHKINS.
© TUNDRA 2000
UH OH! HERE COMES THE LOLLYPOP GUILD...
HEY! YOU STRIKEBREAKERS CROSSED THE PICKET LINE!
LET'S GET 'EM BOYS!
WHIZZ ON THE WIZ!
HEY WIZARD, MUNCH THIS!
MUNCHKINS LOCAL #918 ON STRIKE
SCAB MUNCHKINS?
WIZARD, MUNCH THIS!
LET'S BEAT CHEEKS, MEN!!

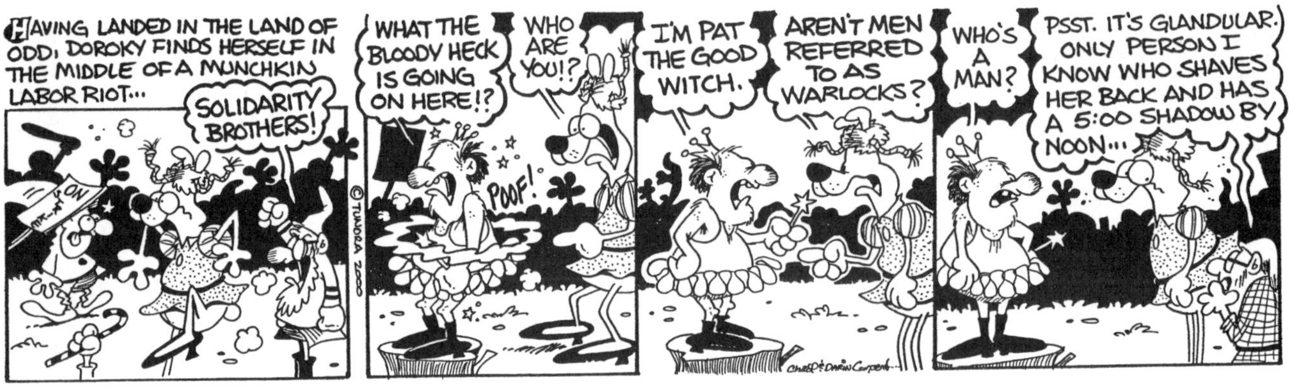
HAVING LANDED IN THE LAND OF ODD, DOROKY FINDS HERSELF IN THE MIDDLE OF A MUNCHKIN LABOR RIOT...
SOLIDARITY BROTHERS!
ON
WHAT THE BLOODY HECK IS GOING ON HERE!?
WHO ARE YOU!?
POOF!
© TUNDRA 2000
I'M PAT THE GOOD WITCH.
AREN'T MEN REFERRED TO AS WARLOCKS?
WHO'S A MAN?
PSST. IT'S GLANDULAR. ONLY PERSON I KNOW WHO SHAVES HER BACK AND HAS A 5:00 SHADOW BY NOON...

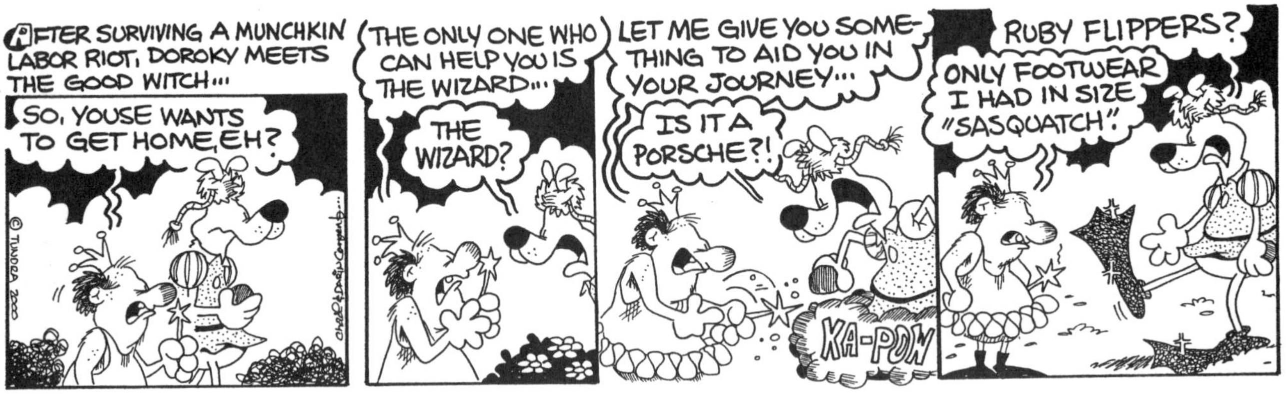
AFTER SURVIVING A MUNCHKIN LABOR RIOT, DOROKY MEETS THE GOOD WITCH...
SO, YOUSE WANTS TO GET HOME, EH?
© TUNDRA 2000
THE ONLY ONE WHO CAN HELP YOU IS THE WIZARD...
THE WIZARD?
LET ME GIVE YOU SOMETHING TO AID YOU IN YOUR JOURNEY...
IS IT A PORSCHE?!
KA-POW
RUBY FLIPPERS?
ONLY FOOTWEAR I HAD IN SIZE "SASQUATCH".

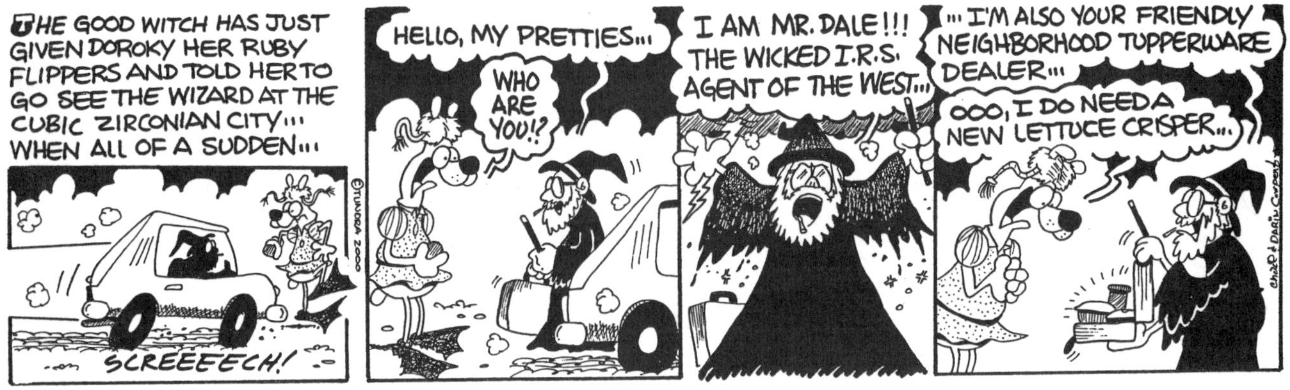
THE GOOD WITCH HAS JUST GIVEN DOROKY HER RUBY FLIPPERS AND TOLD HER TO GO SEE THE WIZARD AT THE CUBIC ZIRCONIAN CITY... WHEN ALL OF A SUDDEN...
SCREEEEECH!
HELLO, MY PRETTIES...
WHO ARE YOU!?
© TUNDRA 2000
I AM MR. DALE!!! THE WICKED I.R.S. AGENT OF THE WEST...
...I'M ALSO YOUR FRIENDLY NEIGHBORHOOD TUPPERWARE DEALER...
OOO, I DO NEED A NEW LETTUCE CRISPER...

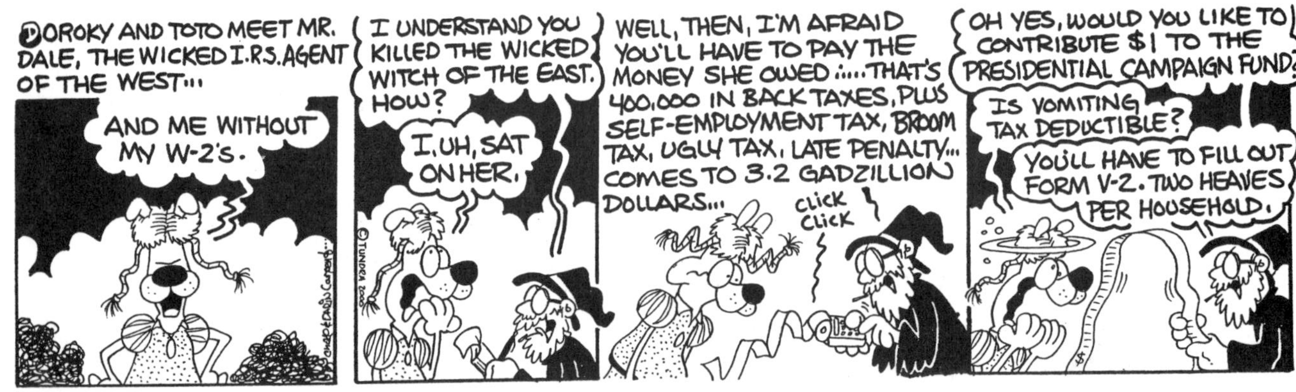
DOROKY AND TOTO MEET MR. DALE, THE WICKED I.R.S. AGENT OF THE WEST...
AND ME WITHOUT MY W-2'S.
I UNDERSTAND YOU KILLED THE WICKED WITCH OF THE EAST. HOW?
I, UH, SAT ON HER.
© TUNDRA 2000
WELL, THEN, I'M AFRAID YOU'LL HAVE TO PAY THE MONEY SHE OWED ..... THAT'S 400,000 IN BACK TAXES, PLUS SELF-EMPLOYMENT TAX, BROOM TAX, UGLY TAX, LATE PENALTY... COMES TO 3.2 GADZILLION DOLLARS...
CLICK CLICK
OH YES, WOULD YOU LIKE TO CONTRIBUTE $1 TO THE PRESIDENTIAL CAMPAIGN FUND?
IS VOMITING TAX DEDUCTIBLE?
YOU'LL HAVE TO FILL OUT FORM V-2. TWO HEAVES PER HOUSEHOLD.

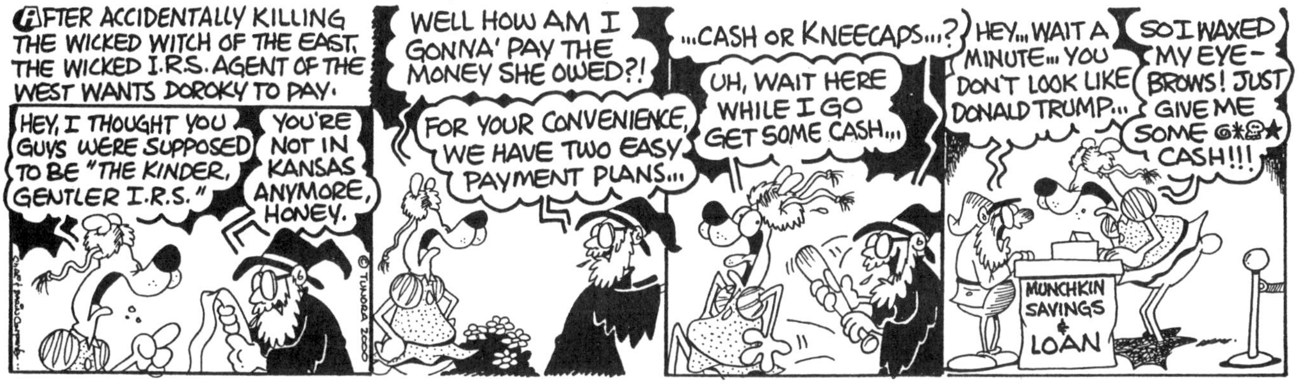
After accidentally killing the Wicked Witch of the East, the Wicked I.R.S. Agent of the West wants Doroky to pay.
HEY, I THOUGHT YOU GUYS WERE SUPPOSED TO BE "THE KINDER, GENTLER I.R.S."
YOU'RE NOT IN KANSAS ANYMORE, HONEY.
WELL HOW AM I GONNA' PAY THE MONEY SHE OWED?!
FOR YOUR CONVENIENCE, WE HAVE TWO EASY PAYMENT PLANS...
...CASH OR KNEECAPS...?
UH, WAIT HERE WHILE I GO GET SOME CASH...
HEY... WAIT A MINUTE... YOU DON'T LOOK LIKE DONALD TRUMP...
SO I WAXED MY EYE-BROWS! JUST GIVE ME SOME @*☺★ CASH!!!
MUNCHKIN SAVINGS & LOAN

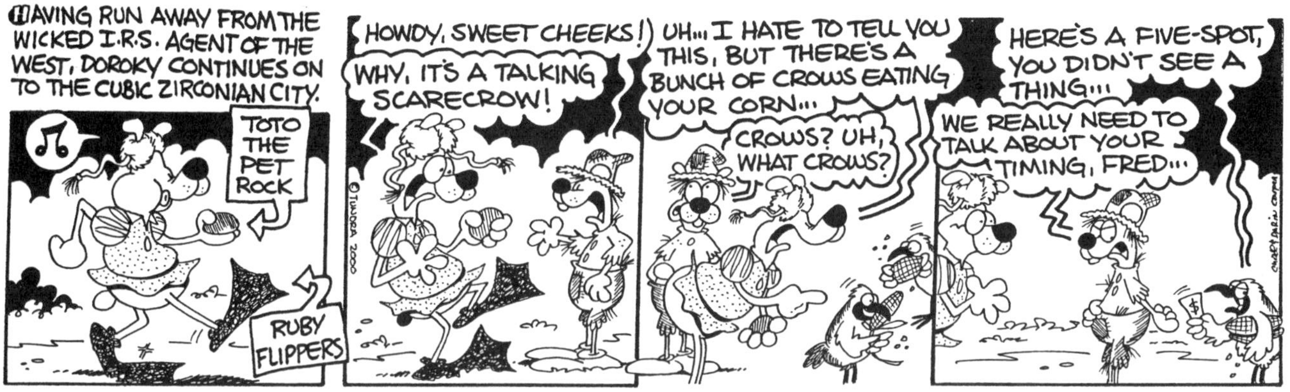
Having run away from the Wicked I.R.S. Agent of the West, Doroky continues on to the Cubic Zirconian City.
TOTO THE PET ROCK
RUBY FLIPPERS
HOWDY, SWEET CHEEKS!
WHY, IT'S A TALKING SCARECROW!
UH... I HATE TO TELL YOU THIS, BUT THERE'S A BUNCH OF CROWS EATING YOUR CORN...
CROWS? UH, WHAT CROWS?
HERE'S A FIVE-SPOT, YOU DIDN'T SEE A THING...
WE REALLY NEED TO TALK ABOUT YOUR TIMING, FRED...

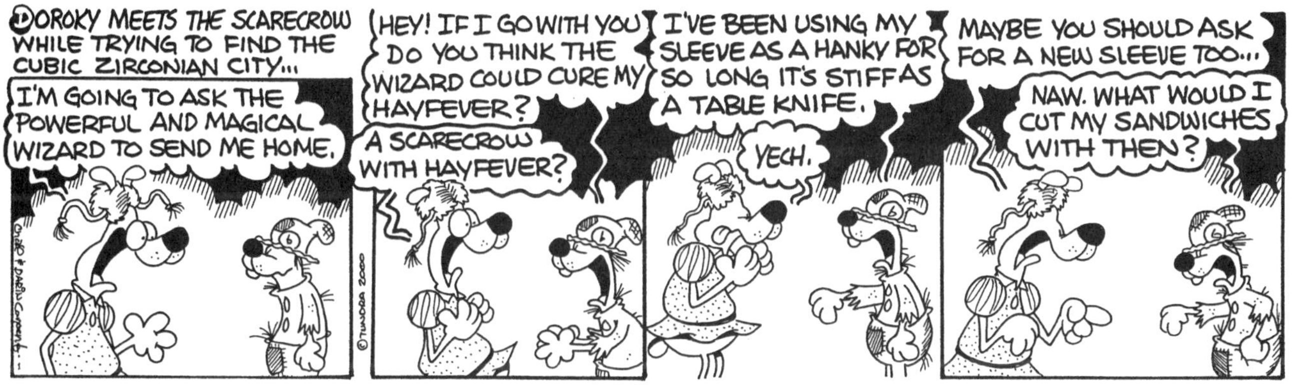
Doroky meets the Scarecrow while trying to find the Cubic Zirconian City...
I'M GOING TO ASK THE POWERFUL AND MAGICAL WIZARD TO SEND ME HOME.
HEY! IF I GO WITH YOU DO YOU THINK THE WIZARD COULD CURE MY HAYFEVER?
A SCARECROW WITH HAYFEVER?
I'VE BEEN USING MY SLEEVE AS A HANKY FOR SO LONG IT'S STIFF AS A TABLE KNIFE.
YECH.
MAYBE YOU SHOULD ASK FOR A NEW SLEEVE TOO...
NAW. WHAT WOULD I CUT MY SANDWICHES WITH THEN?

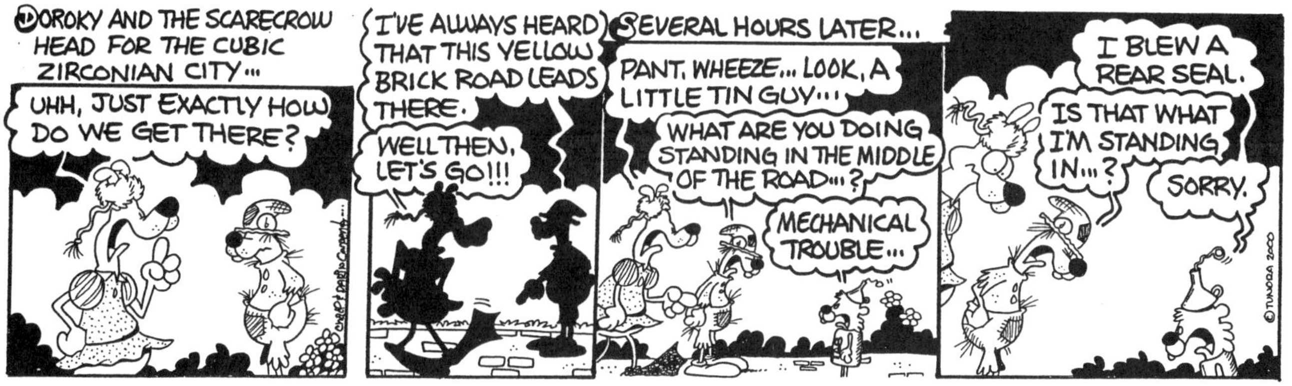
Doroky and the Scarecrow head for the Cubic Zirconian City...
UHH, JUST EXACTLY HOW DO WE GET THERE?
I'VE ALWAYS HEARD THAT THIS YELLOW BRICK ROAD LEADS THERE.
WELL THEN, LET'S GO!!!
Several hours later...
PANT, WHEEZE... LOOK, A LITTLE TIN GUY...
WHAT ARE YOU DOING STANDING IN THE MIDDLE OF THE ROAD...?
MECHANICAL TROUBLE...
I BLEW A REAR SEAL.
IS THAT WHAT I'M STANDING IN...?
SORRY.

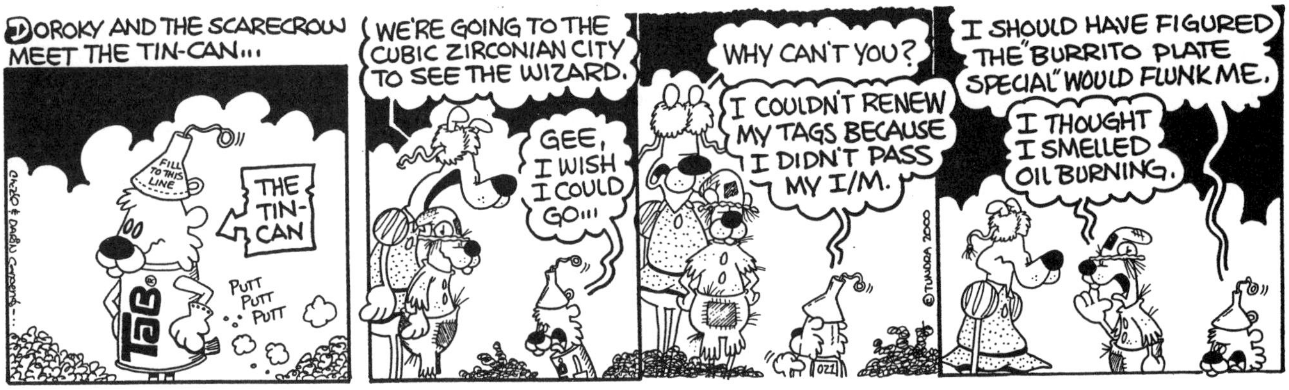
DOROKY AND THE SCARECROW MEET THE TIN-CAN...
FILL TO THIS LINE
THE TIN-CAN
TaB
PUTT PUTT PUTT
WE'RE GOING TO THE CUBIC ZIRCONIAN CITY TO SEE THE WIZARD.
GEE, I WISH I COULD GO...
WHY CAN'T YOU?
I COULDN'T RENEW MY TAGS BECAUSE I DIDN'T PASS MY I/M.
I SHOULD HAVE FIGURED THE "BURRITO PLATE SPECIAL" WOULD FLUNK ME.
I THOUGHT I SMELLED OIL BURNING.

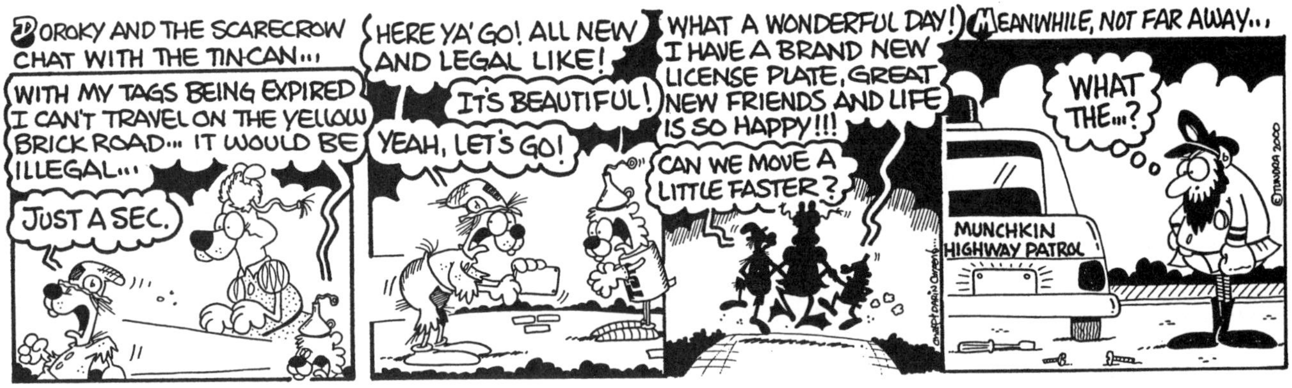
DOROKY AND THE SCARECROW CHAT WITH THE TIN-CAN...
WITH MY TAGS BEING EXPIRED I CAN'T TRAVEL ON THE YELLOW BRICK ROAD... IT WOULD BE ILLEGAL...
JUST A SEC.
HERE YA' GO! ALL NEW AND LEGAL LIKE!
IT'S BEAUTIFUL!
YEAH, LET'S GO!
WHAT A WONDERFUL DAY! I HAVE A BRAND NEW LICENSE PLATE, GREAT NEW FRIENDS AND LIFE IS SO HAPPY!!!
CAN WE MOVE A LITTLE FASTER?
MEANWHILE, NOT FAR AWAY...
WHAT THE...?
MUNCHKIN HIGHWAY PATROL

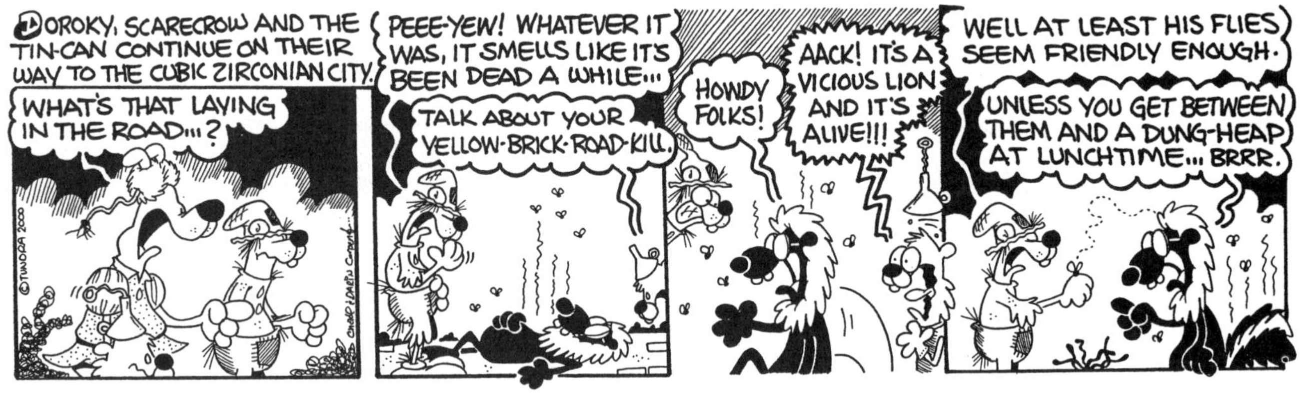
DOROKY, SCARECROW AND THE TIN-CAN CONTINUE ON THEIR WAY TO THE CUBIC ZIRCONIAN CITY.
WHAT'S THAT LAYING IN THE ROAD...?
PEEE-YEW! WHATEVER IT WAS, IT SMELLS LIKE IT'S BEEN DEAD A WHILE...
TALK ABOUT YOUR YELLOW-BRICK-ROAD-KILL.
HOWDY FOLKS!
AACK! IT'S A VICIOUS LION AND IT'S ALIVE!!!
WELL AT LEAST HIS FLIES SEEM FRIENDLY ENOUGH.
UNLESS YOU GET BETWEEN THEM AND A DUNG-HEAP AT LUNCHTIME... BRRR.

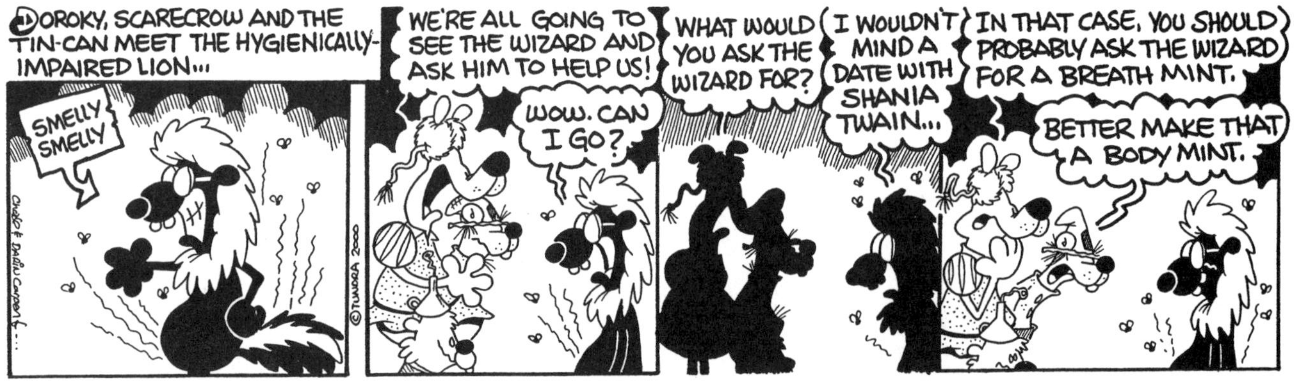
DOROKY, SCARECROW AND THE TIN-CAN MEET THE HYGIENICALLY-IMPAIRED LION...
SMELLY SMELLY
WE'RE ALL GOING TO SEE THE WIZARD AND ASK HIM TO HELP US!
WOW. CAN I GO?
WHAT WOULD YOU ASK THE WIZARD FOR?
I WOULDN'T MIND A DATE WITH SHANIA TWAIN...
IN THAT CASE, YOU SHOULD PROBABLY ASK THE WIZARD FOR A BREATH MINT.
BETTER MAKE THAT A BODY MINT.

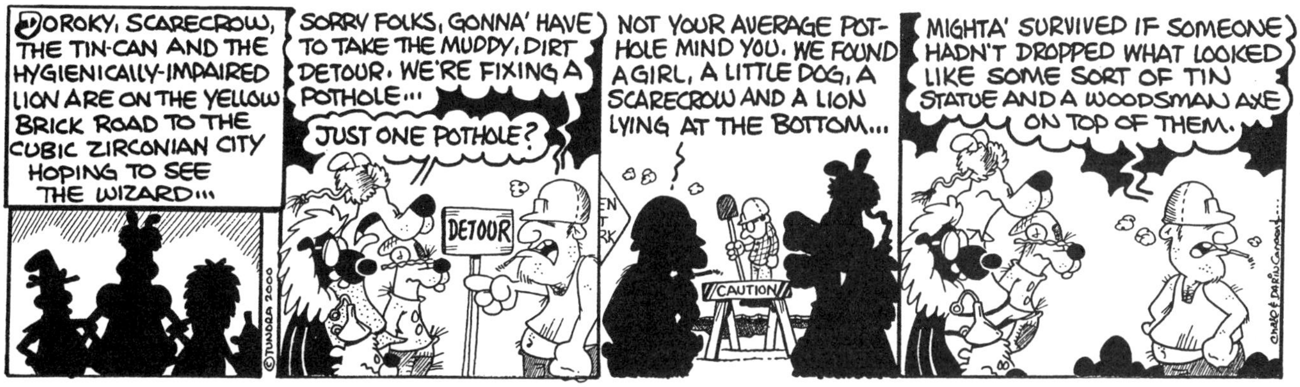
DOROKY, SCARECROW, THE TIN-CAN AND THE HYGIENICALLY-IMPAIRED LION ARE ON THE YELLOW BRICK ROAD TO THE CUBIC ZIRCONIAN CITY HOPING TO SEE THE WIZARD...
SORRY FOLKS, GONNA' HAVE TO TAKE THE MUDDY, DIRT DETOUR. WE'RE FIXING A POTHOLE...
JUST ONE POTHOLE?
DETOUR
NOT YOUR AVERAGE POT-HOLE MIND YOU. WE FOUND A GIRL, A LITTLE DOG, A SCARECROW AND A LION LYING AT THE BOTTOM...
CAUTION
MIGHTA' SURVIVED IF SOMEONE HADN'T DROPPED WHAT LOOKED LIKE SOME SORT OF TIN STATUE AND A WOODSMAN AXE ON TOP OF THEM.

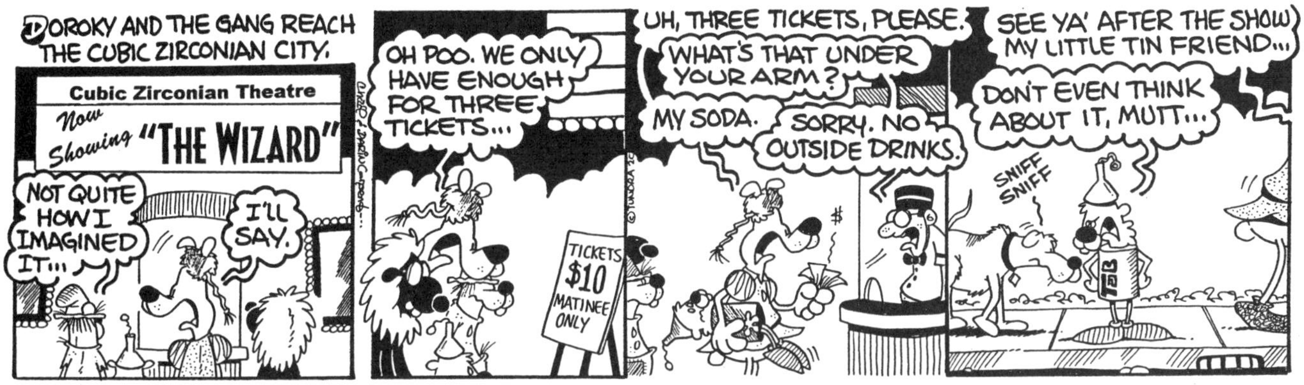
DOROKY AND THE GANG REACH THE CUBIC ZIRCONIAN CITY.
Cubic Zirconian Theatre
Now Showing "THE WIZARD"
NOT QUITE HOW I IMAGINED IT...
I'LL SAY.
OH POO. WE ONLY HAVE ENOUGH FOR THREE TICKETS...
TICKETS $10 MATINEE ONLY
UH, THREE TICKETS, PLEASE.
WHAT'S THAT UNDER YOUR ARM?
MY SODA.
SORRY. NO OUTSIDE DRINKS.
SEE YA' AFTER THE SHOW MY LITTLE TIN FRIEND...
DON'T EVEN THINK ABOUT IT, MUTT...
SNIFF SNIFF

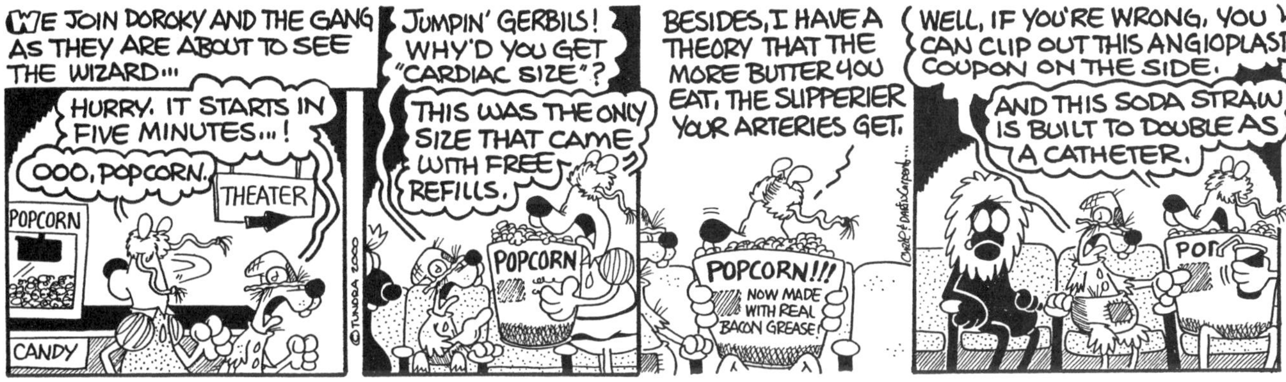
WE JOIN DOROKY AND THE GANG AS THEY ARE ABOUT TO SEE THE WIZARD...
HURRY. IT STARTS IN FIVE MINUTES...!
OOO, POPCORN.
THEATER
POPCORN
CANDY
JUMPIN' GERBILS! WHY'D YOU GET "CARDIAC SIZE"?
THIS WAS THE ONLY SIZE THAT CAME WITH FREE REFILLS.
POPCORN
BESIDES, I HAVE A THEORY THAT THE MORE BUTTER YOU EAT, THE SLIPPERIER YOUR ARTERIES GET.
POPCORN!!! NOW MADE WITH REAL BACON GREASE!
WELL, IF YOU'RE WRONG, YOU CAN CLIP OUT THIS ANGIOPLASTY COUPON ON THE SIDE.
AND THIS SODA STRAW IS BUILT TO DOUBLE AS A CATHETER.

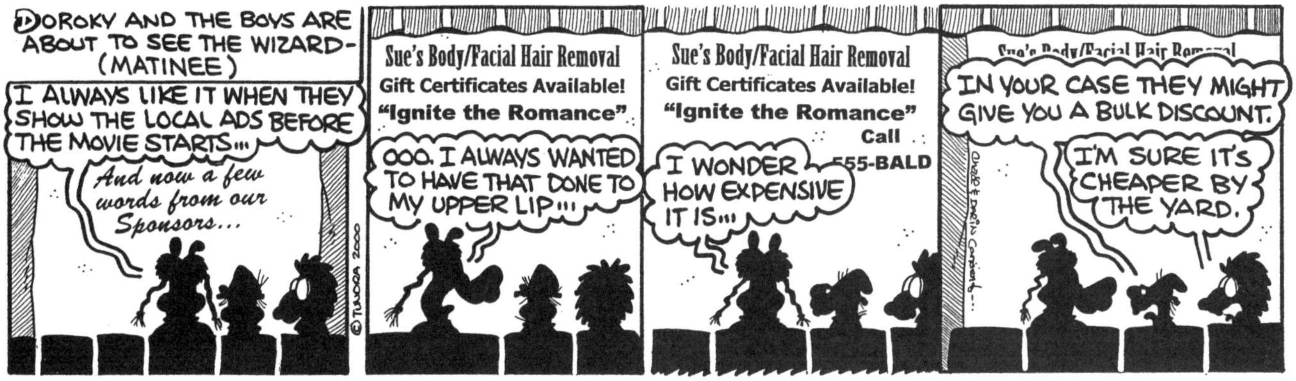
DOROKY AND THE BOYS ARE ABOUT TO SEE THE WIZARD- (MATINEE)
I ALWAYS LIKE IT WHEN THEY SHOW THE LOCAL ADS BEFORE THE MOVIE STARTS...
And now a few words from our Sponsors...
Sue's Body/Facial Hair Removal
Gift Certificates Available!
"Ignite the Romance"
OOO, I ALWAYS WANTED TO HAVE THAT DONE TO MY UPPER LIP...
Sue's Body/Facial Hair Removal
Gift Certificates Available!
"Ignite the Romance"
Call 555-BALD
I WONDER HOW EXPENSIVE IT IS...
IN YOUR CASE THEY MIGHT GIVE YOU A BULK DISCOUNT.
I'M SURE IT'S CHEAPER BY THE YARD.

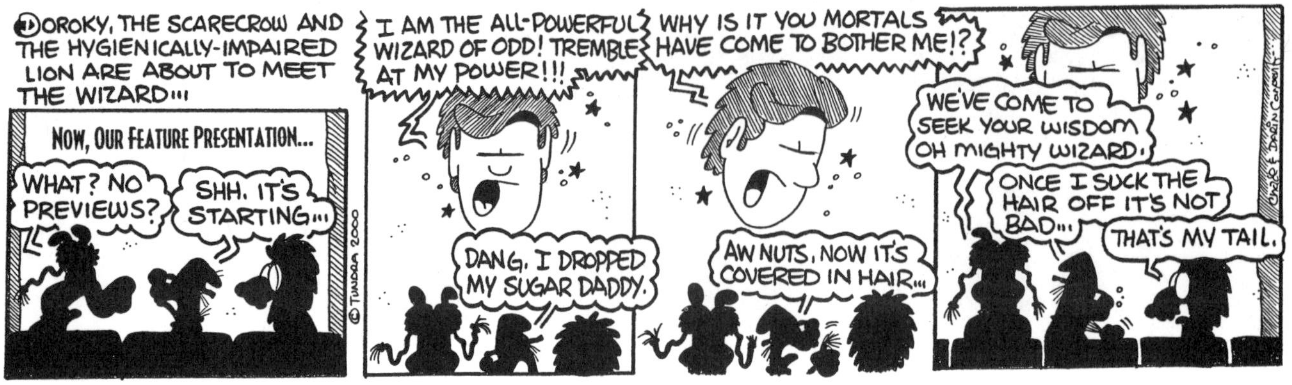
DOROKY, THE SCARECROW AND THE HYGIENICALLY-IMPAIRED LION ARE ABOUT TO MEET THE WIZARD...
NOW, OUR FEATURE PRESENTATION...
WHAT? NO PREVIEWS?
SHH. IT'S STARTING...
© TUNDRA 2000
I AM THE ALL-POWERFUL WIZARD OF ODD! TREMBLE AT MY POWER!!!
DANG. I DROPPED MY SUGAR DADDY.
WHY IS IT YOU MORTALS HAVE COME TO BOTHER ME!?
AW NUTS. NOW IT'S COVERED IN HAIR...
WE'VE COME TO SEEK YOUR WISDOM OH MIGHTY WIZARD.
ONCE I SUCK THE HAIR OFF IT'S NOT BAD...
THAT'S MY TAIL.

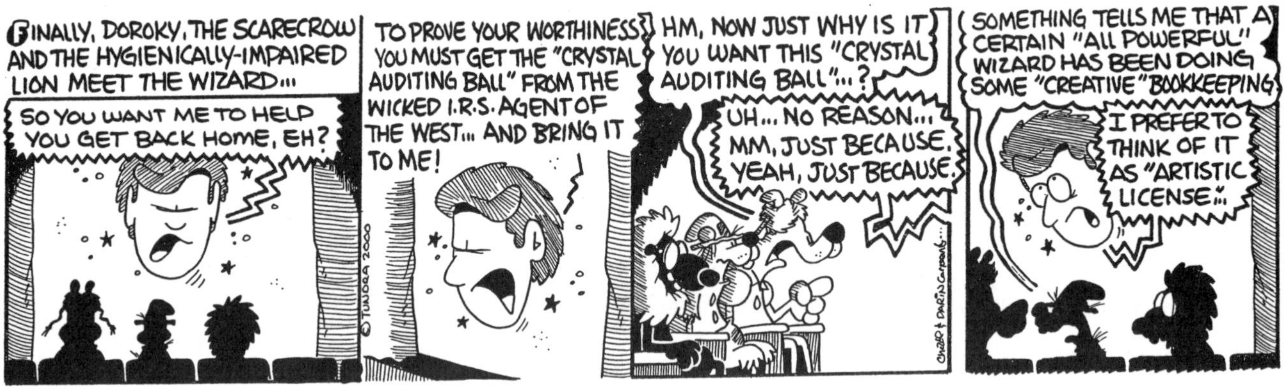
FINALLY, DOROKY, THE SCARECROW AND THE HYGIENICALLY-IMPAIRED LION MEET THE WIZARD...
SO YOU WANT ME TO HELP YOU GET BACK HOME, EH?
TO PROVE YOUR WORTHINESS YOU MUST GET THE "CRYSTAL AUDITING BALL" FROM THE WICKED I.R.S. AGENT OF THE WEST... AND BRING IT TO ME!
© TUNDRA 2000
HM, NOW JUST WHY IS IT YOU WANT THIS "CRYSTAL AUDITING BALL"...?
UH... NO REASON... MM, JUST BECAUSE. YEAH, JUST BECAUSE.
SOMETHING TELLS ME THAT A CERTAIN "ALL POWERFUL" WIZARD HAS BEEN DOING SOME "CREATIVE" BOOKKEEPING
I PREFER TO THINK OF IT AS "ARTISTIC LICENSE"...

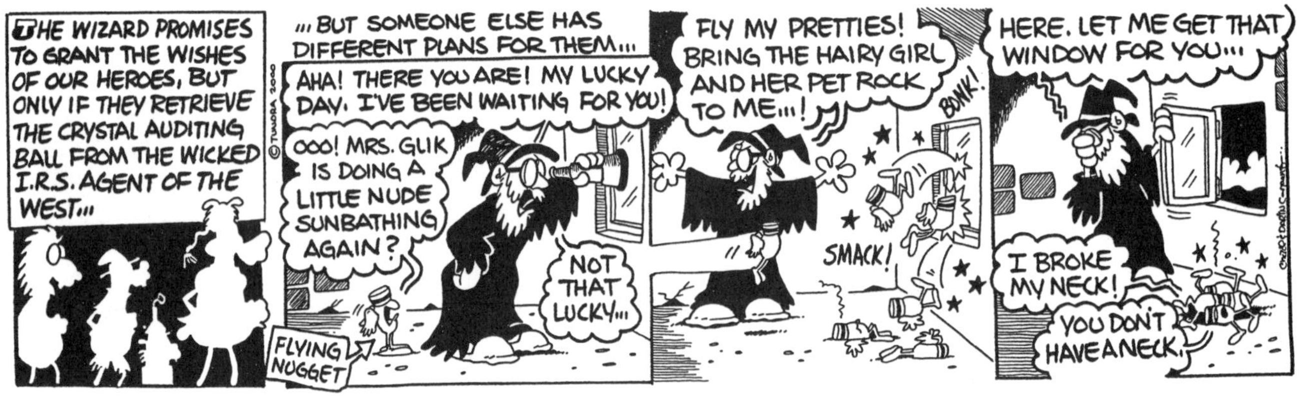
THE WIZARD PROMISES TO GRANT THE WISHES OF OUR HEROES, BUT ONLY IF THEY RETRIEVE THE CRYSTAL AUDITING BALL FROM THE WICKED I.R.S. AGENT OF THE WEST...
© TUNDRA 2000
...BUT SOMEONE ELSE HAS DIFFERENT PLANS FOR THEM...
AHA! THERE YOU ARE! MY LUCKY DAY. I'VE BEEN WAITING FOR YOU!
OOO! MRS. GLIK IS DOING A LITTLE NUDE SUNBATHING AGAIN?
NOT THAT LUCKY...
FLYING NUGGET
FLY MY PRETTIES! BRING THE HAIRY GIRL AND HER PET ROCK TO ME...!
BONK!
SMACK!
HERE. LET ME GET THAT WINDOW FOR YOU...
I BROKE MY NECK!
YOU DON'T HAVE A NECK.

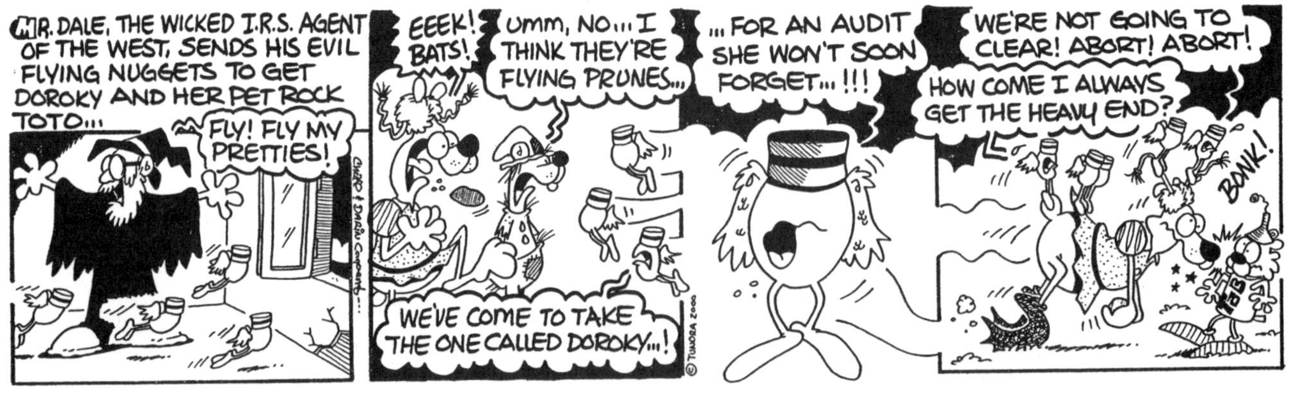
MR. DALE, THE WICKED I.R.S. AGENT OF THE WEST, SENDS HIS EVIL FLYING NUGGETS TO GET DOROKY AND HER PET ROCK TOTO...
FLY! FLY MY PRETTIES!
EEEK! BATS!
UMM, NO... I THINK THEY'RE FLYING PRUNES...
WE'VE COME TO TAKE THE ONE CALLED DOROKY...!
© TUNDRA 2000
...FOR AN AUDIT SHE WON'T SOON FORGET...!!!
WE'RE NOT GOING TO CLEAR! ABORT! ABORT!
HOW COME I ALWAYS GET THE HEAVY END?
BONK!

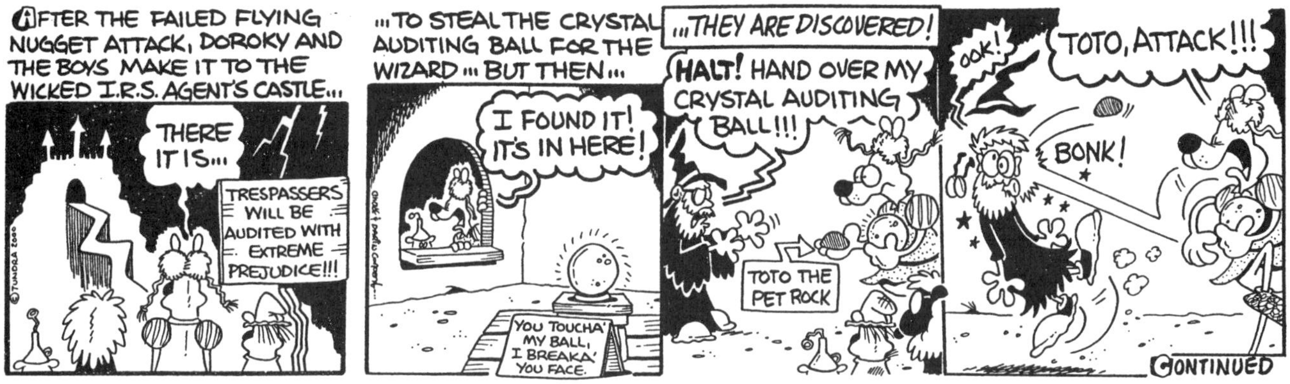
After the failed flying nugget attack, Doroky and the boys make it to the wicked I.R.S. agent's castle...
There it is...
TRESPASSERS WILL BE AUDITED WITH EXTREME PREJUDICE!!!
...to steal the crystal auditing ball for the wizard... but then...
I found it! It's in here!
YOU TOUCHA' MY BALL, I BREAKA' YOU FACE.
...They are discovered!
HALT! Hand over my crystal auditing ball!!!
TOTO THE PET ROCK
OOK!
TOTO, ATTACK!!!
BONK!
Continued

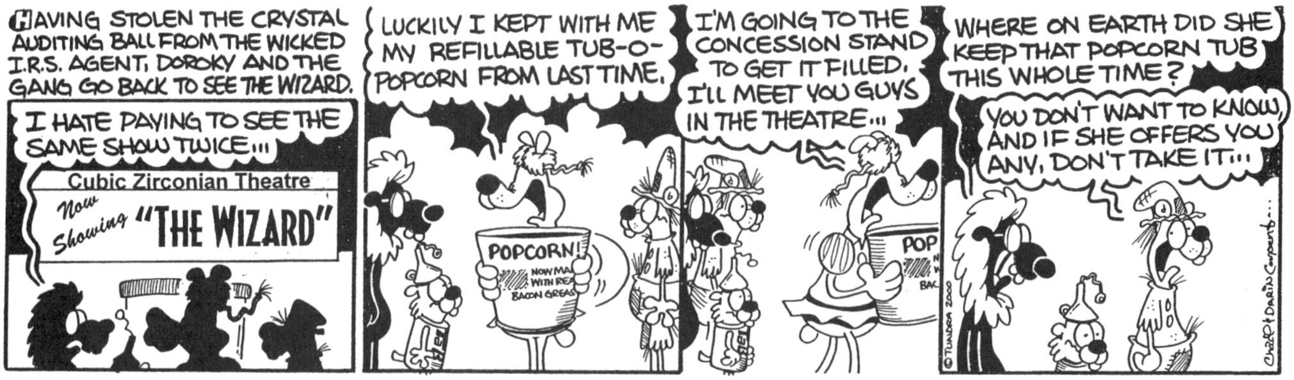
Having stolen the crystal auditing ball from the wicked I.R.S. agent, Doroky and the gang go back to see the wizard.
I hate paying to see the same show twice...
Cubic Zirconian Theatre
Now Showing "THE WIZARD"
Luckily I kept with me my refillable tub-o-popcorn from last time.
POPCORN!
I'm going to the concession stand to get it filled. I'll meet you guys in the theatre...
Where on earth did she keep that popcorn tub this whole time?
You don't want to know, and if she offers you any, don't take it...

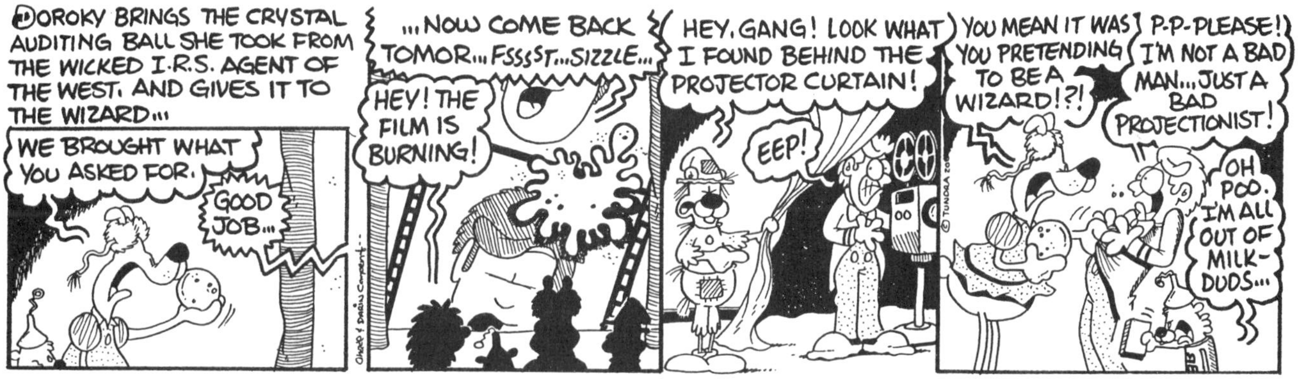
Doroky brings the crystal auditing ball she took from the wicked I.R.S. agent of the west, and gives it to the wizard...
We brought what you asked for.
Good job...
...Now come back tomor... Fsssst... sizzle...
Hey! The film is burning!
Hey, gang! Look what I found behind the projector curtain!
EEP!
You mean it was you pretending to be a wizard!?!
P-p-please! I'm not a bad man... just a bad projectionist!
Oh poo. I'm all out of milk-duds...

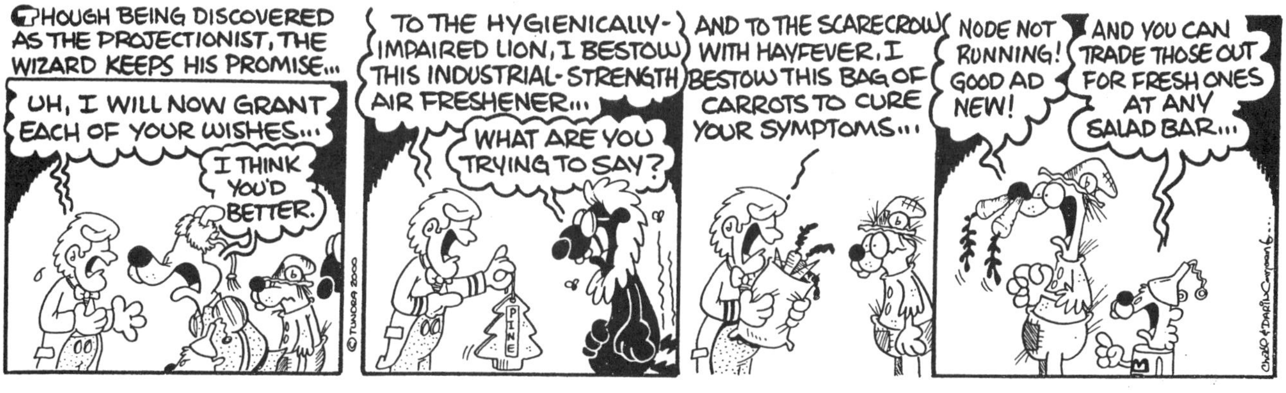
Though being discovered as the projectionist, the wizard keeps his promise...
Uh, I will now grant each of your wishes...
I think you'd better.
To the hygienically-impaired lion, I bestow this industrial-strength air freshener...
What are you trying to say?
PINE
And to the scarecrow with hayfever, I bestow this bag of carrots to cure your symptoms...
Node not running! Good ad new!
And you can trade those out for fresh ones at any salad bar...

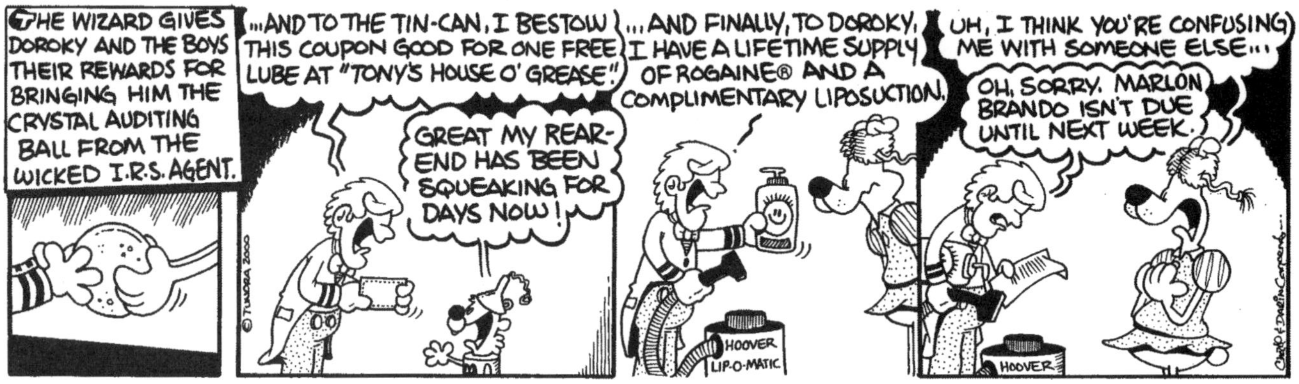
THE WIZARD GIVES DOROKY AND THE BOYS THEIR REWARDS FOR BRINGING HIM THE CRYSTAL AUDITING BALL FROM THE WICKED I.R.S. AGENT.
...AND TO THE TIN-CAN, I BESTOW THIS COUPON GOOD FOR ONE FREE LUBE AT "TONY'S HOUSE O' GREASE".
GREAT MY REAR-END HAS BEEN SQUEAKING FOR DAYS NOW!
...AND FINALLY, TO DOROKY, I HAVE A LIFETIME SUPPLY OF ROGAINE® AND A COMPLIMENTARY LIPOSUCTION.
HOOVER LIP-O-MATIC
UH, I THINK YOU'RE CONFUSING ME WITH SOMEONE ELSE...
OH, SORRY. MARLON BRANDO ISN'T DUE UNTIL NEXT WEEK.
HOOVER

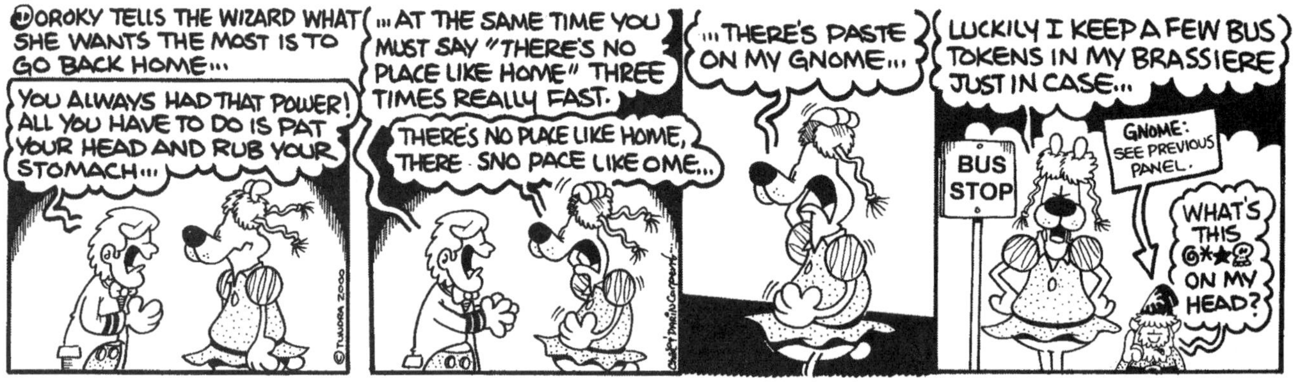
DOROKY TELLS THE WIZARD WHAT SHE WANTS THE MOST IS TO GO BACK HOME...
YOU ALWAYS HAD THAT POWER! ALL YOU HAVE TO DO IS PAT YOUR HEAD AND RUB YOUR STOMACH...
...AT THE SAME TIME YOU MUST SAY "THERE'S NO PLACE LIKE HOME" THREE TIMES REALLY FAST.
THERE'S NO PLACE LIKE HOME, THERE SNO PACE LIKE OME...
...THERE'S PASTE ON MY GNOME...
LUCKILY I KEEP A FEW BUS TOKENS IN MY BRASSIERE JUST IN CASE...
BUS STOP
GNOME: SEE PREVIOUS PANEL.
WHAT'S THIS @*★☠ ON MY HEAD?

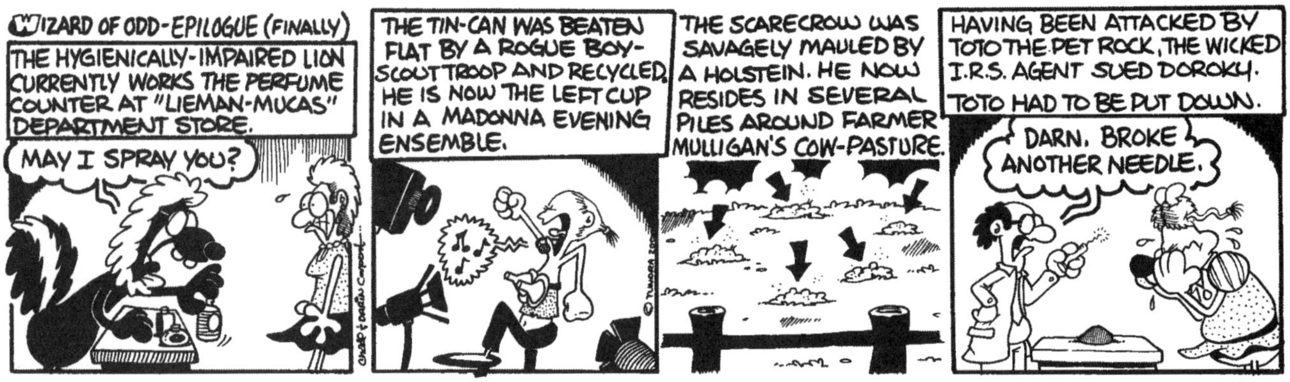
WIZARD OF ODD-EPILOGUE (FINALLY)
THE HYGIENICALLY-IMPAIRED LION CURRENTLY WORKS THE PERFUME COUNTER AT "LIEMAN-MUCAS" DEPARTMENT STORE.
MAY I SPRAY YOU?
THE TIN-CAN WAS BEATEN FLAT BY A ROGUE BOY-SCOUT TROOP AND RECYCLED. HE IS NOW THE LEFT CUP IN A MADONNA EVENING ENSEMBLE.
THE SCARECROW WAS SAVAGELY MAULED BY A HOLSTEIN. HE NOW RESIDES IN SEVERAL PILES AROUND FARMER MULLIGAN'S COW-PASTURE.
HAVING BEEN ATTACKED BY TOTO THE PET ROCK, THE WICKED I.R.S. AGENT SUED DOROKY.
TOTO HAD TO BE PUT DOWN.
DARN. BROKE ANOTHER NEEDLE.

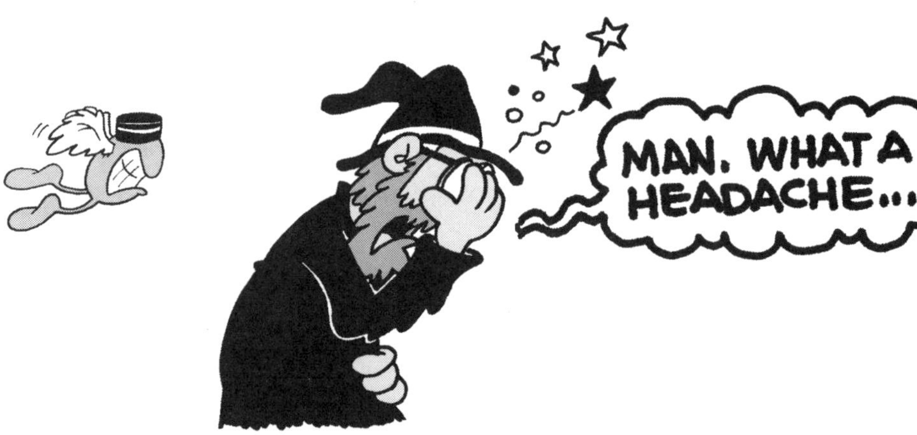
MAN. WHAT A HEADACHE...

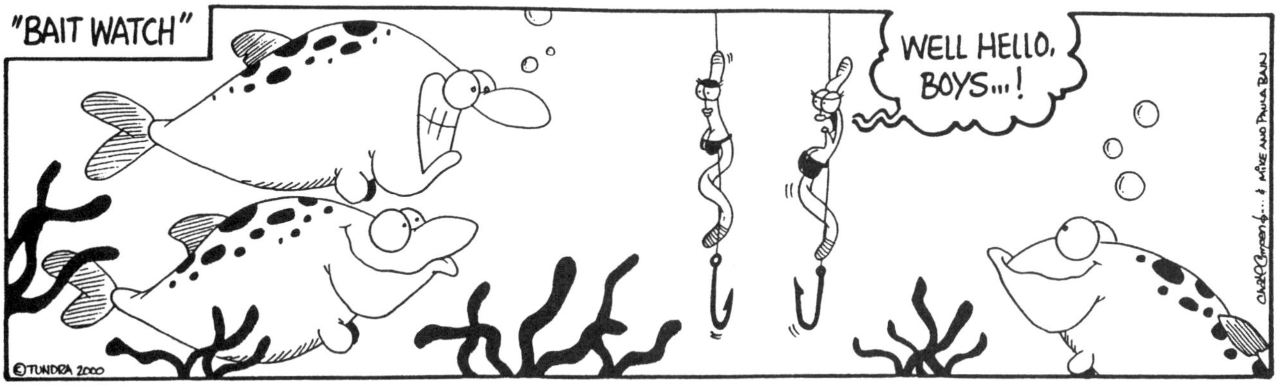
"BAIT WATCH"
WELL HELLO, BOYS...!
©TUNDRA 2000

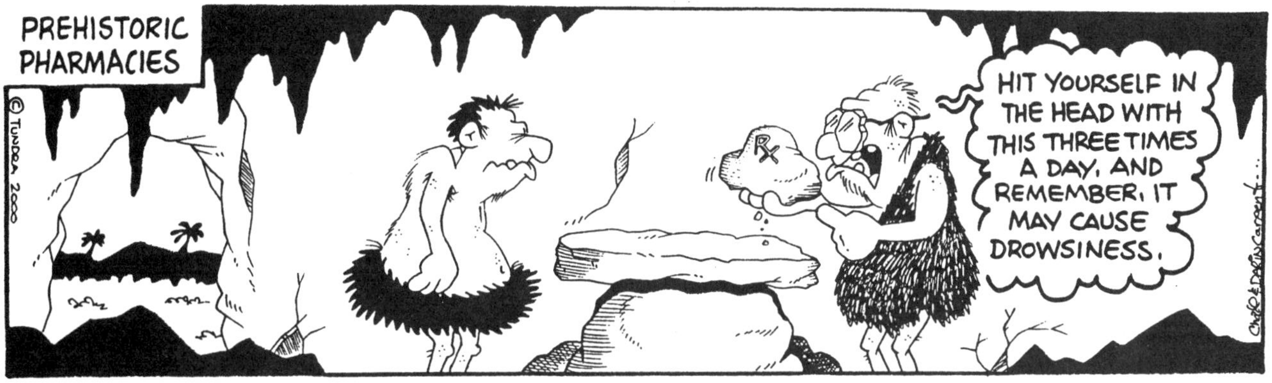
PREHISTORIC PHARMACIES
HIT YOURSELF IN THE HEAD WITH THIS THREE TIMES A DAY, AND REMEMBER, IT MAY CAUSE DROWSINESS.
© TUNDRA 2000

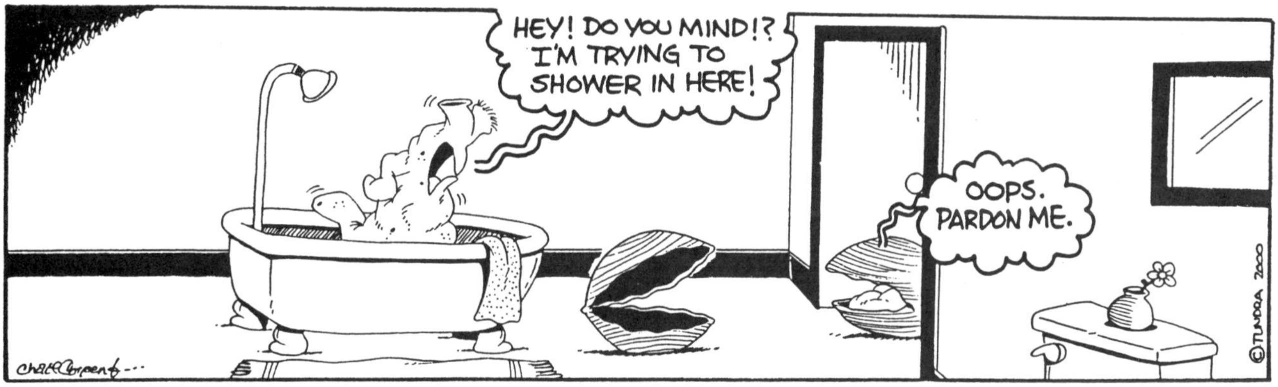
HEY! DO YOU MIND!? I'M TRYING TO SHOWER IN HERE!
OOPS. PARDON ME.
©TUNDRA 2000

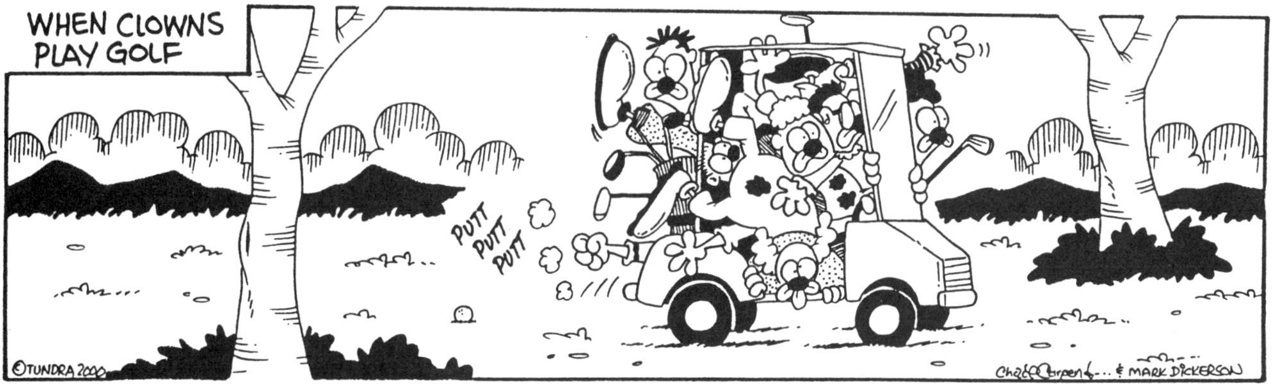
WHEN CLOWNS PLAY GOLF
PUTT PUTT PUTT
©TUNDRA 2000
& MARK DICKERSON

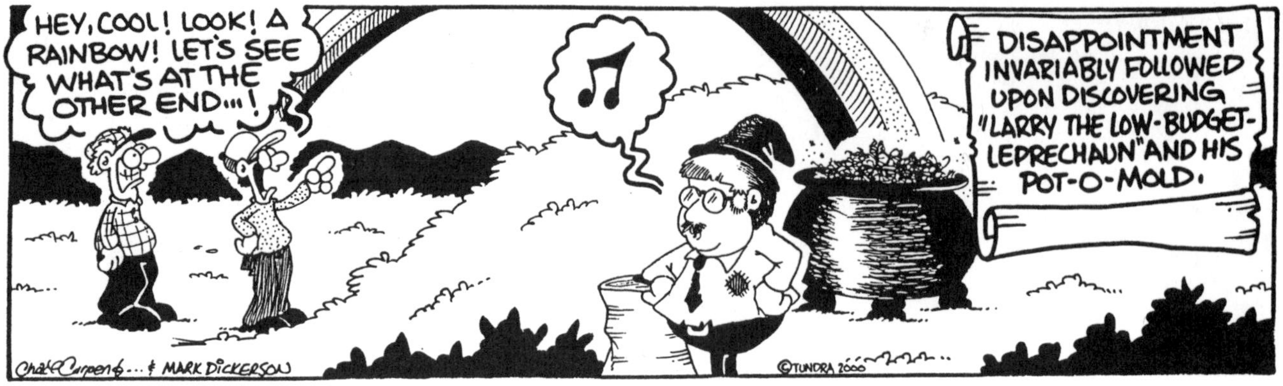
HEY, COOL! LOOK! A RAINBOW! LET'S SEE WHAT'S AT THE OTHER END...!
DISAPPOINTMENT INVARIABLY FOLLOWED UPON DISCOVERING "LARRY THE LOW-BUDGET-LEPRECHAUN" AND HIS POT-O-MOLD.
& MARK DICKERSON
©TUNDRA 2000

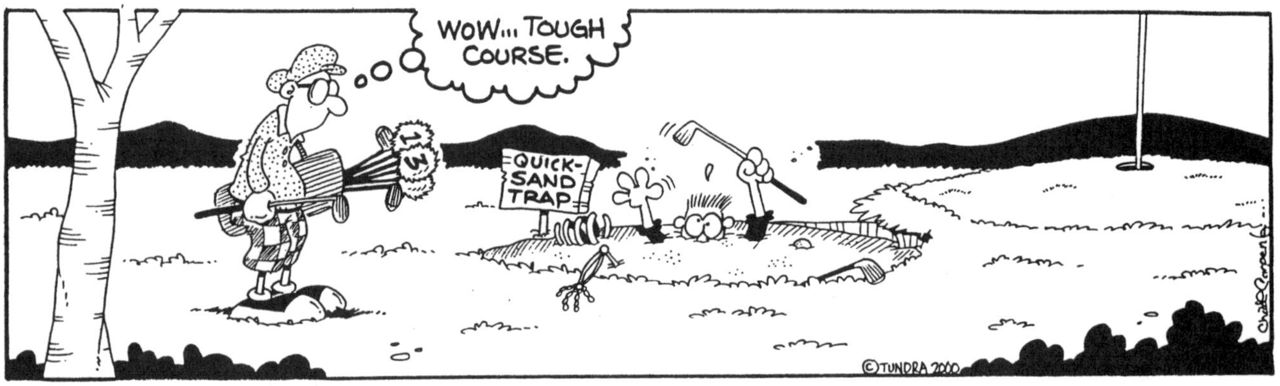
WOW... TOUGH COURSE.
QUICK-SAND TRAP
©TUNDRA 2000

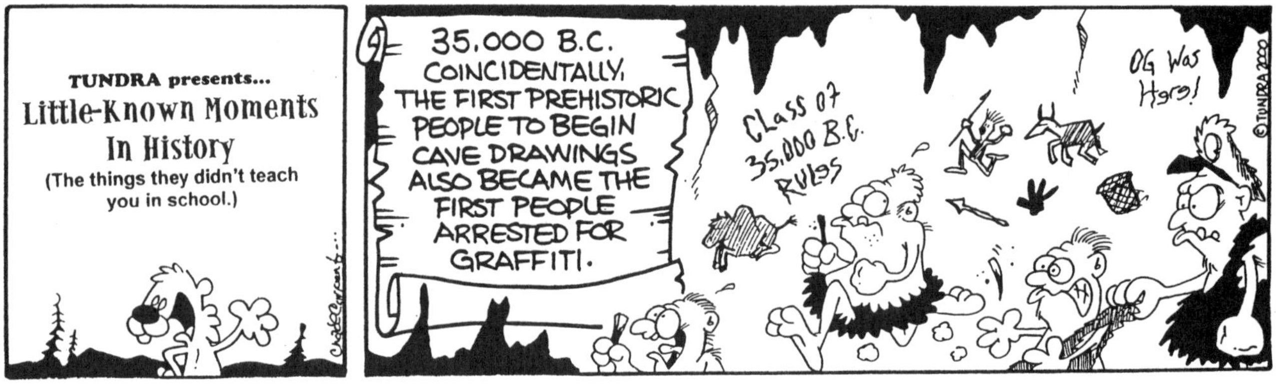
TUNDRA presents...
Little-Known Moments In History
(The things they didn't teach you in school.)
35,000 B.C. COINCIDENTALLY, THE FIRST PREHISTORIC PEOPLE TO BEGIN CAVE DRAWINGS ALSO BECAME THE FIRST PEOPLE ARRESTED FOR GRAFFITI.
Class of 35,000 B.C. Rules
OG Was Here!
©TUNDRA 2000

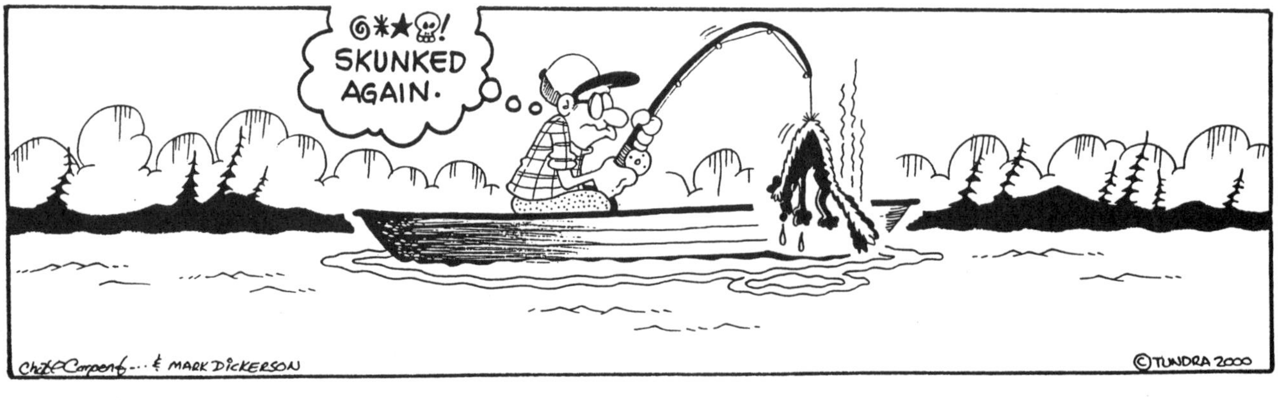
SKUNKED AGAIN.
& MARK DICKERSON
©TUNDRA 2000

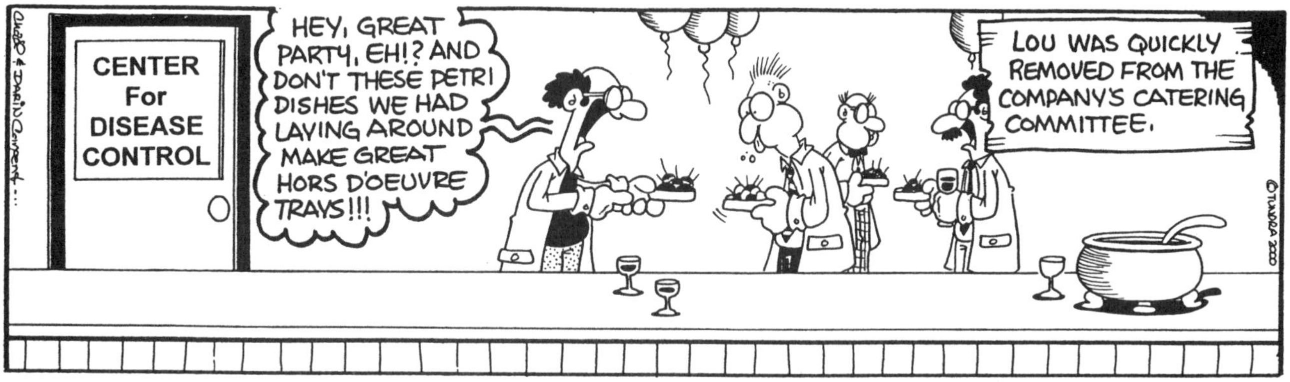
CENTER For DISEASE CONTROL
HEY, GREAT PARTY, EH!? AND DON'T THESE PETRI DISHES WE HAD LAYING AROUND MAKE GREAT HORS D'OEUVRE TRAYS!!!
LOU WAS QUICKLY REMOVED FROM THE COMPANY'S CATERING COMMITTEE.

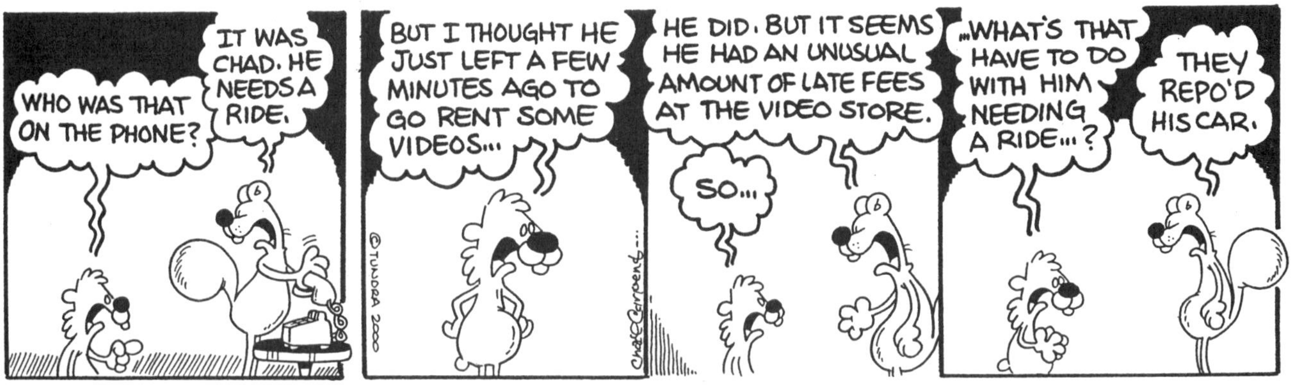
WHO WAS THAT ON THE PHONE?
IT WAS CHAD. HE NEEDS A RIDE.
BUT I THOUGHT HE JUST LEFT A FEW MINUTES AGO TO GO RENT SOME VIDEOS...
HE DID. BUT IT SEEMS HE HAD AN UNUSUAL AMOUNT OF LATE FEES AT THE VIDEO STORE.
SO...
...WHAT'S THAT HAVE TO DO WITH HIM NEEDING A RIDE...?
THEY REPO'D HIS CAR.

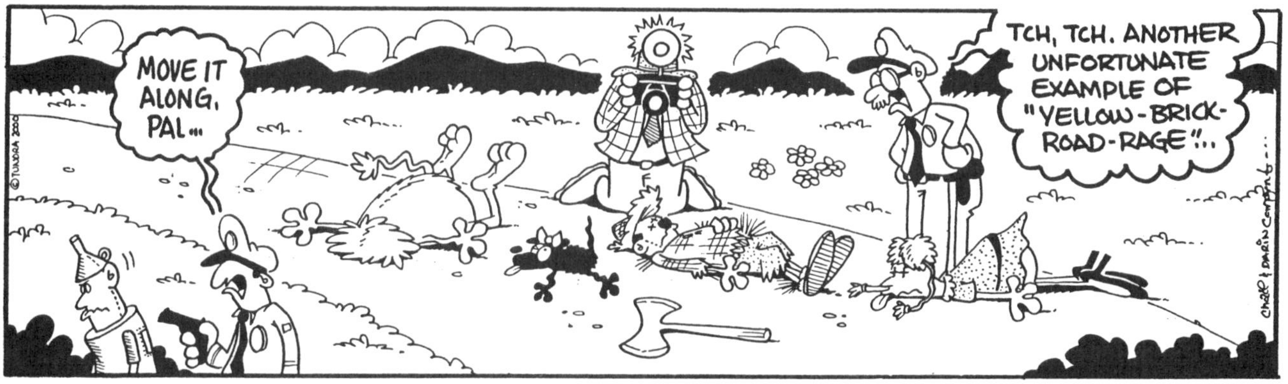
MOVE IT ALONG, PAL...
TCH, TCH. ANOTHER UNFORTUNATE EXAMPLE OF "YELLOW-BRICK-ROAD-RAGE"...

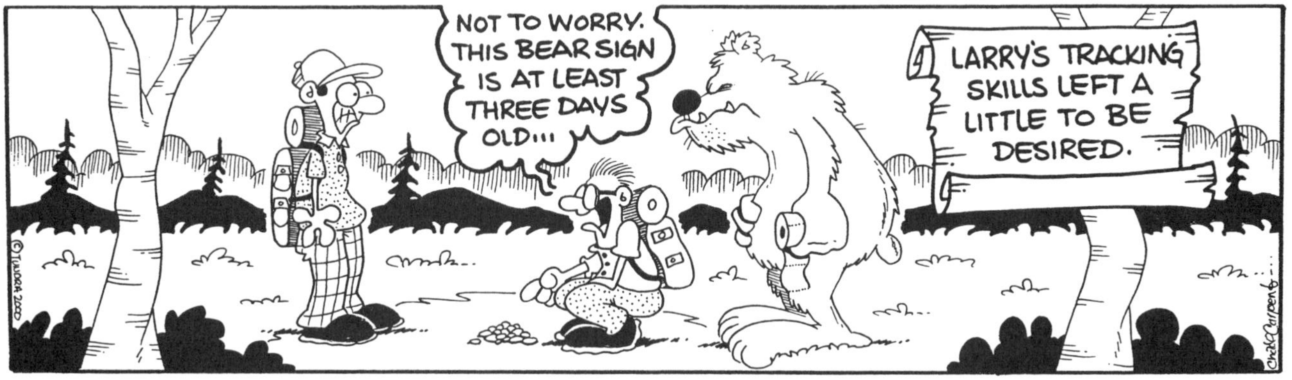
NOT TO WORRY. THIS BEAR SIGN IS AT LEAST THREE DAYS OLD...
LARRY'S TRACKING SKILLS LEFT A LITTLE TO BE DESIRED.

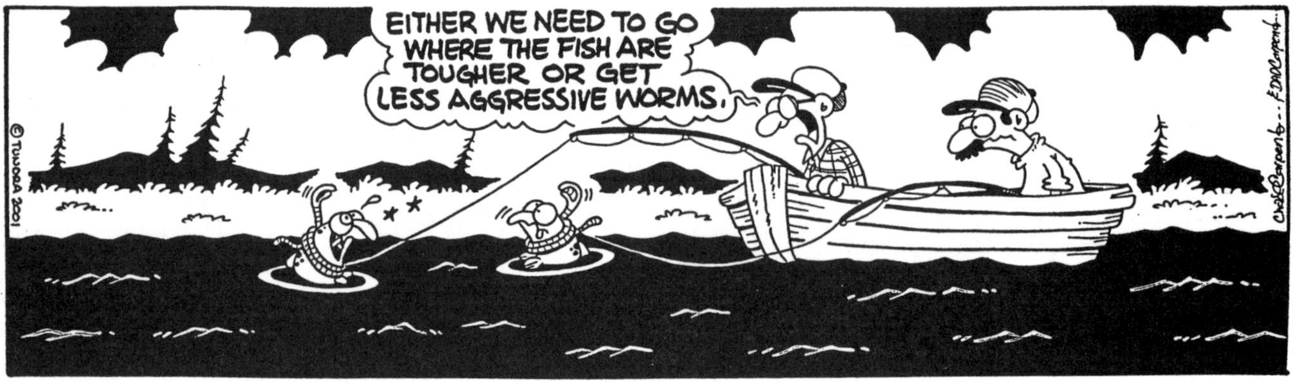
EITHER WE NEED TO GO WHERE THE FISH ARE TOUGHER OR GET LESS AGGRESSIVE WORMS.
© TUNDRA 2001

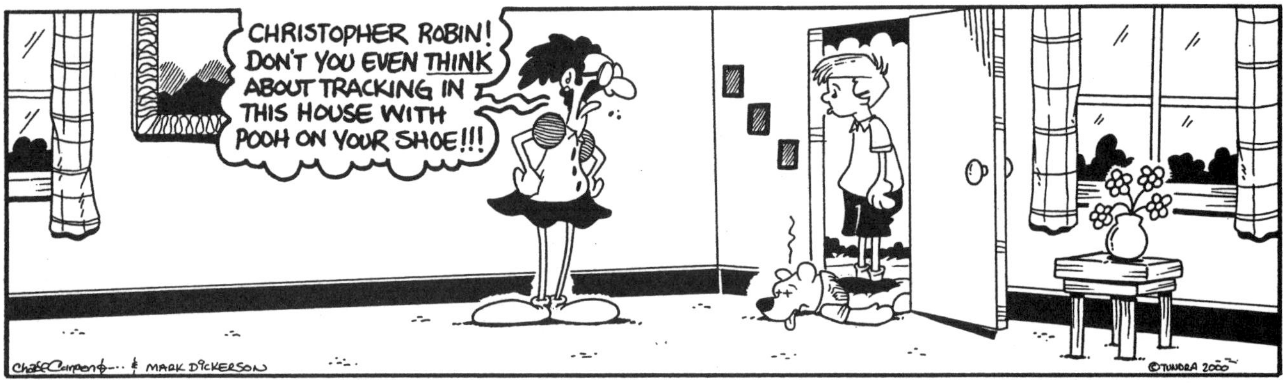
CHRISTOPHER ROBIN! DON'T YOU EVEN THINK ABOUT TRACKING IN THIS HOUSE WITH POOH ON YOUR SHOE!!!
Chad Carpenter & MARK DICKERSON
©TUNDRA 2000

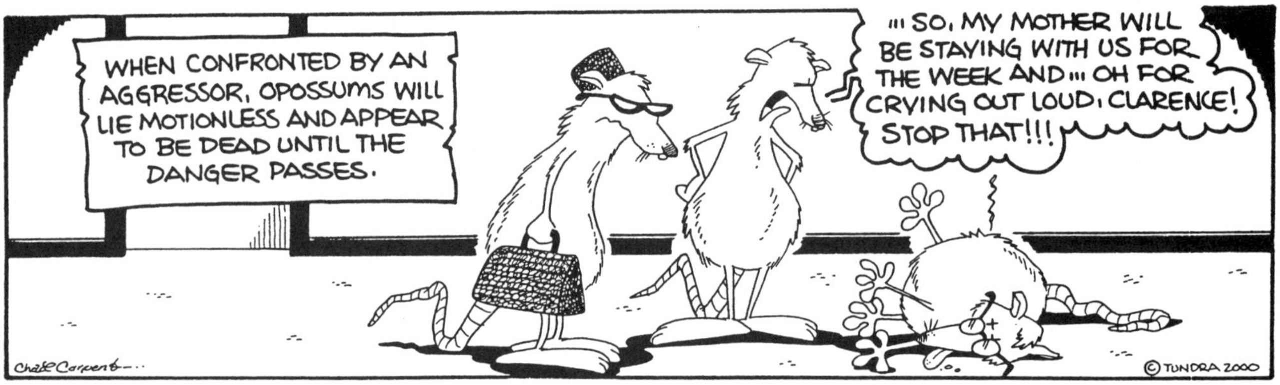
WHEN CONFRONTED BY AN AGGRESSOR, OPOSSUMS WILL LIE MOTIONLESS AND APPEAR TO BE DEAD UNTIL THE DANGER PASSES.
...SO, MY MOTHER WILL BE STAYING WITH US FOR THE WEEK AND... OH FOR CRYING OUT LOUD, CLARENCE! STOP THAT!!!
Chad Carpenter
© TUNDRA 2000

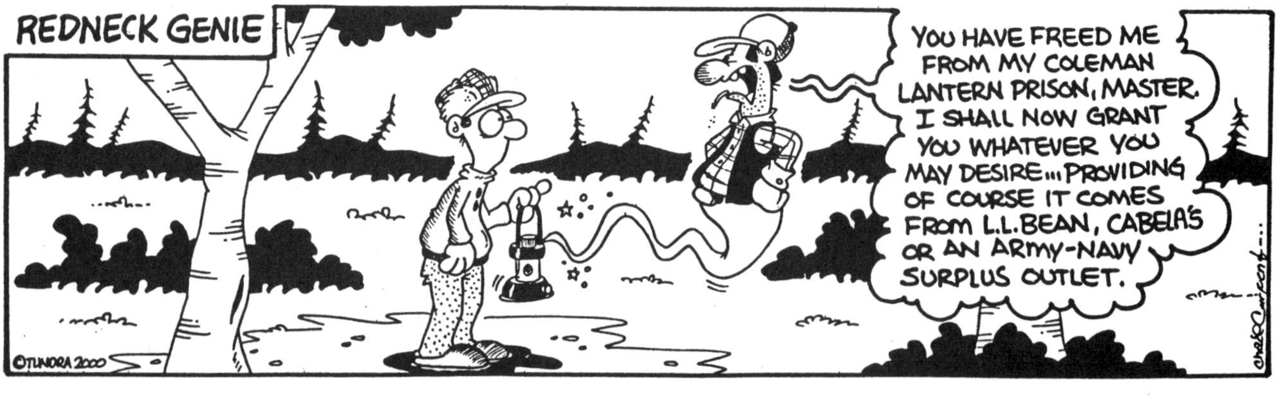
REDNECK GENIE
YOU HAVE FREED ME FROM MY COLEMAN LANTERN PRISON, MASTER. I SHALL NOW GRANT YOU WHATEVER YOU MAY DESIRE... PROVIDING OF COURSE IT COMES FROM L.L.BEAN, CABELA'S OR AN ARMY-NAVY SURPLUS OUTLET.
©TUNDRA 2000

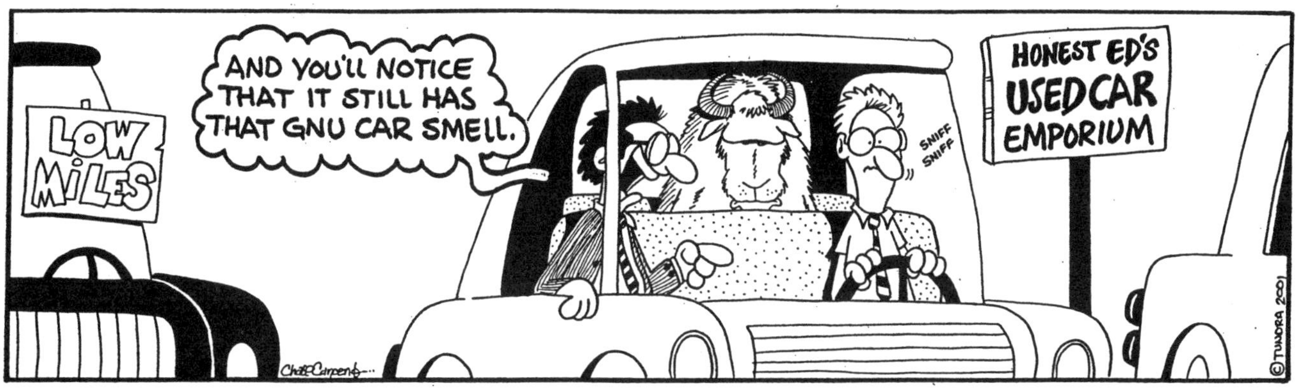
LOW MILES
AND YOU'LL NOTICE THAT IT STILL HAS THAT GNU CAR SMELL.
SNIFF SNIFF
HONEST ED'S USED CAR EMPORIUM
©TUNDRA 2001

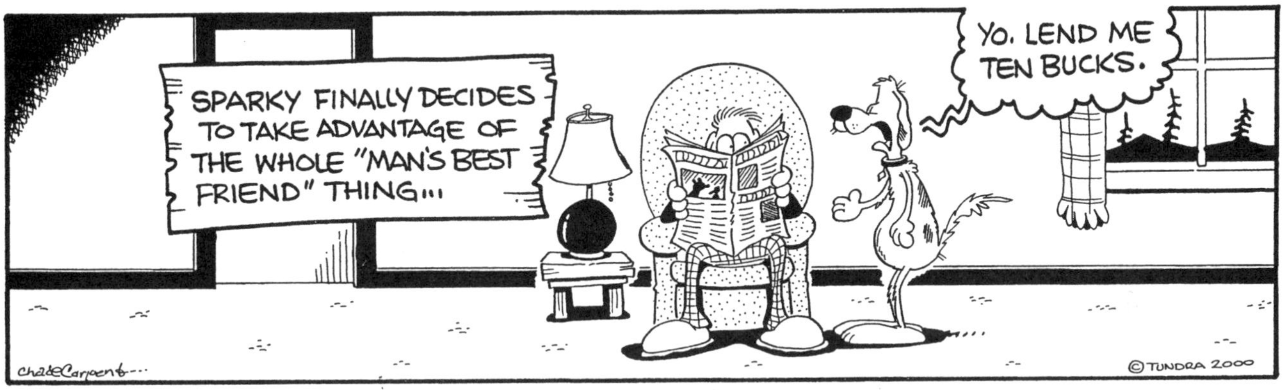
SPARKY FINALLY DECIDES TO TAKE ADVANTAGE OF THE WHOLE "MAN'S BEST FRIEND" THING...
YO. LEND ME TEN BUCKS.
©TUNDRA 2000

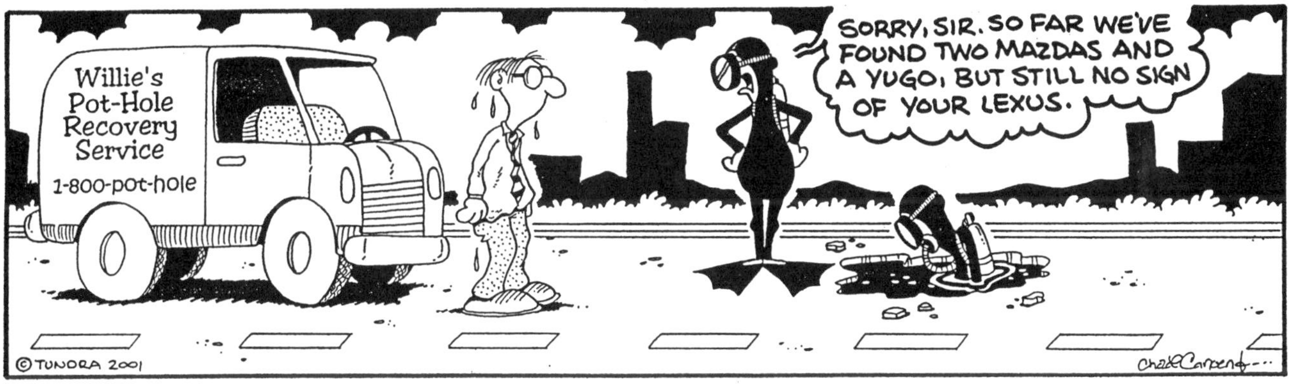
Willie's Pot-Hole Recovery Service 1-800-pot-hole
SORRY, SIR. SO FAR WE'VE FOUND TWO MAZDAS AND A YUGO, BUT STILL NO SIGN OF YOUR LEXUS.
©TUNDRA 2001

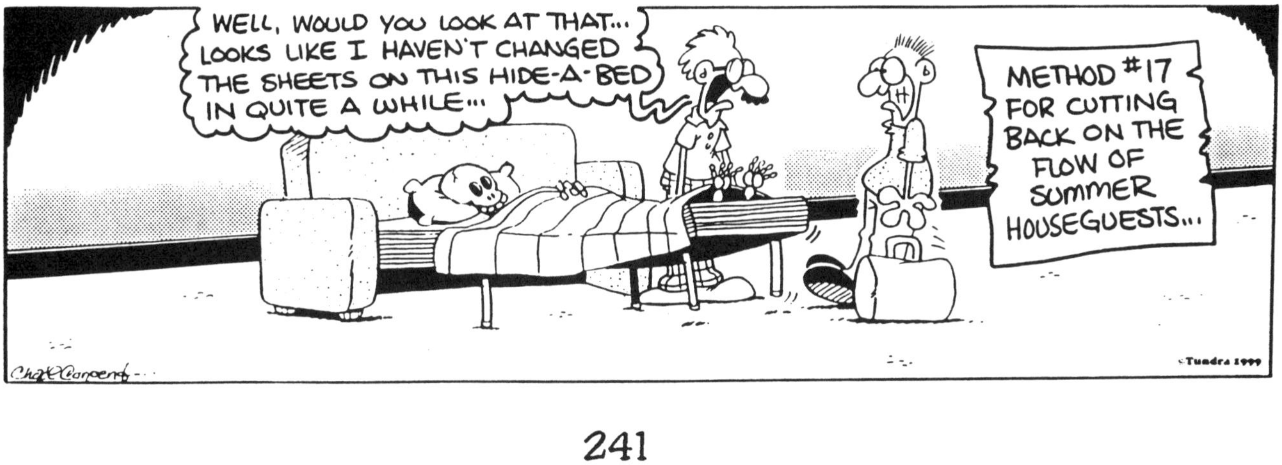
WELL, WOULD YOU LOOK AT THAT... LOOKS LIKE I HAVEN'T CHANGED THE SHEETS ON THIS HIDE-A-BED IN QUITE A WHILE...
METHOD #17 FOR CUTTING BACK ON THE FLOW OF SUMMER HOUSEGUESTS...

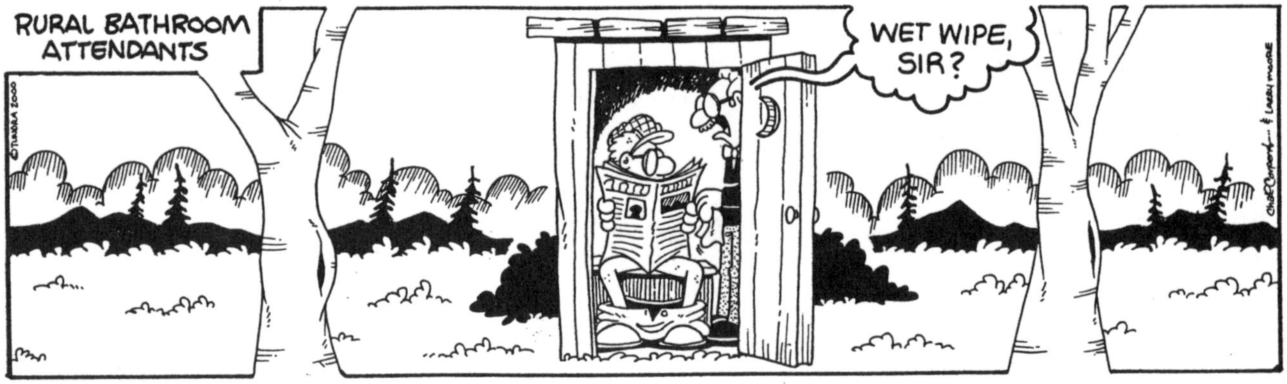
RURAL BATHROOM ATTENDANTS
WET WIPE, SIR?
© TUNDRA 2000

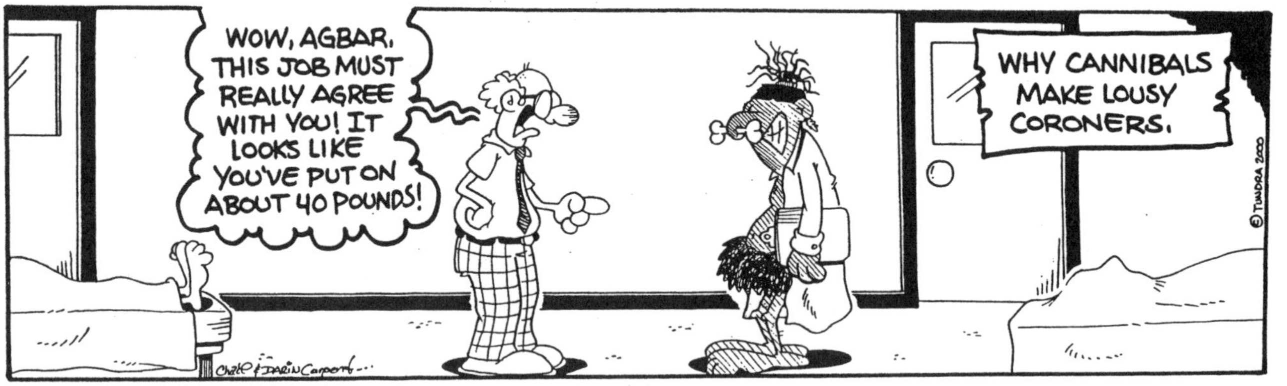
WOW, AGBAR, THIS JOB MUST REALLY AGREE WITH YOU! IT LOOKS LIKE YOU'VE PUT ON ABOUT 40 POUNDS!
WHY CANNIBALS MAKE LOUSY CORONERS.
© TUNDRA 2000

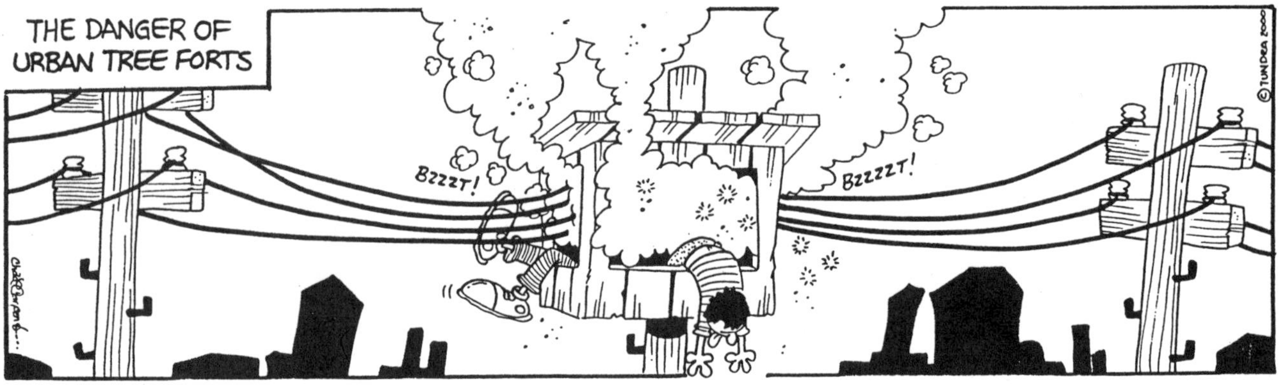
THE DANGER OF URBAN TREE FORTS
BZZZZT!
BZZZZT!
© TUNDRA 2000

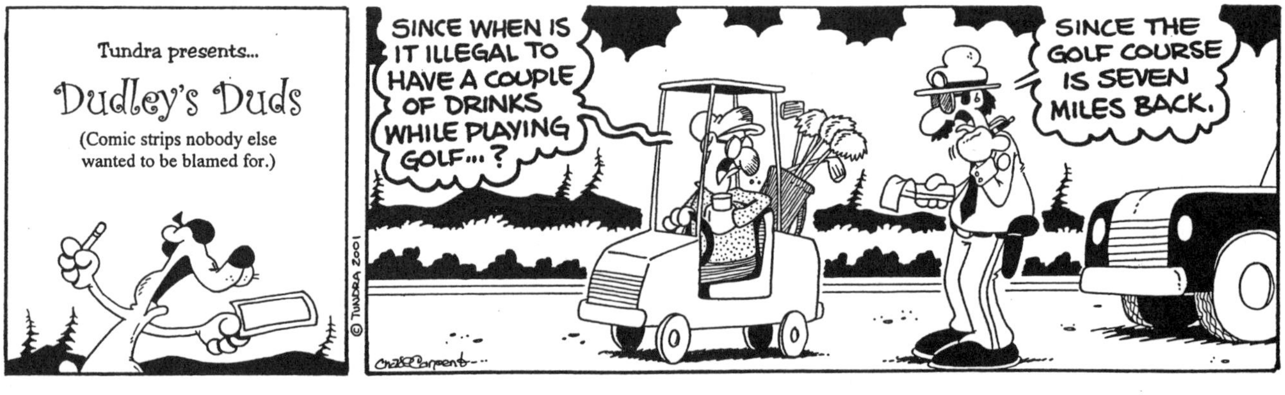
Tundra presents...
Dudley's Duds
(Comic strips nobody else wanted to be blamed for.)
SINCE WHEN IS IT ILLEGAL TO HAVE A COUPLE OF DRINKS WHILE PLAYING GOLF...?
SINCE THE GOLF COURSE IS SEVEN MILES BACK.
© TUNDRA 2001

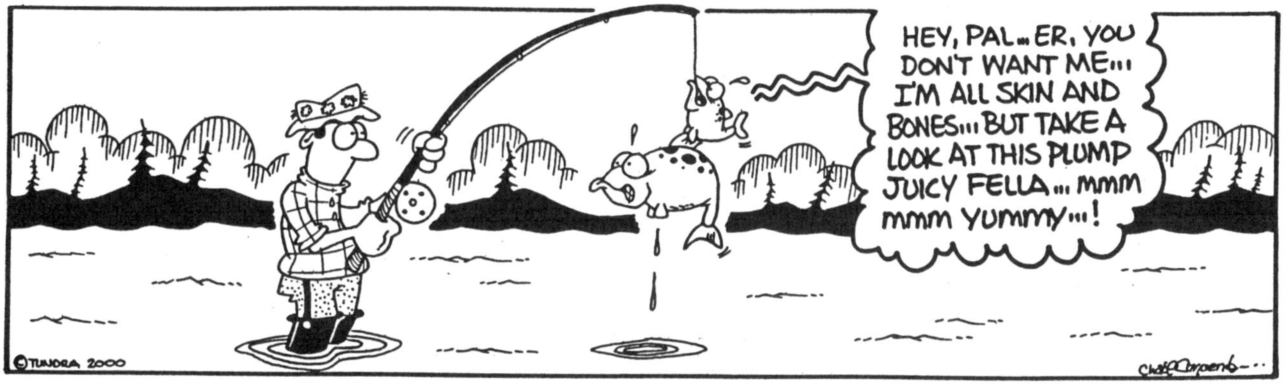
HEY, PAL... ER, YOU DON'T WANT ME... I'M ALL SKIN AND BONES... BUT TAKE A LOOK AT THIS PLUMP JUICY FELLA... mmm mmm yummy...!
©TUNDRA 2000

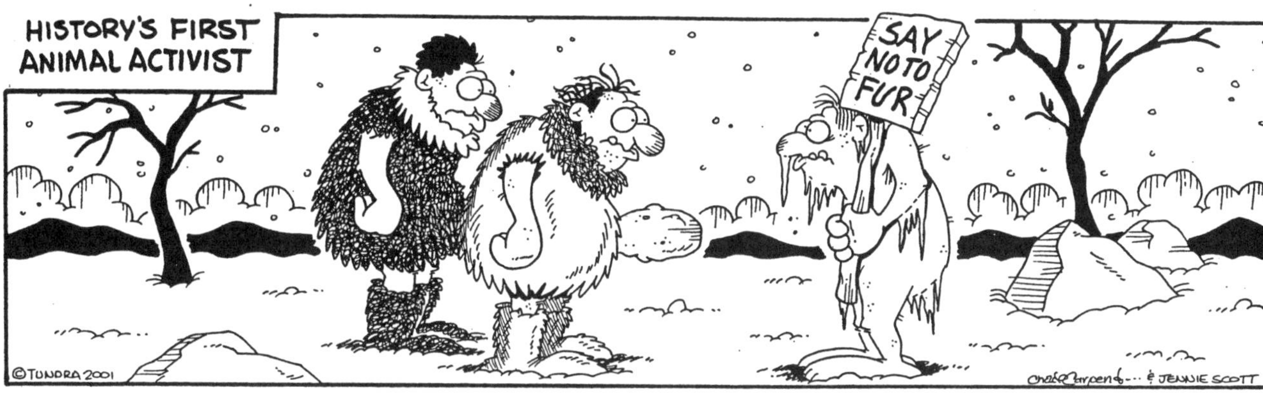
HISTORY'S FIRST ANIMAL ACTIVIST
SAY NO TO FUR
©TUNDRA 2001
& JENNIE SCOTT

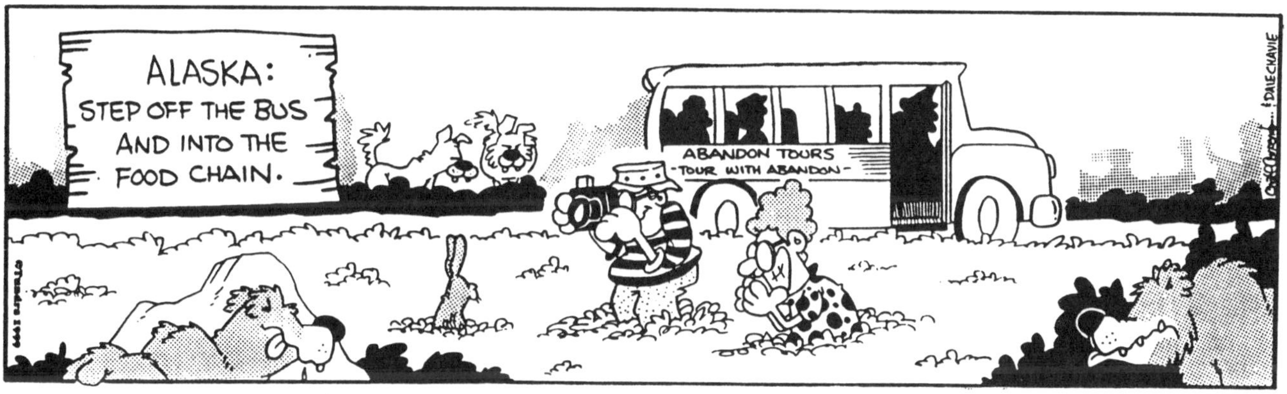
ALASKA: STEP OFF THE BUS AND INTO THE FOOD CHAIN.
ABANDON TOURS
-TOUR WITH ABANDON-

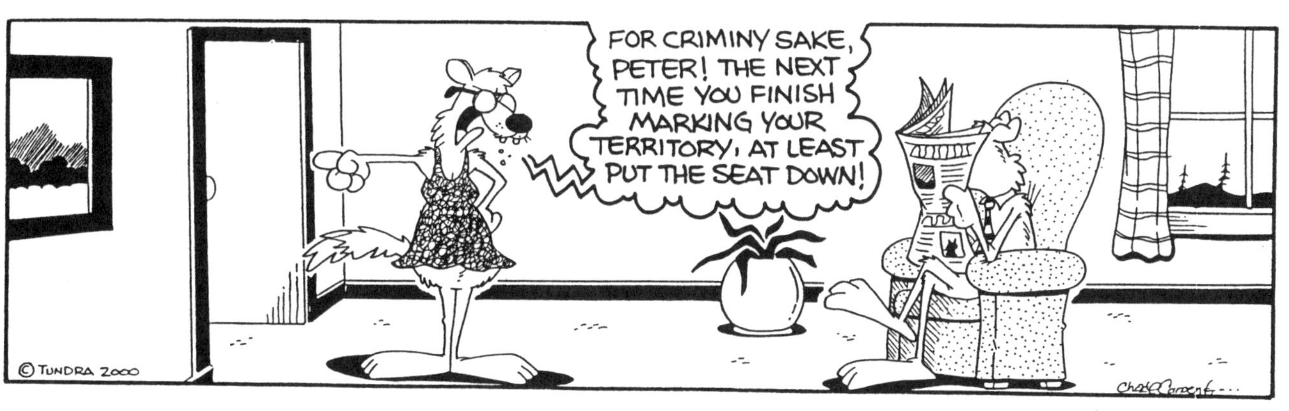
FOR CRIMINY SAKE, PETER! THE NEXT TIME YOU FINISH MARKING YOUR TERRITORY, AT LEAST PUT THE SEAT DOWN!
© TUNDRA 2000

Chad's 10 favorite Tundra strips

I found it interesting that out of the 3,000 Tundra strips I've drawn, my 10 favorites are by no means the most popular ones. In fact, with few exceptions, the best-selling Tundra merchandise (T-shirts, mouse pads, note cards, etc.) usually feature comic strips that I never would have guessed would be so popular. Because of this, I have learned that when it comes to deciding which strips to feature on Tundra merchandise, I take votes from the readers themselves. It has proven to work quite well, especially in view of the fact that I obviously have no concept of what sells.

However, in the following pages I have compiled my 10 favorite strips - regardless of everyone else's good taste. Along with each strip, I have included an explanation or excuse of why I am so fond of it. If a psychiatrist were to study this group of strips, they could probably get a pretty good psychological profile on me, and I'm sure it wouldn't be pretty. That aside, I now present to you (in no particular order) my 10 all-time favorite Tundra strips.

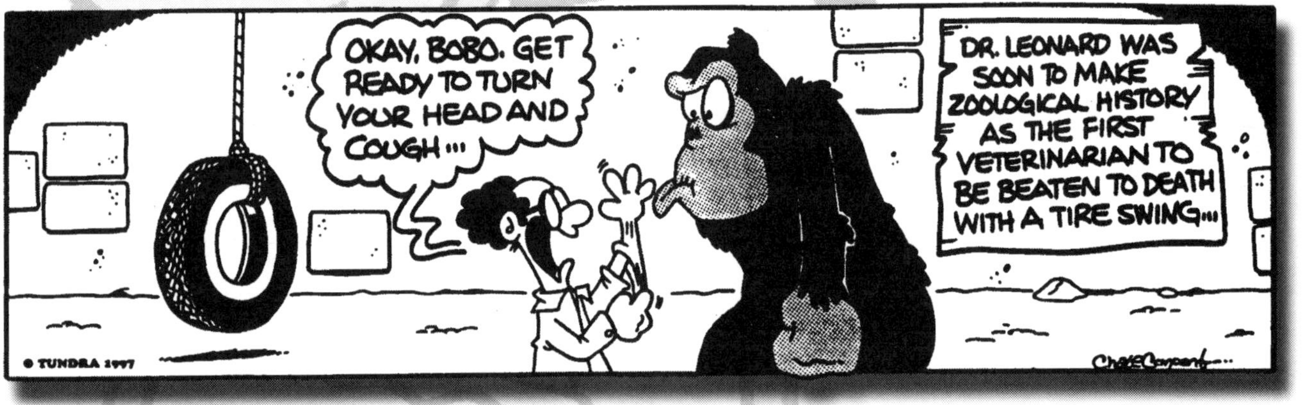
OKAY, BOBO. GET READY TO TURN YOUR HEAD AND COUGH...
DR. LEONARD WAS SOON TO MAKE ZOOLOGICAL HISTORY AS THE FIRST VETERINARIAN TO BE BEATEN TO DEATH WITH A TIRE SWING...
© TUNDRA 1997

This strip seems to run along the theme of a lot of my favorites - toilet humor. I am a big fan of "tastefully done" toilet humor. One thing I've learned over the years is that toilet humor is a lot like Mexican food - some people like it spicy, while others do not. In view of this, I try to keep my toilet humor as moderate as possible without crossing the line of acceptable taste - unfortunately, I have found that there is a small group of vocal people in this world that don't like Mexican food at all.

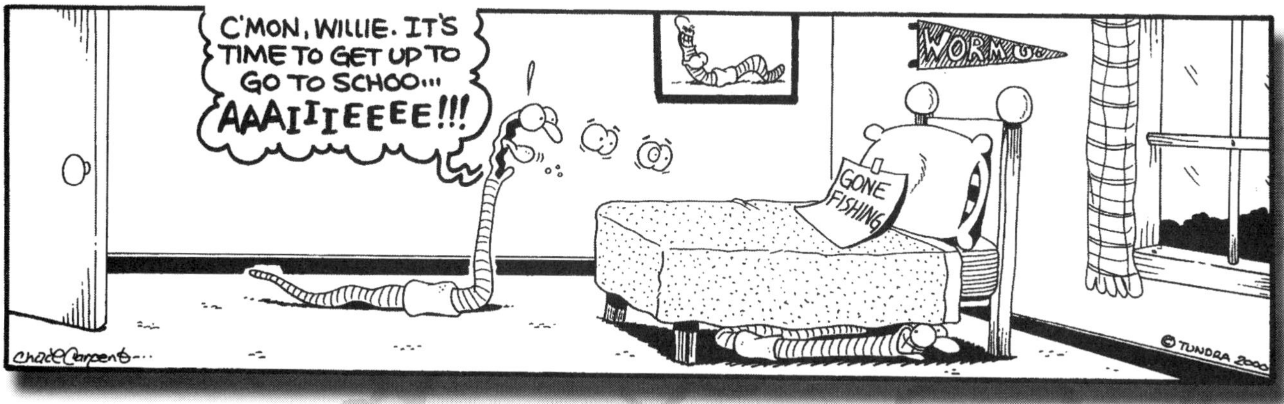
C'MON, WILLIE. IT'S TIME TO GET UP TO GO TO SCHOO... AAAIIIEEEE!!!
GONE FISHING
WORM
Chad Carpenter
© TUNDRA 2000

I love practical jokes. If I were a worm I'd do this.

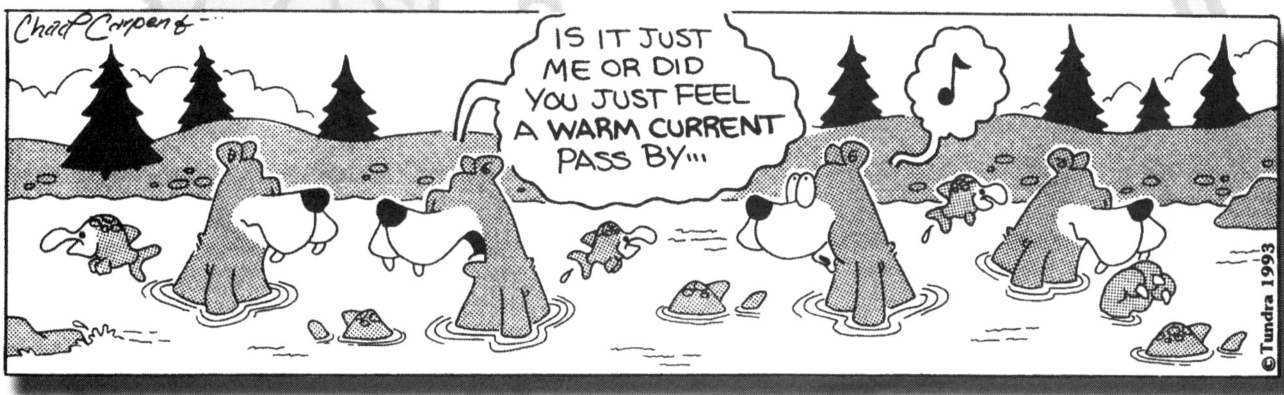
IS IT JUST ME OR DID YOU JUST FEEL A WARM CURRENT PASS BY...
Chad Carpenter
©Tundra 1993

This is something that anyone who has gone swimming with children or immature adults can identify with. It could be why no one is willing to go swimming with me... at least not downstream of me. Incidentally, this is one of my few favorites that also sells well as a T-shirt.

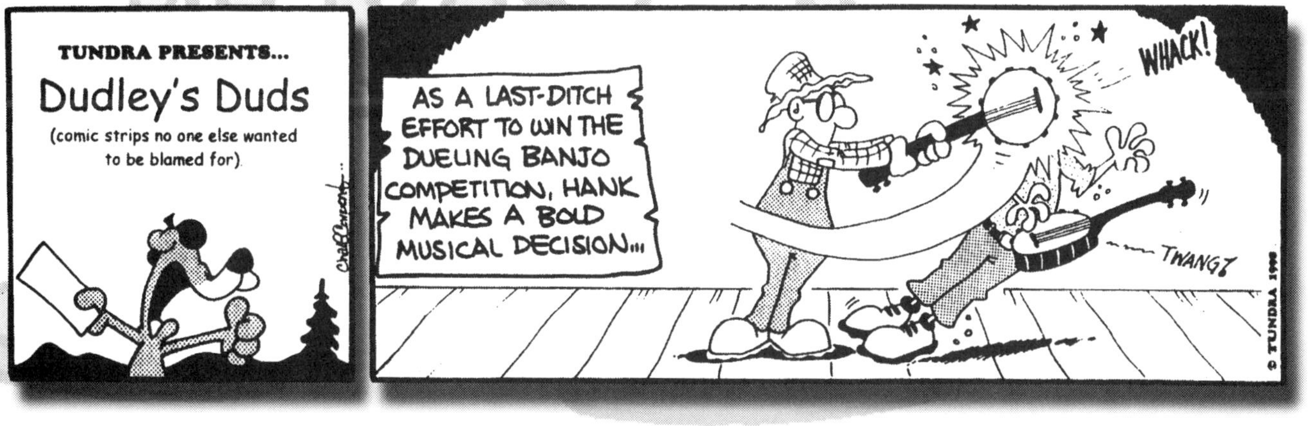
TUNDRA PRESENTS...
Dudley's Duds
(comic strips no one else wanted to be blamed for).
AS A LAST-DITCH EFFORT TO WIN THE DUELING BANJO COMPETITION, HANK MAKES A BOLD MUSICAL DECISION...
WHACK!
TWANG!

How could a banjo cartoon not be funny? Speaking of banjos, what's the difference between a banjo and an onion? No one cries when you cut up a banjo. Har, har!

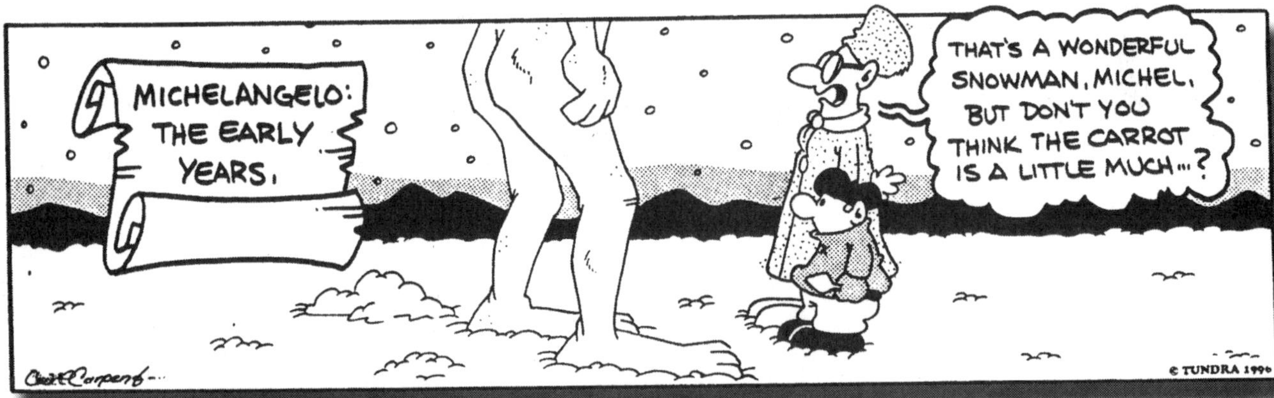
MICHELANGELO: THE EARLY YEARS.
THAT'S A WONDERFUL SNOWMAN, MICHEL, BUT DON'T YOU THINK THE CARROT IS A LITTLE MUCH...?
© TUNDRA 1996

I love doing strips with historical themes - mix that with a little bit of toilet humor and you have what I consider to be a strip that is both informative and entertaining. A few more of these kind of strips and I'm going to start applying for educational grants.

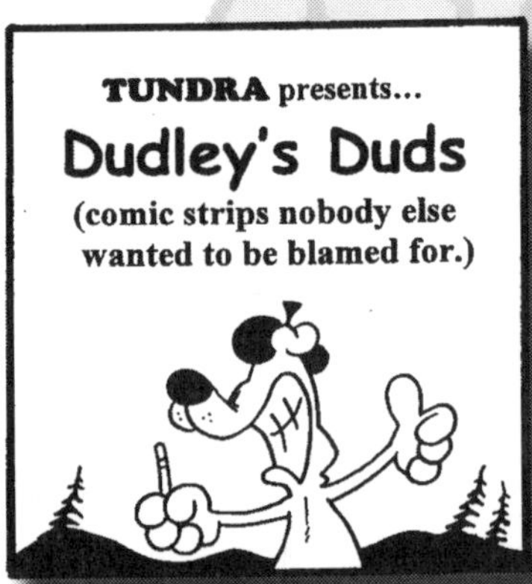
TUNDRA presents...
Dudley's Duds
(comic strips nobody else wanted to be blamed for.)

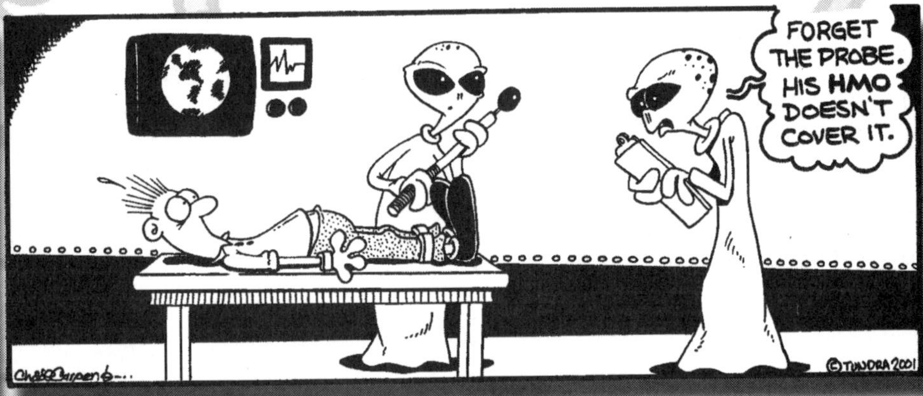
FORGET THE PROBE. HIS HMO DOESN'T COVER IT.
©TUNDRA 2001

I've done a lot of HMO-related cartoons over the years, but I think this one is really swell - mainly because I like to draw aliens.

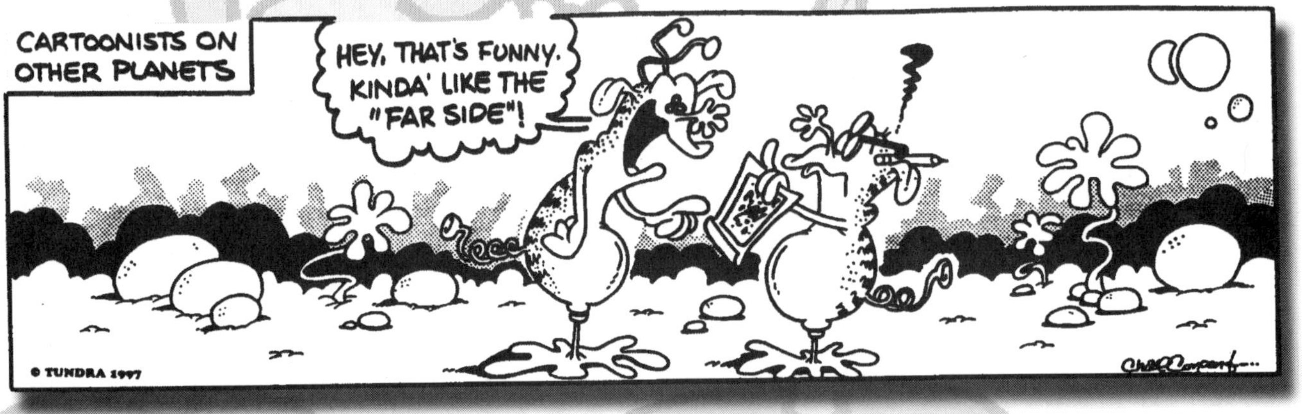
CARTOONISTS ON OTHER PLANETS
HEY, THAT'S FUNNY. KINDA' LIKE THE "FAR SIDE"!
© TUNDRA 1997

First of all I'd like to state for the record that I think Gary Larson's "FAR SIDE" is one of the greatest comic strips in history. However, because of its widespread fame, it is the comic strip to which all other single-panel comic strips are measured. The Far Side is sort of like the Kleenex of the comic world - for example, whenever someone needs to blow their nose, they don't say "Hand me a facial tissue," they almost always say "Hand me a Kleenex," regardless of the brand of facial tissue to which they are referring. It seems that all species of facial tissues will be forever known as Kleenex, just as single-panel comic strips will always be "Kinda' like the Far Side." Because of this, it is my goal to one day have people all over the world saying "Hand me that Tundra strip," whenever they need to blow their nose.

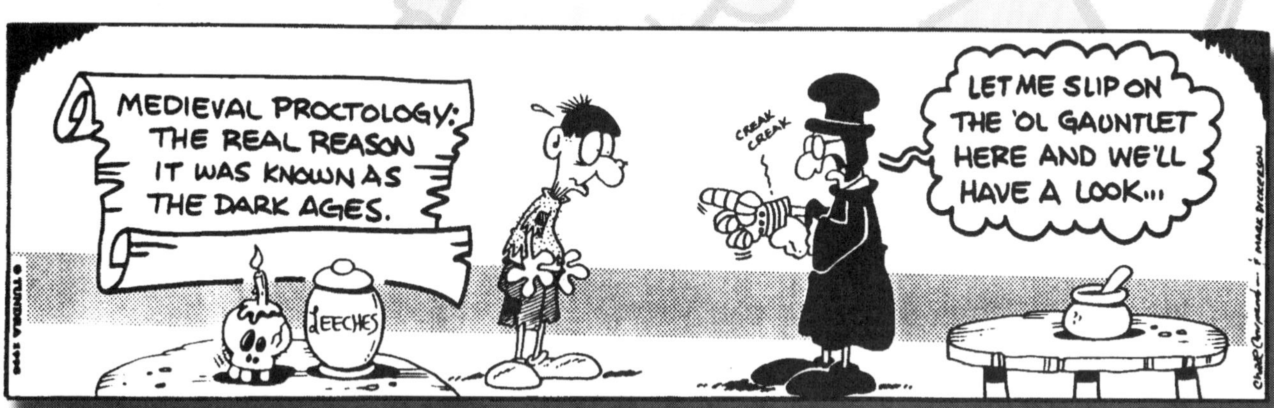
MEDIEVAL PROCTOLOGY: THE REAL REASON IT WAS KNOWN AS THE DARK AGES.
CREAK CREAK
LET ME SLIP ON THE 'OL GAUNTLET HERE AND WE'LL HAVE A LOOK...
LEECHES

I've always found it important to take the most humiliating and embarrassing aspects of the human experience, and make fun of it. One of my favorite quotes is "Life is too important to take seriously." When I was a kid, my mom had a little plaque on her kitchen wall featuring a cutesy cartoon squirrel spouting off those simple words. I'm sure it was originally quoted from some famous, long-dead individual, but now a squirrel is getting the credit. Chances are, if the rightful author of those words were alive today, I'm sure he would be ticked off about the plagiaristic rodent, but then, wouldn't he be missing the wisdom of his own words?

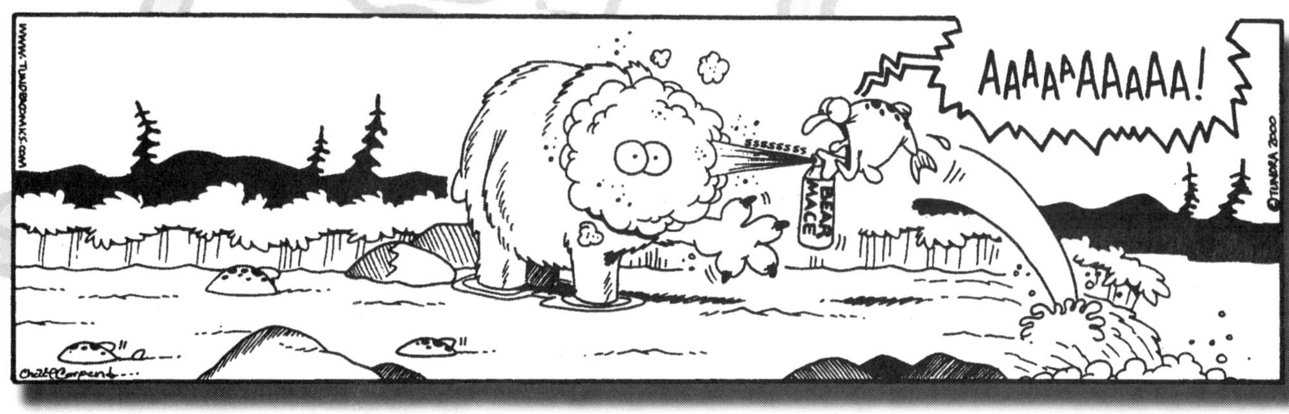
AAAAAAAAAA!
BEAR MACE
SSSSSSSS

Sometimes the best comic strips are those that have the fewest words.

Ah, yes. My all-time favorite Tundra strip. I'm sure I could go into a long explanation as to why this one tickles my pickle so vigorously, (I don't know what that means, I just say it sometimes) but what it really comes down to is, I just think it's really funny.

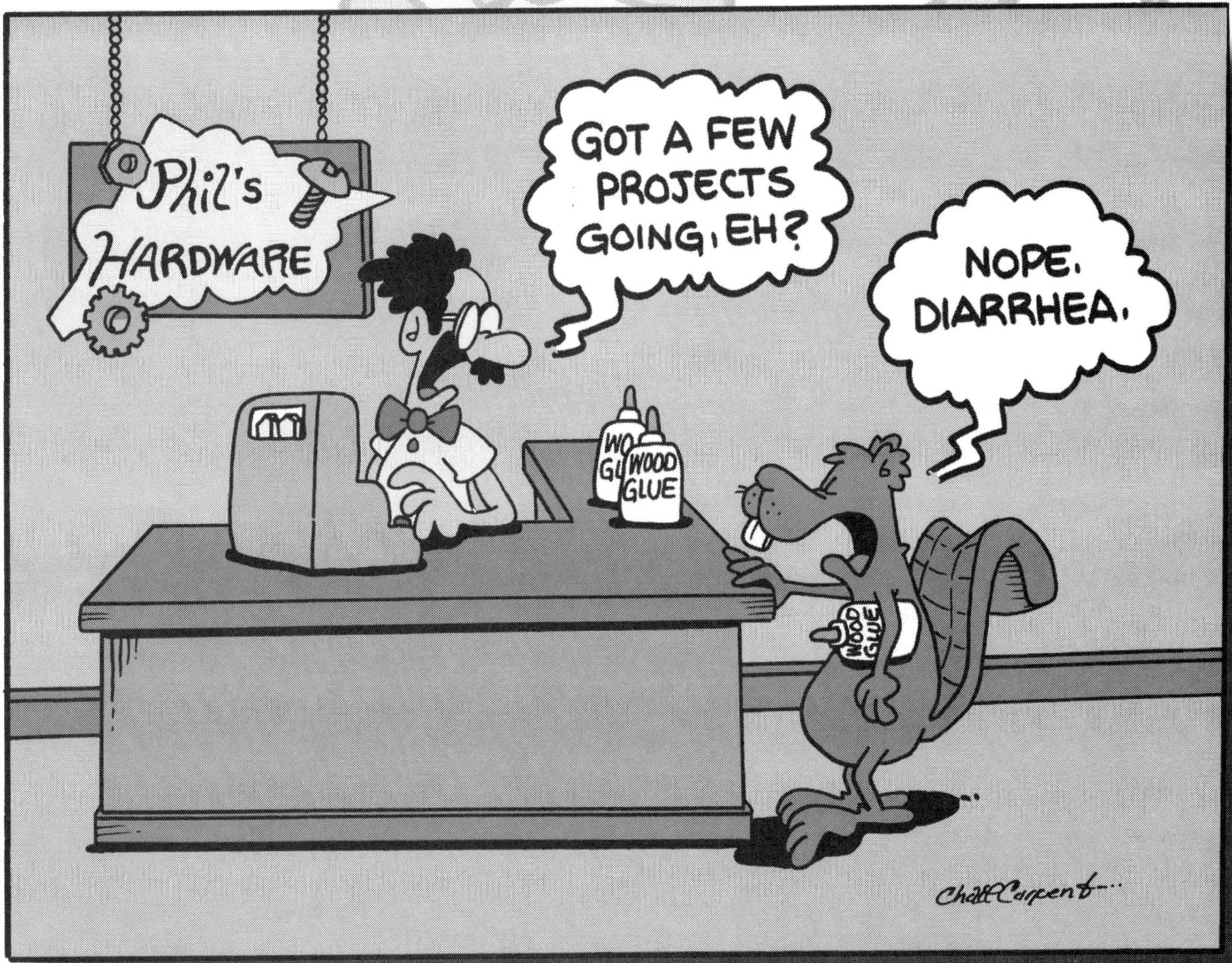
Phil's HARDWARE
GOT A FEW PROJECTS GOING, EH?
NOPE. DIARRHEA.
WOOD GLUE
WOOD GLUE
WOOD GLUE

Incidentally, it was my slowest-selling Tundra T-shirt. Go figure.

The Tundra Pages of Shame

Upon trying to decide which strips to include in this section, I first had to decide what criteria to judge them on. Should I pick out the ones that were the stupidest? The ones that were drawn poorly? Or maybe the ones that didn't make sense. In response to this conundrum, I decided that the best course of action was to pick a few that just plain stunk for whatever reason. Out of the 3,000 Tundra strips I've drawn, I'm not about to insult anybody's intelligence by suggesting that the following strips are the only bad ones I've done. On the contrary, I could probably do a whole other book on the subject. However, since I prefer to try and forget most of my past lame strips, not to mention they wouldn't make a best-selling book, I've chosen to highlight only a few of my cruddy creations. Each strip is followed by a brief explanation of why I feel they are worthy of being so unworthy. My most sincere apologies in advance.

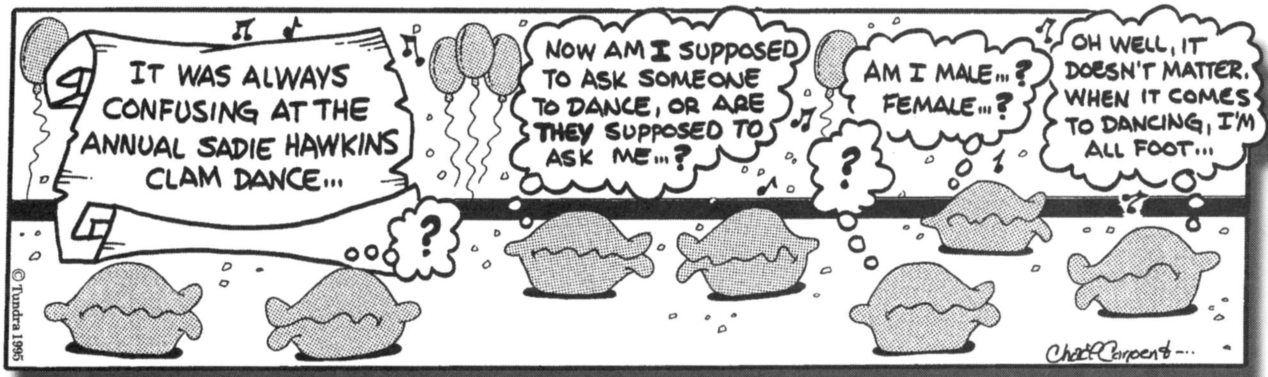
IT WAS ALWAYS CONFUSING AT THE ANNUAL SADIE HAWKINS CLAM DANCE...
?
NOW AM I SUPPOSED TO ASK SOMEONE TO DANCE, OR ARE THEY SUPPOSED TO ASK ME...?
?
AM I MALE...? FEMALE...?
OH WELL, IT DOESN'T MATTER. WHEN IT COMES TO DANCING, I'M ALL FOOT...
© Tundra 1995
Chad Carpenter

What can I say? It's bad. On every level.

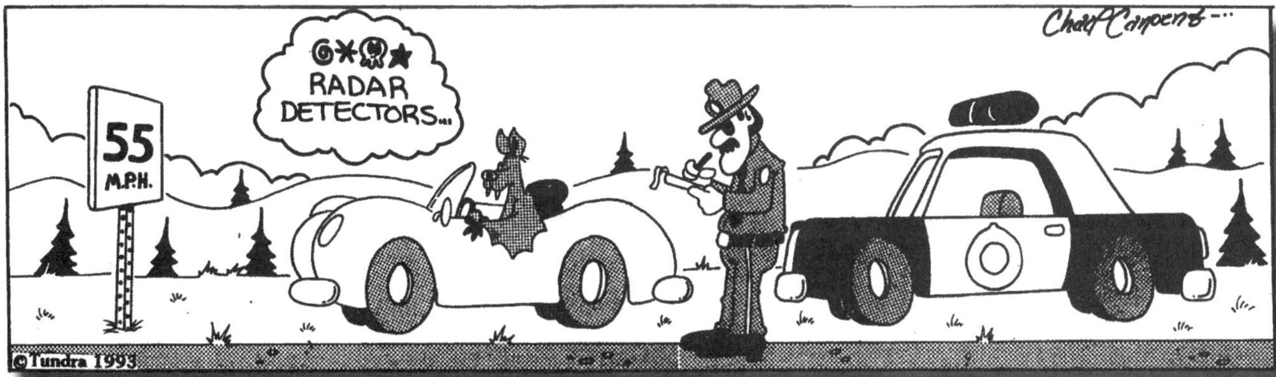
Chad Carpenter
@*☺★ RADAR DETECTORS...
55 M.P.H.
©Tundra 1993

First of all, it's hard to tell what kind of creature is in the car. It's a bat. Secondly, bats don't use radar... they use sonar. Duh.

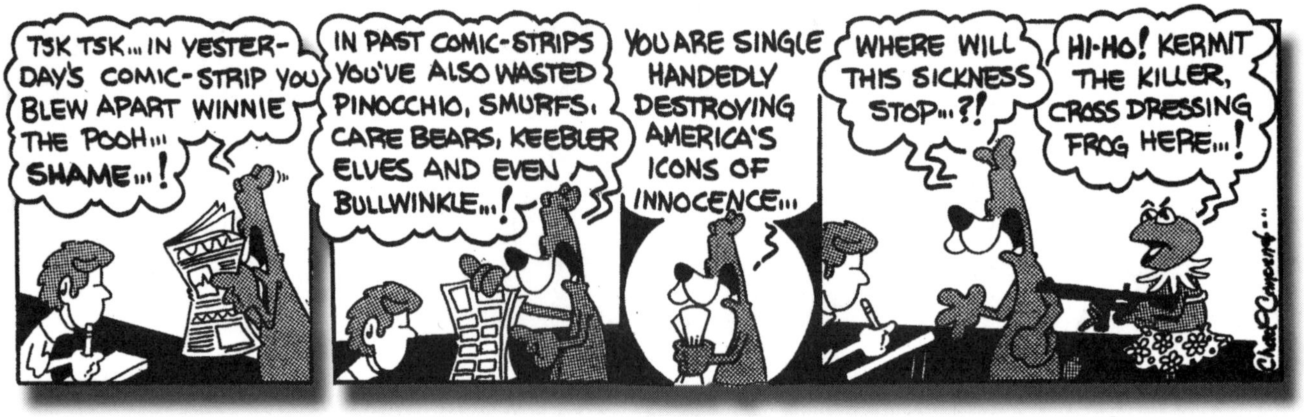
TSK TSK... IN YESTER-DAY'S COMIC-STRIP YOU BLEW APART WINNIE THE POOH... SHAME...!
IN PAST COMIC-STRIPS YOU'VE ALSO WASTED PINOCCHIO, SMURFS, CARE BEARS, KEEBLER ELVES AND EVEN BULLWINKLE...!
YOU ARE SINGLE HANDEDLY DESTROYING AMERICA'S ICONS OF INNOCENCE...
WHERE WILL THIS SICKNESS STOP...?!
HI-HO! KERMIT THE KILLER, CROSS DRESSING FROG HERE...!

This is quite honestly the only strip I've ever done that I've felt the slightest bit guilty about. I've drawn a lot of strips making fun of Disney characters, Care Bears, Smurfs and dozens of other American icons, but Kermit the Frog? That just ain't right.

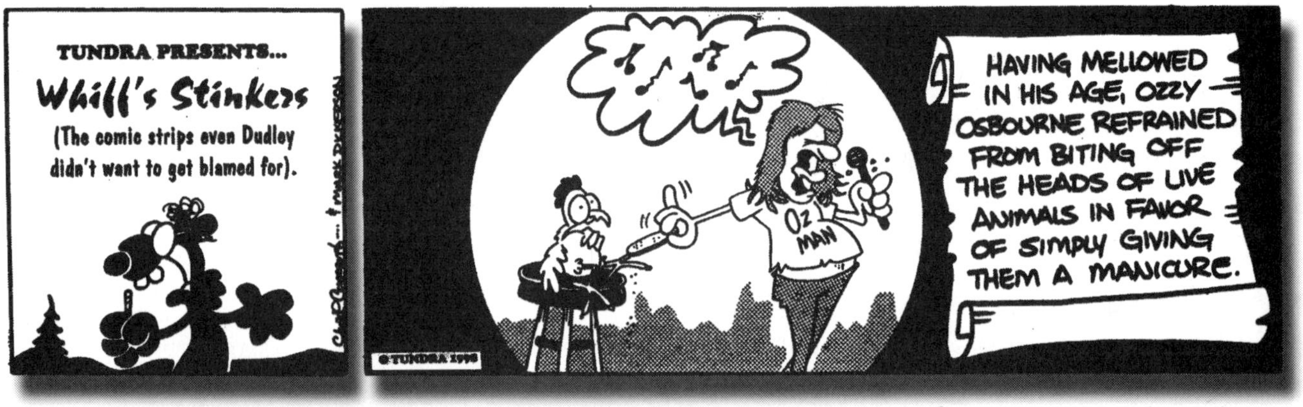
TUNDRA PRESENTS...
Whiff's Stinkers
(The comic strips even Dudley didn't want to get blamed for).
OZ MAN
HAVING MELLOWED IN HIS AGE, OZZY OSBOURNE REFRAINED FROM BITING OFF THE HEADS OF LIVE ANIMALS IN FAVOR OF SIMPLY GIVING THEM A MANICURE.

Talk about reaching. The only excuse I can think of is that at the time I drew this, I was listening to some heavy-metal music that contained some insidious back-masking instructing me to draw a stupid comic strip. Obviously it worked.

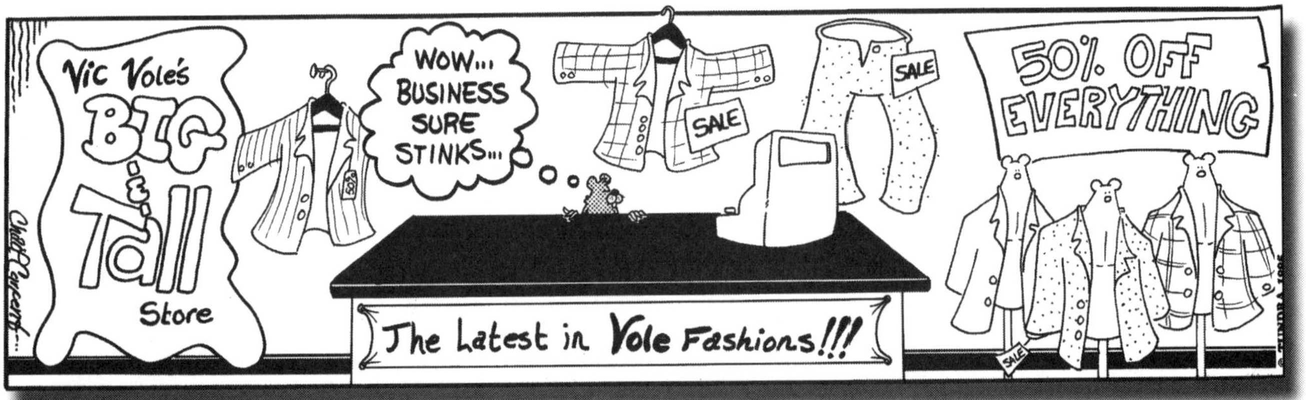
Vic Vole's BIG & Tall Store
WOW... BUSINESS SURE STINKS...
SALE
SALE
50% OFF EVERYTHING
The Latest in Vole Fashions!!!
SALE

I really didn't think that this one was that bad, but my significant other, Jennie, insisted that it was.

I've included the following series of strips into the Pages of Shame not because they aren't funny, but for another reason. A few of them, ever so slightly, are a bit tacky. In fact, thanks to the discerning eyes of several newspaper editors, this series never even made it to the publishing stage... until now...

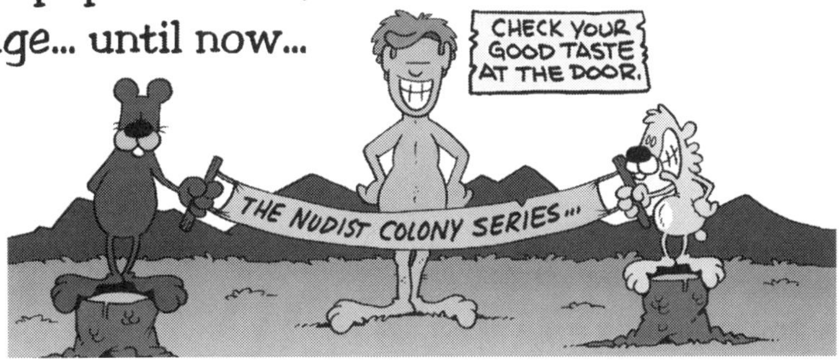
CHECK YOUR GOOD TASTE AT THE DOOR.
THE NUDIST COLONY SERIES...

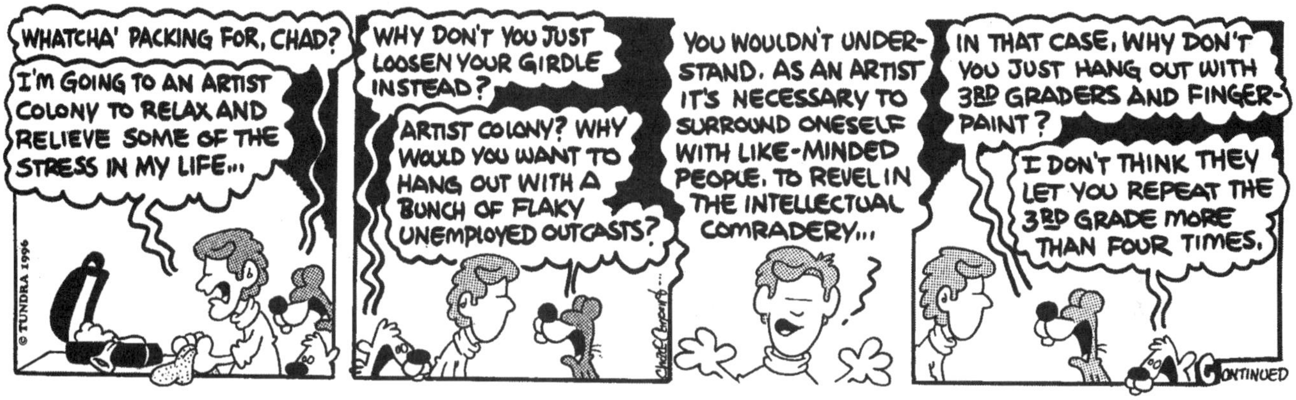
WHATCHA' PACKING FOR, CHAD?
I'M GOING TO AN ARTIST COLONY TO RELAX AND RELIEVE SOME OF THE STRESS IN MY LIFE...
© TUNDRA 1996
WHY DON'T YOU JUST LOOSEN YOUR GIRDLE INSTEAD?
ARTIST COLONY? WHY WOULD YOU WANT TO HANG OUT WITH A BUNCH OF FLAKY UNEMPLOYED OUTCASTS?
YOU WOULDN'T UNDERSTAND. AS AN ARTIST IT'S NECESSARY TO SURROUND ONESELF WITH LIKE-MINDED PEOPLE, TO REVEL IN THE INTELLECTUAL COMRADERY...
IN THAT CASE, WHY DON'T YOU JUST HANG OUT WITH 3RD GRADERS AND FINGER-PAINT?
I DON'T THINK THEY LET YOU REPEAT THE 3RD GRADE MORE THAN FOUR TIMES.
CONTINUED

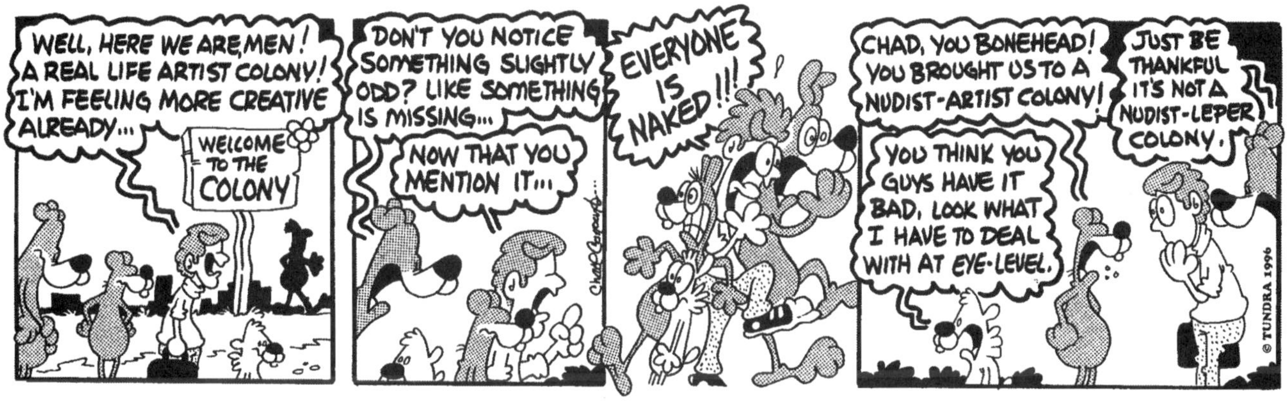
WELL, HERE WE ARE, MEN! A REAL LIFE ARTIST COLONY! I'M FEELING MORE CREATIVE ALREADY...
WELCOME TO THE COLONY
DON'T YOU NOTICE SOMETHING SLIGHTLY ODD? LIKE SOMETHING IS MISSING...
NOW THAT YOU MENTION IT...
EVERYONE IS NAKED!!!
CHAD, YOU BONEHEAD! YOU BROUGHT US TO A NUDIST-ARTIST COLONY!
JUST BE THANKFUL IT'S NOT A NUDIST-LEPER COLONY.
YOU THINK YOU GUYS HAVE IT BAD, LOOK WHAT I HAVE TO DEAL WITH AT EYE-LEVEL.
© TUNDRA 1996

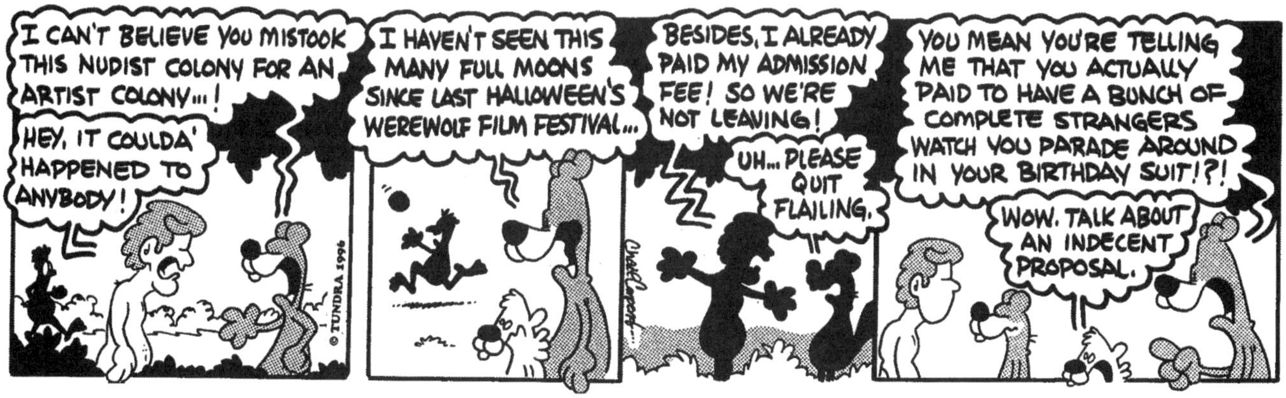
I CAN'T BELIEVE YOU MISTOOK THIS NUDIST COLONY FOR AN ARTIST COLONY...!
HEY, IT COULDA' HAPPENED TO ANYBODY!
© TUNDRA 1996
I HAVEN'T SEEN THIS MANY FULL MOONS SINCE LAST HALLOWEEN'S WEREWOLF FILM FESTIVAL...
BESIDES, I ALREADY PAID MY ADMISSION FEE! SO WE'RE NOT LEAVING!
UH... PLEASE QUIT FLAILING.
YOU MEAN YOU'RE TELLING ME THAT YOU ACTUALLY PAID TO HAVE A BUNCH OF COMPLETE STRANGERS WATCH YOU PARADE AROUND IN YOUR BIRTHDAY SUIT!?!
WOW. TALK ABOUT AN INDECENT PROPOSAL.

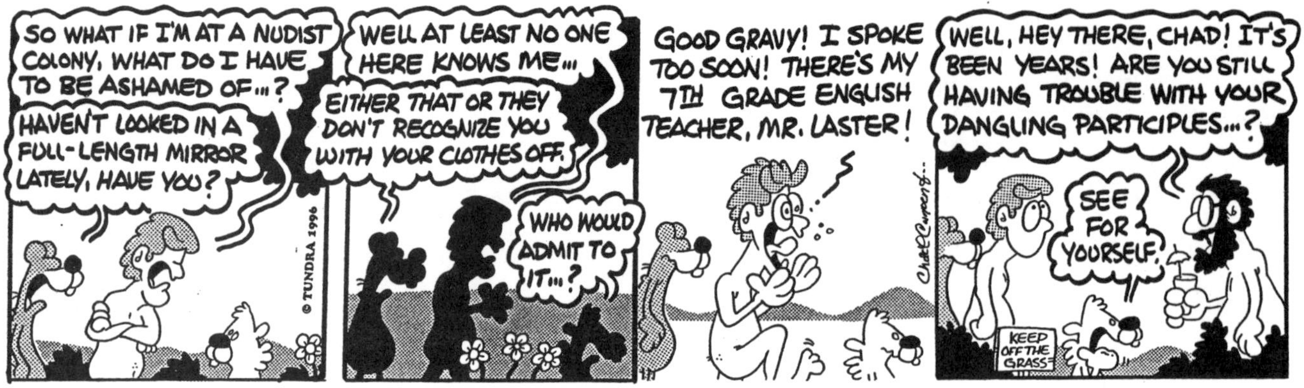
SO WHAT IF I'M AT A NUDIST COLONY, WHAT DO I HAVE TO BE ASHAMED OF...?
HAVEN'T LOOKED IN A FULL-LENGTH MIRROR LATELY, HAVE YOU?
© TUNDRA 1996
WELL AT LEAST NO ONE HERE KNOWS ME...
EITHER THAT OR THEY DON'T RECOGNIZE YOU WITH YOUR CLOTHES OFF.
WHO WOULD ADMIT TO IT...?
GOOD GRAVY! I SPOKE TOO SOON! THERE'S MY 7TH GRADE ENGLISH TEACHER, MR. LASTER!
WELL, HEY THERE, CHAD! IT'S BEEN YEARS! ARE YOU STILL HAVING TROUBLE WITH YOUR DANGLING PARTICIPLES...?
SEE FOR YOURSELF.
KEEP OFF THE GRASS

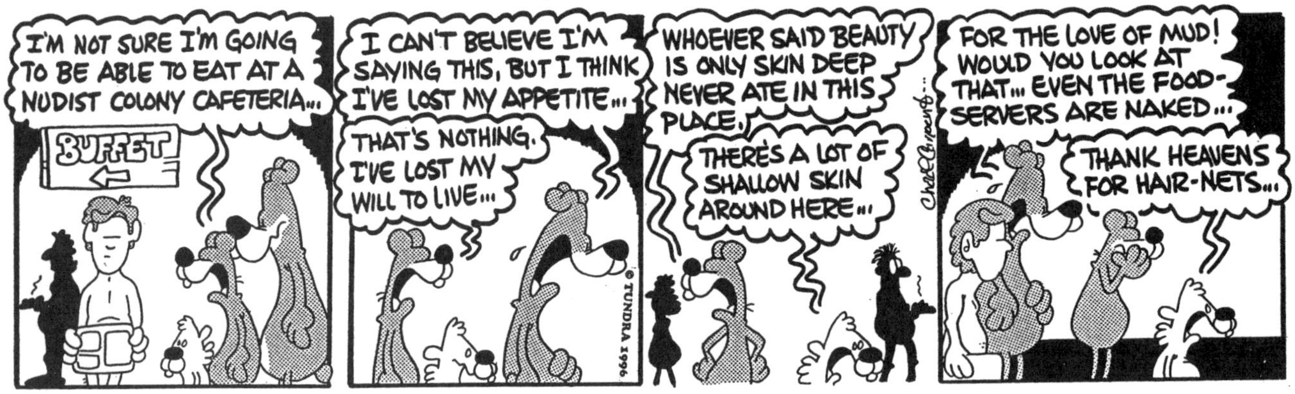
I'M NOT SURE I'M GOING TO BE ABLE TO EAT AT A NUDIST COLONY CAFETERIA...
BUFFET
I CAN'T BELIEVE I'M SAYING THIS, BUT I THINK I'VE LOST MY APPETITE...
THAT'S NOTHING. I'VE LOST MY WILL TO LIVE...
© TUNDRA 1996
WHOEVER SAID BEAUTY IS ONLY SKIN DEEP NEVER ATE IN THIS PLACE.
THERE'S A LOT OF SHALLOW SKIN AROUND HERE...
FOR THE LOVE OF MUD! WOULD YOU LOOK AT THAT... EVEN THE FOOD-SERVERS ARE NAKED...
THANK HEAVENS FOR HAIR-NETS...

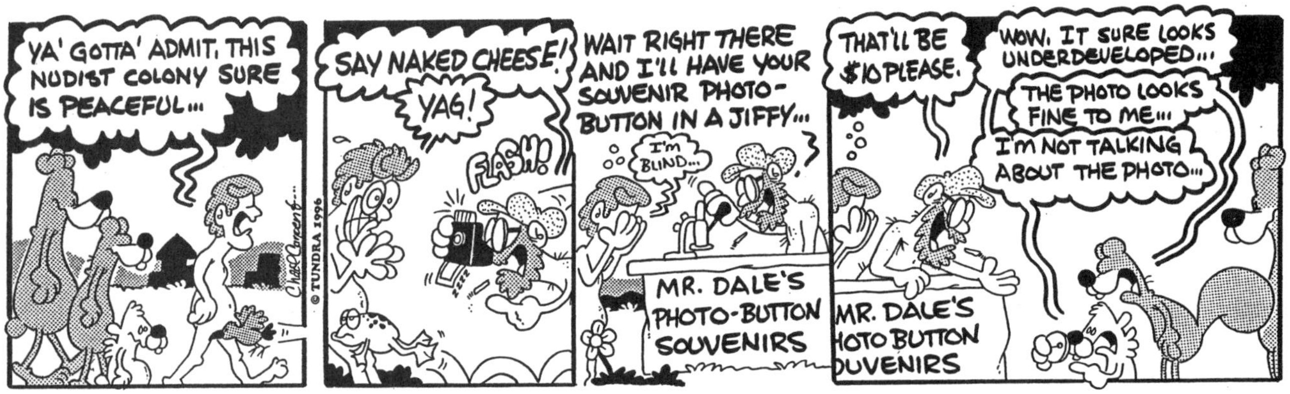
YA' GOTTA' ADMIT, THIS NUDIST COLONY SURE IS PEACEFUL...
© TUNDRA 1996
SAY NAKED CHEESE!
YAG!
FLASH!
WAIT RIGHT THERE AND I'LL HAVE YOUR SOUVENIR PHOTO-BUTTON IN A JIFFY...
I'M BLIND...
MR. DALE'S PHOTO-BUTTON SOUVENIRS
THAT'LL BE $10 PLEASE.
WOW, IT SURE LOOKS UNDERDEVELOPED...
THE PHOTO LOOKS FINE TO ME...
I'M NOT TALKING ABOUT THE PHOTO...
MR. DALE'S HOTO BUTTON UVENIRS

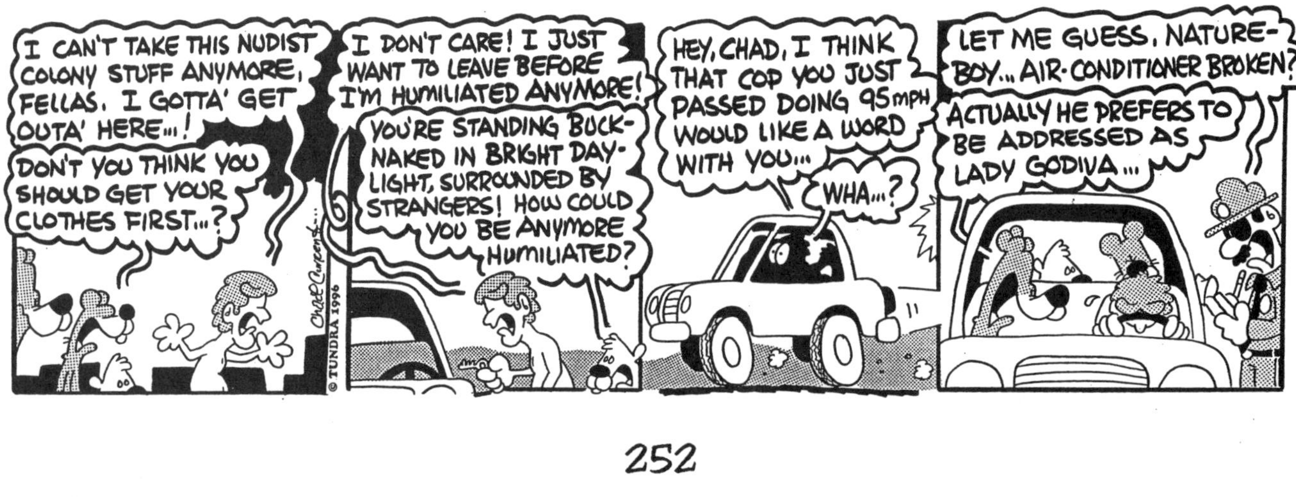
I CAN'T TAKE THIS NUDIST COLONY STUFF ANYMORE, FELLAS. I GOTTA' GET OUTA' HERE...!
DON'T YOU THINK YOU SHOULD GET YOUR CLOTHES FIRST...?
© TUNDRA 1996
I DON'T CARE! I JUST WANT TO LEAVE BEFORE I'M HUMILIATED ANYMORE!
YOU'RE STANDING BUCK-NAKED IN BRIGHT DAY-LIGHT, SURROUNDED BY STRANGERS! HOW COULD YOU BE ANYMORE HUMILIATED?
HEY, CHAD, I THINK THAT COP YOU JUST PASSED DOING 95 MPH WOULD LIKE A WORD WITH YOU...
WHA...?
LET ME GUESS, NATURE-BOY... AIR-CONDITIONER BROKEN?
ACTUALLY HE PREFERS TO BE ADDRESSED AS LADY GODIVA...

Comics that caused trouble...

In the years that I've been drawing Tundra, I've been very fortunate that 99% of the feedback I get from the readers has been positive. However, being a cartoonist has taught me that no matter what, regardless of the innocence of a strip, there is always someone out there capable of being offended by it. In fact, not once has any of the strips that I thought might result in some negative feedback done so. It has always been the strips that I thought were totally "safe" that have caught me off guard.

In the beginning, it used to bother me when I would get a negative email or if someone would confront me personally about a certain comic strip that put their knickers in a twist. But, over time I have realized that there is a certain small but loud faction of folks out there that have a talent for thinking everything is a personal attack against them or their delicate sensibilities.

As I said, 99% of the response I receive is positive, but it's the negative 1% that make the best stories. One member of this 1% Club approached me at a bookstore where I was doing a book signing one day. She let me know that she felt one of my cartoons she had just seen on a T-shirt was inappropriate. (Warm Current, page 245.) She proceeded to inform me that it was something that she wouldn't want her 13-year-old son to see because, as she put it, "We don't talk about elimination in our home." Attempting to hold back my mirthful giggles, I very diplomatically thanked her for her input. I still lose sleep wishing that I had extended my hand to her and asked her to pull my finger.

The following Tundra strips are a few that resulted in some very memorable repercussions. Not surprisingly, when I drew these strips, I never would have guessed that they would cause any sort of disturbance. I was wrong.

Exhibit A - "Chad spreading misinformation"

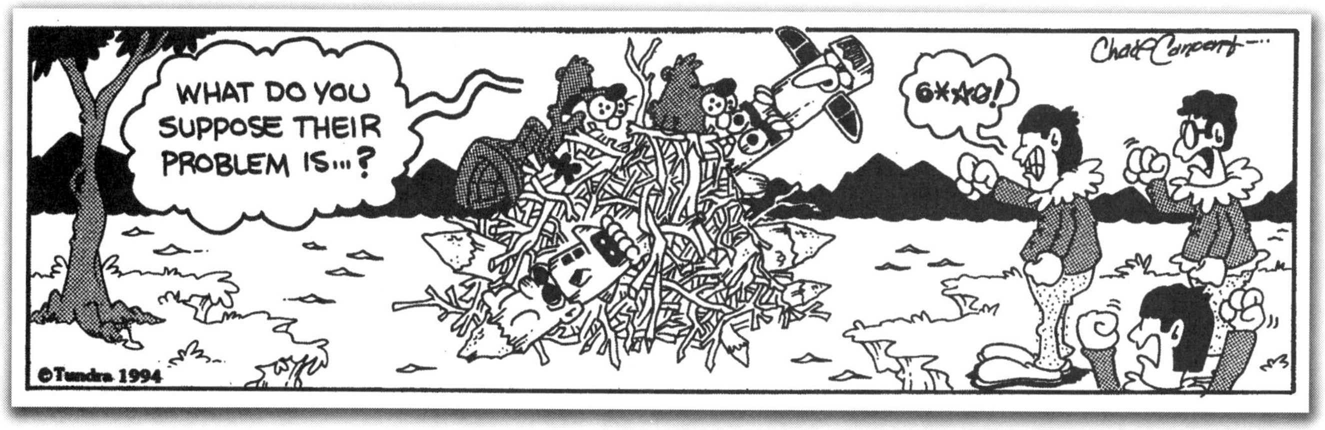
WHAT DO YOU SUPPOSE THEIR PROBLEM IS...?
©Tundra 1994

While I admit this cartoon isn't particularly funny, I was surprised a few days later when the following letter appeared in the editorial section of the Anchorage Daily News.

(The individual's name has been changed so that they don't track me down and beat the stuffing out of me.)

Kenai kings in from the backyard snow bank.

M. Johnson

Cartoon's misinformation

I am, for the most part, a longtime fan of your paper. And from time to time you make changes or print articles I don't agree with but I have never addressed these concerns. However, I do find the Tundra cartoon of Nov. 14 objectionable. The men on the shore are depicted — I think — as Eskimo (the fur ruffs). Eskimo people do not have totem poles. If Chad Carpenter wanted to make the observers Alaska Native, he could have put Athabascan or Tlingit garb on them.

There is enough misinformation generated about Alaska Natives without the Daily News contributing to it.

Thanks for listening.

Another Satisfied Customer

Let us know y

Normally I make it a rule to simply ignore things like this, but I was upset over being accused of doing something in any way degrading towards any ethnic group. It has always been my policy to avoid offending anyone unless I offend everyone - equally. So, a couple of days later, my rebuttal appeared in the editorial section.

Moose nuggets don't talk

I would like to respond to Another Satisfied Customer's Dec. 3 letter in regard to my Nov. 14 "Tundra" cartoon. She stated that she found this particular cartoon objectionable, because the Alaska Native characters within the strip were not clad in garments of Athabascan or Tlingit nature and therefore easily confused with people of Eskimo origin. Because of this, Ms. Get a Life felt that I and the Daily News were responsible for generating misinformation about the Native peoples of Alaska.

This isn't the first time I've been guilty of misrepresentations within my strip. I feel it's time I let the truth be known — *moose nuggets don't really talk*. The charade has gone on long enough. I realize that hundreds, possibly even thousands of my loyal readers (as well as some of my disloyal ones), will be dumbfounded by this revelation. So please, to all of you who have tried in vain to strike up a conversation with our little nugget neighbors ... no more. Go on with your lives. Become productive members of society. I repeat, moose nuggets do not talk (although I did hear one whistle once).

My point is this (if I ever had one), I don't try to make my cartoons "anatomically correct" or "scientifically factual." I strongly feel that the comic pages within a newspaper are meant to be read with a light heart. They should serve as a sort of uplifting interlude from the dark happenings which all too often reside within the bulk of today's newspaper pages. I strive very seriously to create something that makes people happy, if only for a brief moment. To those who can't help but to try to locate the occasional imperfection in these creations ... well, sadly, they miss the whole point.

— Chad Carpenter
Eagle River

Hydee's family healing

On Nov. 14, the Daily News printed a

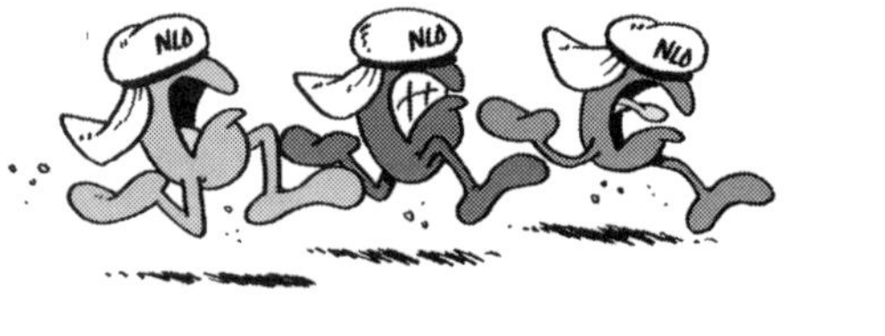

NLD
NLD
NLD

Exhibit B - The "Son of Good Sam" series

The following series of strips appeared in papers during the summer of 1993. The first strip's theme shows my "Chad" character expressing the misery of being stuck behind a motorhome for over two hours. The second strip shows Chad receiving a letter from the president of the local recreational vehicle club, (The Son of Good Sam Club) which contains threats for making offensive comic strips about motorhomes.

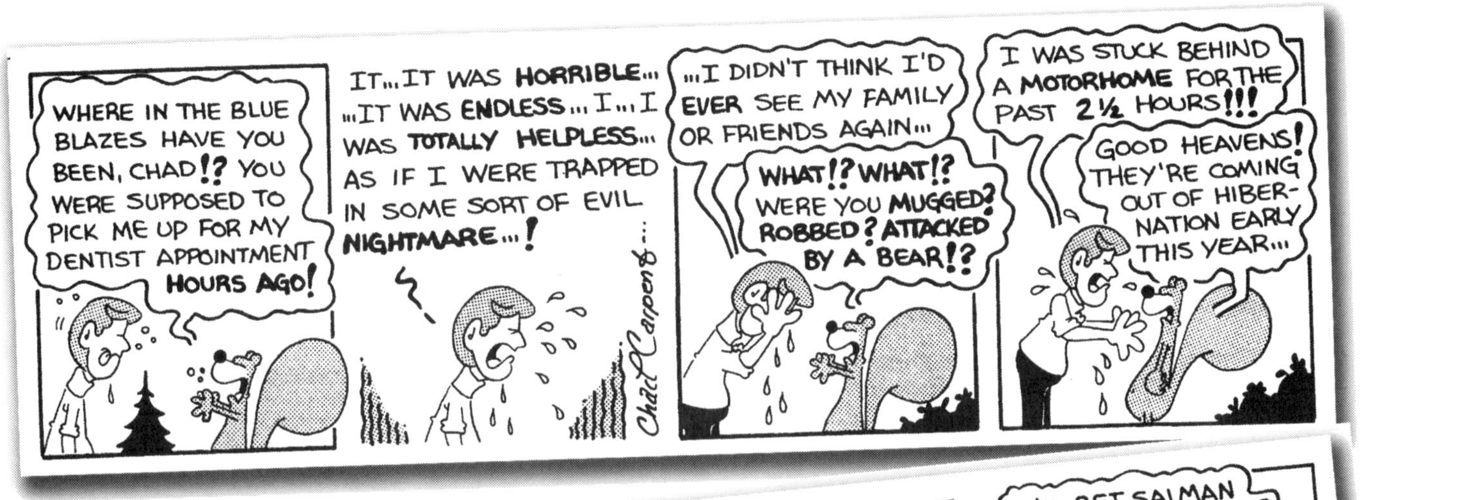
WHERE IN THE BLUE BLAZES HAVE YOU BEEN, CHAD!? YOU WERE SUPPOSED TO PICK ME UP FOR MY DENTIST APPOINTMENT HOURS AGO!
IT...IT WAS HORRIBLE... ...IT WAS ENDLESS... I...I WAS TOTALLY HELPLESS... AS IF I WERE TRAPPED IN SOME SORT OF EVIL NIGHTMARE...!
...I DIDN'T THINK I'D EVER SEE MY FAMILY OR FRIENDS AGAIN...
WHAT!? WHAT!? WERE YOU MUGGED? ROBBED? ATTACKED BY A BEAR!?
I WAS STUCK BEHIND A MOTORHOME FOR THE PAST 2½ HOURS!!!
GOOD HEAVENS! THEY'RE COMING OUT OF HIBERNATION EARLY THIS YEAR...
Chad Carpenter

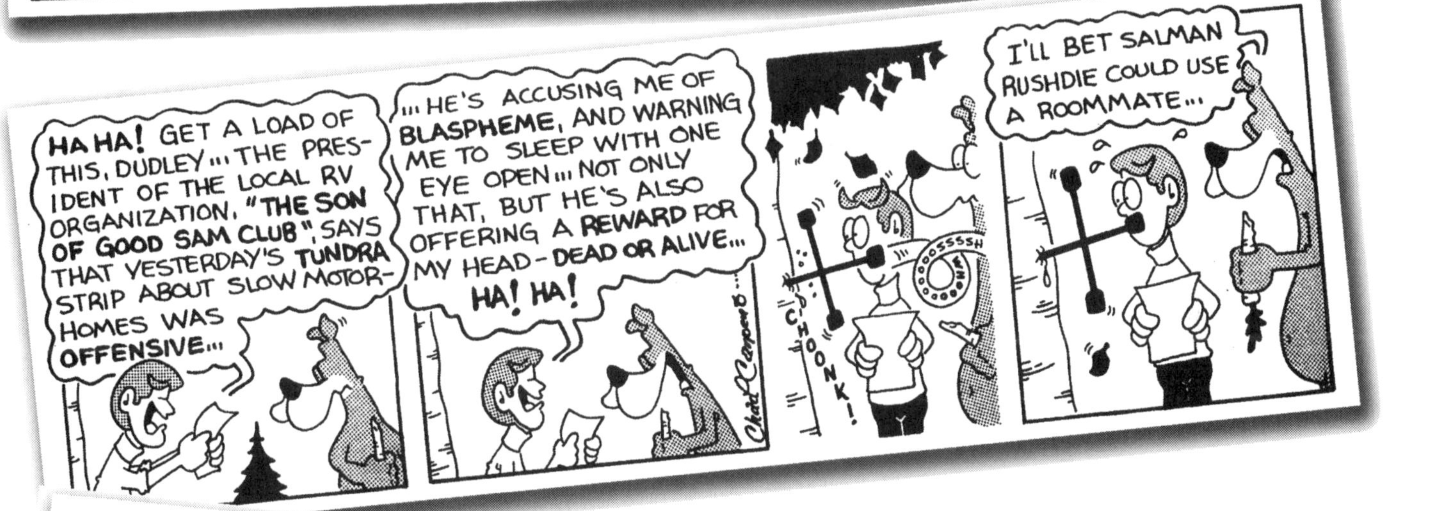
HA HA! GET A LOAD OF THIS, DUDLEY... THE PRESIDENT OF THE LOCAL RV ORGANIZATION, "THE SON OF GOOD SAM CLUB", SAYS THAT YESTERDAY'S TUNDRA STRIP ABOUT SLOW MOTORHOMES WAS OFFENSIVE...
...HE'S ACCUSING ME OF BLASPHEME, AND WARNING ME TO SLEEP WITH ONE EYE OPEN... NOT ONLY THAT, BUT HE'S ALSO OFFERING A REWARD FOR MY HEAD - DEAD OR ALIVE...
HA! HA!
Chad Carpenter
CHOONK!
SSSSSH
I'LL BET SALMAN RUSHDIE COULD USE A ROOMMATE...

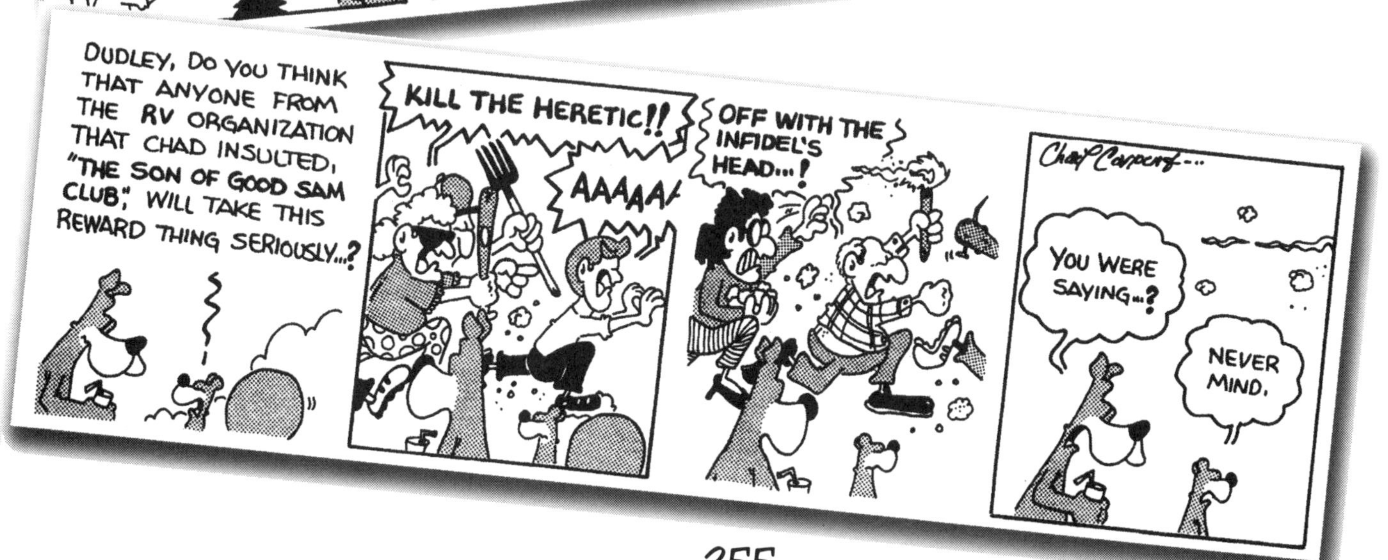
DUDLEY, DO YOU THINK THAT ANYONE FROM THE RV ORGANIZATION THAT CHAD INSULTED, "THE SON OF GOOD SAM CLUB", WILL TAKE THIS REWARD THING SERIOUSLY...?
KILL THE HERETIC!!
AAAAA!
OFF WITH THE INFIDEL'S HEAD...!
Chad Carpenter...
YOU WERE SAYING...?
NEVER MIND.

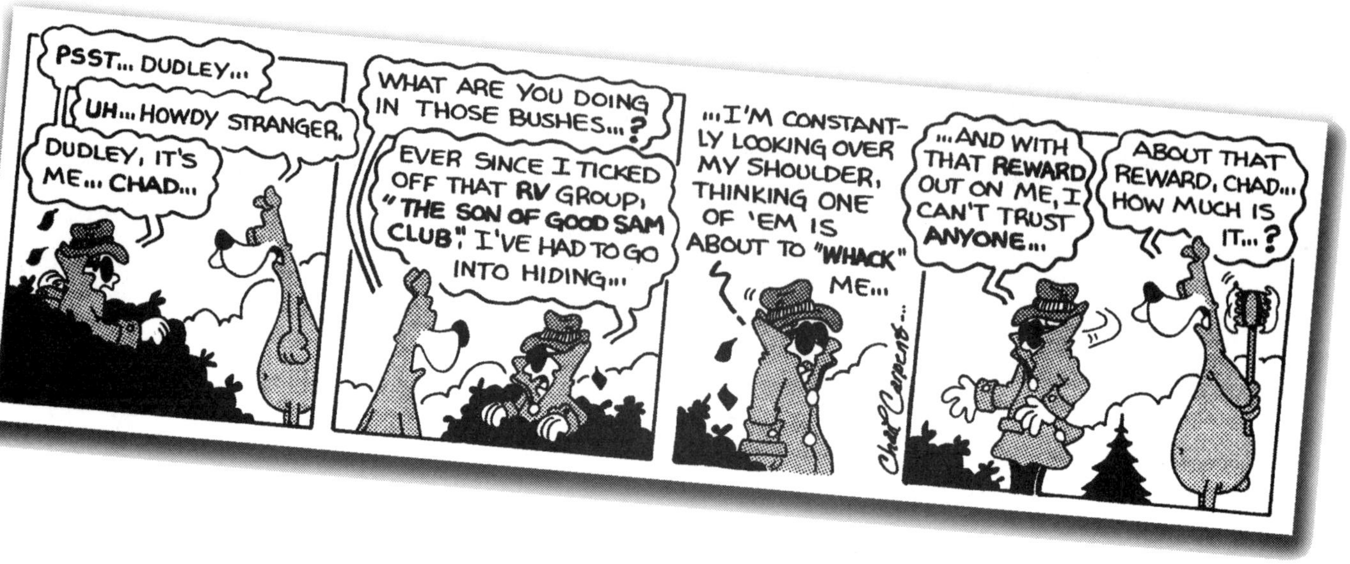
PSST... DUDLEY...
UH... HOWDY STRANGER.
DUDLEY, IT'S ME... CHAD...
WHAT ARE YOU DOING IN THOSE BUSHES...?
EVER SINCE I TICKED OFF THAT RV GROUP, "THE SON OF GOOD SAM CLUB", I'VE HAD TO GO INTO HIDING...
...I'M CONSTANTLY LOOKING OVER MY SHOULDER, THINKING ONE OF 'EM IS ABOUT TO "WHACK" ME...
...AND WITH THAT REWARD OUT ON ME, I CAN'T TRUST ANYONE...
ABOUT THAT REWARD, CHAD... HOW MUCH IS IT...?

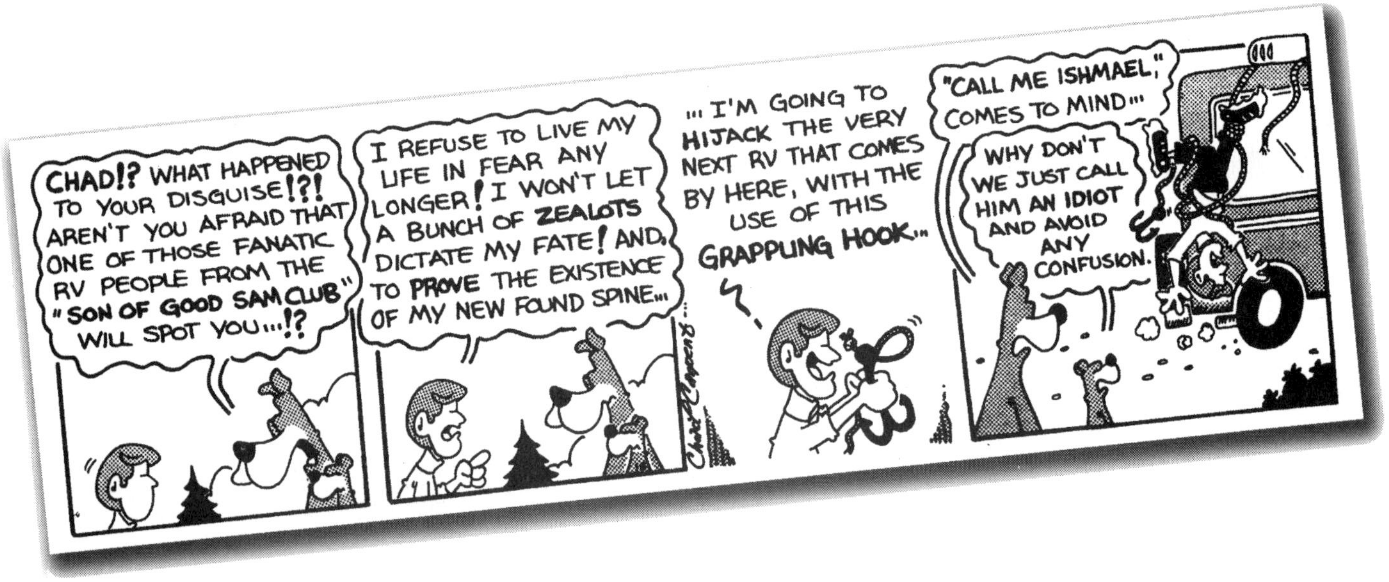
CHAD!? WHAT HAPPENED TO YOUR DISGUISE!?! AREN'T YOU AFRAID THAT ONE OF THOSE FANATIC RV PEOPLE FROM THE "SON OF GOOD SAM CLUB" WILL SPOT YOU...!?
I REFUSE TO LIVE MY LIFE IN FEAR ANY LONGER! I WON'T LET A BUNCH OF ZEALOTS DICTATE MY FATE! AND, TO PROVE THE EXISTENCE OF MY NEW FOUND SPINE...
...I'M GOING TO HIJACK THE VERY NEXT RV THAT COMES BY HERE, WITH THE USE OF THIS GRAPPLING HOOK...
"CALL ME ISHMAEL," COMES TO MIND...
WHY DON'T WE JUST CALL HIM AN IDIOT AND AVOID ANY CONFUSION.

I really didn't expect any negative correspondence from this series. True, I've done a lot of strips poking fun at motorhomes and the people that drive them, but historically, motorhome dwellers have always been the people that seemed to appreciate them the most. Heck, my parents even own a motorhome.

Well, as it turned out, it wasn't the folks that drive motorhomes that didn't see the humor in my little series, it was somebody I never anticipated.

A couple of months after the series ran, I received the following letter in the mail from **The Good Sam Club** headquarters in Camarillo, California. It was sent in a Good Sam envelope on Good Sam stationery and signed by a Good Sam vice president.

(Once again the name has been changed to protect me from the bozo that wrote it.)

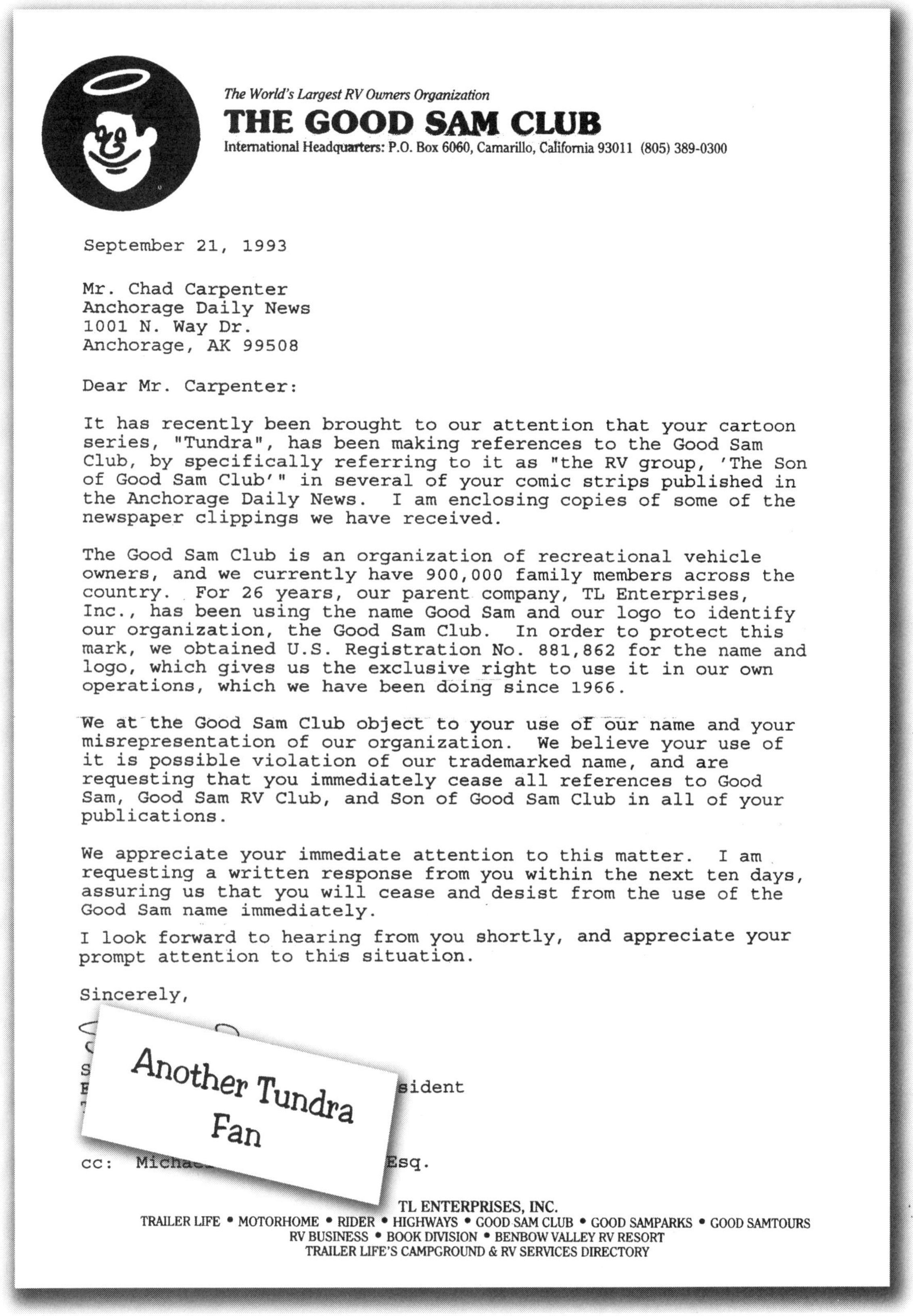

The World's Largest RV Owners Organization

THE GOOD SAM CLUB

International Headquarters: P.O. Box 6060, Camarillo, California 93011 (805) 389-0300

September 21, 1993

Mr. Chad Carpenter
Anchorage Daily News
1001 N. Way Dr.
Anchorage, AK 99508

Dear Mr. Carpenter:

It has recently been brought to our attention that your cartoon series, "Tundra", has been making references to the Good Sam Club, by specifically referring to it as "the RV group, 'The Son of Good Sam Club'" in several of your comic strips published in the Anchorage Daily News. I am enclosing copies of some of the newspaper clippings we have received.

The Good Sam Club is an organization of recreational vehicle owners, and we currently have 900,000 family members across the country. For 26 years, our parent company, TL Enterprises, Inc., has been using the name Good Sam and our logo to identify our organization, the Good Sam Club. In order to protect this mark, we obtained U.S. Registration No. 881,862 for the name and logo, which gives us the exclusive right to use it in our own operations, which we have been doing since 1966.

We at the Good Sam Club object to your use of our name and your misrepresentation of our organization. We believe your use of it is possible violation of our trademarked name, and are requesting that you immediately cease all references to Good Sam, Good Sam RV Club, and Son of Good Sam Club in all of your publications.

We appreciate your immediate attention to this matter. I am requesting a written response from you within the next ten days, assuring us that you will cease and desist from the use of the Good Sam name immediately.

I look forward to hearing from you shortly, and appreciate your prompt attention to this situation.

Sincerely,

S
E sident

Another Tundra Fan

cc: Micha Esq.

TL ENTERPRISES, INC.
TRAILER LIFE • MOTORHOME • RIDER • HIGHWAYS • GOOD SAM CLUB • GOOD SAMPARKS • GOOD SAMTOURS
RV BUSINESS • BOOK DIVISION • BENBOW VALLEY RV RESORT
TRAILER LIFE'S CAMPGROUND & RV SERVICES DIRECTORY

This letter is a perfect example of art imitating life, imitating art. Wow. Obviously this person failed to grasp the irony of what they were doing. I know it's a few years too late, but they can consider this portion of the book my written response.

Exhibit C - This strip is the one that caused the most severe backlash from the 1% Club. In fact it got me thrown out of not just one, but two state capitals.

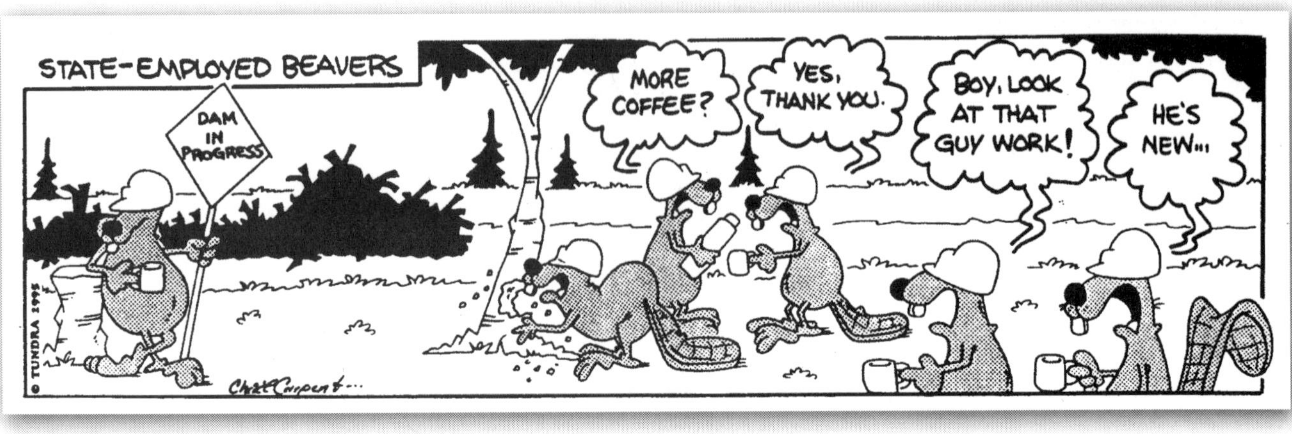
STATE-EMPLOYED BEAVERS
DAM IN PROGRESS
MORE COFFEE?
YES, THANK YOU.
BOY, LOOK AT THAT GUY WORK!
HE'S NEW...
© TUNDRA 1995

This seemingly tame strip ran in newspapers in February of 1997. Almost immediately after its appearance, I knew some folks were unhappy. I received a phone call from one of the editors of the Salem Statesman Journal, Oregon's capital city newspaper. He informed me that his phones were lit up all day from irate state employees wanting Tundra to be axed from the paper. He told me that due to the massive negative public response, he had no choice but to terminate Tundra in their paper. Needless to say, I was not only a little surprised, but also quite disappointed. That same day I also received some extremely angry phone calls from anonymous individuals accusing me of everything from spreading lies about state employees, to being the reason for all of society's animosity towards them. One gentleman even called to inform me that physical harm would be headed my way if he ever saw me in person - of course the way *he* said it was much more colorful, but I'll let you use your imagination for that.

A couple days after all that, I received a letter in the mail from Alaska's state capital newspaper, The Juneau Empire. The letter consisted of one simple sentence from the editor informing me that Tundra was no longer going to be in their newspaper. I decided to call the editor and see if there was something I could do to prevent Tundra's eviction from their comic pages. Upon reaching the editor, she informed me that there had been so many complaints that her mind was made up. Then, just to sugar-coat it, she said that she wanted to throw Tundra out months earlier when she took over as editor, so this seemed like a good opportunity. Ouch.

Later that year, at one of my book signings, I was approached by a young lady who happened to be a state employee. She told me that ***she*** thought the state-employed beaver strip was really funny, but that there were a couple of her fellow employees passing around a petition to get the newspapers to force me to make a public apology. Not only that, but they also wanted me to spend a day with a state employee so that I could see for myself just how hard they work. Don't get me wrong - I think that would be sort of fun. I certainly wouldn't mind spending a day with a state employee, but I wonder if I would have to supply my own lawn chair and coffee? **(Here we go again...)**

The Darin Carpenter Unauthorized Autobiography

My first realization that I may have a gift for "Tooning" came in 1995. I was a stay-at-home dad raising a 2-year-old and a six-month-old daughter. My life consisted of changing diapers, watching Bob Ross paint his "Happy Trees" and being subjected to old Barney re-runs. If things didn't change, someone was going to die. I remembered Chad mentioning to me one time that I should try to write some cartoons for him so he wouldn't have to work so hard. So I took up a pen and notebook and wrote my first Tundra 6-day series. Flush with my first taste of the literary "rush" I sent my masterpiece off to Chad.

I was soon to experience another first - "Cartoon Censorship." The series I had so cleverly written dealt with Sherm and Dud going shopping for a birthday present for Chad. They wanted to buy him a book and while walking around town they came across an adult bookstore. Well, being their typical naive selves and since, logically, Chad is an adult, it would make perfect sense that an adult bookstore would be the perfect place to find him a book. To make a long story short, after I sent this little gem of comedic brilliance to Chad and eagerly began awaiting publication, the phone rings. I answer and it is Chad who informs me that although this particular series was one that would make Larry Flynt proud, it crossed that little gray line we call "Public Decency." The image of some elderly, gray-haired lady choking to death on her bran muffin as she read the morning cartoon section pretty much sent my first attempt to the plain, unmarked file folder in the back of the cartoon closet.

Disappointed but unshaken, I surged on and wrote other series that eventually did manage to see the light of the comics page. The Nursery Rhymes, Shermlock Holmes, Moby Dud, Star Trek, Star Warts and The Wizard of Odd are just a few. If my high school English teacher could have foreseen that I would one day be a published author in some venue other than "Penthouse Forum," she might have taken the doodles on the margins of my test papers a bit more seriously.

Thank you for giving me this chance to entertain you.

Darin L. Carpenter

Going through customs on a recent vacation.

And you thought getting through the Canadian border was tough.

The Unauthorized
Mark Dickerson Biography

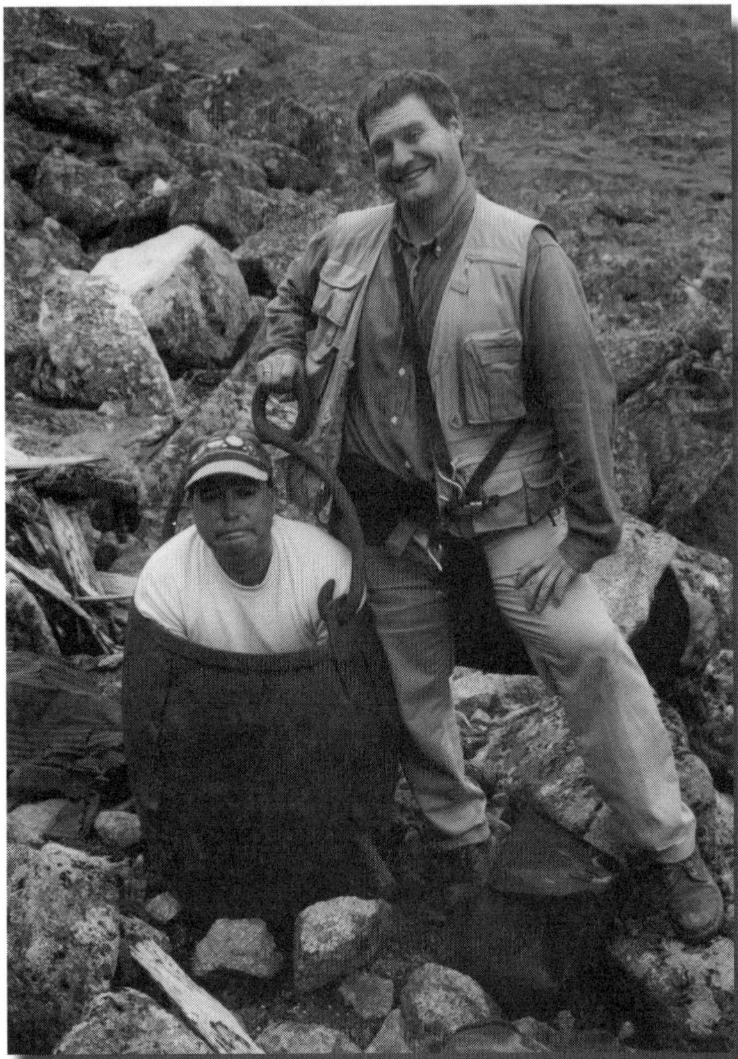

Born to migratory vole herders, the young Mark Dickerson spent his early days catching mosquitoes and making clothing from their pelts.

One day, while Mark was checking his mosquito trap lines, his parents mis-took a wandering fur seal for their son. This of course left poor Mark to fend for himself in the wild.

Years passed until one day, Chad, while on a safari in the Chugach Mountains searching for the elusive hairless yeti, stumbled upon Mark. He was running naked through the woods and quoting Monty Python & Nietzsche. Chad knew instantly that Mark would make the perfect comic strip writer. Acting fast, Chad set a trap and baited it with Thin Mint Girl Scout Cookies. It was only a matter of time before Mark fell into the snare.

Even with hundreds of hours of intense obedience training, Chad found life with Mark a challenge. Chad was finally forced to send him to the Khadaffi School of Etiquette for Wayward Boys. He was eventually sent home after six months of court-ordered electro shock therapy. Not only was Mark's chronic bed-wetting almost completely cured, but his appetite for writing comic strip comedy increased voraciously.

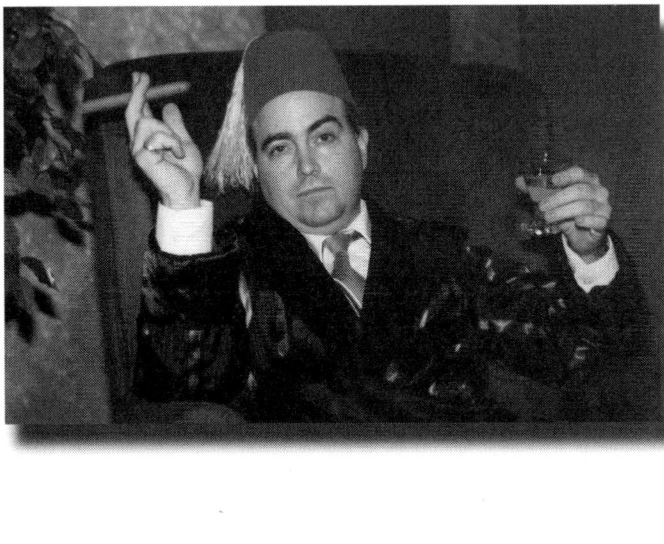

Unfortunately, due to many setbacks which involved various law-enforcement agencies Mark has been forced into hiding. Word has it that he is now residing in a one-room shack deep in the forest and is working on his new book, "Manifestos for Dummies." It is due out next summer at a bookstore near you.

I'd like to take this page to thank Jennie "Bean" Scott for all of her unwavering support. If it wasn't for all of her help, Tundra wouldn't have made it this far.

I would also like to say thank you for putting up with me all the times I've been less than jolly when trying to meet deadlines or struggling with projects such as this book. Thank you for tolerating all the times, when trying to come up with a new cartoon idea, I've gotten frustrated and thrown furniture through windows and slammed my head through walls. Thank you for not holding a grudge when I've locked you in the closet until you promised to laugh at my cartoons. And thank you for helping me through all the bed-wetting & cold-sweats during my "little people in my head" period...

Acually, I haven't really done any of the above things... yet. So, I guess what I'm actually doing is thanking you in advance.

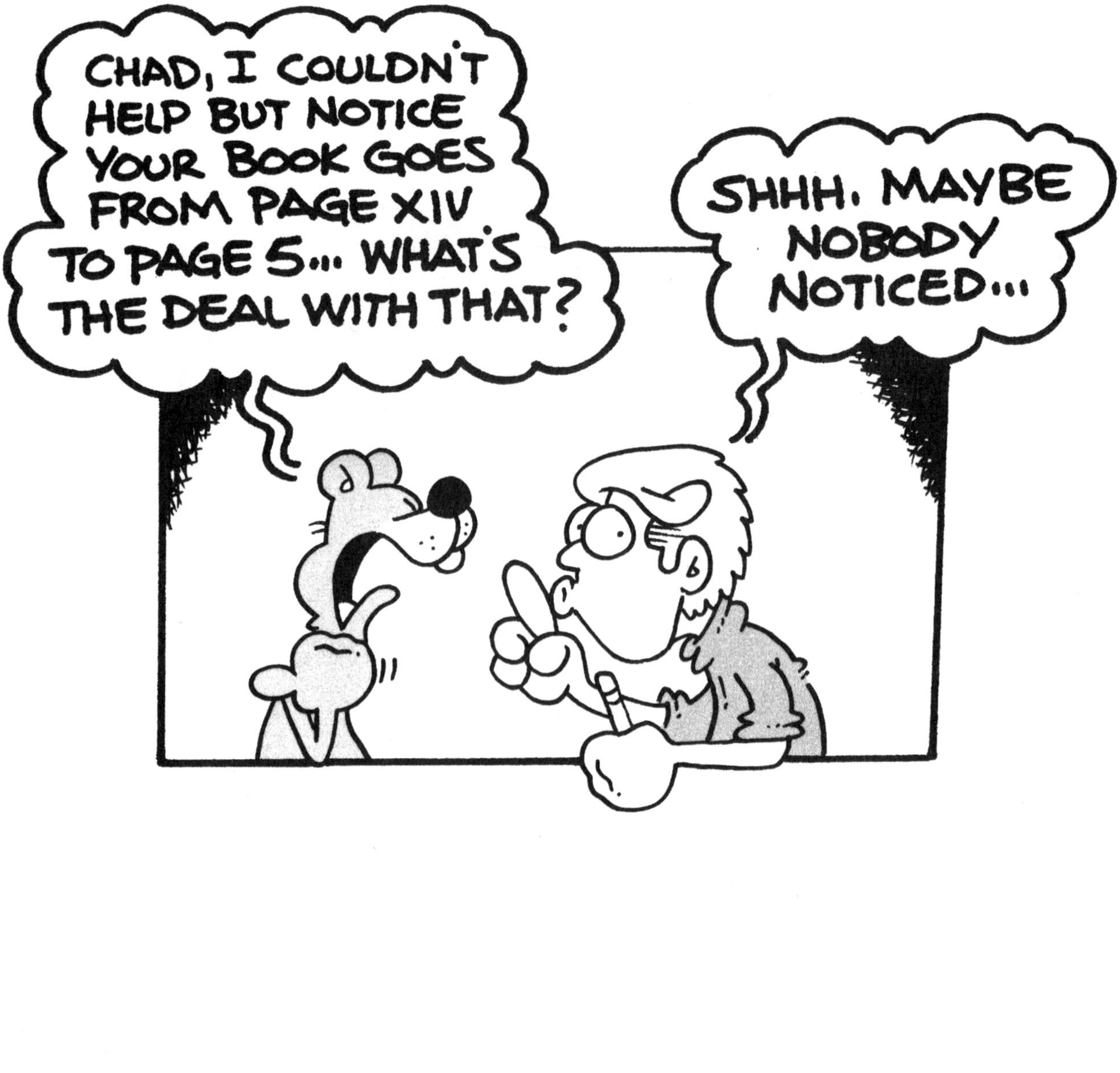
CHAD, I COULDN'T HELP BUT NOTICE YOUR BOOK GOES FROM PAGE XIV TO PAGE 5... WHAT'S THE DEAL WITH THAT?
SHHH. MAYBE NOBODY NOTICED...